2003

Marketing

2003

Marketing

REAL PEOPLE, REAL CHOICES

THIRD EDITION

Michael R. Solomon
Auburn University

Elnora W. Stuart
The American University in Cairo

Upper Saddle River, New Jersey 07458

Library of Congress Cataloging-in-Publication Data
Solomon, Michael R.
  Marketing : real people, real choices / Michael R. Solomon, Elnora W. Stuart. — 3rd ed.
    p. cm.
  Includes bibliographical references and index.
  ISBN 0-13-035134-2
  1. Marketing — Vocational guidance. I. Stuart, Elnora W. II. Title.
HF5415.35 .S65 2002
658.8′0023′73 — dc21

                     2002021822

Senior Editor: Wendy Craven
Editor-in-Chief: Jeff Shelstad
Assistant Editor: Melissa Pellerano
Editorial Assistant: Danielle Serra
Developmental Editor: Audrey Regan
Media Project Manager: Anthony Palmiotto
Marketing Manager: Michelle O'Brien
Marketing Assistant: Amanda Fisher
Managing Editor (Production): Judith Leale
Production Editor: Virginia Somma
Permissions Coordinator: Suzanne Grappi
Associate Director, Manufacturing: Vincent Scelta
Manufacturing Buyer: Arnold Vila
Design Manager: Maria Lange
Designer: Steven Frim
Interior Design: Joanne Chernow
Cover Design: Steven Frim
Cover Illustration/Photo: Ken Fisher/Getty Images
Manager, Print Production: Christy Mahon
Composition: Progressive Information Technologies
Full-Service Project Management: Progressive Publishing Alternatives
Printer/Binder: Courier Kendallville

Credits and acknowledgments borrowed from other sources and reproduced, with permission, in this textbook appear on pages 605 - 607.

Pearson Education LTD.
Pearson Education Australia PTY, Limited
Pearson Education Singapore, Pte. Ltd
Pearson Education North Asia Ltd
Pearson Education, Canada, Ltd
Pearson Educación de Mexico, S.A. de C.V.
Pearson Education–Japan
Pearson Education Malaysia, Pte. Ltd

Prentice Hall

10 9 8 7 6 5 4 3
ISBN 0-13-035134-2

To Gail, Amanda, Zachary, and Alexandra –

my favorite market segment

—M.S.

To Sonny, Patrick, and Marge

—E.S.

Brief Contents

Contents

CHAPTER 6   WHY PEOPLE BUY: CONSUMER BEHAVIOR AND PEER-TO-PEER E-COMMERCE   158

PART IV

COMMUNICATING THE VALUE OFFER   398

Preface

*I*N THIS BOOK, you're the marketer. So before we describe this new edition, you tell us: What is marketing? Which definition of marketing would you choose and why?

Third Edition

MARKETING
Real People, Real Choices

Michael Solomon
Auburn University

Elnora Stuart
American University in Cairo

Option 1: **Marketing** is about memorizing a bunch of terms like *zone pricing* and *merchant wholesaler*.

Option 2: **Marketing** is about the four Ps only – product, price, place, and promotion.

Option 3: **Marketing** is about the four Ps and about the flesh-and-blood people who need to make tough decisions about the best way to develop a hot new product or about how to make that product so irresistible it flies off of store shelves.

We hope you chose option 3. We've been teaching and doing marketing for a long time. If there's one thing *we've* learned, it's that our discipline is fun, exciting and important—when communicated the right way. Sure, this book will give you all the terms you need to know to pass that final exam. But, you'll also see how marketing can come alive when it's being practiced by real people making real choices. To us, marketing is about the creation of value — for customers, companies, and society. We'd like to show you how that's done in the real world.

This book is for students who want to be marketers. It's also for students who don't. If you fall into the first category, we're going to teach you the basics of your field so that you can understand how marketers contribute to the creation of value. If you fall into the second category, maybe at the end of the term, you'll change your mind. Even if you don't, we're going to show you that the principles of marketing apply to many other fields as well, from the arts to accounting. And regardless of your reasons for taking this course, we've worked hard to make the material come alive for you by focusing on marketing decision making. You won't just read about it, you'll do it.

No other book brings students closer to doing real marketing.

Enjoy!

Get Real!

Real People, Real Choices vignettes introduce students to marketers at companies big and small. Vignettes ask students to consider three options the marketer had and then pick the best option.

Decision Making in the New Era of Marketing

3

ETHICS AND THE MARKETING ENVIRONMENT

Real People, Real Choices:

Meet Joe Barstys, a Decision Maker at Subaru of America

www.subaru.com

CURRENT POSITION: Manager of Customer Relationships.

CAREER PATH: B.A. in philosophy, St. Francis College; M.A. theology, Christ the King Theologate; taught high school; commercial photographer, marketing positions at Eaton Corporation. In 1984 became a member of Subaru customer relationships team.

BUSINESS BOOK I'M READING: Re-reading Theodore Levitt's classic The Marketing Imagination.

WHAT I DO WHEN NOT WORKING: Play guitar, long-distance cycling, volunteer work, late-night writing.

HERO: My Dad. A coal miner at 16 and a chemical plant laborer for 50 years. He left this earth at age 85 with four kids doing better than he did, and a wife secure for her remaining days.

MOTTOS: "Carpe diem!" "The cracked ones let in th[...] growth market" is directing me to connect with our [...]

MOTIVATION: I am a tugboat, nudging life's ocean [...] "daily doings" are meaningful.

How Subaru Got Customers to C[...]

The "Holy Grail" for a marketer is to create satis[...] than Joe Barstys. As Manager of Customer Rela[...] tered in Cherry Hill, NJ), Joe's job is to ensure t[...] ages all aspects of relationship building for th[...] program and an owner magazine sent to 650,0[...] drivers are satisfied, Joe is satisfied.

But, in today's competitive business envir[...] there a difference between being *satisfied* with [...] Say the something is a love interest—satisfied w[...] date. But loyalty would mean the big scary C wo[...] stantly trying to get the big C word from cust[...] marketers say, a *New Era* of business relationshi[...]

Joe had to find out what makes consumers [...] pany had been conducting a survey on the pu[...] owners as part of its national Subaru Owner Loy[...] during the warranty period asked Subaru buyers [...] the service they got from local dealers. The com[...] national network of dealers and with Subaru's re[...]

Real People, Other Voices: Advice for Subaru

Miranda Erikkila, Student, Houston Baptist
I would choose option 3 because it will lead the company to higher sales long term and will create an atmosphere among all dealerships that would increase customer loyalty. The short-run costs to rework the system are small compared to the possible long-term profit Subaru stands to gain by focusing on customer loyalty. Only a dramatic rework of the current system will change the company's focus.

Alan Dick, Marketing Professor, University at Buffalo
I would choose option 3. Satisfaction is a *necessary* but not *sufficient* condition for customer loyalty and repeat purchase. To ensure loyalty, you must also be doing a better job than the competition. The only way to know that is to develop measures of loyalty that consider not only your products and services, but also those of your competition. A survey identifying key loyalty indicators and the underlying reasoning for that loyalty would provide Subaru with useful information for building long term relationships with its customers than would information about mere satisfaction.

[...]Communications, Interface Comp[...]
[...]ns do [...]

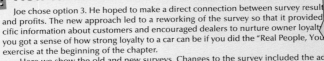

Real People, Real Choices:

How It Worked Out at Subaru of America

Joe chose option 3. He hoped to make a direct connection between survey result[...] and profits. The new approach led to a reworking of the survey so that it provided[...] cific information about customers and encouraged dealers to nurture owner loyalt[...] you got a sense of how strong loyalty to a car can be if you did the "Real People, You[...] exercise at the beginning of the chapter.

Here we show the old and new surveys. Changes to the survey included the ad[...] "loyalty section" to the data reports and the expansion of existing action plannin[...] that Subaru provided to its dealers. The new survey format asked three questions [...] Indicators"): the degree of overall owner satisfaction, how the experience at [...] compared to past car-buying and servicing experiences, and the degree to w[...] would repeat the experience at that dealership. Reports sent to [...] tomers by loyalty types (loyal, vulnerable, and possibl[...] the three key questions [...] dealers [...] actions with an eye [...]

Real People, Real Choices vignettes unify each chapter and place the student in the marketing driver's seat.

Students, faculty, and industry professionals from around the world weigh in on what featured marketers should do to solve their marketing dilemmas.

Students find out the marketer's "real choice" at chapter's end.

New Times

THIS NEW EDITION reflects what's going on in the world of marketing now. It focuses on the creation and transfer of value from manufacturers to consumers. It's organized around the sequence of steps necessary to ensure that the appropriate value exchange occurs and that both parties to the transaction are satisfied (making it more likely they'll continue to do business in the future). These steps include:

- Making Marketing Value Decisions (Part I)
- Identifying Markets and Understanding Customers' Needs for Value (Part II)
- Creating the Value Offer (Part III)
- Communicating the Value Offer (Part IV)
- Delivering the Value Offer (Part V)

We've updated and expanded our coverage of online marketing activities, including everything from virtual communities to new forms of Internet marketing research. The text covers new ways in which marketers are reaching out to customers—and letting them reach back—guerrilla marketing, customer relationship management (CRM), and M-commerce, for instance.

Here's just a sample of what's new:

- Impact of the Internet and new technologies on marketing in every chapter
- "Brand You" (Ch. 1)—students begin by thinking of themselves as a products to be marketed
- New online research practices (Ch. 5)
- Guerilla marketing (Ch. 16)
- E-commerce developments: C2C (Ch. 6), B2B (Ch. 7), B2C (Ch. 18)
- Customer Relationship Management (CRM) and 1:1 marketing (Ch. 8)
- Online dynamic pricing strategies (Ch. 13)
- New coverage of integrated marketing communications (Ch. 14)
- E-commerce and database marketing strategies (Ch. 15)
- Social responsibility and ethical decision-making (Ch. 3)
- Supply chain management and the value chain (Ch. 17)...and much more!

New Topics

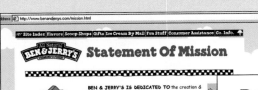

Doing It Right: Ethical Behavior in the Marketplace

In fall, 2001, the public was shaken by the Enron scandal—the largest corporate bankruptcy in U.S. history. With the giant electricity and natural gas trader's collapse in October 2001 came a Justice Department investigation of not only Enron's activities but also its auditor Arthur Andersen. Just a few years prior, Enron's stock had been soaring, and the company had been urging employees to invest their retirement accounts in Enron stock. When Enron filed for Chapter 11 bankruptcy, its stock had fallen from a high of $90.75 per share to .26 per share. Outraged employees filed lawsuits, as did investors who had lost billions. Meanwhile, Enron and Arthur Andersen shredded documents, Wall Street reacted in fear, and investigators tried to ~~what went wrong and when at Enron.~~

ofitability depends on making quality products while acting in an ethical a~~
le manner—anything less and consumers will run, not walk, into the arms
spiring tycoons, don't panic: Marketing still is concerned with the firm's bottom line, bu~~hat went wrong and when at Enron.
w many managers also consider **social profit** which is the net benefit both the firm and soci-
w receive from a firm's ethical practices and socially responsible behavior.[1]

Consumers recognize brand logos with just a single letter— from A to Z. How many can you recognize?

Answers: a. Ali; b. Bubblicious; c. Campbell's; d. Dawn; e. Eggo; f. Frito; g. Gatorade; h. Hebrew National; i. Ice; j. Sugar-free Jell-O; k. Kool-Aid; l. Lysol; m. M&M's; n. Nilla Wafers; o. Oreo; p. Pez; q. Q-Tips; r. Reese's; s. Starburst; t. Tide; u. Uncle Ben's; v. V8; w. Wisk; x. Xtra; y. York; z. Zest

Creating Product Identity: Branding Decisions

Successful marketers keep close tabs on their products' life cycle status, and they plan accordingly. Equally important, though, is giving that product an identity like The Firm is doing with Pony shoes. That's where branding comes in. How important is branding? Well, of the more than 17,000 new products or line extensions introduced each year, 25 percent are new brands. About $127.5 billion per year is spent on introducing these new brands—that's $7.5 million per brand on average.

We said earlier that nearly 40 percent of all new products fail but for new brands the failure rate is even higher—up to 80 to 90 percent![13] Branding is an extremely important (and expensive) element of product strategies. In this next section we will examine what a brand is and how certain laws protect brands. Then we will discuss the importance of branding and how firms make branding decisions.

- *Protest sites*. These sites let consumers "vent" by sharing negative experiences they have had with companies. Many of these sites have links you can find on www.protest.com. In some cases these protest sites pose a public relations problem for companies, so companies try to eliminate them. Dunkin' Donuts bought a site from a disgruntled customer who created the Web page to complain after he could not get skim milk for his coffee.[53] And sometimes these sites spread untrue information about corporations. For example, rumors began spreading on newsgroups that Procter & Gamble's Febreze cleaning product killed dogs. In a preemptive move to minimize problems before they started, P&G registered numerous Web site names so no one else could—including febrezekillspet.com, febrezesucks.com, and ihateprocterandgamble.com.[54] P&G now maintains its own Web site dedicated to fighting rumors: pg.com/rumor.[55]

New Features!

● Real People, Real Choices chapter-opening vignettes

Each chapter opens by introducing students to a real marketer facing a real marketing issue. Students see what options the marketer had and they can decide (during the course of the chapter) the marketer's best option. Students get the answer in the "How It Worked Out" section at chapter's end. Sixteen Real People are new to this edition, ranging from CEOs to brand managers.

● Real People, Your Choices: Think and Do Like a Marketer

Directly following the Real People, Real Choices opener is a short activity with a "hint" to help the student solve the featured marketer's problem. This activity helps students to get in the mindset of a marketer.

● Real People, Other Voices

A marketing professor, marketing executive, and marketing student refer back to the chapter opener and voice the option they would choose if faced with the marketer's dilemma.

● Bookmark It!

This new activity focuses on doing. Each activity is directly keyed to one of the chapter's learning objectives. Students do online research, perform mini-projects, or think about a marketing problem the way a marketer would.

● How It Worked Out

Each chapter concludes with the featured marketer explaining the decision made and the results of that decision.

● Plan It! Developing a Marketing Plan

Students make decisions in order to develop a marketing plan for a small, entrepreneurial company. This new exercise appears at the end of each chapter and allows students to create marketing plans on their own or using professional Marketing Plan Pro software.

New Features Educate, Engage, and Entertain!

Real People, Your Choices: Think and Do Like a Marketer

Real People, Your Choices:

Think and Do Like a Marketer

One exercise a marketing consultant might do to evaluate strategic decisions is to act like a customer—try out the client's service and competing services. With that in mind, do a mini comparative analysis of any of the sites listed below and HotJobs.com. Write down the advantages and disadvantages of each site and why you might choose to place your résumé on one and not the other. Can you offer specific suggestions for areas of improvement?

Online job boards:
www.monster.com
www.ajb.dni.us (American's Job Bank)
www.headhunter.net
www.flipdog.com

the need to attract investor dollars, and [...] Dimitri's problem even more difficult.

Although all of the online firms share [...] people to move their job hunting activitie[...] strategy would be to let industry leader Mon[...] tising to persuade people that matching em[...] preferable to sifting through thousands of p[...] on building awareness of the HotJobs bra[...] that.

Now, join the decision team at HotJo[...] choose and why?

Option 1: Focus on a few major [...] one industry.

Because the biggest job markets (and [...] U.S. cities, Dimitri could spend preci[...] remaining a specialist in technical jobs [...] New York area. But HotJo[...]e's high prices are "highway robbery," an exchange occurs if [...] market conditions. Furthe[...]uy something there—even if they grumble about it for weeks [...] so if Dimitri did not posit[...] window of opportunity. [...]ur for an exchange to take place. A politician can agree to return to the local markets and crush H[...]ange for your vote, or a minister can offer you salvation in

Option 2: Act local [...]

These exercises immediately follow the Real People, Real Choices chapter openers and put students in the featured marketer's shoes.

Bookmark It!

[...]xchanges occur as a monetary transaction in which currency [...]dit card) is surrendered in return for a good or a service. Even [...]ing, as electronic commerce systems (*e-money*) permit sales [...]ver changing hands. Web commerce allows merchants sell-[...]stomers around the world.

[...] CAN BE MARKETED

[...]part of the marketing definition shows us that just about any-[...]ome of the best marketers come from the ranks of services [...]ess or not-for-profit organizations such as Greenpeace. Even [...]rs use marketing to their advantage (just think about that $30 [...]baseball game or rock concert). Ideas, such as political sys-[...]), religion (Christianity, Islam), and art (Realism, Abstract [...]in a "marketplace." In this book, we'll refer to any good, ser-[...] as a **product**, even though what is being sold may not take

[...]ces **Consumer goods** are the tangible products that indi-[...]sonal or family use. **Services** are intangible products that we [...]ervice transactions contribute on average more than 60 per-[...] of all industrialized nations; so as we'll see in Chapter 11, [...]me of the special challenges that arise when marketing an [...]angible good.[7] In both cases, though, keep in mind that the [...]ne underlying value such [...]onveni[...] [...]can come f[...]

1 Bookmark It!

Go through any magazine or newspaper. Find an ad for a product that you think asks too much money in return for the value promised. Find an ad for a second product that you feel gives you good value for your money. What have you learned about the concept of value from this exercise?

product ■ A tangible good, service, idea, or some combination of these that satisfies consumer or business customer needs through the exchange process; a bundle of attributes including features, functions, benefits, and uses.

consumer goods ■ The goods purchased by individual consumers for personal or family use.

services ■ Intangible products that are exchanged directly from the producer to the [...]

Every learning objective in the book is made active through Bookmark It! Activities placed throughout each chapter where relevant.

Plan It! Developing a Marketing Plan

■ PLAN IT!
DEVELOPING A MARKETING PLAN

Marketing PlanPro™

As your instructor directs, create a marketing plan (using Marketing Plan Pro software or a written marketing plan format) to document your marketing decisions or answer these questions in a written or oral report.

CFS needs marketing information and research to build on the current year's marketing plan (see Appendix A) in developing next year's plan.

1. What marketing intelligence would help CFS monitor developments in the external environment?
2. How might management use ethnography to better understand what customers do with CFS products?
[...]hat two scenarios could conceivably emerge in the [...]e of impl[...]nting this year's marketing plan—and [...] these scenarios in planning for

An integrated marketing plan project based on small entrepreneurial company enables students to develop first-hand a marketing plan of their own.

For the Instructor

Instructor's Manual: Contains chapter overview and objectives, plus detailed lecture outlines—incorporating figures and assignments from the text. Includes suggested discussion questions and exercises, plus review questions/answers along with extra projects. Now also includes *Solomon's Marketing Adventure CD-ROM* with suggested activities for both in and out of the classroom. This CD-ROM includes hundreds of the New York Festivals award-winning print advertisements, giving students exciting and relevant examples in every class.

Test Item File: Brand new—completely revamped since the last edition! Includes thousands of questions, consisting of multiple choice, true/false, and short-answer. Page references are provided for each question.

PowerPoint Express: Easily customizable for even the most novice user, this presentation includes basic chapter outlines and key points from each chapter. The best option if you want to incorporate your own material!

PowerPoint Expanded: Includes the basics found in the Express version but also advertisements and art from the text. The best option if you want a complete presentation solution. *Both PowerPoint presentations are available from the Prentice Hall Web site at www.prenhall.com/solomon or on the Instructor Course Organizer CD-ROM.*

Prentice Hall Electronic Test Manager: Windows based Test Manager which creates exams and allows you to evaluate and track students' results. Easily customizable for your needs.

Instructor Course Organizer CD-ROM: One source for all of your supplement needs. This Instructor CD contains all the print and technology supplements on a single CD-ROM. Enjoy the freedom to transport the entire supplements package from home, to the office, and to the classroom. The Instructor CD-ROM enables you to customize any of the ancillaries, print only the chapters or materials you wish to use, or access any item from the package within the classroom.

Guest Lecture Custom Case Videos: Now is your chance to have the Real People highlighted in the text visit your classroom! Issue-based segments include interviews and company footage from Real People at IWON.com, DDB Needham, Federated and more. These custom videos give you an inside look at the real challenges top marketers at real companies face on a day-to-day basis. Also includes segments from many companies not highlighted in the text.

Color Overhead Transparencies: Available as acetates or PowerPoint slides. Includes key figures from the text, key concepts, and additional print advertisements.

Innovative Online Courses: Content for WebCT, Blackboard, and CourseCompass courses is available. No technical expertise needed. Teach a complete online course or a Web-enhanced course. Add your own materials, take advantage of online testing and Gradebook opportunities, and use the bulletin board and discussion board functions. All courses are free to students with purchase of the text.

Bb ®
Blackboard
www.blackboard.com

For the Instructor and Student

Companion Website: Go beyond the text. Our acclaimed Web resource provides professors and students with a customized course Website that features a complete array of teaching and learning material. For instructors: downloadable versions of the Instructor's Resource Manual and PowerPoint slides, plus additional resources such as current events and Internet exercises. Or, try the Syllabus Builder to plan your own course!

For students, an interactive Student Study Guide with quizzes, plus all of the *Bookmark It!* activities from the text. NEW! LiveLab feature gives students additional *Think and Do Like a Marketer* activities from the text and lets them contrast and compare their answers to other students using the text. Also includes behind the scenes "outtake" content, never published before footage from the video library.

www.prenhall.com/solomon

For the Student

Solomon's Marketing Adventure—A one-of-a-kind companion for students. Includes chapter-by-chapter study aids and problems. PLUS a CD-ROM filled with hundreds of New York Festival's award-winning print advertisements with accompanying in and out of class activities.

Marketing Plan Pro and (NEW!) Marketing Plan: A Handbook. Marketing Plan Pro is a highly rated commercial software package that guides students through the entire marketing plan process. The software is totally interactive and features ten sample marketing plans, step-by-step guides and customizable charts. Customize your marketing plans to fit your marketing needs by following easy-to-use plan wizards. *The New Marketing Plan: A Handbook*, by Marian Burk Wood, supplements the in-text marketing plan material with an in-depth guide to what student marketers really need to know. The Software and Handbook are available as value-pack items with this text.

Navigating WebCT or Navigating BlackBoard—A Student's Guide. Beginning with a brief introduction to the Internet and the World Wide Web, these lively guides help students understand and master the basic navigation path through a WebCT or BlackBoard Online Course. Covers WebCT 3.7or BlackBoard 5.0+. The definitive off-line tool for the online student! These guides are available as a value-package option.

Acknowledgments

Many people worked hard to make this 3rd edition a reality. We'd like to thank Wendy Craven, Bruce Kaplan, Michelle O'Brien, Anthony Palmiotto, Suzanne Grappi, Melissa Pellerano, Jeff Shelstad and Virginia Somma at Prentice Hall. As usual, we could not have pulled this off without the steadfast and tenacious support of our favorite "Dragon Lady," (a.k.a. Developmental Editor) Audrey Regan. A special note of thanks goes to the wonderful executives, faculty members and students who participated in the Real People, Real Choices feature. In addition, our Electronic Advisory Board consisting of marketing professors around the country provided invaluable suggestions throughout the process and we are indebted to them for their help.

Advisory Panel Members:

Tony Allred, Weber State University; James Baird, Finger Lakes Community College; Barbara Barrett, St. Louis Community College; Phil Bartos, University of Central Arkansas; Gloria Bemben, Finger Lakes Community College; Robert Berl, University of Memphis; Donald Borbee, St. John Fisher College; Dennis Bredenburg, Southern Utah University; Francine Brion, Alfred State College; Charles Brunner, Manhattan College; Judith Bulin, Monroe Community College; Jeffrey C. Strieter, SUNY Brockport; Joe Cangelosi, University of Central Arkansas; John Christesen, Westchester Community College; Kim Corfman, New York University; Mark Davis, Harding College; Esmerelda DeLosSantos, University of the Incarnate Word; Duane Dean, East Carolina University; Susan Delvecchio, East Carolina University; Kalpesh Desai, SUNY Buffalo; Paul Dholakia, SUNY Buffalo; Bob DiPaolo, Lewis and Clark Community College; Peter Doukas, Westchester Community College; Edward Fitzpatrick, Finger Lakes Community College; Eugene Fram, Rochester Institute of Technology; Robb Frankel, East Carolina University; John Gardner, SUNY Brockport; David Glascoff, East Carolina University; Jonathan Goodrich, Florida International University; Jim Gray, Florida Atlantic University; Linda Gulbransen, Monroe Community College; Neil Hair, Rochester Institute of Technology; Paul Herbig, Tri State University; Jim Hess, Ivy Tech State College; Gene Holland, Columbia Basin College; John Howard, Alfred University; Ken Hunt, Fort Lewis College; Jim Hunt, University of North Carolina at Wilmington; Eva Hyatt, Appalachian State University; Arun Jain, SUNY Buffalo; Micki Johnson, Nova Southeastern University; Andrew Joniak, SUNY Buffalo; Brian Jorgensen, Southern Utah University; Janice Karlen, LaGuardia Community College / CUNY; Pradeep Korgaonkar, Florida Atlantic University; Carl Kranendonk, Florida International University; Russell Laczniak, Iowa State University; Jane Lang, East Carolina University; Robert Lawes, Chaminade University; Dong Lee, Manhattan College; Rick Leininger, Saginaw Valley State University; Chris Lemley, Georgia State University; Paul Londrigan, Mott Community College; Tamara Mangleburg, Florida Atlantic University; John McDade, Tarrant County Junior College; Tom Milton, Mercy College; Cameron Montgomery, Delta State University; Melissa Moore, University of Texas at Brownsville; Ron Mozelewski, St. Louis Community College; Michael Murphy, St. Thomas Aquinas College; Phil Nitse, Idaho State University; Gary Nothnagle, Nazareth College of Rochester; Barbara Oates, Texas A&M University; Marta Ortiz-Buonofino, Florida International University; Terry Paul, Ohio State University; Thom Porter, University of North Carolina at Wilmington; Carmen Powers, Monroe Community College; Carolyn Predmore, Manhattan College; Anne Ranczuch, Monroe Community College; Greg Rose, University of Mississippi; Don Ryktarsyk, Schoolcraft College; Hemant Sashittal, St. John Fisher College; Peter Sattler, SUNY Buffalo; Kenneth Schaefle, North Park University; Louis Seagull, Pace University; Bruce Seaton, Florida International University; Vicky Seiler, Hawaii Pacific University; Thurston Shrader, Southwest Tennessee Community College; Curt Smith, Finger Lakes Community College; Lois Smith, University of Wisconsin-Whitewater; Brent Snow, Dixie State College of Utah; Michael Stoll, Genesee Community College; Steve Stovall, Fort Lewis College; Bill Swinyard, Brigham Young University; Wm. Thompson, University of Texas; John Tiberio, Monroe Community College; Philip Tyler, Rochester Institute of Technology; Edward VanDuzer, SUNY Brockport; Margie Vance, Albuquerque Technical Vocational Institute; Robert Veryzer, Rensselaer Polytechnic Institute; Peter Waasdorp, University of Rochester; Edward Wesneske, Monroe Community College; Seungoog Weun, University of North Carolina at Wilmington; Julian Yudelson, Rochester Institute of Technology; Gerard Zappia, Nazarath College of Rochester; Mary Ellen Zuckerman, SUNY Geneseo

Reviewers:

Ruth Clottey, *Barry University;* Robert M. Cosenza, *Christian Brothers University;* Elizabeth Ferrell, *Southwestern Oklahoma State University;* Jon Freiden, *Florida State University;* John Heinemann, *Keller Graduate School of Management;* Mark B. Houston, *University of Missouri-Columbia;* Jack E. Kant, *San Juan College;* Laura M. Milner, *University of Alaska;* John E. Robbins, *Winthrop University;* Kimberly A. Taylor, *Florida International University;* Susan L. Taylor, *Belmont University;* John Thanopoulos, *University of Piraeus, Greece;* Jane Boyd Thomas, *Winthrop University;* Judee A. Timm, *Monterey Peninsula College;* Steve Wedwick, *Heartland Community College;* Brent M. Wren, *University of Alabama*

Featured Markets:

In addition, 18 busy executives gave generously of their time as the "Real People, Real Choices" feature was written:

Chapter 1: Dimitri Boylan, *President and CEO, Hotjobs.com;* **Chapter 2:** Angela Talley, *VP, Group Strategic Planning Director, DDB Worldwide;* **Chapter 3:** Joe Barstys, *Manager, Customer Satisfaction Subaru of America, Inc.;* **Chapter 4:** Henrik Kaas, *Managing Director, Sony Denmark;* **Chapter 5:** George Terhanian, *Vice President, Internet Research, Harris Interactive;* **Chapter 6:** Jen Dulski, *Senior Brand Manager, Yahoo!;* **Chapter 7:** Steve Schwartz, *Executive Vice President, Lion Apparel;* **Chapter 8:** Landon Pollack, *President, MPower Living;* **Chapter 9:** Dee Dee Gordon, *Co-President, Look-Look, Inc.;* **Chapter 10:** Mario A. Polit, *Senior Manager of Marketing for Sedans, Infinity Division, Nissan, North America, Inc.* **Chapter 11:** Julie Sanoff, *Senior Manager, American Express Consumer Card Services Group;* **Chapter 12:** John Chillingworth, *Senior Sales Consultant, Aithent, Inc.;* **Chapter 13:** Craig Lambert, *Senior VP, Brand Management, Courtyard Marriott;* **Chapter 14:** Leslie Goldfarb, *VP, Price/McNabb Focused Communications;* **Chapter 15:** Bradley Sockloff, *Project Manager, Direct Marketing, Iwon.com;* **Chapter 16:** Melissa Fisher, *VP Marketing & Communications Val-Pak DMS, Inc.;* **Chapter 17:** Mackey McDonald, *President, Chairman & CEO, VF Corporation;* **Chapter 18:** Dawn Robertson, *President & Chief Merchandising Officer, Federated Direct*

Last, but not least, we'd like to thank the students, faculty, and executives from around the world who participated in our "Real People, Other Voices" feature.

Students (in order of appearance)

Kristen Samson, *Rider University;* Cile Smith, *The University of Alabama;* Reem Ezzat Elmenshawy, *The American University in Cairo;* Miranda Erikkila, *Houston Baptist University;* Sophia Zaoudi, *Al Akhawayn University, Ifrane, Morocco;* Katie Finnegan, *University of Illinois;* Meredith Burch, *Berry College;* Joseph Burriss, *Clemson University;* Jarrett Rice, *Middle Tennessee State University; Elise Grant, The University of Colorado-Boulder;* Benjamin Gonzales, *Boston University;* Moatassem Moatez, *The American University in Cairo;* Paola Zuniga, *Florida International University;* Kristin Firkins, *Western Kentucky University;* Aimee Hale, *Illinois State University;* Anise He, *Shanghai University;* Joseph Goodman, *University of Texas at Austin;* Marissa Contreras, *San Diego State University;* Michelle Carelis, *Bentley College;* Shi Qing, *Shanghai Univeristy;* Eli Gelber, *University of North Carolina at Greensboro;* Jennifer Lau, *Temple University;* Camilo Montoya, *Pennsylvania State University*

Faculty (in order of appearance)

Richard Robinson, *Marquette University;* Margaret A. Young, *New Mexico Highlands University;* Alan Dick, *SUNY Buffalo;* Karin Braunsberger, *University of South Florida St. Petersburg;* Basil Englis, *Berry College;* Judy F. Graham, *St. John Fisher College;* Ronald Picker, *St. Mary of the Woods College;* Sal Veas, *Santa Monica College;* Jeff. Gutenberg, *SUNY Geneseo;* Michael Munro, *Florida International;* Kathy Winsted, *Pace University;* Tina Bardsley, *Manhattanville College;* Stephen Gould, *Baruch College;* Cele Otnes, *University of Illinois at Urbana-Champaign;* Marvin G. Lovett, *University of Texas at Brownsville;* Randall Hansen, *Stetson University;* Robert Cosenza, *Christian Brothers University*

Executives (in order of appearance)

John Chillingworth, *Senior Sales Consultant, Aithent, Inc.;* Suzanne Beckmann, *Strategic Planning Director, Saatchi & Saatchi Kongens, Denmark;* Joyce LaValle, *Senior VP of Marketing & Communications, Interface Companies;* Anna Olofsson, *CEO Analys;* Richard Bernstein, *Vice President, Eric Marder Associates;* Melissa Fisher, *VP Marketing & Communications Val-Pak DMS, Inc.;* Bunny Richardson, *Assistant Manager, Media Relations, BMW Manufacturing Corp.;* Michelle Albert, *Senior Director, Strategic Marketing Alliances, Columbia Records;* Michael Hodapp, *Production Manager Dillards, Inc.;* Angela Talley, *VP, Group Strategic Planning Director, DDB Worldwide;* Subha Ramesh, *VP of Real Estate - IBI The Limited;* Joe Barstys, *Manager, Customer Satisfaction Subaru of America, Inc.;* George Terhanian, *Vice President, Internet Research, Harris Interactive;* Bradley Sockloff, *Project Manager, Direct Marketing, Iwon.com;* Leslie Goldfarb, *VP, Price/McNabb Focused Communications;* Brian Kurtz, *VP Marketing Boardroom;* Steve Schwartz, *VP, Lion Apparel;* Jen Dulski, *Senior Brand Manager, Yahoo!;* Martha Garnica, *Principal-Associate Media Director, Optimedia International*

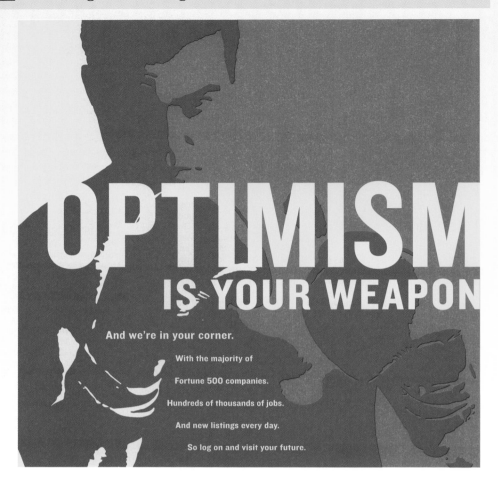

OPTIMISM IS YOUR WEAPON

And we're in your corner.

With the majority of

Fortune 500 companies.

Hundreds of thousands of jobs.

And new listings every day.

So log on and visit your future.

Bookmark It!

OBJECTIVES:

1 Know what marketing is all about.
2 Define the marketing mix.
3 Understand the basics of marketing planning.
4 Describe the evolution of the marketing concept.
5 Explain why marketing is important to all of us.

WELCOME TO THE WORLD OF MARKETING

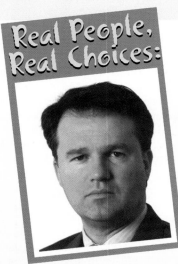

Real People, Real Choices:

Meet Dimitri Boylan, a Decision Maker at HotJobs.com

www.HotJobs.com

CURRENT POSITION: President and CEO, HotJobs.com

CAREER PATH: Formerly managing director of recruiting for OTEC, Inc.

FIRST JOB OUT OF SCHOOL: Carpenter.

CAREER HIGH: HotJobs profit report, 2nd quarter, 2001.

MOTTO: No one ever exceeds their own expectations.

MANAGEMENT STYLE: Hands-on, entrepreneurial.

PET PEEVE: People who think they have finished a job when it's only 90 percent done.

WHAT I DO WHEN I'M NOT WORKING: Home improvement.

EDUCATION: B.S. Biophysics, University of Pennsylvania; M.A. Biophysics, University of Illinois.

How Did HotJobs Heat Up the Industry?

So you're almost ready to start looking for a job. Do you even think of turning to the boring old classifieds without going online to popular job posting sites? Didn't think so . . . But there was a time, way back oh a few years, when online job hunting and seeking were "Jetsonian" to most of us . . .

HotJobs.com started in 1997 as an online job board focusing on high-tech careers, primarily in Northern California. It was the first job board site to provide a résumé database and an online application process—now the industry standard. The online recruiting process at the time was still in its infancy, but it had huge potential. Major newspapers were generating up to half a billion dollars in employment advertising annually in their local markets, but job seekers and recruiters still could not match jobs with job hunters outside of each paper's region. The Web represented a new marketing tool that could revolutionize the recruiting industry.

In a crowded field of competitors, HotJobs' management estimated that they ranked about 15th by the end of 1998. The company needed to break out of the pack. In January of 1999 HotJobs ran an ad during the Super Bowl in a bold attempt to cut through the clutter and make more people aware of the company. The ad helped to catapult HotJobs into the Top 10, but it still left the company one among many in a national job-recruiting market dominated by Monster.com, Career Mosaic, and several other better-funded competitors.

HotJobs offered a more sophisticated system than competitors offered. It had better functionality—a résumé database, an online application process, and the ability for job seekers to block their current employer from finding their résumé posted on the site. Still, Dimitri realized these features would not differentiate HotJobs forever. He knew building a well-recognized brand name was essential, but that he needed to act quickly.

In Spring 2000, Dimitri and his team set out to create an advertising campaign aimed at making HotJobs the number two (to Monster.com) name in the national market for site traffic, brand awareness, and revenue. Dimitri's challenge was formidable, especially because many firms were reluctant to seek employees online. The online companies were still fighting for a small share of the total recruiting market. Limited name recognition, lack of funds, the need to attract investor dollars, and a cluttered media landscape made Dimitri's problem even more difficult.

Although all of the online firms shared a common need to convince more people to move their job hunting activities to the Internet, Dimitri felt a smart strategy would be to let industry leader Monster.com spend <u>its</u> money on advertising to persuade people that matching employers with job seekers online is preferable to sifting through thousands of paper résumés. Dimitri could focus on building awareness of the HotJobs brand name. The question was how to do that.

Now, join the decision team at HotJobs.com. Which option would you choose and why?

Option 1: Focus on a few major cities or on employment in one industry.

Because the biggest job markets (and potential revenue) are in a handful of U.S. cities, Dimitri could spend precious advertising dollars selectively by remaining a specialist in technical jobs only or by focusing exclusively on the New York area. But HotJobs' profits would be limited and vulnerable to local market conditions. Furthermore, online companies were attracting investors, so if Dimitri did not position HotJobs as a national player, he might miss his window of opportunity. Well-funded competitors would go national, then return to the local markets and crush HotJobs.

Option 2: Act local, look national.

By focusing advertising on the country's top seven markets, Dimitri could concentrate his sales force in HotJobs' regional territories (especially New York where the national media is strong), hitting each with short blasts of a multimedia and telemarketing campaign. This option would include limited spending on national television advertising, giving Dimitri more bang for his advertising buck while establishing HotJobs as a premium player. It would also allow messages to be customized to each city. However, a poorly planned and executed advertising message could make HotJobs seem like a low-budget, regional player—making larger companies and job seekers reluctant to sign up for a company they perceived as too small.

Option 3: Advertise aggressively to position HotJobs as a national brand.

By coming out fighting on a national level in this new industry, HotJobs would get a head start by establishing itself as a leader in the business for years to come. But, HotJobs' main competitor Monster.com was better funded and already had an established public image. With much less money to invest, Dimitri could end up with no brand image while exhausting his limited advertising dollars.

Welcome to Brand You

YOU are a product. That may sound weird, but companies like HotJobs couldn't exist if you weren't. After all, you have "market value" as a person—qualities that set you apart from others and features other people want and need. After you finish this course, you'll have even more value because you'll know about the field of marketing and how this field relates to you, both as a future businessperson and as a consumer. In addition to learning about how marketing influences each of us, you'll have a better understanding of what it means to be BRAND YOU.

Although it may seem strange to think about the marketing of people, in reality we often talk about ourselves and others in marketing terms. It is common for us to speak of "positioning" ourselves for job interviews, or to tell our friends not to "sell themselves short." Some people who are cruising for potential mates even refer to themselves as "being on the market." In addition, many consumers hire personal image consultants to devise a "marketing strategy" for them, while others undergo plastic surgery, physical conditioning, or cosmetic makeovers to improve their "product images." The desire to package and promote ourselves is the reason for personal goods and services markets ranging from cosmetics and exercise equipment to resumé specialists and dating agencies.[1]

So, the principles of marketing apply to you, just as they apply to peas, Porsches, and computer processors. Sure there are differences in how we go about marketing each of these, but the general idea remains the same: Marketing is a fundamental part of our lives, both as consumers and as players in the business world. We'll tell you why throughout this book. But first, as a place to begin, we need to answer the basic questions of marketing: Who? What? How? When? and Why? Let's start with Who.

Marketers are drawn from many different backgrounds—remember that Dimitri Boylan of HotJobs majored in biophysics! Although many marketers have earned marketing degrees, others have backgrounds in areas such as engineering or agriculture. Retailers and fashion marketers may have training in merchandising or design. Advertising copywriters often have degrees in English. **E-marketers** use e-commerce in their strategies, and may have studied computer science.

e-marketers ■ Marketers who use e-commerce in their strategies.

And, although you may assume that the typical marketing job is in a large, consumer-oriented company such as Yahoo! or Nissan, marketers work in other types of organizations, too. In fact, there are also many exciting marketing careers in companies that sell to other businesses. In small organizations, one person (perhaps the owner) may handle all of the marketing responsibilities (and then also lock up at night). In large organizations, marketers work on different aspects of the marketing strategy.

Marketers might work in consumer-goods companies such as Coca-Cola or Subaru, or at service companies such as HotJobs.com. You'll see them in retail organizations like Bloomingdales or JCPenney, and you'll find them helping to develop entertainment products with firms such as Columbia Records or MTV. You'll see them in financial institutions such as American Express and at advertising agencies such as DDB Worldwide.

At the beginning of each chapter, we'll introduce you to marketing professionals like Dimitri Boylan in a feature we call "Real People, Real Choices." We'll tell you about a tough decision the marketer had to make and give you the possible options he or she considered. We've also included short exercises that ask you to "think" and "do" like a marketer—to get you into the mind-set of our featured executive. Then, to conclude each chapter, we'll tell you what option the marketer chose and why, as well as what happened. Along the way we'll share some other people's opinions about our featured marketer's decision in our "Real People, Other Voices" box. In each chapter, you'll meet a different marketing professor, a marketing executive, and even a marketing student or two like yourself who will each offer an opinion. Okay, now that you've gotten a glimpse of how this book works, it's time to see what marketing *is*.

What Is Marketing?

Marketing. Lots of people talk about it, but what is it? When you ask people to define marketing, you get many answers. Some people say, "That's what happens when a pushy salesman tries to sell me something I don't want." Other people say, "Oh, that's simple—TV commercials." Students might answer, "That's a course I have to take before I can get my business degree!" Finally, the guy in the front row chimes in, "**Marketing** is the process of planning and executing the conception, pricing, promotion, and distribution of ideas, goods, and services to create exchanges that satisfy individual and organizational objectives."[2] Guess which one of these definitions is correct?

Each of these responses has a grain of truth to it, but the final definition is the most accurate. This response is the official definition of marketing by the American Marketing Association, and it's a real mouthful. Let's break down this definition to better understand the basic idea of marketing, and that's what we'll do throughout this chapter. We'll start at the definition's end and work backward.

marketing ■ The process of planning and executing the conception, pricing, promotion, and distribution of ideas, goods, and services to create exchanges that satisfy individual and organizational objectives.

MARKETING SATISFIES NEEDS

The most important part of our definition is ". . . satisfy individual and organizational objectives." It tells us about the central aspect of marketing: satisfying the needs of both consumers

New Lipfinity with PermaTone.
Lipcolor that stays. Topcoat that shines.
The first to last through linguine.

the world's first **foodproof** lipcolor

MAXFACTOR★
the make-up of make-up artists

Max Factor is a company that recognizes the need to create and market products that satisfy customer needs better than the competition.

consumer ■ The ultimate user of a good or service.

marketing concept ■ A management orientation that focuses on identifying and satisfying consumer needs to ensure the organization's long-term profitability.

need ■ Recognition of any difference between a consumer's actual state and some ideal or desired state.

want ■ The desire to satisfy needs in specific ways that are culturally and socially influenced.

and producers. A **consumer** is the ultimate user of a good or service. Consumers can be individuals or organizations, whether a company, government, sorority, or charity. We like to say that the consumer is king (or queen), but it's important not to lose sight of the fact that the seller also has needs—to make a profit and to remain in business. So products are sold to satisfy both consumers' and marketers' needs—it's a two-way street. When you strip away the big words, marketing is all about satisfying needs.

Most successful firms today practice the **marketing concept**. That is, marketers first identify consumer needs and then provide products that satisfy those needs, assuring the organization's long-term profitability. (We'll talk more about the marketing concept later in this chapter.) A **need** is the difference between a consumer's actual state and some ideal or desired state. When the difference is big enough, the consumer is motivated to take action to satisfy the need. When you're hungry, you buy a snack. If you're not happy with how your hair looks, you get a new hairstyle. When you need a job, maybe you surf the Web at HotJobs.com.

Needs can be related to physical functions (such as eating) or to psychological ones (such as wanting to look good). Levi Strauss & Company does a good job of meeting the psychological needs of consumers to look good (as well as their basic need to be clothed). Levi Strauss' research tells them that people wear Levi's jeans to say important things about themselves and their desired image. Wearing the pants satisfies a need for self-expression. From time to time the company receives a beat-up, handed-down pair in the mail, with a letter from the owner requesting that the jeans be given a proper burial—that's a pretty "deep-seated" attachment to a pair of pants![3]

The specific way a need is satisfied depends on an individual's history, learning experiences, and cultural environment. A **want** is a desire for a particular product used to satisfy a need in specific ways that are culturally and socially influenced. For example, two classmates' stomachs rumble during a lunchtime lecture and both need food. However, how each person satisfies this need might be quite different. The first student may be a health nut who fantasizes about gulping down a big handful of trail mix, while the second person may be equally enticed by a greasy cheeseburger and fries. So, the first student's want is trail mix, while the second student's want is fast food (and some antacid for dessert).

A product delivers a **benefit** when it satisfies a need or want. For marketers to be successful, they must develop products that provide one or more benefits that are important to consumers. The challenge is to identify what benefits people look for, then develop a product that delivers those benefits while also convincing them that their product is better than a competitor's product so that the choice of which product to buy is "obvious." As management expert Peter Drucker wrote, "The aim of marketing is to make selling superfluous."[4]

Take for example the minivan—a staple of suburbia. Soccer moms and dads like minivans because of their roominess, a benefit that means they can carry lots of people, golden retrievers, and soccer gear around. A major complaint about minivans, however, is the difficulty of sliding minivan side doors open and closed when getting in and out. Dodge made this easier for its customers when it developed a remote-control door opener. Push a button on your key chain and a side door opens automatically. Many drivers feel this benefit and other similar conveniences put Dodge ahead of its competitors.

If we succeed in creating a product that meets the needs of the customer, he or she will happily buy it without any "persuasion" from a salesperson. For example, the Swiss firm Ste. Suisse Microelectronique et d'Horlogerie S.A. (SMH) changed the face of the low-priced watch market when it introduced the Swatch watch. These inexpensive pieces of "time-keeping jewelry" satisfy consumers' needs for a reliable timepiece at a reasonable price, and at the same time they give the benefit of wearing a colorful and trendy fashion accessory. Another benefit is that these watches can be bought at drugstores, department stores, and fashion boutiques all around the globe rather than at intimidating, high-end jewelry stores.[5]

Of course, everyone can want your product, but that doesn't ensure sales unless they have the means to obtain it. When desire is coupled with the buying power or resources to satisfy a want, the result is **demand**. So, the potential customers for a snappy, red BMW M3 convert-

After Dodge found that many consumers had difficulty opening minivan doors, it developed an automatic entry system (a benefit) to put them one step ahead of competitors.

While in developed countries, a marketplace may be a large mall or ultramodern supermarket, in developing countries many consumers still shop at small outdoor stands like this one in Egypt.

market ■ All of the customers and potential customers who share a common need that can be satisfied by a specific product, who have the resources to exchange for it, who are willing to make the exchange, and who have the authority to make the exchange.

marketplace ■ Any location or medium used to conduct an exchange.

exchange ■ The process by which some transfer of value occurs between a buyer and a seller.

value proposition ■ A marketplace offering that fairly and accurately sums up the value that will be realized if the product or service is purchased.

ible are the people who want the car *minus* those who can't afford to buy or lease one. A **market** consists of all the consumers who share a common need that can be satisfied by a specific product or service and who have the resources, willingness, and authority to make the exchange.

A **marketplace** used to be a location where buying and selling occurred face-to-face. In today's "wired" world, however, buyers and sellers might not even see each other. The modern marketplace may take the form of a glitzy shopping mall, a mail-order catalog, a television shopping network, or an eBay auction on the Internet. In developing countries, the marketplace may be a street corner or an open-air market where people sell fruits and vegetables much as they did thousands of years ago.

MARKETING IS AN EXCHANGE OF VALUE

The phrase "to create exchanges" in our definition of marketing identifies the heart of every marketing act. An **exchange** occurs when something is obtained for something else in return, which means that some transfer of value occurs between a buyer and a seller. The buyer receives an object, service, or idea that satisfies a need, and the seller receives something he or she feels is of equivalent value.

But, here's a tricky idea: *Value is in the eye of the beholder.* That means that something (or someone) may be worth a lot to one person but not to another. Your mother may believe that you are the greatest, but a prospective employer may form a different conclusion—a big part of marketing is ensuring that the thing being exchanged is appreciated for the value it holds.

Of course, not all consumers agree on value. Software piracy is a huge problem today—the industry estimates it loses about $12 billion a year because of it. In one case, customs agents raided computer networks at five large American universities, busting undergraduates and others in a piracy ring called the DrinkOrDie network. The network distributed bootlegged Windows software and copies of hit movies like *Harry Potter and the Sorcerer's Stone.* It even had its own Web site to boast of their exploits. Some members were industry insiders who stole software from their own companies, believing it should be available to all.[6]

The challenge to the marketer is to create an attractive **value proposition**; a marketplace offering that fairly and accurately sums up the value that will be realized if the product or service is purchased. There are two pitfalls to this basic idea: First, the product can be *oversold*—the value proposition is exaggerated and the buyer doesn't receive the level of satisfaction she was expecting. For example if you were to distort your record of achievements on your résumé and it turns out you don't have the experience you promised, you've oversold yourself. Second, the product can be *undersold*—the value proposition is not properly communicated and there are no takers or the product does not get assigned the worth it deserves. You may be able and willing to do a job, but if you "hide your light under a bushel" an employer may turn to someone else who does a better job of convincing her that he is the right candidate for the position.

This book is organized around the sequence of steps necessary to ensure that the appropriate value exchange occurs and that both parties to the transaction are satisfied—making it more likely they'll continue to do business in the future. These steps include:

- Making Marketing Value Decisions (Section I)
- Understanding Consumers' Value Needs (Section II)
- Creating the Value Proposition (Section III)
- Communicating the Value Proposition (Section IV)
- Delivering the Value Proposition (Section V)

For an exchange to occur, at least two people or organizations must be willing to make a trade, and each must have something the other values. Both parties must agree on the value of the exchange and how it will be carried out. Each party also must be free to accept or reject the other's terms for the exchange. Under these conditions, a gun-wielding robber's offer to "exchange" your money for your life does not constitute a valid exchange. In contrast, though someone may complain that a store's high prices are "highway robbery," an exchange occurs if they still fork over the money to buy something there—even if they grumble about it for weeks to come.

A transfer of value must occur for an exchange to take place. A politician can agree to work toward certain goals in exchange for your vote, or a minister can offer you salvation in return for your faith. Today most exchanges occur as a monetary transaction in which currency (in the form of cash, check, or credit card) is surrendered in return for a good or a service. Even the nature of this basic act is evolving, as electronic commerce systems (*e-money*) permit sales exchanges without paper money ever changing hands. Web commerce allows merchants selling virtually anything to reach customers around the world.

(ALMOST) ANYTHING CAN BE MARKETED

The "ideas, goods, and services" part of the marketing definition shows us that just about anything can be marketed. Indeed, some of the best marketers come from the ranks of services companies such as American Express or not-for-profit organizations such as Greenpeace. Even politicians, athletes, and performers use marketing to their advantage (just think about that $30 T-shirt you may have bought at a baseball game or rock concert). Ideas, such as political systems (democracy, totalitarianism), religion (Christianity, Islam), and art (Realism, Abstract Art), also compete for acceptance in a "marketplace." In this book, we'll refer to any good, service, or idea that can be marketed as a **product**, even though what is being sold may not take a physical form.

Consumer Goods and Services   **Consumer goods** are the tangible products that individual consumers purchase for personal or family use. **Services** are intangible products that we pay for and use but never own. Service transactions contribute on average more than 60 percent to the gross national product of all industrialized nations; so as we'll see in Chapter 11, marketers need to understand some of the special challenges that arise when marketing an intangible service rather than a tangible good.[7] In both cases, though, keep in mind that the consumer is looking to obtain some underlying value such as convenience, security, or status from a marketing exchange. That value can come from a variety of competing goods and services, even those that don't resemble one another on the surface. For example, both a new CD and a ticket to a local concert may cost about the same and each may provide the benefit of musical enjoyment, so consumers often have to choose among competing alternatives if they can't afford (or don't want) to buy them all.

Business-to-Business Marketing   **Business-to-business marketing** is the marketing of goods and services from one organization to another. Although we usually relate marketing to

1 *Bookmark It!*

Go through any magazine or newspaper. Find an ad for a product that you think asks too much money in return for the value promised. Find an ad for a second product that you feel gives you good value for your money. What have you learned about the concept of value from this exercise?

product ■ A tangible good, service, idea, or some combination of these that satisfies consumer or business customer needs through the exchange process; a bundle of attributes including features, functions, benefits, and uses.

consumer goods ■ The goods purchased by individual consumers for personal or family use.

services ■ Intangible products that are exchanged directly from the producer to the customer.

business-to-business marketing ■ Marketing of those goods and services that business and organizational customers need to produce other goods and services, for resale or to support their operations.

What kind of people take blind kids mountain climbing?
The same ones who take paraplegics sailing and amputees horseback riding.

NATIONAL SPORTS CENTER FOR THE DISABLED

To participate, volunteer, or help financially, visit www.nscd.org.

Nonprofit organizations around the world rely on marketing principles to attract customers.

industrial goods ▪ Goods bought by individuals or organizations for further processing or for use in doing business.

e-commerce ▪ The buying of selling of goods and services electronically, usually over the Internet.

not-for-profit organizations ▪ Organizations with charitable, educational, community, and other public service goals that buy goods and services to support their functions and to attract and serve their members.

the thousands of consumer goods begging for our dollars every day, believe it or not more goods are sold to businesses and other organizations than to consumers. These are called **industrial goods**; they are bought by organizations for further processing or for use in their business operations. For example, automakers buy tons of steel to use in the manufacturing process, and they buy computer systems to track manufacturing costs, parts inventories, new car shipments, and other information essential to operations.

Similarly, there is a lot of buzz about **e-commerce** and the buying and selling of products—books, CDs, cars, and so forth—on the Internet. We'll be talking a lot about that in this book. However, just like in the off-line world, much of the real online action is in the area of business-to-business marketing. The total value of goods and services purchased by businesses on the World Wide Web is estimated to increase from \$282 billion in 2000 to 4.3 trillion by 2005.[8] Screaming Media is one company that has used a smart marketing strategy to stand out from the dot-com crowd.[9] It provides a service for dot-coms by supplying them with Web site content tailored to their business. The company has advertised in magazines to skillfully and successfully communicate to potential clients that they can build Web sites that "scream" for attention. We'll talk more about business-to-business marketing in Chapter 7.

Not-for-Profit Marketing   You don't have to be a businessperson to use marketing principles. Many **not-for-profit organizations**, including museums, zoos, and even churches practice the marketing concept. Local governments are getting into the act as they adopt marketing techniques to create more effective taxpayer services and to attract new businesses and industries to their counties and cities. The intense competition for support of civic and charitable activities means that only those not-for-profits that meet the needs of their constituents and donors will survive.

Idea, Place, and People Marketing   Marketing principles also get people to endorse ideas or to change their behaviors in positive ways. Many organizations work hard to convince consumers to use seat belts, not to litter our highways, to engage in safe sex, or to believe that one political system is preferable to another.

Dear all,

How do Thais celebrate the New Year? We splash water on each other !!! This fun unique "Songkran" or water festival comes from the ancient inspiration to cool you down during mid April. Like all our cultural customs, each tradition is shaped from wisdom, beauty and a life in harmony with nature. Come experience them yourself.

See you real soon !

amazing
THAILAND
experience variety

Come and join our fabulous Thailand Grand Festival to celebrate the 220th Anniversary of Bangkok. Let us entertain you with joyous year-round fun!

Contact : Tourism Authority of Thailand, c/o World Publications, 304 Park Avenue South, 8th Floor, New York, N.Y. 10010, U.S.A. Tel. (1 212) 219 4655 Fax. (1 212) 219 4697 E-mail : tatny@aol.com   www.tourismthailand.org

For countries like Thailand that rely on tourism to grow economically, effective marketing strategies that lure tourists and businesses are vital to the future well being of the country and its people.

In addition to ideas, places and people also are marketable. We are all familiar with tourism marketing, whether for resorts like Club Med ("the antidote for civilization") or for states— "Virginia Is for Lovers." For many developing countries such as Thailand, tourism may be the best opportunity available for economic growth.

You may have heard the expression, "Stars are made, not born." There's a lot of truth to that. Mariah Carey may have a killer voice and Sammy Sosa may have a red-hot baseball bat, but talent alone doesn't make thousands or even millions of people buy CDs or stadium seats. Entertainment events do not just happen. People plan them. Whether a concert or a baseball game, the application of sound marketing principles helps to ensure that patrons will continue to support the activity and buy tickets. Today sports and the arts are hotbeds of activity for marketing. That means that many of the famous people you pay to see became famous with the help of shrewd marketing: They and their managers developed a "product" that they hoped would appeal to some segment of the population.

Indeed, some of the same principles that go into "creating" a celebrity apply to you. An entertainer—whether P. Diddy or Pavoratti—must "package" his talents, identify a target market that is likely to be interested, and work hard to gain exposure to these potential customers by appearing in the right musical venues. In the same way everyday people "package" themselves by summing up their accomplishments on a résumé and distributing it at venues like HotJobs.com in order to attract potential buyers.

MARKETING'S TOOLS: THE MARKETING MIX

The "conception, pricing, promotion, and distribution" part of the definition of marketing means that whether it's a box of detergent, a sports medicine clinic, a rap song, or a résumé posted on HotJobs.com, a product must be invented or developed, assigned value and meaning, and made available to interested consumers.

In determining the best way to present a good or a service for consumers' consideration, the marketer has many decisions to make, and so he or she needs many tools. The marketer's strategic toolbox is called the **marketing mix**, which consists of the tools that are used together to create a desired response among a set of predefined consumers. These tools include the product itself, the price of the product, the place where it is available, and the promotional activities that introduce it to consumers. Just as a radio DJ puts together a collection of separate songs (a musical mix) to create a certain mood, the idea of a mix in this context reminds us that no single marketing activity is sufficient to accomplish the organization's objectives.

The elements of the marketing mix are commonly known as the Four Ps: product, price, promotion, and place. As Figure 1.1 shows, each P is a piece of the puzzle that must be combined with other pieces. While we talk about the four Ps as separate parts of a firm's marketing strategy, in reality, nothing could be farther from the truth. Product, price, promotion, and place decisions are totally interdependent. Decisions about any single one of the four are affected by and affect every other marketing mix decision. For example, assume a firm is introducing a superior quality product, one that is more expensive to produce than its existing line of products. The price the firm charges for this new product must cover these higher costs, but in addition, the firm must create advertising and other promotional strategies to convey a top-quality image. At the same time, the price of the product must cover not only the costs of production but also the cost of advertising. Furthermore, the firm must include high-end retailers in its distribution strategy. The elements of the marketing mix work hand in hand.

We'll examine these components of the marketing mix in detail later in this book. For now, let's briefly look at each P to gain some insight into its meaning and role in the marketing mix.

Product   As we've seen, the product is a good, a service, an idea, a place, a person—whatever is offered for sale in the exchange. This aspect of the marketing mix includes the design and packaging of a good, as well as its physical features and any associated services, such as free delivery. So we can see that the product is a combination of many different elements, all of which are important to the product's success. As we said earlier, when it comes to marketing BRAND YOU, you are the product. Everything—your skills, your educational background,

marketing mix ■ A combination of the product itself, the price of the product, the place where it is made available, and the activities that introduce it to consumers that creates a desired response among a set of predefined consumers.

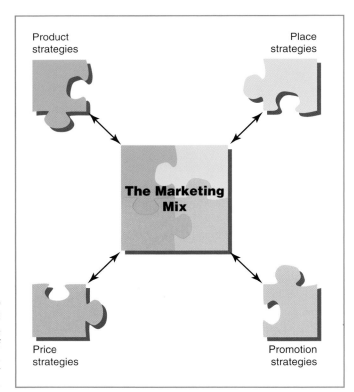

FIGURE 1.1

The Marketing Mix

What marketing is all about! The Marketing Mix is a combination of the four Ps—product, price, place, and promotion—all used together to satisfy customer needs.

often even the way you look and dress—combines to form a value proposition that others choose to "buy" or ignore. That explains why a company like HotJobs can be so successful.

When the British firm Virgin introduced Virgin Cola in the United States, the company attempted to make this new product stand out from the competition through its distinctive packaging. Advertising that introduced the brand told customers about the curved squeezable bottles. "If all you got is Va Va, You got to get some Voom; It's in the curvy bottle, Yeah, Virgin Drinks' got Voom. . . .Virgin puts the Voom in you Va Va."[10] We're not quite sure what that means, but it does get your attention! Whether the focus is on the bottle or some other element, the product is a very important part of the marketing mix. More about this in Section III when we talk about creating the value proposition.

Price Price is the assignment of value, or the amount the consumer must exchange to receive the offering. When BRAND YOU is offered on the job market, for example, a certain value is assigned to that product we call a salary.

The decision about how much to charge for the product is not simple—and of course has a lot to do with market conditions and what people are willing to pay: You may believe BRAND YOU is worth $100,000, but if your competitors are willing to work for $20,000 you may be disappointed!

A price is often used as a way to increase consumers' interest in a product. For example, in 2000 the American cranberry industry faced a dilemma. Its analysts predicted that producers would not be able to sell all of the cranberries that were going to be harvested that year. In fact, the Cranberry Marketing Commmittee recommended that growers reduce the volume of their 2000 crop to keep prices at a reasonable level. Ocean Spray, the dominant firm in the industry, had another idea. Research showed that if the wholesale price of the Ocean Spray cranberry juice were lowered by 30 cents per bottle, volume would grow by 10 percent—just the amount needed to drink up the cranberry surplus and make a profit. The price change would not only make the product more affordable, but it would also lure new customers to the product.[11] So, price is also an important part of creating the value proposition, and we'll return to this concept in Section III.

Promotion **Promotion** includes all of the activities marketers undertake to inform consumers or organizations about their products, and to encourage potential customers to buy these products. Promotions can take many forms including personal selling, television advertising, store coupons, billboards, magazine ads, and publicity releases. There's a reason people pay money to consultants who advise them about job résumés and drop big bucks on "dress for

promotion ■ The coordination of a marketer's marketing communications efforts to influence attitudes or behavior; the coordination of efforts by a marketer to inform or persuade consumers or organizations about goods, services, or ideas.

How did my soul get way out here?

HUMMER. like nothing else.

Sometimes you find yourself in the middle of nowhere. And sometimes in the middle of nowhere you find yourself. The legendary H1.

Makers of the Hummer are using the Internet to promote their product. In the Hummer's advertising campaign, consumers were encouraged to go to the Web site and view movies showing some of the Hummer's many different capabilities.

success" outfits and so on—these actions help to ensure that BRAND YOU is positively represented to prospective buyers. This is part of communicating the value proposition—we'll go into more detail about these important issues in Section IV.

place ■ The availability of the product to the customer at the desired time and location.

2 *Bookmark It!*

The elements of the marketing mix depend on each other. For a product such as an expensive notebook computer, what is the relationship between price and product? Between product and promotion? Between price and place?

Place **Place** refers to the availability of the product to the customer at the desired time and location. If BRAND YOU is not one of the résumés posted on the only job site where an employer is searching, there's no way this product will be considered even if (as we all know) BRAND YOU is superior to the other brands that are posted on that site. As we'll see in Chapter 14, this P is related to the *channels of distribution*, which is the set of firms that works together to get a product from a producer to a consumer. For clothing or electronics, this channel includes local retailers as well as other outlets such as retail sites on the World Wide Web that strive to offer the right quantity of products in the right styles at the right time. In the case of BRAND YOU, an executive recruiter who visits your university might be a channel member.

MARKETING IS A PROCESS

"Marketing is a process of planning and executing." This part of the definition of marketing means that marketing is not a one-shot operation. Just as BRAND YOU isn't something that was developed overnight, building a marketing strategy entails a series of steps involving both careful thought (planning) and action (executing).

The idea of marketing as a process tells us that successful marketing exchanges occur continually over time. For many marketers, it is no longer acceptable to view doing business as a one-time deal in which a company tries to "put one over" on its customers by delivering a minimal product at a maximum price. The concept of **customer relationship management (CRM)** sees marketing as a process of building long-term relationships with customers to keep them satisfied and to keep them coming back. So far we've learned what marketing is—providing products that satisfy customer needs. Now let's move on to see how marketing is done.

customer relationship management (CRM) ▪ A philosophy that sees marketing as a process of building long-term relationships with customers to keep them satisfied and to keep them coming back.

How Is Marketing Done?

When it's done right, marketing is a decision process in which marketing managers determine the strategies that will help the organization meet its long-term objectives. To do this, marketers develop and implement a **marketing plan**. Of course, if we told you exactly how marketing is done right now, we'd "give away the ending," and you wouldn't have any reason to read the rest of this book. So, we'll keep you in suspense. For now, though, we will briefly summarize how marketers go about the business of making decisions and planning their actions. We'll also take a brief look at several key marketing strategies—the strategies marketers use to identify customers and offer goods and services they believe will satisfy the needs and wants of these customers.

marketing plan ▪ A document that describes the marketing environment, outlines the marketing objectives and strategy, and identifies who will be responsible for carrying out each part of the marketing strategy.

MARKETING PLANNING

The first phase of marketing planning is analyzing the marketing environment. This means understanding the organization's current strengths and weaknesses by assessing factors that might help or hinder the development and marketing of products. The analysis must also take into account the opportunities and threats the organization will encounter in the marketplace, such as the actions of competitors, cultural and technological changes, and the economy. These broad issues also apply to BRAND YOU. For example, the demand for people with computer programming skills may rise and fall depending on the health of the software industry and the number of out-of-work, Silicon Valley types competing for jobs. Especially since the events that began on September 11, 2001, many qualified people in industries such as dot-coms, travel, and advertising have unfortunately had a harder time finding a market for their value propositions.

Firms (or individuals) engaging in marketing planning may need to ask such questions as:

- What product benefits will our core customers be looking for in three to five years?
- What capabilities does our firm have that set it apart from the competition?
- What additional customer groups might provide important market segments for us in the future?
- How will changes in technology affect our production process, our communication strategy, and our distribution strategy?
- What changes in social and cultural values are occurring that will impact our market in the next few years?
- How will consumers' awareness of environmental issues affect their attitudes toward our domestic and overseas manufacturing facilities?
- What legal and regulatory issues may affect our business in both domestic and global markets?

Answers to these and other questions provide the foundation for developing an organization's marketing plan.

In the marketing plan, managers set specific marketing objectives and determine how to meet these objectives.

In marketing planning for BRAND YOU, you no doubt began with some objectives—such as getting an exciting job after graduation. In fact, you probably chose your college major to meet those objectives.

A major marketing decision for most organizations is which products to market to which consumers, without turning off other consumers at the same time. Some firms choose to reach

2 *Bookmark It!*

To understand what marketing is all about, pretend you are looking for a job (if you aren't already). You need to market yourself. Using the four Ps, write a description of your product, price, place, and promotion strategies.

mass market ■ All possible customers in a market, regardless of the differences in their specific needs and wants.

market segment ■ A distinct group of customers within a larger market who are similar to one another in some way and whose needs differ from other customers in the larger market.

target market ■ The market segments on which an organization focuses its marketing plan and toward which it directs its marketing efforts.

market position ■ The way in which the target market perceives the product in comparison to competitors' brands.

3 Bookmark It!

We've already applied the four Ps to marketing BRAND YOU. Now, go through the steps in marketing planning and write a brief plan to market yourself to prospective employers.

as many customers as possible by offering their products to a **mass market**, which consists of all possible customers in a market, regardless of the differences in their specific needs and wants. Marketing planning then becomes a matter of developing a basic product and a single strategy for reaching everyone.

Although this approach can be cost-effective, the organization risks losing potential customers to competitors whose marketing plans are directed at meeting the needs of specific groups within the market. The success of an organization's marketing efforts is its ability to find, reach, and satisfy a market. For example, an increasing number of women's Internet sites have popped up on the Web. America Online and NBC have developed the online community iVillage. Other sites aimed at women include Women.com, Women's Financial Network, Totalwoman, bigstar.com, ePregnancy.com, Women's Consumer Network, WomenOutdoors.com, working-woman.com, and SocialNet.[12] These sites don't expect to attract many male surfers, but that's part of the trade-off they make in deciding to appeal to women only.

A **market segment** is a distinct group of customers within a larger market who are similar to one another in some way and whose needs differ from other customers in the larger market. Automakers such as Ford, General Motors, and BMW offer different automobiles for different segments in the marketplace. Depending on its goals and resources, a company may choose to focus on one segment. The chosen market segment becomes the organization's **target market** toward which it directs its efforts. Target marketing is a strategic decision process that determines both the market and the tactics used to reach it. Target marketing has three steps: 1) segmenting the market, 2) selecting a target market, and 3) positioning the product for that market. A product's **market position** is how the target market perceives the product in comparison to competitor's brands.

To achieve a competitive advantage over rivals in the minds of consumers, the marketer carefully blends the Four Ps of the marketing mix. That is, a product is developed to meet the needs of the target market, as are its price, place, and promotion strategies. These strategies may vary from one country to another or may be injected with fresh ideas over time to maintain or change the product's position.

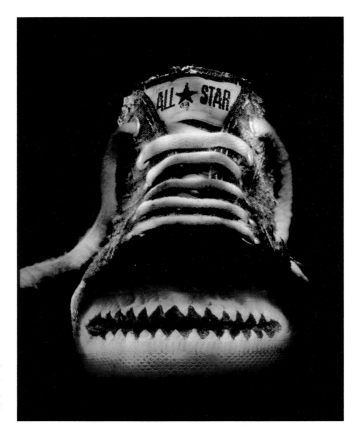

This Thai ad for Converse positions its All Stars as a sneaker for aggressive athletic performance.

LOOKING FOR CUSTOMERS BEYOND YOUR OWN BORDERS

Many companies know that they must look for potential target markets beyond their own geographical borders to compete in today's world economy. Modern marketers are busy meeting the needs of people all around the world, especially when the demand for products at home flattens.

One newly emerging trend for multinational companies is to focus on selling products to developing countries, a trend some refer to as B2-4B—"business to four billion"—which refers to the approximate number of potential customers in these markets.[13] Hewlett Packard, for example, believes that much of the computer firm's future growth could come from developing countries. For several years beginning in 2001, the company plans to sell, lease or donate $1 billion in products and services to governments, development agencies, and not-for-profit groups in these areas. In fact, to satisfy the needs of this market, Hewlett Packard is developing low-power or solar-powered devices that will connect to the Net wirelessly or via satellites. But Hewlett Packard's Third-World efforts are not just philanthropic. It believes that this kind of investment will allow HP to tap into the huge potential markets that will develop in these countries.

Throughout the text, we will emphasize the need for marketers to think globally—even if they act only locally. Smart marketers know that whether in Third-World countries or in developed countries, long-term success means finding customers wherever they are, from Minneapolis to Manila.

When Did Marketing Begin? The Evolution of a Concept

Now that we have an idea of how the marketing process works, let's take a step back and see how this process developed in "the old days." Although it sounds like good ol' common sense to us, the notion that businesses and other organizations succeed when they satisfy customers' needs actually is a pretty recent idea. Before the 1950s, marketing was basically a means of making production more efficient. Let's take a quick look at how the marketing discipline has developed. Table 1.1 tells us about some of the more recent events in this marketing history.

THE PRODUCTION ORIENTATION

Many people say that Henry Ford's Model T changed America forever. Even from the start in 1908, when the "Tin Lizzie," or "flivver" as the T was known, sold for $825, Henry Ford continued to make improvements in production. By 1912, Ford got so efficient that the car sold for $575, a price which even the Ford employees who *made* the car could afford.[14] As the price continued to drop, Ford sold even more flivvers. By 1921, The Model T Ford had 60 percent of the new car market. In 1924, the ten-millionth Model T rolled off the assembly line. The Model-T story is perhaps the most well-known and most successful example of an organization that focuses on the most efficient production and distribution of products.

Ford's focus illustrates a **production orientation**, which works best in a seller's market when demand is greater than supply because it focuses on the most efficient ways to produce and distribute products. Essentially, consumers have to take whatever is available (there weren't a whole lot of other "Tin Lizzies" competing for drivers in the 1920s). Under these conditions, marketing plays a relatively insignificant role—the goods literally sell themselves because people have no other choices. Indeed, in the former Soviet Union, the centralized government set production quotas and weary shoppers lined up (often for hours) to purchase whatever happened to be on a store's shelves at the time.

product orientation ■
Management philosophy that emphasizes the most efficient ways to produce and distribute products.

Firms that focus on a production orientation tend to view the market as a homogeneous group that will be satisfied with the basic function of a product. Sometimes this view is too narrow. For example, Procter & Gamble's Ivory soap has been in decline for some time because P&G viewed the brand as plain old soap, not as a cleansing product that could provide other benefits as well. Ivory soap lost business to newer deodorant and "beauty" soaps containing cold cream that "cleaned up" in this market.[15]

TABLE **1.1**

Marketing Milestones

Year	Marketing Event
1955	Ray Kroc opens his first McDonald's. Marlboro Man makes his debut.
1956	Lever Brothers launches Wisk, America's first liquid laundry detergent.
1957	Ford rolls out Edsel, loses more than $250 million in two years.
1959	Mattel introduces Barbie.
1960	The FDA approves Searle's Enovid as the first oral contraceptive.
1961	Procter & Gamble launches Pampers.
1962	Wal-Mart, Kmart, Target, and Woolco open their doors.
1963	The Pepsi Generation kicks off the cola wars.
1964	Blue Ribbon Sports (now known as Nike) ships its first shoes. Ford launches the Mustang.
1965	Donald Fisher opens The Gap, a jeans-only store in San Francisco.
1971	Cigarette advertising is banned on radio and television.
1973	Federal Express begins overnight delivery services.
1976	Sol Prices opens first warehouse club store in San Diego.
1979	Bernard Marcus and Arthur Blank start Home Depot in Atlanta.
1980	Ted Turner creates CNN.
1981	MTV begins.
1982	Gannett launches *USA Today*.
1983	Chrysler introduces minivans.
1984	AT&T long-distance monopoly ends. Apple Computer introduces Macintosh.
1985	New Coke is launched; Old Coke is brought back 79 days later.
1990	Saturn, GM's first new car division since 1919, rolls out its first car.
1993	Phillip Morris reduces price of Marlboros by 40 cents a pack, loses $13.4 billion in stock market value in one day.
1994	In largest switch in ad history, IBM yanks its business from scores of agencies worldwide and hands its entire account to Ogilvy & Mather.
1997	McDonald's gives away Teenie Beanie Babies with Happy Meals. Consumer response is so overwhelming that McDonald's is forced to take out ads apologizing for their inability to meet demand. Nearly 100 million Happy Meals are sold during the promotion.[a]
1998	Germany's Daimler-Benz acquires America's Chrysler Corp. for more than $38 billion in stock to create a new global automaking giant called Daimler-Chrysler.[b]

Source: Patricia Sellers, "To Avoid Trampling, Get Ahead of the Mass," *Fortune* (1994) 201–202, except as noted.

[a]Tod Taylor, "The Beanie Factor," *Brandweek* (16 June 1997): 22–27.

[b]Jennifer Laabs, "Daimler-Benz and Chrysler: A Merger of Global HR Proportions," *Workforce* (July 1998): 13.

THE SELLING ORIENTATION

When product availability exceeds demand in a buyer's market, businesses may engage in the "hard sell" in which salespeople aggressively push their wares. During the Great Depression in the 1930s when money was scarce for most people, firms shifted their focus from a product orientation to moving their goods any way they could.

selling orientation ■ A managerial view of marketing as a sales function, or a way to move products out of warehouses to reduce inventory.

This **selling orientation** means that management views marketing as a sales function, or a way to move products out of warehouses so that inventories don't pile up. The selling orientation gained in popularity after World War II. During the war, the United States dramatically increased its industrial capacity to manufacture tanks, combat boots, parachutes, and countless other wartime goods. After the war this industrial capacity was converted to producing consumer goods.

Consumers eagerly bought all the things they couldn't get during the war years, but once these initial needs and wants were satisfied, they got more selective. The race for consumers' hearts and pocketbooks was on. The selling orientation prevailed well into the 1950s. But consumers as a rule don't like to be pushed, and the hard sell gave marketing a bad image.

After World War II, the peacetime economy boomed. Americans had plenty of money, and manufacturers used the increased factory capacity created in wartime to turn out an abundance of civilian favorites. As this 1949 Ford ad indicates, suddenly people had a lot of choices and a bounty of products awaited the returning GIs and their young families.

Companies that still follow a selling orientation tend to be more successful at making one-time sales rather than building repeat business. This focus is most likely to be found among companies that sell *unsought goods*—products that people don't tend to buy without some prodding. For example, most of us aren't exactly "dying" to shop for cemetery plots, so some encouragement may be necessary to splurge on a final resting place.

THE MARKETING CONCEPT: A CONSUMER ORIENTATION

At Direct Tire Sales in Watertown, Massachusetts, customers discover an unusual sight: The customer lounge is clean, there is free coffee with fresh cream and croissants, employees wear ties, and the company will even pay your cab fare home if your car isn't ready on time. People don't mind paying 10 percent to 15 percent more for these extra services.[16] Direct Tire Sales has found that it pays to have a **consumer orientation** that satisfies customers' needs and wants.

consumer orientation ■ A management philosophy that focuses on ways to satisfy customers' needs and wants.

As the world's most successful firms began to adopt a consumer orientation, marketers had a way to outdo the competition—and marketing's importance was also elevated in the firm. Marketers did research to segment markets, assisted in tailoring products to the needs of different consumer groups, and did an even better job of designing marketing messages than in the days of the selling orientation.

The marketing world was humming along nicely, but then inflation in the 1970s and recession in the 1980s took their toll on company profits. The marketing concept needed a boost. Firms had to do more than meet consumers' needs—they had to do this better than the competition and do it repeatedly. They increasingly concentrated on improving the quality of their products. By the early 1990s, total quality—a management effort to involve all employees from the assembly line onward in continuous product quality improvement—was well entrenched in the marketing community.

Firms like Avon have a "New Era" orientation. Avon practices social marketing through a variety of activities including its 3-day race to raise money for breast cancer programs.

THE NEW ERA ORIENTATION

Yet another fundamental change in marketing is occurring now, as the goal of long-term growth continues. Although the customer is still number one, many of today's forward-thinking organizations are seeing their commitment to quality as more than simply satisfying consumers' needs. This **New Era orientation** to marketing means a devotion to excellence in designing and producing products that benefit the customer *plus* the firm's employees, shareholders, and communities.

One outgrowth of this new way of thinking is customer relationship management, which we've already mentioned. Another is the social marketing concept, which maintains that marketers must satisfy customers' needs in ways that also benefit society—and that also are profitable for the firm. This perspective is even more important since the terrorist attacks of 2001, which led many people and firms to reexamine their values and redouble their commitments to community and country.

Big and small firms alike practice this philosophy. Their efforts include satisfying society's environmental and social needs for a cleaner, safer environment by developing recyclable packaging, adding extra safety features such as car air bags, voluntarily modifying a manufacturing process to reduce pollution, and sponsoring campaigns to address social problems.

Avon Products is one firm that believes social marketing is good for its customers and good for the company. For nearly 10 years, Avon has supported one and only one cause, breast cancer. Since the inception of the program in 1993, Avon has raised over $55 million for breast cancer programs through a variety of fund-raising channels. These efforts include Avon's "3-Day" event, a long-distance walking event in San Francisco, Boston, Atlanta, Chicago, Los Angeles, and New York.[17]

THE E-MARKETING ERA

We cannot conclude a discussion of the evolution of marketing without discussing today's e-marketing era, a time when more and more firms—like HotJobs—are using the Internet to connect with consumers. Perhaps the Internet provides the ultimate opportunity for implementation of the marketing concept in that it allows a firm to personalize its message and products to better meet the needs of each individual consumer. For example, visitors to Reflect.com can customize their cosmetics order for their specific complexion and beauty needs—and their purchases even come in packages bearing their name.

New Era orientation ■ A management philosophy in which marketing means a devotion to excellence in designing and producing products that benefit the customer plus the firm's employees, shareholders, and communities.

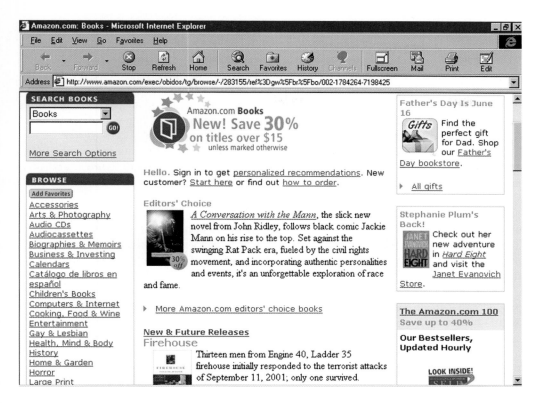

The Internet allows marketers to develop the ultimate in target marketing—strategies geared to segments of one. Sophisticated technology knows when a customer returns to a Web site. This means companies such as Internet book retailer Amazon.com can provide different reading recommendations for each shopper based on that individual's specific literary preferences.

Although in recent years dot-com companies have taken a beating in the marketplace, many analysts believe (and we agree) that this is just a preliminary shakeout—the heyday of the Internet is yet to come. Indeed, some marketing analysts suggest that the Internet has created a *paradigm shift* for business, meaning that companies must adhere to a new model or pattern of how to do business.

Why Is Marketing Important?

The basic principles of marketing apply to the sale of canned peas, to the delivery of food and clothing to needy people, and to the promotion of a symphony orchestra. Because meeting the needs of consumers and society in an efficient way touches on so many aspects of our daily experience, it's important to think about the role marketing plays in our lives.

MARKETING CREATES UTILITY

Marketing activities play a major role in the creation of **utility**, which means that a product provides benefits when it is used. By working to ensure that people have the type of product they want, where and when they want it, the marketing system makes our lives easier.

Form utility is the benefit marketing provides by transforming raw materials into finished products, as when a dress manufacturer combines cotton, thread, buttons, and zippers to create a bridesmaid's gown. *Place utility* is the benefit marketing provides by making products available where customers want them. The most sophisticated evening gown sewn in New York's garment district is of little use to a bridesmaid in Kansas City if it isn't shipped to her in time. *Time utility* is the benefit marketing provides by storing products until they are needed. Some women rent their wedding gowns instead of buying them and wear them only once (they hope!). Finally, *possession utility* is the benefit marketing provides by allowing the consumer to own, use, and enjoy the product. The bridal store provides access to a range of styles and colors that would not be available to a woman outfitting a bridal party on her own.

MARKETING'S ROLE IN THE FIRM

The importance assigned to marketing activities depends on whether the organization has adopted the marketing concept. Top management in some firms is very marketing oriented

4 *Bookmark It!*

Visit several Web sites for some popular retailers— www.eddiebauer.com, www.gap.com, www.landsend.com, www.bananarepublic.com. See if you can find information on the sites that suggest that the firms have adopted the New Era marketing concept.

utility ■ The usefulness or benefit consumers receive from a product.

(especially when the chief executive officer comes from the marketing ranks), whereas in other companies marketing is an afterthought. Sometimes the company uses the term *marketing* when what it really means is sales or advertising. In the case of organizations, particularly not-for-profit ones that are just waking up to the idea of marketing, there may not be anyone in the company specifically designated as "the marketing person." In contrast, some firms that focus on total quality are realizing that the basic marketing concept applies to all aspects of the firm's activities. As a result, there has been a trend toward integrating marketing with other business functions instead of setting it apart as a separate function.

A firm's marketing decisions must affect—and be affected by—its other operations. Marketing managers must work with financial and accounting officers to figure out whether products are profitable, to set marketing budgets, and to determine prices. They must work with people in manufacturing to be sure that products are produced on time and in the right quantities. Anticipating demand is important, especially when marketers do *too good* a job at creating desire for a product and production is unable to keep up. For example, as noted in Table 1.1, a few years ago McDonald's almost had a McMarketing disaster on its hands when the company drastically underestimated how many millions of fanatic collectors would line up for the Teenie Beanie Babies it was giving away—lots of UnHappy Meals resulted.

Marketers also must work with research and development (R&D) specialists to create products that meet consumers' needs. The experience of Stratos Product Development, a Seattle industrial design firm, illustrates how teamwork can create products quickly. When it set about developing a passenger video player for British Airways, Stratos' marketers brought together mechanical specialists, customers, and British Airways personnel in brainstorming sessions where everyone could propose new ideas. The system came together in four months, one-third the time estimated for the project.[18]

MARKETING'S ROLE IN OUR DAILY LIVES: OPERA TO OPRAH

We are surrounded by marketers' creations in the form of advertisements, stores, and products competing for our attention and our dollars. Marketers filter much of what we learn about the world, such as when we see images of rich or beautiful people on TV commercials or magazines. Ads show us how we should act and what we should own. Marketing's influence extends from "serious" goods and services such as health care to "fun" things such as extreme

NASCAR racing is growing in popularity among women as well as men. As a result, more marketers (who are trying to target female consumers) have made sponsoring race drivers and their cars part of their marketing strategy.

skateboarding and hip-hop music (though many people take these products as seriously as their health).

Popular Culture **Popular culture** consists of the music, movies, sports, books, celebrities, and other forms of entertainment that the mass market consumes. Marketers play an important role in providing the materials that become part of this culture. For example, marketers for Nascar racing have worked hard to upgrade its image from a regional attraction to a more mainstream sport. Races now attract millions of fans from around the United States so major advertisers vie to put their logos on the top racers' cars—and pay as much as $15 million for the privilege.[19] While originally a male-only venue, millions of women now enjoy the sport. Advertisers of products targeted toward women, such as Tide laundry detergent, now recognize this and put their logos on top drivers' cars also.

The relationship between marketing and popular culture is a two-way street. The goods and services that are popular at any point in time often mirror changes in the larger society. Consider, for example, some U.S. products that reflected underlying cultural changes at the time they were introduced.

- The TV dinner signaled changes in family structure, such as a movement away from the traditional family dinner hour filled with conversation about the day's events.
- Cosmetics made of natural materials and not animal tested reflected social concerns about pollution and animal rights.
- Condoms marketed in pastel carrying cases intended for female buyers signaled changing attitudes toward sexual responsibility.

Marketing and Myths Marketing messages often communicate myths, stories containing symbolic elements that express the shared emotions and ideals of a culture.[20] Consider, for example, how McDonald's takes on mythical qualities. To some, the golden arches are virtually synonymous with American culture. They offer sanctuary to Americans in foreign lands who are grateful to know exactly what to expect once they enter. Basic struggles of good versus evil are played out in the fantasy world of McDonald's advertising, as when Ronald McDonald confounds the Hamburglar. McDonald's even runs Hamburger University where fast-food majors learn how to make the perfect burger.

MARKETING'S ROLE IN SOCIETY

What about marketing's impact on more serious issues? In many ways we are at the mercy of marketers, because we trust them to sell us products that are safe and perform as promised. We

popular culture ■ The music, movies, sports, books, celebrities, and other forms of entertainment consumed by the mass market.

McDonald's golden arches take on a mythical quality for many consumers worldwide.

also trust them to price and distribute these products fairly. Conflicts often arise in business when the pressure to succeed in the marketplace provokes dishonest business practices—Enron as a case in point. This is why many universities and corporations are teaching and reinforcing ethical behavior.

Ethical Behavior Is Good Business Companies usually find that stressing ethics and social responsibility also is good business, at least in the long run. Some find out the hard way. For example, Chrysler Corporation was accused of resetting the odometers of new cars that managers had actually driven prior to sale. The company admitted the practice only after some managers tried to get out of paying speeding tickets by claiming that their speedometers—and odometers—didn't work because the cables were disconnected![21] These actions caused the company great embarrassment, and it took years of hard work to restore the public's trust.

In contrast, Procter & Gamble voluntarily withdrew its Rely tampons from the market following reports of women who had suffered toxic shock syndrome (TSS). Although scientists did not claim a causal link between the usage of Rely and the onset of TSS, the company agreed with the Food and Drug Administration to undertake extensive advertising notifying women of the symptoms of TSS and asking them to return their boxes of Rely for a refund. The company took a $75 million loss and sacrificed an unusually successful new product that had already captured about one-quarter of the billion-dollar sanitary product market.[22]

Social and Ethical Criticisms of Marketing Whether intentionally or not, some marketers do violate their bond of trust with consumers, and unfortunately the "dark side" of marketing often is the subject of harsh criticism. In some cases, these violations are illegal, such as when a retailer adopts a "bait-and-switch" selling strategy, luring consumers into the store with promises of inexpensive products with the sole intent of getting them to switch to higher-priced goods.

In other cases, marketing practices have detrimental effects on society even though they are not actually illegal—just think about all the "spam" e-mail you get every day. Some alcohol and tobacco companies advertise in low-income neighborhoods where abuse of these products is a big problem. Other alcohol and tobacco companies sponsor commercials depicting groups of people in an unfavorable light to get the attention of a target market. For example, many people complained that Coors beer's "Swedish bikini team" campaign demeaned women in order to appeal to men. Let's consider some of the criticisms of marketing and some responses to those criticisms.

5 Bookmark It!

If you know that a company stresses its ethical practices, are you more likely to give it your business? How is it that you know the company is ethical—does it market itself that way? Find an ad or a Web site for a company in which the marketing of its ethical practices is evident.

5 Bookmark It!

How does marketing make your life better? Are there ways marketing hurts your life? What are some ways marketing might hurt unique groups of people such as the handicapped and the homeless?

The American Association of Advertising Agencies tries to fight the perception that marketers make people buy things they don't want or need.

Real People, Real Choices:

How It Worked Out at HotJobs.com

Dimitri selected option 2. HotJobs.com developed targeted, localized messages that were customized for different cities and for different industries. The messages shared basic design elements, and they all sent a unique message of optimism. HotJobs was able to cut through the clutter and establish awareness with job seekers and credibility with hiring companies. The company also tried innovative and inexpensive media like Elevator News Network, which runs advertisements in the elevators of major corporations. It ran commercials in New York and Los Angeles movie theater lobbies. In addition, a series of billboards touted HotJobs in major cities, tailored to each. Signs in Dallas read "Break from the Herd," while those in San Francisco featured a drawing of the Golden Gate Bridge with the text "Build a Bridge to Your Future."

This focused campaign paid off for HotJobs.com. Monster.com continued to promote the idea of searching for jobs online, helping the market to continue its growth. Meanwhile, HotJobs quickly established itself as the number-one job board site in several key cities like New York, Los Angeles, and San Francisco. Some competitors that instead pursued the national approach ran out of money and dropped out of the race. By September 2001, the firm had pulled ahead of Monster in online "hits" (visitors to its site) per month. According to Media Metrics, a service that tracks Web hits, HotJobs.com is now the number-one online career site.

Unable to shake HotJobs from its rearview mirror, Monster offered to buy HotJobs and gain further control of the number-one position in the category. However, the Federal Trade Commission was concerned that the combination of the number-one and number-two brands would leave companies without a choice for national, online recruitment advertising. The regulatory agency launched a detailed review of situation. During the delay Yahoo! (a major shopping Web site we will learn more about in Chapter 6) decided it wanted to diversify by entering the recruitment business as well. This company made a better offer to HotJobs and Dimitri accepted the Yahoo! deal.

HotJobs created billboards in several major cities that featured a message customized to each place. This billboard appeared in San Francisco.

1. Marketers create artificial needs. The marketing system has come under fire from both ends of the political spectrum. On the one hand, some members of the religious right believe that advertising contributes to the moral breakdown of society by presenting images of sinful pleasure. On the other hand, some members of the left argue that the same promises of material pleasure function to buy off people who would otherwise be revolutionaries working to change the system.[23] The leftists claim that the system creates demand only its products can satisfy.

A RESPONSE: A need is a basic motive, while a want represents one way that society has taught us that the need can be satisfied. For example, although thirst is biologically based, we are taught to want Coca-Cola rather than, say, goat's milk to satisfy that thirst. The need is already there; marketers simply recommend ways to satisfy it. In some circumstances, however, the marketer can engineer an environment to make it more probable that a need will arise. This occurs, for example, when bars supply free peanuts to patrons to stimulate thirst.

2. Marketing teaches us to value people for what they own rather than who they are. Goods are arbitrarily linked to desirable qualities, so we learn that we can be popular, happy, and fulfilled only if we buy these products.

> A RESPONSE: Products meet existing needs, and advertising only helps to communicate their availability. Advertising is an important source of consumer information.[24] It is a service for which consumers are willing to pay because the information it provides reduces the time and effort needed to learn about the product.

3. Marketers promise miracles. Marketing leads consumers to believe that products have magical properties—the products will transform their lives. Marketers provide simplistic answers to complex problems.

> A RESPONSE: Marketers do not know enough about people to manipulate them. In testimony before the Federal Trade Commission, one executive observed that although people think that advertisers have an endless source of magical tricks and scientific techniques to manipulate them, in reality, the industry is successful when it tries to sell good products and unsuccessful when selling poor ones.[25]

Chapter Summary

1. State generally what marketing is all about.

Marketing is the process of planning and executing the conception, pricing, promotion, and distribution of ideas, goods, and services to create exchanges that satisfy individual and organizational objectives. Organizations that seek to assure their long-term profitability by identifying and satisfying customers' needs and wants have adopted the marketing concept. Marketing activities are important to firms that provide goods and services to individual and business consumers, as well as not-for-profit organizations and those that focus on sports, entertainment, places, people, and ideas.

2. Define the marketing mix.

The marketing mix is the four Ps of marketing: product, price, place, and promotion. The product is what satisfies customer needs. Products can be goods, services, or ideas. The price is the assigned value or amount to be exchanged for the product. The place or channel of distribution gets the product to the customer. Promotion is the organization's efforts to persuade customers to buy the product. The four Ps are strongly interrelated, so decisions about one P influence the others as well.

3. Understand the basics of marketing planning.

The strategic process of marketing planning begins with an assessment of factors within the organization and in the external environment that could help or hinder the development and marketing of products. Based on this analysis, marketers set objectives and develop strategies. Many firms use a target marketing strategy in which they divide the overall market into segments and then target the most attractive one. Then they design the marketing mix to gain a competitive position in the target market.

4. Describe the evolution of the marketing concept.

Early in the twentieth century, firms like the Ford Motor Company followed a production orientation in which they focused on the most efficient ways to produce and distribute products. Beginning in the 1930s, some firms adopted a selling orientation that encouraged salespeople to aggressively sell products to customers. In the 1950s organizations adopted a consumer orientation that focused on customer satisfaction. This led to the development of the marketing concept. Today many firms are moving toward a New Era orientation that includes not only a commitment to quality but also a concern for both economic and social profit. Outgrowths of this orientation are relationship marketing, which focuses on building long-term relationships with customers, and social marketing, which advocates social changes and promotes worthy causes. In today's e-marketing era, the

Internet provides the ultimate opportunity for implementation of the marketing concept. With the Internet, marketers can personalize marketing communications, providing different information for each customer based on that individual's specific wants and needs.

5. Explain how marketing is important to all of us.

Marketing of goods and services creates form utility, place and time utility, and possession utility. The importance of marketing within an organization depends on whether the firm has adopted the marketing concept. Firms that haven't may simply see marketing as a sales or advertising function, whereas firms that focus on total quality integrate the marketing concept into all business functions. Marketing influences popular culture, and popular culture influences marketing. Marketing messages are often based on cultural myths, or stories about things or behaviors valued by a society. Although many companies are stressing ethics and social responsibility, some firms have been criticized for creating artificial needs, teaching people to value things too much and promising miracles.

Chapter Review

▇ MARKETING CONCEPTS:
TESTING YOUR KNOWLEDGE

1. Briefly, explain what marketing is.
2. How does marketing facilitate exchange?
3. Define the terms consumer goods, services, and industrial goods.
4. List and describe the elements of the marketing mix?
5. What are target markets? How do marketers select and reach target markets?
6. Explain needs, wants, and demands. What is the role of marketing in each of these?
7. Trace the evolution of the marketing concept.
8. What is the e-marketing era?
9. What is utility? How does marketing create different forms of utility?
10. What is the role of marketing in the firm?
11. How is marketing related to popular culture?
12. What are some criticisms of marketing?

▇ MARKETING CONCEPTS:
DISCUSSING CHOICES AND ISSUES

1. Have you ever pirated software? How about music? Is it ethical to give or receive software instead of paying for it? Does the answer depend on the person's motivation and/or if he or she could otherwise afford to buy the product?
2. In both developed and developing countries, not all firms have implemented programs that follow the marketing concept. Can you think of firms that still operate with a production orientation? A selling orientation? What changes would you recommend for these firms?
3. The marketing concept focuses on the ability of marketing to satisfy customer needs. As a typical college student, how does marketing satisfy your needs? What areas of your life are affected by marketing? What areas of your life (if any) are not affected by marketing?
4. In the chapter we talked about the current e-marketing era. What does the e-marketing era mean to firms? What

does it mean to you as a consumer? Where do you think the future of the e-marketing era will be?
5. We learned in this chapter about how Hewlett Packard and other firms are targeting Third-World countries. Why do you think companies are interested in the Third World? What are some pros and cons of entering Third-World markets?
6. In this chapter a number of criticisms of marketing were discussed. What other criticisms of marketing have you heard? Do you agree or disagree with these criticisms? Why or why not?

▇ MARKETING PRACTICE:
APPLYING WHAT YOU'VE LEARNED

1. An old friend of yours has been making and selling leather handbags and book bags to acquaintances and friends of friends for some time. He is now thinking about opening a shop in a small college town, but he is worried about whether he'll have enough customers who want handcrafted bags to keep a business going. Knowing that you are a marketing student, he's asked you for some advice. What can you tell him about product, price, promotion, and distribution strategies that will help him get his business off the ground?
2. Assume you are employed by your city's chamber of commerce. One major focus of the chamber is to get industries to move to your city. As a former marketing student, you know that there are issues involving product, price, promotion, and distribution that can attract business. Next week you have an opportunity to speak to the members of the chamber and your topic will be "Marketing a City." Develop an outline for that presentation.
3. As a marketing professional, you have been asked to write a short piece for a local business newsletter about the state of marketing today. You think the best way to address this topic is to review how the marketing concept has evolved and to discuss the New Era orientation

and the e-marketing era. Write the short article you will submit to the editor of the newsletter.

4. As college students, you and your friends sometimes discuss the various courses you are taking. One of your friends says to you, "Marketing's not important. It's just dumb advertising." Another friend says, "Marketing doesn't really affect people's lives in any way." As a role-playing exercise, present your arguments against these statements to your class.

5. Are you and your friends a part of the e-marketing era? What about your parents? Conduct a short survey of university students to find out how they use the Internet and what they think about the future of the Internet.

▥ MARKETING MINI-PROJECT:
LEARNING BY DOING

The purpose of this mini-project is to develop an understanding of the importance of marketing to different organizations.

1. Working as a team with two or three other students in your class select an organization in your community that practices marketing. It may be a manufacturer, a service provider, a retailer, a not-for-profit organization—almost any organization will do. Then schedule a visit with someone within the organization who is involved in the marketing activities. Arrange for a short visit in which the person can give your group a tour of the facilities and explain the organization's marketing activities.

2. Divide the following list of topics among your team, and ask each person to be responsible for developing a set of questions to ask during the interview to learn about the company's program:
   - what customer segments the company targets
   - how it determines needs and wants
   - what products it offers, including features, benefits, and goals for customer satisfaction
   - what its pricing strategies are, including any discounting policies it has
   - what promotional strategies it uses and what these emphasize to position the product(s)
   - how it distributes products and whether it has encountered any problems
   - how marketing planning is done and who does it
   - whether social responsibility is part of the marketing program and if so, in what ways

3. Develop a team report of your findings. In each section of the report, share what you learned that is new or surprising to you compared to what you expected.

4. Develop a team presentation for your class that summarizes your findings. Conclude your presentation with comments on what your team believes the company was doing that was particularly good and what was not quite so good.

▥ REAL PEOPLE, REAL SURFERS:
EXPLORING THE WEB

Hotjobs.com is a company that is part of the e-marketing era. Visit HotJobs.com's Web site and visit the Web site of one or more of the company's competitors such as www.monster.com or www.headhunter.com. Follow the links to find out as much as you can about the companies. Then based on your experience, answer the following questions:

1. In your opinion, which firm has the better Web site? What makes it better?

2. Do you think the firms are targeting specific market segments? If so, what market segments? What features of the Web site give you that idea?

3. Do you think there is anything about any of the Web sites that would make it more attractive than the others to employers?

4. What are your major criticisms of each of the Web sites? What would you do to improve each site?

▥ PLAN IT!
DEVELOPING A
MARKETING PLAN

As your instructor directs, create a new marketing plan (using Marketing Plan Pro software or a written marketing plan format) to document your marketing decisions or answer these questions in a written or oral report.

Computer Friendly Stuff (CFS), the company that provided the marketing plan in Appendix A, is a real company marketing real consumer goods to real customers. After more than five years of marketing its computer-related toys and accessories, CFS is poised to dramatically improve sales and distribution as well as introduce new products. Read the current marketing plan and put yourself in the shoes of CFS executives creating a new marketing plan for next year.

1. How can CFS use its product line, in particular, to support customer relationship marketing?

2. How might CFS use the Internet to move toward personalizing its message and products to more effectively satisfy individual consumers' needs?

3. How can the firm incorporate social marketing in its marketing plan?

Key Terms

benefit, (5)
business-to-business marketing,
(7)

consumer, (4)
consumer goods, (7)
consumer orientation, (17)

customer relationship management (CRM), (13)
demand, (5)

MARKETING IN ACTION: CHAPTER 1 CASE

REAL CHOICES AT LEVI STRAUSS & CO.

Robert Haas may be one of the world's most enlightened managers. When he took over Levi Strauss & Company in 1996 it was one of the world's most successful brands. Haas's goal was to show that a New Era company, one driven by social values, could outperform a company interested in profits alone.

Haas made a number of changes in Levi's. He developed programs to teach sewing machine workers teamwork. At Levi's, a factory worker's voice was just as likely to be heard as the CEO's. He developed an employee training program that taught leadership, diversity, and ethical decision making. He personally handed out AIDS leaflets outside the company cafeteria—and he pulled the company out of China to protest human rights' abuses.

But Levi's certainly wasn't making progress on the profits side. Beginning in 1990, before Haas took over, the Levi's brand began losing market share. Indeed, Levi's market share among males 14 to 19 was cut in half between 1990 and 2000. The company hadn't had a successful new product in years. Furthermore, advertising campaigns had been failures. Retailers complained of late deliveries. Levi's was forced to shut plants and lay off thousands of workers as sales plummeted while the sales of more trendy retailers such as the Gap soared.

The reasons for Levi's decline were not difficult to discern. For one thing, the competition had changed. Instead of only competing with Lee, Gap, and Calvin Klein, hundreds of new competitors had entered the market—brands such as JNCO, Mudd, Arizona, Fubu, LEI, Union Bay, and Canyon River Blues.

Internally, the same enlightened management had created its own set of problems. Employees who had left the company complained that the focus on group decision making often meant that everyone got into the process—meaning endless meetings, task forces, and e-mails. Nothing ever got resolved. Many analysts suggested that Levi's simply didn't realize that kids don't wear what their parents do and that cool retailers won't stock the same clothes as JCPenney. No longer can a company make one brand for everyone. Levi's needed to offer new styles or even new brands. One suggestion was that Levi's had to figure out a way to appeal to a small but very influential market of city dwellers who set fashion trends, a group Levi's referred to as the "cultural creatives." But will that be enough to turn Levi's around. Some even asked if Haas's enlightened management was a problem?

Source: Nina Munk, "How Levi's Trashed a Great American Brand," *Fortune*, April 12, 1999, 83–90.

THINGS TO THINK ABOUT

1. What is the decision facing Levi Strauss & Co.?

2. What factors are important in understanding the decision situation?

3. What are the alternatives?

4. What decision(s) do you recommend?

5. What are some ways to implement your recommendation(s)?

Bookmark It!

OBJECTIVES:

1 Explain the strategic planning process.

2 Tell how firms gain a competitive advantage and describe the factors that influence marketing objectives.

3 Describe the steps in the marketing management process.

4 Explain how marketers implement and control the marketing plan.

Strategic Planning

MAKING CHOICES IN A WIRED WORLD

Real People, Real Choices:

Meet Angela Talley, a Decision Maker at DDB Worldwide

www.ddbwm.com

CURRENT POSITION: Vice President, Group Strategic Planning Director

FIRST JOB: 1986–1987 Media Buyer: Bentley, Barnes & Lynne

WHEN I'M NOT WORKING: I'm an avid book reader, traveler, snow skier, language learner, poetry writer, and hockey mom. I'm also a Chicago Marathon finisher.

A MISTAKE I WISH I HADN'T MADE: Concentrating so hard on "getting ahead" rather than my own personal development. Being well-rounded is a key to success.

BUSINESS BOOK I'M READING: <u>Bowling Alone</u> by Robert Putnam

MOTTO: Passion is what makes life worth living.

DON'T DO THIS IN AN INTERVIEW: Use all the marketing buzzwords you learned in school or misrepresent your experience.

PET PEEVE: Meetings that start late and stretch on forever.

EDUCATION: 1986 B.S. Advertising, University of Illinois at Urbana–Champaign 1996 MBA (with honors), University of Chicago, Concentrations in Strategy and Behavioral Science

Decision Time at DDB Worldwide:
How to Give an Old Retailer a New Image

Angela Talley had a big problem. One of DDB Worldwide's most important clients, JCPenney, was fighting for its life in the ferociously competitive world of retailing. Today's consumer has so many choices: catalogs, the Internet, the Home Shopping Channel, malls, department stores, specialty stores, and discount stores. Where was JCPenney in that mix? Pretty much nowhere—a middle-of-the-road department store trying to survive in a world where specialty shops were cooler, discounters were cheaper, and other department stores were classier. Consumers said JCPenney's was boring, out-of-date, and out of touch. Its merchandise wasn't as fashion-forward as it could be. Its stores were crowded and disorganized.

Angela knew that her client had to make big changes. DDB Worldwide had to help create a clear and favorable brand image and to drive traffic into ailing stores. The objective was clear and simple—but also formidable: to stop big sales declines while improving the merchandise and store environment. It would take more than a Band-Aid to correct the problem: A large-scale overhaul and a lot of strategic planning were called for.

The first step was to determine which demographic segments of the market had the most profit potential for JCPenney. JCPenney and DDB spoke to nearly 100,000 consumers to find the answers. The research indicated that working mothers in middle-income families provided the largest current share of spending and the largest profit potential. With the demographic target defined, Angela's task was to decide how to lure these customers back from the competition. These women told DDB that they live by their own rules and standards, they want to be seen as creative, and they want to express their individuality when they buy. After analyzing the findings, Angela considered three options:

Option 1: Focus on value.

In recent years retailing had become an aggressively price-driven business. Consumers had been trained to search for sales and hunt for the lowest prices. With the emergence of discount stores as legitimate fashion outlets, the value message was becoming ever more important to JCPenney's potential customers. Although the store chain couldn't compete price-wise against the Wal-Marts and Targets of the world, it could create a value strategy based on the premise of quality merchandise at an attractive price. But, if JCPenney's became known only as a place to find bargains, it would lose any claim to quality and perhaps over time the chain would be seen as a Wal-Mart wannabe.

Option 2: Form an emotional connection with the customer.

In DDB's conversations with consumers, one theme kept emerging—the ability to express a personal sense of style. Other stores weren't delivering on this need. Specialty shops didn't offer a range of styles; discounters offered only low–quality merchandise; department stores were too expensive. JCPenney could send the message to these women that they could find everything they need to express themselves in its aisles. But if the women didn't believe this message JCPenney's could lose style-oriented shoppers to boutiques and value-oriented shoppers to competitors like Wal-Mart and Kohl's.

Option 3: Focus on brand names.

Consumers told DDB that when they're shopping for themselves and their children, they seek out well-known brands because these are viewed as signs of quality, durability, and style. Retailers Kohl's and Sears were advertising that they carried hundreds of well-known brand names. Although JCPenney could already make the same claim, consumers just weren't thinking of the store when they shopped for brand names. JCPenney could create a position in the retail marketplace as *the* place to shop for the best brand names. But, consumers might not believe this message, especially since Sears relentlessly advertised itself as the place for brand names.

Now, put yourself in Angela Talley's shoes. Which option would you choose and why?

"Plan Well and Prosper"

Angela Talley understands that planning is everything. She should: Her job is to conduct strategic planning for such clients as JCPenney, McDonald's, Kraft Foods, Oscar Mayer, Princess Cruise Lines, Van Kampen Investments, Anheuser-Busch, and even the Library of Congress. Part of the planner's role is to help define a brand's distinctive identity and purpose. Angela makes use of research to develop an understanding and insight into people's behaviors, beliefs, feelings, desires, attitudes, opinions, and frustrations—to see the world through their eyes, to speak their language, to represent their voice. This connection with the consumer inspires strategic choices that enable a company to speak in a clear voice in the marketplace so that customers understand what the firm is and what it has to offer that competitors don't.

Whether a firm is a well-established department store like JCPenney or a relative newcomer like HotJobs.com, planning for the future is a key to prosperity. Sure, it's true that a firm can be successful even if it makes some mistakes in planning. It's also true that some seat-of-the-pants businesses are successful, but without good planning for the future, firms will be less successful than they could be. In the worst-case scenario, a lack of planning can be fatal for both large and small businesses; and, of course there are times when even the best planning cannot anticipate the future accurately. Many businesses, especially those in the travel and tourism industries, had to rethink their plans after the terrorist attack on the World Trade Center on September 11, 2001, as consumers worldwide became fearful of traveling. Still, just like a Boy Scout, it's always better to be prepared.

Planning is an ongoing process of making decisions that guide the firm both in the short term and for the long haul. Planning identifies and builds on a firm's strengths, and it helps managers at all levels make informed decisions in a changing business environment. Planning means that an organization develops objectives before it takes action. In large firms such as IBM, Sony, and Kodak that operate in many markets, planning is a complex process involving many people from different areas of the company's operations. At a small business like Mac's Diner, however, planning is quite different. Mac himself is chief cook, occasional dishwasher, and the sole company planner. With midsize firms, the planning process falls somewhere in between depending on the size of the firm and the complexity of its operations.

In this chapter, we'll look at the different steps in an organization's planning. First, we'll see how managers develop a **business plan** that includes the decisions that guide the entire organization. Then we'll examine the marketing planning process and the stages in that process that lead to the development and implementation of a **marketing plan**—a document that describes the marketing environment, outlines the marketing objectives and strategy, and identifies who will be responsible for carrying out each part of the marketing strategy.

Strategic Planning: Guiding the Business

We all know what planning is—we plan a vacation or a great Saturday night party. Some of us even plan how we're going to study and get our class assignments completed. When businesses plan, the process is more complex. Business planning usually occurs at three levels—strategic, tactical, and operational.

Strategic planning is the managerial decision process that matches the organization's resources (such as its manufacturing facilities, financial assets, and skilled workforce) and capabilities (the things it is able to do well because of its expertise and experience) to its market opportunities for long-term growth. The decisions focus on the firm's ability to respond to changes in its environment. In a strategic plan, top management—usually the chief executive officer (CEO), president, and other top executives—defines the firm's purpose and specifies what the firm hopes to achieve over the next five or so years. For example, a firm's strategic plan may set a goal of increasing the firm's total revenues by 20 percent in the next five years. Good luck!

Many large firms realize that relying on only one product can be risky, so they have become multiproduct companies with self-contained divisions organized around products or brands. These self-contained divisions are **strategic business units (SBUs)**—individual units within the firm, each having its own mission, business objectives, resources, managers, and competitors. The Walt Disney Company, for example, is a firm that has a number of different SBUs. In addition to making movies and running theme parks, Disney now is in the cruise line business; publishes magazines and books; offers TV viewers the Disney channel; runs Disney stores; produces entertainment videos, Disney on Ice, and Broadway musicals; and operates a number of vacation resorts.

As shown in Figure 2.1, for firms such as Disney, strategic planning occurs at two separate levels—at the overall corporate level and at the SBU or business level. Thus, in large firms with many SBUs, strategic planning occurs first as top management establishes a vision or mission for the organization and then sets corporate goals that guide decision making within each SBU. For example Disney's corporate planning expanded its theme park business to Europe and Japan as separate business units. In small firms that are not large enough to have separate SBUs, strategic planning begins at the business unit level.

At the SBU level, top managers typically establish a mission, conduct an analysis of the environment, set business goals, and develop growth strategies. At Disney, the managers of the various SBUs develop separate strategic plans for each of the different Disney businesses.

To look further at strategic planning and the other two levels of planning—tactical and operational—let's think about how a bicycle company called Mike's Bikes might go about the planning process. You can follow along by looking at the steps outlined in Figure 2.1.

In the strategic plan, Mike's might set a goal of increasing revenues by 15 percent over the next five years by developing new bicycles for new markets. The next level is **tactical planning** (sometimes called **functional planning**), which is done by middle-level managers—the vice presidents or department directors. Marketing is one of the functional areas of a firm that does tactical planning; other areas include finance, operations, and human resource management. And so the marketing manager for Mike's Bikes might set an objective to gain 20 percent of the

business plan ■ A plan that includes the decisions that guide the entire organization.

marketing plan ■ A document that describes the marketing environment, outlines the marketing objectives and strategy, and identifies who will be responsible for carrying out each part of the marketing strategy.

strategic planning ■ A managerial decision process that matches an organization's resources and capabilities to its market opportunities for long-term growth and survival.

strategic business units (SBUs) ■ Individual units within the firm that operate like separate businesses, with each having its own mission, business objectives, resources, managers, and competitors.

tactical (functional) planning ■ A decision process that concentrates on developing detailed plans for strategies and tactics for the short term that support an organization's long-term strategic plan.

Strategic Planning		Tactical Planning	Operational Planning
Corporate Level Planning	**Strategic Business Unit (SBU) Planning**	Planning done by Functional Area Managers: *Human Resources Finance Operations Accounting Marketing*	Planning by Supervisory Managers: *Communication manager Sales manager Merchandising manager Marketing research manager*
Planning done by top level corporate managers • Define corporate visions • Set corporate goals • Establish the business portfolio	Planning done by top level SBU managers • Define the business mission • Evaluate the environment (SWOT analysis) • State business objectives • Develop growth strategies	• Evaluate the marketing environment • Set marketing objectives • Develop marketing strategies to achieve corporate objectives	• Develop action plans to implement tactical plans

FIGURE **2.1**

Planning at Different Management Levels

Planning means an organization determines its objectives and then develops courses of action to accomplish them. In very large multi-product corporations, strategic, tactical, and operational planning occur at four distinct levels.

operational planning ■ A decision process that focuses on developing detailed plans for day-to-day activities that carry out an organization's tactical plans.

cross-functional planning ■ An approach to tactical planning in which managers work together in developing tactical plans for each functional area in the firm so that each plan considers the objectives of the other areas.

1 *Bookmark It!*

Do you agree that marketing is a firm's most essential functional area? Suppose you're a marketing planner and your boss claims that marketing is "fluff"—that the company wouldn't need people to push products if the rest of the firm did its job. What arguments might you use to keep your job?

racing bike market by successfully introducing three new models during the coming year. This objective would be part of a tactical plan. Tactical planning typically includes both a broad five-year plan to support the firm's strategic plan and a detailed annual plan for the coming year.

Because marketing is so central to a firm, in many cases strategic planning and marketing planning are almost inseparable. It is the marketing team's responsibility to monitor changes in the marketing environment and to assess the firm's capability to seize opportunities. Thus, the knowledge and understanding of the marketplace and consumer's needs are of paramount importance in developing the achievable business goals.

Still further down the planning ladder are the first-line managers. In the human resources department, there may be a benefits manager, a safety director, and a wage and salary manager. In marketing, sales managers and marketing communications managers might be first-line managers. These managers are responsible for a third level of planning, **operational planning**, which focuses on the day-to-day execution of the tactical plans and includes detailed annual, semiannual, or quarterly plans. Operational plans might show exactly how many units of a product the firm will produce a day or how many television commercials the firm will place on certain networks during a season. At the operational planning level for Mike's Bikes, the marketing communications manager, who works under the marketing director, will develop plans to promote the new bikes to potential customers while the sales manager will develop a quarterly plan for the company's sales force. Both of these activities are forms of operational planning.

Of course, top business planners and marketing managers don't just sit in their offices dreaming up plans without any concern for the rest of the organization. All business planning is an integrated activity even though we've described each layer separately. This means that the organization's strategic, tactical, and operational plans must work together. So, planners must consider good principles of accounting, the value of the company to its stockholders, and the requirements for staffing and human resource management. The different tactical planners within an organization have to make sure that their plans support the overall organization's mission and objectives and that they work well together. For example, if marketing planners want to boost sales during the first quarter of the year, they must make sure that operations can meet the increased production demands required by their sales goals.

In fact, many firms practice **cross-functional planning**, which means that instead of working alone middle managers actually work together as a team to develop tactical plans that consider the objectives of all the functional areas. JCPenney's decision to pursue a value, style, or brand-name strategy would have ramifications for many parts of the company. This decision would influence the type of merchandise JCPenney would carry, what it would charge, and even the physical layout of the stores. Let's take a more detailed look at how firms develop strategic plans.

STRATEGIC PLANNING AT THE CORPORATE LEVEL

As Figure 2.1 shows, the first level of an organization's planning is strategic planning at the corporate level. To develop strategic plans, top-level corporate managers follow three steps: They develop a mission or vision for the total corporation, establish the corporation's long-term goals or objectives, and allocate resources to the different SBUs to maximize growth and profits.

Defining the Organization's Mission   Theoretically, top management's first step in the strategic planning stage is to answer such "soul-searching" questions as: What business are we in? What customers should we serve? How should we develop the firm's capabilities and focus its efforts? In many firms, the answers to questions such as these become the lead items in the organization's strategic plan. They become part of a **mission statement**—a formal document that describes the organization's overall purpose and what it hopes to achieve in terms of its customers, products, and resources. For example, food and cigarette giant Philip Morris's vision is "to be the most successful consumer products company in the world."[1] Figure 2.2 shows examples of some actual mission statements.

Robert Goizueta headed the Coca-Cola Company for 17 years, and during that time sales more than quadrupled from $4 billion to $18 billion—seems like he knew how to sell a bottle of soda or two. When Goizueta took on that job, one of his first actions was to create a mission statement for the company. It began, "Our challenge will be to enhance and protect the Coca-Cola trademark, giving shareholders an above-average return and entering new businesses only if they can perform at a rate substantially above inflation."[2] By focusing all company efforts on building brand value, satisfying customers, and profitability, that mission statement led Coke into two decades of phenomenal worldwide growth (though having a good product and memorable advertising didn't hurt either).

The ideal mission statement is not too broad, too narrow, or too shortsighted. A mission that is too broad will not provide adequate focus for the organization. It doesn't do much good to claim, "We are in the business of making high-quality products"—and it's hard to find a firm that doesn't make this claim. But a mission statement that is too narrow may inhibit managers' ability to visualize possible growth opportunities. If, for example, a firm sees itself in terms of

mission statement ■ A formal statement in an organization's strategic plan that describes the overall purpose of the organization and what it intends to achieve in terms of its customers, products, and resources.

- *Sierra Club*: To explore, enjoy, and protect the wild places of the Earth; to practice and promote the responsible use of the Earth's ecosystems and resources; to educate and enlist humanity to protect and restore the quality of the natural and human environment; and to use all lawful means to carry out these objectives. (www.sierraclub.org/inside.html)
- *MADD*: The mission of Mothers Against Drunk Driving is to stop drunk driving, support the victims of this violent crime, and prevent underage drinking (www.madd.org/about us)
- *Blackhawk Controls Corporation*: The aim of Blackhawk Controls is to provide motion solutions to industry. This includes AC and DC drives, servos, steppers, controllers, and complete systems. We specialize in single and multiple axis applications. We have designed applications for web converting, plastics, profile and sheet lines, wire, boxboard, printing presses, bindery lines, and woodworking machinery. (www.blackhawkcontrols.com)
- *The Quaker Oats Company*: To meet the needs of consumers through innovative marketing and manufacturing of healthful, good-tasting products that contribute to a healthy lifestyle and consumer well-being around the world, yielding above-average returns over time for our shareholders. (www.quakeroats.com/about/goal.htm)
- *First Union Corporation*: Our strategic priorities are to provide our customers unparalleled service, convenience, and responsiveness, balance earnings power through geographic and product diversity; provide the most innovative financing solutions and a broad array of products; increase the production of our specialty businesses; maximize operating efficiency; and emphasize capital strength and loan quality with growth in fee income, deposits, and loans. (www.firstunion.com/profile/strprior/html)

FIGURE **2.2**

Organizational Mission Statements

A mission statement describes the overall purpose of an organization and what it intends to achieve. While different companies may see themselves in unique ways, most mission statements focus on customers, products, and resources.

FIGURE **2.3**

CFS Mission Statement
CFS's mission statement clearly
indicates what business it is in and
the markets that it plans to serve.

CFS's MISSION

The mission of CFS is to design and market integrated computer toys and accessories that offer the benefit of making computers fun to use at home or in the workplace. CFS is targeting two consumer segments, youth aged 7 to 14 and professional women aged 35 to 65. CFS's distinctive competency is the ability to create humorous and imaginative computer toy and accessory combinations.

its product only, consumer trends or technology can make that product obsolete—and the firm is left with no future.

Analysts use the term *marketing myopia* to describe firms that develop shortsighted visions.[3] For example, in the 1980s Kodak faced intense competition from Japanese film and camera companies that had developed electronic cameras capable of storing images digitally on compact disks. The future of filmless photography came a giant step closer— an exciting advancement but not the greatest news for Kodak, which viewed itself as being in only the film business. Abandoning its product-oriented myopic mission, Kodak now says it is in the "imaging" business—a consumer-oriented mission with a focus on products that process and convert images both on film and in the form of electronic data.[4] This broader view led to the development of successful new products, and Kodak now is "off-camera" as it has become involved in electronic publishing, medical and graphics arts imaging, printing, and digital scanning. Figure 2.3 shows the mission statement of Computer Friendly Stuff (CFS), the company whose marketing plan we feature in Appendix A on page 559.

Establishing Corporate Objectives   After constructing a mission statement, top management translates the corporation's mission into goals or objectives. These are specific accomplishments or outcomes that an organization hopes to achieve by a certain time.*

Organizational objectives are a direct outgrowth of the mission statement and broadly identify what the firm hopes to accomplish within the general time frame of the firm's long-range business plan. Philip Morris, for example, is a company that has grown from being simply a manufacturer of tobacco products to a giant food, beer, and tobacco business. Indeed, the company is trying to distance itself from cigarettes in many ways; in late 2001 it even decided to change its name to Altria in hopes that this would help it shed the negative image many people had of "cancer sticks." The company lists these as its objectives or "fundamental strategies:"

> To profitably grow our worldwide tobacco, food, and beer business.
> To enhance shareholder value through a balanced program of dividends and share repurchases.
> To conduct our business as a responsible manufacturer and marketer of consumer products, including those intended for adults.
> To reinvest in our businesses and brands and meet the changing demands of consumers through innovation and new product development.[5]

Planning for Growth: The Business Portfolio   For companies with several different SBUs, strategic planning includes making decisions about how to best allocate resources among these businesses to ensure growth for the total organization. As Figure 2.4 illustrates, each SBU has its own focus within the firm's overall strategic plan, and each has its own target market and strategies for reaching its goals. Just like an independent business, each SBU is

---

*We should note at the beginning that some marketers use the terms *goals* and *objectives* to represent two distinct levels in an organization's goal-setting process, while others use the terms synonymously and refer to only a single level. Because there is no consensus on this, we have chosen to use the two terms, goals and objectives, synonymously throughout this book.

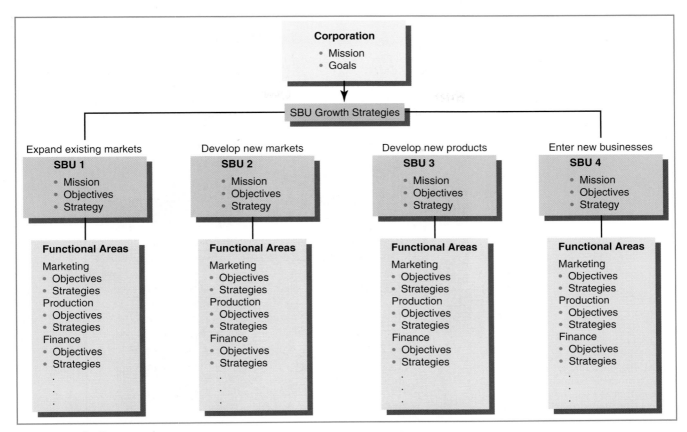

FIGURE 2.4

Role of Strategic Business Units

Very large corporations are normally divided into self-contained divisions organized around products or brands called strategtic business units (SBUs). Each SBU operates as an independent business with its own mission and objectives—and its own marketing strategy.

a separate *profit center* within the larger corporation—that is, each SBU is responsible for its own costs, revenues, and profits.

Just as the collection of different stocks an investor owns is called a portfolio, the range of products that a large firm owns is called its **business portfolio**. Having a diversified portfolio of products reduces the firm's dependence on one product or one group of customers; that's the rationale behind Philip Morris's movement away from a reliance on tobacco products. **Portfolio analysis** is a tool management uses to assess the potential of a firm's products or businesses. It helps management decide which of its current products should receive more—or less—of the firm's resources and which of its lines of business are consistent with the firm's overall mission. Several models are available to assist management in this process. Each model in its own way suggests a strategy for portfolio development based on a product's position relative to competitors.

Let's examine one popular model: The **BCG growth–market share matrix** developed by the Boston Consulting Group (BCG). The BCG method focuses on the potential of a firm's existing successful products to generate cash that the firm can then use to invest in new products. New products are chosen for their potential to become future cash generators. In the BCG matrix, shown in Figure 2.5, the vertical axis represents the attractiveness of the market, the *market growth rate*. Even though Figure 2.5 shows "high" and "low" as measurements, marketers might ask whether the total market for the product is growing 10 percent, 50 percent, 100 percent, or 200 percent annually. The horizontal axis shows the company's current strength in the market through its *relative market share*. Here, marketers might ask whether the firm has 5 percent, 25 percent, or perhaps 75 percent of the current market. Combining the two axes creates four quadrants representing four different types of products or businesses. Each quadrant of the BCG grid uses a symbol to designate products or business units that fall

business portfolio ■ The group of different products or brands owned by an organization and characterized by different income-generating and growth capabilities.

portfolio analysis ■ A management tool for evaluating a firm's business mix and assessing the potential of an organization's strategic business units.

BCG growth–market share matrix ■ A portfolio analysis model developed by the Boston Consulting Group that assesses the potential of successful products to generate cash that a firm can then use to invest in new products.

Philip Morris, once simply a tobacco products company, now sees itself as a consumer products company with a variety of product offerings. Its annual report reflects that shift in strategic orientation.

within a certain range for market growth rate and market share. Let's take a closer look at each cell in the grid.

- *Stars:* Stars are SBUs with products that have a dominant market share in high-growth markets. Like Hollywood movie celebrities, stars command the firm's attention and grab the lion's share of the money. Because the SBU has a dominant share of the market, stars generate large revenues, but they also require large amounts of funding to keep up with production and promotion demands. Because the market has a large growth potential, managers design strategies to maximize market share in the face of increasing competition. The firm aims at getting the largest share of loyal customers so the product will generate profits that can then be

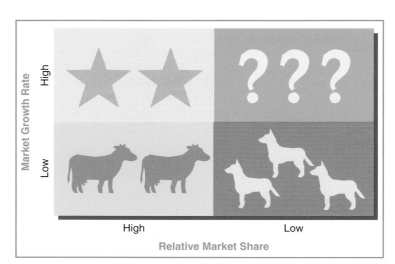

FIGURE 2.5

BCG Growth-Market Share Matrix

The Boston Consulting Group's (BCG) growth–market share matrix is one way a firm can examine its portfolio of different products or SBUs. By categorizing SBUs as stars, cash cows, question marks or dogs, the matrix helps managers make good decisions about how the firm should grow.

plowed into other parts of the company. For example, the BCG matrix might suggest that Viacom should continue to invest in its MTV Networks business that operates MTV: Music Television, M2: Music Television, VH1, Nickelodeon, Nick at Nite, TV Land, MTV Europe, MTV Latin America, Nickelodeon Latin America, Nickelodeon Nordic and VH-1 U.K.[6]

- *Cash Cows:* Cash cows have a dominant market share in a low-growth potential market. Because there's not much opportunity for new products, competitors don't often enter the market. At the same time, the product is well established and enjoys a high market share that the firm can sustain with minimal funding. Firms usually milk cash cows of their profits to fund the growth of other products in a portfolio. Of course, if the firm's goal is to increase revenues, having too many cash cows with little or no growth potential can become a liability. For example, Colgate-Palmolive is a multinational producer of toothpaste, deodorant, and pet food. Colgate's North American business was a cash cow with little growth potential. In the mid-1990s a new management team made sweeping changes. It began to invest in neglected brands such as Colgate toothpaste, Palmolive detergent, Ajax cleanser, and Science Diet pet food. The result: Colgate made a real comeback in its home market and turned its cash cows into stars.[7]

- *Question Marks:* Question marks—sometimes called problem children—are products with low market shares in fast-growth markets. When a business unit is a question mark, it suggests that the firm has failed to compete successfully. Perhaps the product offers fewer benefits than competing products. Maybe its price is too high, its distributors are ineffective, or its advertising is too weak. The firm could pump more money into marketing the product and hope that market share will improve. But the firm may find itself "throwing good money after bad," gaining nothing but a negative cash flow and disappointment. Adolph Coors Co., for example, invested heavily in the launch of its Zima brand beer targeted toward Generation Xers. But Zima sales never materialized—Zima became a question mark. Coors's decision was not to continue high levels of investment in the brand but to provide only minimal support to Zima as a niche product.[8]

- *Dogs:* Dog lovers should not be offended; this label really refers to a mongrel—a product nobody wants. Dogs have a small share of a slow-growth market. They are specialized products in limited markets that are not likely to grow quickly. When possible, large firms may sell off their dogs to smaller firms that may be able to nurture them—or they may take the product off the market. In 2001, General Motors decided to kill its 103-year-old Oldsmobile brand—this "dog" got taken to the auto pound.[9]

1 Bookmark It!

You're in charge of strategic planning at your school. Pick three majors (economics, marketing, art . . .) and classify them as stars, cash cows, question marks, and dogs. Write a short report to your boss about how many resources to devote to each of these major programs and why.

Oldsmobile cars have come a long way since this 1900 model, but after 103 years on the market this brand is being retired.

STRATEGIC PLANNING AT THE SBU LEVEL

So far, we have discussed how strategic planning in large firms occurs at the corporate level. Now it's time to turn to strategic planning for smaller firms without separate SBUs and for specific SBUs within larger firms—the second level of planning shown in Figure 2.1.

As we've noted, a mission statement for a specific business typically focuses on what the business expects to accomplish. Kraft Foods, an SBU of Philip Morris, states this mission: ". . . to be widely recognized as the undisputed leader of the global food and beverage industry. To earn that recognition we strive to be the first choice of our consumers, an indispensable partner to our retailers and other customers, the most desired partner for strategic alliances, the employer of choice in our industry, a responsible citizen in our communities, and a consistent producer of industry-leading financial performance and returns for our investors."[10] Let's see how a firm's strategic business units like Kraft take steps to achieve such ambitious objectives.

Evaluating the Environment: SWOT Analysis   For a small business or a strategic business unit, the second step in strategic planning is to assess its internal and external environments. Managers call this evaluation a **SWOT analysis** because it tries to identify meaningful strengths (S) and weaknesses (W) in the organization's *internal environment,* and opportunities (O) and threats (T) coming from outside the organization—the *external environment.* A SWOT analysis enables a firm to develop strategies that make use of what the firm does best in seizing opportunities for growth, while at the same time avoiding external threats that might hurt the firm's sales and profits.* See Table 2.1 for a sample SWOT analysis.

By **internal environment**, we mean all of the controllable elements inside an organization that influence how well the organization operates. Internal strengths may lie in the firm's technologies. What is the firm able to do well that other firms would find difficult to duplicate? What patents does it hold? A firm's physical facilities can be an important strength or weakness, as can its level of financial stability, its relationships with suppliers, its corporate reputation, and its ownership of strong brands in the marketplace.

Internal strengths and weaknesses often reside in the firm's employees—the firm's human and intellectual capital. What skills do the employees have? What kind of training have they

SWOT analysis ■ An analysis of an organization's strengths and weaknesses and the opportunities and threats in its external environment.

internal environment ■ The controllable elements inside an organization including its people, its facilities, and how it does things that influence the operations of the organization.

TABLE 2.1 A Suggested SWOT Analysis for Nokia		
Strengths	A world–class research, design, and engineering team.	
	Global relationships with all major phone companies worldwide.	
	Nokia is rated as the world's fifth most valuable brand, ahead of Sony, Nike, and Mercedes–Benz.	
	Nokia's strong management team has come through many crises unscathed.	
Weaknesses	Nokia will likely be late in developing third generation (net-enabled) phones.	
Opportunities	The world's biggest phone companies are willing to pay top dollar to offer its customers Nokia's snazzy phones.	
	A growing world market, especially in developing countries such as China and India.	
	In 2002 makers of cellular phones will sell over 140 million phones and within three years the cell-phone market should reach 1 billion units per year.	
Threats	The European market for cellular phones with current technology is nearly saturated.	
	Nokia's key customers, Europe's telcos (telecommunications companies), are $125 billion in debt.	
	Nokia faces well-financed Japanese rivals.	

Adapted from Stephen Baker, John Shinal, and Irene M. Kunii, "Is Nokia's Star Dimming?," *Business Week* (January 22, 2001): 66–72.

1 *Bookmark It!*

Table 2.1 provides a look at Nokia, the giant mobile phone manufacturer. It presents the type of SWOT analysis a consultant might develop for the company. Based on this information, what strategies might Nokia consider?

*It should be noted that some marketing experts have questioned the usefulness of a SWOT analysis, suggesting that a more comprehensive analysis of the marketing environment is needed, (See J. Scott Armstrong, ESSAY—Advice to Marketing Planners: Don't do SWOT, January 11, 2002, accessed at http://elmar.ama.org/); however most firms still rely on the SWOT analysis.

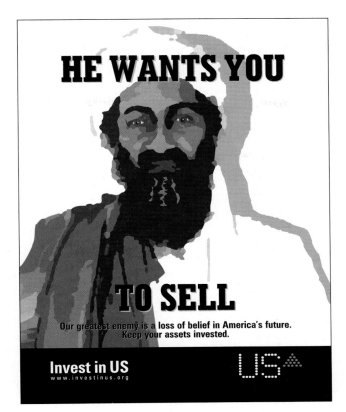

Sudden changes in the external environment, such as the September 11, 2001 terrorist attacks, can dramatically alter consumers' priorities. Following the attacks, many ads such as this one encouraged Americans to continue to buy and invest their money as a patriotic duty.

had? Are they loyal to the firm? Do they feel a sense of ownership? Has the firm been able to attract top researchers and good decision makers? When Jack Welch, widely considered the best manager of the twentieth Century, took over the helm of General Electric, the company had a value of $14 billion. By the time he retired 20 years later, that value had grown to over $400 billion. Welch gave GE a new mission: to be the world's most valuable company. He wanted every SBU within GE to be number one or number two—but he preferred number one. What made Welch such a successful CEO? Many analysts attribute it to his belief that GE's competitive advantage would come from individuals and ideas. Managers of individual businesses were told to take charge and run with their ideas.[11]

The **external environment** consists of elements outside of the organization that may affect it either positively or negatively. The external environment includes consumers, government regulations, competitors, the overall economy, and trends in popular culture. Consider, for example, the problems faced by JCPenney we discussed at the beginning of the chapter. While some of these woes may be traced to the chain's internal environment, in addition some of the blame can be assigned to the fact that traditional retailers in general are experiencing huge problems. A big one is very simple—there are just too many stores competing for the same customers, and this number continues to grow. During the 1990s, the retail industry added three square feet of new floor space for every person in the United States—a growth rate double that of the growth in population during the same period! To compound Penney's problems, shoppers are loaded down with debt, and especially since the terrorist attacks, they are worried about their jobs and not as enthusiastic about shopping in public places.[12] Not a pretty picture.

Opportunities and threats can come from any part of the external environment. Sometimes trends or currently unserved customer needs provide opportunities for growth. On the other hand, if changing customer needs or buying patterns mean customers are turning away from a firm's products, it's a signal of possible danger or threats down the road. During the 1990s, for example, consumers began looking for products that provided good value rather than seeking higher-priced, status-symbol goods. This trend provided an opportunity for lower-priced luxury cars such as the Lexus but was a threat to firms like Mercedes.

external environment ■
The uncontrollable elements outside of an organization that may affect its performance either positively or negatively.

Setting Business Objectives   The next step in crafting an SBU's strategic plan is to set business objectives. Remember that for individual SBUs these objectives must also support the overall objectives of the corporation. Objectives may relate to revenue and sales, profitability, the firm's standing in the market, return on investment (ROI), productivity, innovation, use of resources, product development and introduction, customer relations and satisfaction, or even social responsibility.

Often, objectives are quantitative. For example, a firm might have as an objective a 10 percent increase in profitability. It could reach this objective by increasing productivity, by reducing costs, or by divesting itself of an unprofitable division. Or it might meet this 10 percent objective by developing new products, investing in new technologies, or entering a new market.

In 1990 Campbell Soup Company was hovering near the bottom of the food industry when David W. Johnson became president and CEO. Johnson saw Campbell Soup as a firm that had lost its direction and focus, and his first act was to develop a set of measurable business objectives focusing on growth. He jettisoned business divisions that didn't fit in with Campbell's core products, and he undertook a large-scale restructuring of the company into divisions that unified and coordinated business activities. As a result, within two years Campbell's exceeded its growth goals while launching 122 new products.[13] That ain't just chicken soup.

Creating a Competitive Advantage   In talking about how successful firms plan, it's important to understand that the underlying goal of all business strategies and plans is to create a **competitive advantage** for the firm. A firm has a competitive advantage when it is able to outperform the competition, providing customers with a benefit the competition can't. A competitive advantage gives consumers a reason to choose one product over another again and again.

Andersen Windows boasts of a competitive advantage in its industry. Over the years Andersen developed many choices of window designs to meet customers' ever-changing tastes. Unfortunately, this resulted in too many styles in its product lineup, and Andersen got so many orders wrong that its reputation was at stake. To solve this problem, Andersen created an interactive computerized version of its catalog that allows customers to add, change, or strip away window features. The system also checks the window's dimensions and weight to make sure it will be structurally sound, and then generates a price. Each order is electronically transmitted to the factory, where it receives a unique control number ensuring the order gets built and shipped accurately. As a result, Andersen has cut ordering errors to only one per 200 truckloads shipped—a very good rate in the industry. Customers can select from 188,000 different window possibilities with confidence that Andersen will get their order right—an "open-and-shut case" for competitive advantage.[14]

The Andersen example provides one window onto how a firm can successfully compete—by being more efficient than its rivals. But that's not the only way. How does a firm go about creating a competitive advantage? The first step is to identify what a firm does really well. A **distinctive competency** is a firm's capability that is superior to that of its competition.

For example, Coca-Cola's success in global markets—Coca-Cola ("Coke") commands 50 percent of the world's soft-drink business—is related to its distinctive competencies in distribution and marketing communications. Coke's distribution system got a jump on the competition during World War II. For U.S. soldiers fighting overseas to be able to enjoy a five-cent Coke, the U.S. government assisted Coke in building 64 overseas bottling plants. Coke's skillful marketing communications program, a second distinctive competency, has contributed to its global success. In addition to its glitzy television commercials, Coke has blanketed less developed countries such as Tanzania with its print advertisements so that even people without television will think of Coke when they get thirsty.

The second step in developing a competitive advantage is to turn a distinctive competency into a **differential benefit**—one that is important to customers. Differential benefits set products apart from competitors' products by providing something unique that customers want. Differential benefits provide reasons for customers to pay a premium for a firm's products and exhibit a strong brand preference. For many years loyal Apple computer users benefited from superior graphics capability compared to their PC-using counterparts. Later, when PC manufacturers caught up with this competitive advantage, Apple relied on its inventive product designers to create another

competitive advantage
The ability of a firm to outperform the competition, thereby providing customers with a benefit the competition can't.

distinctive competency
A superior capability of a firm in comparison to its direct competitors.

2 *Bookmark It!*

Think about the different products you buy regularly. Is there one or more products where you are very loyal to one brand? What is that brand's competitive advantage? What is the differential benefit that makes you loyal to it? What might a competitor do to change your loyalty?

differential benefit
Properties of products that set them apart from competitors' products by providing unique customer benefits.

TECHNICALLY SPEAKING, THE BEST NEWS SOURCE IN THE WORLD.

The No.1 best source for technology news, according to Barron's.
For business leaders and investors who recognize the value of up-to-the-second coverage of technology, there is no more informative place to turn. CNET News.com. It's where the people you read about in technology read about technology.

cnet NEWS.COM
TECH NEWS FIRST

CNET's distinctive competency is a sharp focus on technology products.

differential benefit—futuristic looking computers in a multitude of colors. This competitive advantage even caused many loyal PC users to take a bite of the Apple.

Note that a differential benefit does not necessarily mean simply offering something different. For example, Mennen marketed a deodorant with a distinctive feature: It contained Vitamin D. Unfortunately, consumers did not see any reason to pay for the privilege of spraying a vitamin under their arms. Despite advertising claims, they saw no benefit and the product failed. The moral: Effective product benefits must be both different from the competition *and* wanted by customers.

Developing Growth Strategies   Although the BCG matrix helps managers decide which SBUs they should grow, it doesn't tell them much about *how* to make that growth happen. Should the growth of an SBU come from finding new customers, from developing new variations of the product, or from some other growth strategy? Part of the strategic planning at the SBU level entails evaluating growth strategies.

Marketers use the Product–Market Growth Matrix (Figure 2.6) to analyze different growth strategies. The vertical axis represents opportunities for growth, either in existing markets or in new markets. The horizontal axis considers whether the firm would be better off putting its resources into existing products or if it should acquire new products. The matrix provides four different fundamental marketing strategies: market penetration, market development, product development, and diversification.

- **Market penetration** strategies seek to increase sales of existing products to current customers, nonusers, and users of competing brands. For example, a soup company like Campbell can advertise new uses for soup in lunches and dinners, encourage current customers to eat more soup, and prod nonusers to find reasons to buy and

market penetration ■
Growth strategies designed to increase sales of existing products to current customers, nonusers, and users of competitive brands in served markets.

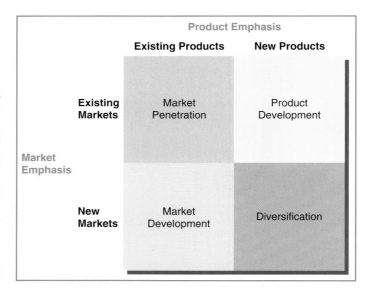

FIGURE 2.6

Product-Market Growth Matrix

When managers have determined that they want to grow a business, they must then decide on the best way to accomplish that growth. The product-growth matrix points to four different strategies based on the market and product emphases.

Source: Adapted from Igor H. Ansoff, "Strategies for Diversification," Harvard Business Review, 30, September–October 1957, 113–124, in Roger A. Kerin, Vijay Mahajan, P. Rajan Varadaarajan, Strategic Market Planning (Boston, Allyn and Bacon: 1990), p. 230.

market development ■ Growth strategies that introduce existing products to new markets.

product development ■ Growth strategies that focus on selling new products in served markets.

diversification ■ Growth strategies that emphasize both new products and new markets.

slurp. The firm might try to increase sales by cutting prices, improving distribution, or conducting promotions aimed at attracting users of competitor brands of soup.

- **Market development** strategies introduce existing products to new markets. This can mean reaching new customer segments within an existing geographic market, or it may mean expanding into new geographic areas. After 40 years in business, IKEA, Sweden's $5.8 billion home-furnishings giant, launched a big expansion into children's furniture and toys while expanding geographically to sites ranging from Warsaw, Poland, to Schaumberg, Illinois.[15]

- **Product development** strategies create growth by selling new products in existing markets. Product development may mean that the firm improves a product's performance, or it may mean extending the firm's product line by developing new variations of the item. Of course, not all growth strategies are successful. In 1959, Xerox, known for decades as "the copier company," launched the first automatic plain-paper office copier. Although this became the top-selling industrial product of all time, Xerox was forced to move beyond copiers to sustain its business growth after its patents expired beginning in the early 1970s.[16] Instead of commercializing on breakthroughs in its own R&D department, the most noteworthy of which is the personal computer, Xerox bought itself into the mainframe computer business, property and casualty insurance, and other financial services businesses—all big mistakes. By January 2001, Xerox was facing bankruptcy.

- **Diversification** strategies emphasize both new products and new markets to achieve growth. Feeling that it may be maxing out in the hamburger business, McDonald's is seeking to attract different customers with new products while building on its distinctive competency: its ability to successfully manage a restaurant chain. In recent years, McDonald's has purchased Donatos Pizza (148 outlets), Aroma Café (23 coffee bars in London), and a controlling interest in Chipotle Mexican Grills. In late 1999, along with other companies including Kraft Foods and Blockbuster, McDonald's bought a stake in an Internet–food delivery firm called Food.Com.[17]

Many firms ultimately rely on more than one of these strategies to achieve growth. Harley-Davidson, for example, was able to grow with a market development strategy that successfully targeted rich urban bikers and with a market penetration strategy that called for redesigning and improving the quality of its bikes to generate sales among existing HOGs (Harley Owner Groups). When the firm realized that its customers not only wanted to ride Harleys but also wanted to let others know this as well, it embarked on a product development strategy. By expanding its line of Motorclothes and souvenirs, Harley dealers sell more of its products to the same customers.[18]

To review what we've learned, strategic planning for the business or strategic business unit includes developing a mission statement, assessing the internal and external environments—called a SWOT analysis, setting objectives, creating a competitive advantage, and planning for

McDonald's product development strategy led it to be one of several firms to invest in Food.Com, a nationwide Internet restaurant food ordering service.

growth. In the next section we'll look at marketers' tactical plans. Then we'll describe how firms implement and control these plans.

Tactical Planning: The Marketing Management Process

An organization's mission statement, the resources it has available, and top management's view of the business environment (SWOT analysis), all influence the firm's objectives. The strategic plan, however, does not specify how to reach the objectives. It "talks the talk," but it puts the pressure on lower-level managers to "walk the walk" by developing the tactical and operational plans—the nuts and bolts—to achieve organizational objectives. Let's see how marketers develop their tactical plans—the next step in planning in Figure 2.1.

The 4 Ps we discussed in Chapter 1 remind us that a successful firm has a viable product at a price consumers are willing to pay, the means to get that product to the place consumers want it, and a way to promote the product to the right consumers. The marketing management process, shown in Figure 2.7, includes planning, implementation, and control. The steps in marketing planning are analyzing the marketing environment, setting marketing objectives, preparing a marketing plan, and developing marketing strategies.

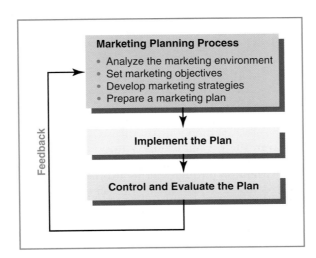

FIGURE 2.7

The Marketing Management Process

Successful marketing programs don't just happen—they are the result of a superior marketing management process that includes planning, implementation, control and evaluation.

3 Bookmark It!

As a marketing director trying to find a niche for a new brand of children's shampoo, you need to assess the competitive environment. Go to drugstore.com (or visit a drug store) and search for baby shampoo. Write down the common themes found in the marketing communication for baby shampoos, as well as their prices. Do you see any market opportunities?

ANALYZING THE MARKETING ENVIRONMENT

The first step in marketing planning is to conduct a comprehensive analysis of the marketing environment. To do this, marketing managers build on the company's SWOT analysis by searching out information about the environment that specifically affects the marketing plan.

For example, to develop effective marketing communications programs marketing managers must know about how their competitors are communicating with customers. It's not enough to have a general understanding of the target market—marketing managers need to know what television shows potential customers watch, whether a coupon, a rebate, or a sweepstakes is most likely to make them buy, and whether they prefer buying their jeans at Kmart or on the Internet. Figure 2.8 shows what CFS found in its marketing environment.

SETTING MARKETING OBJECTIVES

Once marketing managers have a thorough understanding of the marketing environment, the next step in the planning process is to develop marketing objectives. How are marketing objectives different from business objectives? Generally, marketing objectives support the more general business objectives and are more specific to specific brands, sizes, product features, and so forth. Marketing objectives state what the marketing function must accomplish if the firm is to achieve its overall objectives.

Many marketing objectives are quantitative; that is, they are stated in terms like dollars, unit sales, or percentage of market share. When General Motors (GM) developed a new model of its midsize sport-utility vehicle, the Blazer, it set a quantitative objective of a sales increase from 226,000 to 300,000 units annually.[19] To achieve this growth, a qualitative marketing objective during the early stages of product development was to identify ways to make the Blazer more attractive to customers by finding out what its existing customers wanted in a midsized sport-utility vehicle.

With quantitative objectives, marketers can easily determine whether or not the marketing plan has met its goals. In some cases, however, marketing has important objectives that are more difficult to quantify such as "to improve the image of our brand" or "to improve customer loyalty." Still, even these "fuzzy" objectives are measurable. Marketing researchers can assess improvement in brand image, for example, by polling customers to determine whether their feelings about a brand have changed or stayed the same. For example, Angela Talley at DDB Worldwide used consumer research data from several ongoing studies conducted by her agency to help her understand the motivations of working women. These included DDB's Life Style, Brand Capital, Fashion Style, and World Values studies that are used by the agency to probe many different aspects of consumers on behalf of its roster of clients.

Regardless of the overall organizational strategies, marketing objectives normally include one or more sales objectives. After all, without sales there are no profits, and without profits there is no business. Some examples of sales objectives for a company like Hasbro might be "to increase sales of our deluxe toy model by 15 percent during the next 12 months," "to increase our toy market share by 5 percent each year for the next three years," and "to sell 1 million toys during the holiday season."

FIGURE 2.8

CFS Competitive Environment Analysis

The CFS marketing plan includes an analysis of its internal (company background, products, previous results, and channels) and external (market, competitive, economic, demographic, social and cultural, political and legal, and technological) environments. Here is a section of its assessment of the competitive environment.

COMPETITIVE ENVIRONMENT

The closest competing product is a Warner Brothers Taz Mousepad and Screen Saver. The Warner Brothers product enjoys high brand awareness, due to the popularity of the Taz licensed character. It also benefits from national distribution through Warner Brothers Studio Stores and other outlets. Other screen savers featuring brand name licensed characters (but no computer toy) sell for about $20.

MARKETING OBJECTIVES:

- To increase the number of retail outlets carrying CFS products by 100 percent within one year.
- To improve market penetration by boosting the number of additional products purchased by existing customers by 25 percent within two years.
- To increase gross sales by 50 percent within one year and by 100 percent within two years.

FIGURE 2.9

CFS Marketing Objectives

Marketing objectives should clearly state what the marketing function must accomplish. Here are some of the CFS marketing objectives.

If a firm has decided that its growth strategy is to focus on product development (new or improved products for existing customers), it will develop product objectives. Because it is more profitable to retain customers than it is to replace them, firms often set objectives for improvements in quality or service to develop customer loyalty. In the breakfast cereal market where consumers tend to be fickle and like to experiment with new taste varieties each morning, firms such as Kellogg and General Mills may set objectives for developing new brands to suit the tastes of everyone—children, teens, and adults. Or they may set goals for a new product to retain customers who are being lured away by a competitor's new and improved fruit-and-fiber cereal. In other cases, a firm may decide to modify a product by taking advantage of trends, as when Frito-Lay developed its line of "lite" snacks for people who were looking to reduce their fat intake. Figure 2.9 shows the marketing objectives that CFS is focusing on.

DEVELOPING MARKETING STRATEGIES

In the next stage of the marketing planning process, marketing managers develop their actual marketing strategies—that is, they make decisions about what activities they must accomplish to achieve the marketing objectives. Usually this means deciding which markets to target and how to develop the marketing mix (product, price, promotion, and distribution) to reach that market.

Selecting a Target Market The target market is the market segment selected because of the firm's belief that its offerings are most suited to winning those customers. The firm assesses the potential demand—the number of consumers it believes are willing and able to pay for its products—and decides it has the distinctive competencies that will create a competitive advantage in the minds of these consumers. Recall that Angela Talley's team specifically targeted working women as the best prospects to woo back to JCPenney stores. As Figure 2.10 shows, CFS has selected a few target markets.

Developing Marketing Mix Programs Marketing mix decisions identify how marketing will accomplish its objectives in the firm's target markets. As we'll see in later chapters, typically marketers tailor the marketing mix—product, price, promotion, and place—to meet the needs of each target market.

Product Strategies: Because the product is the most fundamental part of the marketing mix—firms simply can't make a profit without something to sell—carefully developed product strategies are essential to achieving marketing objectives. Product strategies include decisions about the best product design, its packaging, branding—even if it will offer a warranty. Product strategy decisions also determine what support services (such as maintenance) will accompany the product, how the product will be positioned relative to the competition, if there will be variations of the product, and what product features will provide the unique benefits targeted customers want. For example, product planners for a number of airlines have tried to increase their attractiveness through improved in-flight cuisine with larger portions of tastier, even exotic, dishes. Passengers may dine on such fare as cranberry brisket, Vermont

FIGURE 2.10

CFS Target Markets
CFS has clearly identified both its consumer and organizational markets.

TARGET MARKETS

Consumer segments
The segment of youngsters, aged 7 to 14, is estimated at 35 million. The segment of professional women, aged 35 to 65, is estimated at 11 million.

Organizational segments
To reach the two targeted consumer segments, CFS is targeting three reseller markets: computers, toys, and gifts. These can be identified by their NAICS/SIC codes. Toy stores are NAICS code 45112 (SIC 5945); gift stores are NAICS code 45322 (SIC 5947); and computer and software stores are NAICS code 44312 (SIC 5734).

---

maple carrots, Starbucks coffee, Pepperidge Farm cookies, bigger bagels, bite-size candy bars, or Mrs. Field's brownies.[20] Now if they could just make those seats a little wider . . .

Pricing Strategies: In a nutshell, the pricing strategy determines what specific price a firm charges for a product. Of course, that price has to be one that customers are willing to pay. If not, all of the other marketing efforts are worthless. In addition to setting prices for the final consumer, pricing strategies must establish prices that will be charged to wholesalers and retailers. A firm's pricing strategies may be based on costs, demand, or the prices of competing products.

Southwest Airlines, "the little airline that could," uses a pricing strategy to successfully target customers who could not previously afford air travel. Southwest's ads show that it does more than compete on low price—it also provides dependable service while keeping costs down. The airline flies point-to-point instead of to a central hub, its planes are never idle at the gate waiting for connections, and few routes are longer than 500 miles. Southwest gets high ratings from its passengers for its on-time service and baggage handling. What's more, even passengers of other airlines win because competing airlines have been forced to match this upstart's low fares.[21]

Promotion Strategies: A promotion strategy is how marketers communicate product benefits and features to the target market. Marketers use promotion strategies to develop the product's message, and the mix of advertising, sales promotion, public relations, and personal selling that will deliver the message.

Promotion strategies also affect the other marketing mix strategies. For example, if the product will have multiple features, then advertising must deliver a more complex message. If the product will sell at a high price, the promotion must communicate a high-quality, luxury image.

A critical part of promotion strategy is creating a brand image that will set the brand apart from the competition. Office Depot licensed the comic-strip character Dilbert to create a brand image and to buy "star power" with its $100-million-plus marketing budget. By the way, Office Depot sales rose 12 percent during the first quarter that the Dilbert ads ran, which explains why competitor Office-Max has banned Dilbert products from its stores.[22]

Distribution Strategies: The distribution (or "place") strategy outlines how, when, and where the firm will make the product available to targeted customers. In developing a distribution strategy, marketers must decide whether to sell the product directly to the final customer or to sell through retailers and wholesalers. And, the choice of which retailers should be involved depends on the product, pricing, and promotion decisions. For example, if the firm is producing a high-quality, top-of-the-line product, it would make more sense to place it in specialty stores rather than in discount stores.

Cappuccino grande to go? Starbucks Coffee, for instance, has stolen market share from companies such as Kraft, P&G, and Nestlé through a distribution strategy that makes its gourmet coffees available to customers in stores, on planes, and in their homes. The retail chain went from 50 stores in 1989 to over 4,900 retailers in North America, Europe, the Middle East, and the Pacific Rim in 2001.[23] Avid Starbucks fans also can have regular shipments of their favorite coffee blends delivered to their doors. At the same time, Starbucks protects its gourmet image by refusing to be sold in convenience stores such as 7-Eleven.[24] For a look at CFS's marketing mix strategies, see Figure 2.11.

MARKETING MIX STRATEGIES

Product Strategies
Early on, CFS management realized that large retailers prefer buying from companies that offer multiple products. For this reason, the company moved beyond its original Computer Bug characters to develop new products, starting with Monitor Morphs. Today, the three existing products, Computer Bug, Monitor Morphs, and Computer Rear View Mirror, are in the maturity stage of the product lifecycle.

Pricing Strategies
In managing wholesale and retail prices, CFS considers production costs, competitive prices, retail and wholesale margins, and consumer reaction. By testing, CFS has confirmed that a slight increase in retail price will not adversely affect consumer demand. CFS uses price lining, assigning different prices to different products in the product line. Therefore, CFS has set wholesale and retail prices for its existing product line as follows:

Product	Wholesale Price	Suggested Retail Price
Computer Bug w/CD-ROM	$8.99	$17.99
Monitor Morphs w/CD-ROM	9.99	19.99
Computer Rear View Mirror	3.99	7.99

Channel (Place) Strategies
CFS plans to increase its selective distribution among toy, computer, and gift stores that can display the product appropriately and reach the targeted consumer segments. This will achieve the goals of increasing the number of retail outlets carrying CFS products by 100 percent and placing CFS products in 10 major U.S. chains during this year. To obtain distribution in these large national chains, CFS plans to support its products with pricing allowances, trade promotions, and consumer promotions.

Promotion Strategies
Personal selling. CFS will continue to evaluate agents on a bimonthly basis to ensure efficient, appropriate coverage of the reseller market. CFS will revise its incentive program of bonuses and promotions for the independent salespeople.
Consumer sales promotion. To support the release of the new Monitor Morph product, CFS will distribute 50,000 in-store point-of-sale flyers to participating resellers this year. In addition, CFS is using sampling—putting demonstration versions of all products on every CD-ROM—to support the market penetration goal of boosting the number of additional products purchased by existing customers by 25 percent within two years. Within three months, CFS plans to design new point-of-purchase displays to improve product placement and encourage more impulse buying in stores.
Trade sales promotion. CFS is allocating $12,000 as push money to encourage sales of Monitor Morphs at computer chains . . . $75,000 to cover the cost of exhibiting at trade shows . . . and up to $32,000 on cooperative promotions through major retailers.
Advertising. CFS will . . . concentrate on co-op advertising, partnering with resellers that stock the product to share the costs of local advertising (including television, newspapers, magazines, and direct mail).
Public relations. In the coming year, CFS will expand the public relations effort to include the top children's magazines; the top working women's magazines; the 50 largest U.S. newspapers; the top children's cable networks; all national television morning shows; and local morning television shows in the top 20 U.S. markets.

FIGURE 2.11

CFS Marketing Mix Strategies
Marketing strategies involve what activities marketers must accomplish to achieve their marketing objectives. Here are some exerpts from CFS's marketing mix strategies.

PREPARING A MARKETING PLAN

The final stage of the marketing planning process (yes, we're getting to the end) is preparing the formal marketing plan. This document describes the marketing environment, outlines the marketing objectives and strategy, and identifies who will be responsible for carrying out each part of the marketing strategy. In large firms, top management often requires a written plan

Reem Ezzat Elmenshawy, Student, The American University in Cairo

If I were in Angela Talley's shoes, I would choose option 2—form an emotional connection with the customer. The target market said that they live by their own rules, want to be seen as creative, and want to express their individuality when they buy. Other stores do not fulfill this important need. Stores like Wal-Mart focus on bargains and stores like Sears focus on selling brand names. JCPenney can seize this opportunity and establish itself as a store that offers its customers products that help them express themselves. The only problem is that women may not believe JCPenney's message. JCPenney can avoid this problem through creative advertising and by conducting frequent interviews with the women to find their product needs.

Cecile Smith, Student, University of Alabama

I would choose option 2 for four reasons. First, the market segment that JCPenney knew would provide the largest profit share was working middle-class mothers. Given this target group, emotional appeals have proven an effective means of product differentiation. Second, if JCPenney could stress that they offer stylish merchandise for self expression, they would fulfill the desires of their target market. Third, it would be difficult to establish a value-added approach because it would mean building an image of superior quality from an image of lower quality or it would mean competing with the Wal-Marts of the marketplace on low price. Fourth, for JCPenney to focus on product differentiation, it would not be in their best interest to follow the likes of Sears and Kohl's by carrying top brand names.

Margaret A. Young, Marketing Professor, New Mexico Highlands University

I would choose option 2. It is the only option that would allow JCPenney to develop a clear market advantage. Research identified that working mother's need for an emotional connection was not being met in the market. Wal-Mart took the value strategy, and the Sears took the brand name strategy. An "Express Yourself" strategy could succeed for JCPenney because they have the right product lines and pricing ranges to appeal to a style-oriented but value-conscious working woman. Their biggest challenge will be how to send the message.

Suzanne Beckmann, Strategic Planning Director, Saatchi & Saatchi Kongens, Denmark

I would choose option 2 because of the target group's nature: working mothers have to meet their own and other people's expectations. Their roles are career woman, mother, wife, friend, housewife, and last but not least woman. A wide selection in the medium-price segment supports these women's needs for variety and individuality. Also, option 2 best supports JCPenney's unique selling point (USP), namely offering a range of styles of good quality for reasonable prices. Combined with the right communication campaign and internal strategy such as considerably improving the store environment, allows the USP to turn into an ESP—"emotional" selling point. However, to convince the target group, I would choose a "light" version of option 3 to achieve the objectives of option 2.

Weigh in with your thoughts! Visit the Live Laboratory at www.prenhall.com/solomon for extended Other Voices replies, exercises, and more.

because it encourages marketing managers to formulate concrete objectives and strategies. In small entrepreneurial firms such as Computer Friendly Stuff (CFS), our running case introduced in the beginning of this book, a well-thought-out marketing plan is often a key factor in attracting investors who will help turn the firm's dreams into reality. To see what CFS's marketing plan looks like, see Appendix A.

As you would expect, the parts of the written marketing plan correspond to the earlier steps in the planning process. The first part of the plan, called a **situation analysis** or a business review, is a thorough description of the firm's current circumstances, including an analysis of its internal and external environments. Then, based on the situation analysis, the plan describes the marketing problems and opportunities and outlines the marketing objectives.

situation analysis ■ The first part of a marketing plan that provides a thorough description of the firm's current situation including its internal and external environments. (Also called a business review.)

I. Mission Statement
II. Situation Analysis
    a. Internal environment
        i. Company background
        ii. Products
        iii. Previous results (company)
        iv. Channels
    b. External environment
        i. Markets
        ii. Competitive environment
        iii. Economic environment
        iv. Demographic environment
        v. Social and cultural environments
        vi. Political and legal environment
        vii. Technological environment
    c. SWOT Analysis
    d. Critical issues
III. Marketing Objectives (including sales objectives)
IV. Marketing strategies
    a. Target market(s)
    b. Product strategies
    c. Pricing strategies
    d. Promotion strategies
    e. Distribution strategies
V. Implementation and Control
    a. Budgets
    b. Schedules
    c. Research
    d. Evaluation and control

FIGURE 2.12

A Marketing Plan

The final stage in the marketing planning process is to prepare a formal written marketing plan. Here are the parts of a typical marketing plan.

The next part of the plan details specific strategies and action plans (or tactics), selection of target markets, and the elements of the marketing mix: product, price, place, and promotion. Finally, the plan outlines how and by whom it is to be implemented and controlled—including budgets and schedules. Sometimes firms require that marketing plans include contingency plans—directions for strategy changes should monitoring of marketing activities show that the objectives are not being met. Figure 2.12 is an outline for a typical marketing plan.

Operational Planning: Executing the Marketing Plan

So far, we've discussed the job of marketing planning—how marketing planners examine the marketing environment, set objectives, and develop product, price, place, and promotion strategies before writing the formal marketing plan. But talk is cheap: The best plan ever written is useless if it's not properly carried out. And that requires some planning too. In the final stage called operational planning (refer back to Figure 2.1), supervisory managers such as the marketing communication manager and the sales manager develop action plans to implement tactical plans. Operational plans generally cover a shorter period of time than strategic and tactical plans—perhaps only one or two months—and they include detailed directions for the specific activities to be carried out, who will be responsible for them, and time lines for accomplishing the tasks.

In this section, we'll look at some of the critical issues in implementing and controlling the tactical marketing plan. What are some reasons why the best-laid plans never materialize as they are expected to?

Take for example, Rubbermaid, the manufacturer of a gazillion household products, mostly made out of plastic. After 78 years in business, Rubbermaid went from Fortune's No. 1

rank to No. 100 and was taken over by a company most people never heard of. The reason for Rubbermaid's failure? The firm could no longer "keep the lid on" its manufacturing and marketing processes. Its products cost more than competitors did, and it couldn't seem to get them to the retailers on time.[25] Clearly, something happened between planning and execution, where "the rubber meets the road."

When top managers who don't have a clear understanding of the day-to-day operations of the firm develop a marketing plan, it will most likely be difficult to carry out. Top managers may be out of touch with what happens on the factory floor or in the store, so the objectives they set up may be more easily said than done. Another problem in implementing the marketing plan occurs when marketers devise short-term objectives for their personal gain. Because management rewards (such as a fat raise) are often tied to short-term profit objectives, implementation of the marketing plan may focus too heavily on short-term results to the detriment of the firm's long-term goals.

In this section, we'll look at two key factors in the successful implementation of marketing plans: the marketing budget and the organization of the marketing function. We'll also look at the ways in which marketing managers control and evaluate the marketing plan. These activities assess the performance of the marketing function, and they also provide valuable feedback for the development of future marketing plans.

IMPLEMENTING THE MARKETING PLAN

Implementation means putting plans into action—bringing the company's strategies to life on a day-to-day basis. The implementation sections of a marketing plan contain a marketing budget, the development of specific action plans, and the assignment of major areas of responsibility to individuals or teams.

marketing budget ■ A statement of the total amount to be spent on marketing and the allocation of money for each activity under the marketer's control.

The Marketing Budget The **marketing budget** is a statement of the total amount a firm spends on marketing and an allocation of money for each activity under the marketer's control. The best, most carefully thought-out marketing strategies are not much good if there isn't money to support them. Usually top level executives and finance managers make the decisions about the allocation of funds within the organization. Just like kids in a family, all of the different functional area managers need financial resources and all usually feel that their needs are the most important. This is one reason why it is critical for marketing managers to understand the other functional areas of the company and to communicate to other functional managers the importance of marketing activities to the success of the overall organizational objectives.

Generally, the budgeting process in medium-sized and large organizations goes through a series of steps. First, marketing managers need to have a basic understanding of how much money they'll have to spend. It makes no sense to develop strategies above budget. In reality, the starting point for planning the marketing budget often matches the amount allocated to marketing during the previous budget planning period—usually a year. From this starting point, marketing managers determine their needs for such marketing activities as new-product development, for developing and maintaining channels of distribution, and for the various promotional activities included in the marketing plan. If the overall organizational goals are to grow revenues through introduction of new products, the marketing department will require larger budgets. For example, when Robert Louis-Dreyfus became president of Adidas, the amount earmarked for marketing was only 6 percent of sales.[26] Louis-Dreyfus believed in the power of marketing enough to double the budget and develop new ads. But if a firm's overall objectives are to control costs, it will be difficult to justify increasing marketing budgets in the short term.

Of course, marketing budgets don't always go up from one year to the next. For example, in 1998 Nike cut its global marketing budget by $100 million as CEO Phil Knight blamed ineffective marketing for sales declines.[27] Although it's hard to understand how spending less on marketing makes a firm's marketing efforts more effective, performance-based cuts such as that often are the reality marketing managers must face.

Organizing the Marketing Function Another element of successful marketing-plan implementation is the organization of the marketing function—that is, how a firm divides marketing tasks into different jobs and assigns people to departments or geographic territories. There are several philosophies about the best way to do this.

A *functional structure* separates marketing into distinct components, such as advertising, sales promotion, sales force management, and marketing research. Some firms feel that customer needs differ by geographic region, so they prefer a *geographic structure,* perhaps setting up one marketing department for Eastern Europe and another for Western Europe. Alternatively, firms choosing a *product structure* may have a number of different brand managers and product group or product line managers, each of whom is responsible for an entire brand. Proctor & Gamble, a firm that reaches around the globe, divides its marketing operations into different product category divisions in different geographic markets. For example, each of the separate dish-care divisions, laundry detergent divisions, and hard-surface cleaning divisions in North America, Latin America, and Asia are managed by individual product category managers who do the marketing planning for their product category in that region of the world.[28]

CONTROLLING THE MARKETING PLAN

Controlling the marketing plan means measuring actual performance, comparing it to planned performance, and making necessary changes in plans and implementation. This process requires that marketing managers obtain feedback on whether activities are being performed well and in a timely manner. Gathering such feedback allows managers to determine whether they should continue with the marketing plan, activate the contingency plan, or go back to the drawing board. It also provides feedback for the next year's planning activities. Let's briefly review some of the tools and techniques that help managers control the marketing plan.

Trend Analysis   Sometimes firms develop trend analyses to better understand patterns of change in their company, the industry, or the market. A *trend* is a general direction, pattern, or change in events or conditions. For example, consumers' attitudes toward advertising stressing patriotic themes changed dramatically after the September 2001 terrorist attacks; in one survey over half of the respondents said that businesses should focus a great deal on contributing to the nation's spirit of patriotism in their ads.[29] In a **trend analysis**, marketers use data such as industry sales and company sales over a period of years to understand past directions that may continue into the future. By industry sales we mean the total sales for a specific industry such as the automobile industry or the soft drink industry. A trend analysis may show that industry sales have been rising, have been falling, or have remained about the same. An understanding of industry trends helps in setting sales goals, developing strategies, and measuring company performance while a company's own sales trends show whether the overall marketing program is on track. Figure 2.13 shows what controls CFS uses to track its progress.

Actions taken by the Lotus Development Corp. illustrate how a company uses trend analysis. Lotus saw its spreadsheet-software market share plummet from 80 percent to 55 percent in the late 1980s. Though the firm had shown an ability to quickly update software products such as its popular spreadsheet application Lotus 1-2-3, people were changing the way they used these products. By analyzing industry sales data, Lotus identified a trend toward demand for groupware (software tools to support groups of people working together, often at different locations) and unified software packages (software suites or groups of applications designed to work together). As a result, Lotus marketers scrapped their old plans and developed new marketing plans that included successful software products designed for these markets. Today, Lotus is focusing on providing e-business solutions to meet the unique needs of a variety of industries.[30]

4 Bookmark It!

A company makes computer software that businesses use. Thinking as a marketer, what type of marketing structure do you think would be best for that company and why: a functional, geographic, or product structure?

controlling the marketing plan ■ Measuring actual performance, comparing it to planned performance and making necessary changes in plans and implementation.

trend analysis ■ An analysis of past industry or company sales data to determine patterns of change that may continue into the future.

CONTROLS

CFS will use several tools to evaluate and control activities implemented under this marketing plan . . . monthly trend analyses . . . will monitor customer and reseller feedback . . . [and] will conduct a marketing audit in mid-year and again at year-end to evaluate the effectiveness and efficiency of the marketing programs.

FIGURE **2.13**

CFS Control Plan

Control means measuring actual performance and comparing it to planned performance. Here is a section of the CFS plan on controls.

Marketing Research *Marketing research* is the process by which firms collect feedback from customers and others. These efforts range from simple interviews with customers to complicated statistical analyses of thousands of responses to questionnaires. As we'll see in Chapter 5, feedback can come from many sources, including a company's employees. For example, Honda enlisted its factory workers to call more than 47,000 Accord owners to see if they were happy with their cars and to get ideas for improvements.[31]

Another kind of feedback comes from an examination of the firm's internal practices. While many people dread an audit of their taxes by the Internal Revenue Service, this close examination can be a positive thing for a company (unless it's been keeping two sets of books!). The **marketing audit** is a comprehensive review of a firm's marketing function. It can also give feedback on specific marketing plans. The purpose of the audit is to determine if a firm can improve its marketing programs.

Because a marketing audit should be objective and unbiased, it is best conducted by an independent consulting organization rather than by the firm itself. Alternatively, employee teams drawn from nonmarketing positions can conduct the audit. In either case, those who conduct the audit systematically examine the marketing environment to identify opportunities and threats of which the marketing manager may not have been aware, as well as the objectives, strategies, and activities spelled out in the marketing plan. Auditors interview managers, customers, and salespeople. Table 2.2 shows the areas of the firm's marketing function that a marketing audit can evaluate.

marketing audit ■ A comprehensive review of a firm's marketing function.

TABLE 2.2

Information Gathered in a Marketing Audit

1. Marketing philosophy
   Support organizational objectives
   Focus on customer needs
   Social responsibility included in decision making
   Different offerings for different segments
   A total system perspective

2. Marketing organization
   Integration of different marketing functions
   Integration of marketing with other functional areas of the organization
   Organization for new-product development
   Qualifications and effectiveness of marketing management personnel

3. Marketing information systems
   Effective use of marketing research
   Current study data available
   Timely communication of relevant information to marketing planners
   Knowledge of sales potential and profitability for various market segments, territories, products, channels, and order sizes
   Monitor effectiveness of marketing strategies and tactics
   Cost-effectiveness studies

4. Strategic orientation
   Formal marketing planning
       Objectives
       Environmental scanning
       Sales forecasting
       Contingency planning
   Quality of current marketing strategy
       Product strategies
       Distribution strategies
       Promotion strategies
       Pricing strategies
   Contingency planning

5. Operations
   Communications and implementation of planning
   Effective use of resources
   Ability to adapt to changes

Source: Adapted from Philip Kotler, "From Sales Obsession to Marketing Effectiveness," *Harvard Business Review* (November–December 1977): 70–71.

How It Worked Out at DDB Worldwide

Angela selected Option 2. She reasoned that JCPenney offered no real, tangible benefit over its competition. It would never be able to match the discounters in terms of price, and communicating brand names was something the competition was already doing well. You probably came to the same conclusion after visiting other stores or surfing to their Web sites. For example, JCPenney would have a hard time competing on a purely price basis with the likes of Wal-Mart.

The store needed a positioning that rang true with consumers today, did not over promise, and was relevant to the consumer. Angela felt it made the most sense to create an emotional connection to the customer. So, the new positioning for JCPenney became: *JCPenney is the one store that fuels self-expression.* This strategic decision led directly to DDB's "It's All Inside" advertising campaign, and it also set a tone throughout the JCPenney organization. Direct-mail pieces, newspaper inserts, catalogs, the Web site, and in-store signage all had a new and consistent look and feel.

The changes implemented in the stores, along with its new positioning, did wonders for JCPenney. Indeed, while one of the corporate objectives was to stop sales declines, in fact JCPenney posted its best sales year ever. In comparison to a decline in sales of more than 2% in 2000, sales in 2001 grew by almost 3.5%. This dramatic increase shows how clear and thoughtful strategic planning can pay off at the cash register for a firm like JCPenney.

To summarize what we've discussed in this chapter, planning, a key element of a firm's success, occurs in several different stages. Strategic planning takes place at both the corporate and the SBU level in large firms and in a single stage in smaller businesses. Marketing planning, one of the functional planning areas, comes next. Operational planning assures proper implementation and control of the marketing plan. In the next chapter, we'll see how firms strive for both economic and social profit in a complex environment.

Chapter Summary

1. Explain the strategic planning process.

Business planning includes strategic planning by top-level managers at the corporate and at the strategic business unit (SBU) level. Tactical planning is done by middle managers, and operations planning by lower-level managers. At the corporate level, strategic planning means establishing a vision or mission and developing corporate goals or objectives. Decisions about the firm's portfolio of strategic business units are often made with the help of such planning tools as the Boston Consulting Group matrix, which assesses SBUs on market growth potential and the firm's relative market share. Strategic planning for SBUs or smaller businesses begins with defining the firm's business mission. From the firm's mission statement and an evaluation of the firm's internal strengths and weaknesses as well as its external opportunities and threats (called a SWOT analysis), planners develop objectives that identify what the business hopes to achieve. Managers may determine the business growth strategy with the product–market growth matrix that identifies four strategies for market penetration, market development, product development, and diversification.

2. Tell how firms gain a competitive advantage and describe the factors that influence marketing objectives.

Creating a competitive advantage is the strategic focus of an organization's marketing planning process. A competitive advantage means that a firm has developed reasons for customers to select its product over others in the market. A firm gains a competitive advantage when it has distinctive competencies or capabilities that are stronger than those of the competition. These distinctive competencies are used to create differential benefits or product benefits, which are uniquely different from the competition.

3. Describe the steps in the marketing management process.

Marketing planning is one type of tactical or functional planning. Marketing planning begins with an evaluation of the internal and external environments. Marketing managers then set quantitative and qualitative market objectives such as desired levels of sales, the development of new or improved products, or growth in new or existing markets. Next, marketing managers select the target market(s) for the organization and decide what marketing mix strategies they will use. Product strategies include decisions about products and product characteristics that will appeal to the target market. Pricing strategies state the specific prices to be charged to channel members and final consumers. Promotion strategies include plans for advertising, consumer and trade sales promotion, the sales function, publicity, point-of-purchase materials, and other marketing communications activities to reach the target market. Distribution strategies outline how the product will be made available to targeted customers when and where they want it. The final step in the marketing planning process is the development of a written market ing plan.

4. Explain how marketers implement and control the marketing plan.

In operational planning, supervisory managers develop action plans to implement tactical plans. Implementation, or putting the plan into action, includes development of the marketing budget. Also essential to successful implementation is effective organization of the marketing function—that is, how the work is broken up into different jobs and assigned to different people. Control is the measurement of actual performance and comparison with planned performance. Planners may use trend analyses or other forms of marketing research to obtain performance feedback. A comprehensive review of the marketing system is sometimes conducted using a marketing audit.

Chapter Review

▪ MARKETING CONCEPTS:
TESTING YOUR KNOWLEDGE

1. What is strategic, tactical, and operational planning? What is cross-functional planning?
2. What is a mission statement? Why is a mission statement important to an organization?
3. What is marketing myopia? What are the negative consequences when a firm suffers from marketing myopia?
4. What is a SWOT analysis? What role does it play in the planning process?
5. What is a strategic business unit (SBU)?
6. Explain the BCG model for portfolio analysis. What is the BCG model used for?
7. What does it mean for a firm to have a competitive advantage? What gives a firm a competitive advantage?
8. What are marketing objectives? What types of marketing objectives do firms typically include in marketing planning?
9. Describe the four businesss growth strategies: market penetration, product development, market development, and diversification.
10. What are some of the factors that firms consider when developing product strategies? What are some influences on pricing strategies? What are some of the issues involved in developing promotion strategies? What do firms consider when developing distribution strategies?
11. What are the elements of a formal marketing plan?
12. What are the differences between a functional structure, a geographic structure and a product structure in the organization of the marketing function?
13. How do firms control their marketing plans?

▪ MARKETING CONCEPTS:
DISCUSSING CHOICES AND ISSUES

1. The Boston Consulting Group matrix identifies products as stars, cash cows, question marks, and dogs. Do you think this is a useful way for organizations to examine their businesses? What are some examples of products that fit in each category?
2. In this chapter we talked about how firms do strategic, tactical, and operations planning. Yet, some firms are successful without formal planning. Do you think planning is essential to a firm's success? Can planning ever hurt an organization?
3. Do you agree with the idea that marketing is a firm's most essential functional area, or do you think a firm's success depends equally on all of its functional areas? Explain your reasoning.

4. Do you think firms should concentrate on developing products that are better in some way than competitors' products, or should each firm focus on making the best product it can without regard to competing products? As a consumer, which approach is more likely to produce products that satisfy you most?

5. Most planning involves strategies for growth. But is growth always the right direction to pursue? Can you think of some organizations that should have contraction rather than expansion as their goal? Do you know of any organizations that have planned to get smaller rather than larger in order to be successful?

6. Sometimes analysis of a company's products using the BCG model suggests that a product should be dropped. But what if the product is still wanted and needed by a small group of consumers. Should firms abandon these consumers? What criteria should they use for the decision?

MARKETING PRACTICE:
APPLYING WHAT YOU'VE LEARNED

1. Assume that you are the marketing director for a small firm that manufactures children's clothing. Your boss, the company president, has decided to develop a mission statement. He's admitted that he doesn't know much about developing a mission statement and has asked that you help guide him in this process. Write a memo outlining what exactly a mission statement is, why firms develop such statements, how firms use mission statements, and your thoughts on what the firm's mission statement might be.

2. As a marketing student, you know that large firms often organize their operations into a number of strategic business units (SBUs). A university might develop a similar structure in which different academic schools or departments are seen as separate businesses. Working with a small group of four to six classmates, consider how your university might divide its total academic units into separate SBUs. What would be the problems with implementing such a plan? What would be the advantages and disadvantages for students and for faculty? Present your analysis of university SBUs to your class.

3. Working in a small group with four to six classmates, select a product that you all use, such as toothpaste or shampoo. Identify the different brands of the product used by each person in the group, and find out what product features and benefits caused each person to choose the particular brand. Then combine your responses to create a list of all possible product attributes a manufacturer might consider in developing a new brand for that product.

4. Assume you are the new marketing assistant in a small metropolitan hospital whose market consists of the residents in the city district and the students and faculty of a large nearby university. You have been asked for ideas that the organization might use in promotional activities to draw clients who might otherwise choose a larger facility across town. Develop a list of the consumer segments in the hospital's market (for example, elderly, children, college athletes, international students, and so on), and for each segment, identify possible features and benefits the hospital might emphasize in its promotions to attract that segment.

5. Successful firms have a competitive advantage because they are able to identify distinctive competencies and use these to create differential benefits for their customers. Consider your business school or your university. What distinctive competencies does it have? What differential benefits does it provide for students? What is its competitive advantage? What are your ideas as to how your university could improve its competitive position? Write an outline of your ideas.

6. An important part of planning is a SWOT analysis, understanding an organization's strengths, weaknesses, opportunities, and threats. Choose a business in your community that you are familiar with. Develop a brief SWOT analysis for that business.

MARKETING MINI-PROJECT:
LEARNING BY DOING

The purpose of this mini-project is to gain an understanding of marketing planning through actual experience.

1. Select one of the following for your marketing planning project:
   - yourself (in your search for a career)
   - your university
   - a specific department in your university

2. Next, develop the following elements of the marketing planning process:
   - a mission statement
   - a SWOT analysis
   - objectives
   - a description of the target market(s)
   - a brief outline of the marketing mix strategies—the product, pricing, distribution, and promotion strategies—that satisfy the objectives and address the target market.

3. Prepare a formal, but brief, marketing plan using Appendix A as a guide.

REAL PEOPLE, REAL SURFERS:
EXPLORING THE WEB

Visit the home pages of one or more of the firms whose mission statements are given in Figure 2.2. Follow the links to find out about the company's products, pricing, distribution, and marketing communications strategies. Do a search of the World Wide Web for other information about the company. Based on your findings, answer the following questions:

1. What is the organization's business? What is the overall purpose of the organization? What does the organization hope to achieve?

2. What customers does the business want to serve?

3. What elements of the Web page specifically reflect the business of the organization? How is the Web page designed to attract the organization's customers?
4. Do you think the marketing strategies and other activities of the firm are consistent with its mission? Why do you feel this way?

Develop a report based on your findings and conclusions about the firm. Present your report to your class.

▨ PLAN IT! DEVELOPING A MARKETING PLAN

As your instructor directs, continue documenting your marketing plan using Marketing Plan Pro software or a written

marketing plan format; alternatively, explain your decisions in a written or oral report.

As you continue to prepare next year's marketing plan for CFS, review the SWOT analysis, issue analysis, objectives, and product strategies in the current year's marketing plan (see Appendix A, pages 559–568).

1. Assuming that the company achieves this year's objectives, what specific strengths and weaknesses not emphasized in this year's plan might influence next year's plan?
2. What other opportunities and threats should management research and factor into next year's planning process?
3. In planning for growth, should CFS pursue a market penetration, market development, product development, or diversification strategy, and why?

Key Terms

BCG growth–market share matrix, (35)
business plan, (31)
business portfolio, (35)
competitive advantage, (40)
controlling the marketing plan, (51)
cross-functional planning, (32)
differential benefit, (40)
distinctive competency, (40)

diversification, (42)
external environment, (39)
internal environment, (38)
market development, (42)
market penetration, (41)
marketing audit, (52)
marketing budget, (50)
marketing plan, (31)
mission statement, (33)

operational planning, (32)
portfolio analysis, (35)
product development, (42)
situation analysis, (48)
strategic business units (SBUs), (31)
strategic planning, (31)
SWOT analysis, (38)
tactical (functional) planning, (31)
trend analysis, (51)

MARKETING IN ACTION: CHAPTER 2 CASE

REAL CHOICES AT MCDONALD'S

As far back as 1965, Ray A. Kroc, the founder of McDonald's Corp., declared, "I don't know what we'll be serving in the year 2000, but we'll be serving more of it than anybody." True, in 2000, McDonald's was the number one fast-food chain with a total of 13,000 restaurants in the United States and 28,000 McDonalds in 121 countries worldwide.

Kroc's prediction was on the money, and McDonald's has dominated the fast-food business for more than 30 years. But as the new century approached, cracks were appearing in the golden arches.

The first McDonald's restaurant opened in 1937 in a parking lot east of Pasadena, California, where happy customers ate hot dogs (the most popular item on the menu) served by teenage carhops. When America's tastes changed, the golden arches changed, too. Carhops were replaced by indoor restaurants. And in the 1960s, the Big Mac made McDonald's stand out from other burger joints. When consumers became tired of beef in the early 1980s, McDonald's introduced bite-size chunks of fried chicken. McDonald's gave consumers what they wanted—seemingly before they knew what they wanted. And in the process, McDonald's became a global icon.

But it's not easy to remain top dog. By the late 1990s Burger King and Wendy's were closing in. McDonald's seemed to have lost its competitive advantage. McDonald's last successful new product had been the Chicken McNugget, introduced in 1983. In the 1990s, McDonald's had experimented with pizza and veggie burgers and had unsuccessfully tried to enter the adult fast-food market with the ill-fated Arche Deluxe, an adult burger with Dijon mustard sauce. Then, to make matters worse, McDonald's had confused customers with a series of discounting strategies. Even though McDonald's still had a large percent of the U.S. fast-food burger market, the data verified that McDonald's faced serious problems. Profits in fall 2000 dropped for the fifth consecutive quarter due, according to the company, to a weakening global economy and a lingering fear of mad-cow disease. But some research suggested otherwise. In an annual study by the University of Michigan in 2000, McDonald's was rated lowest of all national fast-food restaurants by consumers—for the eighth consecutive time.

McDonald's had tried a number of strategies to improve its status. In 1998, McDonald's had required all U.S. restaurants to install a made-to-order cooking system designed to improve the taste of burgers and compete with rivals, but many franchises complained that the system slowed down delivery of food to customers.

Some members of the McDonald's marketing team suggested that the company needed a product development strategy—that there ought to be ways to squeeze new profits by adding items to the current menu. Another idea that had been thrown around was to build on McDonald's brand value to sell totally different products—for example, take advantage of McDonald's popularity with kids to sell a line of toys. Some thought that McDonald's could continue expansion into international markets. McDonald's earned over half of its profits from its international division. But new international expansion meant going past the "easy" markets such as London and Moscow into more challenging markets such as Germany and Japan. And there was substantial anti-American feeling in some countries.

Of course, none of these strategies would solve the problem many felt to be the primary reason for McDonald's low growth—customer satisfaction. While McDonald's had focused on building more stores, what Americans really wanted was better food and more variety. Many consumers who eat fast food at least once a month said that Wendy's and Burger King offer better-tasting food. In a *Business Week*/Harris poll, McDonald's ranked 87th out of 91 in the taste of their food—just behind Hooters. These same consumers ranked taste and quality as very important factors in restaurant choice, whereas they rated convenience and speed as much less important. As the new millenium approached, McDonald's had to figure out its recipe for continued McProfits.

Source: Makc Ballon, "McDonald's Looking for a Break," *Los Angeles Times,* December 15, 2001, Part 3, Page 1; David Leonhardt, "McDonald's: Can It Regain Its Golden Touch?" *Business Week* 9 (March 1998): 70–77; Cyndee Miller, "McDonald's Shifts Strategy as Competitors Get Stronger," *Marketing News* 28 (April 1997): 1, 10.

THINGS TO THINK ABOUT

1. What is the decision facing McDonald's?
2. What factors are important in understanding the decision situation?
3. What are the alternatives?
4. What decision(s) do you recommend?
5. What are some ways to implement your recommendations?

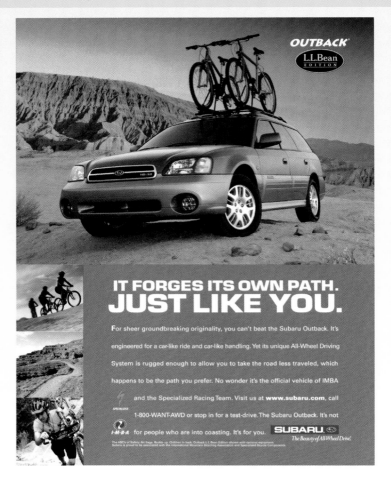

Bookmark It!

OBJECTIVES:

1. Explain how organizations adopt a New Era marketing orientation on ethics and social responsibility.
2. Describe the New Era emphasis on quality.
3. Discuss some of the important elements of an organization's internal environment.
4. Explain why marketers scan an organization's external business environment.

Decision Making in the New Era of Marketing

3

ETHICS AND THE MARKETING ENVIRONMENT

Real People, Real Choices:

Meet Joe Barstys, a Decision Maker at Subaru of America

www.subaru.com

CURRENT POSITION: Manager of Customer Relationships.

CAREER PATH: B.A. in philosophy, St. Francis College; M.A. theology, Christ the King Theologate; taught high school; commercial photographer, marketing positions at Eaton Corporation. In 1984 became a member of Subaru customer relationships team.

BUSINESS BOOK I'M READING: Re-reading Theodore Levitt's classic <u>The Marketing Imagination</u>.

WHAT I DO WHEN NOT WORKING: Play guitar, long-distance cycling, volunteer work, late-night writing.

HERO: My Dad. A coal miner at 16 and a chemical plant laborer for 50 years. He left this earth at age 85 with four kids doing better than he did, and a wife secure for her remaining days.

MOTTOS: "Carpe diem!" "The cracked ones let in the light." Right now "Intelligence is the next growth market" is directing me to connect with our customers.

MOTIVATION: I am a tugboat, nudging life's ocean liners to better paths. Seen from this angle "daily doings" are meaningful.

How Subaru Got Customers to Commit

The "Holy Grail" for a marketer is to create satisfied customers. No one believes this more than Joe Barstys. As Manager of Customer Relationships for Subaru of America (headquartered in Cherry Hill, NJ), Joe's job is to ensure that Subaru's customers are happy. He manages all aspects of relationship building for the company, including an after-sale survey program and an owner magazine sent to 650,000 Subaru owners quarterly. When Subaru drivers are satisfied, Joe is satisfied.

But, in today's competitive business environment is it enough just to be satisfied? Is there a difference between being *satisfied* with something and being *loyal* to something? Say the something is a love interest—satisfied would mean asking the person out on another date. But loyalty would mean the big scary C word—a commitment. Well, marketers are constantly trying to get the big C word from customers, especially today when we are in, as marketers say, a *New Era* of business relationships.

Joe had to find out what makes consumers loyal to a brand of car. Since 1985, his company had been conducting a survey on the purchase and service experiences of Subaru owners as part of its national Subaru Owner Loyalty Program. Forms sent after purchase and during the warranty period asked Subaru buyers to rate their contentment with their car and the service they got from local dealers. The company shared these responses with Subaru's national network of dealers and with Subaru's regional and district managers.

But Joe realized that despite its name the survey wasn't measuring loyalty, just *satisfaction*. In fact, virtually <u>all</u> of the industry's attempts to track customers' reactions

59

focused on satisfaction, including the influential J.D. Power Customer Satisfaction Index (CSI) that published consumers' evaluations of many different car models. Moreover, Subaru, along with most of its industry competitors, had assumed that there is only a short leap from satisfaction to loyalty. If consumers were satisfied with Subaru's service and products, surely they would continue to buy a Subaru in the future—right?

Not necessarily so, say many consumer behavior researchers. Customer repurchases are an outcome of *loyalty* rather than just satisfaction, they say. Satisfaction is simply a positive feeling when there is a match between expectations and experience. Loyalty goes farther. It is a bond with a product that is hard for competitors to shake. Loyal customers will buy the same brand over and over, and refer their friends as well.

Subaru, along with the entire automobile industry, had to face a grim reality. Although 90 percent of car buyers were satisfied with their purchase and service experience, loyalty toward any particular automaker averaged only around 40 percent. The Subaru survey allowed dealers to fix "things gone wrong," but it didn't motivate them to change their business practices to build long-term loyalty.

Historically, the auto business has operated with a short-term approach to business planning—usually making decisions in 10-day cycles. Dealers are more used to thinking in terms of short-term success than in the value of developing relationships over the long haul. The dealer focus is on the profit margin inherent in the sale price and any supplements the factory may choose to provide. Joe needed to rethink the survey and how owner feedback could be used to help dealers build strong bonds with customers. Joe had three options:

Option 1: Maintain the current survey program.

Subaru could maintain the current survey program and supplement it with targeted training for dealership personnel that would help them understand the difference between providing adequate service and exemplary service. This option would introduce some incremental costs, of course, but it would not require any changes in the current survey and report formats.

Option 2: Provide incentives to dealers.

Subaru could provide factory incentives to dealers whose performance improved according to the survey. This option would cost more, but like option #1 it would not require substantial changes to the program administration and support materials.

Option 3: Completely re-work the current program.

Subaru could try to identify a set of key loyalty indicators and try to convince dealers that if their customers scored higher on these measures they would be rewarded with repeat business over time. Although requiring a complete re-work of the current program, the new focus would mean dealer performance improvement would be motivated more by increasing Subaru's share of loyal customers than from a factory incentive. This was a risky proposition, since dealers were not used to thinking in these terms. Getting them to change their mindsets would be an uphill battle.

Now, join the Subaru decision team: Which option would you choose, and why?

Welcome to the New Era of Marketing

Change is in the wind. Marketers recognize that a truly global marketplace beckons them. Businesses seek to attract customers in that global marketplace through e-commerce. Marketers also need to recognize that the attacks on September 11, 2001—and the resulting war on terrorism—have led consumers to assess what's truly important in their lives. Is it family? Is it spirituality? How about patriotism? What about materialism? Marketers have had to figure out the right message to send during this time of heightened sensitivity. Such changes make today's marketers like Joe Bartsys of Subaru more aware than ever that long-term

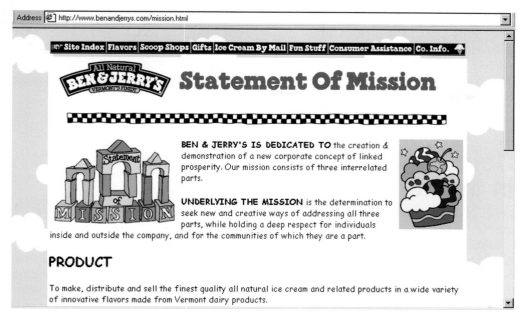

Address http://www.benandjerrys.com/mission.html

Site Index | Flavors | Scoop Shops | Gifts | Ice Cream By Mail | Fun Stuff | Consumer Assistance | Co. Info.

Statement Of Mission

BEN & JERRY'S IS DEDICATED TO the creation & demonstration of a new corporate concept of linked prosperity. Our mission consists of three interrelated parts.

UNDERLYING THE MISSION is the determination to seek new and creative ways of addressing all three parts, while holding a deep respect for individuals inside and outside the company, and for the communities of which they are a part.

PRODUCT

To make, distribute and sell the finest quality all natural ice cream and related products in a wide variety of innovative flavors made from Vermont dairy products.

Ben & Jerry's Ice Cream is a New Era firm that proudly displays its focus on improving the quality of life of employees and the community.

profitability depends on making quality products while acting in an ethical and socially responsible manner—anything less and consumers will run, not walk, into the arms of competitors. Aspiring tycoons, don't panic: Marketing still is concerned with the firm's bottom line, but now many managers also consider **social profit** which is the net benefit both the firm and society receive from a firm's ethical practices and socially responsible behavior.[1]

Creating social profit is so important to Ben & Jerry's, the Vermont super-premium ice-cream firm, that part of its mission statement reads, "To improve the quality of life of our employees and a broad community—local, national, and international."[2] That's why the firm gives 7.5 percent of pretax profits to a foundation that supports social and environmental causes. Ben & Jerry's even recycles part of the waste from its ice-cream factories by feeding it to some happy Vermont pigs that think they died and went to hog heaven.

We call efforts to do business right and do it well the New Era of Marketing. Figure 3.1 shows that New Era firms create both economic and social profit through a commitment to ethical business behavior, social responsibility, total quality, and through a clear understanding of their internal and external environments.

social profit ■ The benefit an organization and society receive from the organization's ethical practices, community service, efforts to promote cultural diversity, and concern for the natural environment.

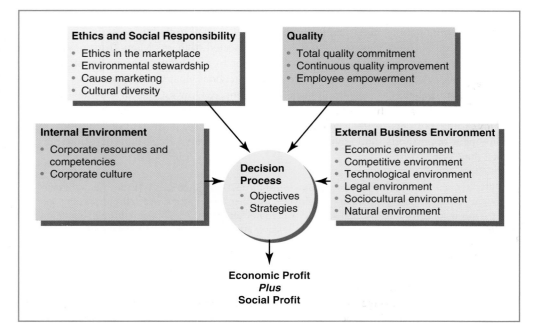

Ethics and Social Responsibility
- Ethics in the marketplace
- Environmental stewardship
- Cause marketing
- Cultural diversity

Quality
- Total quality commitment
- Continuous quality improvement
- Employee empowerment

Internal Environment
- Corporate resources and competencies
- Corporate culture

Decision Process
- Objectives
- Strategies

External Business Environment
- Economic environment
- Competitive environment
- Technological environment
- Legal environment
- Sociocultural environment
- Natural environment

Economic Profit
Plus
Social Profit

FIGURE 3.1

Decision Model for Firms in the New Era of Marketing

New Era firms create both economic profit and social profit by focusing on quality while being socially responsible—and by understanding their internal and external environments.

In this chapter we'll look at companies such as Subaru that practice this philosophy. First, we'll focus on doing it right by talking about ethics and social responsibility. Next we'll examine how New Era firms do it well by producing quality goods and services they can be proud to sell. Then, in the second half of the chapter, we'll take a look at the elements of a firm's internal and external environments and how they influence decision making in the New Era.

Doing It Right: Ethical Behavior in the Marketplace

In fall, 2001, the public was shaken by the Enron scandal—the largest corporate bankruptcy in U.S. history. With the giant electricity and natural gas trader's collapse in October 2001 came a Justice Department investigation of not only Enron's activities but also its auditor Arthur Andersen. Just a few years prior, Enron's stock had been soaring, and the company had been urging employees to invest their retirement accounts in Enron stock. When Enron filed for Chapter 11 bankruptcy, its stock had fallen from a high of $90.75 per share to .26 per share. Outraged employees filed lawsuits, as did investors who had lost billions. Meanwhile, Enron and Arthur Andersen shredded documents, Wall Street reacted in fear, and investigators tried to figure out what went wrong and when at Enron.

The fallout from the Enron case and the scandals at WorldCom, Global Crossing, and ImClone are sure to be ongoing. For our purposes it raises the issue of how damaging unethical practices can be to society at large. Issues of accountability, corporate accounting practices, and government regulation fill the business press as the public and corporate America reassess what comprises ethical behavior.

Ethics are rules of conduct—how most people in a culture judge what is right and what is wrong. **Business ethics** are basic values that guide a firm's behavior. These values govern decisions managers make about what goes into their products, how they are advertised and sold, and how they are disposed of. Developing good business ethics is the first step toward creating social profit.

business ethics ■ Rules of conduct for an organization.

Of course, notions of right and wrong differ among organizations and cultures. Some businesses, for example, believe it is okay for salespeople to persuade customers to buy, even if it means giving them partly true, or even false, information, while other firms practice nothing less than total honesty with customers. Because each culture has its own set of values, beliefs, and customs, ethical business behaviors vary in different parts of the world. While specifically forbidden by law in the United States, bribery is not only accepted in countries including many of the developing nations in Africa, it is expected if you want to do business.

So, how do business managers know what is expected of them? Many firms develop their own **code of ethics**—a written standard of behavior to which everyone in the organization must subscribe. These documents eliminate confusion about what the firm considers to be ethically acceptable behavior for employees. For example, Dow's Code of Business Conduct (available through its Web site [www.dow.com] in 15 different languages) includes ethical principles and policies to deal with issues such as bribery, political contributions, equal employment opportunity, and environment, health and safety.[3] Regarding questionable payments, the Code states:

codes of ethics ■ Written standards of behavior to which everyone in the organization must subscribe.

> It is against Dow policy to make unlawful, improper, or other kinds of questionable payments to customers, government employees, or other third parties. We sell our products on the merits of price, quality, and service. We do not seek business obtained through deviation from this principle. We will not offer expensive gifts, bribes, or any other kind of payment or benefit to representatives of customers, suppliers, competitors, government, or governmental agencies. This applies to any individual or organization at any level, whether domestic or foreign.

To help member firms adhere to ethical behavior in their marketing efforts, the American Marketing Association (AMA) developed its own code of ethics, as shown in Figure 3.2.[4]

Members of the American Marketing Association are committed to ethical, professional conduct. They have joined together in subscribing to this Code of Ethics embracing the following topics:

Responsibilities of the Marketer
Marketers must accept responsibility for the consequences of their activities and make every effort to ensure that their decisions, recommendations, and actions function to identify, serve, and satisfy all relevant publics: customers, organizations, and society.

Marketers' professional conduct must be guided by:
1. The basic rule of professional ethics: not knowingly to do harm;
2. The adherence to all applicable laws and regulations;
3. The accurate representation of their education, training and experience; and
4. The active support, practice, and promotion of this Code of Ethics.

Honesty and Fairness
Marketers shall uphold and advance the integrity, honor, and dignity of the marketing profession by:
1. Being honest in serving consumers, clients, employees, suppliers, distributors, and the public;
2. Not knowingly participating in conflict of interest without prior notice to all parties involved; and
3. Establishing equitable fee schedules including the payment or receipt of usual, customary, and/or legal compensation for marketing exchanges.

Rights and Duties of Parties in the Marketing Exchange Process
Participants in the marketing exchange process should be able to expect that:
1. Products and services offered are safe and fit for their intended uses;
2. Communications about offered products and services are not deceptive;
3. All parties intend to discharge their obligations, financial and otherwise, in good faith; and
4. Appropriate internal methods exist for equitable adjustment and/or redress of grievances concerning purchases.

It is understood that the above would include, but is not limited to, the following responsibilities of the marketer:
In the area of product development and management,
- disclosure of all substantial risks associated with product or service usage;
- identification of any product component substitution that might materially change the product of impact on the buyer's purchase decision;
- identification of extra cost-added features.

In the area of promotions,
- avoidance of false and misleading advertising;
- rejection of high pressure manipulations, or misleading sales tactics;
- avoidance of sales promotions that use deception or manipulation.

In the area of distribution,
- not manipulating the availability of a product for purpose of exploitation;
- not using coercion in the marketing channel;
- not exerting undue influence over the reseller's choice to handle a product.

In the area of pricing,
- not engaging in price fixing;
- not practicing predatory pricing;
- disclosing the full price associated with any purchase.

In the area of marketing research,
- prohibiting selling or fundraising under the guise of conducting research;
- maintaining research integrity by avoiding misrepresentation and omission of pertinent research data;
- treating outside clients and suppliers fairly.

Organizational Relationships
Marketers should be aware of how their behavior may influence or impact on the behavior of others in organizational relationships. They should not demand, encourage, or apply coercion to obtain unethical behavior in their relationships with others, such as employees, suppliers, or customers.
1. Apply confidentiality and anonymity in professional relationships with regard to privileged information;
2. Meet their obligations and responsibilities in contracts and mutual agreements in a timely manner;
3. Avoid taking the work of others, in whole, or in part, and represent this work as their own or directly benefit from it without compensation or consent of the originator or owner;
4. Avoid manipulation to take advantage of situations to maximize personal welfare in a way that unfairly deprives or damages the organization of others.

Any AMA member found to be in violation of any provision of this Code of Ethics may have his or her Association membership suspended or revoked.

FIGURE 3.2

AMA Code of Ethics

The American Marketing Association helps its members adhere to ethical standards of business through its Code of Ethics.

Source: American Marketing Association.

THE HIGH COSTS OF UNETHICAL MARKETPLACE BEHAVIOR

Ethical business is good business. New Era marketers understand that unethical practices can wind up costing dearly in the long run—both financially and to a firm's reputation. Honda found this out the hard way, when a lawsuit made known how former executives of the car company allegedly accepted bribes from dealers in exchange for preferential treatment. Sixteen former employees pleaded guilty in a federal investigation to receiving "gifts" including such goodies as a helicopter tour of Hawaii and a $25,000 shopping spree in Hong Kong. To ensure that this type of activity does not re-occur, Honda set up a financial disclosure policy for its senior executives and established a corporate ethics committee. In addition, employees must sign Honda's revised business ethics and conflict of interest policy every year to certify that their conduct is appropriate.[5] Such policies go a long way to keep a firm's behavior ethical and to maintain customers' trust and loyalty.

Consumers appreciate companies that practice ethical behavior, but sometimes we forget that ethics in the marketplace is a two-way street: Experts estimate that crimes committed by consumers against businesses cost more than $40 billion per year. These violations include shoplifting, employee pilferage, arson, and insurance fraud. A retail theft is committed every five seconds, and one out of every three small business bankruptcies is due to customer and employee theft. Many retailers also lose sales to "retail borrowing" where the consumer purchases an item such as a party dress or an expensive business suit, wears it for a special occasion, and returns it the next day as if it had not been worn. Consumers ultimately pay for such practices when retailers and manufacturers raise prices to cover their losses. In fact, a family of four spends over $300 extra per year because of markups taken by stores to compensate for stolen or damaged merchandise.[6] Although marketers work hard to prevent such behavior, they often must overlook dishonest customers in order to provide return policies and a pleasant retail shopping environment necessary to satisfy honest ones.

CONSUMERISM: FIGHTING BACK

Organized activities that bring about social and political change are not new to the American scene. Women's right to vote, child labor laws, the minimum wage, equal employment opportunity, and the ban on nuclear weapons testing all have resulted from social movements where citizens, public and private organizations, and businesses work to change society. **Consumerism** is the social movement directed toward protecting consumers from harmful business practices.

The modern consumerism movement began in the 1960s when the publication of books—such as Rachel Carson's *Silent Spring*, which attacked the irresponsible use of pesticides, and Ralph Nader's *Unsafe at Any Speed*, which exposed safety defects in General Motors' Corvair automobiles—put pressure on businesses to mend their ways. Consumers organized to call for safer products and honest information—and to boycott companies that did not comply with their demands. Consumerism also prompted the establishment of government regulatory agencies and legislation such as the Cigarette Labeling Act of 1966 and the Child Protection and Safety Act of 1969.

In his 1961 inaugural speech, President John F. Kennedy outlined what became known as the **Consumer Bill of Rights**, which includes:

- *The right to be safe*: Products should not be dangerous when used as intended. Organizations such as the Consumer Products Safety Board and *Consumer Reports* magazine regularly announce products they find to be unsafe. Product safety was an important issue when a number of serious accidents, some fatal, were connected to the sudden loss of tread on Firestone Wilderness AT tires installed as original equipment on Ford SUVs. An engineering analysis conducted by the National Highway Traffic Safety Administration (NHTSA) found that the tires were defective, leading Firestone to recall over 10 million tires. The company stated that while they did not agree with the finding, they were recalling the tires to avoid a long confrontation with the NHTSA.[7]
- *The right to be informed*: Businesses should provide consumers with adequate information to make intelligent product choices. This right means that product information provided by advertising, packaging, and salespeople should be honest and complete.
- *The right to be heard*: Consumers should have the means to complain or express their displeasure in order to obtain redress or retribution from companies. Government agencies and industry self-regulatory groups should respond to every customer complaint.
- *The right to choose freely*: Consumers should be able to choose from a variety of products. No one business should be allowed to control the price, quality, or availability of goods and services.

1 *Bookmark It!*

Business ethics often differ from one country to another. In some countries, for example, bribery is an accepted and expected practice, like a tip. But in the United States it is illegal. How can New Era marketers compete in a global marketplace when competitors based in other countries are allowed to play by different rules?

consumerism ■ A social movement that attempts to protect consumers from harmful business practices.

Consumer Bill of Rights ■ The rights of consumers to be protected by the federal government.

1 *Bookmark It!*

In the aftermath of the 2001 terrorist attacks, many firms "wrapped themselves in the flag" by telling customers it was their patriotic duty to spend as much as possible to keep the economy healthy. Is this sort of appeal to patriotism an ethical marketing practice? Why or why not?

ETHICS IN THE MARKETING MIX

As we've seen in previous chapters, marketing mix strategies are crucial to a firm's success in achieving its objectives. Marketing managers are responsible for determining the most ethical way to price, package, promote, and distribute their offerings to reach profit and market-share objectives. Let's see how ethical considerations can influence marketing mix decisions.

Making a Product Safe A key ethical decision concerns product safety. It can be tempting to cut costs on design, safety testing, and production to rush a new product to market. One infamous example is the case of the Ford Pinto, which was designed with an unprotected gas tank that exploded in rear-end crashes. Consumer watchdog Ralph Nader claimed that Ford had tested a safe fuel system as early as 1970 but had not installed it because it increased production costs. In 1978 Ford recalled 1.5 million Pintos made between 1971 and 1976 to install two plastic shields to protect the cars' gas tanks in rear-end collisions—but not before the company had to pay $7 million to settle a rash of lawsuits.[8]

Horizontal window blinds are another product that has seen two separate recalls in recent years.[9] Between 1991 and 2000, there were 130 infant and young child deaths caused by window blinds. In 1995, the U.S. Consumer Products Safety Commission worked with manufacturers to redesign blinds to eliminate the outer loops on window blind pull cords that were the cause of 114 child deaths. In 2000, a similar program eliminated the inner cords used to raise the slats in blinds that were responsible for 16 of the 132 deaths. In both cases, owners of existing blinds were provided with repair kits to eliminate the hazard.

Pricing the Product Fairly The potential for unethical pricing strategies is so great that many shady pricing practices are illegal. U.S. marketers face laws that prevent greedy firms from hurting consumers or other business with pricing practices that are deceptive, are unfair, or that discriminate against some customers. We'll talk more about specific legal considerations in pricing in Chapter 13.

Some pricing practices, while not illegal, are unfair to customers. This was the case when customers found out about Amazon.com's test run of **discriminatory pricing**, a practice where a seller sets different prices for different customers based on their assumed ability or willingness to pay. Amazon.com's random price test charged some regular customers an additional 3 to 5 percent on DVD movies, which worked out to be about $3.10 per DVD. After the public's negative response, Amazon.com apologized and refunded the $3.10 to more than 6,000 customers.[10] We'll talk more about discriminatory pricing in Chapter 13.

discriminatory pricing ■
A pricing practice in which different customers are charged different prices.

New Era firms price their products fairly—and they have been known to cut their prices in times of need. When Hurricane Andrew hit southern Florida in 1992, many local firms selling building materials raised their prices, knowing that residents would pay anything to protect what was left of their possessions. Home Depot, however, did just the opposite—the hardware stores sold materials for restoring walls and roofs at cost. In the process, Home Depot gained the loyalty of many Floridians and others around the country who heard the story.[11]

Numerous stories of similar selfless acts abounded after the terrorist attacks on New York and Washington DC in September 2001. That morning, a Burger King near the World Trade Center immediately started handing out drinks to people running/walking by, a Starbucks gave free coffee to the rescue workers, and many restaurants in lower Manhattan donated hot meals to the rescue workers.

Promoting the Product Ethically Marketing management's decisions on how to promote the firm's products are likely to draw the most criticism—and government regulation. To protect consumers from being misled, the U.S. Federal Trade Commission (FTC) has specific rules regarding unfair or deceptive advertising.[12] Some deceptive ads make statements that can be proven false. The FTC fined Volvo and its ad agency $150,000 each for an ad containing a "rigged" demonstration. The Volvo "Bear Food" ad campaign showed a monster truck running over a row of cars and crushing all but the Volvo station wagon. The

Nino's Italian restaurant became a 24-hour, 7 days a week rescue shelter, serving hot food and beverages to relief workers at Ground Zero, NYC, after the terrorist attack on the World Trade Center.

Volvos, however, had been structurally reinforced while the structural supports in some of the other cars had been cut.[13]

In 1998, the Federal Trade Commission found personal computer manufacturer Gateway guilty of deceptive advertising when it made claims about a money-back guarantee with a full refund and on-site warranty service.[14] The FTC found that Gateway deducted the cost of shipping PCs to consumers from the "full refund," a cost of approximately $62, and would not provide on-site service until Gateway diagnosed the problem over the phone and determined that the consumer could not make the needed repairs. Gateway settled with the FTC for $290,000.

In addition to fining firms for deceptive advertising, the FTC also has the power to require firms to run **corrective advertising**, messages that clarify or qualify previous claims. For example, an FTC ruling required Warner-Lambert to state in corrective advertising that its Listerine mouthwash would "not help prevent colds or sore throats or lessen their severity"—a claim the company had been making for years.[15]

corrective advertising ■ Advertising that clarifies or qualifies previous deceptive advertising claims.

Other ads, although not illegal, create a biased impression of products with the use of **puffery**—claims of superiority that neither sponsors nor critics of the ads can prove are true or untrue. For example, Nivea bills itself as ". . . the world's #1 name in skin care," Neutrogena claims that its cream cleanser produces "the deepest feeling clean" and DuPont says its Stainmaster Carpet is "a creation so remarkable, it's practically a miracle."

puffery ■ Claims made in advertising of product superiority that cannot be proven true or untrue.

Does this mean that puffery is an unethical marketing practice? Not really. In fact, both advertisers and consumers generally accept puffery as a normal part of the advertising game. Although a little exaggeration may be reasonable, for New Era firms the goal is to create marketing communications that are both honest and that present their products in the most positive way possible. This approach works to the firm's advantage in the long run, since it prevents consumers from becoming overly cynical about the claims it makes.

Getting the Product Where It Belongs The steps companies take to make their products available to consumers also can create ethical dilemmas. For example, because their size gives them great bargaining power when negotiating with manufacturers, many large retail chains force manufacturers to pay a **slotting allowance**—a fee paid in exchange for agreeing to place the manufacturer's products on the retailer's valuable shelf space. Although the retailers claim that such fees pay the cost of adding products to their inventory, many manufacturers feel slotting fees are more akin to highway robbery. Certainly, the practice prevents smaller manufacturers that cannot afford the slotting allowances from getting their products into the hands of consumers.

slotting allowance ■ A fee paid by a manufacturer to a retailer in exchange for agreeing to place products on the retailer's shelves.

Doing It Right: A Focus on Social Responsibility

So far, we've learned how New Era firms gain social profit by practicing business ethics when making marketing mix decisions. The second part of social profit is **social responsibility**, a management philosophy in which organizations engage in activities that have a positive effect on society and promote the public good. These activities include environmental stewardship, cause marketing, and cultural diversity. Firms that believe in social responsibility possess a value system that goes beyond the short-term bottom line. Instead, they consider the short- and long-term effects of decisions on the company, its employees, consumers, the community, and the world at large. In a survey released in 2002 that asked over 20,000 people to rate corporate reputations, the companies receiving the highest marks for social responsibility were Johnson & Johnson, Coca-Cola, Wal-Mart, Anheuser-Busch, and Hewlett-Packard.[16]

social responsibility ■ A management practice in which organizations seek to engage in activities that have a positive effect on society and promote the public good.

SERVING THE ENVIRONMENT

New Era firms assume a position of **environmental stewardship** when they make socially responsible business decisions that also protect the environment. Sometimes these choices occur in tandem with other trends so they just make good sense. For example, many people believe that the use of the Internet for shopping makes commerce more efficient, reducing the use of natural resources. Normally, when the Gross Domestic Product (GDP) of a country increases, there is a proportionate increase in energy consumption. But, during 1997 and 1998, years during which e-commerce was rapidly growing, energy consumption remained nearly the same while GDP grew 8 percent. How does e-commerce reduce energy consumption? As an example, it takes 10 times less energy for an e-marketer to truck books from a warehouse to consumers than it does for those consumers to drive their gas-guzzling SUVs to the mall to buy books at the local retail store.[17]

environmental stewardship ■ A position taken by an organization to protect or enhance the natural environment as it conducts its business activities.

Many firms preserve the environment by following a strategy called **green marketing**, which describes efforts to choose packages, product designs, and other aspects of the marketing mix that are earth friendly but still profitable. Green marketing practices can indeed result in black ink for a firm's bottom line. For example, Electrolux found that profits from its solar-powered lawn mowers, chain saws lubricated with vegetable oil, and water-conserving washing machines actually were 3.8 percent higher than the money made from the company's conventional products.[18] Here's how some other firms are "turning green:"

green marketing ■ A marketing strategy that supports environmental stewardship by creating an environmentally founded differential benefit in the minds of consumers.

- Pencil manufacturer Dixon Ticonderoga introduced a crayon made from soybeans. This is a "green" alternative to crayons made of paraffin wax, which is a by-product of oil drilling—and the firm claims the colors are "brighter and richer with a smoother texture."[19]
- Boeing changed its factory lighting from incandescent to fluorescent. This saved 100,000 tons of carbon dioxide per year, which is one of the main contributors to global warming.[20]
- When 3M upgraded its lighting systems, the company saved $4.3 million a year and reduced carbon dioxide emissions by 143 million pounds.[21] Additionally, upgrading motor systems in its St. Paul, Minnesota, headquarters saved 3M $800,000 annually and reduced CO_2 emissions by 13 million pounds.
- Shaklee, the consumer products company, and Interface Inc., a 1.3 billion floor-covering company, are paying to upgrade public school boilers from coal to natural gas, which produces fewer greenhouse emissions.[22]
- Royal Dutch/Shell is reducing emission of greenhouse gases at its plants by 2002 to a projected 25 percent below its 1990 levels. The savings would be equal to taking every car in New England off the road for five years.[23]
- In 1997 Toyota unveiled its new super energy-efficient car, the Prius. The Prius has both an internal combustion engine and an electric motor, which turn on and off independently to provide peak efficiency. Because the Prius gets as much as 66 miles per gallon, owners can save money while they're doing their part to save the planet.[24] The Honda Insight introduced a few years later gets 61–70 mpg and boasts even lower emissions.[25]

Powerful marketing communications can help to change people's attitudes and behaviors about environmental issues. This novel billboard is sponsored by the Muir Land Trust, which works to save open spaces and support environmental education programs.

Do New Era firms practice environmental stewardship because they're "righteous" or because they will benefit financially? The answer is a little of both. There are many business leaders who simply believe in doing the right thing, but most also need to see financial benefits from these decisions. Customers who are concerned about the future of the planet will buy green products even if the price is higher. But many marketers are wary of some environmental stewardship practices. For example, auto manufactureres estimate that government fuel efficiency requirements will add as much as $1,000 to the cost of an automobile, an amount many consumers may be unwilling to pay.

SERVING SOCIETY: CAUSE MARKETING

cause marketing ■
Marketing activities in which firms seek to have their corporate identity linked to a good cause through advertising, public service, and publicity.

Cause marketing is a strategy of joining forces with a not-for-profit organization to tackle a social problem. In the past, this practice usually meant running a short-term promotion and then donating profits to a charity. Marketing historians generally credit the American Express campaign to raise money for the renovation of the Statue of Liberty in 1983 as the beginning of this promotion-only form of cause marketing.[26]

The problem was that consumers often saw these programs as gimmicky and insincere—especially when there was no apparent connection between the company and the cause. The result was that sales increased during the promotion, but there were no long-term benefits to either the sponsoring firm or the cause it was trying to help. What to do?

Today, New Era firms have abandoned this one-shot approach and instead make a long-term commitment to tackle a social problem such as illiteracy or child abuse. New Era firms believe that sales of their products increase as a result of cause marketing activities. According to one survey of 2,000 American adults, they are right: 84 percent said that cause marketing creates a positive image of a company, and 78 percent said they would be more likely to buy a product associated with an important cause.[27]

Avon's Breast Cancer Awareness Crusade is a well-known example of cause marketing. Since its inception in 1993, the program has raised $25 million through the sale of its breast cancer awareness pin, a pink enameled ribbon similar to the red ribbons worn for AIDS awareness.[28] Avon's program began with educating its 415,000 U.S. sales representatives about breast cancer and the importance of early detection. Through its sales reps, Avon has even distributed 80 million of its brochures titled *10 Facts Every Woman Should Know About Breast Cancer*. Of course, Avon hopes that its long-term involvement with breast cancer awareness will result both in health benefits for women and increased goodwill for the company—a win-win situation.

SERVING THE COMMUNITY: PROMOTING CULTURAL DIVERSITY

One day two groups of hungry Secret Service agents walked into a Denny's restaurant. The all-white group said they got served right away. The other group, made up of African Americans, said they waited . . . and waited . . . and waited. The African-American agents filed a lawsuit, charging unequal treatment of minorities at Denny's.[29] Although Denny's had written policies concerning equal and fair treatment of customers and employees, the lawsuit suggested the policies were ineffective. Negative press had a substantial effect on Denny's sales and on employee morale.[30]

As the Denny's organization discovered, promotion of **cultural diversity** is not only the right thing to do—it's also important to the long-term financial health of the organization. When a firm adopts cultural diversity programs, it makes sure that marketing policies and hiring practices give people an equal chance to work for the company and buy its products. This philosophy also extends to the disabled, a consumer market with a discretionary income of $176 billion. Smart marketers view the disabled as both customers and valued employees.

cultural diversity ◼ A management practice that actively seeks to include people of different sexes, races, ethnic groups, and religions in an organization's employees, customers, suppliers, and distribution channel partners.

God, Allah, Krishna, Waheguru, Jehovah bless America.

America's diversity is united under one ideal. And TIME is there. TIME's trusted insight, perspective, and analysis helps people understand this changing world by getting inside the issues and events that surround them. So, subscribe now and you'll get 28 issues for just $1.20 an issue.

SAVE 67% OFF THE COVER PRICE.
TO ORDER, CALL TOLL-FREE
1-800-442-6566
OR TIME.COM

Since the events of September 11, 2001, Americans have been more sensitive than ever to the issue of cultural diversity. Many magazines and advertisers shifted focus to emphasize the importance of tolerance and of understanding the perspectives of those who are different from ourselves.

Denny's shows a strong commitment to diversity in every aspect of its business.

Hertz, for example, offers cars that disabled people can drive at most Hertz rental locations and has worked to make shuttle buses and vans lift-equipped to transport these customers.[31]

To foster diversity, New Era firms actively recruit people of different sexes, races, ethnic groups, and religions to be customers, suppliers, and employees. After the 1993 incident, Denny's initiated a number of diversity programs. The results: In 1996 Denny's spent $80 million with minority vendors, 28 percent of Denny's managers were minorities, and 160 Denny's restaurants were minority owned—numbers Denny's is now pleased to share.

TJX, parent company of off-price clothing retailers T.J. Maxx and Marshalls, has developed a program to help another minority group—people who have been on welfare. With over 1,000 stores in 47 U.S. states, the company has hired over 16,000 former welfare recipients. And, those hires have stayed with TJX. After a year, 61 percent have kept the same jobs compared with an average in the retail industry of only 43 percent. Next, TJX plans to recruit immigrants and people with developmental disabilities.[32]

We've seen that New Era firms create social profit by adhering to ethical business practices. New Era firms also create social profit when they practice social responsibility—protecting the environment, promoting diversity, and serving their communities through cause marketing. In the next section, we'll see how New Era firms—like Subaru—focus on quality.

quality ■ The level of performance, reliability, features, safety, cost, or other product characteristics that consumers expect to satisfy their needs and wants.

Doing It Well: A Focus on Quality

To borrow a phrase often used by the Ford Motor Company, "Quality is Job 1" in the New Era of Marketing. **Quality** is the level of performance, reliability, features, safety, cost, or other product characteristics that consumers expect to satisfy their needs and wants.

Although the concept of quality is not new, its importance has mushroomed in the past few decades. Because companies today must compete in a global marketplace in which they face a vast number of competitors, it is imperative that firms understand what quality means to their customers—and that they supply it. If they don't, someone else will.

For marketers this means continuously monitoring the changing wants and needs of customers and prospective customers and then making sure that they are giving those customers the quality they expect. For example, Subaru recently announced its commitment to a companywide culture change as part of a long-term strategic renewal called The Subaru Difference. This focus on quality includes greater attention to such issues as service quality provided by dealers and retail redesign (showroom and service area refurbishment).[33]

TOTAL QUALITY MANAGEMENT

In 1980, just when the economies of Germany and Japan were finally rebuilt from World War II and were threatening American markets, an NBC documentary on quality guru W. Edwards Deming called *If Japan Can Do It, Why Can't We?* demonstrated to the American public—and to American CEOs—the poor quality of American products.[34] So began the TQM revolution in American industry.

Many New Era firms with a quality focus have adopted the principles and practices of **total quality management (TQM)**, a philosophy that calls for companywide dedication to the development, maintenance, and continuous improvement of all aspects of the company's operations. Indeed, many of the world's most admired, successful companies—firms such as Merck (pharmaceuticals), Wal-Mart Stores (retailing), 3M (scientific, photo, and control equipment), and Coca-Cola (beverages)—have adopted a total quality focus.

TQM seeks to assure customer satisfaction by involving all employees, regardless of their function, in efforts to continually improve quality. For example, TQM firms encourage employees, even the lowest-paid factory workers, to suggest ways to improve products—and rewards them for good ideas.

But how do you know when you've attained your goal of quality? Other than increased sales and profits, a few key award programs recognize firms that are doing the job well. For instance, in 1987 the U.S. Congress established the Malcolm Baldrige National Quality Award to recognize excellence in U.S. firms. Major purposes for the award are "helping to stimulate American companies to improve quality and productivity for the pride of recognition while obtaining a competitive edge through increased profits" and "recognizing the achievements of those companies that improve the quality of their goods and services."[35] Table 3.1 shows recent winners of the Baldrige award in manufacturing, education, small business, and service.

total quality management (TQM) ■ A management philosophy that focuses on satisfying customers through empowering employees to be an active part of continuous quality improvement.

2 Bookmark It!

Quality is defined in terms of consumer expectations. What expectations do you have of your school? Go to your school's Web site and find its promise of quality or mission statement (or similar statement). How good a job does your university do in providing the quality it promises?

Year	Award Category	Company
2001	Manufacturing	Clarke American Checks, Inc.
	Education	Chugach School District
	Education	Pearl River School District
	Education	University of Wisconsin-Stout
	Small Business	Pal's Sudden Service
2000	Manufacturing	Dana Corporation—Spicer Driveshaft Division
	Manufacturing	KARLEE Company, Inc.
	Service	Operations Management International, Inc.
	Small Business	Los Alamos National Bank
1999	Manufacturing	ST Microelectronics, Inc.—Region Americas
	Service	The Ritz-Carlton Hotel Company, L.L.C.
	Service	BI
	Small Business	Sunny Fresh Foods
1998	Manufacturing	Boeing Airlift and Tanker Programs
	Manufacturing	Solar Turbines Incorporated
	Small Business	Texas Nameplate Company, Inc.

TABLE 3.1

Malcolm Baldrige Award Winners

To receive the prestigious Malcolm Baldrige Quality Award, companies must demonstrate excellence in seven areas: strategic planning, leadership, information and analysis, customer and market focus, human resources focus, process management, and business results. Winners come from five general categories: service, manufacturing, education, healthcare, and small business.

To read why these companies won, visit the National Institute of Standards and Technology's Web site:

www.nist.gov/public_affairs/releases/g01-110.htm

The Malcolm Baldrige Award logo can be proudly displayed in winners' advertising and other communications as a sign of superior product quality.

ISO 9000 ■ Criteria developed by the International Organization of Standardization to regulate product quality in Europe.

ISO 14000 ■ Standards of the International Organization of Standardization concerned with "environmental management" aimed at minimizing harmful effects on the environment.

Of course, recognition of the benefits of TQM programs is not limited to the United States. Around the world, many companies look to the uniform standards of the International Organization of Standardization (ISO) for quality guidelines. This Geneva-based organization developed a set of criteria in 1987 to improve and standardize product quality in Europe. The broad set of guidelines, known as **ISO 9000**, sets established voluntary standards for quality management.[36] Quality management is what the organization does to ensure that its products conform to the customer's requirements. In 1996, ISO developed **ISO 14000**, standards, which concentrate on "environmental management," meaning the organization works to minimize any harmful effects it may have on the environment.[37] Because members of the European Union and other European countries prefer suppliers with ISO 9000 certification, U.S. companies must comply with these standards to be competitive overseas.

ADDING A DOSE OF QUALITY TO THE MARKETING MIX

Marketing people research the level of quality consumers want and need in their products, and what price they are willing to pay for them. Marketing also has to inform consumers about product quality through the firm's marketing communications.

But keeping on top of what customers want is just the beginning. Marketing programs also have to deliver a (customer-perceived) quality product at the right place and at the right price. Instead of being satisfied with doing things the same way year after year, New Era marketers continuously seek ways to improve product, place, price, and promotion. Let's see how quality concerns affect the marketing mix.

- *Product*: One way New Era firms offer quality for their customers is by improving the customer service support they offer. For example, Entergy Corporation, which owns public utility companies in many regions of the United States, needed to improve its customer service. The company needed to increase customer loyalty after utilities were deregulated and opened to competition.[38] Entergy previously provided customer support through 13 help desks in a four-state area. It found that consolidating its help desks, which serve 2.3 million external customers and over 10,000 internal company customers, greatly improved its service. When power interruptions occurred, Entergy was able to answer calls quickly and provide customers with assurance that the company was concerned about their inconvenience.

- *Place*: Clark-Reliance Corporation produces industrial products such as high-tech electronic sensors used by utility companies and refineries. Clark-Reliance relies on teamwork to improve its distribution. Sales and production departments met and reviewed how customers obtained the company's products, and employees came up with ways to boost the firm's on-time delivery rate from 30 percent to 90 percent.[39]
- *Price*: Taco Bell Corp., a subsidiary of PepsiCo Inc., is the largest Mexican fast-food restaurant in the world. In Taco Bell restaurants, making a burrito is "a high-tech happening" that uses the TACO (total automation of company operations) system. When a customer places an order, the cashier enters it into a register. The order is immediately displayed on several screens in the food preparation area so that workers can prepare the food. This system means that Taco Bell restaurants can accurately fill a larger number of food orders with minimal workers, reducing labor and food waste costs; this in turn allows Taco Bell to keep down prices that consumers pay. As a fringe benefit of the system, Taco Bell can monitor exactly what it sells in each of its 4,000 restaurants. The monitoring helps the company reduce costs by supplying each store with the right mixture of taco shells, quesadillas, and hot sauce for its clientele.[40] Olé!
- *Promotion*: New Era firms realize that customers want information when they need it, not when it's convenient for the marketer.[41] The Gap Inc. exemplifies this philosophy. At Gap's Old Navy stores, salespeople wear headsets so they can quickly get the information to answer customers' questions—and fold clothes, stock shelves, and ticket items.

 **Advice for Subaru**

Miranda Erikkila, Student, Houston Baptist

I would choose option 3 because it will lead the company to higher sales long term and will create an atmosphere among all dealerships that would increase customer loyalty. The short-run costs to rework the system are small compared to the possible long-term profit Subaru stands to gain by focusing on customer loyalty. Only a dramatic rework of the current system will change the company's focus.

Alan Dick, Marketing Professor, University at Buffalo

I would choose option 3. Satisfaction is a *necessary* but not *sufficient* condition for customer loyalty and repeat purchase. To ensure loyalty, you must also be doing a better job than the competition. The only way to know that is to develop measures of loyalty that consider not only your products and services, but also those of your competition. A survey identifying key loyalty indicators and the underlying reasoning for that loyalty would provide Subaru with useful information for building long term relationships with its customers than would information about mere satisfaction.

Joyce LaValle, Senior VP of Marketing and Communications, Interface Companies

I would chose option 3 because the other options do not go deep enough to really understand "loyalty". The first step is to find out what programs would matter to this customer base—perhaps it would not be "exemplary service" but rather a superior purchasing experience. Without marketing data, we might never create "loyalty." This would require new thinking and new behavior. Dealers might be more willing to change if they understood what creates "loyal" customers. This is deep work, but in the end it's more sustainable over a quick fix.

Weigh in with your thoughts! Visit the Live Laboratory at www.prenhall.com/solomon for extended Other Voices replies, exercises, and more.

The Internal Business Environment

So far, we've learned about ethics and social responsibility as well as how firms practice total quality management. Now we'll take a look at the other inputs into New Era decision making—understanding the environments in which the firm operates. First, we'll examine the elements of a firm's internal environment—the strengths and weaknesses within the company.

New Era marketers examine the internal environment to see how their firms' positive attributes can help create both economic and social profit. Figure 3.1 shows us that the important elements in the firm's internal environment include the resources and competencies of the firm and its corporate culture. Let's briefly examine these elements.

CORPORATE RESOURCES AND COMPETENCIES

As we discussed in Chapter 2, a firm's resources include its money, people, reputation, brand image, and physical facilities. *Competencies* are what the organization does well. Accurate appraisals of these two parts of a firm's internal environment are essential to making good marketing decisions. When firms underestimate their resources and competencies, they miss opportunities. But overestimating resources and competencies can lead a firm to develop objectives that are doomed to fail. For example, after General Electric began manufacturing large mainframe computers in the 1960s, the firm found it simply didn't have the financial resources to sustain that business along with its other investments, and GE was forced to bail out of the computer business. That's what happens when you "byte" off more than you can chew. As we discussed in Chapter 2, successful firms, those that achieve superior economic and social profit, continuously evaluate their resources and competencies, make improvements where needed and where possible, and develop plans that use the resources and competencies to create a competitive advantage.

CORPORATE CULTURE

corporate culture ■ The set of values, norms, and beliefs that influence the behavior of everyone in the organization.

A firm's **corporate culture** is made up of the values, norms, and beliefs that influence the behavior of everyone in the organization. Corporate culture may dictate whether new ideas are welcomed or discouraged, the importance of individual ethical behavior, and even the appropriate dress for work. For many years, IBM was known as "the white shirt company" because of its unwritten rule that all employees must wear white shirts. Fortunately, corporate cultures do evolve over time and even radical changes such as blue shirts now are tolerated at "Big Blue."

3 *Bookmark It!*

Think about a job you had or have. What was or is the corporate culture? How do you think that culture affected the company's image? (If you have never worked, apply this question to a campus organization that you know.)

Risk-Taking Cultures Some corporate cultures are more inclined to take risks than others. These firms value individuality and creativity, recognizing that nurturing these characteristics often leads to the creation of important competitive advantages. A risk-taking culture is especially important to the marketing function because firms must continually improve their product, their distribution channel, and their promotion programs to remain successful in a competitive environment. A risk-taking culture is also important if managers are to feel free to adopt a philosophy of social responsibility. In firms with more traditional corporate cultures, getting managers to buy into a new way of doing things is like inviting the board of directors to go on a skydiving mission.

Profit-Centered Versus People-Centered Cultures If the firm's business mission is only economic profit and its chief objectives are increasing revenues and decreasing costs, management attitudes will be profit centered, often at the expense of employee morale. In New Era firms, where the business mission includes a concern for employees, customers, and society, as well as shareholder profits, the internal atmosphere is quite different. Managers build employee satisfaction through training and incentive programs, and often include amenities like day-care centers and family leave time. *Fortune Magazine* publishes an annual list of the best companies to work for based on a variety of criteria including company philosophy and practices, employee trust in management, pride in work and the company, and camaraderie. In

THE CODERNAUTS FIND AN ENVIRONMENT THAT SUPPORTS 35 PLATFORMS. HAIL, OPEN WORLD!

WEBSPHERE® FOR MANKIND

| THE FASTEST GROWING E-BUSINESS PLATFORM ON THE PLANET |

e business software   **ibm.com**/websphere/mankind

IT'S A DIFFERENT KIND *OF* WORLD.
YOU NEED A DIFFERENT KIND *OF* SOFTWARE.

IBM, once regarded as a conservative company, has updated its image with offbeat ads like this one.

2001, the top five companies were Edward Jones, the Container Store, SAS Institute, TD Industries, and Synovus Financial Corp.[42]

Scanning the External Business Environment

In addition to keeping its own house in order, New Era firms know that they must also keep up with what's happening in their external environment and try to respond to trends in ways that bring about economic and social profit. Figure 3.1 also shows the major elements of the external business environment. One of these environments is the natural environment, which we discussed earlier in this chapter. Others include the economic, competitive, technological, legal, and sociocultural environments. Let's examine each of these now.

THE ECONOMIC ENVIRONMENT

Assessing the economic environment means evaluating factors that influence consumer and business buying patterns, such as the amount of confidence people have in the health of the economy. This "crystal ball" must be a global one because events in one country can impact the economic health of other countries. For instance, the economic impact of the terrorist attacks on the United States in September 2001 affected the fortunes of businesses around the

The Container Store was listed by *Fortune Magazine* as one of the top five companies to work for in 2001. Companies that ranked in the top offer employees services such as day care for children and dry-cleaning pick up. Employees of these companies feel they are respected and treated as adults.

world. Consumers everywhere became fearful of traveling, creating disastrous declines in the travel and tourism industries of all countries. For many American consumers, the events of 9/11/01 caused changes in basic values—"things" became less important while family and friends gained importance. This in turn created additional declines in spending, intensifying the negative impact on the world's economy that no one could have predicted.

The Business Cycle: What Goes Around, Comes Around

The state of the economy in which a firm does business is vital to the success of its marketing plans. The overall pattern of changes or fluctuations of an economy is called the **business cycle**. All economies go through cycles of prosperity (high levels of demand, employment, and income), recession (falling demand, employment, and income), and recovery (gradual improvement in production, lowering unemployment, and increasing income).

business cycle ■ The overall patterns of change in the economy—including periods of prosperity, recession, depression, and recovery—that affect consumer and business purchasing power.

A severe recession is a *depression*, a period in which prices fall, but there is little demand because few people have money to spend and many are out of work. *Inflation* occurs when prices and the cost of living rise, while money loses its purchasing power because the cost of goods escalates. For example, between 1960 and 2001, prices increased over 5 percent a year so that an item worth $1.00 in 1960 would cost $6.00 in 2001.[43] During inflationary periods, dollar incomes may increase, but real income—what the dollar will buy—decreases because goods and services cost more.

The business cycle is especially important to marketers because of its direct effect on customer purchase behavior. During times of prosperity, both consumers and business customers buy more goods and services. Marketers are busy trying, first, to grow the business and, second, to maintain inventory levels to meet customer demand. Marketers may also develop new versions of existing products or entirely new products to take advantage of customers' willingness to spend. Prosperity is especially kind to businesses that provide vacations, entertainment, and other luxury products because many customers want to enjoy the good life and have the money to do so.

During periods of recession, consumers and business customers simply buy less. The challenge to most marketers is to effectively maintain their firm's level of sales by convincing the few customers who are buying to select the firm's product over the competition's. Of course, even recessions aren't bad for all businesses. Although it may be harder to sell luxury items, firms that make basic necessities are not likely to suffer losses. Sales of used products and do-it-yourself items may actually increase.

The Power of Expectations   Many economists suggest that changes in the economy are primarily a self-fulfilling prophecy. When consumers feel that the economy is getting better, they spend money to buy goods and services, industry flourishes and lo and behold, the economy improves! Similarly, if consumers fear a recession will occur in the next year or so, they may begin saving their money and stop making purchases. In that case, inventories of goods grow, industries slow production, and the recession begins—simply because people expected it to. Consumer beliefs about what the future holds determine **consumer confidence**, or the extent to which people are optimistic or pessimistic about the future health of the economy and how they personally will fare down the road.

consumer confidence ■ An indicator of future spending patterns as measured by the extent to which people are optimistic or pessimistic about the state of the economy.

Government and private research firms periodically conduct surveys of consumer confidence and make forecasts that wise marketers heed. One such ongoing study is conducted by a business organization called the Conference Board. (www.conference-board.org/). This survey attempts to "take the pulse" of consumers to let companies know what people will be in the mood to buy—if, in fact, they're in a buying mood at all.

THE COMPETITIVE ENVIRONMENT

A second important element of a New Era firm's external environment is the competitive environment. In the race for consumer dollars, successful firms take home the gold by keeping ahead of the competition. For products ranging from toothpaste to computers to SUVs, firms must keep abreast of what the competition is doing so they can develop new product features, new pricing schedules, or new advertising to maintain or gain market share.

Analyzing the Competition   Before a firm can begin to develop strategies that will create a competitive advantage in the marketplace, it has to know who its competitors are and

The Conference Board is one of a number of companies that regularly survey consumers to find out what they want—to "take the pulse" of the market place.

competitive intelligence (CI) ■ The process of gathering and analyzing publicly available information about rivals.

what they're doing. Marketing managers size up the competitors according to their strengths and weaknesses, monitor their marketing strategies, and try to predict their moves.

An increasing number of firms around the globe engage in **competitive intelligence (CI)** activities, the process of gathering and analyzing publicly available information about rivals. Most information companies need to know about their competitors is available from rather mundane sources including the news media, the Internet, and publicly available government documents such as building permits and patent grants. Successful CI means that a firm learns about a competitor's new products, its manufacturing, or the management styles of its executives. Then the firm uses this information to develop superior marketing strategies.[44]

Although gathering CI does not mean hiring James Bond to snoop around or steal trade secrets, some firms are quite aggressive in their efforts to learn about the activities of other companies—sometimes too aggressive. For example, Procter & Gamble recently launched a covert operation to learn about competitors' plans to introduce new hair-care products. These efforts included "dumpster diving" in a trash bin located outside a Unilever office (the bin was on public property, so technically no laws were broken). After Unilever discovered P&G's operation, P&G reassigned some executives and negotiated a settlement with Unilver that will restrict its ability to use the information it gathered from the dumpster.[45]

Dumpster diving aside, good competitive intelligence can save a company millions of dollars. For example, when Nutrasweet's industrial customers told their sales reps that the U.S. Food and Drug Administration was preparing to approve an artificial sweetener made by rival Johnson & Johnson, Nutrasweet prepared a massive advertising blitz in response. However, the company found through other sources that this approval was just a rumor. Due to good CI, Nutrasweet shelved its plan and saved itself $84 million. That's a sweet deal.

Competition in the Microenvironment

To be successful in a competitive marketplace, marketers must have a clear understanding of exactly who their competition is. Competition in the microenvironment means the product alternatives from which members of a target market may choose, and we can think of these choices at three different levels. At a broad level, many marketers compete for consumers' **discretionary income**: the amount of money people have left after paying for necessities such as housing, utilities, food, and clothing. Few consumers are wealthy enough to buy anything and everything, so each of us is constantly faced with choices: whether to plow "leftover" money into a new CD player, donate it to charity, or perhaps "turn over a new leaf" and invest in a healthy lifestyle. Thus, the first part of understanding who the competition is means understanding the alternatives consumers consider for their discretionary income.

discretionary income ■ The portion of income people have left over after paying for necessities such as housing, utilities, food, and clothing.

A second type of choice is **product competition**, in which competitors offering different products attempt to satisfy the same consumer's needs and wants. For example, if our couch potatoes opt to clean up their acts, they may choose to buff up by joining a health club, or they may purchase a Soloflex machine and pump iron at home.

product competition ■ When firms offering different products compete to satisfy the same consumer needs and wants.

The third type of choice is **brand competition**, in which competitors offering similar goods or services vie for consumer dollars. So, if our flabby friends decide to join a gym, they still must choose among competitors within this industry such as Gold's Gym or the YMCA. Some marketers make the mistake of thinking only about brand competition; they fret so much about their immediate competitors that they lose out when consumers choose a completely different way to satisfy the same need. Understanding the big picture is important.

brand competition ■ When firms offering similar goods or services compete based on their brand's reputation or perceived benefits.

Competition in the Macroenvironment

When we talk about examining competition in the macroenvironment, we mean that marketers need to understand the big picture—the overall structure of their industry. This structure can range from one firm having total control to numerous firms that compete on an even playing field. Four different structures describe differing amounts of competition. Let's review each structure, beginning with total control by one organization.

A **monopoly** exists when one seller controls a market. Because the seller is "the only game in town," it feels little pressure to keep prices low or to produce quality goods or services. In "the old days," the U.S. Postal Service had a monopoly on the delivery of written documents, but the days of a "snail mail" monopoly are over because the U.S. Postal Service now battles fax machines, e-mail, and couriers such as FedEx for market share.

monopoly ■ A market situation in which one firm, the only supplier of a particular product, is able to control the price, quality, and supply of that product.

In most U.S. industries today, the government attempts to limit monopolies by prosecuting firms for violations of antitrust legislation. Of course, these laws may generate controversy as powerful firms argue that they dominate a market simply because they provide a product most people want. This is at the heart of the mammoth battle fought by Microsoft in recent years. The U.S. Department of Justice brought suit against Microsoft based on the Sherman Anti-Trust Act, saying the software giant abused its Windows monopoly. Originally the Justice Department sought to break up Microsoft into several smaller companies. While the breakup lawsuit was eventually dismissed, an appeals court claimed that Microsoft's bundling of its Internet Browser with its Windows operating system was illegal. As of October 2001, the Government was still demanding that Microsoft share technical information about Windows with other software companies and offer PC makers the option of unbundling these components. Many people expect the appeals process to continue for years.[46]

In an **oligopoly** there are a relatively small number of sellers, each holding substantial market share, in a market with many buyers. Because there are few sellers in an oligopoly, each seller is very conscious of other sellers' actions. Oligopolies most often exist in industries requiring substantial investments in equipment or technology to produce a product—industries in which only a few competitors have the resources to enter the game. The auto industry is an oligopoly. An entrepreneur with little start-up cash is not likely to be successful entering the auto industry. Instead, a few large firms such as General Motors, Ford, Chrysler, Toyota, and Nissan dominate the market. Relatively smaller firms like Subaru succeed by offering products only for select niches rather than trying to compete in every category.

In **monopolistic competition** there are many sellers who compete for buyers in a market. Each firm, however, offers a slightly different product and each has only a small share of the market. In this type of market structure, many shoe manufacturers including Nike, Reebok, and Adidas vigorously compete with one another to offer consumers some unique benefit. For

oligopoly ■ A market structure in which a relatively small number of sellers, each holding a substantial share of the market, compete in a market with many buyers.

monopolistic competition ■ A market structure in which many firms, each having slightly different products, offer unique consumer benefits.

Companies that manufacture comparable products (such as Avia, Adidas, and Skechers) compete with each other to offer consumers something unique within their product base.

example, although every major athletic shoe manufacturer sells many types of basketball shoes, an NBA wannabe can obtain Air Jordans only from Nike. Thus, in the shoe industry, characterized as monopolistic competition, there are many different manufacturers, far more than in an oligopoly. But as in a monopoly, an individual shoe style is produced by just one manufacturer.

Finally, **perfect competition** exists when there are many small sellers, each offering basically the same good or service. In such industries no single firm has a significant impact on quality, price, or supply. Although true conditions of perfect competition are rare, agricultural markets in which there are many individual farmers each producing the same corn, soybeans, or jalapeño peppers come the closest. Even in the case of food commodities, though, there are opportunities for marketers to distinguish their offerings. Eggland's Best, Inc., for example, says it feeds its hens a high-quality, all-vegetarian diet, so the eggs they lay contain less cholesterol and six times more vitamin E than regular eggs.[47] Each egg is branded with a red "EB" seal. The company has scrambled the competition by creating an "egg-straordinary" difference where none existed before.

perfect competition ■ A market structure in which many small sellers, all of whom offer similar products, are unable to have an impact on the quality, price, or supply of a product.

THE TECHNOLOGICAL ENVIRONMENT

It took 38 years for 50 million people to become users of radio.
It took 13 years for 50 million people to become users of television.
It took only four years for 50 million people to become users of the Internet.

While the Internet may be one of the most important technological advances in today's world, it is not the first technological invention to radically change people's lives. However, comparing the history of the Internet to the history of radio and TV points out the Internet's phenomenal growth rate.

How many Netizens (people using the Internet) are there today and exactly who are they? That depends on what day you are asking the question because the number of users changes daily, making the total number of surfers a moving target. Here are the latest numbers as of Spring 2002:

- Half of all American adults use the Internet.
- 75 million U.S. surfers log on at home.
- 39 percent of surfers are 18–34 years old.
- 38 percent of surfers are 35–49 years old.
- Sales of downloaded music by 2.2 million buyers total $53 million, or nearly 10 percent of the total music recording market.[48]

New Era firms see technology as an investment the firm can't afford *not* to make. That's why today there are very few companies that do not have Web sites. But technology goes much further—from improved manufacturing processes using robotics to the use of satellite communication technology to track the movement of goods to a sophisticated e-commerce program—technology provides many firms with important competitive advantages.

Many technological developments profoundly affect marketing activities. Toll-free telephone numbers, easy computer access to customer databases, and of course, the Internet have made it possible for people to buy virtually anything they want (and even some things they don't want) without ever leaving their homes. Physical distribution has improved due to automated inventory control afforded by such advancements as bar codes and computer light pens.

Changes in technology can dramatically transform an industry, as when transistors revolutionized data processing and consumer electronics. Successful marketers continuously scan the external business environment in search of ideas and trends to spark their own research efforts. They also monitor ongoing research projects in government and private organizations. When inventors feel they have come across something exciting, they usually want to protect their exclusive right to produce and sell the invention by applying for a **patent**. A patent is a legal document issued from a country's patent office that gives inventors—or individuals and firms—exclusive rights to produce and sell a particular invention in that country. Marketers monitor government patent applications to discover innovative

patent ■ Legal documentation granting an individual or firm exclusive rights to produce and sell a particular invention.

products they can purchase from the inventor. And there are also other ways marketers keep in touch with technology. Many of the most important inventions are part of government-funded research grants. Clever marketers keep track of what government grant goes to whom for what research, hoping to be the first to identify and obtain exclusive rights to potentially profitable ideas.

THE LEGAL ENVIRONMENT

The legal environment refers to the local, state, national, and global laws and regulations that affect businesses. Legal and regulatory controls can be prime motivators for many business decisions. U.S. laws governing business have two purposes. Some, such as the Sherman Antitrust Act and the Wheeler-Lea Act, make sure that businesses compete fairly with each other. Others, such as the Food and Drug Act and the Consumer Products Safety Commission Act, make sure that businesses don't take advantage of consumers. Although some business-people argue that excessive legislation only limits competition, others say that laws ultimately help firms by maintaining a level playing field for businesses and supporting troubled industries. Table 3.2 lists some of the major federal laws that protect and preserve the rights of U.S. consumers and businesses. We'll also discuss issues related to the international legal environment in the next chapter.

4 *Bookmark It!*

Assume a firm that manufactures personal computers has hired you. What are the environmental factors that are important to your firm? Write down some recommendations for marketing strategies—the 4 Ps—to adapt to these environmental conditions.

TABLE 3.2

Overview of the Legal Environment

Law	Purpose
Sherman Antitrust Act (1890)	Developed to eliminate monopolies and to guarantee free competition. Prohibits exclusive territories (if they restrict competition), price fixing, and predatory pricing.
Food and Drug Act (1906)	Prohibits harmful practices in the production of food and drugs.
Clayton Act (1914)	Prohibits tying contracts, which require a dealer to take other products in the seller's line. Prohibits exclusive dealing if it restricts competition.
Federal Trade Commission Act (1914)	Created the Federal Trade Commission to monitor unfair practices.
Robinson-Patman Act (1936)	Prohibits price discrimination (offering different prices to competing wholesalers or retailers) unless cost-justified.
Wheeler-Lea Amendment to FTC Act (1938)	Revised the FTC Act. Makes deceptive and misleading advertising illegal.
Lanham Trademark Act (1946)	Protects and regulates brand names and trademarks.
Fair Packaging and Labeling Act (1966)	Ensures that product packages are labeled honestly.
National Traffic and Motor Vehicle Safety Act (1966)	Sets automobile and tire safety standards.
Cigarette Labeling Act (1966)	Requires health warnings on cigarettes.
Child Protection Act (1966) Child Protection and Toy Safety Act (1969)	Bans dangerous products used by children. Sets standards for child-resistant packaging.
Consumer Credit Protection Act (1968) Fair Credit Reporting Act (1970)	Protects consumers by requiring full disclosure of credit and loan terms and rates. Regulates the use of consumer credit reporting.
Consumer Products Safety Commission Act (1972)	Created the Consumer Product Safety Commission to monitor and recall unsafe products. Sets product safety standards.
Magnuson-Moss Consumer Product Warranty Act (1975)	Regulates warranties.
Children's Television Act (1990)	Limits the amount of television commercials aired on children's programs.
Nutrition Labeling and Education Act (1990)	Required that new food labeling requirements be set by the FDA.

The Watchdogs of Business: Regulatory Agencies Federal and state governments have created a host of regulatory agencies—governmental bodies that monitor business activities and enforce laws. Let's review some of the agencies whose actions affect marketing activities.

- The Food and Drug Administration (FDA) enforces laws and regulations on foods, drugs, cosmetics, and veterinary products. For example, marketers of pharmaceuticals, over-the-counter medicines, and a variety of other related products must get FDA approval before they can introduce new products to the market.
- The Federal Trade Commission (FTC) enforces laws relating to several areas of business practice. It is responsible for enforcing laws against deceptive advertising and product-labeling regulations. Marketers must constantly keep abreast of changes in FTC regulations to avoid costly FTC fines.
- The Federal Communications Commission (FCC) regulates telephone, radio, and television. FCC regulations directly affect the marketing activities of companies in the communications industries, and they have an indirect effect on all firms that use broadcast media for marketing communications.
- The Interstate Commerce Commission (ICC) regulates interstate bus, truck, rail, and water operations. The ability of a firm to efficiently move products to its customers depends on ICC policies and regulations.
- The Consumer Product Safety Commission (CPSC) protects the public from potentially hazardous products. Firms want to make products that are safe. Through regulation and testing programs, the CPSC helps firms make sure their products won't cause harm to their customers.
- The Environmental Protection Agency (EPA) develops and enforces regulations aimed at protecting the environment. Such regulations have a major impact on the materials and processes that manufacturers use in their products and, thus, on the ability of companies to develop products that meet customer wants and needs.

Adapting to a Regulatory Environment Many times firms loudly object if a government's watchdog activities put a stop to their marketing plans. Warner-Lambert, the manufacturer of Lysol cleaner and disinfectant, coped a bit more creatively with government regulation. Way back in 1966 the FTC objected to Lysol's claim that it helped to prevent the spread of colds because the firm lacked data to substantiate the claim. The company stopped making this claim in its advertising, but it also funded research at a leading medical school on the topic. Warner-Lambert used the resulting data to convince the FTC that Lysol does in fact inhibit the spread of colds, and commercials making this claim began to reappear in 1983.[49]

New Era firms know that the best of all possible worlds is one where no government regulation is needed because firms work together to make sure everyone plays fairly. In fact, there are a number of nongovernment organizations that serve as watchdogs on marketing activities. The most active of these is the National Advertising Division (NAD) of the Better Business Bureau. The NAD receives and investigates complaints from both consumers and other businesses about advertising. If the NAD investigation determines that a complaint is legitimate, the complaint is moved up to a National Advertising Review Board (NARB) panel that may make a recommendation to the offending advertiser to change or cease the advertising. As a voluntary, independent entity, the NARB has no power to enforce its recommendations to advertisers. Most advertisers, however, comply because they believe it is in the best interest of all advertisers to clean their own house rather than having the government step in and do it for them.

Another important arm of the Better Business Bureau is the Children's Advertising Review Unit (CARU). CARU was established in 1974 to help promote truthful, accurate, and socially responsible advertising for children. CARU reviews advertising directed to children under the age of 12 by systematically monitoring thousands of advertisements from print, broadcast, and online media.[50]

How It Worked Out at Subaru of America

Joe chose option 3. He hoped to make a direct connection between survey results and sales and profits. The new approach led to a reworking of the survey so that it provided more specific information about customers and encouraged dealers to nurture owner loyalty. Hopefully you got a sense of how strong loyalty to a car can be if you did the "Real People, Your Choices" exercise at the beginning of the chapter.

Here we show the old and new surveys. Changes to the survey included the addition of a "loyalty section" to the data reports and the expansion of existing action planning materials that Subaru provided to its dealers. The new survey format asked three questions ("Key Loyalty Indicators"): the degree of overall owner satisfaction, how the experience at the dealership compared to past car-buying and servicing experiences, and the degree to which the owner would repeat the experience at that dealership. Reports sent to dealers categorized their customers by loyalty types (loyal, vulnerable, and possibly lost) based on how they responded to the three key questions, allowing the dealers to review the feedback and then prioritize their actions with an eye to retaining customers rather than just fixing "things gone wrong."

In addition, data about car buyers who responded to the survey, such as information about their interests and activities (a carryover from the previous survey) and their backgrounds were now supplemented with the loyalty information. This made it easier to effectively influence customer product and service purchase behavior through "smart" communications during the ownership cycle. For example, selective binding in Subaru's owner magazine allowed the company to customize the publication for each owner based on what they do or don't own and the emotional reactions they have to Subaru as revealed in their survey responses.

Senior management at Subaru declared the Subaru Owner Loyalty Program the primary feedback instrument for owner evaluations and initiated a dealer recognition and staff compensation program in 2002 based on the results.

Will this loyalty focus increase repeat business for Subaru? The book is still out on that, but Joe and his team are confident they have started a cultural change in the company that will pay off in the long term. But, in the short term, the most positive signal that this relationship-building approach is worthwhile is the fact that many of his counterparts at other companies are requesting details about the program. Imitation is the sincerest form of flattery!

Old Survey

SUBARU.

Dealer Service Experience Report

Dealer: 070-999 Hometown Subaru
Sales Group: Subaru Sales 250-499
District: 001
Region: Mid-America

Report Date: July 10, 1996
Quarter: Apr-Jun, 1996

Service Experience Results by Customer

Customer Name Phone # Warranty Claim VIN	Service Representative									Service Department												Fax
	5a	5b	5c	5d	5e	5f	5g	5h	5i	6a	6b	6c	6d	6e	6f	6g	6h	6i	6j	6k	6l	
J MCCGRATH JR. 815/555-1234 12345678901234567	50	50	75	50	25	50	50	75	75	0	50	75	50	50	50	25	50	50	50	50	50	Yes
R M BRIGGS 815/555-2345 1234567890ABCDEFG	75	75	100	75	75	75	75	50	75	75	75	75	75	75	75	75	75	75	75	75	75	No
I T CLARK 815/555-1234 12345678901234567	100	100	100	100	100	100	100	100	100	100	100	100	100	100	100	100	100	100	100	100	100	No
R J KNOXVILLE 815/555-2345 1234567890ABCDEFG	75	75	100	75	75	75	75	50	75	75	75	75	75	75	75	75	75	75	75	75	75	No
Question Average:	75	75	95	75	70	75	75	65	80	65	75	80	75	75	75	70	75	75	75	75	75	

Number of surveys scored may vary from number of surveys returned. See Reference Guide.
Scoring Key: 100 = Very Satisfied, 75 = Satisfied, 50 = Neutral, 25 = Dissatisfied, 0 = Very Dissatisfied

SUBARU

Dealer Service Experience Report

02 D's Inc.
Subaru Sales of 500+
DSM District 0, DFOM District 0; DSOM Area 1
Subaru Distributors Corp.

Report Date: October 15, 2000
Quarter: Jul-Sep, 2000
Current Quarter Returns: 24

Service Visit Review

Service Advisor / Customer Name / Phone # / Repair Order # / VIN	SOLI Satis. (1)	Comp. (3)	Intent (5)	2a	2b	2c	2d	2e	2f	2g	2h	2i	2j	2k	2l	2m	2n	2o	2p	4a	4b	4c	4d	4e	4f	4g	4h	4i	4j	Intent (6)
Advisor Unidentified (Percent Top Box) SOLI=67	85	80	69	88	81	69	75	69	75	33	75	80	93	71	93	73	80	73	50	64	67	79	87	80	71	67	58	73	73	69
Loyal Customers																														
George S (000) 000-0000 A JF1SF635XWH78	1	1	1	1	1	1	1	1	1	7	2	1	1	2	2	1	1	1	1	1	2	1	1	1	1	1	7	2	1	1
Vulnerable Customers																														
Harold P (516) 000-0000 89 JF1SF6353Y	n/a	2	2	1	1	1	1	1	1	7	1	1	1	1	1	2	1	2	6	2	7	n/a	1	1	n/a	2	7	1	1	2
Possible Lost Customers																														
Scott B 4S3BD4354X	7	7	7	6	7	5	3	4	4	7	7	4	2	4	1	3	2	7	6	4	2	4	3	4	4	6	7	7	4	7

George S — Comment: The only disappointment was that I was told I could not have a loaner car and had to call a taxi to get home. Otherwise, I think your service people are great and am also happy with my repairs. (Transportation Provided, –; Staff General, +)

Scott B — Comment: Dealer was notified of the problems and should have had parts available to fix. Instead the dealer had to notify us when the parts came in but never did. It took over 1 month to fix the problem once diagnosed. (Availablity of Parts, –; Communication of Parts Availability, –)

😐 = Less than top box rating. Names of customers who fulfill the SOLI criteria are bolded

THE SOCIOCULTURAL ENVIRONMENT

In both consumer and business-to-business markets, an understanding of social and cultural factors is a must. By the sociocultural environment, we mean the characteristics of the society, the people who live in that society, and the culture that reflects the values and beliefs of the society. We'll focus on these issues in detail in Chapters 6 and 8.

For now, just keep in mind that the first step toward understanding the characteristics of a society is to look at its **demographics**. These are statistics that measure observable aspects of a population, such as size, age, gender, ethnic group, income, education, occupation, and family structure. The information revealed in demographic studies is of great value to marketers in predicting the size of markets for many products, from home mortgages to brooms and can openers.

demographics ■ Statistics that measure observable aspects of a population, including size, age, gender, ethnic group, income, education, occupation, and family structure.

Understanding consumers' attitudes, beliefs, and ways of doing things in different parts of the country or the world is especially important when developing marketing strategy. The consequences of ignoring these issues became evident during the 1994 soccer World Cup, when both McDonald's and Coca-Cola made the mistake of reprinting the Saudi Arabian flag, which includes sacred words from the Koran, on disposable packaging used in promotions. Despite their delight at having a Saudi team in contention for the cup, Muslims worldwide protested this borrowing of sacred imagery, and both companies had to scramble to rectify the situation.[51] Marketers can avoid this type of mistake through a better understanding of consumer values and beliefs.

Chapter Summary

1. Explain how organizations adopt a New Era marketing orientation on ethics and social responsibility.

Firms in the New Era of Marketing emphasize social profit as well as economic profit. This means that New Era companies practice business ethics; that is, they behave according to basic values, respond to consumerism issues, and respect the rights of consumers in order to avoid both financial and reputational costs. Ethical marketing means making products safe, pricing products fairly, promoting products honestly, and treating channel members fairly.

Social responsibility means that New Era firms act in ways that benefit the public, the community, and the natural environment. New Era marketers assume social responsibility through environmental stewardship, in which the firm's actions either improve or do not harm the natural environment, and cause marketing, which focuses on marketing strategies that promote the public good. New Era firms also practice social responsibility by promoting cultural diversity—that is, by including people of different races, ethnic groups, and religions as customers, suppliers, employees, and distribution channel members.

2. Describe the New Era emphasis on quality.

Quality-focused firms in the New Era of Marketing strive to provide goods and services that meet customer expectations and result in economic profit. Total quality management (TQM) is a management philosophy that focuses on satisfying customers through such programs as continuous quality improvement and employee empowerment. Marketing activities in quality-focused firms center around defining consumer perceptions of quality and developing superior marketing-mix strategies that, along with other company programs, meet worldwide standards of quality.

3. Discuss some of the important aspects of an organization's internal environment.

Success in the New Era of Marketing rests heavily on an organization's resources and competencies. This includes the corporate culture, the set of shared values, attitudes, and beliefs that influence its decisions and practices. New Era firms have more risk-taking and people-centered cultures.

4. Explain why marketers scan an organization's external business environment.

Understanding the economic environment is essential to marketing planning. The business cycle (prosperity, recession, recovery, and depression) and inflation affect customer purchase behavior and business activities. Consumer expectations about the general economy and their income can create changes in the business cycle.

In a firm's competitive environment, brand competition, product competition, and the more general competition for consumers' limited discretionary income affect the development of marketing strategies that give the firm a competitive advantage. The amount of competition within a specific industry is determined by whether that industry is a monopoly, an oligopoly, or an example of perfect competition or "imperfect" monopolistic competition.

Changes in the technological environment, especially those related to the growth of the Internet, affect every aspect of marketing. Marketers must be knowledgeable about technological changes, often monitoring government and private research findings.

The legal environment includes local, state, national, and global laws. U.S. laws make sure businesses compete fairly and protect consumers from harmful business practices.

The sociocultural environment helps marketers understand important trends and predict consumer purchasing preferences. Consumer demographics segment a population according to such characteristics as age, gender, family structure, ethnic group, income, occupation, and education.

Chapter Review

■ MARKETING CONCEPTS:
TESTING YOUR KNOWLEDGE

1. What is meant by the New Era of marketing? What are business ethics? What are some ways that marketers practice ethical behavior in the marketing mix?
2. What are some of the problems marketers face with unethical consumer behavior?
3. What is consumerism? What is the Consumer Bill of Rights?
4. What is social responsibility? What is cause marketing? How do marketers promote cultural diversity?
5. What is total quality management? How do marketers add quality to the marketing mix?
6. What is the Baldridge Award? What is ISO 9000?
7. What is corporate culture? What are some ways that the corporate culture of one organization might differ from that of another? How does corporate culture affect marketing decision making?
8. Describe the business cycle. What is consumer confidence? How do consumer expectations affect the business cycle?
9. Explain the types of competition marketers face: discretionary income competition, product competition, and brand competition. Why are all important to marketers?
10. What is competitive intelligence?
11. What are some important changes in the technological environment that have affected marketing?
12. Describe the important elements in marketing's legal environment.
13. What is the role of the NAD and the NARB in the regulation of advertising?
14. What is the sociocultural environment? What are demographics?

■ MARKETING CONCEPTS:
DISCUSSING CHOICES AND ISSUES

1. Calvin Klein's products often are advertised with a healthy dose of sexual innuendo. A few years ago Klein took this approach one daring step farther, when the company unveiled a controversial advertising campaign featuring very young-looking models in racy settings. In one spot, an old man with a gravelly voice says to a scantily clad young boy, "You got a real nice look. You work out? I can tell." The campaign ended when the chairman of Dayton Hudson asked that the stores' names be removed from the ads, and *Seventeen* refused to carry them.[51] By that time, of course, Klein had reaped invaluable volumes of free publicity as teens and adults hotly debated the appropriateness of these images. What's your opinion?
2. Think about a company's cause marketing program with which you are familiar. Why do you think the firm chose

the specific cause? Do you think the firm's customers became more loyal to the company because it sponsored the program? Why or why not?
3. Catalog marketers and others who practice direct marketing have been using discriminatory pricing strategies for years. Are these pricing strategies ethical? What do you think will be the long-term benefits or problems that firms will reap from discriminatory pricing?
4. When New Era firms seek to create social profit, they practice environmental stewardship. Environmental stewardship may mean taking some products off the market and changing other products. What are some products that have a good chance of being removed from the market? What are some products that are likely to be positively affected by environmental stewardship? What are some ideas for new products that would be in tune with these trends?
5. The technological environment has changed marketing in some important ways. What are some of these? What are your predictions for how technology will change marketing in the future?

■ MARKETING PRACTICE:
APPLYING WHAT YOU'VE LEARNED

1. As an employee of a business consulting firm that specializes in helping people who want to start small businesses, you have been assigned a client who is interested in starting a video/DVD delivery service, in which customers call in their video/DVD orders for home delivery. As you begin thinking about the potential for success for this client, you realize that understanding the external environment for this business is essential. First, decide which environmental factors are most important to this client. Then choose one of these factors and use your library to identify the current and future trends in this area. Finally, in a role-playing situation, present all of your recommendations to the client.
2. Assume you are employed in the marketing department of a medium-sized firm in the furniture industry—a manufacturer of case goods, such as end tables, cocktail tables, wall units, dining room chairs, and so on. Your firm has recently been purchased, and the new owner is terribly concerned about social responsibility. As a member of the marketing department, you have been asked to put together a report on how this firm can become a more socially responsible organization. Develop your report for the new owner of the firm.
3. Assume you have recently been employed by the marketing department of a firm that manufactures bicycles. Who are your competitors? Make a list of ways you might seek to gain competitive intelligence for your firm.

4. Assume you have been hired by a firm that markets heavy construction equipment in a global marketplace. You have been asked to develop a code of ethics for the company. Develop a draft of the code you would recommend.

MARKETING MINI-PROJECT:
LEARNING BY DOING

This mini-project is designed to help you find out more about the New Era of Marketing focus on ethics and social responsibility.

1. With one or several other students in your class, select a demographic group of consumers to study. You may wish to study college females, college males, young professionals, retail employees, young mothers, older citizens, or a specific ethnic group.

   a. Develop a brief questionnaire that will allow you to obtain information from members of this group about their experiences with businesses. You might want to ask about some or all of the following:
   - their best experience with a business
   - their worst experience with a business
   - opinions about the ethical behavior of business in general
   - how businesses ought to behave
   - the responsibility of businesses to the environment
   - the responsibility of businesses to promote cultural diversity
   - such consumer behaviors as shoplifting, returning used merchandise, and so on
   - the ethical behavior of retail employees

   b. Obtain responses to your questionnaire from members of your selected demographic group.

2. Analyze the responses to your survey and prepare a report for your class on what you have learned. In what ways might the unique perspectives or characteristics of the group you selected have influenced their responses?

3. What are your recommendations for marketers on ways to improve their dealings with this group? For government? For consumers? For retail stores? For your marketing instructors?

REAL PEOPLE, REAL SURFERS:
EXPLORING THE WEB

There are a number of not-for-profit organizations and government agencies that are important in a firm's legal and ethical environment. Some of these are:

Better Business Bureau www.bbb.org

The American Marketing Association www.marketing power.com

The Federal Trade Commission www.ftc.gov

The Federal Communications Commission www.fcc.gov

Spend some time investigating the Web sites of these organizations or agencies and answer the following questions for each organization's site.

1. What is the major purpose of the organization or agency? What services does it provide?

2. In what ways does the organization or agency influence the behavior of marketers?

3. In what ways does the organization or agency benefit consumers? In what ways does it benefit marketers?

4. Consider the design of the Web site(s). Is the design conducive to use by consumers? By businesses? Does the Web site provide a way for consumers to voice complaints? If so, is the complaint vehicle easy to find and understand?

PLAN IT!
DEVELOPING A
MARKETING PLAN

As your instructor directs, create a marketing plan (using Marketing Plan Pro software or a written marketing plan format) to document your marketing decisions or answer these questions in a written or oral report.

In Chapter 1 you considered how CFS can incorporate social marketing in next year's marketing plan. Now review your ideas and look at the current year's plan in Appendix A as you continue working on next year's plan.

1. How might CFS use green marketing in making and marketing its products?

2. How do you expect the economic and competitive environment to influence CFS's plans for next year?

3. What legal and regulatory issues should CFS examine more closely during the planning process?

Key Terms

brand competition, (78)
business cycle, (76)
business ethics, (62)
cause marketing, (68)
codes of ethics, (62)
competitive intelligence (CI), (78)
Consumer Bill of Rights, (64)

consumer confidence, (77)
consumerism, (64)
corporate culture, (74)
corrective advertising, (66)
cultural diversity, (69)
demographics, (84)
discretionary income, (78)

discriminatory pricing, (65)
environmental stewardship, (67)
green marketing, (67)
ISO 9000, (72)
ISO 14000, (72)
monopolistic competition, (79)
monopoly, (78)

MARKETING IN ACTION: CHAPTER 3 CASE

REAL CHOICES AT NICKELODEON

Nickelodeon is a cable network just for kids that doesn't kid around. It offers many types of children's programming including animation, comedy, adventure, live action, music, and magazine shows for kids ages 2 to 15. The weekly schedule includes syndicated reruns of older shows during Nick at Nite, plus the usual kid fare of cartoon shows such as Bullwinkle and Gumby. According to Nickelodeon's president, Geraldine Layborne, "The major role we can play in kids' lives is to give them back their childhood in an era when there are lots of pressures on kids to grow up fast. If we can provide them with an environment that's filled with humor that's appropriate to their age and to their lives and can help raise self-esteem, then that's a major accomplishment."

As a result of this philosophy, programming isn't limited to cartoons and other fun shows. It also includes many innovative programming ideas focusing on what's good for kids. The award-winning Nick News, a nationally syndicated program that provides children-focused world news, recently aired "Faces of Hope: Kids of Afghanistan" to help American children understand more about the war against terrorism. The network's Big Help program encourages kids to perform volunteer services in their communities.

Nickelodeon's biggest competitive advantage is its ability to make kids feel respected, listened to, appreciated, and important. To help assure that programming is "kid tested and kid approved," Nick sponsored an online panel of 70 kids who signed on via CompuServe three times a week to talk with each other and with Nickelodeon staff. In fact, just about everything the company has done is based on the belief that kids' television should put kids first and that what's good for kids is good for business.

Nickelodeon has adopted the New Era marketing orientation in its business practices. The corporate culture supports the focus on customers and encourages the creation of customer loyalty by satisfying kids (and their parents). Network executives believe that their long-term success has been closely tied to the company's emphasis on ethical behavior and social responsibility toward kids. Nickelodeon supports cultural diversity in its hiring practices and has focused many of its programs on dispelling the kind of sex-role stereotyping that prevents little girls from dreaming about being firefighters and little boys from realizing that men do become nurses. At times, though, it has had difficulty finding producers who can develop quality programs for kids of different ethnic backgrounds.

Like any other New Era firm, Nickelodeon has to keep its eye on the bottom line. Because the network's biggest source of revenue is its advertisers, management knows that keeping its young customers happy means television programming that is in line with the advertisers' marketing strategies. Today's marketers of children's products are well aware of the dramatic shifts underway in the U.S. population and are gearing up for the tide to change. Especially in the lucrative toy market, for example, product development and promotional strategies will be increasingly aimed at Latino, African-American, and Asian children.

To balance the high costs of original programming, Nickelodeon must continue to rely on reruns and cartoons for a healthy part of its air time. But that's hard to do if Nick wants to keep up with the needs of sponsors, one of its important publics. Most of the old shows don't include people of color, let alone children, and even when they do, the children are rarely cast as heroes and heroines. Nickelodeon's progress toward committing itself to minority programming has also been slowed by a number of other hurdles.

The question of how much of its resources to put into developing original programs that meet the needs of minority kids is clearly tied to Nickelodeon's basic business philosophy. Is it ethically and socially responsible, for instance, to keep these costs down by force-fitting minority children into existing program formats designed for white children? This question raises others about the direction and focus for the programs and the best way for Nick to maintain its standards for meaningful, quality programs that kids want to see. Then there's the question of how much air time should be given over to minority programming and when—without the risk of losing its current primarily white audience of older kids.

Sources: www.nickjr.com/grownups/teachers. Accessed 5/22/02. Tibbett Speer, "Nickelodeon Puts Kids Online," *American Demographics/The 1994 Directory*, pp. 16–17; " 'Addicted' to Research, Nick Shows Strong Kids' Lure," *Advertising Age* 10 (February 1992) S2, S22; "Netting the Numbers," *Advertising Age* 10 (February 1992) S2, S22; "Viacom's Nickelodeon Sets Venture to Make Children's Products," *Wall Street Journal*, 11 May 1995, B2.

THINGS TO THINK ABOUT

1. What is the decision facing Nickelodeon?
2. What factors are important in understanding the decision situation?
3. What are the alternatives?
4. What decision(s) do you recommend?
5. What are some ways to implement your recommendation(s)?

Bookmark It!

OBJECTIVES:

1. Understand the big picture of international marketing: trade flows, how firms define the scope of their markets, and how firms develop a competitive advantage in global marketing.

2. Understand how economic, political, legal, and cultural issues influence global marketing strategies and outcomes.

3. Explain the strategies a firm can use to enter global markets.

4. Understand the arguments for standardization versus localization of marketing strategies in global markets, and understand how elements of the marketing mix apply in foreign countries.

MARKETING IN A MULTINATIONAL ENVIRONMENT

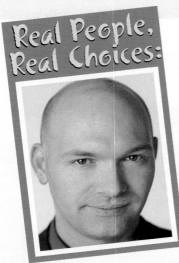

Real People, Real Choices:

Meet Henrik Kaas, a Decision Maker at Sony Nordic

www.sony.com

CURRENT POSITION: CEO

CAREER PATH: 2000–2001 Deputy Managing Director, Sony Nordic/Managing Director Sony Denmark.

1998–2000 Marketing Director, Sony Nordic.

1993–1998 Marketing Manager, GTE Sylvania Lighting, then TV Sony Nordic.

1987–1990 Marketing Manager, Intensa Lighting.

1993 M.B.A., Copenhagen Business School.

WHAT I DO WHEN NOT WORKING: Friends and fitness.

FIRST JOB OUT OF SCHOOL: Working with my dad in the lighting business.

BUSINESS BOOK I'M READING NOW: <u>The Other 90%</u> by Robert K. Cooper.

MOTTO: Treat others as you would like them to treat you.

WHAT DRIVES ME: Challenges.

MY MANAGEMENT STYLE: To set the target and fix the framework.

How Can Sony Reconnect Its Connectivity Campaign?

A few years ago, Sony released the Sony Memory Stick, a new product that would allow integration of all the company's electronics products. Consumers could connect the Memory Stick to a Sony digital camera, then connect the Memory Stick to a Sony VAIO computer and download the images. They could also download music to the Memory Stick on a computer, connect the Memory Stick to a Sony Walkman, and play the downloaded songs.

As Deputy Managing Director of Sony Nordic (headquartered in Copenhagen), Henrik Kaas was responsible for the company's activities in Denmark, Norway, Sweden, Finland, and the Baltic countries of Estonia, Latvia, and Lithuania. Henrik knew connectivity was a great concept, but one that's hard to explain unless someone actually demonstrates how it works. Consumers would have to be given hands-on lessons.

To introduce Sony connectivity products, Sony Nordic created the Sony Experience Tour for its "Go Create" campaign. This Tour was part promotion, part educational event: A specially outfitted bus with workstations featuring VAIO laptops, digital cameras, and networked Walkmans would travel around the Nordic countries to teach consumers about the power of connectivity. The bus also provided online connections via satellite to the Sony Experience Web site. By visiting the site, while using the Memory Stick users could "go create." They could upload pictures, produce slide shows, and use a slide builder for mailing images to friends and family. Henrik estimated that 15,000 to 20,000 people would take the Tour during the summer, so he knew it had to be well planned.

The tour aimed to reach people who spoke numerous languages. Danish, Swedish, and Norwegian are all fairly similar languages, though the pronunciation and some words are different. Finnish and the three Baltic languages are different from the other three. However, the target market group in all of these countries generally spoke English as a second language. For this reason, Sony Nordic decided to produce the Web site in English.

The Sony Experience tour crew included staff from a Danish agency as well as local staff who were a mix of Sony salespeople and freelancers. All were fluent in their native language and English. The plan was to station the local staff in each country outside the bus to hand out leaflets and entice passersby into the bus. The Danish staff would be waiting inside the bus to explain the Sony products.

As soon as the crew made its first stop in Oslo, they realized they had a serious language problem. The staff in the bus did not feel that they communicated well enough with the Norwegian visitors who came in to learn more about Sony products. The Danes tried to speak English instead, but the visitors preferred to receive the information in their native language. Unfortunately some visitors gave up and left the bus. Obviously, the tour needed retooling. Henrik considered his options:

Option 1: Place locals inside the bus; Danish staff outside the bus.

Stop the tour for a while and place the local, native-speaking employees inside the bus and the Danish event staff outside to hand out the leaflets. However, this option would require training the local staff about Sony products and delaying the Tour, which had been planned months ahead. Sony had chosen some sites at yearly music festivals, where dates were fixed and fees already paid to place the bus in these venues.

Option 2: Use only native-speaking staff.

Change to only native-speaking staff. The language problem would be solved. However the new staff would need training and days of touring would be lost. The whole crew would have to change with each new country. Each new crew would have to "start over" in learning how to communicate about Sony's products with the public.

Now join Henrik and the decision team at Sony Nordic. Which option would you choose and why?

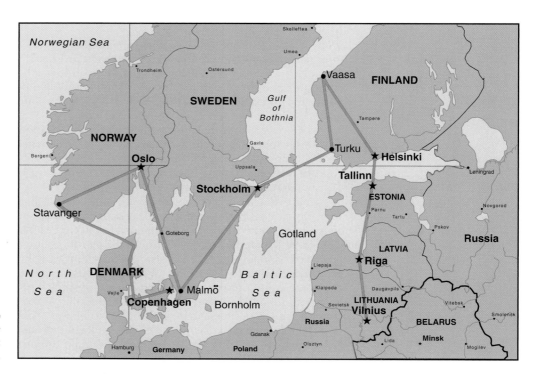

Sony Tour Map: The Sony Experience route through Nordic and Baltic countries.

Playing on a Global Stage

The global game is exciting, but it is not easy to play. Competition comes from both local and foreign firms, and differences in national laws, customs, and consumer preferences can make your head spin. Henrik Kaas of Sony discovered that there are many challenges when marketing to more than one country at a time, even when those countries are fairly close to one another both geographically and culturally. As the title of this chapter suggests, the successful global business needs to set its sights on diverse markets around the world, but it needs to act locally by being willing to adapt business practices to unique conditions in other parts of the globe.

For example, in the mid-1990s U.S. athletic shoe giant Nike had to adjust its global strategy to grow its business in foreign markets. The company set as a top priority appealing to soccer fans worldwide and actively pursued new customers from France to Chile. This was a real change for a company that has made its mark in such "American" sports as basketball and football. Nike's president commented, "Once we set our sights on being a global company, we had to focus on soccer." Today, Nike faces fierce competition in the global soccer market from entrenched companies such as Adidas. Still, Nike's global operations are their most successful. While Nike's 2001 footwear revenues for the United States were down 5 percent, revenues for footwear in the European region (including Africa) increased 10 percent and Asian footwear sales increased 9 percent.[1]

In this chapter, we'll look at the "big picture" of international marketing and zero in on the opportunities and pitfalls of doing business in a world that seems to be getting smaller by the minute. Figure 4.1 presents the major factors that marketers need to consider before making the leap to foreign markets. First, we'll learn that world trade is influenced by a complicated set of relationships among countries and regions, and we'll review some of these connections. Then we'll examine some of the environmental factors a marketer must consider before venturing out into another country, including economic, political, legal, and cultural factors. Finally, we'll get to the crucial questions for marketers: How can we make our company global? What changes (if any) do we need to make to the marketing mix for our product to compete effectively?

In examining its domestic demand, Nike realized that there is little if any growth in the U.S. market for athletic shoes. Thus, as this Chilean ad shows, Nike decided to expand its global marketing strategy by going after the worldwide soccer market—a growth opportunity based on a large global market potential.

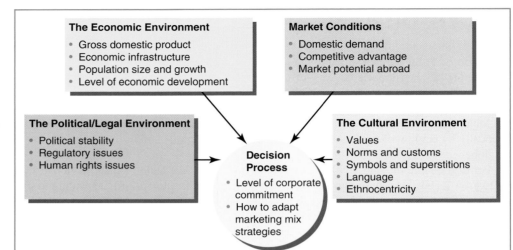

FIGURE 4.1

Decision Model for Entering Foreign Markets

Entering global markets involves a complex decision process. Marketers must fully understand market conditions and environmental factors in order to determine the best strategy for entering the market and to create a successful marketing mix.

The Economic Environment
• Gross domestic product
• Economic infrastructure
• Population size and growth
• Level of economic development

Market Conditions
• Domestic demand
• Competitive advantage
• Market potential abroad

The Political/Legal Environment
• Political stability
• Regulatory issues
• Human rights issues

The Cultural Environment
• Values
• Norms and customs
• Symbols and superstitions
• Language
• Ethnocentricity

Decision Process
• Level of corporate commitment
• How to adapt marketing mix strategies

---

1 *Bookmark It!*

Make a list of 20 products that you own—clothes, toiletries, furniture, appliances, automobiles. Divide the list in two—domestic products (produced by U.S. firms) and foreign-made products. What percentage of the list is "made in America"?

countertrade ■ Type of trade in which goods are paid for with other items instead of with cash.

WORLD TRADE

World trade refers to the flow of goods and services among different countries—the value of all the exports and imports of the world's nations. World trade activity is steadily increasing year by year. In 2000, merchandise exports of all countries totaled $6.2 trillion, up 12.5 percent from 1999. Even with a declining world economy sent into a tailspin by the September 2001 terrorist attacks on the United States, world merchandise trade was expected to increase by 2 percent for 2001.[2] Of course, not all countries participate equally in the trade flows among nations. Understanding the "big picture" of who does business with whom is important to marketers when they devise global trade strategies. Figure 4.2 shows the amount of merchandise traded by North America with its major trade partners around the world.

Having customers in far-reaching places is important, but it requires some flexibility since business must be done differently to adapt to local social and economic conditions. For example, firms engaged in global marketing must be able to accommodate the needs of trading partners when those foreign firms can't pay cash for the products they want to purchase. Believe it or not, the currency of as many as 70 percent of all countries is not convertible; it cannot be spent or exchanged outside the country's borders. In other countries sufficient cash or credit is simply not available, so trading firms work out elaborate deals in which they trade their products with each other (called *barter*), or even supply goods in return for tax breaks from the local government. This **countertrade** accounts for about 25 percent of all world trade. For instance, PepsiCo has been selling its drinks in Russia for years in exchange for Stolichnaya vodka, which it then sells in the United States to those who want a different kind of refreshment break.[3]

FIGURE 4.2

North American Trade Flows

Knowing who does business with whom is essential for overseas marketing strategies. As this figure shows, North America trades most heavily with Asia, Western Europe, and Latin America.

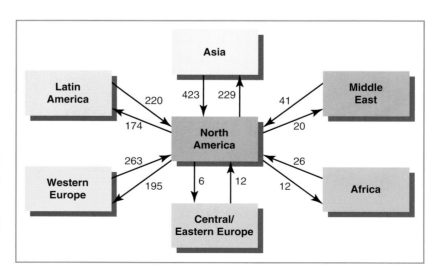

PAS DE PANIQUE, ON VOUS EXPLIQUE.

Pour y voir plus clair il suffit de jeter un coup d'œil à notre programme marketing.
Un programme en continu qui vous en dira plus long sur nous et ce que nous offrons.
Un programme qui vous dénombrera mois par mois comment vous servir au maximum de MTV, l'une des plus célèbres marques de la planète. Efficacement. Avantageusement.
Pour commencer, il y a notre dossier "AU FIL DE L'ONDE" Vous devriez déjà l'avoir reçu. Dans le cas contraire ou si vous désirez de plus amples renseignements, appelez dès maintenant le (16) (1) 42.93.82.85.

As this French ad shows, MTV Europe tailors its messages to local markets.

How "Worldly" Can a Company Be?   Not all companies that engage in world trade are alike. Let's look at one global company, MTV. Like it or not, it's an MTV world. Few other companies have the clout to host a concert for 200,000 young Russian people in Red Square as MTV did in 1999. Viacom, MTV's parent company, estimates that about 1.2 million people who don't live in the United States watch the channel every second.

The MTV concept is spreading as new foreign outposts continue to open in Asia, Australia, and Latin America. MTV understands that it's now very much a global company, but the network also realizes that it can't compete with other music alternatives around the world from its offices in New York only. MTV figured out that it had to divide and conquer: In 1995 the company created regional "feeds" to cater to different markets (for example, one feed just for the United Kingdom and Ireland, another just for Italy). While as much as 60 percent of its programming originates in the United States, the rest is produced in cooperation with local producers who create specialized products ranging from MTV Kitchen, which combines music and cooking in Italy, to Erotica, a Brazilian show that features a panel of young people discussing sex.[4] Also, it's no longer a matter of exporting American music to these markets; global trade in music is very much a two-way street as U.S. markets search for new groups and musical styles, from ska to World Beat. Hint: Go to www.mtveurope.com and check out the different regional Web sites you'll see linked there including MTV events in Germany, Denmark, and so on.

But not all firms define the scope of their markets as MTV does. Some firms remain domestic in scope and confine their sales and marketing efforts to their home markets. The simplest and easiest way to enter the global marketplace is by exporting. Exporting firms expand sales by exporting the same product sold in their domestic markets to other countries. Firms that export generally use the same marketing strategies wherever they do business. For example, Harley-Davidson exports about a quarter of its choppers to avid bikers around the world. Bikers can buy the same Harley bike, helmet, and jacket in Tokyo and in Melbourne that they buy in Kansas City.

Ministry of Sound, a British dance music label well known in Europe, is seeking to find growth opportunities past its domestic market by trying to make a name for itself in the United States.

Multinational or global firms view the entire world as their markets. Some global firms adapt their basic strategies to local conditions while others try to do the same thing everywhere. For example, whereas Kraft adds lemon, egg, or mustard to its mayonnaise to please different European palettes, Gillette sells the same razor everywhere.[5] As Gillette's CEO said, "The most important decision I made was to globalize. We decided not to tailor products to any marketplace, but to treat all marketplaces the same. And it worked in most countries."[6] Nestlé (based in Switzerland), Coca-Cola, and Caterpillar are also global firms that sell the same basic product in all of their markets.

Market Conditions   Of course, we do not mean that all firms can or should go global. The first step in deciding whether and how to go global is to examine some basic market conditions: domestic demand, the market potential abroad, and a firm's ability to have a competitive advantage in foreign markets.

Many times, a firm's decision to go global is based on conditions where domestic demand is declining while demand in foreign markets is growing. For example, the market for personal computers has leveled off in the United States where most sales come from people replacing an old or obsolete machine than from those buying a new PC for the first time. In examining the market potential abroad for computers however, the demand is much greater in some other parts of the world where consumers and businesses are only now beginning to explore the power of the Web.

Competitive Advantage   In Chapter 2 we saw how firms seek to create competitive advantage, a means to outperform the competition. When competing in a global marketplace, this challenge is even greater because there are more players involved and typically some of these local firms have a "home court advantage." It's kind of like soccer—increasing numbers of Americans play the game, but they are up against an ingrained tradition of soccer fanaticism in Europe and South America where kids start dribbling a soccer ball when they start to walk.

Firms need to capitalize on their home country's assets and avoid competing in areas in which they are at a disadvantage. For example, German firms have trouble keeping production costs down due to the high wages, short workweeks, and long vacations that their skilled factory workers enjoy, so they compete better on high quality than on low price. Developing countries typically have a large labor force and low wages but relatively little in the way of highly trained workers or high-tech facilities, so they are better prospects for handmade crafts and low-cost manufacturing.

Some of the most significant U.S. exports are foods, industrial supplies, and services including tourism and entertainment—industries in which U.S. products are particularly valued by customers in other countries. The success of these industries shows that a firm's prospects for success depend not only on its own abilities but on its home country's competitive advantage, barriers to trade, and memberships in economic communities (which we'll discuss shortly).

Professor Michael Porter proposed a model to explain which companies and industries are likely to become leaders or followers in the global market.[7] The model showed that successful global firms were able to beat the competition in foreign markets because they were able to continually innovate and improve, often by taking advantage of assets in their home countries. U.S. assets include access to advanced technology, high agricultural productivity, and a sophisticated marketing orientation. These assets have allowed U.S. companies like Hewlett Packard, IBM, and Intel, for example, to be leaders in supplying the world with computer hardware.

Porter describes four keys to a nation's competitive advantage relative to other countries:

1. *Demand conditions*: The number and sophistication of domestic customers for a product can be an important key to a nation's competitive advantages. Firms that have been successful in meeting domestic demand have developed expertise, processes, or abilities that create an important competitve advantage in global markets. The French pride themselves on a long heritage of wine making, so they are very demanding when it comes to evaluating vintners. This forces the domestic wine industry to maintain a tradition of high quality that can then be exported to connoisseurs elsewhere.

2. *Related and supporting industries*: Companies must have access to suppliers and other supporting firms that provide the high-quality goods and services they require to turn out their own competitive products. U.S. computer makers have access to the world's leading experts and suppliers of hardware and software, most of whom are centrally located in Silicon Valley. As a result the world's markets for computers have been dominated for years by American firms.

3. *Factor conditions*: The quality of a country's resources—including its infrastructure, the educational level of its people, and the availability of raw materials—can create a competitive advantage for firms. Argentina is a leader in cattle production, aided by its vast pampas plains that are ideal for grazing. These conditions mean that Argentinian producers of fine leather goods and great steaks can find success around the globe (even though Argentina's domestic economy in general is in serious trouble).

4. *Company strategy, structure, and rivalry*: The way a country's businesses are organized and managed, and the intensity of competition that creates pressure to innovate also influence competitive advantages. Intense rivalry, for example, forces firms to continually innovate in order to survive, meaning that these firms tend to be more competitive in international markets. Microsoft is such a firm. In the United States, hundreds, if not thousands, of small firms work to get a share of Microsoft's business. This means Microsoft must innovate to stay on top, a characteristic that makes Microsoft successful in global markets, too.

BORDERS, ROADBLOCKS, AND COMMUNITIES

Not only are the conditions at home necessary for global success but conditions overseas must also be right. Even the best of competitive advantages may not allow a firm to be successful in foreign markets if the opportunities for success are not available. We like to think of the world as one big, open marketplace, where companies from every country are free to compete for business by meeting customers' needs better than the next guy. Although the world seems to be moving toward such an ideal of free trade, in reality we're not quite there yet. Often a company's efforts to expand into foreign markets are hindered by roadblocks designed to favor local businesses over outsiders.[8]

Protected Trade   In some cases a government adopts a policy of **protectionism** in which it enforces rules on foreign firms designed to give home companies an advantage. It may shield its own industries from foreign competition with red-tape tactics, including import quotas, embargoes, and tariffs. For example, South Korean customs officials delay approval of foreign shipments of fresh fruits and vegetables for up to four months (not too fresh at that point, are they?).[9] Western distillers saw huge potential in the Russian vodka market when the Soviet Union collapsed. However, the Russian government was determined to protect the local vodka

protectionism ■ Policy adopted by a government to give domestic companies an advantage.

import quotas ■ Limitations set by a government on the amount of a product allowed to enter or leave a country.

embargo ■ A quota completely prohibiting specified goods from entering or leaving a country.

tariffs ■ Taxes on imported goods.

General Agreement on Tariffs and Trade (GATT) ■ International treaty to reduce import tax levels and trade restrictions.

World Trade Organization (WTO) ■ An organization that replaced GATT, the WTO sets trade rules for its member nations and mediates disputes between nations.

1 *Bookmark It!*

The U.S. textile industry believes the U.S. government should protect it against less expensive imports from developing countries. For the U.S. textile industry, what are the pros and cons of such protection? See the Web site for the American Textile Manufacturers Institute, www.atmi.org, for an industry perspective.

economic communities ■ Groups of countries that band together to promote trade among themselves and to make it easier for member nations to compete elsewhere.

industry. It allowed foreign companies only 1 percent share in the market by setting high import duties and banning alcohol advertising on Russian television.[10]

Many governments set **import quotas** on foreign goods to reduce competition for their domestic industries. Quotas are limitations on the amount of a product allowed to enter or leave a country. Quotas can make goods more expensive to a country's citizens because the absence of cheaper foreign goods reduces pressure on domestic firms to lower prices. The United States sets import quotas on products such as sweetened candy, milk, cream, and some types of cotton.[11]

An **embargo** is an extreme quota that prohibits specified foreign goods completely. Much to the distress of hard-core cigar smokers in the Unites States, the U.S. government prohibits the import of Cuban cigars because of political differences with its island neighbor.

Governments also use **tariffs**, or taxes on imported goods, to give domestic competitors an advantage in the marketplace by making foreign competitors' goods more expensive than their own goods. For example, tariffs on rice in Japan prevent U.S. rice growers from establishing a strong presence in that country.

Established under the United Nations after World War II, the **General Agreement on Tariffs and Trade (GATT)** did a lot to reduce the problems protectionism creates. This regulatory group is now known as the **World Trade Organization (WTO)**. The WTO was established during GATT's 1986–1994 Uruguay Round, and effectively replaced GATT in 1995. During the 50-plus years of GATT/WTO, world trade exports increased by 6 percent annually. With over 140 members (and over 30 more negotiating membership now) the WTO member nations account for over 90 percent of world trade. WTO decisions are made by the entire membership, and all participating governments must ratify agreements.

Through a series of trade negotiations (known as *rounds*) that set standards for how much countries are allowed to favor their own products and services, the WTO has become a global referee for trade.[12] The objective of the WTO is to "help trade flow smoothly, freely, fairly, and predictably." It acts as forum for negotiations among countries, settles trade disputes, and even assists developing countries with training programs to give them a stronger position in the world marketplace.[13]

One of the important issues that the WTO tackles is protection of copyright and patent rights. This protection will help firms prevent pirated versions of their software, books, and music CDs from being sold in other countries. This is a serious problem for U.S. companies as their profits are eroded by illegal sales. According to a senior Microsoft executive based in Asia, "Piracy is clearly our number one competitor, and not only Microsoft's number one competitor but also a big impediment to the growth of the local software industry."[14]

Of course, not everyone believes free trade is a good thing. In November of 1999, thousands of protestors disrupted the meeting of the WTO in Seattle and further demonstrations have more recently occurred in Europe. Many environmentalists, labor groups, and some politicians feel that the price of globalization is too high. Some, such as the U.S. group United for a Fair Economy, suggest that the removal of trade barriers results in a loss of American jobs.[15]

Others complain that globalization efforts have ignored environmental and human rights issues.[16] Specifically, the WTO seeks to remove both tariff and non-tariff barriers to trade. Non-tariff barriers include a country's right to ban another country's products because of how products are produced or processed. Environmentalists argue that removing such bans weakens health and environmental safety standards.[17] Certainly, New Era firms should consider such concerns and the impact of greater world trade on the global community. Many New Era managers feel that companies have large ethical responsibilities to treat foreign lands and foreign labor fairly. For example, New Era managers may question whether their firm should open markets in developing countries such as China that support questionable human rights policies.

ECONOMIC COMMUNITIES

Groups of countries may also band together to promote trade among themselves and make it easier for member nations to compete elsewhere. These **economic communities** coordinate trade policies and ease restrictions on the flow of products and capital across their borders. Economic communities are important to marketers because they set policies in such areas as product content, package labeling, and advertising regulations that influence strategic decisions when doing business in these areas.

TABLE 4.1

Major Economic Communities Around the World

Economic communities are organizations of countries that band together to promote trade among themselves and make it easier for member countries to trade elsewhere. Economic communities, only some of which are shown here, exist all around the globe and the number continues to grow.

Community	Member Countries
ALADI	
Latin American Integration Assoc.	Argentina, Bolivia, Brazil, Chile, Colombia, Ecuador, Mexico, Paraguay, Uruguay, Venezuela
ANDEAN and MERCOSUR are sub-communities of ALADI that address special market needs. www.aladi.org	
ANDEAN	Bolivia, Colombia, Ecuador, Peru, Venezuela
This community is becoming more open to foreign trade and investment. www.comunidadandina.org	
ASEAN	
Association of South East Asian Nations	Brunei, Cambodia, Indonesia, Laos, Malaysia, Myanmar, Philippines, Singapore, Thailand, Vietnam
Economies in this community are growing at high rates, even though their GDPs are lower than most industrial nations. www.aseansec.org	
COMESA	
Common Market for Eastern and Southern Africa	Angola, Burundi, Comoros, Democratic Republic of Congo, Djibouti, Egypt, Eritrea, Ethiopia, Kenya, Madagascar, Malawi, Mauritius, Namibia, Rwanda, Seychelles, Somalia, Sudan, Swaziland, Tanzania, Uganda, Zambia, Zimbabwe
Economic communities in Africa such as COMESA tend to trade more with industrial nations than with each other. www.comesa.int	
MERCOSUR	Argentina, Brazil, Paraguay, Uruguay
Although smallest in number of countries, this economic community accounts for more than 80 percent of South America's GNP. www.mercosur.org	
NAFTA	
North American Free Trade Agreement	Canada, Mexico, United States
NAFTA is the world's largest economic community. www.nafta-sec-alena.org	
EU	
European Union	Austria, Belgium, Denmark, Finland, France, Germany, Greece, Ireland, Italy, Luxembourg, The Netherlands, Portugal, Spain, Sweden, The United Kingdom
Twelve of the 15 EU countries are members of a monetary union in which the Euro is the primary currency. Europa.eu.int	

Table 4.1 illustrates the economic communities that have now been created around the world. In South America the group called MERCOSUR currently includes Argentina, Paraguay, Brazil, and Uruguay.[18] South America also has two other economic communities, known as the Andean Group and the Latin American Integration Association (ALADI). The Association of Southeast Asian Nations (ASEAN) includes ten nations: Malaysia, Indonesia, the Philippines, Thailand, Singapore, Brunei Darussalam, Myanmar, Laos, and Cambodia.[19] The economic communities in Europe and North America are the European Union and NAFTA.

In 1957, the Treaty of Paris created the **European Union (EU)**, which at that time consisted of six member countries—Belgium, France, Germany, Italy, Luxembourg, and the Netherlands. This community now includes most of Western Europe—the original six, plus

European Union (EU) ■
Economic community that now includes most of Western Europe.

„Was für mich die Goldmedaille ist, wird der Euro für Europa."

Heike Drechsler, Olympiasiegerin

This German ad reassures people concerned about switching over to the Euro. An Olympic athlete says, "What the gold medal is to me, the Euro will be in Europe."

Austria, Denmark, Finland, Greece, Ireland, Portugal, Spain, Sweden, and the United Kingdom. The EU now represents about 350 million consumers from 15 countries.[20]

The EU has begun many initiatives to improve the quality of products available to Europeans in member countries. These initiatives include standardizing regulations regarding information that companies must share with consumers, encouraging environmentally friendly consumption, and strengthening the rights of consumers who are dissatisfied with products and services.[21] As of January 1, 2002, twelve of the European Union countries (all except Britain, Sweden, and Denmark) abandoned their own currencies and converted to a common currency, the *Euro*, which will (it is hoped) create one strong $6.4 trillion economy.[22]

North American Free Trade Agreement (NAFTA)

■ The world's largest economic community composed of the United States, Canada, and Mexico.

The **North American Free Trade Agreement (NAFTA)** formed the world's largest economic community. It is comprised of the United States, Canada, and Mexico. NAFTA became a unified trading bloc in 1994.[23] This extended the cooperative arrangement already established by the United States and Canada in 1989 under the Canada–United States Free Trade Agreement.

NAFTA is controversial. Some critics claim it diverts jobs from the United States to Mexico, where cheaper labor rates prevail. However, the agreement appears to be stimulating economic growth as foreign investors are pumping money into North American markets. For example, Sei Woo Rubber Works, a Singapore company, chose Mexico in which to open its first foreign plant so it could manufacture rubber components for pagers and telephones sold to the U.S. market.[24]

An even larger American free trade zone might be in the making. Talks are expected to conclude in 2005 for development of the Free Trade Area of the Americas (FTAA). The FTAA, when in place, will include 34 countries with a population of 800 million and combined output of $11 trillion.[25] The results would be that firms in these 34 countries would operate in the "largest free-trade zone on the planet—a vast market marked by nonexistent or very low tariffs, streamlined customs regulations, and the gradual disappearance of quotas, subsidies, and other impediments to trade."[26]

The Global Marketing Environment

Now we've seen the "big picture" of world trade a firm must consider as it decides in which regions of the world it holds a competitive advantage. To complicate matters, companies that enter foreign markets need to consider how—and whether—to adapt to local conditions in a country or region. Environmental scanning of a foreign market is difficult because marketers usually aren't familiar with its economy, politics, laws, and culture. As we saw with the folks at Sony Nordic, even launching programs in other countries that are nearby and fairly similar can create problems due to differences in language or customs. It may be a small world, but it's not a simple one. In this section, we'll see how economic, political, and cultural factors affect marketers' global strategies.

THE ECONOMIC ENVIRONMENT

Countries vary in their level of economic development, and a firm thinking about marketing overseas needs to understand what its potential customers can afford. A maker of fine crystal will find it rough going in a country where few can afford its products.

Indicators of Economic Health One way to gauge the market potential for a product is to look at a country's economic health. The most commonly used measure of economic health of a country is the **gross domestic product (GDP)**, the total dollar value of goods and services a country produces within its borders in a year. A similar but less frequently used measure of economic health is the **gross national product (GNP)**, which measures the value of all goods and services produced by a country's individuals or organizations whether located within the country's borders or not. Table 4.2 shows the GDP and other economic and demographic characteristics of a sampling of countries. In addition to total GDP, marketers may also compare countries based on the *per capita GDP:* the total GDP divided by the number of people in a country. Still such comparisons may not tell the whole story. Per capita GDP can be deceiving because the wealth of a country may be concentrated in the hands of a few. Furthermore, the costs of the same goods and services are much lower in some global markets. For example, goods and services valued at $30,000 in the United States would only cost $5,100 in Uganda.[27]

Of course, GDP alone does not provide the information needed by marketers in deciding if a country's economic environment makes for an attractive market. A country's demographic characteristics also play an important role in determining its citizens' buying power. Birth rates and the size of different age groups are particularly important for forecasting market potential because they tell us what types of products are likely to be in demand. For example,

gross domestic product (GDP) ■ The total dollar value of goods and services produced by a nation within its borders in a year.

gross national product (GNP) ■ the value of all goods and services produced by a country's citizens or organizations, whether located within the country's borders or not.

2 Bookmark It!

Pretend you are a marketing manager for a firm that makes household appliances. Use the data in Table 4.2 to evaluate the attractiveness of five countries for your firm's global expansion plans. Which would be the best prospect for you?

TABLE 4.2

Comparisons of Several Countries on Economic and Demographic Characteristics

	Ecuador	China	Hungary	Spain	Japan	U.S.A.
Total GDP	$372 billion	$4.5 trillion	$113.9 billion	$720.8 billion	$3.15 trillion	$9.963 trillion
Per Capita GDP	$2,900	$3,600	$11,200	$18,000	$24,900	$36,200
Percentage population below poverty level	50%	10%	8.6%	NA	NA	12.7%
Inflation rate	96%	0.4%	9.8%	3.4%	–0.7%	3.4%
Unemployment rate	13%	10%	9.4%	14%	4.7%	4%
Population	13,183,978	1,273,111,290	10,106,017	40,037,995	126,771,662	278,058,881
Birth rate per 1000 population	25.99	15.95	9.32	9.26	10.04	14.2
Percentage population aged 0–14	36%	25%	17%	15%	15%	21%
Percentage population aged 15–64	60%	68%	69%	68%	68%	66%
Percentage population aged 65 and over	4%	7%	15%	17%	18%	13%

Source: Adapted from World Trade Organization, "International Trade Statistics 2001".

the European and U.S. populations are growing older—the proportion of U.S. citizens aged 55 and older will grow by over 60 percent by 2015. This difference means that great opportunities exist for products and services catering to older people, from retirement homes to health care.

Marketers also need to consider whether they can conduct "business as usual" in another country. The **economic infrastructure** is the quality of a country's distribution, financial, and communications systems. For example, Argentina boasts many modern conveniences, but its antiquated phone system is just starting to work properly after years of neglect by the government.

Modern marketers must add another factor to their list of worries: If using the World Wide Web is part of their marketing strategy, they need to be sure that adequate numbers of people will be online. Indeed, the future of e-commerce is in the global marketplace. According to a report by the Computer Industry Almanac, over 490 million people around the world will have Internet access by 2002.[28] By 2003, 46 percent of the world's e-commerce will occur outside the United States. In Western Europe, e-commerce sales are expected to increase enormously from $5.6 billion in 1998 to $430 billion in 2003.[29] E-commerce in Latin America is expected to generate $8 billion in sales by 2003, up from $170 million in 1998 with Brazil, Argentina, Chile, Colombia, Mexico, and Venezuela as the strongest markets.[30] Table 4.3 shows Internet users in the top 15 countries for 2000.

Thus far, we've discussed some of the issues a marketer must think about when determining if a country will be a good prospect. But there are other economic conditions that marketers must understand as well. In the next section, we'll look at the broader economic picture of a country, called its *level of development*.

Level of Economic Development When marketers scout the world for opportunities, it helps if they consider a country's level of economic development to understand the needs of people who live there and the infrastructure conditions with which they must contend. Economists look past simple facts such as growth in GDP to decide this; they also look at what steps are being taken to reduce poverty, inequality, and unemployment. Economists describe the following three basic levels of development.

economic infrastructure ■
The quality of a country's distribution, financial, and communications systems.

TABLE 4.3

Top 15 Wired Countries as of January 2001

Rank	Country	Weekly Internet Users (Number in millions)	All Internet Users (Number in millions)
1	U.S.	114.4	134.6
2	Japan	25.4	33.9
3	Germany	14.9	19.9
4	Canada	13.1	15.4
5	U.K.	12.6	16.8
6	South Korea	12.4	19.0
7	China	11.3	22.5
8	Italy	9.3	12.5
9	France	6.3	9.0
10	Australia	5.3	7.6
11	Taiwan	4.5	7.0
12	Netherlands	4.1	5.5
13	Sweden	3.8	4.4
14	Spain	3.6	5.6
15	Russia	3.0	7.5
—	Top 15 Countries	244.0	321.2
—	West Europe	54.6	73.7
—	Worldwide	299.6	413.7

Source: "U.S. has 33% Share of Internet Users Worldwide Year-end 2000 According to the Computer Industry Almanac" accessed through www.c-i-a.com/200103iu.htm, April 24, 2001.

Less Developed Countries: A country at the lowest stage of economic development is a **less developed country (LDC)**. In most cases, its economic base is agricultural. Many nations in Africa and South Asia such as Chad and Sri Lanka are considered LDCs. Their **standard of living** is low, as are literacy levels. Opportunities to sell many products, especially luxury items such as diamonds and caviar, are minimal because most people don't have spending money. They grow what they need and barter for the rest. These countries are attractive markets for staples and inexpensive items. They may export important raw materials such as minerals or rubber to industrial nations.

In 1996, sub-Saharan Africa attracted less than $1 of every $20 invested in less developed countries. Now signs of change are in the air: Unilever, Nestlé, Eveready, and Coca-Cola have aggressively undertaken marketing efforts in Kenya, and the end of apartheid has brought many firms back to South Africa.[31] Weight Watchers has moved in, too—the company noticed that obesity-related diseases such as hypertension are rising with the influx of processed foods and American style fast-food restaurants. Sometimes economic development is a mixed blessing!

Developing Countries: When an economy shifts its emphasis from agriculture to industry, standards of living, education, and the use of technology rise. These countries are **developing countries**. In such locales there may be a visible middle class, often largely composed of entrepreneurs working hard to run a successful small business.

Because 77 percent of the world's population lives in developing countries, the sheer number of potential customers and the presence of a skilled labor force attract many firms to these areas. And, the economy of the developing world continues to expand. Throughout Latin America, Eastern Europe, and the Pacific Rim (generally, Asia excluding Japan), new crops of consumers are panting for their share of Western-style products.[32]

Eastern Europe, with its 300 million-plus consumers, is an important region that includes a number of developing countries. In the 1990s transition from communism to a free market economy brought with it a hunger for Western goods that continues to grow. In Russia, for example, big retailers from all around Europe, including Ikea of Sweden, Auchan from France, Kesko from Finland, and Spar from the Netherlands are all opening stores there. Moscow designated 20 sites on the outskirts of the city for new shopping malls. As the director of Ramenka, a Turkish mall development company that has opened ten centers in the country noted, "This is the main country in the world that the retail chains haven't entered yet—this market is empty."[33] Not for long.

less developed country (LDC) ■ A country at the lowest stage of economic development.

standard of living ■ An indicator of the average quality and quantity of goods and services consumed in a country.

developing countries ■ Countries in which the economy is shifting its emphasis from agriculture to industry.

In developing countries such as Egypt, the agricultural nature of the economy is slowly giving way to industrialization. For marketers this means growing markets for consumer goods that Egyptians were unable to purchase before.

Developing countries like China are attractive markets for companies such as the Dutch electronics firm Philips. With a growing middle class eager for home appliances, demand is steadily increasing for global suppliers of these products.

The countries of Latin America are emerging from decades of state control, and their economies are opening to foreign business.[34] In 1997, Latin America's economies grew by about 5 percent, and both exports and imports are surging—exports expanded by 13 percent in one year. Mexico and Brazil are the two biggest traders in the region.[35] A construction boom is also rebuilding roads, bridges, and other parts of the infrastructure required to move goods through these countries efficiently.

The Pacific Rim countries of China, South Korea, Malaysia, Indonesia, Thailand, Singapore, and Hong Kong are nicknamed the "Dragons of Asia" because of their tremendous economic growth, despite a serious tumble in 1997 and 1998. Starbucks is pushing ahead in Asia with its first overseas expansion. It plans to have 200 stores in the near future—even if the traditional menu of grande cappuccinos and lattes has to include such local favorites as calamansi juice (a traditional fruit drink) in the Philippines.[36]

developed country ■ A country that boasts sophisticated marketing systems, strong private enterprise, and bountiful market potential for many goods and services.

Developed Countries: A **developed country** boasts sophisticated marketing systems, strong private enterprise, and bountiful market potential for many goods and services. Such countries are economically advanced and offer a wide range of opportunities for international marketers. The United States, the United Kingdom, Canada, France, Italy, Germany, and Japan are the most economically developed countries in the world.

THE POLITICAL AND LEGAL ENVIRONMENT

When entering a foreign market, a firm must carefully weigh political and legal risks. A company's fortunes often are affected by political and legal issues that may be beyond its control. Some successful American companies such as McDonald's are feeling the effects of being too successful in their efforts to capture foreign markets. When the United States engages in activities that some people overseas don't like such as invading Afghanistan in 2001, it's common for symbols of American culture like the golden arches to be the first target of demonstrations, vandalism, and in some cases destruction.

McDonald's has more than 29,000 outlets in 120 countries and is highly vulnerable to anti-American sentiment. Although the company claims it's sensitive to local cultures and adapts to each (for example, it sells a vegetarian Maharaja Mac instead of a Big Mac in India, and its spokesman in Japan where the "r" sound is rarely pronounced is named Donald McDonald), for many the company is the ultimate symbol of American capitalism.[37] A changing, unstable world creates a lot of McHeadaches for companies like McDonald's.

Political Issues   Political actions taken by a government can drastically affect the business operations of outsiders. At the extreme, of course, it goes without saying that when two countries go to war the business environment changes dramatically. Short of war, though, a country may impose **economic sanctions** that prohibit trade with another country (as the United States does with several countries including Cuba and Libya), so access to some markets may be cut off.

In some situations internal pressures may prompt the government to take over the operations of foreign companies doing business within its borders. It is called **nationalization** when the domestic government reimburses a foreign company (often not for the full value) for its assets after taking it over, and it is called **expropriation** when a domestic government seizes a foreign company's assets (and that firm is just out of luck). To keep track of the level of political stability or instability in foreign countries, firms often engage in formal or informal analyses of the potential political risk in various countries. For example, Amoco Corporation, before it merged with British Petroleum, maintained its own foreign intelligence office that monitored political and economic developments in about 50 countries. Other firms retain consultants who specialize in advising companies on the risk of doing business in foreign countries.[38]

economic sanctions ▨ Trade prohibitions imposed by one country against another.

nationalization ▨ A domestic government's takeover of a foreign company for its assets with some reimbursement, though often not for the full value.

expropriation ▨ A domestic government's seizure of a foreign company's assets without any compensation.

Regulatory Issues   Governments and economic communities impose numerous regulations about what products should be made of, how they should be made and what can be said about them. For example, sometimes a company has no choice but to alter product content to comply with local laws. Heinz 57 Sauce tastes quite different in Europe, simply because of different legal restrictions on preservatives and color additives.[39]

Other regulations are less focused on ensuring quality and more focused on ensuring that the host country gets a piece of the action. **Local content rules** are a form of protectionism stipulating that a certain proportion of a product must consist of components supplied by industries in the host country or economic community. For example, under NAFTA rules, cars built by Mercedes-Benz in Alabama must have 62.5 percent of their components made in North America to be able to enter Mexico and Canada duty-free.[40] That helps to explain why Japanese automakers such as Toyota have already beefed up their local presence by opening manufacturing plants in the United States and hiring local workers to run them.

local content rules ▨ A form of protectionism stipulating that a certain proportion of a product must consist of components supplied by industries in the host country.

Product content regulations can also cause headaches for marketers in their home markets, especially when a product's country of origin is part of its sales appeal. For example, New Balance Athletic Shoe, Inc. ran into problems because its advertising claimed the shoes are "made in the U.S.A." The U.S. Federal Trade Commission cracked down on the company because, although it is true that its shoes are sewn and glued in the United States, most of the soles and some of the presewn uppers are imported from China.[41] To avoid the possibility of the FTC taking further action, New Balance deleted the claim in its advertising.

Countries also regulate the promotion of products by foreign firms, sometimes because they fear that their own culture will be corrupted. The French have been the most outspoken opponents of the Americanization of their culture. They have even tried to ban the use of such "Franglish" terms as *le drugstore, le fast food* and *le marketing*.[42] Many nations impose quotas on foreign TV programming, and in some cases television networks are state controlled and may not accept any foreign advertising. In Russia, the Inspectorate for the Control of the Condition of Advertising and Artistic Decorations (how's that for a serious name?) clamped down on the overabundance of Western marketing messages by requiring all stores to display promotional signs in Russian only.[43]

Human Rights Issues   Some governments and companies are especially vigilant about denying business opportunities to countries that mistreat their citizens. They are concerned about conducting trade with local firms that exploit their workers in barbaric factories, or that keep costs down by employing young children or prisoners for slave wages. The Generalized System of Preferences is a set of regulations that allows developing countries to export goods duty-free to the United States. The catch is that each country must constantly demonstrate it is making progress toward improving the rights of its workers.[44]

On the other side of the coin, U.S. firms looking to expand their operations overseas often are enticed by the very low wages they can pay to local workers. Although they provide needed jobs, some companies have been criticized for exploiting workers by paying wages that fall below even local poverty levels, for damaging the environment, and for selling poorly made or unsafe items to foreign consumers. This issue has become quite volatile, as companies such as Nike and Alcoa have had to vigorously defend themselves against charges of abuse. Negative media coverage of these problems has been a public relations nightmare for these firms.

One exception: Levi Strauss & Co. operates in more than 60 countries worldwide, and it has been singled out for its dedication to what CEO Robert Haas calls "responsible commercial success." This philosophy emphasizes the adoption of ethical business practices that encourage workforce diversity, honesty, and a concern for human rights. A company task force developed guidelines for doing business abroad, taking into account working conditions, the environment, and human rights. In Bangladesh, Levi Strauss grew concerned about child labor violations when it discovered that girls as young as 11 were working full-time sewing its Dockers pants. While allowing the children to keep their jobs to support their families, the company arranged to pay for their school tuition, books, and uniforms.[45] However, even Levi Strauss was the target of criticism when in 1998 it reversed an earlier decision not to manufacture in China because of pervasive human rights violations there.[46]

THE CULTURAL ENVIRONMENT

After a firm clears the political and legal issues that can hamper entry into foreign markets, it still needs to understand and adapt to the customs, characteristics, and practices of its citizens. Basic beliefs about such cultural priorities as the role of family or proper relations between the sexes affect people's responses to products and promotional messages. In the late 1970s, Procter & Gamble introduced Pampers diapers in Japan. Although successful in the United States, this product did not sell well in Japan because P&G neglected some important cultural differences between American and Japanese parents. One was that the typical Japanese mom changes her baby's diaper about 14 times a day, twice as often as her American counterpart. Pampers were too expensive for a Japanese mother to use so many. The company also learned to promote a white unisex diaper in Asia despite the popularity of color-coded ones in the United States. When women chose a pink package, they admitted they had a daughter—but male children are much more desirable in many Asian cultures.[47]

cultural values ■ A society's deeply held beliefs about right and wrong ways to live.

collectivist culture ■ Culture in which people subordinate their personal goals to those of a stable community.

individualist culture ■ Culture in which people tend to attach more importance to personal goals than to those of the larger community.

2 *Bookmark It!*

Talk with someone in your community who is from a foreign country. What differing cultural values do they see between their home country and the United States? What are some ways these values might affect U.S. marketing strategies in their country?

Values Every society has a set of **cultural values**, or deeply held beliefs about right and wrong ways to live, that it imparts to its members.[48] For example, cultures differ in their emphasis on collectivism and individualism. In **collectivist cultures** such as those found in Venezuela, Pakistan, Taiwan, Thailand, Turkey, Greece, and Portugal people subordinate their personal goals to those of a stable community. In contrast, consumers in **individualist cultures** such as the United States, Australia, Great Britain, Canada, and the Netherlands tend to attach more importance to personal goals, and people are more likely to change memberships when the demands of the group become too costly.[49]

Consistent with this difference, a study by the research firm Wirthlin Worldwide found that the most important values to Asian executives are hard work, respect for learning, and group loyalty. In contrast, North American businesspeople emphasize the values of personal freedom, self-reliance, and freedom of expression.[50] These differences are vital for marketers to understand. For example, a perfume slogan like "Cachet. As individual as you are," which successfully appeals to American women, would not go over as well in a collectivist culture.

Values can show up in strange ways. For example, Japanese culture is well-known for its emphasis on the value of cleanliness. When Japanese people give money as a wedding gift, they often iron the bills before placing them in the envelope. Some laundromats even allow customers to rinse out the inside of a machine before using it. Tokyo bus drivers and cabdrivers wear immaculate white gloves while working. Pentel sells a germ-free pen in Japan that is decorated with a medical blue cross; the popular brand is advertised with the slogan: "The pen is mightier than the bacterium." Japan's Sanwa Bank literally "launders money" for its customers in specially designed ATM machines that spit out sanitized bills.[51] Following the bioterrorism scares of 2001, we may see similar products and services popping up in the United States and other countries as well.

The Japanese emphasis on the value of cleanliness is evident in the spotless white gloves worn by cab drivers.

Norms and Customs   Values are general ideas about good and bad behaviors. From these values flow **norms**, or specific rules dictating what is right or wrong, acceptable or unacceptable. Some specific types of norms include:[52]

- A **custom** is a norm handed down from the past that controls basic behaviors, such as division of labor in a household.
- **Mores** are customs with a strong moral overtone. Mores often involve a *taboo*, or forbidden behavior, such as incest or cannibalism. Violation of mores often meets with strong punishment from other members of a society.
- **Conventions** are norms regarding the conduct of everyday life. These rules deal with the subtleties of consumer behavior, including the "correct" way to furnish one's house, wear one's clothes, host a dinner party, and so on.

All three types of norms may determine what behaviors are appropriate in different countries. For example, mores may tell us what kind of food is permissible to eat. A meal of dog may be taboo in the United States, whereas Hindus would shun a steak, and Muslims avoid pork products. A custom dictates the appropriate hour at which the meal should be served—many Europeans and Latin Americans do not begin dinner until around 9:00 P.M., and they are amused by American visitors whose stomachs are growling by 7:00. Conventions tell us how to eat the meal, including such details as the utensils, table etiquette, and even the appropriate apparel to be worn at dinnertime.

Aside from marketing the proper products in the proper ways, a global marketer must learn about the characteristics of people in different countries and adapt to local practices to avoid insulting local business partners. A vice president at Caterpillar, Inc., a company that exports over $3 billion in farm and industrial products per year, certainly demonstrated a willingness to understand unfamiliar customs. While toasting a new business relationship with a Saudi sheik, he was expected to eat what the Saudis regard as the choicest part of a lamb: its eyes. His reaction sums up what you sometimes must do to succeed in foreign cultures: "You just swallow hard and do it."[53]

Careful analysis of cultural differences can lead to success, even in foreign markets considered difficult to crack. Until 1995, Procter & Gamble didn't even sell dish soap in Japan, but now its Joy brand is the top seller. P&G offered new technology and packaging that let crowded Japanese grocery stores make more money (providing the soap in cylinders instead of fat-necked bottles that took up more space), and spent heavily on oddball commercials that created a buzz. The company even sent researchers to watch how Japanese homemakers wash their dishes. They found that most women squirted out more detergent than was needed—a clear

norms ■ Specific rules dictating what is right or wrong, acceptable or unacceptable.

custom ■ A norm handed down from the past that controls basic behaviors.

mores ■ A custom with a strong moral overtone.

conventions ■ Norms regarding the conduct of everyday life.

sign of frustration with the weak products available—and P&G cornered the market by convincing consumers that Joy was more powerful than other soaps.[54]

Conflicting customs can be a problem when U.S. marketers try to conduct business in other countries where executives have different ideas about what is proper or expected. These difficulties even include body language; people in Latin countries tend to stand much closer to each other than do Americans, and they will be insulted if their counterpart tries to stand farther away.

Consider the problem of "spreading the grease." In Japan, it's called *kuroi kiri* (black mist), in Germany, it's *schmiergeld* (grease money), whereas Mexicans refer to *la mordida* (the bite), the French say *pot-de-vin* (jug of wine), and the Italians speak of the *bustarella* (little envelope). They're all talking about *baksheesh*, the Middle Eastern term for tip or gratuity. In many cultures, business success depends as much on *baksheesh* as on luck or ability. *Bribery* occurs when someone voluntarily offers payment to get an illegal advantage. *Extortion* occurs when payment is extracted under duress by someone in authority.[55] Bribes are given to speed up required work, to secure a contract, or to avoid having one canceled, and they are a way of life in many countries. The Foreign Corrupt Practices Act of 1977 (FCPA) puts U.S. businesses at a disadvantage, because it bars them from paying bribes to sell overseas.[56] It should be noted, however, that the FCPA does allow payments for "routine governmental action . . . such as obtaining permits, licenses, or other official documents; processing governmental papers, such as visas and work orders; providing police protection . . ." but does not include ". . . any decision by a foreign official to award new business or to continue business with a particular party."[57]

Symbols and Superstitions   On the surface, many marketing images have virtually no literal connection to actual products. What does a cowboy have to do with a bit of tobacco rolled into a paper tube? How can a celebrity such as basketball star Michael Jordan enhance the image of a cologne? The meanings we impart to these symbols are largely influenced by our culture, so marketers need to take special care that the symbol they use in a foreign market has the meaning they intended. Even the same product may be used quite differently and take on a different meaning to people. In parts of rural India, for example, the refrigerator is a status symbol, so people want a snazzy-looking one that they can keep in the living room to show off to visitors.[58]

semiotics ■ Field of study that examines how meanings are assigned to symbols.

For assistance in understanding how consumers interpret the meanings of symbols, some marketers are turning to a field of study known as **semiotics**, which examines how people assign meanings to symbols.[59] For example, although the American cowboy on packs of Marlboro cigarettes is a well-known symbol of the frontier spirit in many countries, people in Hong Kong see him as a low-status laborer. Philip Morris has to make sure he's always pictured riding a white horse, which is a more positive symbol in that country. Even something as simple as a color takes on very different meanings around the globe. Pepsodent toothpaste found this out when it promised white teeth to people in Southeast Asia, where black or yellow teeth are status symbols.

Marketers also need to be concerned about taboos and superstitions. For example, the Japanese are superstitious about the number four. *Shi*, the word for "four," is also the word for "death," so Tiffany sells glassware and china in sets of five in Japan. In some Arab countries, alcohol and pork are forbidden to Islamic consumers (even stuffed pig toys are taboo), and advertisers may refrain from showing nudity or even the faces of women in photos, which some governments prohibit.[60]

Language   As Henrik Kass discovered during the Sony Experience Tour, language barriers can be big obstacles to marketers breaking into foreign markets. These barriers affect product labeling and usage instructions, advertising, and personal selling. It's vital for marketers to work with local people who understand the subtleties of language to avoid the confusion that may result.

For example, the meaning of a brand name—one of the most important signals a marketer can send about the character and quality of a product—can get mangled as it travels around the world. Local product names often raise eyebrows to visiting Americans, who may be surprised to stumble upon a Japanese coffee creamer called Creap or a Mexican bread named Bimbo.[61]

Ethnocentrism   Even if a firm succeeds in getting its products to a foreign market, there's no guarantee local consumers will be interested. Sometimes a willingness to try products made elsewhere comes slowly. In marketing, the tendency to prefer products or people of one's own culture over those from other countries is called **ethnocentrism**. For example, the French tend to be a bit finicky about their cuisine, and they evaluate food products from other countries critically. However, the upscale British department store Marks & Spencer is making inroads in France selling English-style sandwiches like egg and watercress on whole wheat bread and ethnic dishes such as chicken *tikka masala* that are not popular in Paris. Viewed as convenience foods for young office workers, these foreign choices are less expensive than the traditional French loaf split down the middle and lathered with butter and ham or Camembert cheese. So, ethnocentrism can be overcome, but it does take time.

ethnocentrism ▪ The tendency to prefer products or people of one's own culture.

Consumers often look for information about a product's country-of-origin when evaluating its quality and characteristics.

In addition, ethnocentric consumers are likely to feel it is ethically wrong to buy products from other countries because they want to support their domestic economy. Ethnocentric Americans, for example, are likely to agree with statements such as:

- Purchasing foreign-made products is un-American.
- The United States should place restrictions on all imports.
- American consumers who purchase products made in other countries are responsible for putting their fellow Americans out of work.[62]

Marketing campaigns stressing the desirability of "buying American" are more likely to appeal to this consumer segment. In the 1990s it seemed likely that ethnocentrism would become less of a problem over time as people became more accustomed to the idea of living in a global society. After the tragic events of September 11, 2001, marketing campaigns invoking strong American patriotism increased dramatically and feelings of ethnocentrism increased in many segments of the population.

I'd Like to Buy the World a Coke: Exporting American Culture   The National Basketball Association is fast becoming the first truly global sports league. About $500 million of licensed merchandise is sold outside of the United States in a typical year. One factor that makes it easy for some U.S. firms such as Levi Strauss and Harley-Davidson to go global is the special appeal American products have around the world. These products benefit from their strong association with innovation, rebellion, and a casual lifestyle fueled by icons such as Elvis Presley and James Dean.[63] As a Japanese woman noted when she was interviewed while filling her shopping cart at an American warehouse store that opened a branch in that country, "Shopping at Costco is like taking a trip to America."[64]

The laid-back American lifestyle (or at least the way it's portrayed on TV) is desired by many consumers around the world. That explains the popularity, for example, of homes being built in Buenos Aires, Argentina, by Pulte Homes, the second-largest home builder in the United States. Pulte is exporting suburban American home models with names such as Stanford and Cambridge to Argentina, featuring the same floor plans, shingle roofs, and tiny lawns you might see in a typical U.S. community. Of course, some adjustments need to be made to make these homes compatible with the Argentinian lifestyle. In addition to amenities like whirlpool baths and granite countertops, these homes come with a bidet in the bathroom and a rear patio big enough to accommodate a big grill Argentinians use to cook their famous steaks called a *parilla*. And, each gated subdivision also includes a regulation-size soccer field.[65] So much for "Leave it to Beaver."

The American appeal is so strong that some non-U.S. companies go out of their way to assume an American image. A British ad for Blistex lip cream, for example, includes a fictional woman named "Miss Idaho Lovely Lips" who claims Blistex is "America's best-selling lip cream."[66] In other cases, local entrepreneurs are adapting American pastimes to local habits. For example, the Western sport of bowling is now a big craze in China, and it's estimated that a new bowling center opens in China every other week. Bowling's presence as an exhibition sport in the 1988 Seoul Olympics sparked interest in the game, caught the fancy of Koreans, and spread to the rest of Asia.[67]

Cultural Change Marketers need to understand cultural differences, but they also must realize that the global landscape is constantly changing. Just as it's important to engage in political risk assessment, it's also imperative to monitor changes in cultural values and behaviors to ensure that marketing strategies are keeping up.

Since 1978, the Europe-based Research Institute on Social Change (RISC) www.risc-int.com/ has conducted international measurements of social change in more than 40 countries. Surveys include questions on values and attitudes, behavior, and media usage. Ongoing tracking like that provided by RISC and other systems allows marketers to pinpoint which values are most important to consumers in a particular country or region. For example, the RISC system allows analysts to assign people to different segments such as those that primarily value environmentalism, materialism, and so on. This type of comprehensive, ongoing research provides a broad understanding of cultural currents, which makes it possible to anticipate changes in one country before these spread to others. Thus, widespread concern for the environment first appeared in Sweden in the early 1970s, in France in the beginning of the 1980s and this interest finally surfaced in Spain in the early 1990s.[68]

While few Chinese can read or speak English, American symbols, such as this rendition of Disney character Daisy Duck, signify American luxury to Chinese consumers.

How "Global" Should a Global Marketing Strategy Be?

Understanding all the economic, legal, and cultural differences around the world can be a daunting task, not to mention understanding the complexity of world trade. But if a firm decides to expand beyond its home country, it must make important decisions about how to structure its business and whether to adapt its product marketing strategy to accommodate local needs.

First, the company must decide on the nature of its commitment, including whether it will partner with another firm or go it alone. Then it must make specific decisions about the marketing mix for a particular product or service. In this final section, we'll consider issues related to global strategy at these two levels: the company and the product.

COMPANY-LEVEL DECISIONS: CHOOSING A MARKET ENTRY STRATEGY

In 2001, General Electric was named the world's most respected company for the fourth straight year in a worldwide survey of chief executives conducted by the *Financial Times* and accounting firm PricewaterhouseCoopers.[69] Much of GE's success has come from its global operations.

General Electric made the decision to go global, and the company has never looked back. GE's strategy for shifting its "center of gravity" from the industrialized world of the United States to Asia and Latin America made it a local assembler of low-tech goods in some countries and a manufacturer of appliances and other products for export in others.[70] GE tailors the type and extent of its commitment to local conditions in each market it chooses to enter. As GE says in its *2000 Annual Report*, the company is without boundaries. "Globalization has transformed a heavily U.S.-based Company to one whose revenues are now 40% non-U.S. Even more importantly, it has changed us into a Company that searches the world, not just to sell or to source, but to find intellectual capital: the world's best talent and greatest ideas."[71]

Just like a romantic relationship, a firm deciding to go global must determine the level of commitment it is willing to make to operate in another country. This commitment can range from a casual involvement to a full-scale "marriage." At one extreme, the firm can simply export its products, while at the other it can directly invest in another country by buying a foreign subsidiary or opening its own stores. The decision about the extent of commitment entails a trade-off between control and risk. Direct involvement gives the firm more control over what happens in the country, but risk also increases if the operation is not successful. Let's review four strategies representing increased levels of involvement: exporting, contractual arrangements, strategic alliances, and direct investment. These are summarized in Figure 4.3.

export merchant ■ An intermediary used by a firm to represent it in another country.

Exporting If a firm chooses to export, it must decide whether it will attempt to sell its products on its own or rely on intermediaries to represent it in the target country. These representatives are specialists known as **export merchants** who understand the local market and can find

---

FIGURE **4.3**

Market Entry Strategies

Choosing a market entry strategy is a critical decision for companies that want to go global. Choosing whether to operate the new venture versus sharing responsibility with organizations in the local market involves a tradeoff between control and risk.

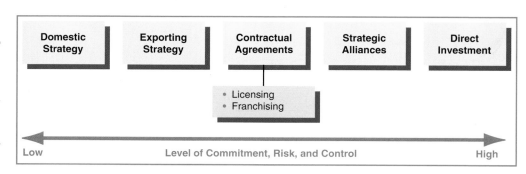

buyers and negotiate terms.[72] An exporting strategy allows a firm to sell its products in global markets and cushions the firm against downturns in its domestic market. Because the exported products are made at home, the firm is able to maintain control over design and production decisions.[73]

In some cases, however, these advantages may be offset by foreign barriers to entry, such as tariffs, or negated by local content laws requiring that the products have a proportion of components made in the importing country. For example, Japan's Nippon Telephone & Telegraph Company used product specifications as a trade barrier when it was forced by the Japanese government to accept bids from foreign firms. The communications giant got around this rule by creating specifications that fit only existing Japanese products—and neglected to provide details in any language but Japanese.[74] Exporting firms find it hard to meet that kind of challenge.

Contractual Agreements   The next level of commitment a firm can make to a foreign market is a contractual agreement with a company in that country to conduct some or all of its business there. These agreements can take several forms. Two of the most common are licensing and franchising.

In a **licensing** agreement a firm (the licenser) gives another firm (the licensee) the right to produce and market its product in a specific country or region in return for royalties. Because the licensee produces the product in its home market, it can avoid many of the barriers to entry that the licenser would have encountered. For example, Mitsubishi Heavy Industries and Kawasaki Heavy Industries produce McDonnell Douglas's F-15 fighter plane for the Japanese military, so the local government cooperates to a far greater extent than if Americans were building the aircraft. However, the licenser also loses control over how the product is produced and marketed, so if the licensee does a poor job the company's reputation may be tarnished.

Franchising is a form of licensing that gives the franchisee the right to adapt an entire way of doing business in the host country. McDonald's, a major franchiser, is the world's largest fast food retailer with about 28,000 restaurants in 121 countries.[75] Asia is a major growth area for the chain. A local franchisee might buy the rights to use McDonald's logo, menu items, production process, and even access to the formula for its "secret" Big Mac sauce. More than 400 U.S. franchising companies, including Coca-Cola, 7-Eleven, Mrs. Fields, Century 21, and Tiffany operate about 40,000 outlets internationally. Again, there is a risk to the parent company if the franchisee does not use the same quality ingredients or procedures, so firms like McDonald's monitor these operations carefully.

Firms seeking an even deeper commitment to a foreign market develop a **strategic alliance** with one or more domestic firms in the target country. These relationships often take the form of a **joint venture**: a new entity owned by two or more firms is created to allow the partners to pool their resources for common goals. Strategic alliances also allow companies easy access to new markets, especially because these partnerships often bring with them preferential treatment in the partner's home country. We tend to think of the international auto industry as fiercely competitive, but in reality many companies actually own pieces of each other. For example, General Motors has major alliances with Fiat Auto SpA, Fuji Heavy Industries Ltd., Isuzu Motors Ltd., and Suzuki Motor Corp.[76]

One downside to a strategic alliance is the difficulty two companies—especially traditional rivals—can have in developing cooperative agreements based on trust when they must suddenly work together. The blending of different corporate cultures can cause problems in willingness to share company secrets and technology, to take risks, and to adopt similar employee policies.

Direct Investment   A deeper level of commitment occurs when a firm expands internationally by buying a business outright in the host country. Instead of starting from scratch in its quest to become multinational organizations, direct investment allows a foreign firm to take advantage of a domestic company's political savvy and market position in the host country. Merrill Lynch & Co. acquired Mercury Asset Management Group, a British firm, for $5.3 billion in 1997 to give the brokerage firm added reach in the global financial services market, while Hoechst of Germany acquired U.S. pharmaceutical company Marion Merrill Dow Inc. for $7.3 billion in 1995.[77]

licensing (in foreign markets) ■ Agreement in which one firm gives another firm the right to produce and market its product in a specific country or region in return for royalties.

franchising ■ A form of licensing involving the right to adapt an entire system of doing business.

strategic alliance ■ Relationship developed between a firm seeking a deeper commitment to a foreign market and a domestic firm in the target country.

joint venture ■ Strategic alliance in which a new entity owned by two or more firms is created to allow the partners to pool their resources for common goals.

3 Bookmark It!

The automobile industry has seen many global strategic alliances. Search the Web site of one of the major automakers (for example, www.ford.com, www.chrysler.com, www.gm.com, or www.bmw.com) and see what information you can get about their global operations (try the annual report).

Ownership gives a firm maximum freedom and control, and it also dodges import restrictions. For example, the United States bans the import of so-called Saturday night specials (cheap, short-barreled pistols)—but it permits their sale. So, the Italian gun manufacturer Beretta got around this restriction by opening a manufacturing plant in Maryland.[78] But direct investment also carries greater risk. Firms that own businesses in foreign countries could suffer partial or complete losses of their investment if economic conditions deteriorate or if political instabilty leads to nationalization or expropriation.

PRODUCT-LEVEL DECISIONS: CHOOSING A MARKETING MIX STRATEGY

When top management makes a company-level decision to expand internationally, the firm's marketers next have to answer a crucial question: How necessary is it to develop a customized marketing mix for each country—a localization strategy? Gillette decided to offer the same products in all of its markets—a standardization strategy. Gillette has 91 percent of the market in Latin America and 69 percent in India and over one billion people use Gillette products world wide—that's a lot of blades.[79] In contrast, Proctor & Gamble adopted a localized strategy in Asia, where consumers like to experiment with different brands of shampoo. Most of P&G's shampoos sold in Asia are now packaged in single-use sachets to encourage people to try different kinds.[80] Toyota follows both localization and standardization strategies. It specifically designs and produces some vehicles to suit the needs of markets in Thailand, Indonesia, the Philippines, and Taiwan while maintaining the Corolla as a "world car" concept for all of its markets.[81]

Standardization Versus Localization   Advocates of standardization argue that the world has become so small with tastes so homogenized that basic needs and wants are the same everywhere.[82] A focus on the similarities among cultures certainly is appealing. After all, if a firm didn't have to make any changes to its marketing strategy to compete in foreign countries, it would realize large economies of scale because it could spread the costs of product development and promotional materials over many markets. Reebok, realizing this, created a new centralized product development center to develop shoe designs that can easily cross borders.[83] Widespread, consistent exposure also helps create a global brand by forging a strong, unified image all over the world—Coca-Cola signs are visible on billboards in London or on metal roofs deep in the forests of Thailand.

In contrast, those in favor of localization feel that the world is not *that* small, and products and promotional messages should be tailored to local environments. They argue that even in an area of the world like Scandinavia there are big cultural differences among Nordic people that we Americans would have trouble identifying—and certainly Henrik Kaas of Sony would agree. These marketers feel that each culture is unique and that each country has a *national character*—a distinctive set of behavioral and personality characteristics.[84] Snapple failed in Japan because consumers there didn't like the drink's cloudy appearance. Similarly, Frito-Lay Inc. stopped selling Ruffles potato chips (too salty for Japanese tastes) and Cheetos (the Japanese didn't appreciate having their fingers turn orange after eating a handful).[85]

Sometimes a company will compromise by producing ads with the same "look and feel" but with different actors and situations that communicate the same underlying message. That's what Exxon Mobil did in 2001 when it launched a $150 million global campaign. The company produced five hours of commercial footage that included as many as six different casts acting out the same story lines but with adjustments for local customs. For example, actors alternated using their right and left hands in scenes where they were eating since in some regions the right hand is the hand people use to eat, while in others, people use the left hand or even both hands. Local managers can use this "library" to select the ads they want to use in their region. Exxon Mobil aired the commercials in 100 countries.[86]

Product Decisions   A firm seeking to sell a product in a foreign market has three choices: Sell the same product in the new market, modify it for that market, or develop a brand-new product to sell there. Let's take a closer look at each possibility.

- A *straight extension strategy* retains the same product for domestic and foreign markets. L'Oreal did this when it decided to sell one of its products in Japan. For generations, proper etiquette in Japan was for girls to bow and never raise their eyes to a man.[87] However, the new generation of Japanese women wants to look straight at you, showing their eyes and eyelashes. Japanese eyelashes are very short, so they have to be curled to show. To meet this need, L'Oreal introduced its Maybelline brand Wonder Curl that dramatically thickens and curls lashes as it is applied. The launch was such a success in Japan that local TV news showed Japanese girls standing in line to buy the product. Within 3 months Wondercurl had captured 18 percent of the market.
- A *product adaptation strategy* recognizes that in many cases people in different cultures do have strong and different product preferences. Sometimes these differences can be subtle, yet important. That explains why Kellogg had to remove the green "loops" from its Froot Loops cereal in European markets after research showed that Europeans felt they were too artificial looking. Americans like the green loop just fine.[88]

  In other cases, products must be adapted because living conditions or customs require different designs. When the Electrolux appliance company began selling refrigerators in Europe, it found that Northern Europeans want large refrigerators because they shop once a week in supermarkets, whereas Southern Europeans want them small because they shop daily in open-air markets. Northerners like freezers on the bottom, southerners like them on the top. And the British are avid purchasers of frozen foods, so they insist on a unit with 60 percent freezer space.[89]
- A *product invention strategy* means a company develops a new product as it expands to foreign markets. Ford's "world cars," such as its Probe model are sold around the globe. In some cases, a product invention strategy takes the form of *backward invention*. A firm may find it needs to offer a less complex product than it sells elsewhere, such as a manually operated sewing machine or a hand-powered clothes washer to people without access to a reliable source of electricity.

In some cases, U.S. marketers develop a product for an overseas market and then discover it could do well at home too. Häagen-Dazs discovered this when it began serving an ice cream

De Probe is er.

The Ford Probe was developed to be a "world car," an example of a product invention strategy.

flavor called *dulce de leche* at its only store in Buenos Aires. The flavor, named after the caramelized milk that is an Argentine favorite, quickly became the outlet's top seller. U.S. executives realized the flavor might appeal to the vast numbers of Latino consumers in its home market. Sure enough, Häagen-Dazs sold $1 million worth of the new flavor a month (twice as much as any other flavor) when it imported *dulce de leche* to Miami.[90]

Promotion Decisions   Marketers must also decide whether it's necessary to change product promotions in a foreign market. Some firms endorse the idea that the same message will appeal to everyone around the world. The advertising director for the Unisys Corporation, a company that specializes in computers, explained the decision to launch a standardized global campaign: "Now they are seeing the same message, the same company, the same look wherever they go. That really stretches my advertising dollars."[91]

Unisys's decision to adopt a global message illustrates one key to the success of a standardized strategy: It is more likely to work if there are not unique cultural factors affecting the purchase—computer buyers tend to have more in common than, say, perfume buyers. This "one world, one message" promotional strategy also has a greater chance of success if the firm's target customers live in cosmopolitan, urban areas where they regularly see images from different countries.

For such a campaign to succeed, the message should focus on basic concepts such as romance or family ties because these are likely to be understood everywhere. For example, Unilever promotes its Impulse Body Spray worldwide by employing the theme "boy meets girl," and Nescafé dwells on the warmth of a shared cup of coffee around the world.[92] Fans of a localization strategy also feel that most messages must have a local frame of reference because people in different countries—or even parts of the same country—do not always agree on what is funny, glamorous, or admirable. Advertisers in Canada, for example, know that when they target consumers in French-speaking Quebec, their messages must be different than messages to consumers in English-speaking Canada. Ads in Montreal tend to be a lot racier than those in Toronto, reflecting differences in attitudes toward sexuality.[93]

Price Decisions   Costs associated with transportation, tariffs, differences in currency exchange rates, and even bribes paid to local officials often make the product more expensive for the company to make for foreign markets than in its home country.

For example, Chrysler Corporation had a hard time offering its Jeep Cherokee to Japanese consumers at a competitive price. Chrysler priced the vehicle at about $19,000 when it left the

Some promotions, such as this ad for Diesel jeans, are not tailored to specific foreign markets.

plant in Toledo, Ohio. By the time it was sitting in a Tokyo showroom, the price had mushroomed to over $31,000. Chrysler fell victim to a number of factors, including the currency exchange rate, the cost of adapting the Jeep to comply with Japanese regulations, tariffs, and profits taken by local distributors.[94] To ease the financial burden of tariffs on companies that import goods, some countries have established *free trade zones*. These are designated areas where foreign companies can warehouse goods without paying taxes or customs duties until the goods are moved into the marketplace.

One danger of pricing too high is that competitors will find ways to offer their product at a lower price, even if this is done illegally. A **gray market** exists when an unauthorized party imports products and then sells them for a fraction of the price charged for the authorized imports. ("Hey mister, wanna buy a watch?"). Goods such as watches, cameras, and perfumes often move through the gray market. At one point, Seiko estimated that one out of every four of its watches brought into the United States was unauthorized![95]

A company can also run into trouble if it tries to price a product too low to establish a foothold in a foreign market. Some countries outlaw a practice called **dumping**, in which a company prices its products lower than they are offered at home—often removing excess supply from home markets and keeping prices up there. In one case, Eastman Kodak accused Japanese rival Fuji Photo Film of selling color photographic paper in the United States for as little as a quarter of what it charges in Japan.[96]

gray market ▨ An unauthorized party imports products and then sells them for a fraction of the price of the authorized imports.

dumping ▨ A company tries to get a toehold in a foreign market by pricing its products lower than they are offered at home.

Distribution Decisions   Getting the product to consumers in a remote location is half the battle. Thus, establishing a reliable distribution system is essential if a marketer is to succeed in a foreign market. Marketers used to dealing with a handful of large wholesalers or retailers may have to rely instead on thousands of small "mom and pop" stores or distributors, some of whom transport goods to remote rural areas on oxcarts or bicycles. In less developed countries, they may run into problems finding a way to package, refrigerate, or store goods for long periods of time.

Even the retailing giant Wal-Mart stumbled at first. When Wal-Mart attempted to ease its entry into the German market by buying local retailers, it underestimated problems it would face in dealing with local distributors. When the chain tried to force the distributors to switch from supplying individual stores to utilizing Wal-Mart's new centralized warehouse system,

The physical transportation systems used for moving goods and services from producer to customer may not be the same in foreign markets. In Venice, where transportation means moving through the city's maze of canals, even medical services must be delivered by boat.

How It Worked Out at Sony Nordic

Henrik chose option 1. The Danish-speaking crew was moved outside to distribute the vouchers and the local freelancers were given an intensive training course on the products and the Web site. As a result of these changes, the Sony Experience Tour was a great success. Far exceeding expectations, a total of 60,000 visitors entered the Sony Experience bus and had hands-on experience with all the latest Sony connectivity products. Some 30,000 visitors went to the Web site, including 6,000 people who uploaded pictures and produced slide shows.

Even with extensive knowledge of local markets, it can be difficult to predict customers' behavior. From your research you've probably discovered that there are greater differences among consumers in neighboring countries than you may have thought. Henrik realized that the spoken language of the tour should be local even if English is widely spoken in Nordic countries and even if the Sony Experience Web site is in English, the language of the Internet. When a company has to develop promotional programs to reach people who speak many different languages, the key to success is localization—people all over want to hear such promotions in their own language. Sony learned its lesson: Think globally, but act locally. You can Go Create at www.sony.dk/experience.

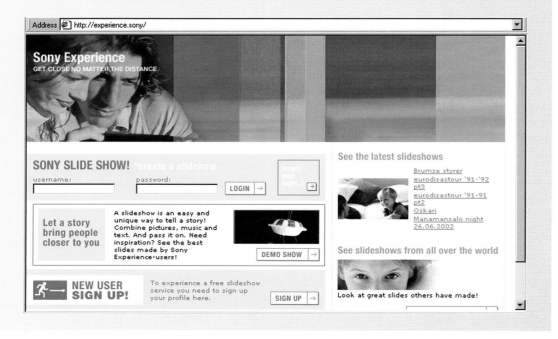

they refused and left Wal-Mart with empty shelves. Now Wal-Mart is working hard to understand local business cultures and to work more closely with suppliers. The retailer's efforts are paying off and it's adding about 120 stores worldwide.[97]

Chapter Summary

1. Understand the big picture of international marketing: trade flows, how firms define the scope of their markets, and how firms develop a competitive advantage in global marketing.

The increasing amount of world trade, the flow of goods and services among countries, may take place through cash or credit payments or through countertrade. While some firms choose to remain domestic in scope, some become exporting forms while others become multinational firms. A company's prospects for success in foreign markets are helped if it has a competitive advantage, which occurs when conditions in its home country make it easier to compete. Some governments adopt policies of protectionism with rules designed to give home companies an advantage. Such policies may include trade quotas, embargos, or tariffs that increase the costs of foreign goods. The World Trade organization works to reduce such protectionism and encourage free trade. Many countries have banded together to form economic communities to promote free trade. These economic communities include MERCOSUR, the Andean Group, and ALADI in South America, the Association of Southeast Asian Nations (ASEAN), the European Union (EU) and the economic alliance produced by the North American Free Trade Agreement (NAFTA).

2. Understand how economic, political, legal, and cultural issues influence global marketing strategies and outcomes.

In evaluating potential foreign markets, firms may examine the economic health of a country using its gross domestic product (GDP), its economic infrastructure, and its level of economic development to classify it as less developed, developing, or developed. A country's political and legal environment includes the presence of economic sanctions and the prospects for nationalization or expropriation of foreign holdings, regulations such as local content rules, and labor and human rights regulations. Marketers also examine a country's cultural environment, that is, its values, norms and customs, symbols, superstitions, language, and ethnocentricity.

3. Explain the strategies a firm can choose to enter global markets.

Different foreign market-entry strategies represent varying levels of commitment for a firm. Exporting of goods entails little commitment but allows little control over how products are sold. Contractural agreements such as licensing or franchising allow greater control. With strategic alliances through joint ventures, commitment increases. Finally, the firm can choose to invest directly by buying an existing company or starting a foreign subsidiary in the host country.

4. Understand the arguments for standardization versus localization of marketing strategies in global markets, and understand how elements of the marketing mix apply to foreign countries.

Firms that operate in two or more countries can choose to standardize their marketing strategies by using the same approach in all countries, or choose to localize by adopting different strategies for each market. The firm needs to decide whether to sell an existing product, change an existing product, or develop a new product. In many cases the promotional strategy must be tailored to fit the needs of consumers in another country. The product may need to be priced differently, especially if income levels are not the same in the new market. Finally, different methods of distribution may be needed, especially in countries lacking a solid infrastructure that provides adequate transportation, communications, and storage facilities.

Chapter Review

▪ MARKETING CONCEPTS:
TESTING YOUR KNOWLEDGE

1. What are domestic firms, exporting firms, and multinational firms?
2. Describe the market conditions that influence a firm's decision to enter foreign markets.
3. Based on Porter's model, what are the four areas that may give a nation an important competitive advantage for companies wishing to enter foreign markets?

4. What is protectionism? Explain import quotas, embargos, and tariffs?
5. How is the WTO changing the global marketplace?
6. What are economic communities? How have they changed global marketing opportunities?
7. Briefly describe the categories of economic development in less developed countries, developing countries, and developed countries.

8. What aspects of the political and legal environment influence a firm's decision to enter a foreign market? Why are human rights issues important to firms in their decisions to enter global markets?

9. What is the difference between collectivist and individualistic cultures? Why is an understanding of these two types of cultures important to marketers?

10. What is ethnocentricity? How does it affect a firm that seeks to enter a foreign market?

11. How is a firm's level of commitment related to its level of control in a foreign market? Describe the four levels of involvement that are options for a firm: exporting, contractual agreements, strategic alliances, and direct investment.

12. What are the arguments for standardization of marketing strategies in the global marketplace? What are the arguments for localization? What are some ways a firm can standardize or localize its marketing mix?

▨ MARKETING CONCEPTS:
DISCUSSING CHOICES AND ISSUES

1. Do you think U.S. firms should be allowed to use bribes to compete in countries where bribery is an accepted and legal form of doing business? Why or why not?

2. Some countries have been critical of the exporting of American culture by U.S. businesses. What about American culture might be objectionable? Can you think of some products that U.S. marketers export that can be objectionable to some foreign markets?

3. Trade regulations and protectionism are important political issues in the United States. What do you think are the positive and negative aspects of protectionist policies for U.S. firms? Do economic communities increase or decrease protectionism? More and larger economic communities are in the planning stages. What impact on world trade do you think these will have?

4. Every society has its own unique cultural environment. People in developed countries such as the United States are often critical of the values and customs of less developed countries, where it is legal for children to work long hours in factories that abound with health and safety hazards and where the rights of women and minorities are not protected. Government leaders in these countries often argue that in developing countries, children must work to survive—pulling out of these markets will only cause more hardship to local citizens. What position do you think U.S. firms should take on such issues? Do firms that wish to do business in these countries need to accept all such cultural differences without question, should they work to change the culture, or should firms in the United States and other developed countries totally avoid markets in which there are human rights violations? What are the pros and cons of entering such markets?

5. In recent years, terrorism and other types of violent activities around the globe have made the global marketplace seem very unsafe. How concerned should firms that have international operations be about such activities? Should they consider abandoning some of their global markets? How should firms weigh their concerns about terrorism against the need to help the economies of developing countries? Would avoiding countries such as those in the Middle East make good sense in terms of economic profit? What about in terms of social profit?

▨ MARKETING PRACTICE:
APPLYING WHAT YOU'VE LEARNED

1. Assume you are a marketing manager for a U.S. manufacturer of personal computers. Your company is considering strategic opportunities abroad, and your boss has asked you to assess the possibilities for entering the following countries: Japan, Spain, China, and Ecuador.
   a. Based on what you've read in this chapter, identify the pros and cons of marketing your products in each of the four countries. You may wish to use the data included in Table 4.1.
   b. Tell which country you think should be the primary target for your company and why.

2. Assume your firm is interested in the global market potential for weight loss centers in the following countries: France, Russia, and Argentina.
   a. Prepare a summary of the demographic, economic, and cultural differences you expect to find in these countries.
   b. Tell how the differences might affect marketing strategies for weight loss centers.

3. Tide laundry detergent, Pizza Hut meals, and IBM computers are very different U.S. products that are marketed globally.
   a. Outline the reasons each of these companies might choose to:
      1. standardize its product strategies
      2. localize its product strategies
      3. standardize its promotion strategies
      4. localize its promotion strategies
   b. Organize a debate in your class to argue the merits of the standardization perspective versus the localization perspective.

4. Although most large corporations have already made the decision to go global, many small to mid-size firms are only now considering such a move. Consider a small firm that manufactures gas barbecue grills.
   a. What type of market-entry strategy (exporting, contractual agreement, strategic alliance, or direct investment) do you feel would be best for the firm? Why?
   b. How would you recommend that the firm implement the strategy? That is, what type of product, price, promotion, and distribution strategies would you suggest? What role can the Internet play?

MARKETING MINI-PROJECT:
LEARNING BY DOING

The purpose of this mini-project is to begin to develop an understanding of a culture other than your own and how customer differences lead to changes in the ways marketing strategies are implemented in that culture.

1. As part of a small group, select a country you would like to know more about and a product you think could be successful in that market. As a first step, gather information about the country. Many campuses have international students from different countries. If possible, find a fellow student from the country and talk with him or her about the country. You will probably also wish to investigate other sources of information such as books and magazines found in your library, or access information from the World Wide Web.

2. Prepare a summary of your findings that includes the following:

   a. An overall description of the country, including such factors as its history, economy, religions, and so on, that might affect marketing of the product you have selected.

   b. The current status of this product in the country.

   c. Your prediction for the future success of the product in the country.

   d. Your recommendations for a product strategy (product design, packaging, brand name, price, and so on).

   e. Your recommendations for promotional strategies.

3. Present your findings and recommendations to the class.

REAL PEOPLE, REAL SURFERS:
EXPLORING THE WEB

For this exercise you must first select a less developed or developing country of interest to you. Assume you are the director of marketing for a firm that manufactures small household appliances such as mixers, coffee makers, toasters, and so forth. You are considering entering the market in _____ (the country you have selected). You recognize that businesses must carefully weigh opportunities for global marketing. Use the Internet to gather information that would be useful in your firm's decision. Although there are many governments, not-for-profit organizations, and businesses that have Web sites with information on international markets, the following sites may be useful to you.

- The U.S. Department of Commerce site on big emerging markets: www.stat-usa.gov/itabems.html
- I-Trade, a commercial site that also provides much free information of international trading: www.i-trade.com/
- TradePort, a free site that provides a large number of links to country-specific Web sites: www.tradeport.org

Write a report that answers the following questions.

1. What are the physical characteristics of the country (geography, weather, natural resources, and so forth)?
2. Describe the economy of the country.
3. What is the country's investment climate?
4. What trade regulations will your firm face in entering the country?
5. What is the country's political climate? Are there obvious political risks?
6. Based on this information, what overall strategy do you recommend for your firm—exporting, a contractual agreement, a strategic alliance, or direct investment?
7. What are your specific recommendations for implementing the strategy?
8. As a final part of your report, describe the Internet sites you used to gather this information. Which sites were most useful and why?

PLAN IT!
DEVELOPING A MARKETING PLAN

As your instructor directs, create a marketing plan (using Marketing Plan Pro software or a written marketing plan format) to document your marketing decisions or answer these questions in a written or oral report.

CFS is planning for global expansion beyond North and Latin America, New Zealand, Asia, and Western Europe. Review this year's plan in Appendix A as you do more work on next year's plan.

1. What additional information about political and legal issues in Asia and Latin America would be helpful as CFS targets those regions?
2. How might language barriers affect the company's ability to sell its products in particular countries?
3. Considering CFS's resources, would you recommend it use exporting, contractual agreements, strategic alliances, or direct investment to enter additional global markets?

Key Terms

collectivist cultures, (106)
conventions, (107)
countertrade, (94)
cultural values, (106)

custom, (107)
developed country, (104)
developing countries, (103)
dumping, (117)

economic communities, (98)
economic infrastructure, (102)
economic sanctions, (105)
embargo, (98)

MARKETING IN ACTION: CHAPTER 4 CASE

REAL CHOICES AT THE WALT DISNEY COMPANY

When Michael Johnson took over as head of Walt Disney International operations in 2000, he had a formidable challenge. For many major companies, international operations have been the path to growth in recent years. Coca-Cola and Gillette, for example, received two-thirds of their revenues from overseas—not so for the Walt Disney Co.

Disney's global operations began in 1988 when CEO Michael Eisner visited Paris and decided that Europe would be the cornerstone of the company's global business. That year he told his board of directors, "We must be in television in all countries."

But 12 years later, as Disney and the world entered a new millennium, that still was not true. The Disney Channel had only entered France in 1997 and was not yet in Latin America or Japan. While Warner's Cartoon Network was seen by 54 million foreign households, there were only 11 million Disney Channel subscribers, less than 5 percent of the cable and satellite market in Europe, Asia, and Latin America. And 80 percent of Disney's revenues were still from the 5 percent of the world's population that lived in the United States. The average per capita spent on Disney products was only 10 to 15 cents in India and China and about $15 in Italy, Germany, and Spain, far lower than the $60 plus per capita spent in the United States. Worldwide licensing revenue alone had declined by $159 million.

Johnson's job was to find out what the problems were and fix them. In some countries, low levels of discretionary income to pay extra for the Disney channel were at least part of the problem. Another suggestion was that the management structure of overseas operations wasn't effective in growing Disney business. Local country managers were assigned only one Disney division instead of all Disney lines so, for example, they were unable to coordinate movie releases with licensed merchandise. And the country managers had never been given the authority to operate autonomously.

Was Disney not being aggressive enough in exploring new markets? China, for example was fast developing a strong middle-class population and would soon be a member of the World Trade Organization. And the Chinese people were familiar with Disney after years of pirating Disney movies. After the failure of the movie *Mulan* that the Chinese criticized for having characters that were too western, success in that market would surely depend on acquiring local partners.

As Johnson began his new job, he felt the opportunities were definitely there. The question was how to develop them.

Source: Mark Lacter, "Mickey Stumbles at the Border," *Forbes* (June 12, 2000): 58; Richard Verrier, "China Seeks to Add China to Its World Media: Its Familiar Name and Theme Park Plans Give the Company a Head Start Over Its Rivals," *Los Angeles Times*, September 16, 2001, Home Edition, Page 1.

THINGS TO THINK ABOUT

1. What is the decision facing the Walt Disney Co.?

2. What factors are important in understanding the decision situation?

3. What are the alternatives?

4. What decision(s) do you recommend?

5. What are some ways to implement your recommendation(s)?

Bookmark It!

OBJECTIVES:

1 Understand the role of the marketing information system and the marketing decision support system in marketing decision making.

2 Describe the marketing research process.

3 Understand the differences among exploratory, descriptive, and causal research, and describe some research techniques available to marketers.

4 Describe the different types of data collection methods and types of samples that researchers use.

5 Understand the growing use of online research.

Marketing Information and Research

5

ANALYZING THE BUSINESS ENVIRONMENT OFF-LINE AND ONLINE

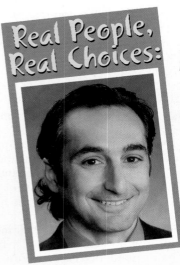

Real People, Real Choices:

Meet George Terhanian, a Decision Maker at Harris Interactive

www.harrisinteractive.com

CURRENT POSITION: Senior vice president of research and methodology.

CAREER PATH: Joined Harris Interactive in 1996.

1993–1996: Research Associate, Center for Research and Evaluation of Social Policy, University of Pennsylvania; 1988–1993 Teacher.

EDUCATION: University of Pennsylvania, Ph.D. Education 2000.
Harvard University, Ed.M. Administration, Planning, and Social Policy, 1992.
Haverford College, B.A. Political Science, 1986.

FIRST JOB OUT OF SCHOOL: Teaching fifth grade and tutoring inmates at a Washington, DC, prison.

CAREER HIGH: Teaching English to high school students in the "badlands" section of Philadelphia.

MANAGEMENT STYLE: Identify, hire, and retain smart, tenacious, passionate people. I then push them to work with minimal supervision.

BIGGEST MISTAKE: Two of my closest friends were killed on September 11, 2001. I deeply regret not having spent more time with them over the past few years.

HEROES: My grandparents, who escaped from Armenia to America.

How Can Harris Find America on the Internet?

Harris Interactive has been conducting marketing research studies for major companies such as Johnson & Johnson since 1958. Although the company is known best for the Harris poll, one of the nation's longest-running, nonpartisan surveys of public opinion, it actually generates most of its revenues through research in the health care, strategic marketing, advertising, automotive, and financial services industries.

In 1997, Gordon Black, chairman and CEO of Harris Interactive, asked several employees to develop a plan for conducting research through the Internet—research that had to be on a sample that was representative of the overall U.S. population. George Terhanian's job was to direct this effort. George recognized that the Internet offered many advantages compared to the telephone, including faster turnaround time, greater convenience, and the ability to present visual materials to respondents worldwide.

But George also recognized that less than 50 percent of the nation could access the Internet at the time, a fact that would no doubt complicate his task because it wasn't clear that the people who were surfing the Web could necessarily be compared to those who weren't. In George's view, the advantages of the Internet vastly outweighed the disadvantages. But finding a large number of users who would be interested in participating in studies—and who were a representative sample of U.S. consumers—was a huge challenge. This project was something few market research firms were willing to take on due to the potential expense and risk. George considered the following options.

125

Option 1: Recruit Internet users.

Recruit Internet users to participate in Internet surveys through direct mail and telephone. In theory, those recruited would constitute a random, representative sample of Internet users. This recruiting method was an industry standard practice that would lead to quicker acceptance by prospective clients. On the negative side, the recruiting costs would be high—approximately $15 per participant, which is about 50 percent higher than the norm. Moreover, the panel would include only Internet users, making it difficult to represent the opinions of the entire adult population through Internet surveys.

Option 2: Recruit regardless of Internet use.

Recruit participants for Internet surveys through mail and telephone regardless of whether they were currently Internet users. Equip non-Internet users with a computer and provide them Internet access. The pros: The resulting sample, in theory, would constitute a random, representative sample, and George would be able to project findings to the entire population. The cons: Recruiting costs would be extraordinarily high—roughly $350 per participant.

Option 3: Recruit users, but at a lower cost.

Recruit Internet users through less expensive means including online banner ads and promotions linked to a registration form. George would also conduct periodic parallel telephone surveys to compare the two pools of respondents. If the online respondents didn't represent the same sample as the telephone respondents, George could then make adjustments to the online surveys to try to correct the imbalance. If George chose this option, the recruitment costs would be very low—about $2 per participant. Furthermore, Harris would derive all the benefits of a small, random telephone survey at a lower cost because finding respondents is cheaper this way. And, if the approach worked in the United States, it would work in other markets.

However, the results would be worthless if there was no significant overlap between the characteristics of online panelists and telephone respondents. Furthermore, few clients would be familiar with this new research methodology, possibly requiring an expensive marketing campaign to convince them to take the plunge into uncharted waters.

Now, put yourself in George Terhanian's shoes. Which option would you choose, and why?

Knowledge Is Power

In Chapter 1 we talked about how marketing is a decision process in which marketing managers determine the strategies that will help the organization meet its long-term objectives. In Chapter 2 we said that successful planning means that managers made good decisions for guiding the organization. But how do marketers make good decisions? How do they go about developing marketing objectives, selecting a target market, positioning—or repositioning—their product, and developing product, price, promotion, and place strategies? The answer is information. To make good decisions, marketers must have information that is accurate, up-to-date, and relevant. In this chapter we will talk about some of the tools that marketers use to get the information they need.

THE MARKETING INFORMATION SYSTEM

marketing information system (MIS) ■ Procedure developed by a firm to continuously gather, sort, analyze, store, and distribute relevant and timely marketing information to its managers.

Firms develop a **marketing information system (MIS)** to meet the information needs of marketing managers. The MIS is a process that first determines what information managers need and then gathers, sorts, analyzes, stores, and distributes relevant and timely marketing information to system users. The MIS system includes three important components: (1) data, (2) computer hardware and software to analyze the data and create reports, and (3) MIS experts who actually handle the necessary report generation.

Where do the data come from? Information to feed the system comes from several major sources: internal company data, marketing intelligence data on competition and other elements

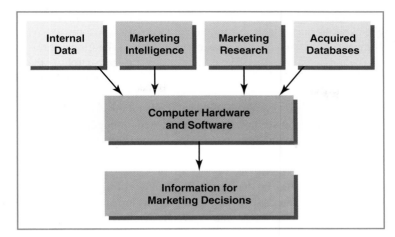

FIGURE **5.1**

The Marketing Information System

A firm's marketing information system (MIS) stores and analyzes data from a variety of sources and turns the data into information useful for marketing decision making.

in the firm's business environment, information gathered through marketing research, and acquired databases.

These data are stored and accessed through computer hardware and software. Based on an understanding of managers' needs, MIS personnel generate a series of regular reports for various decision makers. Frito-Lay's MIS generates daily sales data by product line and by region that its managers use to evaluate the market share of different Frito-Lay products compared to each other and to competing snack foods in each region.[1] Figure 5.1 shows the elements of an MIS.

Internal Data System The internal data system uses a variety of information from within the company to produce reports on the results of sales and marketing activities. Internal data include a firm's internal records of sales—information such as which customers buy which products in what quantities and at what intervals, what items are in stock, and which ones are back-ordered because they are out of stock, when items were shipped to the customer, and what items have been returned because they are defective.

Often an MIS allows salespeople and sales managers in the field to access the internal records using laptop computers through a company **intranet**. An intranet is an internal corporate communication network that uses Internet technology to link company departments, employees, and databases. Intranets are secured so that only authorized employees have access. When the MIS is made available to salespeople and sales managers, they can serve their customers better by having immediate access to information on pricing, inventory levels, production schedules, shipping dates, and the customer's sales history. But equally important, because salespeople and sales managers are the ones in daily direct contact with customers, their reports, entered directly into the system via the company intranet, can provide an important source of information on changes in sales patterns or new sales opportunities.

From the internal data, marketing managers can get daily or weekly sales data by brand or product line. They can also get monthly sales reports to measure progress toward sales goals and market share objectives. Wal-Mart's marketing managers, for example, use up-to-the-minute sales information obtained from store cash registers around the country so they can detect problems with products, promotions, and even the firm's distribution system.

Marketing Intelligence As we discussed in Chapter 3, to make good decisions marketers need to have information about the marketing environment. Thus, a second important element of the MIS is the **marketing intelligence system**, a method by which marketers get information about everyday happenings in the marketing environment. Although the name *intelligence* may suggest cloak-and-dagger spy activities, in reality nearly all the information companies need about their environment including the competitive environment is available by monitoring everyday sources: newspapers, trade publications, or simple observations of the marketplace. Because salespeople are the ones "in the trenches" every day, talking with customers, with distributors, and with prospective customers, they can be an invaluable source of marketing intelligence.

intranet ■ An internal corporate communication network that uses Internet technology to link company departments, employees, and databases.

marketing intelligence system ■ A method by which marketers get information about everyday happenings in the marketing environment.

In recent years, the World Wide Web has become a major source of marketing intelligence. Tremendous amounts of information are available on company Web pages (including those of competitors), through news sources from around the globe, through government reports, and on trade association sites. The ease of accessing and searching the World Wide Web and individual sites makes the Internet an even more attractive source of marketing intelligence.

Sometimes companies engage in specific activities to gain intelligence. For example, retailers often hire "mystery shoppers" to visit their stores (and those of their competitors) posing as customers to see how people are treated—imagine being paid to shop for a living! Other information may come from purchasing competitors' products and from attending trade shows.

Marketing managers may use marketing intelligence data to predict fluctuations in sales due to economic conditions, political issues, and events that heighten consumer awareness, or to forecast the future so that they will be on top of developing trends. For example, knowledge of demographic trends such as a declining birthrate and an aging population allows a firm such as Gerber that makes baby food to expand its focus to include new nutritional products aimed at the unique needs of the elderly.

Indeed, some marketing researchers, known as *futurists*, specialize in predicting consumer trends to come. They try to forecast changes in lifestyles that will affect the wants and needs of customers in the coming years. Futurists try to imagine different **scenarios**, or possible future situations, that might occur and assign a level of probability to each.

A scenario can be shaped by a number of key outcomes. For example, deregulation laws could shape the future of the banking industry or the telecommunications industry. In those cases the futurist might develop different scenarios for different levels of deregulation, including forecasts assuming no deregulation, moderate deregulation, and complete deregulation. Each scenario allows marketers to consider the impact of different marketing strategies and come up with plans based on which outcomes it considers most likely to happen. No one can predict the future—especially sudden, momentous events that change our lives like large-scale terrorist attacks—but it's better to make an educated guess than no guess at all and be caught totally unprepared.

The liquor company Heublein developed a set of scenarios and tried to predict consumers' preferences down the road for different forms of alcohol. This approach helped the company to anticipate a movement away from preferences for colored liquors, such as scotch and bourbon, in favor of wine. Heublein shifted its product emphasis in the wine direction while rival Schenley suffered because it did not predict this movement.[2]

Of course, collecting marketing intelligence is just the beginning. An effective MIS must include procedures to ensure that the intelligence data are translated and combined with internal data and other marketing information to create useful reports for marketing managers.

Marketing Research   A third type of information that is a part of a company MIS is data gathered through marketing research. Whether their business is selling cool stuff to teens or coolant to factories, firms succeed by knowing what customers want, when they want it, where they want it—and what competing firms are doing about it. In other words, the better a firm is at obtaining valid marketing information, the more successful it will be. The gathering of this information is called **marketing research**, the process of collecting, analyzing, and interpreting data about customers, competitors, and the business environment to improve marketing effectiveness. Although marketing intelligence information is collected continuously to keep managers abreast of happenings in the marketplace, marketing research is called for when unique information is needed for specific decisions. Virtually all companies rely on some form of marketing research, though the amount and type of research vary dramatically.

In general, marketing research data available in an MIS includes **syndicated research** reports and **custom research** reports. Syndicated research firms collect fairly general data on a regular basis and sell the information to many firms, while custom research is conducted for a single firm to provide answers to specific questions. The syndicated research firm Marketing Evaluations/TVQ Inc. reports on consumers' perceptions of 1,500 performers such as Carol Burnett and Bill Cosby for companies that are interested in using a performer in their advertising.[3] Other examples of syndicated research reports include the Nielsen's television ratings and

scenarios ■ Possible future situations that futurists use to assess the likely impact of alternative marketing strategies.

1 Bookmark It!

Pretend you are a marketing manager for a large national firm that makes frozen pizzas and other Italian foods. Make a list of the internal information and marketing intelligence information that you think should be gathered and stored in the company's MIS. Now make a list of the reports that you, as a marketing manager, would find useful.

marketing research ■ The process of collecting, analyzing, and interpreting data about customers, competitors, and the business environment in order to improve marketing effectiveness.

syndicated research ■ Research by firms that collect data on a regular basis and sell the reports to multiple firms.

custom research ■ Research conducted for a single firm to provide specific information its managers need.

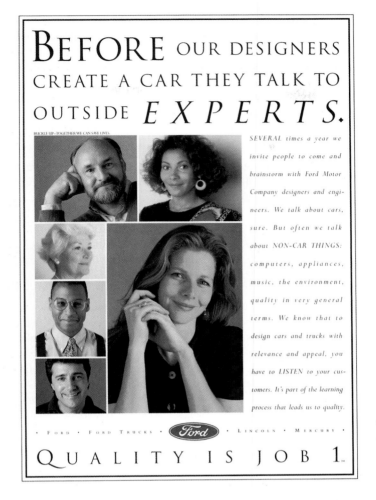

Automakers such as Ford conduct extensive market research on consumers' car preferences.

Arbitron's radio ratings. Simmons Market Research Bureau (SMRB) and Mediamark Research, Inc. (MRI) are two syndicated research firms that combine information about consumers' buying behavior and their media usage with geographic and demographic characteristics.

As valuable as it may be, syndicated research doesn't provide all of the answers to marketing questions because the information collected typically is broad but shallow; it gives good insights about general trends such as who is watching what TV shows or what brand of perfume is hot this year. Often firms need to undertake custom marketing research, especially when they need to know more about *why* these trends have surfaced.

Some firms maintain an in-house research department that conducts studies on its behalf. Many firms, however, hire outside research companies that specialize in designing and conducting projects based on the needs of the client. These custom research reports are another kind of information that is included in the MIS.

Marketers may use marketing research to identify opportunities for new products, to promote existing ones, or to provide data about the quality of their products, who uses them, and how. Sometimes a company will even do research to counter a competitor's claim. For example, Procter & Gamble (P&G) challenged rival Revlon's claim that its ColorStay line of cosmetics won't rub off. P&G researchers wanted to answer a specific question—was ColorStay's claim true? That kind of question can't be answered by buying a syndicated report, so Procter & Gamble commissioned 270 women to provide the specific information needed to support its case against Revlon. The women rubbed their cheeks against their shirts while wearing ColorStay and reported that, in fact, most of the shirts did get stained. But Revlon countered that P&G's test was flawed because the women may have been encouraged to rub too hard. They did their own test on 293 women who were told to use "the pressure they use when caressing someone else's face." This time the women found few stains. To avoid further controversy Revlon now says that ColorStay won't rub off under "normal circumstances."[4] Aren't you relieved?

Acquired Databases   A large amount of information that can be useful in marketing decision making is available in the form of external databases. Firms may acquire databases from any number of sources. For example, some companies are willing to sell their customer database to noncompeting firms. Government databases, including the massive amounts of economic and demographic information compiled by the U.S. Census Bureau, are available at little or no cost. State and local governments may make information such as automobile license data available for a fee.

MARKETING DECISION SUPPORT SYSTEMS

marketing decision support system (MDSS) ■ The data, analysis software, and interactive software that allow managers to conduct analyses and find the information they need.

As we have discussed, a firm's MIS generates regular reports to decision makers on what is going on in the internal and external environment. But sometimes these reports are inadequate. Different managers may want different information and in some cases the problem that must be addressed is too vague or unusual to be easily answered by the MIS process. As a result many firms beef up their MIS with a **marketing decision support system (MDSS)**. An MDSS includes analysis and interactive software that allows managers, even those who are not computer experts, to access MIS data and conduct their own analyses, often over the company intranet. Figure 5.2 shows the elements of an MDSS.

Typically an MDSS includes sophisticated statistical and modeling software tools. Statistical software allows managers to examine complex relationships among factors in the marketplace. For example, a manager who wants to know how consumers perceive her brand in relation to the competition might use a sophisticated statistical technique called *multidimensional scaling* to create a perceptual map, a graphic presentation of the various brands in relationship to each other. You'll see an example of a perceptual map in Chapter 8. Modeling software (no, it doesn't show pictures of supermodels) allows decision makers to examine possible or preconceived ideas about relationships in the data—to ask "what-if" questions. For example, media modeling software allows marketers to see what would happen if they made certain decisions about where to place their advertising versus other possibilities. A manager may be able to use sales data and a model to find out how many consumers stay with his brand and how many switch, thus developing projections of brand share over time. Table 5.1 presents some examples of the different questions that might be considered by an MIS versus an MDSS.

SEARCHING FOR GOLD: DATA MINING

data mining ■ Sophisticated analysis techniques to take advantage of the massive amount of transaction information now available.

As we have discussed, most MIS systems include internal customer transaction databases and many include acquired databases. Often these databases are extremely large. To take advantage of the massive amount of data now available, sophisticated analysis techniques called **data mining** are becoming a priority for many firms. Data mining is a process in which analysts sift through massive amounts of data (often measured in terabytes—much larger than kilobytes or even gigabytes) to identify unique patterns of behavior among different customer groups.

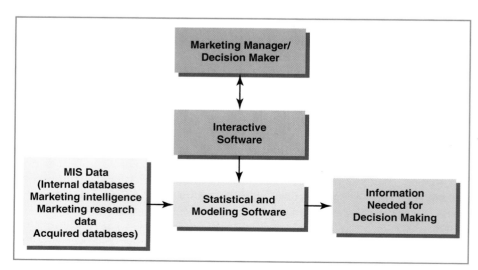

FIGURE 5.2

The Marketing Decision Support System

Although an MIS provides many reports managers need for decision making, it doesn't answer all their information needs. The marketing decision support system (MDSS) is an enhancement to the MIS that makes it easy for marketing managers to access the MIS system and find answers to their questions.

Questions Answered with an MIS	Questions Answered with an MDSS
What were our company sales of each product during the last month and the last year?	Have our sales declines simply reflected changes in overall industry sales or is there some portion of the decline that cannot be explained by industry changes?
What changes are happening in sales in our industry and what are the demographic characteristics of consumers whose purchase patterns are changing the most?	Are the same trends seen in our different product categories? Are the changes in consumer trends very similar among all of our products? What are the demographic characteristics of consumers who seem to be the most and the least loyal?
What are the best media for reaching a large proportion of heavy, medium, or light users of our product?	If we change our media schedule by adding or deleting certain media buys, will we reach fewer users of our product?

TABLE 5.1

Examples of Questions That Might Be Answered by an MIS and an MDSS

American Express, for example, uses data mining to understand shopping patterns. By mining the data, the company can identify customer segments whose shopping patterns indicate they may respond to different types of offers. If its data show that some of its female cardholders buy a lot of clothes at Saks Fifth Avenue, American Express might offer these women a discount if they also buy shoes at the store and whip out their Amex card to pay for them.[5]

Data mining uses supercomputers that run sophisticated programs so different databases can be combined to understand relationships among buying decisions, exposure to marketing messages, and in-store promotions. These operations are so complex that often companies need to build a *data warehouse* (sometimes costing more than $10 million!) simply to store the data and process it.[6]

Data mining has four important applications for marketers.[7]

- *Customer acquisition*: Many firms work hard to include demograhic and other information about customers in their database. For example, a number of supermarkets offer weekly special price discounts for store "members." And, of course, the membership application form requires that customers indicate their age, family size, address, and so on. With this information the firm can determine which of its current customers respond best to specific offers and then send the same offers to noncustomers who share the same characteristics.
- *Customer retention*: The firm can identify big-spending customers and then target them for special offers and inducements other customers won't receive.
- *Customer abandonment*: Strange as it may sound, sometimes a firm wants customers to take their business elsewhere because they actually cost the firm too much to service them. A department store may use data mining to identify unprofitable customers— those who are not spending enough or who return most of what they buy. For example, data mining has allowed Federal Express to identify customers as "the good, the bad, and the ugly."[8] As a result, FedEx strategizes to keep the "good" consumers as profitable customers and make "bad" customers (those who cost the company more than they generate in revenues) more profitable by charging them higher shipping rates. For the "ugly" customers who spend very little, FedEx is saving money by no longer trying to attract their business. After all, beauty is only skin deep—but ugly is to the bone.
- *Market basket analysis*: The firm can develop focused promotional strategies based on its records of which customers have bought certain products. For example, the Fingerhut catalog company analyzes which of its 25 million customers have recently bought outdoor patio furniture and targets them to receive mailings about gas grills.

So far, we have looked at the MIS and the MDSS, the overall systems that provide the information marketers need to make good decisions. We've seen how the data included in the MIS and MDSS include internal records, marketing intelligence data gathered by monitoring everyday sources, acquired databases, and information gathered to address specific marketing decisions through the marketing research process. In the rest of the chapter we'll look at the steps that marketers must take when they conduct marketing research.

1 *Bookmark It!*

Pretend you are a director of marketing for a large department store chain. What information would you hope to find in your customer database? How would data mining help the store become more profitable? What might be some ways to collect this information from customers without invading their privacy?

Questions and Answers: Steps in the Marketing Research Process

The collection and interpretation of strategic information is hardly a one-shot deal that managers engage in "just out of curiosity." Ideally, marketing research is an ongoing *process*, a series of steps marketers take to learn about the marketplace. Whether a company conducts the research itself or hires another firm to do it, the goal is the same—to help managers make informed marketing decisions. Figure 5.3 shows the steps in the research process, and we'll go over each of these now.

DEFINE THE PROBLEM

The first step in the marketing research process is to clearly understand what information managers need that the research is to provide. This step is referred to as defining the research problem. You should note that the word *problem* here does not refer to something that is wrong but to the overall questions for which the firm needs answers—kind of like the word problems you had in your math class. Defining the problem as precisely as possible allows marketers to research for the right answers to the right questions.

For example, a manager may need to understand whether nonusers of his brand would respond to a new flavor of soft drink. Advertising research may seek to determine if planned humorous advertising will get the target audience's attention and cause a change in attitudes toward the brand. A maker of dry cereal may wish to find out if a drop in price will significantly increase sales of the product.

Defining the problem has three components:

- *Specifying the research objectives*: What questions will the research attempt to answer?
- *Identifying the consumer population of interest*: What are the characteristics of the consumer groups of interest?
- *Placing the problem in an environmental context*: What factors in the firm's internal and external business environment might be influencing the situation?

Providing the right kind of information for each of these pieces of the problem is not as simple as it seems. For example, suppose a luxury car manufacturer wants to find out why its sales have fallen off dramatically over the past year. The research objective could revolve around any number of possible questions: Is the firm's advertising failing to reach the right consumers? Is the right message being sent? Do the firm's cars have a particular feature (or lack of one) that is turning customers away? Is there a problem with the firm's reputation for providing quality service? Do consumers believe the price is right for the value they get? The particular objective chosen depends on a variety of factors such as the feedback the firm is getting from its customers, the information it receives from the marketplace, and sometimes even the intuition of the people designing the research.

Often the focus of a research question is driven by feedback the firm gets from the marketplace that identifies a possible problem. For example, Mercedes-Benz continually monitors drivers' perceptions of its cars. When the company started getting reports from its dealers that people were viewing the cars as "arrogant" and "unapproachable," even to the point at which they were reluctant to sit in showroom models, the company undertook a research project to better understand the reasons for this perception.

The research objective determines the consumer population that will be studied. The research might focus on current owners to find out what they especially like about the car. Or the research might study nonowners to understand their lifestyles, what they look for in a luxury automobile, or their beliefs about the company itself that keep them from choosing the cars. For example, research conducted for Mercedes-Benz showed that although people rated its cars very highly on engineering quality and status, many were too intimidated by the elitist Mercedes image to consider buying one. Mercedes dealers reported that a common question from visitors to showrooms was, "May I actually *sit* in the car?" Based on this

2 *Bookmark It!*

Assume that you have been hired by your university as a marketing researcher. The university wants to recruit more students and needs to have information to be successful. Write a description of the research problem.

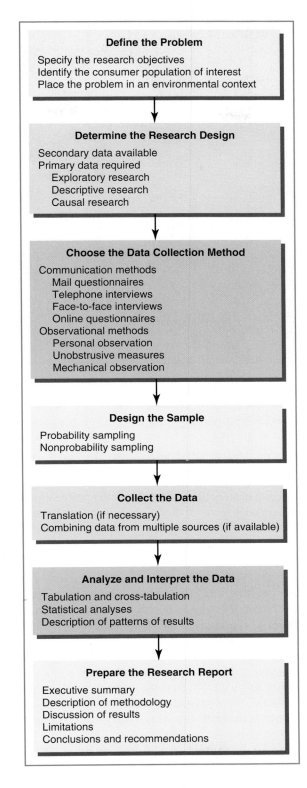

Define the Problem

Specify the research objectives
Identify the consumer population of interest
Place the problem in an environmental context

Determine the Research Design

Secondary data available
Primary data required
    Exploratory research
    Descriptive research
    Causal research

Choose the Data Collection Method

Communication methods
    Mail questionnaires
    Telephone interviews
    Face-to-face interviews
    Online questionnaires
Observational methods
    Personal observation
    Unobstrusive measures
    Mechanical observation

Design the Sample

Probability sampling
Nonprobability sampling

Collect the Data

Translation (if necessary)
Combining data from multiple sources (if available)

Analyze and Interpret the Data

Tabulation and cross-tabulation
Statistical analyses
Description of patterns of results

Prepare the Research Report

Executive summary
Description of methodology
Discussion of results
Limitations
Conclusions and recommendations

FIGURE 5.3

Steps in the Marketing Research Process

The marketing research process includes a series of steps that begins with defining the problem or the information needed and ends with the finished research report for managers.

research, Mercedes softened its image by projecting a slightly more down-to-earth image in its advertising.[9]

Placing the problem in the context of the firm's environment helps researchers structure the research, determine the specific types of questions to ask, and identify factors that will need to be taken into account when measuring results. Environmental conditions also matter. For example, when the economy is tight and sales of luxury cars are generally declining, the population to be studied might be narrowed down to a select group of consumers who are still

Fun

Mercedes-Benz tried to project a friendly, more approachable image by running ads such as this one featuring a cute rubber ducky sporting a Mercedes logo.

willing and able to indulge in a luxury vehicle. Today many consumers are moving away from status-conscious materialism, a trend that began in the late 1990s and then picked up speed after the terrorist attacks in 2001. Thus, a research question might be to see how consumers react to different promotional strategies for luxury goods that go beyond "snob appeal."

DETERMINE THE RESEARCH DESIGN

research design ■ A plan that specifies what information marketers will collect and what type of study they will do.

Once marketers have isolated specific problems, the second step of the research process is to decide on a "plan of attack." This plan is the **research design**, which specifies what information marketers will collect and what type of study they will do. All marketing problems do not call for the same research techniques, and marketers can solve some problems effectively with a number of alternative techniques.

Secondary Versus Primary Research   The very first question to ask in determining the research design is whether or not the information required to make a decision already exists. For example, a coffee producer who needs to know the differences in coffee consumption among different demographic and geographic segments of the market may find that the information needed is available from a study conducted by the National Coffee Association (www.ncausa.org) for its members or even from the U.S. Department of Agriculture (www.ars.usda.gov). Data that have been collected for some purpose other than the problem at hand are called **secondary data**. If secondary data are available, it saves the firm time and money because the expense of designing and implementing a study has already been paid.

secondary data ■ Data that have been collected for some purpose other than the problem at hand.

Secondary Data Sources   Sometimes the data marketers need may be "hiding" right under the organization's nose in the form of company reports; previous company research studies; feedback received from customers, salespeople, or stores; or even in the memories of longtime employees. More typically, though, researchers need to look elsewhere for secondary data. They may obtain reports published in the popular and business press, studies that private research organizations or government agencies conduct, and published research on the state of the industry from trade organizations.

For example, many companies subscribe to *Simmons Study of Media & Markets*, a national survey conducted semiannually by Simmons Market Research Bureau (SMRB, www.smrb.com), the syndicated research firm mentioned earlier. Simmons publishes results that it then sells to

The American Marketing Association is one of many organizations that provides industry data online to aid marketing researchers.

marketers, advertising agencies, and publishers. This information is based on the self-reports of consumers in over 20,000 U.S. households who complete monthly logs detailing their purchases of products from aspirin to snow tires. Simmons data can give a brand manager a profile of who is using a product, identify heavy users, or even provide data on what magazines a target market reads. Marketers can also turn to the Internet for external information sources such as these:

- Find/SVP (www.findsvp.com) provides access to a catalog of more than 300 industry reports.
- U.S. Census Bureau (www.census.gov) publishes separate reports on specific industries (such as agriculture, construction, and mining) as well as on housing, population growth and distribution, and retail trade.
- Marketing Tools (www.marketingtools.com) is a site run by *American Demographics* magazine that lets users search for marketing books and articles.
- The American Marketing Association (www.marketingpower.com) provides many resources to its members on a variety of industry topics.
- DIALOG (www.dialog.com) sorts companies by location, size, and industry. The user can request telemarketing reports, preaddressed mailing labels, and company profiles.
- LEXIS-NEXIS (www.lexis-nexis.com) is a large database featuring information from such sources as Dun & Bradstreet, the *New York Times*, CNN, and National Public Radio transcripts.

Of course, secondary research is not always the answer. When the company needs to make a specific decision, it most often needs to conduct research to collect **primary data**, that is, information collected directly from respondents to specifically address the question at hand. Primary data include demographic and psychological information about customers and prospective customers, customers' attitudes and opinions about products and competing products, as well as their awareness or knowledge about a product and their beliefs about the people who use those products.

primary data ■ Data from research conducted to help in making a specific decision.

In the next few sections, we'll talk briefly about the various designs useful in conducting primary research. Figure 5.4 summarizes many of the types of research designs in the researcher's arsenal. If you go on to take a course in marketing research, you'll learn a lot more about these issues.

Exploratory Research   Marketers use **exploratory research** to generate topics for future, more rigorous studies, ideas for new strategies and opportunities, or perhaps just to get a better handle on a problem they are currently experiencing with a product. Because the studies are usually small scale and less costly than other techniques, marketers may use exploratory research to test their hunches about what's going on without too much risk.

exploratory research ■ Technique that marketers use to generate insights for future, more rigorous studies.

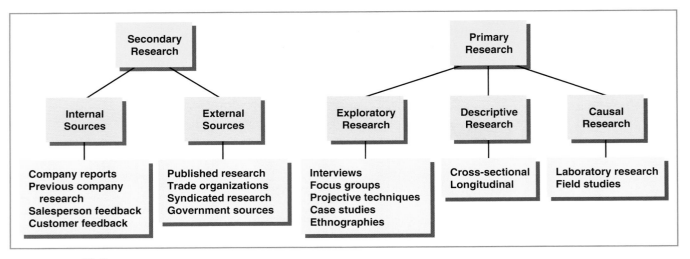

FIGURE 5.4

Marketing Research Designs

For some research problems, the secondary research may provide the information needed. At other times, one of the primary research methods may be needed.

Exploratory studies often involve in-depth probing of a few consumers who fit the profile of the "typical" customer. Researchers may interview consumers, salespeople, or other employees about products, services, ads, or stores. They may simply "hang out" and watch what people do when choosing among competing brands in a store aisle. Or they may locate places where the consumers of interest tend to be and ask questions in these settings. For example, some researchers find that members of Generation X are too suspicious or skeptical in traditional research settings, so they may interview young people waiting in line to buy concert tickets or in clubs.[10] Some firms such as Look-Look (www.look-look.com) send young "coolhunters" armed with videocameras to urban areas to interview people about the latest styles and trends.

Exploratory research can be very useful in helping marketers understand how consumers feel about products. DuPont asked consumers to develop a collage to indicate how they feel about panty hose.

Most exploratory research provides *qualitative data*, in which the researcher collects detailed verbal or visual information about consumers' attitudes, feelings, and buying behaviors in the form of words rather than in numbers. For example, when DuPont wanted to know how women felt about panty hose, marketers asked research particpants to collect magazine clippings that expressed their emotions about the product.[11]

Exploratory research can take many forms. **Consumer interviews** are one-on-one discussions in which an individual shares her thoughts in person with a researcher. When Kimberly-Clarke, maker of Huggies disposable diapers, was thinking about producing training pants, it sent researchers into women's homes and asked them to tell of their frustrations with toilet training.[12] Many women expressed feelings of failure and a horror at having to admit to other parents that their child was "still in diapers." Based on the research, Kimberly-Clark introduced Pull-Ups disposable training pants and sold $400 million worth a year before the competition caught up.

Intuit, the software company that produces personal finance software Turbo-Tax and Quicken, used personal interviews to better understand consumers' frustrations with installing and using its products. When customers told researchers that the software itself should "tell me how to do it," they took this advice literally and developed software that used computer audio to give verbal instructions. Intuit's research went one step beyond interviews when it left respondents microcasette recorders so that whenever they were having problems, they could simply push a button and tell the company of their frustration.[13]

The **focus group** is the technique marketing researchers use most often for collecting exploratory data. Focus groups typically consist of five to nine consumers who have been recruited because they share certain characteristics. These people sit together to discuss a product, ad, or some other marketing topic introduced by a discussion leader. Typically, the leader video- or audio-tapes these group discussions, which may be held at special interviewing facilities that allow for observation by the client, who watches from behind a one-way mirror. In addition to getting insights from what the participants say about a product, a good moderator can sometimes learn by carefully observing other things such as body language. While conducting focus groups on bras, an analyst noted that small-chested women typically reacted with hostility when discussing the subject. The participants would unconsciously cover their chests with their arms as they spoke and complained that they were ignored by the fashion industry. To meet this overlooked need, the company introduced a line of A-cup bras called "A-OK" that depicted these women in a positive light.[14]

Many researchers use **projective techniques** to get at people's underlying feelings, especially when they think that people will be unable or unwilling to express their true reactions. A projective test asks the participant to respond to some object, often by telling a story about it. For example, the manufacturer of Brawny paper towels was locked in a struggle with ScotTowels for the number-two market position behind Bounty. The company decided to reexamine its brand identity, which was personified by a 60-foot character named Brawny who holds an ax. Managers were afraid that Brawny was too old-fashioned, or that women were confused about why a man was selling paper towels in the first place. Researchers asked women in the focus groups questions such as, "What kind of woman would he go out with?" and "What is his home life like?" Then the researchers asked the women to imagine how he would act in different situations, and even to guess what would happen if they were locked in an elevator with him for 20 minutes! Responses were reassuring—the women saw Brawny as a knight in shining armor who would get them out of the elevator—a good spokesman for a product that's supposed to be reliable and able to get the job done. Brawny kept his job.[15]

The **case study** is a comprehensive examination of a particular firm or organization. In business-to-business marketing research in which the customers are other firms, for example, researchers may try to learn how one particular company makes its purchases. The goal is to identify the key decision makers, to learn what criteria they emphasize when choosing among suppliers, and perhaps to learn something about any conflicts and rivalries among these decision makers that may influence their choices.

An **ethnography** is a different kind of in-depth report. It is a technique used by anthropologists who go to "live with the natives" for months or even years. This approach has been adapted by some researchers, who visit people's homes or participate in real-life consumer activities to get a handle on how products really are used.

consumer interviews ■ One-on-one discussions between a consumer and a researcher.

focus group ■ A product-oriented discussion among a small group of consumers led by a trained moderator.

projective techniques ■ Tests that marketers use to explore people's underlying feelings about a product, especially appropriate when consumers are unable or unwilling to express their true reactions.

case study ■ A comprehensive examination of a particular firm or organization.

ethnography ■ A detailed report based on observations of people in their own homes or communities.

And five minutes is all the time you'll need to completely breakdown, or set up, thanks to Columbia Information Systems' new Model III Wireless PERCEPTION ANALYZER™.

We've taken the most advanced, integrated group testing device on the market and made it faster and easier to use than ever before.

We've totally eliminated the wires

between the dials and the console. Now, you can set up as many as 50 stations in as little as five minutes.

In fact, the new Model III is so convenient and lightweight, it actually fits into a single piece of luggage.

To find out more about the Model III, PERCEPTION ANALYZER give us a call at Columbia Information Systems, 1-800-769-0906. And start spending more time analyzing and less time agonizing.

Columbia Information Systems is a research and development/Perception Analyzer marketing subsidiary of Market Strategies, Inc.

After spending hours with a focus group from Hell, we think you're entitled to a complete 5-minute breakdown.

Focus groups are a very popular type of exploratory research. This ad offers researchers a product designed to make focus groups easier to conduct.

3 *Bookmark It!*

Conduct an ethnographic study by observing people in a fast-food restaurant. Make notes about their behavior. What have you learned from the ethnography that would be useful to a store manager who wanted to improve the experience diners had at his restaurant?

Of course, because marketing researchers usually don't have months or years to devote to a project, they devise shortcuts to get the information they need. For example, Warner-Lambert hired a firm to study how consumers actually use its Fresh Burst Listerine mouthwash. The firm paid families who use Fresh Burst and families who use Scope to set up cameras in their bathrooms so researchers could watch how they used each of the competing products. Although both groups said they used mouthwash to make their breath smell good, observers saw that Scope users swished and spit out more quickly than the Listerine users. (One Listerine user told the researchers he kept it in his mouth until he got in his car, then spit it out in a sewer a block away!) Researchers interpreted the results to mean that despite its best efforts Listerine hadn't managed to shake its medicine-like image because people seemed to be using the mouthwash to kill germs rather than freshen breath.[16]

Descriptive Research   We've seen that marketers have many tools in their arsenal, including focus groups and observational techniques, to help them better define a problem or opportunity. These are usually modest studies of a small number of people, enough to get some indication of what is going on but not enough for the marketer to feel confident about generalizing what she observes to the rest of the population.

The next step in marketing research, then, often is to conduct **descriptive research**, which probes systematically into the marketing problem and bases its conclusions on a large sample of participants. Descriptive research is typically expressed in quantitative terms—averages, percentages, or other statistics summarizing results from a large set of measurements. Quantitative data can be as simple as counting the number of Listerine bottles sold in a month in different regions of the country or as complex as statistical analyses of responses to a survey mailed to thousands of consumers. In each case, marketers conduct the descriptive research to answer a specific question in contrast to the "fishing expedition" that may occur in exploratory research.

descriptive research ■ Tool that probes more systematically into the problem and bases its conclusions on large numbers of observations.

Marketing researchers who employ descriptive techniques most often use a **cross-sectional design**. This approach involves the systematic collection of quantitative information (such as responses to a consumer survey or data summarized from store register receipts) from one or more samples of respondents at one point in time. The data may be collected on more than one occasion but generally not from the same pool of respondents.

In contrast to these one-shot studies, a **longitudinal design** tracks the responses of the same sample of respondents over time. Market researchers often create *consumer panels* to get information; a sample of respondents representative of a larger market agrees to provide information about purchases on a weekly or monthly basis. When 3M wanted to find out how it should market its Buf-Puf Sponge facial scrub pads, the company recruited a teen advisory board by running ads in *Seventeen*, *Sassy*, and *Teen*. 3M periodically consults these consumer panel members about their use of personal care products and their concerns about appearance.[17]

Causal Research   It's a fact that purchases of both diapers and beer peak between 5:00 P.M. and 7:00 P.M. Can we say that purchasing one of these products caused shoppers to purchase the other as well—and, if so, which caused which? Or is the answer simply that this happens to be the time that young fathers stop at the store on their way home from work for brew and Pampers?[18]

The descriptive techniques we've examined do a good job of providing valuable information about *what* is happening in the marketplace, but descriptive research, by its very nature, can only describe a marketplace phenomenon—it cannot tell us *why*. Sometimes marketers need to know if something they've done has brought about some change in behavior. For example, does placing one product next to another in a store mean that people will buy more of each? We can't answer this question through simple observation.

Causal research attempts to understand cause-and-effect relationships. Marketers use causal research techniques when they want to know if a change in something (for example, placing cases of beer next to a diaper display) is responsible for a change in something else (for example, a big increase in diaper sales). They call the factors that might cause such a change *independent variables* and the outcomes *dependent variables*. In this example, then, the beer display is an independent variable and sales data for the diapers are a dependent variable.

To rule out alternative explanations, researchers must carefully design **experiments** that test specified relationships among variables in a controlled environment. Because this approach tries to eliminate competing explanations for the outcome, respondents may be brought to a laboratory so the researcher can control precisely what respondents should see. For example, a study testing whether the placement of diapers in a grocery store influences the likelihood that

cross-sectional design ■
Type of descriptive technique that involves the systematic collection of quantitative information.

longitudinal design ■
Technique that tracks the responses of the same sample of respondents over time.

causal research ■
Technique that attempts to understand cause-and-effect relationships.

experiments ■ Techniques that test prespecified relationships among variables in a controlled environment.

Some marketing research firms such as Decision Insight are developing sophisticated in-store simulations that allow respondents to navigate around a "virtual store" to select merchandise. Clients can use this technique to conduct marketing research on such issues as package designs, pricing changes, and optimal placement of merchandise.

telemarketing ■ The use of the telephone to sell directly to consumers and business customers.

male shoppers will buy them might bring a group of men into a testing facility and show them a "virtual store" on a computer screen. Researchers would ask the men to fill a grocery cart as they click through the "aisles." The experiment might vary the placement of the diapers—next to shelves of beer in one scenario, near paper goods in a different scenario. The objective is to see which placement gets the guys to put diapers into their carts.

Although a laboratory allows researchers to exert control over what test subjects see and do, marketers don't always have the luxury of conducting this kind of "pure" research. But it is possible to conduct *field studies* in the real world, as long as the researchers can control the independent variables.

For example, a diaper company might choose two grocery stores that have similar customer bases in terms of age, income, and so on. With the cooperation of the grocery store's management, the company might place its diaper display next to the beer in one store and paper goods in the other and then record diaper purchases made by men over a two-week period. If a lot more diapers were bought by guys in the first store than in the second (and the company was sure that nothing else was different between the two stores (such as a dollar-off coupon for diapers being distributed in one store and not the other), the diaper manufacturer might conclude that the presence of beer in the background does indeed result in increased diaper sales.

CHOOSE THE METHOD FOR COLLECTING PRIMARY DATA

When the researcher decides to collect primary data, the next step in the marketing research process is to figure out just how to collect it. The two main primary data collection methods can be broadly described as communication and observation.

Communication methods involve some kind of interview or other direct contact with respondents who answer questions. Questionnaires can be administered on the phone, in person, through the mail, or over the Internet as George Terhanian and Harris Interactive do. Table 5.2 provides a summary of the advantages and disadvantages of different methods for collecting communication data.

Questionnaires differ in their degree of structure. With a totally unstructured questionnaire, the researcher loosely determines the questions in advance. Questions may evolve from what the respondent says to previous questions. At the other extreme the researcher uses a completely structured questionnaire. She asks every respondent the exact same questions and each participant responds to the same set of fixed choices. You have probably experienced this kind of questionnaire, where you might have had to respond to a statement by saying if you "strongly agree," somewhat agree," and so on. Moderately structured questionnaires ask each respondent the same questions but the respondent is allowed to answer the questions in his own words.

Mail questionnaires are easy to administer and offer a high degree of anonymity to respondents. On the downside, because the questionnaire is printed and mailed, researchers have little flexibility in the types of questions they can ask and little control over the circumstances under which the respondent is answering them. Mail questionnaires also take a long time to get back to the company and are likely to have a much lower response rate than other types of data collection methods because people tend to ignore them. This problem has become even more acute since the 2001 anthrax scares; many people won't open letters from addresses they don't recognize.

Telephone interviews usually consist of a brief phone conversation in which an interviewer reads a short list of questions to the respondent. There are several problems with using telephone interviews as a data collection method. One problem with this method is that the growth of **telemarketing**, in which businesses sell directly to consumers over the phone, has eroded the consumers' willingness to participate in phone surveys—especially when too many calls interrupt dinner or leisure time. In addition to aggravating people by barraging them with obnoxious telephone sales messages, some unscrupulous telemarketers have "poisoned the well" for real researchers by hiding their pitches behind an illusion of doing research. They contact consumers under the pretense of doing a research study, when, in fact, their real intent is to sell the respondent something or to solicit funds for some cause. The respondent also may not feel comfortable speaking directly to an interviewer, especially if the survey is about

TABLE **5.2**

Advantages and
Disadvantages of Data
Collection Methods

Date Collection Method	Advantages	Disadvantages
Mail Questionnaires	Respondents feel anonymous Low cost Good for ongoing research	May take a long time for questionnaires to be returned Low rate of response and many may not return questionnaires Inflexible questionnaire Length of questionnaire limited by respondent interest in the topic Unclear if respondents understand the questions
Telephone Interviews	Fast High flexibility in questioning Low cost Limited interviewer bias	Decreasing levels of respondent cooperation Limited questionnaire length High likelihood of respondent misunderstanding Respondents cannot view materials Cannot survey households without phones Consumers screen calls with answering machines and caller ID
Face-to-Face Interviews	Flexibility of questioning Can use long questionnaires Can determine if respondents have trouble understanding questions Can use visuals or other materials	High cost Interviewer bias a problem Take a lot of time
Online Questionnaires	Instantaneous data collection and analysis Questioning very flexible Low cost No interviewer bias Lack of geographic restrictions	Unclear who is responding No assurance respondents are being honest Limited questionnaire length Unable to determine respondent understanding of question Self-selected samples

a sensitive subject. Finally, increasing numbers of people use answering machines and caller ID to screen calls, further reducing the response rate.

In *face-to-face interviews*, a live interviewer asks questions of one respondent at a time. Although in "the old days" researchers often went door-to-door to ask questions, that's much less common today due to fears about security and because the large numbers of working women make it less likely to find people at home during the day. Typically, today's face-to-face interviews occur in a "mall-intercept" study in which researchers recruit shoppers in malls or other public areas. You've probably seen this going on in your local mall where shoppers are stopped by a smiling person holding a clipboard.

Mall-intercepts offer good opportunities to get feedback about new package designs, styles, or even reactions to new foods or fragrances. However, because only certain groups of the population frequently shop at malls, a mall-intercept study does not provide the researcher with a representative sample of the population (unless the population of interest is mall shoppers). In addition to being more expensive than mail or phone surveys, respondents may be reluctant to answer questions of a personal nature in a face-to-face context.

As we learned from George Terhanian, online research is growing in popularity as more consumers are hooking up to the Web. Even though most consumers feel we have come a long way with successful use of the Internet, experts tell us that this technology is still in its infancy and many questions linger about the quality of responses the firm will receive—particularly because (as with mail and phone interviews) no one can be really sure who is typing in the responses, and it's uncertain how representative of the general population these "wired" consumers are.[19] However, these concerns are rapidly evaporating as research firms devise new ways to verify identities, present surveys in novel formats including the use of

Mall intercepts are a common way to collect data from shoppers.

images, sound, and animation, and recruit more diverse respondents.[20] More about this later in the chapter.

As we said earlier, the second major primary data collection method is observation. Observation is a type of data collection that uses a *passive instrument* in which the consumer's behaviors are simply recorded—often without his knowledge. Researchers do this through personal observation, unobtrusive measures, and mechanical observation.

When researchers use *personal observation*, they watch consumers in action to understand how they react to marketing activities. For example, "traffic analysis" can pay off by pinpointing "dead spots" in stores. After Frito-Lay found that shoppers spend twice as much time in the coffee aisle as in the snack foods section, it began to advertise its chips near the coffee cans instead.[21] Advertising agency Ogilvy & Mather's research division sends researchers into homes with handheld video cameras to get pictures of how people use products and why.[22] The hours of footage are then condensed into a documentary-type video that helps marketers make decisions about future strategies.

Researchers use *unobtrusive measures*, which measure traces of physical evidence that remain after some action has been taken, when they suspect that people will probably alter their behavior if they know they are being observed. For example, instead of asking a person to report on the alcohol products currently in her home, the researcher might go to the house and perform a "pantry check" by actually counting the bottles in her liquor cabinet. Another option for collecting primary data is to sift through garbage, searching for clues about each family's consumption habits. The "garbologists" can tell, for example, which soft drink accompanied what kind of food. As one garbologist noted, "The people in this study don't know that we are studying their garbage so the information is totally objective."[23] Smelly, too!

Mechanical observation is a primary data collection method that relies on nonhuman devices to record behavior. For example, some grocery stores use infrared sensors in their ceilings to track the movements of shopping carts.[24] Another application of mechanical observation is A. C. Nielsen's use of people meters, boxes attached to the television sets of selected viewers, to record patterns of television watching. Data obtained from these devices indicate who is watching which shows. These "television ratings" help the networks determine how much to charge advertisers for commercials and which shows to cancel or renew. Finally, many research firms are developing techniques to measure which Web sites are being visited and by whom. As we'll see shortly, there are ways for companies to tell where you've traveled in virtual space, so be careful which sites you surf to!

"Garbologists" search for clues about consumption activities unobtrusively.

DATA QUALITY: GARBAGE IN, GARBAGE OUT

We've seen that a firm can collect data in many ways, including focus groups, ethnographies, observational studies, and controlled experiments. But how much faith should it place in what it finds?

All too often, marketers who have commissioned a study assume that because they have a massive report full of impressive-looking numbers and tables they must have the "truth." Unfortunately, there are times when this "truth" is really just one person's interpretation of the facts. At other times, the data used to generate recommendations are flawed. As the expression goes, "Garbage in, garbage out!"[25] Typically, three factors influence the quality of research results—validity, reliability, and representativeness.

Validity   **Validity** is the extent to which the research actually measures what it was intended to measure. This was part of the problem underlying the famous New Coke fiasco in the 1980s in which Coca-Cola underestimated people's loyalty to its flagship soft drink after it replaced "Old Coke" with a new, sweeter formula. The company assumed that blind taste testers' preferences for one anonymous cola over another was a valid measure of consumers' preferences for a cola brand. Coca-Cola found out the hard way that measuring taste only is not the same as measuring people's deep allegiances to their favorite soft drink. Sales eventually recovered after the company brought back the old version as "Coca-Cola Classic."[26]

validity ■ The extent to which research actually measures what it was intended to measure.

Reliability   **Reliability** is the extent to which the research measurement techniques are free of errors. Sometimes, for example, the way a researcher asks a question creates error by biasing people's responses. Imagine that an attractive female interviewer working for Trojans condoms stopped male college students on campus and asked them if they used contraceptive products. Do you think their answers might change if they were asked the same questions on an anonymous survey they received in the mail? Most likely they would be different because people are reluctant to disclose what they actually do when their responses are not anonymous. Researchers try to maximize reliability by thinking of several different ways to ask the same questions, by asking these questions on several occasions, or by using several analysts to interpret the responses.

Reliability is a problem when the researchers can't be sure the consumer population they're studying even understands the questions. For example, kids are difficult subjects for

reliability ■ The extent to which research measurement techniques are free of errors.

FIGURE 5.5

Completion Test

It can be especially difficult to get accurate information from children. Researchers often use visuals such as this completion test to encourage children to express their feelings.

market researchers because they tend to be undependable reporters of their own behavior, they have poor recall, and they often do not understand abstract questions.[27] In many cases, the children cannot explain why they prefer one item over another (or they're not willing to share these secrets with grown-ups).[28] For these reasons, researchers have had to be especially creative when designing studies on younger consumers. Figure 5.5 shows part of a *completion test* used to measure children's preferences for TV programming. The test asked boys to write in the empty balloon what they think the boy in the drawing will answer when the girl asks, "What program do you want to watch next?" Reliability is increased because the children are able to respond to pictures depicting a familiar scenario.

representativeness ■ The extent to which consumers in a study are similar to a larger group in which the organization has an interest.

sampling ■ The process of selecting respondents who statistically represent a larger population of interest.

Representativeness   **Representativeness** is the extent to which consumers in the study are similar to a larger group in which the organization has an interest. This criterion for evaluating research underscores the importance of **sampling**, the process of selecting respondents for a study. The issue then becomes how large or small the sample should be and how these people are chosen. We'll talk more about sampling in the next section.

DESIGN THE SAMPLE

Once the researcher has defined the problem, decided on a research design, and determined how to collect the data, the next step is to decide from whom to obtain the needed data. Of course, the researcher *could* collect the information from every single customer or prospective customer, but this would be extremely expensive and time consuming, if possible at all. Instead, researchers collect most of their data from a small proportion or *sample* of the population of interest. Based on the answers of this sample, researchers hope to generalize to the larger population. Whether such inferences are accurate or inaccurate depends on the type and quality of the study sample. There are two main types of samples: probability and non-probability samples.

probability sample ■ A sample in which each member of the population has some known chance of being included.

Probability Sampling   With a **probability sample**, each member of the population has some known chance of being included in the sample. Using a probability sample ensures researchers that the sample is representative of the population and that inferences about the population made from the sample are justified. For example, if a larger percentage of males than females in a probability sample say they prefer action movies to "chick flicks," one can infer with confidence that a larger percentage of males than females in the general population also would rather see a character get sliced and diced.

The most basic type of probability sample is a *simple random sample* in which every member of a population has a known and equal chance of being included in the study. For example, if we simply take the names of all 40 students in your class and put them in a hat and draw one out, each member of your class has a 1 in 40 chance of being included in the sample. In most studies the population from which the sample will be drawn is too large for a hat so marketers generate a random sample from a list of members of the population using a computer program.

Sometimes researchers use a *systematic sampling procedure* to select members of a population in which they select the *n*th member of a population after a random start. For example, if we want a sample of 10 members of your class, we might begin with the second person on the role and select every fourth name after that, that is, the second, the sixth, the tenth, the fourteenth, and so on. Researchers know that studies that use systematic samples are just as accurate as with simple random samples. Unless a list of members of the population of interest is already in a computer data file, it's a lot simpler to create a systematic sample.

Yet another type of probability sample is a *stratified sample* in which a researcher divides the population into segments that are related to the study's topic. For example, imagine that you are interested in studying what movies are most liked by members of a population. You know from previous studies that men and women in the population differ in their attitudes toward different types of movies—men like action flicks and women like romances. To create a stratified sample, you would first divide the population into male and female segments. Then respondents from each of the two segments would be selected randomly in proportion to their percentage of the population. In this way, you have created a sample that is proportionate to the population on a characteristic that you know will make a difference in the study results.

Nonprobability Sampling   Sometimes researchers do not feel the time and effort required to develop a probability sample are justified, perhaps because they need an answer quickly or they just want to get a general sense of how people feel about a topic. They may choose a **nonprobability sample**, which entails the use of personal judgment in selecting respondents— in some cases just asking whomever they can find! With a nonprobability sample, some members of the population have no chance at all of being included in the sample. Thus, there is no way to ensure that the sample is representative of the population. Results from nonprobability studies can be generally suggestive of what is going on in the real world but not necessarily definitive.

A *convenience sample* is a nonprobability sample composed of individuals who just happen to be available when and where the data are being collected. For example, if you simply stand in front of the student union and ask students who walk by to complete your questionnaire, that would be a convenience sample.

In some cases firms even use their own employees as a convenience sample or as "guinea pigs." When Gap Inc. was developing the concept for its chain of Old Navy stores, the company gave employees who fit the desired Old Navy customer profile $200 apiece. They set them loose on a shopping spree and then interviewed them about what they had bought so these products would be on Old Navy's shelves when the stores opened (nice work if you can get it!).[29]

Finally, researchers may also use a *quota sample* that includes the same proportion of individuals with certain characteristics as is found in the population. For example, if you are studying attitudes of students in your university, you might just go on campus and find freshmen, sophomores, juniors, and seniors in proportion to the number of members of each class in the university. The quota sample is much like the stratified sample except that with a quota sample, individual members of the sample are selected through personal judgment as they are in a convenience sample.

nonprobability sample ▪
A sample in which personal judgment is used in selecting respondents.

4 *Bookmark It!*

Many college newspapers contain a section where individual students are asked their opinion about current issues, usually using a convenience sample. Find out if your newspaper has this section. How representative are these sections' responses? Are certain types of students more or less likely to respond?

COLLECT THE DATA

At this point the researcher has determined the nature of the problem that needs to be addressed. She has decided on a research design that will specify how to investigate the problem and what kinds of information (data) she will need. The researcher has also selected the data collection and sampling methods. Once these decisions have been made, the next task is to actually collect the data.

Although collecting data may seem like a simple process, researchers are well aware of its critical importance to the accuracy of research. When interviewers are involved, researchers know that the quality of research results is only as good as the poorest interviewer collecting the data. Careless interviewers may not read questions exactly as written or they may not record respondent answers correctly. So marketers must train and supervise interviewers to make sure they follow the research procedures exactly as outlined. In this section we'll talk about some of the problems in gathering data and some solutions.

Gathering Data in Foreign Countries   Conducting market research around the world is big business for U.S. firms. Among the top 50 U.S. research firms, over 40 percent of revenues come from projects outside the United States.[30] However, market conditions and consumer preferences vary worldwide, and there are big differences in the sophistication of market research operations and the amount of data available to global marketers. For example, there are still large areas in Mexico where native Indian tribes speak languages other than Spanish, so researchers may bypass these groups in surveys.[31]

For these reasons and others, choosing an appropriate data collection method is difficult. In some countries many people may not have phones, or low literacy rates may interfere with mail surveys. Local customs can be a problem as well. Offering money for interviews is rude in Latin American countries.[32] Saudi Arabia bans gatherings of four or more people except for family or religious events, and it's illegal to stop strangers on the street or knock on the door of someone's house![33]

Cultural differences also affect responses to survey items. Both Danish and British consumers, for example, agree that it is important to eat breakfast, but the Danish sample may be thinking of fruit and yogurt while the British sample is thinking of toast and tea. Sometimes marketers can overcome these problems by involving local researchers in decisions about the research design.

Another problem with conducting marketing research in global markets is language. Sometimes translations just don't come out right. A sign at a Tokyo hotel once read, "You are invited to take advantage of the chambermaid," and a dry cleaner in Majorca urged passing customers to "drop your pants here for best results."[34] It is not uncommon for researchers to mistranslate questionnaires, or for entire subcultures within a country to be excluded from research.

back-translation ■ The process of translating material to a foreign language and then back to the original language.

To overcome language difficulties, researchers use a process called **back-translation**, which requires two steps. First, a native speaker translates the questionnaire into the target market's language. Then this new version is translated back into the original language to ensure that the correct meanings survive the process. Even with precautions such as these, however, researchers must interpret data obtained from other cultures with care.

Single-Source Data   One research issue that marketers have been trying to solve for years is knowing what impact each piece of their marketing mix is having on their total marketing strategy. Short of moving in with a family for a few months, marketers had no way to determine the effect of multiple promotional activities. Today, though, sophisticated technology allows researchers to gather data from actual store transactions that they can then trace to different components of the marketing mix.

single-source data ■ Information that is integrated from multiple sources, to monitor the impact of marketing communications on a particular customer group over time.

The term **single-source data** refers to information that is integrated from multiple sources. In single-source systems, data on purchasing behavior and advertising exposure are measured for members of a consumer panel using electronic television meters, retail scanners, and split-cable technology in which different customers on a television cable system can be exposed to different ads. Because single-source systems can measure the impact of a number of different marketing activities in combination, they allow marketers to monitor the impact of many marketing communications on a particular customer group over time. For example,

Checkout scanners enable marketers to collect single-source data.

a firm that sells laundry detergent might use single-source systems to answer the following questions:

- Which consumer segments are more likely to be brand loyal and what segments frequently switch brands of laundry detergent?
- Are coupons or price-off packs more likely to increase sales?
- Does increased advertising exposure influence brand switching?
- What is the total effect of increased advertising and the use of coupons?

A lot of single-source data come from checkout scanners in stores. In addition to speeding up your checkout time, those funny-looking little machines are storing a record of just how many bags of munchies you bought and what brands you chose. Combined with records from the store's other customers (and buyers at other locations), this is a potential pot of gold for firms willing to invest in the research needed to track all those millions of transactions. This technology is becoming so popular that up to 90 percent of apparel, electronics, and grocery purchases in the United States are scanned, and some companies are following up on the wealth of information sitting in their databases. For example, the grocery chain Safeway tracks the purchases of regular customers who show a Savings Club card when they get to the register. Every other week, these shoppers get a mail packet with coupons tailored to their individual purchases. So heavy users of hot dogs might be delighted to find cents-off coupons for mustard in their mailboxes.

ANALYZE AND INTERPRET THE DATA

Once marketing researchers have collected the data, what's next? It's like a spin on the old "if a tree falls in the woods" question: "If results exist but there's no one to interpret them, do they have a meaning?" Well, let's leave the philosophers out of it and just say that marketers would answer "no." Data need analysis for them to have meaning.

To understand the important role of data analysis, let's take a look at a hypothetical research example. In our example, a company that markets frozen foods wishes to better understand consumers' preference for varying levels of fat content in their diets. They have conducted a descriptive research study in which they collected primary data via telephone interviews.

TABLE 5.3

Examples of Data Tabulation
and Cross-Tabulation Tables

Fat Content Preference
(Number and percentages of responses)

Questionnaire Response	Number of Responses	Percentage of Responses
Do you prefer a meal with high fat content, medium fat content, or low fat content?		
High fat	21	6
Medium fat	179	51
Low fat	150	43
Total	350	100

Fat Content Preference by Gender
(Number and percentages of responses)

Questionnaire Response	Number Females	Percentage of Females	Number Males	Percentage of Males	Total Number	Total Percentage
Do you prefer a meal with high fat content, medium fat content, or low fat content?						
High fat	4	2	17	10	21	6
Medium fat	68	39	111	64	179	51
Low fat	103	59	47	27	150	43
Total	175	100	175	100	350	100

Because they recognize that gender is related to dietary preferences, they have used a stratified sample that includes 175 males and 175 females.

Typically, marketers first tabulate the data as shown in Table 5.3—that is, they arrange the data in a table or other summary form so they can get a broad picture of the overall responses. The data in this table show that 43 percent of the sample prefers a low-fat meal. In addition there may be a desire to cross-classify or cross-tabulate the answers to questions by other variables. *Cross-tabulation* means that the data are examined by subgroups, in this case males and females separately, to see how results vary between categories. The cross-tabulation in Table 5.3 shows that 59 percent of females versus only 27 percent of males prefer a meal with low fat content. In addition, researchers may wish to apply additional statistical tests, which you'll learn about in subsequent courses (something to look forward to).

Based on the tabulation and cross-tabulations, the researcher must then interpret or draw conclusions from the results and make recommendations. For example, the study results shown in Table 5.3 may lead to the conclusion that females are more likely than males to be concerned about a low-fat diet. The researcher might then make a recommendation to a firm that it should target females in the introduction of a new line of low-fat foods.

PREPARE THE RESEARCH REPORT

The final step in the marketing research process is to prepare a report of the research results. In general, a research report must clearly and concisely tell the readers—top management, clients, creative departments, and many others—what they need to know in a way that they can easily understand. In general, a research report will include these sections:

- An executive summary of the report that covers the high points of the total report
- An understandable description of the research methodology
- A complete discussion of the results of the study, including the tabulations, cross-tabulations, and additional statistical analyses
- Limitations of the study (no study is perfect)
- Conclusions drawn from the results and the recommendations for managerial action based on the results

Online Research

The growth of the Internet is rewriting some of the rules of the marketing research process. As more and more people have access to the Web, many companies such as Harris Interactive are finding that the Internet is a superior way to collect data—it's fast, it's relatively cheap, and it lends itself well to forms of research from simple questionnaires to online focus groups. General Mills, for example, is a true believer in online research. General Mills conducted 60 percent of its research online in 2000, up from 20 percent in 1999.[35] These developments are happening quickly and it's worth taking some time at the end of this chapter to see how this is working.

The Web is revolutionizing the way many companies collect data and use them to guide their strategic decisions. There are two major types of online research. One type is information gathered by tracking consumers while they are surfing. The second type is information gathered through questionnaires on Web sites, through e-mail, or from moderated focus groups conducted in chat rooms.

ONLINE TRACKING

The Internet offers an unprecedented ability to track consumers as they search for information—we'll talk more about this process in the next chapter. Marketers can better understand where people go to look when they want to learn about products and services—and which advertisements they stop to browse along the way. How can marketers do this? One way is by the use of cookies. Beware the Cookie Monster! **Cookies** are text files inserted by a Web site sponsor into a user's hard drive when the user connects with the site. Cookies remember details of a visit to a Web site, typically tracking which pages the user visits. Some sites request or require that visitors "register" on the site by answering questions about themselves and their likes and dislikes. In such cases, cookies also allow the site to access these details about the customer.

cookies ■ Text files inserted by a Web site sponsor into a Web surfer's hard drive that allow the site to track the surfer's moves.

This technology allows Web sites to customize services, such as when Amazon.com recommends new books to users based on what books they have ordered in the past. Most consumers have no idea that cookies allow Web sites to gather and store all this information. You can block cookies or curb them, although this can make life difficult if you are trying to log on to many sites such as online newspapers or travel agencies that require this information to admit you.

Amazon.com uses sophisticated software called "collaborative filtering" to keep track of shoppers' book choices and recommend new books based on past patterns.

Who Owns Your Cookies? This information generated from tracking consumers' online journeys has become a product as well—companies sell this consumer data to other companies that are trying to target prospects. But consumers have become increasingly concerned about the sharing of these data. In a study of 10,000 Web users, 84 percent objected to the reselling of their information to other companies. Although Internet users can delete cookie files manually or install anticookie software on their computers, there are many people who feel there is a need for privacy regulation and for cookie regulation in order to limit potential abuses.

To date, the Federal Trade Commission (FTC) has relied on the Internet industry to develop and maintain its own standards instead of developing extensive privacy regulations, but many would like to see that situation changed. Privacy rights proponents feel that:

- Information about a consumer belongs to the consumer.
- Consumers should be made aware of information collection.
- Consumers should know how information about them will be used.
- Consumers should be able to refuse to allow information collection.
- Information about a consumer should never be sold or given to another party without the permission of the consumer.

ONLINE TESTING, QUESTIONNAIRES, AND FOCUS GROUPS

The Internet offers a faster, less expensive alternative to traditional communication data collection methods. Here are some ways companies are using the Internet to get feedback from consumers:

- New-product development: Procter & Gamble spent more than five years testing products such as Febreze, Dryel, and Fit Fruit & Vegetable Wash the old-fashioned way before launching nationally. Using online tests, the Crest MultiCare Flex & Clean toothbrush was launched in less than a year. General Motors and Nissan are two automakers that now gather online consumer reactions to upcoming products. Such research allows manufacturers to learn what consumers want in future vehicles.[36]

Some online research firms collect consumers' responses to a variety of proposed new product styles before the items are actually produced. This advance feedback is invaluable to manufacturers because it gives them important guidance regarding which of the new styles are likely to catch on in the marketplace and which will gather dust on store shelves. This study by Mind/Share, Inc. tested clothing styles for a major manufacturer.

Address http://fafnir.berry.edu/LifeStyle/LifeStyle.mv?915686907+kc17592968439489.dat+cat+3+out038+path

Additional information about the product (for example, pricing, model, options, brand, and so on) can appear here.

Yes - Choose This Item

No - Show Selections Again

Experts predict that as much as 25 percent of all consumer market research will be online by 2002.[37]

- Estimating market response: Both Mercury Records and Virgin Records have used online research to test music for performers including Bon Jovi and the Spice Girls.[38] In a typical test, respondents listen to the songs and then click on buttons to indicate how much they like or dislike the music.

- Exploratory research: Conducting focus groups online has mushroomed in popularity in recent years. For example, Procter & Gamble's Web site (www.pg.com) includes a Try & Buy New Products section that sells P&G products still being test-marketed and directs consumers to virtual, real-time focus groups.[39] Of course, with online groups it is impossible to observe body language, facial expressions, and vocal inflection. But marketers continue to develop new ways to talk to consumers in virtual space, including software that allows online focus group participants to indicate nonverbal responses. For example, an online participant can register an expression of disgust by clicking on the command to "roll eyes."[40]

Many marketing research companies are running, not walking, to the Web to conduct studies for clients. Why? For one thing, replacing traditional mail consumer panels with Internet

Real People, Other Voices: Advice for Harris Interactive

Meredith Burch, Student, Berry College

I would choose option 3. Recruiting Internet users through non-standard approaches would reduce costs and conducting parallel telephone and online surveys would result in a more representative sample of the entire population—despite the need for an expensive marketing campaign to tout this new methodology and the possible ineffectiveness of the data if there were no similarities found between the online or phone surveys.

Richard Bernstein, Vice President, Eric Marder Associates

I would choose option 3. At stake is not only research quality, but also Harris' corporate image. Option 1 does not change the market research process. Option 2 would produce a good sample, but from a practical and business standpoint is unwieldy and expensive. Few (if any) clients would bear the expense. Given that Harris wants to 'own' online research, option 3, is the best choice. The novel recruiting approach will allow Harris to harness the promise of the Internet. Parallel studies will allow them to develop 'Internet correction factors' which can effectively counter client concerns about sample quality. Given this option and sufficient investment, the Harris name could be synonymous with Internet research.

Basil Englis, Marketing Professor, Berry College

Option 3 is the best compromise given the costs of constructing a truly representative national panel. Even if a sample could pass this test, there is no guarantee that all of the contacts would agree to participate. Option 3 directly compares an accepted methodology (telephone survey with random-digit dialing) with a less accepted methodology (Internet recruitment through several methods). The telephone survey results could be a benchmark against which the Internet sample could be matched demographically. Then, the polling data from each sample could be compared. George could then argue that his Internet sampling method yields a representative national sample. However, this solution is only as good as its telephone methodology. George should also match the demographic profiles of his telephone and Internet survey samples to Census Bureau data, which means he may not need to use a telephone sampling method at all!

Weigh in with your thoughts! Visit the Live Laboratory at www.prenhall.com/solomon **for extended Other Voices replies, exercises, and more.**

panels allows marketers to collect the same amount of data in a weekend that used to take six to eight weeks. And consumers can complete surveys when it is convenient—even at 3 A.M. There are other advantages: Even large studies can be conducted at low costs. International borders are not a problem, either, since in many countries (for example, in Scandinavia) Internet use is very high and it's easy to recruit respondents. Web-based interviews eliminate interviewer bias or errors in data entry.[41]

However, no data collection method is perfect and online research is no exception—though many of the criticisms of online techniques also apply to off-line techniques. One potential problem is the representativeness of the respondents. Although the number of Internet users continues to grow, many segments of the consumer population, mainly the poor and elderly, do not have equal access to the Internet. Also, in many studies (just as with mail surveys or mall intercepts) there is a *self-selection bias* in the sample: Respondents have agreed to receive invitations to take part in online studies, which means they tend to be the kind of people who like to participate in surveys. As with other kinds of research such as live focus groups, it's not unusual to encounter "professional respondents"—people who just enjoy taking part in studies (and getting paid for it). Online firms such as Harris Interactive address this problem by monitoring their participants and regulating how often they are allowed to participate in different studies over a period of time.

There are other disadvantages of online research. Hackers can actually try to influence research results. Even more dangerous may be competitors who can learn about a firm's marketing plans, products, advertising, and so forth by intercepting information used in research. One company, E-Poll, uses a methodology to prevent some of these problems.[42] To preview TV pilots, commercials, and ad campaigns, E-Poll sends respondents a CD-ROM. The CD guides respondents to a secure area on the E-Poll site, which requires them to enter a password before they can watch the research content and answer the questionnaire.[43]

Despite the potential drawbacks, online research has a bright future. Indeed, it has the potential to take off even faster as a result of the 2001 terrorist attacks, since many people are more hesitant to answer questions from strangers, drive to focus group facilities, or open mail surveys from sources they don't recognize. Firms such as Harris Interactive are on the cutting edge of an exciting new industry.

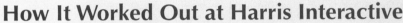

Real People, Real Choices: How It Worked Out at Harris Interactive

After testing the approach internally for nine months, George and Harris Interactive chose option 3. Results from hundreds of parallel telephone and online studies indicated that the approach would allow Harris Interactive to collect credible, trustworthy information through the Internet at a significantly reduced cost (approximately 35 percent, all else being equal) as compared with the other options. You may have discovered in your research that the Internet does allow marketers to locate reasonably representative samples that will generalize to the typical buying public—especially if the client wishes to reach relatively younger and more affluent consumers.

Penetration of the Internet among consumer segments continues to rise. More than 67 percent of all U.S. adults now access the Internet from home, work, or another location. And evidence of the effectiveness of the approach has continued to accumulate. For example, Harris Interactive produced the most accurate forecast of the national race for president in 2000 and more accurate forecasts of state election results than all traditional telephone pollsters. Harris also outperformed Knowledge Networks, an organization that (similar to option 2) recruits people and provides them with Internet access.

The company's financial fortunes have been equally impressive. Harris Interactive raised $110 million for expansion, primarily through an IPO in late 1999, and has generated more than $70 million in revenue through Internet research. Over all, company revenues have increased eleven-fold since 1997, and Harris Interactive has become the world's fastest-growing market research organization.

Chapter Summary

1. Understand the role of the marketing information system and the marketing decision support system in marketing decision making.

A marketing information system (MIS) is composed of internal data, marketing intelligence, marketing research data, acquired databases, and computer hardware and software. Firms use an MIS to gather, sort, analyze, store, and distribute information needed by managers for marketing decision making. The marketing decision support system (MDSS) allows managers to use analysis software and interactive software to access MIS data and to conduct analyses and find the information they need.

2. Describe the marketing research process.

The research process begins by defining the problem and determining the research design or type of study. Next, researchers choose the data collection method, that is, whether there is secondary data available or if primary research with a communication study or through observation is necessary. Then researchers determine what type of sample is to be used for the study and then collect the data. The final steps in the research are to analyze and interpret the data and prepare a research report.

3. Understand the differences among exploratory, descriptive, and causal research, and describe some research techniques available to marketers.

Exploratory research typically uses qualitative data collected by individual interviews, focus groups, or observational methods such as ethnography. Descriptive research includes cross-sectional and longitudinal studies. Causal research goes a step further by designing controlled experiments in order to understand cause-and-effect relationships between marketing independent variables, such as price changes, and dependent variables, such as sales.

4. Describe the different types of data collection methods and types of samples that researchers use.

Researchers may choose to collect data using mail questionnaires, telephone interviews, face-to-face interviews, or online questionnaires. A study may utilize a probability sample such as a simple random or stratified sample in which inferences can be made to a population based on the sample results. Nonprobability sampling methods include a convenience sample and a quota sample. The research tries to ensure that the data are valid, reliable, and representative. Validity is the extent to which the research actually measures what it was intended to measure. Reliability is the extent to which the research measurement techniques are free of errors. Representativeness is the extent to which consumers in the study are similar to a larger group in which the organization has an interest.

5. Understand the growing use of online research.

Marketers increasingly are using the Internet for online research. Online tracking uses cookies to record where consumers go on a Web site. Consumers have become increasingly concerned about privacy and how this information is used and made available to other Internet companies. The Internet also provides an attractive alternative to traditional communication data collection methods because of its speed and low cost. Many firms use the Internet to conduct online focus groups.

Chapter Review

■ **MARKETING CONCEPTS:**
TESTING YOUR KNOWLEDGE

1. What is a marketing information system (MIS)? What types of information are included in a marketing information system? How does a marketing decision support system (MDSS) allow marketers to easily get the information they need?

2. What are the steps in the marketing research process? Why is defining the problem to be researched so important?

3. What is the goal of exploratory research? What techniques are used to gather data in exploratory research?

4. What is descriptive research? What techniques are used in descriptive research?

5. What is causal research?

6. What are some advantages and disadvantages of telephone interviews, mail questionnaires, face-to-face interviews, and online interviews? What unique data collection problems exist in foreign markets?

7. How do probability and nonprobability samples differ? What are some types of probability samples? What are some types of nonprobability samples?

8. What are single-source data? What are some ways that marketers use single-source data?

9. What is meant by reliability, validity, and representativeness of research results?

10. What are online tracking studies? What are some strengths and weaknesses of Internet focus groups?

MARKETING CONCEPTS:
DISCUSSING CHOICES AND ISSUES

1. Some marketers attempt to disguise themselves as marketing researchers when their real intent is to sell something to the consumer. What is the impact of this practice on legitimate researchers? What do you think might be done about this practice?

2. Do you think marketers should be allowed to conduct market research with young children? Why or why not?

3. Are you willing to divulge personal information to marketing researchers? How much are you willing to tell, or where would you draw the line?

4. What is your overall attitude toward marketing research? Do you think it is a beneficial activity from a consumer's perspective? Or do you think it merely gives marketers new insights on how to convince consumers to buy something they really don't want or need?

5. Sometimes firms use data mining to identify and abandon customers who are not profitable because they don't spend enough to justify the service needed or because they return a large proportion of the items they buy. What do you think of such practices? Is it ethical for firms to prune out these customers?

6. Many consumers are concerned about online tracking studies and their privacy. Do consumers have the right to "own" data about themselves? Should governments limit the use of the Internet for data collection?

7. One unobtrusive measure mentioned in the chapter involved going through consumers' or competitors' garbage. Do you think marketers should have the right to do this? Is it ethical?

MARKETING PRACTICE:
APPLYING WHAT YOU'VE LEARNED

1. Your firm is planning to begin marketing a consumer product in several global markets. You have been given the responsibility of developing plans for marketing research to be conducted in South Africa, in Spain, and in China. In a role-playing situation, present the difficulties you expect to encounter, if any, in conducting research in each of these areas.

2. As an account executive with a marketing research firm, you are responsible for deciding on the type of research to be used in various studies conducted for your clients. For each of the following client questions, list your choices.
   a. Will television or magazine advertising be more effective for a local bank to use in its marketing communication plan?
   b. Could a new package design for dry cereal do a better job at satisfying the needs of customers and, thus, increase sales?
   c. Are consumers more likely to buy brands that are labeled as environmentally friendly?
   d. How do female consumers determine if a particular perfume is right for them?
   e. What types of people read the local newspaper?
   f. How frequently do consumers switch brands of soft drinks?
   g. How will an increase in the price of a brand of laundry detergent affect sales?
   h. What are the effects of advertising and sales promotion in combination on sales of a brand of shampoo?

3. Your marketing research firm is planning to conduct surveys to gather information for a number of clients. Your boss has asked you and a few other new employees to do some preliminary work. He's asked each of you to choose three of the topics that will be included in the project and to prepare an analysis of the advantages and disadvantages of mail questionnaires, telephone interviews, face-to-face interviews, online questionnaires, or observation for each.
   a. The amount of sports nutrition drinks consumed in a city
   b. Why a local bank has been losing customers
   c. How heavily the company should invest in manufacturing and marketing home fax machines
   d. The amount of money being spent "over the state line" for lottery tickets
   e. What local doctors would like to see changed in the hospitals in the city
   f. Consumers' attitudes toward several sports celebrities.

MARKETING MINI-PROJECT:
LEARNING BY DOING

The purpose of this mini-project is to familiarize you with marketing research techniques and to help you apply these techniques to managerial decision making.

1. With a group of three other students in your class, select a small retail business or fast-food restaurant to use as a "client" for your project. (Be sure to get the manager's

permission before conducting your research.) Then choose a topic from among the following possibilities to develop a study problem:

- employee–customer interactions
- the busiest periods of customer activity
- customer perceptions of service
- customer likes and dislikes about offerings
- customer likes and dislikes about the environment in the place of business
- the benefits customers perceive to be important
- the age groups that frequent the place of business
- the buying habits of a particular age group
- how customer complaints are handled

2. Develop a plan for the research:
   a. Define the problem as you will study it.
   b. Choose the type of research you will use.
   c. Select the techniques you will use to gather data.
   d. Develop the mode and format for data collection.

3. Conduct the research.

4. Write a report (or develop a class presentation) that includes four parts.
   a. Introduction: a brief overview of the business and the problem studied
   b. Methodology: the type of research used, the techniques used to gather data (and why they were chosen), the instruments and procedures used, the number of respondents, duration of the study, and other details that would allow someone to replicate your study
   c. Results: a compilation of the results (perhaps in table form) and the conclusions drawn
   d. Recommendations: a list of recommendations for actions management might take based on the conclusions drawn from the study

REAL PEOPLE, REAL SURFERS:
EXPLORING THE WEB

As discussed in this chapter, monitoring changes in demographics and other consumer trends is an important part of the marketing intelligence included in an MIS. Today much of this information is gathered by government research and is available on the Internet.

The U.S. Census Bureau provides tabled data for cities and counties across the nations at its site, www.census.gov. The *Statistical Abstract of the United States* is available at www.census.gov/prod/2/gen/96statab.96statab.html. In addition, most states produce their own statistical abstract publication that is available on the Web. For example, the *New York Statistical Abstract* is available at www.columbia.edu/cu/libraries/indiv/dsc/nys/html, the *California Statistical Abstract* is at www.dof.ca.gov/html/fs_data/stat-abs/sa_home.htm, and the *South Carolina Statistical Abstract* is at www.state.sc.us/drss/pop. You should be able to locate the statistical abstract for your state by using a search engine. Using both state data and U.S. Census data, develop a report on a city or county of your choice that answers these questions:

1. What is the total population of the city or county?
2. Describe the population of the area in terms of age, income, education, ethnic background, marital status, occupation, and housing.
3. How does the city or county compare to the demographic characteristics of the entire U.S. population?
4. What is your opinion of the different Web sites you used? How useful are they to marketers? How easy were they to navigate? Was there information that you wanted that was not available? Was there more or less information from the sites than you anticipated? Explain.

PLAN IT!
DEVELOPING A MARKETING PLAN

As your instructor directs, create a marketing plan (using Marketing Plan Pro software or a written marketing plan format) to document your marketing decisions or answer these questions in a written or oral report.

CFS needs marketing information and research to build on the current year's marketing plan (see Appendix A) in developing next year's plan.

1. What marketing intelligence would help CFS monitor developments in the external environment?
2. How might management use ethnography to better understand what customers do with CFS products?
3. What two scenarios could conceivably emerge in the course of implementing this year's marketing plan—and how can you use these scenarios in planning for next year?

Key Terms

back-translation, (146)
case study, (137)
causal research, (139)
consumer interviews, (137)

cookies, (146)
cross-sectional design, (139)
custom research, (128)
data mining, (130)

descriptive research, (138)
ethnography, (137)
experiments, (139)
exploratory research, (135)

MARKETING IN ACTION: CHAPTER 5 CASE

REAL CHOICES AT GENERAL MOTORS

In the early 1990s, General Motors faced several potentially disastrous situations. First, GM's Oldsmobile division was fighting for its life, and GM was only beginning to recover from embarrassing stumbles in small and midsize cars, minivans, and sport-utility vehicles. GM had been doing well in trucks and the large luxury-car segments, but making great cars for older people who'd be moving on out of the market was not a very good prognosis for long-term success. What GM needed to do was to put the customer first, not the sheet metal.

Vince Barabba, general manager of GM's strategic decision center, believed that the answer to GM's problems was research into customer needs. With the right research GM would be able to allocate capital spending and produce vehicles that would not merely satisfy but delight customers—and, in the process, make a large profit for GM. In 1988 Barabba began working with Applied Decision Analysts, a marketing research firm, using conjoint measurement—a sophisticated research technique that allows marketers to estimate the relative preferences people have for different vehicle attributes. With conjoint analysis researchers are able to address such questions as how much fuel economy a customer would be willing to trade for better acceleration or how much a customer would pay to get more cargo space.

GM used this needs-based research to assess the needs and desires of more than a million consumers. This research showed that potential owners of a Chevrolet Lumina, for example, wanted a good-looking car but wouldn't trade functionality or value for appearance. They wanted more interior space, but because these buyers had economic constraints, the overall size would have to be kept down to keep the price in line. The car would also have to deliver a high level of performance based on miles per gallon and be troublefree to keep maintenance costs down.

Potential drivers of a Pontiac Grand Prix wanted a car that made them feel like they owned the road and wouldn't sacrifice high style for driving performance. Because these drivers are primarily interested in their own driving pleasure and excitement, roominess and passenger comfort were of little importance. And there were other drivers who wanted something in between. These potential customers had been a prime target for GM's ailing Oldsmobile division; they wanted a car that had really great styling and room for passengers.

These and other findings revealed overall consumer trends that confirmed the decline of the big-car market and the growth of the small and midsize car markets. They also had implications for developing new cars that specifically fit the desires of the consumer segments studied. But as the manager of GM's strategic decision center, Barabba questioned whether or not such a strategy would overfragment the company's market. Perhaps the real problem stemmed from GM's inability to focus adequately on the needs of any particular group because of the overabundance of different GM product lines and models. Although a true believer in marketing research, Barabba wondered whether the needs-based research was, in fact, pointing the firm in the right direction or whether more traditional methods should be used to research the attitudes of existing customers.

Source: Phil Frame, "GM Guru Returns to Building Blocks," *Advertising Age* (April 3, 1995): S8.

THINGS TO THINK ABOUT

1. What is the decision facing GM?
2. What factors are important in understanding the decision situation?
3. What are the alternatives?
4. What decision(s) do you recommend?
5. What are some ways to implement your recommendation(s)?

Bookmark It!

OBJECTIVES:

1. Define consumer behavior and explain the reasons why consumers buy what they buy.

2. Explain the prepurchase, purchase, and postpurchase activities consumers engage in when making decisions.

3. Describe how internal factors influence consumers' decision-making processes.

4. Understand how situational factors at the time and place of purchase may influence consumer behavior.

5. Describe how consumers' relationships with other people influence their decision-making processes.

6. Understand how the Internet offers consumers opportunities for peer-to-peer marketing.

Why People Buy
CONSUMER BEHAVIOR
AND PEER-TO-PEER E-COMMERCE

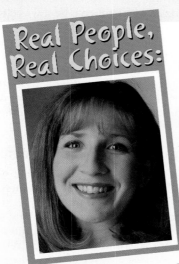

Real People, Real Choices:

Meet Jennifer Dulski, a Decision Maker at Yahoo! Inc.

www.yahoo.com/shopping

CURRENT POSITION: Senior Brand Manager.

CAREER PATH: 1999–2000 Brand Manager, Yahoo! Shopping.

1996–1997 Special Projects Manager, Grable Foundation.

EDUCATION: 1993 B.A. in Psychology, Cornell University.

1999 M.B.A., Cornell University.

WHAT I DO WHEN I'M NOT WORKING: Spend time with my husband and daughter.

FIRST JOB OUT OF SCHOOL: Founder and Executive Director of Summerbridge, a nonprofit, academic program for at-risk students in Pittsburgh.

BUSINESS BOOK I'M READING: <u>Circle of Innovation</u> by Tom Peters.

HERO: Jim Henson.

MOTTO: "Chance favors the prepared mind."—Louis Pasteur.

DON'T DO THIS WHEN INTERVIEWING WITH ME: Ask no questions.

A Portal with a Problem

Yahoo! Shopping is successful because it has established itself as a major portal for online shopping. In other words, it makes money by organizing and presenting information on approximately 10,000 stores and 7,000 products. A consumer deciding to make a purchase often goes through an elaborate process of searching for information, narrowing down alternatives, and evaluating the relative attractiveness of each alternative, as we'll see in this chapter. A portal helps to simplify this process by identifying possible products and providing information about each. Indeed, how could anyone visit thousands of stores in person? For an online shopper, then, a portal is the first stop on a journey that often makes several other stops before it ends (hopefully) in a purchase from a merchant's Web site.

A portal such as Yahoo! makes its money by selling advertising space to businesses that want to reach these surfers. The company also shares a percentage of revenue from each transaction that goes through Yahoo! Shopping. As long as surfers browse the portal to search for product information, advertisers have their attention. Because the advertiser pays Yahoo! only if enough eyeballs are attracted to the site (measured in hits) and only if people buy something as a result, it's a constant challenge for managers like Jennifer to ensure that people keep visiting the portal.

Jennifer's challenge always intensifies during the holiday season, which is as critical for online retailers as it is for off-line retailers. Yahoo! Shopping is under pressure to drive up sales in the fourth quarter every year. Jennifer has to do this on a limited marketing budget. During 2000, the Yahoo! team was in discussions with *USA WEEKEND* magazine about an opportunity that would allow Yahoo! Shopping to inexpensively reach a large number of readers (45 million) during the critical post-Thanksgiving weekend. According to the agreement, Yahoo! would write an editorial and design the layout for a special pull-out section about online shopping for the holidays. This would be a barter deal in which Yahoo! would receive national exposure and *USA WEEKEND* magazine would sell the advertising space in the section. (Yahoo! would not share in the advertising revenue.)

But there was a catch: For the section to be editorially neutral, it would have to mention and provide URLs (Web addresses) for the company's major competitors. Yahoo! would also have to provide the direct URLs for merchants when it would otherwise send consumers to its Yahoo! Shopping site to find those merchants. On the good side, Jennifer knew from Yahoo!'s consumer research and data from third-party sources that portals attract a lot of buyers and drive strong sales for their merchant partners. Indeed, Forrester (an independent online research firm) reported in March 2001 that portals generated 26 percent of Web traffic and nearly 20 percent of online sales to merchants. It was clear, too, that Yahoo! attracted more visitors—and visitors who bought more once they found a site they liked—than such rival portals as AOL, MSN, and Lycos (see Figure 6.1).

But on the bad side, Jennifer also knew that once online shoppers find store sites they like, they'll often go directly to these sites instead of returning to the portal that sent them there. Jennifer was concerned about the possibility that this editorial section would drive people directly to merchant sites, eliminating the need for Yahoo! and diluting her valuable customer base. She considered her options:

Option 1: Pay for an ad or multiple ads in the magazine instead of doing the pull-out section.

Yahoo! could use the entire space to promote Yahoo! Shopping and its features. Because a paid ad would allow Yahoo! to completely control the content of the message, the company wouldn't have to promote its competitors or encourage people to go directly to merchant sites. But this ad would be more expensive than the pull-out section. In addition, the information would not appear to be as neutral because it would be clear that Yahoo! paid to place the ad in the paper.

Option 2: Run the editorial section.

This would be an inexpensive way to achieve significant national exposure to *USA WEEKEND*'s 23.5 million households. It would position Yahoo! as an unbiased, trustworthy source by providing information about competitors' offerings as well as its own. Still, choosing this option meant that Yahoo! would also be promoting its major competitors. And it could teach people to go directly to stores rather than to start at the Yahoo! Shopping site.

Option 3: Do nothing; continue to promote Yahoo! through other avenues including online advertising and public relations efforts.

Obviously, this choice would be easier on Jennifer's advertising budget. And Yahoo! would avoid having to promote competitors or encourage people to go directly to merchant sites. But Yahoo! would miss out on exposure during a key period when consumers were trying to decide what to buy for the holidays.

Now, put yourself in Jennifer Dulski's shoes: Which option would you choose, and why?

The top three portals attract more valuable shoppers than other intermediary sites.

US Traffic*		BPI Traffic ●	
Yahoo!	81	Yahoo!	102
MSN	76	MSN	100
AOL	53	AOL	66
Lycos	31	BizRate.com	55
Excite	23	Lycos	49
BizRate.com	8	Excite	29
mySimon.com	7	mySimon.com	14
Dealtime.com	5	Dealtime.com	14

The Buying Power Index (BPI™), a proprietary comScore calculation, represents the value of a site's audience. It is a relative measure of the buying power of a site's visitors compared with Web users in general. A high BPI means that the average visitor to that site spends more across all merchants online than the average Web user.

BPI Traffic—BPI x unique visitors—credits sites based on the value of their visitors instead of the number of visitors.

*Millions of unique Web visitors

Source: comScore, December 2000

Source: Forrester Research, Inc.

FIGURE 6.1

Portals Attract Web Shoppers

Decisions, Decisions

Compelling new products, clever packaging, and creative advertising surround us, clamoring for our attention—and our money. This clamoring doesn't change online either, as Jennifer Dulski of Yahoo! knows. But consumers don't all respond in the same way. Each of us is a unique person, with our own reasons for choosing one product over another. Recall that the focus of the marketing concept is to satisfy consumers' wants and needs. To do that, we need to understand what those wants and needs are.

Consumer behavior is the process individuals or groups go through to select, purchase, or use goods, services, ideas, or experiences. Marketers recognize that consumer decision making is an ongoing process—it's more than what happens at the moment a consumer forks over the cash and in turn receives a good or service.

Although it seems as if we make some purchases spontaneously (and we may regret our rashness later), in reality we make these buying decisions only after we have undergone a series of steps. Figure 6.2 presents these steps: problem recognition, information search, evaluation of alternatives, product choice, and postpurchase evaluation.

Traditionally, researchers have tried to understand how consumers make decisions by assuming that people carefully collect information about competing products, determine which products possess the characteristics or product attributes important to their needs, weigh the pluses and minuses of each alternative, and arrive at a satisfactory decision. But how accurate is this picture of the decision-making process?

Although it does seem that people do undergo these steps when making an important purchase, is it realistic to assume that they do this for everything they buy? If so, they need to get a life! Researchers now realize that decision makers actually possess a set of approaches

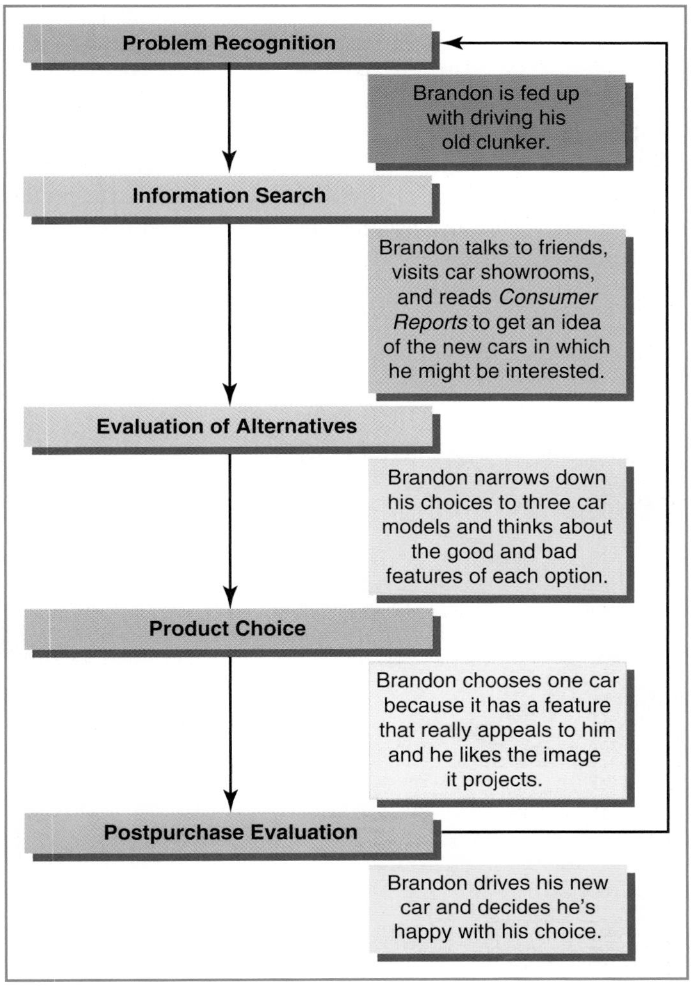

consumer behavior ■ The process involved when individuals or groups select, purchase, use, and dispose of goods, services, ideas, or experiences to satisfy their needs and desires.

FIGURE 6.2

The Consumer Decision-Making Process

The consumer decision-making process involves a series of steps that is summarized here.

FIGURE 6.3

Extended Problem Solving Versus Habitual Decision Making

A number of different factors in consumers' lives influence the consumer decision-making process. Marketers need to understand these influences and which ones are important in the purchase process in order to make effective marketing decisions.

	Extended Problem Solving	*Habitual Decision Making*
Product	New car	Can of soda
Level of involvement	High	Low
Perceived risk	High	Low
Information processing	Careful processing of information	Respond to environmental cues
Learning model	Cognitive learning	Behavioral learning
Needed marketing actions	Provide information via advertising, salespeople, brochures, Web sites. Educate consumers to product benefits, risks of wrong decisions, etc.	Provide environmental cues at point of purchase such as product display

ranging from painstaking analysis to pure whim, depending on the importance of what is being bought and how much effort the person is willing to put into the decision.[1] They have found it convenient to think in terms of an "effort" continuum, which is anchored on one end by *habitual decision making* (such as deciding to purchase a can of soda) and at the other end by *extended problem solving* (such as deciding to purchase a new car). Figure 6.3 provides a summary of the differences between extended problem solving and habitual decision making.

Many decisions fall somewhere in the middle and are characterized by *limited problem solving*, which means that consumers do work to make a decision. We often rely on simple "rules of thumb" instead of painstakingly learning all the ins and outs of every product alternative. Life is too short!

Just how much effort do we put into these decisions? The answer depends on our level of **involvement**—the importance of the perceived consequences of the purchase to the person. As a rule, we are more involved in the decision-making process for products that we think are risky in some way. **Perceived risk** may be present if the product is expensive or complex and hard to understand, such as a new PC or a new sports car.

Perceived risk can also be a factor in product choice if choosing the wrong product results in embarrassment or social rejection. For example, a person who wears a pair of Doc Martens (www.drmartens.com) on a job interview may commit "fashion suicide" and jeopardize the job if the interviewer doesn't approve of this footwear.

involvement ■ The relative importance of perceived consequences of the purchase to a consumer.

perceived risk ■ The belief that choice of a product has potentially negative consequences, either financial, physical, or social.

Business consumers may experience a high level of perceived risk for expensive items. Advertising such as this by Minolta for its copier seeks to reduce that risk.

When perceived risk is low, as in buying a pack of gum, the consumer feels low involvement in the decision-making process—she is not overly concerned about which option she chooses because it is not especially important or risky. In low-involvement situations, the consumer's decision is often a response to environmental cues, such as when a person decides to try a new type of chewing gum because it's prominently displayed at a store checkout counter. Under these circumstances, managers must concentrate on how products are displayed at the time of purchase to influence the decision maker. For example, a chewing gum marketer may decide to spend extra money to be sure its gum stands out at a checkout display or to change the color of the gum wrapper to a bright pink so consumers notice it.

For high-involvement purchases, such as buying a house, a car, or an interview suit, the consumer is likely to carefully process all of the available information and to have thought about the decision well before going to buy the item. The consequences of the purchase are important and risky, especially because a bad decision may result in significant financial losses, aggravation, or embarrassment. Most of us would not just walk into a realtor's office at lunchtime and casually plunk down a deposit on a new house. For high-involvement products, managers must start to reduce perceived risk by educating the consumer about why their product is the best choice well in advance of the time that the consumer is ready to make a decision.

To understand each of the steps in the decision-making process, in the next section we'll follow the fortunes of a consumer named Brandon, who is in the market for a new car—a highly involving purchase decision to say the least.

PROBLEM RECOGNITION

Problem recognition occurs whenever the consumer sees a significant difference between her current state of affairs and some desired or ideal state. The consumer needs to solve a problem, which may be small or large, simple or complex. A woman whose 10-year-old Hyundai lives at the mechanic's shop has a problem, as does the man who thinks he'd have better luck getting dates if he traded his Hyundai for a new sports car. Brandon falls into the latter category—his old clunker runs okay, but he wants to sport some wheels that will get him admiring stares instead of laughs.

Do marketing decisions have a role in buyers' problem recognition? Although most problem recognition occurs spontaneously, marketers can develop creative advertising messages that stimulate consumers to recognize that their current state—that old car—just doesn't equal a shiny, new convertible. Figure 6.4 provides examples of marketing activities for problem recognition and the other stages of the consumer decision process.

problem recognition ■ The process that occurs whenever the consumer sees a significant difference between his or her current state of affairs and some desired or ideal state; this recognition initiates the decision-making process.

INFORMATION SEARCH

Once Brandon recognizes his car problem, he needs adequate information to resolve it. **Information search** is the part of the decision-making process in which the consumer checks his memory and surveys his environment to identify what options are out there that might solve his problem. Advertisements in newspapers, on TV, or even in the Yellow Pages of the telephone directory often provide valuable guidance during this step. Brandon might rely on television ads about different cars, recommendations from his friends, and additional research found in *Consumer Reports*, *Car & Driver*, or brochures from car dealerships.

Increasingly, consumers are using Internet search engines, portals, or "shopping bots" for information search. Search engines are sites such as AltaVista (www.altavista.com), Excite (www.excite.com), and WebCrawler (www.webcrawler.com) that find information on the Web by searching sites for keywords. As we saw in the case of Jennifer Dulski and Yahoo! Shopping, portals offer many Netizens a good place to enter the Web. They simplify searches because they organize information from a lot of separate Web sites according to common themes.

Some portals, such as Spanish-language YupiMSN.com, focus on specific customer segments. This unique portal makes it easy for readers to access Spanish-language Web sites that provide information on education, entertainment, sports, politics, music, and local and international news. Having recognized the enormous and rapidly growing Spanish-speaking market, Bill Gates's Microsoft empire acquired the once independent Yupi.com as part of its global expansion. And with the strength and prestige of Microsoft, YupiMSN.com has created a major link among all Spanish-speaking countries worldwide. For marketers, portals provide good

information search ■ The process whereby a consumer searches for appropriate information to make a reasonable decision.

FIGURE 6.4

Stage in the Decision Process	Marketing Strategy	Example
Problem Recognition	Encourage consumers to see that existing state does not equal desired state	TV commercials showing the excitement of owning a new car
Information Search	Provide information when and where consumers are likely to search	Targeted advertising on TV programs with high target market viewership
		Sales training that ensures knowledgeable salespeople
		Make new car brochures available in dealer showrooms
		Design exciting, easy to navigate, and informative Web sites
Evaluation of Alternatives	Understand the criteria consumers use in comparing brands and communicate own brand superiority	Conduct research to identify most important evaluative criteria
		Create advertising that includes reliable data on superiority of a brand (e.g., miles per gallon, safety, comfort)
Product Choice	Understand choice heuristics used by consumers and provide communication that encourages brand decision	Advertise "Made in America" (country of origin) Stress long history of the brand (brand loyalty)
Postpurchase Evaluation	Encourage accurate consumer expectations	Provide honest advertising and sales presentations

FIGURE 6.4

Marketers' Responses to Decision Process Stages

When they understand the stages of the consumer decision process, marketers can develop strategies to lead consumers to a choice that pleases both the consumer and the marketer.

opportunities to advertise because of the large amount of "hits" (visitors to the site) they get in return.

Robots, also called "shopbots" or "intelligent agents" are software programs used by some Web sites that find Internet retailers selling a particular product. The programs troll the Web for information, and then "report" it back to the host site. Some of these sites also provide information on competitors' prices, and they may even ask customers to rate the various retailers that they have listed on their site so consumers have recommendations of other consumers on which sellers are good and which are less than desirable. We should note, however, that some sites do not wish to compete on price and don't give bots access. Brandon might check with Autobytel.com, an auto shopbot, in his search for the best deal on a specific model car. And sites such as Autobytel often list prices the dealers pay for cars, which gives consumers unprecedented bargaining power when they make an offer to buy one. The role of marketers during the information search phase of the decision process is to make sure information about their brand is available when and where consumers look. Most automakers make sure information about their newest models is on the Web, is advertised frequently in magazines and TV, and, of course, is available in dealer showrooms.

EVALUATION OF ALTERNATIVES

Once Brandon starts identifying the alternatives, it's time to narrow them down and decide which are preferable. There are two components to this stage of the decision-making process. First, a consumer armed with information identifies the set of products in which he is interested. Then he narrows down his choices by deciding which of all the possibilities are feasible and by comparing the pros and cons of each remaining option.

Jeeves is more than just a pretty face. Advertising with Jeeves puts the power of the Web's #1 ranked search engine brand to work for you. That means you can reach your consumers when they are most receptive to your message.

Jeeves' allure reaches to properties beyond Ask.com. Ask Jeeves and its network extends targeted keyword ad impressions to over 40 premier search sites. One of the many reasons to fall in love with Jeeves.

To meet your sales goals, call 1 877 4 JEEVES or contact us at advertise@ask.com.

Ask Jeeves is a popular search engine for Web surfers.

Brandon has always wanted a red Ferrari, but after allowing himself to daydream for a few minutes, he returns to reality and reluctantly admits that an Italian sports car is probably not in the cards for him right now. As he looks around, he decides that the cars he likes in his price range are the Saturn coupe, Ford Focus, and Honda Civic. He's narrowed down his options by considering only affordable cars that come to mind or that his buddies suggest.

Now Brandon has to choose. It's time for him to look more systematically at each of the three possibilities and identify the important characteristics, or **evaluative criteria**, he will use to decide among them. The criteria may be power, comfort, the style of the car, or even safety. Keep in mind that marketers often play a role in educating consumers about *which* product characteristics they should use as evaluative criteria—usually, they will emphasize the dimensions in which their product excels. For example, ads for the Saturn might stress the peace of mind you get from driving a really safe car. To make sure customers like Brandon come to the "right" conclusions in their evaluation of the alternatives, marketers must understand what criteria consumers use and which are more and which are less important. With this information, salespeople and advertising can point out a brand's superiority on the most important criteria.

evaluative criteria ■ The dimensions used by consumers to compare competing product alternatives.

PRODUCT CHOICE

Now it's time to "put the pedal to the metal." Deciding on one product and acting on this choice is the next step in the decision-making process. Brandon has spent several weeks thinking about the alternatives, and he's finally ready to take the plunge and buy. After agonizing over his choice, he decides that even though the Civic and the Saturn have attractive qualities, the Focus's carefree image is just the way he wants others to think about him. All of this thinking about cars is "driving" him crazy, and he's relieved to make a decision to buy the Focus and get on with his life.

How to Decide? Rules of Thumb Choices such as Brandon's often are complicated because it's hard to juggle all of the product characteristics in your head. One car may offer better gas mileage, another is $2,000 cheaper, while another boasts a better safety record. How do we make sense of all these characteristics and arrive at a decision?

Consumers often rely on decision guidelines when weighing the claims that companies make. These **heuristics**, or rules, help simplify the decision-making process. One such heuristic

heuristics ■ A mental rule of thumb that leads to a speedy decision by simplifying the process.

is "price = quality," so many people willingly buy the more expensive brand because they assume that if it costs more, it *must* be better.

brand loyalty ■ A pattern of repeat product purchases, accompanied by an underlying positive attitude toward the brand, which is based on the belief that the brand makes products superior to its competition.

Perhaps the most common heuristic is **brand loyalty**, which assumes that people buy from the same company over and over because they believe that the company makes superior products. Consumers feel that it's not worth the effort to consider competing options. The creation of brand loyalty is a prized goal for marketers. People form preferences for a favorite brand and then may never change their minds in the course of a lifetime, making it extremely difficult for rivals to persuade them to switch. Kodak (www.kodak.com) is marketing its Kodak Max One-Time Use camera to "tweens," consumers aged 8 to 12. Kodak thinks that this age group will respond to the low-priced fun offered by the one-time use cameras. In addition to selling the camera, Kodak's major goal is to develop brand loyalty at an early age and be sure those "tweens" are still buying Kodaks when they're taking pictures of *their* kids.[2]

Still another heuristic is based on *country of origin*. We assume that a product has certain characteristics if it comes from a certain country. Our evaluations of cars are often strongly influenced by their countries of origin. Brandon assumed that the Japanese-made Honda would be a bit more reliable than the Ford or Saturn, so he factored that into his decision.

Sometimes a marketer wants to encourage a country association even when none exists. Consider, for example, the craze for high-tech Japanese toys made by companies such as Takara, Bandai, and Tomy. A company called C |biko Inc. hopes to cash in on this craze with its C |biko pocket organizer and wireless communicator that kids 10 to 14 years old love for its ability to send messages, play games, and download pictures of rock stars. Commercials plugging the product spout Japanese in the background. There's one small catch: The company is not Japanese, it's American. It has no Japanese partners, investors, or even an office in Japan. The president of the company admits, "The kids like the name. It sounds like something that they want to play—some high-tech gadget out of Asia."[3]

POSTPURCHASE EVALUATION

In the last stage of decision making, the consumer evaluates the quality of the decision he made. After mulling over the alternatives and picking one, now he evaluates just how good a choice it was. Everyone has experienced regret after making a purchase, and (hopefully) we have all been pleased with something we've bought. The evaluation of the product results in a level of **consumer satisfaction/dissatisfaction**, which is determined by the overall feelings, or attitude, a person has about a product after purchasing it. In this case, fortunately, Brandon's feelings couldn't be better as he cruises down the highway with tunes blaring and a smile on his face.

consumer satisfaction/ dissatisfaction (CS/D) ■ The overall feelings or attitude a person has about a product after purchasing it.

Just how do consumers decide if they're satisfied with their purchases? One answer would be, "That's easy. The product is either wonderful or it isn't." However, it's a little more complicated than that. When we buy a product, we have some expectations of product quality. How well a product or service meets or exceeds these expectations determines customer satisfaction. In other words, consumers assess product quality by comparing what they have bought to a performance standard created by a mixture of information from marketing communications, informal information sources such as friends and family, and their own experience with the product category. That's why it's very mportant that marketers create accurate expectations of their product in advertising and other communications.

So, even though Brandon's new Focus is not exactly as powerful as a Ferrari, he's still happy with the car because he never *really* expected a fun little car to eat up the highway like a high-performance sports car costing ten times as much. Brandon has "survived" the consumer decision-making process by recognizing a problem, conducting an information search to resolve it, identifying the (feasible) alternatives available, making a product choice, and then evaluating the quality of his decision. It was not easy to do, but when he's tooling down the road on a sunny day, somehow it all seems worth it.

Apart from understanding the mechanics of the consumer decision-making process, marketers also try to ascertain what influences in consumers' lives affect this process. There are three main categories: internal, situational, and social influences. In Brandon's case, for example, the evaluative criteria he used to compare cars and his feelings about each car were influenced by internal factors such as the connection he learned to make between a name like

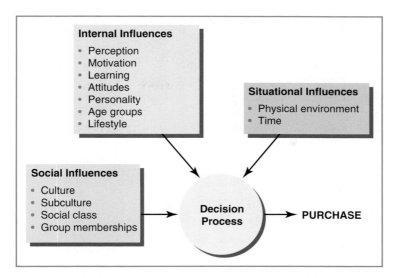

FIGURE 6.5

Influences on Consumer Decision Making

A number of different factors in consumers' lives influence the consumer decision-making process. Marketers need to understand these influences and which ones are important in the purchase process to make effective marketing decisions.

2 Bookmark It!

Locate a friend who has recently purchased an auto or another high-involvement product. Ask her to detail the steps she went through in making the decision. List these activities according to the steps in the consumer decision-making process.

Saturn and an image of "slightly hip yet safe and solid," situational factors such as the way he was treated by the Honda salesperson, and social influences such as his prediction that his friends would be impressed when they saw him cruising down the road in his new wheels. Figure 6.5 shows the influences in the decision-making process and emphasizes that all of these factors work together to affect the ultimate choice each person makes. Let's consider how each of these three types of influences work, starting with internal factors.

Internal Influences on Consumer Decisions

People associate the textures of fabrics and other surfaces with product qualities, and some marketers are exploring how touch can be used in packaging to arouse consumer interest. Some new plastic containers for household beauty items incorporate "soft touch" resins that provide a soft, friction-like resistance when held. Focus group members who tested one such package for Clairol's new Daily Defense shampoo described the sensations as "almost sexy" and were actually reluctant to let go of the containers![4] That's a powerful impact for a piece of plastic. Let's see how internal factors relating to the way people absorb and interpret information influence the decision-making process.

PERCEPTION

Perception is the process by which people select, organize, and interpret information from the outside world. We receive information in the form of sensations, the immediate response of our sensory receptors—eyes, ears, nose, mouth, and fingers—to such basic stimuli as light, color, and sound. Our impressions about products often are based on their physical qualities. We try to make sense of the sensations we receive by interpreting them in light of our past experiences. For example, Brandon chose the color red for his new car because he associated this color with excitement and adventure.

Consumers are bombarded with information on products—thousands of ads, in-store displays, special offers, opinions of their friends, and on and on. The perception process has implications for marketers because, as consumers absorb and make sense of the vast quantities of information competing for their attention, the odds are that any single message will get lost in the clutter. And, if they do notice it, there's no guarantee that the meaning they give it will be quite the same one the marketer intended. The issues that marketers need to understand during this process include exposure, perceptual selection, and interpretation.

- *Exposure*: The stimulus must be within range of people's sensory receptors to be noticed. For example, the lettering on a highway billboard must be big enough for a passing motorist to read easily or the message will be lost. Many people believe that

perception ■ The process by which people select, organize, and interpret information from the outside world.

Critics of subliminal perception claim that hidden messages lurk in ice cubes and elsewhere. This Pepsi ad borrows from that idea.

even messages they *can't* see will persuade them to buy advertised products. Claims about subliminal advertising of messages hidden in ice cubes (among other places) have been surfacing since the 1950s. A survey of American consumers found that almost two-thirds believe in the existence of subliminal advertising, and over one-half are convinced that this technique can get them to buy things they do not really want![5] The Disney Corporation is one of the most recent victims of concerns about subliminal messages. The company recalled 3.4 million copies of its animated video *The Rescuers* because the film included a very brief image of a topless woman. (She appeared in two frames of a 110,000-frame film, each for 1/30th of a second.) This picture was embedded as a prank in the master negative way back in 1977 but "the naked truth" surfaced only recently.[6] Despite an occasional joke like this, there is very little evidence to support the argument that this technique actually has any effect at all on our perceptions of products.

- *Perceptual Selection*: Consumers choose to pay attention to some stimuli but not to others. Consumers are more likely to be aware of messages that speak to their current needs. A newspaper ad for a fast-food restaurant that would go unnoticed after lunch may grab your attention if you sneak a glance at the paper during a class that ends at lunchtime.
- *Interpretation*: Consumers assign meaning to the stimulus. This meaning is influenced by prior associations they have learned and assumptions they make. Extra Strength Maalox Whip Antacid flopped, even though a spray can is a pretty effective way to deliver this kind of tummy ache relief. But to consumers aerosol whips mean dessert toppings, not medication.[7] If we don't interpret the product the way it was intended due to prior experiences, the best marketing ideas will be "waisted."

MOTIVATION

Motivation is an internal state that drives us to satisfy needs. Once we activate a need, a state of tension exists that drives the consumer toward some goal that will reduce this tension by eliminating the need.

For example, think about Brandon and his old car. Brandon began to experience a gap between his present state (owning an old, unimpressive car) and a desired state (having a car that gets him noticed and is fun to drive). The need for a new car is activated, which motivates Brandon to test different models, to talk with friends about different makes, and finally to buy a new car.

Psychologist Abraham Maslow developed an influential approach to motivation.[8] He formulated a **hierarchy of needs** that categorizes motives according to five levels of importance, the more basic needs being on the bottom of the hierarchy and the higher needs at the top. The hierarchy suggests that before a person can meet needs in a given level, she must first meet the lower level's needs. As illustrated in Figure 6.6, people start at the lowest level with basic needs for food, clothing, and shelter and then progress to higher levels to satisfy more complex needs, such as the need to be accepted by others or to feel good about themselves. Ultimately, people can reach the highest-level needs, and they will be motivated to attain such goals as spiritual fulfillment. As the figure shows, if marketers understand the level of needs relevant to consumers in their target market, they can tailor their products and messages to them.

LEARNING

Learning is a change in behavior caused by information or experience. Learning about products can occur deliberately, as when we set out to gather information about different CD players before buying one brand. We also learn even when we are not trying. Consumers recognize many brand names and can hum many product jingles, for example, even for products they themselves do not use. Psychologists who study learning have advanced several theories to explain the learning process, and these perspectives are important because a major goal for marketers is to "teach" consumers to prefer their products. In this section, we'll briefly review the most important perspectives on how people learn.

Behavioral Learning **Behavioral learning theories** assume that learning takes place as the result of connections that form between events that we perceive. In one type of behavioral

motivation ■ An internal state that drives us to satisfy needs by activating goal-oriented behavior.

hierarchy of needs ■ An approach that categorizes motives according to five levels of importance, the more basic needs being on the bottom of the hierarchy and the higher needs at the top.

learning ■ A relatively permanent change in behavior caused by acquired information or experience.

behavioral learning theories ■ Theories of learning that focus on how consumer behavior is changed by external events or stimuli.

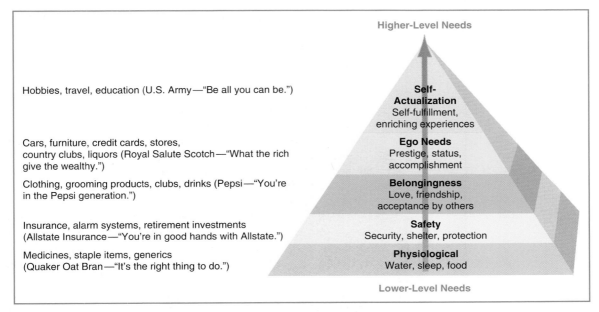

Higher-Level Needs

Hobbies, travel, education (U.S. Army—"Be all you can be.")

Self-Actualization
Self-fulfillment, enriching experiences

Cars, furniture, credit cards, stores, country clubs, liquors (Royal Salute Scotch—"What the rich give the wealthy.")

Ego Needs
Prestige, status, accomplishment

Clothing, grooming products, clubs, drinks (Pepsi—"You're in the Pepsi generation.")

Belongingness
Love, friendship, acceptance by others

Insurance, alarm systems, retirement investments (Allstate Insurance—"You're in good hands with Allstate.")

Safety
Security, shelter, protection

Medicines, staple items, generics (Quaker Oat Bran—"It's the right thing to do.")

Physiological
Water, sleep, food

Lower-Level Needs

FIGURE 6.6

Maslow's Hierarchy of Needs and Related Products
Abraham Maslow proposed a hierarchy of needs that categorizes motives. Savvy marketers know they need to understand the level of needs that motivates a consumer to buy a particular product or brand.

learning, **classical conditioning**, a person perceives two stimuli at about the same time. After a while, the person transfers his response from one stimulus to the other. For example, an ad shows a product and a breathtakingly beautiful scene, so (the marketer hopes) you will transfer the positive feelings you get from looking at the scene to the advertised product. Another common form of behavioral learning is called **operant conditioning**, which occurs when people learn that their actions result in rewards or punishments. This feedback influences how they will respond in similar situations in the future. Just as a rat in a maze learns the route to a piece of cheese, consumers who receive a reward, such as a prize in the bottom of a box of cereal, will be more likely to buy that brand again. That feedback acts as a reinforcement for the behavior.

These learned associations in classical and operant conditioning also have a tendency to transfer to other similar things in a process called **stimulus generalization**. This means that the good or bad feelings associated with a product will "rub off" on other products that resemble it. For example, some marketers create *product line extensions* in which new products share the name of an established brand so that people's good feelings about the current product will transfer to the new one. Dole (www.dole.com), which is associated with fruit, was able to introduce refrigerated juices and juice bars, while Sun Maid (www.sunmaid.com) branched out from raisins to raisin bread.

Cognitive Learning   In contrast to behavioral theories of learning, **cognitive learning theory** views people as problem solvers who do more than passively react to associations between stimuli. Supporters of this viewpoint stress the role of creativity and insight during the learning process. Cognitive learning cocurs when consumers make a connection between ideas or by observing things in their environment. *Observational learning* occurs when people watch the actions of others and note what happens to them as a result. They store these observations in memory and at some later point use the information to guide their own behavior, especially when they admire or identify with these people in some way. Many promotional strategies center around endorsements by athletes, movie stars, and music idols whose fans have observed their successes.

Now we've discussed how the three internal processes of perception, motivation, and learning influence how consumers absorb and interpret information. But the results of these

Observational learning means
we learn by observing the
behavior or the experiences of
others. In this ad, a guitar
company wants to encourage
observational learning by
associating the Alvarez guitar
with singer Ani DiFranco.

processes—the interpretation the consumer gives to a marketing message—differ depending on unique consumer characteristics. We'll talk next about some of these characteristics: existing consumer attitudes, the personality of the consumer, and consumer age groups.

ATTITUDES

An **attitude** is a lasting evaluation of a person, object, or issue.[9] Consumers have attitudes toward brands, such as whether McDonald's or Wendy's has the best hamburgers, as well as toward more general consumption-related behaviors, for example, whether high-fat foods including hamburgers are a no-no in a healthy diet.

A person's attitude has three components: affect, cognition, and behavior. In a marketing context, *affect*, the feeling component of attitudes, refers to the overall feeling a person has about a product. You, like Brandon, may simply like the Ferrari. *Cognition*, the knowing component, is the beliefs and knowledge the person has about the product. You may believe that a Mercedes is built better than most cars or that a Volvo is very safe. *Behavior*, the doing component, is what happens when the person takes action by deciding to buy or use the product.

Depending on the nature of the product, one of these three components—feeling, knowing, or doing—will be the dominant influence in creating an attitude toward a product. Affect is usually dominant for expressive products such as perfume, in which the way the product makes us feel determines our attitude toward it. Cognition is more important for complex products, such as computer systems, that require us to process technical information. Behavior often determines attitudes for commonly purchased, low-involvement items such as chewing gum, for which we often form an attitude based simply on how the product tastes or performs.

PERSONALITY

Personality is the set of unique psychological characteristics that consistently influences the way a person responds to situations in the environment. One adventure-seeking consumer may always be on the lookout for new experiences and cutting-edge products, while another is happiest in familiar surroundings, using the same brands over and over. As we noted in Chapter 4, a research firm estimates that 12 percent of American adults are thrill seekers who like to break the rules and who are strongly attracted to extreme sports such as sky surfing or bungee jumping. This information led Isuzu to position its Rodeo sport-utility vehicle as a car that lets a driver break the rules. Advertising for the Rodeo showed kids jumping in mud puddles, running with scissors, and coloring out of the lines.[10]

For marketers, differences in personality traits such as thrill seeking underscore the potential value of considering personality when crafting marketing strategies. Some specific personality traits relevant to marketing strategies include innovativeness, self-confidence, and sociability.

- *Innovativeness*: The degree to which a person likes to try new things. Cutting-edge products such as radical new hairstyles and fashions might appeal to an innovative woman.
- *Self-confidence*: The degree to which a person has a positive evaluation of her abilities, including the ability to make good product decisions. People who don't have much self-confidence are good candidates for services such as image consultants, who assist in making the right choices.
- *Sociability*: The degree to which a person enjoys social interaction. A sociable person might, for example, respond to entertainment-related products that claim to bring people together or make parties more fun.

The Self: Are You What You Buy?   The notion that consumers buy products that are extensions of their personality traits makes sense. Marketers try to create *brand personalities* that will appeal to different types of consumers. For example, consider the different "personalities" invented by fragrance marketers: A brand with a "wholesome, girl-next-door" image such as White Linen would be hard to confuse with the sultry, exotic personality radiated by Obsession, or the sophisticated image of Chanel No. 5.

A person's **self-concept** is his attitude toward the self. The self-concept is composed of a mixture of beliefs about one's abilities and observations of one's own behavior and feelings

attitude ■ A learned predisposition to respond favorably or unfavorably to stimuli based on relatively enduring evaluations of people, objects, and issues.

personality ■ The psychological characteristics that consistently influence the way a person responds to situations in his or her environment.

self-concept ■ An individual's self-image that is composed of a mixture of beliefs, observations, and feelings about personal attributes.

(usually both positive and negative) about one's personal attributes such as body type or facial features. The extent to which a person's self-concept is positive or negative can influence the products he buys and even the extent to which a person fantasizes about changing his life.

Kenra (www.kenra.com), a marketer of hair and grooming products, recognized that many African American women have developed a poor self-concept because society tells them that only straight hair is beautiful.[11] A Kenra ad campaign said to these women, "All your life, you've been told there's one kind of beautiful. And you're not it. Haven't we fought too hard for freedom to become slaves to fashion? Wear your hair any way you want."

On the more positive side, *self-esteem advertising* attempts to stimulate positive feelings about the self.[12] This technique is used in ads for Clairol ("You're not getting older, you're getting better"), Budweiser ("For all you do, this Bud's for you"), McDonald's ("You deserve a break today"), and L'Oréal ("Because I'm worth it").

AGE GROUPS

A person's age is another internal influence on purchasing behavior. Many of us feel we have more in common with those of our own age because we share a common set of experiences and memories about cultural events, whether these involve World War II or the 2001 World Trade Center attack.

Indeed, marketers of products from cookies to cars are banking on nostalgia to draw in customers, as people are attracted to products and services that remind them of past experiences. One trend is vacations that allow middle-aged men to relive the madness of spring break from their college days (their wives think they're away on a golf outing). Myrtle Beach, South Carolina, boasts about a dozen bars that cater to aging party animals. They offer bikini contests, 75-cent draft beer, and hairy-chest competitions.[13] Warning: Do not attempt this at home.

Products and services often appeal to a specific age group. Although there are exceptions, it is safe to assume that most buyers of Lil' Kim's CDs are younger than those who buy Frank Sinatra discs. Many marketing strategies appeal to the needs of such different age groups as children, teenagers, the middle-aged, and the elderly. As we age, our needs change. The young adult who spends a lot of time in bars, clothing stores, or perhaps backpacking across Europe grows into the newlywed who must focus on setting up house—and perhaps anticipating the time when a baby's diapers and toys will fill it up.

Young people are among the most enthusiastic users of the Internet. According to one study, 62 percent of teenagers say they log on from home for 4.2 hours a week while 46 percent spend 2.3 hours a week using a computer outside the home.[14] For many teenagers, this activity has replaced "old-fashioned fun" such as watching the tube or hanging out at the mall. Teens spend over $1 billion online each year, so many firms are working hard to develop Web sites that will capture their interest. Iturf.com, a network of Web sites for teenagers, has the largest traffic numbers among teen-oriented sites. A subsidiary of Delia's (the catalog company that sells youth-oriented fashions), the site logs more than 1.5 million visitors per month.[15] What do teens do online? As shown in Table 6.1, approximately three

		Percentage of Teens Reporting Participation in Activity	
TABLE 6.1	*Activity*	*Male*	*Female*
Research	71	78
Send/receive e-mail	59	68
Download	58	40
Browse	57	42
Chat	41	49
Play games	32	27
Check out stuff to buy	28	20
Buy stuff	14	9

TABLE 6.1

What Teens Do Online

Percentages of Teens Reporting Various Online Activities.

Source: Jennifer Gilbert, "New Teen Obsession," *Advertising Age*, February 14, 2000, 38.

out of four do research and nearly two out of three use it for e-mail, while far fewer use the Internet for finding or buying products. For marketers, this means that the Internet may be a great way to get information about their goods and services to teens but not so good for sales.

And so the process goes until we reach old age, at which time our priorities may shift from saving for our kids' college educations to buying a retirement home in Florida. Indeed, our purchase preferences depend on our current position in the **family life cycle**—the stages through which family members pass as they grow older. Dramatic cultural changes affecting people's living arrangements have forced marketers to change their concept of the traditional family life cycle. Marketers try to take into account such alternative lifestyles as single-parent families, childless couples, and homosexual relationships in their marketing strategies.

One consumer trend among younger couples is the desire to settle into more sedate home environments, as the lifestyle changes caused by divorce, technology, and so on are leading many to yearn for tradition and stability. For some couples intimate dinner parties are replacing dance clubs as a favored activity. As one 26-year-old writer observed, "Nesting means you get to trade a crazy public space for a place where you can define who you are." Marketers such as Williams-Sonoma are revising their product lines to appeal to younger homebodies. The cooking store offers cookbooks on CD-ROMs and coffee makers in young, lively colors.[16]

LIFESTYLES

The final influence on consumer decisions that we will discuss is lifestyles. A **lifestyle** is a pattern of living that determines how people choose to spend their time, money, and energy and that reflects their values, tastes, and preferences. Lifestyles are expressed in a person's preferences for activities such as sports, interests such as music, and opinions on politics and religion. Marketers often develop marketing strategies that recognize that people can be grouped into common market segments based on similarities in lifestyle preferences.[17]

No one knows this better than American's most famous homemaker, Martha Stewart. Her empire, built on the perfect homemaker image, includes magazines (*Martha Stewart Living* and *Martha Stewart Weddings*) books, network TV, cable TV, and Martha Stewart.com.[18] Many women respond to the Martha Stewart brand personality by buying products that help them to be better homemakers. So, consumers often choose goods, services, and activities that are associated with a certain lifestyle. For example, our friend Brandon may drive a Ford Focus, hang out in Internet cafes, and go extreme skiing during spring break because he views these choices as part of a cool college student lifestyle.

If lifestyles are so important, how do marketers identify them so that they can reach consumers who share preferences for products they associate with a certain lifestyle? Demographic characteristics, such as age and income, tell marketers *what* products people buy, but they don't reveal *why*. Two consumers can share the same demographic characteristics yet be different people—all 20-year-old, male college students are hardly identical to one another!

To breathe life into demographic analyses, marketers turn to **psychographics**, which groups consumers according to psychological and behavioral similarities. One way to do this is to describe people in terms of their activities, interests, and opinions (known as AIOs). These AIOs are based on preferences for vacation destinations, club memberships, hobbies, political and social attitudes, tastes in food and fashion, and so on. Using data from large samples, marketers create profiles of customers who resemble each other in terms of their activities and patterns of product use.[19]

For example, marketers at the beginning of the walking shoe craze assumed that all recreational walkers were just burned-out joggers. Subsequent psychographic research that examined the AIOs of these walkers showed that there were actually several psychographic segments within the larger group who engaged in the activity for very different reasons, including walking for fun, walking to save money, and walking for exercise. This research resulted in the creation of walking shoes aimed at different segments, from Footjoy Walkers to Nike Healthwalkers.

family life cycle ■ A means of characterizing consumers within a family structure based on different stages through which people pass as they grow older.

lifestyle ■ The pattern of living that determines how people choose to spend their time, money, and energy and that reflects their values, tastes, and preferences.

psychographics ■ The use of psychological, sociological, and anthropological factors to construct market segments.

3 Bookmark It!

Suppose you want to market products to college students and need to study their lifestyle. Make a list of products that have fit in well with the "college" lifestyle and products that haven't. Note why you think the products either succeeded or failed. Now, think of a new product that would be successful with the college market. Create a slogan for it, too.

3 Bookmark It!

Some consumers think that the perfect vacation means backpacking deep into a wilderness area. Others want to spend their holiday by the pool in a fancy island resort. What psychographic differences do you think there might be between these two types of consumers?

Situational Influences on Consumer Decisions

We've seen that internal factors such as how people perceive marketing messages, their motivation to acquire products, and their unique personalities influence the decisions they make. In addition, when, where, and how consumers shop—what we call situational influences—shape their purchase choices. Situational cues include our physical surroundings, time pressures, and the people who are in our surroundings at the point of purchase. That's why some clubs hire bouncers to admit only the "cool" people! Marketers know that dimensions of the physical environment, including such factors as décor, smells, and even temperature, can significantly influence consumption. If you don't believe this, consider that one study found that pumping certain odors into a Las Vegas casino actually increased the amount of money patrons fed into slot machines.[20]

THE PHYSICAL ENVIRONMENT

It's no secret that people's moods and behaviors are strongly influenced by their physical surroundings. Despite all their efforts to presell consumers through advertising, marketers know that the store environment influences many purchases. For example, consumers decide on about two out of every three of their supermarket product purchases in the aisles (so always eat *before* you go to the supermarket). The messages they receive at the time and their feelings about being in the store influence their decisions.[21]

Two dimensions, arousal and pleasure, determine if a shopper will react positively or negatively to a store environment. In other words, the person's surroundings can be either dull or exciting (arousing) and either pleasant or unpleasant. Just because the environment is arousing

Physical surroundings in a shopping environment provide important cues that influence purchase choices. Dramatic point-of-purchase displays often influence people's buying decisions in the store.

doesn't necessarily mean it will be pleasant—we've all been in crowded, hot stores that are anything but pleasant! Maintaining an upbeat feeling in a pleasant context is one factor behind the success of theme parks such as Disney World, which tries to provide consistent doses of carefully calculated stimulation to visitors.[22]

The importance of these surroundings explains why many retailers focus on packing as much entertainment as possible into their stores. (1) Vans Inc., a Los Angeles–based sporting goods retailer, opened a huge skate park and off-road bicycle track at the Ontario Mills Mall in California. As one enthusiastic teenager observed, "All malls should have this. They kick us out of every place else to skate—they might as well make it legal." (2) Bass Pro Shops, a chain of outdoor sports equipment stores, features giant aquariums, waterfalls, trout ponds, archery and rifle ranges, putting greens, and free classes in everything from ice fishing to conservation.[23] (3) The Easy Everything cafe in London welcomes about 5,000 people every day, including Europe-crossing backpackers who can check their e-mail on the cafe's computers. This cyber-hangout, like others around the world, is trying to increase traffic with computer game competitions, training seminars, and wine tastings. Some of the cafes even feature live stock exchange feeds to attract a day trader clientele.[24] Whether entertainment, e-mail, or information, providing surroundings that consumers want increases sales.

In-store displays are a marketing communication tool that attracts attention. Although most displays consist of simple racks that dispense the product or related coupons, some marketers have used elaborate performances and scenery such as these:[25]

- *Timex*: A still-ticking watch sitting in the bottom of a filled aquarium.
- *Kellogg's Corn Flakes*: A button with a picture of Cornelius the Rooster placed within the reach of children near Corn Flakes. When a child presses the button, he hears the rooster cock-a-doodle-do.
- *Elizabeth Arden*: The company introduced "Elizabeth," a computer and video makeover system that allows customers to test out their images with different shades of makeup, without having to actually apply the products first.

Advertisers also are being more aggressive about hitting consumers with their messages, wherever they may be. *Place-based media* is a growing way to target consumers in nontraditional places. These days messages can pop up in airports, doctors' offices, college campuses, and health clubs. Turner Broadcasting System began a number of place-based media ventures such as Checkout Channel for grocery stores and Airport Channel, and it even tested McDTV for McDonald's restaurants.[26] Although the Checkout Channel and McDTV didn't make it, the Airport

As consumers are exposed to more and more advertising, advertisers must work harder than ever to get their attention. Place-based media, in this case, a message strategically put on a bathroom wall, offers a way to reach consumers when they are a "captive audience."

4 Bookmark It!

You are the marketing consultant for a new bank. What recommendations for the interior design of the bank would you make if the target market is senior citizens? If the target market is young adults?

Channel entertains bored passengers in many locales. A company called Privy Promotions even sells ad space on restroom walls in stadiums. According to the company's president, "It's a decided opportunity for an advertiser to reach a captive audience."[27] Guess so . . .

TIME

In addition to the physical environment, another situational factor is time. Marketers know that the time of day, the season of the year, and how much time one has to make a purchase affect decision making. Time is one of consumers' most limited resources. We talk about "making time" or "spending time," and Americans are frequently reminded that "time is money."

Indeed, many consumers believe they are more pressed for time than ever before.[28] This sense of *time poverty* makes consumers responsive to marketing innovations that allow them to save time, including such services as one-hour photo processing, drive-through lanes at fast-food restaurants, and ordering products on the World Wide Web.[29] CDNow (www.cdnow.com), for example, sells music over the Web only. The company has been successful because consumers can go to CDNow's Web page, browse through thousands of titles, listen to selections, and order and pay for them—all without setting foot inside a store. This saves the customer time, plus the "store" is always open.

Social Influences on Consumer Decisions

Our discussion of consumer behavior so far has focused on factors that influence us as individuals, such as the way we learn about products. Although we are all individuals, we are also members of many groups that influence our buying decisions. Families, friends, and classmates often influence our decisions, as do larger groups with which we identify, such as ethnic groups and political parties. Now let's consider how social influences such as culture, social class, and influential friends and acquaintances affect the consumer decision-making process.

CULTURE

Think of **culture** as a society's personality. It is the values, beliefs, customs, and tastes produced or valued by a group of people. A consumer's culture influences his buying decisions. For example, cultures have their own *rituals*, such as weddings and funerals, which have specific activities and products associated with them. Although it may be customary for a funeral to be somber and reflective in most parts of the United States, in New Orleans the deceased is given a grand farewell, complete with a gravesite jazz band. As we saw in Chapter 4, very often these cultural expectations are so deeply ingrained that we don't realize how much they affect our consumer behavior.

As we also saw in Chapter 4, cultural values are deeply held beliefs about right and wrong ways to live.[30] For example, one culture might feel that being a unique individual is preferable to subordinating one's identity to a group, while another culture may instead emphasize the importance of the group over individuality. American cultural values include freedom, youthfulness, achievement, materialism, and activity. That's not so say, however, that values can't change. A recent study showed that both baby boomer women (born between 1946 and 1964) and Generation X men (born between 1965 and 1976) and Generation Y men (born after 1976) are more likely to seek balance than to seek only material success[31] (see Table 6.2).

Marketers who understand a culture's values can tailor their product offerings accordingly. For example, cigarette brands Salem Pianissimo and Virginia Slims One, which emit less smoke than other brands, flopped in the United States yet sell well in Japan. Why? Because the Japanese culture values the welfare of others more than it values individual pleasure. The cigarettes that emit less smoke will not offend others, especially nonsmokers, so the Japanese prefer to buy them. An industry executive observed, "Japanese are much more concerned about people around them. If you develop a product which helps them address these concerns, then you have a good chance of developing a hit product."[32]

SUBCULTURES

A **subculture** is a group coexisting with other groups in a larger culture whose members share a distinctive set of beliefs or characteristics. Each of us belongs to many subcultures. These subcultures could be religious groups, ethnic groups, or regional groups, as well as those that form around music groups such as the Dave Matthews Band, media creations such as Trekkers (*Star Trek* fans), or leisure activities such as raves or extreme sports. The hip-hop subculture has had enormous influence as many marketers relied on young trendsetters to help decide what brands were *off the hook* (good) and which were *wack* (bad). Sprite took on a hip-hop persona and went from seventh to fourth among the industry's top brands. The drink's brand manager noted, "Hip-hop epitomizes self-expression, which is the mantra of Sprite."[33]

For marketers, some of the most important subcultures are racial and ethnic groups because many consumers identify strongly with their heritage and are influenced by products that appeal to this aspect of their identities. Some racial differences in consumption preferences can be subtle but important. When Coffee-Mate discovered that African Americans are more

culture ■ The values, beliefs, customs, and tastes valued by a group of people.

subculture ■ A group within a society whose members share a distinctive set of beliefs, characteristics, or common experiences.

TABLE 6.2

Ideas of Success Among Different Consumer Groups

Baby boomer women (born 1946–1964) define success:
  "Home life and being with friends and family are of the utmost importance. Work is just a monetary thing."
  "I'm starting to demand a certain quality of relationships."
  "More responsibility gives us more stress, and there's more confusion when we have more choices."
  "I don't think about work as much as I used to. I just think about having more fun."

Generation X men (born 1965–1976) and Generation Y men (born after 1976) define success:
  "The main goal is being at peace with myself. People come in and out of your life, but if you're at peace with yourself, that's the most important thing."
  "I want to make sure that I have a job I enjoy, a personal life, and the opportunity to enjoy things outside of work. I want to have a mix of everything."
  "The most important thing in my whole life, even if I don't become successful, is to be happy."

Source: Adapted from Becky Ebenkamp, "Chicks, Checks and Balances," *Brandweek* (12 February 2001): 16.

Joseph Burriss, Student, Clemson University

I would choose option 2. At a time when the pressure is on fourth quarter sales and the marketing budget is somewhat restricted, it makes sense for Yahoo! to run the editorial section. Any confident company would jump at the chance to reach 23.5 million households while at the same time appearing unbiased and trustworthy. Listing competitors is risky, but it gives people a chance to experience the major shopping portals and ultimately decide which is best.

Judy F. Graham, Marketing Professor, St. John Fisher College

I would choose Option 2. Consumers are so skeptical of advertising messages, especially the young, sophisticated, and demanding online shopper—*Yahoo! Shopping*'s target market. Editorial content is likely to be more positively received by this group. In addition, consumers establish and maintain a relationship with a specific portal based on its ability to organize and simplify information on the Web. Choosing to run this editorial section affords *Yahoo!* tremendous exposure on a limited budget, and establishes *Yahoo!*'s prominence as a trustworthy and expert source for online shopping.

Melissa Fisher, VP, Marketing & Communications Val-Pak DMS, Inc.

Option 2. Putting Yahoo in a newspaper editorial lends credibility to positioning its site as a consumer reference portal. By controlling the editorial content flow and design enables Yahoo to control the weighted media exposure of key merchant URLs and it's competition's relative exposure. Clearly, major competitors such as AOL, MSN & Lycos are already well known by the on-line buying audience and will be heavily advertising in USA Weekend separately regardless of Yahoo having it's own pull-out section. The added teaching ability created by having the pull-out section be "trusted" editorial may garner added support of loyal users while spurring trial and conversion during the holiday shopping season of soft supporters.

Weigh in with your thoughts! Visit the Live Laboratory at www.prenhall.com/solomon **for extended Other Voices replies, exercises, and more.**

likely than other ethnic groups to drink their coffee with sugar and cream, the company mounted a promotional blitz using black media and in return benefited from double-digit increases in sales volume and market share within this segment.[34]

SOCIAL CLASS

social class ■ The overall rank or social standing of groups of people within a society according to the value assigned to such factors as family background, education, occupation, and income.

Social class is the overall rank of people in a society. People who are within the same class work in similar occupations, have similar income levels, and usually share common tastes in clothing, decorating styles, and leisure activities. These people also share many political and religious beliefs, as well as ideas regarding valued activities and goals.

Many products and stores are designed to appeal to people in a specific social class.[35] Working-class consumers tend to evaluate products in more utilitarian terms such as sturdiness or comfort rather than style or fashionability. They are less likely to experiment with new products or styles, such as modern furniture or colored appliances, because they tend to prefer predictability to novelty.[36] Marketers need to understand these differences and develop product and communication strategies that appeal to the different groups.

Luxury goods often serve as status symbols, visible markers that provide a way for people to flaunt their membership in higher social classes (or at least to make others believe they do). The desire to accumulate these "badges of achievement" is evident in the popular bumper sticker "He who dies with the most toys wins." However, it's important to note that over time the importance of different status symbols rises and falls. For example, many people got turned off to materialistic things following the terrorist attacks of September 11, 2001, and instead started to emphasize such priorities as family time. For some people, activities such as volunteering in the community replaced traditional goods as status symbols.

GROUP BEHAVIOR

Most of us enjoy belonging to groups, and we may even derive comfort from knowing what others are thinking or doing as we try to make up our own minds. Anyone who's ever "gone along with the crowd" knows that people act differently in groups than they do on their own. There are several reasons for this phenomenon. With more people in a group, it becomes less likely that any one member will be singled out for attention and normal restraints on behavior may be reduced (think about the last party you attended). Decisions that groups make differ from those each individual would make. In many cases, group members show a greater willingness to consider riskier alternatives following group discussion than they would if each member made the decision with no discussion.[37]

Even shopping behavior changes when people do it in groups. For example, people who shop with at least one other person tend to make more unplanned purchases, buy more, and cover more areas of a store than those who go alone.[38] Group members may be convinced to buy something to gain the approval of the others, or they may simply be exposed to more products and stores by pooling information with the group. For these reasons, retailers are well advised to encourage group shopping activities.

REFERENCE GROUPS

A **reference group** is a set of people a consumer wants to please or imitate. Unlike a larger culture, the "group" can be composed of one person, such as your spouse, or someone you've never met, such as a statesman like Martin Luther King, a singer like Shaggy, or a suave and sophisticated man of the world like (fictional) movie hero Austin Powers. The group can be small, such as your immediate family, or it could be a large organization, such as People for the Ethical Treatment of Animals.

Conformity   Consumers often change their behavior to gain acceptance into a particular reference group. **Conformity** is at work when a person changes as a reaction to real or imagined group pressure. For example, a male student getting dressed to go to a fraternity rush may choose to wear clothing similar to what he knows the brothers will be wearing so he's accepted by the group.

Home shopping parties, as epitomized by the Tupperware party, capitalize on group pressures to boost sales. A company representative makes a sales presentation to a group of people who have gathered in the home of a friend or acquaintance. Participants model the behavior of others who can provide them with information about how to use certain products, especially because the home party is likely to be attended by a relatively homogeneous group (for example, neighborhood homemakers). Pressures to conform may be particularly intense and may escalate as more and more group members begin to "cave in" (this process is sometimes termed the *bandwagon effect*). Even though Tupperware has moved into new sales venues including a Web site (www.tupperware.com), Home Shopping Network, and mall kiosks, it hopes the venerable shopping party remains a popular means of generating sales.[39]

Sex Roles   Some of the strongest pressures to conform come from our **sex roles**, society's expectations regarding the appropriate attitudes, behaviors, and appearance for men and women. These assumptions about the proper roles of men and women, flattering or not, are deeply ingrained in marketing communications.[40] For example, men are far less likely than women to see a doctor regularly and 25 percent say they would delay seeking help as long as possible. Experts suggest that this may be because boys playing sports are taught to "ignore pain and not ask for help."[41]

Many products take on masculine or feminine attributes, and consumers often associate them with one gender or another.[42] For example, many women downplay their femininity at work by wearing masculine clothing such as pants suits. These women feel that feminine dress

5 *Bookmark It!*

Culture continues to change. What values, beliefs, and customs of your culture do you see changing? How are these changes affecting marketing? Make a list of products (don't forget about services) that might be hits because they're linked to an emerging value in your culture.

reference group ■ An actual or imaginary individual or group that has a significant effect on an individual's evaluations, aspirations, or behavior.

conformity ■ A change in beliefs or actions as a reaction to real or imagined group pressure.

sex roles ■ Society's expectations regarding the appropriate attitudes, behaviors, and appearance for men and women.

in the workplace hurts their chances of being promoted—that the corporate world still rewards men more than women. Pants suits, in this case, take on a masculine attribute.

Marketers play a part in teaching us how society expects us to act as men and women. As consumers we see women and men portrayed differently in marketing communcations and in products promoted to the two groups. And these influences "teach" us what the "proper" role of women or men is and, in addition, which products are appropriate for each gender. Some of these "sex role" products have come under fire from social groups. For example, the Barbie doll has been criticized for reinforcing unrealistic ideas about what women's bodies should look like even though a newer version of the doll isn't quite as skinny and buxom. Other Barbie protests erupted when Mattel introduced a shopping-themed Barbie doll called Cool Shoppin' Barbie. The doll comes with all the equipment kids need to pretend Barbie is shopping— including a Barbie-sized MasterCard. When the card is pressed into the card scanner, her voice says "credit approved!" Although Mattel includes a warning about sticking to a budget, some critics fear the doll sends the wrong message to girls about the desirability of shopping.[43]

Opinion Leaders   If, like Brandon, you are in the market for a new automobile, is there someone you know you would seek out for advice? Some individuals are particularly likely to influence others' product decisions. An **opinion leader** is a person who influences others' attitudes or behaviors because others perceive her as possessing expertise about the product.[44] Opinion leaders usually exhibit high levels of interest in the product category and may continuously update their knowledge by reading, talking with salespeople, and so on.

Because of this involvement, opinion leaders are valuable information sources and, unlike commercial endorsers who are paid to represent the interests of just one company, they have no "axe to grind and can impart *both* positive and negative information about the product." In addition, opinion leaders often are among the first to buy new products, so they absorb much of the risk, reducing uncertainty for others who are not as courageous.

opinion leader ■ A person who is frequently able to influence others' attitudes or behaviors by virtue of his or her active interest and expertise in one or more product categories.

A German ad for Schick razors challenges our sex role expectations (these are men).

Peer-to-Peer E-Commerce

One of the most exciting aspects of the new digital world is that consumers can interact directly with other people who live around the block or around the world. Peer-to-peer, or as it is more commonly referred to, **consumer-to-consumer (C2C)** e-commerce refers to online communications and purchases that occur among individuals without directly involving the manufacturer or retailer. Picture a small group of local collectors who meet once a month at a local diner to discuss their shared interests over coffee. Now multiply that group by thousands, and include people from all over the world who are united through the Internet by a shared passion for sports memorabilia, Harley-Davidson motorcycles, or refrigerator magnets—all are participating in C2C e-commerce.

Yes, group membership has entered cyberspace in a big way, as "Netizens" around the world are forming virtual communities of consumption. These are groups of people who meet online and share their enthusiasm for a product, recording artist, art form, celebrity, and so on.[45] These groups allow consumers to remain anonymous while they form around an incredibly diverse set of interests—everything from Barbie dolls to fine wine. Marketers who target these online communities know that members are more likely to buy products that other group members find of value.

It's been estimated that over 40 million people worldwide participate in virtual communities. These loyal consumers help one another evaluate the quality of choices in the marketplace. For example, on the official *X-Files* homepage (http://thex-files.com) fans debate the merits of each episode, but Fox Mulder groupies also critique and promote the most recently licensed *X-Files* merchandise. On newsgroup boards such as alt.tv.x-file they share pricing and quality hints and issue "rip-off alerts" about new products they deem offensive or inferior.

Companies such as Warner Bros. also are actively promoting virtual communities related to their products. The company noticed that many fans of Bugs Bunny, Batman, and the Tazmanian Devil were including images and sound clips on their personal Web pages and then selling ad space on those pages. Instead of suing its fans, Warner created an online community called ACME City that builds homepages for registered members.[46] Let's look at some specific types of brand communities that are shaking up the ways businesses operate.

Virtual communities come in different forms:

- *Multi-User Dungeons.* Originally, these communities were environments where players of fantasy games met. Now they refer to any cyber environment in which people socially interact through role and game playing. In a game called EverQuest, more than 50,000 people around the globe pay to roam around a fantasyland in

consumer-to-consumer (C2C) e-commerce ■
Communications and purchases that occur among individuals without directly involving the manufacturer or retailer.

After the September 11, 2001, attack on the World Trade Center, many Americans became interested in learning more about Islam. Islamonline.net provides a virtual community for Muslims all over the world and a source of information about Islam for non-Muslims.

cyberspace (www.EverQuest.com). This game combines the stunning graphics of advanced gaming with the social scene of a chat room. Players create a character as a virtual alter ego, which may be a wise elf or a backstabbing rogue. If a character is powerful enough, it can sell on eBay for $1,000 or more! Players can travel around this cyberworld in groups of six. In many cases they settle into a regular group and spend two to three hours each night online with the same people. One couple even held a virtual wedding while playing. The bride reported, "We only had one death, a guest who was killed by the guards. It was a lot of fun."[47]

Realizing that the average online player logs 17 hours per week, firms such as Sony, Microsoft, and Sega are building virtual worlds to get a piece of the action. As one game company executive put it, "This is not a genre of game but a breakthrough new medium. It provides a completely new social, collaborative, shared experience. We're basically in the Internet community business."[48] This new medium opens up many possibilities for marketers, since participants often render judgments on a variety of topics such as hot new bands or movies that can influence the opinions of other participants.

- *Rooms, rings, and lists.* These virtual communities include Internet relay chat (IRC), otherwise known as *chat rooms*. *Rings* are organizations of related homepages and *lists* are groups of people on a single e-mail list who share information. For example, ICQ maintains rings devoted to many topics such as music, electronics, geneaology, and so on. For fan sites devoted to Kid Rock, Limp Bizkit, and others, visit http://web.icq.com/channels/music/rock/.
- *Boards.* Boards are online communities organized around interest-specific electronic bulletin boards. Active members read and post messages sorted by date and subject. There are boards devoted to musical groups, movies, wine, cigars, cars, comic strips, and even fast-food restaurants. Ponder the case of Widespread Panic. The band has never had a music video on MTV or cracked the Billboard Top 200. But it's one of the top 40 touring bands in the United States. How did it get to be so successful? Simple—the group built a virtual community of fans. Fans send messages to its recording studio and hardcore followers can find out vital information, such as what band members ate for lunch.[49]
- *Auction sites.* Auction sites let consumers buy, sell, and barter with each other. The best-known auction site is eBay, where you can buy anything from a rare Beatles poster to an antique iron. At one point, an eBay member even tried to sell a human kidney ("You can choose either kidney. . . . Of course, only one is for sale, as I need the other one to live"). Bidding went to over $5.7 million before the company ended the auction.[50]

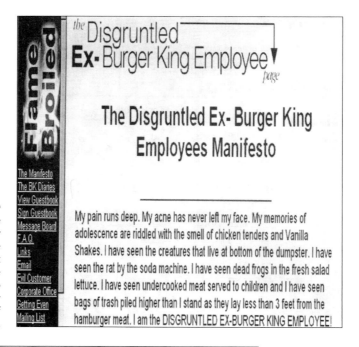

A former Burger King employee who was obviously unhappy about an experience with the company created this protest site. Because (almost) anyone can create a Web page for all to see, corporations have difficulty controlling the content of these sites.

- *Product rating sites.* Sites such as Deja.com give people a forum for their opinions and let them rate products.[51] One product-rating site called Epinions.com even rates and rewards product reviewers. Anyone can sign up to give advice on products that fit into the site's 12 categories, and shoppers can rate the reviews on a scale from not useful to very useful. Reviewers earn royalties of between $1 to $3 for every 10 times their review is read. When recommendations result in a sale, the company earns a referral fee from merchants. One of the site's founders observes that the site relies on a "web of trust," and he claims, "It mimics the way word of mouth works in the real world."[52]

- *Protest sites.* These sites let consumers "vent" by sharing negative experiences they have had with companies. Many of these sites have links you can find on www.protest.com. In some cases these protest sites pose a public relations problem for companies, so companies try to eliminate them. Dunkin' Donuts bought a site from a disgruntled customer who created the Web page to complain after he could not get skim milk for his coffee.[53] And sometimes these sites spread untrue information about corporations. For example, rumors began spreading on newsgroups that Procter & Gamble's Febreze cleaning product killed dogs. In a preemptive move to minimize problems before they started, P&G registered numerous Web site names so no one else could—including febrezekillspet.com, febrezesucks.com, and ihateprocterandgamble.com.[54] P&G now maintains its own Web site dedicated to fighting rumors: pg.com/rumor.[55]

6 *Bookmark It!*

Surf the Web and locate some other product protest sites from protest.com. Do you think sites such as these provide a service to consumers? Why or why not? Do you think sites such as these hurt companies in the long run?

Real People, Real Choices:

How It Worked Out at Yahoo!

Jennifer selected option 2—producing the special section—because she decided it was worth the risk, given her limited budget and the amount of mass consumer exposure Yahoo! would receive. This choice worked out well because it drove a lot of people to the Yahoo! Shopping site who may not have gone there otherwise. As you may have found when you investigated portals, these sites recommend sites we hadn't thought of—many people like to click around just on impulse to see what they're missing.

In fact, sales on the Yahoo! Shopping site were 52 percent higher the week the section came out than the week before. As Figure 6.7 shows, there was a 47 percent increase in the Yahoo! Shopping Buzz (as tracked by the Yahoo! Buzz Index, which measures people searching for words on Yahoo!), the single biggest peak for the entire year. And many of the merchants listed in the *USA WEEKEND* magazine also saw an increase in the Buzz Index, so everyone benefited from the additional exposure. Once again, Yahoo! demonstrated the value of a portal in simplifying the search process for consumers as they underwent the decision-making process.

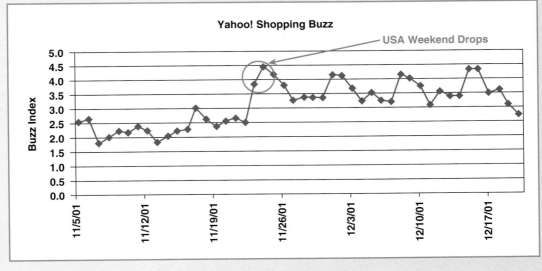

FIGURE 6.7

Yahoo! Site Usage

Chapter Summary

1. Define consumer behavior and explain the reasons why consumers buy what they buy.

Consumer behavior is the process individuals go through to select, purchase, or use goods, services, ideas, or experiences to satisfy their needs and desires. Consumer decisions differ greatly ranging from habitual, almost mindless, repeat (low-involvement) purchases to complex, extended problem-solving activities for important, risky (high-involvement) decisions.

2. Explain the prepurchase, purchase, and postpurchase activities consumers engage in when making decisions.

First, consumers recognize that there is a problem to be solved. The search for information in memory and in the marketplace reduces consumers' risk of making a wrong choice. The set of alternatives, those which will be actively considered, are judged based on various dimensions or evaluative criteria. Consumers may simplify the process by using mental shortcuts or heuristics. Following the purchase, consumer perceptions of product quality lead to satisfaction or dissatisfaction.

3. Describe how internal factors influence consumers' decision-making processes.

Several internal factors influence consumer decisions. Perception is how consumers select, organize, and interpret stimuli. Steps in perception include exposure, perceptual selection, and interpretation. Learning is a change in behavior that results from information or experience. Behavioral learning results from external events while cognitive learning refers to internal mental activity.

An attitude is a lasting evaluation of a person, object, or issue and includees three components: affect, cognition, and behavior. Personality traits such as innovativeness, self-confidence, and sociability may be used to develop market segments. Marketers seek to understand a consumer's self-concept in order to develop product attributes that match some aspect of the consumer's self-concept.

The age of consumers, their family life cycle classification, and lifestyle are strongly related to consumption preferences. Marketers may use psychographics to group people according to activities, interests, and opinions that may explain reasons for purchasing products.

4. Understand how situational factors at the time and place of purchase may influence consumer behavior.

The physical and social environments at the time of purchase create differences in consumer behavior. Retailers often create themed environments and in-store displays to influence customers to make purchases. Time (or the lack of it) influences which products are selected and characteristics of the decision-making process.

5. Describe how consumers' relationships with other people influence their decision-making processes.

Consumers' overall priorities for products and activities are determined by the culture of the society in which the consumers live. Consumer decisions may be influenced by cultural values, which are the enduring beliefs of the culture. Consumers within the same culture may also be members of different religious, ethnic, or regional subcultures.

Social class and reference groups are other types of social influence that have an impact on product and store choices. One way social influences are felt is in the expectations of society regarding the proper roles for men and women, which have led to many sex-typed products. Consumers are motivated to please or imitate people whom they know or respect. Purchases often result from conformity to real or imagined group pressure. Opinion leaders are especially influential people.

6. Understand how the Internet offers consumers opportunities for peer-to-peer marketing.

Peer-to-peer or consumer-to-consumer (C2C) e-commerce includes marketing communication and purchases between individuals. C2C activities include virtual brand communities, auction sites, product rating sites, and protest sites.

Chapter Review

■ MARKETING CONCEPTS:
TESTING YOUR KNOWLEDGE

1. What is consumer behavior? Why is it important for marketers to understand consumer behavior?
2. How does the decision process differ under conditions of high involvement and low involvement? What are the steps in the decision process, and what activities occur in each?
3. What is perception? Explain the parts of the perception process: exposure, perceptual selection, and interpretation. For marketers, what are the implications of each of these components?
4. How has Maslow's hierarchy of needs contributed to an understanding of consumer behavior?
5. What is behavioral learning? What is cognitive learning? How is an understanding of behavioral and cognitive learning useful to marketers?
6. What are the three components of attitudes? What is personality? How is consumer behavior influenced by an individual's personality and self-concept?
7. Explain the family life cycle concept. Why is family life cycle sometimes more meaningful in understanding consumer behavior than age alone?
8. Explain what is meant by lifestyle. What is the significance of lifestyle in understanding consumer behavior and purchasing decisions?
9. How do culture and subculture influence consumer behavior? What is the significance of social class to marketers?
10. What are reference groups, and how do they influence consumers? What are opinion leaders?
11. How does the physical environment influence consumer purchasing behavior?
12. What is peer-to-peer e-commerce? How do consumers communicate and purchase using the Internet?

■ MARKETING CONCEPTS:
DISCUSSING CHOICES AND ISSUES

1. Some consumer advocates have criticized marketing messages that link products to idealized people and situations and encourage the belief that the products will change consumers' lives. Tell whether you agree with these critics and explain why or why not.
2. Demographic or cultural trends are important to marketers. What are some big trends that may affect the marketing of the following products?
   a. housing
   b. health care
   c. newspapers
   d. textbooks
   e. travel and tourism
3. What are the core values of your culture? What subcultures are you a member of? What distinctive beliefs, characteristics, or experiences are a part of the subcultures?

4. Affect, cognition, and behavior are three components of attitudes. Explain each of these components. Why is an understanding of all three components important to marketers?
5. Consumers often buy products because they feel pressure from reference groups to conform. Does conformity exert a positive or negative influence on consumers? With what types of products is conformity more likely to occur?
6. The Internet provides a unique opportunity for consumers to communicate and make purchases from each other. What do you think the future of this C2C e-commerce is? How do you think it will affect traditional marketing firms?

■ MARKETING PRACTICE:
APPLYING WHAT YOU'VE LEARNED

1. Assume you are an account executive with an advertising agency. Your current client is a firm that makes swimwear. You know that swimwear purchases are often influenced by a variety of social or "other people" factors. Write a report that lists these social influences, explain why each is important, and outline how you might use these influences in developing an advertising campaign.
2. This chapter indicated that consumers go through a series of steps (from problem recognition to postpurchase evaluation) as they make purchases. Write a detailed report describing what you would do in each of these steps when deciding to purchase one of the following products:
   a. automobile
   b. computer
   c. vacation
3. Using one of the products in question 2, what can marketers do to make sure that consumers going through each step in the consumer decision process move toward the purchase of their brand? Hint: Think about product, place, price, and promotion strategies.
4. Sometimes advertising or other marketing activities cause problem recognition to occur by showing consumers how much better off they would be with a new product or by pointing out problems with products they already own. For the following product categories, what are some ways marketers might try to stimulate problem recognition?
   a. life insurance
   b. mouthwash
   c. clothing
   d. fast food
5. Assume you are a marketing manager for a firm that markets expensive watches. You are concerned about the effects of current consumer trends, including changing ethnic populations, changing roles of men and women, increased concern for time and for the environment, and

decreased emphasis on owning status goods. Others in your firm do not understand or care about these changes. They believe that the firm should continue to do business just as it always has. Develop a role-playing exercise with a classmate to discuss these two different points of view for your class. Each of you should be sure to include the importance of each of these trends to your firm and offer suggestions for marketing strategies to address these trends.

■ MARKETING MINI-PROJECT:
LEARNING BY DOING

The purpose of this mini-project is to increase your understanding of the roles of personal, social, and situational factors in consumer behavior.

1. With several other members of your class, select one of the following product categories (or some other product of your choice):
   - hair styling
   - large appliances such as refrigerators or washing machines
   - children's clothing
   - banking
   - fine jewelry
2. Visit three stores or locations where the product may be purchased. (Try to select three that are very different from each other.) Observe and make notes on all the elements of each retail environment.
3. At each of the three locations, observe people purchasing the product. Make notes about their characteristics (for example, age, race, gender, and so on), their social class, and their actions in the store in relation to the product.
4. Prepare a report for your class describing the situational variables and individual consumer differences between the three stores and how they relate to the purchase of the product.
5. Present your findings to your class.

■ REAL PEOPLE, REAL SURFERS:
EXPLORING THE WEB

Visit some of the portals and virtual malls listed at the beginning of this chapter. Try to search for the same product at each site. Based on your experience with these sites, answer the following questions:

1. What is your overall opinion of the sites?
2. Would the different sites attract different types of consumers? Explain.
3. How easy or difficult is it to navigate each site?
4. How does the choice of merchandise compare at the different sites?
5. What do you think of the sites' ability to attract consumers to come back again and again?
6. Is there anything about the virtual mall sites that you would recommend Yahoo! Shopping should adopt for its site?

■ PLAN IT!
DEVELOPING A MARKETING PLAN

As your instructor directs, create a marketing plan (using Marketing Plan Pro software or a written marketing plan format) to document your marketing decisions or answer these questions in a written or oral report.

Although consumers buy different CFS products for different reasons, fun plays a role in their perceptions, attitudes, and behavior. Reread the current plan in Appendix A and then continue working on next year's marketing plan by considering the following issues:

1. What level of involvement are consumers likely to have with CFS's products—and what are the implications for CFS's marketing activities?
2. How might personality and lifestyles affect consumer behavior toward CFS's products—and what can CFS do as a result?
3. What might CFS do to bring opinion leaders into its marketing efforts?

Key Terms

attitude, (171)
behavioral learning theories, (169)
brand loyalty, (166)
classical conditioning, (170)
cognitive learning theory, (170)
conformity, (179)
consumer behavior, (161)
consumer satisfaction/dissatisfaction (CS/D), (166)
consumer-to-consumer (C2C) e-commerce, (181)

culture, (177)
evaluative criteria, (165)
family life cycle, (173)
heuristics, (165)
hierarchy of needs, (169)
information search, (163)
involvement, (162)
learning, (169)
lifestyle, (173)
motivation, (169)
operant conditioning, (170)
opinion leader, (180)

perceived risk, (162)
perception, (167)
personality, (171)
problem recognition, (163)
psychographics, (173)
reference group, (179)
self-concept, (171)
sex roles, (179)
social class, (178)
stimulus generalization, (170)
subculture, (177)

REAL CHOICES AT PLAYBOY ENTERPRISES, INC.

Playboy Enterprises, Inc. is one of the best-known companies in America because of its famous *Playboy* magazine. The organization had its beginnings in the 1950s when founder Hugh Hefner (who still controls 70 percent of the company's common stock) introduced the innovative magazine, produced on a shoestring budget. The shock waves from this humble issue—which featured Marilyn Monroe on the cover and, you guessed it, in the centerfold—launched *Playboy* magazine to success, bunny and all. The controversy over the morality of the magazine, the ensuing notoriety, and the changing attitudes of the 1960s and 1970s all helped turn the company into an entertainment giant with revenues in excess of $200 million annually.

In the 1960s and 1970s circulation of *Playboy* magazine surged. At the same time one of the hottest status symbol products in New York, Atlanta, or Dallas was a Playboy Club key, a key-shaped token required for entry into any one of the Playboy Clubs where drinks and meals were served to members by scantily clad Playboy "bunnies." Department stores sold key chains and T-shirts and even men's boxer shorts adorned with the Playboy bunny logo.

In the 1980s and early 1990s, things began to change. The original Playboy fans were getting older, and the clubs lost their intrigue. In fact the cultural climate seemed to lessen the desire to identify with an organization that some still consider to be morally offensive and that others see to be degrading to women. Similarly, the maturing market for men's magazines was less interested in centerfolds and more interested in reading articles about issues important to men. By 2000, circulation was less than half what it was in the 1970s.

In 1997 Playboy introduced an online magazine offering consumers articles, pictures, and licensed merchandise at a cost of $60 a year. But the online venture was a financial failure, most experts felt, because of the availability of free pornography on the Internet that was far more revealing than Playboy's more modest site. Other ventures in the 1990s included expansion into TV production and soft-core movie channels. Then in 2001 Playboy announced it was moving away from its historic soft-core image and buying three X-rated cable movie channels.

But is this move away from Playboy's more wholesome image one that consumers will accept? Will this new venture be met with the same lukewarm reception the magazine and Playboy's Internet operations have had in recent years? Should Playboy consider other options that meet the needs of a broader consumer market? For example, in the United States it can choose to focus on producing home videos and promoting Playboy-branded videos of popular vintage movies. The company could also decide to pursue its experiments in producing Playboy interviews on CD-ROM and other Internet operations. Success, though, depends a lot on the bunny—and how people perceive her.

Source: Adapted from Keith J. Kelly, "Playboy's Fortunes Tied to the Bunny," *Advertising Age* (24 October 1994); Kevin Peraino, "Playboy Goes XXX," *Newsweek* (16 July 2001): 36; Pallavi Gogoi, "Playboy's Not-So-Energized Bunny," *Business Week* (4 December 2000): 44.

THINGS TO THINK ABOUT

1. What is the decision facing Playboy Enterprises?
2. What factors are important in understanding the decision situation?
3. What are the alternatives?
4. What decision(s) do you recommend?
5. What are some ways to implement your recommendation(s)?

Bookmark It!

OBJECTIVES:

1. Describe the general characteristics of business-to-business markets and business buying practices.
2. Tell how marketers classify business or organizational markets.
3. Explain the business buying situation and describe business buyers.
4. Understand the stages in the business buying decision process.
5. Understand the growing role of B2B e-commerce.

Why Organizations Buy

BUSINESS-TO-BUSINESS MARKETS AND B2B E-COMMERCE

Real People, Real Choices:

Meet Steve Schwartz, a Decision Maker at Lion Apparel

www.lionapparel.com

CURRENT POSITION: Executive Vice President, Lion Apparel.

EDUCATION: Northwestern, M.B.A., 1987–1989.

Swarthmore, B.S., Mechanical Engineering, 1980–1984.

FIRST JOB OUT OF COLLEGE: Start-up computer networking company founded by a friend. I was vice president of operations in a two-employee company.

A MISTAKE I WISH I HADN'T MADE: When preparing a proposal, I made a simple mistake that could have been caught had I worked with team members more closely.

HERO: Thomas Edison.

MANAGEMENT STYLE: I focus on future planning and priorities, surround myself with great people, and am not afraid to make personnel changes. I do not micromanage.

PET PEEVE: People who say, "it can't be done" or "we have always done it this way."

GREATEST WORRY: That one day I will be making statements like the above.

How Lion Became King

Not too long ago, a large European city fire brigade wanted to reoutfit its firefighters. Typically, the brigade's research staff would publish a detailed garment specification document for interested bidders. Bidding suppliers would then produce a sample that met this specification. Because the brigade knew exactly what it wanted, the company that came in with the lowest price (rather than the best value) was supposed to get the contract. (This is different than doing this sort of business in the United States, where the pluses and minuses of each bidder tend to carry more weight.)

However, the brigade's chief had a vision. He wanted to evaluate each bidder as a potential long-term supplier, not just as a company that would fill an immediate need. The winner would be rewarded with long-term business, and the brigade would not have to start over each time it wanted to buy new gear. This is the basis of relationship marketing, a concept we first introduced in Chapter 1.

Lion Apparel had recently opened a small office in London to sell its firefighter turnout gear (clothing that firefighters wear while fighting fires) to international markets. Steve Schwartz knew he had to win the contract in order to funnel enough business into this operation to justify the cost of maintaining an overseas office.

To compete successfully for the contract, Steve had to answer two key questions: First, where would Lion produce the gear? At that time, all of Lion's production facilities were in the United States. Brigade leaders had visited them and were impressed. But producing them at home and sending them overseas would bring on export duties, reducing Lion's ability to compete on price. Even though they talked a good game, Steve could not be sure the decision makers would be willing to pay a higher price even if Lion's gear was superior to local gear.

Second, how would Lion handle the maintenance conditions of the proposal? European legislation put legal responsibility for the condition of work clothing on the employer, in this

Think and Do Like a Marketer

To better understand Steve's problem, learn more about how the uniform industry works. Who are the major players? In what kinds of product categories do they compete? What criteria do purchasers use when choosing a vendor?

Visit the Web sites of trade organizations that represent uniform manufacturers. Three organizations are the Textile Rental Service Association (www.trsa.org), the Uniform and Textile Service Association (www.utsa.com), and the National Association of Uniform Manufacturers and Dealers (www.naumd.com). Fire Equipment Manufacturers Association at www.femsa.org lists fire equipment companies. The codes used to regulate the design of firefighter's turnout gear, buildings, and electrical systems can be found at www.nfpa.org. A site that explains more about firefighters' protective apparel is www.dupont.com/nomex.

case the brigade. Maintenance for turnout gear includes both its special cleaning, which removes potentially dangerous residues, and inspection and repair to ensure that the clothing's protective envelope is not compromised. Steve wasn't sure how much responsibility Lion should assume for maintenance; he didn't want it to seem that Lion was passing the buck by subcontracting these duties (especially since the brigade seemed to be looking for a total service package) but perhaps a local firm could maintain the equipment more efficiently. Steve and his staff considered their options.

Option 1: Make the products in Europe and manage all the maintenance.

Lion could market itself as a "local manufacturer," getting support from local offices of its U.S.-based supply partners. It could also team up with the brigade's current supplier, which had a strong product reputation but no service experience, and was in the midst of management turmoil.

Turnout gear must conform to a set of European performance guidelines called the EN369 standards. These standards vary greatly from the U.S. N.F.P.A. (United States National Fire Protection Association) standards. Although Lion made U.S.-style clothing, it was a newcomer to the production of European-standard clothing, so a local supplier with this experience would be an important resource. Lion already had a division called the Lion Uniform Group that designed complete uniform programs, subcontracted with other companies to make the garments, and shipped the uniforms to service businesses such as gas stations and private security firms. However, Lion had no experience in the cleaning and repair of firefighter garments and would have to learn quickly how to perform these tasks and credibly demonstrate it could do so. Finally, Lion would lose control of the manufacturing process because its "local" partner would manage that piece. Lion would only have quality control and inspection oversight.

Option 2: Make the products in the United States, export them to Europe, and subcontract all of the required maintenance work to a European company.

By basing production in the United States, Lion could maximize production resources, control the sources and raw materials more closely, and take advantage of its existing world-class manufacturing facility. However, overseas shipping costs would be high and this might cause trade problems in the importing countries. It also might be difficult to control the service end of the deal if maintenance were left to a subcontractor. Improperly maintained turnout gear could pose a real safety hazard to firefighters, so Lion couldn't afford to fall down on the job.

Option 3: Make the product in Europe and subcontract out the maintenance work to a local company.

As with option 1, Steve felt that by manufacturing in Europe, Lion could be considered a "local" manufacturer with a U.S. touch. Plus, it would be much simpler and less costly not to get involved with maintaining the clothing. This option would not require Lion to invest so much of its resources in setting up infrastructure for a concept that other European fire brigades might not adopt. But Steve was worried that the brigade would not feel that Lion would have adequate control over maintenance, which is more important than the initial delivery of the suits.

Now, join the Lion Apparel decision team: Which option would you choose, and why?

Business Markets: Buying and Selling When Stakes Are High

You might think most marketers spend their days dreaming up the best way to promote cutting-edge Web browsers or funky shoes. Not so. Many marketers know that the "real action" more likely lies in lead pipes, office supplies, safety shoes, meat lockers, or the fire-fighting uniforms sold by Lion Apparel. In fact, some of the most interesting and lucrative jobs for young marketers are in industries you've never heard of because they're not in the consumer market.

A consumer may decide to buy two or three T-shirts at one time, each emblazoned with a different design. *Fortune* 500 companies such as Exxon, Pepsi-Cola, and Texaco buy hundreds, even thousands, of employee uniforms embroidered with their corporate logos in a single order—and sometimes these products have to meet rigorous standards, like the turnout gear that protects the lives of firefighters. Like an end consumer, a business buyer makes decisions—with an important difference: The purchase may be worth millions of dollars, and both the buyer and seller have a lot at stake (maybe even their jobs!).

In this chapter we'll look at the big picture of the business marketplace, a world in which the fortunes of business buyers and sellers can hang in the balance of a single transaction. Then we'll examine how marketers categorize businesses and other organizations to develop effective business marketing strategies. We'll look at business buying behavior and the business buying decision process. Finally, we'll talk about the important world of business-to-business e-commerce.

To begin, consider these transactions: Dassault makes business jets to sell to corporate customers. Procter & Gamble sells cases of Tide to Certified Grocers, a midwestern wholesaler. The Metropolitan Opera buys costumes, sets, and programs. Mac's Diner buys a case of canned peas from BJ's Wholesale Club. The U.S. government places an order for 3,000 new IBM computers. The Peoria Public Library buys a Canon copier.

All of these exchanges have one thing in common—they're part of **business-to-business marketing**. This is the marketing of goods and services that businesses and other organizations buy for purposes other than personal consumption. Firms may resell these goods and services or they may use them to produce still other goods and services to sell to businesses or to support their own operations. Business-to-business customers include manufacturers, wholesalers, retailers, and a variety of other organizations such as hospitals, universities, and government agencies. Another name for business-to-business markets is **organizational markets**. Business customers create vast opportunities for marketers. When measured in dollars, the market for organizational goods and services is *four* times larger than the consumer market.[1]

To put the size and complexity of business markets into perspective, let's consider a single product—a pair of jeans. A consumer may browse through several racks of jeans and ultimately purchase a single pair, but the store at which the consumer shops has purchased many pairs of jeans in different sizes, styles, and brands from different manufacturers. Each of these manufacturers purchases fabrics, zippers, buttons, and thread from other manufacturers that in turn purchase the raw materials to make these components. In addition, all of the firms in this chain need to purchase equipment, electricity, labor, computer systems, office supplies, packing materials, and countless other goods and services.

Thus, even a single purchase of the latest style of Diesel jeans is the culmination of a series of buying and selling activities among many organizations—many people have been keeping busy while you're out shopping!

business-to-business marketing ■ Marketing of those goods and services that business and organizational customers need to produce other goods and services for resale or to support their operations.

organizational markets ■ Another name for business-to-business markets.

CHARACTERISTICS THAT MAKE A DIFFERENCE IN BUSINESS MARKETS

In theory, the same basic marketing principles hold in both consumer and business markets—firms identify customer needs and develop a marketing mix to satisfy those needs. For example, take the company that made the desks and chairs in your classroom. Just like a firm that markets consumer goods, the classroom furniture company first must create an important competitive advantage for its target market of universities. Next the firm develops a marketing mix strategy beginning with a product—classroom furniture that will withstand years of use by thousands of students while providing a level of comfort required of a good learning environment (and you thought those hard-back chairs were intended just to keep you awake during class). The firm must offer the furniture at prices universities will pay. Then the firm must develop a sales force or other marketing communication strategy to make sure your university (and hundreds of others) consider—and hopefully choose—its products when furnishing classrooms.

Many companies make products designed exclusively for other companies to buy. Dassault is a French firm that focuses on building the "best" jets for corporate buyers.

Although marketing to business customers does have a lot in common with consumer marketing, there are differences that make this basic process more complex.[2] Figure 7.1 provides a quick look at some of these differences. Let's review some now.

Multiple Buyers   In business markets, products often have to do more than satisfy an individual's needs. They must meet the requirements of everyone involved in the company's purchase decision. If you decide to buy a new chair for your room or apartment, you're the only one who has to be satisfied. For your classroom, the furniture must satisfy not only students but also faculty, administrators, campus planners, and the people at your school who actually do the purchasing. If your school is a state institution, the furniture may also have to meet certain state-mandated engineering standards.

Number of Customers   Organizational customers are few and far between compared to end consumers. In the United States there are about 100 million consumer households but less than half a million businesses and other organizations. But unless your name is Trump or Gates, each organizational buyer has much more to spend than you do as an individual consumer. Business marketers have a narrow customer base and a small number of buyers. Kodak's business division that markets sophisticated medical products to hospitals, HMOs, and other medical groups has a limited number of potential customers compared to its consumer film division. This means that business marketing strrategies may be quite different from consumer markets. For example, in consumer markets Kodak may use TV advertising, but in its business markets a strong salesforce is a far better means of promoting the product.

Size of Purchases   Business-to-business products can dwarf consumer purchases, both in the quantity of items ordered and in the price of individual purchases. A company that rents uniforms to other businesses, for example, buys hundreds of large drums of laundry detergent

Organizational Markets	Consumer Markets
● Purchases made for some purpose other than personal consumption	● Purchases for individual or household consumption
● Purchases made by someone other than the user of the product	● Purchases usually made by ultimate user of the product
● Decisions frequently made by several people	● Decisions usually made by individuals
● Purchases made according to precise technical specifications based on product expertise	● Purchases often made based on brand reputation or personal recommendations with little or no product expertise
● Purchases made after careful weighing of alternatives	● Purchases frequently made on impulse
● Purchases made based on rational criteria	● Purchases made based on emotional responses to products or promotions
● Purchasers often engage in lengthy decision process	● Individual purchasers often make quick decisions
● Interdependencies between buyers and sellers; long-term relationships	● Buyers engage in limited-term or one-time-only relationships with many different sellers
● Purchases may involve competitive bidding, price negotiations, and complex financial arrangements	● Most purchases made at "list price" with cash or credit cards
● Products frequently purchased directly from producer	● Products usually purchased from someone other than producer of the product
● Purchases frequently involve high risk and high cost	● Most purchases are low risk and low cost
● Limited number of large buyers	● Many individual or household customers
● Buyers often geographically concentrated in certain areas	● Buyers generally dispersed throughout total population
● Products: often complex; classified based on how organizational customers use them	● Products: consumer goods and services for individual use
● Demand derived from demand for other goods and services, generally inelastic in the short run, subject to fluctuations, and may be joined to the demand for other goods and services	● Demand based on consumer needs and preferences, is generally price elastic, steady over time and independent of demand for other products
● Promotion emphasizes personal selling	● Promotion emphasizes advertising

FIGURE 7.1

Differences Between Organizational and Consumer Markets

There are a number of major and minor differences between organizational and consumer markets. To be successful, marketers must understand these differences and develop strategies that can be effective with organizational customers.

each year to launder its uniforms in contrast to a consumer household that buys a box of detergent every few weeks. Organizations purchase many products, such as a highly sophisticated piece of manufacturing equipment or computer-based marketing information systems that can cost a million dollars or more. Recognizing such differences in the size of purchases allows marketers to meet business customers' needs. Although it makes perfect sense to use mass-media advertising to sell laundry detergent to consumers, selling thousands of dollars worth of laundry detergent or a million-dollar machine tool is best handled by a strong personal sales force. More on that in Chapter 16.

Geographic Concentration   Another difference between business markets and consumer markets is geographic concentration, meaning that many business customers are located in a small geographic area rather than being spread out across the country. Whether they live in the heart of New York City or in a small fishing village in Oregon, consumers buy and use toothpaste and televisions. Not so for business-to-business customers who may be almost exclusively located in a single region of the country. Silicon Valley, a 50-mile-long corridor along

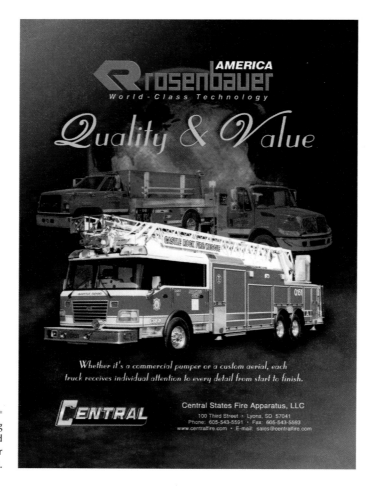

1 *Bookmark It!*

Pretend you are a marketer for a firm that sells computers to both consumers and business customers. Based on the characteristics of B2B markets, write down how your promotion strategies might differ for the two markets.

the California coast, is home to over 7,000 electronics and software companies because of its high concentration of skilled engineers and scientists.[3] This "California dreamin" aside, fully 80 percent of America's industrial buying power and 43 percent of the country's manufacturing plants are located in the Northeast because of the proximity to important resources, such as a skilled workforce and means of transportation.[4]

Of course, the downside to this kind of concentration was illustrated by the plight of the nation's financial services industry following the terrorist attacks in September 2001. It was estimated that approximately 20 percent of the city's office space was destroyed and an additional 30 percent was made temporarily noninhabitable by dust and debris.[5] In a single blow many of the country's leading banks and brokerages had to relocate to other parts of the city or elsewhere while Wall Street struggled to rebound.

BUSINESS-TO-BUSINESS DEMAND

Demand in business markets differs from consumer demand. Most demand for business-to-business products is derived, inelastic, fluctuating, and joint. Understanding these differences in business-to-business demand is important for marketers in forecasting sales and in planning effective marketing strategies. Let's look at each of these concepts now.

Derived Demand   Consumer demand is a direct connection between a need and the satisfaction of that need. But business customers don't purchase goods and services to satisfy their own needs. Business-to-business demand is **derived demand** because a business's demand for goods and services comes either directly or indirectly from consumers' demand. For example, the demand for hospital equipment and supplies depends on consumer need for medical care. During the flu season, hospitals will order increased quantities of antibiotics, oxygen masks, and even ventilators to take care of patients who develop pneumonia and other complications of flu.

derived demand ■ Demand for business or organizational products derived from demand for consumer goods or services.

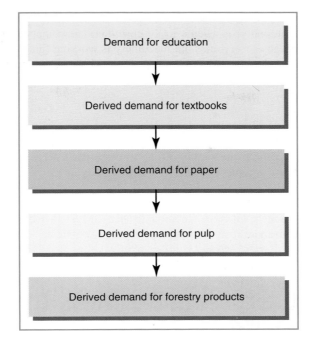

FIGURE 7.2

Derived Demand

Business-to-business demand is derived demand; that is, it is derived directly or indirectly from consumers' demand for another good or service. The demand for forestry products is derived indirectly from the demand for education.

Consider Figure 7.2. Demand for forestry products comes from the demand for pulp that makes paper used to make textbooks. The demand for textbooks comes from the demand for education (yes, that's the product you're buying!). As a result of derived demand, the success of one company may depend on another company in a different industry. The derived nature of business demand means that marketers must be constantly alert to changes in consumer trends that ultimately will have an effect on business-to-business sales.

Inelastic Demand   **Inelastic demand** means that it doesn't matter if the price of a business-to-business product goes up or down—business customers still buy the same quantity. Demand in business-to-business markets is mostly inelastic because a component usually is just one of the many parts and materials that go into producing the consumer product. It is not unusual for a large increase in a business product's price to have little effect on the final consumer product's price.

For example, in 2002, a BMW Z3 Roadster 2.5i was selling for just over $30,000.[6] To produce the car, BMW purchases thousands of different parts. If the price of tires, batteries, or stereos goes up—or down—BMW will still buy enough to meet consumer demand for its cars. As you might imagine, increasing the price by $30 or $40 or even $100 won't change consumer demand for Beemers and so demand for parts remains the same.

But business-to-business demand isn't always inelastic. Sometimes producing a consumer good or service relies on only one or a few materials or component parts. If the price of the part increases, demand may become elastic if the manufacturer of the consumer good passes the increase on to the consumer. Steel, for example, is a large component of automobiles. Automobile manufacturers will need to pay a lot more for steel should its price rise. An increase in the price of steel can drive up the price of automobiles so greatly that consumer demand for the automobiles drops, decreasing the demand for steel. This means that steel makers must consider the long-term impact of price increases carefully so they don't put themselves out of business.

Fluctuating Demand   Even small changes in consumer demand can create large increases or decreases in business demand, as explained by the **acceleration principle** (also called the *multiplier effect*). Take for example, air travel. Even a small increase in demand for air travel can cause airlines to order new equipment, creating a dramatic increase in demand for planes.

A product's life expectancy is another reason for fluctuating demand. Business customers tend to purchase certain products infrequently. Some types of large machinery may need to be

inelastic demand ■ Demand in which changes in price have little or no effect on the amount demanded.

acceleration principle (multiplier effect) ■ A marketing phenomenon in which a small percentage change in consumer demand can create a large percentage change in business-to-business demand.

replaced only every 10 or 20 years. Thus, demand for such products fluctuates—it may be very high one year when a lot of customers' machinery is wearing out but low the following year because everyone's old machinery is working fine. One solution for keeping production more constant is to use price reductions to encourage companies to order products before they actually need them.

joint demand ■ Demand for two or more goods that are used together to create a product.

Joint Demand   **Joint demand** occurs when two or more goods are necessary to create a product. For example, General Motors needs tires, batteries, and spark plugs to turn out the latest cars. If the supply of one of these parts decreases, GM will be unable to manufacture as many automobiles and so it will not buy as many of the other items it needs to make its cars. In this case, the sale of B.F. Goodrich tires to General Motors partly depends on the availability of batteries and spark plugs, even though the tire manufacturer has nothing to do with these products. Of course, companies like GM try to avoid not having the parts they need by dealing with more than one supplier whenever possible.

Classifying Business-to-Business Markets

Many firms buy products in business markets so they can produce other goods. Other business-to-business customers resell, rent, or lease goods and services. Still other customers, including governments and not-for-profit institutions such as the Red Cross or a local church, serve the public in some way.

As Figure 7.3 shows, business-to-business customers can be placed into such categories as producers, resellers, and organizations. Grouping customers makes marketers more effective because they can develop similar strategies when dealing with customers who belong to the same category (more on this in the next chapter). In this section we will look at four major classes of business-to-business customers and then we will look at how marketers classify specific industries.

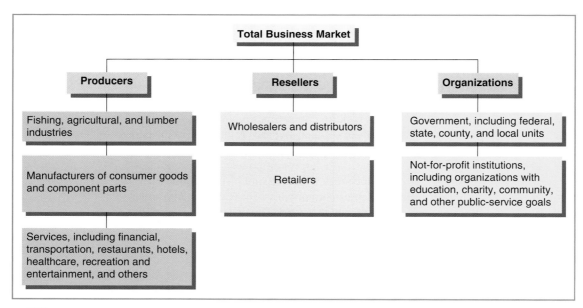

FIGURE 7.3

The Business Marketplace

The business marketplace consists of three major categories of customers: producers, resellers, and organizations. Business-to-business marketers need to understand the different needs of these customers if they are to build successful relationships.

PRODUCERS

Producers purchase products for the production of other goods and services that they in turn sell to make a profit. Producers are customers for a vast number of products from raw materials to goods manufactured by other producers. For example, DuPont buys resins and uses them to manufacture insulation material for sleeping bags. Alcoa buys aluminum ingots that it turns into sheet aluminum. Ford buys a variety of component parts—from transmissions to carpeting—to put into its vehicles. Luxury hotels buy linens, furniture, and food to produce the accommodations and meals their guests expect.

producers ■ The individuals or organizations that purchase products for use in the production of other goods and services.

RESELLERS

Resellers buy finished goods for the purpose of reselling, renting, or leasing to other businesses. Although resellers do not actually produce goods, they do provide their customers with the time, place, and possession utility we talked about in Chapter 1 by making the goods available to consumers when and where they want them.

resellers ■ The individuals or organizations that buy finished goods for the purpose of reselling, renting, or leasing to others to make a profit and to maintain their business operations.

GOVERNMENTS

Government markets make up the largest single business and organizational market in the United States. The U.S. government market includes more than 3,000 county governments, 35,000 municipalities and townships, 28,000 special district governments, 50 states and the District of Columbia, plus the federal government. State and local government markets alone account for 15 percent of the U.S. gross national product. Despite ongoing political efforts to curb spending, federal government expenditures total about $1.86 trillion annually.[7]

Governments are just about the only customers for certain products—jet bombers and firefighting gear, for instance. But much of government expenditures are for more familiar and less

government markets ■ The federal, state, county, and local governments that buy goods and services to carry out public objectives and to support their operations.

Producers of goods and services make up one type of business-to-business market. QualComm uses advertising and other marketing communication tools to tell manufacturers of wireless communication devices about its superior product.

The federal government buys millions of dollars worth of goods and services each year. To find out about these purchases, marketers must check the Web site www.FedBizOpps.com.

2 *Bookmark It!*

From a marketer's perspective, what do you think are some of the advantages and disadvantages of having government organizations as customers? Resellers as customers? Producers as customers? Not-for-profit institutions as customers?

expensive items. In one year the government purchased more than 5 million bed sheets, nearly 2 million note pads, and 3.5 million paintbrushes.[8]

For business marketers, selling goods and services to governments is different from selling to producer or reseller markets. Taking a prospective buyer to lunch may be standard practice in the corporate world, but in government markets this practice may be in conflict with ethical (and legal) standards for government personnel.[9] Because governments make purchases with taxpayer money, the law requires them to adhere to strict regulations. Generally, these regulations require that government buyers develop detailed specifications for even the simplest purchases. These often include the requirement to obtain **competitive bids** in which potential suppliers must submit detailed proposals and the firm making the best offer wins the business. Government agencies are usually required by law to accept the lowest bid from a qualified vendor.

To inform possible vendors about purchases they are about to make, governments regularly make information on upcoming purchases available to potential bidders. The federal government provides information on business opportunities through its Web site: www.FedBizOpps.gov. All federal government buyers can post information directly to FedBizOpps.com via the Internet and vendors can easily search, monitor, and retrieve opportunities at no cost. As we saw in the case of Lion Apparel, these regulations can vary dramatically in different countries, so companies seeking to do business in other markets need to stay on top of these (often complex) requirements.

NOT-FOR-PROFIT INSTITUTIONS

Not-for-profit institutions are organizations with charitable, educational, community, and other public service goals—such as hospitals, churches, universities, museums, and nursing homes. The institutional market also includes charitable and cause-related organizations such as the Salvation Army and the Red Cross. Not-for-profit institutions tend to operate on low budgets. In all but the largest not-for-profits, nonprofessional part-time buyers who have other duties—or who are volunteers—often make purchases. Such customers rely on marketers to provide more advice and assistance before and after the sale than professional business buyers require.

NORTH AMERICAN INDUSTRY CLASSIFICATION SYSTEM (NAICS)

In addition to looking at business-to-business markets within these four general categories, marketers identify their customers using the **North American Industry Classification System**

Major NAICS Sectors	11	Agriculture, Forestry, Fishing, and Hunting
	21	Mining
	22	Utilities
	23	Construction
	31-33	Manufacturing
	42	Wholesale Trade
	44-45	Retail Trade
	48-49	Transportation and Warehousing
	51	Information
	52	Finance and Insurance
	53	Real Estate and Rental and Leasing
	54	Professional, Scientific, and Technical Services
	55	Management of Companies and Enterprises
	56	Administrative and Support and Waste Management and Remediation Services
	61	Education Services
	62	Health Care and Social Assistance
	71	Arts, Entertainment, and Recreation
	72	Accommodation and Food Service
	81	Other Services (except Public Administration)
	92	Public Administration

Paging Equipment Example

Sector (two digits)	Subsector (three digits)	Industry Group (four digits)	Industry (five digits)	U.S. Industry (six digits)
51	**512**	**5121**	**51213**	**512132**
Information	Motion picture and sound recording industries	Motion picture and video industries	Motion picture and video exhibition	Drive-in motion picture theatres

FIGURE 7.4

The North American Industrial Classification System

The North American Industrial Classification System (NAICS) identifies industries using a six-digit code that breaks the 20 sectors down into subsectors, industry groups, industries, and specific country industries.

(NAICS). This is a numerical coding of industries developed by the United States, Canada, and Mexico. NAICS replaced the U.S. Standard Industrial Classification (SIC) system in 1997 so the North American Free Trade Agreement (NAFTA) countries could compare economic and financial statistics.[10] Like the SIC system, the NAICS reports the number of firms, the total dollar amount of sales, the number of employees, and the growth rate for industries, all broken down by geographic region. Many firms use the NAICS to assess potential markets and to determine how well they are doing compared to their industry group. (See Figure 7.4.)

Firms may also use the NAICS to find new customers. A marketer might first determine the NAICS industry classifications of his current customers and then evaluate the sales potential of other firms occupying these categories. For example, a firm may determine that several large customers are in the wireless communication industry. To find new customers, the marketers could examine other firms in the same industrial group.

North American Industry Classification System (NAICS) ■ The numerical coding system that the United States, Canada, and Mexico use to classify firms into detailed categories according to their business activities.

The Nature of Business Buying

So far we've talked about how business-to-business markets are different from consumer markets and about the different types of customers that make up business markets. In this section we'll discuss some of the important characteristics of business buying.

Being successful in business-to-business markets means developing marketing strategies that meet the needs of organizational customers better than the competition. To do this, marketers must understand business buying behavior. Armed with this knowledge, they are able to participate in the buyer's decision process from the start. Take a firm that sells equipment to hospitals. Understanding that physicians who practice at the hospital (rather than the employ-ees who actually purchase medical supplies) often initiate new equipment purchases means that the firm's salespeople will make sure that the physicians and the hospital's buyers know about new and improved products.

In this section we'll first look at the different types of buying situations found in business markets. Then we'll examine the role of professional purchasers and buying centers in business buying.

THE BUYING SITUATION

Like end consumers, business buyers spend more time and effort on some purchases than on others. Devoting such effort to a purchase decision usually depends on the complexity of the product and how often the decision has to be made. A **buy class** framework identifies the degree of effort required of the firm's personnel to collect information and make a purchase decision. These classes, which apply to three different buying situations, are called straight rebuys, modified rebuys, and new-task buys.

buy class ■ One of three classifications of business buying situations that characterizes the degree of time and effort required to make a decision.

Straight Rebuy Buyers are only human—when a purchase has low risk, they often rely on strategies that simplify the process, such as using a fixed set of trusted suppliers for routine purchases. Products such as computer paper, shipping cartons, and cleaning compounds are low risk. Being successful in such markets means keeping prices down and developing selling policies to keep the buying process as simple as possible. A **straight rebuy** is the purchase of items that a business-to-business customer regularly needs. The buyer has purchased the same items many times before and routinely reorders them when supplies are low, often from the same suppliers. Reordering takes little time. Buyers typically maintain a list of approved ven-dors that have demonstrated their ability to meet the firm's criteria for pricing, quality, service, and delivery.

straight rebuy ■ A buying situation in which business buyers make routine purchases that require minimal decision making.

Delivery and shipping services constitute a straight rebuy purchase for most business-to-business customers.

Because straight rebuys can mean a steady income to a firm, many business marketers go to great lengths to cultivate and maintain relationships with customers who submit reorders on a regular basis. Salespeople, for example, regularly call on these customers to personally handle orders and to see if there are additional products the customer needs. They may attempt to obtain long-term contracts. Rebuys keep a supplier's sales volume up and selling costs down.

Modified Rebuy   Alas, straight rebuy situations do not last forever. A **modified rebuy** occurs when a firm wants to shop around for suppliers with better prices, quality, or delivery times. A modified rebuy can also occur when the organization has new needs for products it already buys. A buyer who has purchased many office printers in the past, for example, may have to evaluate several lines of copiers if the firm has a new need for office equipment.

Modified rebuys require more time and effort than straight rebuys. The buyer generally knows the purchase requirements and a few potential suppliers. Marketers know that modified rebuys can mean that some vendors get added to a buyer's approved supplier list while others may be dropped. Astute marketers routinely call on buyers to detect and define problems that can lead to winning or losing in such situations.

New-Task Buy   A first-time purchase is a **new-task buy**. Uncertainty and risk characterize buying decisions in this classification, and they need the most effort because the buyer has no previous experience on which to base a decision.

Your university, for example, may decide (if it hasn't done so already) to go into the "distance learning" business, which is delivering courses to off-site students. Buying the equipment to set up classrooms with two-way video transmission will be an expensive and complex new-task buy for your school. The buyer has to start from scratch to gather information on

modified rebuy ■ A buying situation classification used by business buyers to categorize a previously made purchase that involves some change and that requires limited decision making.

new-task buy ■ A new business-to-business purchase that is complex or risky and that requires extensive decision making.

The purchase of new printers is a modified rebuy for most business-to-business customers. Although they have purchased printers before, they will probably shop around for what is new on the market, for better prices, or for the best quality.

purchase specifications, which may be highly technical and complex and require detailed input from others. In new-task buying situations, buyers not only lack experience with the product, but they also are often unfamiliar with firms that supply the product. Supplier choice, then, is critical, and buyers gather much information about quality, pricing, delivery, and service from several potential suppliers.

A prospective customer's new-task buying situation represents both a challenge and an opportunity. Although a new-task buy can be significant in and of itself, many times the chosen supplier gains the added advantage of becoming an "in" supplier for more routine purchases that will follow (which is what Steve Schwartz was hoping to accomplish).

A growing business that needs an advertising agency for the first time, for example, may seek exhaustive information from several firms before selecting one and will continue to use the chosen agency's services for future projects without exploring other alternatives. Marketers know that to get the order in a new-buy situation, they must develop a close working relationship with the business buyer. Such relationships mean that buyers can count on business marketers to help develop product specifications and terms for the purchase that are in the best interests of the customer's organization and its needs.

THE PROFESSIONAL BUYER

Just as it is important for marketers of consumer goods and services to understand their customers, it is essential that business-to-business marketers understand who handles the buying for business customers. Trained professional buyers typically carry out buying in business-

Centralized purchasing is one way Wal-Mart keeps "dropping" prices for its customers. With centralized purchasing, one buyer makes purchases for all Wal-Mart stores and this volume usually results in the lowest prices from suppliers.

to-business markets. These professional buyers can go by the titles of purchasing agents, procurement officers, directors of materials management—or even fire brigade chief.

Unlike consumers who may spend only a few hours a month making purchase decisions, professional purchasers do it all day, every day. Professional buyers focus on economic factors beyond the initial price of the product, including transportation and delivery charges, accessory products or supplies, maintenance, and other ongoing costs. They are responsible for selecting quality products and ensuring their timely delivery.

Big firms with many facilities in different locations often practice **centralized purchasing**. This means that even when others in the organization participate in the decision of what to buy, one department does all the buying for the company.[11] With centralized purchasing, a firm has more buying power and can get the best prices. Wal-Mart can offer its customers lower prices than other stores because its centralized purchasing department buys large quantities of items and can demand volume discounts from suppliers.

The professional buyers who work in centralized purchasing offices often become experts at the ins and outs of certain types of products and each may have a specialized role in the purchasing function. In the buying departments for retail chains, for example, an individual buyer (and several assistant buyers) may be responsible for buying only women's sleepwear or only junior tops. These type buyers require expert salespeople who understand their customers' needs and who can develop strong customer relationships.

centralized purchasing ■ A business buying practice in which a single department does the buying for all the company's facilities.

THE BUYING CENTER

Whether or not a firm's buying is a centralized process, several people may need to work together to reach a decision. Depending on what they need to purchase, these participants may be production workers, supervisors, engineers, secretaries, shipping clerks, or financial officers. In a small organization, everyone may have a voice in the decision. The group of people in the organization who participate in the decision-making process is referred to as the **buying center**.

buying center ■ The group of people in an organization who participate in a purchasing decision.

The Fluid Nature of the Buying Center Although the term *buying center* may conjure up an image of offices buzzing with purchasing activity, a buying center is not a place at all. Instead, it is a cross-functional team of decision makers. Generally, the members of a buying center have some expertise or interest in the particular decision, and as a group they are able to make the best decision.

Hospitals, for example, frequently make purchase decisions through a large buying center. When making a decision to purchase disposable oxygen masks, one or more physicians, the director of nurses, and purchasing agents may work together to determine quantities and select the best products and suppliers. A separate decision regarding the types of pharmaceutical supplies to stock might need a different cast of characters to advise the purchasing agent. Marketers must continually identify which employees in a firm take part in every purchase and develop relationships with them all.

Roles in the Buying Center   Depending on the complexity of the purchase and the size of the buying center, a participant may assume one, several, or all of the six roles shown in Figure 7.5. Let's review them here.

The *initiator* begins the buying process by first recognizing that the firm needs to make a purchase. A production employee, for example, may notice that a piece of equipment is not working properly and notify a supervisor. At other times, the initiator may suggest purchasing a new product because it will improve the firm's operations. Depending on the initiator's position in the organization and the type of purchase, the initiator may or may not influence the actual purchase decision. For marketers it's important to make sure individuals who might initiate a purchase are aware of improved products they offer.

The *user* is the member of the buying center who needs the product. The user's role in the buying center varies. For example, an administrative assistant may give his input on the features needed in a new copier that he will be "chained to" for several hours a day. Marketers need to inform users of their products' benefits, especially if the benefits outweigh competitors.

The *gatekeeper* is the member who controls the flow of information to other members. Typically the gatekeeper is the purchasing agent who gathers information and materials from salespeople, schedules sales presentations, and controls suppliers' access to other participants in the buying process. For salespeople, developing and maintaining strong personal relationships with gatekeepers is critical to being able to offer their products to the buying center.

An *influencer* affects the buying decision by dispensing advice or sharing expertise. By virtue of their expertise, engineers, quality control specialists, and other technical experts in the firm generally have a great deal of influence in purchasing equipment, materials, and component parts used in production. The influencers may or may not wind up using the product. Marketers need to identify key influencers in the buying center and work to persuade them of their product's superiority.

The *decider* is the member of the buying center who makes the final decision. This person usually has the greatest power within the buying center and often has power within the organization to authorize spending the company's money. For a routine purchase, the decider may be

3 *Bookmark It!*

At your school, who do you think should be included in the buying center for a purchase of new computers? For textbooks? For a new library database? Make a list of how each person in the buying center would approach these purchases.

FIGURE 7.5

Roles in the Buying Center

A buying center is a group of individuals brought together for the purpose of making a purchasing decision. Marketers need to understand that the members of the buying center play a variety of different roles in the process.

Role	Potential Player	Responsibility
● Initiator	● Production employees, sales manager, almost anyone	● Recognizes that a purchase needs to be made
● User	● Production employees, secretaries, almost anyone	● Individual(s) who will ultimately use the product
● Gatekeeper	● Buyer/purchasing agent	● Controls flow of information to others in the organization
● Influencer	● Engineers, quality control experts, technical specialists, outside consultants	● Affects decision by giving advice and sharing expertise
● Decider	● Purchasing agent, managers, CEO	● Makes the final purchase decision
● Buyer	● Purchasing agent	● Executes the purchase decision

When a firm needs to select a location for a company meeting, the needs and wants of the users—the meeting participants—are usually a priority. Resorts that provide good meeting facilities and opportunities for recreational activities are usually on top of the list of possible locations.

the purchasing agent. If the purchase is complex, a manager or CEO may be the decider. Quite obviously, the decider is key to a marketer's success and deserves a lot of attention in the selling process.

The *buyer* is the person who has responsibility for executing the purchase. Although the buyer often has a role in identifying and evaluating alternative suppliers, this person's primary function is handling the details of the purchase. The buyer obtains competing bids, negotiates contracts, and arranges delivery dates and payment plans. Once a firm makes the purchase decision, marketers turn their attention to negotiating the details of the purchase with the buyer. Successful marketers are well aware that providing exemplary service in this stage of the purchase can be key to future sales.

The Business Buying Decision Process

We've seen there are a number of players in the business buying process, beginning with an initiator and ending with a buyer. To make matters even more challenging to marketers, members of the buying team go through several stages in the decision-making process. The business buying decision process, as Figure 7.6 shows, is a series of steps similar to those in the consumer decision process. To help understand these steps, let's say you've just started working at the Way Radical Skateboard Company and you've been assigned to be in the buying center for the purchase of new Web page design computer software, a new-task buy for your firm.

PROBLEM RECOGNITION

As in consumer buying, the first step in the business buying decision process occurs when someone sees that a purchase can solve a problem. For straight rebuy purchases, this step may

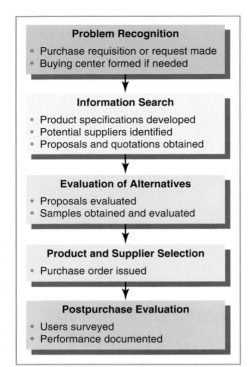

FIGURE 7.6

Steps in the Business Buying Decision Process

The steps in the business buying decision process are the same as those in the consumer decision process. But for business purchases, each step may be far more complex and require more attention from marketers.

---

result because the firm has run out of paper, pens, or garbage bags. In these cases the buyer places the order and the decision-making process ends. Recognition of the need for modified rebuy purchases often comes from wanting to replace outdated existing equipment, from changes in technology, or from an ad, brochure, or some other marketing communication that offers the customer a better product or one at a lower price.

The need for new-task purchases often occurs because the firm wants to enhance its operations in some way or when a smart salesperson tells the business customer about a new product that will increase the efficiency of the firm's operations. In the case of Way Radical's new software purchase, your marketing department has previously had its Web page designed and maintained by an outside agency. The company has become dissatisfied with the outside supplier and has decided to move the design function in-house. Now new software is needed to create a truly Radical Web site.

INFORMATION SEARCH

In the second step of the decision process (for purchases other than straight rebuys) the buying center searches for information about products and suppliers. Members of the buying center may individually or collectively refer to reports in trade magazines and journals, seek advice from outside consultants, and pay close attention to marketing communications from different manufacturers and suppliers. As in consumer marketing, it's the job of marketers to make sure that information is available when and where business customers want it—by placing ads in trade magazines, by mailing brochures and other printed material to prospects, and by having a well-trained, enthusiastic sales force regularly calling on customers. For Way Radical's purchase, you may try to find out what software your outside supplier has been using (if the supplier will tell you), you may talk to the information technology experts in your firm, or you may review ads and articles in trade magazines.

product specifications
■ A written description of the quality, size, weight, and so forth required of a product purchase.

Developing Product Specifications Business buyers often develop **product specifications**, that is, a written description of the quality, size, weight, color, features, quantity, training, warranty, service terms, and delivery requirements for the purchase. When the product needs are complex or technical, engineers and other experts (such as professional firefighters) are the key players in identifying specific product characteristics and determining whether standardized, off-the-shelf or customized, made-to-order goods and services will do. Although there is excellent Web design software available, for some computer applications custom-designed software is necessary.

Obtaining Proposals   Once the product specifications are in hand, the next step may be to obtain written or verbal proposals, or bids, from one or more potential suppliers. For standardized or branded products in which there are few, if any, differences in the products of different suppliers, this may be as simple as an informal request for pricing information, including discounts, shipping charges, and confirmation of delivery dates. At other times the potential suppliers will receive a formal written request for proposal or request for quotation that requires detailed proposals or price quotations for supplying the product. For the Way Radical software, which is likely to be a standardized software package, you will probably just ask for general pricing information.

EVALUATION OF ALTERNATIVES

In this stage of the business buying decision process, the buying center assesses the proposals. Total spending for goods and services can have a major impact on the firm's profitability, so all other things being equal, price is the primary consideration. Pricing evaluations, of course, take into account discount policies for certain quantities, returned goods policies, the cost of repair and maintenance services, terms of payment, and the cost of financing large purchases. For capital equipment, cost criteria also include the life expectancy of the purchase, the expected resale value, and disposal costs for the old equipment. In some cases the buying center may negotiate with the preferred supplier to match the lowest bidder.

Although a bidder often is selected because it offers the lowest price, there are times when the buying decision is based on other factors. For example, American Express wins bids for its travel agency business by offering extra services other agencies don't typically offer, such as a corporate credit card and monthly reports that detail the company's total travel expenses.

The more complex and costly the purchase, the more time buyers spend searching for the best supplier—and the more marketers must do to win the order. Marketers often make formal presentations and product demonstrations to the buying center group. In the case of installations and large equipment, marketers sometimes arrange for buyers to speak with or even visit other customers to examine how the product performs. For the Way Radical Web site, your buying center may ask salespeople from various companies to demonstrate their software for your group so that you can compare the capabilities of different products.

PRODUCT AND SUPPLIER SELECTION

Once buyers have assessed all proposals, it's time for the rubber to hit the road. The next step in the buying process is the purchase decision—the selection of the best product and supplier to meet the firm's needs. Although price is usually a factor, in firms that have adopted a total quality management approach, the quality, reliability, and durability of materials and component parts are paramount. Reliability and durability rank especially high for equipment and systems that keep the firm's operations running smoothly without interruption. For some purchases warranties, repair service, and regular maintenance after the sale are important. For Way Radical, the final decision may be based not only on the capabilities of the software itself but also the technical support provided by the software company. What kind of support is available and at what cost to the company?

A supplier's ability to make on-time deliveries is the critical factor in the selection process for firms that have adopted an inventory management system called **just in time (JIT)**. JIT systems reduce stock to very low levels or even zero and ensure a constant inventory through deliveries just when needed. The advantage of JIT systems is the reduced cost of warehousing. For both manufacturers and resellers that use JIT systems, the choice of supplier may come down to one whose location is nearest. To win a large customer, a supplier may even have to be willing to set up production facilities close to the customer to guarantee JIT delivery (recall that Lion Apparel considered this option when expanding overseas).[12]

One of the most important decisions of a buyer is how many suppliers can best serve the firm's needs. Sometimes one supplier is more beneficial to the organization than multiple suppliers. **Single sourcing**, in which a buyer and seller work quite closely, is particularly important

just in time (JIT) ■ Inventory management and purchasing processes that manufacturers and resellers use to reduce inventory to very low levels and ensure that deliveries from suppliers arrive only when needed.

single sourcing ■ The business practice of buying a particular product from only one supplier.

multiple sourcing ■ The business practice of buying a particular product from many suppliers.

4 *Bookmark It!*

Make a list of the ways the business-to-business decision process is different from the consumer decision process. Then make a list of how the two are alike. Find an ad in a trade magazine (check the library) and tell what part of the business buying process it is targeting. Which type of decision maker is it targeting?

reciprocity ■ A trading partnership in which two firms agree to buy from one another.

outsourcing ■ The business buying process of obtaining outside vendors to provide goods or services that otherwise might be supplied in house.

reverse marketing ■ A business practice in which a buyer firm attempts to identify suppliers who will produce products according to the buyer firm's specifications.

when a firm needs frequent deliveries or specialized products. But reliance on a single source means that the firm is at the mercy of the chosen supplier to deliver the needed goods or services without interruption.

Multiple sourcing means buying a product from several different suppliers. Under this system, suppliers are more likely to remain price competitive. And if one supplier has problems with delivery, the firm has others to fall back on. However, using one or a few suppliers rather than many has its advantages. A firm that buys from a single supplier becomes a large customer with a lot of clout when it comes to negotiating prices and contract terms. Having one or a few suppliers also lowers the firm's administrative costs because it has fewer invoices to pay, fewer contracts to negotiate, and fewer salespeople to see than if it used many sources.

Sometimes supplier selection is based on **reciprocity**, which means that a buyer and seller agree to be each other's customers by saying essentially, "I'll buy from you and you buy from me." For example, a firm that supplies parts to a company that manufactures trucks would agree to buy trucks from only that firm.

The U.S. government frowns on reciprocal agreements and often determines that such agreements between large firms are illegal because they limit free competition—new suppliers simply don't have a chance against the preferred suppliers. Reciprocity between smaller firms, that is, firms that are not so large as to control a significant proportion of the business in their industry, is legal in the United States if it is noncoercive and voluntarily agreed to by both parties. In other countries reciprocity is a practice that is common and even expected in business-to-business marketing.

Outsourcing occurs when firms obtain outside vendors to provide goods or services that might otherwise be supplied in-house. For example, Aramark provides a wide range of services for business and organizational customers—including uniforms for Wal-Mart, child care for the Pentagon, and even serving "mystery meat" in hundreds of university cafeterias.

Yet another type of buyer–seller partnership is **reverse marketing**. Instead of sellers trying to identify potential customers and then "pitching" their products, buyers try to find suppliers capable of producing specific needed products and then attempt to "sell" the idea to the suppliers. The seller aims to satisfy the buying firm's needs. Often large poultry producers practice reverse marketing. Perdue supplies baby chickens, chicken food, financing for chicken houses, medications, and everything else necessary for farmers to lay "golden eggs" for the company. The farmer is assured a market and Perdue is guaranteed a supply of chickens.

So we see that even the final product and supplier selection for business-to-business customers can be quite complex. By understanding the various requirements and options that business customers might require, marketers can develop products and services that meet their needs.

POSTPURCHASE EVALUATION

Just as consumers evaluate purchases, an organizational buyer assesses whether the performance of the product and the supplier is living up to expectations. The buyer surveys the users to determine their satisfaction with the product as well as with the installation, delivery, and service provided by the supplier. By reviewing supplier performance, a firm decides whether to keep or drop the supplier. Many suppliers recognize the importance of conducting their own performance reviews on a regular basis. Measuring up to a customer's expectations can mean winning or losing a big account. Many a supplier has lost business because of a past history of late deliveries or poor equipment repairs and maintenance.

Electronic Business-to-Business Commerce

The Internet has brought about the most important changes in organizational buying behavior in recent years. Electronic commerce, or e-commerce, is the buying and selling of products electronically via the Internet. We see e-commerce in consumer markets—sites such as Amazon.com or alloy.com that sell books or cool clothes (more on that subject in

Chapter 18). Here we're concerned with e-commerce in business markets: **Business-to-business (B2B) e-commerce** refers to the Internet exchanges between two or more businesses or organizations. B2B e-commerce includes exchanges of information, products, services, and payments. It's not as glitzy as consumer e-commerce, but it sure has changed the way businesses operate.

In truth, firms have used electronic data interchange (EDI) systems to communicate with business partners for several decades. EDI allows for limited communication through the exchange of computer data between two companies. But EDI is expensive and transmits only rigidly formatted electronic documents such as purchase orders and invoices.

Today many firms have replaced their EDI systems with Internet tools that allow them to electronically transfer all kinds of data—even engineering drawings—as well as to make EDI-type exchanges. In a typical year General Electric buys $1 billion worth of supplies over the Internet, saving an estimated 20 percent on the purchase price because the Internet allows GE to reach a broader base of suppliers than is possible with other means of communication. For sellers, too, e-commerce provides remarkable advantages. Boeing, for example, received orders for $100 million in spare parts in the first year its Web site was in operation.[13]

Using the Internet for e-commerce allows business marketers to link directly to suppliers, factories, distributors, and their customers, radically reducing the time necessary for order and delivery of goods, tracking sales, and getting feedback from customers. Forrester Research, a leading Internet research firm, projects that by 2004 total B2B sales will reach $2.7 trillion. Half of those transactions will take place through auctions, bids, and exchanges.[14]

In the simplest form of B2B e-commerce, the Internet provides an online catalog of products and services that businesses need. Companies find that their Internet site is important for delivering online technical support, product information, order status information, and customer service to corporate customers.

Dell discovered early on that it could serve the needs of its customers more effectively by tailoring its Internet presence to different customer segments, that is, consumers interested in computers for home and office use, small businesses, medium and large businesses, state and local governments, the federal government, educational institutions, and health care organizations. Dell's Internet site allows shoppers to get recommendations based on their customer segment. The computer giant saves millions of dollars a year by replacing hard-copy manuals with electronic downloads. For its larger customers, Dell provides customer-specific, password-protected pages that allow business customers to obtain technical support or to place an order.

business-to-business (B2B) e-commerce ▪ Internet exchanges between two or more businesses or organizations.

Dell has learned that it can do a better job of serving its business-to-business customers by developing sections of its Internet site tailored to the needs of each segment such as small business, government, and so on. Prospective customers who visit the Dell homepage have the option of going to the area that is especially designed for them.

INTRANETS, EXTRANETS, AND PRIVATE EXCHANGES

Although the Internet is the primary means of B2B e-commerce, many companies maintain intranets, which provide more secure means of conducting business. As we said in Chapter 5, an intranet is an internal corporate computer network that uses Internet technology to link company departments, employees, and databases. Intranets give only authorized employees access. They allow companies to process internal transactions with greater control and consistency because of some of the security measures possible. We will talk about these later in this section. Businesses also use intranets for videoconferencing, distributing internal documents, communicating with geographically dispersed branches, and training employees.

When a company allows certain suppliers, customers, and others outside the organization to access its intranet, the system is known as an **extranet**. A business customer who has been authorized to use a supplier's extranet can place orders online. Extranets can be especially useful for companies that need to have secure communications between the company and its dealers, distributors, and/or franchisees.

Tricon Restaurant International, parent company of Taco Bell, has found extranets a good way to communicate with franchisees.[15] Taco Bell had been spending hundreds of thousands of dollars a year sending informational update packages—everything from recipes to tie-ins to a popular ad campaign featuring a Spanish-speaking Chihuahua—to its 2,800 independent franchised restaurants around the world. Now thousands of documents are on Taco Bell's extranet where franchisees can wake up to new information every morning. Tricon plans to extend its extranet operations to its other two restaurant chains, KFC and Pizza Hut.

As you can imagine intranets and extranets are very cost-efficient. Prudential Health Care's extranet allows its corporate customers to enroll new employees and check eligibility and claim status themselves, which saves Prudential money because fewer customer service personnel are needed, there are no packages of insurance forms to mail back and forth, and Prudential doesn't even have to input policyholder data into the company database.[16]

extranet ■ Private, corporate computer network that links company departments, employees, and databases to suppliers, customers, and others outside the organization.

The popularity of online systems to connect buyers and sellers fuels demand for sophisticated software systems to manage these linkages.

In addition to saving companies money, extranets allow business partners to collaborate on projects (such as product design) and to build relationships. Hewlett-Packard and Procter & Gamble swap marketing plans and review ad campaigns with their advertising agencies through extranets. This way they can exchange ideas quickly, without having to spend money on travel and meetings. General Electric's extranet, called the Trading Process Network (TPN), connects GE with large buyers such as Con Edison.[17]

Some of the most interesting online activity in the B2B world is taking place on **private exchanges**. No, these aren't "adult sites" but rather they are systems that link a specially invited group of suppliers and partners over the Web. A private exchange allows companies to collaborate with suppliers they trust—without sharing sensitive information with others.

private exchanges ■
Systems that link an invited group of suppliers and partners over the Web.

Wal-Mart, IBM, and Hewlett-Packard are among the giant firms already operating private exchanges. Many other companies are getting on board as well. For example, the director of inventory control for Ace Hardware can click his mouse and instantly get an up-to-the minute listing of the screwdrivers, hammers, and other products his suppliers have in stock. In addition, suppliers he has invited to participate in his private exchange (and only those suppliers) can submit bids when he sees that Ace stores are running low on hammers. In the "old days" before this process, it would take 7 to 10 days to purchase more hammers, and Ace's suppliers could only guess how many they should have on hand to supply the store chain at any given time. The system benefits everyone because Ace keeps tighter controls on its inventories, and its suppliers have a more accurate picture of the store's needs so they can get rid of unneeded inventory and streamline their costs.

Indeed, IBM estimates that it saved almost $400 million in 2000 by relying on a private exchange system. Small wonder that one research firm estimates the world's biggest firms will soon spend between $50 million to $100 million total to build private exchanges.[18]

It all sounds great—perhaps too great. Is there a downside to B2B e-commerce? Let's see.

Internet security is a major problem for B2B marketers. e Security Online LLC, an Ernst & Young LLP company, offers a Web-based application that enables firms to asses and manage security risks.

SECURITY ISSUES

There are several security issues with B2B e-commerce. You may be concerned about someone obtaining your credit card number and charging even more to your account than you do, but companies have even greater worries. When hackers break into company sites, they can destroy company records and steal trade secrets. Both B2C and B2B e-commerce companies worry about *authentication* and ensuring that transactions are secure. Authentication means making sure that only authorized individuals are allowed to access a site and place an order.

Maintaining security also requires firms to keep the information transferred as part of a transaction, such as a credit card number, from criminals' hard drives.

Well meaning but careless employees can create security problems as well. They can give out unauthorized access to company computer systems by being careless about keeping their

Real People, Real Choices:

How It Worked Out at Lion Apparel

Steve selected option 1. He gambled that the brigade's new approach to buying and managing turnout gear would be a market-changing event leading to similar business opportunities elsewhere. This strategy created new barriers to the competition because (1) the new contracts were long term (five to seven years) instead of six months to one year, and (2) it required a deep relationship between the supplier and brigade that would be hard to undo at the end of such a long-term contract. Steve realized that Lion could not credibly market itself as an expert in this long-term relationship if it did not control the service end. And he understood that Lion had to position itself as a "local" provider if his company was to have any chance in convincing local authorities that its operations meet local standards. In fact, Lion was able to go one better by partnering with a local agency in the apparel manufacturing business that employed the disabled.

Lion beat out four European and two U.S. competitors for the contract with what it named its TotalCare™ product. In the process, the company "changed the rules" of marketing to European fire brigades. Before this contract, the customer's focus was on initial product quality only, and even that focus was weak. Now service delivery is on an equal footing with product quality, and Lion has mastered both. As a result, in a three-year period, Lion won five TotalCare™ contracts with other fire brigades in the same country and its business has expanded to three other European countries. Lion was able to grow its European business in part because the company focused its marketing efforts on doing free internal "risk assessments" with prospective customers that highlighted the poor practices and procedures currently used, creating incentives to change to TotalCare.™

This experience sold Steve on the benefits of embracing an innovative marketing strategy in a business-to-business setting, even in an environment that tended to be fairly traditional and not very open to change. Lion embraced and developed the product delivery and service concept while competitors resisted it. This approach forced Lion to view itself as a solution provider instead of a product supplier, a difficult transition for a company that had always regarded itself as only a manufacturer. The experience transformed Lion into the first truly multinational provider of turnout gear. Lion is "on fire overseas" and expects to establish sales groups with local manufacturing located on each major continent by 2006.

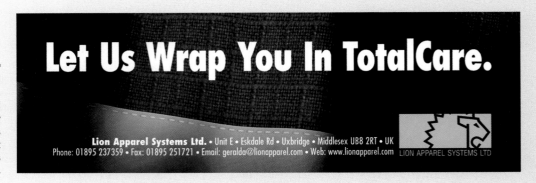

Building on its initial success in Europe, Lion Apparel successfully developed its TotalCare™ product for fire brigades overseas.

passwords into the system a secret. For example, hackers can guess at passwords that are easy—nicknames, birth dates, hobbies, a spouse's name. To increase security of their Internet sites and transactions, most companies now have safeguards in place—firewalls and encryption devices, to name the most common two.

Firewalls A **firewall** is a combination of hardware and software that ensures only authorized individuals gain entry into a computer system. The firewall monitors and controls all traffic between the Internet and the intranet to restrict access. Companies may even place additional firewalls within their intranet when they wish only designated employees to have access to certain parts of the system. Although firewalls can be fairly effective (even though none are totally foolproof), they require costly, constant monitoring.

Encryption *Encryption* means scrambling a message so that only another individual (or computer) that has the right "key" for deciphering it can unscramble it. Otherwise, it looks like gobbledygook. The message is inaccessible without the appropriate encryption software—kind of like a decoder ring you might find in a cereal box. Without encryption, it would be easy for unethical people to get your credit card number by creating a "sniffer" program that intercepts and reads messages. A sniffer program finds messages with four blocks of four numbers, copies the data, and voila! Someone else has your credit card number. Even with basic encryption software, hackers have been able to steal thousands of credit card numbers from companies including Creditcards.com, Western Union, and online music retailer CD Universe. In these cases, the hackers threatened to post the stolen credit card numbers online unless extortion money was paid.[19]

firewall ■ A combination of computer hardware and software that ensure only authorized individuals gain entry into a computer system.

Chapter Summary

1. **Describe the general characteristics of business-to-business markets and business buying practices.**

   Business-to-business markets include business or organizational customers that buy goods and services for purposes other than for personal consumption. Business customers are usually few in number, may be geographically concentrated, and often purchase higher-priced products in larger quantities. Business demand is derived from the demand for another good or service, is generally not affected by price increases or decreases, is subject to great fluctuations, and may be tied to the demand and availability of some other good.

2. **Tell how marketers classify business or organizational markets.**

   Business customers include producers, resellers, governments, and not-for-profit organizations. Producers purchase materials, parts, and various goods and services needed to produce other goods and services to be sold at a profit. Resellers purchase finished goods to resell at a profit, as well as other goods and services to maintain their operations. Governments and other not-for-profit organizations purchase the goods and services necessary to fulfill their objectives. The North American Industry Classification System (NAICS), a numerical coding system developed by NAFTA countries, is a widely used classification system for business and organizational markets.

3. **Explain the business buying situation and describe business buyers.**

   The business buy class identifies the degree and effort required to make a business buying decision. Purchase situations can be straight rebuy, modified rebuy, and new-task buying. Business buying is usually handled by trained professional buyers. A buying center is a group of people who work together to make a buying decision. The roles in the buying center are initiator, user, gatekeeper, influencer, decider, and buyer.

4. **Understand the stages in the business buying decision process.**

   The stages in the business buying decision process are similar to but more complex than the steps in consumer decision making. These steps include problem recognition, information search during which buyers develop product specifications and obtain proposals from prospective sellers, evaluating the proposals, selecting a supplier, and formally evaluating the performance of the product and the supplier. A firm's purchasing options include single or multiple sourcing. In outsourcing, firms obtain outside vendors to provide goods or services that otherwise might be supplied in-house. Other business buying activities are reciprocity and reverse marketing.

5. Understand the growing role of B2B e-commerce.

Business-to-business (B2B) e-commerce refers to Internet exchanges of information, products, services, or payments between two or more businesses or organizations and allows business marketers to link directly to suppliers, factories, distributors, and their customers. An intranet is a secure internal corporate network used to link company departments, employees, and databases. Extranets link a company with authorized suppliers, customers, or others outside the organization. Companies address security issues by using firewalls and encryption. Firewalls consist of hardware and software that ensure only authorized individuals gain entry into a computer system. Encryption means scrambling a message so that only another individual (or computer) that has the right "key" for deciphering it can unscramble it.

Chapter Review

■ MARKETING CONCEPTS:
TESTING YOUR KNOWLEDGE

1. How do business-to-business markets differ from consumer markets? How do these differences affect marketing strategies?
2. How is business-to-business demand different from consumer demand? What are some of the factors that cause business demand to fluctuate?
3. Describe new-task buys, modified rebuys, and straight rebuys. What are some different marketing strategies called for by each?
4. How are business-to-business markets generally classified? What is the NAICS?
5. What are the characteristics of business buyers?
6. What is a buying center? What are the roles of the various people in a buying center?
7. What are the stages in the business buying decision process? What happens in each stage?
8. What is single sourcing? Multiple sourcing? Outsourcing? Explain how reciprocity and reverse marketing operate in business-to-business markets.
9. Explain the role of B2B e-commerce in today's marketplace.
10. What are some of the security issues that B2B marketers face? How can a firm protect itself against security risks?
11. How do intranets and extranets facilitate efficient B2B activities?

■ MARKETING CONCEPTS:
DISCUSSING CHOICES AND ISSUES

1. Do you agree with the idea that business-to-business marketing is more important to a country's economy than consumer marketing? Which one do you think

provides better career opportunities for new college graduates? Explain your answers.
2. E-commerce is dramatically changing the way business-to-business transactions take place. What are the advantages of B2B e-commerce to companies? To society? Are there any disadvantages of B2B e-commerce?
3. The practice of buying business products based on sealed competitive bids is popular among all types of business buyers. What are the advantages and disadvantages of this practice to buyers? What are the advantages and disadvantages to sellers? Should companies always give the business to the lowest bidder? Why or why not?
4. When firms engage in outsourcing, they relinquish control over how goods and services are produced. What are the advantages of outsourcing to a firm? What are some of the hazards of outsourcing? What can firms do to make sure that outsourcing benefits both them and the outsourcing firm?
5. E-commerce presents a number of security issues. Should firms limit their e-commerce operations because of the threat of hackers?

■ MARKETING PRACTICE:
APPLYING WHAT YOU'VE LEARNED

1. You are looking for a part-time job and being considered by a small, weekly newspaper. Knowing that you are a marketing student, the editor has asked you to provide a sample article that explains business demand in a way that will be interesting to the owners of small local shops and businesses. Write that article and circulate it among three classmates, asking each to provide brief written comments and suggestions.
2. Assume you are a new employee of a marketing consulting firm. One of the company's clients is a medium-sized

manufacturer of uniforms worn by employees of delivery, cleaning, and other type service firms. The company is considering moving online with B2B e-commerce. Your boss has asked you to prepare a list of advantages and risks the company will face in this move to the Web. Prepare the list and discuss each point with a classmate who assumes the client's role.

3. As a new director of materials management for a textile firm that manufactures sheets and towels, you are hoping to simplify the buying process where possible, thus reducing costs for the firm. You have first examined each purchase and classified it as a straight rebuy, a modified rebuy, or a new-task purchase. Your next job is to outline the procedures or steps in the purchasing process for each type of purchase. Indicate the type of purchase and outline the steps that must be taken in the purchase of each of the following items.
   a. computer paper
   b. textile dyes for this year's fashion colors
   c. new sewing robotics
   d. new software to control the weaving processes

MARKETING MINI-PROJECT: LEARNING BY DOING

The purpose of this mini-project is to gain knowledge about one business-to-business market using the NAICS codes and other government information.

1. Select an industry of interest to you and use the NAICS information found on the Internet (www.census.gov/pub/epcd/www/naics.html) or in your library.
   a. What are the codes for each of the following classifications?
      NAICS Sector (two digits)
      NAICS Subsector (three digits)
      NAICS Industry Group (four digits)
      NAICS Industry (five digits)
      U.S. Industry (six digits)
   b. What types of products are or are not included in this industry?

2. Locate the U.S. Industrial Outlook or Standard & Poor's Industry Surveys in your library to find the answers to the following.
   a. What was the value of industry shipments (sales) for the United States in the latest year reported?
   b. What were worldwide sales for the industry in the most recent year reported?

3. The U.S. Census Bureau publishes a number of economic censuses every five years covering years ending in 2 and 7. These include the following publications: *Census of Retail Trade, Census of Wholesale Trade, Census of Service Industries, Census of Transportation, Census of Manufacturers, Census of Mineral Industries,* and *Census of Construction Industries.* Use the *Census*

of Manufacturers to determine the value of shipments in your industry for the most recent year reported.

4. *Ward's Business Directory* provides useful industry-specific information. Use it to find the names and addresses of the top four public companies in the industry and their sales revenues.

5. Compact Disclosure provides information from company annual reports on CD-ROM. Use it to provide the following for the four companies listed in question 4.
   a. income statements
   b. net sales, gross profits, and income before tax

6. *The Statistical Abstract of the United States* provides information on the economic, demographic, social, and political structures of the United States. It provides data on the sales of products in consumer markets. Use it to complete the following.
   a. Find a product in the consumer market that is produced by your industry (or is down the chain from your industry, for example, automobiles from the steel industry).
   b. Determine the sales of the consumer product category for the most recent year reported.

REAL PEOPLE, REAL SURFERS: EXPLORING THE WEB

Lion Apparel isn't the only company that makes firefighter protective apparel. Some other companies include Quaker Safety Products Corp. (www.quakersafety.com), Fire-Gear Inc. (www.firegear.com), Fire-Dex Inc. (www.firedex.com), Globe Firefighter Suits (www.globefiresuits.com), Cairns Protective Clothing (www.carinsclothing.com), and Quest Protective Clothing (www.questhq.com). Visit Lion Apparel's Web site (www.lionapparel.com). Then explore the Web sites of one or more other firefighter protective clothing manufacturers.

Based on your experience, answer the following questions:

1. In general, how do the Web sites compare? Which are easier to navigate and why? Which are more innovative and attractive and why?

2. Evaluate each site from the perspective of a fire department chief. What feature in each site would be useful? What information is available that a fire chief might need? Over all, which site do you feel would be most useful to the fire chief? Why?

PLAN IT! DEVELOPING A MARKETING PLAN

As your instructor directs, create a new marketing plan (using Marketing Plan Pro software or a written marketing plan format) to document your marketing decisions or answer these questions in a written or oral report.

According to the marketing plan in Appendix A, CFS markets through resellers such as wholesalers and retailers.

1. In thinking about next year's marketing plan, how might CFS use the NAICS to identify potential channel members?
2. If CFS targets retailers it hasn't worked with before, would the retailers consider this buying situation a straight rebuy, a modified rebuy, or a new–task buy—and what are the implications for the marketing plan?
3. Why does CFS need to know whether resellers use centralized or decentralized purchasing?

Key Terms

acceleration principle (multiplier effect), (195)

business-to-business (B2B) e-commerce, (209)

business-to-business marketing, (191)

buy class, (200)

buying center, (203)

centralized purchasing, (203)

competitive bids, (198)

derived demand, (194)

extranet, (210)

firewall, (213)

government markets, (197)

inelastic demand, (195)

intranet, (210)

joint demand, (196)

just in time (JIT), (207)

modified rebuy, (201)

multiple sourcing, (208)

new-task buy, (201)

North American Industry Classification System (NAICS), (199)

not-for-profit institutions, (198)

organizational markets, (191)

outsourcing, (208)

private exchanges, (211)

producers, (197)

product specifications, (206)

reciprocity, (208)

resellers, (197)

reverse marketing, (208)

single sourcing, (207)

straight rebuy, (200)

MARKETING IN ACTION: CHAPTER 7 CASE

REAL CHOICES AT PITNEY BOWES

In 1920 Arthur H. Pitney convinced U.S. postal officials that postage meters were a good idea. For over 75 years after that, the company, cofounded by Pitney and Walter H. Bowes, held a near monopoly in the postage meter business. They had 85 percent of the U.S. market for postage meters with 1.3 million in use. And they were one of the country's most profitable companies with a 22 percent return on equity.

But in 1997 problems loomed on the horizon. Although there had been attempts to undermine Pitney Bowes's position over the years, none had constituted a real threat. With technological changes during the 1990s and greater global competition, things began to change. During the previous year, the company had lost 2 percent of its mechanical meter customers to competitors that offered electronic machines—and the migration to electronic machines had barely begun.

Surprisingly, however, an even bigger threat came from the U.S. Postal Service (USPS). The USPS was also facing increased competition as it saw its mail delivery service being undermined by United Parcel Service, Federal Express, and other carriers. To add to the problem, e-mail was rapidly replacing "snail mail" in many people's lives. Because the demand for postage meters was derived demand, depending on people's use of the USPS, this meant less need for Pitney Bowes's products.

Postmaster General Marvin Runyon decided to fight back. He wanted more innovative postage meter equipment—postage meters that businesses could refill by phone instead of having to stand in line at a local post office. Runyon also was demanding the development of a digital postmark similar to the UPC codes on product packaging. A digital postmark would allow the USPS to link data about the sender and recipient of a piece of mail together in a database, aggregate those data into neighborhood blocks as the Census Bureau does, and sell it to savvy marketers who wanted to know which neighborhoods read *Ski* magazine and which order from Fredericks of Hollywood. The digital postmark would also allow the USPS to schedule its workers and vehicles more efficiently. For businesses, the digital postmark would certify that mail was from whom it said it was from and that it had not been altered along the way. What's more, the USPS wanted digital postage meters to replace older mechanical meters within two years, providing a made-to-order opportunity for Pitney Bowes's competitors.

To make matters worse for Pitney Bowes, a company called E-Stamp was working to develop a product called PC Postage that would allow businesses to stamp their own mail using a personal computer and a standard office printer. Postage for the system would be sold by the USPS over the Internet.

Although Pitney Bowes had an enviable record of success in the business-to-business market, it had never promoted its business aggressively, fearful of government antitrust action because of its monopoly status. But in the current climate, would business as usual be sufficient to guarantee the company a successful future?

Pitney Bowes's chief executive, Michael Critelli, thought that the direction of the company ought to change—Pitney Bowes should go from being a manufacturer of precision machines to one that solves a company's postal problems. The company was already doing some of this. Over 1,000 companies including large firms such as NationsBank had outsourced their entire mailroom operations to Pitney Bowes. Pitney Bowes could go even further in that direction by developing such products as seminars or a CD to help businesses and other organizations be more successful with direct mail.

Some at Pitney Bowes thought the company ought to focus on the small business and home office market. Pitney Bowes was already selling a small unit called the personal post office that printed a promotional message on envelopes along with postage and could be refilled by phone.

Of course, if Pitney Bowes allocated resources to new directions instead of its core meter business, it risked losing market share. Pitney Bowes needed to make decisions quickly.

Source: Damon Darlin, "Data-Mining the Mail," *Forbes*, February 24, 1997, 112; Damon Darlin, "Innovate or Die," *Forbes*, February 24, 1997, 108–112.

THINGS TO THINK ABOUT

1. What is the decision facing Pitney Bowes?
2. What factors are important in understanding the decision situation?
3. What are the alternatives?
4. What decision(s) do you recommend?
5. What are some ways to implement your recommendation(s)?

Bookmark It!

OBJECTIVES:

1. Understand the need for market segmentation in today's business environment.

2. Know the different dimensions marketers use to segment consumer and industrial markets.

3. Explain how marketers evaluate and select potential market segments.

4. Explain how marketers develop a targeting strategy.

5. Understand how a firm develops and implements a positioning strategy.

6. Know how marketers practice customer relationship management to increase long-term success and profits.

TARGET MARKETING STRATEGIES AND CUSTOMER RELATIONSHIP MANAGEMENT

Real People,
Real Choices:

Meet Landon Pollack, a Decision Maker at MPower Living

CURRENT POSITION: President, MPower Living.

CAREER PATH: Business experience includes owning and operating a personal training consulting business, an exotic animal import/export business, a retail sports store, a mail-order business specializing in sports memorabilia, and a fitness center.

WHAT I DO WHEN I'M NOT WORKING: I work 15 hours a day. Business is life and life is business. I spend free time with my dogs Zeus, Zena, and Pookie.

FIRST JOB: Before school, selling cookies and lemonade on the streets of Greenwich Village in New York City, making over $500 a week. At age 11, I was a nationally established dealer of sports memorabilia.

A MISTAKE I WISH I HADN'T MADE: How I treated my body when I was training to be a professional baseball player. I trained too hard and too much, causing numerous injuries.

BUSINESS BOOK I'M READING: <u>Emotional Marketing</u> by Scott Robinette and Claire Brand.

HERO: As much as it might be a cliché, my mom and dad. My mom taught me about honesty and sincerity; my dad about heart, dogged determination, and not taking "no" as the final answer.

DON'T DO THIS WHEN INTERVIEWING WITH ME: Fidget, not pay attention, or ask pointless questions.

Getting Energized at MPower Living

Each year, Americans spend $300 billion on products and services to help them be healthy. As an entrepreneur with experience in the wellness industry, Landon Pollack saw an opportunity. He knew that there were already several well-established players—The Zone, Atkins Diet, Body for Life, Weight Watchers, Jenny Craig, OneBody, and GNC. However, he also saw a fragmented marketplace with a lot of companies offering specific products but no one-stop, personalized solution for consumers and professionals in the wellness industry.

In 1999 Landon started MPower, a healthy-living and aging-solutions company. Landon recruited health experts to help him construct a sound program, including a former surgeon general of the United States and former presidents of the American Psychological Association and the American Heart Association. He also enlisted the help of a panel of business advisors (including the first author of this book) to help him build and market a unique new program. As he planned out the MPower business, Landon had to answer a key question: Who would be his target market? What people would be the most interested in getting involved, and who would be motivated enough to follow through?

Landon polled his panel of advisors. He researched the wellness industry and obtained data about current users of competitors' products. He conducted numerous consumer interviews and focus groups. Landon identified his core audience as baby boomers between the ages of 35 to 54 with incomes greater than $40,000 per year. Industry studies and interviews showed that they were the most motivated to retain their health and that they spent money to do so. Landon broke this group down more finely:

- *Doers* are successful in taking action and are interested in making additional improvements in their lives.

Think and Do Like a Marketer

How will Landon's target market perceive MPower compared to other exercise or dieting alternatives? Talk to some people like the ones he wants to attract as customers. How do they feel about attaining a healthy lifestyle? What are they doing to achieve this goal? What barriers stand in their way? What do their answers tell you about the best way to reach this group?

- *Contemplators* are either seriously thinking of taking action or are trying to take action.
- *Noncontemplators* are not concerned about their health and are unlikely to be interested in healthy-living products and services.

Landon estimated that about 40 percent of baby boomers are doers while another 20 percent are contemplators. He picked doers as his primary target and hoped to attract many contemplators. Based on current patterns in the industry, he estimated that about two-thirds of his clientele would be women. Although these prospective customers were distributed around the country, Landon also predicted that he would attract more attention among people living on the East and West Coasts where interest in healthy lifestyles tends to be more prevalent.

Once the target was identified, the challenge was to figure out the best way to deliver MPower products. Landon knew he wanted to sell products and services at off-line and online locations, but he struggled with the right combination. These were the options he considered:

Option 1: Offer the personalized healthy-living programs online only but sell the needed products through an MPower retail store chain.

These retail settings would allow MPower personnel to follow up with participants in person. Health coaches would be available online, by telephone, and in the stores. But it is expensive to open and operate bricks-and-mortar facilities. MPower would also risk being perceived as a store that was trying to push its products rather than as a comprehensive health program.

Option 2: Offer the personal program at the retail store and sell additional products on a Web site.

The company would maintain the site for customer accounts and proprietary product sales and a call-in center staffed by health professionals. This strategy would allow MPower to concentrate on its core competency—the ability to develop a scientifically based, personalized healthy-living program. The downside was that Landon could miss out on customers who just wanted to purchase products without signing up for the entire program.

Option 3: Structure MPower as a retail store only, offering products such as supplements, printed media and software, active wear, skin care products, and other self-help products.

To attract customers, the store would also offer such amenities as a juice bar and a free personalized healthy-living plan to assist in product selection. Customers would easily identify the business because it would be visible. MPower could develop its own line of branded products to solidify its identity and differentiate itself from other companies.

But Landon couldn't be sure that the MPower concept would be clear or powerful enough to separate it from other retail stores such as GNC. And this setup would not enable MPower to offer any of the online features Landon envisioned for the company such as a personalized exercise program tailored to the precise needs of each subscriber.

Now join the decision team at MPower. Which option would you choose and why?

Feast or Famine: Selecting and Entering a Market

By now, we've heard over and over that the goal of the marketer is to satisfy needs, but in our modern, complex society it is naive to assume that everyone's needs are the same. Landon Pollack knows that even a "weighty" decision such as whether to gain or lose some pounds depends on many factors, including the stage of life the consumer is in, how important it is to look good to others, having motivation to give up those Oreos for tofu, and so on.

market fragmentation ■
Creation of many consumer groups due to a diversity of distinct needs and wants in modern society.

Understanding these factors gets even more complex today because technological and cultural advances in modern society have created a condition of **market fragmentation**. This condition occurs when people's diverse interests and backgrounds divide them into numerous

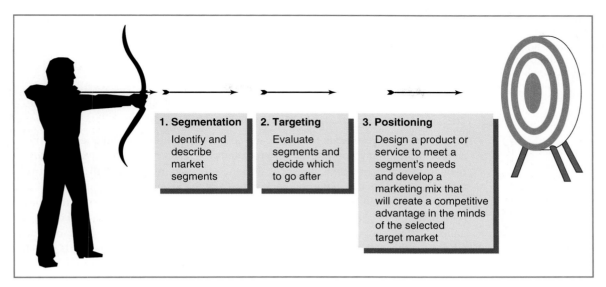

FIGURE 8.1

Steps in the Target Marketing Process

Target marketing strategy consists of three separate steps. Marketers first divide the market into meaningful segments, then select segments, and finally design a unique marketing mix for each segment.

different groups with distinct needs and wants. Because of this diversity, the same good or service will not appeal to everyone.

Consider, for example, the effects of fragmentation in the health and fitness industry. Back in the days when Pritikin was a best-selling diet, health-conscious consumers thought that just cutting fat would yield a lean body and good health. Today's consumers, however, have a whole litany of competing diets from which to choose. There's the Atkins diet or the Pritikin diet. There are Weight Watchers, Jenny Craig, Slim Fast, FitAmerica, and dozens of herbal remedies for people with weight problems. There are physicians who will even wire your jaw shut to keep you from inhaling those treats. And there are diets for every personailty.

Marketers must balance the efficiency of mass marketing, serving the same items to everyone, with the effectiveness of offering each individual exactly what she wants. Mass marketing is certainly the most efficient plan. It costs much less to offer one product to everyone, because that strategy eliminates the need for separate advertising campaigns and distinctive packages for each item. Consumers see things differently; from their perspective the best strategy would be to offer the perfect product for each individual. Unfortunately, that's often not realistic. Even Burger King's longtime motto, "Have It Your Way," was only true to a point: "Your way" is fine as long as you stay within the safe confines of familiar condiments such as mustard or ketchup. Don't dream of topping your burger with salsa, blue cheese, or some other "exotic" ingredient, and forget about ordering that "Diet Whopper" if you've decided to clean up your act!

Instead of trying to sell something to everyone, marketers such as MPower select a **target marketing strategy** in which they divide the total market into different segments based on customer characteristics, select one or more segments, and develop products to meet the needs of those specific segments. The three-step process of segmentation, targeting, and positioning is illustrated in Figure 8.1, and it's what we're going to check out in this chapter. Let's start with the first step—segmentation.

target marketing strategy
■ Dividing the total market into different segments based on customer characteristics, selecting one or more segments, and developing products to meet the needs of those specific segments.

Segmentation

Segmentation is the process of dividing a larger market into smaller pieces based on one or more meaningful, shared characteristics. Segmentation is a way of life for marketers. The truth: You can't please all the people all the time, so you need to take your best shot. Just how do marketers segment a population? How do they divide the whole pie into smaller slices they can "digest?" Segmenting the market is often necessary in both consumer and industrial markets.

segmentation ■ The process of dividing a larger market into smaller pieces based on one or more meaningful, shared characteristics.

In each case, the marketer must decide on one or more useful **segmentation variables**, that is, dimensions that divide the total market into fairly homogeneous groups, each with different needs and preferences. In this section we'll take a look at this process, beginning with the types of segmentation variables that marketers use to divide up end consumers.

ONE SIZE DOESN'T FIT ALL: DIMENSIONS FOR SEGMENTING CONSUMER MARKETS

At one time it was sufficient to divide the sports shoe market into athletes and nonathletes. But a walk through any sporting goods store today will reveal that the athlete market has fragmented in many directions, as shoes designed for jogging, basketball, tennis, cycling, cross-training, and even skateboarding beckon us from the aisles.

During the 1990s, obscure makers of athletic footwear geared to **Generation Y** (people born between 1977 and 1994), makers such as Vans, Airwalk, and DC, chalked up annual sales gains of 20 percent to 50 percent. Known to their peers as shredders, riders, or skaters, the kids who wear these shoes can be seen riding skateboards down the handrails and steps of city parks. They coast downhill and shoot into the air on snowboards. During mud season, they twist their stunt bikes down slippery hills, and in summer they flip and glide on wakeboards pulled by powerboats. Over the next few years, sports marketers expect the skateboard and snowboard populations to double and wakeboarders to soar sixfold. That growth brings with it the potential to sell many new products in a market that barely existed a few years ago.

generation Y ■ The group of consumers born between 1977 and 1994.

Several segmentation variables can slice up the market for all the shoe variations available today. First, not everyone is willing or able to drop $150 on the latest Air Jordans, so marketers consider income. Second, men may be more interested in basketball shoes while women snap up the latest aerobics styles, so marketers also consider gender. Because not all age groups are going to be equally interested in buying specialized athletic shoes, the larger consumer "pie"

Young shredders are a profitable market segment today.

can be sliced into smaller pieces in a number of ways, including demographic, psychological, and behavioral differences. Let's consider each variable in turn.

Segmenting by Demographics Demographics are measurable characteristics such as gender and age. Demographics are vital to identify the best potential customers for a good or service. These objective characteristics are (usually!) easy to identify and then it's just a matter of tailoring messages and products to relevant groups. IBM develops separate marketing messages to appeal to African American, Latino, Asian, Native American, disabled, gay and lesbian, and senior citizen groups. Each message uses copy and spokespeople likely to appeal to members of a specific segment. Ads for IBM's VoiceType software, which allows users to control the PC by voice, featured Curtis Mayfield, who was a Grammy award-winning soul singer and a quadraplegic. The demographic dimensions that marketers usually look at are age, gender, family structure, income and social class, race and ethnicity, and geography (or where people live). Let's take a quick look at how marketers can use each of these dimensions to slice up the consumer pie.

Age: Consumers of different age groups have different needs and wants. Members of a generation tend to share the same outlook and priorities. Levi Strauss has been successful in developing the idea that it is a "brand for life" by introducing products such as Dockers to meet the needs of consumers as they age.

Children have become an attractive age segment for marketers. Although kids obviously have a lot to say about purchases of toys and games, they influence other family purchases as well. By one estimate, American children aged 4 to 12 have a say in family-related purchases of more than $130 billion a year.[1] Kodak is one of many firms scrambling to attract kids. The company discovered that only 20 percent of children aged 5 to 12 own cameras, and they shoot an average of just one roll of film a year. Click! An opportunity to create a new market "developed" for Kodak. In a campaign called "Big Shots," ads portrayed photography as cool and a way to rebel against authority. Kodak packaged cameras with an envelope so it could mail developed film directly back to the young photographers. This way parents couldn't see the photos—and, presumably, ground the kid![2]

In a similar effort to target these kids' slightly older brothers and sisters, Polaroid launched its tiny I-Zone Instant Pocket Camera, which creates postage-stamp size photos or photo stickers aimed at the 12- to 17-year-old market.[3] Growing nearly twice as fast as the general population, this age group is expected to number 30 million by 2005—and teens spend an average of $3,000 per year.[4] Much of this money goes toward "feel-good" products: cosmetics, posters, and fast food—with the occasional nose ring thrown in as well.

Because they are so interested in many different products and have the resources to obtain them, many marketers, especially retailers such as Abercrombie & Fitch and Alloy, avidly court the teen market.[5] And, of course, there are subgroups within the teen market with their own musical idols, distinctive styles, and so on.

For example, Japanese youth are very style conscious and currently there are several niches or "tribes," each with very well-defined looks and rules.[6] A popular look for Japanese girls is called the "Gals"; they are easily recognized by their bleached yellow hair, salon-tanned skin, chalk-white lipstick, and seven-inch platform heels. Other groups include the Sports Clique (low-heeled Air Mocs and Gap clothing) and the Back-Harajuku Group (baggy sweatshirts, colorful jeans, sneakers, and long scarves).

As we said, Generation Y are those consumers born between the years 1977 and 1994. Sometimes referred to as the baby "boomlet," Generation Y is made up of the 71 million children of the baby boomers.[7] They are the first generation to grow up online and they are more ethnically diverse and larger in number than Generation X.

Generation Y is an attractive market for a host of consumer products because of their size (approximately 26 percent of the population) and because of their free-spending nature—as a group they spend about $200 billion annually. But Generation Y consumers are also hard to reach because they resist reading and increasingly turn the TV off. As a result, many marketers have had to develop other ways of reaching Generation Y, including online chat rooms, email promotions, and some of the more unusual "guerilla" marketing techniques we'll talk about in Chapter 16.

The group of consumers born between 1965 and 1976 consists of 46 million Americans sometimes known as **Generation X**, slackers or busters. Many of these people have a cynical attitude toward marketing—a chapter in a book called *Generation X* is "I am not a target market!"[8] As

generation X ■ The group of consumers born between 1965 and 1976.

one 20-year-old Japanese Xer commented, "I don't like to be told what's trendy. I can make up my own mind."[9]

Despite this tough reputation, members of Generation X who now are in their late twenties and thirties have mellowed with age. One study revealed that Xers are already responsible for 70 percent of new start-up businesses in the United States. An industry expert observed, "Today's Gen Xer is both values-oriented and value-oriented. This generation is really about settling down."[10] Many people in this segment seem to be determined to have stable families after being latchkey children themselves. Seven out of ten regularly save some portion of their income, a rate comparable to their parents'. Xers tend to view the home as an expression of individuality rather than material success. More than half are involved in home improvement and repair projects.[11] So much for slackers . . .

baby boomers ■ Segment of people born between 1946 and 1964.

Baby boomers, consumers born between 1946 and 1965 and who are now in their thirties, forties, and fifties, are an important segment to many marketers—if for no other reason than there are so many of them who are making a lot of money. Time-Warner formed a separate unit to publish magazines, including *Health, Parenting*, and *Cooking Light*, that specifically address baby boomers' interests in staying young, healthy—and sane—as they have kids of their own. To appeal to the many boomers who are trying to keep those bodies looking (somewhat) young, Quaker recently introduced Propel "fitness water," a flavored water with vitamins advertised with the line, "I don't live to exercise, I exercise to live."[12] And, of course, that's the age group Landon Pollack is going after with the MPower concept.

According to the 2000 census, there are 35 million Americans aged 65 or older—a 12 percent increase in this age segment since 1990.[13] Many consumers in their sixties and seventies are enjoying leisure time but are in declining health. Marketers are offering new products and services to these aging consumers, and some are adding product features convenient for older people. For example, Whirlpool sells kitchen ranges with side controls to allow wheel chair accessibility. Anheuser-Busch is testing a low-carbohydrate, low-calorie beer called Michelob Ultra in areas such as Florida and Arizona that have large numbers of aging party animals.[14] McDonald's has even focused on the romance of people growing old together. One commercial, called "Golden Years," features an older couple who fell in love over a McDonald's meal. Romance under the arches? Now that's what we'd call a cheap date.[15]

Gender: Many products, from fragrances to footwear, appeal to men or women either because of the nature of the product or because the marketer chose to appeal to one sex or the other. Segmenting by sex starts at a very early age—even diapers come in pink for girls and blue for boys. As proof that consumers take these differences seriously, market researchers report that most parents refuse to put male infants in pink diapers![16] In some cases, manufacturers develop parallel products to appeal to each sex. For example, male grooming products have traditionally been Gillette's priority since the company's founder introduced the safety razor in 1903. Today the company considers women a major market opportunity and continues to develop new shaving products for women.

Family Structure: Because family needs and expenditures change over time, one way to segment consumers is to consider the stage of the family life cycle they occupy (see Chapter 6). Not surprisingly, consumers in different life cycle segments are unlikely to need the same products, or at least they may not need these things in the same quantities.[17] For example, Procter & Gamble introduced Folger's Singles to people who live alone and don't need to brew a full pot of coffee at a time.[18]

As families age and move into new life stages, different product categories ascend and descend in importance. Young bachelors and newlyweds are the most likely to exercise, to go to bars, concerts, and movies, and to consume alcohol (in other words, party while you can). Older couples and bachelors are more likely to use maintenance services, and older people are a prime market for resort condominiums and golf products. Marketers need to discern the family life cycle segment of the target consumers by examining purchase data by family life cycle group.

Income and Social Class: The distribution of wealth is of great interest to marketers because it determines which groups have the greatest buying power. It should come as no surprise that many marketers yearn to capture the hearts and wallets of high-income consumers. Perhaps that explains a recent fashion trend featuring clothes made with real gold, including pinstriped suits selling from

$10,000 to $20,000.[19] At the same time other marketers target lower-income consumers, who make up about 40 percent of the U.S. market (as defined by households with incomes of $25,000 or less). Discount stores such as Target and Wal-Mart have done quite well by catering to this segment.

Race and Ethnicity: A consumer's national origin is often a strong indicator of his preferences for specific magazines or television shows, foods, apparel, and choice of leisure activities. Marketers need to be aware of these differences and sensitivities, especially in light of the terrorist attacks of September 11, 2001. Even overseas American restaurants must adapt to local customs. In the Middle East, rules about the mixing of the sexes and the consumption of alcohol are quite strict. Chili's Grill & Bar is known simply as Chili's and the chain offers a midnight buffet during Ramadan season when Muslims are required to fast from dawn to dusk. McDonald's in Saudi Arabia offers separate dining areas for single men and women and children. Booths must have screens because women can't be seen eating meat.[20]

These cultural/religious issues also abound within the U.S. market. Burger King had to modify a commercial it aired on African American radio stations in which a coffeehouse poet reads an ode to a Whopper with bacon. In the original spot, the poet's name is Rasheed and he uses a common Islamic greeting. The Council on American-Islamic Relations issued a press release noting that Islam prohibits the consumption of pork products. In the new version the poet was introduced as Willie.[21]

African Americans, Hispanic Americans, and Asian Americans are the three fastest-growing ethnic groups in the United States. The Census Bureau projects that by the year 2050 non-Hispanic whites will make up only 50.1 percent of the population (compared to 74 percent in 1995) as these other groups grow.[22] Let's take a closer look at each ethnic segment.

African Americans account for about 12 percent of the U.S. population. A new generation of magazines is springing up to meet the demands of this growing market, including *The Source* and *Vibe* magazines.[23] There are even multicultural romance novels that feature African American heroes and heroines. The basic elements of a romance novel remain, but these books provide numerous references to African American culture, and the heroine is more likely to possess "curly brown locks" than "cascading blond hair."[24] These new books and magazines demonstrate the opportunities that await those who develop specialized products that connect with segments of consumers who share an ethnic or racial identity. The Hispanic American population is a sleeping giant, a segment that mainstream marketers largely ignored until recently. Because of this segment's high birthrate, the U.S. Census Bureau projects that Hispanics will outnumber African Americans as the nation's largest minority group by the year 2005.

In addition to its rapid growth, four other factors make the Hispanic segment attractive to marketers. (1) Hispanics tend to be brand-loyal, especially to products made in their country of origin.[25] (2) They tend to be highly concentrated by national origin, which makes it easy to fine-tune the marketing mix to appeal to those who come from the same country. That's why some companies are trying to appeal to Mexican Americans, who make up about 60 percent of Hispanic Americans, by developing promotions celebrating Cinco de Mayo, a holiday commemorating Mexico's triumph over France in 1862. McDonald's once added fajitas to its regular menu during the holiday.[26] (3) This segment is young (the median age of Hispanic Americans is 23.6, compared with the U.S. average of 32), which is attractive to marketers because it is a great potential market for youth-oriented products such as cosmetics and music. (4) The average Hispanic household contains 3.5 people, compared to only 2.7 people for the rest of the United States. For this reason, Hispanic households spend 15 percent to 20 percent more of their disposable income than the national average on groceries and other household products.[27]

But appeals to these consumers need to take into account cultural differences. For example, the California Milk Processor Board discovered that its hugely successful "Got milk?" campaign was not well received by Hispanics, because biting, sarcastic humor is not part of the Hispanic culture. In addition, the notion of milk deprivation is not funny to a Hispanic mother because running out of milk means she has failed her family. To make matters worse, "Got milk?" translates as "Are You Lactating?" in Spanish. So, new Spanish-language versions were changed to, "And you, have you given them enough milk today?" with tender scenes centered around cooking flan (a popular pudding) in the family kitchen.[28]

One of the most notable characteristics of the Hispanic market is its youth: Many of these consumers are "young biculturals" who bounce back and forth between hip-hop and rock en

Packaged goods companies are doing more to grab a share of the Hispanic youth market. Frito-Lay discovered that Hispanics are only half as likely as the general market to eat salty snacks, so it looked for a way to appeal to this growing segment. In focus groups, young Hispanics said that Frito-Lay products tasted too mild and they wanted bolder flavors. This research led to the development of new products to capture these consumers, such as Frito's Chile and Lime Sabritones.

Espanol, blend Mexican rice with spaghetti sauce, and spread peanut butter and jelly on tortillas.[29] Latino youth are changing mainstream culture. By the year 2020, the U.S. Census Bureau estimates that the number of Hispanic teens will grow by 62 percent compared with 10 percent growth in teens over all. They are looking for spirituality, stronger family ties, and more color in their lives—three hallmarks of Latino culture. Music crossovers from the Latin charts to mainstream are leading the trend, including pop idol Ricky Martin and Big Pun, the first Latino hip-hop artist to go platinum.[30]

Though their numbers are still relatively small, Asian Americans are the fastest-growing minority group in the United States. The Asian American population is projected to grow from 11.3 million in 2000 to 19.6 million in 2020.[31] U.S. marketers are just beginning to recognize the potential of this segment, and some are beginning to adapt their products and messages to reach this group. WonderBra even launched a special line sized for a slimmer Asian body.[32]

Geography: Recognizing that people's preferences often vary depending on where they live, many marketers tailor their offerings to appeal to different regions. Heileman Distilleries sells different brands of beer in different parts of the country, so drinkers in Texas buy the company's Lone Star brand, while those in Boston order Samuel Adams. As the company's marketing vice president once explained in an article, "The primary objective of being a regional brand is to make the consumer think that 'this product is mine' . . . People tend to think positively about their hometowns, and a product strongly identified with this aura is likely to strike a responsive chord."[33]

geodemography ▪
Segmentation technique that combines geography with demographics.

When marketers want to segment regional markets even more precisely, they sometimes combine geography with demographics by using a technique called **geodemography**. A basic assumption of geodemography is that "birds of a feather flock together"—people who live near one another share similar characteristics. Sophisticated statistical techniques identify geographic areas that share the same preferences for household items, magazines, and other products. Through geodemography, marketers construct segments of households with a common pattern of preferences. This way the marketer can home in on those customers who are most likely to be interested in its specific offerings, in some cases so precisely that families living on one block will be included in a segment while those on the next block will not.

Companies can even customize Web advertising by geocoding, so that people who log on in different places will see ad banners for local businesses. For example, the Weather Channel (www.weather.com) can link localized ads to 1,300 U.S. weather-reporting stations so a surfer can get both the local weather forecast and obtain information about businesses in an area.[34]

One widely used geodemographic system is called PRIZM, a large database developed by Claritas, Inc. (www.claritas.com). This system classifies every U.S. zip code into one of 62 "clusters" based on analyses of demographics and lifestyles that define neighborhood types. The 62 clusters range from the highly affluent "Blue-Blood Estates" to the poor "Inner Cities" or "Hard

Scrabble" neighborhoods. This system tells marketers which product categories and specific brands people in each cluster are likely to use. For example, Big Sky Families (see Table 8.1) are likely to be rodeo fans, own a cat, watch QVC, and read *Soap Opera Digest* while Urban Gold Coast consumers are likely to attend the theater, use olive oil, bank online, and read *Self*. Armed with this knowledge, a marketer can identify precisely which zip codes will be the best prospects for a product, while avoiding other nearby zip codes where residents aren't likely to be so interested. Go to the company's Web site, tell them your zip code, and they'll tell you which cluster you live in!

Segmenting by Psychographics   Demographic information is useful, but it does not always provide enough information to divide consumers into meaningful segments. Although we can use demographic variables to discover, for instance, that the female college student segment uses perfume, we won't be able to tell whether certain college women prefer perfumes that express an image of, say, sexiness rather than athleticism. Psychographic data are useful to understand differences among consumers who may be statistically similar to one another but whose needs and wants vary.

For example, most of us are happy driving the speed limit (okay, a few miles over the limit) on the freeway but some of us crave danger. For this psychographic segment there is a variety of unique product offerings including a tour of the sunken *Titanic* at 12,500 feet below the surface of the ocean or getting behind the wheel of a Formula One race car running at 120 mph.[35]

Psychographics segments markets in terms of shared attitudes, interests, and opinions.[36] Psychographic segments usually include demographic information such as age or sex, but the richer descriptions that emerge go well beyond these characteristics. That's why Landon Pollack at MPower decided to further divide his target market of baby boomer women into psychographic groups based on their attitudes toward exercise and healthy eating. Web-based services such as geocities.com allow people to sort *themselves* into lifestyle communities based on specific, shared interests. These selections allow marketers to identify segments that want products and services that enable them to act on their passions, whether these passions include skiing or watching *Star Trek*.

Although some advertising agencies and manufacturers develop their own psychographic techniques to classify consumers, other agencies choose to subscribe to larger services that divide the entire U.S. population into segments and then sell pieces of this information to clients for specific strategic applications. The most well known of these systems is **VALS™ (Values and Lifestyles)** developed by SRI Consulting Business Intelligence (www.sric-bi.com). VALS™ divides U.S. adults into eight groups that are determined both by psychological characteristics, such as "willingness to take risks," and "resources," which include such factors as income, education, energy levels, and eagerness to buy.

As Figure 8.2 (page 229) shows, three self-orientations are key to the system. Consumers with a principle orientation base decisions on abstract, idealized criteria rather than on feelings or a desire for societal approval. People with a status orientation strive for a clear social position and make decisions based on the perceived opinions of a valued social group. Action-oriented individuals are motivated by a desire to make an impact on the physical world or to affect others and resist social controls on their behavior.

The VALS™ system helps to identify consumers who are most likely to be interested in certain types of products, services, or experiences. For example, VALS™ data show that 12 percent of American adults are thrill seekers, who tend to fall into the system's experiencer category and who are likely to agree with statements such as "I like a lot of excitement in my life" and "I like to try new things." VALS™ helped Isuzu market its Rodeo sport-utility vehicle by focusing on experiencers, many of whom believe it is fun to break rules in ways that do not endanger others. The company positioned the car as a vehicle that lets a driver break the rules by going off-road. Isuzu created advertising to support this idea. One ad showed a kid jumping in mud puddles. Another ad showed a school child coloring out of the lines.[37] Isuzu sales increased significantly after this campaign.[38]

Segmenting by Behavior   People may use the same product for different reasons, on different occasions, and in different amounts. So, in addition to demographics and psychographics, it is useful to study what consumers actually *do* with a product. **Behavioral segmentation**

VALS™ (Values and Lifestyles) ■ Psychographic system that divides the entire U.S. population into eight segments.

2 Bookmark It!

Visit the VALS Web site and take the VALS survey (www.sric-bi.com/VALS/ presurvey.shtml). Do you think your VALS type accurately describes you?

behavioral segmentation ■ Technique that divides consumers into segments on the basis of how they act toward, feel about, or use a good or service.

TABLE 8.1

Some PRIZM Clusters

Cluster Name	Demographics	Most Likely To	Neighborhood Examples
Urban Gold Coast	Elite urban singles Age group: 45–64 Professional Average household income: $73,500	Attend the theater Use olive oil Bank online Watch *Mystery* Read *Self*	Marina Del Rey, CA Lincoln Park, Il Upper East Side, NY
Starter Families	Young, middle-class families Age group: under 18, 25–34 Blue-collar/service occupations Average household income: $25,300	Belong to a book club Be boxing fans Use caller ID Watch *Nightline* Read *Bride's Magazine*	Woodland, CA Sioux Falls, SC Lowell, MA
Rural Industrial	Low-income, blue-collar families Age group: under 18 Blue-collar/service occupations Average household income: $27,900	Be auto racing fans Belong to a fraternal order Have veterans' life insurance Watch TNN Read *Field and Stream*	Gas City, IN Wheeler, AR Worthington, KY
Young Literati	Upscale urban singles and couples Age group: 25–44 Professional occupations Average household income: $63,400	Plan for large purchases Take vitamins Use a discount broker Watch *Bravo* Read *GQ*	Hermosa Beach, CA Diamond Heights, CA Edgewater, NJ
Inner Cities	Inner-city, single-parent families Age group: under 18, 18–34 Blue-collar/service occupations Average household income: $16,500	Buy baby food Buy soul/r&b/black music Pay bills by phone Watch pay-per-view sports Read *National Enquirer*	Detroit, MI Hyde Park, IL Morningside, NY
Hispanic Mix	Urban Hispanic singles and families Age group: under 18, 18–34 Blue-collar/service occupations Average household income: $19,000	Be pro basketball fans Use caller ID Use money orders Watch BET Read *Ebony*	Pico Heights, CA El Paso TX Bronx, NY
New Eco-topia	Rural white/blue-collar/farm families Age group: 45+ White-collar/blue-collar/farming occupations Average household income: $39,000	Go cross-country skiing Own a dog Have a Keogh account Watch *Jeopardy* Read *Prevention*	Sutter Creek, CA East Chatham, NY Grafton, VT
Golden Ponds	Retirement town seniors Age group: 65+ White-collar/blue-collar/service occupations Average household income: $28,300	Shop at Wal-Mart Go bowling Eat Grape Nuts Watch QVC network Read *Golf*	Forest Ranch, CA Dollar Bay, MI Kure Beach, NC
Norma Rae-Ville	Young families, biracial mill town Age group: under 18, 18–34 Blue-collar/service occupations Average household income: $20,500	Travel by bus Shop at Payless Shoes Buy Sears tires Watch *Oprah* Read *Seventeen*	Yazoo City, MS Americus, GA Salisbury, NC
Blue Chip Blues	Upscale blue-collar families Age group: 35–64 White-collar/blue-collar occupations Average household income: $47,500	Shop online Belong to a religious club Drink Coke Watch *Days of Our Lives* Read *Car Craft*	Redford, MI Oakville, CT Barrington, NJ
Executive Suites	Upscale white-collar couples Age group: 45–64 Professional occupations Average household income: $68,500	Belong to a health club Visit Japan/Asia Have an airline travel card Watch *Friends* Read *Entrepreneur*	Irving, CA Aurora, IL Mount Laurel, NJ

Source: Adapted from www.yawyl.claritas.com

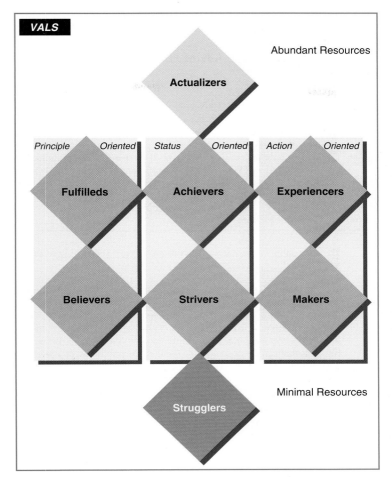

FIGURE 8.2

VALS

VALS uses lifestyles to segment the U.S. market into eight unique groups.

Source: SRI International, Menlo Park, CA.

slices consumers on the basis of how they act toward, feel about, or use a product. Mephisto (see ad on page 231), for example, targets people who prefer comfort over fashion when they choose footwear.

One way to segment based on behavior is to divide the market into users and nonusers of a product. Users have acted to make a purchase, which is a *behavior*. Then marketers may attempt to reward current users or try to win over new ones. In addition to distinguishing between users and nonusers, current customers can further be segmented into groups of heavy, moderate, and light users.

Many marketers abide by a rule of thumb called the **80/20 rule**: 20 percent of purchasers account for 80 percent of the product's sales (this ratio is an approximation, not gospel). This means that it often makes more sense to focus on the smaller number of people who are really into a product rather than on the larger number who are just casual users. Kraft Foods began a $30 million campaign to remind its core users not to "skip the zip" after its research showed that indeed 20 percent of U.S. households account for 80 percent of the usage of Miracle Whip. Heavy users consume 17 pounds of Miracle Whip a year.[39]

Another way to segment a market based on behavior is to look at **usage occasions**, or when consumers use the product most. Many products are associated with specific occasions, whether time of day, holidays, business functions, or casual get-togethers. Businesses often divide up their markets according to when and how their offerings are in demand.

For example, consider how the Biltmore Estate in Asheville, North Carolina, went about increasing attendance during its annual Christmas celebration. Set on 8,000 acres and featuring four acres of lavishly decorated floor space under one roof, the Biltmore is the largest private home in America. Although 750,000 people visited the house annually, in the early 1990s attendance was starting to stagnate. Then the estate's marketers mixed things up by developing four separate strategies to target different types of visitors (for example, heavy users such as those who have made a Christmas pilgrimage an annual family tradition versus light users who

80/20 rule ■ A marketing rule of thumb that 20 percent of purchasers account for 80 percent of a product's sales.

usage occasions ■ Indicator used in one type of market segmentation based on when consumers use a product most.

Elise Grant, Student, University of Colorado of Boulder

I would choose option 2. Despite the high start-up costs of building bricks-and-mortar stores, they would help MPower to increase customer awareness of the brand, create a higher demand for this specific program, and ultimately compete with the growing slate of national competitors in this diverse industry. Additionally, a reliance solely on the Internet would be risky due to the age of the target market. Many people in the target market associate personalization with face-to-face service. To avoid alienating a segment, while still being able to use the Internet's convenience for others, MPower could establish a Web site as a supplementary resource that offers products, information, and consulting services for current and potential MPower customers.

MICHELLE ALBERT, SENIOR DIRECTOR, STRATEGIC MARKETING ALLIANCES, COLUMBIA RECORDS

I would choose a modified version of option 2. Option 2 allows MPower to give its primary target demographic all the information and services they need to succeed in the healthy living program without having to incur the enormous cost of establishing free-standing stores. For the doers that do not like group activities, MPower could alter option 2 by offering the healthy living program online with support from their call-in center—doers can participate in the program and obtain products without having to go into the store. Option 2 gives Mpower both an off line and online business that can be targeted at its focus demographic while allowing room to grow into a dedicated retail chain if and when the business demands it.

Sal Veas, Marketing Professor, Santa Monica College, Santa Monica, California

Option 2 seems like the best choice given the specifics of MPower and the target market back in 1999. This option offers the flexibility of delivering the product both on ground and online. The retail stores will allow MPower to establish a presence in the market to deliver their personalized services. A handful of stores should be established in geodemographic locations such as Santa Monica and Burlingame, California, where demand for services such as MPower has already been identified. MPower can then focus on developing additional outlets. Their web presence can be further enhanced as described in Option 1. MPower might consider opening outlets in existing service providers as a complement to their offerings. For example, Burke-Williams (www.burkewilliamsspa.com) is a respected day spa, but they do not offer MPower type solutions. A joint venture or licensing should be a consideration.

Weigh in with your thoughts! Visit the Live Laboratory at www.prenhall.com/solomon for extended Other Voices replies, exercises, and more.

have visited only once). Each segment received a different invitation offering a customized package calculated to appeal to that segment. As a result, visits increased by 300 percent in one season, resulting in a Merry Christmas for the Biltmore.[40]

SLICING UP THE BUSINESS PIE: DIMENSIONS FOR SEGMENTING INDUSTRIAL MARKETS

We've reviewed the segmentation variables marketers use to divide up the consumer pie, but how about all those business-to-business marketers out there? Segmentation also helps them to slice up the pie of industrial customers. Though the specific variables may differ, the underlying logic of classifying the larger market into manageable pieces that share relevant characteristics is the same whether the product being sold is pesto or pesticides.

Organizational demographics also help an industrial marketer to understand the needs and characteristics of its potential customers. These classification dimensions include the size of the firms either in total sales or number of employees, the number of facilities, whether they are a domestic or a multinational company, and the type of business they are in. Business-to-business

Mephisto targets consumers who want a shoe that is comfortable for walking—part of the "Mephisto Movement."

markets may also be segmented based on the production technology they use and whether the customer is a user or a nonuser of the product. DuPont's Apparel & Textile Science Division (the folks who bring you Lycra and nylon) divides customers for its fibers (such as textile mills) into segments based on the types of products they make such as legwear (stockings), activewear, or home textiles.

Many industries use the North American Industry Classification System (NAICS) discussed in Chapter 7 to obtain information about the size and number of companies operating in a particular industry. Business-to-business marketers often consult information sources on the Web. For example, Hoovers Online (www.hoovers.com) provides subscribers with up-to-date information on private and public companies worldwide.

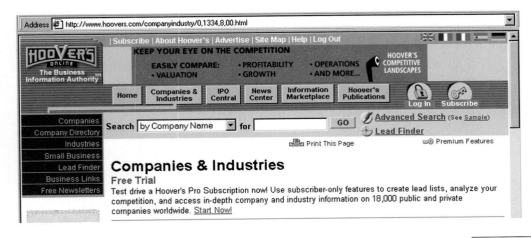

Business-to-business marketers use a variety of resources to classify their prospective customers. Hoovers Online is one resource that provides marketing intelligence on both private and public companies.

Targeting

We've seen that the first step in target marketing is segmentation in which the firm divides the market into smaller groups that share certain characteristics. Just as Landon Pollack considered potential customers for MPower, the next step is targeting in which marketers evaluate the attractiveness of each potential segment and decide which of these groups they will try to turn into customers. The customer group or groups selected are the firm's **target market**. In this section, we'll review how marketers assess these customer groups, and we'll discuss selection strategies for effective targeting.

target market ■ Group or groups that a firm selects to turn into customers as a result of segmentation and targeting.

EVALUATING MARKET SEGMENTS

Just because a marketer identifies a segment does not necessarily mean that it's a useful one to target. A viable target segment should satisfy the following requirements.

1. Are members of the segment similar to each other in their product needs and wants and, at the same time, different from consumers in other segments? Without real differences in consumer needs, firms might as well use a mass-marketing strategy. For example, it's a waste of time to develop two separate lines of skin care products for working women and nonworking women if both segments have the same complaints about dry skin.
2. Can marketers measure the segment? Marketers must know something about the size and purchasing power of a potential segment before deciding if it is worth their efforts.
3. Is the segment large enough to be profitable now and in the future? For example, a graphic designer hoping to design Web pages for Barbie doll collectors must decide whether there are enough hard-core aficionados to make this business worthwhile.
4. Can marketing communications reach the segment? It is easy to select television programs or magazines that will efficiently reach older consumers, consumers with certain levels of education, or residents of major cities because the media they prefer are easy to identify. It is unlikely, however, that marketing communications can reach only left-handed blondes with tattoos who listen to the Backstreet Boys.
5. Can the marketer adequately serve the needs of the segment? Does the firm have the expertise and resources to satisfy the segment better than the competition? Some years ago Exxon made the mistake of trying to enter the office products business, a growing segment. Unfortunately the company's expertise at selling petroleum products did not transfer to copying machines, and the effort ran out of gas.

> **3 Bookmark It!**
>
> You are a marketing manager for a firm that makes hair care products. Your firm is considering segmenting based on hair color—blondes, brunettes, redheads, and so on. Would these be meaningful segments? Why or why not? What about segmenting on the basis of age? Ethnic background? Other segments? Write a memo to your boss explaining your reasons for agreeing or disagreeing with the hair color segments.

DEVELOPING SEGMENT PROFILES

Once a marketer has identified a set of usable segments, it is helpful to generate a profile of each to really understand segment members' needs and to look for business opportunities. This segment profile is a description of the "typical" customer in that segment. A **segment profile** might, for instance, include customer demographics, location, lifestyle information, and a description of how frequently the customer buys the product.

segment profile ■ A description of the "typical" customer in a segment.

When the R.J. Reynolds Company made plans to introduce a new brand of cigarettes called Dakota that would be targeted to women, it created a segment profile of a possible customer group it called the "Virile Female." The profile included these characteristics: Her favorite pastimes are cruising, partying, going to hot-rod shows and tractor pulls with her boyfriend, and watching evening soap operas. Her chief aspiration is to get married in her early twenties.[41] Anyone you know?

CHOOSING A TARGETING STRATEGY

A basic targeting decision is how finely tuned the target should be: Should the company go after one large segment or focus on meeting the needs of one or more smaller segments? Let's look at four targeting strategies. Figure 8.3 summarizes these strategies.

Undifferentiated Marketing A company such as Wal-Mart that selects an **undifferentiated targeting strategy** is appealing to a broad spectrum of people. If successful,

undifferentiated targeting strategy ■ Appealing to a broad spectrum of people.

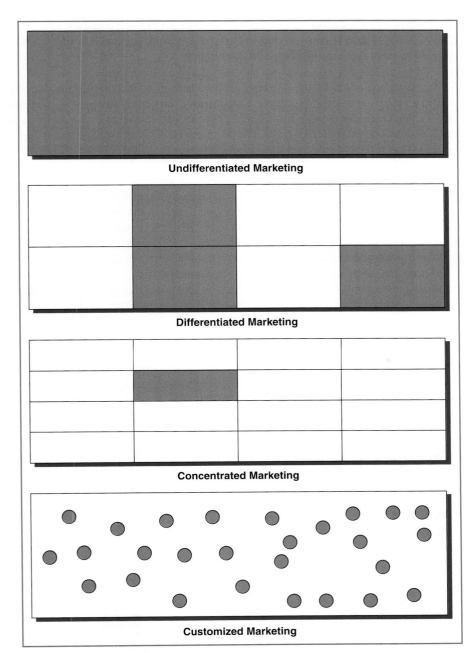

Undifferentiated Marketing

Differentiated Marketing

Concentrated Marketing

Customized Marketing

FIGURE 8.3

Choosing a Target Marketing Strategy

After the market is divided into meaningful segments, marketers must decide on a target marketing strategy. Should the company go after one total market, one or several market segments, or even target customers individually?

this type of operation can be very efficient, especially because production, research, and promotion costs benefit from *economies of scale*—it's cheaper to develop one product or one advertising campaign than to choose several targets and create separate products or messages for each. But the company must be willing to bet that people have similar needs, or that any differences among them will be so trivial that they will not matter, so that the same product and message will appeal to many customers.

Differentiated Marketing A company that chooses a **differentiated targeting strategy** develops one or more products for each of several customer groups with different product needs. A differentiated strategy is called for when consumers are choosing among brands that are well known in which each has a distinctive image in the marketplace, and in which it's possible to identify one or more segments that have distinct needs for different types of products. The cosmetics giant L'Oréal follows this philosophy. The company has the resources to offer

differentiated targeting strategy ■ Developing one or more products for each of several distinct customer groups and making sure these offerings are kept separate in the marketplace.

several product lines at a variety of prices. It targets the luxury market with such brands as Lancôme and Helena Rubinstein, while less expensive offerings such as Elseve and L'Oréal are targeted to large department stores and discounters.[42]

Concentrated Marketing   When a firm focuses its efforts on offering one or more products to a single segment, it is using a **concentrated targeting strategy**. A concentrated strategy is often useful for smaller firms that do not have the resources or the desire to be all things to all people. For example, the cosmetics company Hard Candy sells its funky line of nail polish and other products only to twentysomething women (or to those who wish they still were).

Customized Marketing   Ideally, marketers should be able to define segments so precisely that they can offer products and services that exactly meet the needs of every individual or firm. This level of concentration does occur (we hope!) in the case of personal or professional services we get from doctors, lawyers, and hair stylists. A **custom marketing strategy** is common in industrial contexts in which a manufacturer often works with one or a few large clients and develops products and services that only these clients will use.

Of course, in most cases this level of segmentation is neither practical nor possible when mass-produced products such as computers or cars enter the picture. However, advances in computer technology, coupled with the new emphasis on building solid relationships with customers, have focused managers' attention on devising a new way to tailor specific products and the messages about them are tailored to individual customers. Thus, some forward-looking, consumer-oriented companies are moving toward mass customization in which they modify a basic good or service to meet the needs of an individual. Even a giant automaker such as Buick asks, "Can we build one for you?"

Dell uses **mass customization** in which they modify a basic good or service to meet the needs of an individual.[43] Dell does this by offering customized computer products

concentrated targeting strategy ■ Focusing a firm's efforts on offering one or more products to a single segment.

custom marketing strategy ■ Approach that tailors specific products and the messages about them to individual customers.

mass customization ■ Approach that modifies a basic good or service to meet the needs of an individual.

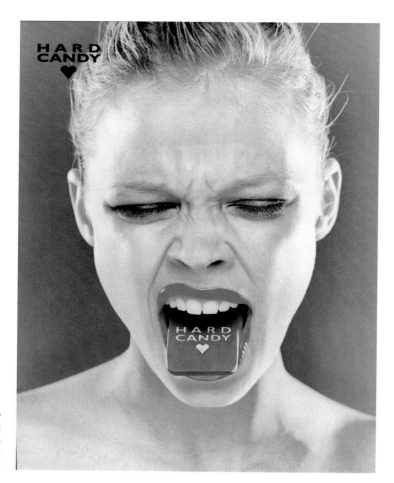

Hard Candy uses a concentrated targeting strategy as the company targets twentysomething women.

over the Internet at Dell.com. Users can create their own computers—everything from personal computers to networking systems.[44] We'll return to the issue of customization shortly when we review new advances in the management philosophy of customer relationship management.

Positioning

The final stage of the target marketing process is to provide consumers who belong to a targeted market segment with a good or service that meets their unique needs and expectations. **Positioning** means developing a marketing strategy aimed at influencing how a particular market segment perceives a good or service *in comparison* to the competition. Developing a positioning strategy entails gaining a clear understanding of the criteria target consumers use to evaluate competing products and then convincing them that your product will meet those needs.

This can be done in many ways. Sometimes it's just a matter of making sure that cool people are seen using your product. That's exactly what BC Ethic did. This apparel manufacturer is known for repopularizing the style of retro, button-down bowling shirt worn by *Seinfeld's* Kramer.[45] Instead of paying millions of dollars to hire a popular rock star for its ads, BC Ethic created shirts with customized, embroidered band logos and offered them free to nationally known music artists such as Barenaked Ladies, Cypress Hill, Sevendust, and Dick Dale. For some outdoor and print advertising, the company used the brand's color scheme—black and red—to develop stylized tinted likenesses of some of the groups and even created posters that became popular merchandising material for retailers including Nordstrom.

4 *Bookmark It!*

Hair color products are not just for women. Visit a retail store that sells men's hair color products and examine the choices available. Based on what you see, how do targeting strategies differ between men's and women's hair color products?

positioning ■ Developing a marketing strategy aimed at influencing how a particular market segment perceives a good or service in comparison to the competition.

BC Ethic positioned its shirts as "cool" by providing popular music groups with custom-designed shirts and then using the groups in its advertising.

DEVELOPING A POSITIONING STRATEGY

The success of a target marketing strategy hinges on marketers' abilities to identify and select an appropriate market segment. Then marketers must devise a marketing mix that will effectively target the segment's members by positioning their products to appeal to that segment.

A first step is to analyze the competitors' positions in the marketplace. To develop an effective positioning strategy marketers must understand the current lay of the land. What competitors are out there, and how are they perceived by the target market? Aside from direct competitors in the product category, are there other products or services that provide the same benefits people are seeking? For example, when a company such as Coca-Cola develops a new drink, it must consider how to compete against many alternatives in addition to those offered by archrival Pepsi. The surprise success of Jolt, which is fortified with caffeine, led Coca-Cola to develop Surge in order to target students, athletes, and people who don't like the taste of coffee but who need to "Feel the Rush."[46]

The next task is to offer a good or service with a competitive advantage to provide a reason why consumers will perceive the product as better than the competition. If the company offers only a "me-too product," it can induce people to buy for a lower price. Other forms of competitive advantage offer a superior image (Giorgio Armani), a unique product feature (Levi's 501 button-fly jeans), better service (Cadillac's roadside assistance program), or even better-qualified people (the legendary salespeople at Nordstrom's department stores).

Once a positioning strategy is set, marketers must finalize the marketing mix by putting all of the pieces into place. The elements of the marketing mix must match the selected segment. This means that the good or service must deliver benefits that the segment values, such as convenience or status. Furthermore, marketers must price this offering at a level these consumers will pay, make the offering available at places consumers are likely to go, and correctly communicate the offering's benefits in locations where consumers are likely to take notice. These decisions are at the heart of MPower's problem: how to develop a wellness offering that people see as unique and desirable—and deliver its products and services in the places the target market will most likely use them (e.g., on the Web versus in a retail store environment).

Finally, marketers must evaluate the target market's responses so they can modify strategies as needed. Over time the firm may find that it needs to change which segments it targets or even redo a product's position to respond to marketplace changes. A classic example of such a makeover, a strategy called **repositioning**, is Marlboro cigarettes. Believe it or not, this brand was positioned as a women's cigarette when it was first introduced—complete with a red-tipped filter to hide lipstick stains. The brand really took off, however, when Marlboro "adjusted" its image as a male product, complete with the "macho" Marlboro cowboy.

repositioning ■ Redoing a product's position to respond to marketplace changes.

BRINGING A PRODUCT TO LIFE: THE BRAND PERSONALITY

Brands are almost like people in that we can often describe them in terms of personality traits. We may use adjectives such as *cheap, elegant, sexy, cool,* or *nerdy* when talking about a store, a perfume, a car, and so on. That's why a positioning strategy often tries to create a **brand personality** for a good or service—a distinctive image that captures its character and benefits. An advertisement for *Elle* magazine once said: "She is not a reply card. She is not a category. She is not shrink-wrapped. *Elle* is not a magazine. She is a woman."

Products as people? It seems funny to say, yet marketing researchers find that most consumers have no trouble describing what a product would be like "if it came to life." People often give clear, detailed descriptions, including what color hair the product would have, the type of house it would live in, and even whether it would be thin, overweight, or somewhere in between.[47] If you don't believe us, try doing this yourself.

Part of creating a brand personality is developing an identity for the product that the target market will prefer over competing brands. How do marketers determine where their product actually stands in the minds of consumers? One solution is to ask consumers what characteristics are important and how competing alternatives would rate on these attributes, too. Marketers use this information to construct a **perceptual map**, which is a vivid way to construct a picture of where products or brands are "located" in consumers' minds.

brand personality ■ A distinctive image that captures a good or service's character and benefits.

perceptual map ■ A vivid way to construct a picture of where products or brands are "located" in consumers' minds.

We often think of products as if they were people. In this Brazilian ad for engine oil, this product begs for help.

For example, suppose you wanted to construct a perceptual map of women's magazines as perceived by American women in their twenties to give you some guidance while developing an idea for a new magazine. After interviewing a sample of female readers, you might determine questions women ask when selecting a magazine: (1) Is it "traditional," that is, oriented toward family, home, or personal issues, or is it "fashion forward," oriented toward personal appearance and fashion? (2) Is it for "upscale" women who are older and established in their careers, or for relatively "downscale" women who are younger and just starting out in their careers?

The perceptual map in Figure 8.4 illustrates how these ratings might look for certain major women's magazines. The map provides some guidance as to where your new women's magazine

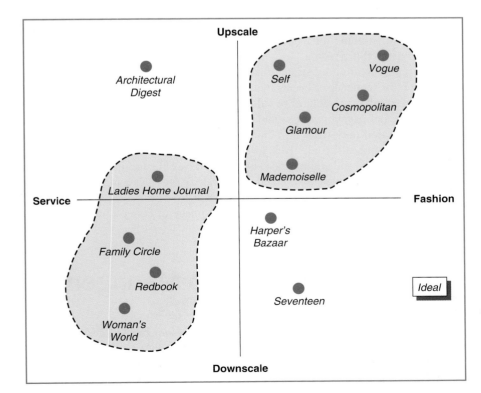

FIGURE 8.4

Perceptual Map

Perceptual mapping allows marketers to identify consumers' perceptions of their brand in relation to the competition.

Brand personalities often are reflected in logos. This clothing ad from Chile pits a shark against the more familiar crocodile—with bloody results.

might be positioned. You might decide to compete directly with either the cluster of "service magazines" in the lower left or the traditional fashion magazines in the upper right. In this case, you would have to determine what benefits your new magazine might offer that these existing magazines do not. Condé Nast, for example, positioned *Allure* to compete against fashion magazines by going into more depth than others do on beauty issues, such as the mental, physical, and emotional dangers of cosmetic surgery.

You might try to locate an unserved area in this map. There may be room for a magazine targeted to "cutting-edge" fashion for college-age women. An unserved segment is the "Holy Grail" for marketers: With luck, they can move quickly to capture a segment and define the standards of comparison for the category. This tactic has paid off for Chrysler, which first identified the minivan market, and Liz Claiborne, which pioneered the concept of comfortable, "user-friendly" clothing for working women. In the magazine category, perhaps *Marie Claire* comes closest to this position.

Creating a positioning strategy is the last step in the target marketing process. We can summarize this sequence of events by looking at the strategy developed by the SoBe Beverage Co., a small drink manufacturer based in Connecticut. The company segmented the market in terms of age and psychographics and then targeted a segment of 18- to 35-year-olds whose profiles indicated they were into "new-age" beverages that would give them a feeling of energy without unhealthy additives. SoBe created XTC, a drink inspired by "herbal ecstasy" cocktails of extracts and amino acids popular at "raves" featuring all-night gyrations to techno music. As an industry executive noted, this strategy provides a unique position for the elixir: "People are taking something that provides a four-times-removed high without having to get arrested or wrecking their bodies. It carries the image of being a little further out there without carrying the risk."[48]

5 *Bookmark It!*

Manufacturers of automobiles take great care to position their models. How do you think Mercedes has positioned itself? Ford? Lexus? Volvo? Toyota?

Customer Relationship Management: Toward a Segment of One

We've talked about identifying a unique group of consumers and developing products specifically to meet their needs. And we talked about how marketers can build products to meet the needs of individual consumers with mass customization. Today many marketing experts advocate customer relationship management (CRM) programs that allow companies to talk to individual customers and adjust elements of their marketing programs in light of how each customer reacts to elements of the marketing mix. The CRM trend has been referred to as one-to-one (1:1) marketing, relationship marketing, and customer-relationship management.[49]

Don Peppers, a leading writer and consultant in this area, defines CRM as ". . . managing customer relationships. If I'm managing customer relationships, it means I'm treating different customers differently, across all enterprises. . . . The relationship develops a context over time, it drives a change in behavior . . . [this] means that I have to change my behavior as an enterprise based on a customer."[50] A CRM strategy allows a company to identify its best customers, stay on top of their needs, and increase their satisfaction.

Is CRM for all companies? Should producers of consumer goods that target the entire market adopt CRM strategies? Of course, CRM seems to make more sense for firms such as business-to-business companies and consumer products companies that have a limited number of customers. But, as we'll see in the next section, even soft-drink and auto companies have used CRM to build customer relationships and brand loyalty.

CRM: A NEW PERSPECTIVE ON AN OLD PROBLEM

CRM is about communicating with customers and customers being able to communicate with a company one-to-one. CRM systems are applications that, through computers, CRM computer software, databases, and often the Internet, automate interactions between customers and companies. They include everything from Web sites that let you check on the status of a bill or package to *call centers* that solicit your business. When you log on to the Federal Express Web site to track a lost package, that's a CRM system. When you get a phone message from the dentist reminding you about that filling appointment tomorrow, that's a CRM system. And, when you get a call from the car dealer asking how you like your new vehicle, that's also CRM.

To appreciate the value of a CRM strategy, consider the experience of financial services firm such as Salomon Smith Barney and Fidelity Investments, both of which have adopted this new perspective. In general, an investment banker needs to manage accounts as well as open new ones—often 30 to 50 per month. Just opening the account can take 45 minutes, not a satisfying process for the banker or for the customer. But with an automated CRM system the banker can open an account, issue a welcome letter, and produce an arbitration agreement in 10 minutes. She can create a unique marketing campaign for each client based on that person's life cycle—including such variables as when a person opened an account, his annual income, family situation, desired retirement age, and so on. The marketer can generate a happy anniversary letter to clients (to commemorate when they joined the firm, not when they got married) and include an invitation to update their investment objectives.

These firms have found that this level of individualized attention results in a much higher rate of customer retention and satisfaction, so CRM creates a win-win situation for everyone.[51]

That success helps to explain why CRM is hot: Industry sources estimate that by 2005 companies will be spending $14 billion to purchase sophisticated software that will let them build these electronic bridges.[52] Even the Internal Revenue Service is buying a CRM software system worth more than $10 million. The system will allow taxpayers to obtain tax records and other information around the clock. An agency spokesman commented that this purchase is part of the IRS's ongoing effort to become more customer friendly. By 2004, the agency hopes the system will be fully operational, which will allow many disgruntled taxpayers to receive quick (and hopefully accurate) answers automatically rather than sitting on the phone for hours.[53]

Power companies in California, rocked by financial and supply problems and deregulation in the last few years, are also concerned about customer relations and are investing heavily in CRM systems. These systems help customers deal with rolling blackouts by automating crucial information and reducing call volume—and in the process those nasty "holds" we're all accustomed to.[54]

In addition to mollifying angry customers, marketers can also use CRM systems to keep better track of enthusiastic ones. Here are ways that marketers of youth products are integrating CRM technology into their efforts:[55]

- Sprite staged a "Rocket Cash" sweepstakes promotion by sending out legions of marketing representatives with handheld touch-screen devices. They hung out at concerts and on street corners and enticed young people to enter the sweepstakes by

FedEx uses Internet technology to communicate with customers worldwide. From Chile to China, customers can track their packages and know where they are and when they will arrive.

tapping their names, e-mail addresses, and birthdays into the devices on the spot. Every evening, data were uploaded to Sprite's Web site and entrants were kept informed by e-mail of their status in the sweepstakes. Needless to say, in return Sprite wound up with a great list of consumers with whom it could continue to communicate in the future.

- Bacardi held a similar sweepstakes, but in this case the rum marketer also took digital photos of drivers' licenses to verify consumers' ages (so lose those fake IDs).
- Ford sponsored a recent concert tour called Area One on behalf of its youth-oriented Focus model. At each of the tour's 17 stops, attendees could have their pictures taken next to a souped-up version of the Focus. If you wanted to see your photo, you registered your e-mail address with Ford and went to a special Web site (focus247.com) where you could download your picture in a special frame (branded with Focus information) and e-mail the picture to your friends. Successful? Ford reported that 87 percent of the people who had their photos taken visited the Web site to retrieve them. And Ford was able to use the e-mail addresses to build relationships with these prospective customers.

CRM is also a more efficient way to reach new customers who may have been overlooked by prior marketing efforts. Many experts are excited about this possibility. Consider this: Although African Americans have $447 billion in purchasing power, the average African American household receives only one catalog per week during the holiday season as compared with 10 catalogs per Caucasian household per week. Similarly, the average Hispanic household ($350 billion in purchasing power) gets 20 pieces of direct mail annually compared to 300 pieces for non-Hispanic households. That explains why some companies are working hard to compile lists of ethnic households and develop new relationships in the race to make "new friends."[56]

Perhaps the most important aspect of CRM is that it presents a new way of looking at how to effectively compete in the marketplace. This begins with looking at customers as partners. CRM proponents suggest that the traditional relationship between customers and marketers is an adversarial one where marketers try to sell their products to customers and customers seek to avoid buying.[57] The customer relationship perspective sees customers as partners, with each partner learning from the other every time they interact. Successful firms compete by establishing relationships with individual customers on a one-to-one basis through dialogue and feedback. What does *this* customer really want?

And, of course, when we say customers we don't just mean end consumers—CRM is widely used to strengthen business-to-business relationships as well. To understand the importance of this kind of thinking, consider the experience of Dow, a giant corporation that sells $30 billion worth of chemicals, plastics, and agricultural products each year in more than 170 countries. Although Dow uses cutting-edge manufacturing technology every day, until recently it had literally no centralized mechanism to keep track of its many customers.

Eventually, Dow launched a major effort to install a companywide CRM system that would be a central repository for customer information and would allow its customers to interact with Dow more efficiently—letting them access information automatically without having to deal with a large corporate bureaucracy. The result? A Web-based interface called MyAccount@Dow that lets customers log on (with a secure password, of course), enter new orders, check on the status of old orders, pay invoices electronically, and collaborate with others throughout the system. As a result, Dow lowered its customer support costs by $15 million and is taking electronic orders of $100 million per month.[58]

CHARACTERISTICS OF CRM

In addition to having a different mind-set, companies that successfully practice CRM have different goals, use different measures of success, and look at customers in some different ways. So, CRM marketers look at their share of the customer, at the lifetime value of a customer, at customer equity, and at focusing on high-value customers.

Share of Customer   Historically, marketers have measured success in a product category by their share of market. For example, if there are 100 million pairs of athletic shoes sold each year, a firm that sells 10 million of them has a 10 percent market share. If the shoemaker's marketing objective is to increase market share, it may lower the price of its shoes, increase its advertising, or offer customers a free basketball with every pair of shoes purchased. Such tactics may increase sales in the short run but, unfortunately, they may not do much for the long-term success of the shoemaker. In fact such tactics may actually *decrease* the value of the brand by cheapening its image with giveaways.

Because it is always easier and less expensive to keep an existing customer than to get a new customer, CRM firms focus on increasing their **share of customer**, not share of market. Let's say that a consumer buys six pairs of shoes a year—two pairs from each of three different manufacturers. Let's assume one shoemaker has a CRM system that allows it to send letters to its current customers inviting them to receive a special price discount or a gift if they buy more of the firm's shoes during the year. If the firm can get the consumer to buy three or four or perhaps all six pairs from it, it has increased its share of customer. And that may not be too difficult because the customer already buys and supposedly likes the firm's shoes. Without the CRM system, the shoe company would probably use traditional advertising to increase sales, which would be far more costly than the customer-only direct-mail campaign. So the company can increase sales and profits at a much lower cost than it would spend to get one, two, or three new customers.

share of customer ■ The percentage of an individual customer's purchase of a product that is a single brand.

Lifetime Value of the Customer   With CRM, a **customer's lifetime value** is identified and is the true goal, not an individual transaction. It just makes sense that a firm's profitability and long-term success are going to be far greater if it develops long-term relationships with its customers so those customers buy from it again and again. Costs will be far higher and profits lower if each customer purchase is a first-time sale.

customer's lifetime value ■ The potential profit generated by a single customer's purchase of a firm's products over the customer's lifetime.

How do marketers calculate the lifetime value of a customer? They first estimate a customer's future purchases across all products from the firm over the next 20 or 30 years. The goal is to try to figure out what profit the company could make from the customer in the future. For example, an auto dealer might calculate the lifetime value of a single customer by first calculating the total revenue that could be generated by the customer over his lifetime: the number of automobiles he would buy times their average price, plus the service the dealership would provide over the years, and even possibly the income from auto loan financing. The lifetime value of the customer would be the total profit generated by the revenue stream.

customer equity ■ The financial value of a customer relationship throughout the lifetime of the relationship.

Customer Equity   Today an increasing number of companies are considering their relationships with customers as financial assets. Such firms measure success by calculating the value of their **customer equity**—the financial value of customer relationships throughout the lifetime of the relationships.[59] To do this, firms compare the investments they make in acquiring customers, retaining customers, and relationship enhancement with the financial return on those investments. The goal is to reap a high return on the investments made in customer relationships and maximize the value of a firm's customer equity.

A Greater Focus on High-Value Customers   Using a CRM approach, customers must be prioritized and communication customized accordingly. For example, any banker will tell you that not all customers are equal—when it comes to profitability. So, some banks (about one out of every eight at this point) now use CRM systems to generate a profile of each customer based on factors such as value, risk, attrition, and interest in buying new financial products. This automated system helps the bank decide which current or potential customers it will target with certain communications or how much effort to expend on retaining a person's account—all the while cutting its costs by as much as a third.[60] It just makes sense to use different types of communication contacts based on the value of each individual customer.

TABLE 8.2

Four Steps of One-to-One Marketing

Step	Suggested Activities
Identify	Collect and enter names and additional information about your customers.
	Verify and update, deleting outdated information.
Differentiate	Identify top customers.
	Determine which customers cost the company money.
	Find higher-value customers who have complained about your product or service more than once.
	Find customers who buy only one or two products from your company but a lot from other companies.
	Rank customers into A, B, and C categories based on their value to your company.
Interact	Call the top three people in the top five percent of dealers, distributors, and retailers that carry your product and make sure they're happy.
	Call your own company and ask questions; see how hard it is to get through and get answers.
	Call your competitors and compare their customer service with yours.
	Use incoming calls as selling opportunities.
	Initiate more dialogue with valuable customers.
	Improve complaint handling.
Customize	Find out what your customers want.
	Personalize your direct mail.
	Ask customers how and how often they want to hear from you.
	Ask your top 10 customers what you can do differently to improve your product or service.
	Involve top management in customer relations.

Source: Adapted from Don Peppers, Martha Rogers, and Bob Dorf, "Is Your Company Ready for One-to-One Marketing?" *Harvard Business Review*, January–February 1999, reprint # 99107.

For example, personal selling may constitute 75 percent of all contacts with high-volume customers while direct mail or telemarketing is more often the best way to contact low-volume customers.

STEPS IN CRM MARKETING

There are four steps in CRM marketing.[61] The first step is to identify customers and get to know them in as much detail as possible. Next, marketers need to differentiate these customers in terms of both their needs and their value to the company. Third, CRM marketers must interact with customers and find ways to improve cost efficiency and the effectiveness of the interaction. Finally, marketers need to customize some aspect of the products or services they offer to each customer. This means treating each customer differently based on what has been learned through customer interactions. Table 8.2 gives suggests some activities for implementing these four steps.

Real People, Real Choices: How It Worked Out at MPower

Landon chose option 1 and decided to offer online programs supported by products available at MPower stores. MPower's product offerings, to be developed with input from his panel of distinguished experts, will be available both online and off-line and will include skin care products, health-related publications, audiotapes, videotapes, self-help tools, sports and fitness accessories, active living wear, software, and supplements.

In your discussions with Landon's target market—health-conscious baby boomers—you may have noticed that they are willing to spend the money but not necessarily the time to achieve their goals. Landon reasoned that these people would respond well to an interactive online program that would allow them to pursue their healthy-living goals without spending too much time at stores talking to salespeople. These targeted consumers could have their (local) cake and eat it, too: access to the information they needed to pursue a healthy lifestyle without leaving home and face-to-face reinforcement if and when they needed it.

To promote the program, plans are in the works to develop a syndicated column and publish a book that will inform baby boomers about this healthy-living option. Landon hopes to open his first retail store and launch the MPower Web site within a year after receiving investor funding for the concept.

Chapter Summary

1. Understand the need for market segmentation in today's business environment.

Market segmentation is often necessary in today's marketplace because of market fragmentation, that is, the splintering of a mass society into diverse groups due to technological and cultural differences. Most marketers can't realistically do a good job of meeting the needs of everyone, so it is more efficient to divide the larger pie into slices in which members of a segment share some important characteristics and tend to exhibit the same needs and preferences.

2. Know the different dimensions marketers use to segment consumer and industrial markets.

Marketers frequently find it useful to segment consumer markets based on demographic characteristics including age, gender, family life cycle, social class, race or ethnic identity, and place of residence. A second dimension, psychographics, uses measures of psychological and social characteristics to identify people with shared preferences or traits. Consumer markets may also be segmented based on how consumers behave toward the product, for example, their brand loyalty, usage rates (heavy, moderate, or light), and usage occasions. Industrial markets are often segmented based on industrial demographics, type of business based on the North American Industry Classification (NAICS) codes, and geographic location.

3. Explain how marketers evaluate and select potential market segments.

To choose one or more segments to target, marketers examine each segment and evaluate its potential for success as a target market. Meaningful segments have wants that are different from those in other segments, can be identified, can be reached with a unique marketing mix, will respond to unique marketing communications, are large enough to be profitable, have future growth potential, and possess needs that the organization can satisfy better than the competition.

4. Explain how marketers develop a targeting strategy.

After the different segments have been identified, the market potential of each segment is estimated. The relative attractiveness of segments also influences the firm's selection of an overall marketing strategy. The firm may choose an undifferentiated, differentiated, concentrated, or custom strategy based on the company's characteristics and the nature of the market.

5. Understand how a firm develops and implements a positioning strategy.

After the target market(s) and the overall strategy have been selected, marketers must determine how they wish the brand to be perceived by consumers relative to the competition; that is, should the brand be positioned like, against, or away from the competition? Through positioning, a brand personality is developed. Brand positions may be compared using such research techniques as perceptual mapping. In developing and implementing the positioning strategy, firms analyze the competitors' positions, determine the competitive advantage offered by their product, tailor the marketing mix in accordance with the positioning strategy, and evaluate responses to the marketing mix selected. Marketers must continually monitor changes in the market that might indicate a need to reposition the product.

6. Know how marketers practice customer relationship management to increase long-term success and profits.

Companies using customer relationship management (CRM) programs establish relationships and differentiate their behavior toward individual customers on a one-to-one basis through dialogue and feedback. Success is often measured one customer at a time using the concepts of share of customer, lifetime value of the customer, and customer equity. In CRM strategies, customers are prioritized according to their value to the firm and communication is customized accordingly.

Chapter Review

▪ MARKETING CONCEPTS:
TESTING YOUR KNOWLEDGE

1. What is market segmentation and why is it an important strategy in today's marketplace?
2. List and explain the major demographic characteristics frequently used in segmenting consumer markets.
3. Explain consumer psychographic segmentation.
4. What is behavioral segmentation?
5. What are some of the ways marketers segment industrial markets?
6. List the criteria used for determining whether a segment may be a good candidate for targeting.
7. Explain undifferentiated, differentiated, concentrated, and customized marketing strategies. What is mass customization?
8. What is product positioning? Describe the three approaches that marketers use to create product positions.
9. What is CRM? How do firms practice CRM?
10. Explain the concepts of share of customer, lifetime value of a customer, and customer equity.

▪ MARKETING CONCEPTS:
DISCUSSING CHOICES AND ISSUES

1. Some critics of marketing have suggested that market segmentation and target marketing lead to an unnecessary proliferation of product choices, which wastes valuable resources. These critics suggest that if marketers didn't create so many different product choices, there would be more resources to feed the hungry and house the homeless and provide for the needs of people

Classifying Products

So far, we've learned that a product may be a tangible good or an intangible service or idea and that there are different layers to the product. Now we'll build on that idea by looking at how products differ from one another. Marketers classify products into categories because the categories represent differences in how consumers and business customers feel about products and how they purchase different products. Such an understanding helps marketers develop new products and a marketing mix that satisfy customer needs. Figure 9.2 summarizes these categories.

Generally, products are either *consumer products* or *business products*, although sometimes the same products—such as toilet paper, vacuum cleaners, and lightbulbs—are bought by consumers and businesses. Of course, as we saw in Chapters 6 and 7, customers differ in how they make the purchase decision depending on whether the decision maker is a consumer

---

Consumer Products

Classified by how long they last

Durable (benefit over a long period)
- Refrigerator

Nondurable (benefits only a short time)
- Toothpaste

Classified by how consumers buy them

Convenience Products—frequently purchased with little effort
- Staples *Milk*
- Impulse products *Candy bar*
- Emergency products *Drain opener*

Shopping Products—considerable time and effort in selection
- Attribute based *Shoes*
- Price based *Water heater*

Specialty Products—unique characteristics important to the buyer
- *Favorite restaurant*
- *Rolex watch*

Unsought Products—little interest until need arises
- *Retirement plan*

Business-to-Business Products

Classified by how organizational customers use them

Equipment
- Capital equipment *Buildings*
- Accessory equipment *Computer terminals*

Maintenance, repair, and operating (MRO) equipment
- *Computer paper*

Business services
- *Accounting*

Raw materials
- *Iron ore*

Processed materials
- *Sheets of steel*

Component parts
- *Automobile water pump*

FIGURE 9.2

Classification of Products

Marketers classify products as a means of better understanding how consumers make purchase decisions. The goal is to do a better job of satisfying customers than the competition.

or a business purchaser. Let's first consider differences in consumer products based on how long the product will last and on how the consumer shops for the product. Then we will discuss the general types of business-to-business products.

CONSUMER PRODUCT CLASSES DEFINED BY HOW LONG A PRODUCT LASTS

Marketers classify consumer goods as durable or nondurable depending on how long the product lasts. You expect a refrigerator to last many years, but a gallon of milk will last only a week or so until it turns into a science project. **Durable goods** are consumer products that provide benefits over a period of months, years, or even decades, such as cars, furniture, and appliances. In contrast, **nondurable goods** such as newspapers and food are consumed in the short term.

Durable goods are more likely to be purchased under conditions of high involvement (as we discussed in Chapter 6) while purchases of nondurable goods are more likely to be low-involvement decisions. When consumers buy a computer or a house, they will spend a lot of time and energy on the decision process. For these products marketers need to understand consumers' desires for different product benefits and the importance of warranties, service, and customer support. So marketers must be sure that consumers can find the information they need. One way to do this is by providing a Frequently Asked Questions (FAQ) section on a company Web site.

Customers usually don't "sweat the details" so much when choosing among nondurable goods. There is little if any search for information or deliberation. Sometimes this means that consumers buy whatever brand is available and reasonably priced. In other instances, the purchase of nondurable goods is based largely on past experience. Because a certain brand has performed satisfactorily in the past, customers see no reason to consider other brands and choose the same one out of habit. For example, some consumers buy that familiar orange box of Tide

durable goods ■ Consumer products that provide benefits over a long period of time such as cars, furniture, and appliances.

nondurable goods ■ Consumer products that provide benefits for a short time because they are consumed (such as food) or are no longer useful (such as newspapers).

Consumers spend a lot of time and energy in making the decision to buy a computer monitor but very little to grab a package of soup at the supermarket.

laundry detergent again and again. In such cases, marketers can probably be less concerned with developing new-product features to attract customers and should focus more on pricing and distribution strategies.

CONSUMER PRODUCT CLASSES DEFINED BY HOW CONSUMERS BUY THE PRODUCT

Marketers also classify products based on where and how consumers buy the product. Both goods and services can be thought of as convenience products, shopping products, specialty products, or unsought products. In Chapter 6 you will recall that we talked about how consumer decisions differ in terms of effort from habitual decision making to limited problem solving to extended problem solving. Classifying products based on how consumers buy them is tied to these differnces in consumer decision making. Through understanding how consumers buy products, marketers have a clearer vision of the buying process and they can develop effective marketing strategies.

Convenience Products   A **convenience product** typically is a nondurable good or service that consumers purchase frequently with a minimum of comparison and effort. As the name implies, consumers expect these products to be handy and will buy whatever brands are easy to obtain. In general, convenience products are low priced and widely available. You can buy a gallon of milk or a loaf of bread at grocery stores, at convenience stores, and even at many service stations. Consumers generally know all they need or want to know about a convenience product, devote little effort to purchases, and willingly accept alternative brands if their preferred brand is not available in a convenient location. Most convenience products purchases are the results of habitual consumer decision making. What's the most important thing for marketers of convenience products? You guessed it—make sure the product is in stores where it's convenient for customers.

But all convenience product purchases aren't alike. You may stop by a local market on your way home from school or work to pick up that gallon of milk because milk is something you always keep in the refrigerator. As long as you're there, why not grab a candy bar for the drive home? Later that night you dash out to buy something to unclog your kitchen drain—also a convenience product. Marketers classify convenience products as staples, impulse products, and emergency products.

Staples such as milk, bread, and gasoline are basic or necessary items that are available almost everywhere. Most consumers don't perceive big differences among brands. When selling staples, marketers must offer customers a product that consistently meets their expectations for quality and make sure it is available at a price comparable to the competition's prices.

Consider this situation: You are standing in the checkout line at the supermarket and notice a copy of *People* magazine featuring a photo of Alanis Morissette with a provocative headline. You've got to check out that article! This magazine is an *impulse product*—something people often buy on the spur of the moment. With an impulse product, marketers have two challenges: to create a product or package design that is enticing, that "reaches out and grabs the customer," and to make sure their product is highly visible, for example, by securing prime end-aisle or checkout lane space.

Emergency products are those products we purchase when we're in dire need. Bandages, umbrellas, and something to unclog the bathroom sink are examples of emergency products. Because we need the product badly and immediately, price and sometimes product quality may be irrelevant to our decision to purchase. If you're caught out in a sudden downpour of rain, any umbrella at any price will do.

What are the challenges to marketers of emergency products? As with any other product, emergency products are most successful when they meet customer needs—you won't sell a drain cleaner that doesn't unclog a drain more than once. And emergency products need to be offered in the sizes customers want. If you cut your finger in the mall, you don't want to buy a box of 100 bandages—you want a box of 5 or 10. Of course, making emergency products available when and where an emergency is likely to occur is the real key to success. This was the challenge facing pharmaceutical companies after the anthrax scares in 2001, when antibiotics like Cipro suddenly were in short supply.

convenience product ■ A consumer good or service that is usually low priced, widely available, and purchased frequently with a minimum of comparison and effort.

Cut your finger? A blister on your foot? A Band-Aid is an emergency product you expect to find whenever and wherever you need it.

shopping product ■ A good or service for which consumers spend considerable time and effort gathering information and comparing alternatives before making a purchase.

Shopping Products   In contrast to convenience products, a **shopping product** is a good or service for which consumers will spend time and effort gathering information on price, product attributes, and product quality. They are likely to compare alternatives before making a purchase. The purchase of shopping products is typically a limited problem-solving decision. Often consumers have little prior knowledge about these products. Because they gather new information for each purchase occasion, consumers are only moderately brand loyal and will switch whenever a different brand offers new or better benefits. They may visit several stores and devote considerable effort to comparing products. For most consumers, a pair of shoes, a color television set, and a house-cleaning service are examples of shopping products.

Some of the latest entrants into the computer category are handheld minicomputers. These computers are a good example of a shopping product because they are relatively new to the market so consumers don't know a lot about the different models and features. Consumers shopping for them may ask, "Does it recognize handwriting? How large is the keyboard? Will it need accessories to handle e-mail? Does the screen light up in the dark?" Designing successful shopping products means making sure they have the attributes that customers want. And product packaging that points out those features helps consumers make the right decisions.

Some shopping products have different characteristics. For these *attribute-based shopping products*, such as a new party dress or a pair of designer jeans, consumers spend time and energy finding the best possible product selection. At other times, when choices available in the marketplace are just about the same, products are considered shopping products because of differences in price. For these *price-based shopping products*, determined shoppers will visit numerous stores in hopes of saving an additional $10 or $20.

In B2C e-commerce, shopping is easier when consumers use "shopbots" or "intelligent agents" which are computer programs that find sites selling a particular product. Some of these programs also provide information on competitors' prices, and they may even ask customers to

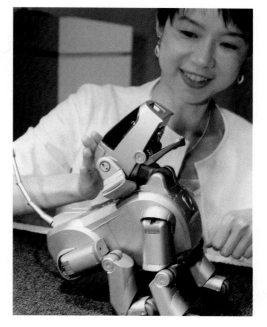

At $1,500, the second generation AIBOs are smarter, more playful, and $1,000 cheaper than the original AIBO introduced in 1999. Sony says the entertainment robot has emotions and instinct programmed into its brain. It can respond to 40 voice commands including "take a picture" (there is a digital camera installed in AIBO's nose). AIBO also chases a ball, performs tricks, and sulks when ignored—and you don't have to feed it.

rate the various e-businesses that they have listed on their site so consumers have recommendations of other consumers on which sellers are good and which are less than desirable. It should be noted, however, that some sites do not wish to compete on price and don't give bots access.

Specialty Products   Who would pay $2,500 for a robot dog? Apparently a lot of people—Sony's AIBOs learn to do many of the things that real live dogs and cats can do—and you don't need a pooper scooper. Despite its hefty price tag, the robots quickly sold out. The AIBO is a good example of a **specialty product**, as are a Big Bertha golf club, a Rolex watch, or the Fetish perfume we've been reading about. Specialty products have unique characteristics that are important to buyers at any price. A specialty service could be a favorite restaurant—one where you're willing to stand in line an hour before being served.

Consumers usually know a good deal about specialty products, are loyal to specific brands, and spend little if any time comparing alternatives. Generally, specialty products are bought with much consumer effort, an extended problem-solving purchase. For specialty products, firms create marketing strategies that make their product stand apart from the rest. For example, advertising for a specialty product such as a big-screen TV may talk about the brand's unique characteristics, attempting to convince prospective customers that savvy shoppers won't accept a substitute for the "real thing."

Unsought Products   A fourth category of consumer products is the unsought product. **Unsought products** are goods or services (other than convenience products) for which a consumer has little awareness or interest until a need arises. For college graduates with their first "real" jobs, retirement plans and disability insurance are unsought products. It requires a good deal of advertising or personal selling to interest people in unsought products—just ask any life insurance salesperson. Marketers are challenged to find convincing ways to interest consumers in unsought products. One solution may be to make pricing more attractive; for example, reluctant consumers may be more willing to buy an unsought product for "only pennies a day" than if they have to think about their yearly or lifetime cash outlay.

specialty product ■ A good or service that has unique characteristics, is important to the buyer, and for which the buyer will devote significant effort to acquire.

unsought product ■ A good or service for which a consumer has little awareness or interest until the product or a need for the product is brought to his or her attention.

2 Bookmark It!

What are some examples of successful convenience products, shopping products, and specialty products? What marketing strategies make these successful?

BUSINESS-TO-BUSINESS PRODUCTS

Although consumers purchase products for their own use, as we saw in Chapter 7, organizational customers purchase products to use in the production of other goods and services or to facilitate the organization's operation. Marketers classify business-to-business products based on how organizational customers use them. As with consumer products, when marketers know how their business customers use a product, they are better able to design products and the entire marketing mix.

Equipment refers to the products an organization uses in its daily operations. Heavy equipment, sometimes called *installations* or *capital equipment*, includes items such as buildings and robotics used to assemble automobiles. Installations are big-ticket items and last for a number of years. Computers, photocopy machines, and water fountains are examples of *light* or *accessory equipment*. Accessory equipment is movable, costs less, and has a shorter life span than capital equipment. Equipment marketing strategies usually emphasize personal selling and may mean custom designing products to meet a customer's specific needs.

Maintenance, repair, and operating (MRO) products are goods that a business customer consumes in a relatively short time. MRO products do not become a part of other goods and services. *Maintenance products* include lightbulbs, mops, cleaning supplies, and the like. *Repair products* are such items as nuts, bolts, washers, and small tools. *Operating supplies* include computer paper and oil to keep machinery running smoothly. Although some firms use a sales force to promote MRO products, others rely on catalog sales, the Internet, and telemarketing to keep prices as low as possible.

Raw materials are products of the fishing, lumber, agricultural, and mining industries that organizational customers purchase to use in their finished products. For example, a firm may use soybeans as raw materials and transform them into a finished product, tofu, whereas a steel manufacturer takes iron ore and changes it into large sheets of steel used by other firms in the manufacture of automobiles, washing machines, and lawn mowers.

Processed materials are produced when firms transform raw materials from their original state. Organizations purchase processed materials to manufacture their own products. Cement used in the manufacture of cement blocks and aluminum ingots used to make aluminum soda cans are examples of processed materials.

Some business customers purchase **specialized services** from outside suppliers. Specialized services may be technical such as equipment repair or nontechnical such as market research and legal services. These services are essential to the operation of an organization but are not part of the production of a product.

Component parts are manufactured goods or subassemblies of finished items that organizations need to complete their own products. For example, a computer manufacturer needs silicon chips to make a computer and an auto manufacturer needs batteries, tires, and fuel injectors. As with processed materials, marketing strategies for component parts usually involve nurturing relationships with customer firms and on-time delivery of a product that meets the buyer's specifications.

To review, we now understand what a product is. We also know how marketers classify consumer products based on how long they last and how they are purchased, and we've seen how they classify business-to-business products according to how they are used. In the next section we'll learn about the marketing of new products, or innovations.

It's "New and Improved!" Understanding Innovations

"New and improved!" What exactly do we mean when we use the term *new product*? The Federal Trade Commission says (1) that a product must be entirely new or changed significantly to be called new and (2) that a product may be called new for only six months.

That definition is fine from a legal perspective. From a marketing standpoint, though, a new product or an **innovation** is anything that customers *perceive* as new and different. Innovations may be a cutting-edge style such as tongue piercings, a fad such as Razor scooters, a new communications technology such as DVD players, or a new product such as personal digital assistants. It may be a completely new product that provides benefits never available before such as personal computers when they were first introduced, or it may simply be an existing product with a new style, in a different color, or with some new feature. If an innovation is successful, it spreads throughout the population. First, it is bought and used by only a few people, and then more and more consumers adopt it.

---

equipment ■ Expensive goods an organization uses in its daily operations that last for a long time.

maintenance, repair, and operating (MRO) products ■ Goods that a business customer consumes in a relatively short time.

raw materials ■ Products of the fishing, lumber, agricultural, and mining industries that organizational customers purchase to use in their finished products.

processed materials ■ Products created when firms transform raw materials from their original state.

specialized services ■ Services purchased from outside suppliers that are essential to the operation of an organization but are not part of the production of a product.

component parts ■ Manufactured goods or subassemblies of finished items that organizations need to complete their own products.

innovation ■ A product that consumers perceive to be new and different from existing products.

THE IMPORTANCE OF UNDERSTANDING INNOVATIONS

Understanding innovations can be critical to the success of firms for at least two reasons. First, technology is advancing at a dizzying pace. Products are introduced and become obsolete faster than ever before. In many industries, firms are busy developing another new-and-better product before the last new-and-better product even hits store shelves. Nowhere is this more obvious than with personal computers, for which a steady change in technology makes consumers want a bigger, better machine before the dust even settles on the old one. Another reason why understanding new products is important is the high cost of developing new products and the even higher cost of new products that fail. In the pharmaceutical industry, the cost of bringing each new drug to market is in the hundred-millions.[3] Even the most successful firms can't afford many product failures with that kind of price tag.

Marketers must understand what it takes to develop a new product successfully. They must do their homework and learn what it is about existing products consumers find less than satisfactory and exactly what it will take to do a better job satisfying customer needs. Savvy marketers know they'll waste a ton of investment money if they don't.

Finally, new-product development is an important contribution to society. We would never suggest that everything new is good, but many new products, some of which are listed in Table 9.2, allow us to live longer, happier lives of better quality than before. Although there are some who disagree, most of us feel that our lives are better because of telephones, televisions, CD players, microwave ovens, and computers—except, of course, when these items break down!

TABLE 9.2

Innovations That Have Changed Our Lives

Products that have changed how we play		*Products that have changed our homes*	
1900	Kodak Brownie camera	1907	Vacuum cleaner
1948	Polaroid camera	1918	Frigidaire refrigerator
1976	JVC videorecorder	1928	Home air conditioner
1982	Philips/Sony CD player	1942	Permacel duct tape
Products that have changed how we work		1946	Tupperware
1900	Paper clip	1967	Amana microwave oven
1959	Xerox photocopier		
1966	Xerox fax machine	*Products that have changed the way we communicate*	
1971	Intel microprocessor		
1980	3M Post-it Notes	1921	RCA radio
1984	Apple Macintosh	1935	RCA television
Products that have changed how we travel		1939	The paperback book
1903	Harley-Davidson motorcycle	1991	World Wide Web
1908	Ford Model T	*Products that have changed our clothing*	
1936	DC-3	1913	Zipper
1950s	Skateboard	1914	Bra
1957	Boeing 707	1936	Bass penny loafer
Products that have changed our health and grooming		1939	Nylons
1903	Safety razors	1954	Velcro
1921	Johnson & Johnson Band-Aid	1959	Lycra
1928	Penicillin	1961	P&G Pampers
1931	Tampax tampon		
1960	Searle birth control pill		
1988	Eli Lilly Prozac		

Source: Adapted from Christine Chen and Tim Carvell, "Products of the Century," *Fortune*, November 22, 1999, pp. 133–136.

New medical products help to keep us from breaking down: In the near future, doctors will be able to replace or assist almost every part of the body with bionic products such as replacement spinal discs, insulin pumps that mimic a natural pancreas in diabetes patients by automatically testing blood-glucose levels, microdetectors implanted into retinas allowing patients with retinal damage to see light, and bionic ears that allow the deaf to hear.[4] Truly useful new products benefit the users and the companies that make them.

TYPES OF INNOVATIONS

Innovations differ in their degree of newness, and this helps to determine how quickly the products will be adopted by a target market. Because innovations that are more novel require greater effort and more changes in behavior, they are slower to spread throughout a population than new products that are similar to what is already available.

Marketers classify innovations into three categories based on their degree of newness, but it is better to think of these three types as ranges along a continuum that goes from a very small change to a totally new product. The three types of innovations are based on the amount of disruption or change they bring to people's lives. For example, when the first automobiles were produced, they caused tremendous changes in the lives of their owners, far greater changes than when auto manufacturers introduced "new and improved" autos with automatic transmissions, air conditioning, and driving directions provided via satellite.

continuous innovation ■
A modification of an existing product that sets one brand apart from its competitors.

Continuous Innovations A **continuous innovation** is a modification to an existing product, such as when Cheerios introduced Honey Nut and Frosted versions of its cereal. This type of modification can set one brand apart from its competitors. For example, Saturn unveiled a new car design in 2001 featuring a third door that made it look different from any other car.

The consumer doesn't have to learn anything new to use a continuous innovation. From a marketing perspective, this means that it is far easier to convince consumers to adopt this kind of new product. A typewriter company, for example, many years ago modified the shape of its product to make it more "user friendly" to secretaries. One simple change was curving the tops of the keys, like we see on today's computer keyboards. The reason is that secretaries complained that flat surfaces were hard to use with long fingernails. Today computer manufacturers have gone a step farther by building ergonomic keyboards that are less likely to cause painful wrist ailments.

Physicians have traditionally performed endoscopies, examination of the small intestine, by inserting fiber-optic tubes anally or orally. Many of these procedures can be less painful for patients because of a new wireless video pill. The M2A is an innovation that passes through the gastrointestinal system and snaps two pictures a second for 24 hours (*Newsweek*, June 25, 2001, p. 52).

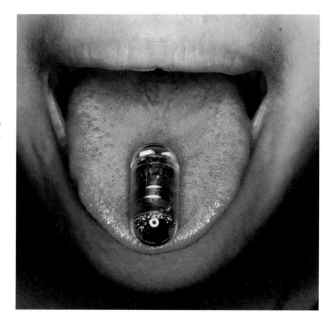

How different does a new product have to be from existing products? We've all heard that "imitation is the sincerest form of flattery," but decisions regarding how much (if at all) one's product should resemble those of competitors often are a centerpiece of marketing strategy. Sometimes marketers feel that the best strategy is to follow the competition. For example, the packaging of "me-too" or look-alike products can create instant market success because consumers assume that similar packaging means similar products.

A **knockoff** is a new product that copies, with slight modification, the design of an original product. Firms deliberately create knockoffs of clothing, jewelry, or other items, often with the intent to sell to a larger or different market. For example, companies may copy the *haute couture* clothing styles of top designers and sell them at lower prices to the mass market. It is difficult to legally protect a design (as opposed to a technological invention) because it can be argued that even a very slight change—different buttons or a slightly wider collar on a dress or shirt—means the knockoff is not an exact copy.

knockoff ■ A new product that copies with slight modification the design of an original product.

Dynamically Continuous Innovations
A **dynamically continuous innovation** is a pronounced modification to an existing product that requires a modest amount of learning or change in behavior to use it. The history of audio equipment is a series of dynamically continuous innovations. For many years, consumers enjoyed listening to their favorite Frank Sinatra songs on record players. Then in the 1960s, that same music became available on a continuous-play eight-track tape (requiring the purchase of an eight-track tape player, of course). Then came cassette tapes (oops, now a cassette player is needed). In the 1980s consumers could hear Metallica songs digitally mastered on compact discs (that, of course, required the purchase of a new CD player). In the 1990s, recording technology moved one more step forward with MP3 technology, allowing music fans to download Limp Bizkit from the Internet or to exchange electronic copies of the music with other fans. Even though each of these changes required learning how to operate the new equipment, consumers were willing to buy the new products because of the improvements in music reproduction, the core product benefit. Hopefully the music will continue to improve, too.

dynamically continuous innovation ■ A change in an existing product that requires a moderate amount of learning or behavior change.

One of the most talked about changes in the future of the digital world is convergence. Convergence has already begun providing consumers with a host of new products that may be classified as dynamically continuous innovations. **Convergence** means the coming together of two or more technologies to create new systems that provide greater benefit than the original technologies alone. In the case of e-commerce, experts predict that in the future the Internet, television, radio, and telephones will all be combined into a single technology.

convergence ■ The coming together of two or more technologies to create a new system with greater benefits than its parts.

People are already beginning to drop out of their local radio markets and instead tune in to far away online radio stations. The advantage for the consumer, of course, is that even small

Imitation products are legal knockoffs of popular brands.

groups of fans of diverse types of music can listen to their favorite songs or other radio programming of their choice. For example, Brazilian top 40 station JB can be heard at jb.fm on the Web. Listeners can hear news out of Beijing via Joy FM's English-language service and you can hear Chubby Checker on louisianaradio.com. Today Web radio requires a computer and an Internet connection, but experts predict that as wireless Internet connections continue to develop, even Web radio will be wireless in the very near future. We'll be able to listen to our favorite Web radio stations on small, inexpensive wireless receivers, something like a kitchen or bedside radio.[5]

discontinuous innovation
◼ A totally new product that creates major changes in the way we live.

3 *Bookmark It!*

What are some new products that have made your life better? How? What are some new products that have been harmful to the quality of life? How?

Discontinuous Innovations   A **discontinuous innovation** creates major changes in the way we live. To use a discontinuous innovation, consumers must engage in a great amount of learning because no similar product has ever been on the market. Major inventions such as the airplane, the car, and the television have radically changed modern lifestyles. Another discontinuous innovation, the personal computer, is changing the way we shop and is allowing more people to work from home or anywhere else.

Understanding the degree of newness of innovations helps marketers develop effective marketing strategies. For example, if marketers know that consumers may resist adopting a new and radically different product, they may offer a free product trial or place heavier emphasis on a personal selling strategy to convince consumers that the new product offers benefits worth the hassle. Business-to-business marketers often provide in-service training for employees of their customers who invest in new products.

Developing New Products

Building on our knowledge of different types of innovations, we'll now turn our attention to how firms go about developing new products such as Fetish perfume. Product development doesn't simply mean creating totally new products never before on the market. Of course, a lot of companies do that but, for many other firms, product development is a continuous process of looking for ways to make an existing product better or finding just the right shade of purple for this year's new pants styles.

For several reasons, new-product development is increasingly important to firms. First, technology is changing at an ever-increasing rate so that products are developed, get adopted, and then are replaced by better products faster and faster. In addition, competition in our global marketplace makes it essential for firms to continuously offer new choices for consumers if they are to compete with companies all around the world rather than just down the street. Firms need to stay on top of current developments in popular culture, religion, politics, and so on to

Lonnie Johnson walked into the slick conference room of the Larami Corporation, smiled mischievously, opened his pink, battered Samsonite suitcase and took out a gizmo that looked a bit like a phaser gun from *Star Trek*. Holding this combination of a handheld pump apparatus, PVC tubing, Plexiglas, and plastic soda bottles, Lonnie aimed . . . and fired! A giant stream of water shot across the room. A year later, the Super Soaker became the most successful water gun in U.S. retail history.

Phases in Development	Outcome
● Idea generation	Identify product ideas that will provide important customer benefits compatible with company mission.
● Product concept development and screening	Expand product ideas into more complete product concepts and estimate the potential commercial success of product concepts.
● Marketing strategy development	Develop preliminary plan for target markets, pricing, distribution and promotion.
● Business analysis	Estimate potential for profit. What is the potential demand, what expenditures will be required, and what is the cost of marketing the product?
● Technical development	Design the product and the manufacturing and production process.
● Market testing	Develop evidence of potential success in the real market.
● Commercialization	Implement full-scale marketing plan.

FIGURE 9.3

Phases in New Product Development

Firms engage in a series of orderly steps in order to maximize the chance of a new product being successful.

develop products that are consistent with consumers' mind-sets. Sometimes new hit products are based on careful research but in many cases being at the right place at the right time doesn't hurt. For example, Hasbro developed a new version of its G.I. Joe toy as a search-and-rescue firefighter prior to the September 11, 2001 attacks, and renewed respect for fire-fighters lit the fire under sales the following Christmas.[6] Unfortunately, most new-product introductions need a bit more than good timing to score big in the marketplace.

Indeed, if anything, successful new-product introductions are becoming more and more difficult. First, the costs of research and development are often so huge that firms must limit the number of new products in development. Because products are outdated faster than ever, firms have less time to recover their research and development costs. And with so many products competing for limited shelf space, retailers often charge manufacturers exorbitant fees to stock a new product, increasing manufacturers' costs even more.[7] Firms must reduce the time it takes to get good products to market and increase the speed of adoption to quickly recover these costs. New-product development generally occurs in seven phases as shown in Figure 9.3.

IDEA GENERATION

In the first phase of product development, **idea generation**, marketers use a variety of sources to come up with great new-product ideas that provide customer benefits and that are compatible with the company mission. Sometimes ideas come from customers. Ideas also come from salespeople, service providers, and others who have direct customer contact.

Often firms use marketing research activities such as focus groups in their search for new-product ideas. For example, a company such as Cable News Network (CNN) interested in developing new channels might hold focus group discussions to get ideas about types of programs not currently available.

idea generation ■ The first step of product development in which marketers brainstorm for products that provide customer benefits and are compatible with the company mission.

PRODUCT CONCEPT DEVELOPMENT AND SCREENING

The second phase in developing new products is **product concept development and screening**. Although ideas for products initially come from a variety of sources, it is up to marketers to expand these ideas into more complete product concepts. Product concepts describe what features the product should have and the benefits those features will provide for consumers.

When screening marketers and researchers examine the chances that the product concept might achieve technical and commercial success, weeding out concepts that have little chance of success. Estimating *technical success* is assessing whether the new product is technologically feasible—is it possible to build this product? Estimating *commercial success* is deciding

product concept development and screening ■ Second step of product development in which marketers test product ideas for technical and commercial success.

whether or not anyone is likely to buy the product. The marketing graveyard is piled high with products that sounded interesting but that failed to catch on, including jalapeño soda, aerosol mustard, and edible deodorant![8]

The achievment of technical success but not commercial success confounded Burger King when the chain invested heavily to develop a new french fry.[9] This innovation was a potato stick coated with a layer of starch to make it crunchier and keep the heat in to stay fresh longer. Burger King created 19 pages of specifications for its new item, including a requirement that there must be an audible crunch present for seven or more chews. The $70 million dollar rollout of the new product included a "Free Fryday" when 15 million orders of fries were given to customers free, advertising on the Super Bowl, and official proclamations by the governors of three states.

Unfortunately, the new fry was a "whopper" of a product failure. Burger King blamed the product failure on inconsistent cooking by franchisees and a poor potato crop but a more likely explanation is that consumers simply did not like the fry as well as those they might find at certain (golden) archrivals. Just because it's new doesn't always make it better.

MARKETING STRATEGY DEVELOPMENT

The third phase in new-product development is to develop a marketing strategy that can be used to introduce the product to the marketplace. This means that marketers must identify the target market, estimate its size, and determine how the product can be positioned to effectively address the target market's needs. And, of course, marketing strategy development includes planning for pricing, distribution, and promotion expenditures both for the introduction of the new product and for the long run.

 **Advice for Lambesis**

Benjamin Gonzales, Student, Boston University, School of Management

I would choose option 1 because it combines the best design and functionality to meet the needs of the target market—teenage girls. Girls at this age want products to display that are deemed cool and prestigious by their friends and other groups while still being affordable and functional. Option 1 gives teenage girls the choice of clipping the vial to clothing and bags or leaving it standing on a dresser by itself. In addition, the colorful designs are attractive and collectible, positioning the perfume with other designer products girls at this age purchase and want to show to their friends. Option 1 may also be the cheapest alternative, as it does not require a separate plastic container to display the product.

Jeff Gutenberg, Marketing Professor, SUNY Geneseo

I would choose option 1 because according to the research the reactions to it are more positive, and its futuristic design and multiple uses meet additional consumer criteria. Equally important, it has more potential than the other two designs to stimulate multiple purchases from a single customer. This is important if the sales goals are to be met. However, the research is just exploratory and all three designs apparently have some appeal to the target audience, so it's not easy to choose.

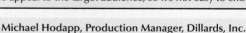

Michael Hodapp, Production Manager, Dillards, Inc.

I would choose option 1 because of the simple, narrow packaging. While all the packages could have other uses, the base that holds the vial/tube makes it functional and decorative for the dressing table and when clipped to clothing or bags. Option 1 is the only option that adds brand identification to the actual vial. Because the product will be clipped to clothing or bags, it will serve as a conversation piece among the target market's peers. As a collectible, the packaging should be offered in multiple colors to entice repeat purchases. The other options offer a more bulky package that is attractive, but practicality wins with option 1.

 Weigh in with your thoughts! Visit the Live Laboratory at www.prenhall.com/solomon for extended Other Voices replies, exercises, and more.

BUSINESS ANALYSIS

Once a product concept passes the screening stage, the next phase is to conduct a **business analysis**. Even though marketers have evidence that there is a market for the product, they still must find out if the product can be a profitable contribution to the organization's product mix. How much potential demand is there for the product? Does the firm have the resources that will be required for successful development and introduction of the product?

The business analysis for a new product begins with assessing how the new product will fit into the firm's total product mix. Will the new product increase sales or will it simply cannibalize sales of existing products? Are there possible synergies between the new product and the company's existing offerings that may improve visibility and the image of both? And what are the marketing costs likely to be?

business analysis ■ Step in the product development process in which marketers assess a product's commercial viability.

TECHNICAL DEVELOPMENT

If it survives the scrutiny of a business analysis, a new-product concept then undergoes **technical development** in which a firm's engineers work with marketers in refining the design and production process. For example, when Airbus wanted to develop a new double-decker, 555-passenger megaliner, it had to find the materials that would provide the strength necessary for such a big plane and overcome the problem of safe emergency evacuation (airplane international certification requires that a plane must permit the evacuation of all passengers within 90 seconds).[10]

Typically, a company's research and development (R&D) department will develop one or more physical versions or **prototypes** of the product. These prototypes may be evaluated by prospective customers—the better a firm understands how customers will react to a new product, the better its chances of commercial success.

Those involved in the technical development process must determine which parts of a finished good the company will make and which ones will be bought from other suppliers. If goods are to be manufactured, the company may have to buy new production equipment or modify existing machinery. Someone has to develop work instructions for employees and train them to produce the product. In developing service processes, technical development includes such decisions as which activities will occur within sight of customers and whether parts of the service can be automated to make delivery more efficient.

Technical development sometimes requires application for a patent. Because patents legally prevent competitors from producing or selling the invention, a patent may reduce or eliminate competition in a market for many years, allowing a firm "breathing room" to recoup investments in technical development.

In September and October 2001, when the anthrax spores were sent through the mail with the potential to infect thousands of people, Bayer held the U.S. patent on Cipro, the drug of choice for preventing anthrax infection. Thus, the government was prevented from legally buying Cipro from non-U.S. manufacturers that sold the product at a lower cost than Bayer. To respond to this, Bayer agreed to dramatically reduce its price from $1.75 to $0.95 per tablet.[11]

technical development ■ Step in the product development process in which a new product is refined and perfected by company engineers and the like.

prototypes ■ Test versions of a proposed product.

MARKET TESTING

The next phase of new-product development includes **test marketing**. This means the firm tries out the complete marketing plan—the distribution, advertising, sales promotion—but in a small geographic area that is similar to the larger market it hopes to enter.

There are both pluses and minuses to test marketing. On the negative side, test marketing is extremely expensive. It can cost over a million dollars to conduct a test market even in a single city. A test market also gives the competition a free look at the new product, its introductory price, and the intended promotional strategy—and an opportunity to get to the market first with a competing product. On the positive side, by offering a new product in a limited area of the market, marketers can evaluate and improve the marketing program. Sometimes test marketing uncovers a need to improve the product itself. At other times, test marketing indicates product failure, allowing the firm to save millions of dollars by "pulling the plug."[12]

Because of the problems with test marketing, marketers sometimes conduct *simulated test marketing* that imitates the introduction of a product into the marketplace using special computer software as we saw in Chapter 5. These simulations allow the company to see the likely impact

test marketing ■ Testing the complete marketing plan in a small geographic area that is similar to the larger market the firm hopes to enter.

DON'T THROW GOOD MONEY AT A BAD IDEA.

Before you launch your new product, see if anyone wants it.

Pretest your new concept — online — with the company that pioneered marketing research on the Internet. Our panel of more than one million consumers from all across the Internet, the largest of its kind, includes exactly the people you want to reach.

Join the Research Revolution!™ Contact the world's most experienced Internet marketing research company for studies online, on time, on target and on budget.

www.greenfield.com 888.291.9997

Greenfield *Online*
Leading the Research Revolution®

New online technologies let marketers test consumer reactions to product ideas faster and more cheaply than ever before.

---

of price cuts and new packaging—or even to determine where in the store the product should be placed to maximize sales. The process entails gathering basic research data on consumer perceptions of the product concept, the physical product, the advertising, and other promotional activity. The test market simulation model uses that information to predict the product's success much less expensively (and more discreetly) than a traditional test market. As this simulated test market technology improves, traditional test markets may become a thing of the past.

commercialization ■ Final step in the product development process in which a new product is launched into the market.

COMMERCIALIZATION

The last phase in new-product development is **commercialization**. This means the launching of a new product and requires full-scale production, distribution, advertising, sales promotion—the works. For this reason commercialization of a new product cannot happen overnight. A launch requires planning and careful preparation. Marketers must implement trade promotion plans, which offer special incentives to encourage dealers, retailers, or other members of the channel to stock the new product so that customers will find it on store shelves the very first time they look. They must also develop consumer promotions such as coupons. Marketers may arrange to have point-of-purchase displays designed, built, and delivered to retail outlets. If the new product is especially complex, customer service employees must receive extensive training and preparation.

As launch time nears, preparations gain a sense of urgency—like countdown to blast-off at NASA. Sales managers explain special incentive programs to salespeople. Soon the media announce to prospective customers why they should buy and where they can find the new product. All elements of the marketing program—ideally—come into play like a carefully planned lift-off of the space shuttle.

4 *Bookmark It!*

You are the director of marketing for a firm that markets cosmetics and personal care products. Your firm is interested in developing new products targeted to teenage girls. Describe the steps that your firm would go through to develop an innovation in this market.

Adoption and Diffusion Processes

In the previous section, we talked about the steps marketers take to develop new products from generating ideas to launch. Moving on, we'll look at what happens after that new product hits the market—how an innovation spreads throughout a population.

A painting is not a work of art until someone views it. A song is not music until someone sings it. In the same way, new products do not satisfy customer wants and needs until the customer uses them. **Product adoption** is the process by which a consumer or business customer begins to buy and use a new good, service, or an idea. The term **diffusion** describes how the use of a product spreads throughout a population.

After months or even years spent developing a new product, the real challenge to firms is getting consumers to buy and use the product and to do so quickly to recover the costs of product development and launch. To accomplish this, marketers must understand the product adoption process. In the next section we'll discuss the stages in this process. We'll also see how consumers and businesses differ in their eagerness to adopt new products and how the characteristics of a product affect its adoption rate.

product adoption ■ The process by which a consumer or business customer begins to buy and use a new good, service, or an idea.

diffusion ■ The process by which the use of a product spreads throughout a population.

STAGES IN A CUSTOMER'S ADOPTION OF A NEW PRODUCT

Whether the innovation is better film technology or a better mousetrap, individuals and organizations pass through six stages in the adoption process. Figure 9.4 shows how a person goes from being unaware of an innovation through the stages of awareness, interest, evaluation, trial, adoption, and confirmation. At every stage, people drop out of the process, so the proportion of consumers who wind up using the innovation on a consistent basis is a fraction of those who are exposed to it.

FIGURE **9.4**

Adoption Pyramid

Consumers pass through six stages in the adoption of a new product—from being unaware of an innovation to becoming loyal adopters. The right marketing strategies at each stage help ensure a successful adoption.

Reinforcing the customer's choice through advertising, sales promotion and other communications — **Confirmation**

Making the product available / Providing product use information — **Adoption**

Demonstrations, samples, trial size packages — **Trial**

Providing information to customers about how the product can benefit them — **Evaluation**

May use teaser advertising — **Interest**

Massive advertising — **Awareness**

Awareness Learning that the innovation exists is the first step in the adoption process. To make consumers aware of a new product, marketers may conduct a massive advertising campaign, called a media blitz. This was the case when McDonald's introduced its Arch Deluxe sandwich with a nationwide rollout accompanied by heavy TV and newspaper advertising. At this point, some consumers will say, "So there's a new sandwich out there. So what?" and they will fall by the wayside, out of the adoption process. But this strategy works for new products when consumers see a new product as something they want and need and just can't live without. Unfortunately, the Arch Deluxe didn't "meat" this test and it became just another resident of the new-product graveyard.

Interest For some of the people who become aware of a new product, a second stage in the adoption process is *interest*. By interest, we mean that a prospective adopter begins to see how a new product might satisfy an existing or newly realized need. Interest also means that consumers look for and are open to information about the innovation. Marketers often design teaser advertisements that give prospective customers just enough information about the new product to make them curious and to stimulate their interest. Despite marketers' best efforts, though, some consumers drop out of the process at this point.

Evaluation In the evaluation stage, a prospect weighs the costs and benefits of the new product. On one hand, for complex, risky, or expensive products, people think about the innovation a great deal before trying it. For instance, a firm will carefully evaluate spending hundreds of thousands of dollars on manufacturing robotics prior to purchase. Marketers for such products help prospective customers see how such products can benefit them.

But little evaluation may occur with an impulse purchase. As an example, consumers may do very little thinking before buying a virtual pet such as the Tamagotchi (Japanese for "cute little egg"). For these products, marketers design the product to be eye-catching and appealing to get consumers to notice the product quickly. Some potential adopters will evaluate an innovation positively enough to move on to the trial stage. Those who do not think the new product will provide adequate benefits drop out.

Trial The next stage in the adoption process, *trial*, means the potential adopters will actually experience or use the product for the first time. Often marketers stimulate trial by providing opportunities for consumers to sample the product. America Online (AOL), for example, allowed consumers to sample its Internet service by including a sample program disk in newspapers.

Based on the trial experience, some potential buyers move on to adoption of the new product. Sometimes prospective customers will not adopt a new product because it costs too much. This was the case with the digital camera. When first on the market, they were simply high-priced toys. A year later, when prices had dropped to below $1,000, consumers were more willing to buy and sales took off.[13]

Internet-ready cell phones allow consumers to receive friends' e-mails and news headlines. In gadget-crazy Japan, 3 million consumers purchased the phones and signed up with mobile carriers within seven months of their introduction.

Adoption   In the *adoption* stage, a prospect chooses a product. If the product is a consumer or business-to-business good, this means buying the product and learning how to use and maintain it. If the product is an idea, this means that the individual agrees with the new idea.

Does this mean that all individuals or organizations that first choose an innovation are permanent customers? That's a mistake many firms make. Some potential customers, even after initial adoption, do not go on to the final stage of confirmation. Marketers need to provide follow-up contacts and communications with adopters to ensure they are satisfied and remain loyal to the new product over time.

Confirmation   After adopting an innovation, a customer weighs expected versus actual benefits and costs. Favorable experiences contribute to new customers becoming loyal adopters, as their initially positive opinions result in *confirmation*. Of course, nothing lasts forever—even loyal customers may decide that a new product is not meeting expectations and reject it. Some marketers feel that *reselling* the customer in the confirmation stage is important. They provide advertisements, sales presentations, and other communications to reinforce a customer's choice.

THE DIFFUSION OF INNOVATIONS

Diffusion describes how the use of a product spreads throughout a population. Of course, marketers would prefer that their entire target market would immediately adopt a new product, but this is not the case. Consumers and business customers differ in how eager or willing they are to try something new, lengthening the diffusion process by months or even years. Based on adopters' roles in the diffusion process, experts have classified them into five categories.

Adopter Categories   Some people like to try new products. Others are so reluctant you'd think they're afraid of anything new. As Figure 9.5 shows, there are five categories of adopters: innovators, early adopters, early majority, late majority, and laggards.[14] To understand how the adopter categories differ, we'll study the adoption of one specific product, the microwave oven.

Innovators are roughly the first 2.5 percent of adopters. This segment is extremely adventurous and willing to take risks with new products. Innovators are typically well educated, younger, better off financially than others in the population, and worldly. Innovators who were into new technology knew all about microwave ovens before other people were aware they

innovators ■ The first segment (roughly 2.5 percent) of a population to adopt a new product.

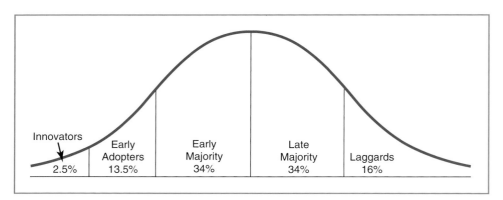

FIGURE **9.5**

Categories of Adopters

Because consumers differ in how willing they are to buy and try a new product, it often takes months or years for an innovation to be adopted by most of the populaton.

early adopters ■ Those who adopt an innovation early in the diffusion process but after the innovators.

early majority ■ Those whose adoption of a new product signals a general acceptance of the innovation.

late majority ■ The adopters who are willing to try new products when there is little or no risk associated with the purchase, when the purchase becomes an economic necessity, or when there is social pressure to purchase.

laggards ■ The last consumers to adopt an innovation.

existed. Because innovators pride themselves on trying new products, they probably purchased microwaves when they were first introduced to the market in the 1960s.

Early adopters, approximately 13.5 percent of adopters, buy product innovations early in the diffusion process but not as early as innovators. Unlike innovators, early adopters have greater concern for social acceptance. Typically, they are heavy media users and often are heavy users of a new-product category. Others in the population often look to early adopters for their opinions on various topics, making early adopters key to a new product's success. For this reason, marketers often target them in developing advertising and other communications efforts. After reading articles in *Consumer Reports* and other sources of information on new products, early adopters of the microwave made their first purchase in the early 1970s.

The **early majority**, roughly 34 percent of adopters, avoid being either first or last to try an innovation. They are typically middle-class consumers and are deliberate and cautious. Early majority consumers have slightly above average education and income levels. When the early majority adopts a product, it is no longer considered new or different—it is, in essence, already established. Early majority microwave owners made their purchase in the early 1980s by which time there were 10 to 15 different brands of microwaves sold by a wide variety of retailers.

Late majority adopters, about 34 percent of the population, are older, more conservative, and typically have lower than average levels of education and income. The late majority adopters avoid trying a new product until it is no longer risky. By that time, the product has become an economic necessity or there is pressure from peer groups to adopt. Late majority homes did not have a microwave until their friends began asking, "How can you survive without a microwave?" By that time, the price of the ovens had gone down and the inno-vators, early adopters, and even many of the early majority were purchasing a second or even a third microwave. To attract late majority buyers, marketers may offer lower-priced models of a product.

Laggards, about 16 percent of adopters, are the last in a population to adopt a new product. Laggards are typically lower in social class than other adopter categories and are bound by tradition. By the time laggards adopt a product, it may already be superseded by other innovations.

By understanding these adopter categories, marketers are able to better develop strategies that will speed the diffusion or widespread use of their products. For example, early in the diffusion process, marketers may put greater emphasis on advertising in special-interest magazines to attract innovators and early adopters. Later they may lower the product's price or come out with lower-priced models with fewer "bells and whistles" to attract the late majority. We will talk more about strategies for new and existing products in the next chapter.

Product Factors Affecting the Rate of Adoption

Not all products are successful. Crystal Pepsi, Premier smokeless cigarettes, the Betamax video player, the Ford Edsel automobile, AT&T Picturephone, and Snif-T-Panties (women's underwear that smelled like bananas, popcorn, whiskey, or pizza), all litter the marketing graveyard.[15] The reason for such product failures is very simple—consumers did not perceive that they satisfied a need better than competitive products on the market.

Product Factors Affecting Rate of Adoption	Product Rated High on Factor	Product Rated Low on Factor	Rating of Microwave Oven on the Factors
Relative Advantage	faster	slower	low until lifestyles changed
Compatibility	faster	slower	low—no metal in oven
Complexity	slower	faster	cooking process seen as highly complex
Trialability	faster	slower	low until cooking schools begun
Observability	faster	slower	on kitchen cabinet: moderately low

TABLE 9.3

Adoption Rate Factors
A variety of product factors cause adoption of the innovation by consumers to be faster or slower. Understanding these factors means marketers can develop strategies to encourage people to try a new product.

If you could predict which new products will succeed and which will fail, you'd quickly be in high demand as a consultant by companies worldwide. That's because companies make large investments in new products, but failures are all too frequent. Experts suggest that between one-third and one-half of all new products fail. As you might expect, there is much research devoted to making us smarter about new-product successes and failures.

Researchers have identified five characteristics of innovations that affect the rate of adoption: relative advantage, compatibility, complexity, trialability, and observability.[16] Whether or not a new product has each of these characteristics affects the speed of diffusion. As we've discussed, it took many years for the microwave to diffuse or spread throughout the U.S. population—from the mid-1960s to the late 1980s. Examining these five factors shown in Table 9.3 helps to explain both why the new product was not adopted during its early years and why adoption sped up later.

Razor scooter sales zoomed away when young consumers saw their friends racing around.

Relative advantage is the degree to which a consumer perceives that a new product provides superior benefits. In the case of the microwave oven, consumers in the 1960s did not feel that the product provided important benefits that would improve their lives. But by the late 1970s, that perception had changed because more women had entered the workforce. The 1960s' woman had all day to prepare the evening meal so she didn't have a need for the microwave. But in the 1970s when many women left home for work at 8:00 A.M. and returned home at 6:00 P.M., an appliance that would "magically" defrost a frozen chicken and cook it in 30 minutes provided a genuine advantage.

Compatibility is the extent to which a new product is consistent with existing cultural values, customs, and practices. Did consumers see the microwave oven as being compatible with existing ways of doing things? Hardly. Cooking on paper plates? If you put a paper plate in a conventional oven, you'll likely get a visit from the fire department. By anticipating compatibility issues early in the new-product development stage, marketing strategies can address such problems in planning communications programs or there may be opportunities for altering product designs to overcome some consumer objections.

Complexity is the degree to which consumers find a new product or its use difficult to understand. Many microwave users today haven't a clue about how a microwave oven cooks food. But when the product was introduced, consumers asked and marketers answered—microwaves cause molecules to move and rub together, creating friction, which produces heat. *Voilà!* Cooked pot roast. But that explanation was complex and confusing for the homemaker of the Ozzie and Harriet days.

Trialability is the ease of sampling a new product and its benefits. Marketers took a very important step in the 1970s to speed up adoption of the microwave oven—product trial. Just about every store that sold microwaves invited shoppers to visit the store and sample an entire meal cooked in the microwave.

Observability is how visible a new product and its benefits are to others who might adopt it. The ideal innovation is easy to see. For example, scooters such as the Razor became the hippest way to get around as soon as one preteen saw his friends flying by. The microwave was moderately observable. Only close friends and acquaintances who visited someone's home could see whether or not she owned a microwave.

5 Bookmark It!

Experts predict that the not-so-distant future will bring us one product that will allow us to talk on the phone, listen to the radio, watch TV or a movie, and check our e-mail. What factors do you think are likely to speed the adoption of such a product? What factors will slow its adoption?

ORGANIZATIONAL DIFFERENCES AFFECT ADOPTION

Just as there are differences among consumers in their eagerness to adopt new products, businesses and other organizations are not alike in their willingness to buy and use

The Italian motorcycle company Ducati introduced its 2000 model over the Internet. The limited-production product (only 500 were made) was sold out within 31 minutes.

new industrial products.[17] Firms that welcome product innovations are likely to be younger companies in highly technical industries with younger managers and entrepreneurial corporate cultures. Early adopter firms are likely to be market-share leaders that adopt new innovations and try new ways of doing things to maintain their leadership. Firms that adopt new products only when they recognize they must innovate to keep up are in the early majority. Late majority firms tend to be oriented toward the status quo and often have large financial investments in existing production technology. Laggard firms are probably already losing money.

Business-to-business products, like consumer products, also may possess characteristics that will increase their likelihood of adoption. Organizations are likely to adopt an innovation that helps them increase gross margins and profits. It is unlikely that firms would have adopted new products like voice mail unless they provided a way to increase profits by reducing labor costs. Organizational innovations are attractive when they are consistent with a firm's ways of doing business.

Cost is also a factor in the new products firms will adopt. Firms are more likely to accept a new product if they perceive the improvement to be large in relation to the investment they will have to make. This was the case when the U.S. Army adopted the John Deere Gator. At under $10,000, or about an eighth of the price of a Humvee, the Gator is an inexpensive off-road utility vehicle that's just right for rescuing wounded soldiers from foxholes. Although the Gator hasn't replaced the Humvee altogether, the military is able to buy fewer of the expensive Humvees and save big taxpayer bucks.

Real People, Real Choices: How It Worked Out at Lambesis

Dee Dee and her colleagues decided to merge the strongest features of options 1 and 2. The final design appears in the advertisement developed for the fragrance (shown here). In the first month following the Fetish product launch, the fragrance sold 500 percent faster than any other new product in Dana's history. Based on this promising early start, the company increased its sales goals by 50 percent.

This ad for Fetish shows the design option that was selected by Lambesis for the new perfume.

Chapter Summary

1. Explain the layers of a product.

A product may be anything tangible or intangible that satisfies consumer or business-to-business customer needs. Products include goods, services, ideas, people, and places. The core product is the basic product category benefits and customized benefit(s) the product provides. The actual product is the physical good or delivered service including the packaging and brand name. The augmented product includes both the actual product and any supplementary services such as warranty, credit, delivery, installation, and so on.

2. Describe the classifications of products.

Marketers generally classify goods and services as either consumer or business-to-business products. They further classify consumer products according to how long they last and by how they are purchased. Durable goods provide benefits for months or years whereas nondurable goods are used up quickly or are useful for only a short time. Consumers purchase convenience products frequently with little effort. Customers carefully gather information and compare different brands on their attributes and prices before buying shopping products. Specialty products have unique characteristics that are important to the buyer. Customers have little interest in unsought products until a need arises. Business products are for commercial uses by organizations. Marketers classify business products according to how they are used, for example, equipment, maintenance, repair, and operating (MRO) products, raw and processed materials, component parts, and business services.

3. Explain the importance of new products.

Innovations are anything consumers perceive to be new. Understanding new products is important to companies because of the fast pace of technological advancement, the high cost to companies for developing new products, and the contributions to society that new products can make. Marketers classify innovations by their degree of newness. A continuous innovation is a modification of an existing product, a dynamically continuous innovation provides a greater change in a product, and a discontinuous innovation is a new product that creates major changes in people's lives.

4. Describe how firms develop new products.

In new-product development, marketers first generate product ideas from which product concepts are first developed and then screened. Next they develop a marketing strategy and conduct a business analysis to estimate the profitability of the new product. Technical development includes planning how the product will be manufactured and may mean obtaining a patent. Next the effectiveness of the new product may be assessed in an actual or a simulated test market. Finally, the product is launched and the entire marketing plan is implemented.

5. Explain the process of product adoption and the diffusion of innovations.

Product adoption is the process by which an individual begins to buy and use a new product whereas the diffusion of innovations is how a new product spreads throughout a population. The stages in the adoption process are awareness, interest, trial, adoption, and confirmation. To better understand the diffusion process, marketers classify consumers according to their readiness to adopt new products as innovators, early adopters, early majority, late majority, and laggards.

Five product characteristics that have an important effect on how quickly (or if) a new product will be adopted by consumers are relative advantage, compatibility, product complexity, trialability, and observability. Similar to individual consumers, organizations differ in their readiness to adopt new products based on characteristics of the organization, its management, and characteristics of the innovation.

Chapter Review

MARKETING CONCEPTS:
TESTING YOUR KNOWLEDGE

1. What is a product? What is meant by the core product, the actual product, and the augmented product?
2. What differences are there in how consumers go about buying durable and nondurable goods?
3. What are the main differences among convenience, shopping, and specialty products?
4. What types of products are bought and sold in business-to-business markets?
5. What is a new product? Why is understanding new products so important to marketers?
6. List and explain the steps in developing new products.
7. What is a test market? What are some pros and cons of doing test markets?
8. Explain the different types of innovations based on their degree of newness.
9. List and explain the categories of adopters.
10. Describe the product factors that affect the speed of adoption.

MARKETING CONCEPTS:
DISCUSSING CHOICES AND ISSUES

1. Technology is moving at an ever increasing speed and this means new products enter and leave the market faster than ever. What are some products you think technology might be able to develop in the future that you would like? Do you think these products could add to a company's profits?
2. In this chapter we talked about the core product, the actual product, and the augmented product. Does this mean that marketers are simply trying to make products that are really the same seem different? When marketers understand these three layers of the product and develop products with this concept in mind, what are the benefits to consumers? What are the hazards of this type of thinking?
3. Discontinuous innovations are totally new products—something seldom seen in the marketplace. What are some examples of discontinuous innovations introduced during this century? Why are there so few discontinuous innovations? What do you think the future holds for new products?
4. In this chapter we explained that knockoffs are slightly modified copies of original product designs. Should knockoffs be illegal? Who is hurt by knockoffs? Is the marketing of knockoffs good or bad for consumers in the short run? In the long run?
5. It is not necessarily true that all new products benefit consumers or society. What are some new products that have made our lives better? What are some new products that have actually been harmful to consumers or to society? Should there be a way to monitor new products that are introduced to the marketplace?

MARKETING PRACTICE:
APPLYING WHAT YOU'VE LEARNED

1. Assume that you are the director of marketing for a major producer of mobile (cellular) phones. Your company has just developed a new mobile phone that is also a digital camera and an Internet communication device. Consumers can use the phone to take digital photos and e-mail them to their friends. As opposed to phones that do nothing but make telephone calls, this product could be classified as a dynamically continuous innovation. What recommendations do you have for marketing the new phone that would address the problems of convincing consumers to adopt such an innovation?
2. Assume that you are employed in the marketing department of the firm that is producing the world's first practical, battery-powered automobile. In developing this product, you realize that it is important to provide a core product, an actual product, and an augmented product that meets the needs of customers. Develop an outline of how your firm might provide these three product layers in the battery-powered car.
3. Firms go to great lengths to develop new-product ideas. Sometimes new ideas come from brainstorming in which groups of individuals get together and try to think of as many different, novel, creative—and hopefully profitable—ideas for a new product as possible. With a group of other students, participate in brainstorming for new-product ideas for one of the following (or some other product of your choice).
   a. an exercise machine
   b. computer software
   c. a new type of university
   Then, with your class, screen one or more of the ideas for possible further product development.
4. As a member of a new-product team with your company, you are working to develop an electric car jack that would make changing tires for a car easier. You are considering conducting a test market for this new product. Outline the pros and cons for test marketing this product. What are your recommendations?

MARKETING MINI-PROJECT:
LEARNING BY DOING

What product characteristics do consumers think are important in a new product? What types of service components do they demand? Most important, how do marketers know how to develop successful new products? This mini-project is designed to let you make some of these decisions.

1. Create (in your mind) a new-product item that might be of interest to college students such as yourself. Develop a written description and possibly a drawing of this new product.
2. Show this new-product description to a number of your fellow students who might be users of the product. Ask

them to tell you what they think of the product. Some of the questions you might ask them are:

  a. What is your overall opinion of the new product?

  b. What basic benefits would you expect to receive from the product?

  c. What about the physical characteristics of the product? What do you like? Dislike? What would you add? Delete? Change?

  d. What do you like (or would you like) in the way of product packaging?

  e. What sort of services would you expect to receive with the product?

  f. Do you think you would try the product? How could marketers influence you to buy the product?

3. Develop a report based on what you found. Include your recommendations for changes in the product and your feelings about the potential success of the new product.

■ REAL PEOPLE, REAL SURFERS: EXPLORING THE WEB

For a fragrance such as Fetish, the core product is the fragrance itself but the augmented product is often the bottle the perfume arrives in. Check out several Web sites for makers of designer fragrances such as www.esteelauder.com, www.dior.com, www.chanel.com, and www.ralphlauren.com. Based on your experience with the sites answer the following questions:

1. Describe the core product, the actual product, and the augmented product for each fragrance.

2. How do the firms try to make something that can't really be described (a fragrance) more tangible?

3. What is your evaluation of each Web site? Does the Web site provide easy access to the information you want? Is the Web site designed in such a way to encourge visitors to return again and again to the site?

4. How might the sites be improved?

■ PLAN IT! DEVELOPING A MARKETING PLAN

As your instructor directs, create a marketing plan (using Marketing Plan Pro software or a written marketing plan format) to document your marketing decisions or answer these questions in a written or oral report.

CFS is considering a new line of stuffed animals under the Chubby Stubby brand. Review the current marketing plan and then consider these issues as you plan for next year:

1. What type of innovation does this line represent, and what are the implications for the next marketing plan, assuming that the products will be introduced late in next year?

2. What type of screening methods and business analysis should CFS use in developing this line?

3. What should CFS do to build awareness and interest as part of the adoption process for this new product line?

Key Terms

MARKETING IN ACTION: CHAPTER 9 CASE

REAL CHOICES FOR MATTEL'S BARBIE

Mattel's Barbie may be the most successful toy of all time with over a billion dolls sold. By the late 1990s, as Barbie approached her fortieth birthday, she enjoyed a 90 percent penetration rate with 2.5 dolls sold every second.

Many felt the success of Barbie was fundamental: All girls worldwide share a dream of their future, of achievement, glamour, romance, and adventure. Barbie fulfills a need to play out what it is like or might be like to live in a grown-up world.

The long-term success of Barbie was also due to Mattel's overall product strategy—to satisfy the timeless emotional needs of children while at the same time continuously updating them to current fads or trends. For example, over the years Barbie had been a teacher, a fashion model, a girlfriend, an astronaut, a big sister, a nurse, a doctor, and a pilot. When the aerobics workout craze hit, Mattel introduced Great Shape Barbie. In 1997, Paleontologist Barbie was introduced followed by Chilean Barbie in 1998.

In the late 1990s, Barbie's looks were changed, at least in part, because of criticisms that Barbie gave young girls unrealistic expectations for their bodies—expectations that could lead to eating disorders. She gained a bigger smile, used less makeup, and had a more athletic looking body with smaller breasts and a larger waist. In 2000, Barbie had her first belly button.

But as the twenty-first century began, Barbie and her maker Mattel were facing a less sure future. Worldwide sales of Barbie had peaked in 1997 at $1.9 billion and declined for the next two years after which they remained flat at $1.2 billion annual sales. In 1999, Mattel had purchased computer games producer, The Learning Co., for $3.5 billion. The idea behind the purchase was to enhance brands like Barbie with software extensions such as a Barbie CD-ROM that designs fingernail stickers. Unfortunately, the popularity of computer games was quickly waning causing the Learning Co. purchase to be a disaster. Mattel suffered a $3 billion loss when the unit was sold in 2000.

Although Barbie certainly wasn't Mattel's biggest problem, most at Mattel thought Barbie had to be a big part of the solution. Despite any declines in popularity, Barbie accounted for approximately a third of Mattel's sales and an even larger percentage of the company's profits. Therefore, the company's marketing managers needed to find a way to reinvigorate Barbie sales. The question was how.

Some attempts had already been made as Mattel had instituted a number of new initiatives in an attempt to invigorate sales. For one, the company had introduced more nondoll Barbie items such as the Barbie Lip Gloss Maker Activity Set, a Sit-n-Style Barbie for hair makeovers, Hollywood Nails Barbie, and electronics such as the Secret Talking Electronic Scrapbook. And in 2000, along with a new logo and packaging, Barbie got a new advertising slogan, "It's a great time to be a girl."

A Barbie clothing line had been introduced in 1998 that included items such as hip-hugging skirts and slacks, jeans, and pajamas for girls size 4 to 6X. Barbie boutiques were opened in over 200 Toys "R" Us stores. And in 2000 the first of a number of planned Barbie stores opened. Mattel considered expansion of the clothing line to include toddlers, 7- to 14-year-olds, teenagers, and even grown-ups.

But an important question needed to be answered: Was Barbie facing a true decline in her product life cycle that was unalterable? Could growth of the product be reclaimed? Would a continuation of Barbie brand extensions reap the rewards Mattel needed? Could Mattel be successful at making Barbie into a designer brand, the Calvin Klein of little girls? And what about the potential popularity of other Barbie products? Would little girls and their parents be willing to adopt Barbie Home furnishings, Barbie cosmetics, Barbie electronics, Barbie sporting goods, Barbie books, and Barbie stationery? Would Mattel be better off to invest in new properties such as the Harry Potter toys that many at Mattel thought would have a long-lasting and international appeal?

Sources: Kelly Barron, "Toy Story," *Forbes*, June 12, 2000, pp. 140, 144; Alice Z. Cuneo and Laura Petrecca, "Barbie Has to Work Harder to Help Out Sagging Mattel," *Advertising Age*, March 6, 2000, 4, 63; Lauren Goldstein, "Barbie's Secret Plan for World Domination," *Fortune*, November 23, 1998, 38–40; Christopher Palmeri, "Barbie, You Look Bodacious," *Business Week*, July 24, 2000, 43; Christopher Palmeri, "Mattel: Up the Hill Minus Jill," *Business Week*, April 9, 2001, 53–54; Gene Del Vecchio, "Keeping It Timeless, Trendy," *Advertising Age*, March 23, 1998.

THINGS TO THINK ABOUT

1. What is the decision facing Mattel?
2. What factors are important in understanding this decision situation?
3. What are the alternatives?
4. What decision(s) do you recommend?
5. What are some ways to implement your recommendation(s)?

Bookmark It!

OBJECTIVES:

1 Explain the different product objectives and strategies a firm may choose.

2 Explain how firms manage products throughout the product life cycle.

3 Discuss how branding creates product identity and describe different types of branding strategies.

4 Explain the roles packaging and labeling play in developing effective product strategies.

5 Describe how organizations are structured for new and existing product management.

Managing the Product

Meet Mario A. Polit, a Decision Maker at Nissan North America, Inc.

www.nissandriven.com

CURRENT POSITION: Senior Manager of Marketing for Sedans, Infiniti Division.

EDUCATION: BS, Business Management, University of Tampa; M.I.M., International Management, American Graduate School of International Management.

WHAT I DO WHEN I'M NOT WORKING: Enjoy the company of friends and family, tennis, alpine skiing, and building and flying radio controlled sailplanes.

CAREER HIGH: Leading a team in crafting the marketing strategy for the Xterra.

HEROES: My father and mother.

MOTTO: The definition of luck: when preparation meets opportunity.

MANAGEMENT STYLE: Instead of allowing employees the "freedom to fail" I believe in encouraging the "freedom to succeed." Challenging people to maximize their effectiveness is my ultimate goal.

DON'T DO THIS WHEN INTERVIEWING WITH ME: Don't wait for me to extract everything that may be relevant. Tell me why you're a good fit for the job and how you can take it to a new level.

PET PEEVE: I hate hot copies from the copier being brought to a meeting. It shows a lack of preparation.

The Rubber Hits the Road at Nissan North America, Inc.

In 1998, Nissan North America began preparations for the launch of the Nissan Xterra, its new SUV. The product concept and positioning were all set, but there was considerable debate on the best way to communicate the image of this vehicle to potential buyers. But, first, a little background.

The Xterra would be an entirely new product in the Nissan lineup, and it would be the second SUV model, following the more upscale Nissan Pathfinder. To the company, the Xterra represented an opportunity to connect with a new group of consumers who were not passionate about any Nissan products.

Critical to the debate was Xterra's position in the SUV market, which industry feedback indicated was beginning to split off into two groups: (1) mini-car/van–based SUVs (industry insiders called these vehicles "posers" or "pretenders") and (2) full-sized and luxury SUVs. Mario and his colleagues on Nissan North America's product planning team saw an emerging opportunity for a truck-based SUV with a "back to basics" approach. Xterra's product concept focused on an "authentic and affordable" SUV, a functional, tough, and rugged piece of "gear" based on Nissan's Frontier pickup truck. By leveraging the Frontier's platform, the model would offer authenticity, affordability, and hardiness rather than luxury amenities. Product features would include a roof rack with gear basket, a first-aid kit, water-resistant seat covers, and an interior bike rack—all for the outdoor enthusiast.

Challenged with managing the marketing strategy for both the Pathfinder and the Xterra, Mario set out to differentiate the two vehicles' positioning in all marketing communications. The Pathfinder had been positioned as "premium equipment." The Xterra was positioned as "tough (and affordable) gear that helps you attack life."

Mario aimed the launch at two types of drivers: (1) true outdoor enthusiasts and (2) those who want to be outdoor enthusiasts. Targeting these two groups called for a unique creative and media approach. The marketing team needed to decide the best way to introduce the Xterra to the market in order to connect with both true outdoor types and "weekend warriors." Mario pondered several options:

Option 1: Pursue a targeted, integrated media and creative strategy.

Such a strategy would almost ensure that Nissan would reach the targeted consumer with the right message, it would be more cost-effective, and it would clearly differentiate Xterra from Pathfinder. However, a campaign of this kind would be risky. Targeted "edgy" imagery could alienate some SUV consumers. Nissan would be placing all its "eggs in one basket," which would not be the case in a diversified, broad-based strategy. A strategy this targeted was relatively untested and unproven for Nissan.

Option 2: Pursue a wide-reaching media and creative strategy to launch Xterra.

Nissan had taken this tack before with very good results. However, Nissan could risk alienating the target consumer. If positioned as a mass-market SUV, Xterra faced the risk of compromising its authenticity and credibility with hard-core enthusiasts and might result in a cannibalizing of Pathfinder sales. Also, such an approach would certainly be more costly than a targeted campaign.

Option 3: Use the strategy laid out in option 1 but also offer consumers popular options and/or accessory equipment, such as a leather interior.

This strategy would likely broaden the appeal of Xterra to the large segment of consumers with SUVs that were so equipped. However, this might damage the Xterra's rugged image that was so critical to the target consumer audience. It would also narrow the product and price differentiation with Pathfinder.

Now join the decision team at Nissan North America: Which option would you choose and why?

Make It and Manage It: Using Product Objectives to Decide on a Product Strategy

In December 2001, a new form of transportation was introduced to the market with much fanfare. The press had been buzzing about it for months, referring to the new device only by such code names as IT or Ginger. According to inventor Dean Kamen, the Segway™ Human Transporter will revolutionize the way city dwellers get around by replacing the automobile. The scooter is described as the first self-balancing, electric-powered transportation machine that can go any place a pedestrian can walk.[1] Investors are pouring millions into the device that Apple CEO Steve Jobs claimed will change the way cities are designed. The project has received so much attention that a publisher paid an author an advance of $250,000 to write a book about how the Segway™ was developed.

Will the Segway™ really change our lives? A lot depends on how this innovative device is marketed and managed once the hype dies down. What makes one product fail and another succeed? It's worth repeating what we said in Chapter 2: Firms that plan well succeed. Product planning plays a big role in the firm's *tactical marketing plans*. The strategies outlined in the product plan spell out how the firm expects to develop a product that will meet marketing

Develop Product Objectives
- for individual products
- for product lines and mixes

Design a Product Strategy

Make Tactical Product Decisions
- product branding
- packaging and labeling design

FIGURE **10.1**

Steps in Managing Products
Effective product strategies come
from a series of orderly steps.

objectives. In Chapter 9 we talked about what a product really is and about how new products are developed and introduced into the marketplace.

Today successful product management is more important than ever. As more and more competitors enter the global marketplace and as technology moves forward at an ever increasing pace, products are created, grow, reach maturity, and decline at faster and faster speeds. This means that good product decisions are more critical than ever. Marketers just don't have the time to try one thing, find out it doesn't work, and then try something else. In this chapter we'll finish the product part of the story by seeing how companies manage products and examine the steps in product planning, as Figure 10.1 outlines. These steps include developing product objectives and the strategies required to successfully market products as they evolve from "new kids on the block" to tried-and-true favorites. Next, we'll discuss branding and packaging, two of the more important tactical decisions product planners make. Finally, we will examine how firms organize for effective product management. Let's start by seeing how firms develop product-related objectives.

When marketers develop product strategies, they make decisions about product benefits, features, styling, branding, labeling, and packaging. But what do they want to accomplish? Clearly stated product objectives provide focus and direction. Product objectives should support the broader marketing objectives of the business unit in addition to supporting the overall mission of the firm. For example, the objectives of the firm may focus on return on investment. Marketing objectives then may concentrate on market share and/or the unit or dollar sales volume necessary to attain that return on investment. Product objectives need to specify how product decisions will support or contribute to reaching a desired market share or level of sales.

To be effective, product-related objectives must be measurable, clear, and unambiguous—and feasible. Also, they must indicate a specific time frame. Consider, for example, how a frozen entrée manufacturer might state its product objectives:

- "In the upcoming fiscal year, modify the product's fat content to satisfy consumers' health concerns."
- "Introduce three new items to the product line to take advantage of increased consumer interest in Mexican foods."
- "During the coming fiscal year, improve the chicken entrées to the extent that consumers will rate them better tasting than the competition."

Planners must keep in touch with consumers or business customers so that objectives accurately respond to customer needs. An up-to-date knowledge of competitive product innovations also is important in developing product objectives.

Above all, product objectives should consider the *long-term implications* of product decisions. Planners who sacrifice the long-term health of the organization to reach short-term sales or financial goals may be on a risky course. Product planners may focus on one or more individual products at a time, or they may look at a group of product offerings as a whole. In this section we will briefly examine these different strategies. We will also look at one important product objective: product quality.

OBJECTIVES AND STRATEGIES FOR INDIVIDUAL PRODUCTS

The Volkswagen Beetle is a product that triumphed over great obstacles. In the beginning almost every U.S. dealer in the country had the opportunity to sell the Beetle but many felt it was too ugly to sell. Soon enough, many of them were kicking themselves because the Beetle took off—dealers who did accept the challenge sold over 21 million Beetles. Customers adored the car's simple engineering and funky image. In 1997 Volkswagen decided to capitalize on baby boomers' warm memories of the original Beetle by introducing a new version. The product strategy seems to be working again, reinforced in 2000 and 2001 with introduction of the Beetles in hot new colors with names such as Isotope, Vortex, and Vapor—some available only when ordered over the Web to reinforce the exclusive, cutting-edge image of the car.

Some product strategies, such as that for the new Beetle, focus on a single new product. Strategies for individual products may be quite different for new products, for regional products, and for mature products. For new products, not surprisingly the objectives relate to successful introduction. And, once after a firm has experienced considerable success with a product in a local or regional market, it may decide that the time is ripe to introduce it nationally. Dr Pepper, for example, started out as a regional soft drink sold only in Texas and Mexico.[2]

For mature products like Cracker Jacks, product objectives may focus on breathing new life into a product long taken for granted while holding onto the traditional brand personality. In the case of Cracker Jacks, this means keeping consumer perceptions of the product positive. The images of Sailor Jack and his dog Bingo have been updated at least four times since the original design of 1893.[3]

OBJECTIVES AND STRATEGIES FOR MULTIPLE PRODUCTS

Although a small firm might make a go of focusing on one product, a larger company often will market a set of related products. This means strategic decisions will affect two or more products simultaneously. The firm must think in terms of its entire portfolio of products (see Chapter 2). Product planning means developing *product line* and *product mix* strategies encompassing multiple offerings. Figure 10.2 illustrates how this works for Procter & Gamble.

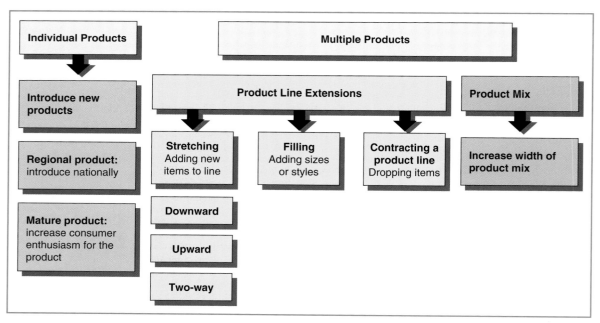

FIGURE 10.2

Objectives for Single and Multiple Products

Product objectives provide focus and direction for product strategies. Objectives can focus on a single product or a group of products.

Product Line Strategies A **product line** is a firm's total product offering designed to satisfy a single need or desire of a group of target customers. For example, Procter & Gamble's line of cleaning products includes three different liquid dish detergent brands. Dawn stresses grease-cutting power, Ivory emphasizes mildness, and Joy is for people who want shiny dishes. To do an even better job of meeting varying consumer needs, each of the three brands comes in more than one formulation. For example, in addition to regular Dawn, there is an antibacterial Dawn and Dawn Special Care that promises to be easy on hands. That's a lot of choices just to wash some dishes! The number of separate items within the same category determines the length of the product line. (See Figure 10.3.)

A large number of variations in a product line is described as a *full line* that targets many customer segments to boost sales potential. A *limited-line strategy* with fewer product variations can improve the firm's image if it is perceived as a specialist with a clear, specific position in the market. Rolls-Royce Motor Cars, for example, makes expensive, handcrafted cars built to each customer's exact specifications and for decades has maintained a unique position

product line ■ A firm's total product offering designed to satisfy a single need or desire of target customers.

Width of Product Mix			
Laundry and Cleaning Products	**Health Care Products**	**Beauty Products**	**Food and Beverage Products**
Bold	Living Better	Cover Girl	Crisco
Bounce	Metamucil	Max Factor	Folgers
Cascade	Pepto Bismol	Old Spice	Hawaiian Punch
Cheer	Attends	Secret	Jif
Comet	Crest	Sure	Pringles
Joy	Fixodent	Giorgio Beverly Hills	Sunny Delight
Dawn	Gleem	Hugo Boss	Millstone
Ivory Dish	Scope	Laura Bisgiioti-roma	Olean
Downy	Vicks Vapo Rub	Red	Tender Leaf Tea
Dreft	Chloraseptic	Venezia	
Mr. Clean	DayQuil	Wings	
Spic and Span	NyQuil	Head & Shoulders	
Tide	Sinex	Ivory Hair Care	
Era	Vicks 44	Pantene	
Gain		Pert	
Ivory Snow		Rejoy/Rejoice	
Oxydol		Vidal Sassoon	
		Camay	
		Clearasil	
		Coast	
		Ivory soap	
		Muse	
		Oil of Olay	
		Safeguard	
		Zest	

Length of Product Line

FIGURE 10.3

Product Line Length and Product Mix Width

A product line is a firm's total offerings that satisfy one need while the product mix includes all the products that a firm offers.

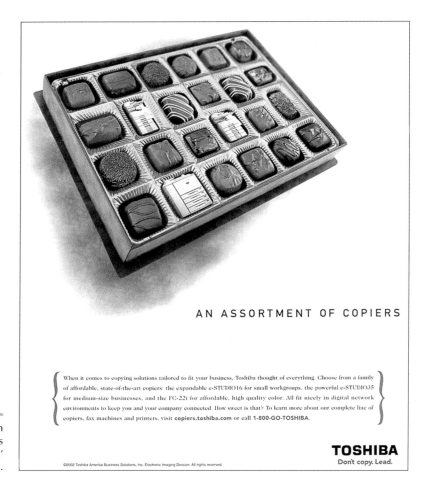

AN ASSORTMENT OF COPIERS

When it comes to copying solutions tailored to fit your business, Toshiba thought of everything. Choose from a family of affordable, state-of-the-art copiers: the expandable e-STUDIO16 for small workgroups, the powerful e-STUDIO35 for medium-size businesses, and the FC-22i for affordable, high quality color. All fit nicely in digital network environments to keep you and your company connected. How sweet is that? To learn more about our complete line of copiers, fax machines and printers, visit copiers.toshiba.com or call 1-800-GO-TOSHIBA.

TOSHIBA
Don't copy. Lead.

A product line consists of an assortment of different products tailored to different consumers' needs.

in the automobile industry. The only three Rolls-Royce models are the Silver Seraph, the Corniche, and the Park Ward.[4]

Organizations may decide to extend their product line by adding more brands or models when they develop product strategies. For example, popular clothing makers Patagonia, Gap, and Lands' End extended their reach by adding children's clothing. When a company stretches its product line, it must decide which is the best direction to go. If a firm's current product line includes middle and lower-end items, an *upward line stretch* adds new items—higher priced and claiming more quality, bells and whistles, and so on.

Folgers and Maxwell House took this route by adding new coffee varieties such as Gourmet Supreme, Columbian Supreme, French Roast, and Italian Espresso Roast. Hyundai decided it could tap the market for bigger, more luxurious cars and so it introduced its XG 300, a car as big as Toyota's Avalon and larger than Nissan's Maxima but selling for thousands of dollars less.[5]

Conversely, a *downward line stretch* augments a line by adding items at the lower end. Here the firm must take care not to blur the images of its higher-priced, upper-end offerings. Rolex, for instance, may not want to run the risk of cheapening its image with a new watch line to compete with the lower-priced Swatch watch.

In some cases, a firm may decide that it is targeting too small a market. In this case the product strategy may call for a *two-way stretch* that adds products at both the upper and lower ends. Marriott Hotels, for example, added Fairfield Inns and Courtyard at the lower end and Marriott Marquis Hotels at the upper end to round out its product line.

A *filling-out strategy* may mean adding sizes or styles not previously available in a product category. PepsiCo tried this with its eight-ounce Pepsi Mini cans and its wide-mouth Big Slam.[6] In other cases the best strategy may be to *contract* a product line, particularly when some of the items are not profitable. When sales of the once popular Chevrolet Chevelle slowed in the 1980s, Chevrolet dropped the midsize car.

We've seen that there are many ways a firm can modify its product line to meet the competition or take advantage of new opportunities. To further explore these strategic decisions, let's return to dish detergents. What does Procter & Gamble (P&G) do if the objective is to increase market share? One possibility would be to expand its line of liquid dish detergents. If the line extension meets a perceived consumer need currently not being addressed, this would be a good strategic objective.

But whenever a product line or a product family is extended, there is risk of **cannibalization**, which occurs when sales of an existing brand are eaten up by the new item as the firm's current customers switch to the new product. That may explain why P&G met consumer demands for an antibacterial dish liquid by creating new versions of existing brands Joy and Dawn.

Product Mix Strategies Product planning can go beyond a single product item or a product line to entire groups of products. A firm's **product mix** is its entire range of products. For example, in addition to a deep line of shaving products, Gillette offers toiletries such as Dry Idea and Right Guard deodorant, Paper Mate and Flair writing instruments, Oral B toothbrushes, Braun oral care products, Duracell batteries, and Cricket cigarette lighters.

In developing a product mix strategy, planners usually consider the *width of the product mix*, that is, the number of different product lines produced by the firm. By developing several different product lines, firms can reduce the risk associated with putting all their eggs in one or too few baskets. Normally, firms develop a mix of product lines that have some things in common, be it distribution channels or manufacturing facilities.

Nike's entry into the golf equipment market is an example of a successful product mix expansion strategy.[7] When golf star Tiger Woods began using Nike's Tour Accuracy balls, its market share increased from 0.9 percent to 3.9 percent. Cashing in on this success, Nike continued the strategy with Tiger Woods golf clubs retailing for $850.

cannibalization ■ The loss of sales of an existing brand when a new item in a product line or product family is introduced.

product mix ■ The total set of all products a firm offers for sale.

1 *Bookmark It!*

What are some product categories in which a firm might think it is best to have a full-line strategy? What are some in which a limited-line strategy might be best? What are the risks a firm takes when it stretches its product line?

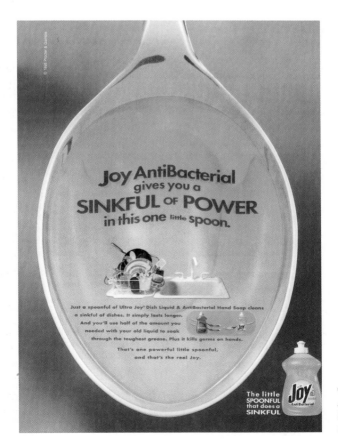

Adding new versions to existing brands helps Procter & Gamble meet new customer demands.

QUALITY AS A PRODUCT OBJECTIVE

Product objectives often focus on product quality, which is the overall ability of the product to satisfy customers' expectations. Quality is tied to how customers *think* a product will perform and not necessarily to some technological level of perfection. Product quality objectives coincide with marketing objectives for higher sales and market share and to the organization's objectives for increased profits.

Dimensions of Product Quality   As we saw in Chapter 3, quality has many meanings (see Figure 10.4). In some cases, product quality means durability; for example, athletic shoes shouldn't develop holes after their owner shoots hoops for a few weeks. Reliability also is an important aspect of product quality—just ask Maytag and its lonely repairman. For other products, quality means a high degree of precision; for example, high-tech audio equipment promises clearer music reproduction with less distortion. Quality, especially in business-to-business products, is also related to ease of use, maintenance, and repair. Yet another crucial dimension of quality is product safety. Finally, the quality of products such as a painting, a movie, or even a wedding gown relates to the degree of aesthetic pleasure they provide. Or course, evaluations of aesthetic quality differ dramatically among people: To one person quality television may mean *Masterpiece Theater* while to another it's MTV's *Jackass*.

Marketing planners often focus product objectives on one or both of two key aspects of quality: level and consistency. Customers often determine the *level of quality* of a product by comparison with other brands in the same product category. A handcrafted Rolls-Royce boasts higher quality than an assembly-line Ford Mustang, but this may be irrelevant to a Mustang buyer inclined to compare it to a Mazda Miata and not an elite luxury car.

Consistency of quality means that customers experience the same level of quality in a product time after time, bringing repeat business and free word-of-mouth advertising. Consistent quality is also one of the major benefits of adopting total quality management practices. Consumer perceptions can change overnight when quality is lacking. Ask anybody who's ever bought a new car that turned out to be a lemon.

The Impact of E-Commerce on Quality as a Product Objective   The Internet has made product quality even more important in product strategies. One of the most exciting aspects of the new digital world is that consumers can interact directly with other people—around the block or around the world. But as we discussed in chapter 6, this new form of communication cuts both ways since it lets people praise what they like and slam what they don't to an audience of thousands.

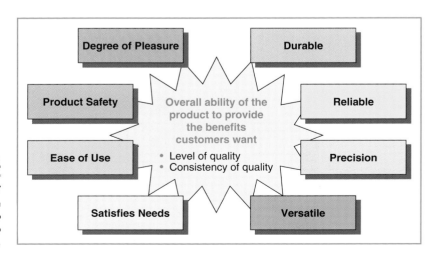

FIGURE 10.4

Product Quality

Some product objectives focus on quality or the ability of a product to satisfy customer expectations—no matter what those expectations are.

Maytag used the "lonely repairman" in its ads for decades to tout its products' superior reliability. Today the repairman remains in Maytag ads for new superior products.

Marketing Throughout the Product Life Cycle

The zipper is an example of a humble, low-tech product that has managed to live an exceptionally long life. Although invented in the 1800s, the zipper was not used in men's clothing until the 1930s. These "hookless fasteners," as they once were called, originally were intended for use on high-buttoned shoes. Claims that this "newfangled gadget" could cause embarrassing and painful injuries kept the zipper out of men's trousers for many years. In 1936 the Prince of Wales adopted the zipper and was the first monarch to "sit on a throne bezippered."

Many products like the zipper have very long lives, while others like the "pet rock" are "here today, gone tomorrow." The **product life cycle (PLC)** is a useful way to explain how product features change over the life of a product. In Chapter 9 we talked about how marketers go about introducing new products, but the launch is only the beginning. Product marketing strategies must evolve and change as they continue through the product life cycle.

This concept relates to either a product category or, less frequently, to a specific brand. Some individual brands may have short life expectancies even though the product lives on in other successful brands. Who can remember the Nash car or Evening in Paris perfume? Other brands seem almost immortal: A Boston Consulting Group study found that 27 of 30 brands that were number one in 1930 were still number one over 50 years later. These brands included Ivory soap, Campbell's soup, and Gold Medal flour.[8]

product life cycle ■ Concept that explains how products go through four distinct stages from birth to death: introduction, growth, maturity, and decline.

THE INTRODUCTION STAGE

In Chapter 8 we talked about the idea that brands have personalities. And, like people, products are born, they "grow up" (well, most people grow up anyway), and eventually they die. We can divide the life of a product into four separate stages. The first stage, shown in Figure 10.5, is

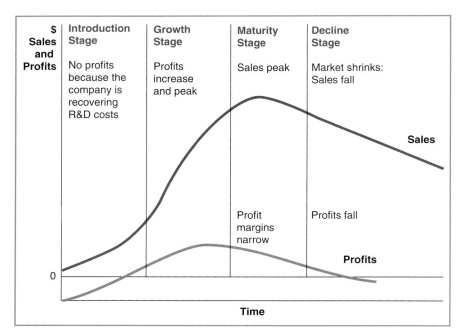

FIGURE 10.5

The Product Life Cycle

The product life cycle helps marketers understand how a product changes over its lifetime and suggests how marketing strategies should be modified accordingly.

introduction ■ The first stage of the product life cycle in which slow growth follows the introduction of a new product in the marketplace.

introduction. Here customers get the first chance to purchase the good or service. During this early stage, a single company usually produces the product. If it clicks and is profitable, competitors will follow with their own versions.

During the introduction stage, the goal is to get first-time buyers to try the product. Sales (hopefully) increase at a steady but slow pace. As is also evident in Figure 10.5, the company does not make a profit during this stage. Why? Two reasons: Research and development (R&D) costs and heavy spending for advertising and promotional efforts cut into revenue. (See Figure 10.6.)

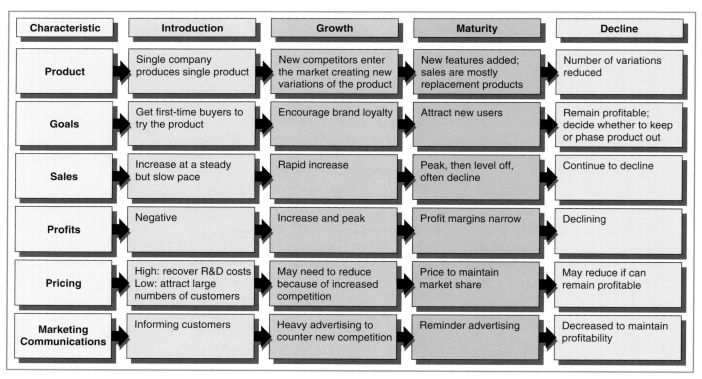

FIGURE 10.6

Marketing Strategies Through the Product Life Cycle

Marketing strategies—the 4 Ps—change as a product moves through the life cycle.

During the introduction stage of the PLC, pricing may be high to recover the research and development costs (demand permitting) or low to attract large numbers of consumers. (See Figure 10.6). For example, the Panasonic digital Palmcorder had a suggested retail price about double that of nondigital Palmcorders, and it was designed to appeal to consumers who are willing to pay dearly for the latest technological advances. The high cost helped Panasonic recover its R&D costs.

How long does the introduction stage last? As we saw in Chapter 9's microwave oven example, it can be quite long. A number of factors come into play, including marketplace acceptance and the producer's willingness to support its product during start-up. In the case of the microwave, sales in countries like Japan were much stronger, helping to support the product through a long introduction stage in the United States.

Not all products make it past the introduction stage. For a new product to be successful, consumers must first know about it. Then they must believe that it is something they want or need. Marketing during this stage often focuses on informing consumers about the product, how to use it, and its promised benefits. Nearly 40 percent of all new products fail.[9]

Ford's Edsel is probably the best-known example of an early flop. Introduced in 1957 and named after the only son of Henry Ford, the Edsel was designed to compete with such cars as the Chrysler New Yorker. It boasted high horsepower, tail fins, three-tone paint jobs, wraparound windshields, a "horse-collar" grille, and a push-button gearshift. The problem was that consumers didn't like the Edsel (many considered it just plain ugly) and only 110,847 were built before Ford abandoned the project.[10]

THE GROWTH STAGE

The **growth stage** is the second stage in the PLC in which sales increase rapidly while profits increase and peak. Marketing's goal here is to encourage brand loyalty by convincing the market that this brand is superior to others in the category. In this stage, marketing strategies may include the introduction of product variations to attract market segments and grow market share. The cellular telephone is an example of a product that continues to be in its growth stage as worldwide sales continue to increase. It is useful to note that for strategic planning considerations, products such as the cellular telephone would be classified as stars in the Boston Consulting Group portfolio analysis discussed in Chapter 2.

When competitors appear, marketers must use heavy advertising and other types of promotion. Price competition may develop, driving profits down. Some firms may seek to capture a particular segment of the market by positioning their product to appeal to a certain group. And, if pricing has initially been set high, it may be reduced to meet the increasing competition.

growth stage ■ The second stage in the product life cycle during which the product is accepted and sales rapidly increase.

THE MATURITY STAGE

The **maturity stage** of the PLC is usually the longest. Sales peak and then begin to level off and even decline while profit margins narrow. Competition grows intense when remaining competitors fight for their share of a shrinking pie. Price reductions and reminder advertising may be used to maintain market share. Because most customers have already accepted the product, sales are often to replace a "worn-out" item or to take advantage of product improvements. For example, almost everyone owns a television set, which means a large share of sales are replacements. During the maturity stage, firms will try to sell their product through as many outlets as possible because availability is crucial in a competitive market. Consumers will not go far to find one particular brand if satisfactory alternatives are close at hand.

To remain competitive and maintain market share during the maturity stage, firms may tinker with the marketing mix. Competitors may add new "bells and whistles" as when producers of potato chips and other snack foods modify their products. When consumers turned from high-fat snacks, chip makers gave them baked, "low-fat" products. Then Frito-Lay introduced its WOW! line of fat-free chips.

Attracting new users of the product can be another strategy that marketers use in the maturity stage. Market development, as discussed in Chapter 2, means introducing an existing

maturity stage ■ The third and longest stage in the product life cycle in which sales peak and profit margins narrow.

Paola Zuniga, Student, Florida International University

I would choose option 3 because it accurately targets the Xterra's consumer market. After all, business is about giving consumers what they want. The consumer who chooses extras on the car is the one who incurs an extra cost in the purchase of the vehicle. Adopting this promotional strategy makes the launch of this new product appealing to a larger population. As for concerns about the Xterra taking away from Pathfinder sales, if the markets for each one start to integrate, the options and body of the car will be what differentiate them.

Moatassem Moatez, Student, The American University in Cairo

I support the first option. It will target Generation X and young, adventurous youth. In this way, Mario will be able to clearly identify the characteristics of his target market and convey an effective message. He will establish a strong position for the Xterra among other SUVs—especially the Pathfinder. Focusing on this target market will build customer loyalty. Such a tailored strategy will allow Mario to build a detailed, creative campaign to give the target market the feeling that the Xterra goes with their outdoor, adventurous lifestyles. I believe in the saying, "If you work on trying to please everyone, you end up pleasing no one."

■ MICHAEL MUNRO, MARKETING PROFESSOR, FLORIDA INTERNATIONAL

I would choose option 1 because the Xterra is a niche product aimed specifically at outdoor enthusiasts. This target market can be efficiently reached through a narrower, efficient media strategy and a distinctive creative strategy. I would not be concerned with SUV consumers seeking luxury and creature comforts since the Xterra's product design focuses on functional performance and power. Attempting to appeal to a broader SUV consumer base via media and creative executions would be ineffective and defuse the brand's core character. There must be an opportunity to buy some accessory packages but they should not include leather seats or anything inconsistent with the brand's rugged image.

Angela Talley, VP, Group Strategic Planning Director, DDB Worldwide

I would eliminate option 3. One of the strengths of the Xterra is its clear market position. Offering popular options such as leather interior would compromise its position and make it difficult to distinguish from the Pathfinder. Option 1 is a more sound decision in that it reinforces Xterra's "edgy" imagery and clearly targets the core user. However, option 2 is an even better strategy. With projected sales of 50,000 units, Nissan will need to reach a large audience. Hard-core outdoor enthusiasts are a small market. Therefore, it is essential to reach "wannabes"—not only "weekend warriors," but also couch potatoes that want the outdoor enthusiast lifestyle. Because of Nissan's high sales goals, pursuing a wide-reaching media and creative strategy seems the best course.

Weigh in with your thoughts! Visit the Live Laboratory at www.prenhall.com/solomon for extended Other Voices replies, exercises, and more.

product to a market that doesn't currently use it. Many U.S. firms are finding new markets in developing countries such as China for products whose domestic sales are lagging. For example, in the early 1990s, when IBM personal computers lost popularity in the United States, the company was able to capture a large percentage of the exploding Eastern European computer market.

THE DECLINE STAGE

decline stage ■ The final stage in the product life cycle in which sales decrease as customer needs change.

The **decline stage** of the product life cycle is characterized by a decrease in product category sales. The reason may be obsolescence forced by new technology—where do you see a new typewriter in this computer age? Although a single firm may still be profitable, the market as

Remember the simple
pleasures of being a kid?

They're back.
Introducing new LAY'S® WOW!®
potato chips. Remember
when all you cared about was
taste? And you didn't know what a calorie was?
New LAY'S® WOW!® potato chips taste as good as–
some say even better than–regular LAY'S® chips. And
because they're made with OLEAN,® they have half the calories®
and are 100% fat free. Hey, now you can eat like a kid again.

*Regular LAY'S® potato chips: 150 cal./oz. LAY'S® WOW!® potato chips: 75 cal./oz.

New LAY'S® WOW!®   **Life Tastes Good Again.®**

By meeting the needs of customers looking for "fat-free" snacks, Lay's gave new life to the mature potato chip product with its WOW chips.

a whole begins to shrink, profits decline, there are fewer variations of the product available, and suppliers pull out. In this stage, there are usually many competitors with none having a distinct advantage.

A firm's major product decision in the decline stage is whether or not to keep the product. An unprofitable product drains resources that could be better used developing newer products. If the decision is to keep the product, advertising and other marketing communications may be decreased to cut costs, and prices may be reduced if the product can remain profitable. If the decision is to drop the product, elimination may be handled in two ways: phase it out by cutting production in stages and letting existing stocks run out, or simply drop the product immediately. If the established market leader anticipates that there will be some residual demand for the product for a long time, it may make sense to keep the product on the market. The idea is to sell a limited quantity of the product with little or no support from sales, merchandising, advertising, and distribution and just let it "wither on the vine."

Some products have been able to hang in there with little or no marketing support. A classic example is the Pilot Stapler, which has been on the market for 70 years. Despite sleeker and less costly competitors, the Pilot sustains its reputation as *the* heavy-duty stapler for a small but loyal group of fans still very "attached" to it.[11]

Sometimes marketers attempt to breathe new life into a mature brand or even to bring a brand back from the dead. That's what The Firm, a music management company that represents Limp Bizkit, Korn, N*SYNC and other groups, is doing with Pony athletic shoes. Pony was popular in the 1970s but went out of business in the early 1980s. The Firm thinks it can bring Pony back as a new, hot youth product by using the same techniques the company employs to plug a new band. Pony T-shirts are showing up on influential people in the music business (including one of the members of Limp Bizkit). And, The Firm created a Web site (pony.com) that features the shoes as well as music from bands represented by the company. The Firm hopes to turn Pony into a new fashion statement that will compete with bigger rivals Reebok and Nike.[12]

2 *Bookmark It!*

What are some of the factors that allow one product to enjoy a very long life cycle while others have a very short one? What are some products that you use that have had a long PLC? What are some products you have used with a short PLC?

The Firm, a music management company, thinks it can bring the Pony brand back to life as a hot new youth product.

Creating Product Identity: Branding Decisions

Successful marketers keep close tabs on their products' life cycle status, and they plan accordingly. Equally important, though, is giving that product an identity like The Firm is doing with Pony shoes. That's where branding comes in. How important is branding? Well, of the more than 17,000 new products or line extensions introduced each year, 25 percent are new brands. About $127.5 billion per year is spent on introducing these new brands—that's $7.5 million per brand on average.

We said earlier that nearly 40 percent of all new products fail but for new brands the failure rate is even higher—up to 80 to 90 percent![13] Branding is an extremely important (and expensive) element of product strategies. In this next section we will examine what a brand is and how certain laws protect brands. Then we will discuss the importance of branding and how firms make branding decisions.

WHAT'S IN A NAME (OR A SYMBOL)?

How do you identify your favorite brand? By its name? By the logo (how the name appears)? By the packaging? By some graphic image or symbol, such as Nike's swoosh? A **brand** is a name, a term, a symbol, or any other unique element of a product that identifies one firm's product(s) and sets it apart from the competition. Consumers easily recognize the Coca-Cola logo, the Jolly Green Giant (a *trade character*), and the triangular blue Nabisco logo (a *brand mark*) in the corner of the box. Branding provides the recognition factor products need to succeed in regional, national, and international markets.

Choosing a Brand Name, Mark, or Character There are several important considerations in selecting a brand name, brand mark, or trade character. First, it must have a positive connotation and must be memorable. Consider Toro's experience when it introduced a lightweight snow thrower called the "Snow Pup." Sales were disappointing because "pup" conveyed a small, cuddly animal—not a desirable image for a snow thrower. Renamed the "Snow Master," its sales went up markedly.[14]

A brand name is probably the most used and most recognized form of branding. Kool-Aid and Jell-O are two of the first words kids learn. Smart marketers use brand names to maintain relationships with consumers "from the cradle to the grave." For example, Jell-O now markets "Sparkling" versions of its gelatin dessert to appeal to adult tastes.

brand ■ A name, a term, a symbol, or any other unique element of a product that identifies one firm's product(s) and sets them apart from the competition.

3 *Bookmark It!*

Why do firms create brand characters? Do brand characters influence consumer attitudes about products? Do they affect consumer purchase behavior? Can brand characters have a negative impact on the brand?

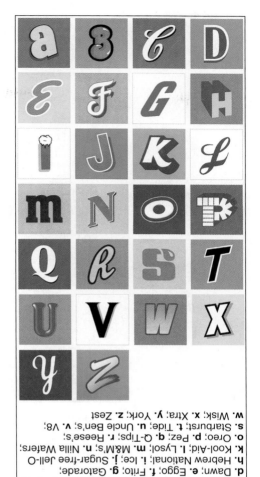

Answers: a. All; **b.** Bubblicious; **c.** Campbell's; **d.** Dawn; **e.** Eggo; **f.** Frito; **g.** Gatorade; **h.** Hebrew National; **i.** Ice; **j.** Sugar-free Jell-O **k.** Kool-Aid; **l.** Lysol; **m.** M&M's; **n.** Nilla Wafers; **o.** Oreo; **p.** Pez; **q.** Q-Tips; **r.** Reese's; **s.** Starburst; **t.** Tide; **u.** Uncle Ben's; **v.** V8; **w.** Wisk; **x.** Xtra; **y.** York; **z.** Zest

Consumers recognize brand logos with just a single letter— from A to Z. How many can you recognize?

A good brand name may position a product by conveying a certain image or personality (Ford Mustang) or by describing how it works (Drano). Brand names such as Caress and Shield help to position these very different brands of bath soap by saying different things about the benefits they promise. The Nissan Xterra combines the word *terrain* with the letter *X*, which is associated by many young people with extreme sports to give the brand name a cutting-edge, off-road feel.

How does a firm select a good brand name? Good brand designers say there are four "easy" tests: *easy to say, easy to spell, easy to read, and easy to remember*. Consider P&G's Tide, Cheer, Dash, Bold, Gain, Downy, and Ivory Snow. And the name should also "fit" four ways: *fit the target market, fit the product's benefits, fit the customer's culture, and fit legal requirements*.

When it comes to graphics for a brand symbol, name, or logo, the rule is that it must be recognizable and memorable. No matter how small or how large, the triangular Nabisco logo in the corner of the box is a familiar sight. And it should have visual impact. That means that from across a store or when you are quickly flipping the pages in a magazine, the brand will catch your attention. Some successful marketers enhance brand recognition by creating a trade character such as the Pillsbury Dough Boy or the Jolly Green Giant.

Trademarks A **trademark** is the legal term for a brand name, brand mark, or trade character. The symbol for legal registration in the U.S. is a capital R in a circle: ®. Marketers register trademarks to make their use by competitors illegal. In the U.S., trademark protection

trademark ■ The legal term for a brand name, brand mark, or trade character; trademarks legally registered by a government obtain protection for exclusive use in that country.

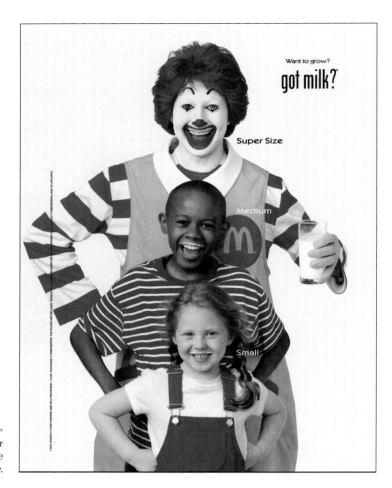

Want to grow?

got milk?

Super Size

Medium

Small

Ronald McDonald is a popular trade character and has become a celebrity.

3 *Bookmark It!*

A trademark protects a brand name only in a single country. To protect brands internationally, firms must register them in every country in which they might wish to do business. Should there be a means for international trademark protection? Who would be responsible for enforcing such an international trademark?

brand equity ■ The value of a brand to an organization.

was established by the Lanham Act of 1946 and updated by the Trademark Revision Act of 1989. Because trademark protection only applies in individual countries where the brand has been registered, unauthorized use of marks on counterfeit products is a huge headache for many companies.

It is possible for a firm to have protection for a brand even if it has not legally registered it. In the U.S. *common-law protection* exists if the firm has used the name and established it over a period of time (sort of like a common-law marriage). Although a registered trademark prevents others from using it on a similar product, it may not bar its use for a product in a completely different type of business. For instance, Chrysler has its Cirrus automobile and MasterCard owns the Cirrus ATM network. The concern for MasterCard is that if the Cirrus car turns out to be an Edsel, it might hurt the reputation of the MC Cirrus network.[15]

THE IMPORTANCE OF BRANDING

Marketers spend huge amounts of money on new-product development, advertising, and promotion to develop strong brands. If it works, this investment creates **brand equity**, which is a brand's value to its organization. If we look at how customers feel about products, we can identify different levels of loyalty or the lack of it. At the lowest level, customers really have no loyalty to a brand and will change brands for any reason, often jumping ship if they find something else at a lower price. At the other extreme, some brands command fierce devotion and loyal users will go without rather than buy a competing brand.

Brand equity means that a brand enjoys customer loyalty, perceived quality, and brand name awareness. For a firm, brand equity provides a competitive advantage because it gives the brand the power to capture and hold onto a larger share of the market and to sell at prices with higher profit margins. For many years the Cadillac automobile had significant brand equity—

many consumers formed a lifetime preference for the brand and would drive nothing else. Today, that brand equity appears to have declined as BMW, Audi, Mercedes, Lexus, and other luxury car makers offer more attractive alternatives for consumers who want a prestigious luxury car.

What makes a brand successful? Kevin Keller, professor of marketing at Dartmouth College, has developed a list of ten characteristics of the world's top brands:[16]

1. The brand excels at delivering the benefits customers truly desire.
2. The brand stays relevant.
3. The pricing strategy is based on consumers' perceptions of value.
4. The brand is properly positioned.
5. The brand is consistent.
6. The brand portfolio and hierarchy make sense.
7. The brand makes use of and coordinates a full repertoire of marketing activities to build equity.
8. The brand's managers understand what the brand means to consumers.
9. The brand is given proper support, and that support is sustained over the long run.
10. The company monitors sources of brand equity.

Products with strong brand equity provide opportunities. A firm may leverage a brand's equity with **brand extensions**, new products sold with the same brand name. For example, in fall 2001 Alka-Seltzer came out with Alka-Seltzer Morning Relief to treat hangovers. A commercial for the extension features a young man (the new product's target market) in bed—he has a flashback to the wild events of the night before and a voiceover asks, "Wish you could undo what you did last night?"[17]

Because of the existing brand equity, the firm is able to sell the brand extension at a higher price than if it had given it a new brand, and the brand extension will attract new customers immediately. Of course, if the brand extension does not live up to the quality or attractiveness of the original brand, brand equity will suffer, as will brand loyalty and sales.

McDonald's opened its first two moderately priced, four-star Golden Arch Hotels in Switzerland.[18] Like McDonald's restaurants, prices for rooms are listed on a glowing sign behind the front desk, 24-hour room service offers guests the familiar McDonald's food, and each room has a Big Mac bed. It remains to be seen if the food chain's reputation for the ultimate French fry will carry over to a McHotel.

brand extensions ■ A new product sold with the same brand name as a strong existing brand.

When Kellogg Co. found overall cereal sales declining, it began to reposition itself as a snack-food company emphasizing portable "convenience foods." In Europe, Kellogg now sells Cereal & Milk Bars, while American brand extensions include Rice Krispies Treats, Pop-Tarts, Snak-Stix, Snack 'Ums, supersize versions of Froot Loops, and Corn Pops in cans.

BRANDING STRATEGIES

Because brands are important to a marketing program's success, branding strategies are a major part of product decision making. Marketers have to determine whether to create individual or family brands, national or store brands, co-brands—it's not that easy!

Individual Brands Versus Family Brands   Part of developing a branding strategy is deciding whether to use a separate, unique brand for each product item—an *individual brand strategy*—or market multiple items under the same brand name—a **family brand** or *umbrella brand* strategy. Individual brands may do a better job of communicating clearly and concisely what the consumer can expect from the product. The decision of whether to use an individual or family branding strategy often depends on characteristics of the product and whether the company's overall product strategy calls for introduction of a single, unique product or for the development of a group of similar products. The H. J. Heinz Company's Weight Watchers name establishes that these products are for consumers who try to maintain a healthy diet and control caloric intake. Under the Weight Watchers umbrella brand are individual brands such as Smart Ones, Brick Oven Style pizza, Ultimate 200, Stir-Fry, Breakfast-on-the-Go, and Sweet Celebrations.[19]

family brand ■ A brand that a group of individual products or individual brands share.

National and Store Brands   Retailers today often are in the driver's seat when it comes to deciding what brands to stock and push. In addition to choosing from producers' brands, called **national or manufacturer brands**, retailers decide whether or not to offer their own versions. **Private-label brands**, also called store brands, are the retail store's or chain's exclusive trade name. Wal-Mart, for example, sells store brand Sam's Cola and Sam's cookies along with national brands such as Coke and Oreos. Store brands are gaining in popularity for many value-conscious shoppers. Retailers continue to develop new ones and some are adding services to the mix: Safeway even offers its own private-label banking to shoppers wishing to apply for a loan while buying their lemons and limes.[20]

national or manufacturer brands ■ Brands that the manufacturer of the product owns.

private-label brands ■ Brands that are owned and sold by a certain retailer or distributor.

Retailers choose a private-label branding strategy because they generally make more profit on these than on national brands. Private-label strategies are also important when retailers seek to maintain a consistent store image; for example, clothing retailers such as Ann Taylor, Gap, and Lands' End protect their image by offering only private-label brands.[21]

Department store shoppers also are being turned on by discount retailers such as Wal-Mart and Target, which have lured millions of customers away from more upscale department stores with exciting private-label clothing and other merchandise.[22] In an attempt to regain some of this market, many department stores have followed the discount retailers by beefing up their own private-label offerings.

Generic Brands   An alternative to either national or store branding is generic branding, which is basically no branding. Generic branded products are typically packaged in white with black lettering that name only the product itself (e.g., "green beans"). Generic branding is one strategy to meet customers' demand for the lowest prices on standard products such as dog food or paper towels. Generic brands were first popularized during the inflationary period of the 1980s when consumers became especially price conscious due to rising prices. However, today generic brands account for very little of consumer spending.

licensing (of a name) ■ Agreement in which one firm sells another firm the right to use a brand name for a specific purpose and for a specific period of time.

Licensing   Some firms choose to use **licensing** to brand their products. In these cases, a licensing agreement means that one firm sells another firm the right to use a legally protected brand name for a specific purpose and for a specific period of time. Firms choose a licensing strategy for a variety of reasons. Licensing can provide instant recognition and consumer interest in a new product and licensing may be important to positioning a product for a certain target market. For example, bourbon maker Jack Daniels licensed its name to T. Marzetti for producing Jack Daniels bourbon-flavored mustard.

Much better known, however, is the licensing of entertainment names such as when movie producers license their properties to manufacturers of a seemingly infinite number of products. When the blockbuster movie *Jurassic Park* hit the screens, stores filled with Jurassic Park

The phenomenal success of the Harry Potter books and the movie have made it a hot property. Characters popped up all over in numerous licensed products.

candy, Jurassic Park key chains, Jurassic Park miniature figures, and Jurassic Park clothing. More recently, we have seen a rush of Harry Potter toys, clothing, and even tattoos.

Co-Branding   Frito Lay sells K.C. Masterpiece–flavored potato chips and Post sells Oreo O's cereal. Strange marriages? No, these are examples of **co-branding**—a marketing tool some regard as one of the "preeminent marketing strategies" today.[23]

Co-branding benefits both partners when combining the two brands provides more recognition power than either enjoy alone. Co-branding has even extended into the auto market.[24] Ford makes the Eddie Bauer Explorer and recently Subaru of America teamed with L.L. Bean Inc. to introduce the L.L. Bean special edition Outback sport utility wagon. In return, Subaru will become the official car of the outdoor clothing and will appear in the L.L. Bean catalogs.

A new and fast-growing variation on co-branding is **ingredient branding** in which branded materials become "component parts" of other branded products.[25] Consumers, for example, can buy Aunt Jemima waffles with Quaker oatmeal, Beech-Nut baby foods with Chiquita bananas, and Post's Morning Traditions Cranberry Almond Crunch cereal, Kraft's Stove Top Stuffing, and Fat Free Cranberry Newtons all with Ocean Spray cranberries.[26]

The practice of ingredient branding has two main benefits. First, it attracts customers to the host brand because the ingredient brand is familiar and has a strong brand reputation for quality. Second, the ingredient brand's firm can sell more of its product, not to mention the additional revenues it gets from the licensing arrangement.[27]

co-branding ■ An agreement between two brands to work together in marketing a new product.

ingredient branding ■ A form of co-branding in which branded materials are used as ingredients or component parts of other branded products.

Creating Product Identity: Packaging and Labeling Decisions

So far we've talked about how marketers create product identity with branding. In this section we'll learn that packaging and labeling decisions also are important in creating product identity.

How do you know if the soda you are drinking is "regular" or "caffeine free"? How do you keep your low-fat grated cheese fresh after you have used some of it? Why do you always leave your bottle of Hugo perfume out on your dresser so everyone can see it? The answer to all these questions is effective packaging and labeling. In this section we will talk about the strategic functions of packaging and some of the legal issues of package labeling.

PACKAGING FUNCTIONS

package ■ The covering or container for a product that provides product protection, facilitates product use and storage, and supplies important marketing communication.

A **package** is the covering or container for a product but, as we saw in Chapter 9's discussion of the Fetish perfume bottle, it's also a lot more. Marketers who want to create great packaging that meets and exceeds consumers' needs and that creates a competitive advantage must understand all the things a package does for a product. Figure 10.7 shows how packaging serves a number of different functions.

First, packaging protects the product. For example, packaging for computers, television sets, and stereos protects the units from damage during shipping, storage, and shelf life. Cereal, potato chips, or packs of grated cheese wouldn't be edible for long if packaging didn't provide protection from moisture, dust, odors, and insects. The chicken broth in Figure 10.7 is protected (before opening) from spoilage by a multilayered, soft box.

In addition to protecting the product, effective packaging makes it easy for consumers to handle and store the product. One example of creative customer-oriented packaging is Hungry Jack Microwave Ready pancake syrup. The product comes in a short, fat jug that fits easily into the microwave. It has a handle that stays cool, a special closure that automatically releases steam, and a label that says "hot" when the syrup is ready to serve.[28]

Over and above these utilitarian functions, the package plays an important role in communicating brand personality. Effective product packaging uses colors, words, shapes, designs, and pictures to provide brand and name identification for the product. In addition, packaging provides specific information consumers want and need, such as information about the specific

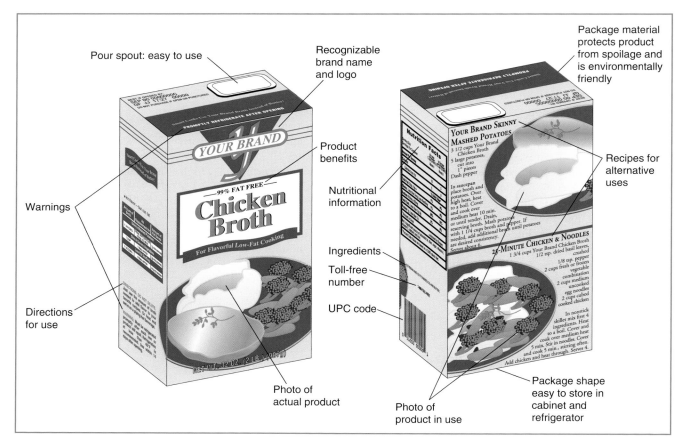

FIGURE 10.7

Functions of Packaging

Great packaging provides a covering for a product and it also creates a competitive advantage for the brand.

variety, flavor or fragrance, directions for use, suggestions for alternative uses (e.g., recipes), product warnings, and product ingredients. Packaging may also include warranty information and a toll-free telephone number for customer service.

In an effort to make its packaging more user friendly, Ben & Jerry's Ice Cream redesigned its package.[29] Because the top is the first thing customers see in a coffin-type freezer, the photo of Ben and Jerry on the carton lid was replaced with text identifying the flavor. Other changes included a more upscale look of a black-on-gold color scheme and enticing realistic watercolors of the product's ingredients.

A final communication element is the **Universal Product Code (UPC)**, which is the set of black bars or lines printed on the side or bottom of most items sold in grocery stores and other mass-merchandising outlets. The UPC is a national system of product identification. Each product has a unique 10-digit number assigned to it. These numbers supply specific information about the type of item (grocery item, meat, produce, drugs, or a discount coupon), the manufacturer (a five-digit code), and the specific product (another five-digit code). At checkout counters, electronic scanners read the UPC bars and automatically transmit data to a computer controlling the cash register, allowing retailers to track sales and control inventory.

DESIGNING EFFECTIVE PACKAGING

Designing effective packaging involves a multitude of different decisions. Should the package have a zip-lock closing, an easy-to-pour spout, be compact for easy storage, be short and fat so it won't fall over, or tall and skinny so it won't take up much shelf space?

Planners must consider the packaging of other brands in the same product category. For example, dry cereal usually comes in tall rectangular boxes. Quaker, however, has introduced a line of cereal packaged in reclosable plastic bags. Quaker offers its cereals at prices that are 25 percent to 35 percent less than well-known brands packaged in boxes. Not all customers are willing to accept a radical change in packaging and retailers may be reluctant to adjust their shelf space to accommodate such packages.

In addition to functional benefits, the choice of packaging material has aesthetic and environmental considerations. Enclosing a fine liqueur in a velvet or silk bag may enhance its image. A fine perfume packaged in a beautifully designed glass bottle means consumers are buying not only the fragrance but an attractive dressing table accessory—or in the case of Fetish perfume a "trophy" to be proudly displayed on a teen's shelf.

Firms seeking to act in a socially responsible manner also consider the environmental impact of packaging. Shiny gold or silver packaging transmits an image of quality and opulence but certain metallic inks are not biodegradable and are harmful to the environment. Some firms are developing innovative *green packaging* that is less harmful to the environment than other materials. Of course, there is no guarantee that consumers will accept such packaging. They didn't take to plastic pouch refills for certain spray bottle products even though the pouches may take up less space in landfills than the bottles do. They didn't like pouring the refill into their old spray bottles. Still, customers have accepted smaller packages of concentrated products such as laundry detergent, dishwashing liquid, and fabric softener.

What about the shape: Square? Round? Triangular? Hourglass? How about an old-fashioned apothecary that consumers can reuse as an attractive storage container? What color should it be? White to communicate purity? Yellow because it reminds people of lemon freshness? Brown because the flavor is chocolate? Sometimes these decisions trace back to irrelevant personal factors. The familiar Campbell's Soup label is red and white because a company executive many years ago liked the football uniforms at Cornell University!

Finally, what graphic information should the package show? Should there be a picture of the product on the package? Should cans of green beans always show a picture of green beans? Should there be a picture of the results of using the product, such as beautiful hair? Should there be a picture of the product in use, perhaps a box of crackers showing crackers with delicious-looking toppings arranged on a silver tray? Should there be a recipe or coupon on the back? Of course, all of these decisions rest on a marketer's understanding of consumers, ingenuity, and perhaps a little creative luck.

4 Bookmark It!

Millions of consumers hate the plastic jewel boxes that house compact disks, complaining that they are hard to open and that their hinges snap. Do you agree? Can you recommend an improved package design?

Universal Product Code (UPC) ■ The set of black bars or lines printed on the side or bottom of most items sold in grocery stores and other mass-merchandising outlets. The UPC, readable by scanners, creates a national system of product identification.

LABELING REGULATIONS

The Federal Fair Packaging and Labeling Act of 1966 controls package communications and labeling in the United States. This law aims at making labels more helpful to consumers by providing useful information. More recently, the requirements of the Nutrition Labeling and Education Act of 1990 have forced food marketers to make sweeping changes in how they label products. Since August 18, 1994, the U.S. Food and Drug Administration (FDA) has required most foods sold in the United States to have labels telling, among other things, how much fat, saturated fat, cholesterol, calories, carbohydrates, protein, and vitamins are in each serving of the product. These regulations are forcing marketers to be more accurate than before in describing their products. Juice makers, for example, must state how much of their product is real juice rather than sugar and water.[30]

Organizing for Effective Product Management

Of course, firms don't create great packaging, brands, or products—people do. Like all elements of the marketing mix, the effectiveness of product strategies depends on marketing managers. In this section we'll talk about how firms organize for the management of existing products and for the development of new products.

MANAGEMENT OF EXISTING PRODUCTS

In small firms, the marketing function is usually handled by a single marketing manager responsible for new-product planning, advertising, working with the company's few sales representatives, marketing research, and just about everything else. But in larger firms such as Nissan, there are a number of managers like Mario A. Polit responsible for different brands, product categories, or markets. Depending on the organization, product management may include brand managers, product category managers, and market managers. Let's take a look at how each operates.

brand manager ■ An individual who is responsible for developing and implementing the marketing plan for a single brand.

Brand Managers   Sometimes a firm has different brands within a single product category. For example, General Foods produces quite a few different brands of coffee including Brim, Maxim, Maxwell House, International Coffees, Sanka, and Yuban. In such cases, each brand may have its own **brand manager**.

Procter & Gamble brand managers once acted independently and were responsible for coordinating all marketing activities for a brand: positioning, identifying target markets, research, distribution, sales promotion, packaging, and evaluating the success of these decisions. Today P&G's brand managers function more like team leaders. They still are responsible for positioning of brands and developing brand equity, but they are likely to work with sales, finance, and logistics staff members as a part of customer business teams working with major retail accounts.[31]

The brand management system is not without its own problems, however. Acting independently, brand managers may fight for increases in short-term sales for their own brand. They may push too hard with coupons, cents-off packages, or other price incentives to a point at which customers will refuse to buy the product without them. That can hurt long-term profitability.

product category manager ■ An individual who is responsible for developing and implementing the marketing plan for all of the brands and products within a product category.

Product Category Managers   Some larger firms have such diverse product offerings that there is a need for extensive coordination. Take Eastman Kodak. Best known for its cameras, film, and other photography supplies, it also markets X-ray film and equipment, printers, motion picture film, and batteries.

In such cases, organizing for product management may include **product category managers** who coordinate the mix of product lines within the more general product category and who consider the addition of new-product lines. In recent years, both Procter & Gamble and

Lever Brothers have consolidated brands under product category managers who are responsible for profit (or losses) within the category.[32]

Market Managers Some firms have developed a **market manager** structure in which different managers focus on specific customer groups rather than on the products the company makes. This type of organization can be useful when firms offer a variety of products that serve the needs of a wide range of customers. Take, for example, Raytheon, a company that specializes in consumer electronics products, special-mission aircraft, and business aviation. Raytheon sells some products directly to consumer markets, others to manufacturers, and still others to the government.

> **market manager** ■ An individual who is responsible for developing and implementing the marketing plans for products sold to a particular customer group.

ORGANIZING FOR NEW-PRODUCT DEVELOPMENT

In Chapter 9 we discussed the importance of new products to the long-term health of an organization. Because launching new products is so important, the management of this process is a serious matter. In some instances, one person handles new-product development, but within larger organizations new-product development almost always needs many people. One person, however, may be assigned the role of new-product manager. Often individuals who are assigned to manage new-product development are especially creative people with entrepreneurial skills.

The challenge in large companies is to get specialists in different areas to work together in **venture teams**. These teams focus exclusively on the new-product development effort. Sometimes the venture team is located away from traditional company offices, usually in a remote location called a "skunk works." This colorful term suggests that the group avoids opponents of change within the firm who might stop a project that challenges the status quo. Having team members with different areas of knowledge—design, engineering, and marketing—contributes to creativity. Sometimes you have to make a stink to make a difference.

5 *Bookmark It!*

Some firms find that the brand management structure is a good option while others do not. What are some products for which you think a brand management system would be effective? What are some products for which it would not be effective?

> **venture teams** ■ Groups of people within an organization who work together focusing exclusively on the development of a new product.

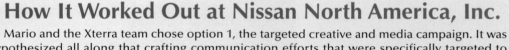

Real People, Real Choices: **How It Worked Out at Nissan North America, Inc.**

Mario and the Xterra team chose option 1, the targeted creative and media campaign. It was hypothesized all along that crafting communication efforts that were specifically targeted to the "pure" outdoor enthusiasts and their lifestyle would not only clearly speak to the target, but would resonate with other consumers outside the target who viewed the Xterra as empowering them to own a piece of the outdoor enthusiasts' life style. The campaign entailed significant prelaunch and launch marketing activities, many of which were a first for an automotive brand.

Nissan parked Xterras at trail heads, surfing beaches, ski resorts, coffee houses, and night spots to gain exposure among target consumers and to generate word-of-mouth "buzz." The company also sponsored the Xterra America Tour, a series of three off-road triathlons that included swimming, off-road biking, and off-road running and culminated in the Xterra Championship in Hawaii, aired on ESPN and CBS.

Nissan also established a unique Xterra Web site several months prior to launch where consumers could get advance incremental Xterra product information and register as "handraisers" (defined as those consumers who entered the Xterra database by providing their e-mail/mail addresses to be "kept in the loop" on updated product/launch information). And, finally, Nissan placed teaser ads with response cards in outdoors lifestyle-oriented printed media. After the launch, Nissan used television, print, and radio ads to market the product, as well as outdoor venues, such as billboards and bus shelters. The prelaunch and launch campaigns were extremely targeted and focused, and the launch budget was relatively small, approximately two-thirds of what Jeep spends to support the established Cherokee model and about 5 percent of total SUV marketing dollars.

The result: Xterra launched very successfully. Sales were 133.8 percent of projections, and Nissan's SUV share more than doubled, from 4.3 percent to 8.9 percent. The positioning strategy was also successful because there was no apparent cannibalization of Pathfinder sales. Xterra has

continued

continued to sustain its sales volume, market share, and profitability despite competitive launches of the Toyota RAV 4, Ford Escape, Mazda Tribute, and Jeep Liberty. Annual sales are currently exceeding 80,000 units. And in model year 2002 Xterra received a considerable facelift and turbo-charged engine. Marketing support and positioning have been sustained, building Xterra and Nissan brand equity with consumers. At launch, Mario was aware of at least 25 Xterra Web sites created by outdoor enthusiasts, and there are, at last count, 15 Xterra owners clubs in the United States. Nissan reaped the benefits of a well integrated plan and "turbo-charged" product launch.

This ad for the Xterra was distributed prior to launch to build awareness and interest. It establishes the strategic positioning of the vehicle as a "no frills" SUV and is targeted to outdoors enthusiasts who participate actively in such sports as biking, mountain climbing, and kayaking.

Chapter Summary

1. Explain the different product objectives and strategies a firm may choose.

Objectives for individual products may be related to introducing a new product, expanding the market of a regional product, or rejuvenating a mature product. For multiple products, firms may decide on a full- or a limited-line strategy. Often companies decide to extend their product line with an upward, downward, or two-way stretch, with a filling-out strategy, or they may decide to contract a product line. Firms that have multiple product lines may choose a wide product mix with many different lines or a narrow one with few. Product quality objectives refer to the durability, reliability, degree of precision, ease of use and repair, or degree of aesthetic pleasure.

2. Explain how firms manage products throughout the product life cycle.

The product life cycle explains how products go through four stages from birth to death. During the introduction stage, marketers seek to get buyers to try the product and may use high prices to recover research and development costs. During the growth stage characterized by rapidly increasing sales, marketers may introduce new-product variations. In the maturity stage sales peak and level off. Marketers respond by adding desirable new-product features or with market development strategies. During the decline stage, firms must decide whether to phase a product out slowly, to drop it immediately, or, if there is residual demand, to keep the product.

3. Discuss how branding creates product identity and describe different types of branding strategies.

A brand is a name, term, symbol, or other unique element of a product used to identify a firm's product. A brand should be selected that has a positive connotation and is recognizable and memorable. Brand names need to be easy to say, spell, read, and remember and should fit the target market, the product's benefits, the customer's culture, and legal requirements. To protect a brand legally, marketers obtain trademark protection. Brands are important because they help maintain customer loyalty and because brand equity or value means a firm is able to attract new customers. Firms may develop individual brand strategies or market multiple items with a family or umbrella brand strategy. National or manufacturer brands are owned and sold by producers whereas private-label or store brands carry the retail or chain store's trade name. Licensing means a firm sells another firm the right to use its brand name. In co-branding strategies, two brands form a partnership in marketing a new product.

4. Explain the roles packaging and labeling play in developing effective product strategies.

Packaging is the covering or container for a product and serves to protect a product and to allow for easy use and storage of the product. The colors, words, shapes, designs, pictures, and materials used in package design communicate a product's identity, benefits, and other important product information. Package designers must consider cost, product protection, and communication in creating a package that is functional, aesthetically pleasing, and not harmful to the environment. Product labeling in the United States is controlled by a number of federal laws aimed at making package labels more helpful to consumers.

5. Describe how organizations are structured for new and existing product management.

To successfully manage existing products, the marketing organization may include brand managers, product category managers, and market managers. Large firms, however, often give new-product responsibilities to new-product managers or to venture teams, groups of specialists from different areas who work together for a single new product.

Chapter Review

▪ MARKETING CONCEPTS: TESTING YOUR KNOWLEDGE

1. What are some reasons a firm might determine it should expand a product line? What are some reasons for contracting a product line? Why do many firms have a product mix strategy?
2. Why is quality such an important product strategy objective? What are the dimensions of product quality? How has e-commerce affected the need for quality product objectives?
3. Explain the product life cycle concept. What are the stages of the PLC?
4. How are products managed during the different stages of the product life cycle?
5. What is a brand? What are the characteristics of a good brand name? How do firms protect their brands?
6. What is a national brand? A store brand? Individual and family brands?
7. What does it mean to license a brand? What is co-branding?

8. What are the functions of packaging? What are some important elements of effective package design?
9. What should marketers know about package labeling?
10. Describe some of the different ways firms organize the marketing function to manage existing products. What are the ways firms organize for the development of new products?

MARKETING CONCEPTS:
DISCUSSING CHOICES AND ISSUES

1. Brand equity means that a brand enjoys customer loyalty, perceived quality, and brand name awareness. What brands are you personally loyal to? What is it about the product that creates brand loyalty and, thus, brand equity?
2. Quality is an important product objective but quality can mean different things for different products, such as durability, precision, aesthetic appeal, and so on. What does quality mean for the following products?
   a. automobile
   b. pizza
   c. running shoes
   d. hair dryer
   e. deodorant
   f. college education
3. Many times firms take advantage of their popular, well-known brands by developing brand extensions because they know that the brand equity of the original or parent brand will be transferred to the new product. If a new product is of poor quality, it can damage the reputation of the parent brand while a new product that is of superior quality can enhance the parent brand's reputation. What are some examples of brand extensions that have damaged and that have enhanced the parent brand equity?
4. Sometimes marketers seem to stick with the same packaging ideas year after year, regardless of whether they are the best possible design. Following is a list of products. For each one, discuss what, if any, problems you have with the package of the brand you use. Then think of ways the package could be improved. Why do you think marketers don't change the old packaging? What would be the results if they adopted your package ideas?
   a. dry cereal
   b. laundry detergent
   c. frozen orange juice
   d. gallon of milk
   e. potato chips
   f. loaf of bread

MARKETING PRACTICE:
APPLYING WHAT YOU'VE LEARNED

1. The Internet allows consumers to interact directly with other people so they can praise products they like and slam those they don't. With several of your classmates, conduct a brief survey of students and of older consumers. Find out if consumers complain to each other about poor product quality. Have they ever used a Web site to express their displeasure over product quality? Make a report to your class.
2. You may think of your college or university as an organization that offers a line of different educational products. Assume that you have been hired as a marketing consultant by your university to examine and make recommendations for extending its product line. Develop alternatives that the university might consider:
   a. upward line stretch
   b. downward line stretch
   c. two-way stretch
   d. filling-out strategy
   Describe how each might be accomplished. Evaluate each alternative.
3. Assume you are the vice president of marketing for a firm that markets a large number of specialty food items (gourmet sauces, marinades, relishes, etc.).
   Your firm is interested in improving its marketing management structure. You are considering several alternatives: a brand manager structure, having product line managers, or focusing on market managers. Outline the advantages and disadvantages of each type of organization. What is your recommendation?
4. Assume you are working in the marketing department of a major manufacturer of athletic shoes. Your firm is introducing a new product, a line of disposable sports clothing. You wonder if it would be better to market the line of clothing with a new brand name or use the family brand name that has already gained popularity with your existing products. Make a list of the advantages and disadvantages of each strategy. Develop your recommendation.
5. Assume you have been recently hired by Kellogg, the cereal manufacturer. You have been asked to work on a plan for redesigning the packaging for Kellogg's cereals. In a role-playing situation, present the following report to your marketing superior:
   a. Discussion of the problems or complaints customers have with current packaging
   b. Several different package alternatives
   c. Your recommendations for changing packaging or for keeping the packaging the same

MARKETING MINI-PROJECT:
LEARNING BY DOING

In any supermarket in any town you will surely find examples of all of the different types of brands discussed in this chapter: individual brands, family brands, national brands, store brands, and co-branded and licensed products. This mini-project is designed to give you a better understanding of branding as it exists in the marketplace.

1. Go to a typical supermarket in your community.
2. Select two product categories of interest to you: ice cream, cereal, laundry detergent, soup, paper products, and so on.

3. Make a list of the brands available in each product category. Identify what type of brand each is. Count the number of shelf facings (the number of product items at the front of each shelf) for each brand.

4. Arrange to talk with the store manager at a time that is convenient with him or her. Ask the manager to discuss:
   a. How the store decides which brands to carry
   b. Whether the store is more likely to carry a new brand that is an individual brand versus a family brand
   c. What causes a store to drop a brand
   d. The profitability of store brands versus national brands
   e. Other aspects of branding that the store manager sees as important from a retail perspective

5. Present a report to your class on what you learned about the brands in your two product categories.

▇ REAL PEOPLE, REAL SURFERS: EXPLORING THE WEB

As we discussed in this chapter and in Chapter 9, companies protect their products by obtaining patents and legal protection for their brands with trademarks. The U.S. Patent and Trademark Office issues both of these forms of protection. Visit the Patent Office Web site at www.uspto.gov. Use the Internet site to answer the following questions.
1. What is a patent? What can be patented?
2. Who may apply for a patent? Can foreign individuals or companies obtain a U.S. patent? Explain.
3. What happens if someone infringes on a patent?
4. What does the term *patent pending* mean?

5. What is a trademark? What is a service mark?
6. Who may file a trademark application? Do firms have to register a trademark? Explain.
7. What do the symbols TM, SM, and ® mean?
8. What are the benefits of federal trademark registration?
9. What are common-law rights regarding trademarks?
10. How long does a trademark registration last? How long does a patent last?
11. How would you evaluate the Patent and Trademark Office Web site? Was it easy to navigate? Was it useful? What recommendations do you have for improving the Web site?

▇ PLAN IT! DEVELOPING A MARKETING PLAN

As your instructor directs, create a marketing plan (using Marketing Plan Pro software or a written marketing plan format) to document your marketing decisions or answer these questions in a written or oral report.

Now that CFS is introducing more products (see Appendix A), its future marketing plans must take product management into account.
1. What product line and product mix strategies are being used by CFS, and what are the implications for next year's marketing plan?
2. Where in the product life cycle are the Computer Bug, Monitor Morphs, and Monster Morphs—and what does this mean for next year's marketing activities?
3. How can CFS make the most of the Chubby Stubby brand if it introduces this product line next year?

Key Terms

MARKETING IN ACTION: CHAPTER 10 CASE

REAL CHOICES AT FUJI

Fujifilm, the photo products brand of the Fuji Photo Film Co., is the world's second largest producer of photographic film and paper. Fujifilm has 70 percent of Japan's $3.6 billion market for photo film and paper and over 25 percent of the U.S. market. With its easily recognizable kelly-green packaging, Fujifilm continues to give market leader Kodak a run for its money.

Financially, Fuji is a strong company. Although only one-fifth the size of Sony, Fuji profits in 1998 were $1.6 billion compared to Sony's $3.2 billion. Fuji has an average operating profit margin of 12.4 percent, far above that of most Japanese manufacturers.

In recent years, the photo products market has seen some dramatic changes as the world is fast moving from film to digital photography. Digital photography began in the labs of Bell Telephone in 1969. In 1985, Sony was the first to commercialize the chips and put them into a camcorder.

Although some Fuji managers would have preferred to ignore the onrush of the digital age, Fuji became committed to the digital camera market when Minoru Ohnishi, Fuji's CEO, personally forced the company forward. Since 1980, Fuji has put over $2 billion into research and manufacturing of digital products. Fuji's philosophy is that the company must be ready for industry challenges that come from technology.

And the move into digital makes sense for a Japanese company. Japan is a country populated with such an incredible number of gadget fanatics that 40 percent of all worldwide consumer digital camera sales take place there. Fuji has a 28 percent share of that market. Still, most experts suggest that the long-term success of Fuji will be measured in terms of U.S. sales where Sony, Eastman Kodak, and Olympus are the market leaders.

Beginning in 1999, Fuji has regularly introduced a vast number of new digital camera models. But with digital cameras, Fuji is like a company selling razors but not the razor blades because Fujifilm doesn't make the memory chips that store the digital images. Although only a small portion of Fuji sales comes from its digital camera products, the company has an overriding aim to be number one. And success in the digital camera market surely means that Fujifilm must cannibalize its main source of revenue, film.

Fuji has made a number of significant developments in the digital photography industry. For example, Fuji's research has led to a Super CCD (supercharged couples device), a half-inch chip that is the "eye" of a digital camera. It is this CCD chip that determines the sharpness of digital pictures. The Super CCD has a top resolution of 2,832 by 2,128 pixels and can produce a 6-megapixel picture. Fujifilm is seen as the leader in CCD development and hopes this research will lead to greater sales of its chips to other digital product manufacturers. In addition to the CCDs, Fuji makes its own lenses, image processors, and signal-processing chips.

Still Fuji's future is not as secure as managers and investors would like it to be. Total worldwide sales of photographic film and paper have declined since 1992. And Kodak, considered a "hip" brand by younger camera enthusiasts, is making inroads into the Japanese digital camera market. Although the global market for photo film and photographic paper is a duopoly shared by Fuji and archrival Kodak, the digital market is far more chaotic and crowded with new companies entering the market regularly—the U.S. market now includes Sony, Olympus, and 18 other manufacturers—and profits are far from certain. Thus, the decisions regarding new products and the direction the company should take are especially important.

Fuji has already made some forays into new opportunities. For example, Fuji's existing photo centers cater to owners of its own cameras by preparing prints or postcards, creating photo indexes, or loading customers' images onto compact disks. In the United States, Fuji has partnered with Wal-Mart Stores, Inc. to store and transmit photos for customers. The PrinCam, a digital camera with a built-in printer to produce instant photos, came out in 1999. And Fuji continues to innovate in the traditional camera film market. The company created a renewed interest in single-use cameras with its introduction of panoramic and zoom lens disposables.

Perhaps Fuji should follow the lead of its biggest competitor, Kodak and develop new digital products. Kodak says its sales of digital products and services could reach up to $4 billion by 2004. In 1999, Kodak introduced a printer that functions as a home photo-processing unit. Just pop out a memory card from a Kodak camera and plug it directly into the printer.

There are a number of dot-com companies that earn profits by storing consumers' picture libraries and giving access to friends and families. Some suggest that Fuji needs to be more aggressive in areas that combine digital photography with consumers' home pages. And other digital markets include calculators, cell phones, and notebook computers. Nokia wants to put digital cameras into cell phones, and both Sony and Toshiba sell laptops featuring digital cameras.

Of course, such ventures may be too risky and perhaps Fuji should stay where it is—in the film and paper industry. There is still a market for paper because millions of digital camera owners need to print their pictures out on home printers. And experts say conventional film won't totally disappear even when digital photography produces images of similar quality. Thus, Fujifilm could continue to focus its efforts on innovations in traditional film.

Sources: Irene M. Junii, Geoffrey Smith, and Neil Gross, "Fuji: Beyond Film," *Business Week*, November 22, 1999; Peter H. Lewis, "Cool Tools," *Fortune*, May 14, 2001, accessed at www.fortune.com/indexw.jhtml?channel=artcol.jhtml&doc_id=202214 on April 4, 2002.

THINGS TO THINK ABOUT

1. What is the decision facing Fuji?

2. What factors are important in understanding this decision situation?

3. What are the alternatives?

4. What decision(s) do you recommend?

5. What are some ways to implement your recommendation(s)?

Bookmark It!

OBJECTIVES:

1. Explain the marketing of people, places, and ideas.
2. Describe the four characteristics of services and understand how services differ from goods.
3. Explain how marketers create and measure service quality.
4. Explain marketing strategies for services.

Marketing What Isn't There

11

INTANGIBLES AND SERVICES

Meet Julie Sanoff, a Decision Maker at American Express

http://home3.americanexpress.com/rewards/explore/explore.asp

CURRENT POSITION: Senior Manager, Business Alliances Division, American Express Consumer Card Services Group.

CAREER PATH: 1992 B.S. in Marketing, Rutgers University.

May 1992–January 1993: Account Executive with a small New Jersey computer company

January 1993–December 1994: Assistant Marketing Analyst, Morgan Stanley

December 1994–August 1998: Manager, Sales Promotion, L'Oréal USA. In charge of all in-store advertising and promotion of the Lancome brand for northeastern U.S. retail stores and specialty accounts (Saks Fifth Avenue, Neiman Marcus, Bloomingdale's, and Nordstrom) across the country.

August 1998–Present: American Express

WHAT I DO WHEN I'M NOT WORKING: Spend time with my husband and young twins.

FIRST JOB OUT OF SCHOOL: Sales rep for a computer company.

HERO: My father.

MOTTO: Live for the moment!

MANAGEMENT STYLE: Autonomy. Give it to people and watch them flourish!

PET PEEVE: Being late.

The Rewards of Membership: Don't Leave Home Without Them!

The AMEX Membership Rewards Program has given enrollees the opportunity to earn points for every dollar they charge on their American Express credit card. They can then redeem these points for travel, retail products, and gift certificates good at participating retail merchants. Enrollees pay a fee to join the program, which has been selectively marketed to about 4 million high-spending card members.

Membership Rewards is a valuable way for American Express to create and maintain loyalty both among the merchants who accept American Express and the cardholders—important in the highly competitive credit card industry. The roster of participating merchants is crucial to the success of the program, because cardholders won't be motivated to participate (and use their American Express cards) if their points can't be redeemed for products and services they want. The participating retail merchants have included Saks Fifth Avenue, Linens-n-Things, Gap, Coach, Tourneau, Dell, and Crate and Barrel.

However, the problem was that most enrollees were redeeming their points for travel rewards, which are much more expensive to American Express than retail rewards because the company tends to get greater discounts from the retailers than from the airlines. Julie Sanoff had to find a way to make the retail category more attractive to cardholders. She needed to understand whether members were not redeeming enough points with the participating retailers because there were not enough choices or if something else was causing the problem.

Julie and her team researched how enrollees make decisions about redeeming points and what products and services they might add to the program. They sent cards listing product rewards to a sample of about 350 enrollees, including some who had never redeemed points for rewards. Julie asked enrollees to rank these rewards in order of interest. A number of respondents liked the idea of adding restaurant and entertainment awards to AMEX's current mix of retailers.

Based on these results, Julie considered her options:

Option 1: Add new rewards categories.

Expand into new categories such as dining and entertainment to satisfy the respondents interested in these types of rewards. Doing so would give the program more breadth and depth and bring it in line with competitors' programs that are for smaller-ticket items, meaning that competitors' members need less points to get rewards. And if more consumers were attracted to these new categories, it might pull them away from more expensive travel rewards. But Julie wasn't sure it would be worth the time and cost to sign on these new merchants if not enough members would redeem their points in these categories.

Option 2: Focus marketing efforts on the most popular rewards.

Streamline the existing rewards to reduce overlap and lack of appeal of certain rewards, redirecting marketing resources to promote the most popular offerings. Julie discovered significant duplication across reward categories (for example, both Sony and Toshiba offered stereos) and realized she could optimize American Express's offerings by removing certain rewards from the program altogether and including only the most appealing ones. But removing some partners might inadvertently take away some specialized products that appealed to American Express's highest spenders, such as the Richard Petty Driving Experience at Disney World. Although this reward interests only a few high spenders, it adds to the appeal of the program and cements the strong relationship AMEX has with Disney.

Option 3: Reduce breadth of reward selection while increasing the depth of certain reward categories.

Streamline the partners in the program and just offer more rewards from this select group. This would make the program a bit more manageable, and it would be less expensive to market a smaller group of partners. However, the program would lose some breadth and its reputation of having many choices for enrollees. Competitive programs might benefit by seeming to provide more offerings. In addition, dropping a member from the Membership Rewards program might alienate a company that has a strong relationship with American Express.

Now, put yourself in Julie Sanoff's shoes: Which option would you pick, and why?

Marketing What Isn't There

At one level, American Express is just selling a little piece of plastic you keep in your wallet. But, of course, this particular little card is much more than that—for some, it's the ticket to a dream, for others a way to show off. Julie Sanoff understands the challenges of marketing what people can't see. As an executive for a major financial services company, she realizes that a customer's decision to patronize one firm's card over others is a complex one that includes the company's image, its "snob appeal," incentives to be loyal (such as membership rewards), pricing, and emotional attachment to a trusted company.

These challenges apply to many different kinds of consumer experiences. For example, what do a Pearl Jam concert, a college education, and a football game have in common? Like the AMEX Membership Rewards Program, each is a product that combines experiences with physical goods to create an event that the buyer consumes. You can't have a concert without instruments, a college education without textbooks (frat parties don't count), or a pigskin showdown without the pigskin. But these tangibles are secondary to the primary product, which is some act that, in these cases, produces enjoyment, knowledge, or excitement.

This chapter will consider some of the challenges and opportunities facing marketers such as Julie Sanoff whose primary offerings are **intangibles**, experience-based products that cannot

intangibles ■ Experience-based products that cannot be touched.

be touched. The marketer whose job it is to build and sell a better football, automobile, or MP3 player—all tangibles—must deal with different issues than someone such as Julie who must find ways to make a credit card more attractive.

We will spend a lot of time on services, a type of intangible that also happens to be the fastest-growing sector in our economy. As we'll see, all services are intangible, but not all intangibles are services. So let's start by considering some types of intangibles other than services before moving into the nuts and bolts of services marketing.

DOES MARKETING WORK FOR INTANGIBLES?

Obviously, the credit cards you keep are more than mere pieces of plastic. They are tickets to a dream because you can use them to obtain many things. But they can also be free admission to a nightmare if you charge yourself into debt! Even the color of the card becomes a status symbol—that green card is cool to have, but not quite as cool as that gold one, and just watch the eyebrows rise around the table when that lucky guy whips out his platinum! These complex meanings attached to a little piece of plastic remind us that we need to expand the marketing concept and recognize that it applies to many types of "products," including politicians, the arts, and the places we live and visit.

Even an intangible such as electric power, normally thought of as a commodity, is now branded and marketed directly to consumers. In an increasing number of states, customers are allowed to pick an electricity supplier from several competitors as deregulation of the industry continues. The first national energy brand was EnergyOne, introduced in 1995 by UtiliCorp United. Cinergy Corp. of Cincinnati paid $6 million to gain brand exposure by renaming the city's Riverfront Stadium to Cinergy Field.[1] Energy company Enron, at the time the seventh largest firm in the United States, later paid to have a stadium in Houston named after it. The subsequent bankruptcy and scandal surrounding the energy giant prompted the Astros in 2002 to pay Enron $2.1 million to buy back the naming rights to the stadium. The Enron name had to be removed from all brochures, the stadium Web site, and all publicity photos of the Astros team.[2] (The only consolation is that the firm's demise may have been the fault of the accountants, the CEO, and the former CEO, but not the marketers.)

Sound marketing concepts don't apply only to companies looking to make a buck or two. Indeed, not-for-profit organizations including symphonies, charities, zoos, museums, and youth organizations increasingly are thinking about branding and image building. The

The babies are here.
BRONX ZOO

Today many not-for-profit organizations have found they need to adopt marketing strategies to successfully attract local support.

not-for-profit sector consists of 546,000 organizations with 9.7 million employees, so competition for customers and donors is fierce. These organizations have to come up with new marketing strategies all the time. When Goodwill wanted to increase donations to its clothing bins, it redesigned its smiling face logo and added a new headline, "Helping Create a Better Community." Clothing donations increased by 10 percent after the change.[3]

The Internet is becoming an increasingly important way to market some charities. The American Red Cross raised nearly $140,000 for Turkey's earthquake victims in one day and Catholic Relief Services raised $350,000 from 2,000 donors for Kosovar refugees in only two weeks.[4] How do these organizations use the Internet? Most will use a variety of news media vehicles to inform potential donors of a need and to request donations. Without the Internet, it can be a complicated process to give a donation—you first have to find out who and how and where to send money and then you have to write a check or send cash to the designated address. The Internet makes it easy for donors to contribute as much or as little as they want 24 hours a day.

Still, some producers of intangibles have been slow to accept the idea that what they do *should* be marketed. Many people who work in health care, the legal profession, or the arts resist the notion that the quality of what they produce and the demand for their services are affected by the same market forces driving the fortunes of paper producers, food canners, or even power utilities.

Let's take a quick look at how some basic marketing concepts would apply to an artistic product. Suppose a local theater company wanted to increase attendance at its performances. Remembering the basics of developing a strategic plan (Chapter 2) here are some marketing actions the organization might take to realize its goals.[5]

- The organization could develop a *mission statement*, such as "We seek to be the premier provider of quality theater in the region."
- A *SWOT analysis* could include an assessment of the organization's strengths and weaknesses and the environmental threats and opportunities. The arts marketer is, after all, competing for the consumer's discretionary dollar against other theater groups. The marketer is also up against other forms of entertainment the consumer might desire instead of going to a play at all, from attending a Destiny's Child concert to a Tom Cruise movie to a pro wrestling match.
- The theater company should use information obtained in the SWOT analysis to develop a number of concrete measurable *objectives*, such as to "increase the number of season ticket holders by 20 percent over the next two years."
- Next, the organization must develop marketing strategies. For example, it must consider which *target markets* it wishes to attract. If audience levels for its plays have been fairly stable for several years, it should consider developing new markets for its performances. This might lead to product modifications, as some opera companies do when they project English translations above the stage to draw new patrons who are unfamiliar with opera's foreign tongues.

MARKETING PEOPLE, PLACES, AND IDEAS

As we've discussed, even a small theater company can benefit by applying some basic marketing principles to its activities. In addition to the arts, people, places, and ideas often need to be "sold" by someone and "bought" by someone else. Let's consider how marketing is relevant to each of these.

Marketing People   As we saw in Chapter 1, people are products, too. If you don't believe that, you've never been on a job interview, nor spent a Saturday night in a singles bar. Many of us find it distasteful to equate people with products. In reality, though, a sizable number of people hire personal image consultants to devise a marketing strategy for them, and others undergo plastic surgery, physical conditioning, or cosmetic makeovers to improve their "market position" or "sell" themselves to potential employers, friends, or lovers.[6] Let's briefly touch upon a few prominent categories of people marketing.

Politicians are created and marketed by sophisticated consultants who "package" candidates and compete for "market share" of votes. This perspective can be traced back to the 1952

These clips are taken from the classic "flower girl" commercial of the Lyndon Johnson presidential campaign. The atomic explosion in the background was meant to arouse fears about what might happen if conservative rival Barry Goldwater was elected instead.

and 1956 presidential campaigns of Dwight Eisenhower, when advertising executive Rosser Reeves repackaged the bland but amiable Army general by inventing jingles, slogans, such as "I like Ike," and contrived man-on-the-street interviews to improve the candidate's market position.[7] For better or worse, Reeves's strategies revolutionized the political landscape as people realized that the same selling tactics used to sell soap could sell candidates. A famous 1964 political ad on behalf of presidential candidate Lyndon Johnson juxtaposed a child plucking the petals from a daisy with an atomic explosion to reinforce the belief that opponent Barry Goldwater would be too quick to start a nuclear war. That's a strong fear appeal.

From actors and musicians to superstar athletes and supermodels, the famous and near-famous jockey for market position in popular culture. Celebrities are carefully packaged by agents who connive to get them exposure on television shows such as *Oprah*, starring roles in movies, recording contracts, or product endorsements.[8]

Like other products, celebrities even rename themselves to craft a "brand identity" using the same strategies marketers use to ensure that their products make an impression on consumers, including memorability (Evel Knievel), suitability (fashion designer Oscar Renta reverted to his old family name of de la Renta because it sounded more elegant), and distinctiveness (Steveland Morris Hardaway became Stevie Wonder).

In addition to these branding efforts, there are other strategies marketers use to "sell" a celebrity as shown in Figure 11.1.[9] One such strategy is the *pure selling approach* in which an agent presents a client's qualifications to potential "buyers" until he finds one who is willing to act as an intermediary. The agent might send a singer's tapes to talent scouts at record companies or photos of an aspiring model to beauty magazines. In this case, the celebrity is sold to distributors, just as the representative of a snack foods company tries to get grocery retailers to give her product adequate shelf space.

Marketing Approach	Implementation
Pure Selling Approach	*Agent presents a client*
	to record companies
	to movie studios
	to TV production companies
	to talk show hosts
	to advertising agencies
	to talent scouts
Product Improvement Approach	*Client is modified*
	New name
	New image
	Voice lessons
	Dancing lessons
	Plastic surgery
	New back-up band
	New music genre
Market Fulfillment Approach	*Agent looks for market opening*
	Identify unmet need
	Develop a new product (band, singer) to the specifications of consumer wants

FIGURE 11.1

Strategies to Sell a Celebrity
There is more than one approach to selling an intangible—even for selling a celebrity. Successful marketing has to determine the best approach to take for each product.

Another strategy is the *product improvement approach* in which the agent works with the client to modify certain characteristics that will increase market value. This means changing the person's repertoire or image to conform to whatever is currently in demand. For example, Madonna's image changed over consecutive albums from East Village punk to lacy virgin to Marilyn Monroe clone, to country cowgirl, and she continues to change with each succeeding release.[10]

Yet another strategy is the *market fulfillment approach*. The agent scans the market to identify unmet needs. After identifying a need, the agent finds a person or a group that meets a set of minimum qualifications and develops a new "product." These "manufactured stars" are

Madonna successfully employs a product improvement approach, changing her image to match, and sometimes introduce, trends.

common, for example, in the music world. The Monkees, The New Kids on the Block, The Spice Girls, and more recently O-Town, Nsync, and the Back Street Boys were successfully formed by auditioning hundreds of photogenic young singers and musicians until producers discovered the right combination of teen idols.

Marketing Places   **Place marketing** strategies regard a city, state, country, or other locale as a brand and attempt to position this location so that consumers choose to visit. Because of the huge amount of money associated with tourism, the competition to attract people is fierce. There are about 1,600 visitors bureaus in the United States alone that try to brand their locations. In addition almost every town or city has an economic development office charged with luring new businesses or residents.

These efforts have intensified in the wake of September 11, 2001, because many Americans now are more interested in going to smaller towns with simpler (and presumably safer) lifestyles. So, in some cases what used to be a negative factor now is viewed as a competitive advantage. The city of Buffalo, New York, decided to revamp its brand image to change perceptions that it's just a place covered in snow. Researchers found that the area's biggest advantage is the quality of its workforce: It boasts one of the lowest turnover and absentee rates in the country. Its 30 colleges turn out well-trained graduates ready to take on skilled jobs. The city's tag line, "Buffalo Niagara: Available. Productive. People" now emphasizes these assets. Web sites such as www.iambuffaloniagarajobs.com tell people more about employment possibilities.[11]

In turn, big cities are fighting back: After the attack on the World Trade Center, New York City unveiled a new tourism advertising campaign in November with the slogan "The New

place marketing ■
Marketing activities that seek to attract new businesses, residents, or visitors to a town, state, country, or some other site.

Buffalo decided to market itself by emphasizing the quality of its workforce to businesses looking for a place to relocate or expand.

York Miracle: Be a Part of It." The campaign included six 30-second TV commercials and some of New York's biggest celebrities—Woody Allen and Robert DeNiro, to name a few.[12]

idea marketing ■ Marketing activities that seek to gain market share for a concept, philosophy, belief, or issue by using elements of the marketing mix to create or change a target market's attitude or behavior.

Marketing Ideas You can see people. You can stand in a city. So how do you market something you can't see, smell, or feel? **Idea marketing** is about gaining market share for a concept, philosophy, belief, or issue. As we saw in Chapter 3, this means using elements of the marketing mix to create or change a target market's attitude or behavior.

A project conducted in Latin America by the Johns Hopkins School of Public Health illustrates how marketing tools can bring about dramatic changes in how people conduct their daily lives. To promote sexual responsibility among young people, the popular Latin pop duo Tatiana and Johnny sang a song promoting abstinence. The record was produced by researchers and went on to become a Top 10 hit in Latin American countries. The record jacket folded out to become a poster with information about obtaining birth control.[13]

In a more recent and controversial cause marketing effort, Italian clothing maker Benetton campaigned aginst the death penalty by using portraits of American death row inmates in its advertising. The series, called "Looking Death in the Face," had little to do with fashion but was created to ignite debate about capital punishment—even at the potential cost of turning off American customers who support the death penalty.[14]

Even religious organizations market ideas about faith and desirable behavior by adopting secular marketing techniques to attract young people. Evangelists use the power of television to convey their messages. So-called "megachurches" are huge steel and glass structures, with acres of parking and slickly produced services complete with live bands and professional dancers to draw huge audiences. Some even offer aerobics classes, bowling alleys, and multimedia Bible classes inspired by MTV to attract "customers" turned off by traditional approaches to religion.[15] Of course, not all religious leaders endorse the use of such marketing techniques. One official at a divinity school rejected the marketing concept by stating, "Church is not supposed to be a place where everybody's needs are met. It's supposed to be a place where we're transformed by God's grace into something we're not."[16] What do you think?

Many religious organizations use a variety of marketing strategies to grow their organizations.

What Is a Service?

So far we've seen that marketing can help sell all kinds of intangibles, from theater performances to ideas about birth control. Now that (hopefully) you are convinced that marketing is equally as important for a dance company as it is for a company that sells ballet slippers, it's time to look more specifically at an important type of intangible.

Services are acts, efforts, or performances exchanged from producer to user without ownership rights. Like other intangibles, a service satisfies needs by providing pleasure, information, or convenience. Services generate 74 percent of the U.S. gross domestic product and account for 79 percent of all jobs. According to the Bureau of Labor Statistics, service occupations will be responsible for *all* job growth through the year 2005.[17] If you pursue a marketing career, it's likely that you will work in some aspect of services marketing. Got your interest?

Of course, the service industry includes services provided for consumers such as dry cleaning and a great rock concert. But it also includes a vast number of services provided for organizations. Some of the more commonly used business services include vehicle leasing, insurance, security, legal advice, food services, consulting, cleaning, and maintenance. In addition, businesses also purchase some of the same services as consumers such as electricity, telephone service, and gas.

The market for business services has grown rapidly because it is often more cost-effective for organizations to hire outside firms that specialize in these services than to try to hire a workforce and handle the service themselves. In other instances, firms buy business services because they do not have the expertise necessary to provide the service.

services ■ Intangible products that are exchanged directly from the producer to the customer.

CHARACTERISTICS OF SERVICES

Services come in many forms, from those done to you, such as a massage or a teeth cleaning, to those done to something you own, such as having your CD player repaired or getting a new paint job on your classic 1965 Mustang. Regardless of whether they affect our bodies or our possessions, all services share four characteristics: intangibility, perishability, inseparability, and variability. Figure 11.2 shows how marketers can meet the potential problems related to these characteristics.

Characteristic	Marketing Response
Intangibility	Provide tangibility through
	Physical appearance of the facility
	Furnishings
	Employee uniforms
	Logo
	Web sites
	Packaging
	Advertising
Perishability	Adjust pricing to influence demand
	Capacity management: adjusting services to match demand
Variability	Gap analysis for identifying gaps in quality
	Employee empowerment
	Improving service delivery processes
	Service guarantees
Inseparability	Employee training
	Disintermediation

FIGURE 11.2

Marketing Strategies for Different Service Characteristics

By understanding the characteristics of services, marketers are better able to develop strategies to lead to success.

2 *Bookmark It!*

Choose a service that you regularly purchase (hair styling, banking, dry cleaning). List the ways that the service provider uses physical cues to make the service more tangible. Then suggest some other physical cues that the provider might use.

capacity management ■
The process by which organizations adjust their offerings in an attempt to match demand.

Intangibility   Service intangibility means that customers can't see, touch, or smell good service. Unlike the purchase of a good, services cannot be inspected or handled before the purchase is made. This makes many services much more difficult for consumers to evaluate. Although it may be easy to evelute your new hair cut, it is far less easy to determine if the dental hygienist has done a great job cleaning your teeth. And how is a manufacturer to know that its security service is doing a good job?

Because they're buying something that isn't there, customers look for reassuring signs before purchasing, and marketers must ensure that these signs are available when consumers look for them. That's why the service provider's appearance and the "look" of the facility, its furnishing, logo, employee uniforms, and even the packaging you carry your dry cleaning home in can make or break a service business. As we'll see shortly, when we talk about how customers decide if a service is giving them what they want, marketers overcome the problem of intangibility by providing physical cues to reassure the buyer. These cues include uniforms, brand logos, and carefully designed Web sites.

Perishability   Service perishability means that a firm can't store its services—it's a case of use it or lose it. When rooms go unoccupied at a ski resort, there is no way to make up for the lost opportunity to rent them for the weekend. Marketers try to avoid these problems by using the marketing mix to encourage demand for the service during times when it would otherwise be low. One option a service provider has to address the perishability problem is to reduce prices to increase demand. Airlines do this by offering more lower-priced seats in the final weeks before a flight. TV stations offer advertisers low-priced airtime at the last minute. We'll talk more about these pricing tactics in Chapter 13.

Capacity management is the process by which organizations adjust their services in an attempt to match demand. This, of course, means accurate forecasting of the need for services, something that is not always easy to accomplish. In the summer, for example, the Winter Park Ski Resort in Colorado combats its perishability problem by opening its lifts to mountain bikers

One means to counter the effects of perishability of services is to increase capacity during low demand period. Airlines such as American offer consumers last minute sale fares over the Internet hoping to fill less popular flights.

who tear down the sunny slopes.[18] Some service providers find pricing strategies an effective tool for demand management. Airlines, for example, offer specially priced tickets on days of the week when business travel is low and many hotels offer special weekend packages to increase weekend occupancy rates.

Variability   Service variability refers to the inevitable differences in a service provider's performances from one day to the next, just as an NFL quarterback may be "hot" one Sunday and ice cold the next. Even the same service performed by the same individual for the same customer can vary. It's rare when you get *exactly* the same cut from a hair stylist.

It is difficult to standardize services because service providers and customers vary. Your experience in college classes is an example. A college can standardize its offerings to some degree—course catalogs, course content, and classrooms are fairly controllable. Professors, however, vary in their training, life experiences, and personalities, so there is little hope of being able to make teaching uniform (not that this would necessarily be desirable anyway). And because students with different backgrounds and interests vary in their needs, the lecture that one finds fascinating might put another to sleep (trust us on this). The same is true for organizational services customers. Differences in the quality of security guards or cleaning personnel mean variability in these services.

For many services purchased by both consumers and organizational customers, standardization is not even desirable. Most of us want a hairstyle that fits our face and personality and a personal trainer who will address our personal physical training needs. And businesses such as McDonald's, Wendy's, and Burger King want unique advertising campaigns. Because of the nature of the tasks performed in services, customers often appreciate the firm that customizes its service for each individual (as Burger King used to promise, "Have it your way . . ."). Of course, all customers want the same level of quality. Thus, service firms need to make sure that customized services have consistency in quality.

One solution to the problem of variability is to institute total quality management programs for continuous improvement of service quality. And offering a guarantee assures consumers that if service quality fails, they will be compensated. We'll talk later in the chapter about how service marketers can provide greater quality and consistency in service delivery through gap analysis and employee empowerment.

Services differ in their level of quality because people who provide the services differ. Some service companies provide their employees with uniforms to give a perception of less variability among employees. Others allow their employees to wear whatever they want.

Inseparability   Although a firm can manufacture goods prior to sale, a service can only take place at the time the service provider performs an act on either the customer or the customer's possession. It's hard to take notes on a lecture when the professor doesn't show! In some cases, of course, the service can be sold prior to delivery, such as a ticket to a Lilith Fair concert months before attending the event.

Still, the expertise, skill, and personality of a provider, or the quality of a firm's employees, facilities, and equipment cannot be detached from the offering itself. The central role played by employees in making or breaking a service underscores the importance of the **service encounter**, or the interaction between the customer and the service provider.[19] The most expertly cooked meal is just plain mush if a surly or incompetent waiter brings it to the table. We'll talk more about the service encounter later in this chapter.

To minimize the potentially negative effects of bad service encounters and to save on labor costs, some service businesses are experimenting with **disintermediation**, which eliminates the need for customers to interact with people. Examples include self-service gas tanks and bank ATM machines. Even salad and dessert bars reduce reliance on a waiter or waitress. Although some consumers resist dealing with machines, pumping their own gas, or fixing their own salad, most prefer the speed and efficiency provided by disintermediation. The remaining consumers who want the personal attention or a Ceasar salad prepared table-side by a salad chef or a fill-up that includes an oil check and a clean windshield provide marketing opportunities for full-service restaurants and a few gas stations that provide these higher levels of service at a higher price.

The Internet has provided some opportunities for disintermediation, especially in the financial services area. Banking customers can access their accounts, transfer frunds from one account to another, and pay their bills with the click of a mouse. Many busy consumers can check out mortgage interest rates and even apply for a loan at their convenience—a lot better option than taking an afternoon off from work to sit in a mortgage company office. Online brokerage services are increasingly popular as many consumers seek to handle their investments themselves and cut out much of the high cost associated with traditional brokerage firms.

service encounter ■ The actual interaction between the customer and the service provider.

disintermediation (of service delivery) ■ Eliminating the interaction between customers and salespeople so as to minimize negative service encounters.

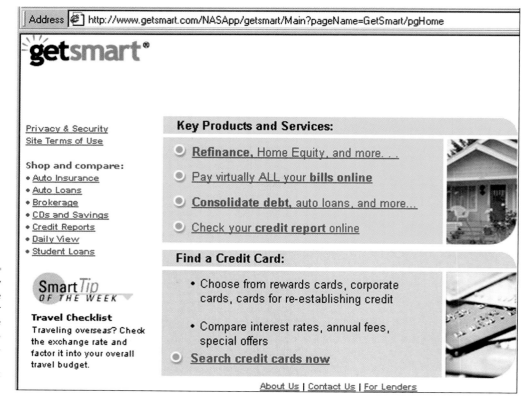

Many financial services are now available online to provide greater convenience for consumers. The site www.getsmart.com helps consumers manage their bills online, consolidate debt, and find a good deal on a credit card.

CLASSIFICATION OF SERVICES

By understanding the characteristics of different types or classifications of services, marketers are better able to develop marketing strategies that will provide customer satisfaction and success for the service provider firm. As shown in Figure 11.3, services may be classified as to their inputs and whether the service consists of tangible or intangible actions. Inputs may be the customers themselves or their possessions. Customers themselves receive tangible services to their bodies—a haircut or a heart transplant. The education you are receiving in this course is an intangible service directed at the consumer. The customer's possessions are the recipient of such tangible services as repair of a favorite carpet. Intangible services directed at a consumer's possessions include insurance and a house security service.

THE GOODS/SERVICES CONTINUUM

In reality, most products are a *combination* of goods and services. The purchase of a "pure good" like a Porsche still has service components, such as bringing it to the dealer for maintenance work. The purchase of a "pure service" like a makeover at a department store has product components, for example, lotions, powders, and lipsticks the cosmetologist uses to create the "new you."

The service continuum in Figure 11.4 shows that some products are dominated by either tangible or intangible characteristics, for instance, salt versus teaching, whereas others tend to include a mixture of goods and services, such as flying in an airplane. A product's placement on this continuum gives some guidance as to which marketing issues are likely to be most relevant. As the product approaches the tangible pole of this continuum, there is fairly little emphasis on service. The physical product itself is the focal point and people will choose one over others based on the product's function or image. But, as the product gets near the intangible pole, the service encounter plays a key role in shaping the service experience. In the middle of the continuum, both goods and services contribute substantially to the quality of the product because these products rely on people to satisfactorily operate equipment that will deliver quality service. Let's consider each of these three positions as we move from products dominated by tangibles to those dominated by intangibles.

2 Bookmark It!

Think about the different services that your school buys. Which of these are equipment based and which are people based?

Good-Dominated Products Many tangible products are accompanied by supporting services, even if this only means that the company maintains a toll-free telephone line for questions or provides a 30-day warranty against defects. Including a service with the purchase of a physical good is termed **embodying**.[20] Embodying is a strategy in the computer industry, especially for companies that are trying to break into international markets saturated with cheap products but with insufficient guidance in their use. As millions of people buy their first computers, they are apt to find it difficult to navigate the maze of setup instructions and next to impossible to cope with machines that crash. Indeed, a survey by *PC Magazine* found that 28 percent of its readers needed technical support in the first year of owning a personal computer. What's more, in grading manufacturers' service performance, they gave two-thirds of them C's and D's. Companies with the resources to do so find that embodying follow-up service is a potent marketing tool when competing with "clone" manufacturers. As an executive at Compaq observed, "The bad guys give us an opportunity to differentiate."[21]

embodying ■ The inclusion of a service with a purchase of a physical good.

	Tangible Services	Intangible Services
Customer	Hair cut	College education
	Plastic surgery	A religious service
	Manicure	A TV program
	Personal trainer	A flower arranging course
		Marriage counseling
Possessions	Dry cleaning	Banking
	Auto repair	Accounting services
	Housecleaning	Insurance
	Package delivery	Home security service

FIGURE 11.3

Classification of Services by Inputs and Tangibility

Services can be classified according to whether the customer or his possessions are the recipient of the service and as to whether the service itself consists of tangible or intangible elements.

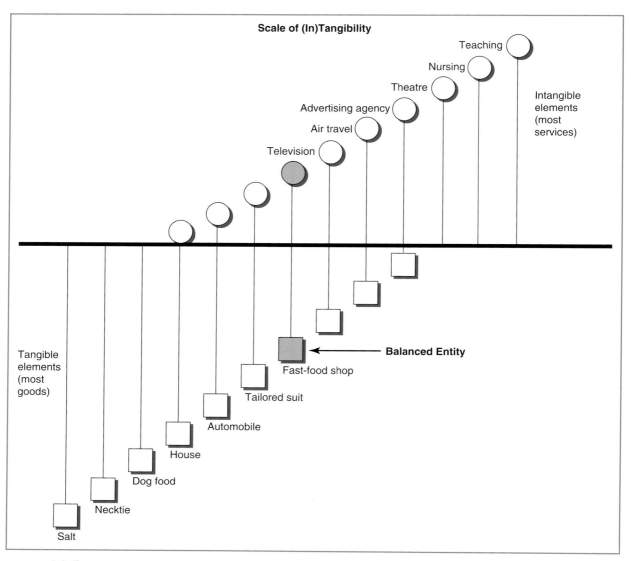

Scale of (In)Tangibility

Teaching

Nursing

Theatre

Advertising agency

Air travel

Television

Intangible elements (most services)

Tangible elements (most goods)

Balanced Entity

Fast-food shop

Tailored suit

Automobile

House

Dog food

Necktie

Salt

FIGURE 11.4

The Service Continuum

Products vary in their level of tangibility. Salt is a tangible product, teaching is an intangible product, and the products offered by fast-food restaurants include both tangible and intangible elements.

Source: Adapted from G. Lynn Shostack, "How to Design a Service," *European Journal of Marketing* 16, no. 1 (1982): 52.

Equipment- or Facility-Based Services   As seen in Figure 11.4, some products require a mixture of tangible and intangible elements. Many hospitals and restaurants fall in the middle of the continuum because they rely on expensive equipment or facilities and skilled personnel to deliver a product. Facility-driven services, such as automatic car washes, amusement parks, museums, movie theaters, health clubs, tanning salons, and zoos, must be concerned with the three factors.[22]

* *Operational factors*: Technologies must move customers smoothly through the service. Clear signs and other guidelines must show customers how to use the service. In particular, firms need to minimize waiting times. Marketers have developed a number of tricks to give impatient customers the illusion that they aren't waiting too long. One hotel chain, responding to complaints about the long wait for elevators, installed mirrors in the lobby: People tend to check themselves out until the elevators arrive, and lo and behold protests decreased.[23] Burger King's research showed that multiple lines create stress in customers—especially if one moves faster than the

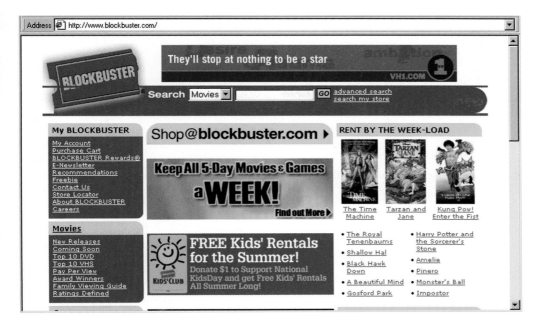

For frequently purchased items, location is very important. Blockbuster says 70 percent of the U.S. population lives near a Blockbuster outlet.

others—so it shifted to single lines in which customers at the head of the line order at the next available register.

- *Locational factors*: These are especially important for frequently purchased services, such as dry cleaning or retail banking, that are obtained at a fixed location. Blockbuster Entertainment estimates that 70 percent of the U.S. population lives within a 10-minute drive of a Blockbuster store.[24]
- *Environmental factors*: Service managers who operate a storefront service requiring people to come to their location realize they must create an attractive environment to lure customers. That's why NFL stadiums are upgrading their facilities by offering plush "sky boxes" to well-heeled patrons and a better assortment of food and merchandise to the rest of us. One trend is for such services to adopt a more retail-like philosophy, borrowing techniques from clothing stores or restaurants to create a pleasant environment. Banks, for example, are creating signature looks for their branches through the use of lighting, color, and art.

People-Based Services At the intangible end of the continuum are people-based services. Take the Great American Backrub store in Manhattan, for instance. To experience this service (no appointment necessary), customers sit in a specially designed chair and for $7.95 get a massage that lasts exactly 8 minutes. The owner of the store explained, "To get Americans to buy massages, I realized you had to solve three problems. You had to come up with something that was quick, inexpensive and most important, and you had to find a way to do it without asking people to take their clothes off."[25] In effect, the Great American Backrub has created a competitive advantage by providing a benefit consumers want.

Because people have less and less time to perform various tasks, the importance of people-based services is increasing. Self-improvement services such as those offered by wardrobe consultants and personal trainers are becoming increasingly popular, and in some cities even professional dog walkers do a brisk business. Many of us hire someone to do our legal work, repair our cars and appliances, and do our tax returns.

CORE AND AUGMENTED SERVICES

Another issue in defining a service is understanding that when we buy a service, we may in fact be buying a *set* of services. The **core service** is a benefit that a customer gets from the service. For example, H&R Block stresses the benefit of the peace of mind you'll get by letting the

2 *Bookmark It!*

Assume you are the marketing manager for a health club. Make a list of the ways you would design operational factors, locational factors, and environmental factors to improve the service received by the customer.

core service ■ The basic benefit of having a service performed.

company prepare your tax return, so peace of mind is the core service. In most cases, though, the core service alone just isn't enough. To attract customers, a service firm often tries to offer **augmented services**, which are additional service offerings that differentiate the firm from the competition.

For example, think about the core service bought with an airline ticket: transportation. Yet airlines rarely stress the basic benefit of arriving safely at your destination (other than making you wait in long lines to get through antiterrorist security checks). Instead, they emphasize augmented services such as frequent flyer miles, speedy checkin, laptop connections and inflight movies. In addition, augmented services may be necessary to deliver the core service. In the case of air travel, airports have added attractions to encourage travelers to fly to one site rather than another.[26] Here are some augmented services now available at airports around the world:

- London Gatwick: Internet café, Planet Hollywood restaurant, personal shopper services
- Amsterdam Schiphol: casino, airport television station, sauna, dry cleaner, grocery store
- Frankfurt International: supermarket, disco, sex shop
- Singapore Changi: fitness center, karaoke lounge, putting green

If differentiation is so important, how can a service stand out? One obvious way to compete by offering superior augmented services is to develop conveniences or innovations competitors lack. The highly competitive market for air passengers has caused competitive airlines to experiment with various innovations in an attempt to make their services stand out. For a while Northwest Airlines provided a buffet meal service in which passengers could choose their own meals instead of distributing the same "gourmet fare" to everyone.[27]

Safe transportation is an airline's core benefit. But to remain competitive, airlines offer a host of other benefits as augmented products.

SERVICES ON THE INTERNET

From video rentals to fine restaurant cuisine, anything that can be delivered can be sold on the Web. In some cities, Web site companies will arrange to have your dry cleaning picked up, your family photos developed, or your shoes repaired.[28]

Here are some of the most popular Web services:

- Cyberbanking customers can check their account and credit card statements, pay bills, transfer money, and balance their accounts 24 hours a day whether they're at home or traveling around the globe. Some banks offer Internet customers higher rates on deposits, lower rates on loans, free electronic bill payment, products from mortgage companies, and insurance carriers and brokerage services.[29]
- Online-only travel and tourism companies, such as travelocity.com and expedia.com, provide information and purchase tickets for consumers and corporate customers. With priceline.com, consumers bid the price they want to pay for airline tickets, hotel rooms, and other travel products. Many believe travel agencies as we know them eventually will disappear.
- Online real estate brokers, such as datatrac.net, offer consumers assistance in buying and selling a house, maps, mortgage rate comparisons, and even automates the closing of real estate transactions.
- Stock trading: Online discount brokerage houses such as etrade.com offer lower fees for consumers. Other sites give consumers information on stocks and allow them to keep track of their personal portfolios online.
- Career-related sites: Employment agencies and recruiting firms such as hotjobs.com (remember Chapter 1) provide important job services and a less expensive way for applicants and employers to advertise their availability.
- Distance learning: Many think it's an important part of our future. Columbia, Stanford, Chicago, Carnegie Mellon, and the London School of Economics have teamed up to create Unext.com, a new Internet university.[30]
- Medical care online: An increasing number of physicians are available to patients through e-mail. Nearly 40 percent of all physicians now have some kind of Web presence and 25 percent of them use e-mail to communicate with patients.[31]

To remain competitive, marketers of such services must adjust their strategies in a number of important ways. If current or prospective customers want services available on the Internet, they must develop an Internet presence; effective Internet sites not only allow customers to access the services online but also provide information for those customers who still want a personal contact. Because customers seek access to Internet-based services for convenience, firms must make sure Internet sites are fast, simple, and easy to navigate to meet customer's needs and they must be continuously updated to provide customer satisfaction. In addition, service providers such as banks must continue to offer their traditional services for those consumers who are not interested in cyber services. And information about the firm's cyber service offerings must be included in all marketing communications.

THE SERVICE ENCOUNTER

The moment of truth for services is when the customer comes into contact with the organization through its employees or the results of its employees' activities. It is this contact that causes that consumer to have a positive or negative impression of the service. Our interactions with service providers can range from the most superficial, such as buying a movie ticket, to telling a psychiatrist (or bartender) our most intimate secrets. In each case, though, the quality of the service encounter can play a big role in determining how we feel about the service we receive.

Service Encounter Dimensions   The service encounter has several dimensions.[32] First, there is the social contact dimension—one person interacting with another person. As such there are certain social expectations. Customers expect employees to be courteous and some even expect employees to engage in friendly small talk. For example, although many banking customers like the speed of ATM transactions, others like to deal directly with a teller who knows them by name and inquires about their health, their children, and so on. The service encounter also has an economic dimension, as there is an exchange of economic value. And there is the production dimension. Something is produced whether it is a haircut, a good meal, or a successful advertising campaign.

Elements of the Service Encounter: Employees and Customers Although a service encounter may include a variety of equipment, supplies, and the impact of physical surroundings, the two most important elements of the service encounter are the employee and the customer. Because services are intimately tied to company employees who deliver the service, the quality of a service is only as good as its poorest employee. The employee represents the organization. The actions, words, physical appearance, courtesy, professionalism—or a lack of it—are seen by the customer as those of the organization. Customers entrust themselves and/or their possessions into the care of the employee so it is important that employees look at the encounter from the customer's perspective.

The customer is also an important element of the service encounter—the most important element. And the customer often has an important role in ensuring that a quality service will be the result of the encounter.

The customer must supply the service provider with correct information, follow directions, and provide the needed input. When you visit a doctor, the quality of the health care you receive depends not only on the physician but also on your ability to accurately and clearly communicate the problems you are experiencing. When you need a haircut, you must be able to explain to the stylist exactly how you'd like your hair to look or suffer the consequences. The business customer must provide accurate information to the accounting firm. And even the best personal trainer is not going to make the desired improvements in a client's body condition if the client refuses to stay on the exercise and diet regimen prescribed for her.

Providing Quality Service

If a service experience isn't positive, it could turn into a disservice with nasty consequences. That's why the Saturn Corporation is serious about its goal "to be the friendliest, best-liked car company in the United States." When it recalled some Saturns for faulty wiring, the automaker converted this potential negative into a publicity bonanza by extending its dealerships' hours, providing door-to-door pickups, and giving away free car washes, coffee, doughnuts, and soft

Customers play a part in the service encounter. To get the right haircut, they must be able to explain exactly what they want.

drinks to customers while repairing their cars. In this way, Saturn turned an aggravating experience into a pleasurable one. The company's strategy of creating loyal customers by providing a better experience than expected has paid off in surveys showing high customer satisfaction among Saturn owners.[33]

JUDGING SERVICE QUALITY

Saturn's strategy illustrates the power of expectations. Many of us have come to expect nothing but aggravation when dealing with a car company, so a pleasant experience comes as a nice surprise that can leave a lasting impression. As we saw in Chapter 3's profile of Subaru, satisfaction or dissatisfaction is more than a reaction to the actual performance quality of a product or service. It is influenced by prior expectations regarding the level of quality.[34] When an offering is as we expected it, we may not think much about it. If, though, it fails to live up to expectations, we will not be happy. And on those rare occasions when it is better than we expect, we turn into loyal customers. We expect a waiter at a fine restaurant to be attentive to our every culinary need, but when we get the same (unexpected) treatment at a local greasy spoon we're customers for life.

Quality Is About Exceeding Expectations   Quality service ensures that customers are satisfied with what they have paid for. However, as we've seen, satisfaction is relative because the service recipient compares the current experience to some prior set of expectations. That's what makes delivering quality service tricky. What may seem like excellent service to one customer may be mediocre to another person "spoiled" by earlier encounters with an exceptional service provider. So, marketers must identify customer expectations and then work hard to exceed them.

Meeting or exceeding expectations is not always so easy. These expectations can be influenced by stories people hear from friends and acquaintances, and they are not always realistic in the first place.[35] In some cases, there is little marketers can do to soothe ruffled feathers. Exaggerated customer expectations, such as providing a level of personal service impossible for a large company to accomplish, account for about 75 percent of the complaints reported by service businesses. However, providing customers with logical explanations for service failures and compensating them in some way can reduce dissatisfaction substantially.[36]

Ironically, the employees who have the biggest impact on service perceptions are among the lowest-ranking individuals in the company. This makes it extra important for management to engage in **internal marketing** in which efforts are made to sell the firm's own employees on the idea that they work for a superior company of which they can be proud. If the service provider doesn't believe in the job and the company, this attitude will quickly be apparent to the customer.

The Ritz-Carlton hotel chain is legendary for anticipating guests' desires and one reason is the company's extensive internal marketing efforts. New employees receive an intensive two-day orientation, 100 additional hours of training, plus a daily appearance inspection. In 1992 the chain became the first hotel to win the Malcolm Baldrige National Quality Award we discussed in Chapter 3. To ensure that attentiveness to guests' needs remains at a peak, the company regularly surveys customers and even hires outside auditors to pose as guests.[37]

Evaluative Dimensions of Service Quality   Because services are inseparable in that they are not produced until the time they are consumed, it is difficult to make a prepurchase evaluation of quality. Most service businesses cannot offer a free trial. Because services are variable, it is hard to predict consistency of quality and there is little or no opportunity for comparison shopping. The selection process for services is somewhat different than with goods, especially for services that are highly intangible, such as those on the right end of the continuum in Figure 11.1.[38] Service marketers have to come up with creative ways to illustrate the benefits their service will provide.

Search qualities are the characteristics of a product that the consumer can examine prior to purchase. These include color, style, price, fit, smell, and texture. Tangible goods, of course, are more likely to have these characteristics, so services need to build them in by paying attention to such details as the style of flight attendants' uniforms or the decor of

internal marketing ■
Marketing activities aimed at employees in an effort to inform them about the firm's offerings and their high quality.

search qualities ■ Product characteristics that the consumer can examine prior to purchase.

Service marketers such as this Italian undertaker have come up with creative ways to illustrate the benefits their service will provide.

a hotel room. The "Service Experience Blueprint™" shown in Figure 11.5 illustrates how one design firm tried to build in such cues for a grocery chain. The company planned an upgraded, freshly painted parking lot that included a special preferred parking space for expectant mothers (complete with a stork logo) to signal that the company cares.[39] Attention to detail makes a difference.

experience qualities ■
Product characteristics that customers can determine during or after consumption.

Experience qualities are product characteristics that customers can determine during or after consumption. For example, we can't really predict how good a vacation we'll have until we have it, so marketers need to reassure customers before the fact that they are in for a positive experience. A travel agency may invest in a slick presentation complete with alluring images of a tropical resort and perhaps even supply enthusiastic recommendations from other clients who had a positive experience.

credence qualities ■
Product characteristics that are difficult to evaluate even *after* they have been experienced.

Credence qualities are attributes we find difficult to evaluate even *after* we've experienced them. For example, most of us don't have the expertise to know if our doctor's diagnosis is correct.[40] Evaluations here are difficult, and to a great extent the client must trust the

FIGURE **11.5**

Service Experience Blueprint

Firms often build in cues their customers can easily see because service quality is often difficult to determine. Grocery stores such as this one often use a variety of cues to convince consumers of superior quality.

Source: Lewis P. Carbone and Stephan H. Haeckel, "Engineering Customer Experiences," *Marketing Management* 3, Winter 1994, reprint, Exhibit 4.

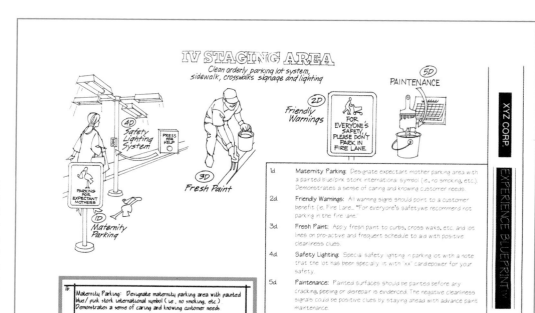

service provider. That is why tangible clues of professionalism, such as diplomas or an organized office, count toward purchase satisfaction.

MEASURING SERVICE QUALITY

Because the customer's experience of a service is crucial to determining future patronage, service marketers feel that measuring positive and negative service experiences is the "Holy Grail" for the services industry. Indeed, one-third of the business of marketing research firms is now devoted to measuring customer satisfaction *after* the sale.[41]

Marketers can gather consumer responses in a variety of ways (see Chapter 5). For example, some companies hire "mystery shoppers" to check on hotels and airlines and report back. These shoppers usually work for a research firm, although some airlines reportedly recruit "spies" from the ranks of their most frequent flyers. Some firms also locate "lost customers" (former patrons) so they can find out what turned them off and correct the problem.

Gap Analysis **Gap analysis** (no, nothing to do with a Gap clothing store!) is a measurement tool that gauges the difference between a customer's expectation of service quality and what actually occurred. By identifying specific places in the service system where there is a wide gap between what is expected and what is received, services marketers can get a handle on what needs improvement. Some major gaps include:[42]

- *Gap between consumer expectations and management perceptions.*
  A major quality gap can occur when the firm's managers don't understand what its customers' expectations are. Many service organizations have an operations orientation rather than a customer orientation. For example, a bank may close its branches at midday to balance transactions because that's more efficient, even though it's not convenient for customers who want to go to the bank on their lunch hour.
- *Gap between management perception and quality standards set by the firm.*
  Quality suffers when a firm fails to establish a quality control program. Successful service firms, such as American Express and McDonald's, develop written quality goals. American Express found that customers complained most about its responsiveness, accuracy, and timeliness. The company established 180 specific goals to correct these problems, and it now monitors how fast employees answer phones in an effort to be more responsive.
- *Gap between established quality standards and service delivery.*
  One of the biggest threats to service quality is poor employee performance. When employees do not deliver the service at the level specified by the company, quality suffers. Teamwork is crucial to service success. Unfortunately, many companies don't clearly specify what they expect of employees. Merrill Lynch addressed this problem by assembling its operations personnel into quality groups of 8 to 15 employees each to foster teamwork among workers and clarify its expectations for how the workers should interact with clients.
- *Gap between service quality standards and consumer expectations.*
  Sometimes a firm makes exaggerated promises or does not accurately describe its service to customers. When the Holiday Inn hotel chain developed an advertising campaign based on the promise that guests would receive "No Surprises," many operations personnel opposed the idea, saying that *no* service organization, no matter how good, can anticipate every single thing that can go wrong. Sure enough, the campaign was unsuccessful. A services firm is better off communicating exactly what the customer can expect and what will happen if the company doesn't deliver on its promises.
- *Gap between expected service and perceived service.*
  Sometimes consumers misperceive the quality of the service. Thus, even when communications accurately describe what service quality is provided and can be expected, consumers are less than satisfied. Some diners at fine restaurants are so demanding that even their own mothers couldn't anticipate their every desire!

3 Bookmark It!

Assume you are the marketing manager of a local bank. Make a list of the search, experience, and credence qualities of banking services. What recommendations can you make to improve these aspects of the service you provide?

gap analysis ■ A marketing research methodology that measures the difference between a customer's expectation of a service quality and what actually occurred.

critical incident technique
■ A method for measuring service quality in which marketers use customer complaints to identify critical incidents, specific face-to-face contacts between consumers and service providers that cause problems and lead to dissatisfaction.

The Critical Incident Technique   The **critical incident technique** is another way to measure service quality.[43] The company collects and closely analyzes very specific customer complaints. It can then identify *critical incidents*—specific contacts between consumers and service providers that are most likely to result in dissatisfaction.

Some critical incidents happen when the expectations of customers cannot be met by the service organization. For example, it is impossible to satisfy a passenger who says to a flight attendant: "Come sit with me. I don't like to fly alone."

In other cases, though, the firm is capable of meeting these expectations but fails to do so. For example, the customer might complain to a flight attendant, "My seat won't recline."[44] A potentially dissatisfied customer can be turned into a happy one if the problem is addressed, or perhaps even if the customer is told why the problem can't be solved at this time. Customers tend to be fairly forgiving if they are given a reasonable explanation for the problem.

Strategies for Developing and Managing Services

We've seen that quality is the goal of every successful service organization. What can the firm do to maximize the likelihood that a customer will choose its service and become a loyal customer?

With services differing from goods in so many ways, decision makers struggle to market something that isn't there. However, many of the same strategic issues apply. For example, Table 11.1 illustrates how three different types of health care practitioners can devise

TABLE 11.1

Health Care Marketing Strategies

	Psychologist	Orthodontist	Chiropractor
Marketing Objective	Add 10 billable hours per week	Attract five new adult patients; increase awareness of practice in community to generate referrals	Increase new patients by 50% within one year
Target Markets	Inactive clients	Primary market: Women 25–55, middle income and above Secondary market: Male executives over 40	25- to 50-year-olds, 65% blue collar, 60% female within a four-mile radius of my office
Benefits Offered	Feel happy Solve problems	Beauty Professional self-confidence	Relief of back, neck, shoulder, head pain; convenience
Strategy	Write a letter to former patients; remind them that if they have learned the basics of turning their lives around, they may just need some short-term assistance now	Talk to 200 people in two days at a local health fair; position myself as the community specialist in cosmetic dentistry	Change location to a new shopping center—locate between a supermarket and a fitness center that attracts a large female clientele. Give seminars at the health club and place articles in its newsletter

Source: Adapted from Alan L. Bernstein, *The Health Professional's Marketing Handbook* (Chicago: Year Book Medical Publishers, 1988).

marketing strategies to improve their practices. In this section, we'll review ways that a service business can determine its best prospects and design a service experience that will be distinctive.

SERVICE FAILURE AND RECOVERY

Of course, sometimes service quality does fail. Some failures, such as when your dry cleaner places strategic red spots on your new white sweater, are easy to see at the time the service is performed. Others, such as when the dry cleaner shrinks your sweater, are less obvious and are only recognized at a later time when you're running late and get a "surprise."

But no matter when or how the failure is discovered, the important thing is that the firm takes fast action to resolve the problem. Quick action means that the problem won't occur again (hopefully) and that the customer's complaint will be satisfactorily resolved. The key is speed; research shows that customers whose complaints are resolved quickly are far more likely to buy from the same company again than when complaints take longer to be resolved.[45]

To make sure service failures are at a minimum and that recovery is fast, managers should first understand the service and the potential places where failures are most likely to occur and then make plans ahead of time to recover.[46] In addition, employees should be trained to listen for complaints and be empowered to take appropriate actions immediately.

SERVICES AS THEATER

One way to think about developing a services strategy that lets the firm stand out from the competition is to think about a service as a show put on for an audience. Whether it's a visit to a doctor's office or a meal at a fine restaurant, each service contact can be thought of as a dramatic performance—complete with actors, props, and costumes. A *service performance* often takes place in two areas, the *back stage* and the *front stage*. The back stage is behind the scene where the service is produced and the front stage is where it gets delivered to the customer.

Think of the activities that occur in a fancy restaurant. On the front stage, waiters, wine stewards, and the maitre'd "perform" for diners by reciting daily specials, opening bottles with a flourish, or even bringing flaming delicacies to the table without burning down the place. The fine restaurant will take great care to elegantly set its tables and play appropriate music softly in the background. Back stage in the kitchen is another story. The elegant waiter with the French accent may slip in to grab a smoke and make jokes about the diners (maybe even revert back to his "real" accent!).

In addition, like the scenes in a play, a service usually happens in steps, so service marketers can anticipate the points at which problems may arise. A look at the flowchart of a hotel service in Figure 11.6 shows the many different operations on stage and behind the scenes.

TARGETING AND POSITIONING STRATEGIES FOR SERVICES

Like any other product, perhaps the most crucial strategic decisions for a service revolve around its definition in the market: Who are the target customers, and how do they perceive the service? As we saw in Chapter 8, the target marketing process is an essential part of many marketing strategies. Let's see how these concepts apply to service businesses.

Targeting: Defining the Service Customer or Audience Most service companies can identify a target customer that they can serve well, and in some cases a company may develop a separate strategy for multiple segments. To understand how this process works, consider how a local theater troupe might go about identifying desirable market segments and targeting them. Depending on the strategic goal of the troupe, here are some targeting actions it might take:[47]

4 *Bookmark It!*

Using the flowchart in Figure 11.6 as a model, make a flowchart for the services provided by a service provider you frequently use. Fill in as much as you can of the back stage column by asking employees what goes on "behind the scenes."

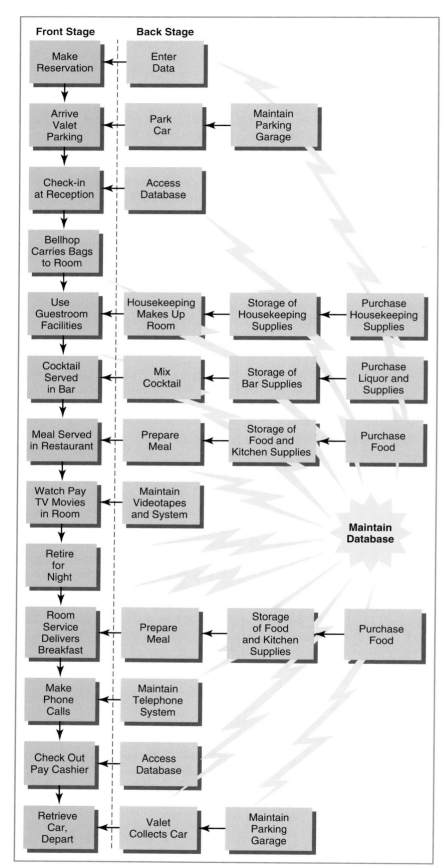

Front Stage

Make Reservation → Arrive Valet Parking → Check-in at Reception → Bellhop Carries Bags to Room → Use Guestroom Facilities → Cocktail Served in Bar → Meal Served in Restaurant → Watch Pay TV Movies in Room → Retire for Night → Room Service Delivers Breakfast → Make Phone Calls → Check Out Pay Cashier → Retrieve Car, Depart

Back Stage

Enter Data

Park Car ← Maintain Parking Garage

Access Database

Housekeeping Makes Up Room ← Storage of Housekeeping Supplies ← Purchase Housekeeping Supplies

Mix Cocktail ← Storage of Bar Supplies ← Purchase Liquor and Supplies

Prepare Meal ← Storage of Food and Kitchen Supplies ← Purchase Food

Maintain Videotapes and System

Prepare Meal ← Storage of Food and Kitchen Supplies ← Purchase Food

Maintain Telephone System

Access Database

Valet Collects Car ← Maintain Parking Garage

Maintain Database

FIGURE 11.6

Flowcharting a Hotel Visit

By developing a flowchart of the services it provides, a firm can identify both the back stage and front stage activities that go into the production of the service encounter. Understanding these different operations allows firms to improve service quality.

Source: Christopher H. Lovelock, *Services Marketing*, 2nd ed. (Upper Saddle River, NJ: Prentice Hall, 1991): 22, Fig. 2.4.

- *Audience maintenance*: Encourage current customers to deepen their commitment by developing newsletters for subscribers or sending letters thanking them for their patronage.
- *Audience enrichment*: Enhance the experience of attendees to ensure their ongoing loyalty by improving augmented services, such as parking, lighting, or temperature control in the theater.
- *Audience expansion*: The troupe can conduct research to generate a profile of the people who now attend and target others with similar characteristics. The manager might attach a postage-paid survey to the back of a play program and ask audience members to complete and return it so she can build a profile.
- *Audience development*: Convince nonattenders that the productions are something they would enjoy. The troupe could expose people to productions through school programs, corporate events, and group sales. The Canadian Opera Company went a step farther by running racy ads to entice people to try the opera. An ad for a production of Strauss's *Elektra* suggested that the troubled characters from the Greek tragedy would feel at home on the *Jerry Springer Show*.[48]

 **Advice for American Express**

 Kristin Firkins, Student, Western Kentucky University

I would choose option 1 because the customer's perception of service quality is related to expectations; streamlining the existing rewards or partners could result in a service gap. AMEX consumers are used to receiving particular rewards; not providing options could result in disappointed or lost customers. The market research reveals some consumers desire to have the dining and entertainment option added. Indeed, one can only have so many stereos or pieces of luggage but can never have enough memories. Instead of running full force with the addition, Julie might do some market testing. She could continue to run the existing rewards, add the new category in small increments, then analyze this demand before investing significant time and money.

 Kathy Winsted, Marketing Professor, Pace University

Julie's best choice is option 1. The membership rewards program is an important customer relationship management tool for American Express. The last thing American Express should do is to "disenfranchise" some customers by taking away their favorite rewards. By offering more rewards, rather than less, American Express can exceed cardholders' expectations. A customization program could offer the biggest spenders the opportunity to contact a customer service rep and request something not in the catalog. To deal with the limited marketing "real estate" issue, specialized catalogs could be tailored to customer preferences and distributed to select groups based on type of rewards preferred. Additionally, cardholders could be directed to the Internet to look at any rewards that can't be put in the printed catalogs.

SUBHA RAMESH, VICE PRESIDENT OF REAL ESTATE, IBI THE LIMITED

I would choose option 1 because 1) the other two options modify current award choices (travel or products), while option 1 is a substantive change, which may catch the attention of the card user; 2) consumer research suggests card members would like dining and entertainment awards, although this finding needs more research; and 3) dining and entertainment, presumably, require less points than travel to claim awards—thus, more frequent cashing of points, resulting in increased loyalty. Regardless of the option, I recommend streamlining awards and doing more research on what awards consumers value.

 Weigh in with your thoughts! Visit the Live Laboratory at www.prenhall.com/solomon for extended Other Voices replies, exercises, and more.

Positioning: Defining the Service to Customers   As we saw in Chapter 8, positioning is a process of creating a specific image for a product that differentiates it from competitors.

Researchers have identified five dimensions that successfully position a service, whether it's a theater troupe, a baseball team, or a credit card company like American Express.[49]

- *Tangibles*: As we touched on earlier, services often rely heavily on **physical evidence**, such as apparel, facilities, graphics, and other visible signals of product quality to communicate a desired position. Such cues as the facility (modern decor versus traditional), distinctive colors (the dependable dark brown of UPS versus the bright purple and orange of Federal Express), and logos (the lion of the Dreyfus Corporation versus the bull of Merrill Lynch) all communicate the underlying characteristics of the service organization. One of the most powerful ways to create physical evidence for a service is to adopt a *branding strategy*, much as a marketer

Real People, Real Choices: How It Worked Out at American Express

Julie chose a combination of all three options. She eliminated those partners that had little or no interest to card members as well as many of the rewards that overlapped and didn't add incremental value to the program. And she targeted certain marketing efforts and rewards to different segments of the enrollee population based on their profiles. American Express is able to track card member spending behavior—where they shop and how much they spend at specific merchants. The company then is able to target certain rewards to certain customer segments based on demographics, geography, card type, and so on.

Since Julie made these changes, American Express has seen an increase in retail redemptions. Ironically, the events of September 11, 2001, significantly affected these decisions because more people are redeeming their points for retail rewards than for travel rewards. Over time, though, Julie thinks that travel will regain its popularity and that she must stay alert to changing preferences to keep cardholders from defecting to other credit card loyalty programs. Staying alert is just one of the challenges of marketing what isn't there.

This "magalog" developed by American Express contains information about retail partners and the rewards they provide in exchange for points accumulated by using the card.

of a tangible product would do. Services marketers such as American Express, the tax preparation firm H&R Block, and the Century 21 realty company have essentially branded their services to create a unique identity. Consumers feel as if they "know" the service.

- *Reliability*: Firms that perform their designated service accurately and dependably create an important competitive advantage. Lawyers that call back when they say they will, resturants that cook your steak just the way you want it, dry cleaners that get your favorite sweater clean the first time, and banks that you can count on to keep your account free from errors are always winners.
- *Responsiveness*: Some services emphasize the speed and care with which they respond to customers' requests. Domino's Pizza was known for its promise to deliver a pizza within 30 minutes—until a jury awarded more than $78 million to a woman who was hit by a driver rushing to make a delivery.[50] So, don't overdo it.
- *Empathy*: An organization that says it genuinely cares about its customers' welfare can gain a competitive edge. Recall the long-standing motto of State Farm insurance: "Like a good neighbor, State Farm is there." And health insurance company Cigna promotes itself with "The Power of Caring." Of course, for such appeals to work, the company's actions have to support the image created. Following the World Trade Center attack in 2001, most of the financial services companies that had offices there got a lot of favorable press by rushing to take care of their employees—but a few got black eyes when they instead acted callously toward the families of employees killed in the bombing.
- *Assurance*: An organization can emphasize the competence of its employees. This is a good strategy to minimize risk, especially for services in which the customer finds it difficult to evaluate quality. For years Texaco proudly proclaimed, "You can trust your car to the man who wears the star."

Chapter Summary

1. **Explain the marketing of people, places, and ideas.**

   Managers follow the steps for marketing planning when marketing intangibles as well. People, especially politicians and celebrities, are often packaged and promoted. Place marketing aims to create or change the market position of a particular locale, whether a city, state, country, resort, or institution. Idea marketing (gaining market share for a concept, philosophy, belief, or issue) seeks to create or change a target market's attitude or behavior. The marketing of religion, aimed at both increasing primary demand and at individual "brand" choice, has gained in popularity as evidenced by the increased use of religious broadcasts and religious advertising.

2. **Describe the four characteristics of services and understand how services differ from goods.**

   Services are products that are intangible and that are exchanged directly from producer to customer without ownership rights. Generally services are acts that accomplish some goal and may be directed either toward people or toward an object. Both consumer services and business-to-business services are important parts of the economy. Important service characteristics include (1) intangibility (they cannot be seen, touched, or smelled), (2) perishability (they cannot be stored), (3) variability (they are never exactly the same from time to time) and (4) inseparability from the producer (most services are produced, sold, and consumed at the same time). In reality, most products are a combination of goods and services. Some services are goods dominant (i.e., tangible products are marketed with supporting services). Some are equipment or facility based (i.e., elaborate equipment or facilities are required for creation of the service). Other services are people based (i.e., people are actually a part of the service marketed). Like goods, services include both a core service or the basic benefit received and augmented services including innovative features and convenience of service delivery.

3. Explain how marketers create and measure service quality.

The customer's perception of service quality is related to prior expectations. Because services are intangible, evaluation of service quality is more difficult and customers often look for cues to help them decide whether they received satisfactory service. Gap analysis measures the difference between customer expectations of service quality and what actually occurred. Using the critical incident technique, service firms can identify the specific contacts between customers and service providers that create dissatisfaction.

4. Explain marketing strategies for services.

As with strategies for marketing physical goods, service strategies include targeting segments of service customers and positioning the service to differentiate it from competitors' offerings. This can be done by emphasizing such dimensions as tangibles (including employee appearance, design of facilities, and company logos), responsiveness, empathy, and assurance. Internet marketing is often an effective way to market a service because it's an easy way for consumers to compare core and augmented services.

Chapter Review

▪ MARKETING CONCEPTS: TESTING YOUR KNOWLEDGE

1. What are intangibles? How do basic marketing concepts apply to the marketing of intangibles?
2. What do we mean by marketing people? Marketing places? Marketing ideas?
3. What is a service? What are the important characteristics of services that make them different from goods?
4. What types of services are used by organizational customers?
5. What is the goods/services continuum? What are product-related services, equipment- or facility-based services, and people-based services?
6. How do marketers create augmented services to increase market share?
7. Describe the growth of the marketing of services on the Internet.
8. What dimensions do consumers and business customers use to evaluate service quality? How do marketers work to create service quality?
9. What is gap analysis? What is the critical incident technique of measuring service quality?
10. How does target marketing apply to the marketing of services?

▪ MARKETING CONCEPTS: DISCUSSING CHOICES AND ISSUES

1. Sometimes service quality may not meet customers' expectations. What problems have you experienced with quality in the delivery of the following services? What do you think is the reason for the poor quality? (a) hotel accommodations, (b) dry cleaning, (c) a haircut, (d) your college education.
2. There have been a lot of criticisms of the way politicians have been marketed in recent years. What are some of the ways marketing has helped our political process? What are some ways the marketing of politicians might have an adverse effect on our government?
3. Many not-for-profit and religious organizations have found that they can be more successful by marketing their ideas. What are some ways that these organizations market themselves that are similar to and different from the marketing by for-profit businesses?
4. Many businesses purchase services rather than provide the services themselves. What are the benefits to the business of this practice? What criteria should an organization use to decide whether to purchase services or provide them itself?

▪ MARKETING PRACTICE: APPLYING WHAT YOU'VE LEARNED

1. Because of increased competition in its community, you have been hired as a marketing consultant by a local bank. You know that the characteristics of services (intangibility, perishability, and so on) create unique marketing challenges. You also know that these challenges can be met with creative marketing strategies. Outline the challenges for marketing the bank created by each of the four characteristics of services. List your ideas for what might be done to meet each of these challenges.

2. Assume you are a physician. You are opening a new family practice clinic in your community. You feel that you have the best chance of being successful if you can create a product that is superior to that offered by competing businesses. Put together a list of ways in which you can augment the basic service offering to develop a better product. List the advantages and disadvantages of each.

3. You are currently a customer for a college education, a very expensive service product. You know that a service organization can create a competitive advantage by focusing on how the service is delivered after it has been purchased—making sure the service is efficiently and comfortably delivered to the customer. Develop a list of recommendations for your school for improving the delivery of its service. Consider both classroom and nonclassroom aspects of the educational product.

4. Assume you have been hired as a campaign manager for a local candidate for mayor. In other words, you have been asked to create and manage a plan for marketing a person. Prepare an outline for your marketing plan. First list the special problems and challenges associated with marketing a person rather than a physical product. Then outline your ideas for product, price, and promotion strategies.

5. Assume you have been recently hired by your city government to head up a program to create 100 percent compliance with recycling regulations. Develop a presentation for the city council in which you will outline the problems in "selling" recycling. Develop an outline for the presentation. Be sure to focus on each of the four Ps.

MARKETING MINI-PROJECT:
LEARNING BY DOING

1. Select a service that you will purchase in the next week or so.

2. As you experience the service, record the details of every aspect, including (a) people, (b) physical facilities,

(c) location, (d) waiting time, (e) hours, (f) transaction, (g) other customers, (h) tangible aspects, (i) search qualities, and (j) credence qualities.

3. Recommend improvements to the service encounter.

REAL PEOPLE, REAL SURFERS:
EXPLORING THE WEB

Fast-food restaurants fall in the middle of the goods/services continuum—half goods and half services. To be successful in this highly competitive market, fast-food chains must carefully develop targeting and positioning strategies. Visit the Web sites of the three top fast-food chains: McDonald's (www.mcdonalds.com), Wendy's (www.wendys.com), and Burger King (www.burgerking.com). Thoroughly investigate each site.

1. How is the Web site designed to appeal to each restaurant's target market?

2. How does each restaurant position its product? How is this positioning communicated through the Web site?

3. What changes or improvements would you recommend for each Web site?

PLAN IT!
DEVELOPING A MARKETING PLAN

As your instructor directs, create a marketing plan (using Marketing Plan Pro software or a written marketing plan format) to document your marketing decisions or answer these questions in a written or oral report.

Although CFS markets tangible products, it must provide customer service for any problems that resellers or consumers experience with the software and toys—which has implications for next year's marketing plan.

1. Where on the service continuum would you place CFS's products?

2. How can CFS use the critical incident technique to check on the quality of its customer service?

3. How can CFS use internal marketing to support superior service delivery among its customer service representatives?

Key Terms

REAL CHOICES FOR O-TOWN

(This case was written by Vassilis Dalakas and Mary Jo Thornton, Berry College, Rome, Georgia.)

It's reality TV with a twist: a television show that has documented the conception, birth, and development of O-Town, a musical pop group rising to stardom. The idea was simple—show how a musical group was selected and lived as a television program in the tradition of reality TV shows that MTV's "Real World" made so popular. Here's how O-Town became a reality.

In the late 1990s, "boy bands," reminiscent of 1970s' groups the Monkees and the Archies, reemerged in the pop music scene. Nsync and the Backstreet Boys became teen idols overnight. The market seemed right for the development of new products patterned after these success stories.

Louis Pearlman saw the potential of creating a new band for this market through a unique and unusual way. The first step was to get hundreds of young men to audition for the opportunity to be part of the new band. The lucky finalists would live together. They would practice their music, but more importantly film crews would record the time they spent together. The resulting footage would be broadcast every week on the ABC prime network television show *Making the Band*. This program became quite successful and was the number-one program in its Friday night time slot among women ages 18 to 34 years old.

During the course of selecting the band members, and before releasing their first song, O-Town made numerous public appearances. They attended the MTV Music Video Awards, were guests on the popular MTV show *Total Request Live*, and sang at the Miss America Pageant. As a result, fans became even more aware of them and eagerly anticipated their album. The new band quickly became a household name among its loyal fan base of young women.

Aided by this advance publicity, O-Town's first single called "Liquid Dreams" entered the Hot 100 singles sales chart at number one, a music success story never before achieved by a new artist. Their debut album called simply "O-Town" sold 145,000 copies the first week and 790,000 copies in 19 weeks. A second single, "All or Nothing" reached number three on the Hot 100. In January 2002 the television show devoted to the band began airing on MTV.

Despite the band's favorable start, keeping its success moving forward remained a challenge. Given the way it originated, O-Town is viewed by many as a manufactured band, an image that may keep the band from being able to sustain success in the long run. Skeptics also pointed to the fact that the O-Town musicians don't write their own songs or play any instruments. Moreover, given how previous boy bands (like New Kids on the Block) faded out of the music scene, the future remained uncertain.

Several options might help extend the product life cycle of O-Town. One possible route would be to gain even more TV exposure through development of an O-Town TV show, a formula that fueled the Monkees' incredible popularity three decades earlier. Of course, although the popularity of O-Town had been driven almost exclusively by television, most new music artists rely on radio programmers to give them the exposure they need to stay in front of the public. Perhaps O-Town's marketers should consider this more traditional route and court these influential programmers. Or it might be necessary to try to reinvent the band as fans become fickle and develop an appetite for new "hunk" idols.

Sources: Edna Gundersen, "Pop Acts Turned to Success Without Radio," *USA Today,* 11 June 2001, accessed via www.usatoday.com/life/music/2001-06-12-pop-tv.htm on March 29, 2002.

Richard Huff, "ABC's Boy Band O-Town Gets an Encore," *New York Daily News,* August 30, 2000.

http://archive.nextwerk.com/newsarchive21.nsf/237c30a68537751c862567e6002558ae/8625666b000ce7b18625694d0036f4e1? OpenDocument

"Making the Band, Moving to MTV," *St. Petersburg Times,* October 25, 2001: Floridian: 5D.

"Making the Band Makes the Scene," *Zap2it,* April 17, 2001; accessed, via http://triton.libs.uga.edu/cgi-bin/door/homepage.cgi?_id=42141c15-1038126891-9045&_cc=1

James Poniewozik, "Inventing Stardom," *The New York Times,* April 2, 2001, 69–70.

GUCCI
timepieces

available at Saks Fifth Avenue

Gucci knows that its high price is a signal of quality for many consumers.

based on the suggested retail price printed on the package, will give the retailer a 30 percent markup, will the retailer be willing to add the product to its stock? Sure it will. The new product will give the retailer a margin that will cover its costs and profit goals with an extra 10 percent to spare.

Price and Product   Obviously, the price of the product must cover the costs of doing business but price also sends a *signal* about product quality. The relationship between place and price also means that marketers select retail channels that match their product's price and image. For example, a shopper would not expect to find a Rolex watch in Sears or Wal-Mart, or expect to see Timex watches on display at Tiffany's.

The sky-high price of a Rolex watch tells consumers a lot about the timepiece, and it also signals that those who can afford one are probably in an upper-income class (or they have gone deeply into debt to make it look like they are). And although experts and the media often try to tell women that most makeup and skin care products have identical ingredients and are pretty much the same, the premium prices charged for certain brands continue to convince consumers that higher price means a better product.

The stage of the product's life cycle also affects pricing. Early in the life cycle, a single firm may be the only producer of a highly desirable product. At this point the firm is a *monopoly supplier*, so it's able to charge a premium price. Later, as competitors enter the market and costs of production decrease, prices often go down. For example, when small handheld calculators were introduced into the market in the late 1960s, the price tag was about $200. Around 1970, the price was cut in half and thousands of consumers were thrilled to be able to buy a great little handheld calculator that added, subtracted, multiplied, and divided for $89.99. Today a calculator that also calculates a variety of statistical and trigonometric functions is sold for less than $20.

1 *Bookmark It!*

Have a discussion with your parents or other consumers who are older than you are. Ask them to tell you about some product whose price is much lower today than it was a few years ago. What do you think are other causes of reductions in prices of goods and services?

Price and Promotion Pricing is strongly related to promotional activities, if for no other reason than the firm needs to be sure it has enough revenue to pay for the promotion.

It is just as important that the advertising strategies justify the cost of the product. For example, an ad for an expensive fragrance should project luxury, quality, and status imagery to convince shoppers that they are getting "quality" for their money. Even ads for high-end building materials such as countertops can create a luxury appeal through advertising.

Developing Pricing Objectives

Taking the importance of price and its relation to the other three Ps into consideration, we can now start to learn how marketers determine prices. Figure 12.1 shows the steps in price planning beginning with *developing pricing objectives*. These must support the broader objectives of the firm (such as maximizing shareholder value) as well as its overall marketing objectives (such as increasing market share). Consider, for example, the different pricing decisions of the three major rivals in the dry breakfast cereal market.

From 1983 to 1988, major cereal producers increased net prices more than 6 percent per year for a total of more than a 30 percent increase in the five-year period. Then came the low-priced supermarket brands, which by 1994 captured a whopping 9 percent of the market. In 1993, the top two cereal makers announced very different pricing strategies. General Mills *cut* prices on three of its major brands in the large sizes in an effort to increase its market share. Kellogg's response, however, was a 2.6 percent price *increase* on its cereals. Kellogg planned to soften the impact with discount coupons, the idea being to hold customers and to increase profits with frequent price-oriented promotions.[5]

Three years later, in 1996, Post announced it was "changing the way the entire cereal category works" with an across-the-board price rollback and a new advertising campaign announcing this change.[6] Each of these pricing strategies had an objective: General Mills sought to increase market share, Kellogg tried to increase profits, and Post hoped to increase consumers' total consumption of cereal. Table 12.1 provides examples of different types of pricing objectives.

SALES OR MARKET SHARE OBJECTIVES

Often the objective of pricing strategy is to maximize sales (either in dollars or in units) or to increase market share. Does setting a price intended to increase unit sales or market share, one that focuses on sales objectives, simply mean pricing the product lower than the competition? Sometimes this is the case. Long-distance telephone companies such as MCI, Sprint, and

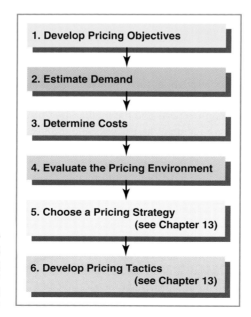

FIGURE 12.1

Steps in Price Planning

Successful price planning includes a series of orderly steps beginning with setting pricing objectives.

1. Develop Pricing Objectives

2. Estimate Demand

3. Determine Costs

4. Evaluate the Pricing Environment

5. Choose a Pricing Strategy (see Chapter 13)

6. Develop Pricing Tactics (see Chapter 13)

Type of Objective	Example
Sales or Market Share	Institute pricing strategy changes to support a 5 percent increase in sales.
Profit	During the first six months, set a price to yield a target profit of $200,000.
	Or
	Set prices to allow for an 8 percent profit margin on all goods sold.
Competitive Effect	Alter pricing strategy during first quarter of the year to increase sales during introduction of new product.
	Or
	Maintain low end pricing policies to discourage new competitors from entering the market.
Customer Satisfaction	Simplify pricing structure to simplify decision process for customers.
	Or
	Alter price levels to match customer expectations.
Image Enhancement	Alter pricing policies to reflect the increased emphasis on the product's quality image.

TABLE 12.1

Pricing Objectives

AT&T relentlessly make rate adjustments to keep them ahead in the "telephone wars" (and have paid for numerous commercials to promote these changes!).

But lowering prices is not always necessary to increase market share. If a company's product has a competitive advantage, keeping the price at the same level as other firms may satisfy sales objectives. (See Table 12.1.)

PROFIT OBJECTIVES

As we discussed in Chapter 2, often a firm's overall objectives relate to a certain level of profit. When pricing strategies are determined by profit objectives, the focus is on a target level of profit growth or a desired net profit margin. A profit objective is important to firms that see profit as what motivates shareholders and bankers to invest in a company.

Although profits are an important consideration in the pricing of all goods and services, they are critical when the product is a fad. Fad products have a short market life, making a profit objective essential to allow the firm to recover its investment in a short period of time. In such cases, the firm must harvest profits before customers lose interest and move on to the next pet rock or hula hoop.

COMPETITIVE EFFECT OBJECTIVES

Competitive effect objectives mean the pricing plan is intended to have a certain effect on the marketing efforts of the competition. Sometimes a firm may deliberately seek to pre-empt or reduce the effectiveness of one or more competitors. So, for example, a retailer such as Toys "R" Us may launch a price offensive by distributing coupons for popular products just before Christmas, hoping to catch competitors such as Wal-Mart off guard and steal their customers.

CUSTOMER SATISFACTION OBJECTIVES

Many quality-focused New Era firms believe that profits result from making customer satisfaction the primary objective. These firms believe that by focusing solely on short-term profits a company loses sight of keeping customers for the long term.

Events in the auto industry illustrate this difference between short-term and long-term pricing philosophies. One reason people hate to buy a new car is because they feel the dealers are untrustworthy hucksters. Saturn started a trend to combat this perception that other car companies have copied. With Saturn's value pricing strategy, customers get one price and one price only—no haggling, no negotiation, no "deals." Customers can even go to Saturn's Web

site to get detailed price information without needing a salesperson. This objective has worked for the company. It is also generating a new breed of car salespeople who use low-pressure sales tactics and promise customer satisfaction and long-term service.

IMAGE ENHANCEMENT OBJECTIVES

Consumers often use price to make inferences about the quality of a product. In fact, marketers know that price is often an important means of communicating not only quality but also image to prospective customers.

The image enhancement function of pricing is particularly important with prestige or luxury products. Most of us would agree that the high price tag on a Rolex watch or

Purex's pricing objectives focus on the competition. The number-two–selling detergent sets its price lower than the best-selling brand.

a Rolls-Royce car, although representing the higher costs of producing the product, is vital to shaping an image of an extraordinary product with ownership limited to only wealthy consumers.

Another example of image pricing comes from Spoetzl Brewery, a small, independently owned, regional beer maker in Texas. Priced below Miller Lite, Spoetzl beer was positioned to compete on price—without much success. Then Spoetzl got a new owner and a turnaround began. The first step was to improve the product, so there could be a stronger appeal to customers than simply low price. After investing in new equipment and making other changes, the firm emerged with a "premium" beer and raised the six-pack price from $3.00 to $4.50, positioning it above Budweiser and Miller Lite but below the superpremiums. The strategy worked: Sales revenue tripled, and the 80-year-old brewery returned to profitability.

FLEXIBILITY OF PRICE OBJECTIVES

It is important that pricing objectives be flexible. Often it is necessary to develop pricing objectives (and strategies) tailored to different geographic areas and time periods. For instance, there may be varying levels of competition in different parts of the country. If so, it may be necessary to lower prices in the areas with the heaviest competition. Some geographic regions may have greater sales potential, making it wise for firms to develop pricing objectives aimed at obtaining a larger market share in those areas. Mortgage lenders may do this by offering lower rates in areas where new housing starts are booming.

Market conditions can change during the year, requiring price adjustments for seasonal and other reasons. Villa rental rates in Naples, Florida, are much higher during the winter than during the summer while rates on the Carolinas' Hilton Head Island and Myrtle Beach are higher during the summer vacation months.

2 Bookmark It!

Some critics of marketing might suggest that charging a high price for a product just to communicate a high-quality image is unethical because the company reaps excessive profits. They contend that these products' prices should reflect the costs of production. What do you think? Is an image enhancement pricing strategy unethical?

Of course, pricing objectives are only one part of price planning. Before any prices can be set, marketers must understand two factors: demand and costs. In the next two sections we will examine these factors.

Estimating Demand: How Demand Influences Pricing

The second step in price planning is to estimate demand. Demand refers to customers' desire for products: How much of a product do consumers want and how much are they willing to buy as the price of the product goes up or down? Obviously, the answer to this question is good to know before prices are set. Therefore, one of the earliest steps that marketers take in price planning is to estimate demand for their products.

DEMAND CURVES

The effect of price on the quantity demanded is often illustrated on a graph using a demand curve. The demand curve (which can be a curved or straight line) shows the quantity of a product that customers will buy in a market during a period of time at various prices if all other factors remain the same.

Figure 12.2 shows demand curves for normal versus prestige products. The vertical axis for the demand curve represents the different prices that a firm might charge for a product (P). The horizontal axis shows the number of units or quantity (Q) of the product. The demand curve for most goods (shown on the left side of Figure 12.2) slopes downward and to the right. As the price of the product goes up (P_1 to P_2), the number of units that customers are willing to buy goes down (Q_1 to Q_2). If prices decrease, customers will buy more. This is known as the *law of demand*. For example, if the price of bananas in the grocery store goes up, customers will probably buy fewer of them. And, if the price really gets high, customers will eat their cereal without bananas.

Although this type of price–quantity relationship is typical, there are exceptions. There are situations in which (otherwise sane) people desire a product more as it *increases* in price. For **prestige products**, such as luxury cars or jewelry that have a high price tag and appeal to status-conscious consumers, an increase in price may actually result in an *increase* in the quantity demanded because consumers see the products as more valuable. In such cases, the demand curve slopes upward. If the price decreases, consumers perceive the product to be less desirable

prestige products ■
Products that have a high price and appeal to status-conscious consumers.

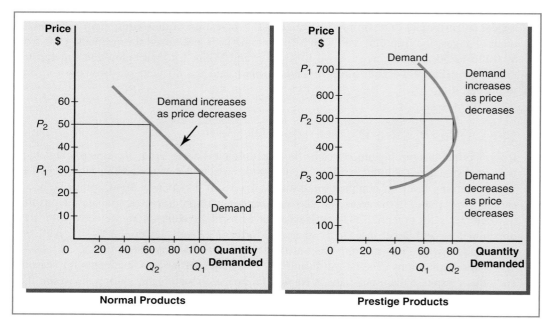

FIGURE 12.2

Demand Curves for Normal and Prestige Products

For normal products, there is an inverse relationship between price and demand. For prestige products, demand will increase—to a point—as price increases, or decrease as price decreases.

and demand may decrease. Figure 12.2 shows the "backward-bending" demand curve associated with prestige products.

Still, the higher-price/higher-demand relationship has its limits. If the firm increases the price too much, making the product simply out of range for buyers, demand will begin to decrease, as shown by the backward direction taken by the top portion of the backward-bending curve.

Shifts in Demand   The demand curves we've shown assume that all factors other than price stay the same. But what if they don't? What if the product is improved? What happens when there is a glitzy new advertising campaign that turns a product into a "must-have" for a lot of people? What if a stealthy photographer catches Russell Crowe using the product at home? Any of these things could cause an *upward shift* of the demand curve. An upward shift in the demand curve means that at any given price, demand is greater than before the shift occurs.

Figure 12.3 shows the upward shift of the demand curve as it moves from D_1 to D_2. At D_1, before the shift occurs, customers will be willing to purchase the quantity Q_1 at the given price, P. For example, customers at a particular store may buy 80 barbecue grills at $60 a grill. But then the store runs a huge advertising campaign, featuring Queen Latifah on her patio using this barbecue grill. The demand curve shifts from D_1 to D_2. (The store keeps the price at $60.) Take a look at how the quantity demanded has changed to Q_2. In our example, the store is now selling 200 barbecue grills. From a marketing standpoint, this shift is the best of all worlds. Without lowering prices, the company can sell more of its product. As a result, total revenues go up and, unless the new promotion costs as much as the increase in revenues it triggers, so do profits.

In the real world, factors other than the price and marketing activities influence demand. If it rains, the demand for umbrellas increases and the demand for tee times on a golf course is a wash. Demand for airline tickets decreased drastically after the September 11, 2001, hijackings. Because the airlines bought less jet fuel in reaction to this slowdown, gasoline prices fell at service stations around the country. In addition, the development of new products may influence demand for old ones. Even though some firms may still produce and sell phonographs, the introduction of the cassette tape, the compact disk, and now MP3 has all but eliminated the demand for new vinyl records and turntables to play them on except for connoissuers of the Old School sound.

Estimating Demand   Understanding and estimating demand is extremely important for marketers. For one, a firm's production scheduling is based on anticipated demand that must be estimated well in advance of when products are brought to market. That explains the shortage on gas masks and American flags after the anthrax scare of 2001—companies that make these items had no way to know that they suddenly would be in such high demand. In addition, all marketing planning and budgeting must be based on reasonably accurate estimates of potential sales.

3 *Bookmark It!*

What are some examples of products you buy that have a normal demand curve? What are some products you buy that probably have a backward-bending demand curve because they are prestige products?

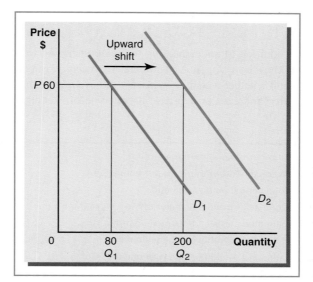

FIGURE 12.3

Shift in Demand Curve

Changes in the environment or in company efforts can cause a shift in the demand curve. A great advertising campaign, for example, can shift the demand curve upward.

The tragic events of September 11, 2001, created an unprecedented wave of patriotism causing the demand for American flags to increase exponentially.

So how do marketers reasonably estimate potential sales? The first step in estimating a product's demand is to identify demand for an entire product category in the markets the company serves. PepsiCo, for example, will estimate the entire demand for soft drinks in domestic and international markets. Table 12.2 shows how a small business, such as a start-up pizza restaurant, will estimate demand only in markets it expects to reach. Marketers predict total demand first by identifying the number of buyers or potential buyers and then multiplying that estimate times the average amount each member of the target market is likely to purchase.

For example, the pizza entrepreneur may estimate that there are 180,000 consumer households in his market who would be willing to buy his pizza and that each household would purchase an average of six pizzas a year. The total annual demand is 1,080,000 pizzas (hold the anchovies on at least one of those, please!).

Once the marketer estimates total demand, the next step is to predict what the company's market share is likely to be. The company's estimated demand is then its share of the whole (estimated) pie. In our pizza example, the entrepreneur may feel that he can gain 3 percent of this market, or about 2,700 pizzas a month—not bad for a new start-up business. Of course, such projections need to take into consideration other factors that might affect demand, such as new competitors entering the market, the state of the economy, and changing consumer tastes.

THE PRICE ELASTICITY OF DEMAND

In addition to understanding the relationship between price and demand, marketers also need to know how sensitive customers are to *changes* in the price. In particular, it is critical to understand whether a change in price will have a large or a small impact on demand. How much can a firm increase or decrease its price before seeing a marked change in sales? If the price of

TABLE **12.2**		
Estimating Demand for Pizza	Number of families in market	180,000
	Average number of pizzas per family per year	6
	Total annual market demand	1,080,000
	Company's predicted share of the total market	3%
	Estimated annual company demand	32,400 pizzas
	Estimated monthly company demand	2,700
	Estimated weekly company demand	675

a pizza pie goes up $1, will people switch to subs and burgers? What would happen if the pizza pie went up $2? Or even $5?

Price elasticity of demand is a measure of the sensitivity of customers to changes in price: If the price changes by 10 percent, what will be the percentage change in demand for the product? The word *elasticity* reminds us that changes in price usually cause demand to stretch or retract like a rubber band.

Price elasticity of demand is calculated as follows:

$$\text{Price elasticity of demand} = \frac{\text{percentage change in quantity demanded}}{\text{percentage change in price}}$$

price elasticity of demand
■ The percentage change in unit sales that results from a percentage change in price.

Elastic and Inelastic Demand   Sometimes customers are very sensitive to changes in prices, and a change in price results in a substantial change in the quantity demanded. In such instances, we have a case of **elastic demand**. In other situations, a change in price has little or no effect on the quantity that consumers are willing to buy and demand is said to be **inelastic**.

For example, using the formula, suppose the pizza maker finds (from experience or from marketing research) that lowering the price of his pizza 10 percent (from $10 per pie to $9) will cause a 15 percent increase in demand. He would calculate the elasticity of demand as 15 divided by 10. The price elasticity of demand would be 1.5. If the price elasticity of demand is greater than 1, demand is elastic; that is, consumers respond to the price decrease by demanding more. Or, if the price increases, consumers will demand less. Table 12.3 shows these calculations.

When demand is elastic, changes in price and in total revenues (total sales) work in opposite directions. If the price is increased, revenues decrease. If the price is decreased, there will be an increase in total revenues. With elastic demand, the demand curve shown in Figure 12.4 is more horizontal. With an elasticity of demand of 1.5, a decrease in price will increase the pizza maker's total sales.

elastic demand ■ Demand in which changes in price have large effects on the amount demanded.

inelastic demand ■ Demand in which changes in price have little or no effect on the amount demanded.

TABLE 12.3

Price Elasticity of Demand

Elastic demand

Price changes from $10 to $9.

$10 − 9 = $1

1/10 = 10% change in price

Demand changes from 2,700 per month to 3,100 per month   3,100
                                                          − 2,700

Increase   400 pizzas

Percentage increase   400/2,700 = .148 ~ 15% change in demand

$$\text{Price elasticity of demand} = \frac{\text{percentage change in quantity demanded}}{\text{percentage change in price}}$$

$$\text{Price elasticity of demand} = \frac{15\%}{10\%} = 1.5$$

Inelastic demand

Price changes from $10 to $9

$10 − 9 = $1

1/10 = 10% change in price

Demand changes from 2,700 per month to 2,835 per month   2,835
                                                          − 2,700

Increase   135 pizzas

Percentage increase   135/2,700 = 0.05 ~ 5% change in demand

$$\text{Price elasticity of demand} = \frac{5\%}{10\%} = 0.5$$

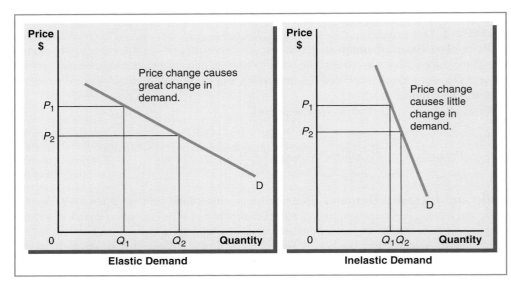

FIGURE 12.4

Price Elastic and Inelastic Demand Curves

Price elasticity of demand represents how demand responds to changes in prices. If there is little change in demand, then demand is said to be price inelastic. If there is a large change in demand, demand is price elastic.

As we noted earlier, in some instances demand is inelastic so that a change in price results in little or no change in demand. For example, if the 10 percent decrease in the price of pizza resulted only in a 5 percent increase in pizza sales, then the price elasticity of demand calculated would be 5 divided by 10, which is 0.5 (less than 1), and our pizza maker faces inelastic demand. When demand is inelastic, price and revenue changes are in the same direction; that is, increases in price result in increases in total revenue while decreases in price result in decreases in total revenue. With inelastic demand, the demand curve shown in Figure 12.4 becomes more vertical. Generally, the demand for necessities is inelastic. Even large price increases do not cause us to buy less food or to give up our telephone (though we may switch to a lower-priced alternative).

If demand is price inelastic, can marketers keep raising prices so that revenues and profits will grow larger and larger? And what if demand is elastic? Does it mean that marketers can never raise prices? The answer to these questions is no. Elasticity of demand for a product often differs for different price levels and with different percentages of change.

As a general rule, pizza makers and other companies can determine the *actual* price elasticity only after they have tested a pricing decision and calculated the resulting demand. Only then will they know whether a specific price change will increase or decrease revenues. To estimate what demand is likely to be at different prices for new or existing products, marketers often do research.

One approach is to conduct a study in which consumers tell marketers how much of a product they would be willing to buy at different prices. For example, researchers might ask participants if they would rent more movies if the price were reduced from $4.00 to $3.00, or how many bags of their favorite chocolate chip cookies they would buy at $3.00, $4.00, or $5.00. At other times, researchers conduct *field studies* in which they vary the price of a product in different stores and measure how much is actually purchased at the different price levels.

Procter & Gamble once learned about price elasticity the hard way when it launched a price war for its disposable diapers. The strategy was to grow market share for Luvs, P&G's lower-priced brand that it had repositioned as a middle-price, no-frills brand. P&G wanted to stem the growth of private-label disposable diapers. It succeeded, but in the process Luvs also cut into sales of P&G's premium brand, Pampers.[7] Because of the sensitivity of customers to price changes—that is, the elasticity of demand—firms such as P&G that have more than one item in a product line must be careful that pricing strategies don't cannibalize sales of other company products.

Influences on Price Elasticity of Demand
Other factors can affect price elasticity and sales. Consider the availability of *substitute* goods or services. If a product has a close substitute, its demand will be elastic; that is, a change in price will result in a change in demand, as consumers move to buy the substitute product. For example, Coke and Pepsi may be considered

close substitutes by all but the most die-hard cola fans. If the price of Pepsi goes up, many people will buy Coke instead. Marketers of products with close substitutes are less likely to compete on price, recognizing that doing so could result in less profit as consumers switch from one brand to another.

Price elasticity also depends on the time period marketers are considering. Demand that is inelastic in the short term may become elastic in the long term. In general, the longer the time period, the greater the likelihood that demand will be more elastic. Here again, the role of substitutes matters because longer time periods make it possible for substitutes to enter the market. If the price of oil increases, there may not be much immediate change in the quantity demanded. However, in the long term, demand will build for alternative home-heating fuels such as gas, electric, and solar power. Utilities may build more electric power plants, and auto manufacturers will develop viable electric cars such as the Prius model.

There is also an **income effect** on demand. This means changes in income affect demand for a product, even if its price remains the same. For products such as clothing and housing (which economists call **normal goods**) and for luxury goods demand is *income elastic*, meaning that as income increases the amount purchased increases. For necessities such as salt, toilet tissue, and toothpaste, demand is *income inelastic* because changes in income do not have much impact on demand. Consumers can't do without these products. For some goods known as **inferior goods**, as income increases, demand decreases. For example, if in a period of economic recession household income decreases, there is likely to be an increase in sales of dried beans (an inexpensive source of protein) while the number of steaks consumed goes down. But if the economy improves and incomes rise, consumers will be able to afford and demand steaks instead of beans.

income effect ■ The effect of changes in income on demand for a product, even if its price remains the same.

normal goods ■ Products for which demand increases as income increases.

inferior goods ■ Products for which demand decreases as income increases.

The gasoline/electric hybrid Prius. It drives efficiently even when you don't. It combines a super-efficient gas engine with an advanced electric motor that never needs to be plugged in. It idles less, so it wastes less energy. It even comes with available GPS navigation. All of which makes Prius a more intelligent way to drive. So you can concentrate on other things.

GET THE FEELING. TOYOTA.
toyota.com/prius

52/45 MPG¹ PRIUS | genius

¹All figures based on 2001 EPA estimates. City/hwy MPG. Actual results may vary. SULEV-certified for California and some Northeastern states. ULEV-certified for the rest of the country. For more information, please see www.arb.ca.gov ©2001 Toyota Motor Sales, U.S.A., Inc.

In the short run the demand for gasoline is inelastic. In the long term, though, introduction of automobiles such as the Prius that runs on electricity may change that.

Finally, the changes in prices of other products affect the demand for an item, a phenomenon called **cross-elasticity of demand**. When products are substitutes for each other, as we've seen, an increase in the price of one will increase the demand for the other. For example, if the price of bananas goes up, consumers may instead buy more strawberries, blueberries, or apples. However, when products are complements—that is, when one product is essential to the use of a second—then an increase in the price of one decreases the demand for the second. For example, if the price of gasoline goes up, consumers may drive less and, thus, demand for tires will also decrease.

Determining Cost

Estimating demand helps marketers develop possible prices to charge for a product. It tells them how much they think they'll be able to sell at different prices. Knowing this brings them to the third step in determining a product's price—making sure the price will cover costs. Before marketers can determine price, they must understand the relationship of cost, demand, and revenue for their product.

In this next section we'll talk about different types of costs that marketers must consider in pricing. Then we'll show two types of analyses that marketers use in making pricing decisions.

TYPES OF COSTS

Here's a revelation: The cost of a product is important in determining what to charge for it. If a firm prices a product lower than the cost to produce it, it doesn't take a rocket scientist to figure out that it will lose money. How much the price exceeds the cost determines the amount of profit the firm may earn, everything else being equal. Before looking at how costs influence pricing decisions, it is necessary to understand the different types of costs that firms incur. If a college student wants to build a bookcase in her dorm, the only costs would be for the lumber, nails, and paint. If after graduation she decides to make a business of producing and selling bookcases, this young entrepreneur would have to worry about other costs such as renting a factory, hiring employees, and paying for utilities, insurance, and so on. Let's consider how these costs affect pricing decisions.

Variable Costs First, a firm incurs **variable costs** in producing a product. Variable costs are the per-unit costs of production that will fluctuate depending on how many units or individual products a firm produces. If it takes 25 cents' worth of nails—a variable cost—to build one bookcase, it will take 50 cents' worth for two, 75 cents' worth for three, and so on. For the production of bookcases, variable costs would also include the cost of lumber and paint, and there would also be the cost of factory workers (unless you get your roommates to work for free).

Table 12.4 shows some examples of the variable cost per unit or average variable cost and the total variable costs at different levels of production (for producing 100, 200, and 500 bookcases). If the firm produces 100 bookcases, the average variable cost per unit is $50.00 and the total variable cost is $5,000 ($50.00 × 100). If production is doubled to 200 units, the total variable cost now is $10,000 ($50.00 × 200).

In reality, calculating variable costs is usually more complex than what we've shown here. As the number of bookcases the factory produces increases or decreases, average variable costs may change. For example, if the company buys just enough lumber for one bookcase, the lumberyard will charge top dollar. If it buys enough for 100 bookcases, it'll get a better deal. And if it buys enough for thousands of bookcases, it may cut variable costs even more. Even the cost of labor goes down with increased production as manufacturers are likely to invest in labor-saving equipment that allows workers to produce bookcases faster. Table 12.4 shows this to be the case. By purchasing wood, nails, and paint at a lower price (because of a volume discount) and by providing a means for workers to build bookcases more quickly, the cost per unit of producing 500 bookcases is reduced to $40.00 each.

TABLE 12.4

Variable Costs at Different Levels of Production

Variable Costs for Producing 100 Bookcases		Variable Costs for Producing 200 Bookcases		Variable Costs for Producing 500 Bookcases	
Wood	$13.25	Wood	$13.25	Wood	$9.40
Nails	0.25	Nails	0.25	Nails	0.20
Paint	0.50	Paint	0.50	Paint	0.40
Labor (3 hours × $12.00 hr)	$36.00	Labor (3 hours × $12.00 hr)	$36.00	Labor (2½ hrs × $12.00 hr)	$30.00
Cost per unit	$50.00	Cost per unit	$50.00	Cost per unit	$40.00
Multiply by number of units	100	Multiply by number of units	200	Multiply by number of units	500
Cost for 100 units:	$5,000	Cost for 200 units:	$10,000	Cost for 500 units:	$20,000

One bookcase = one unit.

Of course, variable costs don't always go down with higher levels of production. Using the bookcase example, at some point the demand for the labor, lumber, or nails required to produce the bookcases may exceed the supply. The bookcase manufacturer may have to pay employees overtime to keep up with production. The manufacturer may have to buy additional lumber from a distant supplier that will charge more to cover the costs of shipping. The cost per bookcase rises. You get the picture.

fixed costs ■ Costs of production that do not change with the number of units produced.

Fixed Costs   **Fixed costs** are costs that do *not* vary with the number of units produced—the costs that remain the same whether the firm produces 1,000 bookcases this month or only 10. Fixed costs include rent or the cost of owning and maintaining the factory, utilities to heat or cool the factory, and the costs of equipment such as hammers, saws, planers, and paint sprayers used in the production of the product. The salaries of a firm's executives and marketing managers (such as John Chillingworth at Aithent) also are fixed costs. All these costs are constant no matter how many items are manufactured.

Average fixed cost is the fixed cost per unit produced, that is, the total fixed costs divided by the number of units (bookcases) produced. Although total fixed costs remain the same no matter how many units are produced, the average fixed cost will decrease as the number of units produced increases. Say, for example, that a firm's total fixed costs of production are $30,000. If the firm produces one unit, the total $30,000 is applied to the one unit. If it produces two units, $15,000 or one-half of the fixed costs is applied to each unit and so on. As we produce more and more units, average fixed costs go down and so does the price we must charge to cover fixed costs.

Of course, like variable costs, in the long term total fixed costs may change. The firm may find that it can sell more of a product than it has manufacturing capacity to produce, so it builds a new factory, its executives' salaries go up, and more money goes into manufacturing equipment.

Combining variable costs and fixed costs yields **total costs** for a given level of production. As a company produces more and more of a product, both average fixed costs and average variable costs may decrease. Average total costs may decrease, too, up to a point. As we said, as output continues to increase, average variable costs may start to increase. These variable costs ultimately rise faster than average fixed costs decline, resulting in an increase to average total costs. As total costs fluctuate with differing levels of production, the price that producers have to charge to cover those costs changes accordingly. Therefore, marketers need to calculate the minimum price necessary to cover all costs—the break-even price.

4 Bookmark It!

Arrange to interview someone who works for the financial planning division of your school's administration. What are the fixed costs for your school? What are the variable costs?

average fixed cost ■ The fixed cost per unit produced.

total costs ■ The total of the fixed costs and the variable costs for a set number of units produced.

BREAK-EVEN ANALYSIS

Break-even analysis is a technique marketers use to examine the relationship between cost and price and to determine what sales volume must be reached at a given price before the company will completely cover its total costs and past which it will begin making a profit. Simply put, the break-even point is the point at which the company doesn't lose any money

break-even analysis ■ A method for determining the number of units that a firm must produce and sell at a given price to cover all its costs.

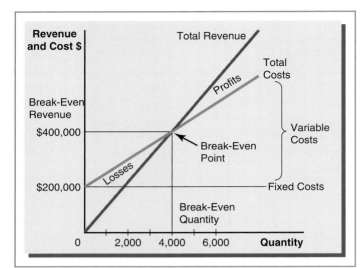

FIGURE 12.5

Break-Even Analysis

Using break-even analysis, marketers can determine what sales volume to reach before the company makes a profit. This company needs to sell 4,000 bookcases at $100 each to break even.

and doesn't make any profit. All costs are covered, but there isn't a penny extra. A break-even analysis allows marketers to identify how many units of a product they will have to sell at a given price to be profitable.

Figure 12.5 uses our bookcase manufacturing example to demonstrate break-even analysis. The vertical axis represents the amount of costs and revenue in dollars, and the horizontal axis shows the quantity of goods produced and sold. In this break-even model, we assume that there is a given total fixed cost and that variable costs do not change with the quantity produced.

In this example, let's say that the total fixed costs (the costs for the factory, the equipment, and electricity) are $200,000 and that the average variable costs (for materials and labor) are constant. The figure shows the total costs (variable costs plus fixed costs) and total revenues if varying quantities are produced and sold. The point at which the total revenue and total costs lines intersect is the **break-even point**. If sales are above the break-even point, the company makes a profit. Below that point, the firm will suffer a loss.

break-even point ■ The point at which the total revenue and total costs are equal and beyond which the company makes a profit; below that point, the firm will suffer a loss.

contribution per unit ■ The difference between the price the firm charges for a product and the variable costs.

To determine the break-even point, the firm first needs to calculate the **contribution per unit**, or the difference between the price the firm charges for a product (the revenue per unit) and the variable costs. This figure is the amount the firm has after paying for the wood, nails, paint, and labor to contribute to meeting the fixed costs of production. For our example, we will assume that the firm sells its bookcases for $100 each. Using the variable costs of $50 per unit that we had before, contribution per unit is $100 − $50 = $50. Using the fixed cost for the bookcase manufacturing of $200,000, we can now calculate the firm's break-even point in units of the product.

$$\text{Break-even point (in units)} = \frac{\text{total fixed costs}}{\text{contribution per unit to fixed costs}}$$

$$\text{Break-even point (in units)} = \frac{\$200,000}{\$50} = 4,000 \text{ units}$$

We see that the firm must sell 4,000 bookcases at $100 each to meet its fixed costs and to break even. We can also calculate the break-even point in dollars. This shows us that to break even, the company must sell $400,000 worth of bookcases.

$$\text{Break-even point (in dollars)} = \frac{\text{total fixed costs}}{1 - \dfrac{\text{variable cost per unit}}{\text{price}}}$$

$$\text{Break-even point (in dollars)} = \frac{\$200,000}{1 - \dfrac{\$50}{\$100}} = \frac{\$200,000}{1 - 0.5} = \frac{\$200,000}{0.5} = \$400,000$$

After the firm's sales have met and passed the break-even point, it begins to make a profit. How much profit? If the firm sells 4,001 bookcases, it will make a profit of $50. If it sells 5,000 bookcases, the profit would be calculated as follows:

Profit = quantity above break-even point × contribution margin
     = 1,000 × 50,
     = $50,000

Often a firm will set a *profit goal*, which is the dollar profit figure it desires to earn. The break-even point may be calculated with that dollar goal included in the figures. In this case, it is not really a "break-even" point we are calculating because we're seeking profits. It's more of a "target amount." If our bookcase manufacturer feels it is necessary to realize a profit of $50,000, his calculations would be as follows:

$$\frac{\text{Break-even point}}{\text{(in units with target amount included)}} = \frac{\text{total fixed costs} + \text{target profit}}{\text{contribution per unit to fixed costs}}$$

$$\text{Break-even point (in units)} = \frac{\$200,000 + \$50,000}{\$50} = 5,000 \text{ units}$$

Sometimes the target return or profit goal is expressed as a *percentage of sales*. For example, a firm may say that it wants to make a profit of at least 10 percent on sales. In such cases, this profit is added to the variable cost in calculating the break-even point. In our example, the company would want to earn 10 percent of the selling price of the bookcase, or $10\% \times \$100 = \$10$ per unit. We would simply add this $10 to the variable costs of $50 and calculate the new target amount as we calculated the break-even point before. The contribution per unit becomes:

Contribution per unit = selling price − (variable costs + target profit)
         = $100 − ($50 + $10) = $40

$$\text{Break-even point (in units)} = \frac{\text{total fixed costs}}{\text{contribution per unit to fixed costs}}$$

$$\text{Break-even point (in units)} = \frac{\$200,000}{\$40} = 5,000 \text{ units}$$

Break-even analysis does not provide an easy answer for pricing decisions. It provides answers about how many units the firm must sell to break even and to make a profit but, without knowing whether demand will equal that quantity at that price, companies can make big mistakes. It is, therefore, useful for marketers to estimate the demand for their product and then perform a marginal analysis.

MARGINAL ANALYSIS

Marginal analysis provides a way for marketers to look at cost and demand at the same time. Specifically, it examines the relationship of **marginal cost** (the increase in total costs from producing one additional unit of a product) to **marginal revenue** (the increase in total income or revenue that results from selling one additional unit of a product). Marginal analysis allows marketers to identify the output and the price that will generate the maximum profit.

Figure 12.6 provides a look at the various cost and revenue elements considered in marginal analysis. Like Figure 12.5, the vertical axis in Figure 12.6 represents the cost and revenues in dollars and the horizontal axis shows the quantity produced and sold. Figure 12.6 shows the average revenue, average cost, marginal revenue, and marginal cost curves. Note that the average revenue curve is also the demand curve.

Table 12.5 presents the data that might result from a marginal analysis that considers profits at different price levels. If only one unit is produced, the average total cost per unit is the same as the marginal cost per unit. However, after the first unit, the cost of *producing each additional unit* (marginal cost) at first decreases and then increases in response to the decrease and subsequent increase in total costs discussed in our bookcase example earlier in this chapter.

As the price of a product goes down, the amount that will be sold (demand) increases (assuming that demand does not track the prestige product curve discussed earlier). Thus, total revenues increase even though prices decrease. Notice, however, that the amount of added revenue for each

marginal analysis ■ A method that uses cost and demand to identify the price that will maximize profits.

marginal cost ■ The increase in total cost that results from producing one additional unit of a product.

marginal revenue ■ The increase in total revenue (income) that results from producing and selling one additional unit of a product.

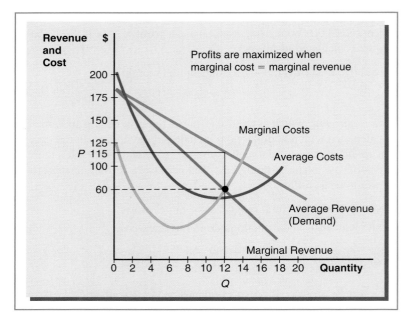

FIGURE 12.6

Marginal Analysis

Marginal analysis allows marketers to consider both costs and demand in calculating a price that maximizes profits.

additional unit sold (marginal revenue) decreases at each lower price level. If the price drops far enough, total revenue would start to fall.

Profit is maximized at the point at which marginal cost is *exactly* equal to marginal revenue. To find the selling price at which profit will be maximized, look in Table 12.5 to see the point at which marginal cost equals marginal revenue. In this example both marginal cost and marginal revenue are $60 at the 12-unit level. Based on the demand in this example, the firm will sell 12 units if the price per unit is set at $115. Given these costs and this demand, the firm

TABLE 12.5

Profit Maximization with Marginal Analysis

1	2	3	4	5	6	7	8	9	10	11
Quantity (Q)	Total Fixed Costs	Total Variable Costs	Average Variable Cost (3) / (1)	Total Cost (2) + (3)	Average Total Cost (5) / (1)	Marginal Cost	Price	Total Revenue (1) × (8)	Marginal Revenue	Total Profit (9) − (5)
0	$300	$ 0	$ 0	$ 300	—					
1	300	170	170	470	$470	$470	$170	$ 170	$170	−$300
2	300	282	141	582	291	112	165	330	160	−252
3	300	348	116	648	216	66	160	480	150	−168
4	300	396	99	696	174	48	155	620	140	−76
5	300	425	85	725	145	29	150	750	130	25
6	300	438	73	738	123	13	145	870	120	132
7	300	441	63	741	106	3	140	980	110	239
8	300	448	56	748	94	7	135	1,080	100	332
9	300	468	52	768	85	20	130	1,170	90	402
10	300	500	50	800	80	32	125	1,250	80	450
11	300	528	48	828	75	28	120	1,320	70	492
12	300	588	49	888	74	60	115	1,380	60	492
13	300	689	53	989	76	101	110	1,430	50	441
14	300	938	67	1,238	88	249	105	1,470	40	232
15	300	1,200	80	1,500	100	262	100	1,500	30	0

will maximize profits at that point. If the firm continues to lower the price, more units of the product will be sold, but total profits will decrease.

One word of caution in using marginal analysis: Although the procedure is straightforward, in the real world things seldom are. Production costs may vary unexpectedly due to shortages, inclement weather, unexpected equipment repairs, and so on. Revenues may also unexpectedly move up and down due to the economy, what the competition is doing, or a host of other reasons. Predicting demand, an important factor in marginal analysis, is never an exact science. This makes marginal analysis a less than perfect way to determine the best price for a product. Indeed, it is theoretically more sound than break-even analysis, but most firms find the break-even approach more useful.

Evaluating the Pricing Environment

In addition to demand and costs, marketers look at factors in the firm's external environment when they are making pricing decisions. Thus, our fourth step in developing pricing strategies is to examine and evaluate the pricing environment. Whether they are pricing a pair of Levi jeans, that expensive Rolex watch, or Aithent's software, marketers need to understand what's going on in the marketplace. Only then can marketers develop pricing that not only covers costs but also provides a competitive advantage—pricing that meets the needs of customers better than the competition. This section will discuss some important external influences on pricing strategies—the economic environment, competition, consumer trends, and some unique aspects of international trade.

THE ECONOMY

Economic trends tend to direct pricing strategies. The business cycle, inflation, economic growth, and consumer confidence all help to determine whether one pricing strategy or another will succeed. But the upswings and downturns in a national economy do not affect all product categories or all regions equally. Marketers need to understand how economic trends will affect their particular business.

Trimming the Fat: Pricing in a Recession During recessions, consumers grow more price sensitive. They switch to generic brands to get a better price and patronize discount stores and warehouse outlets. Even wealthy households, relatively unaffected by the recession, tend to cut back on conspicuous consumption—if for no other reason than to avoid calling attention to themselves. As a result, during periods of recession, many firms find it necessary to cut prices to levels at which costs are covered but the company doesn't make a profit to keep factories in operation. Unfortunately, price sensitivity tends to persist for a time even when a recession ends as it takes a while for consumers to gain confidence in the improved economic environment.[8] During such periods, marketers need to consider what pricing policies will be helpful in regaining prerecession sales and profit levels.

Many people of diverse backgrounds benefited from the explosive gains of the stock market in the late 1990s, to the point where stereotypes of rich people no longer held. One study defined the typical millionaire (note that wealth is measured in terms of assets as well as annual salary) as a 57-year-old man who is self-employed, earns a median household income of $131,000, has been married to the same wife for most of his adult life, has children, has never spent more than $399 on a suit or more than $140 for a pair of shoes, and drives a Ford Explorer.[9] So much for living large . . . so much for the booming stock market, too.

Recession had a great impact on Japanese consumers in the early 1990s. Unlike consumers in the United States, the Japanese were used to paying high prices all the time to satisfy an inefficient, multilayered distribution system. However, the early 1990s' recession opened the door to discount retailing. Specialty retailers bought directly from manufacturers and were able to sell goods at least a third below department stores. The trend has since gained momentum and bargain-hunting is a consumer sport in Japan.[10]

Men's women's & children's fashion & designer clothing 40-75% off every day. Located in New York City: Manhasset, NY; Paramus, Elizabeth, East Hanover and Wayne, NJ; Philadelphia; Potomac Mills Mall, Virginia. **DAFFY'S**

When the economy is hurting, consumers are more interested in paying lower prices—and they're more skeptical about high-priced status symbols.

Increasing Prices: Responding to Inflation   There are also some economic trends that allow firms to increase prices, altering what consumers see as an acceptable or unacceptable price range for a product. Inflation may give marketers causes to either increase or decrease prices. First, inflation gets customers used to price increases. They may remain insensitive to price increases, even when inflation goes away, allowing marketers to make real price increases, not just those that adjust for the inflation. Of course, during periods of inflation, consumers may grow fearful of the future and worry about whether or not they will have enough money to meet basic needs. In such a case, they may cut back on purchases. Then, as in periods of recession, inflation may cause marketers to lower prices and temporarily sacrifice profits in order to maintain sales levels.

THE COMPETITION

Marketers try to anticipate how the competition will respond to their pricing actions. They know that consumers' expectations of what constitutes a fair price depends on what the competition is charging. Marriott, for example, monitors the room rates of other hotel chains such as Hilton and Hyatt.

In the cutthroat fast-food industry, when Burger King trotted out its 99-cent Whopper, McDonald's retaliated with a 55-cent Big Mac, and third-place Wendy's increased promotion of its 99-cent chicken nuggets and Double-Stack cheeseburgers.[11] It's not always a good idea to fight the competition with lower and lower prices. Pricing wars such as those in the fast-food industry can change consumers' perceptions of what is a "fair" price, leaving them unwilling to buy at previous price levels.

In addition, when firms focus on price competition, they often ignore the need to satisfy other customer wants. For instance, many consumers have become dissatisfied with traditional burgers at any price and are looking for restaurants that offer better-tasting meals. To be successful, marketers must continuously monitor consumer preferences and adjust not only pricing strategies but also product strategies to maintain a competitive advantage—to provide the benefit consumers want at a price they are willing to pay, and do it better than the competition.

The type of competitive environment in which an industry operates—that is, whether it's an oligopoly, monopolistic competition, or pure competition—also influences price decisions.

Generally, firms that do business in an oligopoly (in which the market has few sellers and many buyers) are more likely to adopt *status quo* pricing objectives in which the pricing of all competitors is similar. Such objectives are attractive to oligopolistic firms because avoiding price competition allows all players in the industry to remain profitable. The American beer industry is largely an oligopoly in which a few firms, such as brewing giant Anheuser-Busch, control most of the market.

In a state of monopolistic competition, in which there are a lot of sellers each offering a slightly different product, it is possible for firms to differentiate products and to focus on non-price competition. A shopper can buy Bloomingdale's private-label brand of sweaters only at Bloomingdale's, and competitors such as Macy's or Bergdorf Goodman offer their own sweaters. The sweaters are not national brands and are not 100 percent comparable, so consumers are likely to choose which sweater to purchase by considering nonprice factors such as color or style. Therefore, each firm prices its sweater on the basis of its cost without much concern for matching the exact price of competitors' sweaters.

As we discussed in Chapter 3, firms in a purely competitive market have little opportunity to raise or lower prices. Rather, the price of soybeans, corn, or fresh peaches is directly influenced by supply and demand. When bad weather hurts crops, prices go up. And prices for almost any kind of fish have increased dramatically since health-conscious consumers began turning away from beef and other red meat.

CONSUMER TRENDS

Another environmental influence on price is consumer trends. Culture and demographics determine how consumers think and behave and so have a large impact on all marketing decisions. For example, many consumers have grown disinterested in fancy stores with big markups. Marketers of everything from autos to suits are scrambling to find ways to offer value

5 *Bookmark It!*

When companies get into price wars, what are the benefits and hazards for the companies? What are the benefits and hazards for consumers?

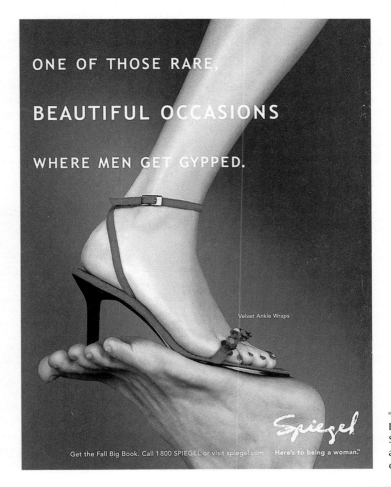

ONE OF THOSE RARE, BEAUTIFUL OCCASIONS WHERE MEN GET GYPPED.

Velvet Ankle Wraps

Spiegel

Get the Fall Big Book. Call 1 800 SPIEGEL or visit spiegel.com   Here's to being a woman.™

Like many other retailers, Spiegel sells unique products and styles that no other retailers offer.

and build bonds with customers who are weary of glitzy promotions and overpriced merchandise. Instead, chic discount is in. Think about Target stores: Referred to as "tar-jay" by its many fans, it is a Kmart for yuppies. Target's bright red bull's eye logo has become a fashion statement for affordable chic.[12]

Still many people are willing to drop large amounts of money for things they consider to be important. Take, for example, the buying habits of the women who opted for a career in their twenties but who are hearing the ticking of their biological clocks as they enter their late thirties and forties. The couples having babies later in their lives are often better off financially than younger parents, and they are far more willing to spend whatever it costs to give their babies the best. For producers of products for babies and children, this means that price resistance is rather low within the group. Such parents have no problem spending $50 or more for a Beatrix Potter musical crib mobile and don't even flinch at the $75 price tag on a Wedgwood china Peter Rabbit Christmas cereal bowl and mug.

Real People, Real Choices: How It Worked Out at Aithent

John chose option 1. Aithent developed the entire risk management software system called FPI (Fraud Prevention and Investigation). As luck would have it, Aithent showed Bank of Boston a prototype of this new system at a meeting. This bank had an immediate need for such a system and bought it even before Aithent presented it to Chase.

Aithent is now developing a Web-based version of this product. Because users can maintain and update the software anywhere, anytime across the globe, fraud investigations can be closed quickly and investigators can work on the same case even though they are based in different locations. FPI has taken off and has now been established as a specific business division within Aithent. John was designated as the brand champion of the FPI system and he now oversees a team of developers dedicated exclusively to expanding on the FPI brand. Then there was the icing on the cake: Chase bought the software system as well. The bank was very pleased with Aithent's efforts and impressed that Aithent took the step to develop the prototype for Chase. The solution is now in use at JP Morgan/Chase Manhattan. John's success with this new software product illustrates the importance of understanding the value of a product or service. Monetary price is only part of the value equation; figuring out how much time, effort, and "brain power" are required to create something clients will value is no easy task—even for computer whizzes.

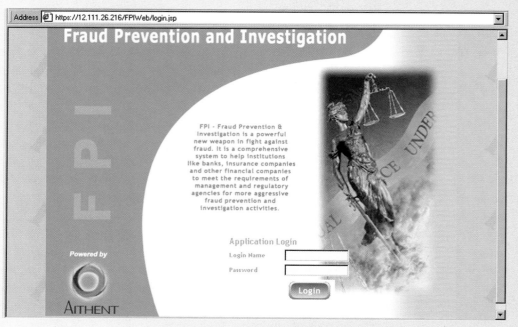

This trend is even more pronounced in China. In a land where one-child families are the rule, Chinese parents spare few expenses when bringing up baby. They want to show off their pampered child and are eager to surround their "little emperors and empresses" with status goods. To meet this need, foreign companies are rushing in, hawking the staples of Western baby care from disposable diapers to Disney crib sheets. These items are expensive luxuries in China, and plenty of families are splurging. Chinese families spend one-third to one-half of their disposable income on their children, according to industry estimates.[13]

INTERNATIONAL ENVIRONMENTAL INFLUENCES

Firms conducting international trade need to monitor the currency exchange rates when making pricing decisions. In quite a number of countries, the exchange rate may differ as much as 100 percent in only a year or two. If products are priced in terms of local currency but the product or its components are being imported, any profit can quickly be eaten up by the exchange rate changes so that the foreign firm is making no profit or may even be losing money. This is especially hazardous in industries in which long-term contracts are the norm.

National or local government policies may lead to differences in the prices companies charge for products in different countries. Government **price subsidies** to domestic industries, either in the form of an outright payment or as tax relief, allow some firms to sell their products at prices often below production costs.

For example, the American company Boeing competes directly with Europe's Airbus. Because airplane manufacturing is considered such an important industry to both the economy and the defense of Europe, the governments of Great Britain, France, Germany, and Spain offer subsidies to their domestic manufacturers. On one occasion, Boeing's costs were actually 18 percent less than Airbus's actual costs on a 50-plane deal, but subsidies wiped out Boeing's advantage, causing it to lose the business.[14] Minor U.S. subsidies to Boeing weren't enough to make a difference.

price subsidies ▪
Government payments made to protect domestic businesses or to reimburse them when they must price at or below cost to make a sale. The subsidy can be a cash payment or tax relief.

Chapter Summary

1. **Explain the importance of pricing and how prices can take both monetary and nonmonetary forms.**

   Price, the amount of outlay of money, goods, services or deeds given in exchange for a product, may be monetary or nonmonetary. Bartering occurs when consumers or businesses exchange one product for another. Pricing is important to firms because it creates profits and influences customers to purchase or not. Pricing decisions are tied to decisions about the rest of the marketing mix. Prices must allow channel members to cover their costs and make a profit. For the product, price is an indicator of quality. Prices vary during stages in the product life cycle. Prices must cover the cost of promotions, and promotions must justify the product price.

2. **Understand the pricing objectives that marketers typically have in planning pricing strategies.**

   Effective pricing objectives are designed to support corporate and marketing objectives and are flexible. Pricing objectives often focus on sales (to maximize sales or to increase market share), or they may specify a desired level of profit growth or profit margin. At other times, firms may develop pricing objectives to compete effectively, to increase customer satisfaction, or to communicate a certain image to prospective customers. Pricing objectives need to be flexible to adapt to different geographic areas and time periods.

3. **Explain how customer demand influences pricing decisions.**

   For most products lower prices increase demand, but with some prestige products demand increases as price goes up. External influences or company efforts may create a shift in the demand curve. Price elasticity of demand is the sensitivity of customers to changing prices. With elastic demand, changes in price create large changes in demand, whereas when demand is inelastic, price increases have little effect on demand and total revenue increases.

4. Describe how marketers use costs, demands, and revenue to make pricing decisions.

Marketers often use break-even analysis and marginal analysis to help in deciding on the price for a product. Break-even analysis uses fixed and variable costs to identify how many units will have to be sold at a certain price in order to begin making a profit. Marginal analysis uses both costs and estimates of product demand to identify the price that will maximize profits. In marginal analysis profits are maximized at the point at which the revenue from producing one additional unit of a product equals the costs of producing the additional unit.

5. Understand some of the environmental factors that affect pricing strategies.

Like other elements of the marketing mix, pricing is influenced by a variety of external environmental factors. This includes economic trends such as inflation and recession, and the firm's competitive environment, that is, whether the firm does business in an oligopoly, a monopoly, or a more competitive environment. Pricing may also be influenced by changing consumer trends, by product production costs, and by differences in international market environments.

Chapter Review

■ MARKETING CONCEPTS:
TESTING YOUR KNOWLEDGE

1. What is price and why is it important to a firm? What are some examples of monetary and nonmonetary prices?
2. How are pricing decisions interrelated with other elements of the marketing mix?
3. What are some of the more commonly used pricing objectives?
4. How is demand influenced by price? What is elastic demand? What is inelastic demand?
5. What external influences affect demand elasticity?
6. Explain variable costs, fixed costs, average variable costs, average fixed costs, and average total costs.
7. What is break-even analysis? How do marketers use break-even analysis?
8. What is marginal analysis? How do marketers use marginal analysis?
9. How does recession affect consumers' perceptions of prices? How does inflation influence perceptions of prices?
10. What are some consumer trends that affect pricing?

■ MARKETING CONCEPTS:
DISCUSSING CHOICES AND ISSUES

1. Governments sometimes provide price subsidies to specific industries; that is, they reduce a domestic firm's costs so that they can sell products on the international market at a lower price. What reasons do governments (and politicians) use for these government subsidies? What are the benefits and disadvantages to domestic industries in the long run? To international customers?

Who would benefit and who would lose if all price subsidies were eliminated?
2. Agricultural price supports are often hotly debated in Congress. Farmers say they can't get along without them. Opponents say that agricultural prices need to be left to the natural pressures of supply and demand. In what ways are price supports good for farmers? For consumers? For our country? What are some ways they hurt us? If you were in Congress, how do you think you would vote?
3. Critics of business often accuse marketers of taking advantage of consumers by setting prices that are far above the cost of producing the good or service—sometimes 10 or 20 or more times the cost. How do you feel about this? What reasons might a manufacturer of luxury products have for setting very high prices? Why might a pharmaceutical firm set the prices of its life-saving medicines higher than the cost of production?
4. Most firms use break-even analysis in examining their pricing structure. Is this a mistake? Why don't firms use marginal analysis, which also considers demand?
5. During times of inflation, consumers get used to price increases. Marketers sometimes take advantage of this to increase prices when their own costs do not increase. Is this an ethical action?

■ MARKETING PRACTICE:
APPLYING WHAT YOU'VE LEARNED

1. Assume you are the director of marketing for a firm that manufactures potato chips. You feel the time is right for your company to increase the price of its chips but you are concerned that increasing the price might not be profitable.

You feel you should examine the elasticity of demand. How would you go about doing this? What findings would lead you to increase the price? What findings would cause you to rethink the decision to increase prices?

2. Assume that you are the assistant director of marketing for a firm that manufactures a line of hair care products (shampoos, conditioners, etc.). This morning your boss came into your office and announced that she is going to recommend a dramatic price increase. You respond by saying, "Well, I guess that means we need to totally revamp our marketing plan." To this she replies, "No, all we're going to do is to raise the price. We're not going to mess with anything else."

After she leaves you think, "I've got to convince her that we can't make pricing decisions without considering the other elements of the marketing mix. It's all interrelated." In a role-playing situation with one of your classmates, explain to your boss why you think the marketing department should consider the implications of the price increase on the other marketing mix elements, what you feel these implications are, and what recommendations for change might be suggested.

3. Again, assume that you are the assistant director of marketing for a firm that manufactures a line of hair care products. This morning your boss came into your office and announced that she is going to recommend a dramatic price decrease. "If we decrease the price, we should be able to sell a lot more of our products and actually increase our total revenue and our bottom line as well."

You respond by asking, "That's true if indeed our demand is elastic. But do we know that? Demand for our product may be fairly inelastic." To this your boss replies, "Elastic-ballastic. What difference does it make? Everyone knows that if you cut prices you sell more and you make more money." After she leaves you think, "I've got to convince her that we have to know the effects of price changes on demand before we can make a move that could be a disaster."

Again, in a role-playing situation with one of your classmates, explain elastic and inelastic demand to your boss. Discuss your recommendations for measuring the elasticity of demand for your product.

4. Assume you and your friend have decided to go into business together manufacturing wrought iron birdcages. You know that your fixed costs (rent on a building, equipment, etc.) will be $60,000 a year. You expect your variable costs to be $12.00 per birdcage.

   a. If you plan on selling the birdcages to retail stores for $18.00, how many must you sell to break even; that is, what is your break-even quantity?

   b. Assume that you and your partner feel that you must set a goal of achieving a $20,000 profit with your business this year. How many units would you have to sell to make that amount of profit?

   c. What if you feel that you will be able to sell no more than 5,000 birdcages? What price will you

have to charge to break even? To make $30,000 in profit?

MARKETING MINI-PROJECT: LEARNING BY DOING

Organizations develop pricing strategies to meet pricing objectives. These objectives may be related to sales, profit, the competition, customer satisfaction, or the image of the product. The purpose of this mini-project is to help you understand how different pricing objectives are important in marketing planning.

1. First, with two or three of your classmates, arrange to visit the owner or manager of a business that many of your classmates patronize—a local restaurant, dry cleaner, bookstore, and so on. Talk with the business owner about his pricing.

   a. How does he determine what prices to charge?

   b. What costs go into his pricing?

   c. How does he know if he is charging enough, too much, or too little?

   d. How does demand affect his pricing strategy?

2. Next talk with students in your school to find out:

   a. What are students' attitudes toward the prices of the business you visited?

   b. What do they feel the business's costs are?

   c. How important are prices to them for the product of this business?

3. Develop a report that includes your findings and the recommendations you would make to the business. What pricing strategies do your findings seem to suggest? Present your results to your class.

REAL PEOPLE, REAL SURFERS: EXPLORING THE WEB

Barter exchanges are organizations that facilitate barter transactions between buyers and sellers. Many of these exchanges are members of the National Association of Trade Exchanges (NATE).

First, visit the NATE Web page at www.nate.org. Using links on that page to NATE member exchanges or an Internet search engine, locate and explore several barter exchange Web pages. Based on your Internet experience, answer the following questions:

1. What is NATE?

2. What are the benefits to a business of joining a barter exchange?

3. What types of products are bartered?

4. How does a trade actually work with a barter exchange?

5. How does the exchange make its money? Who pays the exchange and how much is charged?

6. Assuming the goal of barter exchange Web sites is to attract new members, evaluate the different Web sites you visited. Which Web site do you think was best? What features of the site would make you want to join if you were the owner of a small business? What features

of the other sites made them less appealing than this one?

PLAN IT!
DEVELOPING A MARKETING PLAN

As your instructor directs, create a marketing plan (using Marketing Plan Pro software or a written marketing plan format) to document your marketing decisions or answer these questions in a written or oral report.

The current marketing plan (see Appendix A) shows the wholesale prices that Computer Friendly Stuff charges resellers, along with its suggested retail prices for consumers.

1. What pricing objective(s) should CFS set for next year—and why?
2. What kind of demand curve do CFS products have, and how is demand likely to change if next year's economy is in deep recession?
3. What are some of the fixed and variable costs that CFS must monitor in determining possible product prices for next year?

Key Terms

MARKETING IN ACTION: CHAPTER 12 CASE

REAL CHOICES AT HALLMARK

Hallmark Cards, Inc., headquartered in Kansas City, Missouri, is the world's largest manufacturer of greeting cards, and it's been on top of the heap for a long time. It all began in 1910, when a teenager named Joyce C. Hall began a mail-order business selling picture postcards to retailers. Since then the company has grown to over $3 billion in annual sales. Hallmark publishes greeting cards in 30 languages and distributes them in over 100 countries. In total, Hallmark has 42 percent of the world's greeting card market. The company also sells other items including gift wrap, Christmas ornaments, jigsaw puzzles, and writing paper.

In the late 1990s, Hallmark's future was beginning to look less rosy. Consumers thought the price of greeting cards was too high. It was true that the price of greeting cards had increased substantially in recent years. But a lot of the increases were due to the fees both Hallmark and the other major greeting card company, American Greetings Corp., had to pay to get mass-market retailers such as Wal-Mart and Kmart to stock their cards. To make matters worse, although some consumers thought cards should cost less, a lot of people thought cards were too expensive at any price. In fact, the greeting card industry had experienced stagnant sales throughout the 1990s.

Growing competition posed another threat. Discount retailers such as Factory Card Outlet, a chain of nearly 200 party goods stores that sold its cards for 39 cents apiece, were making inroads into Hallmark's market share. And electronic and e-mail greetings, often sent for free, were growing in popularity.

To respond to these problems, Hallmark had already begun moderating the prices of its cards. Although the average price of a card had increased 8 percent in the mid 1990s, this figure had dropped to only 3 percent a few years thereafter. Many at Hallmark, however, felt that maintaining current pricing levels or even dropping the price of cards was not enough.

Although one solution for Hallmark might have been to lower the price of its cards, there were other alternatives. For example, advertising could either persuade consumers that Hallmark cards were worth the price or convince them that the current cards weren't really expensive. (Consumers, in general, think cards are about 50 percent higher in price than they are.) After all, 70 percent of Hallmark's cards were priced at less than $2. Or perhaps some other pricing strategy was best. As Hallmark designers were busy creating clever "Welcome to the new millennium" cards, marketing managers were looking for a way to make the new century better than Hallmark's first.

Source: Calmetta Y. Coleman, "Hallmark Spends Millions to Say Cards Are Inexpensive," *The Wall Street Journal Interactive Edition* (12 February 1998): http://interactive.wsj.com/; www.wal-mart.com/newsroom/hallmark.html; www.hallmark.com/.

THINGS TO THINK ABOUT

1. What is the decision facing Hallmark?
2. What factors are important in understanding this decision situation?
3. What are the alternatives?
4. What decision(s) do you recommend?
5. What are some ways to implement your recommendation(s)?

Bookmark It!

OBJECTIVES:

1. Understand key pricing strategies.
2. Explain pricing tactics for single and multiple products.
3. Understand the opportunities for Internet pricing strategies.
4. Describe the psychological aspects of pricing.
5. Understand the legal and ethical aspects of pricing.

Pricing Methods

Real People, Real Choices:

Meet Craig Lambert, a Decision Maker at Marriott International

www.marriott.com

CURRENT POSITION: Senior Vice President, Brand Management.

EDUCATION: Cornell University, School of Hotel Administration.

CAREER PATH: 25 years at Marriott as group sales manager, national sales manager, director of marketing for a 700-room Marriott property, and regional marketing and sales manager, overseeing hotels in the southeast United States, Mexico, and Latin America.

A MISTAKE I WISH I HADN'T MADE: Not being a general manager of a Marriott hotel. This prevented me from qualifying as a "business general manager" versus a marketing or brand expert only.

BUSINESS BOOK I'M READING NOW: Frederich Reichheld's <u>Loyalty Rules</u>.

HERO: Bill Marriott, who has guided Marriott International into the twenty-first century.

MOTTO: "Make a contribution or get out of the way."

PET PEEVE: Big egos. They can sink businesses.

Filling Beds with Heads

Marriott's Courtyard is positioned to offer value to "road warriors" who want more than an economy hotel offers but aren't willing to buy luxury. This division is a billion-dollar-plus business for Marriott, with over 400 hotels in eight countries.

Courtyard was feeling growing pains in the early 1990s. Hotels in many U.S. markets were suffering low occupancy rates after extensive overbuilding during the 1980s. To make matters worse, businesses were spending less on travel in response to a soft economy and anxiety from the Gulf War. Courtyard had just opened 50 new properties and found itself competing with traditional full-service, high-quality hotels that were drastically lowering their rates to fill rooms. Craig soon saw a need to change Courtyard's pricing strategy.

Traditionally, hotels use a top-down pricing strategy in which they quote their highest price first and then reduce the rate when the prospect balks. On average, 8 percent to 15 percent of hotel guests pay the full regular rate, called the rack rate. In fact, most hotels have a rate spread ranging up to 50 percent. But, believing Courtyard's business guests wanted fair value, Craig wondered if the top-down approach was the best way to give it to them. He considered his options:

Option 1: Quote the best price first.

Abandon top-down pricing and instead adopt a bottom-up strategy where the "best" price is quoted up-front. Some customers told Craig that instead of asking for a break on the rack rates, they would shop around for better rates elsewhere. Some customers said they felt that Courtyard was overpriced when they were given the rack rate. However, for a bottom-up strategy to work, Courtyard had to reduce the depth of discounting it offered over all to pare revenues lost from abandoning the rack rate altogether. This strategy might backfire if more customers did not book at the new "regular" rate.

Option 2: Wait out the storm.

Keep the top-down pricing strategy and wait. If a hotel lowers its price too much, it runs the risk of eroding its overall standing and being perceived as an "economy" facility/establishment. Losing even more customers to full-service hotels, Courtyard would risk long-term growth potential—and upper Marriott management would not look favorably on its Courtyard division.

Option 3: Lower the fall-back price.

Keep the top-down pricing strategy but lower the fall-back price quote further to capture more guests who are bargain-hunters. In particular, be prepared to offer deeper discounts to high-volume corporate accounts to gain a greater share of their business and replace customers who were being lost to upscale hotels that also were discounting. The risk is a loss of total revenue—unless occupancy increased enough to offset levels of discounting.

Now, join the Marriott Courtyard decision team: Which option would you choose, and why?

Price Planning: Move and Countermove

For both general guests and corporate travelers, the selection of a hotel depends very much on price. That's why Craig Lambert and other Marriott divisional managers look constantly for ways to improve their pricing strategies. But pricing is a bit like a chess game where one move influences the next.

An old Russian proverb says: "There are two kinds of fools in any market. One doesn't charge enough. The other charges too much."[1] In modern business, there seldom is any one-and-only, now-and-forever, best pricing strategy. Pricing practices, with their moves and countermoves, like good chess, require thinking two and three moves ahead. No pricing decision is set in stone—costs increase, sales decline, the competition changes its prices. This chapter will look at how companies develop and manage pricing strategies, and it will examine specific tactics that put pricing strategies into play. We conclude by examining the psychological and ethical issues in pricing strategies.

You will recall that in Chapter 12 we learned about the first four steps in price planning (refresh your memory with Figure 12.1 if you need to). Marketers first develop pricing objectives in line with overall corporate and marketing objectives. Next, they examine demand, costs, and the pricing environment before moving on to our fifth step in price planning—choosing a pricing strategy.

1. Develop Pricing Objectives
2. Estimate Demand
3. Determine Costs
4. Evaluate the Pricing Environment
5. Choose a Pricing Strategy
6. Develop Pricing Tactics

Some strategies work for certain products, with certain customer groups, in certain competitive markets. When is it best for the firm to undercut the competition and when to just meet the competition's prices? When is the best pricing strategy one that covers costs only, and when is it best to use one based on demand?

Marketers who need to develop pricing strategies will consider many alternatives and try to anticipate their outcomes. The break-even analysis and marginal analysis procedures explained in Chapter 12 almost always figure into this process.

In large firms, pricing analysts may conduct research to estimate demand and demand elasticity. Using costs and demand data, they estimate the revenues and profits that are likely to result.

PRICING STRATEGIES BASED ON COST

Marketing planners often choose cost-based strategies because they are simple to calculate and relatively risk free. They promise that the price will at least cover the costs the company incurs in producing and marketing the product.

Cost-based pricing methods have drawbacks, however. They do not consider such factors as the nature of the target market, demand, competition, the product life cycle, and the product's image. Moreover, although the calculations for setting the price may be simple and straightforward, accurate cost estimating may prove difficult. Think about firms such as 3M, General Electric, Texas Instruments, and Nabisco, all of which produce many products. How does cost analysis allocate the costs for the plant, research and development, equipment, design engineers, maintenance, and marketing personnel so that the pricing plan accurately reflects the cost of producing any one product? For example, how do you allocate the salary of a marketing executive who deals with many different products? Should the cost be divided equally among all products? Should costs be based on the actual number of hours spent working on each product? Or should costs be assigned based on the revenues generated by each product? Answer? There is no one right answer. Even within these limitations, cost-based pricing strategies are often a marketer's best choice.

Cost-Plus Pricing   The most common cost-based approach to pricing a product is **cost-plus pricing** in which a marketer figures all costs for the product and then adds an amount to cover profit and, in some cases, any costs of doing business that are not assigned to specific products.

The most frequently used type of cost-plus pricing is *straight markup pricing*. The price is calculated by adding a predetermined percentage to the cost. Most retailers and wholesalers use markup pricing exclusively because of its simplicity—users need only estimate the unit cost and add the markup.

The first step requires that the unit cost be easy to estimate accurately and that production rates are fairly consistent. For this and the other examples, we will consider how a small manufacturer and a retailer price a line of jeans. As Table 13.1 shows, we will assume the jeans manufacturer has fixed costs (the cost of the factory, advertising, managers' salaries, etc.) of $2,000,000. The variable cost per pair of jeans (the cost of fabric, zipper, thread, and labor) is $20.00. With the current plant, the firm can produce a total of 400,000 pairs of jeans, so the fixed cost per pair is $5.00. Combining the fixed and variable costs per pair means that the jeans are produced at a total cost of $25.00 per pair.

The second step is to calculate the markup. There are two methods for calculating the markup percentage: markup on cost and markup on selling price. Using *markup on cost pricing*, just as the name implies, a percentage of the cost is added to the cost to determine the firm's selling price.

Markup on cost: For markup on cost, the calculation is:

Price = total cost + (total cost × markup percentage)

But how does the manufacturer or reseller know the markup percentage to use? One way is to base the markup on the total income needed for profits, for shareholder dividends, and for investment in the business. In our jeans example, the total cost of producing the 400,000 pairs of jeans is $10,000,000. If the manufacturer wants a profit of $2,000,000, what markup

cost-plus pricing ■ A method of setting prices in which the seller totals all the costs for the product and then adds an amount to arrive at selling price.

TABLE 13.1

Markup on Cost

An Example for a Jeans
Manufacturer

Fixed costs	
Management and other nonproduction-related salaries	$750,000
Rent	600,000
Insurance	50,000
Depreciation on equipment	70,000
Supplies	30,000
Advertising	500,000
Total fixed costs	$2,000,000
Number of units (pairs of jeans) produced	400,000
Fixed costs per unit	$5.00
Variable Costs	
Cost of materials (fabric, zipper, thread, etc.)	$7.00
Cost of production labor	10.00
Cost of utilities and supplies used in production process	3.00
Variable cost per unit (pair of jeans)	$20.00
Total cost (fixed cost per unit plus variable cost per unit)	$25.00
Markup on Cost	
Formula: Price = total cost + (total cost × markup percentage)	
Price = $25.00 + ($25.00 × 0.20) = $25.00 + $5.00 = $30.00	

percentage would it use? The $2,000,000 is 20 percent of the $10 million total cost, so 20 percent. To find the price, the calculations would be:

$$Price = \$25.00 + (\$25.00 \times 0.20) = \$25.00 + \$5.00 = \$30.00$$

(Note that in the calculations, the markup percentage is expressed as a decimal; that is, 20% = 0.20, 25% = 0.25, 30% = 0.30, and so on.)

Markup on selling price: Wholesalers and retailers more generally use markup on selling price. The markup percentage here is the seller's gross margin, the difference between the cost to the wholesaler or retailer and the price needed to cover such overhead items as salaries, rent, utility bills, advertising, and profit. For example, if the wholesaler or retailer knows it needs a margin of 40 percent to cover its overhead and reach its target profits, that margin becomes the markup on the manufacturer's selling price.

So now let's say a retailer buys the jeans from the supplier (wholesaler or manufacturer) for $30 per pair. If the retailer requires a 40 percent markup on its cost, the calculation would be as follows:

$$Price = \frac{cost}{(1.00 - markup\ percentage)}$$

As we see in Table 13.2, the price of the jeans with the markup on selling price is $50.00.

Just to compare the difference in the final prices of the two markup methods, Table 13.2 also shows what would happen if the retailer uses a markup on cost method. Using the same product cost and price with a 40 percent markup on cost would yield $42.00, a much lower

1 *Bookmark It!*

Using the information in Table 13.2, recalculate the price with markup on cost and markup on selling price if the retailer requires a 50 percent markup.

TABLE 13.2

Markup on Cost and Markup
on Selling Price: An Example
of a Retailer's Pricing

Mark-up on Selling Price		Mark-up on Cost	
Retailer's cost for a pair of jeans	$30.00	Retailer's cost for a pair of jeans	$30.00
Markup percentage	40%	Markup percentage	40%
Formula: Price = $\dfrac{cost}{(1.00 - markup\ percentage)}$		Formula: Price = total cost + (total cost × markup percentage)	
Price = $\dfrac{\$30.00}{(1.00-.40)} = \dfrac{\$30.00}{.60} = \$50.00$		Price = $30.00 + ($30.00 × 0.40) = $30.00 + $12.00 = $42.00	

price. The markup on selling price gives you the percentage of the selling price that the markup is. The markup on cost gives you the percentage of the cost that the mark up is. In the markup on selling price the markup amount is $20, which is 40 percent of the selling price of $50. In the markup on cost, the markup is $12, which is 40 percent of the cost of $42.

But what happens when costs go up? Do marketers increase their prices? If they do, consumers are likely to rebel. One solution is to keep the price constant but provide a bit less of the product. Frito-Lay, maker of salty snack foods, offset increasing production costs by cutting the contents by 6.7 to 7.5 percent per bag of Fritos, Cheetos, and potato chips.[2] To keep consumers from complaining that packages aren't full, a company may make the package ever so slightly smaller.

In a similar move, Procter & Gamble once reduced the number of disposable diapers in its Luvs and Pampers packages by an average of 13 percent. Let the buyer beware!

Price-Floor Pricing The cost-based pricing methods we have looked at do not take into account any factors except costs and profits. But there are times when firms wish to consider other factors such as the advantage of having a plant operating at its peak capacity, which keeps a skilled workforce fully employed and holds unit cost down. **Price-floor pricing** is a method for calculating price that considers both costs and what can be done to assure that a plant can operate at capacity.

Price-floor pricing has limited use, usually when the state of the economy or other temporary market conditions make it impossible for a firm to sell enough of its product at a price that covers fixed costs, variable costs, and profit goals to keep its plants operating at full capacity. In such circumstances, it may be possible to sell some units at a lower price, one that covers only the variable costs of production. If the price-floor price can be set above the variable costs, then the firm can use the difference to increase profits or to help cover its fixed costs.

For example, assume the jeans firm, operating at full capacity, can produce 400,000 pairs of jeans a year. The average variable costs per unit are $20.00 and the price that covers fixed costs, variable costs, and a desired level of profits is $30.00 per pair. Let's say that due to a downturn in the economy, the firm finds that it can sell only 350,000 units at this price. Using price-floor pricing, the firm can sell the additional 50,000 pairs of jeans at a price as low as $20.00 (i.e., at the variable cost) and maintain full-capacity operations.

The firm will not make anything on the 50,000 pairs—but it will not lose anything either. If instead it sells the additional 50,000 pairs at $25.00, then it will cover variable costs and fixed costs—50,000 × $5 or $250,000—not a bad deal.

But there are risks with price-floor pricing. If the word gets out, it could jeopardize price levels on the first 350,000 pairs—or at least anger regular customers.

Firms that produce their own national brands and also manufacture private-label brands sold through various retailers and distributors may use price-floor pricing for the private-label end of the business. So Frigidaire may sell 70 percent of its refrigerators under the Frigidaire name and the rest to Sears for sale under the retail chain's own Kenmore brand name.

PRICING STRATEGIES BASED ON DEMAND

Demand-based pricing means that the selling price is based on an estimate of volume or quantity that a firm can sell in different markets at different prices. To use any of the pricing strategies based on demand, firms must determine how much product they can sell in each market and at what price. Often marketers use customer surveys where consumers indicate whether they would buy a certain product and how much of it they would buy at various prices. More accurate estimates may be obtained by some type of field experiment. For instance, a firm might actually offer the product at different price levels in different test markets and gauge the reaction.

One advantage of demand-based pricing strategies is that their use assures a firm that it should be able to sell what it produces at the determined price because the price is based on market research findings about customer demand rather than on the seller's costs. A major disadvantage is the difficulty of estimating demand accurately.

Dell Computers uses demand pricing.[3] Dell revises the price of its computers when necessary to offset decreasing sales. The computer company reviews its prices frequently (often

price-floor pricing ■ A method for calculating price in which, to maintain full plant operating capacity, a portion of a firm's output may be sold at a price that covers only marginal costs of production.

demand-based pricing ■ A price-setting method based on estimates of demand at different prices.

1 Bookmark It!

Conduct a brief survey asking how many medium-size pizzas respondents would buy per month at four or five different prices—at $5.99, $7.99, $10.99, $13.99, and $16.99. What do the results tell you about the demand for pizza?

Dell uses a demand-based pricing strategy. The company regularly reviews sales performance and adjusts its prices accordingly.

a few times a month) in an attempt to keep tabs on customer thinking and give customers the value they want.

Two specific demand–based pricing strategies are target costing and yield management pricing. We'll talk about those next.

Target Costing   Today firms are finding that they can be more successful if they match price with demand using a process called **target costing**.[4] With target costing, a firm first determines the price at which customers would be willing to buy the product and then it works backwards to design the product in such a way that it can produce and sell the product at a profit.

With target costing, a product's cost, and thus its price, are strongly tied to its design— 70 to 80 percent of a product's costs cannot be decreased once a final product design has been determined.

With target costing, firms first use marketing research to identify the quality and functionality needed to satisfy attractive market segments and what price they are willing to pay *before the product is designed.* As Table 13.3 shows, the next step is to determine what margins retailers and dealers require, as well as the profit margin the company requires. Based on this information, managers can calculate the target cost—the maximum it can cost the firm to manufacture the product. In addition, the company may break down this total target cost into different product functions or components, allocating more of the cost to product features consumers consider critical. If the firm can meet customer quality and functionality requirements, and control costs to meet the required price, it will manufacture the product. If not, it abandons the product.

One reason that target costing is practiced more today is the global economy—competitor firms can bring "me too" products to market so quickly, usually within months, that there is little time to recover development costs much less to create brand loyalty. Success is tied to designing costs out of a product.

target costing ■ A process in which firms identify the quality and functionality needed to satisfy customers and what price they are willing to pay *before the product is designed*; the product is manufactured only if the firm can control costs to meet the required price.

TABLE **13.3**

Target Costing Using a Jeans Example

Step 1: Determine the price customers are willing to pay for the jeans. $39.99

Step 2: Determine the markup required by the retailer. 40% = 0.40

Step 3: Calculate the maximum price the retailer will pay, the markup amount.

Price to the Retailer = Selling price × (1.00 − markup percentage)

Price to the Retailer = $39.99 × 0.60 = $23.99

Step 4: Determine the profit required by the firm. 15% = 0.15

Step 5: Calculate the *target cost*, the maximum cost of producing the jeans.

Target Cost = Price to the Retailer × (1.00 − profit percentage)

Target Cost = $23.99 × 0.85 = $20.39

Camera maker Olympus Optical Company has adopted target costing. When Olympus began losing money in the mid 1980s, it first tried to introduce new products. A second initiative was to improve product quality. Its third initiative was to examine production costs. Olympus managers realized that success depended on their ability to manufacture products at a cost that would meet customers' requirments. Olympus determined that a baseline price for a compact camera in the U.S. market was $100. Considering import fees and the margins dealers required, Olympus determined a target cost for any new product. Initially only about 20 percent of proposed new models would meet the target costs on the first pass. But those that did quickly became the most popular—and profitable—compact cameras in the U.S. market.

Yield-Management Pricing   **Yield management pricing**, another type of demand based pricing, is a pricing strategy used by airlines, hotels, and cruise lines. With yield management pricing, firms charge different prices to different customers in order to manage capacity while maximizing revenues. Many service firms practice yield management pricing because they recognize that different customers have different sensitivities to price—some customers will pay top dollar for an airline ticket while others will travel only if there is a discount fare. The goal of yield management pricing is to accurately predict the proportion of customers who fall into each category and allocate the percentages of the airline's or hotel's capacity accordingly so that no product goes unsold.

> **yield management pricing** ■ A practice of charging different prices to different customers in order to manage capacity while maximizing revenues.

For example, an airline may have two prices for seats: the full fare ($899) and the discount fare ($299). The airline must predict how many seats it can fill at full fare and how many can be sold at only the discounted fare. The airline begins months ahead of the date of the flight with a basic allocation of seats—perhaps it will place 25 percent in the full fare "bucket" and 75 percent in the discount fare "bucket." While the seats in the full fare bucket cannot be sold at the discounted price, the seats allocated for the discounted price can be sold at the full fare.

As flight time gets closer, the airline might make a series of adjustments to the allocation of seats in the hope of selling every seat on the plane at the highest price possible. If the New York Mets need to book the flight, chances are some of the discount seats will be sold at full fare, decreasing the number available at the discounted price. If, as the flight date nears, the number of full–fare ticket sales falls below the forecast, some of those seats will be moved to the discount bucket. This process continues until the day of the flight as the airline attempts to have every seat filled when the plane takes off. This is why you may be able to get a fantastic price on an airline ticket through an Internet auction site such as Priceline.com if you wait until the last minute to buy your ticket.

PRICING STRATEGIES BASED ON THE COMPETITION

Sometimes a firm's pricing strategy involves pricing its wares near, at, above, or below the competition's. In the "good old days," when U.S. automakers had the home market to themselves, pricing decisions were straightforward: Industry giant General Motors would announce its new car prices, and Ford, Chrysler, Packard, Studebaker, and the others got in line or dropped out. In such a **price leadership** strategy, which usually is the rule in an industry dominated by a few firms and called an oligopoly, it may be in the best interest of all firms to minimize price competition to make a profit. Price leadership strategies are popular because they provide an acceptable and legal way for firms to agree on prices without ever talking with each other.

> **price leadership** ■ A pricing strategy in which one firm first sets its price and other firms in the industry follow with the same or very similar prices.

Sometimes firms choose to price their products below the competition. Electronics retailers have bargain-priced CDs to get shoppers into their stores in hope of building sales of high-profit electronics equipment.[5]

PRICING STRATEGIES BASED ON CUSTOMERS' NEEDS

When firms develop pricing strategies that cater to customers, they are less concerned with short-term results than with keeping customers for the long term. New Era firms constantly assess customer responses in developing pricing strategies. U.S. Cellular refines its pricing strategies by talking to customers to determine the best blend of minutes, plan features, and price.[6] The firm even designed its FarmFlex Plan to offer farmers one rate during the planting season and a lower rate in the off-season.

Sanyo bases pricing of its rechargeable batteries on customer needs by using a cost-of-ownership strategy. The *cost of ownership* is the price consumers pay for a product, plus the cost of maintaining and using the product, less any resale (or salvage) value. Because Sanyo's batteries are reusable, consumers may see the initial high price in a more favorable light as the recharge expense proves less than purchasing new disposable batteries.

Firms that practice **value pricing**, or **everyday low pricing (EDLP)**, develop a pricing strategy that promises ultimate value to consumers. Here *value* is the "ratio of benefits to the sacrifice necessary to obtain those benefits,"[7] but what this really means is that, in the customers' eyes, the price is justified by what they receive.[8] In 2001, Kmart tried to stop its sales decline by reinitiating its famous "Blue Light Specials" as an everyday low price strategy called "Blue Light Always."[9]

When firms base price strategies solely or mainly on cost, they are operating under the old production orientation and not a marketing orientation. Value-based pricing begins with customers, then considers the competition, and then determines the best pricing strategy. Smart

value pricing ■ A pricing strategy in which a firm sets prices that provide ultimate value to customers.

everyday low pricing (EDLP) ■ See value pricing.

Sanyo bases its pricing on customer needs using a cost-of-ownership strategy.

marketers know that the firm that wins is not necessarily the one with the lowest prices but rather the one that delivers the best combination of price and customer value perceptions.

In practice, when marketers use EDLP strategies, consumers may feel they get more for their money. Marketers hope that customers will see the price as reasonable and remain loyal rather than snapping up whatever happens to be on sale. This may not be the case now because shoppers have been "trained" to choose products because they are "on special" rather than because they are superior to others.

Changing pricing strategies at Procter & Gamble in recent years illustrate value pricing in action. Until about a decade ago, P&G watched as sales dollar volume dropped for its Charmin toilet tissue, Dawn dishwashing liquid, Pringles potato chips, and many other well-established brands. More and more shoppers were buying whatever brand was on sale or had a special promotion offer. To rebuild loyalty, P&G switched to an EDLP pricing strategy. It reduced everyday prices 12 to 24 percent on nearly all U.S. brands by cutting the amount it spent on trade promotions. Like the Saturn pricing policy discussed in Chapter 12, P&G said, in effect, "This really is our best price, and it's a good value for the money. Buy now. There will be no sale next week. We won't do business that way." So far the EDLP strategy has worked for P&G.

1 Bookmark It!

Wal-Mart, Target, and Kmart all claim to offer the lowest prices. Visit the three (or at least two) stores and compare prices on 10 brands that you typically buy. Report the results to your class.

NEW-PRODUCT PRICING

As we discussed in Chapter 9, new products are vital to the growth and profits of a firm, but new products also present unique pricing challenges. When a product is new to the market or when there is no established industry price norm, marketers may use a skimming price strategy, a penetration pricing strategy, or trial pricing when they first introduce the item to the market.

Skimming Price Many college students may not know that milk in its natural, unhomogenized form separates, with the cream rising to the top, leaving nonfat milk below. If your grandmother wanted to make ice cream for a Fourth of July picnic or serve whipped cream on top of the Christmas fruitcake, instead of buying a carton of whipping cream in the grocery store, she would simply "skim" the rich cream off the top of the whole milk.

In the world of pricing, setting a **skimming price** means that the firm charges a high, premium price for its new product with the intention of reducing it in future response to market pressures. For example, in 1996, when Top-Flite introduced its new Strata golf balls with a new dimple design and more solid core for better flight with metal clubs, the price was three times that of regular balls. Pro shops still couldn't keep them in stock.[10]

If a product is highly desirable and offers unique benefits, demand is price inelastic during the introductory stage of the product life cycle, allowing a company to recover research and development and promotion costs. When rival products enter the market, the price is lowered in order for the firm to remain competitive. Firms focusing on profit objectives in developing their pricing strategies often set skimming prices for new products.

In certain circumstances a skimming price is more likely to succeed. First, the product has to provide some important benefits to the target market that make customers feel they must have the product, no matter what the cost. As noted in Chapter 12, when introduced in the late 1960s, handheld calculators were such a product. To the total astonishment of 1960s' consumers, these magic little devices could add, subtract, multiply, and divide with just the push of a button, but—hard to believe now—they commanded prices as high as $200.

Second, for skimming pricing to be successful, there should be little chance that competitors can get into the market quickly. With highly complex, technical products, it may be quite a while before competitors can put a rival product into production. Finally, a skimming pricing strategy is most successful when the market consists of several customer segments with different levels of price sensitivity. There must be a substantial number of initial product customers who have very low price sensitivity. After a period of time, the price can go down and a second segment of the market with a slightly higher level of price sensitivity will purchase, and so on.

skimming price ■ A very high, premium price that a firm charges for its new, highly desirable product.

Penetration Pricing **Penetration pricing** is just the opposite of skimming pricing. This strategy means that a new product is introduced at a very low price, as Intel did with its Pentium chips. Intel's implementation of this strategy underscored the importance of a new product's

penetration pricing ■ A pricing strategy in which a firm introduces a new product at a very low price to encourage more customers to purchase it.

price in determining its chances for success in the marketplace.[11] Earlier, because rivals were way behind in developing competitive chips, Intel set a high price for its 486 CPU. When the Pentium chip, which more than doubled the speed of the 486, was introduced, Intel knew that Motorola was working with IBM and Apple to develop comparable chips. Thus, it set a low price to sell more in a short period of time and complicate Motorola's debut.[12] This strategy worked well for Intel. The low price generated demand and sales early on and, because the marketing objective was to beef up market share, penetration pricing made sense.

Another reason marketers use penetration pricing is to discourage competitors from entering the market. The firm first out with a new product has an important advantage. Experience has shown that a pioneering brand often is able to maintain dominant market share for long periods of time. Penetration pricing may act as a *barrier to entry* for competitors if the prices the market will bear are so low that the company will not be able to recover development and manufacturing costs. Bayer aspirin and Hoover vacuum cleaners are examples of brands that were first to market decades ago and still dominate their industries today. Such pioneering brands don't need to do much talking to tell consumers who they are.

trial pricing ■ Pricing a new product low for a limited period of time in order to lower the risk for a customer.

Trial Pricing   With **trial pricing** a new product carries a low price for a limited period of time to attract the customer. In trial pricing, the idea is to win customer acceptance first and make profits later. A low enough introductory price may be an acceptable alternative to free samples.

CA-Simply Money, a personal finance software package supplier, was initially offered to mail-order customers at a trial price of $7.00, the cost of shipping and handling. Later the software was priced at $69.95. Similarly, Microsoft introduced the Access database program at the short-term promotional price of $99; the suggested retail price was $495. Marketers from both firms hoped many would try the products, the strong benefits of which would build a loyal customer base and generate favorable word-of-mouth communication.

Trial pricing also works for services. Health clubs and other service providers frequently offer trial memberships or perhaps special introductory prices in hopes the initiated will become good customers at regular prices later.

Developing Pricing Tactics

Once marketers have developed pricing strategies, the last step in price planning is to implement them. The methods companies use to set their strategies in motion are their *pricing tactics*, as Figure 13.1 shows.

PRICING FOR INDIVIDUAL PRODUCTS

Once marketers have settled on a product's price, the way they present it to the market can make a big difference. Here are two tactics with examples of each.

- With *two-part pricing*, two separate types of payments are required to purchase the product. For example, golf and tennis clubs charge yearly or monthly fees plus fees for each round of golf or tennis. Likewise, cellular phone service providers offer customers a set number of minutes usage for a monthly fee plus a per-minute rate for extra usage.
- *Payment pricing* seeks to make the consumer think the price is "doable"[13] by breaking up the total price into smaller amounts payable over time. For example, many customers now opt to lease rather than buy a car. The monthly lease amount is an example of payment pricing, which tends to make people less sensitive to the total price of the car (sticker shock).[14]

PRICING FOR MULTIPLE PRODUCTS

A firm may sell several products that consumers typically buy at one time. As fast-food restaurants all know, selling a burger, pizza, or taco for lunch usually invites purchase of a soft drink, fries, or salad as well. The sale of a paper-cup dispenser usually means a package of cups is not far behind. Here are some tactics for pricing multiple products.

Pricing for individual products • Two-part pricing • Payment pricing
Pricing for multiple products • Price bundling • Captive product pricing
Geographic pricing • F.O.B. pricing • Zone pricing • Uniform delivered pricing • Freight absorption pricing
Discounting for members of the channel • Trade or functional discounts • Quantity discounts • Cash discounts • Seasonal discounts
Pricing with electronic commerce

FIGURE 13.1

Pricing Tactics

Before pricing strategies can be implemented, marketers must decide on the specific pricing tactics. There are specific tactics for individual products, for multiple products, for geographic pricing, for members of the channel, and for pricing in electronic commerce.

Price Bundling   **Price bundling** means selling two or more goods or services as a single package for one price. A music buff can buy tickets to an entire concert series for a single price. A PC typically comes bundled with a monitor, a keyboard, and software. Even an all-you-can-eat special at the local diner is an example of price bundling.

From a marketing standpoint, price bundling makes good sense. If products are priced separately, then it is likely that customers will buy some but not all of the items. They might choose to put off some purchases until later or they might buy from a competitor. Whatever revenue a seller loses from the reduced prices, it makes up in increased total purchases.

price bundling ■ Selling two or more goods or services as a single package for one price.

2 *Bookmark It!*

Visit a fast-food restaurant. Calculate how much you actually save by buying the combo meals rather than each food item separately. Then calculate the percentage savings. Are you surprised?

Captive Pricing   **Captive pricing** is a pricing tactic a firm uses when it has two products that work only when used together. The firm sells one item at a very low price and then makes its profit on the second high-margin item. Gillette uses captive pricing to sell its shaving products. When the company introduced the Mach3, a triple-bladed razor, it spent approximately $1 billion on development and introduction of the new product but anticipated that the razor would generate annual revenues of $1 billion by 2001.[15] Although the razor sold for the low price of $6.99, blades for the Mach3 cost a stiff $1.50 or more each. The typical American man buys 30 blades per year. Do the math: If he uses the Mach3 razor, it costs him $45 annually to replenish his supply of blades, compared to the $9 annual cost for generic blades. Although the blade and razor business generates only a third of corporate revenues for Gillette, the company's use of captive pricing tactics in this category delivers a much larger proportion of the company's profits.

captive pricing ■ A pricing tactic for two items that must be used together; one item is priced very low and the firm makes its profit on another, high-margin item essential to the operation of the first item.

GEOGRAPHIC PRICING

Geographic pricing is a pricing tactic that establishes how firms handle the cost of shipping products to customers near, far, and wide. Characteristics of the product, the customers, and the

competition figure in the decision to charge all customers the same price or to vary according to shipping cost.

F.O.B. Pricing Often a price is given as F.O.B. factory or F.O.B. delivered. F.O.B. stands for free on board, which means the supplier will pay to have the product loaded onto a truck or some other carrier. Also—and this is important—*title passes to the buyer* at the F.O.B. location. F.O.B. factory or **F.O.B. origin pricing** means that the cost of transporting the product from the factory to the customer's location is the responsibility of the customer. **F.O.B. delivered pricing** means that the seller pays both the cost of loading and transporting to the customer, which is included in the selling price.

F.O.B. origin pricing ■ A pricing tactic in which the cost of transporting the product from the factory to the customer's location is the responsibility of the customer.

F.O.B. delivered pricing ■ A pricing tactic in which the cost of loading and transporting the product to the customer is included in the selling price and is paid by the manufacturer.

zone pricing ■ A pricing tactic in which customers in different geographic zones pay different transportation rates.

uniform delivered pricing ■ A pricing tactic in which a firm adds a standard shipping charge to the price for all customers regardless of location.

Zone Pricing Another geographic pricing tactic is **zone pricing**. Like F.O.B. factory pricing, zone pricing means that distant customers pay more than customers who are close to the factory. But in zone pricing there are a limited number of different prices charged based on geographic zones established by the seller. All customers located in each zone pay the same transportation charge.

Zone pricing simplifies geographic cost differences, which is important in certain markets. It would be nearly impossible for United Parcel Service to charge one price if a package shipped from Los Angeles went to Miami, another if it went to Fort Lauderdale, and another for Vero Beach, Florida.

Uniform Delivered Pricing In **uniform delivered pricing** an average shipping cost is added to the price, no matter what the distance from the manufacturer's plant—within reason. Internet sales, catalog sales, home television shopping, and other types of nonstore retail sales usually use uniform delivered pricing.

Gillette practices captive pricing with its razors. Once customers have bought the razor, they are a "captive" of the company's blade prices.

Freight Absorption Pricing   **Freight absorption pricing** means the seller takes on part or all of the cost of shipping. This policy is good for high-ticket items, when the cost of shipping is a negligible part of the sales price and the profit margin. Marketers are most likely to use freight absorption pricing in highly competitive markets or when such pricing allows them to enter new markets.

freight absorption pricing ■ A pricing tactic in which the seller absorbs the total cost of transportation.

DISCOUNTING FOR MEMBERS OF THE CHANNEL

So far we've talked about pricing tactics used to sell to end customers. Now we'll talk about some discounting tactics used to implement pricing strategies to members of the channel of distribution—wholesalers, distributors, and retailers.

Trade or Functional Discounts   Whether a firm sells to businesses or directly to consumers, most pricing structures are built around list prices. A **list price**, also referred to as a *suggested retail price*, is the price that the manufacturer sets as the appropriate price for the end consumer to pay. In pricing for members of the channel, marketers recognize that retailers and wholesalers have costs to cover and profit targets as well.

When manufacturers develop pricing tactics for channel intermediaries, they often offer **trade or functional discounts** because the channel members perform selling, credit, storage, and transportation services that the manufacturer would otherwise have to provide. Often setting functional discounts is simplified when a firm uses set percentage discounts off list price for each channel level.

Let's look at a simple example of a channel of distribution that includes a manufacturer that sells to wholesalers that in turn sell to retailers. The manufacturer may state trade discounts as *list price less 40/20*. The first number means that 40 percent of the list price is to cover the overhead and profit requirements for the retailer. Thus, the manufacturer suggests

list price ■ The price the end customer is expected to pay as determined by the manufacturer; also referred to as the suggested retail price.

trade or functional discounts ■ Discounts off list price of products to members of the channel of distribution that perform various marketing functions.

In pricing to retailers, bicycle manufacturers have to consider the amount retailers must have to operate their business and make a profit.

that the wholesalers sell to their retail customers at list less 40 percent. If the list price of a product is $200, the price to the retailers would be:

$$\$200 - (40\% \times 200) = \$200 - \$80 = \$120$$

The second number—the 20—is the discount percentage allowed for wholesalers to cover their costs of doing business and profit. Thus, the manufacturer's selling price to the wholesaler is discounted from the price to the retailer and would be:

$$\$120 - (20\% \times 120) = \$120 - \$24 = \$96$$

A final note: Although we talk about trade discounts being determined by manufacturers, in reality the manufacturer has little if any control over the percentage discounts. In most industries, these are influenced by whatever margins retailers and wholesalers require to cover their overhead and profit targets.

Quantity Discounts   Firms that sell to distribution channel members or end-user business customers often offer **quantity discounts**, or reduced prices for purchases of larger quantities. Marketers commonly use quantity discounts as a way to encourage larger purchases from distribution channel partners.

Sometimes marketers offer buyers **cumulative quantity discounts**, which are based on a total quantity bought within a specified time period, often a year. Cumulative quantity discounts encourage a buyer to stick with a single seller instead of moving from one supplier to another.

Cumulative quantity discounts may be in the form of *rebates*, in which case the firm sends the buyer a rebate check at the end of the discount period. In other cases, the discount is a credit against future orders. In either case, the buyer must wait until the end of the discount period to receive the discount. This delay makes cumulative quantity discounts less attractive because the buyer must pay the nondiscounted price for the goods up-front and not realize the discount until the end of the period. For retailers and others operating on thin gross margins, this can create some financial hardships.

quantity discounts ■
A pricing tactic of charging reduced prices for purchases of larger quantities of a product.

cumulative quantity discounts ■ Discounts based on the total quantity purchased within a specified time period.

Noncumulative quantity discounts are based only on the quantity purchased with each individual order. Noncumulative discounts encourage larger single orders but do little to tie the buyer and the seller together. When a competitor makes a better discount offer, the buyer may switch.

In most cases, noncumulative quantity discounts mean that the buyer pays a reduced price for the goods purchased—a simple cash discount. In other cases the discount offer is made in terms of free goods. For example, a grocer that buys 10 cases of salsa may get one case free.

Sometimes offering quantity discounts can create problems for the manufacturer. For example, a Canadian publisher offered a four-volume set of encyclopedias, for which it developed a pricing structure with steep quantity discounts and a list price of $175 per set. Small, independent bookstores bought the encyclopedias at $125 per set while large chain stores purchased in larger quantities at $75 or $80 a set. When the chain stores decided to give up some of their margin to increase sales and sold the sets at $99, which was way below what the small independents paid the publisher, the manufacturer faced some very unhappy "former" customers.

Cash Discounts Using money costs money, as anyone who's ever taken out a mortgage or a college loan understands. When a firm borrows money, it must pay interest for every day it has the use of the money. Conversely, if a firm has excess cash, it is able to invest that cash and make money from its money. The bottom line: Having cash is an advantage. For this reason many firms try to entice their customers to pay their bills quickly by offering *cash discounts*. For example, a firm selling to a retailer may state that the terms of the sale are "2 percent 10 days, net 30 days." This means that if the retailer pays the producer for the goods within 10 days, the amount due is cut by 2 percent. The total amount is due within 30 days, and after 30 days, the payment is late.

Seasonal Discounts Seasonal discounts are price reductions offered only during certain times of the year. Products such as snowblowers, lawn mowers, and water-skiing equipment are priced in this way. If such products are sold only during a few months of the year, then the manufacturer must either build a large plant that has to be shut down during the off-season or build a large warehouse to store inventory until the season comes around again. Both of these options are unattractive, so in order to entice retailers and wholesalers to buy off-season and store the product at their locations until the right time of the year, a firm may offer seasonal discounts.

Pricing with Electronic Commerce

As we have seen, pricing for "bricks-and-mortar" firms is a complex decision process. But with the advent of the Internet, a whole new set of options appeared. Many experts suggest that technology is creating a pricing revolution that might change pricing forever—and create the most efficient market ever, some say. Because sellers are connected to buyers around the globe as never before through the Internet, corporate networks, and wireless setups, marketers can offer consumers deals tailored to a single person at a single moment.[16]

For firms that want to sell to other businesses (B2B firms), the Internet means that they can change prices rapidly to adapt to changing costs. For consumers who have lots of stuff in the attic they need to put in someone else's attic (C2C e-commerce), the Internet means an opportunity for consumers to find ready buyers. And for B2C firms, firms that sell to consumers, the Internet offers other opportunities. In this section we will discuss some of the more popular Internet pricing strategies.

DYNAMIC PRICING STRATEGIES

One of the most important opportunities offered by the Internet is **dynamic pricing**, where the price can easily be adjusted to meet changes in the marketplace. Posting merchandise for sale on the Web means the costs of price changes are negligible. If a retail store wants to change prices, new price tags must be placed on items, new store display signage and media advertising must be created and displayed, and new prices input into the store's computer system. For business-to-business marketers, catalogs and price lists must be printed and distributed to salespeople and to customers. These activities can be very costly to a firm, so firms simply don't change their prices very often. Because the cost of changing prices on the Internet is

noncumulative quantity discounts ■ Discounts based only on the quantity purchased with individual orders.

dynamic pricing ■ Pricing strategy in which the price can easily be adjusted to meet changes in the marketplace.

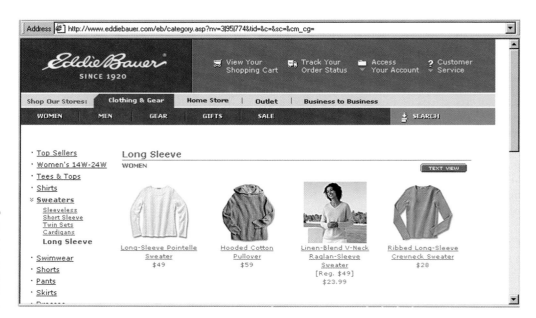

Online retailers have an advantage over bricks-and-mortar retailers in that they can use dynamic pricing. They can easily and quickly change prices to adjust to supply, demand, and costs.

3 *Bookmark It!*

Visit several Web sites that offer airline tickets at discounted prices. Get the lowest price for an available seat to a destination of your choice. How do the sites compare in the flights available, the prices, and the ease of using the site?

online auctions ■
E-commerce that allows shoppers to purchase products through online bidding.

practically zero, firms are able to respond quickly and, if necessary, frequently, to changes in costs, changes in supply, and/or changes in demand. Tickets.com adjusts concert ticket prices based on supply and demand.

Because it's so easy to change prices on the Internet, firms can test different pricing strategies. For example, if a firm wants to see if a 5 percent increase in price will affect sales, it might try the new pricing strategy on every twentieth customer and then see if the rate of sales decreases among that group of customers. As a result, the company reports it has been able to increase revenue as much as 45 percent.[17]

AUCTIONS

Hundreds of Internet **online auctions** allow shoppers to bid on everything from Beanie Babies to health and fitness equipment to a Mark McGwire home-run ball. Auctions provide a second Internet pricing strategy. Perhaps the most popular auctions are the C2C auctions such as those on eBay. The eBay auction is an open auction, meaning that the buyers all know the highest price bid at any point in time. In many Internet auction sites the seller can set a reserve price, a price below which the item will not be sold.

Many B2B sites offer reverse-price auctions in which buyers ask sellers to submit quotations for a desired product. The supplier with the lowest bid wins the sales. Priceline.com offers customers goods and services in first-price, sealed-bid auctions. This means that potential buyers may offer a single price to a potential seller of a product (such as an airline ticket). In the case of Priceline.com, bidders guarantee their bids with a credit card. Priceline then checks to see if any airline is willing to sell a ticket for or below the bid price.

PRICE DISCRIMINATION

For years, some catalog marketers have sent out more than one catalog version with different prices based on what they know different customer segments are willing to pay. Customers in one zip code may receive a catalog with prices that are 10 or 15 percent higher on many items than customers who live in a different zip code area. This practice, called price discrimination, is even more easily implemented on the Web in situations in which Internet marketers know more about customers who shop on the Web and can segment them easily and quickly.

Price discrimination means that marketers classify customers based on some characteristic that indicates what they are willing or able to pay. Movie theaters offer lower prices to children and *The Wall Street Journal* offers college students lower subscription rates. The downside is that customers who pay the higher price usually aren't thrilled about this if they

Priceline.com uses a "first price" auction strategy for airline tickets, hotel rooms, even cruises. Customers make a bid and Priceline checks to see if any suppliers are willing to sell at that price.

find out. When customers found out that Amazon.com was testing prices using a price discrimination strategy, they were outraged. The random price test charged some customers 3 to 5 percent more than other customers for DVD movies. Amazon.com refunded $3.10 each to more than 6,000 customers.

PRICING ADVANTAGES FOR ONLINE SHOPPERS

The Internet also creates unique challenges for marketers in terms of prices. As we've already discussed, consumers or business customers are gaining more control over the buying process. With the availability of search engines and "shopbots" they are less at the mercy of firms handing out prices that they must accept. The result is that customers have become more price sensitive. For example, online drugstores have been stealing customers from traditional pharmacies by offering drastically lower prices: As one illustration, a comparison study found Rogaine priced at $53.99 at Rite Aid while at the same time the antibaldness product could be purchased online for $47.39 at More.com.[18] (That's a hair-raising difference.)

Detailed information about what products actually cost manufacturers, available from sites such as consumerreports.org, can give consumers more negotiating power when shopping for new cars and other big-ticket items. Finally, e-commerce potentially can lower consumers' costs due to the gasoline, time, and aggravation saved by avoiding a trip to the mall.

Psychological Issues in Pricing

Much of what we've said about pricing depends on economists' notions of a customer who evaluates price in a logical, rational manner. For example, the concept of demand is expressed by a smooth demand curve, which assumes that if a firm lowers a product's price from $10 to $9.50 and then from $9.50 to $9 and so on, then customers will simply buy more and more. In the real world, though, it doesn't always work that way. Let's look at the psychological issues of pricing.

BUYERS' PRICING EXPECTATIONS

Often consumers base their perceptions of price on what they perceive to be the customary or fair price. For example, long ago a candy bar or a pack of gum was priced for many years at 5 cents. Consumers would have perceived any other price as too high or low. It was a nickel candy bar—period. So when costs went up or inflation kicked in, some candy makers tried to

shrink the size of the bar instead of changing the price. Eventually, inflation prevailed, consumers' salaries rose, and that candy bar goes for 10 to 12 times one nickel today—a price that consumers would have found unacceptable a few decades ago.

When the price of a product is above or even sometimes when it's below what consumers expect, they are less willing to purchase the product. If the price is above their expectations, they may think it as a rip-off. If it is below expectations, consumers may think quality is below par. By understanding the pricing expectations of their customers, marketers are better able to develop viable pricing strategies. These expectations can differ across cultures and countries. For example, one study conducted in southern California found that Chinese supermarkets charge significantly lower prices (only half as much for meat and seafood) than mainstream American supermarkets in the same areas.[19]

internal reference price
A set price or a price range in consumers' minds that they refer to in evaluating a product's price.

Internal Reference Prices Sometimes consumers' perceptions of the customary price of a product depend on their **internal reference price**. That is, based on past experience, consumers have a set price or a price range in their mind that they refer to in evaluating a product's cost. The reference price may be the last price paid, or it may be the average of all the prices they know of similar products. No matter what the brand, the normal price for a loaf of sandwich bread is about $1.49. In some stores it may be $1.39 and in others it is $1.59, but the average is $1.49. If consumers find a loaf of bread priced much higher than this—say, $2.99—they will feel it is overpriced and grab a competing brand. If they find bread priced significantly lower—say, at $0.59 or $0.69 a loaf—they may shy away from the purchase, wondering "what is wrong" with the bread. Marriott customers, too, have an internal reference price for what a hotel room should cost.

In some cases, marketers try to influence consumers' expectations of what a product should cost by employing reference pricing strategies. For example, manufacturers may show their price compared to competitors' prices in advertising. Similarly, a retailer will display a product next to a higher-priced version of the same or a different brand. The consumer must choose between the two products with different prices. Two results are likely.

On the one hand, if the prices (and other characteristics) of the two products are fairly close, the consumer will probably feel the product quality is similar. This is called an *assimilation effect*. The customer might think, "The price is about the same, they must be alike. I'll be smart and save a few dollars." And so the customer chooses the item that is priced lower because the low price made it look attractive next to the high-priced alternative. This is why store brands of deodorant, vitamins, pain relievers, and shampoo sit beside national brands, often accompanied by a shelf sign pointing out how much shoppers can save by purchasing the store brands.

On the other hand, if the prices of the two products are too far apart, a *contrast effect* may result in which the customer equates it with a big difference in quality. "Gee, this lower-priced one is probably not as good as the higher-priced one. I'll splurge on the more expensive one." Using this strategy, an appliance store may place an advertised $300 refrigerator next to a $699 model to convince a customer the bottom-of-the-line model just won't do.

Price Quality Inferences Imagine that you are in a shoe store looking for a pair of running shoes. You notice one pair that is priced at $89.99. On another table you see a second pair looking almost identical to the first pair but priced at only $24.95. Which pair do you want? Which pair do you think is the better quality? Many of us will pay the higher price because we believe the bargain-basement shoes aren't worth the risk at any price.

As we saw in Chapter 6, consumers make *price–quality inferences* about a product when they use price as a cue or an indicator of quality. By inference, we mean that something is believed to be true without any direct evidence. If consumers are unable to judge the quality of a product through examination or prior experience, they usually will assume that the higher-priced product is the higher-quality product.

Real People, Other Voices: Advice for Marriott Courtyard

Joseph Goodman, University of Texas at Austin, Student

I recommend option 1. Changing the pricing strategy will differentiate Courtyard by giving the customer a fair market price, every night, and in any city—also enabling Courtyard to build long-term relationships with frequent customers and large corporations. Since Courtyard caters to the business traveler, it can offer a stable pricing strategy that does not need to be as aggressive during peak seasons or for large conferences. Courtyard faces the threat of decreases in perceived value, due to the absence of a high reference price, and in total revenue. To counter this, an effective promotional campaign will be necessary to differentiate Courtyard from the price hagglers. This strategy will allow Courtyard to avoid cannibalization of Fairfield Inn due to larger price cuts suggested in option 3, and Marriott's cannibalization of Courtyard due to a status-quo pricing strategy suggested in option 2.

Ronald Picker, Marketing Professor, St. Mary of the Woods College

I would choose option 3. You want to maintain your "high end" image and still fill empty beds. Option 2 is risky. If the economy stays sluggish, Marriott, Courtyard's parent company, might pull the plug on Courtyard. As far as option 1, this is a potential "win the battle and lose the war" strategy. The marketing graveyard is filled with products that started out high-end, but for some reason fell in price (and sometimes in quality.) Brands like Nautica, Tommy Hilfiger, and Ralph Lauren would lose their high-class appeal if they could readily and inexpensively be purchased at discount retailers. The companies might make an extra quick profit, but at what price in the long run?

George Terhanian, Vice President, Internet Research, Harris Interactive

I would choose option 1, primarily because of the brand-enhancing possibilities it offers. For instance, option 1 would enable Courtyard to (further) appeal to the sensibilities of frequent business travelers who have no interest in haggling about room price, or any other activity that might stand in the way of a good night's sleep. Presumably, Courtyard makes its living by catering to the needs of no-nonsense, hard-core business travelers. For this reason, a pricing approach that is anything other than open and honest would diminish the brand.

Weigh in with your thoughts! Visit the Live Laboratory at www.prenhall.com/solomon for extended Other Voices replies, exercises, and more.

CAFÉ DE QUALITÉ
À UN PRIX BIEN SERRÉ.

CHAT NOIR

Consumers often associate higher prices with higher quality. This Belgian ad for Chat Noir (Black Cat) coffee tries to convince them otherwise. It reads, "Quality coffee. But we've really squeezed the price."

PSYCHOLOGICAL PRICING STRATEGIES

Setting a price is part science, part art. Psychological aspects of price are important for marketers to understand in making pricing decisions.

Odd–Even Pricing   In the U.S. market, we usually see prices in dollars and cents—$1.99, $5.98, $23.67, or even $599.95. We see prices in even dollar amounts—$2.00, $10.00, or $600.00—far less often. The reason? Marketers have assumed that there is a psychological response to odd prices that differs from the responses to even prices. Habit might also play a role here. Research on the difference in perceptions of odd versus even prices supports the argument that prices ending in 99 rather than 00 lead to increased sales.[20]

At the same time, there are some instances in which even prices are the norm or perhaps even necessary. Theater and concert tickets, admission to sporting events, and lottery tickets tend to be priced in even amounts. Professional fees are normally expressed in even dollars. If a doctor or dentist charged $39.99 for a visit, the patient might think the quality of medical care was less than satisfactory. Many luxury items such as jewelry, golf course fees, and resort accommodations use even dollar prices to set them apart. Hotels—and motels—usually price in even dollar amounts.

price lining ■ The practice of setting a limited number of different specific prices, called price points, for items in a product line.

Price Lining   Marketers often apply their understanding of the psychological aspects of pricing in a practice called **price lining**. In price lining, items in a product line sell at different prices, called price points. If you want to buy a new refrigerator, you will find that most manufacturers have one "stripped-down" model for about $400, with an exact price of $379 or $389 or even $419. A better-quality but still moderately priced model will be around $600. A good refrigerator will be about $800 and a large refrigerator with lots of special features will be around $1,000. Recently, some appliance manufacturers have come out with new models, branded and marketed as special premium lines, with price tags of $3,000 or more.

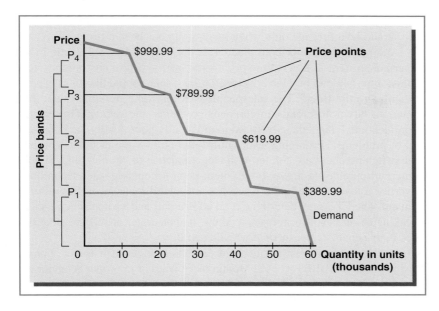

FIGURE 13.2

Price Lining
Sometimes firms will offer products at different price points to sell to more markets.

Now, that's cold! Price lining provides the different ranges necessary to satisfy each segment of the market.

Why is price lining a good practice? From the marketer's standpoint, price lining is a way to maximize profits. In theory, a firm would charge each individual customer the highest price that customer was willing to pay. If the maximum one particular person would be willing to pay for a refrigerator is $550, then that would be the price. If another person would be willing to pay $900, that would be his price. But charging each consumer a different price is really not possible. Having a limited number of prices that generally fall at the top of the range customers find acceptable is a more workable alternative. Firms that use price lining assume that demand is inelastic within certain ranges but that if prices go above that range, demand will become elastic and customers will balk. Figure 13.2 shows an assumed demand curve for a product for which price lining is a good strategy. This figure shows price points within price bands for different refrigerators in a manufacturer's product line.

Legal and Ethical Considerations in Pricing

The free enterprise system is founded on the idea that the marketplace will regulate itself. Prices will rise or fall according to demand. Supplies of goods and services will be made available if there is an adequate profit incentive.

Unfortunately, the business world includes the greedy and unscrupulous. Federal, state, and local governments have found it necessary to enact legislation to protect consumers and to protect businesses from predatory rivals. For example, under current laws in Europe, car companies are allowed to charge wildly different prices for the same vehicle in different countries—prices can vary by as much as 30 percent. New regulations are now being proposed to create a more level playing field among countries belonging to the European Union (EU)—despite fierce opposition by some car manufacturers that want to retain control over their pricing decisions.[21] In this next section we will talk about deceptive prices, unfair prices, discriminatory prices, price fixing, and some regulations to combat them.

DECEPTIVE PRICING PRACTICES

Unscrupulous businesses may advertise or promote prices in a deceptive way. The Federal Trade Commission (FTC), state lawmakers, and private bodies such as the Better Business Bureau have developed pricing rules and guidelines to meet the challenge. They say retailers (or other suppliers) must not claim that their prices are lower than a competitor's unless it's true. A going-out-of-business sale should be the last sale before going out of business. A fire sale should be a fire sale only when there really has been a fire.

Another deceptive pricing practice is the **bait-and-switch** tactic in which a retailer will advertise an item at a very low price—the *bait*—to lure customers into the store. But it is almost impossible to buy the advertised item—salespeople like to say (privately) that the item is "nailed to the floor." The salespeople do everything possible to get the unsuspecting customers to buy a different, more expensive, item—the *switch*. They might tell the customer "confidentially" that "the advertised item is really poor quality, lacking important features and full of problems." Enforcing laws against bait-and-switch tactics is complicated because bait-and-switch practices are similar to the legal practice of "trading up." Simply encouraging consumers to purchase a higher-priced item is an acceptable sales technique, but it is illegal to advertise a lower-priced item when it's not a legitimate, bona fide offer that is available on demand. The FTC may determine if an ad is a bait-and-switch scheme or a legitimate offer by checking to see if a firm refuses to show, demonstrate, or sell the advertised product, disparages it, or penalizes salespeople who do sell it.[22]

Marketers also must not claim a price is reduced if it is not. For example, the Better Business Bureau (BBB) accused Montgomery Ward of improper behavior when it compared the "regular price" of a pair of diamond earrings, $1,199, with Montgomery Ward's sale price of $399. The BBB found no evidence that Ward had ever sold the earrings at the "regular" price.[23]

UNFAIR SALES ACTS

Not every advertised bargain is a bait-and-switch. Some retailers advertise items at very low prices or even below cost and are glad to sell them at that price because they know that once in the store, customers may buy other items at regular prices. This is called **loss leader pricing** and is aimed at building store traffic and sales volume.

Some states consider loss leader practices to be wrong and have passed legislation called **unfair sales acts** (also called *unfair trade practices acts*). These laws or regulations prohibit wholesalers and retailers from selling products below cost. Most of these regulations even include a set percentage markup below which the retailer or wholesaler may not sell the products. This percentage is most commonly 6 percent for retailers and 2 percent for wholesalers.[24] These laws are designed to protect small wholesalers and retailers from larger competitors because the larger competitors have the financial resources that allow them to offer loss leaders or products sold at very low prices—usually something the smaller firms cannot do.

PRICE DISCRIMINATION

The *Robinson-Patman Act* includes regulations against price discrimination in interstate commerce. These price discrimination regulations relate to selling the same product to different retailers and wholesalers at different prices if such practices lessen competition. In addition to regulating the price charged, the Robinson-Patman Act specifically prohibits offering such "extras" as discounts, rebates, premiums, coupons, guarantees, and free delivery to some, but not all, customers.

There are exceptions, however. Robinson-Patman does not apply to final customers—only resellers. A discount to a large channel customer is legal if it is based on the quantity of the order and the resulting efficiencies such as transportation savings. But the quantity discount must be available to any customer who chooses to buy in that quantity. Differences in prices are also allowed if there are physical differences in the product, such as different features. A name-brand appliance may be available through a large national retail chain at a lower price than an almost identical item sold by a higher-priced retailer because that "model" is sold only through that chain.

PRICE FIXING

Price fixing occurs when two or more companies conspire to keep prices at a certain level. For example, General Electric Co. and De Beers Centenary AG were charged with fixing the prices in the $600-million-a-year world market for industrial diamonds used in cutting tools. This type of illicit agreement can take two forms: horizontal and vertical.

Horizontal Price Fixing   *Horizontal price fixing* occurs when competitors making the same product jointly determine what price they each will charge. This kind of price fixing keeps prices high by eliminating competition and is illegal under the Sherman Act. In industries in which there are few sellers, there may be no specific price-fixing agreement but sellers will still charge the same price to "meet the competition." Such parallel pricing is not of itself considered price fixing. There must be an exchange of pricing information between sellers to indicate illegal price-fixing actions.

In 1994, six major airlines settled federal charges that they had fixed prices. The cost to customers from 1988 to 1992 was estimated at almost $2 billion. In this case, price fixing was conducted in a novel manner through an industry-owned, computerized, fare-information system. The airlines had communicated with each other about prospective price changes via coded messages.

Vertical Price Fixing   Sometimes manufacturers or wholesalers attempt to force retailers to charge a certain price for their product. This is called *vertical price fixing*. If the retailer wants to carry the product, for instance, it has to charge the "suggested" retail price. The *Consumer Goods Pricing Act* of 1976 limited this practice, leaving retail stores free to set whatever price they choose without interference by the manufacturer or wholesaler. Today retailers don't need to adhere to "suggested" prices.

There are exceptions, of course. Manufacturers or wholesalers are free to set prices when they own the retail outlet. The same is true for consignment selling in which retailers do not actually ever own the product but simply agree to offer it for sale and to accept a percentage of the selling price for their efforts.

PREDATORY PRICING

Predatory pricing means that a company sets a very low price for the purpose of driving competitors out of business. Later, when they have a monopoly, they will increase prices. The Sherman Act and the Robinson-Patman Act prohibit predatory pricing. For example, in 1999 the Justice Department accused American Airlines of predatory pricing at its Dallas–Ft. Worth hub.[25] In the mid-1990s, three small rivals started flying into the airport. American responded by offering cheap seats to scare the rivals away and then raised its prices. That's a no-no, says Uncle Sam.

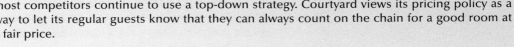

Real People, Real Choices: How It Worked Out at Courtyard by Marriott

Craig chose option 1. He introduced a new strategy called best available rate (BAR), where callers would immediately receive a price quote below the discounted corporate rate at more expensive hotels but higher than the rate they would get at upper-grade–level economy hotels. This strategy is similar to the EDLP (everyday low price) strategy that has been adopted by Procter & Gamble and other manufacturers.

Craig established a weekday goal of selling 85 percent of all rooms at the BAR rate. The remainder of the rooms could be offered to high-volume corporate accounts at discounts of 8 percent to 15 percent under the BAR. He also took steps to establish the idea in customers' minds that Courtyard is always fairly priced and there is no need to play a game to get a good price. Courtyard also instituted several internal practices that forced common price quotes in all distribution channels and ensured that employees would always quote the lowest available price.

After implementing the BAR strategy, Courtyard's market share reached its highest point in the brand's history. BAR pricing continues to be standard policy at Courtyard hotels, even while most competitors continue to use a top-down strategy. Courtyard views its pricing policy as a way to let its regular guests know that they can always count on the chain for a good room at a fair price.

Chapter Summary

1. Understand key pricing strategies.

The most commonly used pricing strategies are based on cost. Though easy to calculate and "safe," cost-based strategies do not consider demand, the competition, the stage in the product life cycle, plant capacity, or product image. Cost-based strategies include cost-plus pricing (either markup on cost or markup on selling price) and price-floor pricing.

Pricing strategies based on demand can require that marketers estimate demand at different prices in order to be certain they can sell what they produce. Such strategies include target costing and yield management pricing.

Strategies based on the competition may represent industry wisdom but can be tricky to apply. A price leadership strategy is often used in an oligopoly.

Firms that focus on customer needs may consider everyday low price (EDLP) or value pricing strategies. If a new product has unique customer benefits and demand is inelastic, then a firm may charge a high skimming price to recover research and development and promotional costs. If the firm needs to encourage more customers and discourage competitors from entering the market, then it may use a very low penetration price. Trial pricing means setting a low price for a limited time.

2. Explain pricing tactics for single and multiple products.

To implement pricing strategies with individual products, marketers may use two-part pricing or payment pricing tactics. For multiple products, marketers may use price bundling, wherein two or more products are sold and priced as a single package. Captive pricing is often chosen when two items must be used together; one item is sold at a very low price and the other at a high, profitable price.

Geographic pricing tactics address differences in how far products must be shipped. F.O.B. origin pricing indicates that the seller will pay only to have the product loaded for shipment. In zone pricing, a firm sets a limited number of different prices based on shipping distances. Uniform delivered pricing means that the same shipping cost is added to the product price no matter how far the product is actually shipped. In freight absorption pricing, the seller absorbs the costs of transportation.

Pricing for members of the channel may include trade or functional discounts, cumulative or noncumulative quantity discounts to encourage larger purchases, cash discounts to encourage fast payment, and seasonal discounts to spread purchases throughout the year or to increase off-season or in-season sales.

3. Understand the opportunities for Internet pricing strategies.

E-commerce may offer firms an opportunity to initiate dynamic pricing—meaning prices can be changed frequently with little or no cost. Auctions offer opportunities for customers to bid on items in C2C, B2C, and B2B e-commerce. The Internet makes it easy to offer different prices to different market segments, a form of price discrimination. The Internet allows buyers to compare products and prices, gives consumers more control over the price they pay for items, and has made customers more price sensitive.

4. Describe the psychological aspects of pricing.

Consumers may express emotional or psychological responses to prices. Customers may use an idea of a customary or fair price as an internal reference price in evaluating products. Sometimes marketers use reference pricing strategies by displaying products with different prices next to each other. A price–quality inference means that consumers use price as a cue for quality. Customers respond to odd prices differently than to even-dollar prices. Marketers can manipulate pricing with price lining strategies, a practice of setting a limited number of different price ranges for a product line.

5. Understand the legal and ethical aspects of pricing.

Most marketers seek to avoid unethical or illegal pricing practices. Deceptive pricing practices include illegal bait-and-switch tactics and superficial discounting. Many states have unfair sales acts, which are laws against loss leader pricing that make it illegal to sell products below cost or, in some states, to sell at a price less than a certain percentage above cost. Federal regulations prohibit predatory pricing, price discrimination, and horizontal or vertical price fixing.

Review Questions

■ MARKETING CONCEPTS: TESTING YOUR KNOWLEDGE

1. Why do firms use cost-based pricing strategies? Explain cost-plus pricing and price-floor pricing.
2. What are the advantages and disadvantages of pricing strategies based on demand? Explain target costing and yield management pricing.
3. Explain how a price leadership strategy works and how it helps all of the firms in an oligopolistic industry.
4. For new products, when is skimming pricing more appropriate and when is penetration pricing the best strategy? When would trial pricing be an effective pricing strategy?
5. Explain how marketers may use two-part pricing, payment pricing, price bundling, and captive pricing tactics.
6. How do marketers use geographic location in pricing strategies?
7. Why do marketers use trade or functional discounts, quantity discounts, cash discounts, and seasonal discounts in pricing to members of the channel?
8. What is dynamic pricing? Why does the Internet encourage the use of dynamic pricing?
9. How do marketers use the Internet for auctions? For price discrimination?
10. Regarding the prices of purchases, what is the advantage of the Internet for consumers?
11. Explain these psychological aspects of pricing: price–quality inferences; odd–even pricing; internal reference price; the practice of price lining.
12. Explain these unethical or illegal pricing practices: bait-and-switch; loss leader pricing; predatory pricing; price discrimination; price fixing.

■ MARKETING CONCEPTS: DISCUSSING CHOICES AND ISSUES

1. Many very successful retailers use a loss leader pricing strategy in which they advertise an item at a price below their cost and sell the item at that price to get customers into their store. They feel that these customers will continue to shop with their company and that they will make a profit in the long run. Do you consider this an unethical practice? Who benefits and who is hurt by such practices? Do you think the practice should be made illegal as some states have done?
2. With a price leadership strategy, firms are able to avoid price competition without getting together to set prices. Although it is legal, is a price leadership strategy ethical? How does it hurt and how does it help an industry?

What benefits does it provide and what problems does it pose for customers?
3. The Internet offers marketers a means to offer different customer segments different prices. How do you feel about that? As a student, should you get special discounted prices on some products? How is that different from price discrimination on the Web?
4. Consumers often make price–quality inferences about products. What does this mean? What are some products for which you are likely to make price–quality inferences? Do such inferences make sense?
5. Retailers sometimes display, side by side, two similar products carrying different prices, hoping for an assimilation effect or for a contrast effect. Give some examples of products that you have noticed displayed in this manner. What factors do you think make it more likely that one effect versus the other will occur? Do such practices help or hurt the consumer?

■ MARKETING PRACTICE: APPLYING WHAT YOU'VE LEARNED

1. Assume you have been hired as the assistant manager of a local store that sells fresh fruits and vegetables. As you look over the store, you notice that there are two different displays of tomatoes. In one display the tomatoes are priced at $1.39 per pound and in the other the tomatoes are priced at $1.29 per pound. The tomatoes look very much alike. You notice that no one is buying the $1.39 tomatoes. Write a report explaining what is happening and give your recommendations for the store's pricing strategy.
2. As the vice president for marketing for a firm that markets computer software, you must regularly develop pricing strategies for new software products. Your latest product is a software package that automatically translates any foreign language e-mail messages to the user's preferred language. You are trying to decide on the pricing for this new product. Should you use a skimming price, a penetration price, or something in between? With a classmate taking the role of another marketing professional with your firm, argue in front of your class the pros and cons for each alternative.
3. Assume that you have recently begun working in the marketing department of a firm that manufactures furnaces and air conditioners. Previously, the firm has priced its products on a cost-plus basis. You are concerned that this is not the most advantageous pricing strategy for the firm. You wish to discuss the issue with your boss. Develop an outline of the discussion you plan. Include the pros and cons of cost-plus pricing, the

advantages and disadvantages of other strategies, and your recommendation.

■ MARKETING MINI-PROJECT:
LEARNING BY DOING

The purpose of this mini-project is to help you become familiar with how consumers respond to different prices by conducting a series of pricing experiments.

For this project you should first select a product category that students such as yourself normally purchase. It should be a moderately expensive purchase such as athletic shoes, a bookcase, or a piece of luggage. You should next obtain two photographs of items in this product category, or if possible, two actual items. The two items should not appear to be substantially different in quality or in price.

Note: You will need to recruit separate research participants for each of the activities listed in the next section.

- **Experiment 1—reference pricing**
  a. Place the two products together. Place a sign on one with a low price. Place a sign on the other with a high price (about 50 percent higher will do). Ask your research participants to evaluate the quality of each of the items and to tell which one they would probably purchase.

  b. Reverse the signs and ask other research participants to evaluate the quality of each of the items and to tell which one they would probably purchase.

  c. Place the two products together again. This time place a sign on one with a moderate price. Place a sign on the other that is only a little higher (less than 10 percent higher). Again, ask research participants to evaluate the quality of each of the items and to tell which one they would probably purchase.

  d. Reverse the signs and ask other research participants to evaluate the quality of each of the items and to tell which one they would probably purchase.

- **Experiment 2—odd–even pricing**

  For this experiment you will only need one of the items from experiment 1.

  a. Place a sign on the item that ends in $.99 (for example, $59.99). Ask research participants to tell you if they think the price for the item is very low, slightly low, moderate, slightly high, or very high. Also ask them to evaluate the quality of the item and to tell you how likely they would be to purchase the item.

  b. This time place a sign on the item that ends in $.00 (for example, $60.00). Ask different research partici-

pants to tell you if they think the price for the item is very low, slightly low, moderate, slightly high, or very high. Also ask them to evaluate the quality of the item and to tell you how likely they would be to purchase the item.

Develop a presentation for your class in which you discuss the results of your experiments and what they tell you about how consumers view prices.

■ REAL PEOPLE, REAL SURFERS:
EXPLORING THE WEB

Courtyard is but one of a number of Marriott brands. Explore the Marriott Internet site www.marriott.com and answer the following questions:

1. Examine the sites of the four or five different Marriott brands. Based on what you see, how does Marriott position each of these brands?
2. What market segments do you think Marriott is targeting with each of these brands?
3. How does Marriott use pricing to support the positioning of the brands?
4. Does Marriott use a price-lining strategy with its hotel brands? Explain.
5. What other pricing tactics can you find on the Web site that Marriott is using?
6. What is your evaluation of the Marriott Web site? Is it useful to consumers? To business customers? What recommendations would you make for improvement of the site?

■ PLAN IT!
DEVELOPING A
MARKETING PLAN

As your instructor directs, create a marketing plan (using Marketing Plan Pro software or a written marketing plan format) to document your marketing decisions or answer these questions in a written or oral report.

In the course of working on CFS's marketing plan for next year, consider which pricing methods would be most appropriate for the company's products.

1. How can CFS use price lining to differentiate each item in its product line?
2. Assuming that the Chubby Stubby products will be introduced next year, would you recommend skimming, penetration, or trial pricing?
3. What discounting tactics would help CFS build distribution for the Chubby Stubby products?

Key Terms

bait-and-switch, (392)
captive pricing, (381)
cost-plus pricing, (373)

cumulative quantity discounts, (384)
demand-based pricing, (375)

dynamic pricing, (385)
everyday low pricing (EDLP), (378)

MARKETING IN ACTION: CHAPTER 13 CASE

REAL CHOICES AT SOUTHWEST AIRLINES

It's not only the makers of disposable diapers and laundry detergent that are jumping on the everyday low price (EDLP) bandwagon. A number of airlines are becoming EDLP carriers, a move that is expected to transform the industry as both large and small carriers compete for low-fare travelers.

Southwest Airlines was the first airline to implement EDLP fares, and so far it has been the most successful. Its strategy has been to reduce costs in order to offer low fares day in and day out. According to Keith Taylor, Southwest's director of revenue management, "We've had a simplified, low-fare structure for 21 years, and we've kept that in place." An indication of cost cutting and of the profitability of Southwest is its load factor. The load factor is the percentage of seats filled. While the industry average requirement to cover costs is a 67 percent load factor, Southwest's is closer to 45 percent.

How does Southwest keep costs down? For one thing, Southwest uses only one type of plane, the Boeing 737. Other major airlines may have 15 or 20 different planes. Using only one plane cuts costs for parts, repairs, and maintenance substantially.

As the airline industry has become more and more competitive, other airlines have attempted to follow Southwest's EDLP strategy. For example, in the early 1990s, Continental Airlines nearly tripled the number of no-frills "Peanuts Fares" to 875 daily departures, more than half of the airline's 1,599 daily flights. It is in this increasingly competitive environment that Southwest must consider its future. Although the airline would like to increase its number of flights in the hope of becoming the first national low-fare carrier, it must consider whether such growth is possible. One problem with larger airlines is that they are saddled with high fixed costs that are not part of the current Southwest financial structure. By increasing in size, would Southwest increase its per-mile costs substantially above what they are now? And although Southwest has secured its position in its current routes, would attempts at expansion cause its market to overlap those of the new EDLP competitors so that new routes would not be profitable?

Sourc: Adam Bryant, "Three Airlines Chart Austerity Course," *The New York Times* (14 June 1995): D1, D4; Jennifer Lawrence, "Major Airlines Look for Lift from Low Pricing," *Advertising Age* (14 February 1994): 8; Bridget O'Brian, "Continental's CALite Hits Some Turbulence in Battling Southwest," *The Wall Street Journal* (10 January 1995): A1, A5.

THINGS TO THINK ABOUT

1. What is the decision facing Southwest Airlines?
2. What factors are important in understanding this decision situation?
3. What are the alternatives?
4. What decision(s) do you recommend?
5. What are some ways to implement your recommendation(s)?

Bookmark It!

OBJECTIVES:

1. Understand the communication model.
2. List and describe the elements of the promotion mix.
3. Explain the stages in developing the promotion plan.
4. Explain the current trend toward interactive promotion strategies.
5. Explain why database marketing is increasingly popular and how databases are developed and managed.
6. Explain how firms implement integrated marketing communications and why some marketers resist it.

PROMOTIONAL STRATEGY, INTERACTIVE MARKETING, AND DATABASE MARKETING

Real People, Real Choices:

Meet Leslie Goldfarb, a Decision Maker at Price McNabb Communications

www.pricemcnabb.com

CURRENT POSITION: Vice President.

CAREER PATH: B.A. in Communications, Syracuse University.

PROFESSIONAL ACHIEVEMENTS: American Marketing Association's EFFIE award, the Citibank Directors award for outstanding achievement in marketing, and a Clio and Silver Lion for outstanding TV advertising.

WHAT I DO WHEN I'M NOT WORKING: A mommy to my five-year-old daughter Jessica.

FIRST JOB OUT OF SCHOOL: Assistant Account Executive at NW Ayer Advertising in New York City. Technically, my first job lasted only three hours. I was hired to work on the Nestlé account, but 24 hours before my start date, the agency lost it.

MOTTO: If you don't know where you're going, you'll end up someplace else.

WHAT DRIVES ME: A happy client who keeps coming back.

MANAGEMENT STYLE: No BS. No politics. I simply want to be with smart people who give it all they've got.

The Name Game

One of Price McNabb's most recent projects was restructuring and redesigning the marketing plan of the Comporium Group, an independent telecommunications company founded in South Carolina in 1894 and now one of the largest independent communications companies in the Southeast. It provides state-of-the-art commercial and residential communications services, including local and long-distance telephone, Internet, wireless, cable television, and security systems.

Family interests have heavily influenced the organizational structure of the privately held company. Business units operate independently along family lines with little or no crossover among them. Deregulation and advances in technology pushed Comporium Group into an increasingly competitive environment. The protected monopoly that they once enjoyed was breaking down and, as more companies came on the scene, the firm decided it needed to contain customers' curiosity about the competition. To do so, the company first needed to transform itself from a group of loosely affiliated, independent businesses into a unified, customer-focused organization.

Price McNabb was brought in to devise a strategy. Leslie Goldfarb's first challenge was to think of a new name for the company that would (1) give the impression of a larger business entity while still providing an identity for the smaller business units, (2) provide a "corporate entity" for philanthropic activities, community relations, employee retention, and morale building, (3) provide a platform to help facilitate divisional cross-selling like selling long-distance, wireless, and cable services to the company's local phone customers, and (4) enhance the corporation's image outside of its region to facilitate national expansion of select business units.

These are the options Leslie and her colleagues presented to their client:

Option 1: Choose an umbrella corporate name.

Choose an endorser strategy in which the parent company provides an umbrella corporate name under which individual operating companies are still marketed independently (CNN, a Time Warner Company, for example). A unifying type-set/symbol and corporate brand name would be used as an "endorser" to the business unit brand name. In this situation, the business units would be named Rock Hill Telephone & Cable TV, a Comporium Group company. On the one hand, this would allow individual units to retain control over their own marketing, while creating a corporate "beacon" to follow. On the other hand, however, individual units might choose to deemphasize or even ignore their relationship to the parent company.

Option 2: Always use the corporate name.

The parent company name becomes the unifying symbol/name across all individual units (Comporium Communications, Comporium Security, Comporium Publishing, Comporium Long Distance). This would create a new corporate identity almost overnight. Such a radical move signals to consumers and others that a real change is taking place at the company. But this would require a significant marketing effort to maintain customer awareness and loyalty. And it might be too bold a move for some of the individual unit heads.

Option 3: Let each unit pick its own name.

Allow the individual units to choose either option. In this way, each unit would have the flexibility to choose how and to what extent it wished to align with the parent company. Some risks are that this method might not send a unified message to customers or employees and might lead to unintentional ranking of units based on how they choose to use the parent company name.

If you were on the decision team, which option would you choose and why? The "How It Worked Out" box shows the finished ad from page 398. We've deleted the company information so as not to give away the chosen option.

Tailoring Marketing Communications to Customers

What's in a name? Shakespeare's Juliet took that question lightly, perhaps, but Leslie Goldfarb believes the answer is far from trivial. Deciding on a naming strategy is one piece in a complex jigsaw puzzle; all of the pieces need to fit to communicate an image of a product, service, or company that is consistent and desirable so that customers want to be *your* customers. It is not an easy task.

The coordination of marketing communications efforts to influence attitudes or behavior is **promotion.** As one of the famous four Ps of the marketing mix, promotion plays a vital role, whether the goal is to sell suits to executives or to encourage government to reduce import tariffs on textiles.

promotion ■ The coordination of a marketer's communications efforts to influence attitudes or behavior.

A promotion can take many forms: quirky television commercials, sophisticated magazine ads, World Wide Web banner ads boasting the latest Java language applications, funky T-shirts, blimps, blinking messages over football stadiums, and so on.

Some promotions push specific products, while others seek to create or reinforce a corporate image.

- Promotion *informs* consumers about new goods and services and where they can purchase them.[1]
- Promotion *reminds* consumers to continue using certain products.
- Promotion *persuades* consumers to choose one product over others.
- Promotion *builds* relationships with customers.

When employing an integrated marketing communications strategy, marketers provide information to consumers when and where they want it. This ad for Lexus provides lots of product details for consumers, and sends them to Lexus.com for a "test drive."

Although promotion used to be a one-sided conversation from marketer to customer, modern technology allows the process to become interactive. The customer can talk back now. As telephone, cable, and entertainment companies unite to offer new ways to reach consumers in their homes, in their cars, or even at the beach via laptops, the face of promotion is changing in exciting ways. In Chapter 8 we talked about customer relationship management (CRM) and how firms try to communicate with individual customers on a one-to-one basis through dialogue and feedback. That same focus is what **integrated marketing communications (IMC)** is all about. Just as customer needs are the focus of the marketing concept and of total quality management programs, the customer is also the focus for companies that are adopting an IMC perspective. In the traditional promotion campaign, there is little effort to look at the communication needs of consumers. With IMC, marketers seek to understand what information consumers want, as well as how, when, and where they want it. That's the philosophy that drives Price McNabb's desire to craft a clear image for its client.

integrated marketing communications (IMC) ■
A strategic business process that marketers use to plan, develop, execute, and evaluate coordinated, measurable, persuasive brand communication programs over time with targeted audiences.

In traditional promotion plans, there is little effort to coordinate the messages consumers receive. The IMC approach argues that consumers see the variety of messages they receive from a firm—a TV commercial, a coupon, an opportunity to win a sweepstakes, and a display in a store—as a whole and as the company speaking to them. In most traditional promotion campaigns, nothing is further from the truth. An advertising campaign typically is run independently of a sweepstakes, which in turn has no relation to a series of billboard ads. These disjointed efforts could send conflicting messages that leave the consumer confused and unsure of the identity of the brand.

Let's see how the rules are changing in the promotions business. To truly understand IMC, we need to examine some of the basics. First, we will review the communication process, then we will discuss the promotion planning process, and finally we will see how IMC has changed the way firms are developing total communication programs.

The Traditional Communications Model

The traditional perspective on communication views the consumer as the final link in a chain of events: A message is transmitted through some medium from a sender to a receiver who (it is hoped) is listening and understands the sender. Regardless of how messages are sent—a hat with a Caterpillar tractor logo on it or a door-to-door sales pitch from a Mary Kay representative—they are designed to capture receivers' attention and relate to their needs.

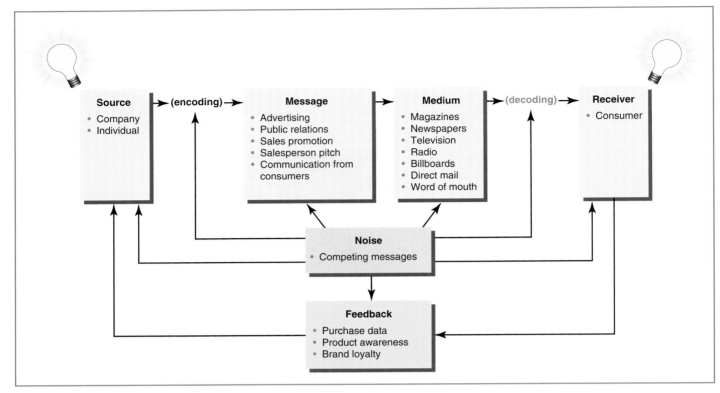

FIGURE 14.1

Communications Model

The communications model explains how ideas are translated into messages and transmitted from the marketer (the source) to the consumer (the receiver) who hopefully understands what the marketer intended.

Any way that marketers reach out to consumers, from a simple highway billboard to a customized message sent via e-mail, is part of the basic communications process. The **communications model** specifies the elements necessary for communication to occur: a source, a message, a medium, and a receiver. Figure 14.1 shows the communications model.

communications model ■
The process whereby meaning is transferred from a source to a receiver.

ENCODING BY THE MARKETER

It is one thing for marketers to form an idea about a product in their own minds and quite another to express it so other people get the same picture. **Encoding** is the process of translating an idea into a form of communication that will convey the desired meaning.

encoding ■ The process of translating an idea into a form of communication that will convey meaning.

For example, consider how financial services companies like to represent themselves with different animal symbols. The Dreyfus Corporation uses a lion in its marketing communications to connote fearlessness and being "king of the jungle." (Of course, this lion must fight it out with other companies' mascots, such as the Merrill Lynch bull and the T. Rowe Price ram.)

THE SOURCE

source ■ An organization or individual that sends a message.

The **source** is the organization or individual sending the message. Marketers often choose a real person (Jared Fogle, the dieting college student for Subway restaurants), hire an actor or model (Cindy Crawford for Pepsi), or create a character (Mr. Peanut for Planters Peanuts) who will represent the source.

THE MESSAGE

message ■ The communication in physical form that goes from a sender to a receiver.

The **message** is the actual communication going from sender to receiver.[2] It must include all the information necessary to persuade, inform, remind, or build a relationship. Messages may include both verbal and nonverbal elements such as beautiful background scenery, celebrity presenters, and so on. Messages used in advertising must be carefully constructed so that they

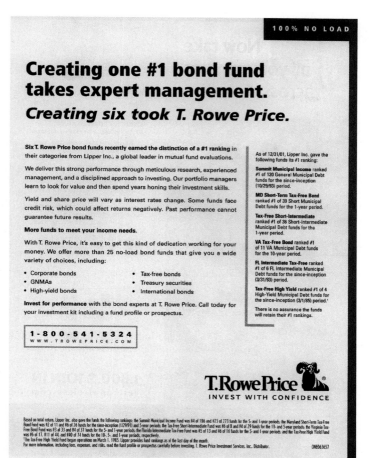

T. Rowe Price hopes that when consumers encode the message in its ads, they will associate the characteristics of the ram with the company.

can connect with a wide variety of consumers or business customers. In contrast, the message delivered by a salesperson can be carefully tailored for each individual customer and the salesperson can respond to questions or objections.

THE MEDIUM

No matter how the message is encoded, it must then be transmitted via a **medium,** a communications vehicle used to reach members of a target audience. This vehicle can be television, radio, a magazine, personal contact, a billboard, or even a product logo printed on a coffee mug. Ideally the attributes of the product should match those of the medium. For example, magazines with high prestige are more effective at communicating messages about overall product image and quality, whereas specialized magazines do a better job of conveying factual information.[3]

medium ■ A communications vehicle through which a message is transmitted to a target audience.

1 *Bookmark It!*

Watch a few hours of television, making notes on commercials presented on different programs and different specialized cable channels. Does the medium match the product for each? Why or why not?

DECODING BY THE RECEIVER

Communication cannot occur unless a **receiver** is there to get the message. Assuming that the customer is even paying attention (a big assumption in our overloaded, media-saturated society!), the meaning of the message is interpreted in light of that individual's unique experiences. **Decoding** is the process whereby a receiver assigns meaning to a message. We hope that the target consumer will decode the message the way we had intended. Effective communication occurs only when the source and the receiver have a *mutual frame of reference.* They must share the same understanding about the world. Grabbing the receiver's attention is more likely if the message source is someone the receiver likes, if the message is creatively executed, and when the medium is one the receiver typically notices. Furthermore, it helps if the subject of

receiver ■ The organization or individual that intercepts and interprets the message.

decoding ■ The process by which a receiver assigns meaning to the message.

the message is something that is personally relevant. The most enticing shampoo ad in the world probably won't be noticed by a bald man!

NOISE

noise ■ Anything that interferes with effective communication.

The communications model also acknowledges that messages can be blocked by **noise**, which is anything that interferes with effective communication. Noise can occur at any stage. It can occur at the encoding stage if the sender uses words or symbols that the receiver will not understand. Or the reciever may be distracted by a nearby conversation. There may be a problem with transmission of the message through the medium. Competing marketing communications cause noise, as do other things going on in the environment that divert the receiver's attention.

Marketers try to minimize noise by placing their messages where there is less likely to be distractions or competition for consumers' attention. Calvin Klein, for example, will often buy a block of advertising pages in a magazine so the reader sees only pictures of its clothing.

For many products, factual information is essential. Magazine advertising provides an opportunity to deliver the desired information.

FEEDBACK

To complete the communications loop the source receives **feedback** (reactions) from receivers. These reactions to the message help to gauge the appeal's effectiveness and fine-tune it. Obtaining feedback reminds us of the importance of conducting marketing research (as we discussed in Chapter 5) to verify that a firm's strategies are working.

However, there are two drawbacks of traditional promotion methods—feedback is often difficult to measure and customers' reactions to prior messages are not sufficiently reflected in subsequent promotions. This is where newer techniques based on more interactive feedback come in, as we'll see shortly.

feedback ■ Receivers' reactions to the message.

Promotional Strategy

As we said earlier, promotion is one of the four Ps. But virtually *everything* an organization says and does is a form of marketing communication or promotion. The ads it creates, the packages it designs, even the uniforms its employees may wear contribute to the impression people have of the company and its products. In fact, in a broad sense it can be argued that every element of the marketing mix is actually a form of communication. After all, the price of a product, where it is sold, and even the nature of the product itself contribute to the impression of the item in people's minds.

THE PROMOTION MIX

Within the marketing mix, we call the communication elements that the marketer controls the **promotion mix.** These elements include advertising, sales promotions, public relations, and

promotion mix ■ The major elements of marketer-controlled communications including advertising, sales promotions, public relations, and personal selling.

Sitting at the
big kids table
is overrated.

Formal dining rooms can be so...formal. Then there are Corian' solid surfaces. Equally at home with hot dogs and filet mignon, the inviting beauty of Corian' is backed by a 10-year limited warranty. For inspiration, visit corian.com or call 800-4CORIAN

CORIAN'

Product design sends a powerful message. To create a consistent brand image, the product and the advertising must be combined effectively. Here, the Corian counter top is strong enough to withstand kids.

personal selling. We'll be diving into each of these topics more deeply in upcoming chapters, so be patient.

The term *mix* implies that a company's promotion strategy is focused on more than one element, so part of the challenge is to combine these different communications tools in an effective way.

Another challenge is to be sure that the promotion mix works in harmony with the overall marketing mix, which combines elements of promotion with place, price, and product information to position the firm's offering in people's minds.

These other Ps also communicate. For example, a product design can send a powerful message, as when Honda Motor Company introduced a model called the City to the Japanese market that was designed to attract young drivers. City featured a very high roof that made it look like a toy. This playful quality appealed to Japan's young consumers, and the design theme was reinforced by carefree promotional messages.[4]

Marketing communications vary in the amount of control that the marketer has over the message. As Figure 14.2 shows, mass media advertising and sales promotion are at one end of the continuum, where the marketer has total control over what message is delivered. At the other end is word-of-mouth communication. Marketers know what consumers hear from one another is a vitally important component of the brand attitudes consumers form—and of their decisions about what and what not to buy. Marketers, however, have little, if any, control over word-of-mouth communication.

Between the ends we find personal selling, where marketers have much but not total control over the message delivered, and public relations, where marketers have even less control. In this section we'll briefly describe the elements of the promotion mix, each of which will be covered in detail in later chapters. Table 14.1 presents some of the pros and cons of each element.

Personal Appeals   The most immediate way for a marketer to make contact with customers is simply to tell them how wonderful the product is. This is part of *personal selling*, direct

FIGURE 14.2

Control Continuum

The elements of the promotion mix differ in the amount of control the marketer has over the message delivered to the consumer.

High				Low
Advertising	Sales Promotion	Personal Selling	Public Relations	Word of Mouth

Promotional Element	Pros	Cons
Advertising	The marketer has control over what the message will say, when it will appear, and who is likely to see it.	Often expensive to produce and distribute. May have low credibility and/or be ignored by audience.
Sales promotion	Provides incentives to retailers to support one's products. Builds excitement for retailers and consumers. Encourages immediate purchase and trial of new products. Price-oriented promotions cater to price-sensitive consumers.	Short-term emphasis on immediate sales rather than a focus on building brand loyalty. The number of competing promotions may make it hard to break through the promotional clutter.
Public relations	Relatively low cost. High credibility.	Lack of control over the message that is eventually transmitted and no gurarantee that the message will ever reach the target. Hard to track the results of publicity efforts.
Personal selling	Direct contact with the customer gives the sales-person the opportunity to be flexible and modify the sales message to coincide with the customer's needs. The salesperson can get immediate feedback from the customer.	High cost per contact with customer. Difficult to ensure consistency of message when it is delivered by many different company representatives. The credibility of salespeople often depends on the quality of their company's image, which has been created by other promotion strategies.

TABLE 14.1

A Comparison of Elements of the Promotion Mix

interaction between a company representative and a customer that can occur in person, by phone, or even over an interactive computer link. Salespeople are a valuable source of communications because customers can ask questions and the salesperson can immediately address objections and describe product benefits.

Personal selling can be tremendously effective, especially for big-ticket consumer items and for industrial products where the "human touch" is essential. It can be so effective that some marketers, if given a choice, might neglect other forms of promotion. This form of promotion is expensive, however.

Mass Appeals   The other pieces of the promotion mix are those messages intended to reach many prospective customers at the same time. Whether a company mails an announcement to a few hundred local residents or airs a television commercial to millions, it is promoting itself to a mass audience.

- *Advertising*: Advertising is for many the most familiar and visible element of the promotion mix. **Advertising** is nonpersonal communication from an identified sponsor using the mass media. Because it can convey rich and dynamic images, advertising can establish and reinforce a distinctive brand identity. This helps marketers bond with customers and boost sales.

    This promotion element is also useful in communicating factual information about the product or reminding consumers to buy their favorite brand. However, advertising sometimes suffers from a credibility problem because cynical consumers tune out

2 Bookmark It!

Think about some products that you and your family have purchased in recent years. Which ones were better promoted with personal appeals? With mass appeals? With a combination of the two?

advertising ■ Nonpersonal communication from an identified sponsor using the mass media.

TESTED FOR THE UNEXPECTED. ⊘ DUNLOP

Advertising often creates and
reinforces a distinctive brand
identity by using rich and
dynamic images.

messages they think are biased or are intended to sell them something they don't need. Advertising can also be expensive, so firms must take great care to ensure their messages are effective.

- *Sales Promotion*: Sales promotions are programs such as contests, coupons, or other incentives that marketers design to build interest in or encourage purchase of a product during a specified time period. Unlike other forms of promotion, sales promotions are intended to stimulate immediate action (often in the form of a purchase) rather than building long-term loyalty.

- *Public Relations*: Public relations techniques portray an organization and its products positively by influencing the perceptions of various publics, including customers, government officials, and shareholders. It includes writing press releases, holding special events, and conducting and publishing consumer surveys about product or company-related issues. It also includes efforts to put a positive spin on negative company news. Unlike sales promotions, public relations components of the promotion mix usually do not seek a short-term increase in sales. Instead they try to craft a long-term positive image for the product or the organization.

DEVELOPING THE PROMOTION PLAN

The marketing manager has many different promotion tools available to identify the specific combination that will meet the company's objectives in the most effective and cost-efficient way. Think of the marketing manager as an artist who must choose just the right blend of "paints" to create a picture of the organization and its products that is pleasing to the public and satisfactory to the client.

Numerous decisions must be made to avoid winding up with a picture of the organization that is a jumble of unrelated events and themes, so the smart manager first develops a "sketch," or a **promotion plan**. This is a framework for developing, implementing, and controlling the firm's promotional activities.[5] Just as with any other strategic decision-making process, the development of this plan includes several stages, as shown in Figure 14.3. Let's review each stage.

promotion plan ■ A framework that outlines the strategies for developing, implementing, and controlling the firm's promotional activities.

As long as sausages cannot be sent by e-mail, we will have to share the road.

Trucks are good for everyone.
a Mercedes-Benz Project

Mercedes-Benz

The marketing manager has many promotional tools available—even the back of a truck, as this German ad for Mercedes-Benz illustrates.

Establish Promotion Objectives The whole point of developing a promotion strategy is to connect the marketing plan to consumers to let them know that the organization has a product to meet their needs in a timely and affordable way. It's bad enough when a product comes along that people don't want or need. But the bigger marketing sin is to have a product that they do want but fail to let them know about it. That's what communications firms such as Price McNabb work hard to avoid.

As creative as some advertisements or salespeople are, it is rare that any single promotion could cause a consumer who's never heard of a product to become aware of it, prefer it over

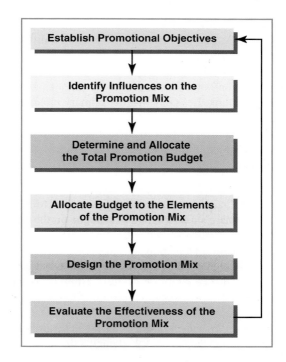

Establish Promotional Objectives

↓

Identify Influences on the Promotion Mix

↓

Determine and Allocate the Total Promotion Budget

↓

Allocate Budget to the Elements of the Promotion Mix

↓

Design the Promotion Mix

↓

Evaluate the Effectiveness of the Promotion Mix

FIGURE 14.3

Stages in Developing the Promotion Mix

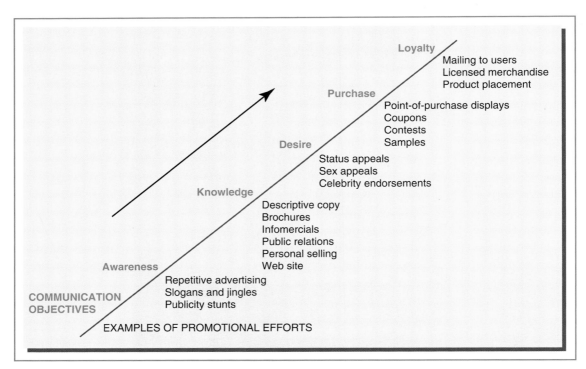

FIGURE 14.4

Up the Promotional Road

Communication objectives seek to move a consumer up the "promotional road" from awareness of the product to becoming a loyal user.

competing products, and buy it on the spot. Exceptions are novelty and impulse items when the product is bought on a whim—but the vast majority of new products require a lot more advance work to get their story across.

Think of this promotion road as an uphill climb, such as the one in Figure 14.4, in which each step is harder than the one before. As the hill steepens, steps that establish a preference for the product and build demand get tougher. Many potential buyers may drop out along the way leaving less of the target group inclined to go the distance and become loyal customers. Each part of this path entails different promotion objectives to "push" people to the next level.

To understand how this process works, consider how a company would have to adjust its promotion objectives as it tries to establish a presence in the market for a new men's cologne called Hunk. Let's say that the primary target market for the cologne is single men aged 18 to 24 who care about their appearance and who are into health, fitness, and working out. The company would want to focus more on some promotion methods (such as advertising) and less on others (such as personal selling). Here are some steps the company might take to promote Hunk.

- *Create awareness.* The first step is to make members of the target market aware that there's a new brand of cologne on the market. This would be accomplished by simple, repetitive advertising in magazines, on television, and on the radio that push the brand name. The company might even undertake a teaser campaign in which interest is heightened by not revealing the exact nature of the product (for example, newspaper ads that simply proclaim, "Hunk is coming!"). The promotion objective might be to create an 80 percent awareness of Hunk cologne among 18- to 24-year-old men in the first two months.
- *Inform the market.* The next step would be to provide prospective users with knowledge about the benefits the new product has to offer, that is, how it is positioned

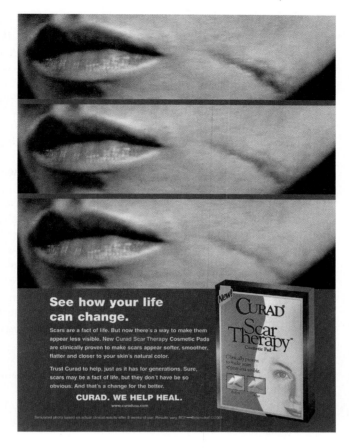

Often a major objective for advertising is to inform consumers about the benefits of a new product. This Curad Scar Therapy ad presents some convincing arguments.

relative to other fragrances (see Chapter 8). Perhaps the cologne has a light, slightly mentholated scent with hints of liniments used after a workout.

Promotion would focus on communications that emphasize this position. The objective at this point might be to communicate the connection between Hunk and muscle building so that 70 percent of the target market develops some interest in the product.

- *Create desire.* The next task is to create favorable feelings toward the product and to convince at least some portion of this group that Hunk is preferable to other men's colognes. Communications at this stage might employ splashy advertising spreads in magazines, perhaps including an endorsement by a well-known celebrity "hunk" such as Arnold Schwarzenegger. The specific objective might be to create positive attitudes toward Hunk cologne among 50 percent of the target market and brand preference among 30 percent of the target market.

- *Encourage trial.* As the expression goes, "How do ya know 'til ya try it?" The company now needs to get some of the men who have formed a preference for the product to splash it on. A promotion plan might encourage trial by mailing samples of Hunk to members of the target market, inserting "scratch-and-sniff" samples in bodybuilding magazines, placing elaborate displays in stores that dispense money-saving coupons, or even sponsoring a contest in which the winner gets to have Arnold Schwarzenegger as his personal trainer for a day. The specific objective now might be to encourage trial of Hunk among 25 percent of 18- to 24-year-old men in the first two months.

- *Build loyalty.* Of course, the real test is loyalty: convincing customers to stay with Hunk after they've gone through the first bottle. Promotion efforts must maintain ongoing communications with current users to reinforce the bond they feel with the product. As before, this will be accomplished with some mix of strategies, including periodic advertising, special events for users, and maybe even the development of

3 *Bookmark It!*

Using the notes you made on TV commercials earlier, what objectives do you believe the marketers had in mind for each commercial? What elements of the commercial prompted your conclusions?

push strategy ■ The company tries to move its products through the channel by convincing channel members to offer them.

pull strategy ■ The company tries to move its products through the channel by building desire for the products among consumers, thus convincing retailers to respond to this demand by stocking these items.

a workout clothing line bearing a Hunk logo. The objective might be to develop and maintain regular usage of Hunk cologne among 10 percent of men from 18 to 24 years old.

Identify Influences on the Promotion Mix   Unfortunately, there is no such thing as one perfect promotion mix that the manager can pull off the shelf for every product. The mix must be carefully tailored to match each situation. The manager must consider how various characteristics of the situation will determine which promotion tools work best each and every time.

One crucial issue in determining the promotion mix is whether the company is relying on a push strategy or a pull strategy.

A **push strategy** means that the company is seeking to move its products through the channel of distribution by convincing channel members to offer them and entice their customers to select these items. In this case, promotion efforts will focus on personal selling, trade advertising and sales promotions such as exhibits at trade shows.

The company relying on a **pull strategy** is counting on consumers to learn about and express desire for its products, thus convincing retailers to respond to this demand by stocking these items. In this case, efforts will focus on media advertising and consumer sales promotion to stimulate interest among end consumers. Very few, if any, companies actually have a strategy that is totally a push or a pull strategy. Most firms combine elements of each.

There are salespeople who have boasted they could sell "ice boxes to Eskimos," and some products do need the personal selling touch. But certain products are best sold by other methods. It would be silly for Colgate to hire door-to-door salespeople to promote its toothpaste. Many consumer products, such as cologne, tend to rely more on advertising, especially when the buyer selects the brand because of an image the manufacturer has carefully created for it.

Using consumer sales promotion techniques such as coupons and premiums is important to Procter & Gamble's sales of Tide detergent, but those same tactics would cheapen the image

The Altoids brand was resurrected by a promotion campaign that made it a cult hit among young people.

of a Rolex watch or a Mercedes ($10 off an S-Class?). To compete for shoppers' attention, many companies allocate some promotional efforts to in-store displays and even live product demonstrations to add some personal touch.

The promotion mix must vary over time because some elements work better at different points than others. As we saw in the Hunk cologne example, the stage of the product life cycle influences the promotion mix.

In the *introduction phase*, the objective is to build awareness and encourage of the product among consumers and to rely on a push strategy. Advertising is the primary promotion tool for creating awareness, and a publicity campaign to generate news reports about the new product may help as well. Sales promotion (free samples and such) may be used to encourage trial. Personal selling is important in this phase in order to get channel members to carry the product. For consumer goods sold through retailers, trade sales promotion may be necessary to encourage retailers to stock the product.

In the *growth phase*, promotions must now start stressing product benefits. Advertising increases here, while sales promotions that encourage trial usually decline because people are more willing to try the product without being offered an incentive.

The opposite pattern often occurs during the *maturity phase* in which many people have already tried or use the product. As sales stabilize, strategy now shifts to persuading brand switching. This can be tough if consumers don't see enough differences to bother. Usually sales promotions, particularly coupons and special price deals, have greater chances of success than advertising.

All bets are off during the *decline phase*. As sales plummet, the company dramatically reduces spending on all elements of the promotion mix. Sales will be driven by the continued loyalty of a small group of users who keep the brand alive until it is sold to another company or discontinued. Alternatively, the company may decide to try to revive the brand and dedicate a modest budget to bringing it back from the dead. Such was the case with the 200-year-old breath mint Altoids, which had a devoted following among smokers and coffee drinkers who hung out in the blossoming Seattle club scene during the 1980s. When Altoid's manufacturer (Callard & Bowers) was bought by Kraft, the brand's marketing manager persuaded Kraft

During the growth stage of the product life cycle, advertising that shows product benefits is required. This Dryel ad tells consumers about the benefits of the product and gives directions for proper use.

(a much larger company) to hire advertising agency Leo Burnett to develop a modest promotion effort. The agency publicized the candy using subway posters containing retro imagery and other low-tech media to avoid making the product seem mainstream and as a result turn off the original audience.[6]

Determine and Allocate the Total Promotion Budget

In an ideal world, setting the budget for promotion would be simple: Spend whatever it takes to accomplish the promotion objectives. In the real world, firms often view communications costs as an expense rather than as an investment leading to greater profits. When sales are declining or the company is operating in a difficult economic environment, it is often tempting to cut costs by reducing spending on advertising, promotions, and other "soft" activities whose contributions to the bottom line are hard to quantify. When this is the case, marketers must work harder to justify these expenses.

Economic approaches to budgeting rely on marginal analysis (discussed in Chapter 12), in which the organization spends money on promotion as long as the revenues realized by these efforts continue to exceed the costs of the promotions themselves. This perspective assumes that promotions are always intended solely to increase sales when in fact these activities may have other objectives, such as enhancing a firm's image.

Also, the effects of promotions often lag over time. For example, a firm may have to spend a lot on promotion when it first launches a product without seeing any immediate return. Because of these limitations, most firms rely on two budgeting techniques: top-down and bottom-up.

Top-down budgeting techniques require top management to establish the overall amount that the organization allocates for promotion activities, and this amount is then divided among advertising, public relations, and other promotion departments.

The most common top-down technique is the **percentage-of-sales method** in which the promotion budget is based on last year's sales or on estimates for the present year's sales. The percentage may be an industry average provided by trade associations that collect objective information on behalf of member companies. The advantage of this method is that it reinforces the idea that spending on promotion does result in profits.

Unfortunately, this method can imply that sales *cause* promotional outlays, rather than viewing sales as the *outcome* of promotional efforts. As sales drop, firms might be reluctant to spend more on promotion even though the drop might be due to environmental changes, such as a change in economic conditions or a rival's recent introduction of a new product. If so, cutting promotion spending might not help the firm in the long run.

The **competitive-parity method** is a fancy way of saying "keep up with the Joneses." In other words, match whatever competitors are spending. Some marketers think this approach simply mirrors the best thinking of others in the business. However, this method often sees each player maintaining the same market share year after year. This method also assumes that the same dollars spent on promotion by two different firms will yield the same results, but spending a lot of money doesn't guarantee a successful promotion. Firms certainly need to monitor their competitors' promotion activities, but they must combine this information with their own objectives and capacities.

The problem with top-down techniques is that budget decisions are based more on established practices than on promotion objectives. Another approach is to begin at the beginning; identify promotion goals and allocate enough money to accomplish them. That is what **bottom-up budgeting techniques** attempt. For example, some marketers devise a payout plan that attempts to project the revenues and costs associated with a product over several years and then matches promotion expenditures to a pattern—such as spending more on promotion in the first year to build market share, and then spending less once the product catches on.

This bottom-up logic is at the heart of the **objective-task method**, which is gaining in popularity. Using this approach, the firm first defines the specific communications goals it hopes to achieve, such as increasing by 20 percent the number of consumers who are aware of the brand. It then tries to figure out what kind of promotional efforts it will take to meet that goal. Although this is the most rational approach, it is hard to implement because it obliges

---

top-down budgeting techniques ■ Allocation of the promotion budget based on the total amount to be devoted to marketing communications.

percentage-of-sales method ■ A method for promotion budgeting that is based on a certain percentage of either last year's sales or on estimates for the present year's sales.

competitive-parity method ■ A promotion budgeting method in which an organization matches whatever competitors are spending.

bottom-up budgeting techniques ■ Allocation of the promotion budget based on identifying promotional goals and allocating enough money to accomplish them.

objective-task method ■ A promotion budgeting method in which an organization first defines the specific communications goals it hopes to achieve and then tries to calculate what kind of promotional efforts it will take to meet these goals.

managers to specify their objectives and attach dollar amounts to them. This method requires careful analysis—and a bit of lucky "guesstimating."

Allocate the Budget to a Specific Promotion Mix   Once the organization decides how much to spend on promotion, it must divide its budget among the elements in the promotion mix. Although advertising used to get most of the promotion budget, sales promotions today are playing a bigger role in marketing strategies. As MasterCard's vice president of promotions observed, marketers who once relied on promotions solely to create a short-term response now see them as "a permanent, integral part of the brand."[7]

For example, although the typical NASCAR racing car is covered with the logos of tobacco and motor oil companies, other marketers such as Hewlett-Packard, Universal Studios, and even banking giant HSBC (Hong Kong and Shanghai Banking Corp.) are changing their promotion mix by sponsoring racing teams. They are joining the race to capture the attention of the 460 million people who watch NASCAR events now broadcast to 201 countries.[8] Several factors influence how companies divide up the promotional pie:

- *Organizational factors*: Characteristics of the specific firm influence how it allocates its money. These characteristics include the complexity and formality of the company's decision-making process, preferences for advertising versus sales promotions or other elements in the promotion mix, past experiences with specific promotion vehicles, and the "comfort level" of the firm's advertising and promotion agencies with different approaches in marketing communications. For example, Nestlé, the giant Swiss company, shifted 20 percent of its advertising budget into sales promotion and direct-response efforts over a two-year period after it determined that promotion dollars would be more effective there.[9]
- *Market potential*: Some consumer groups are more likely to buy the product than others. For example, the marketers of Hunk might find that men in blue-collar occupations would be more interested in the product than men in white-collar occupations. It makes sense for marketers to allocate more resources to areas with more sales potential.
- *Market size*: As a rule, larger markets are more expensive places in which to promote. The costs of buying media (such as local TV spots) are higher in major metropolitan areas, but high population density means it will be easier to reach more consumers at the same time. Advertising is good for mass-market products, while personal selling is good for big-ticket, specialized, or highly technical products.

Designing the Promotion Mix   Developing the promotion mix is the most complicated step in promotion planning. It includes determining the specific communication tools that will be used, what message is to be communicated, and the communication channel(s) to be employed. Planners must ask how advertising, sales promotion, personal selling, and public relations can be used most effectively. Each element of the promotion mix has benefits and shortcomings, all of which must be considered in making promotion decisions.

The message should ideally accomplish four objectives (though a single message can rarely do all of these): It should get *Attention*, hold *Interest*, create *Desire*, and produce *Action*. These communications goals are known as the **AIDA model**. Here we'll review some different forms the message can take, as well as how the information in the message might be structured.

AIDA model ■ The communications goals of attention, interest, desire, and action.

Type of appeal: There are many ways to say the same thing, and marketers must take care in choosing what type of appeal, or message strategy, they will use when encoding the message.

To illustrate, consider two strategies employed by rival car companies to promote similar automobiles: A few years ago, Toyota and Nissan both introduced a large luxury car that sold for more than $40,000. Toyota's advertising for its Lexus model used a rational

By using an emotional appeal, advertisers seek to arouse good feelings that will transfer to the brand—and hopefully result in a purchase. Note the use of the words "Tender" and "Family" in this ad.

3 *Bookmark It!*

Find three magazine ads that have emotional appeals and three magazine ads that have rational appeals. Write a few sentences for each ad describing whether the appeal works well for each product and why or why not.

appeal, which focused on the technical advancements in the car's design. This approach is often effective for promoting products that are technically complex and require a substantial investment.

In contrast, Nissan's campaign for its Infiniti model used an emotional appeal, and sought to generate good feelings in the consumer. The new car was introduced with a series of print and television ads that focused on the Zen-like experience of driving, and featured long shots of serene landscapes. As one executive with the campaign explained, "We're not selling the skin of the car; we're selling the spirit."[10]

Structure of the appeal: Many marketing messages are similar to debates or trials in which someone presents arguments and tries to convince the receivers to shift their opinions. The way the argument is presented can be important. Most messages merely tout one or more positive attributes of the product or reasons to buy it. These are known as *supportive arguments* or *one-sided messages*. An alternative is to use a *two-sided message*, with both positive and negative information. Two-sided ads can be quite effective, but marketers do not use them often.[11]

A related issue is whether the argument should draw conclusions. Should the ad say only "our brand is superior," or should it explicitly tell the consumer to buy it? The answer depends on the degree of a consumer's motivation to think about the ad and the complexity of the arguments. If the message is personally relevant, people will pay attention to it and draw their own conclusions. But, if the arguments are hard to follow or the person's motivation to follow them is lacking, it is best to make these conclusions explicit.

Even the best message is wasted if it is not placed in communication channels that will reach the target audience effectively. Communication channels include the mass media: newspapers, television, radio, magazines, and direct mail. Other media include outdoor display signs and boards and electronic media, the most important of which is the Internet.

Many of the traditional promotion tactics can also be adapted for the Internet. And the Internet provides a unique environment for messages that include text, audio, video, hyperlinking, and personalization, not to mention opportunities for interaction with customers and other stakeholders. Web sites can come alive with the right mix of technical wizardry and good design. One advantage of the Web is that companies can give customers a "feel" for their products or services before they buy. Even nightclubs are going to the Web to draw virtual crowds.[12] Sites such as groovetech.com, thewomb.com, raveworld.net, and digital-clubnetwork.com feature real-time footage of what's happening in the clubs. No more big, beefy bouncers to worry about!

Today many marketers are finding that **viral marketing** is both powerful and cheap. It works like this: A company in essence recruits customers to be sales agents by offering them some incentive, such as free e-mail service, to send other consumers a message about the company. In 18 months, Hotmail, which offers free e-mail service, grew to 12 million users using viral marketing.[13] The approach was simple. Hotmail put the message "Get Your Free E-mail at Hotmail.com" at the bottom of every e-mail sent by a Hotmail user. And that's the idea behind viral marketing—messages spread like the flu from one friend to another until "there's a full-blown epidemic and products are flying off the shelves."[14] For companies such as Hotmail, it's a win-win situation. The more free "customers" they have the more they can charge advertisers who pay to have messages on the Hotmail site.

Although the original users of viral marketing received the word-of-mouth pitches from customers for free, many companies have upped the ante by offering premiums and free products if customers tell friends who become customers. AT&T Wireless San Francisco offered college students a discounted cell phone, a calling plan with free features, and a $25 credit on their bill for every friend who signs up for the service (up to a limit of five).[15] Procter & Gamble generated 2 million referrals when it offered consumers a free styling hair spray and entry into a sweepstakes for every 10 friends who visited the Web site for P&G's new Physique shampoo.[16]

viral marketing ■ Marketing activity in which a company recruits customers to be sales agents and spread the word about the product.

Evaluate the Effectiveness of the Promotion Mix   The final stage in managing the promotion mix is to decide whether the plan is working. The marketer needs to determine whether the promotion objectives are adequately translated into marketing communications that are reaching the right target market.

It would be nice if a marketing manager could simply report, "The $3 million promotion campaign for our revolutionary glow-in-the-dark surfboards brought in $15 million in new sales!" It's not so easy. There are many random factors in the marketing environment: a rival's manufacturing problem, a coincidental photograph of a movie star toting one of the boards, or perhaps a surge of renewed interest in surfing.

Still, there are ways to monitor and evaluate the company's promotional efforts. The catch is that the effectiveness of some forms of promotion is easier to determine than others. As a rule, sales promotions are the easiest to evaluate because they occur over a fixed, usually short period making it easier to link to sales volume. Advertising researchers measure brand awareness, recall of product benefits communicated through advertising, and even the image of the brand before and after an advertising campaign. The firm can analyze and compare the performance of salespeople in different territories, although, again, it is difficult to rule out other factors that make one sales person more effective than another. Public relations activities are more difficult to assess because their objectives relate more often to image building than sales volume.

Interactive Marketing

Some marketers understand that we live in an *attention economy*, in which the amount of information available seems infinite, but our ability to get the exact information we want is limited by the amount of time we can spend looking for it. Interactive media are in the business of getting people's attention by making the information consumers want easy to access.

That's the key to **interactive marketing** in which customized marketing communications yield a measurable response from receivers in the form of a purchase or perhaps a request for more information. Let's learn more about interactive marketing.

For example, as we saw in Chapter 6, competing Web portals such as America Online and Yahoo! make their money by luring Web surfers to their sites where they provide them with ads and product information. The "winner" in this race is the site that draws more surfers and provides information that is of interest to them.[17]

CUSTOMIZING THE MESSAGE

As an executive in charge of exploring interactive marketing applications for Leo Burnett once observed, "Advertising started as . . . one guy with a bullhorn standing 300 yards from the crowd, who had to yell to sell, had to keep his sales pitch real general for the whole audience. . . . Technology brings him closer and closer to the crowd. He can lower his voice now, and talk to the really key customers; and they can talk back, because he's close enough to talk to them without having to yell. So you lower your voice, you target your audience better, you become less manipulative in your advertising."[18]

Although advertising on the Web seemed like a boon to marketers early on, its appeal may be fading. Some marketers have found that targeted e-mail customized for each recipient, can be far more effective as an important component of the brand strategy.[19] Marketers have been able to develop e-mail written in HTML (the same language used to produce Web pages), which means that the message looks and feels like a Web page so that many of the design elements (color, animation, etc.) can be adapted to e-mail messages.

De-Mass Marketing   To improve the abilities of organizations to offer goods and services that better match the characteristics of targeted individuals, companies are slicing the mass market into smaller and smaller pieces. In a truly interactive marketing environment, promotion efforts will look more like door-to-door selling than like television advertising. Even the

Web sites that provide the information consumers need get their attention and make them want to learn more about the product, service, or organization. That's important for interactive marketing.

```
-----Original Message-----
From: Barnes & Noble.com [mailto:BNcom@email.bn.com]
Sent: Tuesday, June 11, 2002 12:51 PM
To: estuart@aucegypt.edu
Subject: Limited Time Offer: Save $10, plus get Free Shipping

        Fiction & Literature

        Mystery & Crime

        Romance

        Computing & Internet

        Science Fiction & Fantasy

        Nonfiction

        See All Subjects

    Dear Barnes & Noble.com Customer:

For a limited time, you can save $10 off your online order of $50 or more. Plus, you'll enjoy even greater savings with our
FREE SHIPPING OFFER when you order two or more items.
```

By creating e-mail using HTML (the same programming language used to create Web pages), firms can send customers messages that look like their corporate Web pages. This helps to communicate a consistent image.

Coca-Cola Company, which long has been known for extravagant network productions, is looking for alternatives to big-budget, mass-market commercials.

One campaign, produced by Creative Artists Agency, had 24 ads developed in many moods and styles for 20 different television networks. These range from one done in a "quick-cut" style for MTV to a *Star Trek*–style spot called "Spaceship," aimed at teenage boys.[20] These changes make sense if recipients identify with the message and go on to reach for a Coke.

Levels of Interactive Response   Recall that the goals of promotion include—but are not limited to—purchases. Others include building awareness, informing, reminding, and building a long-term relationship with the product and the firm. To round out our understanding of what interactive marketing is all about, we need to distinguish between two levels of response.

- *First-order response*: In Chapter 18, we will see that direct-marketing vehicles such as catalogs and home shopping television shows are playing a major role in nonstore retailing. These techniques are interactive. If successful, they result in an order (which is most definitely a response), and the record of these responses is called **transactional data**. So let's think of a product offer that directly yields a transaction as a first-order response.
- *Second-order response*: Customer feedback other than a transaction in response to a promotional message is a second-order response. This may be a request for more information about a good, service, or organization.

transactional data ■ An ongoing record of individuals or organizations that buy a product.

When Heinz wanted to steal dog owners away from Nabisco's Milk-Bone for its Meaty Bone dog biscuits, it ran a television commercial that offered a Meaty Bone Taste Challenge Kit. Callers to a toll-free 800 number received a trial-size box of biscuits, a 50-cent coupon, and a special canine placemat that told puppies to choose brands by placing a paw over a picture of their preferred biscuit. As a company executive noted, "It's as if we poured the names of all our potential customers into a funnel. Thanks to that 800 number we now know the people most likely to buy from us, and we can send them coupons and questionnaires."[21]

It may sound weird, but another kind of second-order response is a request *not* to receive any more information from the company. We assume that a priority of any promotion campaign is to get more customers. Interactive marketers sometimes operate with the opposite goal in mind: to *reduce* their customer base! No, they have not lost their minds. They know that future efforts will be more efficient when they connect with customers who are interested in what they have to promote. The amount of effort required to sell the same item gets

4 *Bookmark It!*

You have been hired as marketing manager for a company in Hawaii that wants to sell flowers to consumers throughout the United States. How can the company use interactive marketing to grow the business?

progressively greater as the target's interest in it gets lower. An expression of no interest is valuable information because it enables the firm to concentrate its resources on customers who are the most likely to buy.

Now, let's see what interactive marketers do with all this feedback.

DATABASE MARKETING

The goal of the interactive marketer is to track responses to its messages and develop a dialogue with the customer. That's what Price McNabb did for Drexel Heritage, a client that manufactures upscale furniture. Beginning with customer lists from a dozen Drexel dealers and adding information about these customers from other sources such as car registration rolls and magazine subscriptions, Price McNabb developed a profile of Drexel's most profitable customers in each market. Price McNabb targets customers who match these best customer profiles and reaches them with customized messages that specifically appeal to these buyers.

The secret to effective interactive marketing is the development of a customer database that allows the organization to learn about the preferences of its customers, fine-tune its offering, and build an ongoing relationship with them. The database evolves over time. For example, a music company found, by mining its database of customers, that a significant proportion of people age 62 and older were buying rap music.[22] No, it wasn't a secret clan of Snoop Doggy Dogg fans; it was seniors buying music for their grandchildren. Because many seniors are on a fixed income, the music company developed a direct-marketing campaign focusing on low price. The campaign is continually updated to reflect both the first-order and the second-order responses of the firm's customers.

Maintaining a customer database is not a new idea. What is new is using the database at the core of the company's marketing communication activities and not merely as a simple repository of information. **Database marketing** is the creation of an ongoing relationship with a set of customers with an identifiable interest in a product or service and whose responses to promotion efforts become part of the ongoing communications process. The following list explains what database marketing can do.[23]

database marketing ■ The creation of an ongoing relationship with a set of customers who have an identifiable interest in a product or service and whose responses to promotional efforts become part of future communications attempts.

- *Database marketing is interactive.* Recall that interactive marketing requires a response from the consumers, be it filling out an order form or calling an 800 number for product information. For example, H.J. Heinz sent a mail piece to female cat owners that asked the provocative question, "Does he sleep with you?" If the woman completes a brief survey that tells the company more about her pet food preferences, she receives a personalized thank-you note that mentions her pet by name.[24] She is also entered into the company's database so that she will receive future communications about her feline friend. This type of interactivity gives marketers more than one opportunity to develop a dialogue with the customer and possibly to create add-on sales by engaging the customer in a discussion about the product and related items or services in which she might be interested.
- *Database marketing builds relationships.* It's easier for the marketer to build promotion programs that continue over time with database marketing because the marketer can best adapt them in light of consumers' responses. The best predictor of who will buy a product is knowing who bought it in the past. That's why *Reader's Digest's* 12 full-time statisticians sort its customers by likelihood of purchase and predict the probability that each will respond to a given offer.[25] Once sophisticated database marketers know who has already purchased, they can keep in touch with these consumers on an ongoing basis. They can reward loyal customers with money-saving coupons, and keep them informed of upcoming prizes and promotions. As one executive whose company tracks big-ticket customers explained, "They are members of a club, but they don't know they are members."[26]
- *Database marketing locates new customers.* In some cases, a marketer can create new customers by focusing communications on likely prospects with characteristics similar

to current users. For example, Dial sent coupon mailings about rust stains to neighbors of people in Des Moines, Iowa, and Omaha, Nebraska, who use its Sno Bol toilet bowl cleaner. The brand's sales volume jumped 81 percent in a 12-week period.[27]

- *Database marketing stimulates cross-selling.* Database marketers can find it easy to offer related products to their customers. Interest in one product category boosts the odds that the customer is a good candidate for similar items. This explains why consumers are bombarded with mail offers for computer software, magazines, or clothing after purchasing a similar product over the phone or through a catalog. Hershey Direct, a division of Hershey Foods Corp. that sells limited-edition collectible elf figurines (not the edible kind), tested its database by sending some mailings to only its most serious collectors while other mailings measure the potential of other database segments.[28] Some mailings have included questionnaires regarding specific collectible interests such as plates and music boxes to help the company decide on future product offerings.

- *Database marketing is measurable.* A common complaint of many marketers is the difficulty in pinpointing the impact a promotion had on the target market. Who can say for sure that a single TV commercial motivated people to switch colas? But the database marketers know exactly who received a specific message so they are able to measure the effectiveness of each communication.

- *Responses are trackable.* The marketer can assess the proportion of message recipients that responded, compare the effectiveness of different messages, and compile a history of which consumers are most likely to respond over time. Farm equipment manufacturer John Deere targeted 20,000 farmers who were loyal to other brands. Using a list of farmers who owned competing equipment, Deere sent prospects a series of four mailings spaced over eight weeks, each with an inexpensive gift such as a stopwatch that was related to the theme of saving time and money by replacing existing equipment. The campaign brought 5,800 farmers into the showroom, yielding a 29 percent response rate. Nearly 700 of these consumers bought new equipment, resulting in more than $40 million in new business.[29]

Putting It All Together: Integrated Marketing Communications

All of this brings us back to integrated marketing communications (see Figure 14.5). As defined by a leading researcher in this area, integrated marketing communications (IMC) is "a strategic business process used to plan, develop, execute and evaluate coordinated, measurable, persuasive brand communication programs over time with consumers, customers, prospects and other targeted, relevant external and internal audiences."[30] In one survey of

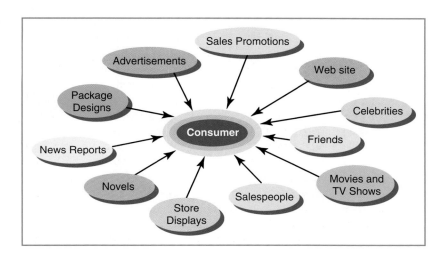

FIGURE 14.5

Integrated Communications Perspective

The integrated marketing communications perspective recognizes that consumers receive information about a product from many different sources, not all of which are under the marketer's control.

marketing executives, IMC was rated the most important factor in marketing strategy—more important than consumer lifestyle changes, economic trends, new retail formats, or globalization.[31]

THE EMERGING IMC PERSPECTIVE

The IMC philosophy recognizes that the customer absorbs information about a product or organization from many sources, not all of which are formal promotion messages or fully under the marketer's control. The basic idea is to take the recipient's perspective by trying to anticipate every occasion in which he will encounter information about the good, service, or organization—from advertising to business cards to employee uniforms—and make sure each of these different exposures communicates the desired message and prompts the intended response.[32] In other words, make sure that everything the company does—including the name given to the product—speaks to the customer with one message and in one voice. This approach still relies on elements in the promotion mix, but it mandates harmony to reach targeted consumers.

Although this idea of communication harmony seems logical, many companies have never considered it before. Public electric and natural gas companies, for example, had long periods of government regulation and in most cases only one company was allowed to operate in a geographic area. Deregulation is changing this, prompting many utilities to examine their communication practices—from advertising to the letters they send late-paying customers—and to start turning to newer marketing and image-building techniques.

Microsoft follows an IMC strategy. The software company's customers receive direct-mail advertising with software user tips, product upgrade deals, and new-product information.

Microsoft is a company that practices integrated marketing communications by coordinating print advertising with other elements of the promotion mix.

Connections with the company are further reinforced by including the company's Windows Showcase catalog inside of product boxes. Microsoft's advertising usually includes an 800 number for obtaining further information. Microsoft also holds many customer seminars, exhibits at trade shows, and spends more than $100 million annually on customer service.[33]

The IMC perspective is still new and evolving. At many companies it still is more of an idea than a reality. However, agencies such as Price McNabb, manufacturers, and other organizations are beginning to develop their own ideas of what an IMC strategy should look like. These approaches tend to share a number of characteristics:

- They focus on customers' need for communications rather than on the message.
- They rely on a customer database to precisely focus their messages.
- They send consistent messages via diverse communications vehicles.
- They plan carefully timed message deliveries to generate a steady stream of consistent information.
- They use several elements of the promotion mix plus product design and packaging to communicate.

THE IMC PLANNING MODEL

So, if IMC is so great, how do you do it? A company wanting to implement an IMC strategy must start with a promotion plan. However, the planning procedure here is a bit different than the traditional approach.[34] This sequence is outlined in Figure 14.6.

Let's take a closer look at what it takes to develop an IMC promotion strategy.

Start with a Customer Database   An IMC plan starts with a marketing database that holds substantial information on current customers and prospects. This is a departure from traditional promotion planning because it means that the *customer*, rather than the firm's profit or sales goals, is the focus of the communications strategy. This approach recognizes that in

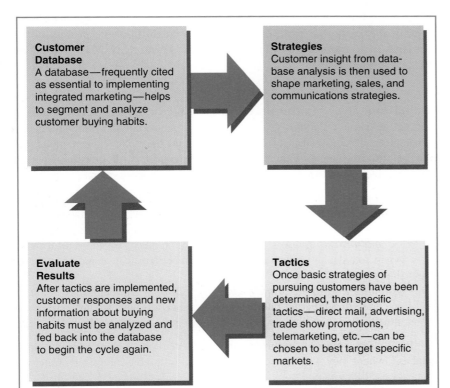

Customer Database
A database—frequently cited as essential to implementing integrated marketing—helps to segment and analyze customer buying habits.

Strategies
Customer insight from database analysis is then used to shape marketing, sales, and communications strategies.

Tactics
Once basic strategies of pursuing customers have been determined, then specific tactics—direct mail, advertising, trade show promotions, telemarketing, etc.—can be chosen to best target specific markets.

Evaluate Results
After tactics are implemented, customer responses and new information about buying habits must be analyzed and fed back into the database to begin the cycle again.

FIGURE 14.6

Integrated Marketing Model
An integrated marketing communications plan begins with a customer database that allows marketers to gain the insight necessary to deliver customized messages to target audiences.

today's competitive world, no firm has the power to transform a market with a catchy jingle, a tempting pricing strategy, or an irresistible sales pitch. Firms depend much more on developing a base of long-term, satisfied customers to bring them profits.

A second difference is that what customers *think* matters less than what they *do*. An important component of the marketing database is that it uses data from past purchases to identify *loyal users* of the brand, *loyal users of competing brands*, and *brand switchers*. Separate communications strategies can then appeal to each group.

contact management ■ A communication strategy that provides communications exposures where and when the targeted customer is most likely to receive them.

Develop Promotion Strategies   Insights from the database are used to devise strategies that reach targeted customers. One strategy is **contact management**, which identifies the best times, places, or situations to reach customers. For example, planners at the advertising agency DDB Worldwide use a technique they call *media mapping*. Planners ask consumers to identify the media (billboards, televisions in bars, etc.) that catch their attention over a given period so that planners can better reach the target audience. They then choose a mix of promotion tools to match their target audience's profile.

Some of the best examples of IMC strategies combine traditional advertising with a company's Web presence. For example, some use TV and radio to drive consumers to their Web sites, leveraging the strengths of each medium. Nike ran a series of TV commercials featuring big-name athletes such as track star Marion Jones and baseball's Mark McGwire.[35] Each ad ended with the message "continued at whatever.nike.com." Web surfers were presented with a choice of seven or eight different endings for the commercials. The campaign generated 4.26 million visitors to the whatever.nike.com Web site.

Implementing Specific Promotion Tactics   The time and place where people will receive a message determines the message and the medium. The planners may want to induce 30 percent of the target market to try the product, or they may want to convince 10 percent of competing brand users to switch. The best promotion mix, therefore, is tailored to the characteristics of the target market. For example, Mountain Dew jumped on a recent youth craze for beepers by inviting its target market of teens to "Do the Dew. Get the Beeper. Join the Network." By sending in proofs of purchase from the soda with $29.99, consumers received a Motorola Renegade pager and six months of free service (a sales promotion). Each of the more than 200,000 pagers ordered through the promotion received weekly messages with a number to call for special offers from Sony, MTV, K2, and other companies (an advertisement).[36]

Evaluating IMC Communications   The IMC perspective takes a broad view: Information about a good or service comes from many sources, and beliefs develop over time. Consequently, traditional measurement techniques that focus on the impact of one message at one point in time can not gauge the impact of an entire communications program. Instead, the following factors are used to conduct a more accurate assessment:[37]

- *First-order responses*: Recall that transactional data, consisting of first-order consumer responses to an offer, form the backbone of a marketing database. The firm can track transactions to determine a campaign's effectiveness.
- *Second-order responses*: Data on customer requests for more information, number of visits to a dealer, or new association memberships can also determine if the campaign has stimulated interest.
- *Attitudes toward the brand and/or organization*: Although they are not always accurate in predicting purchases, customers' attitudes toward an item are important nonetheless, especially when changes in attitudes are tracked over time.

Ideally these pieces of information are collected on an ongoing basis and fed back into the database, where they will be used to update and refine the integrated strategy.[38]

How It Worked Out at Price McNabb

The key to Price McNabb's ultimate decision was to select a strategy that would be most likely to provide the seamless integration of transactions between and services delivered by the individual Comporium business units. With that as the goal, Leslie recommended option 2 and her client agreed. The decision makers came to the conclusion that this strategy would play a significant role in changing how customers and employees viewed the company; they believed the new unified image would move perceptions of the organization from its current position as a local single-product provider to a major business enterprise offering a full range of products and services.

In fact, by employing this strategy and supporting it with a comprehensive communications effort, Price McNabb was able to accelerate customer awareness of the "new and improved" company, create a new corporate culture at Comporium, and lay a strong foundation for joint efforts by the individual business units. Six weeks after the brand launch, research showed that:

- Ninety-five percent of the targets were aware of Comporium's name change and had positive perceptions of the new enterprise.
- Purchase intent increased.
- Likeliness of switching to a competitor decreased.

In addition, an internal survey showed that Comporium salespeople were enthusiastic about the changes and felt the new environment fostered the ability to sell services. This integrated communications strategy clearly "rang a bell" for customers and employees.

The copy for this ad emphasizes that Comporium makes life easier by bringing together in one place all the communications services one needs. The Comporium logo appears as a heading over a list of the full range of products and services (local telephone, long distance wireless, cable TV, Internet, and security) Comporium offers.

WHY DOESN'T EVERYONE ADOPT AN IMC APPROACH?

The idea that one should coordinate the elements of the promotion mix seems so sensible. So, what's the big deal? Why aren't all communications strategies done this way? The truth is that many marketers either resist the IMC approach or have trouble implementing it.[39] Following are some of the barriers to acceptance:

- The approach requires changes in the way marketers plan and implement promotional strategies. Many companies are financially driven rather than customer driven. Also, there is a general resistance to change in organizations. Finally, many executives specialize in one aspect of promotion such as advertising or sales promotion and are reluctant to branch out.
- The IMC approach puts more weight on aspects of promotion other than advertising (such as public relations). Some executives are reluctant to divert part of their communications budget from glamorous ads to coupons, contests, or PR.
- Brand managers and associate brand managers develop promotion strategies at lower levels after senior planners have already developed the larger marketing strategy. But the IMC approach requires upper-level management to view other aspects of the marketing mix (such as packaging or pricing decisions) as part of the communications strategy.
- A successful IMC approach requires a companywide commitment, from the CEO on down, to putting the customer first and communicating interactively with customers in many different channels. Some firms find it hard to change their habits.
- Many advertising agencies feel they should provide "one-stop shopping" for promotional services.[40] Virtually every major agency today has a separate direct-marketing arm. Large agencies are also attempting to buy companies that specialize in other aspects of promotion. For example, Ogilvy & Mather bought Adams & Rinehart, a public relations firm, and A. Eicoff & Co., an infomercial producer, to provide diversified services to its clients. But many marketers doubt that ad agencies will be able to change so quickly. As one executive put it, "You can teach an elephant to dance, but the likelihood of its stepping on your toes is very high."[41]

A survey by the American Association of Advertising Agencies found that 85 percent of clients said they wouldn't trust their agencies to coordinate integrated marketing. To address this problem, some companies are creating a communications "czar," often called a *marcom manager* (for marketing communications), who plans the overall program and coordinates the company's efforts to give the consumer a smooth ride.

6 *Bookmark It!*

Using any Internet search engine (Yahoo!, GoTo.com, AOL search), find some agencies claiming they practice IMC strategies. Based on their services and philosophy, do you think they have implemented true IMC or not? What did you find that leads you to this conclusion?

Chapter Summary

1. Understand the communication model.

The traditional communications model includes a message source that creates an idea, encodes the idea into a message, and transmits the message through some medium. The message is delivered to the consumer, who decodes the message and may provide feedback to the source. Anything that interferes with the communication is called "noise."

2. List and describe the elements of the promotion mix.

Through promotion strategies, marketers inform consumers about new products, remind them of familiar products, persuade them to choose one alternative over another, and build strong customer relationships.

The four major elements of marketing communication are known as the promotion mix. Personal selling provides direct contact between a company representative and a customer. Advertising is nonpersonal communication from an identified sponsor using mass media. Sales promotions stimulate immediate sales by providing incentives to the trade or to consumers. Public relations activities seek to influence the attitudes of various publics.

3. Explain the stages in developing the promotion plan.

The promotion plan begins with promotion objectives, usually stated in terms of communications tasks such as creating awareness, knowledge, desire, product trial, and brand loyalty. Which promotion mix elements will be used depends on the overall strategy (i.e., a push versus a pull strategy, the type of product, and the stage of the product life cycle).

Promotion budgets are often developed from such rules of thumb as percentage-of-sales method, competitive-parity method, and objective-task method. Monies from the total budget are then allocated to various elements of the promotion mix based on characteristics of the organization, the market potential, and market size. Designing the promotion mix includes determining what communication tools will be used and the message that will be delivered.

Marketing messages use a variety of different appeals including those that are rational and others that are emotional in nature. The message may provide one- or two-sided arguments and may or may not draw conclusions.

Communication channels must be selected. The Internet provides both challenges and opportunities for communication including using customers as salespeople in viral marketing activities.

Finally, marketers monitor and evaluate the promotion efforts to determine if the objectives are being reached.

4. Explain the current trend toward interactive promotion strategies.

Today marketers are focusing on interactive marketing in which customized marketing communications elicit a measurable response from receivers. Specialized market segments can now be identified and reached. Increasingly, marketers are tailoring messages to individual consumers, decreasing the use of mass-marketing programs. An important part of interactive marketing is the response of the consumer. Product purchases provide first-order responses but marketers also seek second-order responses such as requests for information or suggestions for product improvements.

5. Explain why database marketing is increasingly popular and how databases are developed and managed.

Database marketing is interactive marketing that utilizes a customer database. Database marketing allows marketers to develop dialogues and build relationships with customers. Marketers use database marketing to create programs that are more flexible, reward loyal users, locate new customers, offer related products to existing customers (cross-selling), and track customer responses.

6. Explain how firms implement integrated marketing communications and why some marketers resist it.

Integrated marketing communication (IMC) is a customer-focused communication strategy that coordinates all communications from a firm. IMC uses customer databases to stay in touch with the market. In an IMC strategy, contact management means that communications occur when customers are receptive. The type of message is influenced by the communication objectives, the characteristics of the customer group, and the exposure situation. The effectiveness of the IMC strategy may be assessed through transactional data, by customers' second-order responses, or by customer attitudes. Some marketers resist IMC because it requires changing accepted ways of doing things, decreases emphasis on advertising, puts an increased focus on communications, and requires major changes within advertising agencies.

Chapter Review

■ MARKETING CONCEPTS:
TESTING YOUR KNOWLEDGE

1. How is integrated marketing communication different from traditional promotion strategies?
2. Describe the traditional communications model.
3. List and describe the elements of the promotion mix.
4. List and explain the steps in the development of a promotion strategy.
5. Why should promotion objectives be phrased in terms of communications tasks? What are some examples of communications task objectives?
6. How does the promotion mix vary with push versus pull strategies? How does it vary in different stages of the product life cycle (PLC)?
7. Explain each of the following budgeting methods: (a) percentage-of-sales method, (b) competitive-parity method, and (c) objective-task method.
8. What are some of the challenges and opportunities for marketing communication on the Internet? What is viral marketing?
9. What is interactive marketing?
10. What is database marketing? What are some reasons that database marketing is growing in popularity?
11. What is integrated marketing communications (IMC)? What is contact management and how is it a part of IMC?

■ MARKETING CONCEPTS:
DISCUSSING CHOICES AND ISSUES

1. The Internet provides some new opportunities for marketing communications. From a consumer perspective, what types of Internet communications are effective?
2. Implementation of IMC strategies requires major changes in the way marketers and agencies think and do business. Why do you think people resist these changes?
3. Consumers are becoming concerned that the proliferation of databases is an invasion of an individual's privacy. Do you feel this is a valid concern? How can marketers use databases effectively and, at the same time, protect the rights of individuals?
4. There are some who argue that there is really nothing new about IMC. What do you think?

■ MARKETING PRACTICE:
APPLYING WHAT YOU'VE LEARNED

1. Visit the Comporium Group Web site (www.comporium.com/comporium-group.htm). Use the hyperlinks to visit the various businesses of Comporium. What elements of the Web site are used to provide a single image of the company? How does Comporium use interactive marketing? What recommendations do you have for improving the Comporium Web site?

2. As a marketing consultant, you are frequently asked by clients to develop recommendations for promotion strategies. Outline your recommendations for the use of different promotion mix elements for one of the following clients: (a) a new online banking service, (b) a health spa and resort, (c) a political candidate, or (d) a brand of photocopy equipment.

3. As the director of marketing for a small firm that markets premium coffees through upscale supermarkets, you are developing a marketing communication plan. With one or more of your classmates, provide suggestions for each of the following items. Then, in a role-playing situation, present your recommendations to the client.
   a. promotion objectives
   b. a method for determining the promotion budget
   c. the use of a push strategy or a pull strategy

4. Assume you are an account executive with an advertising agency. Your assignment is to develop recommendations for a new client, a health and fitness center. Give your recommendations for:
   a. how to use interactive marketing.
   b. how to develop a database for interactive marketing.

5. As a member of the marketing department for a manufacturer of handheld power tools for home improvement, you have been directed to select a new agency to do the promotion for your firm. Of two agencies solicited, one recommends an integrated marketing communications plan, and the other has developed recommendations for a traditional advertising plan. Write a memo to your boss explaining each of the following.
   a. What is different about an integrated marketing communications plan?
   b. Why is the IMC plan superior to conventional advertising?

■ MARKETING MINI-PROJECT:
LEARNING BY DOING

This mini-project is designed to help you understand how organizations use database marketing.

1. Visit your campus admissions office and ask to discuss how it uses database marketing to recruit students. Some of the questions you might ask include:
   a. how the office obtains names for an initial or expanded database.
   b. what information is included in the initial database.
   c. what information is added to the database.
   d. how the office uses the database for communicating with prospective students.

2. Based on what you learn, consider other ways the school might use database marketing for recruiting students.

3. Make a presentation of your findings and recommendations to your class.

REAL PEOPLE, REAL SURFERS: EXPLORING THE WEB

A vast majority of traditional media (television stations, newspapers, magazines, and radio stations) are now using the Internet to build relationships with readers and viewers. For the media, the Internet provides an excellent way to build a database and to communicate one-on-one with customers.

Although individual sites change frequently, some media sites that have provided opportunities for interactive communications with customers and for building a database are:

Business Week (www.businessweek.com)
The New York Times (www.nytimes.com)
Advertising Age (www.advertisingage.com)
Newsweek (www.newsweek.com)

Explore these or other sites that provide opportunities for consumers to register, answer questionnaires, or in some other way use the Internet to build a database. After completing your exploration of each site, answer the following questions:

1. In what ways does each Web site facilitate interactive communications between the firm and customers?
2. How does each firm use the Internet to gather information on customers? What information is gathered? Which site does a superior job of gathering information and why?

3. How do you think the firm might use the information it gathers through the Internet in database marketing activities? How can the information be used to build relationships with customers and prospective customers?
4. What recommendations do you have for each company to improve the interactive opportunities on its Web site?

PLAN IT! DEVELOPING A MARKETING PLAN

As your instructor directs, create a marketing plan (using Marketing Plan Pro software or a written marketing plan format) to document your marketing decisions or answer these questions in a written or oral report.

Review CFS's current promotional strategy in the marketing plan shown in Appendix A.

1. As you move ahead with next year's marketing plan, would you suggest a push or pull strategy to support the company's sales growth—and how will you use this strategy?
2. Next, select one of the CFS products. Based on its stage in the product life cycle, what kind of promotion mix would be most appropriate for this product?
3. Finally, how can CFS use viral marketing to stimulate word-of-mouth about its computer toys?

Key Terms

advertising, (407)
AIDA model, (415)
bottom-up budgeting techniques, (414)
communications model, (402)
competitive-parity method, (414)
contact management, (424)
database marketing, (420)
decoding, (403)
encoding, (402)

feedback, (405)
integrated marketing communications (IMC), (401)
interactive marketing, (418)
medium, (403)
message, (402)
noise, (404)
objective-task method, (414)
percentage-of-sales method, (414)
promotion, (400)

promotion mix, (405)
promotion plan, (408)
pull strategy, (412)
push strategy, (412)
receiver, (403)
source, (402)
top-down budgeting techniques, (414)
transactional data, (419)
viral marketing, (417)

MARKETING IN ACTION: CHAPTER 14 CASE

REAL CHOICES AT KIMBERLY-CLARK

In January 2001, Kimberly-Clark Corp. announced its plans to introduce what it called "the most significant category innovation since toilet paper first appeared in roll form in 1890"—Kleenex Cottonelle Fresh RollWipes moist bath tissue. The result of $100 million on research and development, the actual product was a roll of moist wipes in a plastic dispenser that clipped to a regular toilet-paper holder. Consumer research had shown that 63 percent of adults would use such a product. Kimberly-Clark projected first year sales of $150 million.

Kimberly-Clark was not alone in its enthusiasm for RollWipes. When announced in January, the media greeted the idea with the same excitement and widely reported the planned introduction. But the actual product introduction came much later. Kimberly-Clark had planned to introduce RollWipes in June but production issues delayed things. Finally, in July, RollWipes was launched with a $40 million television, print, and Internet advertising campaign and sampling in public restrooms. Consumers could buy the starter kit that included a dispenser and four rolls of the wipes for $8.99 and the package of four replacement rolls sold for $3.99—three times the price of regular toilet paper.

The projected sales for RollWipes didn't materialize. The product was only successful in a small regional market. Sales were so small that company officials called them "insignificant." Although Kimberly-Clark continued to support RollWipes, growth was much slower than expected.

Why did a product with such high expectations not meet its projected success? Many analysts point to marketing mistakes that Kimberly-Clark made. First, advertising for RollWipes was far less than satisfactory. Analysts suggested that the ads simply did not explain the product, did not show consumers what the product does, and, thus, did not create demand. Instead the ads tried to create a fun image for RollWipes and included humorous shots of people from behind, splashing in the water. Ads carried the slogan, "Sometimes wetter is better." One print ad, for example, featured a close-up of a sumo wrestler from behind.

With a product such as RollWipes, it seems logical that the best way to convince consumers of product benefits is through product trial. But Kimberly-Clark didn't design RollWipes in small trial sizes, which might have been passed out in free samples. Instead, it planned to have a van, outfitted with a mobile restroom and RollWipes, to stop at public places in the Southeast in mid-September. After the terrorist attacks of September 11, 2001, the road trip was canceled.

Another problem may have been a lack of understanding of consumers' response to the product design. Most Americans are more likely than not to blush at discussions of toilet paper. RollWipes, instead of coming in a box like other moist wipes, came in a highly visible dispenser that clipped to the spindle of the regular toilet tissue but was about the size of two rolls of regular toilet paper.

Timing was another problem. Kimberly-Clark announced the product to the media in January 2001, six months before the product launch and six months before the product was available in stores. By that time, many consumers who had been intrigued when they read about RollWipes in their local newspaper had forgotten all about it. And all the introductory product hype and advertising were national while the product itself was available only in select southern U.S. markets.

Unexpected competition also hurt the RollWipes' introduction. Based on the excitement generated by Kimberly-Clark's product announcement in January, Procter & Gamble decided it would enter the same market. Instead of developing its own product, P&G bought Moist Mates, a small private company that produced a similar product that had been successfully marketed in Europe, and repackaged it under the brand name Charmin Fresh Mates. Similar to RollWipes, P&G's Fresh Mates consisted of a plastic dispenser that hung underneath the regular toilet paper. In May 2001, P&G shipped its new product to the same test markets as RollWipes. In July, P&G began advertising on the exact same day.

Kimberly-Clark marketers were left with two major decisions: what to do about RollWipes and how to learn from their mistakes. They wondered just how much of the problem with RollWipes' sales was a result of the product announcement's timing. If the product had not been announced until store shelves were already stocked, would the sales growth have been different? And what next? Should RollWipes be introduced nationally or only in certain regions? And what about advertising? Although a different advertising campaign might convey product benefits more clearly, frank discussions of the product might offend some consumers. Perhaps other means of promoting the product would be more effective.

Sources: Jack Neff, "In Turnaround, P&G Buys Moist Makes," *Advertising Age*, May 7, 2001, accessed at www.adage.com/news.cms?newsId=32341 on April 23, 2002; Jack Neff, "Kimberly-Clark Takes Hit on RollWipes Rollout," *Advertising Age*, October 23, 2001, accessed at www.adage.com/news.cms?newsId=33249 on April 22, 2002; Emily Nelson, "Moistened Toilet Paper Wipes Out After Launch for Kimberly-Clark, *The Wall Street Journal Online*, April 15, 2002, accessed at online.wsj.com/article_email/0,,SB1018817069329538160,00.html on April 15, 2002.

THINGS TO THINK ABOUT

1. What is the decision facing Kimberly-Clark?

2. What factors are important in understanding the decision situation?

3. What are the alternatives?

4. What decision(s) do you recommend?

5. What are some ways to implement your recommendation(s)?

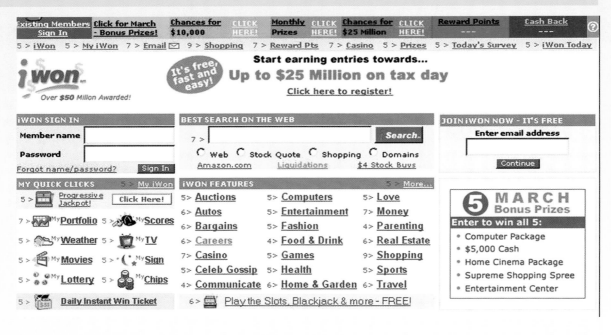

Bookmark It!

OBJECTIVES:

1. Tell what advertising is and describe the major types of advertising.
2. Describe the process of developing an advertising campaign.
3. Explain how marketers evaluate advertising.
4. Understand direct marketing.
5. Explain the future of m-commerce.

Advertising, Direct Marketing, and M-Commerce   15

Meet Brad Sockloff, a Decision Maker at iWon.com

www.iwon.com

CURRENT POSITION: Marketing Manager, Direct Marketing, Excite.com and iWon.com

EDUCATION: B.A., SUNY Albany, M.B.A. Hagan School of Business, Iona College.

WHAT I DO WHEN I'M NOT WORKING: Watch sports and play basketball, softball, and golf.

FIRST JOBS OUT OF SCHOOL: A bartender and high school basketball coach—two jobs that taught me how to work with people.

CAREER HIGH: The launch of the first product that I managed from its inception.

BUSINESS BOOK I'M READING NOW: Ben & Jerry's Double-Dip: How to Run a Values-Led Business and Make Money, Too by Ben Cohen and Jerry Greenfield.

WHAT DRIVES ME: Results—the best thing about direct marketing is that when you work on a marketing campaign, you see the results.

PET PEEVE: Lazy work—it takes less time to do a thorough job than to do a sloppy job and have to redo it.

And the Winner Is . . .

iWon.com is an Internet portal that offers a search engine as well as sweepstakes and rewards programs. In December 2001, iWon bought the Web portal Excite.com after Excite's parent company Excite@Home declared bankruptcy. The acquisition of the much larger Excite operation expanded iWon—the Excite Web site attracts 14 million monthly visitors, and 600,000 people each month register on the portal to receive e-mail and other services.[1] This made iWon's site even more attractive to advertisers who could reach a greater number of Web surfers with their messages.

By registering at iWon.com, users become eligible to participate in cash giveaways. Users earn Reward Points each time they click on certain links. The more entries users accumulate, the more chances they have of winning cash prizes or discounts on all sorts of products in the iWon Cash Points Store. Participation is free to users. The benefit to iWon is that it knows who its users are: It maintains a database with users' membership information obtained during the registration process including postal address, e-mail address, gender, age, activities, and household income. iWon uses this information to target both e-mail and banner ads to specific groups of users. This targeting leads to better response rates for advertisers because they are only paying to show their ads to the users most likely to be interested in what they have to say.

Brad Sockloff oversees various direct-marketing initiatives, including acquiring new users, retaining existing users, and developing and implementing product offers for current users. Although iWon is a successful site, the competitive world of Internet browsers demanded that Brad and his staff keep adding to their registry of users. New users are important, but more important are "quality" users—people who will become loyal iWon members. A large pool of users pushes the brand name (a site with 20 million users is more attractive to advertisers than a site with 10 million users). But only active users actually drive revenue, either by purchasing products from the site or by viewing advertisers' offers.

Users generally find out about iWon through both traditional advertising and online advertising. Online advertising is much more like direct marketing in that results can be carefully tracked. iWon can track exactly how many banners (or e-mails) were sent, how many times a link was clicked through, and then how many new users actually registered. For this reason, most of iWon's advertising took the form of banner ads on other Web sites rather than on TV or radio.

Online advertising generally is sold by the impression (the number of people who visit the site regardless of what they do there). Brad had to figure out what he spent on advertising and how many new members the ads brought in, or "cost per registered user." This meant that Brad had to examine every potential site where iWon might place its advertising. He had to find out the impressions, click-throughs (the percentage of people who actually click on a banner ad), and conversion (the proportion of people who actually bought or registered when visiting a site compared to those who visited but didn't take any further action) for every site and for every banner ad he ran on that site. Brad was ultimately looking to maximize retention: Will these users return to the iWon site and how often? He considered his options:

Option 1: Focus on promoting iWon's services and content.

By stressing iWon's value as an Internet Service Provider, it is more likely to attract people who will use iWon regularly for free e-mail, reading news, playing games, and so on. Brad assumed that people who registered for content would be "quality" users. However, many other sites also offered such features as free e-mail and games. What distinguished iWon was the ability to win cash at its site. By talking about content rather than the sweepstakes component, Brad would be downplaying iWon's core competency.

Option 2: Focus on promoting the sweepstakes and prizes.

By stressing the prize-winning opportunities, iWon would more likely attract a large number of new users. Prizes are an appealing draw for most people. However, these users may not form an attachment to the site. They could lose interest and switch to another site if they don't win.

Option 3: Promote both the content and the prizes.

This strategy would tell users that iWon offers more than just content, more than just prize opportunities. However, it is hard to send multiple messages in a banner ad—there simply isn't enough space. By following this strategy it's possible that neither message—the great content and chance to win prizes—would have enough impact to motivate people to click through to the site. iWon could wind up attracting no one if it tried to do too much in its advertising.

Now join the decision team at iWon.com. Which option would you choose, and why?

It's an Ad Ad Ad Ad World

advertising ■ Nonpersonal communication paid for by an identified sponsor using mass media to persuade or inform.

Wherever we turn, we are bombarded by advertising. Television commercials, radio spots, banner ads for Web sites such as iWon.com, and huge billboards scream "Buy Me!!" **Advertising** is nonpersonal communication paid for by an identified sponsor using mass media to persuade or inform an audience.[2] Advertising can be fun, glamorous, annoying, informative—and even ineffective.

A long-running Virginia Slims cigarettes advertising campaign says, "You've come a long way, baby!" The same could be said about advertising itself. Advertising has been with us a long time. In ancient Greece and Rome, advertisements appeared on walls and were etched on stone tablets. Would the ancients have believed that today we get messages about products almost wherever we are, whether cruising down the road or around the Web? We even hear them on the telephone, courtesy of companies such as the Swedish firm GratisTel International that allowed users to place free telephone calls as long as they were willing to hear a 10-second ad first and then others that chime in during two-minute intervals.[3]

Advertising is also a potent force that creates desire for products by transporting us to imaginary worlds where the people are happy, beautiful, or rich. In this way advertising allows the organization to communicate its message in a favorable way and to repeat the message as often as it deems necessary to have an impact on receivers. Let's look at the different types of advertising.

TYPES OF ADVERTISING

Although almost every business advertises, some industries are bigger spenders than others. Restaurants, toy manufacturers, and household-cleanser companies spend as much as one-fifth of their revenues on advertising, while specialized industrial firms spend considerably less. On average, all U.S. businesses spend between 1 and 3 percent of what they earn on advertising. About 79 percent of this total is on consumer advertising, while the rest is in business-to-business markets.[4] Because so much is spent on advertising, marketers must decide which type of ad will work best given the organizational and marketing goals. The advertisements an organization runs can take many forms, so let's review the most common kinds.

Product Advertising   When people give examples of advertising, they are likely to recall the provocative poses in Calvin Klein ads or Michael Jordan flying through the air for Nike. These are examples of product advertising where the message focuses on a specific good or service. **Product advertising** usually has one of three purposes. If a product is in the introductory stage of the product life cycle, advertising will educate people about a new product and what it does. Other product ads emphasize a brand's features and try to convince the target market to choose it over other options. Finally, many of the ads we see are designed to ensure that people won't forget about the product and the things they already know about it. These messages are often used for products that are already well established.

product advertising ■ An advertising message that focuses on a specific good or service.

Institutional Advertising   Rather than focusing on a specific brand, **institutional advertising** promotes the activities, personality, or point of view of an organization or company. It also builds demand. Unlike many older campaigns that consisted largely of "fluff" ("We're

institutional advertising ■ An advertising message that promotes the activities, personality, or point of view of an organization or company.

Product advertising focuses on a specific good or service. Like many ads, this ad for Lipton Onion Dip mix communicates to customers the features of the brand.

advocacy advertising ■ A type of public service advertising provided by an organization that is seeking to influence public opinion on an issue because it has some stake in the outcome.

public service advertisements (PSAs) ■ Advertising run by the media without charge for not-for-profit organizations or to champion a particular cause.

1 Bookmark It!

Look at TV, radio, magazine, and newspaper ads for each type of advertising: product, advocacy, public service, and retail. Do you think each ad is effective? Why?

advertising campaign ■ A coordinated, comprehensive plan that carries out promotion objectives and results in a series of advertisements placed in media over a period of time.

Company X. Look how wonderful we are!"), today institutional ads are likely to offer one cohesive message, such as Cigna Corporation's ad, "The business of caring."[5]

Some institutional messages state a firm's position on an issue to sway public opinion, a strategy called **advocacy advertising**.[6] For example, the R.J. Reynolds company ran an ad titled "Of Cigarettes and Science," which attempted to refute arguments about the relationship between smoking and health. Other messages called **public service advertisements (PSAs)** are advertisements the media runs free of charge for not-for-profit organizations that serve society in some way or to champion an issue such as increasing literacy or discouraging drunk driving. Advertising agencies usually take on one or more public service campaigns on a *pro bono* (for free) basis.

Retail and Local Advertising   Both major retailers and small, local businesses advertise to encourage customers to shop at a specific store or use a local service. Much local advertising focuses on store hours, location, and products that are available or on sale. Retail advertisers spend more than any other type of advertiser per year (almost $8 billion).

WHO DOES ADVERTISING?

An **advertising campaign** is a coordinated, comprehensive plan that carries out promotion objectives and results in a series of advertisements placed in media over a period of time. Although a campaign may be based around a single ad, most have multiple ads with all ads in the campaign having the same look, feel, and message. For example, the popular campaign for Taco Bell (*"Yo quiero Taco Bell!"*) included both print advertising and a series of humorous television commercials featuring a funky dog that all worked together to elevate the profile of the fast-food chain.

Ford uses institutional advertising to let consumers know about its support of an important cause—the fight against breast cancer.

This is what happens when a fly lands on your food.

Flies can't eat solid food, so to soften it up they vomit on it. Then they stamp the vomit in until it's a liquid, usually stamping in a few germs for good measure. Then when it's good and runny they suck it all back again, probably dropping some excrement at the same time. And then, when they've finished eating, it's your turn.

Cover food. Cover eating and drinking utensils. Cover dustbins.

The Health Education Council

Public service announcements (PSAs) are ads that the media run for free for not-for-profit organizations.

Creating and executing an advertising campaign often means many companies work together, and it requires a broad range of skilled people to do the job right. Some firms may do their own advertising. In many cases, though, the firm will retain one or more outside advertising agencies to develop advertising messages on its behalf. A **limited-service agency** provides one or more specialized services such as media buying or creative development (we'll see what these tasks are a bit later). A **full-service agency** provides most or all of the services needed to mount a campaign, including research, creation of ad copy and art, media selection, and production of the final messages. The five largest American agencies are the Leo Burnett Co., J. Walter Thompson Co., Grey Advertising, McCann-Erickson Worldwide, and DDB Worldwide.[7]

Many different tasks are required to produce a campaign. Big or small, an advertising agency hires a range of specialists to craft a message and make the communications concept a reality.

limited-service agency ■
Agency that provides one or more specialized services such as media buying or creative development.

full-service agency ■
Agency that provides most or all of the services needed to mount a campaign, including research, creation of ad copy and art, media selection, and production of the final messages.

- *Account Management:* The account executive, or account manager, is the "soul" of the operation. This person develops the campaign's strategy for the client. The account executive supervises the day-to-day activities on the account and is the primary liaison between the agency and the client. The account executive has to ensure that the client is happy while verifying that people within the agency are executing the desired strategy.
- *Creative Services: Creatives* are the "heart" of the communications effort. These are the people who actually dream up and produce the ads. They include the agency's creative director, copywriter, and art director. Creatives are the artists who breathe life into marketing objectives and craft messages that (hopefully) will interest consumers.
- *Research and Marketing Services:* Researchers are the "brains" of the campaign. They collect and analyze information that will help account executives develop a sensible

strategy. They assist creatives in getting consumer reactions to different versions of ads or by providing copywriters with details on the target group.

- *Media Planning:* The media planner is the "legs" of the campaign. The media planner helps to determine which communication vehicles are the most effective and recommends the most efficient means for delivering the ad by deciding where, when, and how often it will appear.

As we saw in the last chapter, more and more agencies practice integrated marketing communication (IMC) in which advertising is only one element of a total communication plan. Because IMC includes more than just advertising, client teams composed of people from account services, creative services, media planning, research, public relations, sales promotion, and direct marketing may work together to develop a plan that best meets the communication needs of each client.

Developing the Advertising Campaign

The advertising campaign is about much more than creating a cool ad and hoping people notice it. It should be intimately related to the organization's overall promotional goals. That means the firm (and its outside agency if it uses one) must have a good idea of whom it wants to reach, what it will take to appeal to this market, and where and when the messages should be placed. Let's examine the steps required to do this. (See Figure 15.1.)

IDENTIFY THE TARGET MARKET

The best way to communicate with an audience is to understand as much as possible about them, and what turns them on and off. An ad that uses the latest "hip hop" slang may relate to teenagers but not to their parents—and this strategy may backfire if the ad copy reads like an "ancient" 40-year-old trying to sound like a 20-year-old.

The target market of an advertising campaign is identified from research and segmentation decisions that we discussed in Chapter 8. Researchers try to get inside the customer's head to understand just how to create a message that the customer will understand and respond to. For example, an account executive working on a campaign for Pioneer Stereo was assigned to hang out with guys who were likely prospects to buy car stereos. His observations resulted in an advertising campaign that incorporated the phrases they used to describe their cars: "My car is my holy temple, my love shack, my drag racer of doom. . . ."[8]

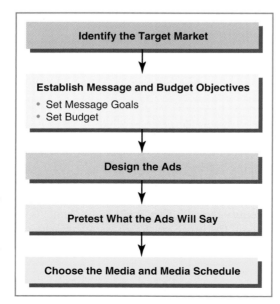

FIGURE 15.1

Steps in Developing an Advertising Campaign

Developing an advertising campaign includes a series of steps that hopefully will ensure that the advertising meets communication objectives.

WOULDN'T IT BE NICE IF YOUR WORK HOURS
WERE AS FLEXIBLE AS YOUR WORK PANTS?

DOCKERS
Exclusively at department stores.

NICE
PANTS

Successful advertising must
speak to the target audience.
The use of people who
represent the target audience
is a good way to do this.

ESTABLISH MESSAGE AND BUDGET OBJECTIVES

Advertising objectives should be consistent with the marketing plan. That means that both the underlying message and its costs need to be related to what the marketer is trying to say about the product and what the marketer is willing or able to spend.

Setting Message Goals Message goals for a campaign can be increasing brand awareness, boosting sales by a certain percentage, or even changing the image of a product. For example, Dr Pepper used advertising to reposition itself from a quirky soft drink to a mainstream beverage. In contrast to its years of showing somewhat unconventional people drinking Dr Pepper, newer ads invoke images of small-town America and family values.[9]

Sometimes the objective is simply to get people to recognize that they need the product. That was the task facing an Indian advertising agency, R K Swamy/BBDO, as it began work on a campaign for its client, Apple Computer. At the time only 5 percent of households in India owned a computer. Apple wanted to motivate its target market, middle-class Indian consumers, to buy a personal computer for household management, children's education, and entertainment.

Apple and R K Swamy/BBDO found that the key consumer expectations for a home PC centered around low price, ease of use, and reliability. The agency developed a campaign for Apple's Macintosh Performa to communicate with potential customers on these terms.[10] The agency positioned the Performa as the ideal computer for the family by highlighting its ease of use, value for the money, and multimedia capability.

Setting the Budget Advertising is expensive! Businesses spend over $44 billion per year on advertising in the United States alone. Procter & Gamble, which leads all U.S companies in advertising expenditures, invests over $2 billion a year in advertising. Other companies that spend well over a billion dollars a year include Philip Morris, General Motors, Sears, and PepsiCo.[11] Did you think Britney Spears plugs Pepsi for free?

Full-service agencies traditionally make a commission of 15 percent of the cost of the media they purchase to run the ads, but this is changing as competition among advertising agencies for clients has increased. More than half of U.S. agencies charge a preset fee instead, whereas a few others peg their rate to how the advertised product sells. For example, Ford Motor Co. pays the agencies that handle its advertising budget (which is over $1 billion a year) based on their contributions to meeting profit goals for the company.[12]

A firm allocates a percentage of its overall communication budget to advertising, depending on how much and what type of advertising the company can afford. Major corporations such as General Motors advertise heavily through expensive media such as television for multiple products throughout the year. Other companies need to be more selective, and smaller firms are more likely to put their advertising dollars into cheaper media outlets such as direct mail or trade publications.

The major approaches and techniques to setting overall promotional budgets such as the percentage-of-sales and objective-task methods discussed in Chapter 14 also set advertising budgets.

DESIGN THE AD

creative strategy ■ The process that turns a concept into an advertisement.

Creative strategy is the process that turns a concept into an advertisement. It's one thing to know what a company wants to say about itself and its product and another to figure out how to say it. The creative process for an advertising campaign has been described as the "spark between objective and execution." As we said in Chapter 14, an effective advertising message should satisfy four requirements that marketers call AIDA: attention, interest, desire, and action.

The first challenge for advertising is to get consumers' attention. Here, a visual that is both attractive and unexpected makes consumers want to know more about the product.

It is unlikely that one ad can do all that, but the goal of an advertising campaign is to present a series of messages and repeat it to a sufficient degree so that the customer will progress through the AIDA stages. To do this, advertising creatives (art directors, copywriters, photographers, and others) must develop a "big idea," a concept that expresses aspects of the product, service, or organization in a tangible, attention-getting, memorable manner.

When designing the ad, advertisers come up with many ingenious ways to express a concept. An **advertising appeal** is the central idea of the ad. Some advertisers use an emotional appeal complete with dramatic color or powerful images, while others bombard the audience with facts. Some feature sexy people or stern-looking experts (even professors from time to time). Different appeals can work for the same product, from a bland "talking head" to a montage of animated special effects. An attention-getting way to say something profound about cat food or laundry detergent is more art than science, but we can describe some common appeals.

advertising appeal ■ The central idea or theme of an advertising message.

- *Reasons Why: The USP.* A **unique selling proposition (USP)** gives consumers a single, clear reason why one product is better at solving a problem. The format focuses on a need and points out how the product can satisfy it. For example, "M&Ms melt in your mouth, not in your hands." In general, a USP strategy is best if there is some clear product advantage that consumers can readily identify and that is important to them.

unique selling proposition (USP) ■ An advertising appeal that focuses on one clear reason why a particular product is superior.

- *Comparative Advertising.* A comparative advertisement explicitly names two or more competitors. Comparative ads can be very effective, but there is a risk of turning off consumers who don't like the negative tone. This is especially a problem in cultures that don't take kindly to impolite messages. For instance, Tokyo's five major television networks pulled a Pepsi comparative ad because Japanese viewers found it offensive to be too blunt.[13] And in many countries comparative advertising that names the competitor is illegal. Americans don't seem to be so bothered by this appeal—it's legal in the United States. Comparative advertising is probably best for brands that have a smaller share of the market and can focus on a clear observable superiority to a larger brand. When market leaders use comparative advertising, there is the risk of consumers feeling they are "picking on" the other guy.
- *Demonstration:* The ad shows a product "in action" to prove that it performs as claimed. "It slices, it dices!" This appeal helps sell products that people "use." Demonstration advertising is most useful when consumers are unable to identify important benefits except through seeing the product in use.
- *Testimonial:* A celebrity, an expert, or a "typical person" states the product's effectiveness. The use of *celebrity endorsers* is a common but expensive strategy. It is particularly effective for mature products that need to differentiate themselves from competitors, such as Coke and Pepsi, which enlist celebrities to tout one cola over another.[14]
- *Slice-of-Life:* A slice-of-life format presents a (dramatized) scene from everyday life. Slice-of-life advertising can be effective for everyday products such as peanut butter and headache remedies that consumers may feel good about if they see "real" people buying and using them. An ad for Spray 'n Wash Stain Stick from Dow Chemical shows a mother and her Down's syndrome child. The mother comments, "The last place we need another challenge is the laundry room." One advertising critic described the spot as "the most crassly contrived slice-of-life in advertising history." But the National Down's Syndrome Congress applauded the ad and awarded Dow its annual media award.[15]
- *Lifestyle:* A lifestyle format shows a person or persons attractive to the target market in an appealing setting. The advertised product is "part of the scene," implying that the person who buys it will attain the lifestyle. For example, a commercial shown on MTV might depict a group of "cool" California skateboarders who take a break for a gulp of milk and say, "It does a body good."

  R K Swamy/BBDO used a lifestyle appeal to sell the Performa by focusing on how the machine empowers children to pursue their potential. R K Swamy/BBDO created print ads and television commercials that plugged the Performa computer by showing parents and children using it to expand their horizons. The goal was to create "feel-good" ads that would humanize the technology behind Apple's products and show potential buyers how the home computer could improve their lives.

A fantasy format is a variation of the lifestyle approach in which the viewer is encouraged to imagine being transported to a novel or exotic situation. In one recent fantasy appeal, a commercial for Holiday Inn Express depicts a bunch of nerdy guys masquerading as the rock group Kiss, makeup and all.[16]

- *Fear Appeals:* This appeal highlights the negative consequences of using or not using a product. Some fear appeal ads focus on physical harm while others seek to create concern for social harm or disapproval. Mouthwash, toothpaste, deodorant, and dandruff shampoo makers have successfully used the fear appeal, as have ads aimed at changing behaviors such as antidrug and antidrinking and driving ads.

- *Sex Appeals:* Some ads appear to be selling sex rather than products. In a Guess jeans ad, a shirtless man lies near an almost shirtless woman. An ad for Timex's glow-in-the-dark wristwatch proclaims "Make Your Husband Really Shine in Bed."[17] These ads and many others rely on sexuality to get consumers' attention. Sex appeal ads are more likely to be effective when there is a connection between the product and sex or at least romance. For example, sex appeals will work well with a perfume but are less likely to be effective in selling a lawn mower.

- *Humorous Appeals:* Humorous ads can be an effective way to break through advertising clutter. But humor can be tricky because what is funny to one person may be offensive or stupid to another. Different cultures also have different senses of humor. A recent Reebok commercial showed women at a basketball game checking out the all-male cheerleading squad—people from countries who don't have cheerleaders (you don't find too many pom-poms at soccer matches) might not "get it." Perhaps the

Lifestyle advertising shows consumers who are attractive to the target market in an appealing setting. Here, Cheer focuses on family living in an appeal for clean laundry.

major benefit of humorous advertising is that it attracts consumers' attention and leaves them with a pleasant feeling.

- *Slogans and Jingles.* Slogans seek to link the brand to a simple linguistic device that is memorable. Jingles do the same but set the slogan to music. Some popular slogans that have been used for successful advertising campaigns are "Please don't squeeze the Charmin," "Double your pleasure, double your fun," "Aren't you glad you use Dial, and "Good to the last drop."

PRETEST WHAT WILL BE SAID

Now that the creatives have worked their magic, how does the agency know if the campaign ideas will work? Advertisers try to minimize mistakes by getting reactions to ad messages before they are actually placed. Much of this **pretesting**, the research that goes on in the early stages of a campaign, centers on gathering basic information that will help planners to be sure they've accurately defined the product's market, consumers, and competitors. This information comes from quantitative sources, such as syndicated surveys, and qualitative sources, such as focus groups.

As the campaign takes shape, the players need to determine how well the advertising concepts will perform. **Copy testing** measures the effectiveness of ads. This process determines whether consumers are receiving, comprehending, and responding to the ad according to plan. Some copy-testing techniques include:

- *Concept testing* helps determine if initial ideas will work. In this technique, respondents who are often drawn from the target market for which the ad is intended evaluate different creative ideas or rough copies of ad layouts.
- *Test commercials* let consumers respond to a rough version of what a television message will look like. This preliminary treatment may take the form of an *animatic* or *storyboard*, which is a series of sketches showing frame by frame what will happen in the finished commercial.
- *Finished testing* means testing audience reactions to a fully produced commercial or print ad to see if it motivates them to buy the product. This occurs before the ad is placed in the media. Because production of a "real" commercial or print ad is so expensive, most testing is conducted prior to this point.

CHOOSE THE MEDIA

Media planning is a problem-solving process for getting a message to a target audience in the most efficient and effective fashion. The decisions to be made include audience selection and where, when, and how frequent the exposure should be. There is no such thing as one perfect

pretesting ■ A research method that seeks to minimize mistakes by getting consumer reactions to ad messages before they appear in the media.

copy testing ■ A marketing research method that seeks to measure the effectiveness of ads by determining whether consumers are receiving, comprehending, and responding to the ad according to plan.

media planning ■ The process of developing media objectives, strategies, and tactics for use in an advertising campaign.

medium for advertising. The choice depends on the specific target audience, the objective of the message, and, of course, the budget. For the advertising campaign to be effective, the media planner must match up the profile of the target market with specific media vehicles. For example, many African American consumers are avid radio listeners, so reaching this segment means a marketer might allocate a larger share of the advertising budget to buying time on radio stations.

The first task for a media planner is to find out when and where people in the target market are most likely to be exposed to the communication. This is called an **aperture**, the best "window" to reach the target market. Many college students read the campus newspaper in the morning (often during class!), so their aperture would include this medium at this time.

aperture ■ The best place and time to reach a person in the target market group.

Where to Say It: Traditional Media

What does the evening news seen on a 52-inch television with Dolby Surround-Sound have in common with a matchbook? Each is a media vehicle that permits an advertiser to communicate with a potential customer. Depending on the intended message, each medium has its advantages and disadvantages. Let's take a look at the major categories of media. Table 15.1 summarizes some of the pros and cons of each type.

Television. Because of television's ability to reach so many people at once, it's the medium of choice for regional or national companies. A television network consists of affiliate stations that agree to carry programming supplied by a central source for at least part of the day. In return, the local stations receive a percentage of the advertising revenue (usually 12 percent to 25 percent) paid to the national network.

Advertising on a television network can be very expensive. The cost to place a 30-second ad on a popular prime-time TV show one time normally ranges between $200,000 and $500,000 depending on the size of the show's audience. Advertisers may prefer to buy local television time rather than network time because it's cheaper or because they have a more localized target market. *Spot TV* is television time advertisers buy from a local station. The station in turn agrees to run a commercial during a certain time of day, called a *daypart*. Another alternative to the expensive networks is cable television. More than half of all U.S. households get cable TV, and satellite TV is becoming increasingly popular. This medium offers many channels, each specializing in a specific programming format (MTV) or audience (Black Entertainment Television) that can mean easy access to a particular market segment.

Radio. Radio as an advertising medium goes back to 1922, when a New York City apartment manager went on the air to advertise apartments for rent. One advantage of radio advertising is flexibility. Marketers can change commercials quickly, often on the spot by an announcer and a recording engineer.[18] Radio is attractive to advertisers seeking low cost and the ability to reach specific consumer segments. And 99 out of every 100 U.S. households have a radio—the average home has at least five of them.[19]

Newspapers. The newspaper is among the oldest media. Retailers in particular have relied on newspaper ads since before the turn of the century to inform readers about sales and deliveries of new merchandise. Newspapers are an excellent medium for local advertising and for events (such as sales) that require a quick response. Many newspapers, such as the Wall Street Journal and the New York Times, now also offer online versions of their papers to expand their exposure.

Magazines. Magazines are an important advertising medium because approximately 92 percent of adults look through at least one magazine per month. Magazines have adapted to changing times by narrowing their segments. New technologies such as selective binding allow publishers to personalize their editions so that advertisements for local businesses can be included in issues mailed to specific locations only. Desktop publishing software allows magazines to close their

TABLE 15.1

Pros and Cons of Media Vehicles

Vehicle	Pros	Cons
Television	Extremely creative and flexible. Network TV is the most cost-effective way to reach a mass audience. Cable TV allows the advertiser to reach a selected group at relatively low cost. A prestigious way to advertise. Messages have high impact because of the use of sight and sound.	The message is quickly forgotten unless it is repeated often. The audience is increasingly fragmented. Although the relative cost of reaching the audience is low, prices are still high on an absolute basis—often too high for smaller companies. A 30-second spot on a prime-time TV sitcom costs well over $250,000. Rising costs have led to more and shorter ads, which cause greater clutter.
Radio	Good for selectively targeting an audience. Is heard out of the home. Relatively low cost, both for producing a spot and for running it repeatedly. Radio ads can be modified quickly to reflect changes in the marketplace. Use of sound effects and music allows listeners to use their imagination to create a vivid scene.	Listeners often don't pay full attention to what they hear. The small audience of individual stations means ads must be placed with many different stations and must be repeated frequently. Not appropriate for products that must be seen or demonstrated to be appreciated.
Newspapers	Wide exposure provides extensive market coverage. Flexible format permits the use of color, different sizes, and targeted editions. Useful for comparison shopping. Allows local retailers to tie in with national advertisers.	Most people don't spend much time reading the newspaper. Readership is especially low among teens and young adults. Short life span—people rarely look at a newspaper more than once. Very cluttered ad environment. The reproduction quality of images is relatively poor.
Magazines	Audiences can be narrowly targeted by specialized magazines. High credibility and interest level provide a good environment for ads. Advertising has a long life and is often passed along to other readers. Visual quality is excellent.	With the exception of direct mail, the most expensive form of advertising. The cost of a full-page, four-color ad in a general-audience magazine typically exceeds $100,000. Long deadlines reduce flexibility. The advertiser must generally use several magazines to reach the majority of a target market.
Outdoor	Most of the population can be reached at low cost. Good for supplementing other media.	Hard to communicate complex messages. Hard to demonstrate a product's effectiveness. Controversial and disliked in many communities.
Direct response	Ads can target extremely narrow audiences. Messages can be timed by the advertiser at his or her convenience. Easy to measure the effectiveness of ads.	High cost per exposure. Target lists must be constantly updated. Ads lack credibility among many consumers.

Source: Adapted from J. Thomas Russell and W. Ronald Lane, *Kleppner's Advertising Procedure*, 11th ed. (Upper Saddle River, NJ: Prentice Hall, 1990); William Wells, John Burnett, and Sandra Moriarty, *Advertising: Principles and Practice*, 3d ed. (Upper Saddle River, NJ: Prentice Hall, 1995).

pages just before going to press—no more long lead times that used to plague advertisers that wanted to hit their market with timely information.

Directories. Directory advertising is the most "down-to-earth," information-focused advertising medium. In 1883, a printer in Wyoming ran out of white paper while printing part of a telephone book and he substituted yellow paper instead. Today, the Yellow Pages has revenues of more than $9.5 billion, and more than 6,000 directories are published in North America alone. Consumers usually look through directories when or just before they are ready to buy, so the advertiser has the opportunity to influence the buyer close to the decision. In a typical week, 60 percent of all American adults use the Yellow Pages.[20]

Out-of-home media. **Out-of-home media** such as blimps, transit ads, and billboards reach people in public places. This medium works best when it tells a simple, straightforward story.[21]

out-of-home media ■ A communication medium that reaches people in public places.

Deciding on the best place for an advertising message is often a key element of any strategy. This Spanish ad for a media company asks, "Is your product in the right place?"

place-based media ■
Advertising media that transmit messages in public places, such as doctors' offices and airports where certain types of people congregate.

For example, four Houston men rented a billboard with the message: "4 Middle Class White Males, 32–39, Seek Wives." These "advertisers" got responses from almost 800 women.[22]

Place-based media. Marketers are constantly searching for new ways to get their messages out to busy people. **Place-based media**, such as "The Airport Channel," which transmit messages in public places, such as doctors' offices and airports where certain types of people congregate, are an effective way to reach a captive audience.

Out-of home media provide an excellent way to reach consumers on the go. Billboards such as this one certainly grab our attention.

Where to Say It: Internet Advertising   Another medium through which advertisers send their messages is the Internet. Internet advertising consists of two major categories of messages: e-mail messages and advertising messages on the World Wide Web. Both dot.com companies such as iWon.com and traditional businesses are finding the Internet an attractive place to advertise. Online advertising offers several advantages. First, the Internet provides new ways to finely target customers. Web user registrations and cookies allow sites to track user preferences and deliver ads based on previous Internet behavior. In addition, because the Web site can track how many times an ad is "clicked," exact response to advertising can be measured. Finally, online advertising can be interactive—it lets consumers participate in the advertising campaign and in some cases they can even offer advertising ideas.

For example, bolt.com, an online teen community, gave cameras to several dozen teens to shoot their own spots for the site.[23] All ads are posted on the Web site where online community members vote on the spots and share with their friends. And a few have even been aired on Fox's teen drama, *American High*.

Specific forms of Internet advertising include banners, buttons, pop-up ads, search engines and directories, sponsorships, and e-mail. Let's take a quick look at each.

- **Banners,** those rectangular graphics at the top or bottom of Web pages, were the first form of Web advertising. Although the effectiveness of banners remains in question (banners now receive less than a 1 percent click-through rate), they still remain the most popular form of Web advertising. One study that tested the impact of banner ads at top Web sites reported a dramatic increase in brand awareness after just one exposure and significant positive impact on intent to purchase.[24] Experts suggest banners that contain animation, effectively use color, call for action (e.g., "click here"), and create a sense of urgency are more effective.
- **Buttons** are small banner-type advertisements that can be placed anywhere on a page. Early in the life of the Internet, buttons encouraging surfers to "Download Netscape Now" became a standard on many Web sites and were responsible for much of Netscape's early success.
- *Sponsorships*, much like the sponsorships of traditional radio and television programming, provide visibility for the company but, unlike banners and buttons, are not aimed at getting Web users to visit their sites. For example, three major companies, Merrill Lynch, Ford Motor Company, and the McKinsey Group, were sponsors of the Wharton School of Business site.[25] iVillage has sponsorships by Ford Motor Company and Johnson & Johnson.[26] Ford sponsors a site that provides answers to women's major concerns about buying cars, safety, maintenance, and leasing rather than buying. Johnson & Johnson and its Huggies brand sponsor a parenting area on iVillage.
- *Search engine and directory listings*. Just as the Yellow Pages and other directories are advertising media, so too are search engines and online directory listings. Increasingly firms are paying search engines for more visible or higher placement on results lists.
- *Pop-up ads*. A pop-up ad is an advertisement that pops up on the screen while a Web page is being loaded or after it is loaded. Because pop-up ads take the center of the screen while surfers are waiting for the desired page to load, they are difficult to ignore. A pop-up ad opens a separate Internet window. Web advertisers are typically charged only if people click through the windows.
- *E-mail*. For advertising, e-mail is becoming as pervasive as radio and television. It is one of the easiest ways of communicating with consumers. In the early years of the Internet, companies found that they could send unsolicited e-mail advertising messages to thousands of users by **spamming**—unsolicited e-mail directed to five or more people not personally known to the sender. Consumers were quick to display their irritation at receiving the unsolicited e-mail messages. Many Internet providers have since developed "acceptable use policies" (AUPs) that prohibit spamming.

    Many Web sites that offer e-mail give surfers the opportunity to refuse unsolicited e-mail. This **permission marketing** gives the consumer the power to opt in or out. By 2004, U.S. marketers will send 200 billion e-mails to consumers and hope that a good portion of these will be welcomed.[27]

banners ■ Internet advertising in the form of rectangular graphics at the top or bottom of Web pages.

buttons ■ Small banner-type advertisement that can be placed anywhere on a Web page.

2 Bookmark It!

When surfing the Web, pay attention to banner advertising. What banner ads get your attention? What makes them more attention getting than other ads? Are there any ads that make you want to "click through?" If so, what made you click?

spamming: ■ Unsolicited e-mail directed to 5 or more people not personally known to the sender.

permission marketing ■ E-mail advertising where online consumers have the opportunity to accept or refuse the unsolicited e-mail.

Many marketers think permission marketing will build relationships with customers. And many surfers agree; they are happy to receive offers from an Internet retailer that they like and know. However, spamming continues to be a problem, especially when the content of the unsolicited e-mail is distasteful to the recipient.

- *Web site design:* An organization's Web site defines the organization and creates an enduring image in the minds of stakeholders. Benetton (Benetton.com) uses its Web presence to nourish an image that has been much maligned. The Italian apparel company even publishes e-mails it receives that are critical of its controversial ads.

Media Scheduling: When to Say It   After choosing the advertising media, the planner then creates a **media schedule** that specifies the exact media to use for the campaign, as well as when and how often the message should appear. Figure 15.2 shows a hypothetical media schedule for the promotion of a new video game. Note that much of the advertising reaches its target audience in the months just before Christmas and that much of the expensive television budget is focused on advertising during specials just prior to the holiday season.

The media schedule outlines the planner's best estimate of which media will be most effective in attaining the advertising objective(s) and which specific media vehicles will do the most effective job. The media planner considers such factors as the match between the demographic and psychographic profile of a target audience and the people reached by a media vehicle, the advertising patterns of competitors, and the capability of a medium to convey the desired information adequately. The planner must also consider such factors as the compatibility of the product with editorial content. For example, viewers might not respond well to a lighthearted ad for a new snack food during a somber documentary on world hunger.

When analyzing media, the planner is interested in assessing **advertising exposure**, the degree to which the target market will see an advertising message in a specific medium. Media planners talk in terms of **impressions**, which measure the number of people who will be exposed to a message placed in one or more media vehicles. For example, if 5 million people watch *MTV Total Request Live* on television, then each time an advertiser runs an ad during that program it receives 5 million impressions. If the advertiser's spot runs four times during the program, the impression count would be 20 million (even though some of these impressions would represent repeated exposure to the same viewers).

To calculate the exposure a message will have if placed in a certain medium, planners consider two factors: reach and frequency. **Reach** is the percentage of the target market that will be exposed to the media vehicle at least one time. This measure is particularly important for widely used products when the message needs to get to as many consumers as possible. **Frequency** is the number of times a person in the target group would be exposed to the message. Frequency is important for products that are complex or are targeted to relatively small markets for which multiple exposures to the message are necessary to make an impact.

Say a media planner wants to get Club Med advertising to college students. The advertiser learns that 25 percent of that target market reads at least a few issues of *Rolling Stone*

media schedule ■ The plan that specifies the exact media to use and when.

advertising exposure ■ The degree to which the target market will see an advertising message placed in a specific vehicle.

impressions ■ The number of people who will be exposed to a message placed in one or more media vehicles.

reach ■ The percentage of the target market that will be exposed to the media vehicle.

frequency ■ The number of times a person in the target group will be exposed to the message.

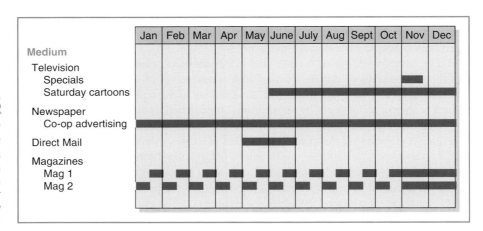

FIGURE 15.2

A Media Schedule for a Video Game

Media planning includes decisions on where, when, and how much advertising will be done. A media schedule such as this one for a video game shows the plan visually.

each year (reach). The advertiser may also determine that these students are likely to see three of the 12 monthly ads that Club Med will run in *Rolling Stone* during the year (frequency). Now the planner calculates the magazine's **gross rating points (GRPs)** by multiplying reach times frequency, which in this case compares the effectiveness of *Rolling Stone* to alternative media. By using this same formula, the planner could then compare this GRP number to another magazine, to the GRP of placing an ad on television or on a bus or any other advertising medium.

gross rating points (GRPs)
■ A measure used for comparing the effectiveness of different media vehicles: average reach times frequency.

Although some media vehicles deliver superior exposure, they may not be cost-efficient. More people will see a commercial aired during the Super Bowl than during a 3:00 A.M. rerun of a Tarzan movie. But the advertiser could run late night commercials every night for a year for the cost of one 30-second Super Bowl spot. To compare the relative cost-effectiveness of different media and of spots run on different vehicles in the same medium, media planners use a measure called **cost per thousand (CPM)**. This figure compares the relative cost-effectiveness of different media vehicles that have different exposure rates and reflects the cost to deliver a message to 1,000 people. A medium's popularity with consumers determines how much advertisers must pay to put their message on it. Television networks are concerned with getting good ratings because their advertising rates are determined by how many viewers their programming attracts. Similarly, magazines and newspapers try to boost circulation to justify raising ad rates.

cost per thousand (CPM) ■
A measure used to compare the relative cost-effectiveness of different media vehicles that have different exposure rates; the cost to deliver a message to 1,000 people or homes.

Media Scheduling: How Often to Say It After deciding where and when to advertise, the planner must decide how often. What time of day? Frequently for a few weeks or occasionally for a long time? Many people consider the classic "1984" television spot that introduced the Apple Macintosh to be the most powerful commercial ever made—even though it was shown only during the third quarter of the 1984 Super Bowl and never again. Most ordinary ads, however, need a bit more exposure than that. After selecting the media schedule, the planner turns to the overall pattern the advertising will follow.

A *continuous schedule* maintains a steady stream of advertising throughout the year. This is most appropriate for products that sell on a regular basis such as shampoo or bread. The American Association of Advertising Agencies, an industry trade group, maintains that

Some consider this 1984 Apple Macintosh commercial the best ever made. It cost just under a million dollars to produce and broadcast. It aired only once during a Super Bowl.

continuous advertising sustains market leadership even if total industry sales fall.[28] On the downside, some messages can suffer from *advertising wearout* because people tune out the same old ad messages.

A *pulsing schedule* varies the amount of advertising throughout the year based on when the product is likely to be in demand. A suntan lotion might advertise year around but more heavily during the summer months. *Flighting* is an extreme form of pulsing in which advertising appears in short, intense bursts alternating with periods of little to no activity. It can produce as much brand awareness as a steady dose of advertising at a much lower cost, if the messages from the previous flight were noticed and made an impact.

Evaluating Advertising

John Wanamaker, a famous Philadelphia retailer, once complained: "I am certain that half the money I spend on advertising is completely wasted. The trouble is, I don't know which half."[29] Now that we've seen how advertising is created and executed, let's step back and consider how we decide if it's working.

The short story is that advertisers can take heart: Research findings generally support the wisdom of spending money on advertising. Studies by media companies and trade groups such as the American Association of Advertising Agencies and the Advertising Research Foundation show that increased advertising boosts sales, and that increased product usage is linked to advertising exposure.[30] Still, there's no doubt that a lot of advertising is ineffective, so it's important for firms to evaluate their efforts to increase the impact of their messages. How can they do that?

POSTTESTING

posttesting ■ Research conducted on consumers' responses to actual advertising messages they have seen or heard.

Posttesting means conducting research on consumers' responses to advertising messages they have seen or heard (as opposed to *pretesting*, which as we've seen collects reactions to messages before they're actually placed in "the real world"). Ironically, many creative ads that are quirky or even bizarre make an advertising agency look good within the industry but are ultimately unsuccessful because they don't communicate what needs to be said about the product itself. As one consultant observed, "There is so much emphasis on the creative aspect of the ads, sort of 'Aren't we clever?' that the message is lost."[31]

unaided recall ■ A research technique conducted by telephone survey or personal interview that asks whether a person remembers seeing an ad during a specified period of time.

In some cases the ads are popular but they send the wrong message to consumers. For example, a lot of people remember Joe Isuzu, the lying car salesman whose television commercials were popular for two years but were no help to Isuzu's car sales during that time.[32] As one advertising executive explained, "The humor got in the way. All you remembered was that car salesmen are dishonest, and the car salesman you remembered most was from Isuzu."[33]

aided recall ■ A research technique that uses clues to prompt answers from people about advertisements they might have seen.

Three ways to measure the impact of an advertisement are *unaided recall, aided recall*, and *attitudinal measures*. **Unaided recall** tests by telephone survey or personal interview whether a person remembers seeing an ad during a specified period of time without giving the person the name of the brand. An **aided recall** test uses the name of the brand and sometimes other clues to prompt answers. For example, a researcher might show a group of consumers a list of brands and ask them to choose which items they have seen advertised within the past week. **Attitudinal measures** probe a bit more deeply by testing consumer beliefs or feelings about a product before and after being exposed to messages about it. If, for example, Pepsi's messages about "freshness-dating" make enough consumers believe that freshness of soft drinks is important, marketers can consider the advertising campaign successful.

attitudinal measures ■ A research technique that probes a consumer's beliefs or feelings about a product before and after being exposed to messages about it.

CHALLENGES FACING THE ADVERTISING INDUSTRY

In addition to evaluating the quality of specific advertising messages, marketers also must think hard about the overall effectiveness of advertising as a promotional strategy, especially as other forms of promotion threaten to overshadow it.

Michelle Carelis, Student, Bentley College

I would choose option 3 because the advertising incorporates both the content and the prizes, which should attract loyal and new registered users. Both of these markets are vital to iWon.com's success. Regular users drive retention and the company's revenue while new members add to the registry of users and attract advertisers. The other two options focus on only one market. Option 3 capitalizes on iWon.com's core competency: users can participate in all activities available on other sites but also have the opportunity to win. Advertising should concentrate on this model, which distinguishes iWon.com from its competitors. Banner advertising offers iWon.com the creative flexibility to send multiple messages. It is possible to design a banner message that focuses on both content and prizes with enough impact to motivate people to click through to the site.

SHI QING, STUDENT, SHANGHAI INTERNATIONAL STUDIES UNIVERSITY

I would choose option 1. If iWon.com focuses on promoting its service and content, it is likely to attract those who will be "qualified" users. Loyal customers contribute a large amount of revenue to companies, and they may give good advice to the company, further strengthening the relationship between customers and the company. The Internet has brought new problems and opportunities, but business fundamentals still apply, one of which is seeking customer loyalty. Once iWon.com acquires these "qualified users" the possibility of losing them is lower than the possibility of losing those who just want to win cash at the site.

Cele Otnes, Marketing Professor, Dept. of Business Administration, University of Illinois at Urbana-Champaign

I would choose option 1 because it is better to target users who are likely to become loyal to iWon, rather than those who might just be looking for a "quick cash fix." Brad Sockloff said active users increase revenue by buying products from sponsors of the site. Moreover, loyal users are likely to be more patient with a rewards program, allowing their points to accumulate and understanding that most of the payoffs from the iWon contests will be generated through repeat use. People tend to only subscribe to one service provider, and do so because it offers the features they want. If iWon can lure customers through promises of service quality and content that just happens to be accompanied by sweepstakes and loyalty points, the company will have a database of customers who are likely to lead to long-term profitability.

Leslie Goldfarb, VP, Price McNabb Focused Communications

I would choose option 2 because the first task is to get people to visit the site. Their experience with that site will determine whether they visit again. (I'm assuming the quality of the site is not Brad's responsibility.) The opportunity to win prizes or earn points is compelling, and it actually created enough interest with me that I visited about a year ago. In fact, the company's "reminder" e-mails caused me to visit a few more times. I did not become a regular user, however, because I did not find the site to be especially unique or helpful. Brad is probably doing everything possible to attract visitors and to encourage a return visit. His job now is to ensure the company makes the site the very best in the industry.

Weigh in with your thoughts! Visit the Live Laboratory at www.prenhall.com/solomon for extended Other Voices replies, exercises, and more.

There was a time in the 1970s and 1980s when advertising agencies could do no wrong. Spurred by the popularity of new-product categories such as personal computers and compact disc players that needed heavy promoting, ad revenues soared. Things slowed down in 1989, when total ad spending grew only 5 percent and then slimmed to 3.8 percent in 1990. Although things started to pick up in the 1990s, the decline in the fortunes of the dot-com industry in 1999 and 2000 meant that less money was spent on advertising. Then, the slowing of the economy in 2001, especially after September 11, 2001, resulted in a one-two punch to the advertising business. It still faces several threats as many marketers are choosing to allocate less of their promotional budget to advertising while shifting money into other areas such as sales promotions. Here are some of these threats.

- *Erosion of brand loyalty.* Consumers are becoming cynical over the constant barrage of advertisements, and buyers are more likely to choose brands based on price rather than image. When consumers buy on the basis of price only, image-oriented advertising that stresses intangible qualities such as sex appeal or style is not effective.
- *Technology gives power back to the people.* Modern technology has given consumers television remotes, VCRs, PCs, and cable television. No longer passive "couch potatoes," they have the power to "zip" through commercials by fast-forwarding, or to "zap" them by channel-surfing on their trusty remote. A VCR sold in Japan even allows users to automatically skip over commercials while taping their favorite shows.
- *Greater emphasis on point-of-purchase factors.* Consumers make many purchase decisions when they are actually shopping. This realization has forced many marketers to shift away from advertising toward other elements of the promotion mix, such as in-store sales promotions and publicity events.
- *The rules are changing.* Although advertising has always been a competitive business, executives in advertising agencies are now finding that they must also compete with other industries for business. Formerly loyal clients such as Coca-Cola are turning to computer wizards and even to Hollywood talent agencies to produce mind-bending commercials using the latest special-effects technology or to recruit movie directors and other specialists who are able to create gripping stories about everyday products.
- *The advertising environment is cluttered.* There are many messages competing for customers' attention. About 40,000 magazines and journals are published every year, and there are more than 10,000 radio stations, most of which depend on advertising revenue to survive. The average household can view 35 television channels. The number of network television commercials has tripled from about 1,800 per week 50 years ago to 6,000 per week today. During prime time, commercials account for 10.5 minutes of each programming hour.[34] Many people feel overwhelmed by the barrage of ads and a lot of messages simply get lost.
- *Some consumers are turned off by advertising.* Some advertising messages are so persistent or obnoxious that people tune them out. One survey said 60 percent of consumers polled agreed with the statement "advertising insults my intelligence."[35] Other people feel that ads have little or no credibility because product claims are untrue or exaggerated.
- *People are looking for substance over style.* Since September 11, 2001, advertisers are reluctant to focus so much on "frivolous" images of sullen, high-fashion models playing with expensive toys. Simplicity and innocence are back, as is domestic contentment. This back-to-basics emphasis won't last forever, but at least for a time it's had a chilling effect on creative advertising and poses new challenges to marketers who still want to sell their products but to do so in a tasteful, understated way.[36]

HOW THE ADVERTISING INDUSTRY IS MEETING THE CHALLENGES

These discouraging factors have forced advertising agencies to demonstrate that advertising can deliver powerful, persuasive messages to vast numbers of consumers in a cost-efficient manner. One solution is to continue to create images that are fun, artistic, or powerful to remind us that "a picture is worth a thousand words." In addition, advertisers are looking to the future to anticipate changes and be sure that their messages will always have a place in society. Here are some ways they're doing this:

- *Global Reach.* Advertisers are trying to establish brand images globally so that customers around the world will respond to their messages and allow firms to expand their markets by appealing to many people with the same messages (see

3 Bookmark It!

Talk with friends who are not business or marketing students. Ask if they are turned off by advertising. What about advertising do they dislike? Is there anything about advertising that they like?

Chapter 4). For example, Dentsu's advertising for Lexus cars in Japan is targeted to higher-income Japanese, but the creative execution depicts a young law professor at Yale as the ideal driver of the car. Even though the person in the ad is a foreigner, the agency is counting on this "yuppie" image to travel across national boundaries.

- *Diversity.* Consumers are becoming quite vocal about advertising they feel singles out a group in a negative way. Even Nike ads starring cartoon character Porky Pig drew fire from the National Stuttering Project, which argued that advertisers that make fun of speech disabilities make it difficult for stutterers to get respect.[37] Advertisers are working hard to better reflect the cultural diversity of their target markets by including people of different races and ethnic groups in their advertising. At the beginning of 2002, the California Milk Processor Board ("Got Milk?") started a new campaign aimed at enticing Hispanic teens to drink more milk. Their new pitchwoman is "La Llorona"—the Crying One—a well-known character in Hispanic myth who murders her children, commits suicide, and roams for all eternity looking for her lost brood. The phantom floats through a house and up to the fridge—only to find an empty milk carton. There's no dialogue, except for a voice at the end that still says, in English, "Got Milk?"[38]
- *Technology.* Many agencies use new technology to deliver advertising messages often with a tasteful touch of personalization. For example, Chrysler Corporation introduced Command, a system that coordinates the company's databases, to learn about customers. This system will allow Chrysler to customize its advertising to customer preferences. Command does this by ensuring that drivers receive ads only for those models in which they're most likely to be interested, so the information they receive is timely and welcome rather than an intrusion.[39]

A company called Emtnetwork.com connects fans with athletes and musicians including the New York Yankees and David Bowie. Users get access to a personalized browser featuring imagery from the person or group and exposure to special promotions.[40] Other marketers are hard at work developing innovative Web sites and CD-ROM magazines, such as *Launch*, which include advertisements you can click on only if you want to see and hear them—and making these messages so interesting you will *want* to see and hear them.

Direct Marketing

Are you one of those consumers who loves to get lots of catalogs in the mail, to pore over them for hours, and then order just exactly what you want without leaving home? Do you order CDs, computer software, and books on the Web? Have you ever responded to an infomercial on TV? All of these are examples of direct marketing, the fastest-growing type of marketing communications. **Direct marketing** refers to "any direct communication to a consumer or business recipient that is designed to generate a response in the form of an order, a request for further information, and/or a visit to a store or other place of business for purchase of a product."[41] That's the business Brad Sockloff is in—iWon.com takes traditional direct marketing and converts it to warp speed by putting it on the Web. In 2000, direct-marketing sales totaled $1.73 trillion and included a growth rate that was 54 percent higher than overall U.S. sales growth.[42]

direct marketing ■ Any direct communication to a consumer or business recipient that is designed to generate a response in the form of an order, a request for further information, and/or a visit to a store or other place of business for purchase of a product.

Let's look at the most popular types of direct marketing, starting with the oldest—buying through the mail.

MAIL ORDER

In 1872 Aaron Montgomery Ward and two partners put up $1,600 to mail a one-page flyer that listed their merchandise with prices, hoping to spur a few more sales for their retail store.[43] The mail-order industry was born. Today consumers can buy just about anything through the mail, and mail orders account for 3 percent of overall retail sales in the United States.[44] Mail order comes in two forms, catalogs and direct mail.

Catalogs A **catalog** is a collection of products offered for sale in book form, usually consisting of product descriptions accompanied by photos of the items. Catalogs came on the scene within a few decades of the invention of moveable type in the fifteenth century, but they've come a long way since then.[45] The early catalogs pioneered by Montgomery Ward and other innovators such as Sears were designed for people in remote areas who lacked access to stores.

Today the catalog customer is likely to be an affluent career woman with access to more than enough stores but who does not have the time or desire to go to them. According to the Direct Marketing Association, over two-thirds of the U.S. adult population order from a catalog at least once a year.[46] Catalog mania extends well beyond clothing and cosmetics purchases. Dell and Gateway 2000, direct-selling computer companies, each have annual sales of over $1 billion. Although established retailers such as Bloomingdale's or JCPenney publish catalogs, others are start-ups by ambitious entrepreneurs who cannot afford to open a store. That's how housewife Lillian Hochberg began—by selling handbags through the mail. Today the Lillian Vernon catalog mails out more than 137 million copies each year.[47]

Many stores such as Neiman-Marcus use catalogs to complement their in-store efforts. This allows the store to reach people who live in areas too small to support a store. Catalogs can be an efficient and expensive way to do business. Catalog retailers mail out 10 to 20 books for every order they receive, and paper and printing costs are rising steadily.

Still, catalog sales are a successful form of nonstore retailing, and U.S. firms are using them to reach overseas markets as well. Companies such as Lands' End and Eddie Bauer are doing brisk sales in Europe and Asia, where consumers tend to buy more products through the mail than do Americans in the first place. Lands' End opened up a central warehouse in Berlin and attacked the German market with catalogs. The company trained phone operators in customer service and friendliness and launched an aggressive marketing campaign to let consumers know of the Lands' End lifetime warranty (German catalog companies require customers to return merchandise within two weeks). Although local competitors protested and even took the company to court, the case was settled in the American company's favor and the Yanks' invasion continues.[48]

Direct Mail Unlike a catalog retailer that offers a variety of merchandise through the mail, **direct mail** is a brochure or pamphlet offering a specific product or service at one point in time.

For example, Saab Cars U.S.A. started a program to sell cars using letters and a coupon for $2,000. A pilot program that cost only $200,000 helped generate sales of $62 million in new Saabs.[49] A direct-mail offer has an advantage over a catalog because it can be personalized. Direct mail also is widely used by charities, political groups, and other not-for-profit organizations.

Just as with e-mail spamming, many Americans get overwhelmed with direct-mail offers and don't open all their "junk mail." This problem was amplified following the anthrax scare of 2001, when a lot of people became more reluctant to open mail from a source they couldn't identify. One solution was to create an industry-wide, nonproprietary Web site (www. whatsmailing.org) so mail recipients can check the legitimacy of packages that cross their desks or land in their home mailboxes.

Even so, after the attacks of September 11, 2001, adjustments had to be made. Procter & Gamble halted shipments of samples of Always Maxi Pads because consumers received lumpy packages without a clearly identified sender. Nissan canceled a direct-mail push for its new Altima model because the unusual packages spurred about 50 calls from fearful consumers.[50] The direct-mail industry is always working on ways to monitor what is sent through the mail and provides some help by allowing consumers to "opt out" of at least some mailing lists (you can learn more about this at the Direct Marketing Association's Web site at www.the-dma.org).

TELEMARKETING

Telemarketing is direct selling conducted over the telephone. Especially compared to door-to-door selling, this method is cheap and easy. Surveys indicate that one out of six Americans find it difficult to resist a telemarketing pitch. However, about one in three complained of feeling

following are some easy tips that will help you participate in environmental protection.

10 Easy Ways You Can Help Protect the Planet

1. **Shop by Mail: "The Greatest Car Pool on Earth"**
Shopping from home and work through catalogs and other forms of direct mail saves gasoline and cuts pollution. In 1995, more than 131 million Americans shopped by mail and phone, helping to reduce auto emissions and gasoline usage. (Simmons Market Research Bureau, 1996).

2. **Support Recycling in Your Hometown**
Towns and cities in many parts of the U.S. are collecting catalogs, direct mail and other "mixed papers" in waste-reducing recycling programs. Contact the new nationwide Environmental Hotline, sponsored by the U.S. Environmental

The Direct Marketing Association (DMA) is an industry trade group that uses the direct mail technique. Among other messages, the group emphasizes that catalogs and other direct mail pieces reduce pollution by cutting down on driving. And the DMA is supporting the recycling of catalogs to improve the environment as well.

cheated at one time by a telemarketer.[51] And do they always have to call during dinner? Telemarketing is more successful and more profitable for organizational markets than for consumer markets. When business-to-business marketers use the telephone to keep in contact with smaller customers, it costs far less than personal sales call and lets small customers know they are important to the company.

DIRECT-RESPONSE TELEVISION

As early as 1950, a channel called Television Department Stores brought the retailing environment into the television viewer's living room by offering a limited number of products the viewer could buy by calling the advertised company. Television sales picked up in the 1970s when two companies, Ronco Incorporated and K-Tel International, began to hawk such products as the Kitchen Magician, the Mince-O-Matic, and the Miracle Broom on television sets around the world.[52] A simple phone call and one of these wonders could be yours. The form of advertising called **direct-response TV** or **DRTV** includes short commercials of less than 2 minutes, 30-minute or longer infomercials and home shopping networks such as QVE and HSN. Top-selling DRTV product categories include exercise equipment, self-improvement products, diet and health products, kitchen appliances, and music. And this is hardly just an American phenomenon—DRTV sales in Japan of $1.5 billion per year equal those in the United States.[53]

direct response TV (DRTV) ■ Advertising on TV that seeks a direct response including short commercials of less than 2 minutes, 30-minute or longer infomercials, and home shopping networks.

Infomercials   Today these primitive sales pitches have been replaced by slick **infomercials**, which are half-hour or hour commercials that resemble a talk show but in actuality are intended to sell something. Although some infomercials still carry a low-class, sleazy stereotype, more than 40 major companies have used this format including heavyweights from American Airlines and Apple Computer to Visa and Volkswagen. A survey by *TV Guide* found that 72 percent of respondents have watched at least one infomercial, and about one-third made a purchase as a result.[54] Top-selling categories include cosmetics, self-improvement products, fitness products, kitchen appliances, music, and videos.

infomercials ■ Half-hour or hour commercials that resemble a talk show but in actuality are intended to sell something.

Home Shopping Networks   Television channels that exist solely to sell products let shopping junkies indulge themselves without leaving their living rooms.[55] In the United States the QVC channel alone sells products at the rate of $39 per second around the clock. To date, the typical American home shopping customer is in a low-income bracket, and the most frequently purchased product is inexpensive jewelry. Some upscale retailers such as Saks Fifth

Avenue and Donna Karan have experimented with this format, but these efforts have largely been unsuccessful.[56]

M-Commerce

m-commerce: ■
Promotional and other e-commerce activities transmitted over mobile phones and other mobile devices such as personal digital assistants (PDAs)

In this age of the Internet, it seems like we just get used to a dozen or so new terms when they are replaced by an equal number of new ones. M-commerce is a new buzzword that many marketers are talking about. The "m" stands for mobile. **M-commerce** is the promotional and other e-commerce activities transmitted over mobile phones and other mobile devices such as personal digital assistants (PDAs).[57]

M-commerce is prevalent in Europe and Asia. Text messaging in the Philippines is replacing traditional phone calls because of convenience and cost savings. According to the Philippine Long Distance Telephone Co., an estimated 1 million text messages are sent everyday.[58]

Slowly but surely, m-commerce is making its way to the United States. Even the MTV Music Video Awards now include a wireless advertising campaign to promote the event. Millions of consumers who use such networks as AT&T, Sprint, Palm, and OmniSky will get messages urging them to tune in.[59]

What's the big attraction?

WIRELESS MOBILE-COMMERCE

Although only a small proportion of the millions of users of mobile phones worldwide use their phones to check e-mail, stock quotes, and so on, that number is expected to grow dramatically in the next few years. Young people in particular are big users of cell phones. At this point about 28 percent of young people own or use a cell phone, which explains why cell phone companies such as Nokia are aggressively advertising on high school campuses.[60]

This high usage will open the door for m-commerce advertising campaigns like those now being conducted in other countries. Consider a campaign for the Kit Kat candy bar that was conducted by Nestlé in the United Kingdom. The firm's ad agency sent text messages to the cell phones of 6,000 consumers ages 18 to 25 that alerted them when ads for the candy would air and invited them to take a quiz about the ad that would in turn enter them into a drawing to win a month's supply of Kit Kats (about 94 percent of British youth have cell phones with wireless messaging capability). This technique, known as *short–messaging system marketing (SMS)*, is becoming a popular way to reach customers in the United Kingdom and throughout Europe.

M-commerce messages can reach specific types of consumers. A campaign for readers of *Men's Health* magazine sent a customized daily menu via cell phone to help interested readers curb calories (doubtful those Kit Kats were on the list).[61]

So what are the advantages of m-commerce to consumers? First, m-commerce provides incredible consumer convenience. You can use your mobile phone to buy tickets for a concert without standing in line. You can even buy soft drinks from a vending machine through the phone—a service already available in Europe.[62]

But the potential for m-commerce is even greater. Perhaps you're in the market for a new computer. You visit a local retailer and decide what you want. While you're there, you use your mobile phone or PDA to check prices of the same computer on the Internet. If you decide you have the best price, you'll be able to handle the transaction on your phone as well, paying for the computer through a secure Internet connection.

For marketers the opportunities for m-commerce are even more exciting. Using sophisticated *location–based technologies* including satellites, a retailer will be able to know when you are only a few blocks away from her store and she can send you messages about a special sale.[63] And as you pass McDonald's, your phone will beep to remind you how great a Big Mac combo would taste right about now. Of course, such opportunities bring a whole host of privacy issues that must be settled before these scenarios can become a reality.

For the time being there are some technological barriers that must be overcome for m-commerce to take off. At present American consumers are put off by the reliability of these services, the difficulty of typing messages on a tiny keypad, and concerns about security and privacy since it's possible for some services to pinpoint the user's location. For these reasons about one in four people who try m-commerce stop after the first few attempts.[64] In addition, U.S. mobile phone standards differ from those in Europe and Asia, which prevents worldwide access.

Still, the future is bright for m-commerce: One study predicts that despite the slow start, about 90 million Americans will be participating in m-commerce by 2007, generating more than $50 billion in revenues.[65] That's opportunity calling!

Real People, Real Choices: How It Worked Out at iWon

Brad and his colleagues conducted extensive testing on both content and sweepstakes advertisements. They did this by using a control banner ad that had been successful in the past and then creating new banners to test against the control. Perhaps you come up with this idea after doing the mini exercise following the first part of this case. Each banner is run in rotation so that they never appear at the same time. This lets iWon determine which banner is the most appealing in terms of click-through, and the firm can also monitor which version leads to greater conversion—sometimes the banner with the strongest click-through does not end up with the strongest conversion rate.

Based on the results of these tests, Brad chose option 3. He developed banner advertisements that talked about both iWon's content and sweepstakes opportunities. This approach allowed him to drive large numbers of users to the site—both users interested in the prizes and users more likely to become loyal, long-term users of iWon. This dual strategy worked: iWon was named by Nielsen as the stickiest portal (i.e., people stay at the site instead of just surfing on) and the fifth most visited site on the Internet in terms of page views.

This banner ad highlights two content areas of iWon, e-mail and travel. A prize opportunity is also mentioned. This hybrid message appealed to users who were interested in content, as well as those users who were interested in prize opportunities.

Chapter Summary

1. Tell what advertising is and describe the major types of advertising.

Advertising is nonpersonal communication from an identified sponsor using mass media to persuade or influence an audience. Advertising informs, reminds, and creates consumer desire. Product advertising is used to persuade consumers to choose a specific product or brand. Institutional advertising is used to develop an image for an organization or company, to express opinions (advocacy advertising), or to support a cause (public service advertising). Advertising begins with the client or advertiser that may be a manufacturer, a distributor, a retailer, or an institution. Most companies rely on the services of advertising agencies.

2. Describe the process of developing an advertising campaign.

Development of an advertising campaign begins with identifying the target market and developing message and budget objectives. Next, advertisers develop a creative strategy, choosing an effective type of advertising appeal. Pretesting advertising before placing it in the media prevents costly mistakes. A media plan determines where and when advertising will appear. Media options include broadcast media (network and spot television and radio), print media (newspapers, magazines, and directories), out-of-home media (outdoor advertising, place-based media), and Internet advertising. A media schedule specifies when and how often the advertising will be seen or heard.

3. Explain how marketers evaluate advertising.

Posttesting research may include recall tests or attitudinal measures that examine whether the message had an influence on the target market. Marketers must also consider the overall effectiveness of advertising threatened by an erosion of brand loyalty, threats from technology, greater emphasis on point-of-purchase communications, new communications industries, a cluttered advertising environment, and increased consumer disapproval of advertising.

4. Understand direct marketing.

Direct marketing refers to any direct communication designed to generate a response from a consumer or business customer. Some of the types of direct-marketing activities are mail order (catalogs and direct mail), telemarketing, and direct-response TV, including infomercials and home shopping networks.

5. Explain the future of m-commerce.

M-commerce is e-commerce done over mobile devices such as phones and personal digital assistants (PDAs). M-commerce can provide great convenience for consumers and gives marketers the opportunity for location-based commerce. In the next few years m-commerce is expected to grow as technological barriers are overcome.

Chapter Review

MARKETING CONCEPTS:
TESTING YOUR KNOWLEDGE

1. What is advertising and what is its role in marketing?
2. What are the types of advertising that are most often used?
3. How is an advertising campaign developed? Describe some of the different advertising appeals used in campaigns.
4. What are the strengths and weaknesses of television, radio, newspapers, magazines, directories, out-of-home media, and the Internet for advertising?
5. What are the ways marketers advertise on the Internet?
6. Describe the media planning process.
7. How do marketers pretest their ads? How do they posttest ads?
8. What are the challenges facing advertising today? How have advertisers responded to these challenges?
9. What is direct marketing? Describe the more popular types of direct marketing.
10. What is m-commerce?

MARKETING CONCEPTS:
DISCUSSING CHOICES AND ISSUES

1. Some people are turned off by advertising because they say it is obnoxious, that it insults their intelligence, and that advertising claims are untrue. Others argue that advertising is beneficial and actually provides value for consumers. What are some arguments on each side? How do you feel?
2. Technology through televison remotes, VCRs, computers, and cable television is giving today's consumers more and more control over the advertising images they see. How has this affected the advertising industry so far, and do you think this will affect it in the future? What are some ways that advertising can respond to this?
3. M-commerce will allow marketers to engage in location commerce where they can identify where consumers are and send them messages about a local store. Do you think consumers will respond positively to this? What do you think the benefits for consumers of m-commerce are?
4. Catalog shopping has been incredibly popular in recent years, but will it be replaced by e-commerce? Why or why not?

MARKETING PRACTICE:
APPLYING WHAT YOU'VE LEARNED

1. As an account executive for an advertising agency, you have been assigned to a new client, a manufacturer of a new sports drink. As you begin development of the creative strategy, you are considering different types of appeals: (a) USP, (b) comparative advertising, (c) a fear appeal, (d) a celebrity endorsement, (e) a slice-of-life ad, (f) sex appeal, and (g) humor. Outline the strengths and weaknesses of using each of these appeals for advertising the sports drink.
2. Assume you want to develop Internet advertising for the client in question 1. What form of Internet advertising would you suggest? Develop an example of what you would do.
3. Spend some time looking through magazines. Find an ad that fits each of the following categories:
   a. USP strategy
   b. testimonial
   c. lifestyle format
   d. humor appeal
   Critique each ad. Tell who the target market appears to be. Describe how the appeal is executed. Discuss what is good and bad about the ad. Do you think the ad will be effective? Why or why not?

MARKETING MINI-PROJECT:
LEARNING BY DOING

The purpose of this mini-project is to give you an opportunity to experience the advertising creative process.

1. With one or more classmates, create (imagine) a new brand of an existing product (such as a laundry detergent, toothpaste, perfume, soft drink, or the like).
2. Decide on an advertising appeal for your new product.
3. Create a series of at least three different magazine ads for your product, using the appeal you selected. Your ads should have a headline, a visual, and copy to explain your product and to persuade customers to purchase your brand.
4. Present your ads to your class. Discuss the advertising appeal you selected, and explain your ad executions.

REAL PEOPLE, REAL SURFERS:
EXPLORING THE WEB

Much of the advertising you see every day on television and in magazines is created by a small number of large advertising agencies. To make their agency stand out from the others, the different agencies develop unique personalities or corporate philosophies. Visit the Web sites of several advertising agencies.

Leo Burnett, www.leoburnett.com
BBDO, www.bbdo.com
Bates USA, http://batesusa.com
DDBNeedham, www.ddbn.com
Fallon, www.fallon.com
J. Walter Thompson, www.jwt.com

If you want to locate other agencies, you can find them in Internet lists of marketing companies such as this one from Yahoo: http://dir.yahoo.com/Business_and_Economy/Companies/Marketing/Advertising. Explore the Web sites to see how they differ. Then answer the following questions.

1. What is the mission of each agency? How does each agency attempt to position itself compared to other agencies?
2. Who are some of the major clients of the agency?
3. How does the site demonstrate the creative ability of the agency? Does the site do a good job of communicating the mission of the agency? Explain.
4. If available, tell a little about the history of the agency.
5. Of the agencies you visited, which would you most like to work for and why?
6. As a client, based on your exploration of the Web sites, which agency would you choose for your business and why?

PLAN IT!
DEVELOPING A MARKETING PLAN

As your instructor directs, create a marketing plan (using Marketing Plan Pro software or a written marketing plan format) to document your marketing decisions or answer these questions in a written or oral report.

Up to now, CFS has not used advertising (see the marketing plan in Appendix A). However, it may soon need advertising to boost sales of its growing product line. Choose one of the company's products.

1. What type of appeal (USP, comparative advertising, demonstration, testimonial, and so on) would be most appropriate for this product—and why?

2. Given CFS's limited promotional budget, what media would you recommend—and why?

3. How might CFS use direct marketing to reach targeted consumer segments?

Key Terms

advertising, (434)

advertising appeal, (441)

advertising campaign, (436)

advertising exposure, (448)

advocacy advertising, (436)

aided recall, (450)

aperture, (444)

attitudinal measures, (450)

banners, (447)

buttons, (447)

catalog, (454)

copy testing, (443)

cost per thousand (CPM), (449)

creative strategy, (440)

direct mail, (454)

direct marketing, (453)

direct-response TV, (455)

frequency, (448)

full-service agency, (437)

gross rating points (GRPs), (449)

impressions, (448)

infomercials, (455)

institutional advertising, (435)

limited-service agency, (437)

m-commerce, (456)

media planning, (443)

media schedule, (448)

out-of-home media, (445)

permission marketing, (447)

place-based media, (446)

posttesting, (450)

pretesting, (443)

product advertising, (435)

public service advertisements (PSAs), (436)

reach, (448)

spamming, (447)

unaided recall, (450)

unique selling proposition (USP), (441)

MARKETING IN ACTION: CHAPTER 15 CASE

REAL CHOICES AT POSTUM

Postum is a 100-year-old coffee substitute of which many of today's consumers have never even heard. In the mid 1990s some stubborn marketers at Kraft planned for that to change. They were engineering a comeback for Postum and were hoping that advertising could convince a new generation to give the venerable old product another try.

Postum was the first product sold by the Post Cereal Company. (Post was later absorbed by General Foods, which was then bought by Kraft Foods.) Made from roasted wheat, bran, and molasses, the powder was added to hot water to make a tasty morning beverage (at least to the 2 million people who bought the product each year). The brand had dominated the market for coffee substitutes for a century with an 87.7 percent share. Postum marketers felt that much of that success could be traced back to early advertising efforts. In 1934, a newspaper ad showed how a husband suffering from indigestion, headaches, and sleeplessness became a "new man" after his wife switched from coffee to Postum. The ad also featured "Mr. Coffee-Nerves," a cartoon character, who grumbled, "Postum, curse it, has driven me out of another home!" This character had been out of work for some time, though. Since 1983 there had been no advertising of any kind for Postum.

Tate Lucy was senior brand manager for Postum at Kraft Foods. When talking about the brand, Lucy used such phrases as "a very stable franchise" and "a lot of loyal users." But another term for Postum is "ghost brand," an older, unadvertised product that survives because a small group of steadfast fans continues to buy it. Even though Postum pretty much "owned" the coffee substitute market, sales of Postum had not increased in recent years and, in fact, had shown a slight decline. Whereas annual sales of popular coffee brands typically ran into several hundred million dollars, Postum's yearly sales had been in the range of $7 million to $8 million.

Kraft wanted to try to breathe new life into Postum. In recent years, as more and more products had been introduced to the market, grocery store shelf space had become increasingly scarce. For packaged goods producers, this meant that venerable, older brands must either grow or die. And many at Kraft felt that Postum deserved a chance. After no advertising or other marketing support for over a decade, though, no one was quite sure what the potential for the brand really was.

Postum's target consumer was at least 55 years old. Existing product users were almost exclusively in the 65 plus range, but Lucy thought advertising could effectively persuade slightly younger consumers to add Postum to their current portfolio of drinks. He felt that "coffee, tea, or Postum?" should be the question consumers asked themselves when thinking of hot beverages. According to Lucy, as people age, "they tend to look for hot beverage alternatives," and he intended to put Postum high on the list.

The only question was how best to convince these consumers to become Postum drinkers. Advertising worked a hundred years ago, and there was reason to believe it would work again. But what media, what message, and what budget? Could the company afford to spend $1 million on a market of less than $8 million? It was do or die for Lucy. Could he craft a wake-up call to revive this dormant brand?

Source: Stuart Elliott, "Advertising," *New York Times*, April 19, 1995, D7.

THINGS TO THINK ABOUT

1. What is the decision facing Postum?

2. What factors are important in understanding this decision situation?

3. What are the alternatives?

4. What decision(s) do you recommend?

5. What are some ways to implement your recommendation(s)?

Valpak's Blue Envelope

- **Early Promotions**

1986 - 2001 Design Version

Initial promotions were instant win cash giveaways. Tailored specially for the Valpak envelope promotions were proprietary and did not co-brand with other products or companies.

Side 2 – Holiday Hundreds Promotion

$100 checks were seeded randomly into envelopes.

Bookmark It!

OBJECTIVES:

1. Explain the role of public relations.
2. Describe the steps in developing a public relations campaign.
3. Explain what sales promotion is and describe some of the different types of trade and consumer sales promotion activities.
4. Explain the important role of personal selling in the marketing effort.
5. List the steps in the personal selling process.
6. Explain the job of the sales manager.

Public Relations, Sales Promotion, and Personal Selling

Real People, Real Choices: Meet Melissa Fisher, a Decision Maker at Cox Target Media

www.coxtarget.com

CURRENT POSITION: Vice President of marketing and communications.

EDUCATION: B.S. in Business Administration, Houghton College; M.A. in Management, Regent University. Pursuing a Ph.D. in Business Leadership and Corporate Communications.

ACCOMPLISHMENTS: Received the 1999 and 2000 Pace Setter Award, 1999 Cable Advertising Award for Strategic Positioning of Cable. Credited with the launch of Comedy Central, ESPN2, HGTV, FX, Sci-Fi, TLC, TV Guide Channel, and TV Land as new networks in the Virginia cable market.

WHAT I DO WHEN I'M NOT WORKING: Garden, cook, watch TV and movies.

FIRST JOB OUT OF SCHOOL: Skip tracer (Division of TRW), found people who falsified information and skipped out of medical, phone, credit card bills. Pay was great!

A MISTAKE I WISH I HADN'T MADE: Speaking my mind in e-mail when I probably should have just hit the delete key.

BUSINESS BOOK I'M READING NOW: <u>Permission Marketing</u> by Seth Godin.

MOTTO: "No one reads your résumé at your funeral."—Barbara Bush

PET PEEVE: Mediocrity—do it well or don't do it at all.

And the Envelope Please . . .

For the last 35 years, Cox Target Media has delivered 500 million light blue Valpak envelopes containing over 15 billion coupons and advertising offers directly to more than 50 million consumers throughout the United States, Canada, Puerto Rico, and the United Kingdom. Local merchants—dry cleaners, dentists, carpet cleaning services, and others—buy space in the envelope and these promotions are sold through a network of over 220 independent Valpak franchises. These franchises purchase the right to sell specific territories to advertisers and Cox Target Media supplies the Valpak inserts and envelopes.

Because the operation is decentralized, Valpak's reputation is uneven because the quality of the package is only as good as the local franchisee that puts it together. The Cox unit wanted to transform Valpak into a truly national brand attractive to large advertisers that want to communicate with consumers in many locations simultaneously. National advertiser research indicated, however, that the envelope's dated design and local nature were turn-offs for image-conscious companies. A new package design supported by an extensive advertising campaign that repositioned Valpak with consumers was planned to launch in January 2002.

As a direct-mail product, Valpak's effectiveness depends on consumers opening the envelope and examining the contents. Independent research studies conducted in the past 10 years claim that 9 out of 10 adults familiar with the Valpak envelope open this direct-mail item. However, opening the envelope doesn't guarantee that all of the advertising merchants' coupons were viewed or that any of them were redeemed. Melissa knew that Valpak franchisees would have a much easier time persuading advertisers to buy into the program if they could be sure that this form of sales promotion would really increase sales.

New consumer research studies conducted by three independent firms indicated that promotional materials such as sweepstakes, instant cash, or movie tickets in the envelopes would create a surprise element for Valpak recipients, enticing them to take a closer look at all of the offers in the envelope.

Melissa also believed that persuading national sponsors to participate in these promotions would generate co-branding opportunities with well-known companies. Through co-branding, national sales could offer added value opportunities to entice new advertisers. Getting nationally known names in the envelope would benefit all of the advertisers, because consumers would be more likely to examine each and every coupon.

However, Valpak was new to the concept of conducting a sophisticated national promotion, such as a sweepstakes. The company had previously conducted only limited promotions for small local businesses through its franchisees or its own instant cash promotion involving randomly inserted $100 checks that lucky consumers could immediately cash at any bank. Melissa needed to figure out how to sell envelope "space" to national advertisers, especially high-profile dining, entertainment, and retail companies. She considered these options:

Option 1: Include more local promotions.

Expand local promotions but hold off on national co-branded promotions until the Valpak rebranding and redesign process was complete. By sponsoring more instant-win promotions, including cash awards or other prizes such as lottery, movie, music, or event tickets, Valpak could continue to reward consumers in selected markets. Costs would increase because the company would have to buy more prizes, but Melissa thought this might be her only chance to make a good impression with national advertisers who would see the impact of these local promotions.

Option 2: Build promotions with high-profile companies.

Create a long-term strategy aimed at building promotional tie-ins whether Valpak would profit from these sponsorships or not. Valpak would even be willing to pay for the products it gave away just to be able to include items from high-profile companies in the promotion.

The idea would be to maximize promotional sales using the success of the 2001 programs. The promotional staff could approach prospective sponsors who might be willing to help underwrite the promotion, for example, convincing Kids "R" Us to sponsor a Cool for School promotion by including a registration form in the Valpak envelope.

Customized promotions would create proof of performance for future sales; if advertisers thought that Valpak didn't have an audience that would interest them, the firm could show, after a promotion, the many thousands who registered to win their products or services. Initially, co-branding with recognized brands might require Valpak to finance all promotional program elements, including the prizes themselves, printing, staff time, prize distribution, and other associated costs. This strategy could be expensive. But offering sponsors tie-ins at little to no cost could jeopardize future sales opportunities because potential sponsors might balk at having to pay for what they had been getting free. For this strategy to work, immediate results offering proof of promotional performance would be crucial.

Option 3: Allow the sales force to direct promotions.

Provide national sales personnel with off-the-shelf promotional templates that they could present to key clients during sales calls. In addition to local franchisees, Valpak's corporate office has a national sales team that calls on about 600 to 1,200 large consumer products companies to persuade them to buy advertising space in Valpak envelopes. The national sales force would be able to market a Valpak promotion, such as a sweepstakes, as another advertising opportunity in addition to any coupons they might insert in the envelope. Dividing the work between the promotions and sales staff would ease the burden of implementing the system. However, providing open-ended opportunities to sales staff risks pitching similar promotions to multiple clients. The first-come, first-served platform for accepting commitments could lead to resentment on the part of some advertisers.

Another risk was the lack of commission opportunities for salespeople, prompting Melissa's concern that sales staff would be reluctant to present these opportunities to clients. Although salespeople might eventually sell more advertising to a national client by enticing it to join in a promotion, failure to meet short-term sales quotas might make them reluctant to exert maximum effort for an uncertain payoff further down the road.

Now, join the decision team at Cox Target Media: Which option would you choose, and why?

Advertising Is Not the Only Game in Town!

Melissa's attempts to encourage coupon redemption by sponsoring sweepstakes and other sales promotions show that when it comes to promoting a product, there's more than one way to skin a cat—or, in one case, a goose: A liquor company once sent attractive models into trendy cigar bars to push Grey Goose, a pricey French vodka being introduced in the U.S. market. To get customers to try it, the women dropped a cherry soaked with the liquor into people's martinis and then gave surprised barflies a sales pitch about the vodka. When word of this "guerrilla marketing" hit the newspapers, the company got some free publicity for its efforts. To paraphrase Agent 007, the company apparently hopes potential customers will be stirred, not shaken. . . .[1]

We saw in Chapter 14 that traditional advertising efforts are steadily being supplemented with other communication methods such as direct mail and sweepstakes as companies work harder and harder to get through the clutter. Grey Goose's strategy to "stir" interest in a new vodka combines three different promotional techniques to make its impact: public relations (free publicity), sales promotion (a focused campaign to get people to try the vodka), and personal selling (the cherry drop in this instance). In this chapter we'll look at these three forms of promotion that are commonly used in addition to advertising in a firm's promotion mix. Let's start with public relations.

Public Relations

Public relations (PR) is the communication function that seeks to build good relationships with an organization's publics including consumers, stockholders, legislators and others who have a stake in the organization. Today PR activities are used to influence the attitudes and perceptions of various groups not only toward companies and brands but also toward politicians, celebrities, not for profit organizations and so forth. The basic rule of good public relations: Do something good, then talk about it. A company's efforts to get in the limelight—and stay there—can range from humanitarian acts to more lighthearted "exposure." Consider, for example, the Homemade Bikini Contest sponsored by the makers of Cruzan Rum: Each year hundreds of competitors nationwide show up in bathing suits made of anything but cloth—including jelly beans, Express Mail tape, dog biscuits, and picnic baskets.[2]

The big advantage of this kind of communication is that when public relations messages are placed successfully, they are more credible than if the same information appeared in a paid advertisement. As one marketing executive observed, "There's a big difference between hearing about a product from a pitchman and from your trusted local anchorman."[3]

Public relations is crucial to an organization's ability to establish and maintain a favorable image. Some types of PR activities, referred to as *proactive PR*, stem from the company's marketing objectives. For example, marketers create and manage **publicity**, which is unpaid communication about an organization that gets media exposure. This strategy helps to create awareness about a product or an event, as when a local newspaper reporting on an upcoming concert features an interview with the band's lead guitarist around the time that tickets go on sale. Although some publicity happens naturally, more typically a "buzz" needs to be created by a firm's publicists. Efforts to win this kind of attention sometimes result in bizarre

public relations ■ Communication function that seeks to build good relationships with an organization's publics, including consumers, stockholders, and legislators.

publicity ■ Unpaid communication about an organization appearing in the mass media.

TABLE 16.1	Sponsor	Stunt
"Wild and Wacky" Publicity Stunts	Wild 107 FM (San Francisco)	Deejay blocked traffic on the Bay Bridge for two hours during morning rush hour while he got a haircut (chosen as winner of the "most poorly timed, dumbest, or most tasteless stunt" award by the local chapter of the Public Relations Society of America).
	KYNG FM (Dallas)	The Fort Worth public library was left in a shambles after the radio station announced that it had hidden $5 and $10 bills in library books. More than 3,000 books were thrown on the floor by frenzied money seekers. The station claimed it wanted to boost interest in the library.
	British Knights	Hosted "World's Smelliest Socks Contest." About 4,600 people sent in their stinky socks to win free sneakers.
	Publishers of the book *Marketing Warfare*	Hired a World War II tank to carry the authors down Fifth Avenue in Manhattan.
	Milton Bradley	Sponsored National College Pigsty Search, a contest for the messiest dorm room.

Sources: Michael J. Ybarra, "Some Publicists Are Good, Some Are Bad, and Some Just Talk Funny," *The Wall Street Journal*, February 28, 1994, B1; "Cash in the Library? Not a Total Fiction," *The New York Times*, April 7, 1994, A16; Lee Berton, "Smelly Socks and Other Tricks from the Public-Relations Trade," *The Wall Street Journal*, November 30, 1993, B1; James Barron, "A Winemaker, a Bird, and the Publicity Game," *The New York Times*, December 2, 1993, B1; "Masses of Messes," *Asbury Park Press*, December 14, 1994, A2.

activities—some even weirder than the noncloth bikini competition we mentioned earlier. Table 16.1 provides some examples of a few such wacky antics publicists have pulled off to get attention in the media.

Public relations is also important when the company's image is at risk due to negative publicity, for example, product tampering.[4] The goal here is to manage the flow of information to address concerns so that consumers don't panic and distributors don't abandon the product. For example, a few years ago PepsiCo was rocked by claims that hypodermic needles had been found in Diet Pepsi cans. The company assembled a crisis team to map out a response and supplied video footage of its bottling process showing that foreign objects could not find their way into cans before they were sealed at the factory. The claims proved false, and PepsiCo ran follow-up ads reinforcing the findings. Pepsi's calm, coordinated response averted a public relations disaster.

When Microsoft found itself with a barrage of bad publicity while the U.S. Department of Justice pressed its antitrust case, it responded with an image strategy that included advertising portraying Microsoft as warm and accessible. Other corporate image ads focused on how the software giant's innovations have improved people's lives.[5] The chief spokesman for the PR campaign was CEO Bill Gates himself, who promised that "the best is yet to come."

The Internet has expanded the capabilities of the traditional PR function.[6] Corporate Web sites post testimonials from customers, make new product announcements, and respond quickly to important events. News releases posted on the company Web site may double as sales vehicles, a new function for PR.

The Internet can be very effective in handling company crises. With a host of Internet news sites, companies can respond to a crisis online in far less time than other forms of communication such as press releases or conferences.[7] When Alaska Airlines Flight 261 crashed off the California coast in January 2000, the company turned its Web site into a crash-information site posting updates hourly, a move most PR professionals would feel is the best way to minimize damage from a disaster.[8]

OBJECTIVES OF PUBLIC RELATIONS

Public relations specialists need to operate at many levels to ensure that various *publics* of a company receive coordinated, positive messages about the firm. These groups include customers, suppliers, employees, the media, stockholders, and government regulators.

Why are all of these publics important in marketing communication? Companies, brands, and customers do not exist in isolation. As we noted in Chapter 14, customers receive

1 *Bookmark It!*

Visit the Web sites of several major companies such as Procter & Gamble (www.pg.com), General Motors (www.gm.com), Microsoft (www.microsoft.com), and Pepsi (www.pepsi.com). What evidence is there that the site is used as a public relations tool? How effective do you think the site is as a PR tool?

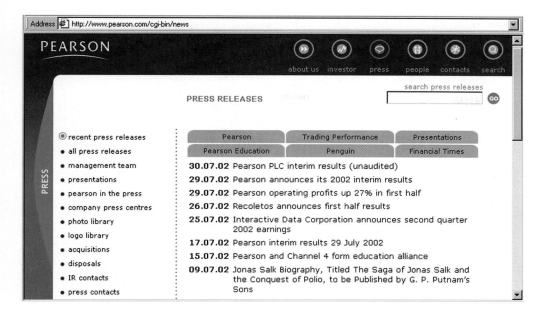

Many company Web sites allow surfers to access its recent press releases. Many of these press releases provide information about products—making the Web site an important sales vehicle.

information about the company and its products from many different sources. Thus, a company must establish and maintain a positive image with all of these publics because they influence market attitudes and consumer behavior, perhaps even more than communications that come directly from corporate headquarters.

Companies that practice integrated marketing communication (IMC) strategies know that PR strategies are best used in concert with advertising, sales promotions, and personal selling to send a consistent message to customers and other stakeholders. As part of the total IMC plan, public relations is often used to accomplish the following objectives:

- *Introducing new products to manufacturers*: When Weyerhaeuser Co. introduced Cellulon, a new biotechnology product, it distributed information kits that clearly explained the technical product and its applications in each of 12 markets to ensure that the trade press properly covered the introduction.[9]
- *Introducing new products to consumers*: When Chrysler Corp. rolled out its trio of LH sedans, the market was already anticipating their arrival. Working months ahead of time, Chrysler's public relations teams exposed journalists to the LH project through factory and laboratory tours, as well as discussions with designers. These efforts were successful in garnering favorable reviews in automotive magazines.[10]
- *Influencing government legislation*: Concerned about attempts to limit the amount that could be reimbursed for prescriptions in health care plans, the Pharmaceutical Manufacturers Association initiated an $8 million print campaign arguing that such drugs represent just 5 percent of national health care expenditures and save lives.[11]
- *Enhancing the image of a city, region, or country*: Faced with international criticism about possible human rights abuses and restriction of trade, the Chinese government established an office in charge of "overseas propaganda" to present a more favorable image of China to the rest of the world.[12]
- *Calling attention to a firm's involvement with the community*: Each year, an estimated 4,500 firms spend some $3.7 billion to sponsor sporting events (two-thirds of all event promotions), rock concerts, museum exhibits, and the ballet. "We're touching customers in their life-style, when they are more relaxed," said the national director of sponsorships and promotions for AT&T's consumer long-distance division.[13] PR specialists work behind the scenes to ensure that sponsored events receive ample press coverage and exposure.

Oscar Mayer created an eye-catching promotion with its Weinermobile—guaranteed to draw attention from hot dog lovers.

PLANNING A PUBLIC RELATIONS CAMPAIGN

A public relations campaign is a coordinated effort to communicate with one or more of the firm's publics. This is a three-step process of developing objectives, executing, and evaluating. Let's review each step.

The organization must first develop clear objectives for the PR program that define the message it wants people to hear. Next, the PR specialists must develop a campaign strategy that includes:

- a statement of objectives
- a situation analysis
- specification of target audiences (publics), messages to be communicated, and specific program elements to be used
- a timetable and budget
- discussion of how the program will be evaluated

For example, the International Apple Institute, a trade group devoted to increasing the consumption of apples, had to decide if a campaign should focus on getting consumers to cook more with apples, drink more apple juice, or buy more fresh fruit. Because fresh apples brought a substantially higher price per pound to growers than apples used for applesauce or apple juice, the group decided to push the fresh fruit angle. It used the theme "An apple a day . . ." (sound familiar?) and mounted a focused campaign to encourage people to eat more apples by placing articles in consumer media extolling the fruit's health benefits.

Execution of the campaign means deciding precisely how the message should be communicated to the targeted public(s). An organization can get out its positive messages in many ways: news conferences, sponsorship of charity events, and other attention-getting promotions.

One of the barriers to greater reliance on public relations campaigns is the difficulty encountered when trying to gauge their effectiveness. Who can say precisely what impact appearances by company executives on talk shows or sponsoring charity events has on sales?

It is possible to tell if a PR campaign is getting media exposure, though it's more difficult to gauge bottom-line impact. Table 16.2 describes some of the most common measurement techniques.

PUBLIC RELATIONS PROGRAM ELEMENTS

Sometimes PR efforts entail lobbying government officials to persuade them to vote a certain way on pending legislation or writing speeches on the topic for company executives to deliver. PR specialists may provide input on corporate identity materials, such as logos, brochures,

TABLE **16.2**

Measuring the Effectiveness of Public Relations Efforts

Method	Description	Pros	Cons
In-house assessments conducted by a public relations manager	Analyze media coverage in publications, looking for number of mentions and prominence of mentions.	Relatively inexpensive because the major cost is the manager's time.	Cannot guarantee objectivity in the analysis; crucial to specify up-front what the relevant indicators are.
Awareness and preference studies	Assess company's standing in the minds of customers relative to competition.	Good for broad-based strategy setting or to demonstrate the progress of a large program.	Difficult to connect results to specific PR events and to identify which actions had what level of impact on awareness; very expensive.
Measurement of print and broadcast coverage generated by PR activities.	The basic measurement tool in PR.	Provides a quantifiable measure of press coverage; relatively inexpensive.	Quantitative only; does not consider the *content* of the press coverage.
Impression counts	Measure the size of the potential audience for a given article.	Because a similar measure is used to assess advertising effectiveness, provides a common measure for comparison.	Usually limited to the circulation of selected publications, so this method does not include pass-along readership; can be expensive.

Source: Adapted from Deborah Holloway, "How to Select a Measurement System That's Right for You," *Public Relations Quarterly*, Fall 1992, 15–17.

building design, and even stationery that communicates a positive image for the firm. Or the organization can simply try to get media exposure for the achievements of an employee who has done some notable charity work or for a product it developed that saved someone's life.

For example, a Canadian pharmaceutical firm called Boerhinger Ingelhim Ltd. sent large dolls wearing respirator masks to Canadian pediatricians. The idea was to help doctors to ease the fears of their young patients about putting a mask over their mouths and noses. Boerhinger won considerable favorable publicity when the campaign was featured in many Canadian newspapers.

The most common way for public relations specialists to communicate is a **press release**, which is a report of some event that an organization writes itself and sends to the media in the hope that it will be published for free. A newer version of this idea is a video news release (VNR) that tells the story in a film format instead. Some of the most common types of press releases include:

press release ■ Information that an organization distributes to the media intended to win publicity.

- *Timely topics* deal with topics in the news, such as Levi Strauss's efforts to promote "casual" Fridays to boost sales of its Dockers and Slates casual dress pants by highlighting how different corporations around the country are adopting a relaxed dress code.
- *Research project stories* published by universities highlighting breakthroughs by faculty researchers.
- *Consumer information releases* provide information to help consumers make product decisions, such as helpful tips from a turkey company about preparing dishes for Thanksgiving dinner.

Internal public relations activities aimed at employees often include company newsletters and closed-circuit television. These sources of information help keep employees informed about company plans, successes, changes, and so on. Often company newsletters are distributed outside the firm to suppliers or other important publics.

Sponsorships are PR activities through which companies provide financial support to help fund an event in return for publicized recognition of the company's contribution.

sponsorship ■ A PR activity through which companies provide financial support to help fund an event in return for publicized recognition of the company's contribution.

Many companies today find that their promotion dollars are far better spent on sponsoring a golf tournament, a NASCAR driver, a symphony concert, or global events such as the Olympics or World Cup soccer competition. These sponsorships are particularly effective because consumers often connect their enjoyment of the event with the sponsor, thus creating brand loyalty.

Because different events cater to different consumers, sponsorships are a good way to target specific market segments. Rolling Rock beer, a product that brags about its roots in Latrobe, a small Pennsylvania town, attracted 35,000 consumers to a Rolling Rock Town Fair complete with headlining rock bands the Red Hot Chili Peppers, Moby, and Fuel.[14] Box office prices for the tickets were $33 but drew bids in excess of $170 on eBay.

Sponsorships also help to build interest in an entire product or activity. In Huntington Beach, California, corporate sponsors are trying to get everyone involved in surfing again. Companies such as Toyota, Washington Mutual, Seagrams, and Microsoft are getting involved in the sport because they want their brand associated with this legendary cool extreme sport.[15]

A few years back, some companies with smaller advertising budgets developed innovative ways of getting consumers' attention. Like the Grey Goose strategy described earlier, these activities—from putting stickers on apples and heads of lettuce, to placing product-related messages on the backs of theater tickets, and flags on a golf course—became known as **guerrilla marketing**. No, this term doesn't refer to marketers making monkeys out of themselves. This strategy involves "ambushing" consumers with promotional content in places they are not expecting to encounter this kind of activity.[16] This form of promotion was pioneered by people in the music business way back in the mid 1970s, when deejays like Kool DJ Herc and Afrika Bambaataa promoted their parties through flyers. To promote hip hop albums, Def Jam and other labels start building a buzz months before a release, leaking advance copies to deejays who put together "mix tapes" to sell on the street. If the kids seem to like a song, street teams then push it to club deejays. As the official release date nears, these groups of fans start slapping up posters around the city. They plaster telephone poles,

guerrilla marketing ■
Promotional strategies that "ambush" consumers with promotional content in places they are not expecting it.

When Pepsi-Cola introduced its new Fruit Works line of beverages, the company used a sampling strategy by distributing free bottles of the new drinks to spring breakers in Florida.

sides of buildings and car windshields with promotions announcing the release of new albums by artists such as Public Enemy or Jay-Z.[17]

Today, big companies are buying into guerrilla marketing strategies big time. Coca-Cola did it for a Sprite promotion; Nike did it to build interest in a new shoe model.[18] When RCA records wanted to create a buzz around teen pop singer Christina Aguilera, the label hired a team of young people to swarm the Web and chat about her on popular teen sites like alloy.com, bolt.com and gurl.com. They posted information casually, sometimes sounding like fans. Just before one of her albums debuted, RCA also hired a direct marketing company to email electronic postcards filled with song snippets and biographical information to 50,000 Web addresses. The album quickly went to Number 1 on the charts.

Guerilla marketing can be used to promote new drinks, cars, clothing styles—or even computer systems. Much to the annoyance of city officials in San Francisco and Chicago, in 2001 IBM painted hundreds of "Peace Love Linux" logos on sidewalks to publicize the company's adoption of the Linux operating system. Even though the company got hit with a hefty bill to pay for cleaning up the "corporate graffiti," one marketing journalist noted that they "got the publicity they were looking for."[19] Given the success of many of these campaigns that operate on a shoestring budget, expect to see even more of this kind of tactic as other companies climb on the guerrilla bandwagon.

Sales Promotion

Sometimes a simple walk through your student union is like running a gauntlet of people eager for you to enter a contest, taste a new candy bar, or take home a free T-shirt with a local bank's name on it. These are examples of **sales promotions**, programs that marketers design to build interest in or encourage purchase of a product or service during a specified time period.[20] As consumers, we are exposed to more and more advertising—some suggest we get bombarded with up to 3,000 marketing messages a day. Marketers have been placing an increasing amount of their total marketing communication budget into sales promotions (like the sweepstakes considered by Valpak) for one simple reason—these strategies deliver results.

Sales promotions sometimes can be elaborate and far-reaching. For example, a successful promotional effort by Diet Coke capitalized on the enormous popularity of the television sitcom *Friends* when the company distributed bottle caps with each of the show's main characters' names on them. Each week, a different character was shown drinking a bottle of Diet Coke in a commercial immediately after the show, and holders of caps with that person's name won a prize.

How does a sales promotion differ from advertising? Both are paid messages from identifiable sponsors intended to change consumer behavior or attitudes. In some cases, the sales promotion itself is publicized using a traditional advertising medium, such as the Diet Coke commercials that ran after *Friends*. But although many advertising campaigns are carefully crafted to create long-term positive feelings about a brand, company, or store, sales promotions tend to focus on more short-term objectives, such as an immediate boost in sales or the introduction of a new product.

Sales promotions are very useful if the firm has an immediate objective, such as bolstering sales for a brand quickly or encouraging consumers to try a new product. The objective of a sales promotion may be to generate enthusiasm among retailers to take a chance on a new product or provide more shelf space for an item they already carry. Thus, like advertising, sales promotions can target channel partners or the firm's own employees in the form of trade promotions as well as end consumers.

However, sales promotion is but one part of a total integrated marketing communication program and, thus, must be coordinated with other promotion activities. For example, if brand packaging and advertising seek to position the product as an expensive, luxury item, a sales promotion activity that reduces the price or involves distribution of free samples by a guy dressed in a clown suit may send conflicting messages to the customer.

Table 16.3 summarizes these techniques. Let's start with trade promotions and then learn about consumer promotions.

sales promotions ∎
Programs designed to build interest in or encourage purchase of a product during a specified time period.

TABLE 16.3

Sales Promotion Techniques:
A Sampler

Technique	Primary Target	Description	Example
Trade show	Industry	Many manufacturers showcase their products to convention attendees.	The National Kitchen and Bath Association organizes several shows a year. Manufacturers display their latest wares to owners of kitchen and bath remodeling stores.
Incentive program	Sales force	A prize is offered to employees who meet a prespecified sales goal or who are top performers in a given time period.	Mary Kay cosmetics awards distinctive pink cars to its top-selling representatives.
Point-of-purchase displays	Trade and consumers	In-store exhibits make retail environments more interesting and attract consumers' attention.	The Farnam Company: As somber music plays in the background, a huge plastic rat draped in a black shroud lies next to a tombstone to promote the company's Just One Bite rat poison.
Push money	Trade	Salespeople are given a bonus for selling a specific manufacturer's product.	A retail salesperson at a formal wear store gets $1.00 every time he or she rents a particular tuxedo for a prom or wedding.
Promotional products	Trade	A company builds awareness and reinforces its image by giving out items with its name on them.	Beer companies send liquor store owners posters of attractive women wearing company T-shirts.
Cooperative promotions	Trade	Companies team up to promote their products jointly.	CompuServe and Universal Pictures ran a promotion for the mystery/thriller film *Sneakers*. CompuServe users were invited to break a series of codes contained in a special "Sneakers" file and win a trip to Hollywood.
Coupons	Consumers	Certificates for money off on selected products, often with an expiration date are used to encourage product trial.	Colgate-Palmolive offers 79 cents off a bottle of Teen Spirit deodorant.
Samples	Trade and consumers	Retailers might get a demonstration product to help in sales presentations; consumers get a free trial size of the product.	A small bottle of Pert shampoo arrives in the mail.
Contests/sweepstakes	Trade and consumers	A sales contest rewards wholesalers or retailers for performance; consumers participate in games or drawings to win prizes; builds awareness and reinforces image.	The Publishers' Clearing House announces its zillionth sweepstakes.
Bonus packs	Consumers	Additional product is given away with purchase; rewards users.	Maxell provides two extra cassettes with purchase of a pack of ten.
Gifts with purchase	Consumers	A consumer gets a free gift when a product is bought; reinforces product image and rewards users.	A free umbrella comes with the purchase of Lagerfeld's Photo cologne.

Source: Some material adapted from Ajay Bhasin, Roger Dickinson, William A. Robinson, and Christine G. Hauri, "Promotion Investments That Keep Paying Off," *Journal of Consumer Marketing*, Winter 1989, 31–36; "One Sneaky Campaign," *Incentive*, November 1992, 93.

TRADE PROMOTIONS

Trade promotions take one of two forms. Discount promotions reduce the cost of the product to the retailer or help defray its advertising expenses. They are designed to encourage stores to stock the item and be sure it's given a lot of attention. Sales promotions that focus on increasing awareness and sales do so by creating enthusiasm among salespeople and customers. Let's take a look at both types in more detail.

Discounts and Deals One form of trade promotion is a *price break*. A manufacturer can reduce a channel partner's costs through sales promotions that discount its products. For example, a manufacturer can offer a **merchandise allowance**, which reimburses the retailer for in-store support such as shelving, or a **case allowance**, which provides a discount to the retailer or wholesaler based on the order volume of a product.

> **merchandise allowance** Reimburses the retailer for in-store support of the product.
>
> **case allowance** A discount to the retailer or wholesaler based on the volume of product ordered.

Allowances and deals have a downside, however. As with all sales promotion activities, the manufacturer's expectation is that they will be of limited duration after which the channel partner will again pay full price for the items. Unfortunately some channel members engage in a practice called *forward buying* in which large quantities of the product are purchased during a discount period, warehoused, and not bought again until another discount is offered. Some large retailers engage in what is known as *diverting*, an even more questionable practice. Here the retailer buys the product at the discounted promotional price, warehouses it, and after the promotion has expired, sells the inventory to other retailers at a price that is lower than the nondiscounted price but high enough to turn a profit. Both forward buying and diverting go against the spirit of the sales promotions, raising the question as to whether or not the practices are ethical.

Industry Boosting and Boasting Other types of trade sales promotions increase the visibility of a manufacturer's products to channel partners. Whether an elaborate exhibit at a convention or a coffee mug with the firm's logo sent out to clients, these efforts seek to keep the company's name topmost when distributors and retailers make decisions about which products to stock and push. These forms of sales promotions include:

- *Trade shows*. The thousands of industry **trade shows** held in the United States and around the world each year are major vehicles for manufacturers to show off their product lines to wholesalers and retailers. Usually, large trade shows are held in big convention centers where many companies set up elaborate exhibits to show their products, give away samples, distribute product literature, and troll for new business contacts. One example of how technology is changing traditional marketing is the advent of online trade shows where potential customers can preview a manufacturer's wares remotely. This idea is growing in popularity, though many industry people are finding it a challenge to "schmooze" in cyberspace. An important benefit of traditional trade shows is the opportunity to develop customer leads that are then given to the company's sales force for follow-up. We'll talk more about the function of the sales force later in this chapter.

> **trade shows** Events at which many companies set up elaborate exhibits to show their products, give away samples, distribute product literature, and troll for new business contacts.

- *Promotional products*. We have all seen them: coffee mugs, visors, T-shirts, key chains, and countless other doodads emblazoned with a company logo. They are examples of promotional products. Unlike licensed merchandise sold in stores, these goodies are given away to build awareness for the sponsor. Although some of these freebies are distributed directly to consumers and business customers, many are intended for channel partners such as retailers and vendors to build name recognition and loyalty.
- *Incentive programs*. Mary Kay cosmetics is famous for giving its more productive distributors pink cars to reward their efforts. In addition to motivating distributors and customers, some promotions are designed to light a fire under the firm's own sales force. These incentives, known as **push money**, may come in the form of cash bonuses, trips, or prizes. For example, Danish shoe manufacturer Ecco recently offered retail shoe salespeople a free pair of its shoes if they sold 10 pairs in a seven-day period. Needless to say, the salespeople made sure every customer knew about the Ecco brand.

> **push money** A bonus paid by a manufacturer to a salesperson for selling its product.

Promotional products are giveaways with the company logo. Companies find that promotional products, such as 3M Post-its, imprinted with their company logo are a good way to keep their name in front of both their customers and channel partners.

CONSUMER PROMOTIONS

Some consumer sales promotions create a buzz in the form of a contest or a special event. For example, Coca-Cola USA toured the country in a trailer that converted into a 25,000-square-foot interactive entertainment center. This road show included a performance stage anchored

Cooking contests (such as the "Bourboncuing" contest sponsored by Jim Bean) are a popular way to let consumers "strut their stuff" and create a buzz about a company's products.

To encourage consumers to buy more Chiquita products, the producer held a sweepstates to win a Ford Windstar.

by two huge Coca-Cola bottles, a video wall with interactive video and sports games, a 16-foot-high observation deck, a scoreboard with field lights for nighttime entertainment, a soft-drink stand, and a retail store offering Coca-Cola merchandise.[21] Coke's efforts illustrate how far major companies will go to create unusual and attention-getting forms of promotion. As is the case with trade promotions, such efforts to boost sales seek to attract consumers with price breaks or novel events. Let's see how they apply both strategies.

Price-Based Consumer Promotions   Many sales promotions target where consumers live: their wallets. They emphasize short-term price reductions or refunds, thus encouraging people to choose a brand—at least while the deal is on. Price-based consumer promotions, however, have a downside similar to the price break trade promotion. If used too frequently, the consumers become conditioned to purchase the product only at the lower promotional price.

- *Coupons.* Try to pick up any Sunday newspaper without spilling some coupons. These certificates, redeemable for money off on a purchase, are the most common price promotion. Indeed, they are the most popular form of sales promotion over all, with billions distributed annually including those distributed by Valpak. Even industries such as pharmaceuticals that never tried this approach before are turning to it in a big way. Coupons that can be redeemed for free supplies of drugs and pharmaceuticals are being mailed and are also available through sites such as viagra.com and purplepill.com. Companies use the coupons to prompt patients to ask for the specific brand instead of the more economical generic version.[22]
- *Price deals, refunds, and rebates.* In addition to coupons, manufacturers often offer a temporary price reduction to stimulate sales. This price deal may be printed on the package itself, or it may be a price-off flag or banner on the store shelf. Alternatively, companies may offer **rebates**, which allow the customer to recover part of the purchasing price via mail-ins to the manufacturer.
- *Frequency (loyalty/continuity) programs.* **Frequency programs**, also referred to as loyalty or continuity programs, offer a consumer a discount or a free product for multiple purchases over time. The airlines were the first to offer these, calling them frequent flyer miles. Today similar programs have been initiated by a host of other firms including retailers, auto rental companies, hotels, and restaurants. For example,

rebates ■ Sales promotions that allow the customer to recover part of the product's cost from the manufacturer.

frequency programs ■ Consumer sales promotion programs that offer a discount or free product for multiple purchases over time; also referred to as loyalty or continuity programs.

TGI Friday's boasts more than a million members in its Friday's Gold Points program, which allows customers to redeem gifts from a variety of cosponsors.[23]

- *Special packs*. Another form of price promotion is to give the shopper more product instead of lowering its price.[24] A *special pack* also can be a separate product given away along with another product, such as National Football League mugs given to gas station customers.

Attention-Getting Consumer Promotions Attention-getting consumer promotions stimulate interest in and publicity for a company's products. Consider some recent imaginative promotions designed to lure passengers in the highly competitive airline industry. After Northwest Airlines announced cheap flights to Memphis on Elvis Presley's birthday, American Airlines countered with a discount to passengers who came to the airport dressed as The King.

Real People, Other Voices: Advice for Cox Target Media

Eli Gelber, Student, University of North Carolina

I would choose option 1 because Valpak is not ready to conduct customized national promotions or develop co-branding alliances. Valpak has only one chance to make a first impression with national advertisers. A strategy that prematurely aims promotional campaigns at companies with powerful brand equity could prove disastrous for Valpak. Advertisers must be confident in Valpak's ability to protect their brand name and to reach their target consumers effectively. Valpak, while aggressively expanding its local promotions, should gather data that prove its advertising reaches the intended target. Learning what is required to implement successful, large-scale promotional campaigns will ensure Valpak is well equipped to "go national" after the debut of its new packaging. Finally, I recommend the creation of a small, centralized promotional staff to gather hard data on Valpak use and oversee local and national expansion.

Marvin G. Lovett, Marketing Professor, University of Texas at Brownsville

I choose option 2. Cox is ready for an aggressive move. The recent development of a new modern package design and repositioning strategies indicates significant progress toward entering the national market. Recent consumer studies indicate strong acceptance of the product. The key for Cox Target Media is to increase sales for its clients. Cox has a proven product; it just has to prove it to the national players. The strategy of allowing new national clients to try the product at Cox's expense is well founded and is referred to as sampling. In fact, Schultz, Robinson & Petrison (1998) report that sampling is the most effective form of sales promotion—even more so when coupled with incentives such as coupons. The national market is a challenging new SBU for Cox. This entrepreneurial venture, like most new significant ventures, will require early nurturing but will later provide for huge revenue potential. (Reference: Don E. Schultz, William A. Robinson, and Lisa A. Petrison, *Sales Promotion Essentials*, 3rd ed., Chicago: NTC Business Books, 1998.)

Brian Kurtz, Vice President, Marketing Boardroom

I would choose option 1 because there are still many untapped possibilities with local advertisers. Valpak's "brand" is about taking care of local businesses, not big, national ones. It's true that Valpak's costs would increase if ". . . the company bought more prizes. . ." but why wouldn't the local advertisers/businesses be allowed to *contribute* "prizes" in exchange for better positions, outer envelope copy, and the like? The win-win possibilities between Valpak and existing local advertisers are abundant—and not all would increase Valpak's costs. With nine out of ten adults already opening the envelopes, the next challenge is making them stay in the envelopes longer. Searching for the promoted prizes and learning more about *all* of the other local possibilities for a longer period of time seems like the obvious next step. The national strategies (options 2 and 3) seem grandiose and could bite the hand(s) that feeds Valpak best.

Weigh in with your thoughts! Visit the Live Laboratory at www.prenhall.com/solomon for extended Other Voices replies, exercises and more.

Soon after, United Airlines awarded a first-class upgrade to passengers willing and able to sing the words to Elvis's song "Jailhouse Rock."[25] Some typical types of attention-getting promotions include:

Contests and sweepstakes. A contest is a test of skill and a sweepstakes is based on chance. Guinness Import Company's "Win Your Own Pub in Ireland" contest gave away an actual pub to the winner of an essay contest titled "Why Guinness Is My Perfect Pint."[26]

The dairy industry's milk mustache advertising campaign was also the basis for a consumer contest.[27] Consumers collected under-the-cap game pieces on gallons of milk and winners of the "Milk Mustache Fame Game" were featured in a milk mustache ad. Chiquita Brands, marketer of Chiquita bananas, included a Ford Windstar, $5,000 in cash, and other items as grand prizes in its "Miss Chiquita's Summer Fun on the Run" contest.[28]

Premiums. **Premiums** are items offered free to people who have bought a product. They usually are novelty items, such as the removable tattoos called Barqtoos that Barq's root beer gave away. The prize in the bottom of the box of cereal—the reason many college students open the box from the bottom—is a premium. A new wrinkle in premiums involves prepaid phone cards. Companies jumping on the phone card bandwagon offer cards emblazoned with pictures of sports heroes, products, and even rock bands. Phone cards make ideal premiums because they are compact, can display brand logos or attractive graphics, provide opportunities for repeat exposure, and the issuer can build databases by tracking card usage.[29]

premiums ■ Items offered free to people who have purchased a product.

Sampling. How many people at one time or another have managed to scrape together an entire meal by scooping up free food samples at their local grocery store? **Sampling** induces people to try a product by distributing trial-size versions in stores, on street corners, or through the

sampling ■ Distributing free trial-size versions of a product to consumers.

Premiums such as this one provide consumers with another reason to choose one brand over the other.

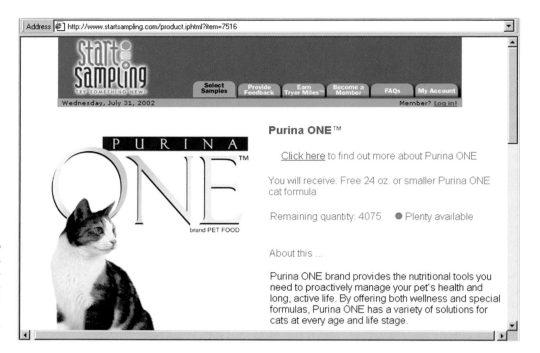

Address http://www.startsampling.com/product.iphtml?item=7516

start:sampling
TRY SOMETHING NEW!

Select Samples | Provide Feedback | Earn Tryer Miles | Become a Member | FAQs | My Account

Wednesday, July 31, 2002   Member? Log in!

Purina ONE™

Click here to find out more about Purina ONE

You will receive: Free 24 oz. or smaller Purina ONE cat formula

Remaining quantity: 4075   ● Plenty available

About this ...

Purina ONE brand provides the nutritional tools you need to proactively manage your pet's health and long, active life. By offering both wellness and special formulas, Purina ONE has a variety of solutions for cats at every age and life stage.

Increasingly the Internet is becoming an effective and low-cost means of delivering sales promotion offers. At this and other product sample sites, customers can request products they want to try.

mail. When Pepsi-Cola introduced a new beverage line called FruitWorks, it used vehicles in Panama City, Florida, and South Padre Island, Texas, to offer spring breakers free tours—and free samples of the new products.[30]

Many marketers are now taking advantage of free sample sites on the Internet.[31] Companies such as Procter & Gamble Co, Unilever, S.C. Johnson & Son, and SmithKline Beecham are readily taking advantage of Web sites such as www.freesamples.com and www.startsampling.com that not only distribute the firms' samples but also follow up with satisfaction surveys.

point-of-purchase (POP) promotion ■ In-store displays or signs.

Point-of-purchase promotion. A **point-of-purchase (POP) promotion** attempts to influence consumers while they are in the store by catching their attention with displays or signs.[32] Marketers are challenged to come up with new and innovative POP displays that will grab attention, such as the promotion Bausch & Lomb ran in Spain. The company wanted to encourage consumers with good vision to buy contact lenses that changed their eye color. The in-store display gave shoppers an advanced peek at how they would look with five different eye colors without actually inserting the contacts.[33]

POP activities also include the use of *in-store media* such as placards on shopping carts or closed-circuit television to promote specific products. As the CEO of one company that produces these in-store messages put it, "Does it make any sense to spend millions of dollars talking to people in their living rooms and cars and then let them wander around a supermarket with 30,000 product choices without something to remind them to buy your product?"[34]

brand placement ■ Getting a brand featured in a movie or television show.

Brand placements. A **brand placement** means getting your brand featured in movies or television shows. When consumers see a brand being used by a popular celebrity or shown in a favorite movie or TV program, they might develop a more positive attitude toward the brand. Successful brand placements have included the BMW Z3 driven by Agent 007, James Bond, the Nike shoes worn by Forrest Gump, and the Ray-Ban sunglasses worn by Tom Cruise in *Risky Business.*

Reality shows have also gotten into the act: The TV show *Lost* was funded by a group of four clients: Coca-Cola, Johnson & Johnson, Lowe's, and Marriott International. The four companies took most of the ad time and their products were easy to spot in the programs. Participants drank Dasani water (Coca-Cola) and opened "survival kits" that came packed in crates from Lowe's.[35]

A cross-promotion lets companies join forces to push their products using a single promotional tool. That's the plan behind the cross-promotion between Hard Candy and Visa.

The next frontier for brand placements? Video games that include real-life brands such as Ford, Radio Shack, General Motors, Toyota, Procter & Gamble, and Sony. Quiksilver, a clothing manufacturer for extreme-sport participants, now puts its shirts and shorts into video games such as Tony Hawk's Pro Skater 3. It's estimated that video game placements will generate $705 million a year by 2005.[36] That's not child's play.

Once marketers have determined the objectives, they must decide what the program will look like. If the objective is to encourage users of a competing product to try the item, a sampling program might work best. If the objective is to encourage loyal customers to increase their interest in the brand, the firm might sponsor a contest or sweepstakes as Valpak considered doing. If the company wants to increase hard-won shelf space, it might try giving a price break to retailers. Many marketers are discovering the virtues of **cross-promotion**, in which suppliers of two or more products or services join forces to create interest using a single promotional tool.

Personal Selling

Both public relations and sales promotions rely on TV, newspapers, and other mass-media vehicles to reach channel partners and customers. The final piece of the promotion pie is personal selling, which is a far more intimate way to talk to the market. **Personal selling** occurs when a company representative contacts a prospect directly regarding a good or service. Many organizations rely heavily on this approach because at times the "personal touch" can carry more weight than mass-media material. For business-to-business marketers such as Xerox, the personal touch builds a lot of sales volume. Many industrial products and services are too complex or expensive to market effectively in an impersonal trade advertisement.

Another advantage of a good sales force is that salespeople are the firm's eyes and ears. They learn who is talking to the customers, what is being offered, what new rival products are on the way—all sorts of competitive intelligence. Personal selling has special importance for students because many graduates with a marketing background will enter sales jobs. The

3 *Bookmark It!*

Find some examples of sales promotions. You probably have some at home and will find others in newspapers, magazines, and at the supermarket. How do the sales promotions influence consumers differently than advertising?

cross-promotion ■ Two or more products or services combine forces to create interest using a single promotional tool.

personal selling ■ The part of the promotion mix that involves direct contact between a company representative and a customer.

Bureau of Labor Statistics has estimated that 17.4 million people will be employed in sales and related occupations by 2010, up from 15.5 million in 2000.[37]

Got your attention? Let's take a close look at how personal selling works and how sophisticated salespeople develop long-term relationships with customers.

THE ROLE OF PERSONAL SELLING

When a man calls an 800 number to order a new desktop PC configured with a snappy CD-ROM drive so his kids can play the latest version of Doom, he is dealing with a company salesperson. When he sits in on a presentation by a computer technician presenting a new spreadsheet software package, he is dealing with a salesperson. And when that same man agrees over dinner at a swanky restaurant to buy a new computer network for his company, he also is dealing with a company salesperson. For many firms, some element of personal selling is essential to land a contract, making this type of promotion an important part of any marketing plan.

Generally, a personal sales effort is more important when a firm engages in a *push strategy*, in which (as we'll see in the next chapter) the goal is to push the product through the channel of distribution so that it is available to consumers. As a vice president at Hallmark Cards observed, "We're not selling to the retailer, we're selling *through* the retailer. We look at the retailer as a pipeline to the hands of consumers."[38]

Personal selling also is likely to be crucial in business-to-business contexts when direct interaction with upper-level management is required to clinch a big deal—and often when intense price negotiations will occur before the deal is signed. In addition, inexperienced buyers may need the hands-on assistance that a professional salesperson can provide. Firms selling products that consumers buy infrequently—computers, lawn mowers, college educations—often rely heavily on personal selling, as do firms selling complex or very expensive products that need a salesperson to explain, justify, and sell them.

If personal selling is so effective, why don't firms just scrap their advertising and sales promotion budgets and hire more salespeople? There are some obvious drawbacks that limit the role played by personal selling in the promotion mix. First, when the dollar amount of individual purchases is low, it doesn't make sense to use personal selling. The cost per contact with a customer is high compared to other forms of communication. In 2000, the average cost for a sales call with consultative selling was $211.56, a cost that includes salary, travel, a company car, and so on.[39] The per contact cost of a national television commercial is miniscule by comparison. A 30-second, prime-time commercial may be $300,000 to $500,000, but with millions of viewers, the cost may be only $10 or $15 per 1,000 viewers.

Salespeople—even the *really* energetic—can make only so many calls a day. Thus, reliance on personal selling is effective only when the success ratio is at its highest. Because the cost of fielding salespeople is high, **telemarketing**, in which person-to-person communication takes place via the telephone or fax machine, is growing in popularity (much to the dismay of many prospects who are interrupted by dinner-time calls).

Of course, the types of salespeople and their functions vary considerably. The person who processes a computer purchase over the phone is an **order taker**, a salesperson whose primary function is to process transactions that the customer initiates. Order takers include both inside and outside salespeople. Most retail salespeople are inside order takers, but often wholesalers, dealers, and distributors also employ salespeople to wait on customers. Manufacturers' reps for companies such as Procter & Gamble and Duncan Hines are outside order takers who call on supermarkets and other retail outlets and do little more than ask how much the supermarket needs this time.

In contrast, a computer technician is a **technical specialist** who contributes expertise in the form of product demonstrations, recommendations for complex equipment, and setup of machinery. The technical specialist's job is to provide *sales support* rather than actually closing the sale. The technical specialist promotes the firm and tries to stimulate demand for a product to make it easier for colleagues to actually make the deal.

Sometimes a person whose job is to lay this groundwork is known as a **missionary salesperson**.[40] Missionary salespeople promote the firm and try to stimulate demand for a product but don't actually complete a sale.

telemarketing ■ The use of the telephone to sell directly to consumers and business customers.

order taker ■ A salesperson whose primary function is to facilitate transactions that the customer initiates.

technical specialist ■ Sales support person with a high level of technical expertise who assists in product demonstrations.

missionary salesperson ■ A salesperson who promotes the firm and tries to stimulate demand for a product, but does not actually complete a sale.

Many firms find that the selling function is best handled by **team selling**. A selling team may consist of a salesperson, a technical specialist, the missionary salesperson who made the initial contact, and someone from the engineering department of the firm who can develop pricing and packages that satisfy the customer's needs. Xerox, for example, competes for big accounts by sending out Team Xerox, a group that includes customer service personnel, financial experts, and even top management.[41]

Finally, the person who actually convinces the customer to shell out for the computer network (probably after several weeks or months of negotiations) is an **order getter**. These salespeople work creatively to develop relationships with customers or to generate new sales. They find new customers, persuade customers to buy, and close sales.

APPROACHES TO PERSONAL SELLING

Personal selling is one of the oldest forms of promotion, but its image was tarnished by smooth-talking pitchmen who would say anything to make a sale. In more recent years, personal selling has redeemed itself as a profession and has moved from a transactional, hard-sell technique to a relationship marketing approach. Let's see how.

Transactional Marketing: Putting on the Hard Sell   The *hard sell* is a high-pressure process. We've all been exposed to the pushy electronics salesperson who puts down the competition by telling shoppers that if they buy elsewhere they will be stuck with an inferior sound system apt to fall apart in six months. These hard-sell tactics are a form of **transactional selling**, a technique that focuses on making an immediate sale with little or no attempt to develop a relationship with the customer. As customers, the hard sell makes us feel manipulated and resentful. This technique also contributes to the negative image many of us have of obnoxious salespeople.

Relationship Selling: Polishing the Tarnished Image   Today's professional salesperson is more likely to practice **relationship selling** than transactional selling. This means that the salesperson seeks to develop a mutually satisfying relationship with the customer.[42] Relationship selling involves winning, keeping, and developing customers. *Winning* a customer means converting an interested prospect into someone who is convinced that the product or service holds value for him. *Keeping* a customer means ensuring that the customer gets what she paid for. *Developing* a customer means satisfying the customer so that he will be counted on to provide future business.[43]

THE ROLE OF PERSONAL SELLING IN THE PROMOTION MIX

The salesperson's job can be made easier with support from publicity and advertising. The business customer, interested after seeing the supplier's advertisements or product releases, is likely to welcome that vendor's representative. Responses to toll-free numbers provided in advertising and sales promotions can provide hot sales leads for prospective customers who have already expressed interest in learning more about the product. Many salespeople obtain valuable leads at industry trade shows attended by hundreds or thousands of prospective customers.

THE SELLING PROCESS

Selling is seldom boring. Every customer, every sales call, and every salesperson are unique. Some salespeople are successful primarily because they know so much about what they sell. Others are successful because they've built strong relationships with customers who look forward to their visits to "chew the fat." Regardless, most salespersons understand and engage in a series of activities necessary to bring about a transaction.

Complex or expensive sales require careful planning, and successful personal selling in these cases is more likely if the salesperson undergoes a systematic series of steps called the **creative selling process**. These steps require the salesperson to seek out customers, analyze their needs, determine how product attributes provide benefits, and then decide how best to

team selling ■ The sales function when handled by a team that may consist of a salesperson, a technical specialist, and others.

order getter ■ A salesperson who works creatively to develop relationships with customers or to generate new sales.

transactional selling ■ A form of personal selling that focuses on making an immediate sale with little or no attempt to develop a relationship with the customer.

relationship selling ■ A form of personal selling in which the salesperson seeks to develop a mutually satisfying relationship with the consumer.

creative selling process ■ The process of seeking out customers, analyzing needs, determining how product attributes might provide benefits for the customer, and then communicating that information.

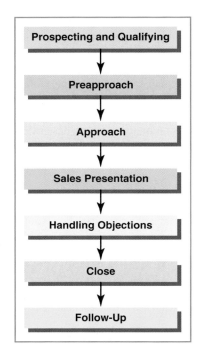

FIGURE 16.1

Steps in the Creative Selling Process

In the creative selling process, salespeople follow an orderly series of steps to ensure a long-term relationship with the customer.

communicate this to the prospects. As Figure 16.1 shows, there are seven steps in the process. Let's examine them.

prospecting ■ A part of the selling process that includes identifying and developing a list of potential or prospective customers.

Prospect Customers **Prospecting** is the process of identifying and developing a list of potential customers, called *prospects* or *sales leads*. Leads can come from existing customer lists, telephone directories, and commercially available databases. The local library usually contains directories of businesses (including those published by state and federal agencies) and directories of association memberships. Sometimes companies generate sales leads through their advertising or sales promotions by letting customers request more information (in Chapter 14, we called this a *second-order response*). As we said earlier, trade shows are often an important source of sales leads.

One way to generate leads is through *cold calling*, when the salesperson simply contacts prospects "cold," without prior introduction or arrangement. It always helps to know the prospect, so salespeople might rely instead on *referrals*. Current clients who are satisfied with their purchase often give referrals—yet another reason to maintain good customer relationships.

qualify prospects ■ A part of the selling process that determines how likely prospects are to become customers.

Qualify Prospects The mere fact that someone is willing to talk to a salesperson doesn't guarantee a sale. Along with identifying potential customers, salespeople need to **qualify prospects** to determine how likely they are to become customers by asking questions such as: Are the people likely to be interested in what I'm selling? Are they likely to switch their allegiance from another supplier or product? Is the potential sales volume large enough to make a relationship profitable? Can they afford the purchase? If they must borrow money to buy the product, what is their credit history?

preapproach ■ A part of the selling process that includes developing information about prospective customers and planning the sales interview.

Do a Preapproach The **preapproach** consists of compiling background information about prospective customers and planning the sales interview. Important purchases are not made lightly, so it is foolish for a salesperson to blindly call on a qualified prospect and risk losing the sale due to a lack of preparation. Salespeople try to learn as much as possible about qualified prospects early on. They may probe prior purchase history, current needs, or, in some cases, information about their interests.

Salespeople can draw information about a prospect from a variety of sources. In the case of larger companies, financial data, names of top executives, and other information about a business may be found in such publications as *Standard & Poor's 500 Directory* or the Dun & Bradstreet's *Million Dollar Directory*. The inside scoop on a prospect, however, often comes from informal sources, such as noncompeting salespeople who have dealt with the prospect before. This background information helps salespeople plan their strategy and set their goals.

Make the Approach After the groundwork has been laid with the preapproach, it is time to **approach**, or contact, the prospect. During these important first minutes when the salesperson initiates contact with the prospective customer, several key events occur. The salesperson tries to learn even more about the prospect's needs, create a good impression, and build rapport. If the salesperson made contact with the prospect through a referral, the salesperson will probably say so up-front: "Kevin Keenan with Hamdy Industries suggested I call on you."

During the approach, the customer is deciding whether the salesperson has something to offer. The old saying, "You never get a second chance to make a good first impression," rings true here. A professional appearance tells the prospect that the salesperson means business and is competent to handle the sale. A good salesperson is well groomed and wears appropriate business dress. He or she doesn't chew gum, use poor grammar or inappropriate language, mispronounce the customer's name, or seem uninterested in the job.

approach ■ The first step of the actual sales presentation in which the salesperson tries to learn more about the customer's needs, create a good impression, and build rapport.

Make the Sales Presentation Many sales calls involve a formal **sales presentation** that lays out the benefits of the product and its advantages over the competition. Some companies such as Tupperware also provide sales information that prospects can view online prior to making a purchase.[44] *Proof statements*, such as data on past sales, testimonials, guarantees, or research results, help to make the salesperson's pitch credible.

Some sales presentations are *canned*, which means a script has been written in advance, and the same message is delivered to many prospects. This technique often provides a series of verbal prompts to which there are expected customer responses. For example, an office supplies salesperson might start off a pitch by saying, "Would you like to see a new line of products that will revolutionize the way you run your office?" A similar approach called a *formulated approach* identifies a buyer's needs and then provides a scripted sales pitch keyed to that kind of buyer. These standardized approaches work fine in some cases, but the most effective sales presentations are those that are tailored to the specific customer. For example, the salesperson instead might say, "Would you be interested in getting better-quality report

sales presentation ■ The part of the selling process in which the salesperson seeks to persuasively communicate the product's features and the benefits it will provide after the sale.

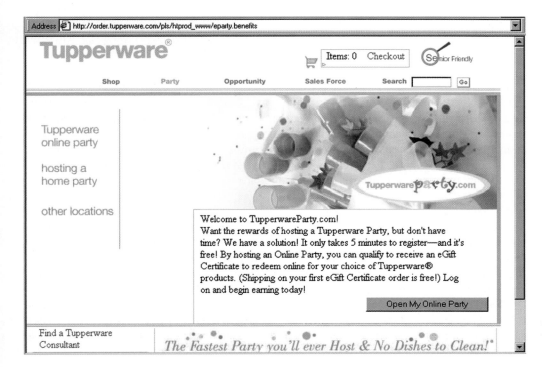

Tupperware parties used to be housebound—not anymore!

binders at a lower price?" if the salesperson discovered during preapproach that the office manager is under pressure to cut costs on office supplies.

Overcome Customer Objections   It is rare when a prospect accepts whatever the salesperson has to say and places an order on the spot. The effective salesperson anticipates *objections*, or reasons why the prospect is reluctant, and is prepared to respond with additional information or persuasive arguments. The salesperson might *welcome* objections because they show the prospect is at least interested enough to have considered the offer and seriously weigh the pros and cons. Handling the objection successfully can move a prospect to the decision stage. For example, the salesperson might say, "Ms. Robbins, you've said before that you don't have room to carry our new line of sleeping bags, although you admit that you may be losing some sales by carrying only one brand with very few different models. If we could determine how much business you're losing, I'd be willing to bet you'd make room for our line, wouldn't you?"

Close the Sale   A common mistake made by salespeople is that they work very hard to open the door for the prospect but don't get the prospect to walk through that door. The toughest stage of the sales process—clinching the deal—is a measure of the effectiveness of the preparatory steps. **Sales closing** occurs when the salesperson asks the customer straight out to buy the product and complete the transaction.

There are a variety of techniques good salespeople use to close the sale. For example, a *last objection close* asks customers if they are ready to purchase, providing any concerns they have about the product can be addressed: "Are you ready to order if we can prove our delivery time frames meet your expectations?" Using a *trial close*, however, the salesperson acts as if the purchase is inevitable with only a small detail or two to be settled: "What quantity would you like to order?" In some cases, the salesperson applies a bit more pressure by using a *standing-room-only close* that suggests the opportunity might be missed if the customer hesitates. No matter what technique is used, it's important to close the sale and not assume that the transaction will happen somehow on its own.

Follow Up After the Sale   **Sales follow-up** includes arranging for delivery, payment, and purchase terms. It also means the salesperson makes sure the customer received delivery and is satisfied. Follow-up also allows the salesperson to *bridge* to the next purchase. Once a relationship develops, the selling process is only beginning. Even as one cycle of purchasing draws to a close, a good salesperson is already laying the foundation for the next one.

SALES MANAGEMENT

Few, if any, firms can succeed with just one star salesperson. Personal selling is a team effort that requires careful planning and salespeople in the field when and where customers need them. **Sales management** is the process of planning, implementing, and controlling the personal selling function. Let's review some of the major decisions sales professionals who oversee this function must make as outlined in Figure 16.2.

Setting Sales Force Objectives   Sales force objectives state what the sales force is expected to accomplish and when. Sales managers develop such sales force performance objectives as "acquire 100 new customers," "generate $100 million in sales," or even "reduce travel expenses by 5 percent." Some firms also state goals for customer satisfaction, new customer development, new-product suggestions, training, or community involvement.

Sales managers also work with their salespeople to develop individual goals. *Performance goals* are measurable outcomes, such as total sales and total profits per salesperson. *Behavioral goals* specify the actions salespeople must accomplish, such as the number of prospects to identify, the number of sales calls, and the number of sales presentations.

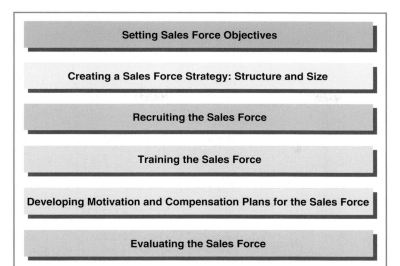

FIGURE 16.2

The Sales Force Management Process

Personal selling is a team effort that requires careful planning to place salespeople in the best locations at the best times.

Creating a Sales Force Strategy   A sales force strategy specifies the structure and size of a firm's sales force. Each salesperson has the responsibility for a set group of customers—the **sales territory**. The territory structure allows salespeople to have an in-depth understanding of customers and their needs through frequent contacts, both business and personal. The most common way to allot territories is geographically, minimizing travel and other field expenses. A *geographic sales force structure* usually is sized according to how many customers are found in a given area.

> **sales territory** ■ A set of customers often defined by geographic boundaries, for whom a particular salesperson is responsible.

If the product line is diverse or technically complex, however, a better approach may be to structure sales territories based on different classes of products to enable the sales force to provide more expertise to a set of customers with similar needs. Still another structure is *industry specialization*, in which salespeople focus on a single industry or a small number of industries. For example, IBM went from a geographic sales force structure to one in which its salespeople were assigned to one of 14 industrial groupings. In making the change, IBM executives cited a need to field salespeople who "speak the language of its customers and understand their industries."[45]

Putting a salesperson out into the field is an expensive proposition, so the number of people out there pounding the pavement has an impact on a company's profitability. Determining the optimal number of salespeople is an important decision. A larger sales force may increase sales, but at what cost? A smaller sales force will keep costs down, but this could backfire if competitors move in with larger sales forces and are able to develop strong customer relationships because each of their salespeople doesn't have to call on as many customers.

Recruiting, Training, and Rewarding Salespeople   Because the quality of a sales force can make or break a firm, a top priority for sales managers is to recruit and hire the right set of people to do the job—people who are strategic thinkers, who have technical knowledge pertaining to the industry, and who have excellent interpersonal skills.[46] Companies screen potential salespeople to reveal these skills, along with useful information about interests and capabilities. Pencil-and-paper tests can determine quantitative skills and competence in areas not easily assessed through interviews.

Although some feel that a successful salesperson is born, not made, even the most skilled communicator still may have much to learn. *Sales training* teaches salespeople about the organization and its products and how to develop the right skills, knowledge, and attitudes. For example, training programs at Xerox focus on ways to identify customer problems. The Xerox Document University, a training facility with 250 classrooms and a curriculum of 180 courses, provides an 11-week training program for new salespeople and continuing training throughout the salesperson's career.[47]

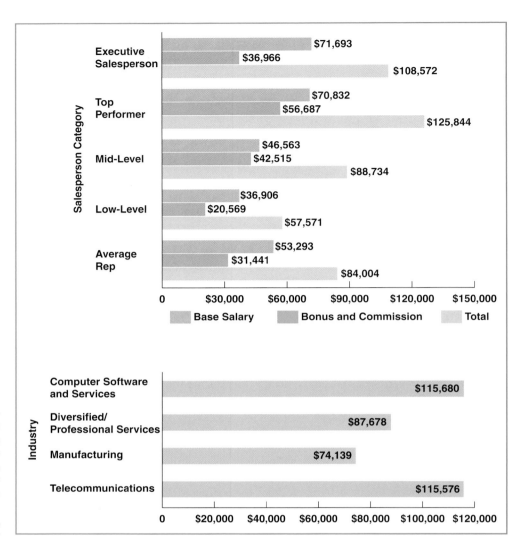

FIGURE **16.3**

Sales Force Compensation

A *Sales and Marketing Management* magazine survey showed 2001's average sales compensation figures by salesperson category and certain industries.

Source: 2001 Salary Survey, Sales and Marketing Management, May 2001, 47–50.

6 *Bookmark It!*

You are a sales manager for a company that sells robotics to textile manufacturers. Your sales force is currently paid on a straight commission basis. You are considering changing to a salary plus commission plan. Make a list of the advantages and disadvantages of each plan.

Of course, a way to motivate salespeople is to pay them well. This can mean tying compensation to performance. A *straight commission plan* is based solely on a percentage of sales the person closes. Under a *commission-with-draw plan*, earnings are based on commission plus a regular payment, or "draw," that may be charged against future commissions if current sales are inadequate to cover the draw. With a *straight salary compensation plan*, the salesperson is paid a set amount regardless of sales performance. Sometimes straight salary plans are augmented by use of a *quota-bonus plan*, in which salespeople are paid salary plus a bonus for sales above an assigned quota.

Some average sales compensation figures are shown in Figure 16.3.

As shown in Figure 16.4, in addition to basic compensation, many managers find that a variety of other incentives can also enhance the sales force effort tremendously. Such incentives can range from a free trip to the Carribbean for the top salesperson and his family to some simple but always appreciated extra cash. Cutler Hammer, a leading manufacturer of electrical equipment, invites the top 5 percent of its salespeople and their spouses to a "Pinnacle Club" three-day trip that includes a sales meeeting in an expensive resort.

Although many salespeople like to work independently, supervision is essential to an effective sales force. Sales managers often require salespeople to develop monthly, weekly, or daily *call reports*, a plan of action detailing which customers were called on and how things went. These reports allow the sales manager to track what the salespeople are doing in the field, and they provide marketing managers with timely information about customers' responses, competitive activity, and any changes in the firm's customer base.

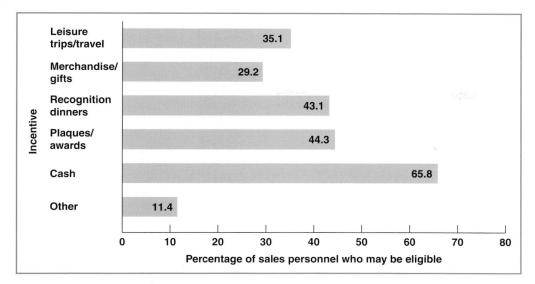

FIGURE 16.4

Incentives Available to Sales People

A 2001 salary survey in *Sales and Marketing Management* magazine found that salespeople are eligible for non-traditional forms of compensation.

Source: 2001 Salary Survey, *Sales and Marketing Management*, May 2001, 47–50.

Evaluating the Sales Force   Of course, the job of sales management isn't complete until the total effort of the sales force is evaluated. First, it is important to determine if the sales function is meeting its quantitative objectives. If not, the sales manager must figure out the causes. Is it due to flaws in the design and/or implementation of the sales force strategy, or are there uncontrollable factors that have contributed? An overall downturn in the economy, such as that of the third quarter of 2001, after the attack on the World Trade Center, can make it impossible for the best of sales force plans to meet sales goals.

Individual salesperson performance is normally measured against sales quotas for individual sales territories, even when compensation plans do not include bonuses or commissions

In addition to regular monetary compensation, salespeople are often motivated by rewards for a good job.

How It Worked Out at Cox Target Media

Melissa chose a combination of options 2 and 3. The marketing staff developed a prospective list of national brands in categories known to be highly interesting to consumers. This information was based on market research commissioned by Valpak from a panel study of over 1,000 U.S. homes that receive the blue envelope.

As a test, Melissa started with a single franchisee in North Carolina. Cox created a local "watch 'n' win" promotion with WACH, the local Fox Television affiliate. They named this sweepstakes Win Kramer's Cash and tied it in with Fox's programming of *Seinfeld*. Unique serial numbers were added to Valpak envelopes before being mailed out to residents. Inserts in the envelope told consumers how to play and Fox ran 30-second on-air announcements prompting viewers to look for lucky Valpak numbers and "watch 'n' win" daily prizes. Fox used the promotion throughout the Nielsen ratings sweeps and jumped from number 5 to number 1 in this market.

Building on this success story, Cox approached 20th Century Fox Studios to seek a movie partnership with *Dr. Dolittle 2* (starring Eddie Murphy). Cox created two promotional versions for Fox: one seeding instant-win tickets in Valpak envelopes for admission to sneak preview events, and another offering movie prize packs and Hollywood studio tours.

Although Cox paid for all print and promotional prize elements, joint press releases promoted the partnership to the trade press. Increased industry awareness prompted calls from WPAX, Universal, Miramax, and Time Warner seeking similar promotional tie-ins.

Valpak continues to find national advertisers that now are interested in cosponsoring promotions. For the launch of the new blue Valpak in early 2002, Cox partnered with CBS Networks and H&R Block. Consumers could register to win either by using entry forms included in Valpak envelopes or by signing up online at the Valpak.com Web site.

CBS promoted its new programming lineup and H&R Block offered to pay up to 10 years of federal taxes for lucky winners. 20th Century Fox asked Valpak early in 2001 to be its exclusive direct-mail partner for its first computer-animated feature, *Ice Age*. Cox plans to seed tickets for sneak previews in Valpak envelopes for U.S. and Canadian markets and it will create sweepstakes offering gifts and trips. Burger King also joined in, offering a gift for every envelope presented (no purchase necessary). With all of these, Cox created self-liquidating or revenue-generating promotions, as Melissa had hoped. As an effective form of direct marketing, the blue envelope is well on its way to realizing Cox's quest for national brand status.

Valpak's promotion with the movie *Dr. Dolittle 2* featured in-store point-of-purchase materials that included Valpak branding. Instant-win tickets were seeded into coupon packages in over 50 markets to admit winners to sneak previews of the movie.

based on the quotas. Other quantitative measures, such as number of sales calls and sales reports, may also be used in the evaluation.

In addition to quantitative measures, many firms also evaluate their sales force on qualitative indicators of performance such as salesperson attitude, product knowledge, and communication skills. Increasingly, as firms focus on relationship management, the level of customer satisfaction is a strong qualitative measure of superior salesperson performance.

Finally, the salesperson's expense account for travel and entertainment (T&E) may be considered since the best sales record can mean little to a company's bottom line if the salesperson is gouging the company with outrageous expenses. You think you're creative when spending money? Here are some expenses submitted in 2001 according to *Sales and Marketing Management Magazine*:[48] Chartering a private plane to make an appointment after missing a regularly scheduled flight; A Jaguar convertible rental car; A $2,300 round of golf for four people; A set of china for a salesperson's wife to use for a client dinner party; A "meeting" in the Virgin Islands during Christmas and New Year's; A $3,100 elk-hunting trip; A three-day houseboat rental with a crew and chef for $30,000; Season baseball tickets for $6,000.

Chapter Summary

1. Explain the role of public relations.

The purpose of public relations is to maintain or improve the image of an organization among various publics. An important part of this is managing publicity. Public relations is useful in introducing new products, influencing legislation, enhancing the image of a city, region, or country, and calling attention to a firm's community involvement.

2. Describe the steps in developing a public relations campaign.

The steps in a public relations campaign begin with setting objectives, creating and executing a campaign strategy, and planning how the PR program will be evaluated. PR specialists often use print or video news releases to communicate timely topics, research stories, and consumer information. Internal communications with employees include company newsletters and internal TV programs. Sponsorships and guerrilla marketing activities can be effective at informing stakeholders about a company and its products.

3. Explain what sales promotion is and describe some of the different types of trade and consumer sales promotion activities.

Sales promotions are short-term programs designed to build interest in or encourage purchase of a product. Trade promotions include merchandise and case allowances, trade shows, promotional products, and incentive programs including push money devices. Consumer sales promotions include coupons, price deals, rebates, frequency programs, special packs, contests and sweepstakes, premiums, sampling programs, point-of-purchase promotions, and brand placements.

4. Explain the important role of personal selling in the marketing effort.

Personal selling occurs when a company representative directly informs a client about a good or service to get a sale. Personal selling is more important for push strategies. Because of the high cost per customer contact for field sales, telemarketing is growing in popularity. Different types of salespeople include inside and outside order takers, technical specialists, missionary salespeople, and order getters. Today's salespeople are less likely to employ old-fashioned hard-sell tactics in favor of relationship selling in which they pursue mutually satisfying relationships with customers.

5. List the steps in the personal selling process.

The steps in the personal selling process include prospecting, qualifying the prospects, the preapproach, the approach, making the sales presentation, overcoming customer objections, closing the sale, and postsale follow-up.

6. Explain the job of the sales manager.

Sales management means planning, implementing, and controlling the selling function. The responsibilities of a sales manager include setting sales force objectives, assigning sales territories, recruiting, training, rewarding, and evaluating salespeople.

Chapter Review

MARKETING CONCEPTS:
TESTING YOUR KNOWLEDGE

1. What is the purpose of public relations? What is proactive public relations? What is reactive public relations?
2. What are the steps in planning a public relations campaign? Describe some of the activities that are a part of public relations.
3. What is sponsorship marketing? What is guerrilla marketing?
4. What is sales promotion?
5. Explain some of the different types of trade sales promotions frequently used by marketers.
6. Explain some of the different types of consumer sales promotions frequently used by marketers.
7. What is the role played by personal selling within the total marketing function?
8. What is the difference between transactional selling and relationship selling?
9. What are order getters, order takers, missionary salespeople, and technical specialists? What is team selling?
10. List the steps in the creative selling process.
11. Describe the major decisions made by sales managers.

MARKETING CONCEPTS:
DISCUSSING CHOICES AND ISSUES

1. Guerrilla marketing tactics were quite successful for small firms unable to pay for big advertising budgets. Do you think they can also be effective for large firms? Why or why not?
2. Some people refer to marketing public relations versus general public relations, suggesting that only PR activities aimed at promoting a product are part of the marketing communication program. What do you think?
3. Some critics denounce public relations specialists, calling them "flacks" or "spin doctors" whose job is to hide the truth about a company's problems. What is the proper role of public relations within an organization? Should PR specialists try to put a good face on bad news?
4. Companies sometimes teach consumers a "bad lesson" with the overuse of sales promotion. As a result, consumers expect the product always to be "on deal." What are some examples of products where this has occurred? How do you think companies can prevent this?
5. In general, professional selling has evolved from hard-sell to relationship selling. Still, is the hard-sell style still used? If so, in what types of organizations? What do

you think the future holds for these organizations? Will the hard-sell continue to succeed?
6. One reason cited by experts for the increase in consumer catalog shopping is the poor quality of service available at retail stores. What do you think about the quality of most retail salespeople you come in contact with? What are some ways retailers can improve the quality of their sales associates?

MARKETING PRACTICE:
APPLYING WHAT YOU'VE LEARNED

1. Assume you are the head of public relations for a textile company that makes sheets and towels. There has been a fire in one of your plants and several people have been seriously injured. As the director of public relations, what recommendations do you have for how the firm might handle this crisis?
2. Assume you and a friend have begun a new Internet business that offers new and used textbooks to university students. You don't have the money for a major advertising campaign and are thinking that you ought to do guerrilla marketing. Make a list of possible guerrilla marketing activities for your new company.
3. As a public relations professional employed by your university, you have been asked to develop strategies for improving your school's public relations program. Write a memo to your university president with your recommendations.
4. Assume you are a member of the marketing department for a firm that produces several brands of household cleaning products. Your assignment is to develop recommendations for trade and consumer sales promotion activities for a new laundry detergent. Develop an outline of your recommendations for sales promotions.
5. Timing is an important part of a sales promotion plan. Marketers must decide when the best time is to mail out samples, to offer trade discounts, to sponsor a sweepstakes. Assume the introduction of the new laundry detergent in question 4 is planned for April 1. Place the activities you recommended in question 4 on a 12-month calendar. In a role-playing situation, present your plan to your supervisor. Be sure to explain why you have included certain types of promotions and the reasons for your timing of each promotion activity.
6. Assume you have just been hired as a field salesperson by a firm that markets university textbooks. As part of your training, your sales manager has asked you to

develop an outline of what you will say in a typical sales presentation. Write that outline.

■ MARKETING MINI-PROJECT: LEARNING BY DOING

The purpose of this mini-project is to help you understand the impact of different sales promotion activities.

1. With several of your classmates, first select a product that most college students buy regularly (e.g., toothpaste, shampoo, pens, pencils, soft drinks, etc.).

2. Develop a questionnaire that describes scenarios in which students find a new brand of the product with different sales promotion offers (e.g., a price-off package, a bonus pack, a coupon, etc.). Ask whether the students would buy the new brand with each offer and how many units of the product they would buy.

3. Report the results to your class along with recommendations you would give a company planning to introduce a new brand to the market.

■ REAL PEOPLE, REAL SURFERS: EXPLORING THE WEB

A problem that has confronted marketers for several years is how to efficiently distribute coupons. Some companies find the Internet to be a useful medium. In fact, a number of Web sites have been developed solely for the purpose of distributing coupons. Some of these follow.

www.hotcoupons.com
www.valupage.com
www.suzicoupon.com
www.couponsonline.com
www.couponcraze.com

Visit several of these Web sites, or use an Internet search engine to identify other coupon sites. Then evaluate the different sites you've visited by answering the following questions.

1. Generally describe each coupon Web site you visited. What kinds of coupons were there? How do consumers take advantage of the offers?

2. What in the design of each Web site is most useful to you as a consumer?

3. Do you think the coupons offered by the Web sites are useful to many consumers? Do you think consumers visit the Web site on a regular basis? What do you think would be some of the characteristics of the type of consumer most likely to be a regular visitor to these sites?

4. As a marketer, would you be likely to try to distribute coupons for your products over the Web sites? Why or why not?

5. How would you improve each of the Web sites you visited?

■ PLAN IT! DEVELOPING A MARKETING PLAN

As your instructor directs, create a marketing plan (using Marketing Plan Pro software or a written marketing plan format) to document your marketing decisions or answer these questions in a written or oral report.

CFS will need strategies for public relations, sales promotion, and personal selling in its marketing plan for next year.

1. How can the company drum up positive publicity about its newer products?

2. What kind of trade promotion can CFS use to attract resellers to its exhibit at the Toy Fair next year, and how will the reseller's buyers, CFS, and CFS's sales reps benefit?

3. What sales force objectives should CFS set for its sales reps for next year, and how will these objectives help the company reach its overall goals?

Key Terms

approach, (483)

brand placement, (478)

case allowance, (473)

creative selling process, (481)

cross-promotion, (479)

frequency programs, (475)

guerrilla marketing, (470)

merchandise allowance, (473)

missionary salesperson, (480)

order getter, (481)

order taker, (480)

personal selling, (479)

point-of-purchase (POP) promotion, (478)

preapproach, (482)

premiums, (477)

press release, (469)

prospecting, (482)

publicity, (465)

public relations (PR), (465)

push money, (473)

qualify prospects, (482)

rebates, (475)

relationship selling, (481)

sales closing, (484)

sales follow-up, (484)

sales management, (484)

sales presentation, (483)

sales promotions, (471)

sales territory, (485)

sampling, (477)

sponsorship, (469)

team selling, (481)

technical specialist, (480)

telemarketing, (480)

trade shows, (473)

transactional selling, (481)

MARKETING IN ACTION: CHAPTER 16 CASE

REAL CHOICES AT COCA-COLA

Coca-Cola is the most recognized brand in the world. Many people believe the name is synonymous with excellent brand stewardship—that the Coca-Cola Company has protected and enhanced its brand name continuously through its 100-plus years in business.

Coca-Cola's reign as the leader in soft drinks began over a century ago when Coke was sold through Atlanta pharmacies for pennies. A century later, the company has about half the total market for carbonated soft drinks compared to Pepsi with only 22 percent of the world market for carbonated soft drinks. Coke is distributed in 200 countries, and overseas sales account for about three-fourths of Coke's profits.

Unfortunately, even the best companies can make mistakes. That is exactly what happened when Coca-Cola, faced by a major crisis, made a public relations blunder that changed the company image from a much admired and trusted leader in Europe to a company that was struggling to retrieve what was left of consumer confidence.

In the summer of 1999, children and adults became ill after drinking Coca-Cola products in Belgium and northern France. Unfortunately, company officials did not take the reports seriously enough. It seemed impossible to them that Coca-Cola could have a product liability problem. And the company seemed not to recognize consumers' level of concern. Thus, at the first reports of the illnesses, Coca-Cola denied that its product could have been the cause.

Only after a delay of seven days did the company make a full-scale response. An apology by CEO M. Douglas Ivester stated that a bad taste and bad smell in some Coke products had caused some people to become ill. The official explanation was that one Coca-Cola plant used a batch of bad carbon dioxide and some chemicals in another factory may have gotten into some cans. Unfortunately, this response was too little too late.

Early on, when Coca-Cola's only response was a denial, people assumed the worst. The press, because it did not have a formal full-scale response from the company, exaggerated the crisis by printing speculation and accusations. In Sweden, the newspaper headline read "200 Poisoned by Coca-Cola." An Italian newspaper headline read, "Alarm Across Europe for Coca-Cola Products." In a move to protect consumers, governments throughout Europe either banned or recalled Coca-Cola soft drinks or all Coca-Cola products before the company had a chance to selectively recall bad shipments.

There were several factors that made the crisis especially expensive for the Coca-Cola Company. First, the crisis occurred during the summer when soft drink sales are highest, which made the economic impact of the crisis greater. And Belgium is a very large market for Coke. Belgians consume 260 eight-ounce servings of Coke per year compared with 203 for Germans, 118 for Britons, and 88 for the French. In all, it is estimated that the crisis cost Coca-Cola $103 billion.

Ultimately Coca-Cola made a number of major responses to regain consumer confidence. The company established a consumer hotline and offered to pay all medical bills of consumers who had become sick. In Belgium, the company developed a Web page—"Coca-Cola Belgium: Your Questions"—and distributed enough coupons to give a Coke to every man, woman, and child in the country.

But for Coca-Cola the question that must be answered is how to protect the company from such financial disasters in the future. What needs to be done to maintain the Coke brand image worldwide? Was the response in Europe adequate to convince consumers that Coca-Cola really does care about their health or is more needed? What can Coca-Cola do to make sure that it takes charge of any future crisis immediately to minimize damage?

One problem that Coca-Cola faces is that it does not produce its own product in many countries. Instead Coca-Cola products are manufactured by independent bottlers who buy syrup from Coca-Cola. Although Coca-Cola does have stringent quality standards to which bottlers are asked to adhere, the truth is that the company lacks control over its product.

Perhaps Coca-Cola should have honestly responded to the crisis by telling consumers that the problem occurred because the company does not have control over bottling standards throughout the world but is making every effort to correct that situation. In recent years, Coca-Cola has bought up many of these independent bottlers, but perhaps the company should do more.

Then again, perhaps this crisis was just a one-time problem. Can Coca-Cola just look at this loss as accidental?

Source: Kathleen V. Schmidt, "Coke's Crisis," *Marketing News*, September 27, 1999.

THINGS TO THINK ABOUT

1. What is the decision facing Coca-Cola?

2. What factors are important in understanding the decision situation?

3. What are the alternatives?

4. What decision(s) do you recommend?

5. What are some ways to implement your recommendation(s)?

Reflections | You need a special occasion to dress up. Being out of milk and oranges counts as a special occasion.

riveted
By Lee®

The Painter Jean. To find a store call 1-800-453-3348 or visit www.rivetedbylee.com

Bookmark It!

OBJECTIVES:

1. Explain what a distribution channel is and what functions distribution channels perform.

2. Describe some of the types of wholesaling intermediaries found in distribution channels.

3. Describe the types of distribution channels and the steps in planning distribution channel strategies.

4. Explain how logistics is used to implement the value chain.

CHANNELS OF DISTRIBUTION, LOGISTICS, AND WHOLESALING

17

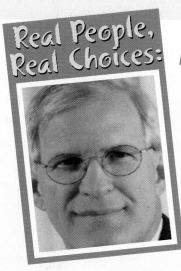

Meet Mackey McDonald, a Decision Maker at VF Corporation

www.vfc.com

CURRENT POSITION: President, Chairman, and CEO.

CAREER PATH: Appointed chairman in October 1998, capping a 16-year career with the company. Joined VF in 1983 as assistant vice president, merchandising services.

EDUCATION: B.A., Davidson College; M.B.A., Marketing Management, Georgia State University.

WHAT I DO WHEN I'M NOT WORKING: Exercise and hang out with my children.

FIRST JOB OUT OF SCHOOL: Pilot for the U.S. Army.

CAREER HIGH: Becoming CEO of VF Corporation.

MOTTO: Find solutions, not problems.

MANAGEMENT STYLE: Collaborative effort from a diversified team.

DON'T DO THIS WHEN INTERVIEWING WITH ME: Camouflage the tough questions.

Are You the Weakest Link?

VF Corporation is the largest apparel manufacturer in the world. It is the parent company of Lee, Wrangler, Vanity Fair, JanSport, The North Face, and other well-known brands. A big corporation like VF relies on its partners to be sure its products make their way from its factories into consumers' shopping bags. These companies devote a great deal of attention to their partners, including suppliers, shipping companies, and retailers, to ensure that they are efficiently moving merchandise down the chain.

JCPenney is a major distributor for VF. VF could always count on the department store to move many of its products, especially garments made by VF's Lee division. In 1997, womenswear accounted for 40 percent of Lee's total retail sales nationwide. Womenswear accounted for 75 percent of Lee's business with JCPenney, and sales were up 22 percent over the past year. In 1998 and 1999, however, Lee's womenswear sales at JCPenney stores started to drop off. This was a puzzling problem since Lee's overall business, including womenswear, was strong (and growing) with its other retail distributors—May Company, Federated Department Stores, Kohl's, and Sears.

As we saw way back in Chapter 2 (seems like yesterday, doesn't it?) at the time JCPenney was not competing well against specialty clothing retailers such as Gap, Old Navy, and The Limited Express, whose product lines were tailored to the lifestyle of the typical shopper at that store. In contrast, shoppers seemed to be visiting Penney's only to find bargains; the chain was struggling to convince its customers that it was a good place to find clothing that defined a specific lifestyle. During this time period, JCPenney allowed individual store managers to select and order products from the manufacturers with which the store did business. As a result, JCPenney was confusing customers by selling different brands at different stores.

When Lee's sales at Penney outlets dropped 20 percent between 1998 and 1999, Mackey knew VF had to take action. The ordering process had to be simplified so that shoppers wouldn't be confused about what they found in each Penney store. That meant paying attention to the way products were distributed as they made their way through the links in the chain that eventually connected VF with end consumers. Mackey and his team needed to strengthen links in the chain to boost sales of womenswear. But how to help? The team considered these options:

Option 1: Use VF's customized delivery program.

Implement VF's already-in-place Retail Floor Space Management program, which it had used successfully at other retail outlets including Wal-Mart and Shopko. VF developed this system to match product selection to the demographics and psychographic profiles of consumers shopping in each store. This customized approach was an innovation in the retail industry. The idea is to centralize product selection and be sure that product assortments available at each store would be clearly focused and easily replenished. However, JCPenney would give up control of its Lee's womenswear inventories. The store chain had balked at this system in the past because it just was not the way it did business. Penney's management felt it could run its business better than could an outside vendor.

Option 2: Deliver a bargain message.

Focus on volume and reduce the price of Lee and other VF national brands at Penney's, delivering a "bargain" message to the consumer. This option would help attract the price-driven consumer and probably boost sales in the short term. But it could reduce JCPenney's operating margins and devalue brand equity by sending the message that the jeans are a discount brand.

Option 3: Institute a pull strategy.

Maintain the status quo. JCPenney would continue to allow individual stores to buy and manage their own product assortments. It would be up to VF to engineer a "pull strategy" to lure consumers into the stores with national brand advertising promoting the availability of Lee products at Penney stores. JCPenney would not have to change its procedures and would maintain control of its inventory. However, the stores would continue to operate with inconsistent product lines, risking consumer loyalty and further eroding the effectiveness of the VF/Penney relationship.

Now, put yourself in Mackey's shoes: Which option would you choose, and why?

Place: The Final Frontier

As VF Corporation knows, you can make the best products in the world but if the right clothes aren't available in the right assortment at the right prices and in the stores where customers are inclined to look for them, you have a problem.

Distribution may be the final "frontier" for marketing success. After years of hype, many consumers no longer believe that "new and improved" products really *are* new and improved. Nearly everyone, even upscale manufacturers and retailers, tries to gain market share through aggressive pricing strategies. Advertising and other forms of promotion are so commonplace they have lost some of their impact. Marketers know that *place* may be the only one of the four Ps offering an opportunity for competitive advantage.

This chapter is about the science and art of getting goods and services to customers. First we'll learn about distribution channels and talk about how marketers make smart decisions in developing distribution strategies. Then we'll look at how marketing channels are a part of the broader concept of value chain management. We'll also consider logistics management, which is the process of actually moving goods through the supply chain.

The Importance of Distribution: You Can't Sell What Isn't There!

So you've created your product. Priced it, too. And you've done the research to understand your target market. Sorry, you're still not done because now you need to get what you make out into the marketplace. That means not only thinking about the end consumer who will take home what you make but also all of the steps in between production and consumption. That's what we mean by a channel of distribution.

WHAT IS A DISTRIBUTION CHANNEL?

In a marketing context a channel is *not* a place on television. A **channel of distribution** is a series of firms or individuals that facilitates the movement of a product from the producer to the final customer. In many cases, these channels include an organized network of producers (also called manufacturers) wholesalers, and retailers that develop relationships and work together to make products conveniently available to eager buyers.

Distribution channels come in different shapes and sizes. The bakery around the corner where you buy your cinnamon rolls is a member of a channel, as is the baked goods section at the local supermarket, the espresso bar at the mall that sells biscotti to go with your double mocha cappuccino, and the bakery outlet store that sells day-old rolls at a discount.

A channel of distribution consists of, at a minimum, a producer—the individual or firm that manufactures or produces a good or service—and a customer. This is a direct channel. For example, when you buy a gallon of strawberries at a farm where they're grown, that's a direct channel. Firms that sell their own products through catalogs, 800 numbers, or factory outlet stores use direct channels.

But life (or marketing) usually isn't that simple: Channels often are *indirect* because they include one or more **channel intermediaries**, firms or individuals such as wholesalers, agents, brokers, and retailers, who in some way help move the product to the consumer or business user. For example, our strawberry farmer may choose to sell his acres of berries to a produce wholesaler that will, in turn, sell cases of the berries to supermarkets and restaurants that in turn sell to consumers.

FUNCTIONS OF DISTRIBUTION CHANNELS

Distribution channels perform a number of functions that make possible the flow of goods from the producer to the customer. These functions must be handled by someone, be it the producer, a channel intermediary, or even the customer, such as when he picks up a new chair from the warehouse instead of having it delivered to his home, but they cannot be eliminated. Channels that include one or more organizations or intermediaries can often accomplish certain distribution functions more effectively and efficiently than can a single organization. This is especially true in international distribution channels where differences in countries' customs, beliefs, and infrastructures can make global marketing a nightmare. Even small companies can be successful in global markets by relying on distributors that know local customs and laws.

Over all, channels provide the time, place, and ownership utility we described in Chapter 1. They make desired products available when, where, and in the sizes and quantities that customers want them. Suppose, for example, you want to buy that perfect bouquet of flowers for a special someone. You *could* grow them yourself or even "liberate" them from a cemetery if

channel of distribution ■
The series of firms or individuals that facilitates the movement of a product from the producer to the final customer.

channel intermediaries ■
Firms or individuals such as wholesalers, agents, brokers, or retailers who help move a product from the producer to the consumer or business user.

1 *Bookmark It!*

Visit a local retailer, perhaps with several of your classmates. Ask the retailer to explain how the products it sells get from the manufacturer to it, that is, to describe the distribution channel of which it is a member. Is there a more efficient way for the retailer to get these products?

Supermarkets like this one are channel intermediaries. They buy fresh fruits and vegetables from farmers and make them available to consumers on a daily basis.

you were really, really desperate (let's hope not!). Fortunately, you can probably just accomplish this task with a simple phone call or a few mouse clicks and "like magic" the flowers are delivered to your honey's door. Just think about what happened behind the scenes to make this possible. Many flowers, for example, are harvested and electronically sorted by growers, auctioned to buyers in Amsterdam, shipped by air to importers in New York where they are inspected for insects and disease, transported to over 170 wholesalers around the country, and finally distributed to local florists who make them available to their customers. The channel members—the growers, the auction house, the importers, the wholesalers, and the local florists—all work together to create just the right bouquet for budding lovers—and save you a lot of time and hassles.

Distribution channels provide a number of logistics or physical distribution functions that increase the efficiency of the flow of goods from producer to customer. How would we buy groceries without our modern system of supermarkets? We'd have to get our milk from a dairy, our bread from a bakery, our tomatoes and corn from a local farmer, and our flour from a flour mill. And forget about specialty items such as Twinkies or Coca-Cola. The companies that make these items would have to handle literally millions of transactions to sell to every individual who craved a junk-food fix.

Distribution channels create *efficiencies* by reducing the number of transactions necessary for goods to flow from many different manufacturers to large numbers of customers. This occurs in two ways. The first is called **breaking bulk**. Wholesalers and retailers purchase large quantities (usually cases) of goods from manufacturers but sell only one or a few at a time to many different customers. Second, channel intermediaries reduce the number of transactions by **creating assortments**—providing a variety of products in one location—so that customers can conveniently buy many different items from one seller at one time.

Figure 17.1 provides a simple example of how distribution channels work. This simplified illustration includes five producers and five customers. If each producer sold its product to each individual customer, 25 different transactions would have to occur, which is not an efficient way to distribute products. But with a single intermediary who buys from all five manufacturers and sells to all five customers, the number of transactions is cut to 10. If there were 10 manufacturers and 10 customers, an intermediary would reduce the number of transactions from 100 to just 20. Do the math: Channels are efficient.

breaking bulk ■ Dividing larger quantities of goods into smaller lots in order to meet the needs of buyers.

creating assortments ■ Providing a variety of products in one location to meet the needs of buyers.

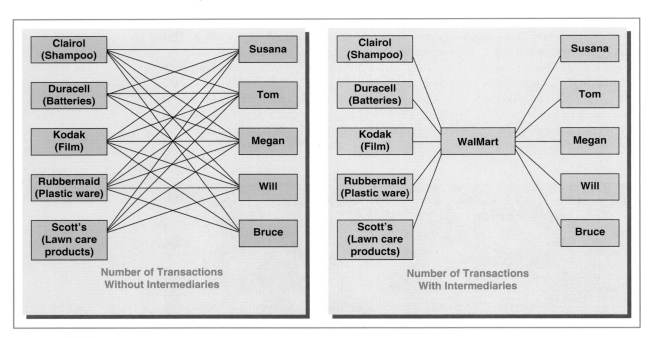

FIGURE 17.1

Reducing Transactions via Intermediaries

One of the functions of distribution channels is to provide an assortment of products. Because the customers can buy a number of different products at the same location, the total costs of obtaining a product are reduced.

Many distribution channel members provide customer services. Appliance and electronic retailers such as Circuit City provide repair and warranty services for the products they sell.

The transportation and storage of goods is another type of physical distribution function. Retailers and other channel members move the goods from the production point to other locations where they can be held until they are wanted by consumers.

Channel intermediaries also perform a number of **facilitating functions**, functions that make the purchase process easier for customers and manufacturers. For example, intermediaries often provide customer services such as offering credit to buyers. Most of us like to shop at department stores because if we are not happy with the product, we can take it back to the store, where cheerful customer service personnel are happy to give us a refund (at least in theory). These same customer services are even more important in business-to-business markets in which customers purchase larger quantities of higher-priced products than in consumer markets.

facilitating functions ■
Functions of channel intermediaries that make the purchase process easier for customers and manufacturers.

Some wholesalers and retailers assist the manufacturer by providing repair and maintenance service for products they handle. An appliance, television, stereo, or computer dealer may serve as an authorized repair center, provide maintenance contracts, and sell essential supplies to customers. And channel members perform a risk-taking function. If a retailer buys a product from a manufacturer and it just sits on the shelf because no customers want it, he is stuck with the item and must take a loss. Perishable items present an even greater risk of spoilage.

Finally, intermediaries perform a variety of communication and transaction functions. Wholesalers buy products to make them available for retailers and sell products to other channel members. Retailers handle transactions with final consumers. Channel members can provide two-way communication for manufacturers. They may supply the sales force, advertising, and other types of marketing communication necessary to inform consumers and persuade them that a product will meet their needs. And the channel members can be invaluable sources of information on consumer complaints, changing tastes, and new competitors in the market.

THE INTERNET IN THE DISTRIBUTION CHANNEL

For those who don't even have time to run out to the grocery store, the Internet is fast becoming an important place for consumers to shop for everything from tulip bulbs to exotic vacations, that is, a channel member. By using the Internet, even small firms with limited resources can enjoy the same competitive advantages as their largest competitors in making their products available to customers around the globe at a very low cost.

E-commerce can result in radical changes in distribution strategies. For example, when Stephen King experimented with distributing his writing on the Internet, 400,000 copies of his *Riding the Bullet* were distributed free the first day while other readers paid $2.50 to download the book.[1] And hosts of consumers find it far more convenient to read their daily newspapers or to receive their magazine subscriptions via the Internet.

Jennifer Lau, Student, Temple University Fox School of Business & Management

I would choose option 1. Switching to a centralized buying system from a decentralized buying system would allow senior corporate buyers with more experience to make good decisions. The inventory at JCPenney would also be better managed. Furthermore, by coupling the centralized buying solution with psychographic profiles of consumers and their trends would allow JCPenney to offer products that meet the needs of the market.

Randall Hansen, Marketing Professor, Stetson University

I would choose option 3 because of the power dynamic within the channel system, the positioning of the company's products, and the availability of other channels besides JCPenney. All companies, channel members included, want to control their business operations, and unless Penney invites VF Corp. to help it solve its image and merchandising problem, option 1 would simply cause more problems for VF. Option 2 would involve a complete repositioning of all VF brands for the sake of one retailer (a major outlet or not) and seems unwise, unless there are many mitigating factors. Maintaining the status quo with JCPenney—until management can redefine its image—while staking out and developing other retail outlets and increasing sales volume in those channels makes the most strategic sense.

Steve Schwartz, Vice President, Lion Apparel

I would choose option 1 because the other two options are not options. Option 2 devalues the brand, and this is a step to take only when desperate. Option 3 is likely to fail because the problem is a lack of JCPenney brand identity rubbing off onto Lee. Also, if Lee gives JCPenney extra media attention, its other better channel partners may be upset. My qualification of option 1 is to consider how to handle the "not invented here" syndrome expressed by JCPenney. Sometimes it is important to prove to the customer you are right through a "test" process rather than through an edict. I would run the program in a test market for a reasonable period of time. I would also get a commitment from JCPenney that if sales results respond to the use of this approach, it will adopt it across all stores. Ultimately, if the sales respond to this program, JCPenney will change its position, or it will become even more clear why it will not be a long-term customer.

Weigh in with your thoughts! Visit the Live Laboratory at www.prenhall.com/solomon for extended Other Voices replies, exercises, and more.

Today most goods are mass-produced, and in most cases end users do not obtain products directly from manufacturers. Rather, goods flow from manufacturers to intermediaries and then on to the final customers. With the Internet, this need for intermediaries and much of what we assume about the need and benefits of channels will change. For example, an increasing number of consumers are adding to their music collections by buying downloadable MP3 albums from Internet retailers, making retail music stores less and less necessary. As more and more consumers have access to faster broadband Internet service, downloadable DVDs may replace the local video store as a means of renting a favorite movie. And the same potential exists for other channel intermediaries in both consumer and business-to-business markets. In the future, channel intermediaries that physically handle the product may become obsolete. Already many traditional intermediaries are being eliminated as companies question the value added by layers in the distribution channel—a process called **disintermediation (of the channel of distribution)** (see Chapter 11). For marketers, disintermediation reduces costs in many ways: fewer employees, no need to buy or lease expensive retail property in high-traffic locations, and no need to furnish a store with fancy fixtures and decor.

So far, we've learned what a distribution channel is and about some of the functions it performs. Now let's find out about different types of channel intermediaries and channel structures.

disintermediation (of the channel of distribution) ■ The elimination of some layers of the channel of distribution in order to cut costs and improve the efficiency of the channel.

The Composition of Channels: Types of Wholesaling Intermediaries

How can you get your hands on a new Phish T-shirt? There are several ways. You could pick one up at your local music store, at a trendy clothing store like Hot Topic, or directly over the Internet. You might buy an "official Phish concert T-shirt" from vendors during a show. Alternatively, you might get a "deal" on a bootlegged, unauthorized version of the same shirt being sold from a suitcase by a shady guy standing *outside* the stadium. It might even be possible to buy it on the Home Shopping Network. Each of these distribution alternatives traces a different path from producer to consumer. Let's look at the different types of wholesaling intermediaries and at different channel structures. We'll focus on retailers, which are usually the last link in the chain, in the next chapter.

Wholesaling intermediaries are firms that handle the flow of products from the manufacturer to the retailer or business user. There are many different types of consumer and business-to-business wholesaling intermediaries. Some of these are independent, but manufacturers and retailers can own them, too. Table 17.1 summarizes the important characteristics of each.

wholesaling intermediaries ■ Firms that handle the flow of products from the manufacturer to the retailer or business user.

TABLE 17.1

Types of Intermediaries

Intermediary Type	Description	Advantages
INDEPENDENT INTERMEDIARIES	Do business with many different manufacturers and many different customers	Used by most small to medium-size firms
Merchant Wholesalers	Buy (take title of) goods from producers and sell to organizational customers; either full or limited function	Allow small manufacturers to serve customers throughout the world while keeping costs low
Rack jobbers	Provide retailers with display units, check inventories, and replace merchandise for the retailers	Useful when retailers require merchandising services from manufacturers
Cash-and-carry wholesalers	Provide products for small business customers who purchase at wholesaler's location	To distribute low-cost merchandise for small retailers and other business customers
Truck jobbers	Deliver perishable food and tobacco items to retailers	For perishable items when delivery and some sales functions are required
Drop shippers	Take orders from and bill retailers for products drop-shipped from manufacturer	Facilitate transactions for bulky products
Mail-order wholesalers	Sell through catalogs, telephone, or mail order	For products sold to small organizational customers at a reasonable price
Merchandise Agents and Brokers	Provide services in exchange for commissions	Sellers do not give up legal ownership of product
Manufacturers' agents	Independent salespeople; carry several lines of noncompeting products	Supply sales function for small and new firms
Selling agents including Export/import agents	Handle entire output of one or more products	Handle all marketing functions for small manufacturers
Commission merchants	Receive commission on sales price of product	Primarily in agricultural products markets
Merchandise brokers	Identify likely buyers and bring buyers and sellers together	In markets where there are lots of small buyers and sellers
Export/import brokers		
MANUFACTURER OWNED INTERMEDIARIES	Operations limited to one manufacturer	For large firms
Sales branches	Like wholesalers, maintain some inventory in different geographic areas	When firms must provide service to customers in different geographic areas
Sales offices	Carry no inventory; in different geographic areas	Reduce selling costs and provide better customer service
Manufacturers' showrooms	Products attractively displayed for customers to visit	When desirable for customers to examine merchandise at a central location

INDEPENDENT INTERMEDIARIES

independent intermediaries ■ Channel intermediaries that are not controlled by any manufacturer but instead do business with many different manufacturers and many different customers.

Independent intermediaries do business with many different manufacturers and many different customers. Because they are not owned or controlled by any manufacturer, they make it possible for many manufacturers to serve customers throughout the world while keeping prices low.

merchant wholesalers ■ Intermediaries that buy goods from manufacturers (take title to them) and sell to retailers and other business-to-business customers.

Merchant Wholesalers   **Merchant wholesalers** are independent intermediaries that buy goods from manufacturers and sell to retailers and other business-to-business customers. Because merchant wholesalers take title to the goods (i.e., they legally own them), they assume certain risks and can suffer losses if products get damaged, become out-of-date or obsolete, are stolen, or just don't sell. At the same time, because they own the products, they are free to develop their own marketing strategies including setting the prices they charge their customers.

- *Full-service merchant wholesalers*, as the name suggests, provide a wide range of services for their customers. These services may include delivery, credit, product-use assistance, repairs, advertising, and other promotion support—even market research. Full-service wholesalers often have their own sales force to call on businesses and organizational customers. Some general merchandise wholesalers carry a large variety of different items while specialty wholesalers carry an extensive assortment of a single product line. For example, a candy wholesaler would carry only candy and gum but have enough different varieties to give your dentist nightmares for a year.

take title ■ To accept legal ownership of a product and the accompanying rights and responsibilities of ownership.

- In contrast, *limited-service merchant wholesalers* provide fewer services for their customers. Like full-service wholesalers, limited-service wholesalers **take title** to merchandise but they are less likely to provide such services as delivery, credit, or marketing assistance to retailers. Specific types of limited-service wholesalers include the following:
  - *Cash-and-carry wholesalers* provide low-cost merchandise for retailers and industrial customers that are too small for other wholesalers' sales representatives to call on. Customers pay cash for products and provide their own delivery. Some popular cash-and-carry product categories include groceries, office supplies, building materials, and electrical supplies.
  - *Truck jobbers* carry their products to small business customer locations for their inspection and selection. Truck jobbers often supply perishable items such as fruit, vegetables, and meats to small grocery stores. For example, a bakery truck jobber calls on supermarkets, checks the stock of bread on the shelf, removes any outdated items, and suggests how much bread the store needs to reorder.
  - *Drop shippers* are limited-function wholesalers that take title to the merchandise but never actually take possession of it. Drop shippers take orders from and bill retailers and industrial buyers but the merchandise is shipped directly from the manufacturer. Because they take title to the merchandise, they assume the same risks as other merchant wholesalers. Drop shippers are important to both the producers and customers of bulky products such as coal, oil, or lumber.
  - *Mail-order wholesalers* sell products to small retailers and other industrial customers, often located in remote areas, through catalogs rather than a sales force. They usually carry products in inventory and require payment in cash or by credit card before shipment. Mail-order wholesalers supply such products as cosmetics, hardware, sporting goods, and general merchandise.
  - *Rack jobbers* supply retailers with such specialty items as health and beauty products, magazines, and books. Rack jobbers get their name because they own and maintain the product display racks in grocery, drug, and variety stores. These wholesalers visit their retail customers on a regular basis to maintain levels of stock and refill their racks with merchandise.

merchandise agents or brokers ■ Channel intermediaries that provide services in exchange for commissions but never take title to the product.

Merchandise Agents or Brokers   **Merchandise agents or brokers** are a second major type of independent intermediary. Agents and brokers provide services in exchange for commissions. They may or may not take possession of the product, but they never take title; that is,

Rack jobbers are full-service merchant wholesalers. These intermediaries own and maintain product display racks in retail stores.

they do not accept legal ownership of the product. Agents normally represent buyers or sellers on an ongoing basis, whereas brokers are employed by clients for a short period of time.

- *Manufacturers' agents*, also referred to as *manufacturers' reps*, are independent salespeople who carry several lines of noncompeting products. They have contractual arrangements with manufacturers that outline territories, selling prices, and other specific aspects of the relationship. These agents have little if any supervision and are compensated with commissions based on a percentage of what they sell. Manufacturers' agents often develop strong customer relationships and provide an important sales function for small and new companies.
- *Selling agents* including export/import agents market a whole product line or one manufacturer's total output. They are often seen as independent marketing departments because they perform the same functions as full-service wholesalers but do not take title to products. Unlike manufacturers' agents, selling agents have unlimited territories and control the pricing, promotion, and distribution of their products. Selling agents are found in such industries as furniture, clothing, and textiles.
- *Commission merchants* are sales agents who receive goods, primarily agricultural products such as grain or livestock, on *consignment*. That is, they take possession of products without taking title. Although sellers may state a minimum price they are willing to take for their products, commission merchants are free to sell the product for the highest price they can get. Commission merchants receive a commission on the sales price of the product.
- *Merchandise brokers*, including export/import brokers, are intermediaries that facilitate transactions in markets such as real estate, food, and used equipment in which there are lots of small buyers and sellers. Brokers identify likely buyers and sellers and bring the two together in return for a fee received when the transaction is completed.

MANUFACTURER-OWNED INTERMEDIARIES

Sometimes manufacturers set up their own channel intermediaries. In this way, they are able to have separate business units that perform all of the functions of independent intermediaries, while at the same time maintaining complete control over the channel.

- *Sales branches* are manufacturer-owned facilities that, like independent wholesalers, carry inventory and provide sales and service to customers in a specific geographic area. Sales branches are found in such industries as petroleum products, industrial machinery and equipment, and motor vehicles.

2 *Bookmark It!*

Visit a real estate broker or stockbroker in your area. Talk to him about his job, what he does, how he works for clients and firms, and how he is compensated (contrary to popular belief most realtors work for the seller, not the buyer). Make a list of the functions this type of channel member performs. Finally, list the advantages and disadvantages of the job for your personal career choice.

Real estate brokers are independent intermediaries whose job it is to identify likely buyers and sellers and bring the two together.

- *Sales offices* are manufacturer-owned facilities that, like agents, do not carry inventory but provide selling functions for the manufacturer in a specific geographic area. Because they allow members of the sales force to be located close to customers, they reduce selling costs and provide better customer service.
- *Manufacturers' showrooms* are manufacturer-owned or leased facilities in which products are permanently displayed for customers to visit. Manufacturers' showrooms are often located in or near large merchandise marts, such as the furniture market in High Point, North Carolina. Merchandise marts are often multiple buildings in which one or more industries hold trade shows and many manufacturers have permanent showrooms. Retailers can come either during a show or all year long to see the manufacturer's merchandise and make business-to-business purchases.

Types of Distribution Channels

Firms face many choices when structuring distribution channels. Should they sell directly to consumers and business users? Would they benefit by including wholesalers, retailers, or both in the channel? Would it make sense to sell directly to some customers but use retailers to sell to other customers? Of course, there is no single best channel for all products. The marketing manager must select a channel structure that creates a competitive advantage for the firm and its products based on the size and needs of the target market. Let's consider some of the factors these managers need to think about.

channel levels ■ The number of distinct categories of intermediaries that populate a channel of distribution.

In developing place or distribution strategies, marketers first consider different **channel levels**, or the number of distinct categories of intermediaries that make up a channel of distribution. Many different factors have an impact on this decision. What channel members are available? How large is the market, how frequently do consumers purchase the product, and what services do they require?

Figure 17.2 summarizes the different structures a distribution channel can take. The producer and the customer are always members so the shortest channel possible has two levels. Using a retailer adds a third level, a wholesaler adds a fourth level, and so on. Different channel structures exist for both consumer and business-to-business markets.

CONSUMER CHANNELS

As we noted earlier, the simplest channel is a direct channel. Why do some producers sell directly to customers? One reason is that a direct channel may allow the producer to serve its customers better and at a lower price than is possible using a retailer. By using a direct

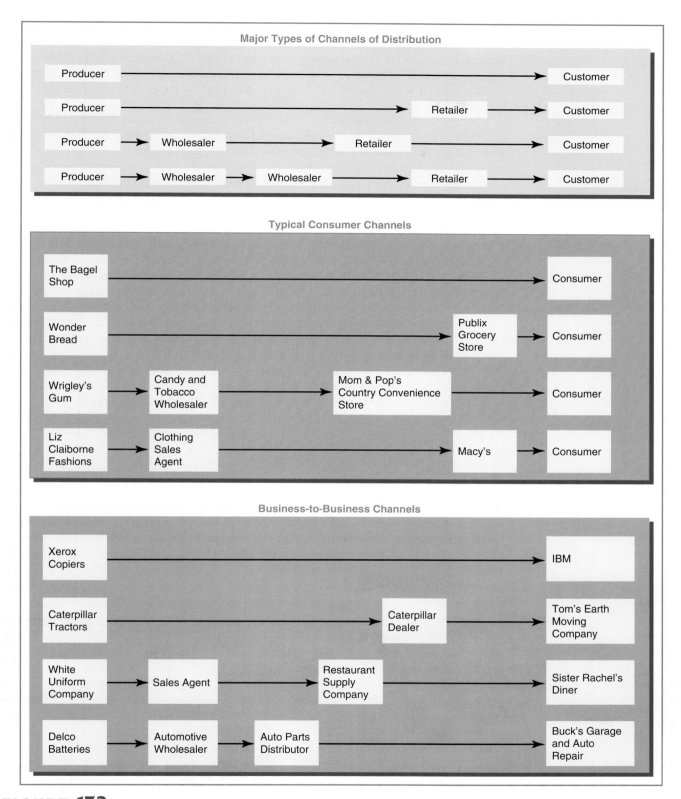

FIGURE 17.2

Different Types of Channels of Distribution

Channels differ in the number of channel members that participate.

channel, the strawberry farmer makes sure his customers have fresher strawberries than if he sells the berries through a local supermarket. Furthermore, if the farmer sells the berries through a supermarket, their price will be higher because of the supermarket's costs of doing business and required profit on the berries. In fact, sometimes this is the *only* way to sell the product because using channel intermediaries may increase the price above what consumers are willing to pay.

For both large and small firms, one of the newest means of selling in a direct channel is the Internet. For example, small entrepreneurs Richard Lodico and Vinny Baribieri, owners of Eastern Meat Farms Italian Market, have found Internet sales are a great way to expand their business to new markets.[2] For years, Lodico and Baribieri shipped sausages and cheeses to customers' relatives across the country but didn't feel there was enough volume to justify the expense of direct marketing. However, when the Internet offered them the opportunity to sell to customers all around the globe with only $1,800 a month in Web charges, www.salami.com was born. The company ships each order using styrofoam and ice packs to ensure that customers from around the globe receive high-quality, fresh products, often for less than half the price they would have to pay for similar delicacies locally. Hot dog!

Another reason to use a direct channel is control. When the producer handles distribution, it maintains control of pricing, service, delivery—all elements of the transaction. Because distributors and dealers carry many products, it can be difficult to get their sales forces to focus on selling one product. In a direct channel, a producer works directly with customers, gaining insights into trends, customer needs and complaints, and the effectiveness of its marketing strategies.

Why do producers choose to use indirect channels to reach consumers? A reason in many cases is that customers are familiar with certain retailers or other intermediaries—it's where they always go to look for what they need. That's why a big company like VF relies so much on well-known retailers. Getting customers to change their normal buying behavior, for example, convincing consumers to buy their laundry detergent or frozen pizza from a catalog or over the Internet instead of from the corner supermarket, would be difficult. In addition, intermediaries help producers in all the ways described earlier. By creating utility and transaction efficiencies, channel members make producers' lives easier and enhance their ability to reach customers.

The *producer–retailer–consumer channel* in Figure 17.2 is the shortest indirect channel. GE uses this channel when its sells small appliances through large retailers such as Wal-Mart or Sears. Because the retailers buy in large volume, they can buy at a low price, which they pass on to shoppers. The size of these retail giants also means they can provide the physical distribution functions such as transportation and storage that wholesalers handle for smaller retail outlets.

Richard Lodico and Vinny Baribieri, owners of Eastern Meat Farms Italian Market, used the Internet to expand their business as salami.com. It's turned out to be a meaty distribution strategy.

The *producer–wholesaler–retailer–consumer channel* is a common distribution channel in consumer marketing. Take ice cream, for instance. A single ice-cream factory can supply, say, four or five regional wholesalers. These wholesalers then sell to 400 or more retailers such as grocery stores. The retailers in turn each sell the ice cream to thousands of customers. In this channel, the regional wholesalers combine many manufacturers' products to supply to grocery stores. Because the grocery stores do business with many wholesalers, this arrangement results in a broad selection of products.

BUSINESS-TO-BUSINESS CHANNELS

Business-to-business distribution channels, as the name suggests, facilitate the flow of goods from a producer to an organizational or business customer. Generally, business-to-business channels parallel consumer channels in that they may be direct or indirect. For example, the simplest indirect channel in industrial markets occurs when the single intermediary—a merchant wholesaler referred to as an *industrial distributor* rather than a retailer—buys products from a manufacturer and sells them to business customers.

Direct channels are more common to business-to-business markets than to consumer markets. This is because business-to-business marketing often means selling high-dollar, high-profit items (a single piece of industrial equipment may cost hundreds of thousands of dollars) to a market made up of only a few customers. In such markets, it pays for a company to develop its own sales force and sell directly to customers at a lower cost than if it used intermediaries.

DISTRIBUTION CHANNELS FOR SERVICES

Because services are intangible, there is no need to worry about storage, transportation, and the other functions of physical distribution. In most cases, the service travels directly from the producer to the customer. However, some services do need an intermediary, often called an *agent*, who helps the parties complete the transaction. Examples include insurance agents, stockbrokers, and travel agents.

DUAL DISTRIBUTION SYSTEMS

Figure 17.2 shows simple distribution channels. Well, life is rarely that simple: Producers, dealers, wholesalers, retailers, and customers alike may actually interact with more than one type of channel. We call these *dual* or *multiple distribution systems*.

The pharmaceutical industry provides a good example of multiple channel usage. Pharmaceutical companies distribute their products in at least three channel types. First, they sell to hospitals, clinics, and other organizational customers directly. These customers buy in quantity, purchasing a wide variety of products. Because pills are dispensed one at a time rather than in bottles of 50, they require different product packaging than when the products are sold to other customers. Pharmaceuticals' second channel is an indirect consumer channel in which the manufacturer sells to large drug retailer chains that distribute the medicines to their stores across the country. Some of us would rather purchase our prescriptions in a more personal manner from the local independent drugstore where we can still get an ice-cream soda while we wait. In this channel, the manufacturer sells to drug wholesalers that in turn supply these independents.

HYBRID MARKETING SYSTEMS

Instead of serving a target market with a single channel, companies have added new channels—direct sales, distributors, retail sales and direct mail. As they add channels and communications methods, they create a **hybrid marketing system**.[3] For example, at one time IBM computers were only available from IBM sales people. Today, IBM personal computers are sold through dealers, catalog operations, direct mail, telemarketing and retailers. Hybrid marketing systems can offer companies certain advantages including increased coverage of the market, lower marketing costs, and a greater potential for customization. In other words, hybrid marketing systems give a firm a competitive advantage.

hybrid marketing systems
■ Marketing systems that use a number of different channels and communication methods to serve a target market.

Pharmaceutical companies usually interact with more than one channel. They may sell directly to hospitals, while consumers buy their prescription medicines from retail drug stores.

Now we know what distribution channels and channel intermediaries are and the role of channel members in the distribution of goods and services. We also know that not all channels are alike. Some channels are direct, but indirect channels can be quite complex. The next section is about how marketers plan channel strategies to meet customer needs better than the competition—the all-important competitive advantage.

Planning a Channel Strategy

Do customers want products in large or small quantities? Do they insist on buying them locally or will they purchase from a distant supplier? How long are they willing to wait to get the product? Intelligent marketers want to know!

Distribution planning is best accomplished when marketers follow the steps in Figure 17.3. In this section we will first look at how manufacturers decide on distribution objectives and then we'll examine what influences distribution decisions. Finally, we'll talk about how firms select different distribution strategies and tactics.

Firms that operate within a channel of distribution—manufacturers, wholesalers, and retailers—may do some distribution planning. In this section, our perspective focuses on distribution planning of producers or manufacturers rather than intermediaries because they, more often than intermediaries, take a leadership role in creating a successful distribution channel.

CHANNEL OBJECTIVES

The first step in deciding on a distribution plan is to develop objectives that support the organization's overall marketing goals. How can distribution work with the other elements of the marketing mix to increase profits? To increase market share? To increase volume of sales?

In general, the overall objective of any distribution plan is to make a firm's product available when, where, and in the quantities customers want and need at a minimum cost. More specific distribution objectives, however, depend on characteristics of the product and the market.

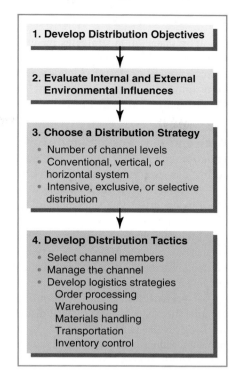

FIGURE 17.3

Steps in Distribution Planning
Distribution planning begins with setting channel objectives and includes developing channel strategies and tactics.

For example, if the product is bulky, a primary distribution objective may be to minimize shipping costs. If the product is fragile, a goal may be to develop a channel that minimizes handling. In introducing a new product to a mass market, a channel objective may be to provide maximum product exposure or to make the product available close to where customers live and work. Sometimes marketers make their product available where similar products are sold so that consumers can compare prices.

EVALUATING THE ENVIRONMENT

After setting the distribution objectives, marketers must consider their internal and external environments to develop the best channel structure. Should the channel be long or short? Is intensive, selective, or exclusive distribution best? Short, often direct, channels may be better suited for business-to-business marketers where customers are geographically concentrated and customers require high levels of technical know-how and service. Expensive or complex products are frequently sold directly to final customers. Short channels with selective distribution also make more sense with perishable products where getting the product to the final user quickly is an important issue. However, longer channels with more intensive distribution are generally best for inexpensive, standardized consumer goods that need to be distributed broadly and where little technical expertise is required.

The organization must also examine such issues as its own ability to handle distribution functions, what channel intermediaries are available, the ability of customers to access these intermediaries, and how the competition distributes its products. Should a firm use the same retailers as its competitors? Sometimes, to ensure customers' undivided attention, a firm sells its products in outlets that don't carry the competitors' products. In other cases a firm uses the same intermediaries as its competitors because customers expect to find the product there. For example, you will only find Harley-Davidson bikes in selected Harley "boutiques," but you can expect to find Coca-Cola, Colgate toothpaste, and a Snickers bar in every store that sells these types of items.

Finally, by studying competitors' distribution strategies, marketers can learn from their successes and failures. If the biggest complaint of competitors' customers is delivery speed, developing a system that allows same-day delivery can make the competition pale in comparison.

3 *Bookmark It!*

You are the marketing manager for a company that sells expensive candies (think Godiva). Would you want a long or a short channel of distribution? Would you use exclusive, selective, or intensive distribution? What elements of the internal and external environment are important in these decisions? Write a report to your boss on your decisions.

CHOOSING A DISTRIBUTION SYSTEM

Planning distribution strategies means making at least three decisions. First, of course, distribution planning includes decisions about the number of levels in the distribution channel. But distribution strategies also involve decisions about channel relationships, that is, whether a conventional system or a highly integrated system will work best. A third decision relates to the distribution intensity or the number of intermediaries at each level of the channel.

Conventional, Vertical and Horizontal Marketing Systems
Participants in any distribution channel form an interrelated system. In general, these systems take one of three forms: conventional, vertical, and horizontal marketing systems.

A **conventional marketing system** is a multilevel distribution channel in which members work independently of one another. Their relationships are limited to simply buying and selling from one another. Each firm seeks to benefit with little concern for other channel members. Even though channel members work independently, most conventional channels are highly successful. For one thing, all members of the channel are working for the same goals—to build demand, reduce costs, and improve customer satisfaction. And the channel members know that it's in everyone's best interest to treat other channel members fairly.[4]

A **vertical marketing system (VMS)** is a channel in which there is cooperation among channel members at two or more different levels, that is, the manufacturing, wholesaling, and retailing levels. Vertical marketing systems were developed as a way to meet customer needs better by reducing costs incurred in channel activities. A single channel member controls channel behavior to avoid conflict and to create economies through size, eliminating duplication of services, and creating buying bargaining power. Often a vertical marketing system can provide a level of cooperation and efficiency not possible with a conventional channel, maximizing the effectiveness of the channel while maximizing efficiency and keeping costs low. Members share information and provide services to other members, recognizing that such coordination makes everyone more successful in reaching a desired target market.

There are three types of vertical marketing systems: administered, corporate, and contractual. In an administered VMS, channel members remain independent but voluntarily work together because of the power of single channel member. Strong brands are able to effect an administered VMS because resellers are eager to work with the manufacturer to carry the product.

In a corporate VMS, a single firm owns manufacturing, wholesaling, and retailing operations. Thus, the firm has complete control over all channel operations. Retail giant Sears Roebuck & Co., for example, owns a nationwide network of distribution centers and retail stores.

conventional marketing system ■ A multiple-level distribution channel in which channel members work independently of one another.

vertical marketing system (VMS) ■ A channel of distribution in which there is cooperation among members at the manufacturing, wholesaling, and retailing levels.

With a conventional marketing system, members work independently. The only relationship between clothing retailers and the clothing makers is that they buy and sell from one another.

In a contractual VMS, cooperation is enforced by contracts (legal agreements) that spell out each member's rights and responsibilities and how they will cooperate. Contractual VMSs mean that the channel members can have more impact as a group than they could alone. In a wholesaler-sponsored VMS, wholesalers get retailers to work together under their leadership in a voluntary chain. Retail members of the chain use a common name, cooperate in advertising and other promotion, and even develop their own private-label products. Examples of wholesaler-sponsored chains are IGA (Independent Grocers' Alliance) food stores and Ace Hardware stores.

In other cases, retailers themselves organize a cooperative marketing channel system. A *retailer cooperative* is a group of retailers that has established a wholesaling operation to help them compete more effectively with the large chains. Each retailer owns shares in the wholesaler operation and is obligated to purchase a certain percentage of inventory from the cooperative operation. Associated Grocers and True Value Hardware Stores are examples of retailer cooperatives.

Franchise organizations are a third type of contractual VMS. In these organizations, channel cooperation is explicitly defined and strictly enforced through contractual arrangements in which a franchiser (a manufacturer or a service provider) allows an entrepreneur to use the franchise name and marketing plan for a fee. In most franchise agreements, the franchiser provides a variety of services for the franchisee, such as helping to train employees, giving access to lower prices for needed materials, and helping pick a location with visibility. In return, the franchiser receives a percentage of revenue from the franchise owner. Usually the franchisees are also allowed to use the franchiser business format, but they are required to follow that format to the letter.[5] For example, a McDonald's franchisee is not allowed to change the menu or the physical decor of the restaurant. It's important that customers know that they can get the same Big Mac in New York City that they will find in Moncks Corner, South Carolina. Some long-standing and some new franchise operations are listed in Table 17.2.

From the manufacturer's perspective, franchising a business is a way to develop widespread product distribution with minimal financial risk while at the same time maintaining control over product quality. From the entrepreneur's perspective, franchises are a popular way to get a start in business.

In a **horizontal marketing system**, two or more firms at the same channel level agree to work together to get their product to the customer. Sometimes these agreements are between unrelated businesses. For example, many supermarkets now have formed a horizontal marketing system with banks that maintain a branch in the store. Customers like this because they can do their food shopping and their banking in one stop.

Most all airlines today are members of a horizontal alliance that allows them to cooperate in providing passenger air service. For example, Delta Airlines is a member of Sky Team, which also includes such international carriers as AeroMexico, Air France, Alitalia, CSA Czech Airlines, and Korean Air. These alliances increase passenger volume for all airlines because travel agents who book passengers on one of the airline's flights will be more likely to

horizontal marketing system ■ An arrangement within a channel of distribution in which two or more firms at the same channel level work together for a common purpose.

Company Name	Description	Start-Up Costs
Kid to Kid Franchise System	sells used children's clothing	$88,000 and up
Record Swap Franchises, Inc.	sells a mix of recycled and new audio disks	$150,000
Heartland Properties, Inc.	assisted living for the elderly (not nursing home care)	$600,000
Mad Science Group, Inc.	after-school programs and birthday party entertainment that make science fun	$57,000
McDonald's	fast-food restaurants	$500,000 (estimated)
Subway	sandwich shops	$34,400
Baskin-Robbins	ice-cream shops	$134,000–150,000
Hardee's	fast-food restaurants	$700,000–$1.7 million
Domino's Pizza	pizza delivery	$76,500–187,500

Source: Adapted from Jeffrey A. Tannenbaum, "Franchisers Are Finding Some New Twists on Old Ideas," *Wall Street Journal*, April 24, 1995, B2; Veronica Byrd, "Hamburgers or Home Decorating? Businesses That Sell," *New York Times*, October 4, 1992, 10.

TABLE 17.2

Established and Emerging Franchises: A Sampler

book a connecting flight on the other airline. To increase customer benefits, they also share frequent-flyer programs and airport clubs. SkyTeam is an alliance dedicated to providing you with greater flight options, improved customer service, and enhanced benefits.[6]

Intensive, Exclusive, and Selective Distribution   How many wholesalers and retailers will carry the product within a given market? This may seem like an easy decision: Distribute the product through as many intermediaries as possible. But guess again. If the product goes to too many outlets, there may be inefficiency and duplication of efforts. For example, if there are too many Honda dealerships in town, there will be a lot of unsold Hondas sitting on dealer lots and no single dealer will be successful. But, if there are not enough wholesalers or retailers carrying a product, total sales of the manufacturer's products (and profits) will not be maximized. If customers have to drive hundreds of miles to find a Honda dealer, they may settle for a Ford or a Chevy. Thus, a distribution objective may either be to increase or decrease the level of market penetration.

The three basic choices are intensive, exclusive, and selective distribution. Table 17.3 summarizes the five decision factors—company, customers, channels, constraints, and competition—and how they help marketers determine the best fit between distribution system and marketing goals.

intensive distribution ■
Selling a product through all suitable wholesalers or retailers that are willing to stock and sell the product.

Intensive distribution aims at maximizing market coverage by selling a product through all wholesalers or retailers that will stock and sell the product. Marketers use intensive distribution for products such as chewing gum, soft drinks, milk, and bread that are quickly consumed and must be frequently replaced. Intensive distribution is necessary for these products because availability is more important than any other consideration in customers' purchase decisions.

exclusive distribution ■
Selling a product only through a single outlet in a particular region.

In contrast to intensive distribution, **exclusive distribution** means limiting distribution to a single outlet in a particular region. Marketers sell pianos, cars, executive training programs, television programs, and many other products with high price tags through exclusive distribution arrangements. These strategies are typically used with products that are high priced, that have considerable service requirements, and when there are a limited number of buyers in any single geographic area. Exclusive distribution enables wholesalers and retailers to recoup the costs associated with long selling processes for each customer and, in some cases, extensive after-sale service.

Of course, not every situation neatly fits a category in Table 17.3. (You didn't *really* think it would be that simple, did you?) For example, consider professional sports. Customers might not shop for games in the same way they shop for pianos. They might go to a game on impulse, and they don't require much individualized service. Nevertheless, professional sports employ exclusive distribution. The team's cost of serving customers is high due to those million-dollar player salaries and multimillion-dollar stadiums.

selective distribution ■
Distribution using fewer outlets than in intensive distribution but more than in exclusive distribution.

The alert reader (and/or sports fan) may note that there are some exceptions to the exclusive distribution of sports teams. New York has two football teams and two baseball teams, Chicago fields two baseball teams, and so on. Market coverage that is less than intensive distribution, but more than exclusive distribution, is called **selective distribution**. Selective

TABLE 17.3

Characteristics That Favor Intensive Over Exclusive Distribution

Decision Factor	Intensive Distribution	Exclusive Distribution
Company	Oriented toward mass markets	Oriented toward specialized markets
Customers	High customer density Price and convenience are priorities	Low customer density Service and cooperation are priorities
Channels	Overlapping market coverage	Nonoverlapping market coverage
Constraints	Cost of serving individual customers is low	Cost of serving individual customers is high
Competition	Based on a strong market presence, often through advertising and promotion	Based on individualized attention to customers, often through relationship marketing

For products such as Rockport shoes, marketers need more than exclusive distribution but less than intensive distribution. This means that you can buy Rockports in some but not all shoe stores.

distribution fits when demand is so large that exclusive distribution is inadequate, but selling costs, service requirements, or other factors make intensive distribution a poor fit. Although a White Sox baseball fan may not believe that the Cubs franchise is necessary (and vice versa), major league baseball and even some baseball fans think the Chicago market is large enough to support both teams.

Selective distribution strategies are suitable for so-called *shopping products* such as household appliances, computers, and electronic equipment for which consumers are willing to spend time visiting different retail outlets to compare product alternatives. For producers, selective distribution means freedom to choose only those wholesalers and retailers that have a good credit rating, provide good market coverage, serve customers well, and cooperate effectively. Wholesalers and retailers like selective distribution because it results in higher sales and profits than are possible with intensive distribution where sellers often have to compete on price.

DEVELOPING DISTRIBUTION TACTICS

As with planning for the other marketing Ps, the final step in distribution planning is developing the distribution tactics necessary to implement the distribution strategy. These decisions are usually about the type of distribution system to use such as a direct or indirect channel, or a conventional or an integrated channel. Distribution tactics relate to the implementation of these strategies such as selecting individual channel members and managing the channel. These decisions are important because they often have a direct impact on customer satisfaction—nobody wants to have to wait for something they've bought! Toyota's plans for its new youth-oriented Scion model include a new way to distribute the cars. The car company's goal is to cut delivery time to its impatient young customers to no more than a week by offering fewer model variations and doing more customization at the dealer rather than at the factory.[7]

Selecting Channel Partners   When firms agree to work together in a channel relationship, they become partners in what is normally a long-term commitment. Like a marriage, it is important to both manufacturers and intermediaries to select channel partners wisely or they'll regret the matchup later. In evaluating intermediaries, manufacturers try to answer questions such as: Will the channel member contribute substantially to our profitability? Does the channel member have the ability to provide the services customers want? What impact will a potential intermediary have on channel control?

For example, what small to midsize firm wouldn't jump at the chance to have its products distributed by retail giant Wal-Mart? With Wal-Mart as a channel partner, a small firm could double, triple, or quadruple its business. Actually, more than one firm, recognizing that size means power in the channel, has decided against selling to Wal-Mart because they are not willing to relinquish control of their marketing decision making.

Another consideration in selecting channel members is competitors' channel partners. Because people spend time comparing different brands when purchasing a shopping product, firms need to make sure their products are displayed near similar competitors' products. If most competitors distribute their electric drills through mass merchandisers, a manufacturer has to make sure its brand is there also.

A firm's dedication to social responsibility may also be an important determining factor in the selection of channel partners. Many firms have developed extensive programs to recruit minority-owned channel members.

Managing the Channel of Distribution   Once a manufacturer develops a channel strategy and aligns channel members, the day-to-day job of managing the channel begins. The **channel leader**, sometimes called a *channel captain*, is the dominant firm that controls the channel. A firm becomes the channel leader because it has power relative to other channel members. This power comes from different sources:

channel leader ■ A firm at one level of distribution that takes a leadership role, establishing operating norms and processes that reduce channel conflicts and costs and enhance delivered customer value.

- A firm has *economic power* when it has the ability to control resources.
- A firm such as a franchiser has *legitimate power* if it has legal authority to call the shots.
- A firm has *reward or coercive power* if it engages in exclusive distribution and has the ability to give profitable products and to take them away from the channel intermediaries.

Although producers have traditionally held the role of channel captain, a firm at any level of distribution may emerge as a channel leader. When retailers were much smaller than they are now, producers tended to assume leadership in consumer goods markets. Procter & Gamble, for instance, developed customer-oriented marketing programs, tracked market trends, and advised retailers on the mix of products most likely to build sales. As large retail chains evolved, giant retailers such as Wal-Mart began to assume a leadership role because of the sheer size of their operations.

Because producers, wholesalers, and retailers depend on one another for success, channel cooperation helps everyone. Channel cooperation is also stimulated when the channel leader takes actions that help make its partners more successful. High intermediary profit margins, training programs, cooperative advertising, and expert marketing advice are invisible to end customers but are motivating factors in the eyes of wholesalers and retailers.[8] Haggar Apparel, for example, finds ways to help its retail channel partners become more successful. By improving the speed and accuracy of reorders, retailers are able to maintain inventory levels necessary to satisfy customers while avoiding ordering errors.

Of course, relations among members in a channel are not always full of sweetness and light. Because each firm has its own objectives, channel conflict may threaten a manufacturer's distribution strategy. Such conflict most often occurs between firms at different levels of the same distribution channel. Incompatible goals, poor communication, and disagreement over roles, responsibilities, and functions cause conflict. For example, a producer is likely to feel the firm would enjoy greater success and profitability if intermediaries carry only its brands, but many intermediaries believe they will do better if they carry a variety of brands.

DISTRIBUTION CHANNELS AND THE MARKETING MIX

How are decisions regarding place related to the other three Ps? For one thing, place decisions affect pricing. Marketers that distribute products through mass merchandisers such as Kmart and Wal-Mart will have different pricing objectives and strategies than will those that sell to specialty stores.

Distribution decisions can sometimes give a product a distinct position in its market. For example, Enterprise Rent-a-Car avoids the cutthroat airport rental car market by instead seeking locations in residential areas and local business centers. This strategy takes advantage of the preferences of those customers who want short-term use of a rental vehicle.[9] And, of course, the choice of retailers and other intermediaries is strongly tied to the product itself. Manufacturers select mass merchandisers to sell mid-price-range products while they distribute top-of-the-line products such as expensive jewelry through high-end department and specialty stores.

So far we've been concerned with the distribution channels firms use to get their products to customers. In the next section, we'll look at the different day-to-day activities of these firms as the product travels from producer to user—activities referred to as physical distribution.

Logistics: Implementing the Value Chain

Marketing textbooks tend to depict the practice of marketing as 90 percent planning and 10 percent implementation. In the real world, many managers would argue that this ratio should be reversed. Marketing success is very much the art of getting the timing right and delivering on promises. That's why marketers place so much emphasis on efficient **logistics**, the process of designing, managing, and improving the movement of products through the supply chain. Logistics includes purchasing, manufacturing, storage, and transport.[10] To understand logistics, we must first examine the concept of supply chain management.

logistics ■ The process of designing, managing, and improving the movement of products through the supply chain.

THE SUPPLY CHAIN

The **supply chain** includes all the firms that engage in activities that are necessary to convert raw materials into a good or service and put it in the hands of the consumer or business customer. Thus, **supply chain management** is the management of flows among the firms in a supply chain to maximize total profitability.

The difference between a supply chain and a channel of distribution is the number of members and their function. A supply chain consists of those firms that supply the raw materials, component parts, and supplies necessary for a firm to produce a good or service *plus* the firms that facilitate the movement of that product to the ultimate users of the product, that is, the channel members.

Figure 17.4 provides a simple example of the supply chain for a computer maker such as Hewlett-Packard. Of course, Hewlett-Packard uses hundreds of suppliers in manufacturing its computers and sells those items through hundreds of online and off-line retailers worldwide. And it is noteworthy that the role of individual firms within the supply chain depends on your perspective. If we are looking at Hewlett-Packard's supply chain, Intel is a supplier and Best Buy is a member of its channel of distribution. From Intel's perspective Hewlett-Packard is a customer. From the perspective of Best Buy, Hewlett-Packard is a supplier.

Another way to look at the supply chain is as a value chain. The **value chain** concept looks at the supply chain from the perspective of adding value.[11] As a product "flows" from the producer to the consumer, other firms add value by providing supporting materials (such as packaging), financing, providing a physical place to store or display the item, and so on. So, every firm in the channel of distribution occupies a position on a value chain whether that firm is "upstream" (it is involved fairly early on in the process) or "downstream" (relatively closer to the point where the product reaches the consumer).

supply chain ■ All the firms that engage in activities necessary to turn raw materials into a good or service and put it in the hands of the consumer or business customer.

supply chain management ■ The management of flows among firms in the supply chain to maximize profitability.

value chain ■ The concept of a supply chain that looks at how each firm receives inputs, adds value to these inputs, and then passes them along to the next firm in the value chain.

A supply chain can be complicated, and sophisticated software often is needed to be sure a link in the chain doesn't break.

Let's see how a value chain works in our computer example. Intel takes raw materials such as silicon and adds value by turning them into Pentium chips. Intel ships these chips to Hewlett-Packard, which combines them with the other components of a computer, again adding value. Best Buy takes the finished product and adds value by providing display, sales support, repair service, financing, and so forth for the customer. Ideally, then, the product a consumer "catches" in the value stream has been transformed as it journeys from the source of the stream to its end.

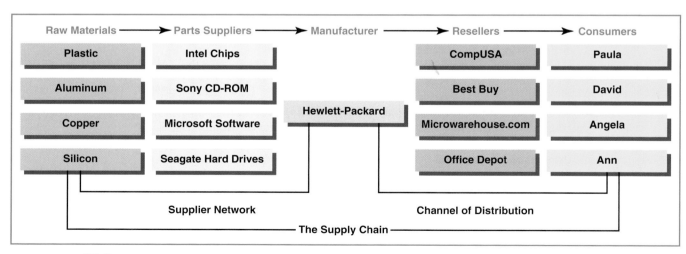

FIGURE 17.4

Supply Chain

The supply chain for computer maker Hewlett-Packard includes firms that supply component parts for the machines as well as retailers such as Best Buy and CompUSA. Each firm in the chain adds value to its inputs to provide the PC the consumer wants at the lowest cost.

FLOORS.
DONE.
MOLDING.
DONE.
PAINT.
DONE.
CEILING?
HMMM...
GO TO THE HOME DEPOT.
HAMPTON BAY.
PERFECT.
NEXT ROOM.

The distinctive styles of Hampton Bay add the finishing touch to any room. Or every room. Available at The Home Depot.

In a value chain, each member firm adds value to the product as it moves downstream. Retailers such as Home Depot provide classes on how to install what customers buy there.

THE LOWDOWN ON LOGISTICS

Logistics was originally a military term used to describe everything needed to deliver troops and equipment to the right place, at the right time, and in the right condition.[12] In business, logistics is similar in that its objective is to deliver exactly what the customer wants—at the right time, in the right place, and at the right price. The application of logistics is essential to the efficient management of the supply chain. Just as it's said "an army travels on its stomach" (meaning it can't function without adequate supplies), so a business relies on efficient planning to be sure it has what it needs to contribute its part to the value chain.

In planning for the delivery of goods to customers, marketers have usually looked at a process termed **physical distribution**, which refers to the activities used to move finished goods from manufacturers to final customers. Physical distribution activities include order processing, warehousing, materials handling, transportation, and inventory control. This process impacts how marketers physically get products where they need to be, when they need to be there, and at the lowest possible cost.

In logistics, the focus is on the customer. When logistics was thought of as physical distribution only, the objective was to deliver the product at the lowest cost. Today, when planning for the logistics function, firms consider the needs of the customer first. The customer's goals become the logistics provider's goals. And this means that with most logistics decisions, firms must compromise between low costs and high customer service.

The focus on the customer is important when customer goals and "lowest price" goals conflict. Take, for example, an industrial customer who demands just-in-time (JIT) delivery. The appropriate goal is not just to deliver what is needed at the lowest cost but rather to provide the product at the lowest cost possible *so long as* the JIT delivery requirements are met. Although it would be nice to transport all goods quickly by air, that is certainly not practical. But sometimes air transport is necessary to meet the needs of the customer, no matter the cost.

4 *Bookmark It!*

With several of your classmates, visit a local pharmacy and talk with the manager. Ask her to explain the steps in a typical pharmaceutical company's supply chain. How does each firm in the supply chain add value?

physical distribution ■ The activities used to move finished goods from manufacturers to final customers including order processing, warehousing, materials handling, transportation, and inventory control.

LOGISTICS FUNCTIONS

In developing logistics strategies, marketers must make decisions related to the five functions of logistics: order processing, warehousing, materials handling, transportation, and inventory control. For each decision, managers must consider how to minimize costs while maintaining the service customers want.

Order Processing *Order processing* includes the series of activities that occurs between the time an order comes into the organization and the time a product goes out the door. After an order is received, it is typically sent electronically to an office for record keeping and then on to the warehouse to be filled. When the order reaches the warehouse, personnel there check to see if the item is in stock. If it is not, the order is placed on *back-order status*. That information is sent to the office and then to the customer. If the item is available, it is located in the warehouse, packaged for shipment, and scheduled for pickup by either in-house or external shippers.

Fortunately, many firms have automated this process. Once an order is in the system, all of the other steps occur automatically. Inventories are continuously updated in computer databases so that a sales representative who calls on customers or telemarketers who take orders by phone know immediately whether the product is in stock.

Warehousing Whether we speak of fresh-cut flowers, canned goods, or computer chips, at some point goods (unlike services) must be stored. Storing goods allows marketers to match supply with demand. For example, toys and other gift items are big sellers at Christmas, but toy factories operate 12 months of the year. **Warehousing**—storing goods in anticipation of sale or transfer to another member of the channel of distribution—enables marketers to provide time utility to consumers by holding onto products until consumers need them.

Part of developing effective logistics means deciding how many warehouses a firm needs and where and what type they should be. A firm determines the location of its warehouse(s) by the location of customers and access to major highways, airports, or rail transportation. The number of warehouses often depends on the level of service customers require. If customers generally require fast delivery (today or tomorrow at the latest), then it may be necessary to store products in a number of different locations where they can be delivered to the customer quickly.

Firms use private and public warehouses to store goods. With *private warehouses*, firms have a high initial investment but they also lose less inventory due to damage. *Public warehouses* are an alternative, allowing firms to pay for a portion of warehouse space rather than having to own an entire storage facility. Most countries offer public warehouses in all large cities and many smaller cities to support domestic and international trade. A *distribution center* is a warehouse that stores goods for short periods of time and that provides other functions, such as breaking bulk.

Materials Handling **Materials handling** is the moving of products into, within, and out of warehouses. When goods come into the warehouse, they must be physically identified, checked for damage, sorted, and labeled. Next they are taken to a location for storage. Finally, they are recovered from the storage area for packaging and shipment. All in all, the goods may be handled over a dozen separate times. Procedures that limit the number of times a product must be handled decrease the likelihood of damage and reduce the cost of materials handling.

Transportation Logistics decisions take into consideration the modes of transportation and the individual freight carriers a firm needs to use to move products among channel members. Again, making transportation decisions entails a compromise between minimizing cost and providing the service customers want. As shown in Table 17.4, modes of transportation including railroads, pipelines, water transportation, motor carriers, and airways differ in the following ways:

- *Dependability*: the ability of the carrier to deliver goods safely and on time.
- *Cost*: the total transportation costs for moving a product from one location to another, including any charges for loading, unloading, and in-transit storage.

warehousing ■ Storing goods in anticipation of sale or transfer to another member of the channel of distribution.

materials handling ■ The moving of products into, within, and out of warehouses.

TABLE 17.4

A Comparison of Transportation Modes

Transportation Mode	Dependability	Cost	Speed of Delivery	Accessibility	Capability	Traceability	Most Suitable Products
Railroads	average	average	moderate	high	high	low	heavy or bulky goods such as automobiles, grain, steel
Water	low	low	slow	low	moderate	low	bulky, nonperishable goods such as automobiles
Trucks	high	high for long distances; low for short distances	fast	high	high	high	a wide variety of products including those that need refrigeration
Air	high	high	very fast	low	moderate	high	high-value items such as electronic goods and fresh flowers
Pipeline	high	low	slow	low	low	moderate	petroleum products and other chemicals
Internet	high	low	very fast	potentially very high	low	high	services such as banking, information, and entertainment

- *Speed of delivery*: the total time for moving a product from one location to another, including loading and unloading.
- *Accessibility*: the number of different locations the carrier serves.
- *Capability*: the ability of the carrier to handle a variety of different products (large and small, fragile and bulky, etc.).
- *Traceability*: the ability of the carrier to locate goods in shipment.

Each mode of transportation has strengths and weaknesses that make it a good choice for different transportation needs. Table 17.4 summarizes the pros and cons of each mode.

Railroads. Railroads are best for carrying heavy or bulky items such as coal and other mining products, agricultural products, forest products, steel, automobiles, and large machines over long distances. Railroads are about average in their cost and provide moderate speed of delivery. Although rail transportation provides dependable, low-cost service to many locations, trains simply cannot carry goods to every community in the country and they can't go over the oceans. These problems with rail transportation have been solved in recent years. *Piggyback services* allow low-cost rail transportation for shipping to a larger number of destinations. Truck trailers are loaded onto trains and carried as close to their destination as possible. Truck, train, and ship transportation has been similarly combined to provide *fishyback services.* Combining truck and air transportation is called *birdyback service.* Problems of excessive handling and damage have been reduced by *containerization* in which large quantities of goods are sealed in large protective containers for transit.

Water. Ships and barges, like railroads, carry large, bulky, nonperishable goods and are very important in international trade. Water transportation is quite low in cost but is very slow.

Trucking. As the bumper sticker says, "America's needs move by truck." Trucks or motor carriers are the most important carrier for consumer goods, especially for shorter hauls. Motor

Transportation by water such as that provided by Maersk Sealand is best for large, bulky, nonperishable goods and is vital to international trade.

carrier transportation allows flexibility because trucks can travel to those locations missed by boats, trains, and planes. Trucks are also able to carry a wide variety of products, including perishable items.[13]

Although costs are fairly high for longer-distance shipping, trucks are economical for shorter deliveries. Because trucks provide door-to-door service, product handling is minimal, reducing the chance of product damage.

Air. Air transportation is the fastest and most expensive transportation mode. It is ideal to move high-value items such as some mail, electronic goods, fresh-cut flowers, and live lobsters. Passenger airlines, air-freight carriers, and express delivery firms such as Federal Express, UPS, and Airborne Express provide air transportation. Air transportation, especially the overnight services provided by express delivery firms, is becoming more and more important in the development of international markets. Ships remain the major mover of international cargo, but air transportation networks are rapidly making the world a smaller place.

Pipeline. Pipelines are used to carry petroleum products such as oil and natural gas and a few other chemicals. Pipelines primarily flow from oil or gas fields to refineries. They are very low in cost, require little energy, and are not subject to disruption by weather.

The Internet. True, scientists haven't yet figured out how to transport goods electronically (not counting the transporter on *Star Trek*). But, as we discussed earlier in this chapter, marketers of services such as banking, news, and entertainment are taking advantage of distribution opportunities provided by the Internet.

Inventory control seeks to make sure the company has only the quantity of goods it needs available. Because of the cost of delivery, gasoline is delivered in whole tanker loads.

Inventory Control   Another component of logistics is **inventory control**, which means developing and implementing a process to ensure that the firm always has goods available to meet customers' demands—no more and no less. Firms store goods (i.e., create an inventory) for many reasons. For manufacturers, the pace of production may not match seasonal demand, and it may be more economical to produce snow skis year around than to produce them only during the winter season. For channel members that purchase goods from manufacturers or other channel intermediaries, it may be economical to order a product in quantities that don't exactly parallel demand. For example, delivery costs make it prohibitive for a retail gas station to place daily orders for just the amount of gas people will use that day. Instead, stations usually order truckloads of gasoline, holding their inventory in underground tanks. The consequences of stockouts may be very negative. Hospitals must keep adequate supplies of blood, IV fluids, drugs, and other supplies on hand to meet emergencies, even if some items go to waste.

Inventory control has a major impact on the costs of logistics. If supplies of products are too low to meet fluctuations in customer demand, a firm may have to make expensive emergency deliveries or lose customers to competitors. If inventories are above demand, unnecessary storage expenses and the possibility of damage or deterioration occur. Manufacturers are turning to quick-response replenishment systems to ensure that their products get to where they are needed.

inventory control ■
Activities to ensure that goods are always available to meet customers' demands.

Real People, Real Choices: How It Worked Out at VF Corporation

Mackey convinced JCPenney to choose option 1. In May 2000, the store chain implemented Lee's Retail Floor Space Management (RFSM) program in its womenswear division. In the six months following the implementation of this program, Lee's womenswear business at JCPenney increased 15 percent. In June 2001, Lee expanded the RFSM to include JCPenney's men's and boys' wear departments. Owing to the success of the rollout, JCPenney expanded implementation of the plan from 300 to 650 stores. JCPenney also began to test the program in men's casuals. Lee's RFSM has proven to be a success for JCPenney as well. For 2000, total brand sales were up over 5 percent. And in 2001 things got even better; Lee ended the year up 15 percent.

Mackey's experience illustrates how retailers and manufacturers within a *channel of distribution* can work together to improve profitability for all channel members: In the flow of value from producer to consumer, fixing one link makes the chain stronger for everyone!

VF Corporation is at the forefront of this new technology.[14] VF makes sure customers find what they're looking for by use of a computerized market-response system that keeps records on what consumers buy so that VF can rapidly restock stores with popular items. The system is hooked up to the computers of large retail customers such as JCPenney. Every night retailers transmit sales data collected at register scanners straight to VF where the market-response system automatically enters an order based on what items have been sold. VF jeans arrive within three days.[15] Manufacturers that provide their channel partners with this type of fast service are way ahead of the competition.

Chapter Summary

1. Explain what a distribution channel is and what functions distribution channels perform.

A distribution channel is a series of firms or individuals that facilitates the movement of a product from the producer to the final customer. Channels provide time, place, and ownership utility for customers and reduce the number of transactions necessary for goods to flow from many manufacturers to large numbers of customers by breaking bulk and creating assortments. Channel members make the purchasing process easier by providing important customer services. Today the Internet is becoming an important player in distribution channels.

2. Describe some of the types of wholesaling intermediaries found in distribution channels.

Wholesaling intermediaries are firms that handle the flow of products from the manufacturer to the retailer or business user. Merchant wholesalers are independent intermediaries that take title to a product and include both full-function wholesalers and limited-function wholesalers. Merchandise agents and brokers are independent intermediaries that do not take title to products. Manufacturer-owned channel members include sales branches, sales offices, and manufacturers' showrooms.

3. Describe the types of distribution channels and the steps in planning distribution channel strategies.

Distribution channels vary in length from the simplest two-level channel to longer channels with three or more channel levels. Consumer distribution channels include direct distribution, in which the producer sells directly to consumers, and indirect channels, which may include a wholesaler and/or a retailer. Business-to-business channels may also be either direct or indirect and often include industrial distributors. Distribution channels for services are usually direct but may include an agent intermediary. Many firms are part of more than one type of channel; that is, they participate in dual or multiple distribution systems. Conventional marketing systems include multiple levels of intermediaries that work independently. Vertical marketing systems (VMSs) are channels in which there is cooperation at the different levels and may be administered, corporate, or contractual. Horizontal marketing systems are composed of firms at one channel level that work together. Intensive distribution means including all possible intermediaries, exclusive distribution means having only one intermediary per region, and selective distribution includes a few but not all outlets in a region.

Marketers begin channel planning by developing channel objectives and considering important environmental factors. The next step is to decide on the type of distribution channel that is best. Distribution tactics include the selection of individual channel members and management of the channel.

4. Explain how logistics is used to implement the value chain.

The supply chain includes all the firms that engage in activities that are necessary to turn raw materials into a good or service for a consumer or business customer including those in the marketing channel of distribution. Every firm occupies a position on a value chain.

Companies add value to inputs received from firms upstream. Logistics is the process of designing, managing, and improving supply chains, including all those activities that are required to move products through the supply chain. Logistics activities include order processing, warehousing, materials handling, transportation, and inventory control.

Chapter Review

■ MARKETING CONCEPTS:
TESTING YOUR KNOWLEDGE

1. What is a channel of distribution? What are channel intermediaries?
2. Explain the functions of distribution channels. What is the role of the Internet in distribution channels?
3. List and explain the types of independent and manufacturer-owned wholesaling intermediaries.
4. What factors are important in determining if a manufacturer should choose a direct or indirect channel? Why do some firms use hybrid marketing systems?
5. What are conventional, vertical, and horizontal marketing systems?
6. Explain intensive, exclusive, and selective forms of distribution.
7. Explain the steps in distribution planning.
8. What is a supply chain and how is it different from a channel of distribuion? What is a value chain?
9. What is logistics? Explain the functions of logistics.
10. What are the advantages and disadvantages of shipping by rail? By air? By ship? By truck?

■ MARKETING CONCEPTS:
DISCUSSING CHOICES AND ISSUES

1. The supply chain concept looks at both the inputs of a firm and the means of firms that move the product from the manufacturer to the consumer. Do you think marketers should be concerned with the total supply chain concept? Why or why not?
2. You have probably heard someone say, "The reason products cost so much is because of all the intermediaries." Do intermediaries increase the cost of products? Would consumers be better off or worse off without intermediaries?
3. Many entrepreneurs choose to start a franchise business rather than "go it alone." Do you think franchises offer the typical businessperson good opportunities? What are some positive and negative aspects of purchasing a franchise?
4. As colleges and universities are looking for better ways to satisfy their customers, an area of increasing interest is the distribution of their product—education. Describe the characteristics of your school's channel(s) of distribution. What types of innovative distribution might make sense for your school to try?

■ MARKETING PRACTICE:
APPLYING WHAT YOU'VE LEARNED

1. Assume you have recently been hired by a firm that manufactures furniture. You feel that marketing should have an input into supplier selection for the firm's products but the purchasing department says that should not be a concern for marketing. You need to explain to him the importance of the value chain perspective. In a role-playing exercise, explain to the purchasing agent the value chain concept, why it is of concern to marketing, and why the two of you should work together.
2. Assume you are the director of marketing for a firm that manufactures cleaning chemicals used in industries. You have traditionally sold these products through manufacturer's reps. You are considering adding a direct Internet channel to your distribution strategy but you aren't sure whether this will create channel conflict. Make a list of the pros and cons of this move. What do you think is the best decision?
3. As the one-person marketing department for a candy manufacturer (your firm makes high-quality, hand-dipped chocolates using only natural ingredients), you are considering making changes in your distribution strategy. Your products have previously been sold through a network of food brokers that call on specialty food and gift stores. But you think that perhaps it would be good for your firm to develop a corporate VMS (i.e., vertical integration). In such a plan, a number of company-owned retail outlets would be opened across the country. The president of your company has asked that you present your ideas to the company executives. In a role-playing situation with one of your classmates, present your ideas to your boss including the advantages and disadvantages of the new plan compared to the current distribution method.
4. Assume that you have recently been given a new marketing assignment by your firm. You are to head up development of a distribution plan for a new product line—a series of do-it-yourself instruction videos for home gardeners. These videos would show consumers how to plant trees, shrubbery, and bulbs, how to care for their plants, how to prune, and so on. You know that in developing a distribution plan, it is essential you understand and consider a number of internal and external environmental factors. Make a list of the information you will need before you can begin developing the distribution plan. How will you adapt your plan based on each of these factors?

■ MARKETING MINI-PROJECT:
LEARNING BY DOING

In the United States, the distribution of most products is fairly easy. There are lots of independent intermediaries (wholesalers, dealers, distributors, and retailers) that are willing to cooperate to get the product to the final customer. Our elaborate interstate highway system combines with rail, air, and water transportation to provide excellent means for moving goods from one part of the country to another. In many other countries, the means for distribution of products are far less efficient and effective.

For this mini-project you and one or more of your classmates should first select a consumer product, probably one you normally purchase. Then use either or both library sources and other people (retailers, manufacturers, dealers, classmates, etc.) to gather information to do the following:

1. Describe the path the product takes to get from the producer to you. Draw a model to show each of the steps the product takes. Include as much as you can about transportation, warehousing, materials handling, order processing, inventory control, and so on.

2. Select another country in which the same or a similar product is sold. Describe the path the product takes to get from the producer to the customer in that country.

3. Determine if the differences between the two countries cause differences in price, availability, or quality of the product.

4. Make a presentation to your class on your findings.

■ REAL PEOPLE, REAL SURFERS:
EXPLORING THE WEB

Visit a Web site for a logistics company such as NYK Line (www2.nykline.com/nykinfo/main/global_home.html). What logistics services does the logistics firm offer its customers? What does the company say to convince prospective customers that its services are better than those of the competition?

■ PLAN IT!
DEVELOPING A
MARKETING PLAN

As your instructor directs, create a marketing plan (using Marketing Plan Pro software or a written marketing plan format) to document your marketing decisions or answer these questions in a written or oral report.

Take another look at the CFS marketing plan in Appendix A to understand how direct and indirect distribution channels are currently being used. Now continue working on next year's marketing plan.

1. From CFS's perspective, how many channel levels would be optimal—and why?

2. Is intensive, exclusive, or selective distribution most appropriate for CFS's Monitor Morphs?

3. What materials handling issues might arise for CFS products that include a CD-ROM?

Key Terms

breaking bulk, (498)
channel intermediaries, (497)
channel leader, (514)
channel levels, (504)
channel of distribution, (497)
conventional marketing
  system, (510)
creating assortments, (498)
exclusive distribution, (512)
facilitating functions, (499)

horizontal marketing system, (511)
hybrid marketing systems (507)
independent intermediaries, (502)
intensive distribution, (512)
inventory control, (521)
logistics, (515)
materials handling, (518)
merchandise agents or
  brokers, (502)
merchant wholesalers, (502)

physical distribution, (517)
selective distribution, (512)
supply chain, (515)
supply chain management, (515)
take title, (502)
value chain, (515)
vertical marketing system
  (VMS), (510)
warehousing, (518)
wholesaling intermediaries, (501)

MARKETING IN ACTION: CHAPTER 17 CASE

REAL CHOICES AT PEAPOD

Who says grocery shopping has to be a time-consuming hassle? Brothers Andrew and Thomas Parkinson had a different idea in 1989 when they founded Peapod, Inc., the country's first online grocery business. If Peapod succeeded, the company would radically change the way the $400 billion U.S. grocery industry operates. Based in Evanston, Illinois, Peapod turned its customers' PCs into grocery carts. For the busy woman with a 60-hour workweek and a family to feed, Peapod provided a virtual supermarket by allowing shoppers to place their orders from home and have them conveniently delivered without ever leaving the house.

Here's how the system works: Each day supermarkets that are partners with Peapod transmit computerized price updates on over 18,000 items from toothpaste to tofu. At-home shoppers can scan entire categories of products, just as they would if they were in the store walking down the grocery aisles. Items can be selected from broader categories (snacks), from more narrow categories (pretzels), or by brand name (Rold Gold). Regular users of the system can save even more time simply by calling up their own personal shopping lists. Because shoppers can sort items in the computer database by cost per ounce or per pound or check to see what's on sale today, it's easy to comparison shop for the most economical brand or size. Customers can indicate if they are willing to accept a substitute product if their selected brand is out of stock, and they can even specify precisely what they want, for example, a ripe avocado, two green bananas, or six large apples.

The Peapod distribution system offers other ways to make shoppers' lives easier as well. The service takes credit cards, checks, or online payments and even accepts coupons. The customer simply places an order, specifies a method of payment, indicates a preferred delivery time, and waits for the order to show up at the door. Once Peapod receives the order, it is forwarded to the closest grocery store partner where the specified items are collected by Peapod employees. These items are checked out at special Peapod counters and taken to a holding area where refrigerated and frozen goods can be safely stored until Peapod delivers them.

Peapod seemed like a great idea, but in January 1997, the jury was still out on whether the company would succeed. The company had never made a profit and in 1996 Peapod suffered a net loss of $9.5 million on revenues of $29.2 million. There were many doubters in the industry who questioned whether Peapod could ever turn the corner to profitability. These critics suggested that Internet grocery shopping was just a novelty distribution system doomed to eventual failure like many other computer shopping ventures. But Microsoft Chairman Bill Gates had predicted that one-third of food sales would be handled electronically by the year 2005. If this high-tech soothsayer is correct, Peapod is off to a good start toward cornering this market.

Indeed, to date Peapod has few competitors. Although this could be seen as a plus, it also could mean that other firms simply were hesitant to invest in such a risky venture. Although consumer surveys repeatedly indicate that shoppers are unwilling to pay extra for the privilege of shopping online, Peapod customers tend to be loyal and don't seem to wince at paying the $29.95 start-up fee, a $4.95 monthly service fee, and a $6.95 base charge per order plus 5 percent of their grocery bill. But to become profitable it seems that Peapod would have to make changes in its marketing strategy, such as raise its prices even more, increase its volume to spread fixed costs over a larger number of customers, or perhaps cut the level of service it provides to customers. Only time will tell if a sufficient number of harried shoppers are willing to write a bigger check to save time at the checkout.

Source: Susan Chandler, "The Grocery Cart in Your PC," *Business Week*, September 11, 1995, 63–64; http://adage.com/interactive/articles/19970609/article2.html;www.webreview.com/96/01/26/biz/olc/index.html.

THINGS TO THINK ABOUT

1. What is the decision facing Peapod?

2. What factors are important in understanding this decision situation?

3. What are the alternatives?

4. What decision(s) do you recommend?

5. What are some ways to implement your recommendation(s)?

Bookmark It!

OBJECTIVES:

1. Define retailing and understand how retailing evolves.
2. Describe how retailers are classified.
3. Describe direct selling and automatic vending, two forms of nonstore retailing.
4. Describe B2C e-commerce, its benefits, limitations, and future promise.
5. Understand the importance of store image to a retail positioning strategy and explain how a retailer can create an image in the marketplace.

Meet Dawn Robertson, a Decision Maker at Federated Direct

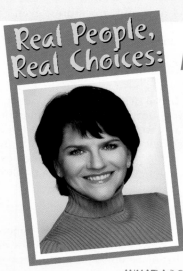

www.macys.com

www.bloomingdales.com

CURRENT POSITION: President and Chief Merchandising Officer.

EXPERIENCE: Before joining Federated, Dawn was president and chief executive officer of McCrae's, a division of Saks, Inc.

FIRST JOB OUT OF SCHOOL: Buyer and executive trainee with Davidson's, then a division of R.H. Macy & Co.

EDUCATION: B.S., Fashion Merchandising, Auburn University, 1977.

WHAT I DO WHEN I'M NOT WORKING: Activities with my daughters, water sports, biking.

BUSINESS BOOK I'M READING NOW: Jack: Straight from the Gut by Jack Welch and John A. Byrne.

MOTTO: "Dream big and dare to fail," Norman Vaughan, the explorer.

DON'T DO THIS WHEN INTERVIEWING WITH ME: Wink at me!

PET PEEVE: Lack of commitment—whatever you do in life, try hard and give it your best.

A Walk Down the (Store) Aisle

Discount stores, catalog companies, and online upstarts have been grabbing business right and left from department stores. Being the president and chief merchandising officer at Federated Direct, the Federated department stores' consumer catalog and e-commerce division, Dawn Robertson looked for ways to outperform these rivals. She saw one opportunity for growth in the bridal business, especially since increasing numbers of baby boomers' kids would be at the age to get married over the next decade. Since Federated added an Internet component to its Bridal Registry operation, the total bridal business (both in-store and online) now reported to her.

Under the right conditions, Dawn was convinced that Federated could acquire new customers and win the lifetime loyalty of millions of brides and grooms. In fact, her research showed that over half of women who get engaged shop at new stores as they prepare for the Big Day—and three years later 96 percent of them still are shopping in those stores. That's a relationship worth cultivating.

Even though Federated Stores, which include Macy's East and West, Bloomingdale's, Rich's, Lazarus, Goldsmiths, Burdines, and The Bon Marche, were recognized as the leaders in Bridal Registry, younger customers in greater numbers were going to newer, cooler specialty stores. To make matters worse, Dawn knew that a poor bridal registry experience could poison the relationship brides, grooms, and their wedding guests have with a store. She also recognized that Federated was not alone in seeing the potential of this business: Competition is fierce as retailers such as Bed, Bath and Beyond, Target, and Crate and Barrel lure droves of engaged couples to their registries.

Two other trends factored into Dawn's thinking: (1) Offering engaged couples personalized bridal consulting, once the advantage of the department store, was eroding as Web-savvy women were doing research online. (2) With the exception of certain brands of china,

527

specialty and discount stores were carrying the same merchandise as traditional department stores at cheaper prices.

So Dawn reviewed customer feedback gathered from 15,000 customer surveys, 10 focus groups, and evaluations of competitors conducted by Federated staff. The research found that consumers liked Federated's bridal merchandise over all, but in-store service and visual displays were in need of work. And, unlike some of its competitors' private-label offerings, Federated store brands did not evoke an emotional connection with its customers. Also, Dawn learned that brides- (and grooms) to-be love using the scanning gun that lets them scan in the items they want to register without the need for a salesperson. However, this cool tool was no longer novel or rare. Many stores, even discounters, offered a self-scan option.

Dawn had three options to enhance Federated's bridal services business:

Option 1: Offer a total bridal solution.

Maintain the existing bridal registry business, meaning the product offerings and service, but invest in buying bridal dress and tuxedo businesses, while developing alliances with a national florist and a bridal magazine to make Federated the "Total Bridal Location." This strategy would differentiate Federated from its competitors by offering a broad selection of services that the bride and groom need. But this option would require a significant investment. And these extra businesses would not be a core competency—it's difficult for big retailers to compete with smaller stores on customer service.

Option 2: Slowly enhance registry offerings.

Improve Federated's bridal offerings slowly without adding significant investment. Focus on providing better in-store training to sales representatives and better merchandise selection, particularly in the china and crystal categories that make up 50 percent of bridal sales. This conservative financial strategy would slightly increase sales and bridal registrations without draining the company of time and money. However, this strategy would not deter competitors from taking away bridal registry market share, and it would not establish Federated as a leader in this category.

Option 3: Completely redo the bridal registry.

Totally revamp Federated's core bridal business and give it a new marketing push. This strategy would require significant change in merchandise selection, pricing policies, and customer service. Such a radical move could either succeed beautifully or fail miserably. It would take management's time away from other initiatives, cost a lot of money, and be difficult to execute across both Federated's bricks-and-mortar and online operations.

Now, put yourself in Dawn Robertson's shoes: Which option would you choose, and why?

Retailing: Special Delivery

Shop 'til you drop! For many people, obtaining the product is half the fun. Others, of course, would rather walk over hot coals than spend time in a store. Marketers like Dawn Robertson need to find ways to deliver products and services that please both types of consumers. **Retailing** is the final stop on the distribution path—the process by which goods and services are sold to consumers for their personal use.

A retail outlet is more than a place to buy something. The retailer adds or subtracts value from the offering with its image, inventory, service quality, location, and pricing policy. In many cases the shopping experience is what is being bought as well as the products we take home. That's what visitors to the Discovery Channel store in Washington, DC, get when they meet up with a life-size model of a *Tyrannosaurus rex* on the main floor of the four-level store. The place feels like a museum with attractions such as a cockpit from a vintage World War II plane.[1] In a way, retailers are a special breed of marketer. The image through which they present products adds to a product's branding strategy.

retailing ■ The final stop in the distribution channel by which goods and services are sold to consumers for their personal use.

This chapter will explore the many different types of retailers, keeping one question in mind: How does a retailer—whether store or nonstore (selling via television, phone, or computer)—lure the consumer? Answering this question isn't getting any easier as the competition for customers has intensified because of the Internet and the growth of global retailers. So this chapter has plenty "in store" for us. Let's start with an overview of where retailing has been and where it's going.

RETAILING: A MIXED (SHOPPING) BAG

Retailing is big business. About one of every five U.S. workers is employed in retailing. There are over 1.2 million retail firms, but only about 8 percent of them have annual sales greater than $2.5 million. Although we tend to associate huge stores such as Wal-Mart and Sears with retailing activity, in reality most retailers are small businesses.[2] Certain retailers such as Home Depot also are wholesalers because they provide goods and services to businesses as well as end consumers.

As we said in Chapter 17, retailers are one of the members of a channel of distribution and as such provide time, place, and ownership utility for customers. Some retailers save people time or money by providing an assortment of merchandise under one roof. Others search the world for the most exotic delicacies, allowing shoppers access to goods they would otherwise never see. Still others, such as Barnes & Noble café/bookstores, provide us with interesting environments in which to spend our leisure time and, they hope, our money.

THE EVOLUTION OF RETAILING

Retailing has taken many forms over time, including the peddler who hawked his wares from a horse-drawn cart, a majestic urban department store, an intimate boutique, and a huge "hyperstore" that sells everything from potato chips to snow tires. But now that horse-drawn cart has been replaced by the cart you see at your local mall, selling new-age jewelry or monogrammed golf balls to passersby. As the economic, social, and cultural times change, different types of retailers emerge—often replacing older, outmoded types. How can marketers know what the dominant types of retailing will be tomorrow or 10 years from now?

The Wheel of Retailing   One of the oldest and simplest explanations for these changes is the **wheel-of-retailing hypothesis**. This states that new types of retailers find it easiest to enter the market by offering goods at lower prices than competitors.[3] After they gain a foothold, they gradually trade up, improving their facilities, increasing the quality and assortment of merchandise, and offering amenities such as parking and gift wrapping. This upscaling results in greater investment and operating costs, so the store must raise its prices to remain profitable, which then makes it vulnerable to still newer entrants that can afford to charge lower prices. And so the wheel turns.

The wheel of retailing helps to explain the development of some, but not all, forms of retailing. For example, some retailers never trade up; they simply continue to occupy a niche as discounters. Others, such as upscale specialty stores, start out at the high end. Of course, some retailers after experiencing success at the high end move down. That's what Crate & Barrel has done in introducing CB2, a cheaper sister chain.[4] Let's take a look at a more satisfying explanation for the evolution of retailing/retailers.

The Retail Life Cycle   Of course, retailers sell products. But in a way retailers also *are* products because they provide benefits such as convenience or status to consumers and they must offer a competitive advantage over other retailers to survive. So another way to understand how retailers evolve is the **retail life cycle**. Like the product life cycle, this explanation recognizes that retailers are born, they live, and eventually they die. The life cycle approach allows us to categorize retail stores by the conditions they face at different points in the cycle.[5]

In the *introduction* stage, the new retailer often is an aggressive entrepreneur who takes a unique approach to doing business. This may mean competing on the basis of low price, as the wheel of retailing suggests. However, the new guy on the block may also enter the market by offering a distinctive assortment or a different way to distribute items, such as through the Internet. In this initial stage, profits are low due to high development costs.

wheel-of-retailing hypothesis ■ A theory that explains how retail firms change, becoming more upscale as they go through their life cycle.

retail life cycle ■ A theory that focuses on the various stages that retailers pass through from introduction to decline.

The wheel of retailing suggests that new retailers enter the market by offering goods at lower prices than competitors.

As the business enters the *growth* stage, the retailer catches on with shoppers, and sales and profits rise. But a new idea doesn't stay new for long. Others start to copy it and competition increases, so the retailer needs to expand what it offers. Often the retailer responds by opening more outlets and developing systems to distribute goods to these new stores, which may cut profits as the firm invests in new buildings and fixtures.

By the time the business reaches the *maturity* stage, many other individual retailers have copied the unique idea of the original entrepreneuer to form an entire industry. The industry has overexpanded, and intense competition makes it difficult to maintain customer loyalty. Profits decline as competitors resort to price cutting to keep their customers. This pattern can be seen in department stores and fast-food chains like McDonald's.

Office supply superstores are entering the mature phase of the retail life cycle, which means they need to find ways of differentiating themselves other than price. Claiming "Business is crazy. Office Depot makes sense" in 1998, one of America's largest office supply chains enlisted the help of cartoon character Dilbert, America's favorite cubicle dweller, to forge a distinctive identity.[6]

In the *decline* stage retail businesses, like the general store or the peddler, become obsolete as newer ways of doing business emerge. Of course, the outmoded retailer does not have to fold its tent at this stage. Marketers that anticipate these shifts can avert decline by changing to meet the times. For example, full-service gas stations had difficulty competing with self-service discount outlets. Many responded by adding variety stores to their retail mix for drivers wanting to buy a tank of gas and groceries at the same location.

THE EVOLUTION CONTINUES: WHAT'S "IN STORE" FOR THE FUTURE?

As our world continues to change rapidly, retailers are scrambling to keep up. Three factors motivate innovative merchants to reinvent the way they do business. These are demographics, technology, and globalization.

Demographics   As we noted in Chapter 8, keeping up with changes in population characteristics is at the heart of many marketing developments. Retailers can no longer afford to stand by and assume that their customer base is the same as it has always been. They are coming up with new ways to sell their products to diverse groups.

For example, although many retailers chase after the same set of affluent customers, others are carving out markets by targeting lower-income households. Stores such as Dollar General, Dollar Tree, and Family Dollar profit by serving the needs of the four-out-of-ten

U.S. households that earn less than $25,000. These "value retailers," operating stores with bare-bones fixtures and offering cash-and-carry checkout only (no credit cards), have total sales of over $8 billion in merchandise per year.

Here are some of the ways changing demographics are altering the face of retailing:

- *Convenience for working women*: Some retailers are expanding their operating hours because many women no longer have time to shop during the day. Other retailers, including dry cleaners and pharmacies, are adding drive-up windows. In areas from financial services to interior decorating, enterprising individuals have turned time shortage into a business opportunity by becoming shopping consultants for busy women. Many major department stores offer in-house consultants at no charge.
- *Catering to specific age segments*: Retailers are seeing the benefits of serving specific age groups. For example, the global furniture superstore IKEA responded to its me-too rivals by developing a new concept called Children's IKEA that sells furniture and related products for kids. The company recruited psychologists to assist in creating 600 new products for this market, from egg-shaped cribs to fabric dolls.[7]
- *Recognizing ethnic diversity*: Although members of every ethnic group can usually find local retailers that cater to their specific needs, larger companies must tailor their strategies to the cultural makeup of specific areas. For example, in Texas, California, and Florida where there are large numbers of customers who speak only Spanish, many retailers make sure that there are sales associates who are Hispanic and speak Spanish.

Technology   In addition to demographics, technology is revolutionizing retailing. As we all know, the Internet has brought us the age of e-tailing. Whether it's a store that sells only on the Web or a traditional retailer such as Federated Department Stores that *also* sells on the Web, in general, retailing has evolved from bricks to clicks. Our personal computers have turned our homes into virtual malls. There are other technological advances that, believe it or not, have little to do with the Internet that are also helping to change our shopping experiences. In-store video channels entertain customers by giving messages about local events or showing ads.[8] Some stores feature talking posters containing a human body sensor that speaks up when a shopper approaches.[9] Other retailers, such as the A&P grocery chain, have installed wireless networks that allow shoppers to scan in their own items as they shop, eliminating the need for checkout lines.[10]

Some of the most profound changes are not even visible to shoppers, such as advanced electronic **point-of-sale (POS) systems**, which contain computer brains that collect sales data and are connected directly into the store's inventory control system. For example, every day 500 gigabytes of data are sent from JCPenney stores across the United States to their corporate headquarters in Dallas. From there, computer programs analyze patterns of demand for different products and automatically send orders to vendors.[11] This makes stores such as Penney's or Macy's more efficient. If shoppers in your area are buying a lot of wide-legged jeans, for example, the company can be sure that its store there will offer an ample selection for every hip-hop shopper.

Other technological innovations will radically change the way we shop in the future. JCPenney International makes these predictions about retailing in the year 2010: "Each consumer will have a personal preference card, so a store will know your tastes, clothing sizes, and even your current household decor. When shopping for furniture, a design consultant will call up a 3-D image of your living room, and show you how your new purchases will actually look in the room. Or, forget about endlessly trying on clothes—holographic imaging will let you 'see' yourself in a new suit or dress."[12] Sophisticated body scanners will be able to read a person's exact dimensions and send this information to machines that produce clothing precisely tailored to individual proportions.

point-of-sale (POS) systems ■ Retail computer systems that collect sales data and are hooked directly into the store's inventory control system.

1 Bookmark It!

Select a retailer that you visit often. What do you predict for retailers in the future based on the changes in demographics and technology that we discuss here? What might that store look like in 2010?

Globalization   As we saw in Chapter 4, the world is becoming a much smaller place. Retailers are busy expanding to other countries and bringing with them innovations and new management philosophies. Toys "R" Us, TGI Friday's, and Blockbuster Entertainment are among the global

success stories for U.S. retailers. Starbucks has become a household name in Japan (it is pronounced STAH-buks-zu). The coffee shops feature comfortable sofas, American hip-hop music, and large servings of gourmet brew. These are relatively new concepts in Japan, where café patrons had been accustomed to sitting in dimly lit shops and sipping from thimble-sized cups.[13]

Globalization is a two-way street. Innovative retailing concepts developed overseas are influencing U.S. retailing. For example, Shiseido operates stores that sell nothing but cosmetics and beauty products made by many companies conveniently organized by category (need 1,000 different shades of lipstick from which to choose?).

Of course, an understanding of global retailing means recognizing that retailing differs from country to country. In many developing countries, the retailing industry is made up of small individual retailers. In many parts of the developing world, kiosks, small street corner stands, sell cigarettes, soft drinks, snacks, cassette tapes, batteries—the products of convenience stores. In Shanghai, Internet orders for water are delivered by a nineteenth-century style pedicart—a kind of bicycle with a cart over the rear wheel.[14]

In planning expansion to other countries, companies must consider the way retailing is done in each country. In China, many independent retailers take their merchandise to open markets in pedicarts.

From Mom-and-Pop to Super Wal-Mart: Classifying Retail Stores

We've seen that exciting things are happening in the world of retailing. But the field of retailing covers a lot of ground—from mammoth department stores to sidewalk vendors to Web sites. This section will provide an overview of the different types of retailers. Retail marketers need to understand the competitive environment so they can decide how to offer their merchandise to the public and compare the productivity of their business to other similar retailers.

CLASSIFYING RETAILERS BY WHAT THEY SELL

One of the most important strategic decisions a retailer makes is *what* to sell—its **merchandise mix**. This choice is similar to settling on a market segment (as discussed in Chapter 8): If a store's merchandise mix is too limited, it may not have enough potential customers, whereas if it is too broad, the retailer runs the risk of being a "jack of all trades, master of none." Because what the retailer sells is central to its identity, we will describe some retail types by merchandise mix.

While we learned in Chapter 10 that a manufacturer's product line consists of product offerings that satisfy a single need, in retailing a *product line* is a set of related products offered by a retailer, such as kitchen appliances or leather goods. The Census of Retail Trade, conducted by the U.S. Bureau of the Census, classifies all retailers by North American Industry Classification System (NAICS) codes (the same system we described in Chapter 7 that is used to classify industrial firms). A retailer that wants to identify direct competition can find other firms that are classified by the same NAICS codes.

However, a word of caution: As retailers experiment with different merchandise mixes, these direct comparisons are getting harder to make. For example, even though marketers like to distinguish between food and nonfood retailers, in reality these lines are blurring. Supermarkets are adding hardware product lines, and some department stores offer gourmet food.

For a while, British shoppers could pick up a pair of cut-rate-priced Levi's jeans while food shopping.[15] In 2001, Levi Strauss sued Tesco, a big U.K. grocery store chain, to prevent it from buying jeans at a low price in the United States, importing them into the United Kingdom, and then selling the jeans at very low prices. Levi's argument was that it allows the sale of its jeans only in selected outlets that agree to provide the service and selection that customers want. Similar situations are common in retailing, such as warehouse stores that are not authorized dealers of designer clothing but are able to obtain the items at a low price and then stack the designer clothing on wooden palettes next to economy-size boxes of pretzels or jars of pickles.

The strategy of carrying a combination of food and nonfood items is called **scrambled merchandising**. This strategy is exemplified by Blockbuster Entertainment Group, which defines its merchandise mix in terms of products a customer might want when spending an evening at home, including food items and other goods. In addition to stocking your favorite James Bond video, the stores sell candy, soda, and even private-label popcorn to complete the couch potato experience.

> **merchandise mix** ■ The total set of all products offered for sale by a retailer, including all product lines sold to all consumer groups.

> **scrambled merchandising** ■ A merchandising strategy that offers consumers a mixture of merchandise items that are not directly related to each other.

CLASSIFYING RETAILERS BY LEVEL OF SERVICE

In Chapter 17 we said level of service to business customers was a way to classify merchant wholesalers. Retailers also differ in the amount of service they provide for consumers. Firms develop strategies for the level of service they will offer recognizing that there is a trade-off between service and low prices. Customers who demand higher levels of service must be willing to pay for that service, and those who want lower prices must be willing to give up services.

Retailers such as Sam's Club that promise bottom dollar prices are often self-service operations. With *self-service retailers*, customers make their product selection without any assistance, they often must bring their own bags or containers to carry their purchases, and they may even handle the checkout process with self-service scanners.

Then there are *full-service retailers*. Many of us prefer to shop at major department stores such as Bloomingdale's and specialty stores such as Victoria's Secret because they provide supporting services such as gift wrapping, and they offer trained sales associates who can assist in making a product selection. Other specialized services are available based on the merchandise offered. For example, many full-service clothing retailers will provide alterations services. Retailers such as Federated Department Stores that carry china, silver, housewares, and other items brides might want offer special bridal consultants and bridal gift registries.

Falling in between self-service and full-service retailers are *limited-service retailers*. Stores such as Wal-Mart, Target, Old Navy, and Kohl's offer credit and merchandise return but little else. Customers select merchandise without much assistance, preferring to pay a bit less rather than be waited on a bit more.

CLASSIFYING RETAILERS BY MERCHANDISE SELECTION

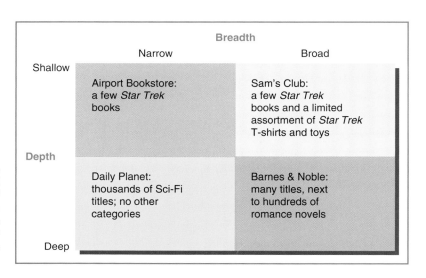

Another way to classify retailers is in terms of the selection they offer. A retailer's **merchandise assortment**, or selection of products sold, has two dimensions: breadth and depth. **Merchandise breadth**, or variety, is the number of different product lines available. A *narrow assortment*, such as that found in convenience stores, means that shoppers will find only a limited selection of product lines such as candy, cigarettes, and soft drinks. A *broad assortment*, such as that in a warehouse store, means there is a wide range of items from eyeglasses to barbecue grills.

Merchandise depth is the variety of choices available for each specific product. A *shallow assortment* means that the selection within a product category is limited, so a factory outlet store may sell only white and blue men's dress shirts (all made by the same manufacturer, of course) and only in standard sizes. In contrast, a men's specialty store may feature a *deep assortment* of dress shirts (but not much else) in varying shades and in hard-to-find sizes. Figure 18.1 illustrates these assortment differences for one product, science fiction books.

Now that we've seen how retailers differ in the breadth and depth of their assortments, let's review some of the major forms these retailers take.

Convenience Stores **Convenience stores** carry a limited number of frequently purchased items including basic food products, newspapers, and sundries. They cater to consumers willing to pay a premium for the ease of buying staple items close to home. In other words, they

---

merchandise assortment
The range of products sold.

merchandise breadth
The number of different product lines available.

merchandise depth The variety of choices available for each specific product line.

convenience stores
Neighborhood retailers that carry a limited number of frequently purchased items, and cater to consumers willing to pay a premium for the ease of buying close to home.

FIGURE 18.1

Retail stores are often classified based on the breadth and depth of their merchandise assortment. In this figure, the two dimensions are used to classify types of bookstores that carry science fiction books.

Convenience stores such as 7–11 offer consumers just that, convenience, by carrying a limited number of frequently purchased items.

meet the needs of those who are pressed for time, who buy items in smaller quantities, or who shop at irregular hours.

Supermarkets   **Supermarkets** are food stores that carry a wide selection of edibles and nonedible products. The modern supermarket first appeared in the 1930s with the opening of the King Kullen store in Brooklyn, New York. At the time, Kullen's large breadth and depth were a radical departure for retailers that, aided by such inventions as the automobile and refrigerator, could now offer shoppers a wider selection of goods at lower prices than "mom and pop" food stores. Although the large supermarket is a fixture in the United States, it has not caught on to the same extent in other parts of the world. Europeans, for example, are used to walking or biking to small stores near their homes. They tend to have smaller food orders per trip and to shop more frequently. Wide variety is less important than quality and local ambiance, though as we'll see shortly, those habits are changing as huge hypermarkets have become popular overseas as well.

supermarkets ■ Food stores that carry a wide selection of edibles and related products.

Specialty Stores   **Specialty stores** have narrow and deep inventories. They do not sell a lot of product lines, but they offer good selection of brands within the lines they do sell. One store in the Mall of America in Minnesota sells nothing but refrigerator magnets (but just about any magnet you'd care to buy), certainly a narrow and deep inventory. Specialty stores can tailor their assortment to the specific needs of a targeted consumer, and they often offer a high level of knowledgeable service.

specialty stores ■ Retailers that carry only a few product lines but offer good selection within the lines that they sell.

Discount Stores   **General merchandise discount stores**, such as Sears, Kmart, and Wal-Mart, offer a broad assortment of items at low prices and with minimal service. Discounters are tearing up the retail landscape because they appeal to price-conscious shoppers who want easy access to a lot of merchandise. Kohl's, for example, is the nation's fastest-growing retailer. These stores increasingly carry designer name clothing at bargain prices as companies such as Liz Claiborne are creating new lines just for discount stores.[16]

The mass-merchandise approach to retailing is exemplified by Sears' motto: "Sears has everything." After an unsuccessful attempt to change its identity to an upscale department store, Sears reverted to its roots, promoting itself as "Brand Central," meaning shoppers could find well-known brand names for appliances and other products within its walls.

Some discount stores, such as Loehmann's, are **off-price retailers**. These stores obtain surplus merchandise from manufacturers and offer these brand-name, fashion-oriented goods at low prices.

general merchandise discount stores ■ Retailers that offer a broad assortment of items at low prices with minimal service.

off-price retailers ■ Retailers that buy excess merchandise from well-known manufacturers and pass the savings on to customers.

warehouse clubs ■
Discount retailers that charge
a modest membership fee to
consumers that buy a broad
assortment of food and nonfood
items in bulk and in a
warehouse environment.

Warehouse clubs such as Costco and BJ's are a newer version of the discount store. These establishments do not even pretend to offer any of the amenities of a full-service store; a bargain mentality is reinforced by merchandise that is displayed (often in its original box) in a cavernous, bare-bones facility. These clubs often charge a modest membership fee to consumers and small businesses, which buy a broad assortment of food and nonfood items in bulk sizes. The typical warehouse shopper is likely to have a large family and a relatively high income and can afford to pay several hundred dollars to "stock up" on staples during one shopping trip.[17] Nothing like laying in a three-year supply of paper towels or 5-pound box of pretzels—even if you have to build an extra room in your house to store all this stuff!

factory outlet store ■   A
discount retailer, owned by
a manufacturer, which sells
off defective merchandise and
excess inventory.

The **factory outlet store** is still another type of discount retailer. These stores are owned by a manufacturer, which uses this outlet to sell off its defective merchandise or excess inventory.[18] Although the assortment is not wide because a store carries only products made by one manufacturer, a recent trend is for different factory outlet stores to cluster together in the same location to form an *outlet mall*. And, in keeping with the wheel-of-retailing idea, we tend to see outlet malls adding amenities such as elaborate food courts and local entertainment.

department stores ■
Retailers that sell a broad range of
items and offer a good selection
within each product line.

Department Stores   **Department stores** such as those operated by Federated sell a broad range of items and offer a deep selection organized into different sections of the store. Grand stores dominated urban centers in the early part of this century. In their heyday, these stores sold airplanes and auctioned fine art. Lord & Taylor even offered its customers a mechanical horse to assure the perfect fit of riding habits.

Department stores have struggled in recent years. Specialty stores have lured department store shoppers away with deeper, more cutting-edge fashion selections and better service. Department stores have also been squeezed by mass merchandisers and catalogs that can offer the same items at lower prices because they don't have the expense of rent, elaborate store displays and fixtures, high salaries for knowledgeable salespeople, and so on. These problems have been compounded since September 11, 2001, because consumers have lost interest in buying pricey status symbols from upscale stores—shoppers are more interested in price and value than in a store's reputation or the way merchandise is presented on the sales floor.[19]

As we saw in Dawn Robertson's situation at Federated, department stores are searching for different strategies to compete. Some retail stores have pruned their assortments to concentrate more on soft goods, such as clothing and home furnishings, and less on hard goods, such as appliances. Macy's dropped its electronics department altogether and used the space instead to create its highly successful Macy's Cellar, which features tastefully displayed cooking items and food.

hypermarkets ■   Retailers
with the characteristics of
both warehouse stores and
supermarkets; hypermarkets
are several times larger than
other stores and offer virtually
everything from grocery items
to electronics.

Some department stores are trying to go upscale by introducing amenities such as valet parking (remember the wheel of retailing); others are competing more directly with discount stores by offering shopping carts. Others such as Nordstrom and Saks Fifth Avenue are cutting prices whereas others such as May Company are trying to grow by targeting specific types of customers such as brides. Federated is trying a different strategy: To increase sales for young women's clothing, the chain is enhancing young women's departments with new sound systems and Internet access. The chain is also placing these departments near the young men's department to create more of a social atmosphere.[20]

2 *Bookmark It!*

Make a list of all the retailers you have shopped with for the past month or so. Then classify each retailer on that list. What types of retailers do you patronize most frequently? What types do you seldom or never shop with? What do you especially like or dislike about each of these retail alternatives?

Hypermarkets   **Hypermarkets** combine the characteristics of warehouse stores and supermarkets. Originally introduced in Europe, these are huge establishments several times larger than other stores. A supermarket might be 40,000 to 50,000 square feet, whereas a hypermarket takes up 200,000 to 300,000 square feet, or four football fields. They offer one-stop shopping, often for over 50,000 items, and feature restaurants, beauty salons, and children's play areas. Hypermarkets, such as those run by the French firm Carrefours, are popular in Europe and Latin America where big stores are somewhat of a novelty. They haven't caught on as well in the United States where so many discount stores, malls, and supermarkets are available. U.S. consumers find the hypermarkets to be too large and shopping in them too time-consuming.[21]

Continente, a Spanish hypermarket, offers one-stop shopping and includes a variety of smaller stores within the store.

Nonstore Retailing

The Buckle succeeds because it puts cool merchandise in the hands of young shoppers who can't get it elsewhere. But competition for shoppers' dollars comes from sources other than traditional stores, ranging from bulky catalogs to dynamic Web sites. Debbie in Dubuque can easily log on to alloy.com at 3:00 A.M. and order the latest belly-baring fashions without leaving home.

Many products are readily available in places other than stores. Think of the familiar Avon Lady selling beauty products to millions of women around the world. Avon allows customers to place orders by phone, fax, catalog, or through a sales representative.

Avon's success at giving customers alternatives to traditional store outlets illustrates the increasing importance of **nonstore retailing**, which is any method a firm uses to complete an exchange that does not require a customer visit to a store. Americans spend almost $60 billion using catalogs, TV shopping channels, the Web, and other nonstore formats.[22] Many retail stores even offer nonstore alternatives to buying their merchandise, such as using catalogs and Web sites. As the founder of the Neiman-Marcus department store acknowledged, "If customers don't want to get off their butts and go to your stores, you've got to go to them."[23]

We talked about direct marketing done through the mail, the telephone, and television in Chapter 15. In this section we'll look at two other types of nonstore retailing, direct selling and automatic vending.

nonstore retailing ■ Any method used to complete an exchange with a product end user that does not require a customer visit to a store.

DIRECT SELLING

Direct selling occurs when a salesperson presents a product to one individual or a small group, takes orders, and delivers the merchandise. This form of nonstore retailing works well for products such as vacuum cleaners, nutritional products, and educational materials—products that require a great deal of information to sell. Most people involved in direct selling are independent agents who buy the merchandise from the company and then resell it to consumers.

direct selling ■ An interactive sales process in which a salesperson presents a product to one individual or a small group, takes orders, and delivers the merchandise.

Door-to-Door Sales   Although door-to-door selling is popular in some countries such as China, it is declining in the United States because few women are home during the day and those who are home are reluctant to open their doors to strangers. Companies that used to rely on door-to-door sales have had to adapt their retailing strategies. Avon now sells to women at the office during lunch and coffee breaks. Similarly, Tupperware features rush-hour office parties at the end of the workday and finds that about 20 percent of its sales come from outside the home. An employee of Mary Kay Cosmetics, which has also adopted this strategy, offered an explanation for its success: "Working women buy more in the office because they are not looking at the wallpaper that needs replacing. They feel richer away from home."[24]

PARTIES AND NETWORKS

About three-quarters of direct sales are made in the consumer's home, sometimes at a home shopping party, at which a company representative makes a sales presentation to a group of people who have gathered in the home of a friend.[25] People who attend may get caught up in the "group spirit," buying things they would not normally buy if alone.[26] This technique is called a **party plan system**.

Another form of nonstore retailing, epitomized by the Amway Company, is called a **multilevel network**, or network marketing. In this system a master distributor recruits other people to become distributors. The master distributor sells the company's products to the people she entices to join and receives commissions on all the merchandise sold by the people she recruits.

One of the advantages of multilevel marketing is that it allows firms to reach consumers who belong to tightly knit groups not easy to reach. Salt Lake City–based Nu Skin Enterprises relies on Mormons to sell its products in Mormon communities. Shaklee (which sells food supplements, cleaning products, and personal care items) recruits salespeople in isolated religious communities including Amish and Mennonite people (who receive "bonus buggies" instead of cars as prizes for superior salesmanship).[27] Despite the growing popularity of this technique, some network systems are illegal. They are really **pyramid schemes** in which the

party plan system ■ A sales technique that relies heavily on people getting caught up in the "group spirit," buying things they would not normally buy if alone.

multilevel network ■ A system in which a master distributor recruits other people to become distributors, sells the company's product to the recruits, and receives a commission on all the merchandise sold by the people recruited.

pyramid schemes ■ An illegal sales technique in which the initial distributors profit by selling merchandise to other distributors, with the result that consumers buy very little product.

Amway uses a multilevel network, one type of direct selling, to sell its many products. Amway's global expansion includes China, where Amway products have gained popularity.

While vending machines are popular for sales of convenience products such as soft drinks, they can also be used for other products. Levi Strauss sells jeans in vending machines to French consumers.

initial distributors profit by selling merchandise to other distributors—very little product ever gets to consumers.[28]

AUTOMATIC VENDING

Coin-operated vending machines are a tried-and-true way to sell convenience goods, especially cigarettes and drinks. These machines are appealing because they require minimal space and personnel to maintain and operate.

Some of the most interesting innovations are state-of-the-art vending machines, which dispense everything from Ore-Ida french fries to software. French consumers can even purchase Levi's jeans from a machine called Libre Service that offers the pants in 10 different sizes. Due to their frenetic lifestyles, the Japanese are avid users of vending machines. These machines, a cluster of which can be found on many Tokyo street corners, dispense virtually all of life's necessities, plus many luxuries people in other countries would not consider obtaining from a machine. The list includes jewelry, fresh flowers, frozen beef, pornography, business cards, underwear, and even the names of possible dates.[29]

In general, vending machines are best suited to the sales of inexpensive merchandise and food and beverages. Most consumers are reluctant to buy pricey items from a machine. New vending machines may spur more interest, however, as technological developments such as video kiosk machines that let people see the product in use, the ability to accept credit cards as payment, and inventory systems that signal the operator when malfunctions or stock-outs occur, loom on the horizon.

3 Bookmark It!

In developed countries such as the United States and countries of the European Union, vending machines are commonplace. However, you seldom find vending machines in developing countries. What do you think are some reasons for this?

B2C E-Commerce

Business-to-consumer (B2C) e-commerce is the online exchange between companies and individual consumers. Forrester Research predicts that by 2004, 49 million households will be online shoppers compared with 17 million in 1999. U.S. consumers will spend $184 billion

business-to-consumer (B2C) e-commerce ■
Online exchanges between companies and individual consumers.

TABLE 18.1

B2C Sales by Product
Category

Product Category	1999 Online Sales (in $millions)	Projected 2004 Online Sales (in $millions)
Computer hardware	1,964	12,541
Computer software	1,240	3,290
Books	1,202	3,279
Music	848	4,286
Videos	326	1,743
General apparel	1,061	22,516
Footwear	121	1,085
Household goods	250	5,755
Toys and video games	253	3,663
Food and beverage	513	16,863
Furniture	268	3,884
Leisure travel	7,798	32,097

Source: Adapted from Seema Williams, David M. Cooperstein, David E. Weisman, and Thalika Oum, *Post-Web Retail*, Forrester Research, Inc., September 1999.

annually (7 percent of all retail sales) or nearly $4,000 per household.[30] That's a lot of CDs and sweaters.

What is powering this online retail growth? As more people shop, more retailers will enter the Web marketplace, making more types of products available. At the same time, enhanced technology and improvements in delivery and security will entice even more consumers to shop online. Table 18.1 shows 1999 and predicted 2004 B2C sales in various product categories.

We are just beginning to see the enormous potential of electronic commerce in retailing. The success of this nonstore format will depend on the ability of retailers to offer sites that are entertaining and informative and that are worth surfing to even after the novelty wears off. Gap, for example, offers a Web site with a page that allows the shopper to mix and match colors and styles on the computer, a service that can't be matched by a conventional catalog.

BENEFITS OF B2C E-COMMERCE

For both consumers and marketers, B2C e-commerce provides a host of benefits and some limitations. Some of these are listed in Table 18.2. E-commerce allows consumers and marketers to easily find and make exchanges in a global marketplace—consumers can choose from hundreds of thousands of sellers worldwide and marketers can tap into consumer and business markets with no geographic limitations.

From the consumer's perspective, electronic marketing has increased convenience by breaking down many of the barriers caused by time and location. You can shop 24 hours a day without leaving home. Electronic marketing makes more products available to consumers. Consumers in even the smallest of communities can purchase funky shoes or a hot swimsuit from Bloomingdales.com just like big city dwellers. In less developed countries, the Internet lets consumers purchase products that may not be available at all in local markets. Thus, the Internet can improve the quality of life without the necessity of developing costly infrastructure such as opening retail stores in remote locations.

Understanding just what online shoppers really desire and why they are shopping online can help marketers to be more successful. For some consumers, online shopping provides an additional benefit by fulfilling their experiential needs, that is, their need to shop for fun.[31] Consumers who are collectors or who enjoy hobbies are most likely to be **experiential shoppers**. While most online consumers engage in goal-directed behavior—they wish to satisfy their shopping goal as quickly as possible—between 20 and 30 percent of online consumers

experiential shopper ■
Consumers who engage in online shopping because of the experiential benefits they receive.

Benefits of E-Commerce	Limitations of E-Commerce	TABLE 18.2
For the consumer	*For the consumer*	Benefits and Limitations of E-Commerce
Shop 24 hours a day	Lack of security	
Less traveling	Fraud	
Can receive relevant information in seconds from any location	Can't touch items	
More product choices	Exact colors may not reproduce on computer monitors	
More products available to less developed countries	Expensive to order and then return	
Greater price information	Potential breakdown of human relationships	
Lower prices so that less affluent can purchase		
Participate in virtual auctions		
Fast delivery		
Electronic communities		
For the marketer	*For the marketer*	
The world is your marketplace	Lack of security	
Decreases costs of doing business	Must maintain site to reap benefits	
Very specialized businesses can be successful	Fierce price competition	
Real-time pricing	Conflicts with conventional retailers	
	Legal issues not resolved	

shop online because they enjoy the "thrill of the hunt" as much or more than the actual acquisition of the item. Experiential shoppers stick to sites longer and are motivated by a desire to be entertained. Consequently, marketers who wish to attract these customers must design Web sites that offer surprise, uniqueness, and excitement. LandsEnd.com gives frequent markdowns on overstock items encouraging bargain-hunter experiential shoppers to visit the site more frequently. How well a site satisfies experiential needs might determine how much money consumers will choose to spend at that site.

Marketers realize equally important benefits from e-commerce. Because marketers can reach such a large number of consumers with electronic commerce, it is possible to develop very specialized businesses that could not be profitable if limited by geographic constraints. For example, although your town may not have enough fanatic dog owners to support a doggie toy store, there are a number of sites on the Web including dogtoys.com and petexpo.net that cater to the needs of pampered pooches.

For companies large and small, the Internet offers opportunities to build relationships with customers. General Mills has a Betty Crocker Web site (www.bettycrocker.com) that offers recipe suggestions.[32] Another General Mills site (www.mycereal.com) offers customized breakfast cereals.[33]

As we discussed in Chapter 12, one of the biggest advantages of e-commerce is that it's easy to get price information. Want to buy a new textbook for your class? Instead of going from store to store to compare prices, students can use search engines or "shop bots" that go out on the Web and get price information from sellers such as Bigwords.com or Textbooks.com in a matter of minutes. With readily available pricing information, shoppers can spend their dollars more efficiently, and less affluent consumers can afford to purchase a greater variety of goods and services.

E-commerce also allows businesses to reduce costs. Compared to traditional bricks-and-mortar retailers, cost for e-tailers is minimal—no expensive mall sites and no need for in-store sales associates.

For some products, such as computer software and digitized music, e-commerce provides fast, almost instantaneous delivery. Many college students have already begun downloading their favorite artists' recordings via highly compressed, CD-quality MP3 music files. This benefit to consumers, in fact, created the first major legal battle of the Internet age.[34] Beginning in

For students at thousands of universities, the Internet means that it's no longer necessary to stand in long lines at the bookstore on a hot August afternoon—or a cold January morning. Ecampus.com is one of many B2C e-commerce sites where students can buy textbooks.

2000, consumers could download music at no charge, thanks to a program created by 19-year-old college dropout Shawn Fanning. Although Napster didn't store music on its own servers, the Napster program allowed its members to download music that other Napster members had on their computers. After being sued by the Recording Industry Association of America as well as heavy-metal band Metallica, Napster closed its service in July 2001 in preparation for a trial with the recording industry.[35] In Napster's place, a number of for-pay download sites, including some owned by record companies themselves, have begun offering downloaded music for a monthly fee. And other free sites such as Morpheus continue to spring up like weeds. No matter what the outcome of the Napster trial, the moral is that the Internet has changed the music industry forever.[36]

LIMITATIONS OF B2C E-COMMERCE

Alas, all is not perfect in the virtual world. E-commerce does have its limitations. One drawback relative to shopping in a store is that customers still must wait a few days to receive the products, which are often sent via private delivery services, so shoppers can't achieve instant gratification by walking out of a store clutching their latest "finds." And many e-commerce sites still suffer from poor design that people find confusing or irritating. One study found that 65 percent of online shoppers empty their carts before they complete their purchase because they find the process hard to follow and there are not "flesh and blood" customer service people available to answer questions. To make matters worse, 30 percent of online shoppers who have problems with a Web site say they won't shop there again and 10 percent say they won't shop online at all anymore.[37]

Security is a concern to both consumers and marketers. We hear horror stories of consumers whose credit cards and other identity information have been stolen. Although an individual's financial liability in most theft cases is limited to $50, the damage to one's credit rating can last for years.

Consumers also are concerned about Internet fraud. Although most of us feel competent to judge a local bricks-and-mortar business by its physical presence, how long it's been around, and from the reports of friends and neighbors who shop there, we have little or no information on the millions of Internet sites offering their products for sale.

Another problem is that people need "touch-and-feel" information before buying many products. Although it may be satisfactory to buy a computer or a book on the Internet, buying clothing and other items where touching the item or trying it on is essential may be less

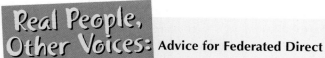

Camilo Montoya, Student, Pennsylvania State University

I would choose option 1 because it would best differentiate Federated's bridal offerings from the competition by repositioning an image of being a department store with bridal merchandise to a "Total Bridal Location." In searching for Federated's most distinctive competitive advantage, it is important to find out why 96 percent of the customers are loyal after three years. Internal and intercompany communication is essential to efficiently and effectively realize the change. Acquiring a national florist and bridal magazine will establish the infrastructure to promote a "one-stop" solution to complicated wedding planning, also making sure to guarantee customer satisfaction with high-quality service and expertise. Initial costs will be high, but repositioning Federated as a complete bridal location as part of a strong IMC strategy will prove beneficial.

Robert Cosenza, Marketing Professor, Christian Brothers University

I would choose option 3. Dawn is very savvy about the emotional and interactive requirements of her younger target audience. Therefore, she should develop a multivariety branding strategy along with alliances with other symbiotic Web retailers that can complement the Federated business model. Although the initial costs are high, these costs could be allocated across Federated stores. Although a change of bricks and mortar culture must take place, the dynamics of supply chain management with e-commerce, plus the fact that Federated would not really incur the costs of brand merchandise inventory, would make this option to be not as risky or expensive as first thought. The ROI potential would be enormous if properly executed with the proper business model.

Jen Dulski, Senior Brand Manager, Yahoo!

I would choose option 2 because it directly addresses the two major needs pointed out in the consumer research (in-store service and visual displays) without requiring a major investment. Although the other two options may have more potential to push Federated into a leadership position, they are too risky to undertake without more consumer insight about whether those directions make sense for Federated's brand and overall corporate strategy. Option 1 not only takes Federated outside of its core competency but also is a significant departure from its brand equity—it could be quite a stretch to get consumers to think of Federated as the "Total Bridal Location." Similarly, option 3 strays from the core attributes that consumers associate with Federated. By putting a heavy marketing push behind the bridal registry and shifting its merchandise mix, Federated could actually detract from its core business and primary consumer base, which might cause more harm than good.

Martha Garnica, Principal, Associate Media Director, Optimedia International

You can tell that Dawn has done her homework. There is definitely an opportunity to boost Federated sales via the bridal department. Based on the facts and the research conducted with store consumers, I would choose option 2. As a marketer you need to understand your category and the needs of your consumers. The research shows that once married, brides are loyal to stores where they have had a good store experience. Federated does have some issues that Dawn has to focus on, which is why I think option 2 is the better option. She is able to slowly improve the bridal department without completely revamping things (Option 3) or adding new services (Option 1). Both of these options do not address the underlying issues of in-store service, visual displays and store brand merchandise. Once Dawn resolves these issues, she can explore the online opportunities.

Weigh in with your thoughts! Visit the Live Laboratory at www.prenhall.com/solomon for extended Other Voices replies, exercises, and more.

attractive. As with catalogs, even though most online companies have liberal return policies, consumers can still get stuck with large delivery and return shipping charges for items that don't fit or simply aren't the right color. Although online sales account for more than a quarter of the personal computers sold, less than 2 percent of apparel sales are transacted this way—and 30 percent of this clothing bought online will be returned.[38] These problems help to explain why companies such as Tupperware, Amway, and Mary Kay discourage Internet sales.

Executives at Tupperware want shoppers to be able to "burp" their plastic containers to appreciate their airtight qualities.[39]

In some cases ingenious businesspeople find ways to combine electronic retailing with traditional shopping to overcome this barrier. For example, peapod.com offers home delivery of groceries that have been selected by a "personal shopper" who fills Internet orders based on customers' exact preferences, even squeezing to be sure they correspond to the person's ripeness specifications.[40] Some retailers have tried to mix things up by showing activity in their physical stores on their Web sites: Stores such as F.A.O. Schwarz and the Canal Jean Company in Manhattan have installed cameras to beam images from their stores over the Internet. Webcams can be pointed at merchandise and photos are sent to remote viewers so they can check out what's on the racks (not to mention who is shopping in the store!) without leaving home.[41]

The giddy, early days of e-commerce (where it seems that start-up e-tailers were doing so well they were printing their own money) may be over. We're now seeing a huge shakeout as many aspiring Jeff Bezoses (the CEO of Amazon.com) find that e-commerce is not quite the paradise it was first cracked up to be. Shares of once high-flying companies such as Value America, CDNow, Etoys, and even the formidable Amazon.com are skidding as investors and venture capitalists are now demanding to see real profits rather than mere promises. Ironically, one reason for this wake-up call is that e-commerce is *too* efficient: True, some costs are reduced because the overhead associated with running a store and paying sales help is sharply reduced. However, e-tailers have to keep their prices very low to please customers who have learned that a better price could be just a click away at the other approximately 30,000 Web sites offering products for sale.

Traditional bricks-and-mortar companies such as Federated are actually *more* likely to be successful in cyberspace than are Internet-only start-ups because they already have established brand names and a base of loyal customers. From Wal-Mart to Circuit City, traditional retailers are going online, many combining their Web retailing with existing stores. For example, at Circuit City and Office Depot, customers can check the inventories of stores near them for availability of an item and then pick the item up at the store.[42]

Catalog companies have had the easiest time making the transition to the Web, since they have the most experience delivering goods directly to consumers. That explains why almost three-quarters of these firms have profitable e-commerce sites, whereas less than 40 percent of other Web retailers are in the black so far.[43]

We're also seeing movement in the opposite direction. Online travel companies like Expedia.com are adding off-line operations and buying traditional travel agencies (in 2002 Expedia paid $48 million to acquire a retail chain called Classic Custom Vacations). These businesses recognize that many shoppers use the Web to research their travel options but then actually purchase their tickets off-line due to concerns about security and privacy. As one online analyst observed, "A lot of folks who used to think we live in a milk-or-meat world are now realizing that travelers aren't kosher. They'll buy the type of travel they want through the channel they want."[44]

Another obstacle to B2C e-commerce is found in developing countries with primarily cash economies. In these countries, few people use credit cards and so they can't easily pay for items they purchase over the Internet. An alternative for payments that may gain popularity in the future is *digital cash*. Currently digital cash is available on prepaid cards and smart cards such as a prepaid phone card. Another alternative is e-cash, developed by Digicash of Amsterdam. E-cash provides secure payments between computers using e-mail or the Internet. You can use e-cash to buy a pizza or to get money from home. To do so you need e-cash client software and a *digital bank account*, a Web-based account that allows you to make payments to Internet retailers directly from the account while online. You withdraw money from your bank account, store it on your computer, and spend it when you need to. When the going gets tough, the tough go shopping!

As major marketers beef up their presence on the Web, they worry that inventory they sell online will cannibalize their store sales. This is a big problem for companies such as bookseller Barnes & Noble, which has to be careful about steering customers toward a Web site and away from its chain of stores bursting with inventory. Barnes & Noble has to deal with competitors such as Amazon.com (with 2.25 million worldwide customers and sales close to $350 million a year), which sells its books and music exclusively over the Web.[45]

4 *Bookmark It!*

With several members of your class, conduct interviews with five or six consumers of different demographic groups. Ask them if they have purchased any products on the Internet. Then ask what they see as benefits and limitations of the Internet for them.

4 *Bookmark It!*

Visit some Web sites that also have retail outlets such as Barnes & Noble (www.bn.com), Gap (www.gap.com), and Wal-Mart (www.walmart.com). How do these sites try to avoid taking customers away from their retail stores? Do you think the Web sites help create loyal customers?

Traditional retailers such as Wal-Mart may find it easy to be successful in cyberspace because they already have established brand names and a base of loyal customers.

B2C's EFFECT ON THE FUTURE OF RETAILING

Does the growth of B2C e-commerce mean the death of bricks-and-mortar stores as we know them? Don't plan any funerals prematurely. Although some argue that virtual distribution channels will completely replace traditional ones because of their cost advantages, this is unlikely. For instance, although a bank saves 80 percent of its costs when customers do business online from their home computers, Wells Fargo found that it could not force its customers to use PC-based banking services. At least in the short term, too many people are accustomed to obtaining goods and services from stores—and, of course, shopping provides a social outlet that (at least now) can't be replaced by solitary surfing. At least in the near future, clicks will have to coexist with bricks.[46]

Stores as we know them will have to continue to evolve to lure shoppers away from their computer screens. In the future, the trend will be "destination retail." Many retailers are already developing ways to make the shopping in bricks-and-mortar stores an experience rather than just a place to pick up stuff. For example, Levi Strauss opened a retail store in San Francisco that features a "shrink-to-fit" hot tub, fabric painting and ornamentation services, and a showcase of new music, art, and Levi's product samples from around the world. The Bass Pro shop in Gurnee, Illinois, allows customers to try out fishing equipment in an in-store trout stream, whereas Sony's Metreon, also in San Francisco, is a high-tech mall featuring futuristic computer games and cutting-edge electronics.[47]

Developing a Store Positioning Strategy: Retailing as Theater

A "destination retail" strategy reminds us that shopping often is part buying, part entertainment, and part social outlet. So far we've seen that stores can be distinguished in several ways, including the types of products they carry, and the breadth and depth of their assortments. But recall that stores themselves are a product that adds to or subtracts from the goods the shopper came to buy. When we are deciding which store to patronize, many of us are less likely to say "I'll go there because their assortment is broad," and more likely to say "That place is so cool.

The REI store in Seattle provides a unique shopping experience that includes a 65-foot high artificial climbing rock, a bike trail, and this pseudo campground.

I really enjoy hanging out there." Stores can entertain us, they can bore us, they can make us angry, or even make us sad (unless it's a funeral parlor, that variety probably won't be in business for long). In today's competitive marketplace, retailers have to do more than offer good inventory at reasonable prices. They need to position their stores so that they offer a competitive advantage over other stores also vying for the shopper's attention—not to mention the catalogs, Web sites, and shopping channels that may offer the same or similar merchandise without having to leave home. Let's see next how bricks-and-mortar retailers are competing.

Walk into REI, a Seattle-based store that sells gear for climbing, cycling, skiing, and camping. REI is more than that, though. The store features a 65-foot-high, artificial climbing rock, a vented area for testing camp stoves, and an outdoor trail to check out mountain bikes. Buying a water pump? Test it in an indoor river. Eyeing that new Gore-tex jacket? See how it holds up in a simulated rainstorm.[48]

In Chapter 11, we saw that staging a service is much like putting on a play. Similarly, many retailers recognize that much of what they do is theater. At a time when it is possible to pick up a phone or log on to a computer to buy many items, a customer must have a reason to make a trip to a store instead. True, you can probably buy that jacket over the Web, but try getting your computer to rain on it.

Shoppers are an audience to entertain. The "play" can cleverly employ stage sets (store design) and actors (salespeople) that together create a "scene." For example, think about buying a pair of sneakers. Athletic shoe stores are a far cry from the old days, when a tired shoe salesman (much like Al Bundy in the TV show *Married with Children*) waded through box after box of shoes as kids ran amok across dingy floors. Now salespeople (actors) are dressed in costumes such as black-striped referee outfits. Stores such as Woolworth's World Foot Locker are ablaze with neon, with the shoes displayed in clear acrylic walls so they appear to be floating.[49] All these special effects make the buying occasion less about buying and more about having an experience. As one marketing strategist commented, "The line between retail and entertainment is blurring."[50] In this section we'll review some of the tools available to the retailing playwright.

STORE IMAGE

When people think of a store, they often have no trouble portraying it in the same terms they might use in describing a person. They might use words such as *exciting, depressed, old-fashioned, tacky,* or *elegant.* **Store image** is how the target market perceives the store—its market position relative to the competition. Even stores operated by the same parent company such as Federated can be

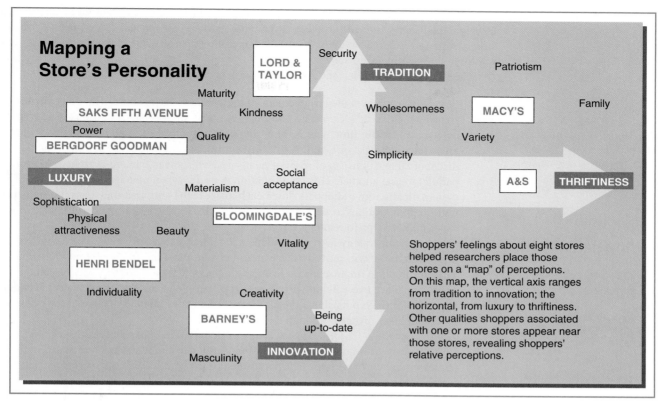

FIGURE 18.2

Mapping a Store's Personality

Marketers can use perceptual mapping to chart the personality of retail stores.

Source: Adapted from BBDO; Stephanie From, "Image and Attitude Are Department Stores' Draw," *New York Times*, August 12, 1993, B1.

quite different from one another: Bloomingdale's department store is seen by many as chic and fashionable, especially compared to a more traditional competitor such as Macy's. These images don't just happen. Just as brand managers do for products, store managers work hard to create a "personality."

In developing a desirable store image, the resourceful retailer has a number of choices. Ideally, all of these elements should work together to create a clear, coherent picture that meets consumers' expectations of what that particular shopping experience should be. Figure 18.2 illustrates one attempt to identify and compare the store images of eight different department stores in the New York City area.

Atmospherics is the use of color, lighting, scents, furnishings, sounds, and other design elements to create a desired setting. Marketers manipulate these to create a certain "feeling" about the retail environment.[51] Kinney's Colorado Stores, which sell high-end outdoor clothing, for example, are designed to make the shoppers feel they're out in nature. The stores pipe in New Age background music, interrupted occasionally by the sound of a thunderstorm or a babbling brook. Motion sensors in the ceiling activate displays as a shopper approaches so, for example, a person who walks near an arrangement of beach shoes may hear the sound of waves crashing.[52] The owners of these stores believe that getting people "in the mood" makes them more likely to buy what they see. Recently, Taco Bell sought to use décor to change its image from cheap fast food to a kind of "Starbucks with a Spanish accent."[53] To attract a wider range of customers, Taco Bell used more wood, natural fibers, and new colors.

atmospherics ■ The use of color, lighting, scents, furnishings, and other design elements to create a desired store image.

Store Design: Setting the Stage The elements of store design should correspond to management's desired image. A bank lobby needs to convey respectability and security because people need to be reassured about the safety of their money. In contrast, a used bookstore might create a disorderly look so shoppers think treasures lie buried beneath piles of tattered novels. Chili's Grill & Bar restaurant recently opened a new restaurant in Denver. Due to heightened competition from other restaurants with similar menus, Chili's is using radical store design (a restaurant in the shape of a huge chili pepper) to woo customers who are looking for a "hot" dining experience.[54]

Here are some other design factors that retailers consider.

traffic flow ■ The direction in which shoppers will move through the store and what areas they will pass or avoid.

- *Store layout.* This is the arrangement of merchandise in the store. The placement of fixtures such as shelves, racks, and cash registers is important because store layout determines **traffic flow**, that is, how shoppers will move through the store and what areas they will pass or avoid. A *grid layout*, usually found in supermarkets and discount stores, consists of rows of neatly spaced shelves that are at right angles or parallel to one another. This configuration is useful when management wants to systematically move shoppers down each aisle, being sure that they pass through such high-margin sections as deli and meat. Figure 18.3 illustrates how a grid layout in a supermarket helps to regulate traffic flow.

  A typical strategy is to place staple goods in more remote areas. The designers know that traffic will move to these areas because these are frequently purchased items. They try to place impulse goods in spots shoppers will pass on their way elsewhere. Then they place eye-catching displays to rope people in, such as the signs for Mountain Dew that PepsiCo puts above the cash registers in convenience stores that look like a mountain biker dropped through the ceiling.[55]

  In contrast, a *free-flow layout* is more often used in department and specialty stores because it is conducive to browsing. A retailer might arrange merchandise in circles or arches, or perhaps in separate areas each with its own distinct image and merchandise mix.

- *Fixture type and merchandise density.* Just as we may form impressions of people from their home décor, our feelings about stores are affected by furnishings, fixtures (shelves and racks that display merchandise), and even how much "stuff" is packed into the sales area. Generally, clutter conveys a store with lower-priced merchandise. Upscale

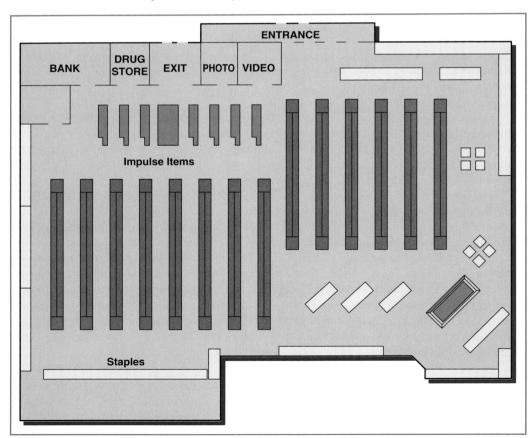

FIGURE **18.3**

Grid Layout

A grid layout encourages customers to move up and down the aisles, passing many different products, and is often used by supermarkets and discount stores.

stores allocate space for sitting areas, dressing rooms, and elaborate displays of merchandise. A shopping center called The Lab in southern California attracts its target audience of mall rats aged 18 to 30 by using unusual furnishings such as concrete walls, a fountain made of oil drums, and an open-air living room filled with thrift-shop furniture to craft a laid-back image its patrons call "the anti-mall."

- *The sound of music.* An elegant restaurant softly playing Mozart in the background is worlds apart from a raucous place such as the Hard Rock Café, where loud rock 'n roll is essential to the atmosphere. The music playing in a store has become so central to its personality that many retailers including Ralph Lauren, Victoria's Secret, Au Bon Pain, Starbucks, and Pottery Barn are even selling the soundtracks specially designed for them.[56]
- *Color and lighting.* Marketers use color and lighting to set a mood. Red, yellow, and orange are warm colors (fast-food chains use a lot of orange to stimulate hunger) whereas blue, green, and violet signify elegance and cleanliness. Light colors make one feel more serene, whereas bright colors convey excitement. Fashion designer Norma Kamali replaced fluorescent lights with pink ones after management found that pink lighting is more flattering and made female customers more willing to try on bathing suits.[57]

The Actors: Store Personnel Store personnel should complement a store's image. Each employee has a part to play, complete with props and costumes. Movie theaters often dress ushers in tuxedos, and many store employees are provided with scripts to use when they present products to customers.

Although the presence of knowledgeable sales personnel is important to shoppers, they generally rate the quality of service they receive from retail personnel as low, often because stores don't hire enough people to wait on their customers.[58] In one survey, 62 percent of shoppers surveyed said they had decided not to buy a product in a store in the past six months because sales clerks were not available to help them.[59] Retailers are working hard to upgrade service quality, though they often find that the rapid turnover of salespeople makes this a difficult goal to achieve. Perhaps they can learn from Japanese retailers. A visitor to a Japanese store is greeted by an enthusiastic, polite, and immaculately dressed employee who bows profusely.[60]

Some U.S. firms have taken customer service and made it into a competitive advantage. Nordstrom's chain of department stores is legendary for its service levels. In fact, some "Nordies" have even been known to warm up customers' cars while they are paying for merchandise! The store motivates its employees by paying them substantially more than the average rate and deducting sales commissions if the merchandise is returned. This encourages the salesperson to be sure the customer is satisfied the first time.[61]

Pricing Policy: How Much for a Ticket to the Show? When consumers form an image of a store in their minds, the *price points*, or price ranges, of its merchandise often play a role. A chain of off-price stores in the Northeast called Daffy's advertises with such slogans as, "Friends Don't Let Friends Pay Retail," implying that anyone who buys at the full, nondiscounted price needs psychiatric help. Discount stores and general merchandisers are likely to compete on a price basis by offering brand names for less.

In recent years department stores have been hurt by consumers' desires for bargains. The response of many department stores was to run frequent sales, a strategy that often backfired because many consumers would buy *only* when the store held a sale. Some stores have instead reduced the number of sales they run in favor of lowering prices across the board. Many, such as Home Depot and Wal-Mart, are adapting an everyday low-pricing (EDLP) strategy in which they set prices that are between the list price suggested by the manufacturer and the deeply discounted price offered by stores that compete on price only (see Chapter 11). Although the store's prices are not the lowest around, the consumer benefits because the retailer spends less money advertising one-time sales and passes these savings on to the customer. In addition, salespeople can spend more time with customers when they are not trying to deal with the throngs who flock to a special sale, and stores can better manage their inventory because it's easier to predict how much they will sell. That makes it less likely that customers will experience **stock-outs** when a desired item is no longer available.[62] EDLP is best suited for product categories that are bought regularly so that consumers have a good idea of what a fair price is.

stock-outs ■ An inventory problem that results when desired items are no longer available.

A price discounting strategy works best when the retailer wants to move merchandise quickly or is looking to generate excitement by sponsoring a really great sale.

BUILDING THE THEATER: STORE LOCATION

Any realtor will tell you the three most important factors in buying a home are: "location, location and location." The same is true in retailing. Wal-Mart's success is not due to only what it is but *where* it is. Wal-Mart was the first mass merchandiser to locate in small and rural markets. When choosing a site, Wal-Mart's planners consider such factors as proximity to highways and major traffic routes. By carefully selecting "undiscovered" areas, the company has been able to negotiate cheap leases in towns with expanding populations, an important strategy for Wal-Mart because it means access to markets hungry for a store that offers such a wide assortment of household goods.[63] This section will review some important aspects of retail locations.

Types of Store Locations   As Figure 18.4 shows, there are four basic types of retail locations. A store can be found in a business district, in a shopping center, as a freestanding entity, or in a nontraditional location.

- *Business districts.* A central business district (CBD) is the traditional downtown business area found in a town or city. Many people are drawn to the area to shop or work, and public transportation is usually available. CBDs have suffered in recent years due to concerns about security, lack of parking, and the lack of customer traffic on evenings and weekends. To combat these problems, many cities provide incentives such as tax breaks to encourage the opening of stores and entertainment areas such as Boston's Quincy Marketplace. These vibrant developments are called *festival marketplaces*, and they have done a lot to reverse the fortunes of aging downtown areas from Boston to Baltimore.

A central business district is often found in downtown areas. Although U.S. retailers have been deserting impoverished center cities in droves for the past 20 years, these downtown areas are now staging a comeback. Sophisticated developments such as the festival marketplaces including New York City's South Street Seaport, Union Station in St. Louis, Harborplace in Baltimore, and Boston's Fanueil Hall (shown here) are contributing to the renaissance of American cities.

A shopping center features one or more anchor stores, usually major department stores that initially attract shoppers, who then discover the other small, specialty stores in the center. Shopping centers have the advantages of (1) providing heavy traffic flows (especially for small stores that would not attract so many people if they were on their own), (2) the sharing of costs (such as advertising and promotion) among tenants, and (3) a clean (and usually safe) environment. It seems likely that large malls will continue to evolve as entertainment centers and for recreational shopping, featuring a greater mix of movie theaters, restaurants, and hobby and bookstores.[a] The Mall of America in Minneapolis features 78 acres of stores, theaters, restaurants, and even an amusement park called Camp Snoopy.

A freestanding store is not located near other stores. This locational strategy, used by some big chains like Kids R Us, has the advantage of offering a lack of direct competition, lower rents, and adaptability. The store has the freedom to alter its selling space to accomodate its own needs. On the other hand, the store had better be popular because it cannot rely on the drawing power of neighbor stores to provide it with customer traffic.

A nontraditional location offers products to shoppers in convenient places—the Baskin-Robbins ice cream chain even puts stores on U.S. Navy ships! McDonald's has located inside Wal-Mart stores to entice customers to take a McBreak from shopping.

[a] Chip Walker "Strip Malls: Plain But Powerful," *American Demographics*, October 1991, 48(4).

FIGURE **18.4**

Types of Store Locations

Different types of store locations are best for different types of retailers. Retailers choose from central business districts, shopping centers, freestanding stores, or nontraditional locations.

- *Shopping centers.* A shopping center is a group of commercial establishments owned and managed as a single property. They range in size and scope from *strip centers* to massive *superregional centers* such as the Mall of America, which offers 4.2 million square feet of shopping plus such attractions as a seven-acre Knott's Camp Snoopy Theme Park. Strip centers offer quick and easy access to basic conveniences such as dry cleaners and video rentals, though shoppers seeking more exotic goods need to look elsewhere. Shopping malls offer variety and the ability to combine shopping with entertainment. Rents tend to be high in shopping malls, making it difficult for many stores to be profitable. In addition, small specialty stores may find it hard to compete with a mall's *anchor stores*, the major department stores that typically draw many shoppers.

  A new form of store location called a *lifestyle center* combines the feel of a neighborhood park with the convenience of a strip mall. Typically located in affluent neighborhoods and featuring expensive landscaping, these more intimate centers are an appealing way for retailers to blend in to residential areas. Retailers including Williams-Sonoma and Talbot's are investing heavily in this concept.[64]

- *Freestanding retailers.* Some stores, usually larger ones such as IKEA, are freestanding, located by themselves in a separate building. These retailers benefit from lower rents and fewer parking problems. However, the store must be attractive enough on its own to be a destination point for shoppers because it can't rely on spillover from consumers visiting other stores at the same place.

- *Nontraditional store locations.* Innovative retailers find new ways to reach consumers. Many entrepreneurs use *carts*; small, movable stores that can be set up in many locations including inside malls, in airports, or in other public facilities, or *kiosks* that are slightly larger and offer storelike facilities including telephone hookups and electricity. Carts and kiosks are relatively inexpensive and a good way for new businesses to get started.

Site Selection: Choosing Where to Build

Sam Walton, the founder of Wal-Mart, used to fly over an area in a small plane until he found a spot that appealed to him. That's a story from the past. Now such factors as long-term population patterns, the location of competitors and the demographic makeup of an area factor into retailers' decisions. The choice of where to open a new store should reflect the company's overall growth strategy. It should be consistent with long-term goals and be in a place that allows the company to best support the outlet. For example, a chain with stores and an extensive warehouse system in the Northeast may not be wise to open a new store in California because the store would be an "orphan" cut off from the company's supply lines.

Location planners look at many factors when selecting a site. They want to find a place that is convenient to customers in the store's **trade area**, the geographic zone that accounts for the majority of its sales and customers.[65] A *site evaluation* considers such specific factors as traffic flow, number of parking spaces available, ease of delivery access, visibility from the street, local zoning laws that determine the types of buildings, parking, and signage allowed, and such cost factors as the length of the lease and the amount of local taxes.

trade area ■ A geographic zone that accounts for the majority of a store's sales and customers.

Planners also consider such population characteristics as age profile (is the area witnessing an influx of new families?), community life cycle (is the community relatively new, stable, or in decline?), and mobility (how often are people moving in and out of the area?). This information is available from a variety of sources, including the U.S. Census Bureau, the buying power index (BPI) published each year by the trade magazine *Sales and Marketing Management*, and by research firms such as Urban Decision Systems and Claritas that analyze many forms of demographic data to create profiles of selected areas.

Planners also have to consider the degree of competition they will encounter by locating in one place versus another. One strategy followed, for example, by fast-food outlets is to locate in a *saturated trade area*. This is a site where a sufficient number of stores already exist so that high customer traffic is present but where the retailer believes it can compete successfully by going head-to-head with the competition. Another strategy is to find an *understored trade area*, where too few stores exist to satisfy the needs of the population (this was Wal-Mart's strategy) and the retailer can establish itself as a dominant presence in

How It Worked Out at Federated Direct

Dawn chose option 3. Federated developed a strategy to revamp its bridal registry business. To attract younger couples and change shoppers' perceptions of its bridal registry, the retailer developed a list of the "Top 10 Reasons to Register with Federated." These reasons were the core of the marketing strategy:

1. Creating your registry is FUN, FAST, and EASY—With the latest technology, including touch-screen kiosks, in-store scanner guns, and online registrations.
2. Personalized Service—Meet with professional bridal consultants at our Premier Stores to customize a registry that fits your lifestyle.
3. Best Selection—Of china, crystal, flatware, housewares, and home textiles under one roof!
4. Locking in Low Registry Prices Is a Piece of Cake!—On the day that you register, you will lock in the lowest price of the last 60 days for the next year to be used by you and your guests.
5. Guests Buy Gifts with Ease . . . And Confidence—By visiting 400 stores of the most highly recognized nameplates across the USA, shopping online, or by calling our toll-free number.
6. Great Brands You Know . . . And Trust—Choose from the most respected national brand names plus our own exclusive brands that you won't find anywhere else.
7. New, Exciting Shower Gifts—A selection of great gift ideas is available through our special shower gift in-store displays.
8. Reliable Delivery—The most popular items are always in stock and shipped to you within 5 days.
9. Special Savings—With our additional 10% off completion program for brides in all Home areas.
10. Hassle-Free Returns—With our one-stop return desk.

Early returns showed a dramatic increase in the number of bridal registrations across the stores. Dawn is hopeful that Federated's revamped courtship of brides and grooms will be a match made in heaven.

Macy's revamped bridal registry offers younger couples what they want.

the community. Over time, these areas may become *overstored*, so that too many stores exist to sell the same goods. Those that can't compete are forced to move or close, as has happened to many small mom-and-pop stores that can't beat the Wal-Marts of the world at their sophisticated retailing games.

A store's targeted consumer segment also determines where it locates. For example, a new, growing community would be appealing for hardware stores that can supply hammers and drywall to homeowners, while upscale dress stores and travel agencies might find better locations in more established areas because people living there have the income to spend on fashion items and vacations. The Buckle, a clothing store chain, successfully sells designer clothing in 200 small towns across the United States. This retailer specifically targets high school and college students who want cutting-edge fashion but who live in relatively isolated areas.[66]

Chapter Summary

1. Define retailing and understand how retailing evolves.

Retailing is the process by which goods and services are sold to consumers for their personal use. The wheel-of-retailing hypothesis suggests that new retailers compete on price and over time become more upscale, leaving room for other new, low-price entrants. The retail life cycle theory suggests retailing institutions are introduced, grow, reach maturity, and then decline. Three factors that motivate retailers to evolve are changing demographics, technology, and globalization.

2. Describe how retailers are classified.

Retailers are classified by NAICS codes based on product lines sold. Retailers may also be classified according to whether they carry items having high or low gross margins and high or low turnover rates, by the level of service offered, and by the merchandise assortment offered. Merchandise assortment is described in terms of breadth and depth, which refer to the number of product lines sold and the amount of variety available for each.

3. Describe direct selling and automatic vending, two forms of nonstore retailing.

Two types of nonstore retailing are direct-selling and automatic vending machines. In direct selling, a salesperson presents a product to one individual or a small group, takes orders, and delivers the merchandise. Direct selling includes door-to-door sales and party or network sales. With state-of-the-art self-service vending machines, products from french fries to blue jeans can be dispensed.

4. Describe B2C e-commerce, its benefits, limitations, and future promise.

B2C e-commerce, online exchanges between companies and consumers, is growing rapidly. B2C benefits include greater convenience and greater product variety for consumers and opportunities for specialized businesses, lower business costs, and instantaneous delivery of some products for marketers. For consumers, the downside of B2C e-commerce is that they have to wait to receive products, security issues, and the inability to touch and feel products. For Internet-only marketers, success on the Internet may be difficult to achieve, whereas cannibalization may be a problem with traditional retailers' online operations.

5. Understand the importance of store image to a retail positioning strategy and explain how a retailer can create an image in the marketplace.

Store image results from many different elements working together to create the most desirable shopping experience and to ensure that shoppers view a store favorably relative to the competition. Color, lighting, scents, furnishings, and other design elements, called atmospherics, are used to create a "feel" for a store environment. Use of atmospherics includes decisions on (1) store layout, which determines traffic flow and influences the desired customer behavior in the store, (2) the use of store fixtures and open space, (3) the use of sound to attract (or repel) certain types of customers, and (4) the use of color and lighting that can influence customers' moods. The number and type of store personnel are selected to complement the store image. Pricing of products sold in the store contributes to shoppers' perceptions. A store's location also contributes to its image. Major types of retail locations include central business districts, shopping centers, freestanding retailers, and nontraditional locations such as kiosks.

Chapter Review

■ MARKETING CONCEPTS:
TEST YOUR KNOWLEDGE

1. How does the wheel-of-retailing hypothesis explain changes in retail outlets? How does the retail life cycle concept explain these changes?
2. What are some of the environmental trends that will have a major impact on the future of retailing?
3. Explain how retail stores differ in terms of their merchandise mix.
4. How do retailers vary in terms of services offered?
5. Describe the differences in merchandise assortments for convenience stores, supermarkets, specialty stores, discount stores, department stores, and hypermarkets.
6. Explain the different types of direct selling. What is the role of automatic vending in retailing?
7. What is B2C e-commerce? What are some benefits of B2C e-commerce for consumers? For marketers?
8. What are some possible effects of B2C e-commerce on traditional retailing?
9. What is meant by store atmospherics? How can the elements of atmospherics be used to increase the store's success? How are store personnel a part of store image?
10. What are some of the different types of store locations? What are their advantages and disadvantages?

■ MARKETING CONCEPTS:
DISCUSSING CHOICES AND ISSUES

1. The wheel-of-retailing theory suggests that the normal path for a retailer is to enter the marketplace with lower-priced goods and then to increase quality, services, and prices. Why do you think this happens? Is it the right path for all retailers? Why or why not?
2. It seems that discount retailers such as Wal-Mart Super Stores are getting larger and larger. Is there an optimal size for retailers? Can retail stores get too large? Why or why not?
3. Owners of stores that make effective use of atmospherics believe that getting people "in the mood" makes them more likely to buy. Do you feel that store atmospherics influence your purchase behavior? Is this sort of planned store setting ethical?
4. Napster was sued by major record companies for offering consumers an opportunity to download music for free. Do you think consumers should be able to download music for free or should they have to pay for it? Were the record companies right to have sued Napster?

■ MARKETING PRACTICE:
APPLYING WHAT YOU'VE LEARNED

1. Assume you are the marketing manager for a company that markets unique cheeses from around the world. Your products have been traditionally sold through specialty food stores. You are considering going online but you recognize there are both benefits and limitations. Write an outline of the pros and cons of going online for your firm. Then develop your recommendations for the firm.
2. All your life you've wanted to be an entrepreneur and to own your own business. Now you're ready to graduate from college and you've decided to open a combination coffee shop and bookstore in a location near your college. You know that to attract both the college student market and other customers from the local community it will be necessary to carefully design the store image. Develop a detailed plan that specifies how you will use atmospherics to create the image you desire.
3. In your job with a marketing consulting firm, you often are asked to make recommendations for store location. Your current client is a local caterer that is planning to open a new retail outlet for selling take-out gourmet dinners. You are examining the possible types of locations: the central business district, a shopping center, freestanding entity, or some nontraditional location. Outline the advantages and disadvantages of each type of location. Present your recommendations to your client.
4. Assume you are the director of marketing for a national chain of convenience stores. Your firm has about 200 stores located in 43 states. The stores are fairly traditional both in design and in the merchandise they carry. Because you want to be proactive in your marketing planning, you are concerned that your firm may need to consider making significant changes due to the current demographic, technological, and global trends in the marketplace. You think it is important to discuss these things with the other executives at your firm. Develop a presentation that includes:
   a. a discussion of the demographic changes that will impact your stores.
   b. a discussion of the technological changes that will impact your stores.

c. a discussion of how global changes may provide problems and opportunities for your organization.

d. your recommendations for how your firm might meet the challenges faced in each of these areas.

■ MARKETING MINI-PROJECT: LEARNING BY DOING

This project is designed to help you understand how store atmospherics play an important role in consumers' perceptions of a retail store.

1. First, select two retail outlets where students in your college are likely to shop. It will be good if you can select two outlets you feel are quite different so far as the store image but that sell the same types of products.

2. Visit each of the stores and write down a detailed description of the store atmosphere—colors, materials used, types of displays, lighting fixtures, product displays, store personnel, and so on.

3. Survey some of the students in your college. Develop a brief questionnaire asking about the perceptions of the two stores you are studying. You may want to ask about such things as the quality of merchandise, prices, competence and friendliness of the store personnel, the attitude of management toward customer service, and so on. What is the "personality" of each store?

4. Develop a report of your findings. Compare the description of the stores with the results of the survey. Attempt to explain how the different elements of the store atmosphere create each store's unique image.

■ REAL PEOPLE, REAL SURFERS: EXPLORING THE WEB

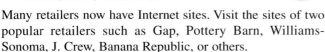

Many retailers now have Internet sites. Visit the sites of two popular retailers such as Gap, Pottery Barn, Williams-Sonoma, J. Crew, Banana Republic, or others.

1. Describe each retailer's Web site. What information is available on each site? How easy was each to navigate? What information did you find interesting and useful on each site? What did you find that you didn't expect to find at a retailer site? What did you find lacking at each site?

2. How is the retailer coordinating its Web site with its traditional bricks-and-mortar stores? Does the site encourage consumers to visit the physical store or just to remain an online shopper?

3. How do the retailers' Web sites communicate the image or personality of their stores? How are they alike? How are they different? If you had no information except that available on the Web, would you know what types of products are sold; whether the products sold are expensive, prestige products, or low-priced products; and what types of consumers each retailer is attempting to attract to its stores? How does each site use graphics or other design elements to represent the "setting" as retailers do in their stores? How do they communicate the type of consumer they consider their primary market?

4. What recommendations would you make to each retailer to improve its Web site?

■ PLAN IT! DEVELOPING A MARKETING PLAN

As your instructor directs, create a marketing plan (using Marketing Plan Pro software or a written marketing plan format) to document your marketing decisions or answer these questions in a written or oral report.

Your final task in developing next year's marketing plan is to consider CFS's retailing and e-commerce strategy.

1. Assuming that Chubby Stubby products are introduced late next year, what type of retailers would be most appropriate for this new product line—and why?

2. Would you recommend that CFS use the party plan system for any or all of its products—and why?

3. What are the advantages and disadvantages of separately selling the software that comes bundled with Computer Bug, Monitor Morphs, and Monster Morphs for download via B2C e-commerce?

Key Terms

atmospherics, (547)

business-to-consumer (B2C) e-commerce, (539)

convenience stores, (534)

department stores, (536)

direct selling, (537)

experiential shopper, (540)

factory outlet store, (536)

general merchandise discount stores, (535)

hypermarkets, (536)

merchandise assortment, (534)

merchandise breadth, (534)

merchandise depth, (534)

merchandise mix, (533)

multilevel network, (538)

nonstore retailing, (537)

off-price retailers, (535)

party plan system, (538)

point-of-sale (POS) systems, (531)

pyramid schemes, (538)

retailing, (528)

retail life cycle, (529)

scrambled merchandising, (533)

MARKETING IN ACTION: CHAPTER 18 CASE

REAL CHOICES AT COSTCO WHOLESALE CORPORATION

Costco Warehouse Clubs is the leading retailer of its type. In 2002, Costco had 386 stores—285 in the United States, 60 in Canada, 11 in the United Kingdom, 5 in Korea, 3 in Taiwan, 2 in Japan, and 20 in Mexico. Although Costco had fewer stores than Wal-Mart Corporation's Sam's Clubs (there were 500 Sam's clubs), it was estimated that Costco revenues were over $1 billion higher than Sam's and operating profits in 2001 were $1.293 billion compared to $1.028 billion for Sam's.

But what makes Costco unique is its product mix. Costco focuses on providing low prices on high-quality merchandise—not the sort of products people expect to find at a wholesale club. Costco carries 4,000 carefully chosen items. In general, the Costco product mix can be described as a broad but shallow selection. Although three-fourths of the products carried are basic items such as paper towels, cans of tuna, and auto tires, the other one-quarter are high-end discretionary items with brand names such as Godiva and Waterford. At any point in time, a Costco shopper might find a $20,000 engagement ring, a large drum of olives, and a Ralph Lauren golf jacket selling for 75 percent below retail list price.

One in four households in the United States has a Costco membership. Costco customers, in general, have a higher-paying occupation and a higher level of education than competitors' customers. In Seattle, Microsoft millionaires pick up their Costco membership cards at the Microsoft "campus."

Costco customers are frequent shoppers. Between 1995 and 1999, the average frequency of a shopper's visit to Costco increased from every 3 weeks to every 10 days. But since the average purchase on each visit remained steady at $95, the Costco shopper was buying more.

Costco seems to be very successful at creating an exciting place to shop. Eighty-six percent of Costco members renew their memberships, the highest percentage in the industry. The only complaints most Costco shoppers have is that they buy too much.

Costco's formula for success includes a variety of customer-pleasing retail practices. First, Costco keeps prices down by carrying a limited number of products (no more than 4,000 at a time), which reduces inventory costs. Also, the company does not advertise.

Costco gives customers what they want in other ways, too. All products carry a return-anything-at-any-time guarantee. The Costco diamond guarantee says that the company will give a member $100 if the diamond is appraised for less than double the Costco price.

Twelve percent of the products sold carry Costco's own Kirkland brand. In fact the Kirkland brand has become so popular that some manufactures have gone into co-branding with Costco. Costco customers can buy "Kirkland Signature by Whirlpool" appliances including refrigerators and dishwashers.

Because some high-end manufacturers, refuse to sell to a warehouse retailer, Costco even uses diverting to get some branded merchandise. Some $200 million in merchandise is obtained this way annually using gray market channels.

Costco also produces knockoffs of expensive designer products. Costco uses offshore factories to create Tumi luggage, Cole Haan loafers, and Coach handbag look-alikes.

Although Costco's success is unquestioned, Costco planners have many questions to consider while trying to continue its success and profitability in the future:

- How will the Internet affect Costco's future? Costco launched its Internet sales site, www.costco.com, in 1999 but the site only carries the company's high-end products. Should Costco offer all of its products on the Web?

- At some point, Costco can expect the domestic market to become saturated. Is Costco's future in international markets? Although most of Costco's global ventures have been successful, this has not been the case in Japan. The Japanese retail market is the second largest in the world at $1 trillion in sales. Four years after opening in Japan, Costco's two Japanese warehouse sites were not yet profitable.
- Perhaps Costco should consider expanding its product line. For example, Wal-Mart superstores carry about 125,000 products compared to Costco's 4,000.

Sources: "Costco Wholesale Corporation," Yahoo Commercial Directory, accessed at dir.yahoo.com/Business_and_Economy/Shopping_and_Services/Retailers/Costco_Wholesale_Corporation/ on April 21, 2002; "Costco Wholesale Corporation Reports March Sales Results," Costco Wholesale Corporation News Release, April 11, 2002, accessed at biz.yahoo.com/bw/020411/110009_1.html on April 1, 2002; Patricia O'Connell, ed., "Costco: Still Finding Its Way in Japan," *Business Week Online*, March 25, 2002, accessed at www.businessweek.com/bwdaily/dnflash/mar2002/nf20020325_4462.htm on April 21, 2002; Shelly Branch, "Inside the Cult of Costco," *Fortune*, September 6, 1999, 84–190.

THINGS TO THINK ABOUT

1. What is the decision facing Costco Wholesale Corporation?
2. What factors are important in understanding the decision situation?
3. What are the alternatives?
4. What decision(s) do you recommend?
5. What are some ways to implement your recommendation(s)?

A Sample Marketing Plan
COMPUTER-FRIENDLY STUFF

Situation Analysis
COMPANY BACKGROUND

Computer Friendly Stuff (CFS) was founded in May 1996 in Chicago with the goal of creating and marketing toys and accessories to make computers more fun to use. CFS is pioneering the integrated computer toy/accessory category, which is expected to grow as computer use expands both domestically and internationally. Currently, little competition exists in this new category, although more competition is anticipated in the coming years.

The initial product, introduced in mid-1997, was the Original Computer Bug computer toy, a plastic character designed to adhere to the side or top of a computer monitor. An integrated add-on product was a series of humorous screen savers and animations featuring the Bug, available on CD-ROM in Windows format. The second product, introduced in 1998, was Monitor Morphs. This product consists of bendable arms that adhere to a computer monitor, plus an integrated series of goofy-face screen savers and animations on CD-ROM in Windows format.

As an entrepreneurial company, CFS has a flat, functional organization structure. Key personnel include:

- *Chris Cole, founder and co-president.* Cole is responsible for the creation, design, packaging, and production management of all CFS products.
- *Bill Martens, co-founder and co-president.* Martens is responsible for international and domestic distribution and marketing.
- *David Winter, chief financial officer.* Winter develops financial strategy and keeps the company's books.
- *Joel Wildman, national sales manager.* Wildman is responsible for maintaining the sales force of independent sales reps. He also handles licensing negotiation and advises on product development and manufacturing.
- *James Knepper, initial financier and consultant.* Along with Bill Martens, Knepper is responsible for initial financing of the company. He also provides legal and accounting/tax services through his other companies. Knepper's shares in CFS were purchased in 1999 by Lucille and Bud Martens.
- *Lucille and Bud Martens, shareholders.* Next to Chris Cole and Bill Martens, Lucille and Bud Martens possess the largest number of shares. They consult and sit on the company's board of directors.

MARKETS

In the broadest sense, the overall consumer market for CFS products is anyone who uses a personal computer (PC). This market is exploding, with over 165 million personal computers in U.S. homes and over 625 million personal computers worldwide at the end of 2001. This sales trend is the result, in part, of tremendous advances in technology and the benefits of economies of scale now enjoyed by manufacturers at all levels of personal computer development. Despite strong domestic sales growth, just over half of all U.S. households own a PC, compared with greater than 90 percent penetration of televisions. As a result, the domestic market for PCs is expected to continue expanding for some time, as are the markets in Asia and other areas around the world. This growth is expected to slow, however, as the current world economic recession runs its course.

Within the U.S. consumer market, CFS is targeting two specific segments. Based on feedback about the strong appeal of the Bug character, one important segment is youngsters, aged 7 to 14. This represents a sizable segment. According to U.S. Bureau of the Census data, the domestic population of boys and girls aged 5 to 14 was just under 40 million as of the year 2000. Therefore, the segment of 7- to 14-year-olds would be slightly smaller, estimated at 35 million.

The second consumer segment being targeted is women aged 30 to 65 who use computers. According to U.S. Bureau of the Census data, the domestic population of women aged 35 to 64 totals almost 55 million. Assuming that 20 percent of those women are employed in a professional work setting, this segment is estimated at 11 million.

To reach the consumer market, CFS is targeting three broad reseller markets: computers, toys, and gifts. CFS sells through wholesalers to selected retailers and, through independent sales reps, sells directly to major national retail chains. CFS products are also available on Web retail sites such as What On Earth and ComputerGear. CFS products are currently available nationally in the U.S. market as well as in Canada, New Zealand, Western Europe, Latin America, and Asia.

COMPETITION

No direct competition currently exists in the integrated computer toy and accessory category. Many screen saver products are available at the retail level, and many are offered without charge on the Web, but none of these products incorporate adhesive toy attachments for the monitor. Thus, the ability to create humorous and imaginative computer toy and accessory combinations is a distinctive competency for CFS.

The closest competing product is a Warner Brothers Taz Mousepad and Screensaver. The Warner Brothers product enjoys high brand awareness, due to the popularity of the Taz licensed character. It also benefits from national distribution through Warner Brothers Studio Stores and other outlets. Other screen savers featuring brand-name licensed characters (but no computer toy) sell for about $20.

In recent years, interactive toys based on licensed characters such as Barney have been introduced, at relatively high price points (approximately $100). Because these are geared primarily toward younger children and are unrelated to PC use, they are not considered competition for CFS products.

From a competitive standpoint, CFS products are positioned as fun, unique, and value-added. They retail at a slightly higher price than the Warner Brothers product but they also provide significantly more in terms of software and innovation. Whereas buyers receive only one Taz screen saver when they buy the Warner Brothers product, they receive 10 screen savers with the CFS product. The CFS characters are humorous, new, and distinctive, and feedback demonstrates their widespread appeal among the market segment of youngsters aged 7 to 14.

Indirect competition from similar toys, and toy and entertainment products in general, has increased since the economic recession began in 2001. There are now fewer consumer dollars available for "nonnecessities" like toys than there were in the previous economic boom. The value-added nature of CFS products keeps them competitive in this larger market.

PRODUCTS

CFS is expanding its line of products that make computers more fun. At present, the product line consists of:

The Original Computer Bug (introduced in 1997). This is a plush character set in a plastic base designed to adhere to the side or top of a computer monitor, without marring the monitor's finish. It is integrated with a CD-ROM containing a series of screen savers, wallpapers, and animations of the Bug, for Windows 95 and later formats. This add-on product can be sold separately or bundled with the Bug toy.

CFS experimented with two packaging designs before settling on a brightly colored blister pack. This package enhances the consumer appeal of the package. It also allows the product to stand on a shelf or hang from a peg, depending on the retailer's merchandising preference. More packaging changes, however, are needed to emphasize the integrated CD-ROM and explain the product.

Monitor Morphs (introduced in 1998). This product comes with two adhesive, bendable arms that attach to the sides of a computer monitor that can hold pens, paper, or other office supplies. The product also includes a CD-ROM for Windows 95 and later formats with an integrated series of screen savers with giant animated faces. When installed, the product appears to transform the user's monitor into a giant head with arms sticking out.

Computer Rear View Mirror (introduced in 1999). This product mounts with an adhesive disc onto the top or side of a monitor. The ball-and-socket mount allows users to angle the mirror in various directions, generally over their shoulder, to see people approaching or standing behind them while they are working. The product includes three stickers with reusable static adhesive and humorous statements such as "bosses in mirror are closer than they appear," à la a car side-view mirror that says, "objects in mirror are closer than they appear."

Monster Morphs (anticipated release date May 2003). A new version of Monitor Morphs but with scary green arms, the product will include a CD-ROM in Windows 2000 format with an integrated series of screen savers with comical monster faces. When installed, the product appears to transform the user's monitor into a monster, similar to Frankenstein.

CHANNELS

CFS's primary emphasis is on the retail channel, specifically toy stores, gift stores, computer and software stores, and catalogs. The company broke into the retail channel by cold-calling single-store retailers; by the second Christmas of operation, CFS products were being carried by 50 small stores. Today, CFS reaches the retail channel using wholesalers for select accounts and independent sales representatives for other accounts. The appointment of a national sales manager has boosted CFS's ability to sell into the retail channel.

To build awareness and generate leads, CFS also participates in industry conventions such as the New York Toy Fair, the Hong Kong Game and Toy Fair, and the Electronic Entertainment Expo. Because the company has a limited budget, it attracts attention at industry events using guerrilla marketing techniques such as having an employee roam the aisles in a seven-foot Computer Bug costume.

To date, CFS's largest retail accounts have been CompUSA (a 250-store chain), Electronics Boutique (a 500-store chain), Fry's Electronics (a chain of 25 megastores), and the What on Earth catalog. CFS's products have also sold in virtually every major retail chain in Western Europe.

The Internet is a secondary channel for CFS. Online retail outlets currently account for 10 percent of CFS's annual sales. This proportion has decreased slightly in the wake of the rash of recent dot-com failures, the downsizing of e-commerce, and the economic recession of 2000. Long term, it is expected that online channels will again play a significant role in the distribution and sales of CFS products.

CFS briefly experimented with direct sales to consumers via a mall kiosk and Christmas fairs in Indiana, Wisconsin, and Michigan. Although labor intensive—and impractical for national markets—this approach allowed management to meet members of the target market face-to-face and learn more about their needs and expectations.

ENVIRONMENT

Economic considerations. CFS products have sold well in periods of prosperity, when the economy is strong and consumer confidence high. The current economic downturn has impacted CFS in many areas, from production to distribution to marketing, and the company has adapted to these changes by streamlining its operations and nurturing the relationships it already has with key distributors.

Demographic considerations. The U.S. population of children aged 7 to 14 is projected to remain stable through 2005, which means this targeted segment will remain at about 40 million. The U.S. population of women aged 35 to 64 is projected to grow to 58 million by 2005.

If 20 percent are assumed to be in professional work settings, this targeted segment will represent nearly 12 million women by 2005.

Social and cultural considerations. The economic boom of the late 1990s, fueled by the technology sector, has created a high level of computer awareness and competency among American adults. This has increased demand for computer products in general. However, this demand has been offset, worldwide, by the economic downturn and the uncertainty of all markets in light of the events of September 11, 2001.

Political and legal considerations. No import/export restrictions currently affect CFS products. Special legal and regulatory guidelines would apply if the products were geared for children under 3 years old, but these are currently not an issue since the target market is children aged 7 and older. Any future television campaigns developed by CFS will have to conform to regulatory guidelines governing advertising targeted at children.

Technological considerations. The consumer market is split into two PC platforms, Windows/IBM-compatible PCs and Apple/Macintosh PCs. The original CFS products were designed for Windows 95. The huge popularity of Apple's iMac, along with a host of new G-series products, makes that platform attractive for future CFS products. Microsoft continues to release newer versions of Windows, but CFS products are designed to be compatible with these newer versions, which means consumers will still be able to run their screen savers after any Windows upgrades (such as Windows XP). An area of possible future concern is an increase in pirating, which could cut into revenues and profits.

PREVIOUS RESULTS

Sales of CFS products peaked in 1999, the third year of operations, and have remained fairly flat since then.

Company sales performance	
1997 gross sales	$ 47,000
1998 gross sales	$105,000 (123% increase over 1997)
1999 gross sales	$400,000 (281% increase over 1998)
2000 gross sales	$375,000 (6% decrease over 1999)
2001 gross sales	figures not yet finalized

Product sales performance	
1997	
Computer bug toy	$ 10,000
Bug and screen saver	37,000
1998	
Computer bug toy	$ 15,000 (50% increase over 1997)
Bug and screen saver	72,000 (95% increase over 1997)
Monitor Morphs	18,000 (introduced October)
1999	
Computer bug toy	$ 40,000 (167% increase over 1998)
Bug and screen saver	275,000 (282% increase over 1998)
Monitor Morphs	85,000 (372% increase over 1998)
2000	
Bug and screen saver	$150,000 (45% decrease from 1998)
Monitor Morphs	175,000 (105% increase over 1999)
Rear View Mirrors	50,000 (introduced September)

Seasonality of sales. To date, 80 percent of product sales have occurred during the year-end holiday season. This seasonality is the direct result of the nature of the product line, which is somewhat gift oriented. Although CFS products sell in gift and toy stores and catalogs, seasonal sales patterns appear consistent across the spectrum of retail outlets.

SWOT and Issue Analysis

Strengths.   One internal strength of CFS is the creative, skilled employee team. All employees apply their creative talents to every project. Employees have appropriate technical skills and have proven their ability to adapt to the ever-changing demands of an entrepreneurial start-up. A second strength is the high-performance organizational culture, which focuses on quality and customer satisfaction—with a sense of humor. A third strength is the flexibility, scalability, and cost savings gained by outsourcing production functions.

Weaknesses.   One internal weakness of CFS is limited financial resources to fund heavy promotional campaigns or large-scale expansion activities to meet unexpectedly high demand. Also, if CFS had an established reputation and a proven product track record, it would be better able to compete for distribution opportunities in major chains. Another weakness of CFS is that its product line may be vulnerable to prolonged economic recession.

Opportunities.   One external opportunity for CFS is the increase in computer use—both domestically and internationally—which is creating a huge potential market for CFS products. Another opportunity is licensing opportunities. Both Marvel Comics and Warner Brothers have expressed interest in licensing their characters for CFS products, an arrangement that could greatly expand the public's awareness of CFS and open new promotion and distribution opportunities. The possible licensing of the Original Computer Bug for a Saturday morning cartoon series is another opportunity. Given the co-founders' experience and connections in the entertainment industry, this opportunity could lead to extremely wide public awareness and much higher sales of tie-in products.

Threats.   The main external threat is the depth and duration of the economic downturn, which has affected all aspects of CFS's product cycle, from production to distribution. Another threat is the relative lack of awareness of CFS brands among the target audiences. In comparison, the Warner Brothers licensed characters enjoy widespread brand awareness, whereas the Original Computer Bug and Monitor Morphs are much less widely known at present. Another threat is vulnerability to imitations produced by companies with more financial resources and larger distribution networks. In addition, CFS products have a limited lifespan because they are designed for desktop PC monitors; as laptops and flat-screen monitors become more popular, CSF will need new products designed specifically for these uses. Finally, the current seasonality of CFS products is problematic for cash flow.

Critical Issues.   One critical short-term issue for CFS is the ability to negotiate favorable licensing arrangements for established characters from Warner Brothers or other sources. Another critical issue is ensuring compatibility of CFS products with future Windows operating systems, as well as designing products for the growing market of laptops and flat-screen monitor users. The third critical issue for CFS is to continue developing new products to stay ahead of any deep-pockets competitors who may imitate CFS's existing products. A fourth critical issue is obtaining suitable distribution in U.S. and world markets to boost sales while spreading sales more evenly throughout the year.

Mission and Objectives

The mission of CFS is to design and market integrated computer toys and accessories that offer the benefit of making computers more fun to use at home or in the workplace. CFS is targeting two consumer segments, youth aged 7 to 14 and professional women aged 35 to 65. CFS's distinctive competency is the ability to create humorous and imaginative computer toy and accessory combinations.

MARKETING OBJECTIVES

- To increase the number of retail outlets carrying CFS products by 100 percent within one year.
- To improve market penetration by boosting the number of additional products purchased by existing customers by 25 percent within two years.
- To introduce a new product (Monster Morphs) by next year.
- To research brand awareness of CFS among targeted segments as a baseline and then set objectives for boosting brand awareness by year-end.
- To improve market development by expanding distribution of current products to at least one new international market by year-end.
- To develop an in-package customer feedback campaign for the Monster Morphs product to test brand loyalty and product cross-over.

SALES OBJECTIVES

- To increase gross sales by 50 percent within one year and by 100 percent within two years.
- To increase sales of Monitor Morphs by 50 percent within one year.
- To maintain sales growth of at least 20 percent for Computer Bug toys for the next year, regardless of the state of the world economy.
- To achieve first-year gross sales of at least $100,000 for the Monster Morphs product after its introduction in October and by the end of the year.

TARGET MARKETS AND POSITIONING

CFS is using a target market strategy to focus only on selected consumer and organizational segments. CFS has segmented the consumer market on the basis of demographics (age and gender) and behavior (computer usage at home or office and propensity to give gifts). CFS has segmented the organizational market on the basis of NAICS/SIC codes.

Consumer segments. The segment of youngsters, aged 7 to 14, is estimated at 35 million. The segment of professional women, aged 35 to 65, is estimated at 11 million. Informal research (feedback from trade shows, Christmas shows, fan mail, and in-store appearances) indicates that the youth segment reacts very positively to the Bug character and the humorous screen savers. Secondary market research shows that professional women buy more gifts than men, so they are a good target for buying CFS products for gift-giving occasions.

Organizational segments. To reach the two targeted consumer segments, CFS is targeting three reseller markets: computers, toys, and gifts. These can be identified by their NAICS/SIC codes. Toy stores are NAICS code 45112 (SIC 5945); gift stores are NAICS code 45322 (SIC 5947); and computer and software stores are NAICS code 44312 (SIC 5734). CFS sells through wholesalers to selected retailers in these segments and, through independent sales reps, sells directly to major national retail chains in these segments. CFS products are also available on retail Web sites that sell toys and gifts.

CFS products are positioned as fun, unique, and value-added, with the major benefit of making computer use more fun. The products have a distinctive and humorous brand personality, which supports this major benefit. The Computer Bug carries the slogan, "I'm the Bug you *want* to have on your computer!" and Monitor Morphs carry the slogan, "Morph your monitor!"

Product Strategies

Early on, CFS management realized that large retailers prefer buying from companies that offer multiple products. For this reason, the company moved beyond its original Computer Bug characters to develop new products, starting with Monitor Morphs. Today, the three existing products, Computer Bug, Monitor Morphs, and Computer Rear View Mirror, are in the maturity stage of the product life cycle.

Although these continue to do well, CFS needs additional new products to maintain steady sales and cash flow in an unstable market, to meet retailers' needs, and to meet sales objectives for the future. New-product sales will also balance a drop in sales that might occur if one or more of the original products drops rapidly in popularity at the end of its life cycle. Given CFS's relationships with Asian manufacturers, management can submit sketches or mock-ups of potential new products and receive finished prototypes within a few weeks. This is a cost-effective way for the company to examine, test, and revise product prototypes before moving into production.

Packaging is another important aspect of product strategy. For consistency across the brand and for the convenience of its channel partners, CFS is adapting its stand-or-hang blister pack for all its products.

CFS plans to develop both the product line and the product mix. The product line will be lengthened by adding new licensed characters and different Computer Bugs and Monitor Morphs (such as Monster Morphs). The product mix will be broadened by adding new products such as Chubby Stubby stuffed animals, cute creatures with stubby legs.

In the future, CFS will build on the product franchise and extend the product life cycle of the Computer Bug by investigating opportunities to license the character for a television cartoon show or for other types of products. In contrast, Monitor Morphs are expected to have a more compressed product life cycle, unless CFS is able to arrange licensing of established characters, a move that would extend the appeal and sales possibilities for this product.

Monster Morphs will be presented as both an extension of Monitor Morphs and as a separate product from it. Key positioning in seasonal outlets is expected to create a niche demand for the product during its peak season (Halloween), while general distribution will keep the product viable through the ensuing Christmas season. CFS will also do its first direct-response product testing, by including an incentive for customers to provide feedback when purchasing Monster Morphs. A survey within the package will test, among other things, what other CFS products that customer owns, and if ownership or product knowledge of Monitor Morphs contributed to the customer's choice to purchase Monster Morphs. This survey will be linked to some incentive—a rebate perhaps—to encourage response.

Pricing Strategies

Pricing is a key ingredient for boosting profits that can be reinvested to support CFS's plans for stable sales growth and resiliency in the face of recession. It also affects consumers' perceptions of product quality and value. In addition, product pricing must cover sufficient gross margin for retailers as well as commissions for the independent sales representatives and wholesalers who sell CFS products; otherwise, CFS will be unable to expand its distribution base.

In managing wholesale and retail prices, CFS considers production costs, sales commissions, marketing and advertising costs, competitive prices, retail and wholesale margins, and consumer reaction. Initially, CFS set its wholesale and retail prices for the first product too low to cover all distributor margins and trade promotion costs. However, the company quickly revised its wholesale and retail prices in line with fixed and variable costs. By testing, CFS has confirmed that a slight increase in retail price will not adversely affect consumer demand. CFS uses price lining, assigning different prices to different products in the product line. Therefore, CFS has set wholesale and retail prices for its existing product line as follows:

Product	Wholesale Price	Suggested Retail Price
Computer Bug w/CD-ROM	$8.99	$17.99
Monitor Morphs w/CD-ROM	9.99	19.99
Computer Rear View Mirror	3.99	7.99

The national sales manager has authority to negotiate with large retail chains that request discounts for volume, advertising allowances, and other pricing adjustments. CFS also plans to use seasonal discounts, coinciding with major holidays and trade shows, to encourage purchasing during specific periods. In addition, pricing in international markets is adjusted sale by sale to account for ever-changing foreign currency rates. As competition develops, CFS plans to consider revising wholesale and retail prices as necessary to support sales growth, product market share, and support distribution objectives.

Channel (Place) Strategies

Distribution is an important component for increasing sales of CFS products domestically and internationally. CFS targets three categories of resellers: toy stores, computer stores, and gift stores. The primary CFS channel strategy involves indirect distribution, selling through wholesaler and manufacturers' agents (independent reps supervised by a CFS national sales manager) to the targeted retailers, which in turn sell to the consumer market. These independent reps have developed relationships with buyers for the top U.S. retail chains, so they can demonstrate CFS products and negotiate orders and pricing.

CFS plans to increase its selective distribution among toy, computer, and gift stores that can display the product appropriately and reach the targeted consumer segments. This will achieve the goals of increasing the number of retail outlets carrying CFS products by 100 percent and placing CFS products in 10 major U.S. chains during this year. To obtain distribution in these large national chains, CFS plans to support its products with pricing allowances, trade promotions, and consumer promotions. For example, CFS will produce and distribute 50,000 consumer promotion flyers to support the release of Monster Morphs. In the coming year, CFS will use its track record with major distributors such as CompUSA to open doors to large toy retailers.

CFS also sells directly to consumers through the Web, although this is currently a secondary strategy. At first, management saw great potential in selling computer-related products to people who use their computers to access the Internet. The company created a fun Web site and invited online orders. However, processing customer orders, authorizing credit card payments, packing products for shipping, and sending orders to customers proved more time-consuming and less profitable than expected. Next, CFS tried an arrangement in which an Internet catalog lists products in exchange for a small percentage of the retail price. Although this approach helped CFS learn more about customer behavior, it was also an inefficient use of company resources. A third approach, wholesaling to online resellers that sell to consumers, proved more efficient.

The challenges to e-commerce over recent years have reduced the immediate effectiveness of online retail channels, but they will again become an important element in CFS's distribution strategy when the economy strengthens. CFS no longer sells products directly to customers. Instead, CFS has moved toward dealing exclusively with Internet retailers that take title to the goods and handle all order processing and shipment.

Promotion Strategies

CFS will use promotion to educate the target audience about the features and benefits of its products, to build brand awareness and preference, to support the distribution strategy, and to build long-term customer relationships. As CFS works toward its distribution goals, it is putting more emphasis on personal selling. Other promotional techniques will include consumer and trade sales promotion, limited advertising, and public relations.

Personal selling. CFS has a network of 32 manufacturers' agents who sell CFS to resellers. These independent salespeople receive a commission of 5 to 10 percent of the wholesale price of all the CFS products they sell. Joel Wildman serves as CFS national sales manager, hiring and managing the agents, approving pricing adjustments, negotiating licensing deals, and working with CFS management to set sales goals. CFS will continue to evaluate agents on a bimonthly basis to ensure efficient, appropriate coverage of the reseller market. These frequent reviews will also allow CFS to monitor sales to key accounts more closely and replace agents quickly if they do not achieve sales goals. To support personal selling tactics, CFS will provide additional promotional materials and product demonstration models earlier in the selling season. CFS will revise its incentive program of bonuses and promotions for the independent salespeople to encourage retention of successful reps.

Consumer sales promotion. To support the release of the new Monster Morph product, CFS will distribute 50,000 in-store, point-of-sale flyers to participating resellers this year. In addition, CFS is using sampling—putting demonstration versions of all products on every CD-ROM—to support the market penetration goal of boosting the number of additional products purchased by existing customers by 25 percent within two years. Within three months, CFS plans to design new point-of-purchase displays to improve product placement and encourage more impulse buying in stores.

Trade sales promotion. In addition to providing resellers with new point-of purchase displays to support sales, CFS is allocating $12,000 as push money to promote sales of Monster Morphs at computer chains. CFS has also budgeted $75,000 to cover the cost of exhibiting at key trade shows in the coming year, including toy industry events in New York, Hong Kong, and Dallas as well as computer and gift shows. In addition, the company will spend up to $32,000 on cooperative promotions through major retailers. To promote its brand during computer industry trade show appearances, the company has distributed small cards with irreverent sayings that attendees can stick to the side of their official show badges. For toy industry events, CFS relies more heavily on an employee wearing the seven-foot Computer Bug costume to draw attention to the company's booth and products.

Advertising. Tests of magazine advertising have resulted in low sales response because CFS products cannot be demonstrated in print media. National television advertising would be ideal for demonstrating the Computer Bug, Monitor Morphs, and Monster Morphs, but the high costs of production and media put this medium out of reach for a young, entrepreneurial company weathering economic recession. CFS will, therefore, concentrate on co-op advertising, partnering with resellers that stock the product to share the costs of local advertising (including television, newspapers, magazines, and direct mail). These advertising messages will emphasize the "fun" benefits and the unique brand personality.

Public relations. CFS has successfully used public relations to showcase products to the consumer audience. To date, CFS products have been featured in the *Chicago Tribune, BUZZ* magazine, and *CBS This Morning*. In the coming year CFS will expand the public relations effort to include the top children's magazines, the top working women's magazines, the 50 largest U.S. newspapers, the top children's cable networks, all national television morning shows, and local morning television shows in the top 20 U.S. markets. Each television show will receive a special package including a customized demonstration CD-ROM (mentioning the program and the anchors by name). When attending trade shows, the Computer Bug Mascot will visit targeted media outlets in the local area. All these public relations tactics will be timed to coincide with specific selling periods, such as back-to-school and Christmas.

Marketing Research, R&D

As CFS products gain wider distribution, more research is needed to better understand brand awareness and perceptions among professional women, one of the two targeted consumer segments. Therefore, CFS will commission exploratory research early this year, using personal interviews and focus groups, to uncover women's attitudes, feelings, and buying behaviors toward CFS products.

Informal marketing research is helpful in assessing children's reactions to existing products and testing ideas for new products. Throughout this year, CFS will insert youth-oriented notices into products sold in toy stores, inviting children to submit their comments through e-mail (after asking their parents' permission). The Web site will also invite children to answer a brief online questionnaire about new products (reassuring parents that no identifying personal data will be collected). Before Monster Morphs are test-marketed, CFS will conduct focus group research to gauge consumer reaction to the product and to various marketing mix strategies.

Controls

CFS will use several tools to evaluate and control activities implemented under this marketing plan. First, CFS will use monthly trend analyses to examine sales by channel, by type of reseller, by chain, by agent, and by geographical area. These analyses will enable CFS to take corrective action when necessary.

Second, CFS will monitor customer and reseller feedback on a weekly basis to quickly identify problems in such areas as product quality and to stay abreast of competitive moves. This will allow CFS to respond more quickly.

Third, CFS will conduct a marketing audit in midyear and again at year's end to evaluate the effectiveness and efficiency of the marketing programs. In this way, CFS will be able to pinpoint areas for improvement and prepare contingency plans for emerging problems.

Marketing Math

To develop marketing strategies to meet the goals of an organization effectively and efficiently, it is essential that marketers understand and use a variety of financial analyses. This appendix provides some of these basic financial analyses, including a review of the income statement and balance sheet as well as some basic performance ratios. In addition, this appendix includes an explanation of some of the specific calculations that marketers use routinely in determining price.

Income Statement and Balance Sheet

The two most important documents used to explain the financial situation of a company are the income statement and the balance sheet. The **income statement** (which is sometimes referred to as the profit and loss statement) provides a summary of the revenues and expenses of a firm—that is, the amount of income a company received from sales or other sources, the amount of money it spent, and the resulting income or loss that the company experienced.

The major elements of the income statement are

Gross sales: the total of all income the firm receives from the sales of goods and services.

Net sales revenue: the gross sales minus the amount for returns and promotional or other allowances given to customers.

Cost of goods sold (sometimes called the *cost of sales*): the cost of inventory or goods that the firm has sold.

Gross margin (also called *gross profit*): the amount of sales revenue that is in excess of the cost of goods sold.

Operating expenses: expenses other than the cost of goods sold that are necessary for conducting business. These may include salaries, rent, depreciation on buildings and equipment, insurance, utilities, supplies, and property taxes.

Operating income (sometimes called *income from operations*): the gross margin minus the operating expenses. Sometimes accountants prepare an *operating statement*, which is similar to the income statement except that the final calculation is the operating income—that is, other revenues or expenses and taxes are not included.

Other revenue and expenses: income and/or expenses other than those required for conducting the business. These may include such items as interest income/expenses and any gain or loss experienced on the sale of property or plant assets.

Taxes: the amount of income tax the firm owes calculated as a percentage of income.

Net income (sometimes called *net earnings* or *net profit*): the excess of total revenue over total expenses.

Table B1 shows the income statement for an imaginary company, DLL Incorporated. DLL is a typical merchandising firm. Note that the income statement is for a specific year and includes income and expenses from January 1 through December 31 inclusive. The following comments explain the meaning of some of the important entries included in this statement.

- DLL Inc. has total or gross sales during the year of $253,950. This figure was adjusted, however, by deducting the $3,000 worth of goods returned and special allowances given to customers and by $2,100 in special discounts. Thus, the actual or net sales generated by sales is $248,850.
- The cost of goods sold is calculated by adding the inventory of goods on January 1 to the amount purchased during the year and then subtracting the inventory of goods on December 31. In this case, DLL had $60,750 worth of inventory on hand on January 1. During the year the firm made purchases in the amount of $135,550. This amount, however, was reduced by purchase returns and allowances of $1,500 and by purchase discounts of $750, so the net purchase is only $133,300.

Gross Sales		$253,950	
Less: Sales Returns and Allowances	$ 3,000		
Sales Discounts	2,100	5,100	
Net Sales Revenue			$248,850
Cost of Goods Sold			
Inventory, January 1, 20XX		$ 60,750	
Purchases	$135,550		
Less: Purchase Returns and Allowances	1,500		
Purchase Discounts	750		
Net Purchases	$133,300		
Plus: Freight-In	2,450	135,750	
Goods Available for Sale		196,500	
Less: Inventory, December 31, 20XX		60,300	
Cost of Goods Sold			$136,200
Gross Margin			112,650
Operating Expenses			
Salaries and Commissions		15,300	
Rent		12,600	
Insurance		1,500	
Depreciation		900	
Supplies		825	
Total Operating Expenses			31,125
Operating Income			81,525
Other Revenue and (Expenses)			
Interest Revenue		1,500	
Interest Expense		(2,250)	(750)
Income Before Tax			80,775
Taxes (40%)			32,310
Net Income			$ 48,465

There is also an amount on the statement labeled "Freight-In." This is the amount spent by the firm in shipping charges to get goods to its facility from suppliers. Any expenses for freight from DLL to its customers (Freight-Out) would be an operating expense. In this case, the Freight-In expense of $2,450 is added to net purchase costs. Then these costs of current purchases are added to the beginning inventory to show that during the year the firm had a total of $196,500 in goods available for sale. Finally, the inventory of goods held on December 31 is subtracted from the goods available, for the total cost of goods sold of $136,200.

For a manufacturer, calculation of the cost of goods sold would be a bit more complicated and would probably include separate figures for such items as inventory of finished goods, the "work-in-process" inventory, the raw materials inventory, and the cost of goods delivered to customers during the year.

- The cost of goods sold is subtracted from the net sales revenue to get a gross margin of $112,650.
- Operating expenses for DLL include the salaries and commissions paid to its employees, rent on facilities and/or equipment, insurance, depreciation of capital items, and the cost of operating supplies. DLL has a total of $31,125 in operating expenses, which is deducted from the gross margin. Thus, DLL has an operating income of $81,525.
- DLL had both other income and expenses in the form of interest revenues of $1,500 and interest expenses of $2,250, making a total other expense of $750, which was subtracted from the operating income, leaving an income before tax of $80,775.

- Finally, the income before tax is reduced by 40 percent ($32,310) for taxes, leaving a net income of $48,465. The 40 percent is an average amount for federal and state corporate income taxes incurred by most firms.

The **balance sheet** lists the assets, liabilities, and stockholders' equity of the firm. Whereas the income statement represents what happened during an entire year, the balance sheet is like a snapshot; it shows the firm's financial situation at one point in time. For this reason, the balance sheet is sometimes called the *statement of financial position*.

Table B2 shows DLL Inc.'s balance sheet for December 31. Assets are any economic resource that is expected to benefit the firm in the short or long term. *Current assets* are items that are normally expected to be turned into cash or used up during the next 12 months or during the firm's normal operating cycle. Current assets for DLL include cash, securities, accounts receivable (money owed to the firm and not yet paid), inventory on hand, prepaid insurance, and supplies: a total of $84,525. *Long-term assets* include all assets that are not current assets. For DLL, these are property, plant, equipment, furniture, and fixtures less an amount for depreciation, or $45,300. The *total assets* for DLL are $129,825.

A firm's *liabilities* are its economic obligations, or debts that are payable to individuals or organizations outside the firm. *Current liabilities* are debts due in the coming year or in the firm's normal operating cycle. For DLL, the current liabilities—the accounts payable, unearned sales revenue, wages payable, and interest payable—total $72,450. *Long-term liabilities* (in the case of DLL, a note in the amount of $18,900) are all liabilities that are not due during the coming cycle.

Assets			
Current Assets			
Cash		$ 4,275	
Marketable Securities		12,000	
Accounts Receivable		6,900	
Inventory		60,300	
Prepaid Insurance		300	
Supplies		150	
Total Current Assets			84,525
Long-Term Assets—Property, Plant and Equipment			
Furniture and Fixtures	$42,300		
Less: Accumulated Depreciation	4,500	37,800	
Land		7,500	
Total Long-Term Assets			45,300
Total Assets			$129,825
Liabilities			
Current Liabilities			
Accounts Payable	$70,500		
Unearned Sales Revenue	1,050		
Wages Payable	600		
Interest Payable	300		
Total Current Liabilities		72,450	
Long-Term Liabilities			
Note Payable		18,900	
Total Liabilities			91,350
Stockholders' Equity			
Common Stock		15,000	
Retained Earnings		23,475	
Total Stockholders' Equity			38,475
Total Liabilities and Stockholders' Equity			$129,825

Stockholders' equity is the value of the stock and the corporation's capital or retained earnings. DLL has $15,000 in common stock and $23,475 in retained earnings for a total stockholders' equity of $38,475. Total liabilities always equal total assets—in this case, $129,825.

Important Financial Performance Ratios

How do managers and financial analysts compare the performance of a firm from one year to the next? How do investors compare the performance of one firm with that of another? Often a number of different financial ratios provide important information for such comparisons. Such *ratios* are percentage figures comparing various income statement items to net sales. Ratios provide a better way to compare performance than simple dollar sales or cost figures for two reasons. They enable analysts to compare the performance of large and small firms, and they provide a fair way to compare performance over time, without having to take inflation and other changes into account. In this section we will explain the basic operating ratios. Other measures of performance that marketers frequently use and that are also explained here are the inventory turnover rate and return on investment (ROI).

OPERATING RATIOS

Measures of performance calculated directly from the information in a firm's income statement (sometimes called an operating statement) are called the *operating ratios*. Each ratio compares some income statement item to net sales. The most useful of these are the *gross margin ratio, the net income ratio, the operating expense ratio*, and *the returns and allowances ratio*. These ratios vary widely by industry but tend to be important indicators of how a firm is doing within its industry. The ratios for DLL Inc. are shown in Table B3.

- The **gross margin ratio** shows what percentage of sales revenues is available for operating and other expenses and for profit. With DLL, this means that 45 percent, or nearly half, of every sales dollar is available for operating costs and for profits.
- The **net income ratio** (sometimes called the *net profit ratio*) shows what percentage of sales revenues is income or profit. For DLL, the net income ratio is 19.5 percent. This means that the firm's profit before taxes is about 20 cents of every dollar.
- The **operating expense ratio** is the percentage of sales needed for operating expenses. DLL has an operating expense ratio of 12.5 percent. Tracking operating expense ratios from one year to the next or comparing them with an industry average gives a firm important information about how efficient its operations are.
- The **returns and allowances ratio** shows what percentage of all sales is being returned, probably by unhappy customers. DLL's returns and allowances ratio shows that only a little over 1 percent of sales are being returned.

INVENTORY TURNOVER RATE

The *inventory turnover rate*, also referred to as the stockturn rate, is the number of times inventory or stock is turned over (sold and replaced) during a specified time period, usually a year.

TABLE **B3**						
Hypothetical Operating Ratios for DLL Inc.	Gross margin ratio	=	$\dfrac{\text{gross margin}}{\text{net sales}}$	=	$\dfrac{\$112,650}{248,850}$	= 45.3%
	Net income ratio	=	$\dfrac{\text{net income}}{\text{net sales}}$	=	$\dfrac{\$48,465}{248,850}$	= 19.5%
	Operating expense ratio	=	$\dfrac{\text{total operating expenses}}{\text{net sales}}$	=	$\dfrac{\$31,125}{248,850}$	= 12.5%
	Returns and allowances ratio	=	$\dfrac{\text{returns and allowances}}{\text{net sales}}$	=	$\dfrac{\$3,000}{248,850}$	= 1.2%

Inventory turnover rates are usually calculated on the basis of inventory costs, sometimes on the basis of inventory selling prices, and sometimes by number of units.

In our example, for DLL Inc., we know that for the year the cost of goods sold was $136,200. Information on the balance sheet enables us to find the average inventory. By adding the value of the beginning inventory to the ending inventory and dividing by 2, we can compute an average inventory. In the case of DLL, this would be

$$\frac{\$60,750 + \$60,300}{2} = \$60,525$$

Thus,

$$\frac{\text{Inventory turnover rate}}{\text{(in cost of goods sold)}} = \frac{\text{costs of goods sold}}{\text{average inventory at cost}} = \frac{\$136,200}{\$60,525} = 2.25\text{ times}$$

RETURN ON INVESTMENT (ROI)

Firms often develop business objectives in terms of return on investment, and ROI is often used to determine how effective (and efficient) the firm's management has been. First, however, we need to define exactly what a firm means by investment. In most cases, firms define investment as the total assets of the firm. In order to calculate the ROI, we need the net income found in the income statement and the total assets (or investment) found in the firm's balance sheet.

Return on investment is calculated as follows:

$$\text{ROI} = \frac{\text{net income}}{\text{total investment}}$$

For DLL Inc., if the total assets are $129,825, then the ROI is

$$\frac{\$48,465}{\$129,825} = 37.3\%$$

Sometimes return on investment is calculated by using an expanded formula.

$$\text{ROI} = \frac{\text{net profit}}{\text{sales}} \times \frac{\text{sales}}{\text{investment}}$$

$$= \frac{\$48,465}{\$248,850} \times \frac{\$248,850}{\$129,825} = 37.3\%$$

This formula makes it easy to show how ROI can be increased and what might reduce ROI. For example, there are different ways to increase ROI. First, if the management focuses on cutting costs and increasing efficiency, profits may be increased while sales remain the same.

$$\text{ROI} = \frac{\text{net profit}}{\text{sales}} \times \frac{\text{sales}}{\text{investment}}$$

$$= \frac{\$53,277}{\$248,850} \times \frac{\$248,850}{\$129,825} = 41.0\%$$

But ROI can be increased just as much without improving performance simply by reducing the investment—by maintaining less inventory, for instance.

$$\text{ROI} = \frac{\text{net profit}}{\text{sales}} \times \frac{\text{sales}}{\text{investment}}$$

$$= \frac{\$48,465}{\$248,850} \times \frac{\$248,850}{\$114,825} = 42.2\%$$

Sometimes, however, differences among the total assets of firms may be related to the age of the firm or the type of industry, which makes ROI a poor indicator of performance. For this reason, some firms have replaced the traditional ROI measures with *return on assets managed* (ROAM), *return on net assets* (RONA), or *return on stockholders' equity* (ROE).

Price Elasticity

Price elasticity, discussed in Chapter 12, is a measure of the sensitivity of customers to changes in price. Price elasticity is calculated by comparing the percentage change in quantity to the percentage change in price.

$$\text{Price elasticity of demand} = \frac{\text{percentage change in quantity}}{\text{percentage change in price}}$$

$$E = \frac{(Q_2 - Q_1)/Q_1}{(P_2 - P_1)/P_1}$$

where Q = quantity and P = price.

For example, suppose the manufacturer of jeans in Chapter 13 increased its price from $30.00 a pair to $35.00. But instead of 40,000 pairs being sold, sales declined to only 38,000 pairs. The price elasticity would be calculated as follows:

$$E = \frac{(38,000 - 40,000)/40,000}{(\$35.00 - 30.00)/\$30.00} = \frac{-0.05}{0.167} = 0.30$$

Note that elasticity is usually expressed as a positive number even though the calculations create a negative value.

In this case, a relative small change in demand (5 percent) resulted from a fairly large change in price (16.7 percent), indicating that demand is inelastic. At 0.30, the elasticity is less than 1.

On the other hand, what if the same change in price resulted in a reduction in demand to 30,000 pairs of jeans? Then the elasticity would be

$$E = \frac{(30,000 - 40,000)/40,000}{(\$35.00 - 30.00)/\$30.00} = \frac{-0.25}{0.167} = 1.50$$

In this case, because the 16.7 percent change in price resulted in an even larger change in demand (25 percent), demand is elastic. The elasticity of 1.50 is greater than 1.

Note: Elasticity may also be calculated by dividing the change in quantity by the average of Q_1 and Q_2 and dividing the change in price by the average of the two prices. We, however, have chosen to include the formula that uses the initial quantity and price rather than the average.

Economic Order Quantity

The amount a firm should order at one time is called the *economic order quantity* (EOQ). Every time a firm places an order, there are additional costs. By ordering larger quantities less frequently, the firm saves on these costs. But it also costs money to maintain large inventories of needed materials. The EOQ is the order volume that provides both the lowest processing costs and the lowest inventory costs. The EOQ can be calculated as follows:

1. Determine the **order processing cost**. This is the total amount it costs a firm to place an order from beginning to end. Typically, this might include the operating expenses for the purchasing department, costs for follow-up, costs of record keeping of orders (data processing), costs for the receiving department, and costs for the processing and paying of invoices from suppliers. The simplest way to calculate this is to add up all these yearly costs and then divide by the number of orders placed during the year.
2. Next, calculate the **inventory carrying cost**. This is the total of all costs involved in carrying inventory. These costs include the costs of capital tied up in inventory, the cost of waste (merchandise that becomes obsolete or unuseable), depreciation costs, storage costs, insurance premiums, property taxes, and opportunity costs.

The formula for calculating EOQ is

$$EOQ = \sqrt{\frac{2 \times \text{units sold (or annual usage)} \times \text{ordering cost}}{\text{unit cost} \times \text{inventory carrying cost (\%)}}}$$

For example, suppose an office supply store sells 6,000 cases of pens a year at a cost of $12.00 a case. The cost to the store for each order placed is $60.00. The cost of carrying the pens in the warehouse is 24 percent per year (this is a typical inventory carrying cost in many businesses.) Thus, the calculation is

$$EOQ = \sqrt{\frac{2 \times 6000 \times \$60}{\$12 \times 0.24}} = \sqrt{\frac{\$720{,}000}{\$2.88}} = 500$$

The firm should order pens about once a month (it sells 6,000 cases a year or 500 cases a month).

Notes

CHAPTER 1

1. John W. Schouten, "Selves in Transition: Symbolic Consumption in Personal Rites of Passage and Identity Reconstruction," *Journal of Consumer Research* (17 March 1991): 412–25; Michael R. Solomon, "The Wardrobe Consultant: Exploring the Role of a New Retailing Partner," *Journal of Retailing* 63 (1987): 110–28; Michael R. Solomon and Susan P. Douglas, "Diversity in Product Symbolism: The Case of Female Executive Clothing," *Psychology & Marketing* 4 (1987): 189–212; Joseph Z. Wisenblit, "Person Positioning: Empirical Evidence and a New Paradigm," *Journal of Professional Services Marketing* 4, no. 2 (1989): 51–82.
2. "AMA Board Approves New Definition," *Marketing News* (1 March 1985): 1.
3. Michael R. Solomon, "Deep-Seated Materialism: The Case of Levi's 501 Jeans," in *Advances in Consumer Research*, ed. Richard Lutz (Las Vegas, NV: Association for Consumer Research, 1986), 13:619–22.
4. Peter F. Drucker, *Management: Tasks, Responsibilities, Practices* (New York: Harper & Row, 1972), 64–65.
5. Kevin Helliker, "Can Wristwatch Whiz Switch Swatch Cachet to an Automobile?" *The Wall Street Journal* (4 March 1994) A1, p. 2; Ferdinand Protzman, "Off the Wrist, Onto the Road: A Swatch on Wheels," *New York Times* (5 March 1994) 39.
6. Philip Shenon, "Internet Piracy is Suspected as U.S. Agents Raid Campuses," 12 December 2001, accessed via www.nytimes.com
7. Lee D. Dahringer, "Marketing Services Internationally: Barriers and Management Strategies," *Journal of Service Marketing* 5 (1991): 5–17.
8. CyberAtlas staff, "B2B E—Commerce Will Survive Growing Pains" www.cyberatlas.internet.com/markets/b2b/article/0, 10091_930251,00.html
9. "Cut to the Chase", *BtoB* (10 April 2000): 56.
10. Gerry Khermouch, "Virgin's 'Va Va' Bottle Has 'Voom'; First Ads via Long Haymes Carr," *Brandweek* (10 July 2000): 13.
11. Sonai Reyes and Gerry Khermouch, "Ocean Spray's Squeeze Play," *Brandweek* (26 June 2000 1): 6.
12. Jennifer Gilbert, "Sites Play to Women's Specialized Interests," *Advertising Age* (1 May 2000): 56, 62.
13. David Kirkpatrick, "Looking for Profits in Poverty," *Fortune* (5 February 2001): 175–178.
14. "Henry Ford and The Model T", *Forbes Greatest Business Stories*, (New York: John Wiley & Sons, Inc., 1996) accessed via www.wiley.com/legacy/products/subject/business/forbes/ford.html.
15. Theodore Levitt, "Marketing Myopia," *Harvard Business Review* (July–August 1960): 45–56.
16. Rahul Jacob, "How to Retread Customers," *Fortune* (autumn/winter 1993): 23–24.
17. Kate Fitzgerald, "Avon Adds 3 Venues to Anti-Cancer Walk," *Advertising Age* (1 May 2000): 54.
18. Ani Hadjian, "Communicate, Innovate," *Fortune* (autumn/winter 1993): 25
19. Laura Petrecca, "Sponsors Press On Despite NASCAR Deaths," *Advertising Age* (26 February 2001), accessed via www.adage.com/news.cms?newsId=32185#.
20. Sal Randazzo, "Advertising as Myth-Maker; Brands as Gods and Heroes," *Advertising Age* (8 November 1993): 32.
21. "Dear Chrysler: Outsiders' Advice on Handling the Odometer Charge," *The Wall Street Journal* (26 June 1987): 19.
22. Larry Edwards, "The Decision Was Easy," *Advertising Age* 2 (26 August 1987): 106. For research and discussion related to public policy issues, see Paul N. Bloom and Stephen A. Greyser, "The Maturing of Consumerism," *Harvard Business Review* (November/December 1981): 130–39; George S. Day, "Assessing the Effect of Information Disclosure Requirements," *Journal of Marketing* (April 1976): 42–52; Dennis E. Garrett, "The Effectiveness of Marketing Policy Boycotts: Environmental Opposition to Marketing," *Journal of Marketing* 51 (January 1987): 44–53; Michael Houston and Michael Rothschild, "Policy-Related Experiments on Information Provision: A Normative Model and Explication," *Journal of Marketing Research* 17 (November 1980): 432–49; Jacob Jacoby, Wayne D. Hoyer, and David A. Sheluga, *Misperception of Televised Communications* (New York: American Association of Advertising Agencies, 1980); Gene R. Laczniak and Patrick E. Murphy, *Marketing Ethics: Guidelines for Managers* (Lexington, MA: Lexington Books, 1985): 117–23; Lynn Phillips and Bobby Calder, "Evaluating Consumer Protection Laws: Promising Methods," *Journal of Consumer Affairs* 14 (summer 1980): 9–36; Donald P. Robin and Eric Reidenbach, "Social Responsibility, Ethics, and Marketing Strategy: Closing the Gap Between Concept and Application," *Journal of Marketing* 51 (January 1987): 44–58; Howard Schutz and Marianne Casey, "Consumer Perceptions of Advertising as Misleading," *Journal of Consumer Affairs* 15 (winter 1981): 340–57; Darlene Brannigan Smith and Paul N. Bloom, "Is Consumerism Dead or Alive? Some New Evidence," in *Advances in Consumer Research*, ed. Thomas C. Kinnear (Provo, UT: Association for Consumer Research, 1984): 11:569–73.
23. William Leiss, Stephen Kline, and Sut Jhally, *Social Communication in Advertising: Persons, Products, and Images of Well-Being* (Toronto: Methuen, 1986); Jerry Mander, *Four Arguments for the Elimination of Television* (New York: Morrow, 1977).
24. George Stigler, "The Economics of Information," *Journal of Political Economy* (1961): 69.
25. William Leiss, Stephen Kline, and Sut Jhally.

CHAPTER 2

1. *2000 Annual Report*, Philip Morris.
2. David Greising, "I'd Like the World to Buy a Coke," *Business Week* (13 April 1998): 70–76.
3. Theodore Levitt, "Marketing Myopia," *Harvard Business Review* (September–October 1975): 1ff.
4. Kodak Corporate Information: Mission Statement, posted 12 April 2000, www.kodak.com/country/US/en/corp/mission/visionMission Values.shtml;
5. 2000 Annual Report, Philip Morris.
6. www.viacom.com/thefacts.tin.
7. Linda Grant, "Outmarketing P&G," *Fortune* (12 January 1998): 150–152.
8. Richard W. Melcher, "Why Zima Faded So Fast," *Business Week* (10 March 1997): 11–14.
9. Bill Sharfman, "One Last Look at Oldsmobile," *Brandweek* (8 Jaunuary 2001): 28–30, 32.
10. "Inside Kraft: A Company Overview," www.kraftfoods.com
11. Geoffrey Colvin, "The Ultimate Manager," *Fortune* (22 November 1999): 185–187.
12. Robert Berner and Gerry Khermouch, "Retail Reckoning," *Business Week* (10 December 2001): 71–77.
13. Jeffrey Zygmont, "In Command at Campbell," *Sky* (March 1993): 52–62.
14. Justin Martin, "Are You as Good as You Think You Are?" *Fortune* (30 September 1996): 142–52.
15. Julia Flynn, "IKEA's New Game Plan," *Business Week* (6 October 1997): 99, 102.
16. Anthony Bianco and Pamela L. Moore, "Downfall X," *Business Week* (5 March 2001): 82–92.

17. Michael Arndt, "Did Somebody Say McBurrito?" *Business Week* (10 April 2000): 166, 170.
18. Dyan Machan, "Is the Hog Going Soft?" *Forbes* (10 March 1997): 114–119.
19. Mike McKesson, "Blazer Aims for High Sales," *Times Union* (8 September 1994): C-12.
20. Karen Schwartz and Ian P. Murphy, "Airline Food Is No Joke," *Marketing News* (13 October 1997): 1, 10.
21. Ian P. Murphy, "Southwest Emphasizes Brand as Others Follow the Low-Fare Leader," *Marketing News* (4 November 1996): 1–2.
22. Gail DeGeorge, "Dilbert to the Rescue," *Business Week* (4 May 1998): 166.
23. "Starbucks Reports November Revenues, Opened 1,000th International Location," press release, November 29, 2001, www.starbucks.com/aboutus/pressdesc.asp?id=219.
24. Ronald Henkoff, "Growing Your Company: Five Ways to Do It Right," *Fortune* (26 November 1996): 78–88.
25. Geoffrey Colvin, "How Rubbermaid Managed to Fail," *Fortune* (23 November 1998): 32–33.
26. Charles P. Wallace, "Adidas: Back in the Game," *Fortune* (18 August 1997): 176–182.
27. Jeff Jensen, "Nike to Slice Marketing by $100 Mil," *Advertising Age* (23 March 1998): 1, 46.
28. www.pg.com
29. David Whelan, "Wrapped in the Flag," *American Demographics* (December 2001): 37–38.
30. "Industry Solutions," www.lotus.com/home.nsf/welcome/industry
31. Terence P. Paré, "How to Find Out What They Want," *Fortune* (autumn/winter supplement 1993): 39–41.

CHAPTER 3

1. *1992 Annual Report*, Rockwell International.
2. www.benjerry.com/mission.html; Ben & Jerry's hand-out available at the factory store (1993); Paul C. Judge, "Is It Rainforest Crunch Time?" *Business Week* (15 July 1996): 70–71.
3. www.dow.com/webapps/lit/litorder.asp?filepath=about/pdfs/noreg/473-00001.pdf&pdf=true
4. Rajendra S. Sisodia, "We Need Zero Tolerance toward Ethics Violations," *Marketing News* (March 1990): 4, 14.
5. "When Gift Giving Goes Too Far," *Sales and Marketing Management* (June 1995): 15.
6. Catherine A. Cole, "Deterrence and Consumer Fraud," *Journal of Retailing* (spring 1989): 107–20; Roy Carter, "Whispering Sweet Nothings to the Shop Thief," *Retail & Distribution Management* (January/February 1986): 36.
7. Kenneth N. Gilpin, "Firestone Will Recall An Additional 3.5 Million Tires," *New York Times*, Online Edition, 5 October 2001.
8. *Facts on File*, 17 March 1978, 185; *Facts on File*, 14 April 1978, 264; *Facts on File*, 19 May 1978, 366; *Facts on File*, 28 July 1978, 569; *Facts on File*, 22 September 1978, 718–19.
9. Consumer Product Safety Council press release, "CPSC, Window Covering Industry Announce Recall to Repair Window Blinds, New Investigation of Children's Deaths Leads to Redesigned Window Blinds," 1 November 2000, accessed via www.cpsc.gov/cpscpub/prerel/prhtml01/01023.html.
10. Melillo, Wendy, "Amazon Price Test Raises Net Privacy Outcry," *Adweek* (2 October 2001) 41 (40): 51 (3).
11. Joan C. Szabo, "Business Pitches in after Andrew," *Nation's Business* (October 1992): 37–39. Joan C. Szabo, "Business Pitches in after Andrew," *Nation's Business* (October 1992): 37–39.
12. Federal Trade Commission, *FTC Policy Statement on Deception*, 14 October 1983, www.ftc.gov/bcp/policystmt/ad-decept.htm; Dorothy Cohen, *Legal Issues in Marketing Decision Making* (Cincinnati, OH: South-Western College Publishing, 1995).
13. Ibid.
14. "Gateway Fined for False Ads," *Advertising Age*, 23 July 1998, accessed via www.adage.com/news.cms?newsId=23418.

15. Ira Teinowitz, "FTC Faces Test of Ad Power," *Advertising Age* (30 March 1998): 26.
16. Ronald Alsop, "Companies Reputations Depends on Service They Give Customers," *The Wall Street Journal Online*, 16 January 2002.
17. Christine Y. Chen and Greg Lindsay, "Will Amazon (.com) Save the Amazon?" *Fortune* (20 March 2000): 224.
18. Ibid.
19. Catherine Arnst, Stanley Reed, Gay McWilliams, and De'Ann Weimer, "When Green Begets Green," *Business Week* (10 November 1997): 98–106.
20. Sharon Begley, "The Battle for Planet Earth," *Newsweek* (24 April 2000): 50–53.
21. www.cool-companies.org/ads/ad5.cfm
22. Ibid.
23. Ibid.
24. Nancy Arnott, "Marketing with a Passion," *Sales & Marketing Management* (January 1994): 64–71.
25. "Insight vs. Prius," www.insightcentral.net/prius.html; Why the Toyota Prius and Honda Insight cannot obtain a carpool lane sticker, www.arb.ca.gov/msprog/carpool/faq.htm
26. Ibid.
27. Nancy Arnott, "Marketing with a Passion"
28. Fiona Gibb, "Avon: Pinning Down an Issue," *Sales & Marketing Management*, (September 1994): 85; www.avonb.com/about/women/crusade/_background
29. Laura Bird, "Denny's TVAd Seeks to Mend Bias Image," *Wall Street Journal* (21 June 1993): B3.
30. Chuck Hawkins, "Denny's: The Stain That Isn't Coming Out," *Business Week* (28 June 1993): 98–99.
31. Patricia Digh, "America's Largest Untapped Market: Who They Are, the Potential They Represent," *Fortune* (2 March 1998): S1–S12; "Hertz Offers a Full Range of Services for the Physically Challenged," accessed via www.hertz.com/serv/us/services_phys.html.
32. Ann Harrington, "How Welfare Worked for T.J. Maxx," *Fortune* (13 November 2000): 453–456.
33. Joe Barstys, Subaru of America, personal communication, 3 January 2002.
34. Geoffrey Colvin, "The Ultimate Manger," *Fortune* (22 November 1999): 185–187.
35. The Malcolm Baldrige National Quality Improvement Act of 1987—Public Law 100–107, www.quality.nist.gov/Improvement_Act.htm
36. "ISO 9000 and ISO 14000 in Plain Language," www.iso.ch/iso/en/iso9000-14000/tour/magical.html
37. John Holusha, "Global Yardsticks Are Set to Measure 'Quality,' " *The New York Times* (23 December 1992): D6.
38. Patrice Rhoades-Baum, "Consolidating Support Functions: This Strategic Move Helps Companies Meet Business Needs," *Fortune* (10 July 1995): S9.
39. Stanley Brown, "Now It Can Be Told," *Sales & Marketing Management* (November 1994): 34, 38.
40. Patrick Bultema, "From Cost Center to Profit Center: The Changing Bent of Support Operations," *Fortune* (10 July 1995): S2–S3.
41. Don E. Schultz, "Maybe We Should Start All Over with an IMC Organization," *Marketing News* (25 October 1993): 8.
42. *Fortune Magazine* (8 January 2001): accessed via the web at www.FORTUNE.COM/INDEXW.JHTML?CHANNEL=LIST_FRAG_CHANNEL.JHTML&SEARCH_ERROR=0&LIST_FRAG=LIST_3COLUMN_BEST_COMPANIES_WORK_FOR.JHTML&_REQUESTID=251066
43. www.russell.com/services/individual/employee/articles/scarticle3b.htm http://woodrow.mpls.frb.fed.us/economy/calc/cpihome.html
44. Stan Crock, Geoffrey Smith, Joseph Weber, Richard A. Melcher, and Linda Himelstein, "They Snoop to Conquer," *Business Week* (28 October 1996): 172–76.
45. Jack Neff, "P&G: Spy Skids," *Advertising Age* (3 September 2001): 3 (2).
46. Michael Brick, "High Court Declines to Hear Microsoft Appeal," *New York Times Online*, 9 October 2001.

47. www.eggland.com/egg.html

48. Roger O. Crockett, "Heard Any Good Computer Files Lately," *Business Week e.biz* (27 September 1999): EB 16.

49. P. Rajan Varadarajan, Terry Clark, and William M. Pride, "Controlling the Uncontrollable: Managing Your Market Environment," *Sloan Management Review*, (winter 1992): 39–47.

50. www.bbb.org

51. "Packaging Draws Protest," *Marketing News* (4 July 1994): 1.

52. Margaret Carlson, "Where Calvin Crossed the Line," *Time* (11 September 1995): 64.

CHAPTER 4

1. Press Release, Nike, "Nike Reports Second Quarter Earnings Up Nine Percent; Worldwide Futures Orders Increase eight Percent," 20 December 2001, accessed via www.nikebiz.com/media/n_q202.shtml, February 18, 2002.

2. Press Release, World Trade Organization, 19 October 2001,"World trade slows sharply in 2001 amid the uncertain international situation," accessed via www.wto.org/english/news_e/pres01_e/pr249_e.htm, February 18, 2002.

3. Sak Onkvisit and John J. Shaw, *International Marketing: Analysis and Strategy*, 2nd ed. (New York: Macmillan, 1993).

4. Brett Pulley and Andrew Tanzer, "Sumner's Gemstone," *Forbes* (21 February 2000): 107 (6).

5. Sara Hope Franks, "Overseas, Its What's Inside That Sells," *Washington Post National Weekly Edition*, 5–11 December 1994, 21.

6. Louis Uchitelle, "Gillette's World View: One Blade Fits All," *New York Times* (4 January 1994): C3.

7. Michael E. Porter, *The Competitive Advantage of Nations* (New York: The Free Press, 1990).

8. Michael R. Czinkota and Masaaki Kotabe, "America's New World Trade Order," *Marketing Management* 1(3) (1992): 47–54.

9. Onkvisit and Shaw, International Marketing.

10. Ernest Beck, "Russians Resist Foreign Vodka, Frustrating Western Distillers," *Wall Street Journal Interactive Edition*, 15 January 1998.

11. Onkvisit and Shaw, International Marketing.

12. "The WTO in Brief," accessed via, www.wto.org/english/thewto_e/whatis_e/inbrief_e/inbr00_e.htm, February 18, 2002.

13. Ibid.

14. Nic Hopkins, "Software piracy Microsoft's Big Threat," CNN.com, 7 February 2001, accessed via www.cnn.com/2001/WORLD/asiapcf/east/02/07/hongkong.microsoft, February 18, 2002.

15. "Curfew in Effect as Seattle Struggles to Control WTO Protests," CNN.com, 30 November 1999, accessed via www.cnn.com/US/9911/30/wto.04/#3, February 14, 2002.

16. Aaron Bernstein, "Backlash," *Business Week* (24 April 2000): 38–44. Rich Miller, "Does Anybody Love the IMF or World Bank?" *Business Week* (24 April 2000): 46–48.

17. "Activists to WTO: Put People Over Profits," CNN.com, 29 November 1999, accessed via www.cnn.com/US/9911/29/wto.seattle.02/, February 7, 2002.

18. "WTO International Trade Statistics, 2001," accessed via www.wto.org/english/res_e/statis_e/statis_e/htm

19. Harvey S. James, Jr. and Murray Weidenbaum, *When Businesses Cross International Borders: Strategic Alliances and Their Alternative* (Westport, CT: Praeger, 1993).

20. "The ABC of the European Union," The European Union Online, accessed via http://europa.eu.int/abc-en.htm, January 25, 2002.

21. Michael Solomon, Gary Bamossy, and Søren Askegaard, *Consumer Behavior: A European Perspective* (London: Prentice Hall International, 1999).

22. Thane Peterson, "The Euro," *Business Week*, (27 April 1998): 90–94.

23. William C. Symonds, "Border Crossings," *Business Week* (22 November 1993): 40(3); "FACT SHEET: North American Free Trade Agreement," July 2001, accessed via www.fas.usda.gov/info/factsheets/nafta.html, February 18, 2002.

24. "Far East Goes Deep South," *Latin Trade* 5 (July 1997): 611, accessed via www.xls.com, 27 August 1998.

25. Geri Smith, Elisabeth Malkin, Johathan Wheatley, Paul Magnusson, and Michael Arnds, "Betting on Free Trade," *Business Week* (23 April 2001): 60–62.

26. Ibid, p. 60.

27. Peter Fuhrman and Michael Schuman, "Where Are the Indians? The Russians?" *Forbes* (17 July 1995): 126(2).

28. "North America is the Leading Region for Internet Users According to the Computer Industry Almanac," *Computer Industry Almanac*, accessed via www.c-i-a.com/199908iu.htm, February 13, 2002.

29. Brian Ploskina, "Globalizing E-Business Can Invite a World of Pain," *E-Business* (6 October 1999): 30, 32.

30. Dana James and Kathleen V. Schmidt, "Brazil Net: Growing Demand Tempered by Privacy Regulations," *Marketing News* (27 September 1999): 40–41.

31. Karen Yates, "Advertising's Heart of Darkness," *Advertising Age* (15 May 1995): I-10, I-15; Cyndee Miller, "Exploring Africa: Untapped Market Scares Most Companies," *Marketing News* (21 July 1997,): 1; Matt Murray, "Weight Watchers Hopes to Fatten Its Ledgers with Zimbabwe Focus," *Wall Street Journal Interactive Edition*, 25 August 1997.

32. Ibid., 62(3).

33. Quoted in Sabrina Tavernise, "Moscow is Getting a Taste of the Mall," *The New York Times on the Web*, 10 August 2001.

34. "Peru: Privatization Is Principal Policy for Attracting Foreign Investment," *Wall Street Journal* (27 October 1993): B7.

35. Press Release, World Trade Organization, 19 March 1998, accessed via www.wto.org/wto/intltrad/internat.htm, 27 August 1998.

36. Normandy Madden, "Starbucks Ships Its Coffee Craze to Pacific Rim," *Advertising Age* (27 April 1998): 28.

37. David Barboza, "When Golden Arches are Too Red, White and Blue," *New York Times on the Web*, October 14, 2001.

38. Onkvisit and Shaw, International Marketing.

39. Sara Hope Franks, "Overseas, It's What's Inside That Sells," *Washington Post National Weekly Edition*, 5–11 December 1994, 21.

40. William C. Symonds, "Border Crossings," *Business Week* (22 November 1993): 40.

41. Michael O'Neal, "Does New Balance Have an American Soul?" *Business Week* (12 December 1994): 86, 90.

42. "French Council Eases Language Ban," *The New York Times* (31 July 1994): 12.

43. Press Release, World Trade Organization, 19 March 1998, accessed via www.wto.org/wto/intltrad/internat.htm, 27 August 1998.

44. Thomas L. Friedman, "U.S. Prods Indonesia on Rights," *The New York Times* (18 January 1994): D1(2).

45. Quoted in Michael Janofsky, "Levi Strauss: American Symbol with a Cause," *The New York Times* (4 January 1994): C4; Russell Mitchell, "Managing by Values," *Business Week*, (1 August 1994): 46(7); Mitchell Zuckoff, "Taking a Profit, and Inflicting a Cost," *Boston Globe* (10 July 1994): 1(2).

46. Joanna Ramey, "Levi's Will Resume Production in China After 5-Year Absence," *Women's Wear Daily*, 9 April 1998, 1(2).

47. Alecia Swasy, "Don't Sell Thick Diapers in Tokyo," *The New York Times* (13 October 1993): F9.

48. Richard W. Pollay, "Measuring the Cultural Values Manifest in Advertising," *Current Issues and Research in Advertising* 6 (1983): 71–92.

49. Daniel Goleman, "The Group and the Self: New Focus on a Cultural Rift," *The New York Times* (25 December 1990): 37; Harry C. Triandis, "The Self and Social Behavior in Differing Cultural Contexts," *Psychological Review* 96 (July 1989): 506; Harry C. Triandis, Robert Bontempo, Marcelo J. Villareal, Masaaki Asai, and Nydia Lucca, "Individualism and Collectivism: Cross-Cultural Perspectives on Self-Ingroup Relationships," *Journal of Personality and Social Psychology* 54 (February 1988): 323.

50. Paul M. Sherer, "North American and Asian Executives Have Contrasting Values, Study Finds," *Wall Street Journal* (8 March 1996): 12B.

51. Quoted in "New Japanese Fads Blazing Trails in Cleanliness," *Montgomery Advertiser*, 28 September 1996, 10A; cf. also Andrew Pollack, "Can the Pen Really Be Mightier Than the Germ?" *The New York Times* (27 July 1995): A4.

52. George J. McCall and J. L. Simmons, *Social Psychology: A Sociological Approach* (New York: The Free Press, 1982).

53. Alison Leigh Cowan, "Caterpillar: Worldwide Watch for Opportunities," *The New York Times*, (4 January 1994): C4.

54. Norihiko Shirouzu, "P&G's Joy Makes a Splash in Japan's Dish Soap Market," *Wall Street Journal Interactive Edition*, 10 December 1997.

55. Philip R. Cateora, *Strategic International Marketing* (Homewood, IL: Dow Jones-Irwin, Inc., 1985).

56. "Capital Wrap-Up: Competitiveness," *Business Week* (1 November 1993): 47.

57. U.S. Department of Justice, "Foreign Corrupt Practices Act Antibribery Provisions," October 24, 2001, accessed via www.usdoj.gov/criminal/fraud/fcpa/dojdocb.htm, January 15, 2002.

58. William Echikson, "The Trick to Selling in Europe," *Fortune* (20 September 1993): 82.

59. See David Mick, "Consumer Research and Semiotics: Exploring the Morphology of Signs, Symbols, and Significance," *Journal of Consumer Research* 13 (September 1986): 196–213.

60. Marian Katz, "No Women, No Alcohol, Learn Saudi Taboos Before Placing Ads," *International Advertiser* (February 1986): 11–12.

61. Steve Rivkin, "The Name Game Heats Up," *Marketing News* (22 April 1996): 8.

62. Items excerpted from Terence A. Shimp and Subhash Sharma, "Consumer Ethnocentrism: Construction and Validation of the CETSCALE," *Journal of Marketing Research* 24 (August 1987): 282.

63. Kevin Kelly and Karen Lowry Miller, "The Rumble Heard Round the World: Harleys," *Business Week* (24 May 1993): 58(2).

64. Quoted in Yuri Kageyama, "Japanese Shoppers Go American When the Going Gets Rough," *Opelika-Auburn News*, 13 August 2001, 8A.

65. Evan Perez, "Argentina's Middle Class Goes Suburban Thanks to Vision of a U.S. Home Builder," *Wall Street Journal Interactive Edition*, 16 January 2002.

66. Dana Milbank, "Made in America Becomes a Boast in Europe," *Wall Street Journal*, 19 January 1994, B1(2).

67. Craig Smith, "Bowling Fever Sweeps China as Sport Picks Up Momentum," *Wall Street Journal Interactive Edition*, 11 November 1997.

68. Solomon, Bamossy, and Askegaard, *Consumer Behavior*.

69. "Business Leaders Again Name GE World's Most Respected Company," GE press release, December 17, 2001, accessed via www.ge.com/cgi-bin/biz-pressroom-list.pl? list=all, February 12, 2002.

70. Tim Smart, "GE's Brave New World," *Business Week* (8 November 1993): 64(7).

71. *GE 2000 Annual Report*, accessed via www.ge.com/annual00/letter/index.html, January 22, 2002.

72. Alexander Hiam and Charles D. Schewe, *The Portable MBA in Marketing* (New York: John Wiley & Sons, 1992).

73. Harvey S. James Jr. and Murray Weidenbaum, *When Businesses Cross International Borders*, (Westport, CT: Praeger, 1993).

74. Onkvisit and Shaw, International Marketing.

75. www.mcdonalds.com/corporate/index.html

76. www.gm.com/company/corp_info/profiles/

77. Ibid.

78. Onkvisit and Shaw, International Marketing.

79. Jeremy Kahn, "The World's Most Admired Companies," *Fortune* (October 26, 1998).

80. Jeremy Kahn, "The World's Most Admired Companies," *Fortune* (October 26, 1998).

81. Ibid.

82. One of the most influential arguments for this perspective can be found in Theodore Levitt, "The Globalization of Markets," *Harvard Business Review* (May–June 1983): 92–102.

83. Juliana Koranteng, "Reebok Finds Its Second Wind as It Pursues Global Presence," *Advertising Age International* (January 1998): 18.

84. Terry Clark, "International Marketing and National Character: A Review and Proposal for an Integrative Theory," *Journal of Marketing* 54 (October 1990): 66–79.

85. Norihiko Shirouzu, "Snapple in Japan: How a Splash Dried Up," *Wall Street Journal*, 15 April 1996, B1(2).

86. Vanessa O'Connell, "Exxon Mobile 'Centralizes' a New Global Campaign," *The Wall Street Journal Interactive Edition*, 11 July 2001.

87. Richard C. Morais, "The Color of Beauty," *Forbes* (November 27, 2000): 170–176.

88. Franks, "Overseas, It's What's Inside That Sells."

89. Echikson, "The Trick to Selling in Europe."

90. Leonhardt, "It Was a Hit in Buenos Aires—So Why Not Boise?" *Business Week* (7 September 1998): 56.

91. Bradley Johnson, "Unisys Touts Service in Global Ads," *Advertising Age* 3(2) (15 February 1993): 59.

92. Ashish Banerjee, "Global Campaigns Don't Work; Multinationals Do," *Advertising Age* (18 April 1994): 23.

93. Clyde H. Farnsworth, "Yoked in Twin Solitudes: Canada's Two Cultures," *New York Times*, 18 September 1994, E4.

94. Sheryl WuDunn, "An Uphill Journey to Japan," *New York Times*, 16 May 1995, D1(2).

95. Onkvisit and Shaw, International Marketing.

96. "Kodak Alleges Fuji Photo is Dumping Color Photographic Paper in the U.S.," *Wall Street Journal*, 22 February 1993, B6.

97. Wendy Zellner, "How Well Does Wal-Mart Travel?" *Business Week* (3 September 2001): 82 (2).

CHAPTER 5

1. Alan J. Greco and Jack T. Hogue, "Developing Marketing Decision Support Systems in Consumer Goods Firms," *Journal of Consumer Marketing* 7 (1990): 55–64.

2. Edward Cornish, *The Study of the Future: An Introduction to the Art and Science of Understanding and Shaping Tomorrow's World* (Washington, DC: World Future Society, 1977); examples provided by Professor Fredric Kropp, personal communication, 12 August 1998.

3. "Performer Q," www.qscores.com/performer-q1.html.

4. Yumiko Ono, "An Ad for Smudge-Proof Makeup Rubs a Big Marketer Wrong Way," *Wall Street Journal* (12 April 1996): B1.

5. Laurie Hays, "Using Computers to Divine Who Might Buy a Gas Grill," *Wall Street Journal* (16 August 1994): B1(2).

6. Peter R. Peacock, "Data Mining in Marketing: Part I," *Marketing Management*, Winter 1998, 9–18.

7. Ibid.

8. Paul C. Judge, "Do You Know Who Your Most Profitable Customers Are?" *Business Week Online*, September 14, 1998, Accessed at www.Businessweek.Com/1998/37/B3595144.Htm?$Se.

9. Robert Baxter, Mercedes-Benz North America, personal communication (June 1996).

10. Cyndee Miller, "Sometimes a Researcher Has No Choice But to Hang Out in a Bar," *Marketing News* (3 January 1994): 16(2).

11. Ronald B. Lieber, "Storytelling: A New Way to Get Close to Your Customer," *Fortune* (3 February 1997): 102–108.

12. Ibid.

13. Ibid.

14. Michael R. Solomon, *Consumer Behavior: Buying, Having and Being*, 5th ed., Upper Saddle River, NJ: Prentice Hall, 2001.

15. Jack Weber, "Absorbing Some Changes," *Quirk's*, Article # 101 (November 1994), accessed via www.quirks.com, 26 January 1998.

16. Leslie Kaufman, "Enough Talk," *Newsweek* (18 August 1997): 48–49.

17. Kelly Shermach, "Art of Communication," *Marketing News* (8 May 1995): 2.

18. Srikumar Rao, "Diaper–Beer Syndrome," *Forbes* (6 April 1998): 128(3).

19. Peter Krasilovsky, "Surveys in Cyberspace," *Marketing Tools*, November/December 1996, 18(4).

20. Basil G. Englis and Michael R. Solomon, *Life/Style OnLine©: A Web–Based Methodology for Visually–Oriented Consumer Research,"*

Journal of Interactive Marketing, 14, 1, (2000) 2–14; Basil G. Englis, Michael R. Solomon, and Paula D. Harveston, "Web–Based, Visually Oriented Consumer Research Tools," in *Online Consumer Psychology: Understanding How to Interact with Consumers in the Virtual World*, Curt Haugtvedt, Karen Machleit, and Richard Yalch, eds. Hillsdale, NJ: Lawrence Erlbaum, in press.

21. Michael J. McCarthy, "James Bond Hits the Supermarket: Stores Snoop on Shoppers' Habits to Boost Sales," *Wall Street Journal* (25 August 1993): B1(2).

22. David Goetzl, "O&M Turns Reality TV into Research Tool," *Advertising Age* (10 July 2000): 6.

23. Mike Galetto, "Turning Trash to Research Treasure," *Advertising Age* (17 April 1995): I–16.

24. McCarthy, "James Bond Hits the Supermarket."

25. Bruce L. Stern and Ray Ashmun, "Methodological Disclosure: The Foundation for Effective Use of Survey Research," *Journal of Applied Business Research* 7 (1991): 77–82.

26. Alan E. Wolf, "Most Colas Branded Alike by Testy Magazine," *Beverage World* (31 August 1991): 8.

27. Janet Simons, "Youth Marketing: Children's Clothes Follow the Latest Fashion," *Advertising Age* (14 February 1985): 16.

28. Gary Levin, "New Adventures in Children's Research," *Advertising Age* (9 August 1993): 17.

29. Stephanie Strom, "How Gap Inc. Spells Revenge," *New York Times* (24 April 1994): 1(2).

30. Jan Larson, "It's a Small World, After All," *Marketing Tools*, September 1997, 47–51.

31. Jack Honomichl, "Research Cultures Are Different in Mexico, Canada," *Marketing News* (10 May 1993): 12.

32. Ibid.

33. Tara Parker–Pope, "Nonalcoholic Beer Hits the Spot in Mideast," *Wall Street Journal* (6 December 1995): B1(2).

34. Steve Rivkin, "The Name Game Heats Up," *Marketing News* (22 April 1996): 8.

35. David J. Lipke, "You've Got Surveys," *American Demographics*, November 2000 42–45.

36. Jean Halliday, "Automakers Involve Consumers," *Advertising Age* (January 31, 2000): 82.

37. Jack Neff, "Safe at Any Speed," *Advertising Age* (24 January 2000) 1, 12.

38. Sue Cummings, "Online Music Surveys Look for Future Hits," *New York Times On Line*, February 2, 2001.

39. Jack Neff, "P&G Weds Data, Sales," *Advertising Age* (23 October 2000): 76

40. James Heckman, "Turning the Focus Online," *Marketing News* (28 February 2000): 15; Judith Langer, " 'On' and 'Offline' Focus Groups: Claims, Questions," *Marketing News* (5 June 2000): H38.

41. Dana James, "Precision Decision," *Marketing News* (27 September 1999): 24–25.

42. Erik Bruenwedel, "Poll Position," *Brandweek* (20 March 2000): 82.

43. Thomas L. Greenbaum, "Focus Groups vs. Online," *Advertising Age* (14 February 2000): 34.

CHAPTER 6

1. James R. Bettman, "The Decision Maker Who Came In from the Cold," Presidential Address, in *Advances in Consumer Research* 20, eds. Leigh McAllister and Michael Rothschild (Provo, UT: Association for Consumer Research, 1990); John W. Payne, James R. Bettman, and Eric J. Johnson, "Behavioral Decision Research: A Constructive Processing Perspective," *Annual Review of Psychology* 4 (1992): 87–131; for an overview of recent developments in individual choice models, see Robert J. Meyer and Barbara E. Kahn, "Probabilistic Models of Consumer Choice Behavior," in *Handbook of Consumer Behavior*, eds. Thomas S. Robertson and Harold H. Kassarjian (Englewood Cliffs, NJ: Prentice Hall, 1991), 85–123.

2. Janice Rosenberg, "Tweens Mesh Latest Fads, Moms & Dads," *Advertising Age* (14 February 2000): 40.

3. Quoted in Elizabeth Stanton, "An International Toy with a Japanese Accent," *The New York Times on the Web*, 30 September 2001.

4. "Touch Looms Large as a Sense That Drives Sales," *BrandPackaging* (May/June 1999): 39–40.

5. Michael Lev, "No Hidden Meaning Here: Survey Sees Subliminal Ads," *The New York Times* (3 May 1991): D7.

6. Bruce Orwall, "Disney Recalls 'The Rescuers' Video Containing Images of Topless Woman," *The Wall Street Journal Interactive Edition*, 11 January 1999.

7. Robert M. McMath, "Image Counts," *American Demographics* (May 1998): 64.

8. Abraham H. Maslow, *Motivation and Personality*, 2nd ed. (New York: Harper & Row, 1970).

9. Robert A. Baron and Donn Byrne, *Social Psychology: Understanding Human Interaction*, 5th ed. (Boston: Allyn & Bacon, 1987).

10. Rebecca Piirto Heath, "You Can Buy a Thrill: Chasing the Ultimate Rush," *American Demographics* (June 1997): 47–51.

11. Mercedes M. Cardona, "Kenra Restyles Idea of 'Good/Bad' Hair," *Advertising Age* (16 August 1999): 27.

12. Jeffrey F. Durgee, "Self-Esteem Advertising," *Journal of Advertising*, 14 (1986) 4–21.

13. Nancy Keates, "Baby-Boomers Relive Spring Break, But MTV Is Conspicuously Absent," *The Wall Street Journal Interactive Edition*, 26 March 1998.

14. Jennifer Gilbert, "New Teen Obsession," *Advertising Age* (14 February 2000): 38.

15. Cate T. Corcoran, "Shares of Teen Hub iTurf Surge on Traffic Numbers," *The Wall Street Journal Interactive Edition*, 24 January 2000.

16. Tamala M. Edwards, "The Young and the Nested," *Time* (10 November 1997): 88–89, quoted on p. 88.

17. Benjamin D. Zablocki and Rosabeth Moss Kanter, "The Differentiation of Life-Styles," *Annual Review of Sociology* (1976): 269–97.

18. Diane Brady, "Martha, Inc.," *Business Week* (17 January 2000).

19. Alfred S. Boote, "Psychographics: Mind Over Matter," *American Demographics* (April 1980): 26–29; William D. Wells, "Psychographics: A Critical Review," *Journal of Marketing Research* 12 (May 1975): 196–213.

20. Alan R. Hirsch, "Effects of Ambient Odors on Slot-Machine Usage in a Las Vegas Casino," *Psychology & Marketing* 12, 7 (October 1995): 585–594.

21. Marianne Meyer, "Attention Shoppers!" *Marketing and Media Decisions* 23 (May 1988): 67.

22. See Eben Shapiro, "Need a Little Fantasy? A Bevy of New Companies Can Help," *The New York Times* (10 March 1991): F4.

23. Janet Ginsburg, "Xtreme Retailing," *Business Week* (20 December 1999): 120 (7).

24. Stephanie Grunier, "An Entrepreneur Chooses to Court Cafe Society (Cyber Version, Actually)," *The Wall Street Journal Interactive Edition*, 24 September 1999.

25. Bernice Kanner, "Trolling in the Aisles," *New York* (16 January 1989): 12; Michael Janofsky, "Using Crowing Roosters and Ringing Business Cards to Tap a Boom in Point-of-Purchase Displays," *The New York Times* (21 March 1994): D9.

26. John P. Cortez, "Media Pioneers Try to Corral On-the-Go Consumers," *Advertising Age* (17 August 1992): 25.

27. Quoted in John P. Cortez, "Ads Head for Bathroom," *Advertising Age* (18 May 1992): 24.

28. John P. Robinson, "Time Squeeze," *Advertising Age* (February 1990): 30–33.

29. Leonard L. Berry, "Market to the Perception," *American Demographics* (February 1990): 32.

30. Richard W. Pollay, "Measuring the Cultural Values Manifest in Advertising," *Current Issues and Research in Advertising* (1983): 71–92.

31. Becky Ebenkamp, "Chicks and Balances," *Brandweek* (12 February 2001): 16.

32. Norihiko Shirouzu, "Japanese 'Hygiene Fanatics' Snap Up Low-Smoke Cigarette," *The Wall Street Journal Interactive Edition*, 8 September 1997.

33. Nicole Crawford, "Getting Street-Smart," *PROMO Magazine* (March 1998): 61 (3), quoted on p. 62.

34. Bob Jones, "Black Gold," *Entrepreneur* (July 1994): 62–65; Fred Thompson, "Blacks Spending Potential Up 54 Percent Since 1990," *Montgomery Advertiser* (9 May 1997): 1.

35. J. Michael Munson and W. Austin Spivey, "Product and Brand-User Stereotypes Among Social Classes: Implications for Advertising Strategy," *Journal of Advertising Research* 21 (August 1981): 37–45.

36. Stuart U. Rich and Subhash C. Jain, "Social Class and Life Cycle as Predictors of Shopping Behavior," *Journal of Marketing Research* 5 (February 1968): 41–49.

37. Nathan Kogan and Michael A. Wallach, "Risky Shift Phenomenon in Small Decision-Making Groups: A Test of the Information Exchange Hypothesis," *Journal of Experimental Social Psychology* 3 (January 1967): 75–84; Arch G. Woodside and M. Wayne DeLozier, "Effects of Word-of-Mouth Advertising on Consumer Risk Taking," *Journal of Advertising* (Fall 1976): 12–19.

38. Donald H. Granbois, "Improving the Study of Customer In-Store Behavior," *Journal of Marketing* 32 (October 1968): 28–32.

39. Jack Neff, "Door-to-door sellers join the party online," *Advertising Age* 27 September 1999, accessed at www.adage.com/news.cms?newsId =1100.

40. Kathleen Debevec and Easwar Iyer, "Sex Roles and Consumer Perceptions of Promotions, Products, and Self: What Do We Know and Where Should We Be Headed," in *Advances in Consumer Research* 13, ed. Richard J. Lutz (Provo, UT: Association for Consumer Research, 1986), 210–214; Lynn J. Jaffe and Paul D. Berger, "Impact on Purchase Intent of Sex-Role Identity and Product Positioning," *Psychology & Marketing* (Fall 1988): 259–271.

41. Becky Ebenkamp, "Battle of the Sexes," *Brandweek* (17 April 2000).

42. Kathleen Debevec and Easwar Iyer, "Sex Roles and Consumer Perceptions of Promotions, Products and Self"; Deborah E. S. Frable, "Sex Typing and Gender Ideology: Two Facets of the Individual's Gender Psychology That Go Together," *Journal of Personality and Social Psychology* 56 (1989): 95–108; Lynn J. Jaffe and Paul D. Berger, "Impact on Purchase Intent of Sex-Role Identity and Product Positioning"; Keren A. Johnson, Mary R. Zimmer, and Linda L. Golden, "Object Relations Theory: Male and Female Differences in Visual Information Processing," in *Advances in Consumer Research* 14, eds. Melanie Wallendorf and Paul Anderson, (Provo, UT: Association for Consumer Research, 1986), 83–87; Leila T. Worth, Jeanne Smith, and Diane M. Mackie, "Gender Schematicity and Preference for Gender-Typed Products," *Psychology & Marketing* 9 (January 1992): 17–30.

43. Kara K. Choquette, "Not All Approve of Barbie's MasterCard," *USA Today* (30 March 1998): 6B.

44. Everett M. Rogers, *Diffusion of Innovations*, 3rd ed. (New York: Free Press, 1983).

45. This section adapted from Michael R. Solomon, *Consumer Behavior: Buying, Having and Being*, 5th ed., Upper Saddle River, NJ: Prentice Hall, 2001.

46. Robert V. Kozinets, "E-Tribalized Marketing?: The Strategic Implications of Virtual Communities of Consumption," *European Management Journal* 17, 3 (June 1999): 252–264.

47. Tom Weber, "Net's Hottest Game Brings People Closer," *The Wall Street Journal Interactive Edition*, 20 March 2000.

48. Quoted in Marc Gunther, "The Newest Addiction," *Fortune* (2 August 1999): 122–124, p. 123.

49. Greg Jaffe, "No MTV for Widespread Panic, Just Loads of Worshipful Fans," *The Wall Street Journal Interactive Edition*, 17 February 1999.

50. Amy Harmon, "Illegal Kidney Auction Pops Up on eBay's Site," *The New York Times on the Web*, 3 September 1999.

51. Ravi S. Achrol and Philip Kotler, "Marketing in the Network Economy," *Journal of Marketing* 63 (Special Issue 1999): 146–163.

52. Bob Tedeschi, "Product Reviews from Anyone with an Opinion," *The New York Times On the Web*, 25 October 1999.

53. "Dunkin' Donuts Buys Out Critical Web Site," *The New York Times on the Web*, 27 August 1999.

54. Bradley Johnson, "febrezekillsdogs.com (and birds, too)," *Advertising Age* (10 May 1999): 8.

55. Nicholas Kulish, "Still Bedeviled by Satan Rumors, P&G Battles Back on the Web, *The Wall Street Journal Interactive Edition*, 21 September 1999.

CHAPTER 7

1. *U.S. Statistical Abstract* (1997): 330.

2. B. Charles Ames and James D. Hlaracek, *Managerial Marketing for Industrial Firms* (New York: Random House Business Division, 1984); Edward F. Fern and James R. Brown, "The Industrial/Consumer Marketing Dichotomy: A Case of Insufficient Justification," *Journal of Marketing* (Spring 1984): 68–77.

3. Andy Reinhardt, Joan O'C. Hamilton and Linda Himelstein, "Silicon Valley: How It Really Works," *Business Week* (25 August 1997): 64–147.

4. Robert W. Haas, *Business Marketing: A Managerial Approach*, 6th ed. (Cincinnati, OH: South-Western College Publishing, 1995).

5. Donna Clapp, "After September 11, 2001: The Impact of Terrorism on Corporate America," *Business Facilities* (October 2001) accessed at www.facilitycity.com/busfac/bf_01_10_cover.asp.

6. www.bmwusa.com/welcome.cfm?page=&bottom=0.

7. *U.S. Statistical Abstract*, 2001, 303.

8. Mark Amtower, "There's Room for Players of All Types and Sizes," *Business Marketing* (July 1994): G-1.

9. Ibid.

10. www.census.gov/pub/epcd/www/naics/html.

11. For a study that examined factors affecting the time taken to make purchase decisions in organizations, see Ruby Roy Dholakia, "Decision-Making Time in Organizational Buying Behavior: An Investigation of Its Antecedents," *Journal of the Academy of Marketing Science*, (fall 1993): 281–292.

12. Faye W. Gilbert, Joyce A. Young, and Charles R. O'Neal, "Buyer-Seller Relationships in Just-in-Time Purchasing Environments," *Journal of Organizational Research* (February 1994): 29, 111–20.

13. Ibid.

14. Steven J. Kafka, Bruce D. Temkin, Matthew R. Sanders, Jeremy Sharrard, and Tobias O. Brown, "eMarketplaces Boost B2B Trade," *The Forrester Report*, Forrester Research, Inc., February 2000.

15. "The Whole Enchilada," *Intranet Design*, http://idm.internet.com/rweb/ tacobell/shtml.

16. Andy Reinhardt, "Log On, Link Up, Save Big," *Business Week* (22 June 1998): 132–138.

17. Ibid.

18. Nicole Harris, "'Private Exchanges' May Now Allow B-to-B Commerce to Thrive After All," *The Wall Street Journal Online* (16 March 2001).

19. "Credit Card Numbers Posted Online," USA *Today Online*, December 13, 2000, www.usatoday.com/life/cyber/tech/cti911.htm#readmorehttp:// www.usatoday.com/life/cyber/tech/cti911.htm#readmore.

CHAPTER 8

1. Conway Lackman and John M. Lanasa, "Family Decision-Making Theory: An Overview and Assessment," *Psychology & Marketing*, 10, (March/April 1993): 81–93.

2. Emily Nelson, "Kodak Aims to Put Kids Behind Its Cameras," *The Wall Street Journal Interactive Edition*, 6 May 1997.

3. Cara Beardi, "Targeting Teens Pays Off for Polaroid," *Advertising Age* (6 March 2000): 16.; Jennifer Gilbert, "New Teen Obsession," *Advertising Age* (14 February 2000): 38.

4. Mary Beth Grover, "Teenage Wasteland," Forbes (28 July 1997): 44–45.

5. Amy Barrett, "To Reach the Unreachable Teen," *Business Week* (18 September 2000): 78–80.

6. Yumiko Ono, "They Say That a Japanese Gal Is an Individualist: Tall, Tan, Blond," *The Wall Street Journal Interactive Edition*, 19 November 1999.

7. Bruce Horovitz, "Gen Y: A Tough Crowd to Sell," *USA Today* (21 May 2002), accessed at www.usatoday.com/money/covers/2002-04-22-geny.htm on June 1, 2002.

8. T. L. Stanley, "Age of Innocence . . . Not," *PROMO* (February 1997): 28–33; Douglas Coupland, *Generation X: Tales for an Accelerated Culture* (New York: St. Martin's Press, 1991).

9. Quoted in Karen Lowry Miller, "You Just Can't Talk to These Kids," *Business Week* (19 April 1993): 104.

10. Robert Scally, "The Customer Connection: Gen X Grows Up, They're in Their 30s Now," *Discount Store News* (25 October 1999): 38 (20), accessed online February 13, 2000.

11. Ibid.

12. Terry Lefton, "Quaker Propels New Water at Older Actives," *Brandweek* (10 April 2000): 6.

13. www.census.gov/dmd/www/2khome.htm

14. Hillary Chura, "DraftCodger," *Advertising Age* (11 February 2002): 4 (2).

15. Charles D. Schewe, "Strategically Positioning Your Way into the Aging Marketplace," *Business Horizons* (May/June 1991): 59–66.

16. Jennifer Lawrence, "Gender-Specific Works for Diapers—Almost Too Well," *Advertising Age* (8 February 1993): S-10.

17. Charles M. Schaninger and William D. Danko, "A Conceptual and Empirical Comparison of Alternate Household Life Cycle Markets," *Journal of Consumer Research* 19 (March 1993): 580–94.

18. Christy Fisher, "Census Data May Make Ads More Single-Minded," *Advertising Age* (20 July 1992): 2.

19. Susan Carey, "Not All That's Gold Glitters in a $14,000 Pinstriped Suit," *The Wall Street Journal Interactive Edition*, 13 December 1999.

20. "Religion Reshapes Realities for U.S. Restaurants in Middle East," *Nation's Restaurant News* (16 February 1998): 32 (7), accessed online February 13, 2000.

21. "Burger King Will Alter Ad That Has Offended Muslims," *The Wall Street Journal Interactive Edition*, 15 March 2000.

22. Tom Morganthau, "The Face of the Future," *Newsweek* (27 January 1997): 58.

23. Michael E. Ross, "At Newsstands, Black Is Plentiful," *The New York Times* (26 December 1993): F6.

24. Eleena DeLisser, "Romance Books Get Novel Twist and Go Ethnic," *The Wall Street Journal* (6 September 1994): B1 (2 pp.).

25. Joe Schwartz, "Hispanic Opportunities," *American Demographics* (May 1987): 56–59.

26. Carolyn Shea, "The New Face of America," *PROMO*, January 1996, 53.

27. Schwartz, "Hispanic Opportunities."

28. Rick Wartzman, "When You Translate 'Got Milk' for Latinos, What Do You Get?" *The Wall Street Journal Interactive Edition*, 3 June 1999.

29. Ibid.

30. Helene Stapinski, "Generacion Latino," *American Demographics* (July 1999): 62–68.

31. Brad Edmondson, "Asian Americans in 2001," *American Demographics* (February 1997): 16–17.

32. Dorinda Elliott, "Objects of Desire," *Newsweek* (12 February 1996): 41

33. Quoted in George Rathwaite, "Heileman's National Impact with Local Brews," *Marketing Insights*, premier issue (1989): 108.

34. Rick E. Bruner, "Sites Help Marketers Think Global, Advertise Local," *Advertising Age* (24 March 1997): 30.

35. Tara Weingarten, "Life in the Fastest Lane," *Newsweek* (21 February 2000): 60–61.

36. See Lewis Alpert and Ronald Gatty, "Product Positioning by Behavioral Life Styles," *Journal of Marketing* 33 (April 1969): 65–69; Emanuel H. Demby, "Psychographics Revisited: The Birth of a Technique," *Marketing News* (2 January 1989): 21; William D. Wells, "Backward Segmentation," in *Insights into Consumer Behavior*, ed. Johan Arndt (Boston: Allyn & Bacon, 1968), 85–100.

37. Rebecca Piirto Heath, "You Can Buy a Thrill: Chasing the Ultimate Rush," *American Demographics* (June 1997): 47–51.

38. Bill Guns, president, SRI Consulting, personal communication 1998.

39. Judann Pollack, "Kraft's Miracle Whip Targets Core Consumers with '97 Ads," *Advertising Age* (3 February 1997): 12.

40. Reported in Michael R. Solomon and Elnora W. Stuart, *Marketing: Real People, Real Choices*, 1st ed. (Upper Saddle River, NJ: Prentice Hall, 1997).

41. Anthony Ramirez, "New Cigarettes Raising Issue of Target Market," *The New York Times* (18 February 1990): 28.

42. William Echikson, "Aiming at High and Low Markets," *Fortune* (22 March 1993): 89.

43. Chip Bayers, "The Promise of One to One (A Love Story)," *Wired* (May 1998) 130.

44. www.dell.com

45. Becky Ebenkamp, "No Dollars for Bowling," *Brandweek* (27 March 2000): 56–58.

46. Ian P. Murphy, "Beverages Don't Mean a Thing If They Ain't Got That Zing," *Marketing News* (14 April 1997): 1.

47. For an example of how consumers associate food brands with a range of female body shapes, see Martin R. Lautman, "End-Benefit Segmentation and Prototypical Bonding," *Journal of Advertising Research* (June/July 1991): 9–18.

48. Ian P. Murphy, "Beverages Don't Mean a Thing If They Ain't Got That Zing."

49. "A Crash Course in Customer Relationship Management," *Harvard Management Update* (March 2000): HBS reprint #U003B.

50. Quoted in Cara B. DiPasquale, "Navigate the Maze," Special Report on 1:1 Marketing, *Advertising Age* (29 October 2001): S1 (2).

51. Jim Middlemiss, "Users Say CRM Is Worth the Effort," www.wallstreetandtech.com (Third Quarter 2001): 17–18.

52. Mel Duvall, "Charting Customers: Why CRM Spending Remains Strong Even in Tight Times," *Interactive Week*, 8, (20 August 2001): 23.

53. Todd R. Weiss, "PeopleSoft Delivers CRM Apps to a Friendlier IRS," *Computerworld*, 35 (27 August 2001): 12 (3).

54. Marc L. Songini, "Dimmed Utilities Plug into CRM," *Computerworld*, 35 (6 August 2001): 1 (2).

55. Kate Fitzgerald, "Events a Big 1st Step," *Advertising Age* (29 October 2001): S4.

56. Rodney Moore, "1-to-1 an Ethnic Star," *Advertising Age*, 29 October 2001: S8.

57. Susan Fournier, Susan Dobscha, and David Glen Mick, "Preventing the Premature Death of Relationship Marketing," *Harvard Business Review* (January-February 1998).

58. Mel Duvall, "Charting Customers: Why CRM Spending Remains Strong Even in Tight Times," 23.

59. Robert C. Blattberg, Gary Getz, and Mark Pelofsky, "What to Build Your Business? Grow Your Customer Equity," *Harvard Management Update* (August 2001) Harvard Business School Publishing Corporation, Article Reprint No. U0108B, 3.

60. Tonia Bruyns, "Banking on Targeted Marketing," *Business 2.0*, www.business2.co.za, (7 November 2001).

61. Don Peppers, Martha Rogers, and Bob Dorf, "Is Your Company Ready for One-to-One Marketing," *Harvard Business Review* (January-February 1999).

CHAPTER 9

1. Information obtained from the Woodstream Corporation.

2. Gabriella Stern, "If You Don't Feel Like Fetching the Rental Car, It Fetches You," *The Wall Street Journal* (9 June 1995): B1 (2).

3. George Anders, "Vital Statistic: Disputed Cost of Creating a Drug," *The Wall Street Journal* (9 November 1993): B1.

4. "The Replacements," *Newsweek* (25 June 2001): 50.

5. Clea Simon, "The Web Catches and Reshapes Radio," *The New York Times* (16 January 2000): S2, 1, 15.

6. F. Keenan, "G.I. Joe Heroics at Hasbro," *Business Week* (26 November 2001):16.

7. Roman G. Hiebing and Scott W. Copper, Instructor's Manual, *The Successful Marketing Plan* (Lincolnwood, IL: NTC Business Books, 1992).

8. James Dao, "From a Collector of Turkeys, A Tour of a Supermarket Zoo," *The New York Times* (24 September 1995): F12.

9. Jennifer Ordonez, "Burger King's Decision to Develop French Fry Has Been a Whopper," *The Wall Street Journal* (16 January 2001): accessed at http://interactive.wsj.com/articles/SB97960472517999878 on January 16, 2001.

10. Stuart F. Brown, "How to Build a Really, Really, Big Plane," *Fortune* (5 March 2001): 144–152.

11. Keith Bradsher, "Bayer Halves Price for Cipro, but Rivals Offer Drugs Free," *The New York Times* (26 October 2001): accessed at www.nytimes.com.

12. "Test Marketing a New Product: When It's a Good Idea and How to Do It," *Profit Building Strategies for Business Owners* (March 1993): 14.

13. Michael J. Himowitz, "At Last, Digital Cameras Worth the Price," *Fortune* (22 June 1998): 148.

14. Everett Rogers, *Diffusion of Innovations* (New York: Free Press, 1983), 247–251.

15. Christine Chen and Tim Carvell, "Hall of Shame," *Fortune* (22 November 1999): 140.

16. Everett Rogers, *Diffusion of Innovations*, Chapter 6.

17. Thomas S. Robertson and Yoram Wind, "Organizational Psychographics and Innovativeness," *Journal of Consumer Research* 7 (June 1980): 24–31.

CHAPTER 10

1. www.ask.com, accessed March 27, 2002.

2. Cara S. Trager, "Goya Foods Tests Mainstream Market's Waters," *Advertising Age* (9 February 1987): S-20.

3. Ian P. Murphy, "All-American Icon Gets a New Look," *Marketing News* (18 August 1997): 6.

4. www.rollsroycemotorcars.co.uk/rolls-royce/index.html, accessed March 24, 2002.

5. Larry Armstrong, "And Now, a Luxury Hyundai," *Business Week* (26 February 2001): 33.

6. Eleena de Lisser, "Pepsi Puts Spotlight on New Packaging," *The Wall Street Journal* (August 11, 1993): B1.

7. Mark Hyman, "Nike: Great Balls Afire. Will Golf Clubs be Next?" *Business Week* (26 February 2001): 109.

8. Richard W. Stevenson, "The Brands with Billion-Dollar Names," *The New York Times* (28 October 1988): A1.

9. Robert J. Thomas, *New Product Development* (New York: John Wiley & Sons, 1993), 17.

10. www.ford.com/archive/edselhistory.html; www.lvrj.com/lvrj home/1998/_Mar-29-Sun=1998/news/; www.theautochannel.com/content/news/date/19960426/news00601.html.

11. Ed Brown, "Thwacking Away for 66 Years," *Fortune* (4 August 1997): 40.

12. Wayne Friedman, "The Firm Runs with Pony," *Advertising Age* (5 November 2001): 8.

13. John Bissell, "What's in a Brand Name? Nothing Inherent to Start," *Brandweek* (7 February 1994): 16.

14. Gail Tom, Teresa Barnett, William Lew and Jodean Selmonts, "Cueing the Consumer: The Role of Salient Cues in Consumer Perception," *Journal of Consumer Marketing* (1987): 23–27.

15. Douglas Lavin, "A Cloudy Issue: Will ATM Users Be Confused by a Car Called Cirrus?" *The Wall Street Journal* (16 February 1994): B1.

16. Kevin Lane Keller, "The Brand Report Card," *Harvard Business Review*, January–February 2000, Harvard Business Publishing Reprint Number R00104.

17. David Goetz, "A Hangover Helper," *Advertising Age* (5 November 2001): 8.

18. "Bedtime at Mickey D's," *Sales & Marketing Management* (June 2001): 18.

19. Julie Liesse, "Weight Watchers Looks to New Items to Spark Rebound," *Advertising Age* (22 February 1993): 36.

20. Bill Virgin, "Safeway Makes Investment In Store-Brand Branch Banks," *Seattle Post–Intelligencer*, 16 March 2002, accessed at www.marketingpower.com/index.php?&Session_ID=f21e39f3e0653e0b590a3414a6850986 on March 26, 2002.

21. Susan Caminiti, "How to Win Back Customers," *Fortune* (14 June 1993): 118.

22. "Overcrowded Retail Market Could Spell End to Some Stores,"*Milwaukee Journal Sentinel*, 24 March 2002, accessed at www.marketingpower.com/index.php?&Session_ID=f21e39f3e0653e0b590a3414a6850986 on March 26, 2002.

23. Betsy Spethmann and Karen Benezra, "Co-Branding or Be Damned," *Brandweek* (21 November 1994): 21–24.

24. Jean Halliday, "L.L. Bean, Subaru Pair for Co-Branding," *Advertising Age* (21 February 2000): 21.

25. D.C. Denison, "The Boston Globe Business Intelligence Column," *The Boston Globe*, May 26, 2002, accessed at http:// marketingpower.yellowbrix.com/pages/marketingpower/Story.nsp?story_id=30186718&ID=marketingpower on June 5, 2002.

26. Stephanie Thompson, "Brand Buddies," *Brandweek* (23 February 1998): 26–30.

27. Stephanie Thompson, "Brand Buddies," *Brandweek* (23 February 1998): 26–30; Jean Halliday, "L.L. Bean, Subaru Pair for Co-Branding," *Advertising Age* (21 February 2000): 21.

28. Wayne Simpson and Terry Lefton, "Seeing Double," *Brandweek* (17 October 1994): 31–36.

29. Ed Brown, "I Scream You Scream–Saaay, Nice Carton!," *Fortune* (26 October 1998): 60.

30. Laura Bird, "New Labels Will Tell Real Story on Juice Drinks," *The Wall Street Journal* (3 May 1994): B1, B6.

31. Jack Neff, "P&G Redefines the Brand Manager," *Advertising Age* (13 October 1997): 1, 18, 20.

32. Pam Weisz, "Lever Plans P&G-Like Moves," *Brandweek* (10 January 1994): 1, 6.

33. Gary Hoover, Alta Campbell, and Patrick J. Spain, *Hoover's Handbook of American Business*, 1994 (Austin, TX: The Reference Press, 1994).

CHAPTER 11

1. Ross Kerber and Benjamin A. Holden, "Power Struggle: Deregulation Sparks Marketing Battle," *The Wall Street Journal* (13 May 1996): B1 (2); Rebecca Piirto Heath, "The Marketing of Power," *American Demographics* (September 1997): 59–63.

2. Associated Press, "Astros airbrush reference to Enron Field," March 16, 2002, accessed at www.marketingpower.com/index.php?&Session_ID=13af9ba667c21450aee9ed04b6b91ba1 on March 29, 2002.

3. Laura Koss Feder, "Branding Culture," *Marketing News* (5 January 1998): 1 (2).

4. Kathleen V. Schmidt, "E-Giving: Charity Begins At the Home Page," *Marketing News* (11 October 1999): 13.

5. Based on a discussion in Gene R. Laczniak, "Product Management and the Performing Arts," in eds. Michael P. Mokwa, William M. Dawson, and E. Arthur Prieve, *Marketing the Arts* (New York: Praeger Publishers, 1980), 124–138.

6. Michael R. Solomon, "The Wardrobe Consultant: Exploring the Role of a New Retailing Partner," *Journal of Retailing*, 63 (Summer 1987): 110–128.

7. Irving J. Rein, Philip Kotler, and Martin R. Stoller, *High Visibility* (New York: Dodd, Mead & Company, 1987).

8. Michael R. Solomon, "Celebritization and Commodification in the Interpersonal Marketplace," unpublished manuscript, Rutgers University, 1991.

9. Adapted from a discussion in Irving J. Rein, Philip Kotler, and Martin R. Stoller, *High Visibility* (New York: Dodd, Mead & Company, 1987).

10. Charla Krupp, "Can Cyndi Lauper Bring Back the Headdress?" *Glamour* (January 1987): 138 (2).

11. Rebecca Gardyn, "Packaging Cities," *American Demographics* (January 2002): 34–41.

12. "New York Rolls Out Tourism Ad Campaign, accessed via http://cnn.com/travel, 8 November 2001.

13. Patricia Braus, "Selling Good Behavior," *American Demographics* (November 1995): 60–64.

14. "Benetton Ads Feature Death-Row Inmates," *The Journal News* (January 9, 2000): 16A.

15. Gustav Niebuhr, "Where Religion Gets a Big Dose of Shopping-Mall Culture," *The New York Times* (16 April 1995): 1 (2).

16. Quoted in "New Church Uses Marketing to Appeal to Baby Boomers," *Marketing News* (12 April 1993): 11.

17. Ronald Henkoff, "Service Is Everybody's Business," *Fortune* (27 June 1994): 48 (6).

18. Marj Charlier, "Bikers Give Ski Resorts Summertime Life," *The Wall Street Journal* (7 July 1994): B1 (2).

19. Cf. John A. Czepiel, Michael R. Solomon, and Carol F. Surprenant, eds., *The Service Encounter: Managing Employee/Customer Interaction in Service Businesses* (Lexington, MA: D.C. Heath and Company, 1985).

20. Lee D. Dahringer, "Marketing Services Internationally: Barriers and Management Strategies," *Journal of Services Marketing* 5, Summer 1991, 5–17, p. 10, Table 2.

21. Quoted in Jim Carlton, "Support Lines' Busy Signals Hurt PC Makers," *The Wall Street Journal* (6 July 1995): B1 (2).

22. Lou W. Turkey and Douglas L. Fugate, "The Multidimensional Nature of Service Facilities: Viewpoints and Recommendations," *Journal of Services Marketing* 6, Summer 1992, 37–45.

23. David H. Maister, "The Psychology of Waiting Lines," in eds. J. A. Czepiel, M. R. Solomon, and C. F. Surprenant, *The Service Encounter: Managing Employee/Customer Interaction in Service Businesses* (Lexington, MA: Lexington Books, 1985), 113–124.

24. www.blockbuster.com/bb/about/0,7710,00.html, accessed March 31, 2002.

25. Michael T. Kaufman, "About New York: The Nail Salon of the 90's: Massages for the Clothed," *The New York Times* (1 December 1993): B3.

26. Jennifer Chao, "Airports Open Their Gates to Profits," *Montgomery Advertiser* (26 January 1997): 16A.

27. Adam Bryant, "An Airborne Battle of Services," *The New York Times* (19 October 1994): D1 (2).

28. Jared Sandbert, "NoChores.com," *Newsweek* (30 August 1999): 64–66.

29. Andrew Osterland, "Nothing But Net," *Business Week* (2 August 1999): 72.

30. John McCormick, "The New School," *Newsweek* (24 April 2000): 60–62.

31. Wayne J. Guglielmo, "Take Two Aspirin and Hit the Send Key: Doctor E-Mail," *Newsweek* (25 June 2001): 61.

32. Cengiz Haksever, Barry Render, Roberta S. Russell and Robert G. Murdick, *Service Management and Operations* (Englewood Cliffs, NJ: Prentice Hall, 2000), 25–26.

33. Ray Serafin, "Saturn Recall a Plus—For Saturn!" *Advertising Age* (16 August 1993): 4.

34. Joe Barstys, Subaru of America, personal communication November 2001; Gilbert A. Churchill Jr. and Carol F. Surprenant, "An Investigation into the Determinants of Customer Satisfaction," *Journal of Marketing Research* 19 (November 1983): 491–504; John E. Swan and I. Frederick Trawick, "Disconfirmation of Expectations and Satisfaction with a Retail Service," *Journal of Retailing* 57 (Fall 1981): 49–67; Peter C. Wilton and David K. Tse, "Models of Consumer Satisfaction Formation: An Extension," *Journal of Marketing Research* 25 (May 1988): 204–12; for a discussion of what may occur when customers evaluate a new service for which comparison standards do not yet exist, see Ann L. McGill and Dawn Iacobucci, "The Role of Post-Experience Comparison Standards in the Evaluation of Unfamiliar Services," in eds. John F. Sherry Jr. and Brian Sternthal, *Advances in Consumer Research* 19 (Provo, UT: Association for Consumer Research, 1992), 570–78.

35. Cynthia Webster, "Influences upon Consumer Expectations of Services," *Journal of Services Marketing* 5, Winter 1991, 5–17.

36. Mary Jo Bitner, "Evaluating Service Encounters: The Effects of Physical Surroundings and Employee Responses," *Journal of Marketing* 54, April 1990, 69–82.

37. Edwin McDowell, "Ritz-Carlton's Keys to Good Service," *The New York Times* (31 March 1993): D1 (2).

38. Michael Selz, "Chain Aims to Hammer Dents Out of Auto-Collision Repair," *The Wall Street Journal Interactive Edition*, 31 July 1998.

39. Lewis P. Carbone and Stephan H. Haeckel, "Engineering Customer Experiences," *Marketing Management* 3, Winter 1994, reprint, Exhibit 4.

40. Valarie A. Zeithaml, "How Consumer Evaluation Processes Differ between Goods and Services," in Christopher H. Lovelock, *Services Marketing*, 2nd ed. (Englewood Cliffs, NJ: Prentice Hall, 1991), 39–47.

41. Kenneth Wylie, "Customer Satisfaction Blooms; Rivalry at Top Grows," *Advertising Age* (18 October 1993): S–1 (2).

42. Valarie A. Zeithaml, Leonard L. Berry, and A. Parasuraman, "Communication and Control Processes in the Delivery of Service Quality," *Journal of Marketing* 52, April 1988, 35–48.

43. Jody D. Nyquist, Mary F. Bitner, and Bernard H. Booms, "Identifying Communication Difficulties in the Service Encounter: A Critical Incident Approach," in eds. John A. Czepiel, Michael R. Solomon, and Carol F. Surprenant, *The Service Encounter: Managing Employee/Customer Interaction in Service Businesses* (Lexington, MA: D. C. Heath, 1985), 195–212.

44. Ibid.

45. Ron Zemke, "The Art of Service Recovery: Fixing Broken Customers—And Keeping Them on Your Side," in Eberhard E. Scheuing and William F. Christopher, (eds.) *The Service Quality Handbook*, New York, American Management Association, 1993.

46. Cengiz Haksever, Barry Render, Roberta S. Russell and Robert G. Murdick, *Service Management and Operations*, 342–343.

47. Adapted from recommendations in eds. Michael P. Mokwa, William M. Dawson, and E. Arthur Prieve, *Marketing the Arts* (New York: Praeger Publishers, 1980).

48. "Opera Company Employs Racy Ads," *Montgomery Advertiser* (28 September 1996): 10A.

49. A. Parasuraman, Valarie A. Zeithaml, and Leonard L. Berry, "SERVQUAL: A Multiple-Item Scale for Measuring Consumer Perceptions of Service Quality," *Journal of Retailing* 64, Spring 1988, 12–40; Zeithaml, Valarie A., A. Parasuraman, and Leonard L. Berry, "Strategic Positioning on the Dimensions of Service Quality," in *Advances in Services Marketing and Management: Research and Practice*, vol. 1, Teresa A. Swartz, David E. Bowen, and Stephen W. Brown, eds. (Greenwich, CT: JAI Press), 207–28.

50. Michael Janofsky, "Domino's Ends Fast-Pizza Pledge after Big Award to Crash Victim," *The New York Times* (22 December 1993): A1 (2).

CHAPTER 12

1. Michael L. Rothschild, "Marketing Communications in Nonbusiness Situations or Why It's So Hard to Sell Brotherhood Like Soap," *Journal of Marketing*, Spring 1979, 11–20.

2. Kenneth Labich, "What Will Save the U.S. Airlines," *Fortune* (14 June 1993): 98–101.

3. Leslie Vreeland, "How to Be a Smart Shopper," *Black Enterprise* (August 1993): 88.

4. Melissa Campanelli, "The Price to Pay," *Sales and Marketing Management* (September 1994): 96.

5. Andrew E. Serwer, "What Price Brand Loyalty?" *Fortune* (10 January 1994): 103–104; Richard Gibson, "General Mills to Cut Prices of 3 Cereals and Curb Discounts," *The Wall Street Journal*, 222, No. 116, (14 December 1993): A10; Richard Gibson, "Kellogg Boosts Prices on Many Cereals; Average 2.6% Rise May Meet Resistance," *The Wall Street Journal* (8 February 1994): A3, A8.

6. Judann Pollack, "Post's Price Play Rocked Category, But Did It Work," *Advertising Age* (1 December 1997): 24.

7. Gabriella Stern, "P&G Gains Little from Diaper Price Cuts," *The Wall Street Journal* (28 October 1993): B12.

8. Rahul Jacob, "The Economy: Girding for Worse," *Fortune* (18 October 1993): 10.

9. Shelly Reese, "The Many Faces of Affluence," *Marketing Tools*, November/December 1997, 44–48.

10. Yumiki Ono, "As Discounting Rises in Japan, People Learn to Hunt for Bargains," *The Wall Street Journal* (31 December 1993): 1, 8.

11. George Burns, "McDonald's: Now It's Just Another Burger Joint," *Business Week* (17 March 1997): 38; Bill McDowell and Laura Petrecca, "Burger King Ads Take Slap at McD's," *Advertising Age* (10 February 1997): 12.

12. Keith Naughton, "Hitting the Bull's-Eye," *Newsweek* (11 October 1999): 64.

13. Quoted in "Western Companies Compete to Win Business of Chinese Babies," *The Wall Street Journal Interactive Edition*, 15 May 1998.

14. Shawn Tully, "Can Boeing Reinvent Itself?" *Fortune* (8 March 1993): 67.

CHAPTER 13

1. Steward Washburn, "Pricing Basics: Establishing Strategy and Determining Costs in the Pricing Decision," *Business Marketing*, July 1985, reprinted in Valerie Kijewski, Bob Donath, and David T. Wilson, eds., *The Best Readings from Business Marketing Magazine* (Boston: PWS-Kent Publishing Co., 1993), 257–269.

2. Greg Winter, "What Keeps a Bottom Line Healthy? Weight Loss," *The New York Times*, 2 January 2001, accessed at www.nytimes.com/ 2001/01/02/business/02WEIG.html, 3 January 2001.

3. Ken Popovich and Mary Jo Foley, "Dell Remains Committed to Pricing Strategy," *eWeek*, 9 April 2001, accessed at www.eweek.com/article/ 0,3658,s=701&a = 9334,00.asp, 22 February 2002.

4. Robin Cooper and W. Bruce Chew, "Control Tomorrow's Costs Through Today's Design," *Harvard Business Review*, January-February 1996, 88–97.

5. Tim Carvell, "The Crazy Record Business: These Prices Really Are Insane," *Fortune* (4 August 1997): 109–116.

6. Nikki, Swartz, "Rate-Plan Wisdom," *Wireless Review*, 15 June 2001, accessed at http://industryclick.com/magazinearticle.asp?releaseid= 2921&magazinearticleid=17552&siteid=3&magazineid=9, 22 February 2002.

7. Zachary Schiller, " 'Value Pricing' Pays Off," *Business Week* (1 November 1993): 32–33.

8. Ibid.

9. Joann Muller and Therese Palmer, "Kmart's Bright Idea," *Business Week Online*, 9 April 2001, accessed through www.businessweek.com, 22 February 2002.

10. Jennifer Merritt, "The Belle of the Golf Balls," *Business Week* (29 July 1996): 6.

11. Sebastian Rupley, "The PowerPC Revolution," *PC/Computing* (February 1994): 129–131; Marc Dodge, "New Power Chips," *PC/Computing* (February 1994): 116–117.

12. Jim Carlton, "Apple to Launch Macintosh PowerPCs Priced at Level to Gain Market Share," *The Wall Street Journal* (14 March 1994): B4.

13. Ibid.

14. Douglas Lavin, "Goodbye to Haggling: Savvy Consumers Are Buying Their Cars Like Refrigerators," *The Wall Street Journal* (20 August 1993): B1, B3.

15. William C. Symonds, "Would You Spend $1.50 for a Razor Blade?" *Business Week* (27 April 1998): 46.

16. Amy E. Cortese and Marcia Stpeanek, "Good-Bye to Fixed Pricing?" *Business Week* (4 May 1998): 71–84.

17. Walter Baker, Mike Marn, and Craig Zawada, "Price Smarter on the Net," *Harvard Business Review*, February 2001, accessed at www.hbsp.harvard.edu/rcpt/filestream.asp?otype=s&key=69541836& prodno=R0102J&order_id=1136431&type=.pdf, 22 February 2002.

18. Jennifer Gilbert, "Drugstores Wage a Pricey Online Battle," *Advertising Age* (30 August 1999): 26.

19. David Ackerman and Gerald Tellis, "Can Culture Affect Prices? A Cross-Cultural Study of Shopping and Retail Prices," *Journal of Retailing* 2001, 77: 57–82.

20. Robert M. Schindler and Thomas M. Kibarian, "Increased Consumer Sales Response Through Use of 99-Ending Prices," *Journal of Retailing*, 1996, 72 (2): 187–199.

21. Edmund L. Andrews, "Europe to Seek Uniformity in Car Pricing," *The New York Times on the Web*, 5 February 2002.

22. Dorothy Cohen, *Legal Issues in Marketing Decision Making* (Cincinnati, OH: Southwestern College Publishing, 1995), 193.

23. Paul Farhi, "The Everlasting Sale—Retailers' Nonstop 'Specials' Stir a Question: When Is a Markdown Real?" *Washington Post* (20 June 1993): 1.

24. Dorothy Cohen, *Legal Issues in Marketing Decision Making*, 219.

25. Adam Bryant, "Aisle Seat Bully?" *Newsweek* (24 May 1999): 56.

CHAPTER 14

1. Leiss et al., *Social Communication*; George Stigler, "The Economics of Information," *Journal of Political Economy* (1961): 69.

2. Frank R. Kardes, "Spontaneous Inference Processes in Advertising: The Effects of Conclusion Omission and Involvement on Persuasion," *Journal of Consumer Research* 15, (September 1988): 225–33.

3. Gert Assmus, "An Empirical Investigation into the Perception of Vehicle Source Effects," *Journal of Advertising* 7, Winter 1978, 4–10; for a more thorough discussion of the pros and cons of different media, see Stephen Baker, *Systematic Approach to Advertising Creativity* (New York: McGraw-Hill, 1979).

4. Katsumi Hoshino, "Semiotic Marketing and Product Conceptualization," in ed. Jean Umiker-Sebeok, *Marketing and Semiotics: New Directions in the Study of Signs for Sale* (Berlin: Mouton de Bruyter, 1987), 41–56, p. 44.

5. George E. Belch and Michael A. Belch, *Introduction to Advertising & Promotion: An Integrated Marketing Communications Perspective*, 2nd ed. (Homewood, IL: Irwin, 1993).

6. Pat Wechsler, "A Curiously Strong Campaign," *Business Week* (21 April 1997): 134.

7. Quoted in Jonathan Berry, "Wilma! What Happened to the Plain Old Ad?" *Business Week* (6 June 1994): 54–55.

8. Tom Buerkle, "Advertisers Find a Formula They Like in Auto Racing," *International Herald Tribune* [online] 10 March 1998, accessed via ssnewslink.

9. Patricia Sellers, "Winning Over the New Consumer," *Fortune* (27 July 1991): 113.

10. Michael Lev, "For Car Buyers, Technology or Zen," *The New York Times* (22 May 1989): D1.

11. Linda L. Golden and Mark I. Alpert, "Comparative Analysis of the Relative Effectiveness of One- and Two-Sided Communication for Contrasting Products," *Journal of Advertising* 16 (1987) 18–25; Robert B. Settle and Linda L. Golden, "Attribution Theory and Advertiser Credibility," *Journal of Marketing Research* 11 (May 1974): 181–85.

12. Khanh T.L. Tran, "Lifting the Velvet Rope: Night Clubs Draw Virtual Throngs with Webcasts," *The Wall Street Journal Interactive Edition*, August 30, 1999.

13. Amanda Beeler, "Virus Without a Cure," *Advertising Age* (17 April 2000): 54, 60.

14. Erin Kelly, "This Is One Virus You Want to Spread," *Fortune* (27 November 2000): 297–300.

15. Ibid.

16. Ibid.

17. John Browning and Spencer Reiss, "Encyclopedia of the New Economy, Part I," *Wired* (March 1998): 105 (8); Laurie Flynn, "A Search Engine That Charges for Top Billing," New York Times News Service, 16 March 1998 [online], 24 paragraphs.

18. Quoted in Beth Spethman, "Closer and Closer to the Crowd," *Mediaweek* (17 October 1994).

19. Daniel London, "Digital Direct: E-Mail Marketing Grows as a Means to Targeted Branding," *B to B* (May 8, 2000): 1, 45; Eileen McCooey, "Making an Impact," *Brandweek* (17 April 2000): 72–74.

20. Patricia Sellers, "The Best Way to Reach Your Buyers," *Fortune* (Autumn/Winter 1993): 15 (4).

21. Quoted in Patricia Sellers, "Winning Over the New Consumer," *Fortune* (27 July 1991): 113.

22. Todd Wasserman, Gerry Khermouch, and Jeff Green, "Mining Everyone's Business," *Brandweek* (28 February 2000): 32–52.

23. Curt Barry, "Building a Database," *Catalog Age* (August 1992): 65–68.

24. Martin Everett, "This One's Just for You," *Sales and Marketing Management* (June 1992): 119–126.

25. Ian P. Murphy, "Reader's Digest Links Profits Directly to Research," *Marketing News* (31 March 1997): 7.

26. Elaine Santoro, "NBO Markets with Style," *Direct Marketing*, February 1992, 28–31, quoted on p. 30.

27. Gary Levin, "Package-Goods Giants Embrace Databases," *Advertising Age* (2 November 1992): 1.

28. Carol Krol, "New Window of Opportunity in Hershey Direct's Elf Push," *Advertising Age* (10 May 1999): 30, 34.

29. Martin Everett, "This One's Just for You."

30. Don E. Schultz and Heidi F. Schultz, "Transitioning Marketing Communications into the Twenty-First Century," *Journal of Marketing Communications* 4 , March 1998, 1, 9–26, quoted on p. 18.

31. Scott Hume, "Integrated Marketing: Who's in Charge Here?" *Advertising Age* (22 March 1993): 3 (2).

32. Don E. Schultz, Stanley I. Tannenbaum, and Robert F. Lauterborn, *Integrated Marketing Communications: Pulling It Together and Making It Work* (Chicago, IL: NTC Business Books, 1993); Melanie Wells, "Purposeful Grazing in Ad Land," *Advertising Age* (11 April 1994): S–12.

33. Bradley Johnson, "In a Millisecond, Microsoft Boots Up Marketing Database," *Advertising Age* (8 November 1993): S–6.

34. Don E. Schultz, Stanley I. Tannenbaum, and Robert F. Lauterborn, *Integrated Marketing Communications.*

35. Chris Warren, "The 360 Brand," *Critical Mass* (Fall 2000): 32–40.

36. Dan Hanover, "Mountain Dew Hits the Bullseye with Its 'Extreme Network' Promotion," *PROMO Magazine* (May 1997): P10.

37. Don E. Schultz, Stanley I. Tannenbaum, and Robert F. Lauterborn, *Integrated Marketing Communications.*

38. John F. Yarbrough, "Putting the Pieces Together," *Sales and Marketing Management* (September 1996): 70.

39. Don E. Schultz, Stanley I. Tannenbaum, and Robert F. Lauterborn, *Integrated Marketing Communications.*

40. Adrienne Ward Fawcett, "Marketers Convinced: Its Time Has Arrived," *Advertising Age* (8 November 1993): S–1 (2).

41. Quoted in Joshua Levin, "Teaching Elephants to Dance," *Forbes* (15 March 1993): 100 (2), p. 105.

CHAPTER 15

1. Saul Hansell, "In Rewritten Internet Fables, the Late Bird Gets the Worm," *The New York Times Online*, 27 December 2001.

2. William Wells, John Burnett, and Sandra Moriarty, *Advertising: Principles and Practice,* 5th ed. (Englewood Cliffs, NJ: Prentice Hall, 2000).

3. Stephen Shipside, "We Interrupt This Call . . . ," *Wired* (August 1998): 58.

4. Kip Cassino, "An Advertising Atlas," *American Demographics* (August 1994): 44–55.

5. Stuart Elliott, "An Increase in Corporate Campaigns Points to a Continuing Recovery for Madison Avenue," *The New York Times* (18 January 1995): D5.

6. Bob D. Cutler and Darrel D. Muehling, "Another Look at Advocacy Advertising and the Boundaries of Commercial Speech," *Journal of Advertising* 20 (December 1991): 49–52.

7. "U.S. Agency Brands Ranked by Gross Income," *Advertising Age* (2 January 1995): 13.

8. Leslie Kaufman, "Enough Talk," *Newsweek* (18 August 1997): 48–49.

9. Kevin Goldman, "Dr. Pepper Wraps Ads in Stars and Stripes," *Wall Street Journal* (4 October 1993): B3.

10. This material adapted from R&D: Relevance and Difference at Work, June 1996, Bombay, India: R K Swami/BBDO, and Praia Raja, Director Client Services, R K Swami/BBDO, personal communication, January 1998.

11. "100 Leading National Advertisers," *Advertising Age* (2 January 1995): 12.

12. Mercedes M. Cardona, "Price Becomes Prime Issue," *Advertising Age* (14 September 1998): 24.

13. Juliette Walker, "Pepsi-Coke Spat Raises Questions about Ad Policies," *Japan Times Weekly*, International Edition (24–30 June 1991): 7.

14. Douglas C. McGill, "Star Wars in Cola Advertising," *The New York Times* (22 March 1989): D1.

15. Kevin Goldman, "Ad with Disabled Child Stirs Controversy," *Wall Street Journal* (3 September 1993): B8.

16. www.sixcontinentshotels.com/hiexpress?_template= exmovies.html& jrunsessionid=1017347262817161659, accessed April 7, 2002.

17. Michael Janofsky, "Naked Bodies. Oh-My-Goodness Words. They Attract Plenty of Attention, But Can They Hold It?" *The New York Times* (4 October 1993): D8.

18. Phil Hall, "Make Listeners Your Customers," *Nation's Business* (June 1994): 53R.

19. Rebecca Piirto, "Why Radio Thrives," *American Demographics* (May 1994): 4(7).

20. Information provided by Yellow Pages Publishers Association, Troy, Michigan.

21. Lisa Marie Petersen, "Outside Chance," *Mediaweek* (15 June 1992): 20–23.

22. Ibid.

23. Laurie Freeman, "User-Created Ads Catch On," *Advertising Age* (18 September 2000): 84.

24. Gene Koprowsky, "Eyeball to Eyeball," *Critical Mass* (Fall 1999): 32 (5).

25. Janis Mara, "The Halo Effect," *Brandweek* (22 May 2000): 86–92.

26. Ibid.

27. Ann M. Mack, "Got E-mail," *Brandweek* (20 March 2000): 84–88.

28. Bristol Voss, "Measuring the Effectiveness of Advertising and PR," *Sales and Marketing Management* (October 1992): 123–24.

29. This remark has also been credited to a British businessman named Lord Leverhulme, cf. Charles Goodrum and Helen Dalrymple, *Advertising in America: The First 200 Years* (New York: Harry N. Abrams, 1990).

30. The research findings reported here are abstracted from Bristol Voss, "Measuring the Effectiveness of Advertising and PR," *Sales and Marketing Management* (October 1992): 123–24.

31. Carol Moog, President, Creative Focus, quoted in Kevin Goldman, "The Message, Clever as It May Be, Is Lost in a Number of High-Profile Campaigns," *Wall Street Journal* (27 July 1993): B1(2).

32. Charles Goodrum and Helen Dalrymple, *Advertising in America: The First 200 Years.*

33. Quoted in Kevin Goldman, "Knock, Knock. Who's There? The Same Old Funny Ad Again," *Wall Street Journal* (2 November 1993): B10.

34. William Wells, John Burnett, and Sandra Moriarty, *Advertising: Principles and Practice*, 5th ed. (Englewood Cliffs, NJ: Prentice Hall, 2000).

35. Ibid.

36. Gina Bellafante, "Sell That Dress: Back to Basics in Spring Advertising," *The New York Times on the Web*, 5 February 2002.

37. Kevin Goldman, "From Witches to Anorexics, Critical Eyes Scrutinize Ads for Political Correctness," *Wall Street Journal* (19 May 1994): B1(2).

38. Eduardo Porter, "New 'Got Milk?' TV Commercials Try to Entice Hispanic Teenagers," *WSJ.com*, December 28, 2001, accessed April 7, 2002.

39. Gary Levin, "Keeping in Touch Easy with Database," *Advertising Age* (28 March 1994): S-8.

40. Elizabeth Weinstein, "E-Marketing's Browser Adds Personal Touch to Web Surfing," *WSJ.com*, September 7, 2000.

41. The Direct Marketing Association, "What Is Direct Marketing," accessed at www.the-dma.org/aboutdma/whatisthedma.shtml#whatis, on April 6, 2002.

42. The Direct Marketing Association, "Despite Slowing Economy, Direct Marketing Revenue Growth Outpaces Overall U.S. Advertising Sales Growth By 54 Percent" May 1, 2001, accessed at www.the-dma.org/cgi/disppressrelease?article=85 on April 5, 2002.

43. Frances Huffman, "Special Delivery," *Entrepreneur* (February 1993): 81 (3).

44. Cacilie Rohwedder, "U.S. Catalog Firms Target Avid Consumers Overseas," *Wall Street Journal Interactive Edition*, 6 January 1998.

45. Paul Hughes, "Profits Due," *Entrepreneur* (February 1994): 74 (4).

46. *1996 Statistical Fact Book* (New York: Direct Marketing Association, 1996).

47. Frances Huffman, "Special Delivery."

48. Cacilie Rohwedder, "U.S. Catalog Firms Target Avid Consumers Overseas."

49. Stuart Elliott, "A Mail Campaign Helps Saab Find, and Keep, Its Customers," *The New York Times* (21 June 1993): D7.

50. C.B. DiPasquale, "Direct Hit After Anthrax Threat," *Advertising Age* (22 October 2001): 1, 60.

51. Linda Lipp, "Telephones Ringing Off the Hook," *Journal and Courier* (19 May 1994). Denise Gillene, "FBI Launches 12-State Telemarketing Sweep," *Los Angeles Times* (5 March 1993): D1.

52. Alison J. Clarke, "'As Seen on TV:' Socialization of the Tele-Visual Consumer," paper presented at the Fifth Interdisciplinary Conference on Research in Consumption, University of Lund, Sweden, August 1995.

53. Gary Arlen, "DRTV: Beyond the Fringe!" *Marketing Tools* (October 1997): 37–42.

54. Tim Triplett, "Big Names Crowd the Infomercial Airwaves," *Marketing News* (28 March 1994): 1 (2).

55. "How Videotex Offers Special Potential in France," *Business Marketing Digest* 17 (1992): 81–84.

56. Scott McMurray, "Television Shopping Is Stepping Up in Class," *The New York Times* (6 March 1994): F5.

57. William Safire, "M-Commerce," *The New York Times Magazine*," accessed at www.nytimes.com/library/magazine/home/20000319mag-onlanguage.html on February 27, 2002.

58. Michael Bociurkiw, "Text messaging thrives in the Philippines," *Forbes* (10 September 2001): 28.

59. "MTV Adds Wireless Ads to Mix," (August 23, 2001). CNN.com, http://cnn.career.printthis.clickability.com/pt/printThis?clickMap=p . . .

60. Sheree R. Curry, "Wireless Trend Taking Hold,"*Advertising Age* (25 June 2001): 2.

61. Dana James, "RU PYNG ATTN?: Europeans Find Text Messaging the Right Marketing Call," *Marketing News* (7 January 2002): 4.

62. Olga Kharif, "Online Extra: Mobile Commerce Is Coming—Modestly, Eventually," *Business Week Online, E-Biz*, May 14, 2001, accessed February 26, 2002.

63. Ibid.

64. "M-commerce Report," *New Media Age* (30 November 2000): 56.

65. Mike Dano, "M-Commerce Will Outperform E-Commerce," RCR Wireless News 20 (2 April 2001): 4.

CHAPTER 16

1. James B. Arndorfer, "Models to Troll Taverns for Pricey French Vodka," *Advertising Age* (5 May 1997): 8.

2. Kate Fitzgerald, "Homemade Bikini Contest Hits Bars, Beach for 10th Year," *Advertising Age* (13 April 1998): 18.

3. Ibid.

4. Willie Vogt, "Shaping Public Perception," *Agri Marketing* (June 1992): 72–75.

5. Tobi Elkin, "Microsoft Tires Soft Sell, Plays Hardball with DOJ," *Advertising Age* (8 May 2000): 26.

6. Steve Jarvis, "How the Internet is Changing Fundamentals of Publicity," *Marketing News* (17 July 2000): 6–7.

7. Dana James, "When Your Company Goes Code Blue," *Marketing News* (6 November 2000): 1, 15.

8. Ibid.

9. Judy A. Gordon, "Print Campaign Generates Sales Leads for Biotechnology Product," *Public Relations Journal*, July 1991, 21.

10. Lindsay Chappell, "PR Makes Impressions, Sales," *Advertising Age* (22 March 1993): S–18, S–32.

11. Patricia Winters, "Drugmaker Portrayed as Villains, Worry about Image," *Advertising Age* (22 February 1993): 1, 42.

12. Ni Chen and Hugh M. Culbertson, "Two Contrasting Approaches of Government Public Relations in Mainland China," *Public Relations Quarterly*, Fall 1992, 36–41.

13. Stephen Kindel, "Gentlemen, Flash Your Logos," *Financial World*, 13 April 1993, 46–48.

14. Gerry Khermouch, "Long Live Roll 'n' Rock!" *Brandweek* (17 July 2000): 20–23.

15. Matt Krantz, (2001, August 6). "Sponsors Get Gnarly Idea: Surf Sells, Dude," *USA TODAY Online*, August 6, 2001. Accessed 08/25/2001.

16. T. L. Stanley, "Guerrila Marketers of the Year," *Brandweek* (27 March 2000): 28; Jeff Green, "Down with the Dirt Devils," *Brandweek* (27 March 2000): 41–44; Stephanie Thompson, "Pepsi Favors Sampling Over Ads for Fruit Drink," *Advertising Age* (24 January 2000): 8.

17. Sonia Murray, "Street Marketing Does the Trick," *Advertising Age* (20 March 2000): s12.

18. Constance L. Hays, "Guerrilla Marketing is Going Mainstream," *The New York Times on the Web* (October 7, 1999).

19. Quoted in Michelle Kessler, "IBM Graffiti Ads Gain Notoriety," *USA Today* (26 April 2001): 3B.

20. Howard Stumpf and John M. Kawula, "Point of Purchase Advertising," in ed. S. Ulanoff, *Handbook of Sales Promotion* (New York: McGraw Hill, 1985); Karen A. Berger, *The Rising Importance of Point-of-Purchase Advertising in the Marketing Mix* (Englewood, NJ: Point-of-Purchase Advertising Institute, no date).

21. Patricia Winters and Scott Donaton, "Coke Takes to Highway to Grab College Crowd," *Advertising Age* (29 March 1993): 8.

22. Gardiner Harris, "Drug Makers Offer Consumers Coupons for Free Prescriptions," *The Wall Street Journal Online* (March 13, 2002).

23. Amanda Beeler, restaurateurs Learn to Savor Loyalty Plans," *Advertising Age* (5 June 2000): 35–36.

24. This section based on material presented in Don E. Schultz, William A. Robinson, and Lisa A. Petrison, *Sales Promotion Essentials*, 2nd ed. (Lincolnwood, IL: NTC Business Books, 1993).

25. Adam Bryant, "When It Comes to Offbeat Promotions to Woo Passengers, Where Will the Airlines Draw the Line?" *The New York Times* (24 January 1994): D9.

26. Kate Fitzgerald, "Guinness Looks to Its Past to Fresh 5th Pub Giveaway," *Advertising Age* (30 March 1998): 46.

27. Stephanie Thompson, "New Milk Effort Promises Fame with Cap Game," *Advertising Age* (24 April 2000): 34.

28. Sonia Reyes, "Chiquita Appeals to Health-Minded Consumers with Ford Giveaway," *Brandweek* (19 March 2001): 15.

29. Kerry J. Smith, "It's for You," *PROMO: The International Magazine for Promotion Marketing*, (August 1994): 41(4); Sharon Moshavi, "Please Deposit No Cents," *Forbes* (16 August 1993): 102.

30. Stephanie Thompson, "Pepsi Favors Sampling Over Ads for Fruit Drink," *Advertising Age* (24 January 2000): 8.

31. Amanda Beeler, "Package-Goods Marketers Tune in Free-Sampling Sites," *Advertising Age* (12 June 2000): 58.

32. *The Point-of-Purchase Advertising Industry Fact Book* (Englewood, NJ: The Point-of-Purchase Advertising Institute, 1992).

33. "Bausch & Lomb Makes Eyes with Consumers in Spain," *PROMO: The International Magazine for Promotion Marketing* (October 1994): 93.

34. Patricia Sellers, "Winning Over the New Consumer," *Fortune* (29 July 1991): 113.

35. Melanie Wells, "Who Really Needs Madison Avenue?" *Forbes* (29 October 2001): 131–134.

36. Karen J. Bannan, "Companies Look to Video Games for Product Placements," *The New York Times on the Web* (March 5, 2002).

37. Bureau of Labor Statistics, "Employment by Major Occupational Group, 2000 and Projected 2010," accessed via http://stats.bls.gov/news.release/ecopro.t02.htm on March 8, 2002.

38. Quoted in Jaclyn Fierman, "The Death and Rebirth of the Salesman," *Fortune* (25 July 1994): 38(7), 88.

39. "What a Sales Call Costs," *Sales and Marketing Management* (1 September 2000): accessed at www.salesandmarketing.com/salesandmarketing/search/search_display.jsp?vnu_content_id=1030753 on April 7, 2002.

40. Dan C. Weilbaker, "The Identification of Selling Abilities Needed for Missionary Type Sales," *Journal of Personal Selling & Sales Management* 10, Summer 1990, 45–58.

41. W. David Gibson, "Fielding a Force of Experts," *Sales and Marketing Management* (April 1993): 88–92; Henry Canaday, "Team Selling Works!" *Personal Selling Power* (September 1994): 53–58.

42. Martin Everett, "This Is the Ultimate in Selling," *Sales and Marketing Management* (August 1989): 28.

43. Maurice G. Clabaugh Jr. and Jessie L. Forbes, *Professional Selling: A Relationship Approach* (New York: West, 1992).

44. Linda Formichelli, (2001, August 24). "Good References". www.tnbt.com. Accessed 09/28/2001.

45. Melissa Campanelli, "Reshuffling the Deck," *Sales and Marketing Management* (June 1994): 83–90.

46. W. David Gibson, "Fielding a Force of Experts," *Sales and Marketing Management* (April 1993): 88–92.

47. Ibid.

48. Adapted from Erin Strout, "The Top 10 Most Outrageous T&E Expenses," *Sales and Marketing Management* (February 2001): 60.

CHAPTER 17

1. David Gates and Ray Sawhill, "A Thriller on the Net," *Newsweek* (27 March 2000): 46–47.

2. Kathy Rebello, "Italian Sausage That Sizzles in Cyberspace," *Business Week* (23 September 1996): 118.

3. Rowland T. Moriarty and Ursula Moran, "Managing Hybrid Marketing Systems," *Harvard Business Review*, November-December 1990, 2–11.

4. Brent H. Felgner, "Retailers Grab Power, Control Marketplace," *Marketing News* 23, 16 January 1989, 1–2.

5. Jeffrey A. Tannenbaum, "Chain Reactions," *The Wall Street Journal* (15 October 1993): R6.

6. www.delta.com/prog_serv/global_alliance/index.jsp, accessed April 13, 2002; Robert L. Rose and Bridget O'Brian, "United, Lufthansa Form Marketing Tie, Dealing a Setback to American Airlines," *The Wall Street Journal*, 4 (October 1993): A4.

7. Norihiko Shirouzu, "Toyota's New Scion Brand to Offer 'New Model' of Auto Distribution," *The Wall Street Journal Online*, March 27, 2002.

8. Allan J. Magrath, "The Gatekeepers," *Across the Board* (April 1992): 43–46.

9. Gabriella Stern, "If You Don't Feel Like Fetching the Rental Car, It Fetches You," *The Wall Street Journal* (9 June 1995): B1(2).

10. Richard Norman and Rafael Ramirez, "From Value Chain to Value Constellation: Designing Interactive Strategy," *Harvard Business Review*, July–August, 1993, accessed through www.hbsp.harvard.edu/rcpt/filestream.asp?otype=s&key=69541836&prodno=93408&order_id=1151389&type=.pdf on March 9, 2002.

11. Ibid.

12. "Transport, Logistics, and All That," The Institute of Logistics and Transport, accessed at www.iolt.org.uk/whoweare/who_fr.htm on 7 March 2002.

13. Christopher Palmeri, "Reefer Man," *Forbes* (25 April 1994): 82–84.

14. Joseph Weber, "Just Get It to the Stores on Time," *Business Week* (6 March 1995): 66–67.

15. Scott Woolley, "Replacing Inventory with Information," *Forbes* (24 March 1997): 54–58.

CHAPTER 18

1. Jennifer Steinhauer, "Interactive Stores Make Shopping an Experience," *New York Times News Service* [Online], 28 February 1998.

2. Michael Levy and Barton A. Weitz, *Retailing Management*, 3rd ed. (Boston: Irwin/McGraw-Hill, 1998).

3. Stanley C. Hollander, "The Wheel of Retailing," *Journal of Retailing*, July 1960, 41.

4. Kate Grossman and Joan Raymond, "Sofas for the Masses," *Newsweek* (5 June 2000): 44.

5. William R. Davidson, Albert D. Bates, and Stephen J. Bass, "The Retail Life Cycle," *Harvard Business Review*, November–December 1976, 89.

6. Gail DeGeorge, "Dilbert to the Rescue," *Business Week* (4 May 1998): 166.

7. Julia Flynn, "IKEA's New Game Plan," *Business Week* (6 October 1997): 99 (2).

8. Robert E. Calem, "Coming to a Cash Register Near You: Multimedia," *The New York Times* (31 July 1994): F7.

9. Marianne Meyer, ", 67 and Attention Shoppers!" *Marketing Media Decisions*, May 1998, 67–70.

10. Gary Robins, "Wireless POS Systems," *STORES*, February 1994, 47 (2).

11. Michael Levy and Barton A. Weitz, *Retailing Management*, 3rd ed.

12. Alfred F. Lynch, "Training for a New Ball Game: Retailing in the 21st Century," *The Futurist*, July/August 1992, 36–40.

13. Belson, K., "As Starbucks Grows, Japan, Too, Is Awash," *The New York Times on the Web*, 21 October, 2001, accessed at http://query.nytimes.com/search/abstract?res=F50F14FF3B5A0C728EDDA90994D9404482 on April 10, 2002.

14. Grace Fan, "Pedicarts Link Shanghai's Streets to the Internet," *The New York Times*, 29 March 2000, accessed at www.nytimes.com/library/tech/00/03/biztech/technology/29fan.html on 2 January 2001.

15. "Levi Wins Designer Shopping Battle," CNN.com, 20 November 2001 accessed at www.cnn.com/2001/WORLD/europe/11/20/designer.goods/index.html.

16. Amy Merrick, "Kohl's Woos Tony Upscale Brands, Jolting Battered Department Stores," *The Wall Street Journal Online*, 12 March 2002.

17. Julie Liesse, "Welcome to the Club," *Advertising Age* (1 February 1993): 3 (2).

18. Debra Hazel, "The Factory Outlets' Best of Times: Belz's and Other Centers Beat the Recession," *Chain Store Age Executive* (November 1992): 39–42.

19. Alice Z. Cuneo, "Retailers Grasping for Right Mix," *Advertising Age* (11 March 2002): S–4.

20. Amy Merrick, Jeffrey A. Trachtenberg and Ann Zimmerman, "Department Stores Fight to Save a Model That May Be Outdated," *The Wall Street Journal Online*, 12 March 2002.

21. Levy and Weitz, *Retailing Management*, 3rd ed.

22. John Browning and Spencer Reiss, "Encyclopedia of the New Economy, Part I," *Wired* (March 1998): 105 (8).

23. Quoted in Stratford Sherman, "Will the Information Superhighway Be the Death of Retailing?" *Fortune* (18 April 1994): 99 (5), 110.

24. Quoted in Kate Ballen, "Get Ready for Shopping at Work," *Fortune* (15 February 1988): 95

25. Levy and Weitz, *Retailing Management*, 3rd ed; Len Strazewski, "Tupperware Locks in New Strategy," *Advertising Age* (8 February 1988): 30.

26. Peter Wilkinson, "For Your Eyes Only," *Savvy Woman* (January 1989): 68.

27. H.J. Shrager, "Close Social Networks of Hasidic women, Other Tight Groups, Boost Shaklee Sales," *The Wall Street Journal Online*, 19 November 2001.

28. Mario Brossi and Joseph Marino, *Multilevel Marketing: A Legal Primer* (Washington, DC: Direct Selling Association, 1990).

29. James Sterngold, "Why Japanese Adore Vending Machines," *The New York Times* (5 January 1992): A1 (2).

30. Seema Williams, David M. Cooperstein, David E. Weisman, and Thalika Oum, "Post-Web Retail," *The Forrester Report*, Forrester Research, Inc., September 1999.

31. Stuart Elliott, "Betty Crocker: Can She Cook in Cyberspace?" *The New York Times Online*, December 13, 2000, accessed at www.nytimes.com/library/tech/00/12/biztech/technology/13elli.html on January 14, 2001.

32. Ibid.

33. Brad Stone, N'Gai Croal, Jennifer Tanaka, Arian Campo-Flores, Jamie Reno, Andrew Murr, and Pat Wingert, "The Noisy War Over Napster," *Newsweek* (5 June 2000): 44–53.

34. Matt Richtel, "Napster Wins One Round in Music Case," *The New York Times*, accessed at www.nytimes.com/2002/02/23/technology/23MUSI.html on February 25, 2002.

35. Amy Kover, "The Hot Idea of the Year," *Fortune*, June 26, 2000, 128–136.

36. Joan Raymond, "No More Shoppus Interruptus," *American Demographics* (May 2001): 39.

37. B. Tedeschi, "Selling Made-to-Order Clothing Online," *The New York Times on the Web*, 5 November 2001.

38. Lisa Napoli, *New York Times News Service Online*, 26 February 1998, accessed via ssnewslink.

39. Michael Krantz, "Click Till You Drop," *Time* (20 July 1998): 34(6).

40. Slatalla, M., "Voyeur-Cams Come to Home Furnishings," *The New York Times on the Web*, 6 July 2000, accessed at www.nytimes.com/library/tech/00/07/circuits/articles/06shop.html on July 6, 2000.

41. Dennis K. Berman, "Stop Online—Pick Up at the Store," *Business Week* (12 June 2000): 169–172.

42. Rebecca Quick, "Hope Springs Anew for Web Retailers: Study Shows Many Are Making Money," *The Wall Street Journal Interactive Edition*, 18 April 2000; Randy Myers, "E-Tailers & Space Invaders," *e-CFO* (April 2000): 47 (7).

43. Quoted in Bob Tedeschi, "Online Travel Agents Expand Offline," *The New York Times on the Web*, 18 March 2002.

44. Michael Krantz, "Click Till You Drop."

45. C. K. Prahalad and Venkatram Ramaswamy, "Co-Opting Customer Competence," *Harvard Business Review*, January/February 2000, 79–87.

46. Kathryn Waskom, "Destination Retail Is on Its Way," *Marketing News* (13 March 2000): 15.

47. Jennifer Steinhauer, "Interactive Stores Make Shopping an Experience."

48. "A Wide World of Sports Shoes: Fixtures Enhance Appeal of World Foot Locker," *Chain Store Age Executive*, January 1993, 176–181.

49. Quoted in Wendy Marx, "Shopping 2000," *Brandweek* (9 January 1995): 20 (2).

50. L. W. Turley and Ronald E. Milliman, "Atmospheric Effects on Shopping Behavior: A Review of the Experimental Evidence," *Journal of Business Research*, 49, 2000, 193–211.

51. "The Sound of Retail," *Chain Store Age* (January 1996): 3C–6C.

52. Louise Dramer, "Taco Bell Tests Improved Taste—in Interior Design," *Advertising Age* (19 July 1999): 1, 26.

53. Emily Nelson, "Chili's Hopes Customers Warm to Pepper-Shaped Restaurant," *Wall Street Journal Interactive Edition*, 8 April 1998.

54. Yumiko Ono, "Food, Beverage Makers Set Up Traps to Increase Number of Impulse Buys," *Wall Street Journal Interactive Edition*, 8 September 1998.

55. Julie Flaherty, "Ambient Music Has Moved to Record Store Shelves," NYT.com, July 4, 2001.

56. Deborah Blumenthal, "Scenic Design for In-Store Try-Ons," *The New York Times* (9 April 1988).

57. "Service: Retail's No. 1 Problem," *Chain Store Age* (19 January 1987).

58. Elaine Underwood, "Mall Busters, Like Crime, a Boon for Home Shopping," *Brandweek* (17 January 1994): 18 (2).

59. Stephanie Strom, "Bold Stroke in Japan's Art of Retailing," *The New York Times* (23 April 1993): D1 (2).

60. Levy and Weitz, *Retailing Management*, 3rd ed.

61. Ibid.

62. Kate Fitzgerald, "All Roads Lead to . . . ," *Advertising Age* (1 February 1993): S–1.

63. Dean Starkman, "Lifestyle Centers Are New Mall Concept: Part Main Street and Part Fifth Avenue," *The Wall Street Journal Online*, 25 July 2001.

64. Levy and Weitz, *Retailing Management*, 3rd ed.

65. Rekha Balu, "The Buckle Finds Rural Kids Will Pay Dearly for Hip Clothes," *Wall Street Journal Interactive Edition*, 14 January 1998.

Glossary

A

acceleration principle (multiplier effect)   A marketing phenomenon in which a small percentage change in consumer demand can create a large percentage change in business-to-business demand.

advertising appeal   The central idea or theme of an advertising message.

advertising campaign   A coordinated, comprehensive plan that carries out promotion objectives and results in a series of advertisements placed in media over a period of time.

advertising exposure   The degree to which the target market will see an advertising message placed in a specific vehicle.

advertising   Nonpersonal communication from an identified sponsor using the mass media.

advocacy advertising   A type of public service advertising provided by an organization that is seeking to influence public opinion on an issue because it has some stake in the outcome.

AIDA model   The communications goals of attention, interest, desire, and action.

aided recall   A research technique that uses clues to prompt answers from people about advertisements they might have seen.

aperture   The best place and time to reach a person in the target market group.

approach   The first step of the actual sales presentation in which the salesperson tries to learn more about the customer's needs, create a good impression, and build rapport.

atmospherics   The use of color, lighting, scents, furnishings, and other design elements to create a desired store image.

attitude   A learned predisposition to respond favorably or unfavorably to stimuli based on relatively enduring evaluations of people, objects, and issues.

attitudinal measures   A research technique that probes a consumer's beliefs or feelings about a product before and after being exposed to messages about it.

augmented services   The core service plus additional services provided to enhance value.

average fixed cost   The fixed cost per unit produced.

B

baby boomers   Segment of people born between 1946 and 1964.

back-translation   The process of translating material to a foreign language and then back to the original language.

banners   Internet advertising in the form of rectangular graphics boxes placed at the top or bottom of Web pages.

BCG growth-market share matrix   A portfolio analysis model developed by the Boston Consulting Group that assesses the potential of successful products to generate cash that a firm can then use to invest in new products.

behavioral learning theories   Theories of learning that focus on how consumer behavior is changed by external events or stimuli.

behavioral segmentation   Technique that divides consumers into segments on the basis of how they act toward, feel about, or use a good or service.

benefit   The outcome sought by a customer that motivates buying behavior—that satisfies a need or want.

bottom-up budgeting techniques   Allocation of the promotion budget based on identifying promotional goals and allocating enough money to accomplish them.

brand   A name, a term, a symbol, or any other unique element of a product that identifies one firm's product(s) and sets them apart from the competition.

brand competition   When firms offering similar goods or services compete based on their brand's reputation or perceived benefits.

brand equity   The value of a brand to an organization.

brand extensions   A new product sold with the same brand name as a strong existing brand.

brand loyalty   A pattern of repeat product purchases, accompanied by an underlying positive attitude toward the brand, which is based on the belief that the brand makes products superior to its competition.

brand manager   An individual who is responsible for developing and implementing the marketing plan for a single brand.

brand personality   A distinctive image that captures a good or service's character and benefits.

brand placement   Getting a brand featured in a movie or television show.

break-even analysis   A method for determining the number of units that a firm must produce and sell at a given price to cover all its costs.

break-even point   The point at which the total revenue and total costs are equal and beyond which the company makes a profit; below that point, the firm will suffer a loss.

breaking bulk   Dividing larger quantities of goods into smaller lots in order to meet the needs of buyers.

business analysis   Step in the product development process in which marketers assess a product's commercial viability.

business cycle   The overall patterns of change in the economy—including periods of prosperity, recession, depression, and recovery—that affect consumer and business purchasing power.

business ethics   Rules of conduct for an organization.

business plan   A plan that includes the decisions that guide the entire organization.

business portfolio   The group of different products or brands owned by an organization and characterized by different income-generating and growth capabilities.

business-to-business (B2B) e-commerce   Internet exchanges between two or more businesses or organizations.

business-to-business marketing   Marketing of those goods and services that business and organizational customers need to produce other goods and services for resale or to support their operations.

business-to-consumer (B2C) e-commerce   Online exchanges between companies and individual consumers.

buttons   Small banner-type advertisements that can be placed anywhere on a Web page.

buy class   One of three classifications of business buying situations that characterizes the degree of time and effort required to make a decision.

buying center   The group of people in an organization who participate in a purchasing decision.

C

cannibalization   The loss of sales of an existing brand when a new item in a product line or product family is introduced.

capacity management   The process by which organizations adjust their offerings in an attempt to match demand.

captive pricing   A pricing tactic for two items that must be used together; one item is priced very low and the firm makes its profit on another, high-margin item essential to the operation of the first item.

case allowance   A discount to the retailer or wholesaler based on the volume of product ordered.

case study   A comprehensive examination of a particular firm or organization.

catalog   A collection of products offered for sale in book form, usually consisting of product descriptions accompanied by photos of the items.

causal research   Technique that attempts to understand cause-and-effect relationships.

cause marketing   Marketing activities in which firms seek to have their corporate identity linked to a good cause through advertising, public service, and publicity.

centralized purchasing   A business buying practice in which a single department does the buying for all the company's facilities.

channel intermediaries   Firms or individuals such as wholesalers, agents, brokers, or retailers who help move a product from the producer to the consumer or business user.

channel leader   A firm at one level of distribution that takes a leadership role, establishing operating norms and processes that reduce channel conflicts and costs and enhance delivered customer value.

channel levels   The number of distinct categories of intermediaries that populate a channel of distribution.

channel of distribution   The series of firms or individuals that facilitates the movement of a product from the producer to the final customer.

classical conditioning   The learning that occurs when a stimulus eliciting a response is paired with another stimulus that initially does not elicit a response on its own but will cause a similar response over time because of its association with the first stimulus.

co-branding   An agreement between two brands to work together in marketing a new product.

codes of ethics   Written standards of behavior to which everyone in the organization must subscribe.

cognitive learning theory   Theory of learning that stresses the importance of internal mental processes and that views people as problem solvers who actively use information from the world around them to master their environment.

collectivist culture   Culture in which people subordinate their personal goals to those of a stable community.

commercialization   Final step in the product development process in which a new product is launched into the market.

communications model   The process whereby meaning is transferred from a source to a receiver.

competitive advantage   The ability of a firm to outperform the competition, thereby providing customers with a benefit the competition can't.

competitive bids   A business buying process in which two or more suppliers submit proposals (including price and associated data) for a proposed purchase and the firm providing the better offer gets the bid.

competitive intelligence (CI)   The process of gathering and analyzing publicly available information about rivals.

competitive-parity method   A promotion budgeting method in which an organization matches whatever competitors are spending.

component parts   Manufactured goods or subassemblies of finished items that organizations need to complete their own products.

concentrated targeting strategy   Focusing a firm's efforts on offering one or more products to a single segment.

conformity   A change in beliefs or actions as a reaction to real or imagined group pressure.

consumer   The ultimate user of a good or service.

consumer behavior   The process involved when individuals or groups select, purchase, use, and dispose of goods, services, ideas, or experiences to satisfy their needs and desires.

Consumer Bill of Rights   The rights of consumers to be protected by the federal government.

consumer confidence   An indicator of future spending patterns as measured by the extent to which people are optimistic or pessimistic about the state of the economy.

consumer goods   The goods purchased by individual consumers for personal or family use.

consumer interviews One-on-one discussions between a consumer and a researcher.

consumer orientation A management philosophy that focuses on ways to satisfy customers' needs and wants.

consumer satisfaction/dissatisfaction (CS/D) The overall feelings or attitude a person has about a product after purchasing it.

consumerism A social movement that attempts to protect consumers from harmful business practices.

consumer-to-consumer (C2C) e-commerce Communications and purchases that occur among individuals without directly involving the manufacturer or retailer.

contact management A communication strategy that provides communications exposures where and when the targeted customer is most likely to receive them.

continuous innovation A modification of an existing product that sets one brand apart from its competitors.

contribution per unit The difference between the price the firm charges for a product and the variable costs.

controlling the marketing plan Measuring actual performance, comparing it to planned performance and making necessary changes in plans and implementation.

convenience product A consumer good or service that is usually low priced, widely available, and purchased frequently with a minimum of comparison and effort.

convenience stores Neighborhood retailers that carry a limited number of frequently purchased items, and cater to consumers willing to pay a premium for the ease of buying close to home.

conventional marketing system A multiple-level distribution channel in which channel members work independently of one another.

conventions Norms regarding the conduct of everyday life.

convergence The coming together of two or more technologies to create a new system with greater benefits than its parts.

cookies Text files inserted by a Web site sponsor into a Web surfer's hard drive that allow the site to track the surfer's moves.

copy testing A marketing research method that seeks to measure the effectiveness of ads by determining whether consumers are receiving, comprehending, and responding to the ad according to plan.

core service The basic benefit of having a service performed.

corporate culture The set of values, norms, and beliefs that influence the behavior of everyone in the organization.

corrective advertising Advertising that clarifies or qualifies previous deceptive advertising claims.

cost per thousand (CPM) A measure used to compare the relative cost-effectiveness of different media vehicles that have different exposure rates; the cost to deliver a message to 1,000 people or homes.

cost-plus pricing A method of setting prices in which the seller totals all the costs for the product and then adds an amount to arrive at selling price.

countertrade Type of trade in which goods are paid for with other items instead of with cash.

creating assortments Providing a variety of products in one location to meet the needs of buyers.

creative selling process The process of seeking out customers, analyzing needs, determining how product attributes might provide benefits for the customer, and then communicating that information.

creative strategy The process that turns a concept into an advertisement.

credence qualities Product characteristics that are difficult to evaluate even *after* they have been experienced.

critical incident technique A method for measuring service quality in which marketers use customer complaints to identify critical incidents, specific face-to-face contacts between consumers and service providers that cause problems and lead to dissatisfaction.

cross-elasticity of demand When changes in price of one product affect the demand for another item.

cross-functional planning An approach to tactical planning in which managers work together in developing tactical plans for each functional area in the firm so that each plan considers the objectives of the other areas.

cross-promotion Two or more products or services combine forces to create interest using a single promotional tool.

cross-sectional design Type of descriptive technique that involves the systematic collection of quantitative information.

cultural diversity A management practice that actively seeks to include people of different sexes, races, ethnic groups, and religions in an organization's employees, customers, suppliers, and distribution channel partners.

cultural values A society's deeply held beliefs about right and wrong ways to live.

culture The values, beliefs, customs, and tastes valued by a group of people.

cumulative quantity discounts Discounts based on the total quantity purchased within a specified time period.

custom marketing strategy Approach that tailors specific products and the messages about them to individual customers.

custom research Research conducted for a single firm to provide specific information its managers need.

custom A norm handed down from the past that controls basic behaviors.

customer equity The financial value of a customer relationship throughout the lifetime of the relationship.

customer relationship management (CRM) A philosophy that sees marketing as a process of building long-term relationships with customers to keep them satisfied and to keep them coming back.

customer's lifetime value The potential profit generated by a single customer's purchase of a firm's products over the customer's lifetime.

D

data mining Sophisticated analysis techniques to take advantage of the massive amount of transaction information now available.

database marketing The creation of an ongoing relationship with a set of customers who have an identifiable interest in a product or service and whose responses to promotional efforts become part of future communications attempts.

decline stage The final stage in the product life cycle in which sales decrease as customer needs change.

decoding The process by which a receiver assigns meaning to the message.

demand Customers' desire for products coupled with the resources to obtain them.

demand-based pricing A price-setting method based on estimates of demand at different prices.

demographics Statistics that measure observable aspects of a population, including size, age, gender, ethnic group, income, education, occupation, and family structure.

department stores Retailers that sell a broad range of items and offer a good selection within each product line.

derived demand Demand for business or organizational products derived from demand for consumer goods or services.

descriptive research Tool that probes more systematically into the problem and bases its conclusions on large numbers of observations.

developed country A country that boasts sophisticated marketing systems, strong private enterprise, and bountiful market potential for many goods and services.

developing countries Countries in which the economy is shifting its emphasis from agriculture to industry.

differential benefit Properties of products that set them apart from competitors' products by providing unique customer benefits.

differentiated targeting strategy Developing one or more products for each of several distinct customer groups and making sure these offerings are kept separate in the marketplace.

diffusion The process by which the use of a product spreads throughout a population.

direct mail A brochure or pamphlet offering a specific product or service at one point in time.

direct marketing Any direct communication to a consumer or business recipient that is designed to generate a response in the form of an order, a request for further information, and/or a visit to a store or other place of business for purchase of a product.

direct response TV (DRTV) Short commercials of less than two minutes, 30-minute or longer infomercials, and home shopping networks.

direct selling An interactive sales process in which a salesperson presents a product to one individual or a small group, takes orders, and delivers the merchandise.

discontinuous innovation A totally new product that creates major changes in the way we live.

discretionary income The portion of income people have left over after paying for necessities such as housing, utilities, food, and clothing.

discriminatory pricing A pricing practice in which different customers are charged different prices.

disintermediation (of service delivery) Eliminating the interaction between customers and salespeople so as to minimize negative service encounters.

distinctive competency A superior capability of a firm in comparison to its direct competitors.

diversification Growth strategies that emphasize both new products and new markets.

dumping A company tries to get a toehold in a foreign market by pricing its products lower than they are offered at home.

durable goods Consumer products that provide benefits over a long period of time such as cars, furniture, and appliances.

dynamic pricing Pricing strategy in which the price can easily be adjusted to meet changes in the marketplace.

dynamically continuous innovation A change in an existing product that requires a moderate amount of learning or behavior change.

E

early adopters Those who adopt an innovation early in the diffusion process but after the innovators.

early majority Those whose adoption of a new product signals a general acceptance of the innovation.

e-commerce The buying or selling of goods and services electronically, usually over the Internet.

economic communities Groups of countries that band together to promote trade among themselves and to make it easier for member nations to compete elsewhere.

economic infrastructure The quality of a country's distribution, financial, and communications systems.

economic sanctions Trade prohibitions imposed by one country against another.

80/20 rule A marketing rule of thumb that 20 percent of purchasers account for 80 percent of a product's sales.

elastic demand Demand in which changes in price have large effects on the amount demanded.

e-marketers Marketers who use e-commerce in their strategies.

embargo A quota completely prohibiting specified goods from entering or leaving a country.

embodying The inclusion of a service with a purchase of a physical good.

encoding The process of translating an idea into a form of communication that will convey meaning.

environmental stewardship A position taken by an organization to protect or enhance the natural environment as it conducts its business activities.

equipment Expensive goods an organization uses in its daily operations that last for a long time.

ethnocentrism The tendency to prefer products or people of one's own culture.

ethnography A detailed report based on observations of people in their own homes or communities.

European Union (EU) Economic community that now includes most of Western Europe.

evaluative criteria The dimensions used by consumers to compare competing product alternatives.

everyday low pricing (EDLP) See *value pricing.*

exchange The process by which some transfer of value occurs between a buyer and a seller.

exclusive distribution Selling a product only through a single outlet in a particular region.

experience qualities Product characteristics that customers can determine during or after consumption.

experiential shopper Consumers who engage in online shopping because of the experiential benefits they receive.

experiments Techniques that test prespecified relationships among variables in a controlled environment.

exploratory research Technique that marketers use to generate insights for future, more rigorous studies.

export merchant An intermediary used by a firm to represent it in another country.

expropriation A domestic government's seizure of a foreign company's assets without any compensation.

external environment The uncontrollable elements outside of an organization that may affect its performance either positively or negatively.

extranet Private, corporate computer network that links company departments, employees, and databases to suppliers, customers, and others outside the organization.

F

F.O.B. delivered pricing A pricing tactic in which the cost of loading and transporting the product to the customer is included in the selling price and is paid by the manufacturer.

F.O.B. origin pricing A pricing tactic in which the cost of transporting the product from the factory to the customer's location is the responsibility of the customer.

facilitating functions Functions of channel intermediaries that make the purchase process easier for customers and manufacturers.

factory outlet store A discount retailer, owned by a manufacturer, which sells off defective merchandise and excess inventory.

family brand A brand that a group of individual products or individual brands share.

family life cycle A means of characterizing consumers within a family structure based on different stages through which people pass as they grow older.

feedback Receivers' reactions to the message.

firewall A combination of computer hardware and software that ensure only authorized individuals gain entry into a computer system.

fixed costs Costs of production that do not change with the number of units produced.

focus group A product-oriented discussion among a small group of consumers led by a trained moderator.

franchising A form of licensing involving the right to adapt an entire system of doing business.

freight absorption pricing A pricing tactic in which the seller absorbs the total cost of transportation.

frequency The number of times a person in the target group will be exposed to the message.

frequency programs Consumer sales promotion programs that offer a discount or free product for multiple purchases over time; also referred to as loyalty or continuity programs.

full-service agency Agency that provides most or all of the services needed to mount a campaign, including research, creation of ad copy and art, media selection, and production of the final messages.

G

gap analysis A marketing research methodology that measures the difference between a customer's expectation of a service quality and what actually occurred.

General Agreement on Tariffs and Trade (GATT) International treaty to reduce import tax levels and trade restrictions.

general merchandise discount stores Retailers that offer a broad assortment of items at low prices with minimal service.

generation X The group of consumers born between 1965 and 1976.

generation Y The group of consumers born between 1977 and 1994.

geodemography Segmentation technique that combines geography with demographics.

good Tangible product we can see, touch, smell, hear, or taste.

government markets The federal, state, county, and local governments that buy goods and services to carry out public objectives and to support their operations.

gray market An unauthorized party imports products and then sells them for a fraction of the price of the authorized imports.

green marketing A marketing strategy that supports environmental stewardship by creating an environmentally founded differential benefit in the minds of consumers.

gross domestic product (GDP) The total dollar value of goods and services produced by a nation within its borders in a year.

gross national product (GNP) The value of all goods and services produced by a country's citizens or organizations, whether located within the country's borders or not.

gross rating points (GRPs) A measure used for comparing the effectiveness of different media vehicles: average reach times frequency.

growth stage The second stage in the product life cycle during which the product is accepted and sales rapidly increase.

guerrilla marketing Promotional strategies that "ambush" consumers with promotional content in places they are not expecting it.

H

heuristics A mental rule of thumb that leads to a speedy decision by simplifying the process.

hierarchy of needs An approach that categorizes motives according to five levels of importance, the more basic needs being on the bottom of the hierarchy and the higher needs at the top.

horizontal marketing system An arrangement within a channel of distribution in which two or more firms at the same channel level work together for a common purpose.

hybrid marketing systems Marketing systems that use a number of different channels and communications methods to serve a target market.

hypermarkets Retailers with the characteristics of both warehouse stores and supermarkets; hypermarkets are several times larger than other stores and offer virtually everything from grocery items to electronics.

I

idea generation The first step of product development in which marketers brainstorm for products that provide customer benefits and are compatible with the company mission.

idea marketing Marketing activities that seek to gain market share for a concept, philosophy, belief, or issue by using elements of the marketing mix to create or change a target market's attitude or behavior.

import quotas Limitations set by a government on the amount of a product allowed to enter or leave a country.

impressions The number of people who will be exposed to a message placed in one or more media vehicles.

income effect The effect of changes in income on demand for a product, even if its price remains the same.

independent intermediaries Channel intermediaries that are not controlled by any manufacturer but instead do business with many different manufacturers and many different customers.

individualist culture Culture in which people tend to attach more importance to personal goals than to those of the larger community.

industrial goods Goods bought by individuals or organizations for further processing or for use in doing business.

inelastic demand Demand in which changes in price have little or no effect on the amount demanded.

inferior goods Products for which demand decreases as income increases.

infomercials Half-hour or hour commercials that resemble a talk show but in actuality are intended to sell something.

information search The process whereby a consumer searches for appropriate information to make a reasonable decision.

ingredient branding A form of co-branding in which branded materials are used as ingredients or component parts of other branded products.

innovation A product that consumers perceive to be new and different from existing products.

innovators The first segment (roughly 2.5 percent) of a population to adopt a new product.

institutional advertising An advertising message that promotes the activities, personality, or point of view of an organization or company.

intangibles Experience-based products that cannot be touched.

Integrated marketing communications (IMC) A strategic business process that marketers use to plan, develop, execute, and evaluate coordinated, measurable, persuasive brand communication programs over time with targeted audiences.

intensive distribution Selling a product through all suitable wholesalers or retailers that are willing to stock and sell the product.

interactive marketing A promotion practice in which customized marketing communications elicit a measurable response from individual receivers.

internal environment The controllable elements inside an organization including its people, its facilities, and how it does things that influence the operations of the organization.

internal marketing Marketing activities aimed at employees in an effort to inform them about the firm's offerings and their high quality.

internal reference price A set price or a price range in consumers' minds that they refer to in evaluating a product's price.

intranet An internal corporate communication network that uses Internet technology to link company departments, employees, and databases.

introduction The first stage of the product life cycle in which slow growth follows the introduction of a new product in the marketplace.

inventory control Activities to ensure that goods are always available to meet customers' demands.

involvement The relative importance of perceived consequences of the purchase to a consumer.

ISO 14000 Standards of the International Organization of Standardization concerned with "environmental management" aimed at minimizing harmful effects on the environment.

ISO 9000 Criteria developed by the International Organization of Standardization to regulate product quality in Europe.

J

joint demand Demand for two or more goods that are used together to create a product.

joint venture Strategic alliance in which a new entity owned by two or more firms is created to allow the partners to pool their resources for common goals.

just in time (JIT) Inventory management and purchasing processes that manufacturers and resellers use to reduce inventory to very low levels and ensure that deliveries from suppliers arrive only when needed.

K

knockoff A new product that copies with slight modification the design of an original product.

L

laggards The last consumers to adopt an innovation.

late majority The adopters who are willing to try new products when there is little or no risk associated with the purchase, when the purchase becomes an economic necessity, or when there is social pressure to purchase.

learning A relatively permanent change in behavior caused by acquired information or experience.

less developed country (LDC) A country at the lowest stage of economic development.

licensing (in foreign markets) Agreement in which one firm gives another firm the right to produce and market its product in a specific country or region in return for royalties.

licensing (of a name) Agreement in which one firm sells another firm the right to use a brand name for a specific purpose and for a specific period of time.

lifestyle The pattern of living that determines how people choose to spend their time, money, and energy and that reflects their values, tastes, and preferences.

limited-service agency Agency that provides one or more specialized services such as media buying or creative development.

list price The price the end customer is expected to pay as determined by the manufacturer; also referred to as the suggested retail price.

local content rules A form of protectionism stipulating that a certain proportion of a product must consist of components supplied by industries in the host country.

logistics The process of designing, managing, and improving the movement of products through the supply chain.

longitudinal design Technique that tracks the responses of the same sample of respondents over time.

loss leader pricing The pricing policy of setting prices very low or even below cost to attract customers into a store.

M

maintenance, repair, and operating (MRO) products Goods that a business customer consumes in a relatively short time.

margin The difference between the cost of a product and the selling price.

marginal analysis A method that uses cost and demand to identify the price that will maximize profits.

marginal cost The increase in total cost that results from producing one additional unit of a product.

marginal revenue The increase in total revenue (income) that results from producing and selling one additional unit of a product.

market All of the customers and potential customers who share a common need that can be satisfied by a specific product, who have the resources to exchange for it, who are willing to make the exchange, and who have the authority to make the exchange.

market development Growth strategies that introduce existing products to new markets.

market fragmentation Creation of many consumer groups due to a diversity of distinct needs and wants in modern society.

market manager An individual who is responsible for developing and implementing the marketing plans for products sold to a particular customer group.

market penetration Growth strategies designed to increase sales of existing products to current customers, nonusers, and users of competitive brands in served markets.

market position The way in which the target market perceives the product in comparison to competitors' brands.

market segment A distinct group of customers within a larger market who are similar to one another in some way and whose needs differ from other customers in the larger market.

marketing The process of planning and executing the conception, pricing, promotion, and distribution of ideas, goods, and services to create exchanges that satisfy individual and organizational objectives.

marketing audit A comprehensive review of a firm's marketing function.

marketing budget A statement of the total amount to be spent on marketing and the allocation of money for each activity under the marketer's control.

marketing concept A management orientation that focuses on identifying and satisfying consumer needs to ensure the organization's long-term profitability.

marketing decision support system (MDSS) The data, analysis software, and interactive software that allow managers to conduct analyses and find the information they need.

marketing information system (MIS) Procedure developed by a firm to continuously gather, sort, analyze, store, and distribute relevant and timely marketing information to its managers.

marketing intelligence system   A method by which marketers get information about everyday happenings in the marketing environment.

marketing mix   A combination of the product itself, the price of the product, the place where it is made available, and the activities that introduce it to consumers that creates a desired response among a set of predefined consumers.

marketing plan   A document that describes the marketing environment, outlines the marketing objectives and strategy, and identifies who will be responsible for carrying out each part of the marketing strategy.

marketing research   The process of collecting, analyzing, and interpreting data about customers, competitors, and the business environment in order to improve marketing effectiveness.

marketplace   Any location or medium used to conduct an exchange.

mass customization   Approach that modifies a basic good or service to meet the needs of an individual.

mass market All possible customers in a market, regardless of the differences in their specific needs and wants.

materials handling   The moving of products into, within, and out of warehouses.

maturity stage   The third and longest stage in the product life cycle in which sales peak and profit margins narrow.

m-commerce   Promotional and other e-commerce activities transmitted over mobile phones and other mobile devices such as personal digital assistants (PDAs).

media planning   The process of developing media objectives, strategies, and tactics for use in an advertising campaign.

media schedule   The plan that specifies the exact media to use and when.

medium   A communications vehicle through which a message is transmitted to a target audience.

merchandise agents or brokers   Channel intermediaries that provide services in exchange for commissions but never take title to the product.

merchandise allowance   Reimburses the retailer for in-store support of the product.

merchandise assortment   The range of products sold.

merchandise breadth The number of different product lines available.

merchandise depth   The variety of choices available for each specific product line.

merchandise mix   The total set of all products offered for sale by a retailer, including all product lines sold to all consumer groups.

merchant wholesalers   Intermediaries that buy goods from manufacturers (take title to them) and sell to retailers and other business-to-business customers.

message   The communication in physical form that goes from a sender to a receiver.

mission statement   A formal statement in an organization's strategic plan that describes the overall purpose of the organization and what it intends to achieve in terms of its customers, products, and resources.

missionary salesperson   A salesperson who promotes the firm and tries to stimulate demand for a product, but does not actually complete a sale.

modified rebuy   A buying situation classification used by business buyers to categorize a previously made purchase that involves some change and that requires limited decision making.

monopolistic competition   A market structure in which many firms, each having slightly different products, offer unique consumer benefits.

monopoly   A market situation in which one firm, the only supplier of a particular product, is able to control the price, quality, and supply of that product.

mores   A custom with a strong moral overtone.

motivation   An internal state that drives us to satisfy needs by activating goal-oriented behavior.

multilevel network   A system in which a master distributor recruits other people to become distributors, sells the company's product to the recruits, and receives a commission on all the merchandise sold by the people recruited.

multiple sourcing   The business practice of buying a particular product from many suppliers.

N

national or manufacturer brands   Brands that the manufacturer of the product owns.

nationalization   A domestic government's takeover of a foreign company for its assets with some reimbursement, though often not for the full value.

need   Recognition of any difference between a consumer's actual state and some ideal or desired state.

New Era orientation   A management philosophy in which marketing means a devotion to excellence in designing and producing products that benefit the customer plus the firm's employees, shareholders, and communities.

new-task buy   A new business-to-business purchase that is complex or risky and that requires extensive decision making.

noise   Anything that interferes with effective communication.

noncumulative quantity discounts   Discounts based only on the quantity purchased with individual orders.

nondurable goods   Consumer products that provide benefits for a short time because they are consumed (such as food) or are no longer useful (such as newspapers).

nonprobability sample   A sample in which personal judgment is used in selecting respondents.

nonstore retailing   Any method used to complete an exchange with a product end user that does not require a customer visit to a store.

normal goods   Products for which demand increases as income increases.

norms   Specific rules dictating what is right or wrong, acceptable or unacceptable.

North American Free Trade Agreement (NAFTA)   The world's largest economic community composed of the United States, Canada, and Mexico.

North American Industry Classification System (NAICS) The numerical coding system that the United States, Canada, and Mexico use to classify firms into detailed categories according to their business activities.

not-for-profit institutions The organizations with charitable, educational, community, and other public service goals that buy goods and services to support their functions and to attract and serve their members.

O

objective-task method A promotion budgeting method in which an organization first defines the specific communications goals it hopes to achieve and then tries to calculate what kind of promotional efforts it will take to meet these goals.

off-price retailers Retailers that buy excess merchandise from well-known manufacturers and pass the savings on to customers.

oligopoly A market structure in which a relatively small number of sellers, each holding a substantial share of the market, compete in a market with many buyers.

online auctions E-commerce that allows shoppers to purchase products through online bidding.

operant conditioning Learning that occurs as the result of rewards or punishments.

operational planning A decision process that focuses on developing detailed plans for day-to-day activities that carry out an organization's tactical plans.

opinion leader A person who is frequently able to influence others' attitudes or behaviors by virtue of his or her active interest and expertise in one or more product categories.

order getter A salesperson who works creatively to develop relationships with customers or to generate new sales.

order taker A salesperson whose primary function is to facilitate transactions that the customer initiates.

organizational markets Another name for business-to-business markets.

out-of-home media A communication medium that reaches people in public places.

outsourcing The business buying process of obtaining outside vendors to provide goods or services that otherwise might be supplied in house.

P

package The covering or container for a product that provides product protection, facilitates product use and storage, and supplies important marketing communication.

party plan system A sales technique that relies heavily on people getting caught up in the "group spirit," buying things they would not normally buy if alone.

patent Legal documentation granting an individual or firm exclusive rights to produce and sell a particular invention.

penetration pricing A pricing strategy in which a firm introduces a new product at a very low price to encourage more customers to purchase it.

perceived risk The belief that the choice of a product has potentially negative consequences, either financial, physical, or social.

percentage-of-sales method A method for promotion budgeting that is based on a certain percentage of either last year's sales or on estimates for the present year's sales.

perception The process by which people select, organize, and interpret information from the outside world.

perceptual map A vivid way to construct a picture of where products or brands are "located" in consumers' minds.

perfect competition A market structure in which many small sellers, all of whom offer similar products, are unable to have an impact on the quality, price, or supply of a product.

permission marketing E-mail advertising where online consumers have the opportunity to accept or refuse the unsolicited e-mail.

personal selling The part of the promotion mix that involves direct contact between a company representative and a customer.

personality The psychological characteristics that consistently influence the way a person responds to situations in his or her environment.

physical distribution The activities used to move finished goods from manufacturers to final customers including order processing, warehousing, materials handling, transportation, and inventory control.

physical evidence A visible signal that communicates not only a product's quality but also the product's desired market position to the consumer.

place marketing Marketing activities that seek to attract new businesses, residents, or visitors to a town, state, country, or some other site.

place The availability of the product to the customer at the desired time and location.

place-based media Advertising media that transmit messages in public places, such as doctors' offices and airports where certain types of people congregate.

point-of-purchase (POP) promotion In-store displays or signs.

point-of-sale (POS) systems Retail computer systems that collect sales data and are hooked directly into the store's inventory control system.

popular culture The music, movies, sports, books, celebrities, and other forms of entertainment consumed by the mass market.

portfolio analysis A management tool for evaluating a firm's business mix and assessing the potential of an organization's strategic business units.

positioning Developing a marketing strategy aimed at influencing how a particular market segment perceives a good or service in comparison to the competition.

posttesting Research conducted on consumers' responses to actual advertising messages they have seen or heard.

preapproach A part of the selling process that includes developing information about prospective customers and planning the sales interview.

premiums Items offered free to people who have purchased a product.

press release Information that an organization distributes to the media intended to win publicity.

prestige products Products that have a high price and appeal to status-conscious consumers.

pretesting A research method that seeks to minimize mistakes by getting consumer reactions to ad messages before they appear in the media.

price The value that customers give up or exchange to obtain a desired product.

price bundling Selling two or more goods or services as a single package for one price.

price elasticity of demand The percentage change in unit sales that results from a percentage change in price.

price fixing The collaboration of two or more firms in setting prices, usually to keep prices high.

price-floor pricing A method for calculating price in which, to maintain full plant operating capacity, a portion of a firm's output may be sold at a price that covers only marginal costs of production.

price leadership A pricing strategy in which one firm first sets its price and other firms in the industry follow with the same or very similar prices.

price lining The practice of setting a limited number of different specific prices, called price points, for items in a product line.

price subsidies Government payments made to protect domestic businesses or to reimburse them when they must price at or below cost to make a sale. The subsidy can be a cash payment or tax relief.

primary data Data from research conducted to help in making a specific decision.

private exchanges Systems that link an invited group of suppliers and partners over the Web.

private-label brands Brands that are owned and sold by a certain retailer or distributor.

probability sample A sample in which each member of the population has some known chance of being included.

problem recognition The process that occurs whenever the consumer sees a significant difference between his or her current state of affairs and some desired or ideal state; this recognition initiates the decision-making process.

processed materials Products created when firms transform raw materials from their original state.

producers The individuals or organizations that purchase products for use in the production of other goods and services.

product A tangible good, service, idea, or some combination of these that satisfies consumer or business customer needs through the exchange process; a bundle of attributes including features, functions, benefits, and uses.

product adoption The process by which a consumer or business customer begins to buy and use a new good, service, or an idea.

product advertising An advertising message that focuses on a specific good or service.

product category manager An individual who is responsible for developing and implementing the marketing plan for all of the brands and products within a product category.

product competition When firms offering different products compete to satisfy the same consumer needs and wants.

product concept development and screening Second step of product development in which marketers test product ideas for technical and commercial success.

product development Growth strategies that focus on selling new products in served markets.

product life cycle Concept that explains how products go through four distinct stages from birth to death: introduction, growth, maturity, and decline.

product line A firm's total product offering designed to satisfy a single need or desire of target customers.

product mix The total set of all products a firm offers for sale.

product orientation Management philosophy that emphasizes the most efficient ways to produce and distribute products.

product specifications A written description of the quality, size, weight, and so forth required of a product purchase.

projective techniques Tests that marketers use to explore people's underlying feelings about a product, especially appropriate when consumers are unable or unwilling to express their true reactions.

promotion The coordination of a marketer's marketing communications efforts to influence attitudes or behavior; the coordination of efforts by a marketer to inform or persuade consumers or organizations about goods, services, or ideas.

promotion mix The major elements of marketer-controlled communications including advertising, sales promotions, public relations, and personal selling.

promotion plan A framework that outlines the strategies for developing, implementing, and controlling the firm's promotional activities; the coordination of a marketer's communications efforts to influence attitudes or behavior.

prospecting A part of the selling process that includes identifying and developing a list of potential or prospective customers.

protectionism Policy adopted by a government to give domestic companies an advantage.

prototypes Test versions of a proposed product.

psychographics The use of psychological, sociological, and anthropological factors to construct market segments.

public relations Communication function that seeks to build good relationships with an organization's publics, including consumers, stockholders, and legislators.

public service advertisements (PSAs) Advertising run by the media without charge for not-for-profit organizations or to champion a particular cause.

publicity   Unpaid communication about an organization appearing in the mass media.

puffery   Claims made in advertising of product superiority that cannot be proven true or untrue.

pull strategy   The company tries to move its products through the channel by building desire for the products among consumers, thus convincing retailers to respond to this demand by stocking these items.

push money   A bonus paid by a manufacturer to a salesperson for selling its product.

push strategy   The company tries to move its products through the channel by convincing channel members to offer them.

pyramid schemes   An illegal sales technique in which the initial distributors profit by selling merchandise to other distributors, with the result that consumers buy very little product.

Q

qualify prospects   A part of the selling process that determines how likely prospects are to become customers.

quality   The level of performance, reliability, features, safety, cost, or other product characteristics that consumers expect to satisfy their needs and wants.

quantity discounts   A pricing tactic of charging reduced prices for purchases of larger quantities of a product.

R

raw materials   Products of the fishing, lumber, agricultural, and mining industries that organizational customers purchase to use in their finished products.

reach   The percentage of the target market that will be exposed to the media vehicle.

rebates   Sales promotions that allow the customer to recover part of the product's cost from the manufacturer.

receiver   The organization or individual that intercepts and interprets the message.

reciprocity   A trading partnership in which two firms agree to buy from one another.

reference group   An actual or imaginary individual or group that has a significant effect on an individual's evaluations, aspirations, or behavior.

relationship selling   A form of personal selling in which the salesperson seeks to develop a mutually satisfying relationship with the consumer.

reliability   The extent to which research measurement techniques are free of errors.

repositioning   Redoing a product's position to respond to marketplace changes.

representativeness   The extent to which consumers in a study are similar to a larger group in which the organization has an interest.

research design   A plan that specifies what information marketers will collect and what type of study they will do.

resellers   The individuals or organizations that buy finished goods for the purpose of reselling, renting, or leasing to others to make a profit and to maintain their business operations.

retail life cycle   A theory that focuses on the various stages that retailers pass through from introduction to decline.

retailing   The final stop in the distribution channel by which goods and services are sold to consumers for their personal use.

reverse marketing   A business practice in which a buyer firm attempts to identify suppliers who will produce products according to the buyer firm's specifications.

S

sales closing   The stage of the selling process in which the salesperson actually asks the customer to buy the product.

sales follow-up   Sales activities that provide important services to customers.

sales management   The process of planning, implementing, and controlling the personal selling function of an organization.

sales presentation   The part of the selling process in which the salesperson seeks to persuasively communicate the product's features and the benefits it will provide after the sale.

sales promotions   Programs designed to build interest in or encourage purchase of a product during a specified time period.

sales territory   A set of customers often defined by geographic boundaries, for whom a particular salesperson is responsible.

sampling (as a type of sales promotion)   Distributing free trial-size versions of a product to consumers.

sampling (in the research process)   The process of selecting respondents who statistically represent a larger population of interest.

scenarios   Possible future situations that futurists use to assess the likely impact of alternative marketing strategies.

scrambled merchandising   A merchandising strategy that offers consumers a mixture of merchandise items that are not directly related to each other.

search qualities   Product characteristics that the consumer can examine prior to purchase.

secondary data   Data that have been collected for some purpose other than the problem at hand.

segment profile   A description of the "typical" customer in a segment.

segmentation   The process of dividing a larger market into smaller pieces based on one or more meaningful, shared characteristics.

segmentation variables   Dimensions that divide the total market into fairly homogenous groups, each with different needs and preferences.

selective distribution   Distribution using fewer outlets than in intensive distribution but more than in exclusive distribution.

self-concept   An individual's self-image that is composed of a mixture of beliefs, observations, and feelings about personal attributes.

selling orientation   A managerial view of marketing as a sales function, or a way to move products out of warehouses to reduce inventory.

semiotics Field of study that examines how meanings are assigned to symbols.

service encounter The actual interaction between the customer and the service provider.

services Intangible products that are exchanged directly from the producer to the customer.

sex roles Society's expectations regarding the appropriate attitudes, behaviors, and appearance for men and women.

share of customer The percentage of an individual customer's purchase of a product that is a single brand.

shopping product A good or service for which consumers spend considerable time and effort gathering information and comparing alternatives before making a purchase.

single-source data Information that is integrated from multiple sources, to monitor the impact of marketing communications on a particular customer group over time.

single sourcing The business practice of buying a particular product from only one supplier.

situation analysis The first part of a marketing plan that provides a thorough description of the firm's current situation including its internal and external environments (also called a business review).

skimming price A very high, premium price that a firm charges for its new, highly desirable product.

slotting allowance A fee paid by a manufacturer to a retailer in exchange for agreeing to place products on the retailer's shelves.

social class The overall rank or social standing of groups of people within a society according to the value assigned to such factors as family background, education, occupation, and income.

social profit The benefit an organization and society receive from the organization's ethical practices, community service, efforts to promote cultural diversity, and concern for the natural environment.

social responsibility A management practice in which organizations seek to engage in activities that have a positive effect on society and promote the public good.

source An organization or individual that sends a message.

spamming Unsolicited e-mail directed to 5 or more people not personally known to the sender.

specialized services Services purchased from outside suppliers that are essential to the operation of an organization but are not part of the production of a product.

specialty product A good or service that has unique characteristics, is important to the buyer, and for which the buyer will devote significant effort to acquire.

specialty stores Retailers that carry only a few product lines but offer good selection within the lines that they sell.

sponsorship A PR activity through which companies provide financial support to help fund an event in return for publicized recognition of the company's contribution.

standard of living An indicator of the average quality and quantity of goods and services consumed in a country.

stimulus generalization Behavior caused by a reaction to one stimulus occurs in the presence of other, similar stimuli.

stock-outs An inventory problem that results when desired items are no longer available.

store image The way a retailer is perceived in the marketplace relative to the competition.

straight rebuy A buying situation in which business buyers make routine purchases that require minimal decision making.

strategic alliance Relationship developed between a firm seeking a deeper commitment to a foreign market and a domestic firm in the target country.

strategic business units (SBUs) Individual units within the firm that operate like separate businesses, with each having its own mission, business objectives, resources, managers, and competitors.

strategic planning A managerial decision process that matches an organization's resources and capabilities to its market opportunities for long-term growth and survival.

subculture A group within a society whose members share a distinctive set of beliefs, characteristics, or common experiences.

supermarkets Food stores that carry a wide selection of edibles and related products.

supply chain management The management of flows among firms in the supply chain to maximize profitability.

supply chain All the firms that engage in activities necessary to turn raw materials into a good or service and put it in the hands of the consumer or business customer.

SWOT analysis An analysis of an organization's strengths and weaknesses and the opportunities and threats in its external environment.

syndicated research Research by firms that collect data on a regular basis and sell the reports to multiple firms.

T

tactical (functional) planning A decision process that concentrates on developing detailed plans for strategies and tactics for the short term that support an organization's long-term strategic plan.

take title To accept legal ownership of a product and the accompanying rights and responsibilities of ownership.

target costing A process in which firms identify the quality and functionality needed to satisfy customers and what price they are willing to pay *before the product is designed*; the product is manufactured only if the firm can control costs to meet the required price.

target market Group or groups that a firm selects to turn into customers as a result of segmentation and targeting.

target marketing strategy Dividing the total market into different segments based on customer characteristics, selecting one or more segments, and developing products to meet the needs of those specific segments.

tariffs Taxes on imported goods.

team selling The sales function when handled by a team that may consist of a salesperson, a technical specialist, and others.

technical development Step in the product development process in which a new product is refined and perfected by company engineers and the like.

technical specialist Sales support person with a high level of technical expertise who assists in product demonstrations.

telemarketing The use of the telephone to sell directly to consumers and business customers.

test marketing Testing the complete marketing plan in a small geographic area that is similar to the larger market the firm hopes to enter.

top-down budgeting techniques Allocation of the promotion budget based on the total amount to be devoted to marketing communications.

total costs The total of the fixed costs and the variable costs for a set number of units produced.

total quality management (TQM) A management philosophy that focuses on satisfying customers through empowering employees to be an active part of continuous quality improvement.

trade area A geographic zone that accounts for the majority of a store's sales and customers.

trade or functional discounts Discounts off list price of products to members of the channel of distribution that perform various marketing functions.

trade shows Events at which many companies set up elaborate exhibits to show their products, give away samples, distribute product literature, and troll for new business contacts.

trademark The legal term for a brand name, brand mark, or trade character; trademarks legally registered by a government obtain protection for exclusive use in that country.

traffic flow The direction in which shoppers will move through the store and what areas they will pass or avoid.

transactional data An ongoing record of individuals or organizations that buy a product.

transactional selling A form of personal selling that focuses on making an immediate sale with little or no attempt to develop a relationship with the customer.

trend analysis An analysis of past industry or company sales data to determine patterns of change that may continue into the future.

trial pricing Pricing a new product low for a limited period of time in order to lower the risk for a customer.

U

unaided recall A research technique conducted by telephone survey or personal interview that asks whether a person remembers seeing an ad during a specified period of time.

undifferentiated targeting strategy Appealing to a broad spectrum of people.

unfair sales acts State laws that prohibit suppliers from selling products below cost to protect small businesses from larger competitors.

uniform delivered pricing A pricing tactic in which a firm adds a standard shipping charge to the price for all customers regardless of location.

unique selling proposition (USP) An advertising appeal that focuses on one clear reason why a particular product is superior.

Universal Product Code (UPC) The set of black bars or lines printed on the side or bottom of most items sold in grocery stores and other mass-merchandising outlets. The UPC, readable by scanners, creates a national system of product identification.

unsought product A good or service for which a consumer has little awareness or interest until the product or a need for the product is brought to his or her attention.

usage occasions Indicator used in one type of market segmentation based on when consumers use a product most.

utility The usefulness or benefit consumers receive from a product.

V

validity The extent to which research actually measures what it was intended to measure.

VALS™ (Values and Lifestyles) Psychographic system that divides the entire U.S. population into eight segments.

value chain The concept of a supply chain that looks at how each firm receives inputs, adds value to these inputs, and then passes them along to the next firm in the value chain.

value pricing A pricing strategy in which a firm sets prices that provide ultimate value to customers.

value proposition A marketplace offering that fairly and accurately sums up the value that will be realized if the product or service is purchased.

variable costs The costs of production (raw and processed materials, parts, and labor) that are tied to, and vary depending on the number of units produced.

venture teams Groups of people within an organization who work together focusing exclusively on the development of a new product.

vertical marketing system (VMS) A channel of distribution in which there is cooperation among members at the manufacturing, wholesaling, and retailing levels.

viral marketing Marketing activity in which a company recruits customers to be sales agents and spread the word about the product.

W

want The desire to satisfy needs in specific ways that are culturally and socially influenced.

warehouse clubs Discount retailers that charge a modest membership fee to consumers that buy a broad assortment of food and nonfood items in bulk and in a warehouse environment.

warehousing Storing goods in anticipation of sale or transfer to another member of the channel of distribution.

wheel-of-retailing hypothesis A theory that explains how retail firms change, becoming more upscale as they go through their life cycle.

wholesaling intermediaries Firms that handle the flow of products from the manufacturer to the retailer or business user.

World Trade Organization (WTO) An organization that replaced GATT, the WTO sets trade rules for its member nations and mediates disputes between nations.

Y

yield management pricing A practice of charging different prices to different customers in order to manage capacity while maximizing revenues.

Z

zone pricing A pricing tactic in which customers in different geographic zones pay different transportation rates.

Credits

CHAPTER 1

xxxiv Courtesy of HotJobs.com, Ltd.; **1** Dmitri Boylan; **4** © The Procter & Gamble Company. Used by Permission; **5** Used with permission of the Dodge Division of DaimlerChrysler Corporation; **6** Elnora Stuart; **8** Used with permission of the National Sports Center for the Disabled; **9** Used with permission of the Tourism Authority of Thailand; **11** © General Motors Corporation. Used with permission of GM Media Archives; **12** Kristen Sampson; **12** John Chillingworth; **12** Richard Robinson; **14** Tactic Marketing Company, LTD.; **17** Ford Motor Company; **18** AP/Wide World Photos; **19** © 2001 Amazon.com, Inc. All rights reserved; **20** © The Procter & Gamble Company; **21** John Eastcott/Yva Monat/The Image Works; **22** Courtesy of the American Association of Advertising Agencies; **23** Courtesy of HotJobs.com, Ltd.

CHAPTER 2

28 AP/Wide World Photos; **29** Used with permission of Angela Talley; **36** Philip Morris Co., Inc.; **37** CORBIS; **39** Used with the permission of Investinus.org and Doremus Ad Agency; **41** Used with permission of CNET Networks, Inc. Copyright 2002. All rights reserved; **43** Used with permission of Food.com; **48** Reem Ezzat Elmenshawy; **48** Cecile M. Smith; **48** Margaret A. Young; **48** Dr. Suzanne C. Beckmann; **53** Used with permission of Angela Talley

CHAPTER 3

58 Used with permission of Subaru America; **59** Used with permission of Joseph F. Barstys; **61** Ben & Jerry's Homemade Holdings, Inc.; **66** Used with the permission of Operation Blessing International; **68** Used with the permission of the Muir Heritage Land Trust; **69** © 2001 Time Inc. Reprinted by permission; **70** Denny's; **72** Used with permission of National Institute of Standards and Technology; **73** Miranda Erikkila; **73** Alan Dick; **73** Joyce LaValle; **75** Used with permission of IBM. Jeff Compton, Art Director. Maggie Powers, Copy Writer. Rob Delahanty, Photographer. Kevin Scully, Advertising Director; **76** Used with permission of The Container Store; **77** Used with permission of The Conference Board; **79** Skechers USA; **83** Used with permission of Joseph F. Barstys; **84** Used with permission of Subaru America

CHAPTER 4

90 Used with permission of Sony Nordic A/S; **91** Henrik Kaas; **93** Nike Advertising; **95** MTV, Music Television; **96** Used with permission of ministryofsound.com; **103** Elnora Stuart; **104** [PUB: Please supply credit line]; **107** J.Nordell/The Image Works; **109** Sophia Zaoudi; **109** Katie Finnegan; **104** Anna Olofsson; **109** Karin Braunsberger; **110** Used with permission of Aurora Writing Instruments and Kenro Industries; **111** Elnora Stuart; **115** Ogilvy & Mather; **116** Paradiset DDB; **117** Elnora Stuart; **118** Henrik Kaas; **118** Used with permission of Sony Nordic A/S

CHAPTER 5

124 © 2002, Harris Interactive Inc. All rights reserved; **125** © 2002, Harris Interactive Inc.; **129** Ad courtesy of Ford Motor Company; **134** Mercedes-Benz USA; **135** Used with permission of Marketing-Power.com and American Marketing Association; **136** Harvard Business School; **138** Columbia Information Systems; **139** Decision Insight, Inc.; **142** Photo by Jeff Greenberg/PhotoEdit; **143** Photo by Louie Psihoyos/Matrix International, Inc.; **144** Reprinted from *Marketing Tools* magazine, January/February, 1998. Copyright 1998. Courtesy of Intertec Publishing Corp., Stamford, Connecticut. All rights reserved. **147** Photo by Paul Shambroom/Photo Researchers, Inc.; **149** Used with permission of Amazon.com; **150** Courtesy of Mind/Share Inc.; **151** Meredith Burch; **151** Richard Bernstein; **151** Basil Englis; **152** © 2002, Harris Interactive Inc.;

CHAPTER 6

158 Reproduced with permission of Yahoo! Inc. © 2000 by Yahoo! Inc. YAHOO! and the YAHOO! Logo are trademarks of Yahoo! Inc.; **159** Used with permission of Jen Dulski; **162** Minolta; **165** Used with permission of Ask Jeeves Inc.; **168** Pepsi-Cola Company; **170** Alvarez; **174** Used with permission of Ducane Gas Grills Co.; **175** Photo by James Leynse/Corbis/SABA Press Photos, Inc.; **176** AP/Wide World Photos; **178** Joseph Burriss; **178** Dr. Judy F. Graham; **178** Melissa Fisher; **180** Schick; **181** IslamOnline.net; **182** Solomon Boovin; **183** Used with permission of Jen Dulski

CHAPTER 7

188 Syracuse Newspapers/Brian Phillips/The Image Works; **189** Lion Apparel Ltd.; **192** Dassault Falcon Jet Corporation; **194** Used with permission of Central States Fire Apparatus; **197** Qualcomm Inc.; **198** Federal Business Opportunities; **200** Federal Express; **201** Used with permission of Minolta Corporation. Images provided by kind courtesy of digitalvisiononline.com; **202** Jarrett Rice; **202** Ronald Picker; **202** Bunny Richardson; **203** Ralf-Finn Hestoft/SABA Press Photos, Inc.; **205** The Scottsdale Plaza Resort; **209** Used with permission of Dell Computer Corporation; **210** Used with permission of Excelon; **211** eSecurityOnline.com; **212** Used with permission of Steve Schwartz; **212** Lion Apparel Ltd.

CHAPTER 8

218 Vic Bider/Photo Edit; **222** Vans, Inc.; **226** Frito-Lay, Inc.; **230** Elise Grant; **230** Sal Veas; **231** Mephisto; **231** Hoover's Online; **234** Hard Candy, Inc.; **235** Used with permission of BC Ethic USA; **237** Esso Lubricants; **238** Maui; **240** FedEx

CHAPTER 9

230 Elle's Color Portraits; **248** Churchill & Klehr Photography; **249** Much and House; **254** Samsung Electronics; **256** Used with permission of Johnson & Johnson; **257** AP/Wide World Photos; **260** Sebastian Gollings Photography; **261** Jessica Wecker Photography; **262** Photo by Ann States/Corbis/SABA Press Photos, Inc.; **264** Benjamin Gonzales; **264** Jeff Gutenberg; **264** Michael Hodapp; **266** Used with permission of Greenfield Online; **267** Clean Shower; **269** AP/Wide World Photos; **271** Used with permission of The Sharper Image®; **272** Ducati North America Inc.; **273** Much and House; **273** Renaissance Cosmetics, Inc.

CHAPTER 10
278 Nissan North America; **279** Mario A. Polit; **284** Used with permission of Toshiba; **285** © The Procter & Gamble Company. Used by permission; **287** Reprinted with permission of The Maytag Company; **290** Paola Zuniga; **290** Moatassem Moatez; **290** Used with permission of Angela Talley; **291** Frito-Lay, Inc.; **292** Courtesy of Pony.com; **293** American Alphabet © 2001 Heidi Cody; **294** Courtesy of Bozell New York; **295** KELLOGG'S and POP-TART PASTRY SWIRLS are registered trademarks of Kellogg Company. All rights reserved. Used with permission; **297** AP/Wide World Photos; **301** Maro A. Polit; **302** Nissan North America

CHAPTER 11
308 Index Stock Imagery, Inc.; **309** Julie Sanoff; **311** Used with permission of Wildlife Conservation Society; **313** Lyndon Baines Johnson Library Collection; **314** AP/Wide World Photos; **314** AP/Wide World Photos; **314** AP/Wide World Photos; **315** Buffalo-Niagara Enterprise; **316** The Richards Group; **318** Used by permission of American Airlines; **319** Lennox Industries Inc.; **320** Used with permission of Providian Financial Corp.; **323** BLOCKBUSTER name, design and related marks are trademarks of Blockbuster Inc. © 2002 Blockbuster Inc. All rights reserved; **324** Used by permission of American Airlines; **326** Photo by Richard T. Nowitz/CORBIS; **328** Eugenio Fabozzi Onoranze Funebri; **328** Lewis P. Carbone and Stephan H. Haeckel, "Engineering Customer Experiences," *Marketing Management* 1994, U.3, 3, Exhibit 4. Courtesy of the American Marketing Association.; **333** Kirstin Firkins; **333** Kathy Winsted; **334** Julie Sanoff; **334** American Express

CHAPTER 12
340 Athient; **341** John Chillingworth; **343** MADD; **345** Gucci America Inc.; **348** Aimee Hale; **348** Tina Bardsley; **348** Used with permission of Joseph F. Barstys; **349** Used with permission of Dial Corp.; **352** Photo by Robert Brenner/PhotoEdit; **355** AP/Wide World Photos; **362** Daffy's; **363** Spiegel; **364** John Chillingworth; **364** Aithent

CHAPTER 13
370 Photo by Dan Ham/Marriott International, Inc.; **371** Marriott International, Inc.; **376** Used with permission of Dell Computer Corporation; **378** General Electric; **382** Suzuki; **383** Used with permission of Gillette Inc.; **384** Mongoose; **386** Used with permission of Eddie Bauer Inc.; **387** Courtesy of Priceline.com; **388** Ikea; **389** Joseph Goodman; **389** Ronald Picker; **389** © 2002, Harris Interactive Inc.; **390** Chat Noir; **393** Marriott International, Inc.

CHAPTER 14
398 Comporium Group; **399** Leslie Goldfarb; **401** Lexus; **403** Courtesy of T. Rowe Price Group; **404** Marissa Contreras; **404** Stephen Gould; **404** Bradley Sockloff; **405** Oreck Direct; **406** Courtesy of

DuPont; **408** BBDO/Duesseldorf; **409** Courtesy of Scholz & Friends; **411** Curad USA; **412** Altoids/Hunter & Associates; **413** © The Procter & Gamble Company. Used by permission; **416** Used with permission of Stouffer's Foods; **418** University of South Carolina; **419** Barnes & Noble.com; **422** Used with permission of Microsoft; **425** Leslie Goldfarb; **425** Comporium Group

CHAPTER 15
432 iWon.com; **433** Bradley Sockloff; **435** Used with the permission of Lipton® and Unilever United States, Inc.; **436** J. Walter Thompson; **437** Saatchi & Saatchi; **439** Dockers courtesy of Levi's; **440** © The Procter & Gamble Company. Used by permission; **442** © The Procter & Gamble Company. Used by permission; **443** Cinemaxx; **446** Leo Burnett/Madrid; **446** SeaWorld; **449** © Apple Computer, Inc. Used with permission. All rights reserved. Apple® and the Apple logo are registered trademarks of Apple Computer, Inc.; **451** Cornelia Otnes; **451** Cele Otnes; **451** Leslie Goldfarb; **455** Used with permission of the Direct Marketing Association; **457** Bradley Sockloff; **457** iWon.com

CHAPTER 16
462 Val-Pak DMS, Inc.; **463** Melissa Fisher; **467** Pearson; **468** Oscar Mayer Foods; **470** Used with permission of Pepsico; **474** Used with permission of 3M; **474** Jim Beam Bourbon/Joseph D'Amore; **475** Used with permission of Chiquita® Brands; **476** Eli Gelber; **476** Marvin G. Lovett; **476** Brian Kurtz; **477** © 2002 Time Inc. Reprinted by permission; **478** Used with permission of StartSampling.com; **479** Steve Hellerstein/Visa USA, Inc.; **483** Used with permission of Tupperware; **487** Used with permission of Omaha Steaks; **488** Melissa Fisher; **488** Val-Pak DMS, Inc.

CHAPTER 17
494 VF Corporation; **495** Mackey McDonald; **497** Photo by David Lassman/The Image Works; **499** Photo by Bob Daemmrich/The Image Works; **500** Jennifer Lau; **500** Randall Hansen; **500** Steve Schwartz; **503** AP/Wide World Photos; **504** Getty Images Inc.; **506** Larry Ford Foto; **506** Salami.com; **508** Courtesy of Shering Plough Corporation; **510** Photo by Jim Bertoglio/Index Stock Imagery, Inc.; **513** Rockport; **516** Used with permission of Business Objects; **517** Used with permission of Home Depot; **520** Maersk Sealand; **521** CORBIS; **521** Photo by Lowell Georgia/CORBIS.

CHAPTER 18
526 Used with permission of Macy's Corporation; **527** Dawn Robertson; **530** Photo by Michael Newman/PhotoEdit; **532** TC(2) Textile/Clothing Technology Corporation; **532** Elnora Stuart; **535** Photo by David Young-Wolff/PhotoEdit; **537** Elnora Stuart; **538** M. Antman/The Image Works; **539** Photo by M. Antman/The Image Works; **543** Camilo Montoya; **543** Dr. Robert Consenza; **543** Jen Dulski; **543** Martha Garnica; **545** Courtesy of Wal-Mart; **546** Photo by David SAmuel Robbins/CORBIS; **550** The Rouse Company; **550** Photo by Jim Mone/AP/Wide World Photos **550** Photo by D. Young-Wolff/PhotoEdit **550** Photo by A. Ramey/PhotoEdit **552** Dawn Robertson; **552** Used with permission of Macy's Corporation

Index

Scottsdale Plaza Resort, 205f
Screaming Media, 8
Sears, 440, 535
Sega, 182
Segman Human Transporter, 280
Sei Woo Rubber Works, 100
7–11, 535f
Shaklee, 67, 538
Sherman Antitrust Act, 81, 393
Sierra Club, 33f
Silent Spring, 64
Simmons Market Research Bureau (SMRB), 129, 134–135
Simmons Study of Media & Markets, 134
Sinatra, Frank, 260
Skechers, 79f
Slim Fast, 221
Smith, Cile, 48
SmithKlineBeecham, 478
Snapple, 114
SoBe Beverage Company, 238
SocialNet, 14
Sockloff, Bradley, 404, 433–434, 457
Sony, 90f, 91–92, 92f, 109, 118, 182, 257, 257f, 545
South Carolina, University of, 418f
Southwest Airlines, 46, 397
Spice Girls, 315
Spiegel, 363f
Spoetzl Brewery, 349
Sprite, 177, 239–240, 471
Stainmaster carpet, 66
Standard & Poor's 500 Directory, 482
Starbucks, 46, 65, 104, 532, 549
State Farm insurance, 335
Ste. Suisse Microelectronique et d'Horlogerie S.A. (SMH), 5
Stewart, Martha, 173
Stouffer's, 416f
Stratos Product Development, 20
Subaru, 58f, 59–60, 71, 73, 79, 83–84, 297
Subway restaurants, 402
Sun Maid, 170
Super Soaker, 262f
Suzuki, 382f
Synovus Financial Corporation, 75

Taco Bell, 73, 210, 436, 547
Talbot's, 551
Talley, Angela, 29–30, 44–45, 53, 289
Target, 296, 534
Taylor, Keith, 397
TD Industries, 75
Terhanian, George, 125–126, 152, 389
Tesco, 533
Texaco, 335
TGI Friday's, 531
Thailand, 9
Thornton, Mary Jo, 338
3M, 67
Tiffany, 108
Time, 477f
Time Warner, 224
Timex, 175, 442
TJX, 70
Top-Flite, 379
Toro, 292
Totalwoman, 14
Toyota, 67, 105, 355f, 415, 513
Toys "R" Us, 531
Trademark Revision Act of 1989, 294
Travelocity.com, 325
Tricon Restaurant International, 210
T. Rowe Price, 403f
True Value Hardware Stores, 511

Tupperware, 179, 483f, 538
Turner Broadcasting System, 175

Unext.com, 325
Unilever, 103, 116, 478
Unisys Corporation, 116
United Airlines, 477
United Parcel Service (UPS), 334, 382
Unsafe at Any Speed, 64
U.S. Census Bureau, 130, 135
U.S. Department of Agriculture, 134
U.S. Postal Service, 78

Valpak, 462f, 463–465, 488f
Vans, 175, 222, 222f
Veas, Sal, 230
VF Corporation, 495–496, 500, 521–522
Viacom, 94
Victoria's Secret, 534, 549
Virgin, 11, 151
Virginia Slims, 177, 434
Visa, 479f
Volkswagen Beetle, 282
Volvo, 65–66

Wall Street Journal, The, 386
Wal-Mart, 67, 71, 117, 127, 203, 203f, 211, 296, 514, 534–535, 545, 549–551
Walt Disney Company, 31, 122–123
Walton, Sam, 551
Ward, Aaron Montgomery, 453
Warner Brothers, 181
Warner-Lambert, 82, 138
WebCrawler, 163
Weight Watchers, 103, 221, 296
Welch, Jack, 38
Wendy's, 362
Western Union, 213
Weyerhaeuser Company, 467
Wharton School of Business, 447
Wheeler-Lea Act, 81
Whirlpool, 224
Widespread Panic, 182
Williams-Sonoma, 173, 551
Winsted, Kathy, 333
Winter Park Ski Resort, 318
Wirthlin Worldwide, 106
Women.com, 14
Women's Consumer Network, 14
Women's Financial Network, 14
WomensOurdoors.com, 14
WonderBra, 226
Wonder, Stevie, 313
Woods, Tiger, 285
Woodstream Company, 250
Workingwoman.com, 14
World Trade Organization (WTO), 98

Xerox, 42, 481, 485
X-Files, 181
Xterra, 279–280, 289, 293, 301–302, 302f

Yahoo!, 158f, 159–160, 160f, 183
Yellow Pages, 445
Young, Margaret A., 48
YupiMSN.com, 163

Zoudi, Sophia, 109
Zuniga, Paola, 289

SUBJECT INDEX

Acceleration principle, 195
Adoption, product
    adopter categories, 269–270, 270f
    definition of, 267

organizational differences affecting, 272–273
    product factors affecting, 270–272, 271t
    stages, 267–269, 268f
Advertising, 433–461
    campaign
        choosing media. *See* Media planning
        designing ad, 440–443
        establishing message, 439
        identifying target market, 438
        overview, 436–438
        pretesting, 443
        setting budget, 439–440
    case study, 460–461
    challenges facing advertising industry, 450–453
    definition of, 407, 434
    direct marketing
        direct-response television, 455–456
        mail order, 453–454
        telemarketing, 454–455
    evaluating, 450
    m-commerce (mobile commerce), 456–457
    overview, 434–435
    types, 435–436
Advertising appeal, definition of, 441
Advertising exposure, definition of, 448
Advocacy advertising, 436
Age groups, 172–173, 172t
AIDA model, 415
Aided recall, 450
American culture, exporting, 110–111, 111f
Aperture, definition of, 444
Approach, definition of, 483
Atmospherics, 547
Attitudinal measures, 450
Auctions, online, 386
Augmented service, 324
Automatic vending, 539
Average fixed cost, definition of, 357

B2B (business-to-business) e-commerce
    extranets, 210–211
    intranets, 210
    overview, 208–209
    private exchanges, 211
    security issues, 212–213
B2C (business-to-consumer) e-commerce
    benefits of, 540–542, 541t
    limitations of, 541t, 542–544
    overview, 539–540, 540t
    predictions for future, 545
Baby boomers, 224
Back-translation, 146
Banners, 447
BCG growth-market share matrix, 35, 36f
Behavioral learning theories, 169–170
Behavioral segmentation, definition of, 227, 229
Benefit, definition of, 5
Borders, 97–98
Bottom-up budgeting techniques, 414
Brand
    competition, 78
    definition of, 292
    equity, 294
    extensions, 295
    loyalty, 166
    personality, 236, 238f
    placement, 478
Branding
    choosing brand name, mark, or character, 292–293
    co-branding, 297
    generic brands, 296
    importance of, 294–295
    licensing, 296–297